The **Rough Guide** to

New Zealand

written and researched by

Laura Harper, Catherine Le Nevez,
Tony Mudd and Paul Whitfield

ROUGH
GUIDES

www.roughguides.com

Contents

Colour section   1

Introduction 6
Where to go 9
When to go 11
Things not to miss 14

Basics   25

Getting there........................... 27
Getting around........................ 31
Accommodation 42
Food and drink 47
The media 52
Festivals and public holidays ... 53
Outdoor activities 55
Spectator sports 64
Culture and etiquette 66
Living in New Zealand.............. 67
Travel Essentials 69

Guide   81

1 Auckland and around 83
2 Northland 149
3 Western North Island 205
4 Central North Island 257
5 The Coromandel, Bay of Plenty
and the East Cape 307
6 Poverty Bay, Hawke's Bay and
the Wairarapa.................... 359
7 Wellington and around 397
8 Marlborough, Nelson and
Kaikoura............................ 429
9 Christchurch and south to
Otago................................ 493
10 Central South Island 545
11 Dunedin to Stewart Island... 575
12 The West Coast................. 619

13 Queenstown, Wanaka and the
Gold Country 667
14 Fiordland.......................... 727

Contexts   759

History 761
Chronology of New Zealand .. 775
Maoritanga............................. 777
Landscapes and wildlife 785
Film and music 795
Books 798

Language   805

Maori 807
Maori place names 808
Pronunciation........................ 809
Glossary................................ 810

Travel store   813

Small print & Index   821

Maori in the modern world colour section
following p.216

Conservation in action colour section
following p.408

Adrenaline heaven colour section
following p.648

◄◄ Crayfish stall, Kaikoura ◄ Moeraki Boulders

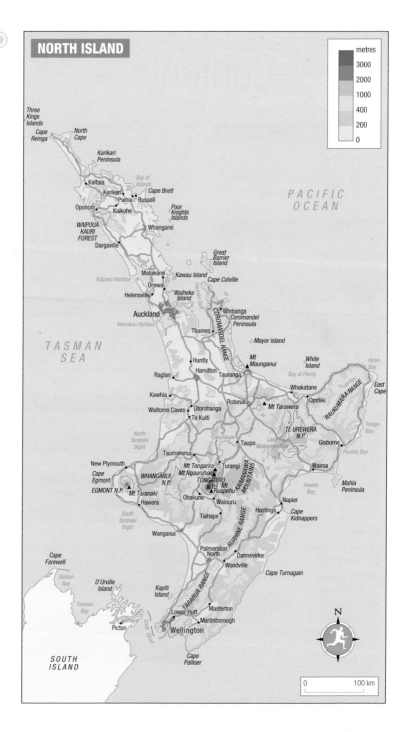

NORTH ISLAND

metres
3000
2000
1000
400
200
0

Three Kings Islands
Cape Reinga
North Cape
Karikari Peninsula
Bay of Islands
Kaitaia
Kerikeri
Paihia
Russell
Cape Brett
Opononi
Kaikohe
Poor Knights Islands
WAIPOUA KAURI FOREST
Whangarei
Dargaville
PACIFIC OCEAN
Great Barrier Island
Matakana
Kawau Island
Cape Colville
Kaipara Harbour
Orewa
Helensville
Waiheke Island
Auckland
Manukau Harbour
Whitianga
Coromandel Peninsula
Hauraki Gulf
COROMANDEL RANGE
Thames
Mayor Island
TASMAN SEA
Huntly
Hamilton
Mt Maunganui
White Island
Hicks Bay
Raglan
Tauranga
Bay of Plenty
Whakatane
East Cape
Kawhia
Rotorua
Opotiki
RAUKUMARA RANGE
Waitomo Caves
Otorohanga
Mt Tarawera
Te Kuiti
TE UREWERA N.P.
Tolaga Bay
North Taranaki Bight
Lake Taupo
Lake Waikaremoana
Gisborne
Taumarunui
Taupo
Poverty Bay
New Plymouth
Mt Tongariro
Turangi
Wairoa
Cape Egmont
Mt.Ngauruhoe
WHANGANUI N.P.
TONGARIRO N.P.
Mt Ruapehu
KAIMANAWA MOUNTAINS
Mahia Peninsula
EGMONT N.P.
Mt Taranaki
Ohakune
Waiouru
Napier
Hawke Bay
Hawera
Waiouru
Hastings
Cape Kidnappers
Taihape
RUAHINE RANGE
Wanganui
Palmerston North
Dannevirke
Cape Farewell
Woodville
Cape Turnagain
Golden Bay
D'Urville Island
Kapiti Island
TARARUA RANGE
Tasman Bay
Masterton
Picton
Lower Hutt
Martinborough
Cook Strait
Wellington
SOUTH ISLAND
Cape Palliser
South Taranaki Bight

N

0   100 km

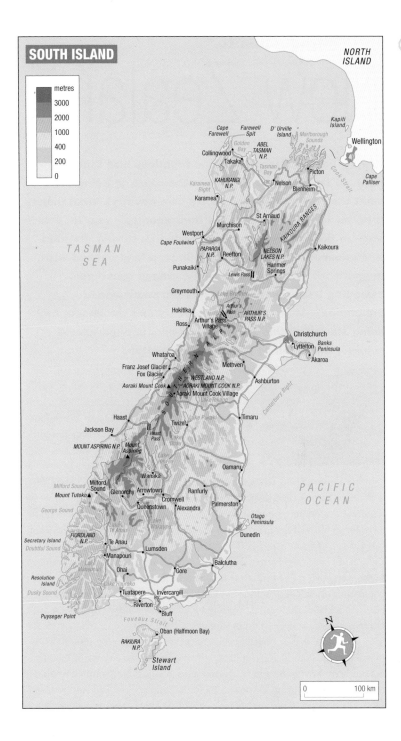

SOUTH ISLAND

metres
3000
2000
1000
400
200
0

NORTH
ISLAND

Cape Farewell
Farewell Spit
D' Urville Island
Kapiti Island
Golden Bay
ABEL TASMAN N.P.
Marlborough Sounds
Wellington
Collingwood
Takaka
Tasman Bay
Picton
Cook Strait
Cape Palliser
KAHURANGI N.P.
Nelson
Blenheim
Karamea Bight
Karamea
St Arnaud
KAIKOURA RANGES
Westport
Murchison
Cape Foulwind
PAPAROA N.P.
Reefton
NELSON LAKES N.P.
Kaikoura
Punakaiki
Lewis Pass
Hanmer Springs
TASMAN SEA
Greymouth
Lake Brunner
Hokitika
Arthur's Pass
ARTHUR'S PASS N.P.
Ross
Arthur's Pass Village
Christchurch
Banks Peninsula
Lyttelton
Whataroa
Methven
Akaroa
Franz Josef Glacier
Fox Glacier
WESTLAND N.P.
Aoraki Mount Cook
AORAKI MOUNT COOK N.P.
Aoraki Mount Cook Village
Ashburton
SOUTHERN ALPS
Lake Tekapo
Haast
Lake Pukaki
Timaru
Jackson Bay
Twizel
Haast Pass
Canterbury Bight
MOUNT ASPIRING N.P.
Mount Aspiring
Lake Hawea
Oamaru
Wanaka
Milford Sound
Milford Sound
Arrowtown
Ranfurly
Mount Tutoko
Glenorchy
Cromwell
PACIFIC OCEAN
George Sound
Queenstown
Alexandra
Palmerston
Otago Peninsula
FIORDLAND N.P.
Secretary Island
Lake Te Anau
Te Anau
Lake Wakatipu
Dunedin
Doubtful Sound
Manapouri
Lumsden
Resolution Island
Ohai
Lake Manapouri
Gore
Balclutha
Dusky Sound
Lake Hauroko
Tuatapere
Invercargill
Puyseger Point
Riverton
Bluff
Foveaux Strait
Oban (Halfmoon Bay)
RAKIURA N.P.
Stewart Island

N

0   100 km

Introduction to

New Zealand

Kiwis – named after the unique flightless bird that is their national emblem – can't believe their luck at being born in what they call "Godzone" (God's own country). What makes it better is that travellers list their country – year in, year out – in the top ten of places they'd like to visit. Perhaps it is because New Zealand is unique, a land packed with magnificent and diverse scenery: craggy coastlines, sweeping beaches, primeval forests, snowcapped mountains, glacier-fed lakes, geysers and volcanoes. And living among all this awesome scenery is unparalleled wildlife, the result of evolution in isolation.

Given this backdrop it is unsurprising that there are boundless diversions, ranging from strolls along moody windswept beaches and multi-day tramps over alpine passes to adrenaline-charged adventure activities like bungy jumping, skiing, sea kayaking and whitewater rafting. Some visitors treat the country as a large-scale assault course, aiming to tackle as many challenges as possible in the time available. The one-time albatross of isolation (even Australia is 2000km away) has become a boon, bolstering New Zealand's clean, **green** image – in truth, more an accident of geography than the conscious policy of any government.

At the top of many travellers' wish lists, New Zealand is incredibly popular and yet remains largely free of crowds and clamour. Almost everything is easily accessible, packed into a land area little larger than Britain but with a population of only 4.3 million – over half tucked away in the three largest **cities**: Auckland, the capital, Wellington, and Christchurch. Elsewhere, you can travel miles through stunning countryside without seeing a soul: there are spots so remote that, it's reliably contended, no human has yet visited them.

Geologically, New Zealand split away from the super-continent of Gondwanaland early, developing a unique **ecosystem** in which birds adapted to fill the role of mammals, many becoming flightless because they had no predators. That all changed with the arrival of Polynesian navigators, about 1000 years ago, when New Zealand became the last major landmass to be settled by humans. On sighting the new land from their canoes, Maori named it **Aotearoa** – "the land of the long white cloud". On disembarking they proceeded to unbalance the fragile ecosystem, dispatching forever the giant ostrich-sized moa, which formed a major part of their diet. The country once again settled into a fragile balance before the arrival of **Pakeha** – white Europeans, predominantly of British origin – who swarmed off their square-rigged ships full of colonial zeal and altered the land forever.

An uneasy coexistence between **Maori** and **European** societies informs the current wrangles over cultural identity, land and resource rights. The British didn't invade as such, and were to some degree reluctant to enter into the 1840 **Treaty of Waitangi**, New Zealand's founding document, which effectively ceded New Zealand to the British Crown while guaranteeing Maori hegemony over their land and traditional gathering and fishing rights. As time wore

Fact file

• Adrift in the south Pacific some 2000km east of Australia, New Zealand was only peopled around 1000 years ago.

• At 268,000 square kilometres, New Zealand is a little larger than the UK and about two-thirds the size of California. With only 4.3 million people, most parts of the country are thinly populated, though Auckland has around 1.3 million inhabitants.

• For an instinctively conservative nation, New Zealand has often been socially progressive. It was the first country with votes for women and workers' pensions, and now pursues a bicultural approach to race relations.

• Traditionally, New Zealand's economy is agricultural, with dairy products, meat and wool remaining central to its prosperity, and forestry and fishing also playing a part. New Zealand has almost 40 million sheep, nine for every inhabitant. There is also a growing "knowledge economy" and, with over two million visitors a year, tourism is a big earner.

• New Zealand's flora and fauna developed independently, giving rise to a menagerie of exotica: tall tree ferns, the kea (the world's only alpine parrot), the reptilian tuatara, the peculiar kiwi, and many more.

▲ Cathedral Square, Christchurch

Location, location, location...

When Peter Jackson filmed his *Lord of the Rings* trilogy in New Zealand the country rejoiced, even appointing a special minister for the project. However, few could have anticipated how completely it would take over the country. For thousands of visitors, no stay in Aotearoa is complete without a tour of film locations.

The next wave of scene-seeking tourists took Disney's *The Lion the Witch and the Wardrobe* as their inspiration, and now there is the prospect of a tsunami of tourists wanting to stand where the hobbits of Peter Jackson's new epic (based on J.R.R Tolkien's *The Hobbit*) will plant their feet as the cameras whir. While this is a good way to see some magnificent scenery, be prepared for disappointment: scenes rarely look as they did in the films. The tourist dollars are good for the country and the knock-on effect on domestic film releases is beneficial, but the land is quite beautiful in its own right without CGI enhancement.

on and increasing numbers of settlers demanded ever larger parcels of land from Maori, antipathy surfaced and escalated into hostility. Once Maori were subdued, a policy of partial integration all but destroyed **Maoritanga** – the Maori way of doing things. Maori, however, were left well outside the new European order, where difference was perceived as tantamount to a betrayal of the emergent sense of nationhood. Although elements of this still exist and Presbyterian and Anglican values have proved hard to shake off, the Kiwi psyche has become infused with Maori generosity and hospitality, coupled with a colonial mateyness and the unerring belief that whatever happens, "she'll be right".

Only in the last forty years has New Zealand come of age and developed a true national self-confidence, something partly forced on it by Britain severing the colonial apron strings in the early 1970s, and by the resurgence of Maori identity. Maori demands have been nurtured by a willingness on the part of most Pakeha to redress the wrongs perpetrated over the last century and a half, as long as it doesn't impinge on their high standard of living or overall feeling of control. More recently, integration has been replaced with a policy of **biculturalism** – promoting two cultures alongside each other, but with maximum interaction. This policy has been somewhat weakened by relatively recent and extensive **immigration** from China, Korea and South Asia.

Despite having and achieving much to give them confidence, Kiwis somehow, unlike their Australian neighbours, retain an underlying shyness that borders on an inferiority complex: you may well find yourself interrogated about your opinions on the country almost before you've even left the airport. Balancing this is an extraordinary enthusiasm for **sports** and **culture**, which generate a swelling pride in New Zealanders when they witness plucky Kiwis taking on and sometimes beating the world.

Where to go

New Zealand packs a lot into a limited space, meaning you can visit many of the main sights in a couple of weeks, but allow at least a month or two for a proper look around. The scenery is the big draw, and most people only pop into the big cities on arrival and departure – easily done with open-jaw air tickets, allowing you to fly into Auckland and out of Christchurch.

Sprawled around the sparkling Waitemata Harbour is go-ahead **Auckland**, looking out over the island-studded Hauraki Gulf. Most people head south from here, missing out on **Northland**, the cradle of both Maori and Pakeha colonization, cloaked in wonderful sub-tropical forest that harbours New Zealand's largest kauri trees. East of Auckland the coast follows the isolated greenery and long, golden beaches of the **Coromandel Peninsula**, before running down to the beach towns of the **Bay of Plenty**. Immediately south your senses are assailed by the ever-present sulphurous whiff of **Rotorua**, with its spurting geysers and bubbling pools of mud, and the volcanic plateau

Paua

Paua is New Zealand's endemic species of abalone and is found in shallow waters, encrusted in limescale. Vigorous polishing removes this and reveals a wonderfully iridescent shell, with swirls of silver, blue, green and purple. Early Maori used slivers as lures to catch fish and

inlaid shaped pieces into carvings, particularly as the eyes of tiki figures. Its later use in tourist trinkets has produced many kitsch items, but to fully appreciate it look for its use in more traditional Maori arts and crafts, perhaps incorporated into a brooch or inlaid in a mirror frame.

centred on the trout-filled waters of **Lake Taupo,** overshadowed by three snow-decorated volcanoes. Cave fans will want to head west of Taupo for the eerie limestone caverns of **Waitomo**; alternatively it's just a short hop from Taupo to the delights of canoeing the **Whanganui River**, a broad, emerald-green waterway banked by virtually impenetrable bush thrown into relief by the cone of **Mount Taranaki**, whose summit is accessible in a day. East of Taupo lie ranges that form the North Island's backbone, and beyond them the **Hawke's Bay wine country**, centred on the Art Deco city of Napier. Further south, the wine region of Martinborough is just an hour or so from the capital, **Wellington**, its centre squeezed onto reclaimed harbourside, the suburbs slung across steep hills overlooking glistening bays. Politicians and bureaucrats give it a well-scrubbed and urbane sophistication, enlivened by an established café society and after-dark scene.

The **South Island** kicks off with the world-renowned wineries of **Marlborough** and appealing **Nelson**, a pretty and compact spot surrounded by lovely beaches and within easy reach of the hill country around the **Nelson Lakes National Park** and the fabulous sea kayaking of the **Abel Tasman National Park**. From the top of the South Island you've a choice of nipping behind the 3000m summits of the Southern Alps and following the West Coast to the fabulous **glaciers** at Fox and Franz Josef, or sticking to the east, passing the whale-watching territory of **Kaikoura** en route to the South Island's largest centre, refined **Christchurch**, a city with its roots firmly in colonial English traditions. From here you can head across country to the West Coast via Arthur's Pass on one of the country's most scenic train trips, or shoot south-west across the patchwork Canterbury Plains to the foothills of the **Southern Alps** and **Aoraki Mount Cook** with its distinctive drooping-tent summit.

The patchwork-quilt fields of Canterbury run, via the grand architecture of **Oamaru**, to the unmistakably Scottish-influenced city of **Dunedin**, a base for

▲ Lake Wakatipu

exploring the wildlife of the **Otago Peninsula,** with its albatross, seal, sea lion and penguin colonies. In the middle of the nineteenth century, prospectors arrived here and rushed inland to gold strikes throughout central Otago and around stunningly set **Queenstown**, now a commercialized activity centre where bungy jumping, rafting, jetboating and skiing hold sway. Just up the road is Glenorchy, a tramping heartland, from which the **Routeburn Track** sets out to rain-sodden **Fiordland**; its neighbour, Te Anau, is the start of many of New Zealand's most famous treks, including the Milford Track. Further south you'll feel the bite of the Antarctic winds, which reach their peak on New Zealand's third landmass, isolated **Stewart Island**, covered mostly by dense coastal rainforest that offers a great chance of spotting a kiwi in the wild.

When to go

▼ Hawke's Bay Farmers' Market, Hastings

With ocean in every direction it is no surprise that New Zealand has a maritime climate, warm in the summer months, December to March, and never truly cold, even in winter. **Weather** patterns are strongly affected by prevailing westerlies, which suck up moisture from the Tasman Sea and dump it on the western side of both islands. The South Island gets the lion's share,

Hot pools, geysers and boiling mud

For many, one of the most enduring memories of New Zealand is laying back in a **natural hot pool** surrounded by bush and gazing up at the stars. New Zealand lies on the Pacific Ring of Fire, and earthquakes and volcanic activity are common. Superheated steam finds its way to the surface as **geysers** (around Rotorua), **boiling**

mud pools (Rotorua and Taupo) and **hot springs**. Blissfully, there are around eighty hot springs across the northern two-thirds of the North Island and another fifteen along a thin thread down the western side of the Southern Alps.

Over thirty are commercial **resorts** offering tepid swimming pools, near-scalding baths, BBQ areas and sometimes mineral mud and hydrothermal pampering. The remainder are **natural pools**, either in the bush, beside a stream or welling up from below a sandy beach. A few are well known, but many more require a little sleuthing: locals like to keep the best spots to themselves. Check out ⓦ**www.nzhotpools.co.nz**, which includes a hot pools map of the country, links to resorts and details of how to get to some of the free natural hot pools. Also read our notes on **amoebic meningitis** on p.75.

To get you started we've picked a handful of the best spots (listed north to south).

Polynesian Spa Commercial resort in Rotorua with something for everyone: mineral pools, family spa, adult-only open-air complex and all manner of body treatments. See p.267

Hot Water Beach Come at low tide, rent a spade and dig a hot pool beside the cool surf. See p.330

Maruia Springs Small resort in the hills 200km north of Christchurch. Particularly magical in winter. See p.552

Welcome Flat Hot Springs Four natural pools sited amid mountain scenery just south of Fox Glacier. It is a six- to seven-hour walk in and you can stay at the adjacent DOC hut. See p.660

with the West Coast and Fiordland ranking among the world's wettest places. Mountain ranges running the length of both islands cast long rain shadows eastward, making those locations considerably drier. The south is a few degrees cooler than elsewhere, and sub-tropical Auckland and Northland are appreciably more humid. In the North Island, warm, damp summers fade imperceptibly into cool, wet winters, while the further south you travel the more the weather divides the year into four distinct seasons.

Most people visit New Zealand in the summer but it is a viable destination at any time, provided you pick your destinations. From December to March

you'll find everything open, though often busy with holidaying Kiwis from Christmas to mid-January. In general, you're better off joining the bulk of foreign visitors during the **shoulder seasons** – October, November and April – when sights and attractions are quieter, and accommodation easier to come by. **Winter** (May–Sept) is the wettest, coldest and consequently least popular time, unless you are enamoured of winter sports, in which case it's fabulous. The switch to prevailing southerly winds tends to bring periods of crisp, dry and cloudless weather to the West Coast and heavy snowfalls to the Southern Alps and Central North Island, allowing for some of the most varied and least-populated **skiing and snowboarding** in the world.

Average monthly temperatures and rainfall

	Jan	Feb	Mar	Apr	May	Jun	July	Aug	Sep	Oct	Nov	Dec
Auckland												
max/min (°C)	23/16	23/16	22/15	19/13	17/11	14/9	13/8	14/8	16/9	17/11	19/12	21/14
max/min (°F)	73/61	73/61	72/59	66/55	63/52	57/48	55/46	57/46	61/48	63/52	66/54	70/57
rainfall (mm)	79	94	81	97	112	137	145	117	102	102	89	79
Wellington												
max/min (°C)	21/13	21/13	19/12	17/11	14/8	13/7	12/6	12/6	14/8	16/9	17/10	19/12
max/min (°F)	70/55	70/55	66/54	63/52	57/46	55/45	54/43	54/43	57/46	61/48	63/50	66/54
rainfall (mm)	81	81	81	97	117	117	137	117	97	102	89	89
Christchurch												
max/min (°C)	21/12	21/12	19/10	17/7	13/4	11/2	10/2	11/2	14/4	17/7	19/8	21/11
max/min (°F)	70/54	70/54	66/50	63/45	55/39	52/36	50/36	52/36	57/39	63/45	66/46	70/52
rainfall (mm)	56	43	48	48	66	66	69	48	46	43	48	56
Hokitika												
max/min (°C)	19/12	19/12	18/11	16/8	14/6	12/3	12/3	12/3	13/6	15/8	16/9	18/11
max/min (°F)	66/54	66/54	64/52	61/46	57/43	54/37	54/37	54/37	55/43	59/46	61/48	64/52
rainfall (mm)	262	191	239	236	244	231	218	239	226	292	267	262
Queenstown												
max/min (°C)	21/10	21/10	20/9	15/7	11/3	9/1	9/0	11/1	14/3	18/5	19/7	20/10
max/min (°F)	70/50	70/50	68/48	59/45	52/37	48/34	48/32	52/34	57/37	64/41	66/45	68/50
rainfall (mm)	79	72	74	72	64	58	59	63	66	77	64	62

30

things not to miss

It's not possible to see everything that New Zealand has to offer in one trip – so don't try. What follows, in no particular order, is a selective taste of the islands' highlights, including outstanding national parks, natural wonders, adventure activities and exotic wildlife. They're arranged in five colour-coded categories, which you can browse through to find the very best things to see and experience. All highlights have a page reference to take you straight into the Guide, where you can find out more.

01 Milford Sound Page **742** • Experience the grandeur and beauty of Fiordland on the area's most accessible fiord, wonderfully atmospheric in the mist but best in bright sunshine.

02 **Wai-O-Tapu** Page **278** • The best of Rotorua's geothermal sites, Wai-O-Tapu offers beautiful, mineral-coloured lakes, a geyser that erupts on cue each morning and pools of plopping mud.

03 **Otago Central Rail Trail** Page **721** • Taking three leisurely days on a bike is the best way to tackle this 150km trail, which follows the route of a former rail line through some ruggedly barren country.

04 **East Cape** Page **351** • A varied coastline, tiny communities and the slow pace of life make the East Cape a place to linger.

05 **Abel Tasman National Park** Page **458** • Visitors flock to the magnificent Abel Tasman National Park, to hike its Coast Track and kayak its coastline.

06 **Moeraki Boulders** Page **543** • Don't pass through the Oamaru area without a visit to the these large, perfectly round, natural spheres with a honeycomb centre, just sitting in the surf.

07 **Surfing at Raglan** Page **216** • A left-hand break that's one of the world's longest, coupled with reliable swells, makes Raglan a prime surfing destination.

08 **Hangi** Page **49** • Sample fall-off-the-bone pork and chicken along with sweet potatoes and pumpkin, disinterred after several hours' steaming in a Maori earth oven.

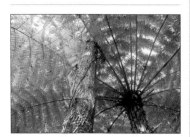

09 **Tree ferns** Page **789** • New Zealand has a unique ecosystem, its ubiquitous tree ferns sometimes reaching up to 10m in height and providing shade for more delicate specimens.

10 **The glaciers** Page **651** • The steep and dramatic Fox and Franz Josef glaciers can be explored by glacier hike, ice climbing and helicopter flights landing on the snowfields above.

11 Tongariro Alpine Crossing Page **298** • A superb one-day hike through the volcanic badlands of the Tongariro National Park, passing the cinder cone of Mount Ngauruhoe, along the shores of turquoise lakes and with long views right across the North Island.

12 Christchurch Art Gallery Page **507** • The South Island's most extensive collection of New Zealand art is housed in a striking modern building in the heart of Christchurch.

14 Wine Page **51** • Spend a day or two sampling fine New Zealand wines and dining overlooking the vines in Hawke's Bay, Martinborough, Marlborough, Central Otago or any of half-dozen other major wine regions.

15 Whanganui River Journey Page **239** • This relaxing three-day canoe trip along a historic waterway takes you far away from roads through some of the North Island's loveliest scenery.

13 Bungy jumping Page **61** • There are some fabulously scenic spots to try New Zealand's trademark adventure sport, few more so than high above the Waikato River in Taupo.

16 The Catlins Coast Page **598** • Seals and dolphins and a laidback approach to life make the Catlins a great place to unwind for a few days.

18 Museum of New Zealand (Te Papa) Page **408** • A celebration of the people, culture and art of New Zealand that's as appealing to kids as it is to adults, with an impressive use of state-of-the-art technology.

19 Hokianga Harbour Page **196** • As a low-key antidote to the commercialization of the Bay of Islands, the sand dunes, quiet retreats and crafts culture of the Hokianga Harbour are hard to beat.

17 Farewell Spit Page **471** • This slender 25km arc of sand dunes and beaches is a nature reserve protecting a host of bird species including black swans, wrybills, curlews and dotterels.

20 Whale watching Page **489** • Whale watching off the Kaikoura Peninsula is justifiably popular, and you don't have to stick to a boat trip to do it, with plane and helicopter rides also on offer.

21 **Jetboating** Page **61** • Jetboating is a countrywide obsession with some superb trips around Queenstown, in Fiordland and just north of Taupo.

22 **The Penguin Place** Page **597** • Watch penguins waddle up the beach to their nests each night from hides and viewing platforms all along the southwestern coast of the South Island.

23 **Ninety Mile Beach** Page **192** • This seemingly endless wave-lashed golden strand is a designated highway, plied by tour buses that regularly stop to let passengers toboggan down the steep dunes.

24 White Island Page **346** • Take an appealing boat trip out to New Zealand's most active volcano, and stroll through the sulphurous lunar landscape to peer into the steaming crater.

25 The Routeburn Track Page **700** • One of the country's finest walks, showcasing forested valleys, rich birdlife, thundering waterfalls, river flats, lakes and wonderful mountain scenery.

26 **Taieri Gorge Railway** Page **590** • Dating back to 1859, the Taieri Gorge Railway penetrates otherwise inaccessible mountain landscapes and is a dramatic journey at any time of the year.

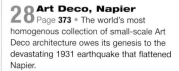

28 **Art Deco, Napier** Page **373** • The world's most homogenous collection of small-scale Art Deco architecture owes its genesis to the devastating 1931 earthquake that flattened Napier.

27 **Caving and cave rafting** Page **221** • Enter Waitomo's labyrinthine netherworld on huge abseils and explore its glowworm-filled cave systems while floating down streams on inner tubes.

29 **Zealandia: the Karori Sanctuary Experience** Page **413** • On the edge of Wellington yet seemingly a million miles from anything urban, this beautiful fenced-in nature reserve is being restocked with purely native flora and fauna.

30 **Diving at the Poor Knights Islands** Page **164** • Two-dive day-trips visit any of several dozen sites at one of the world's best diving destinations. A couple of scuttled navy boats nearby add to the possibilities.

Basics

Basics

Getting there 27

Getting around 31

Accommodation 42

Food and drink... 47

The media 52

Festivals and public holidays.. 53

Outdoor activities... 55

Spectator sports 64

Culture and etiquette 66

Living in New Zealand... 67

Travel Essentials 69

Getting there

The quickest, easiest and cheapest way to get to New Zealand is to fly. It is possible to arrive by sea, but there are no international passenger ferries, so unless you own a boat this means joining a cruise, crewing on a private yacht, or paying for your passage on a cargo ship (a rewarding experience for those who like sea journeys – find out more at ⓦ www.freightertravel.co.nz).

Air **fares** depend on the season, with the highest prices during the NZ summer (Dec–Feb); prices drop during the shoulder seasons (Sept–Nov & March–May) and you'll get the cheapest rates during the low (ski) season (June–Aug).

If New Zealand is only one stop on a longer journey, you might consider buying a **Round-the-World (RTW)** ticket. An "off-the-shelf" RTW ticket will have you touching down in about half a dozen cities (Auckland is on many itineraries), or you can assemble one tailored to your needs, though this is liable to be more expensive.

Arriving in New Zealand, your only real choice, unless you're coming from Australia, is between the international airports at **Auckland** and **Christchurch**. Christchurch receives fewer direct flights but many scheduled airlines have a codeshare shuttle from Auckland at no extra cost. The most desirable option, an **open-jaw ticket** (flying into one and out of the other), usually costs no more than an ordinary return. For **internal flights** within NZ, see box, p.31.

Tourists and those on short-term working visas (see p.68) are generally required by New Zealand immigration to arrive with an **onward ticket** out of the country, so one-way tickets are really only viable for Australian and NZ residents.

If you've purchased a return ticket and find you want to stay longer or head off on a totally different route, it's often possible to **change** the dates (and, in fewer instances, routes) with the airline or travel agent, depending on the conditions of your ticket, though often for a fee. Passenger changes are rarely permitted, so flogging an unused ticket on the internet usually isn't an option.

From the UK and Ireland

Over a dozen airlines compete to fly you **from Britain** to New Zealand for as little as £733, but prices depend upon the time of year, and can be double that amount at Christmas. Going for the **cheapest flight** typically means sacrificing some comfort (multiple stops, longer layovers and so on), which you may regret, given that even the shortest journey will last at least 24 hours including an obligatory refuelling stop. There are no direct flights to New Zealand **from Ireland**, and prices are proportionately higher, since the short hop to London (around £100 return, cheaper with internet deals) has to be added to the fare.

Most **scheduled flights** allow multiple **stopovers** either in North America and the Pacific, or Asia and Australia. The vast majority of direct scheduled flights depart from London Heathrow, though some services operate from London Gatwick, Manchester and Newcastle.

From the US and Canada

Direct trans-Pacific flights to Auckland operate from Los Angeles (with Air New Zealand and Qantas), San Francisco (with Air New Zealand), and Vancouver (with Air New Zealand), a flight of 12–16 hours. Assorted codeshare partners – Air Canada, American Airlines, British Airways, etc – sell tickets to New Zealand, usually offering several connections a day to Wellington and Christchurch.

From the US a direct LA–Auckland or San Francisco–Auckland round-trip **fare** goes for around US$1400 during the southern winter, rising to around US$1700 or more in peak southern summer season. Flights from all other US cities are routed via

California. Off-peak you might expect to pay US$1600–1800 from New York or Chicago, but shopping around for special offers could save you more than a few bucks.

From Canada, Air New Zealand runs direct Vancouver–Auckland flights three days per week, and codeshares with Air Canada for links to provincial capitals. Depending on the season, fares from Vancouver are around CAN$1800; from Toronto, around CAN$2300; and from Montréal, around CAN$2800; substantial savings can often be made through discount travel companies and websites.

Apart from a **RTW** ticket (p.27), an alternative approach from North America is to fly **via Asia**, which may work out cheaper. Korean Air, for example, has flights from Atlanta, Chicago, Dallas, Las Vegas, Los Angeles, New York, San Francisco, Seattle, Toronto, Vancouver and Washington DC, all changing at Seoul (Incheon) before continuing on to Auckland. An equally exotic option is to stop off at a **Pacific island** or two along the way. Air New Zealand visits half a dozen islands and often charges less than US$100 per stopover.

From Australia

Qantas, Jetstar, Air New Zealand and Pacific Blue all fly between **Australia** and New Zealand, as do Thai, Emirates, Aerolineas Argentinas and LanChile. **Prices** vary enormously depending on demand (book well in advance in summer), but the level of competition generally keeps them reasonable – as low as A$366 return from Australia's east coast (including a basic baggage allowance) if you're prepared to go for non-refundable tickets. Return flights from Perth start at around A$1000.

It's a relatively short hop across the Tasman Sea: **flying time** from Sydney or Melbourne to New Zealand is around three hours. Auckland, Christchurch, Dunedin, Hamilton, Rotorua, Queenstown and Wellington international airports all have direct flights to/from Australia.

Six steps to a better kind of travel

At Rough Guides we are passionately committed to travel. We feel strongly that only through travelling do we truly come to understand the world we live in and the people we share it with – plus tourism has brought a great deal of **benefit** to developing economies around the world over the last few decades. But the extraordinary growth in tourism has also damaged some places irreparably, and of course **climate change** is exacerbated by most forms of transport, especially flying. This means that now more than ever it's important to **travel thoughtfully** and **responsibly**, with respect for the cultures you're visiting – not only to derive the most benefit from your trip but also to preserve the best bits of the planet for everyone to enjoy. At Rough Guides we feel there are six main areas in which you can make a difference:

- Consider what you're contributing to the **local economy**, and how much the services you use do the same, whether it's through employing local workers and guides or sourcing locally grown produce and local services.
- Consider the **environment** on holiday as well as at home. Water is scarce in many developing destinations, and the biodiversity of local flora and fauna can be adversely affected by tourism. Try to patronize businesses that take account of this.
- Travel with a purpose, not just to tick off experiences. Consider **spending longer** in a place, and getting to know it and its people.
- Give thought to how often you **fly**. Try to avoid short hops by air and more harmful night flights.
- Consider **alternatives to flying**, travelling instead by bus, train, boat and even by bike or on foot where possible.
- Make your trips "**climate neutral**" via a reputable carbon offset scheme. All Rough Guide flights are offset, and every year we donate money to a variety of charities devoted to combating the effects of climate change.

Top tips for 2010

1. Hunt for 'Old Man snapper' in the fabulous Marlborough Sounds.

2. Take a guided walk on a living glacier.

3. Enjoy a wine tour on Clydesdales.

4. Search for NZ's rarest dolphin in Akaroa.

5. Look for the world's largest buttercup at Aoraki/Mount Cook.

6. Experience a wildlife sanctuary in the heart of the Capital.

Experience New Zealand like a local – wherever your travels take you.

We know all the best things to do, places to stay and ways to get there. Plus we'll take care of the bookings. Start with i-SITE today.

Start with i-SITE

www.i-SITE.org.nz

From Australia, there's a huge variety of **package holidays** to New Zealand. For example, Air New Zealand's holiday subsidiary offers short **city-breaks** (flight and accommodation), winter skiing packages and **fly-drive** deals for little more than the cost of the regular air fare; you can build your own package on the website.

From South Africa

Travelling to New Zealand from **South Africa** invariably involves flying via Australia. Qantas flies Johannesburg–Sydney then on to New Zealand. South African Airways operates the same route as a codeshare with Qantas and Air New Zealand. Expect to pay around R17,000–27,000 depending on the season.

Airlines, travel agents and tour operators

If time is limited and you have a clear idea of what you want to do, numerous companies offer **organized tours**, from backpacker excursions to no-expense-spared extravaganzas. Full "see-it-all" packages, with most meals and transport included, can be good value, considering what you'd be spending anyway. Some companies offer tours specifically for those aged 18–35, such as Contiki (UK ⊛www.contiki.co.uk, US ⊛www.contiki.com); or seniors, such as Exploritas (⊛www.exploritas.org); while others are adventure specialists, like UK-based The Adventure Company (⊛www.primeadventures.co.uk) or US-based Adventures Abroad (⊛www.adventures-abroad.com). You can also find tours to suit your interest (such as hiking or kayaking); check with travel agents, newspapers' travel sections or online. For details of **NZ-based tour operators** see p.60.

A number of companies operate **flexible bus tours**, which you can hop off whenever you like and rejoin a day or two later when the next bus comes through (see p.33 for details of these).

Pretty much all the major tour operators can also book you onto **tramping trips**, including some of the guided Great Walks (see p.57); you'll still need to book way in advance, though. For **skiing** trips, the cheapest option is usually to contact ski clubs at the fields directly: check out contact details at ⊛www.snow.co.nz.

Even if an all-in package doesn't appeal, it still may be worth investigating potential savings by pre-booking some accommodation, tours or a rental vehicle.

Airlines

Aerolineas Argentinas ⊛www.aerolineas.com.ar
Air Canada ⊛www.aircanada.com
Air New Zealand ⊛www. airnewzealand.co.nz
American Airlines ⊛www.aa.com
British Airways ⊛www.ba.com
Cathay Pacific ⊛www.cathaypacific.com
Emirates ⊛www.emirates.com
JAL (Japan Airlines) ⊛www.jal.com
Jetstar ⊛www.jetstar.com
Korean Air ⊛www.koreanair.com
LanChile ⊛www.lan.com
Malaysia Airlines ⊛www.malaysiaairlines.com
Pacific Blue ⊛www.flypacificblue.com
Qantas ⊛www.qantas.com.au
Royal Brunei Airlines ⊛www.bruneiair.com
Singapore Airlines ⊛www.singaporeair.com
South African Airways ⊛www.flysaa.com
Thai Airways ⊛www.thaiair.com

Travel agents

Backpackers World Travel Australia ☎1800/676 763, ⊛www.backpackersworld.com.au.
Educational Travel Center US ☎608/256-5551, ⊛www.edtrav.com. Student/youth discount agent.
North South Travel UK ☎01245/608 291, ⊛www.northsouthtravel.co.uk. Friendly, competitive travel agency, offering discounted fares worldwide. Profits are used to support projects in the developing world, especially the promotion of sustainable tourism.
Quest Worldwide UK ☎0845/263 6963, ⊛www.questtravel.com. Specialist in RTW and Australasian discount fares.
STA Travel UK ☎0871/2300 040, US ☎1-800/781-4040, Australia ☎134 782, NZ ☎0800/474 400, South Africa ☎0861/781 781; ⊛www.statravel.co.uk. Worldwide specialists in independent travel; also student IDs, travel insurance, car rental, rail passes, and more. Good discounts for students and under-26s. Experts on NZ travel with branches in major Kiwi cities.
Trailfinders UK ☎0845/058 5858, Ireland ☎01/677 7888, Australia ☎1300/780 212; ⊛www.trailfinders.com. One of the best-informed and most efficient agents for independent travellers.
Travel Cuts Canada ☎1-866/246-9762, US ☎1-800/592-2887; ⊛www.travelcuts.com. Canadian student-travel organization.
USIT Ireland ☎01/602 1906, Northern Ireland ☎028/9032 7111; ⊛www.usit.ie. Ireland's main student and youth travel specialists.

Getting around

New Zealand is a relatively small country and getting around is easy, with some form of public transport going to most destinations, though sometimes limited to one or two services per day. Most out-of-the-way places are accessible with will, flexibility and a little ingenuity.

Internal **flights** are reasonably priced if booked well in advance, but you'll appreciate the scenery better by travelling at ground level. The cheapest and easiest, though slowest, way to get around is by using **buses** (coaches or shuttle buses). The **rail service**, by contrast, is limited and expensive.

For getting off the beaten track having your own wheels is a boon. Rental **cars** and campervans, particularly the little ones (see p.38), can be remarkably good value for two or more people but if you are staying in the country for more than a couple of months, it's more economical to buy a vehicle. New Zealand's green countryside encourages **cyclists**, but even the keenest vary their transport options.

Competition on the **ferries** connecting the North and South islands means passenger fares are good value, though transporting vehicles is pricey. Planes and boats give limited access to offshore islands and the parts of the mainland that remain stubbornly impenetrable by road, though an increase in specialist **tours** makes getting into the wilds easier.

The regularity of long-distance bus, train and plane services are listed under "Travel details" at the end of each chapter, local buses and trains in the main text.

By air

Many visitors fly into Auckland at the beginning of their trip and out from Christchurch at the end, so don't touch **domestic flights**, but those with a tight timetable wanting to hit a few key sights in a short time might be tempted by reasonable-value internal fares.

By far the biggest domestic operator is Air New Zealand, serving all the main centres and numerous minor ones (25 destinations in all). The main competition is from Qantas, which serves Auckland, Wellington, Christchurch, Rotorua and Queenstown and potentially Dunedin, though this last was not confirmed at time of writing. Air New Zealand runs single-class planes with **fares** that come in three levels, offering lower fares for decreased flexibility: there are fewer low-cost fares at popular times. Qantas has a similar system. For example a one-way standard flight between Auckland and Christchurch is about $399, a Flexi Plus around $279 and a Smart Saver as little as $79. Other flights you might take are scenic jaunts from Auckland to Great Barrier Island, the hop over Cook Strait, or the short trip from Invercargill to Stewart Island.

Internal flights

If you decide to use **internal flights**, booking tickets online and well in advance can save you up to fifty percent. It's also worth looking at **air passes** offered by Air New Zealand (@www.airnewzealand.co.nz), including a variety of cheap one-way flights from Auckland and Christchurch to various destinations, if booked at the same time as an international flight. Alternatively, within the "Domestic Booking" section of its website, you can buy one-way tickets to various destinations at Smart Saver or Flexi Plus rates, and create a multi-stop itinerary within New Zealand. Qantas (@www.qantas.com.au) runs similar multi-destination tickets at less favourable rates.

Air companies

Air New Zealand ☏ 0800/737 000, ⊛ www
.airnewzealand.co.nz.
Great Barrier Airlines & Air Coromandel
☏ 0800/900 600, ⊛ www.greatbarrierairlines
.co.nz. Flights between Auckland, Coromandel and
Great Barrier Island.
Fly My Sky ☏ 0800/222 123, ⊛ www.flymysky
.co.nz. Flights between Auckland and Great Barrier
Island.
Qantas ☏ 0800/808 767, ⊛ www.qantas.com.au.
Soundsair ☏ 0800/505 005, ⊛ www.soundsair
.com. Small planes across Cook Strait.
Stewart Island Flights ☏ 03/218 9129, ⊛ www
.stewartislandflights.com. Scheduled services
between Invercargill and Stewart Island.

By bus

You can get most places on long-distance
buses ("coaches") and smaller **shuttle
buses**, which essentially offer the same
service but are more likely to drop you off
and pick up at hotels, hostels and the like.
Services are generally reliable and reasonably comfortable, and stiff competition
keeps prices competitive. The larger buses
are usually air-conditioned, and some have
toilets, though all services stop every couple
of hours, at wayside tearooms and points of
interest along the way. Most of your fellow
passengers are likely to be visitors to New
Zealand so drivers often give a commentary,
the quality of which varies.

InterCity and Newmans

Easily the biggest operator, **InterCity** runs
high-quality full-size buses all over the
country. They operate closely with
Newmans, who pitch themselves as slightly
more luxurious and target sightseeing excursions. In practice, the two companies share a
timetable and InterCity passes can often be
used on Newmans buses: when we refer to
InterCity we are generally referring to services
run collectively by InterCity and Newmans.

As an example, a standard one-way fare
on the North Island, Auckland to Rotorua, is
$59, while on the South Island, Christchurch
to Queenstown, it's $95.

Prices often plummet during off-peak
periods and a range of **discounted fares** is
available, with an advance-purchase Saver
fare yielding a 25-percent **discount** and a
Super Saver fifty-percent. Extreme Saver
and Web Saver fares are also available:
book early for the best prices. YHA, VIP and
BBH cardholders get fifteen-percent
discounts off Standard rates but you'll often
find cheaper deals by chasing down the
various Saver fares.

InterCity also offers numerous fixed-route
passes such as the Auckland, Bay of
Islands Pass, including Cape Reinga ($205,
backpacker $175); Auckland, Rotorua,
Napier via Taupo, Wellington and back
($251, backpacker $226); Nelson to Queenstown via the west coast ($154, backpacker
$139); and various all-NZ experiences (from
$606, backpacker $545).

Other buses

A host of **bus** and **shuttle bus** companies
compete directly with InterCity/Newmans
on the main routes and fill in the gaps
around the country, often linking with the
major operators, to take you off the beaten
track. Generally they cost less (sometimes
appreciably) and are often more obliging

Backpacker buses

One of the cheapest ways to cover a lot of ground is on a **backpacker bus**, which combines some of the flexibility of independent travel with the convenience of a tour. You typically purchase a ticket for a fixed route (usually valid for 12 months), and then take it at your own pace. You can either stick with the one bus for the entire journey with nights spent at various towns along the route, or stop off longer in places and hop on a later bus. During peak times some buses may be full, so you'll need to plan onward travel several days in advance. Most companies operate year-round, though services are reduced in winter.

The emphasis is on **experiencing the country** rather than travelling from one town to the next, so you'll be stopping off to bungy jump, hike or somesuch. Being part of a group of forty rowdy backpackers arriving at some idyllic spot isn't everyone's idea of a good time and, by using assorted public transport, it is often just as cheap to make your own way around New Zealand. But if you want almost everything organized for you, and a ready-made bunch of like-minded fellow travellers this sort of travel has appeal.

It can be 5–10 percent cheaper to **book before you arrive**, as some deals are not available once you step off the plane: check the websites or with your travel agent. You might also save a few dollars by being a YHA, VIP, BBH or ISIC cardholder. Tickets don't generally cover accommodation, activities (although these are often discounted), side trips, food or travel between the North and South islands.

Operators are listed below. For those interested in multi-day tours and adventure activities check out "Outdoor activities" (p.55), where more intimate and specialized excursions are listed.

Flying Kiwi Wilderness Expeditions (Ⓦ www.flyingkiwi.com). Free-spirited operator which gets off the beaten track and eschews city hostels in favour of camping out. Converted buses are equipped with bikes, canoes, windsurfers, kitchen, awning, fridge, beds, tents and hot shower, and everyone mucks in with domestic chores. Trips operate all year and once on board you stick with the same group. Options range from the Northern Express from Wellington to Auckland via Taupo (2 days; $246) to a full NZ tour (27 days; $3159 including food and camping fees).

Kiwi Experience (Ⓦ www.kiwiexperience.com). With a deserved reputation for attracting high-spirited revellers, Kiwi Experience offers a huge array of passes, from a trip to Cape Reinga starting in Auckland (min 3 days; $194) to the Full Monty (minimum 33 days; $2202).

Magic Travellers Network (Ⓦ www.magicbus.co.nz). The king of the backpacker buses, with a comprehensive selection of trips and guaranteed seats if you book at least 24hr in advance. It works with the YHA, offering substantial discounts to YHA cardholders, and targeting more independent-minded travellers. Its Spirit of New Zealand pass is valid for a year and covers the country in 23 travel days ($1291), while the Northern Discovery heads from Auckland to Rotorua, Taupo, Napier, Wellington and Waitomo before returning to Auckland over a minimum of six days ($439).

Stray (Ⓦ www.straytravel.com). Of late, Stray has been attempting to take the mantle of party bus away from Kiwi Experience. Trips typically include a Round South Island (RON) circuit (minimum 17 days; $895) and a basic North Island circuit (minimum 7 days; $510).

when it comes to drop-offs and pick-ups, though seldom as comfortable over distances. We've listed a number of the operators below, but there are many more mentioned in the appropriate sections of the Guide.

Official (i-SITE) visitor centres carry **timetables** of companies operating in their area, so you can compare frequencies and prices. **Fare structures** are generally straightforward, with fixed prices and no complicated discounts. Auckland to Rotorua, on the North Island, will set you back about $29, while on the South Island, Christchurch to Queenstown will be roughly $40.

Main bus companies

Atomic Shuttles ☎03/349 0697, ⓦwww .atomictravel.co.nz. Major long-distance bus operator in the South Island.
ConneXions ☎03/477 5577, ⓦwww.time2 .co.nz. Linking Dunedin, Queenstown, Invercargill and Wanaka.
InterCity & Newmans Auckland call centre ☎09/583 5780, ⓦwww.intercitycoach.co.nz & www.newmanscoach.co.nz. Long-distance buses nationwide.
NakedBus ☎0900/62533 (premium rate), ⓦwww.nakedbus.com. Cheap, frill-free trips on both islands.
Northliner Express ☎09/623 1503, ⓦwww .northliner.co.nz. Bus travel around Northland, owned by InterCity.
Southern Link ☎0508/458 835, ⓦwww .southernlinkcoaches.co.nz. Routes all over the South Island.

By train

Not much is left of New Zealand's passenger train service besides **commuter train** services in Wellington and Auckland and a few inter-city trains. The **long-distance services** that exist are scenic runs, primarily used by tourists; trains are so slow that they have ceased to be practical transport for

New Zealanders. Minimal investment in infrastructure and rolling stock is beginning to have an effect on standards, but railway travel remains a pleasant experience.

Trains have reclining seats, a buffet car with reasonable, good-value food, beer, panoramic windows, and occasionally a glass-backed observation carriage. You also get a sporadic and not particularly diverting commentary. A ticket guarantees a seat: passengers check in on the platform before boarding and bags are carried in a luggage van.

Long-distance trains are all run by **Tranz Scenic** (☎04/495 0775 & 0800/872 467, ⓦwww.tranzscenic.co.nz), which operates three passenger routes. The longest is the *Overlander* **between Auckland and Wellington**, passing through some of the more rural areas of the North Island as well as the scenic Central Plateau with its volcanic peaks. Interesting stops along the way include Te Awamutu, To Kuiti (where the train is met by a shuttle bus to Waitomo Caves) and National Park (with access to Mount Ruapehu and the Tongariro Alpine Crossing). The service leaves both Auckland and Wellington daily around 7.35am and reaches its destination around 7.20pm.

In the South Island, the *TranzCoastal* runs **between Christchurch and Picton**, a pretty run sometimes hugging the coast. It leaves Christchurch at 7am for the run up through

Travel passes

If you're doing a lot of travelling by bus and train, there are savings to be made with travel passes. Tranz Scenic's **Scenic Rail Pass** (ⓦwww.transzscenic.co.nz) gives unlimited travel on Tranz Scenic trains for a week ($409). The pass also includes one Interislander ferry passage between the North and South islands.

InterCity/Newmans offer their own **Flexi-Pass**, allowing you to buy bus travel by the hour – the more hours you buy the better the savings. You would typically need 45 hours ($469) to cover one of the main islands, 60 hours upwards ($605) for a full tour, and if that's not enough you can top-up your pass with, say, 15 hours ($169). The Flexi-Pass is valid for 12 months and journeys can be booked online or by free-calling ☎0800/222 146. Travellers wanting to move around pretty quickly might be better off with one of the **New Zealand Travel Passes** (ⓦwww.travelpass.co.nz) which make extensive use of InterCity and throw in a ferry journey and a few extras ($606, backpacker $545), and for more money, include a train journey and/or a domestic flight.

Finally, the backpacker tour buses (see p.33) offer lower prices in return for older buses and – often – a more boisterous time.

Kaikoura (10am) and Blenheim (11.45pm) to Picton (12.15pm). It then returns from Picton (1pm) through Blenheim (1.30pm), and Kaikoura (3.30pm) to Christchurch (6.20pm).

The finest rail journey in New Zealand is the *TranzAlpine* **between Christchurch and Greymouth** on the West Coast – it is covered in detail on p.513.

Fares are higher than the comparable bus tickets but with discounts and the use of a travel pass (see below), travelling is still reasonably good value. Most people get the standard or **Flexi fare**, which gives a discount in return for advance booking, limited availability and only a fifty-percent refund if cancelled after the departure time. As an example, a standard, one-way ticket from Auckland to Wellington is about $129, from Christchurch to Greymouth around $161. Seniors (60-plus) can get a thirty-percent discount on standard fares, though most folk do better by going for a Scenic Rail Pass (see box, p.34). Blind and some disabled travellers (see p.79) are entitled to a forty percent discount on the standard fare.

Apart from a couple of short-run steam trains, the only other passenger trains are along the **Taieri Gorge Railway** (see p.590) between Dunedin and Middlemarch, again run almost entirely for the benefit of tourists.

By car

For maximum flexibility, it's hard to beat **driving** around New Zealand: you'll be able to get to places beyond the reach of public transport and to set your own timetable. With the freedom to camp or stay in cheaper places away from town centres this is a very economical option for two or more people.

In order to drive in New Zealand you need a valid **licence** from your home country or an International Driver's Licence (available from your national motoring organization). These are valid for up to a year in New Zealand and you must always carry your licence when driving.

In New Zealand you **drive on the left** and will find **road rules** similar to those in the UK, Australia and the US. The one variation peculiar to New Zealand is that you must give way to all traffic crossing or coming from your right; this means that if you are turning left and another car coming from the

opposite direction wants to turn right into the same side road, you must let them go first. There are proposals to abolish this rule, so it may soon no longer apply, but ask before you drive. All occupants must wear **seatbelts** and drivers must park in the same direction as that in which they are travelling.

The **speed limit** for the open road is 100kmph, reduced to 70kmph or 50kmph in built-up areas. Speeding fines start at $30 and rapidly increase as the degree of transgression (speed over the limit) increases. Some drivers flash their headlights at oncoming cars to warn of lurking police patrols but the advent of hidden cameras makes this pointless. **Drink driving** has traditionally been a problem in New Zealand: as part of a campaign to cut the death toll, random breath tests have been introduced and offenders are dealt with severely.

Road conditions are generally good and **traffic** is relatively light except around Auckland and at rush hour in Wellington. Most roads are sealed (paved), although a few have a metalled surface composed of an aggregate of loose chippings. Clearly marked on most maps, these are slower to drive along, prone to washouts and landslides after heavy rain, and demand considerably more care and attention from the driver. Some rental companies prohibit the use of their cars on the worst metalled roads – typically those at Skippers Canyon and around the northern tip of Coromandel Peninsula. Always check conditions locally before setting off on these routes.

Other **hazards** include one-lane bridges: a sign before the bridge will indicate who has right of way, and on longer examples there'll be a passing place halfway across. Even on relatively major roads you might also come across **flocks of sheep**, slow-moving farm equipment and monstrous logging trucks, all made more of a nuisance by the paucity of passing lanes.

Unleaded and super unleaded **petrol** and diesel are available in New Zealand and in larger towns petrol stations are open 24hr. In smaller towns, they may close after 8pm, so be sure to fill up for long evening or night journeys. At publication, prices were hovering around $1.65 a litre for unleaded, $1.85 for super unleaded, and $1.09 for diesel, with higher prices in more out-of-the-way places.

If you're driving your own vehicle, check if the **New Zealand Automobile Association** (ⓦwww.nzaa.co.nz) has reciprocal rights with motoring organizations from your country to see if you qualify for their cover; otherwise, you can join as an overseas visitor. Apart from a free 24hr **emergency breakdown service** (ⓣ0800/500 222) – excluding vehicles bogged on beaches – membership entitles you to free maps, accommodation guides and legal assistance, discounts on some rental cars and accommodation, plus access to insurance and pre-purchase vehicle inspection services.

Car rental

Visitors driving around New Zealand typically pick up a car in Auckland, tour the North Island to Wellington where they leave the first vehicle, cross Cook Strait, pick up a second car in Picton, then drive around the South Island dropping off the car in Christchurch. The whole thing can be done in reverse, and may work out cheaper.

New Zealand is awash with companies wanting to rent you a car. You'll even see deals for under $30 a day, though only for

older, small cars rented for over a month in winter (June–Aug). Demand is high over the main summer season and prices rise accordingly.

Most of the **major international companies** – Avis, Budget, Hertz, National, Thrifty, etc – are represented here and offer good deals for virtually new cars. **Nationwide firms** offer cheaper rates partly by minimizing overheads and offering older (but perfectly serviceable) vehicles. You may find even cheaper deals with cut-rate local companies, which are fine for short stints, though for general touring nationwide companies are probably the best bet. Their infrastructure helps when it comes to crossing between the North and South islands (see p.401) and they typically offer free breakdown assistance.

In peak season it usually pays to have a car **booked in advance**. At quieter times you can often pick up something cheaper once you arrive; and in winter (except in ski areas) you can almost name your price. Provided your rental period is four days or more the deal will be for **unlimited kilometres**. The rates quoted below are for summer season assuming a two-week rental period, but don't be afraid to haggle at any time.

As a general rule, Ace, Apex, Omega and Pegasus offer reasonably new cars at moderate prices, while the rest of the NZ companies listed below try desperately to undercut each other and offer **low prices**.

Based on a two-week rental in summer, for two people a **small car** (1.3–1.8 litre) might cost $50–70 a day from the majors, $30–60 from national firms. For those requiring a little more comfort, or needing to fit in the kids, a **medium-sized car** (2–3 litre) would be more appropriate. This might cost $80–90 from the majors and $40–80 from national companies. Unless you're here in winter and want to get up to the ski-fields without tyre chains you don't really need a **4WD**, which generally costs $90–130 a day; you'll be better off renting one for short trips in specific areas.

If you are renting for several weeks, there is often no **drop-off fee** for leaving the vehicle somewhere other than where you picked it up. For shorter rental periods you may be charged $150–300, though if you're

travelling south to north, you may be able to sweet-talk your way out of drop-off charges. At different times in the season Wellington, Picton, Christchurch and Queenstown have a glut of cars that are needed elsewhere, and companies will offer **relocation deals**. Look at hostel notice boards, call the firms listed below or phone around companies listed under "Rental Cars" in the Yellow Pages. Some companies want quick delivery, while others will allow you to spend a few more days en route for a reduced rental rate.

Before signing on the dotted line you must have a full, clean **driver's licence** and be over 21; drivers under 25 often pay more for insurance. In most cases insurance is included in the quoted cost but you are liable for any windscreen damage and the first $1000 of any damage. With some of the cheaper companies this excess can be as much as $3000 if the accident is your fault. This can usually be reduced to $250 or zero by paying an additional $10–20 a day Collision Damage Waiver. Usually before giving you a car rental companies take a credit-card imprint or a cash bond from you for $1000. If you have an accident, the bond is used to pay for any damage: in some cases you can pay anything up to the value of the bond; in others you pay the entire bond no matter how slight the damage. Read the small print, look around the car for any visible **defects**, so you won't end up being charged for someone else's mistakes, and check whether there are any restrictions on driving along certain roads.

New Zealand car-rental agencies

A2B Rentals ☏ 0800/616 888, ⊛ www .a2brentals.co.nz.
Ace Rental Cars ☏ 0800/502 277, ⊛ www .acerentalcars.co.nz.
Apex ☏ 0800/939 597, ⊛ www.apexrentals.co.nz.
Bargain Rental Cars ☏ 0800/001 122 ⊛ www .bargainrentals.co.nz.
Jucy ☏ 0800/399 736, ⊛ www.jucy.co.nz
Omega ☏ 0800/525 210, ⊛ www .omegarentalcars.com.
Pegasus ☏ 0800/803 580, ⊛ www.rentalcars.co.nz.

Campervan rental

Throughout the summer, NZ roads seem clogged with **campervans** (small motorhomes). Almost all are driven by foreign visitors who rent them for a few weeks and drive around the country staying in campsites and rest areas (see box below). A small campervan is generally suitable for two adults and perhaps a couple of kids and comes with a fold-down bed and compact kitchen. Larger models sleep four or more and often have a shower and toilet.

Medium to large **campervan rentals** (based on a 3-week rental) average about $200–350 a day during the high season (Dec–Feb), dropping a little for a couple of months either side and plummeting to $150 in winter. The two biggest rental firms are Maui and Britz

(effectively the same company), but a few smaller firms (listed on p.39) offer cheaper rates, saving 20–30 percent.

Small vans are often quite cramped and aimed at backpackers prepared to sacrifice comfort to save money. These typically cost $95 a day during summer, $85 in the shoulder season and $65 in the depths of winter. The current trend is for wildly painted vans, often with arcane, quirky or downright offensive comments graffitied on them: witness Escape Rentals and Wicked Campers. Other good bets are the distinctive orange Spaceships that have been imaginatively converted to suit two adults, possibly more if you're very friendly. For an affordable and slightly offbeat experience go for a restored, classic VW campervan (possibly with a pop-top), from Auckland-based Kiwi Kombis, who charge $150–250 a day, depending on dates and van.

For all campervans there's usually a minimum rental period of 5–7 days, but you get unlimited kilometres, a kitchen kit and perhaps airport transfer. Insurance is often included but you may be liable for the first $1000–5000 and you should seriously consider paying extra fees to get this liability reduced. Most companies have a supply of tents, camping kits, outdoor chairs and tables that can be rented for a few dollars.

No special **licence** is required to drive a campervan, but some caution is needed, especially in high winds and when climbing hills and going around tight corners. Finally, have some consideration for other road users and pull over to let folk pass wherever possible.

Campervan rentals: medium to large

Adventure ☏ 0800/123 555; ⊛ www .nzmotorhomes.co.nz.

Camp clean

One of the pleasures of driving a campervan around New Zealand is the ability to sneak the odd free night in wayside rest areas. This is not strictly legal, but rules have rarely been enforced. However, with increased abuse of this privilege and indiscriminate littering, authorities are cracking down, particularly on smaller campervans with no on board toilet. Consult ⊛ www.camping.org.nz for guidelines on freedom camping, and ask advice from locals. Most of all, be considerate and don't ruin things for those yet to experience New Zealand's beauty.

Backpacker Campervans ☎ 800/200 80801, ⊛ www.backpackercampervans.com.
Britz ☎ 0800/831 900, ⊛ www.britz.com.
Escape ☎ 0800/216 171, ⊛ www.escaperentals.co.nz.
Eurocampers ☎ 0800/489 226, ⊛ www.eurocampers.co.nz.
Freedom Campers ☎ 0800/325 939, ⊛ www.freedomcampers.co.nz.
Jucy (see p.38)
Kea Campers ☎ 0800/520 052, ⊛ www.keacampers.com.
Maui ☎ 0800/651 080, ⊛ www.maui.co.nz

Small vans and conversions

Backpackers Transport ☎ 0800/226 769, ⊛ www.backpackernz.co.nz.
Escape ☎ 0800/216 171, ⊛ www.escaperentals.co.nz.
Ezy ☎ 0800/399 736, ⊛ www.ezy.co.nz.
Kiwi Kombis ☎ 09/533 9335, ⊛ www.kiwikombis.com.
Spaceships ☎ 0800/772 237, ⊛ www.spaceshipsrentals.co.nz.
Wicked Campers ☎ 0800/246 869, ⊛ www.wickedcampers.com.au.

Buying a used vehicle

Buying a **used vehicle** can be cost-effective if you are staying in the country for more than a couple of months. Reselling can recoup enough of the price to make it cheaper than using public transport or renting. Of course, if you buy cheap there's also a greater risk of breakdowns and expensive repairs. The majority of people buy cars in Auckland and then try to sell them in Christchurch, so there's something to be said for buying in Christchurch where you'll often have more choice and a better bargaining position.

Some of the best deals are found on backpacker **hostel notice boards** where older cars and vans are typically offered for $500–4000. Realistically you can expect to pay upwards of $2500 for something half-decent. It may not look pretty and with a **private sale** there's no guarantee the vehicle will make yet another trip around the country, but you might get an added bonus like camping gear thrown in with the car (or offered at a snip). Alternatively, trawl the used-car ads in local papers.

For a little more peace of mind, buy from a **dealership**. There are plenty all over the country, especially in Auckland, Christchurch and Wellington. Prices begin at around $5000 and some yards offer a **buy-back service**, usually paying about fifty percent of the purchase price. If you're confident of your ability to spot a lemon, you can try to pick up a cheap car at an **auction**; they're held weekly in Auckland (see p.122), and Christchurch and are advertised in the local press. Be aware that you'll usually be liable for the **buyer's premium** of ten percent over your bid.

Before you commit yourself, consult the vehicle ownership section of the NZ Transport Agency website (⊛ www.nzta.govt.nz), which has good advice on buying and the pitfalls. The *Buying a used car* factsheet is particularly helpful.

Unless you really know your big end from your steering column you'll want to arrange a mobile **vehicle inspection**, either from the AA (☎ 0800/500 333, ⊛ www.aa.co.nz; members $140, non-members $165), or the equally competitive Car Inspection Services (☎ 0800/500 800 in Auckland and Wellington, ⊛ www.carinspections.co.nz). The inspection may give you enough ammunition to negotiate a price reduction. Finally, before you close a private sale, call AA LemonCheck (☎ 0800/500 333, ⊛ www.aalemoncheck.co.nz) – its staff will fill you in on registration history, possible odometer tampering and any debts on the vehicle ($20 members, $25 non-members).

Before they're allowed on the road, all vehicles must have a **Warrant of Fitness** (WOF), which is a test of its mechanical worthiness and safety. WOFs are carried out and issued by specified garages and testing stations and last for a year if the vehicle is less than six years old, or six months if older. Check the expiry date, as the test must have been carried out no more than one month before sale. The vehicle should also have a current **vehicle licence,** which must be renewed before it expires (6 months $128, 12 months $248 for petrol-driven, private vehicles): post offices and AA offices are the most convenient for this though you can also do it online at ⊛ www.nzta.govt.nz.

You **transfer ownership** with a form (filled in by buyer and seller) at a post office: the licence plates stay with the vehicle. Next you'll need **insurance**, either Comprehensive (which covers your vehicle and any other damaged vehicles) or Third Party, Fire & Theft (which covers your own vehicle against fire and theft, but only pays out on damage to other vehicles in case of an accident). There are dozens of companies listed under "Insurance Companies" in the Yellow Pages: shop around as prices vary widely, but expect to pay, a minimum of $400 for six months' Third Party, Fire & Theft cover.

By motorbike

Visitors from most countries can ride in New Zealand with their normal licence, though it (or your international licence) must specify motorbikes. Helmets are compulsory, and you'll need to be prepared to ride on gravel roads from time to time.

Few people bring their own bike but **bike rental** is available from the companies running guided bike tours (see below). It isn't cheap, and for a 650cc machine in summer you can expect to pay $170–250 a day. Bike Adventure New Zealand (☎0800/498 600, ⓦwww.bikeadventure.co.nz) offers 600cc enduro machines for $95 per day for short periods, dropping to $55 per day for ten weeks. Alternatively, try the same channels as for "Buying a used vehicle" on p.39.

Motorbike tours

The obvious alternative is an organized **tour**, self-guided or guided, usually incorporating top-of-the-range accommodation, restaurants and bikes.
Adventure New Zealand Motorcycle Tours & Rentals ⓦwww.gotournz.com. Nelson-based company providing upmarket, small-group guided or self-guided tours around the South Island, with itineraries tweaked to suit and a luxury coach in your wake. Rates start at $7200 for a standard 10-day trip on a relatively modest bike.
New Zealand Motorcycle Rentals & Tours ⓦwww.nzbike.com. Another specialist top-end company, offering guided all-inclusive tours staying in quality accommodation, semi-guided tours and bike rental. A fully guided 13-day tour will set you back about $9000.
Te Waipounamu Motorcycle Hire & Tours ⓦwww.motorcycle-hire.co.nz. These folk do upscale

tours round the bottom of the South Island and bike rentals including Beamers at $250/day in the high season.

Cycling

If you have bags of time, **cycling** is an excellent way of getting around. Distances aren't enormous, the weather is generally benign, traffic is light, and the countryside is gorgeous. Everywhere you go you'll find hostels and campsites well set up for campers but also equipped with rooms and cabins for when the weather really sucks.

But there are downsides. New Zealand's road network is skeletal, so in many places you'll find yourself riding on main roads or unsealed minor roads. You'll also experience a fair bit of rain and have to climb quite a lot of hills.

Contrary to what you might think, cycling the **South Island** is an easier proposition than the **North Island**. The South Island's alpine backbone presents virtually the only geographical barrier, while the eastern two-thirds of the island comprise a flat plain. In the North Island you can barely go 10km without encountering significant hills – and you have to contend with a great deal more traffic, including intimidating logging trucks.

New Zealand law requires all cyclists to wear a **helmet**. Some **fitness** is important, but distances don't have to be great and you can take things at your own pace. If you'd rather go with a **guided group**, see our recommendations on p.61.

For more **information** get the *Pedallers' Paradise* guides (ⓦwww.paradise-press .co.nz) or Bruce Ringer's *New Zealand by Bike* (see Contexts, p.803).

The bike

Since the vast majority of riding will be on sealed roads with only relatively short sections of gravel, it is perfectly reasonable (and more efficient) to get around New Zealand on a touring bike. But fashion dictates most people use a **mountain bike** fitted with fat but relatively smooth tyres.

On long trips it's cheaper to **bring your own bike**, set up to your liking before you leave home. Most international airlines simply count bikes as a piece of luggage and don't incur any extra cost as long as you don't exceed your baggage limit. However, they do require you use a **bike bag** or box, or at the very least remove pedals and handlebars and wrap the chain. Some airlines will sell you a cardboard bike box at the airport, though your friendly local bike dealer may give you one free. Soft bags are probably the most convenient (they're easy to carry on the bike once you arrive), but if you are flying out from the same city you arrive in you can often store hardshell containers (free or for a small fee) at the backpacker hostel where you spend your first and last nights: call around.

Renting bikes for more than the odd day can be an expensive option, costing anything from $30–50 a day, depending on whether you want a bike with little more than pedals and brakes, a tourer or state-of-the-art mountain bike. Specialist cycle shops do more economical monthly rentals for around $200–250 for a tourer and $300 or more for a full-suspension superbike.

For long-distance cycle touring, it's generally cheaper to **buy a bike**. You're probably looking at paying at least $1000 to get fully kitted out with new equipment, but it is worth checking hostel notice boards for **secondhand bikes** (under $500 is a reasonable deal), often accompanied by extras like wet-weather gear, lights, a helmet and a pump. Some cycle shops offer **buy-back deals**, where you buy at full price and they guarantee to refund about fifty percent of the purchase price at the end of your trip – contact Adventure Cycles, 9 Premier Ave, Western Springs, in Auckland (℡09/940 2453, ⓦwww.adventure-auckland.co.nz /adventurecycles.html). If you're bringing your own bike, the same folk will let you store the bike box you transported your machine in, help organize an emergency

package of spare parts and extra clothing to be forwarded at your request, and give your bike a once-over before you set off, all for around $45. The best bet for servicing and spares in Christchurch is Laurie Dawe Cycles, 838 Colombo St (℡021/366 5639).

Transporting bikes

Lethargy, boredom, breakdowns or simply a need to shift your bike between islands mean you'll need to use **public transport** at some point. You can usually hoick your bike onto a bus (generally $10–15) or train ($10–20 per journey) though space is often limited so book well in advance. Crossing Cook Strait, the Interislander and Blue Bridge ferries charge $10–20.

Bikes usually travel free on buses, trains and ferries if packed in a bike bag and treated as ordinary luggage. Air New Zealand will fly your bike free if it is within your baggage allowance; Qantas will charge you at its normal excess baggage rate, though that doesn't cut into your free allowance.

By ferry

The **ferries** you're most likely to use are vehicle-carrying services plying Cook Strait between Wellington on the North Island and Picton on the South Island. Details are given in the "Crossing Cook Strait" box on p.401.

Passenger ferries link Bluff, in the south of the South Island, to Stewart Island, and both vehicle and passenger ferries connect Auckland with the Hauraki Gulf islands, principally Waiheke, Rangitoto and Great Barrier. Information about these short trips is included in our accounts of Invercargill and Auckland. Most visitors spend more boat time on cruises – whale watching, dolphin swimming, sightseeing – or **water taxis**.

Accommodation

Accommodation will take up a fair chunk of your money while in New Zealand, but the good news is that standards across all categories are excellent. Almost every town has a motel or hostel of some description, so finding accommodation is seldom a problem – though it's essential to book in advance during high summer (from Christmas through to the end of January) and advisable a month or two either side.

Kiwis travel widely at home, most choosing to self-cater at the country's huge number of well-equipped **campsites** (aka motor camps or holiday parks) and **motels**, shunning **hotels**, which cater mainly to package holiday-makers and the business community. The range of **B&Bs**, **homestays**, **farmstays** and **lodges** form an appealing alternative, covering the whole spectrum from a room in someone's suburban home to pampered luxury in a country mansion.

Since the mid-1980s, New Zealand has pioneered the **backpacker hostel**, a less-regimented alternative to traditional YHAs, which have transformed themselves dramatically to compete. Found all over the country, hostels offer superb value to budget travellers.

Wherever you stay, you can expect unstinting hospitality and a truckload of valuable advice on local activities and onward travel. We've included a wide selection of New Zealand's best accommodation throughout the book, and more detail can be gleaned from specialist accommodation guides.

Many places are now accredited using the nationwide **Qualmark** system (ⓦwww .qualmark.co.nz), which grades different types of accommodation – exclusive, hotel, self-contained, guest and hosted, holiday parks and backpackers – from one to five stars. Most fall between three stars (very good) and four plus (at the top end of excellent), but there is no way of knowing whether, for example, a four-star backpacker is superior to rooms at a five-star holiday park. Many places choose not to join the system, but may be just as good or better.

Useful accommodation guides and websites

AA Accommodation Guide ⓦwww.aatravel .co.nz. Annual advertising-based guide for the whole country; concentrates mostly on motels and holiday parks. Available free from most motels and i-SITE offices.
The Bed & Breakfast Book ⓦwww.bnb.co.nz. Annually updated listing of member B&Bs, boutique lodges, homestays and farmstays, covering around 1000 places all over NZ. Entries are submitted by the owners, so it's a good idea to read between the lines. Nominally $20 (plus $10 for international postage) but often much cheaper.

Booking accommodation

You should **book accommodation** at major towns and popular tourist locales at least a few days in advance from December to March. Reserving several weeks ahead is a good idea if you're particular about where you stay. Most Kiwis take two to three weeks off from Christmas onwards, so from **December 26 to mid-January** anywhere near a nice beach or lake is likely to be packed, particularly holiday parks (campsites) and motels, which usually rack up their prices considerably during this period. Places that don't attract Kiwi holiday-makers can be relatively peaceful at this time. Towns near **ski resorts** are typically busiest between July and September, particularly on weekends and during school holidays.

Accommodation price codes

Accommodation listed in this guide has been categorized into one of nine **price bands**. The rates quoted represent the cheapest available double or twin room in high season, though we have generally ignored the short spike in prices around Christmas and New Year. Single rooms usually cost only ten to twenty percent less than doubles or twins, In hostels and campsites where individual dorm beds are available, we have given the full price assuming no discount cards. YHA members get a $3 discount at full YHAs, BBH members typically save $3 at BBH-affiliated establishments and VIP cardholders save $1 a night. DOC hut and camping fees are also per person, unless otherwise stated.

Prices normally include Goods and Services Tax (GST), as do our codes.

❶ $59 and under	❹ $100–129	❼ $200–249
❷ $60–79	❺ $130–159	❽ $250–349
❸ $80–99	❻ $160–199	❾ $350 and over

Charming Bed & Breakfast ⓦ www.bnbnz.com. Glossy B&B guide concentrating on mid-range places. Available through its website for the price of postage and can often be picked up free at B&Bs.

House rental Many Kiwis own a holiday home (aka *bach* or *crib*) which they rent out when they're not using them. Some are in superb locations next to beaches but you'll often have to agree to a minimum stay (perhaps 4 nights). Rates vary enormously, peaking around Christmas (when availability is scarce) and plummeting in winter. Sites to check out include ⓦ www.bookabach.co.nz and www.holidayhouses.co.nz.

Hotels and motels

In New Zealand, **hotel** is a term frequently used to describe old-style pubs, once legally obliged to provide rooms for drinkers to recuperate. Many no longer provide accommodation, but some have transformed themselves into backpacker hostels, while others are dedicated to preserving the tradition. At their best, such hotels (❸–❹) offer comfortable rooms in characterful, historic buildings, though just as often lodgings are rudimentary. Hotel bars are frequently at the centre of small-town life and at weekends in particular can be pretty raucous, so you may find a budget room at a hostel a better bet.

In the cities and major resorts, you'll also come across hotels in the conventional sense, predominantly business- or tour bus-oriented places (❻–❾). Priced accordingly, they're seldom good value, though at quiet times and weekends there can be substantial discounts; it's always worth asking.

Most Kiwi families on the move prefer the astonishingly well-equipped **motels** (❹–❻), which congregate along the roads running into town, making them more convenient for drivers than for those using trains or buses. They usually come with Sky TV, bathroom, some sort of kitchen and tea and coffee, but are often fairly functional concrete-block places with little to distinguish one from another. Rooms range from all-in-one **studios**, with beds, kettle, toaster and a microwave, through **one-bedroom units**, usually with a full and separate kitchen, to two- and three-**bedroom suites**, sleeping six or eight. Suites generally go for the same basic price as a one-bedroom unit, with each additional adult paying $15–25, making them an economical choice for groups travelling together. Anything calling itself a **motor inn** (❺–❼) or similar will be quite luxurious, with a bar, restaurant, swimming pool and sauna but no cooking facilities.

B&Bs, lodges and boutique hotels

While families might prefer the freedom and adaptability of a motel, couples are generally better served by a **bed and breakfast** (B&B; ❸–❾). This might be a simple room with a bathroom down the hall and a modest continental breakfast included in the price. But the term also encompasses luxurious colonial homes with well-furnished en-suite rooms and sumptuous home-cooked breakfasts. Those at the top end are now

43

NZ Backpacker Accommodation

To order a free guide to 325+ backpacker hostels visit

www.bbh.co.nz

fashioning themselves as lodges, boutique hotels and "**exclusive retreats**" (❼–❾), where standards of service and comfort reach extraordinary levels, with prices to match.

Rates drop in the low season, when these places can often be good value. If you're travelling alone and don't fancy hostels, B&Bs can also be a viable alternative, usually charging **lone travellers** 60–80 percent of the double room rate, though some only ask fifty percent.

Homestays and farmstays

Homestays (❹–❺) usually offer a guest room or two in an ordinary house where you muck in with the owners and join them for breakfast the following morning. Staying in such places can be an excellent way to meet ordinary New Zealanders; you'll be well looked after, sometimes to the point of being overwhelmed by your hosts' generosity. It is courteous to **call in advance**, and bear in mind you'll usually have to **pay in cash**. Rural versions often operate as **farmstays** (❹–❺), where you're encouraged to stay a couple of

nights and are welcome to spend the intervening day trying your hand at farm tasks: rounding up sheep, milking cows, fencing, whatever might need doing. Both homestays and farmstays charge for a double room, including breakfast; some cook dinner on request for $25–75 per person, and you may pay a small fee for lunch if you spend the day at the farm or for a packed lunch.

Hostels, backpackers and YHAs

New Zealand has over four hundred budget and self-catering places, pretty much interchangeably known as **hostels** or **backpackers** (❶–❸) and offering a dorm bed or bunk for around $21–30. They're often in superb locations – bang in the centre of town, beside the beach, close to a ski-field or amid magnificent scenery in a national or forest park – and are great places to meet other travellers and pick up local information. Backpacker hostels range in size from as few as four beds up to huge premises accommodating several hundred. Virtually wherever you stay you'll find a fully equipped kitchen, laundry, TV and games room, a travellers' notice board, and a stack of tourist information. Beds are generally fully made up; you should bring your own towel, though you can rent one for a few dollars. **Internet access** (typically a coin-op booth, and increasingly wi-fi) is now pretty standard, though a few rural places intentionally eschew such mod cons. Depending on the area, there may be a pool, barbecue, bike and/or canoe rental and information on local work opportunities. For **security**, many places offer cupboards for your gear, though you'll usually need your own lock. Almost all NZ hostels are affiliated with local and international organizations that offer **accommodation discounts** to members, along with an array of other travel- and activity-related savings.

Some hostels allow you to pitch a tent in the grounds and use the facilities for around $17 a person, but generally the most basic and cheapest accommodation is in a six- to twelve-bunk **dorm** ($21–27), with three- and four-bed rooms (also known as three-shares and four-shares) usually priced a couple of dollars higher. Most hostels also have **double**, **twin** and **family rooms** (❶–❷ for two), the more expensive ones with en-suite bathrooms. Lone travellers who don't fancy a dorm can sometimes get a **single room** for around $35, and many larger places (especially YHAs and Base backpackers) also offer **women-only dorms**.

Around sixty places are classified as **YHA hostels** or associate YHA hostels (@www .yha.co.nz), which, unlike their European counterparts, have abandoned lock-outs, curfews and arcane opening hours, but maintain a predominance of single-sex dorms. Newer hostels have been purpose-built to reflect the YHA's environmental concerns, promoting recycling and energy conservation. YHA and associate YHA hostels are listed on the annual *YHA Backpacker Map* and in the eight regional guides (all free from hostels and organization offices). You should obtain a **Hostelling International Card** in your own country (see above for contact details), but you can buy a $40 annual membership in NZ, which includes a phonecard loaded with around $14 of free calling time. Non-members can pay the additional $3 rate per night. The rest of the hostels are affiliated **associate hostels**, where no membership card is required, though there is often a discount of a dollar or so for members. YHAs request that you don't use your own sleeping bag to avoid bed bugs and the like. You can book ahead either from another hostel or through the YHA National Reservations Centre and through Hostelling International offices in your home country.

YHAs are outnumbered by around six-to-one by other **backpacker hostels**, where the atmosphere is more variable; some are friendly and relaxed, others more party-oriented. Many are aligned with the NZ-based **Budget Backpacker Hostels**, and are listed (along with current prices) in the *BBH Accommodation Guide* (@www .bbh.co.nz), widely available from hostels and visitor centres. The entries are written by the hostels and don't pretend to be impartial. Anyone can stay at BBH hostels, but savings can be made by buying a BBH Club Card ($45), which generally saves the holder $3 on each night's stay in either a dorm or a room. Cards are available from BBH and all participating hostels, and each

card doubles as a rechargeable phonecard loaded with $20 worth of calling time.

Over seventy hostels are members of **VIP Backpacker Resorts** (@www.vip .co.nz), an umbrella organization that offers a dollar off each night's stay to people with a VIP Discount Card ($43, valid in NZ, at VIP hostels worldwide).

For advice on backcountry camping and trampers' huts, see the "Outdoor activities" section on p.55.

Holiday parks, campsites and cabins

New Zealand has some of the world's best **camping** facilities, and even if you've never camped before, you may well find yourself using **holiday parks** (❶–❺; also known as **motor camps**), which are geared for families on holiday, with space to pitch tents, powered sites (or hook-ups) for campervans and usually a broad range of dorms, cabins and motel units. You'll find more down-to-earth camping at wonderfully located DOC sites.

Camping is largely a summer activity (Nov–May), especially in the South Island. At worst, New Zealand can be very wet, windy and plagued by voracious winged **insects**, so the first priority for tent campers is good-quality gear with a fly sheet which will repel the worst that the elements can dish out, and an inner tent with bug-proof ventilation for hot mornings.

Busy times at motor camps fall into line with the school holidays, making Easter and the summer period from Christmas to the end of January the most hectic. Make **reservations** as far in advance as possible at this time, and a day or two before you arrive through February and March. DOC sites are not generally bookable, and while this is no problem through most of the year, Christmas can be a mad free-for-all.

See p.38 for information about responsible overnight stops outside official areas.

Campsites and cabins

Campsites are typically located on the outskirts of towns and are invariably well equipped, with a communal kitchen, TV lounge, games area, laundry and sometimes a swimming pool; non-residents can often get showers for around $2–5. **Campers** usually get the quietest and most sylvan corner of the site and are charged around $10–15 per person; camping prices throughout the Guide are per person unless followed by "per site". There is often no distinction between tent pitches and the **powered sites** set aside for campervans, but the latter usually cost an extra few dollars per person for the use of power hook-ups and dump stations.

In addition, most campsites have some form of on-site accommodation: the basic dorm-style **lodge** ($15–25/person); **standard cabins** (❶–❷ for two, plus $10 for each extra person), often little more than a shed with bunks; larger, fully equipped cabins variously known as **kitchen cabins**, tourist cabins or self-contained (s/c) cabins (❷, plus $15/extra person) have cooking facilities; and if you step up to **tourist flats** (❸ for two, plus $15/extra person), you also get your own bathroom. The flasher places also have self-contained **motel units** (❹–❺ for two, plus $15–20/extra person), usually with a separate bedroom and a TV. Cabins and units generally sleep two to four, but motor camps often have at least one place sleeping six or eight. **Sheets** and **towels** are rarely included, so bring a sleeping bag or be prepared to pay to rent bed linen (typically $5–10). Sometimes pans and plates can be borrowed after handing over a small deposit, though for longer stays it is worth bringing your own.

Campsites are independently run but some have now aligned themselves with nationwide organizations which set minimum standards. Look out for **Top 10** sites (🌐www.top10.co.nz), which maintain a reliably high standard in return for slightly higher prices. By purchasing a $40 club card you save ten percent on each night's stay and get local discounts; the card (valid 2 years) is transferable to Australia.

DOC campsites

Few holiday parks can match the idyllic locations of the several hundred **campsites** operated by the **Department of Conservation** (DOC; 🌐www.doc.govt.nz) in national parks, reserves, maritime and forest parks, the majority beautifully set by sweeping beaches or deep in the bush. This is back-to-nature camping, low-cost and with simple **facilities**, though sites almost always have running water and toilets of some sort. Listed in DOC's free *Conservation Campsites* leaflet (available from DOC offices), the sites fall into one of three categories: **informal** (free), often with nothing but a water supply; the more common **standard** ($6–10, typically $6), all with vehicular access and many with barbecues, fireplaces, picnic tables and refuse collection; and rare **serviced** ($15), which are similar in scope to the regular motor camps. Children aged 5–15 are charged 25–50 percent off the adult price, and only the serviced sites can be booked in advance.

Food and drink

Forget preconceptions about "slam in the lamb" Kiwi cuisine with pavlova for dessert. New Zealand's food scene is brilliant – in terms of the quality of the food, its cooking, presentation and the places where it's served.

Kiwi **gastronomy** has its roots in the British culinary tradition, an unfortunate heritage that still informs cooking patterns for older New Zealanders and occasionally rears its ugly head in some farmstays and guest-houses. Indeed, it is only in the last 25 years or so that New Zealand's chefs have really woken up to the possibilities presented by a fabulous larder of super-fresh, top-quality ingredients, formulating what might be termed **Modern Kiwi** cuisine. Taking its culinary cues from Californian and contemporary Australian cooking, it combines traditional elements such as steak, salmon and crayfish with flavours drawn from the **Mediterranean**, **Asia** and the **Pacific Rim**: sun-dried tomatoes, lemongrass, basil, ginger, coconut, and many more. Restaurateurs feel duty-bound to fill their menu with as broad a spectrum as possible, lining up seafood linguini, couscous, sushi, Thai venison meatballs and a chicken korma alongside the rack of lamb and gourmet pizza. Sometimes this causes gastronomic overload, but often it is simply mouthwatering.

Meat and fish

New Zealanders have a taste for **meat**, the quality of which is superb, with New Zealand lamb often at the head of the menu (due to traveller expectation) but matched in flavour by venison and beef.

With the country's extensive coastline, it's no surprise that **fish** and seafood loom large. The white, flaky flesh of the snapper is the most common saltwater fish, but you'll also come across tuna, John Dory, groper (often known by its Maori name of *hapuku*), flounder, blue cod and the firm, delicately flavoured *terakihi*. Salmon is common, but not trout, which cannot be bought or sold (an archaic law originally intended to protect

sport fishing when trout were introduced to NZ in the nineteenth century), though most hotels and restaurants will cook one if you've caught it. All are also very tasty smoked, though *terakihi*, *hapuku*, blue cod, marlin and smoked eel take some beating.

One much-loved delicacy is whitebait, a tiny silvery fish mostly caught on the West Coast and eaten whole in fritters during the August to November season.

Shellfish are a real NZ speciality. The king of them all is the *toheroa*, a type of clam dug from the sands of Ninety Mile Beach on the rare occasions when numbers reach harvestable levels. They are usually made into soups and are sometimes replaced by the inferior and sweeter *tuatua*, also dug from Northland beaches. On menus you're more likely to come across the fabulous Bluff oysters, scallops and sensational green-lipped mussels, which have a flavour and texture that's hard to beat and are farmed in the cool clear waters of the Marlborough Sounds, especially around Havelock. Crayfish is also available round the coast and should be sought out, particularly when touring Kaikoura and the East Cape.

Fruit, vegetables and dairy produce

New Zealand's **fruit** is a winner, especially at harvest time when stalls line the roadsides selling apples, pears, citrus and stone fruits for next to nothing. Top-quality fruit and dairy products are the starting point for delicious desserts, traditionally variations on the themes of ice cream, cheesecake and pavlova, though today supplemented by rich cakes and modern twists on British-style steamed puddings.

Vegetables are generally fresh and delicious. British favourites such as potatoes, carrots, peas and cabbage, along with pumpkin and squash, are common in Kiwi homes but on restaurant menus you're far more likely to encounter aubergines (eggplant), capsicums (bell peppers) and tomatoes. Pacific staples to look out for are *kumara* (sweet potato), which crops up in *hangi* and deep-fried as *kumara* chips. A delicious crossover point between fruit and vegetables is carrot cake, which comes in many variations; Kiwis have a passion for it and most cafés and restaurants offer up their own special take on it.

New Zealanders eat a lot of **dairy**. Small producers, particularly around the Kapiti Coast (north of Wellington), Blenheim and Banks Peninsula (east of Christchurch), turn out some gorgeous, if expensive cheeses, from traditional hard cheddar styles to creamy blues, via spicy pepper bries. Basic supermarket cheeses tend to be bland so head for the deli counter and get cheese from local specialists. Delicious ice cream of the firm, scooped variety is something of a NZ institution, and is available in a vast range of flavours, including intensely fruity ones and the indulgent hokey pokey – vanilla ice cream riddled with chunks of caramel.

Vegetarian food

The abundance of fresh vegetables and dairy food means that self-catering **vegetarians** will eat well, though in restaurants they are less well served. Outside the major centres you'll find hardly any dedicated vegetarian restaurants and will have to rely on the token meat-free dishes served in most cafés. Salad, sandwiches, vegetarian pizza or pasta are readily available but can get a bit monotonous. **Vegans** can always ask for a simple stir-fry if all else fails but in terms of snacks, you'll develop an unhealthy reliance on nachos and the ubiquitous veggieburger, though these days many new "organic" outlets offer home-made vegan and vegetarian pies.

If you are taking a multi-day expedition on which food is provided, give them plenty of notice of your dietary needs.

Eating out

The quality of **restaurants** in New Zealand is typically superb, portions are respectable,

and many are good value for money – especially **BYO** establishments, where cost shrinks if you "bring your own" wine (corkage fees are typically $5–15). In most restaurants you can expect to pay upwards of $25 for a main course, perhaps $55 for three courses without wine. **Service** tends to be helpful without being forced and there is no expectation of a tip, though a reward for exceptional service is welcomed. However, legislation means that on public holidays you'll be expected to pay a surcharge (15–20 percent) to ensure staff wages compensate for their giving up their statutory holiday.

New Zealand's range of **ethnic restaurants** is constantly improving, with the major influx of East Asian immigrants enlivening the scene and lending a strong Thai, Chinese, Malaysian, Singaporean and Japanese flavour to the larger cities, alongside Indian and Mexican places. **Maori and Polynesian food** isn't widely represented in restaurants, but you shouldn't miss the opportunity to sample it when it's on offer, particularly in Rotorua (p.272), or try a *hangi* (see box opposite) – an earth oven producing delectable, fall-off-the-bone meat and delicately steamed vegetables.

Often there is little between restaurants and the better **café/bars**, which offer food that's just as good and a few dollars cheaper. Dining is less formal and you may well find yourself elbow to elbow with folk just out for a beer or coffee. Other **cafés** might only offer breakfasts and all-day snacks but nearly all serve good coffee.

Cosmopolitan cafés have all but replaced the traditional **tearooms**, self-service cafeteria-style establishments with no atmosphere but cheap food. Most were unlicensed and dished out machine coffee or tea, pre-packaged sandwiches, unsavoury savouries, sticky cakes and other crimes against the tastebud. On tourist routes, long-distance buses usually made their comfort stops at such tearooms but nowadays tend to opt for more modern cafés, though a few "trad" tearooms still hang on.

Most bars now serve **pub meals**, often the best budget eating around, with straightforward steak and chips, lasagne, pizza or burritos all served with salad for under $24.

The hangi

In New Zealand restaurants you'll find few examples of **Maori** or Polynesian cuisine, though the cooking style does now have a foothold in forward-looking eateries. But you can always sample traditional cooking methods at a *hangi* (pronounced nasally as "hungi"), where meat and vegetables are steamed for hours in an earth oven then served to the assembled masses. The ideal way to experience a *hangi* is as a guest at a private gathering of extended families, but most people have to settle for one of the commercial affairs in Rotorua or Christchurch. There you'll be a paying customer rather than a guest but the *hangi* flavours will be authentic, though sometimes the operators may have been creative in the more modern methods they've used to achieve them.

At a traditional *hangi*, first the men light a fire and place river stones in the embers. While these are heating, they dig a suitably large pit, then place the hot stones in the bottom and cover them with wet sacking. Meanwhile the women prepare lamb, pork, chicken, fish, shellfish and vegetables (particularly *kumara*), wrapping the morsels in leaves then arranging them in baskets (originally of flax, but now most often of steel mesh). The baskets are lowered into the cooking pit and covered with earth so that the steam and the flavours are sealed in. A couple of hours later, the baskets are disinterred, revealing fabulously tender steam-smoked meat and vegetables with a faintly earthy flavour. A suitably reverential silence, broken only by munching and appreciative murmurs, usually descends.

The country's ever-burgeoning wine industry has also spawned a number of **vineyard restaurants**, particularly in the growing areas of Hawke's Bay and Marlborough. They're almost all geared to shifting their own vino but provide good, though often expensive, food to soak up the tastings. Most have outdoor seating close to or under the vines, and there may well be an area for a postprandial game of pétanque.

Breakfast, snacks and takeaways

New Zealanders generally take a light "continental" **breakfast** of juice, cereals, toast and tea or coffee. Visitors staying at a homestay or B&B may well be offered an additional "cooked breakfast", probably along the lines of bacon and eggs; if you're staying in motels, hostels or campsites, you'll usually have to fend for yourself. In bigger towns, you'll often find a **bakery** selling fresh croissants, bagels and focaccia, but at weekends New Zealanders tend to go out for breakfast or brunch, at cafés serving anything from a bowl of fruit and muesli to platefuls of Eggs Florentine or Benedict with smoked salmon or bacon.

In the cities you'll also come across **food courts**, usually in shopping malls with a dozen or so stalls selling bargain plates of all manner of ethnic dishes. Traditional **burger bars** continue to serve constructions far removed from the limp international-franchise offerings: weighty buns with juicy patties, thick ketchup, a stack of lettuce and tomato and the ever-present Kiwi favourite, beetroot. **Meat pies** are another stalwart of Kiwi snacking: sold in bakeries and from warming cabinets in pubs everywhere, the traditional steak and mince varieties are now supplemented by bacon and egg, venison, steak and cheese, steak and oyster, smoked fish and *kumara* and, increasingly, vegetarian versions.

Fish and chips (or "greasies") are also rightly popular – the fish is often shark (euphemistically called lemon fish or flake), though tastier species are always available for slightly more, and the chips (fries) are invariably thick and crisp. Look out too for paua fritters, battered slabs of minced abalone that are something of an acquired taste.

Self-catering

If you're **self-catering**, your best bet for cheap supplies is the local supermarket, but the best food is found in small independent outlets, offering predominantly local and/or organic supplies. These represent a better alternative than the plethora of convenience corner shops (or dairies) stocking bog-standard essentials. Sadly, both types of store, along with shops at campsites and those in isolated areas with a captive market, tend to have inflated prices. Supermarkets sell **beer** and **wine**, but for anything else you'll need a **bottle store**, often attached to the local pub.

Drinking

New Zealand boasts many fine wines and beers, which can be sampled in cafés and restaurants all over the land. But for the lowest prices and a genuine Kiwi atmosphere you can't beat the **pub**. It's a place where folk stop off on their way home from work, its emphasis on consumption and back-slapping camaraderie rather than ambience and decor. In the cities, where competition from cafés is strong, pubs tend to be more comfortable and relaxing, but in the sticks little has changed. Rural pubs can initially be daunting for strangers, but once you get chatting, barriers soon drop. A few pubs are still divided into the **public bar**, a joyless Formica and linoleum place where overalls and work boots are the sartorial order of the day, and the **lounge bar**, where you are expected to dress up a bit more. Drinking hours are barely limited at all; you can drink in most bars until at least midnight on weeknights and until 4am or later at weekends. The **drinking age** is 18, though anyone who looks under 25 can expect to be asked for identification and smokers are banished to open air, often in small, purpose-built shelters.

Beer

Beer is drunk everywhere and often. Nearly all of it is produced by two huge conglomerates – New Zealand Breweries and DB – who market countless variations on the lager and Pilsener theme, as well as insipid, deep-brown fizzy liquid dispensed from taps and in bottles as "draught" – a distant and altogether feebler relation of British-style bitter.

Increasingly, Kiwi beer drinkers are turning to lager, especially their beloved Steinlager

and its newer "no-additive" version Pure. There really isn't a lot to choose between the beers except for alcohol content, normally around four percent, though five percent is common for premium beers usually described as "export".

To find something different and better tasting, seek out **boutique beers** such as those brewed near Nelson by Mac's. Try their dark and delicious stout-like Black Mac, the bitter-like Sassy Red or wait around for the Oktober Mac, a light and fresh concoction brewed in September and only available until it runs out. Small, regional brewers and in-house microbreweries are increasingly establishing themselves on the scene – look out for the *Loaded Hog* and *One Red Dog* restaurant/bars, while in other pubs and bars, check for Emersons, from Dunedin, or Founders, from Nelson (to name but a couple of widespread superior ale producers). Recently, in the central North Island, the Waituna Brewing Company have started producing "Maori" beer, available in and around Palmerston North, but they've some catching up to do if they want to compete with other microbreweries.

Most bottle shops stock a fair range of foreign brews and the flashier bars are always well stocked with international bottled beers – at a price. On tap, you will only find New Zealand beer, except for the odd ersatz Irish bar pouring Guinness and the like. A good source of information about all things beery in New Zealand is ⓦwww.brewing.co.nz.

Measures are standard throughout the country: traditionalists buy a one-litre **jug**, which is then decanted into the required number of glasses, usually a **seven** (originally seven fluid ounces, or 200ml), a **ten**, or even an elegantly fluted **twelve**. Despite thirty years under the metric system, handled **pints** (just over half a litre) have now become widespread. Keep in mind that a half-pint will always be served as a ten fluid ounce glass and therefore will be a little over half the price of a pint. Prices vary enormously, but you can expect to pay around $6–9 for a pint. It is much cheaper to buy in bulk from a bottle shop where beer is either sold in six-packs or cartons of a dozen or 24 ($18–25). Serious drinkers go for refillable half-gallon **flagons** (2.25 litres) or their metric variant, the two-litre **rigger**; these can be bought for around a dollar and filled for $11–16 at taps in bottle shops.

Wines and spirits

Kiwis are justifiably loyal to NZ winemakers, who now produce **wines** that are among the best in the world. New Zealand is rapidly encroaching on the Loire's standing as the world benchmark for Sauvignon Blanc, while the bold fruitiness of its Chardonnay and apricot and citrus palate of its Rieslings attracts many fans. Wine menus feature few non-Kiwi **whites**, but reds are often of the broad-shouldered Aussie variety. Nevertheless, there are good New Zealand **reds,** particularly young-drinking varietals using Cabernet Sauvignon, Merlot and, perhaps best of all, Pinot Noir. A liking for **champagne** no longer implies "champagne tastes" in New Zealand: you can still buy the wildly overpriced French stuff, but good Kiwi Méthode Traditionelle (fermented in the bottle in the time-honoured way) starts at around $18 a bottle: Montana's Lindauer Brut is widely available, and justly popular. Another drinking trend is for **dessert wines** (or "stickies") typically made from grapes withered on the vine by the *botrytis* fungus, the so-called "noble rot".

Most bars and licensed restaurants have a tempting range of wines, many sold by the glass ($6–10, $8 and up for dessert wine), while in shops the racks groan under bottles starting from $11 ($14–28 for reasonable quality). "Chateau cardboard" wine bladders are considered passé nowadays, so buy a decent bottle if invited out.

If you want to try before you buy, visit a few wineries, where you are usually free to sample half a dozen different wines. There is sometimes a small fee, especially to try the reserve wines, but it is always redeemable if you buy a bottle. Among the established wine-growing areas, **Henderson and the Kumeu Valley**, 15km west of Auckland, is one of the more accessible, though its urban nature makes it less appealing to tour. On the east coast of the North Island, the area around **Gisborne** is good for a tasting afternoon but wine connoisseurs are better off in **Hawke's**

Bay, where Napier and Hastings are surrounded by almost thirty vineyards open to the public. Further south, **Martinborough** has the most accessible cluster of vineyards, many within walking distance. The colder climate of the South Island limits wine production to the northern part with the exception of the microclimate of **Central Otago** near Queenstown and Alexandra, where excellent Pinot Noir is produced. There are a number of fantastic vineyards in **Marlborough**, close to Blenheim, which competes with Hawke's Bay for the title of New Zealand's top wine region. A good starting point for information on the Kiwi wine scene is ⓦwww .nzwine.com.

New Zealand also produces fruit **liqueurs**; some are delicious, though few visitors develop an enduring taste for the sickly sweet kiwi fruit or feijoa varieties, which are mostly sold through souvenir shops. International spirits are widely available and their dominance is challenged only by one New Zealand-made **vodka** called 42 Below, and two single malt **whiskies**: Milford, made by the New Zealand Malt Whisky Co. (ⓦwww .milfordwhisky.co.nz); and Lammerlaw, made by Dunedin-based Wilson Distillers.

Soft drinks

New Zealand coolers are stocked with just about every international brand of carbonated soft drink, but one home-grown (though not Kiwi-owned) brand to look out for is L&P – originally **Lemon and Paeroa** after the Hauraki Plains town where it was first made – a naturally lemon-flavoured pop. **Milkshakes**, **thickshakes** (usually with a dollop of ice cream) and **smoothies** made with blended fruit are popular and almost any café worth its salt serves glasses of **spirulina**, a thick, green goo made from powdered seaweed and often mixed with the likes of apple juice and avocado. Enthusiasts claim restorative properties when drunk the morning after a bender.

Tea and coffee

Tea is usually a down-to-earth Indian blend (sometimes jocularly known as "gumboot"), though you may also have a choice of a dozen or so flavoured, scented and herbal varieties. **Coffee** drinking has been elevated to an art form with a specialized terminology: an Italian-style espresso is known as a **short black** (sometimes served with a jug of hot water so you can dilute it to taste); a weaker and larger version is a **long black**, which,

with the addition of hot milk becomes a **flat white**; **cappuccinos** come regular or chocolate-laced as a mochaccino; while a milky café **latte** is usually sold in a glass but sometimes in a gargantuan bowl. Better places will serve all these decaffeinated, skinny or even made with soya milk.

The media

For a country of only four million inhabitants, New Zealand has a vibrant media scene. Auckland claims to have more radio stations per capita than any city in the world, and the magazine racks groan with Kiwi-produced weeklies and monthlies. The standard of media coverage sometimes leaves a little to be desired, but for the most part this is a well-informed country with sophisticated tastes. On the web a good starting point is ⓦ www.publicaddress.net, the leading Kiwi blog site, which always features something interesting.

TV

New Zealanders receive five main free-to-air **broadcast channels**, a handful of local channels and Sky TV (which you'll find in most motels). Travellers are always griping about low standards, but while much prime-time viewing is unashamedly populist there is high-quality stuff out there – you just have to look for it.

The biggest broadcaster is the state-owned **TVNZ**, which operates two advertising-heavy channels. TV ONE has slightly older and more information-based programming while TV2 is younger and more entertainment-oriented. In practice there is a lot of crossover, and both channels present a diet of local news, current affairs, sport, drama and entertainment, plus a slew of US, British and Australian programmes: you'll find most of your favourites, often three to six months behind. British readers may be surprised to learn that *Coronation Street* is huge in NZ.

The main opposition comes from **TV3**, which pitches itself roughly between TV ONE and TV2, and **Prime**, backed by Sky TV, which often has quirkier programming.

Lastly there's **Maori TV**, launched in 2004 with substantial government support (though it also has ads). Broadcasting in Maori and English, it is charged with promoting the language and culture but is far from a stuffy educational channel. Along with good movies you might catch Maori cooking shows, lifestyle makeovers, sitcoms and Maori angles on news, current affairs and sport – all well worth dipping into.

Radio

New Zealand has few countrywide radio stations, but syndication means that some commercial stations can be heard in many parts of the country, with local commercials. All websites listed stream the channel over the **internet**.

For news, current affairs and a thoughtful look at the arts and music, tune into the government-funded **Radio New Zealand National** (101.0–101.6 FM; ⓦ www.radionz .co.nz) which is the nearest New Zealand gets to, say, NPR or BBC Radio 4. You'll pick it up most places, though there are blank spots. Its sister station, **Radio New Zealand Concert** (89–100 FM), concentrates on classical music.

Though often amateurish, **student radio stations** provide excellent and varied "alternative" listening, though only in their home cities. In Auckland tune to bFM (95.0; ⓦwww.95bfm.co.nz); in Wellington to Active (89.0; ⓦwww.radioactive.co.nz); in Christchurch to RDU (98.5; ⓦwww.rdu.org.nz); and in Dunedin to Radio One (91.0; ⓦwww.r1.co.nz).

The rest of the airwaves are clogged up by **commercial stations**, perhaps the most interesting being **KiwiFM** (102.1–102.5; ⓦwww.kiwifm.co.nz) playing solely NZ music to Auckland, Wellington and Canterbury.

Print

New Zealand has no national **daily newspaper**, making do with four major regional papers (all published Mon–Sat mornings) and a plethora of minor rags of mostly local interest. All are politically fairly neutral. The North Island is shared between the Auckland-based *New Zealand Herald* (ⓦwww.nzherald.co.nz) and Wellington's *Dominion Post* (ⓦwww.dompost.co.nz), while *The Press* (ⓦwww.stuff.co.nz) covers Christchurch and its environs, and the *Otago Daily Times* (ⓦwww.odt.co.nz) serves the far south of the country. All offer a pretty decent selection of national and international news, sport and reviews, often relying heavily on wire services and syndication deals with major British and American newspapers. On **Sunday**, read the tabloid-style *Sunday News;* the superior, broadsheet *Sunday Star-Times;* or Auckland's *Herald on Sunday*.

Kiwi newspaper journalists get little scope for imaginative or investigative journalism, though the broad-ranging and slightly left-leaning **weekly magazine**, the *Listener* (ⓦwww.listener.co.nz), does its best. With coverage of politics, art, music, TV, radio, books, science, travel, architecture and much more, it is perhaps the best overall insight into what makes New Zealand tick.

Topics are covered in greater depth in the nationwide **monthly** *North and South*, though for an insight into the aspirations of Aucklanders you might be better off with the snappier glossy, *Metro*.

Specialist magazines cover the range: *Wilderness* (ⓦwww.wildernessmag.co.nz) has a good spread of tramping, kayaking, climbing and mountain biking, and *Real Groove* is the best of the general music mags.

The bi-monthly *Mana* (ⓦwww.manaonline.co.nz) pitches itself as "the Maori news magazine for all New Zealanders", and gives an insight into what sometimes seems like a parallel world barely acknowledged by the mainstream media. It is in English, but comes peppered with Maori words and concepts which can make reading a little baffling at first, though it conveniently comes with a back-page glossary.

Festivals and public holidays

In the southern hemisphere, **Christmas** falls near the start of the school **summer holidays**, which run from mid-December until early February. From Boxing Day through to the middle of January Kiwis hit the beaches en masse and during this time you'll find a lot more people about. Motels and campsites can be difficult to book and often raise their prices, though B&Bs and hostels rarely up their rates. To help you chart a path through the chaos, i-SITE visitor centres are open longer hours, as are many other tourist attractions. Other school **holidays** last for two weeks in mid- to late April, a fortnight in early to mid-July and the first two weeks of October, though these have a less pronounced effect.

Public holidays are big news in New Zealand and it can feel like the entire country has taken to the roads, so it's worth staying put rather than trying to travel on these days. Each region also takes one day a year to celebrate its **Anniversary Day**, remembering the founding of the original provinces that made up New Zealand, and generally celebrated with an agricultural show, horse-jumping, sheepshearing, cake-baking and best-vegetable contests and novelty events (such as gumboot throwing). We've listed official dates below, but days are usually observed on the nearest Monday (or occasionally Friday) to make a long weekend.

Public holidays and festival calendar

Many of the festivals listed below are covered in more detail in the relevant section of the Guide. **PH** indicates a public holiday.

January

1 New Year's Day (PH) Whaleboat Racing Regatta, **Kawhia** (@ www.kawhiaharbour.co.nz); **Highland Games**, Waipu (@ www.highlandgames.co.nz).
2 (PH).
First Sat Glenorchy Races (@ www.glenorchy -nz.co.nz).
17 Anniversary Day (PH in Southland).
Third Fri Big Day Out, NZ's biggest one-day music festival, Auckland (@ www.bigdayout.com).
22 Anniversary Day (PH in Wellington).
29 Anniversary Day (PH in Auckland, Northland, Waikato, Coromandel, Taupo and the Bay of Plenty), celebrated with a massive regatta on Auckland's Waitemata Harbour.
Last Sat Harvest Hawke's Bay Wine and Food Festival (@ www.harvesthawkesbay.co.nz).

February

1 Anniversary Day (PH in Nelson).
6 Waitangi Day (PH) formal events at Waitangi; **Rippon Open Air Festival**, Wanaka (@ www .ripponfestival.co.nz), featuring top Kiwi bands.
Second Sat Wine Marlborough Festival, Blenheim (@ www.wine-marlborough-festival.co.nz).
Second weekend Coast-to-Coast multisport race, South Island (@ www.coasttocoast.co.nz).
Third weekend Art Deco Weekend, Napier (@ www.artdeconapier.com); **Devonport Food, Wine & Music Festival** (@ www.devonportwinefestival.co.nz).
Third last Sat Mission Bay Jazz and Blues Streetfest, Mission Bay, Auckland (@ www .jazzandbluesstreetfest.com).
Mid-Feb to early March Wellington Fringe Festival (@ www.fringe.org.nz).

Mid-Feb to mid-March Burst: The Festival of Flowers, Christchurch (@ www.festivalofflowers.co.nz).

March

Late Feb to late March NZ International Arts Festival, Wellington (even-numbered years only; @ www.nzfestival.telecom.co.nz).
First week Golden Shears sheepshearing competition in Masterton (@ www.goldenshears .co.nz).
Second Sat Pasifika Festival, Auckland (@ www .aucklandcity.govt.nz/pasifika); **Wildfoods Festival**, Hokitika (@ www.wildfoods.co.nz); **Te Houtaewa Challenge** and **Te Houtaewa Surf Challenge**, Ahipara (@ www.newzealand-marathon.co.nz).
Mid-March WOMAD world music festival, New Plymouth (@ www.womad.co.nz); **Sounds of Aotearoa**, New Plymouth, featuring NZ's finest musicians (http://soundsaotearoa.com).
Mid-March Round-the-Bays Sunday fun run, Auckland (@ www.roundthebays.co.nz).
Closest Sat to March 17 Ngaruawahia Maori Regatta, near Hamilton (see p.207).
23 Anniversary Day (PH in Otago).
31 Anniversary Day (PH in Taranaki).

April

Late March to late April Good Friday (PH) and Easter Sunday **(PH)**.
Easter week Royal Easter Show, Auckland (@ www.royaleastershow.co.nz); **Warbirds Over Wanaka International Airshow** (even-numbered years only; @ www.warbirdsoverwanaka.com); **National Jazz Festival**, Tauranga (@ www.jazz.org.nz).
25 ANZAC Day (PH).
Late April Five-day Festival of Colour (odd-numbered years only; @ www.festivalofcolour.co.nz) in Wanaka featuring music, dance, theatre and arts.
Mid-April to late April Arrowtown Autumn Festival (@ www.arrowtownautumnfestival.org.nz).

June

First Mon Queen's Birthday (PH).
Middle weekend Fieldays, the southern hemisphere's largest agricultural show, Hamilton (@ www.fieldays.co.nz).
Mid- to late June Matariki, Maori New Year festivities (@ www.taitokerau.co.nz/matariki.htm).
Late June to early July Queenstown Winter Festival (@ www.winterfestival.co.nz).

July

Early July to late Nov New Zealand International Film Festival, held for two weeks

each in the nation's 15 largest cities (@www
.enzedff.co.nz).

Late July to early Aug Taranaki International
Festival of the Arts (odd-numbered years only;
@www.artsfest.co.nz).

September

First full week Gay Ski Week, Queenstown
(@www.gayskiweeknz.com).
Late Sept to early Oct Alexandra Blossom
Festival (@www.blossom.co.nz).
Late Sept to early Oct World of Wearable Art
Awards (WOW), Wellington (@www
.worldofwearableart.com).

October

Fourth Mon Labour Day (**PH**).
31 Halloween. General trick or treating.
Late Oct to early Nov Taranaki Rhododendron &
Garden Festival, New Plymouth (@www.rhodo.co.nz).

November

1 Anniversary Day (**PH** in Hawke's Bay and
Marlborough).
5 Guy Fawkes' Night fireworks.
Second week New Zealand Cup & Show Week,
Canterbury (@www.nzcupandshow.co.nz).
Third Fri Anniversary Day (**PH** in Canterbury).
Third Sun Toast Martinborough Wine, Food &
Music Festival (@www.toastmartinborough.co.nz).

December

1 Anniversary Day (**PH** in Westland).
25 Christmas Day (**PH**).
26 Boxing Day (**PH**).
Late Dec Rhythm and Vines three-day music
festival, culminating on New Year's Eve, Gisborne
(@www.rhythmandvines.co.nz).

Outdoor activities

Life in New Zealand is tied to the Great Outdoors, and no visit to the country
would be complete without spending a fair chunk of your time in intimate contact
with nature.

Kiwis have long taken it for granted that within
a few minutes' drive of their home they can
find a deserted beach or piece of "bush" and
wander freely through it, an attitude enshrined
in a fabulous collection of national, forest and
maritime parks. They are all administered by
the **Department of Conservation** (DOC;
@www.doc.govt.nz), which seeks to balance
the maintenance of a fragile environment with
the demands of tourism. For the most part it
manages remarkably well, providing a superb
network of signposted paths studded with
trampers' huts and operating visitor centres
that present highly informative material
about the local history, flora and fauna.
They also publish excellent leaflets for major
walking tracks.

The lofty peaks of the Southern Alps offer
challenging **mountaineering** and great

skiing, while the lower slopes are ideal for
multi-day **tramps** which cross low passes
between valleys choked with subtropical and
temperate rainforests. Along the coasts
there are sheltered lagoons and calm
harbours for gentle **swimming** and **boating**,
but also sweeping strands battered by some
top-class **surf**.

The country also promotes itself as the
adventure tourism capital of the world. All
over New Zealand you will find places to go
bungy jumping, whitewater or cave rafting,
jetboating, tandem skydiving, mountain
biking, stunt flying or scuba diving – in fact
if you name it someone somewhere
organizes it. While thousands of people
participate in these activities every day
without incident, standards of instructor
training vary. It seems to be a point of

honour for all male (and they are almost all male) river guides, bungy operators and tandem parachute instructors to play the macho card and put the wind up you as much as possible. Such bravado shouldn't be interpreted as a genuine disregard for safety, but the fact remains that there have been a few well-publicized injuries and deaths – a tragic situation that's addressed by industry-regulated codes of practice, an independent system of accreditation and home-grown organizations that insist upon high levels of professionalism and safety instruction.

Before engaging in any adventure activities, check your insurance cover (see p.74).

Tramping

Tramping, trekking, bushwalking, hiking – call it what you will, it is one of the most compelling reasons to visit New Zealand, and for many the sole objective.

Hikes typically last three to five days, following well-worn trails through relatively untouched wilderness, often in one of the country's national parks. Along the way you'll be either camping out or staying in trampers' huts, and will consequently be lugging a pack over some rugged terrain, so a moderate level of fitness is required. If this sounds daunting, you can sign up with one of the guided tramping companies that maintain more salubrious huts or luxury lodges, provide meals and carry much of your gear. Details of these are given throughout the Guide.

The main tramping season is in summer, from October to May, although the most popular tramps – the Milford, Routeburn and Kepler – are in the cooler southern half of the South Island, where the season is shorter by a few weeks at either end.

The tramps

Rugged terrain and a history of track-bashing by explorers and deer hunters has left New Zealand with a web of tramps following river valleys and linking up over passes, high above the bushline. As far as possible, we've indicated the degree of difficulty of all tramps covered in the Guide, broadly following DOC's classification system: a **path** is level, well graded and often wheelchair-accessible; **walking tracks** and **tramping tracks** (usually marked with red and white or orange flashes on trees) are respectively more arduous affairs requiring some fitness and proper walking equipment; and a **route** requires considerable tramping experience to cope with an ill-defined trail, frequently above the bushline. DOC's estimated **walking times** can trip you up: along paths likely to be used by families, for example, you can easily find yourself finishing in under half the time specified, but on serious routes aimed at fit trampers you might struggle to keep pace. We've given estimates for moderately fit individuals and, where possible, included the distance and amount of climbing involved, aiding route planning.

Invaluable information on walking directions, details of access, huts and an adequate map are contained in the excellent DOC tramp **leaflets** (usually $1 apiece). The title of each leaflet relating to an area is included in the appropriate places throughout this book, though we only include the price if it is $2 or over.

Te Araroa – The Long Pathway

Since the mid-1970s it has been a Kiwi dream to have a continuous path from one end of the country to the other. In recent years, **Te Araroa – The Long Pathway** (ⓦ www.teararoa.org.nz), has been championed by the Te Araroa Trust, a private group that intended to have the whole 2900km route, from Cape Reinga to Bluff, open by the end of 2010. Short trails, built with the trust's involvement, link the fragmented network of existing tracks into a continuous whole. A provisional, impressively varied, route exists, much of it running through fairly remote country, although it intentionally visits small communities so that trampers can re-supply.

A handful of hardy souls have already tramped the whole route but it is envisaged that most people will tackle short sections.

The maps in each DOC leaflet should be sufficient for trampers as long as they stick to the designated route, but experienced walkers planning independent routes and folk after a more detailed vision of the terrain should fork out for specialized **maps** that identify all the features along the way. Most trampers' huts have a copy of the local area map pinned to the wall or laminated into the table. In describing tramps we have used **"true directions"** in relation to rivers and streams, whereby the left bank (the "true left") is the left-hand side of the river looking downstream.

Eight of New Zealand's finest, most popular tramps, plus one river journey, have been classified by DOC as **Great Walks** and are covered in detail in the Guide and in the *Adrenaline heaven* colour section. Great Walks get the lion's share of DOC track spending, resulting in relatively smooth, broad walkways, with boardwalks over muddy sections and bridges over almost every stream. In short, they represent a sanitized side of New Zealand tramping.

Access to tracks is seldom a problem in the most popular tramping regions, though it does require planning. Most finish some distance from their start, so taking your own vehicle is not much use; besides, cars parked at trailheads are an open invitation to thieves. Great Walks always have transport from the nearest town, but there are often equally stunning and barely used tramps close by which require a little more patience and tenacity to get to – we've included some of the best of the rest in the Guide, listed under "Tramps" in the index.

Backcountry accommodation: huts and camping

New Zealand's backcountry is strung with a network of almost nine hundred **trampers' huts**, sited less than a day's walk apart, frequently in beautiful surroundings. All are simple, communal affairs that fall into five distinct categories as defined by DOC.

Basic Huts (free) are often crude and rarely encountered on the major tramps. Next up is the **Standard Hut** ($5/person/night): basic, weatherproof, usually equipped with individual bunks or sleeping platforms accommodating a dozen or so, an external

long-drop toilet and a water supply. There is seldom any heating and there are no cooking facilities. **Serviced Huts** ($15) tend to be larger, sleeping twenty or more on bunks with mattresses. Water is piped indoors to a sink, and flush toilets are occasionally encountered. Again, you'll need to bring your own stove and cooking gear, but heating is provided; if the fire is a wood-burning one, you should replace any firewood you use. More sophisticated still are the **Great Walk Huts** – unsurprisingly found along the Great Walks. They tend to have separate bunkrooms, gas rings for cooking (but no utensils), stoves for heating, a drying room and occasionally solar-powered lighting. Children of school age generally pay half the adult fee and, thanks to a DOC initiative, under-18s can now use Great Walk huts and campsites for free – though you should still book in advance.

Hut fees are best paid in advance at the local DOC office, visitor centre or other outlet close to the start of the track. For most tramps you buy a quantity of $5 tickets and give the warden the appropriate number (one for a Standard hut, three for a Serviced hut) or post them in the hut's honesty box. You can sometimes buy tickets direct from wardens, but there is often a 25-percent premium on the price. If you are planning to tramp any of the Great Walks you **must** buy a **Great Walks Hut Pass**, covering the cost of your accommodation for the walk you intend to complete, and carry the confirmation with you, otherwise the wardens will charge you for each hut again. The pass and reservation, made simultaneously, guarantee trekkers a bed on the Kepler, Milford, Routeburn, Abel Tasman and Heaphy. No similar reservation is made with a hut pass bought for the remaining Great Walks, primarily because it's considered very unlikely that each hut will fill up.

The easiest way to make reservations and get Great Walk hut passes is online (@www.doc.govt.nz), or through the relevant/local DOC office (see accounts in the Guide) or, at a push, by using a booking agent, stating which hut you intend to use each night. To get more information about the Great Walks and other NZ tramps you can also log onto @www.tramper.co.nz. In winter (May–Sept) the huts on Great Walks are often stripped of heating and cooking facilities and downgraded to Standard status, so if you have an Annual Hut Pass (see below) you can use them, though possessing the pass or a ticket doesn't guarantee you a bunk. Beds go on a first-come-first-served basis, so if the trail is very busy you may find yourself in an undignified gallop to the next hut.

Should you wish to do a lot of tramping outside the Great Walks system, or on the Great Walks out of season, it's worth buying an **Annual Hut Pass** ($90), which allows you to stay in all Standard and Serviced huts.

Camping is allowed on all tracks except the Milford. Rules vary, but in most cases you're required to minimize environmental impact by camping close to the huts, whose facilities (toilets, water and gas rings where available, but obviously not bunks) you can use.

Equipment

Tramping in New Zealand can be a dangerous and/or dispiriting experience if you're not equipped for both hot, sunny days and wet, cold and windy weather. The best

tramps pass through some of the world's wettest regions, with parts of the Milford Track receiving over 6m of rain a year. It is essential to carry a good waterproof jacket, preferably made from breathable fabric and fitted with a decent hood. Keeping your lower half dry is less crucial and most Kiwis tramp in shorts. Early starts often involve wading through long, sodden grass, so a pair of knee-length gaiters can be useful. Comfortable boots with good ankle support are a must; take suitably broken-in leather boots or lightweight walking boots, and some comfortable footwear for the day's end. You'll also need a warm jacket or jumper, plus a good sleeping bag; even the heated huts are cold at night and a warm hat never goes amiss. All this, along with lighter clothing for sunny days, should be kept inside a robust backpack, preferably lined with a strong waterproof liner such as those sold at DOC offices.

Once on the tramp, you need to be totally self-sufficient. On Great Walks, you should carry **cooking** gear; on other tramps you also need a cooking stove and fuel. **Food** can be your heaviest burden; freeze-dried meals are light and reasonably tasty, but they are expensive, and many cost-conscious trampers prefer pasta or rice, dried soups for sauces, a handful of fresh vegetables, muesli (granola), milk powder and bread or crackers for lunch. Consider taking biscuits, trail mix (known in NZ as "scroggin"), tea, coffee and powdered fruit drinks (the Raro brand is good), and energy-giving spreads. All huts have drinking **water** but DOC advise treating water taken from lakes and rivers to protect yourself from giardia; see p.74 for more on this and water-purification methods.

You should also carry basic supplies: a first aid kit, blister kit, sunscreen, insect repellent; a torch (flashlight) with spare battery and bulb, candles, matches or a lighter; and a compass (though few bother on the better-marked tracks).

In the most popular tramping areas you will be able to **rent equipment**. Most important of all, remember that you'll have to carry all this stuff for hours each day. Hotels and hostels in nearby towns will generally let you leave your surplus gear either free or for a small fee.

Safety

Most people spend days or weeks tramping in New Zealand with nothing worse than stiff legs and a few sandfly bites, but **safety** is nonetheless a serious issue and there are deaths every year. The culprit is usually New Zealand's fickle **weather**. It cannot be stressed too strongly that within an hour (even in high summer) a warm, cloudless day can turn bitterly cold, with high winds driving in thick banks of track-obscuring cloud. Heeding the weather forecast (posted in DOC offices) is some help, but there is no substitute for carrying warm, windproof and waterproof clothing.

Failed **river crossings** are also a common cause of tramping fatalities. If you are confronted with something that looks too dangerous to cross, then it is, and you should wait until the level falls or backtrack. If the worst happens and you get swept away while crossing, don't try to stand up; you may trap your leg between rocks and drown. Instead, lie on your back and float feet first until you reach a place where swimming to the bank is feasible.

If you do get lost or injured, your chances of being found are better if you left word of your intentions with a **friend** or with a **trusted person** at your next port of call, who will realize you are overdue. DOC offices stock **intention forms** for you to declare your planned route and estimated finishing time but by the time they are checked you could have been missing too long for it to matter. While on the tramp, fill in the hut logs as you go, so that your movements can be traced, and when you return check in with the folk you told about the trip.

Animals are not a problem in the NZ bush, the biggest irritants being sandflies whose bites itch, or kea, alpine parrots that delight in pinching anything they can get their beaks into and tearing it apart to fulfil their curiosity.

Swimming, surfing and windsurfing

Kiwi life is inextricably linked with the beach, and from Christmas to the end of March (longer in warmer northern climes), a weekend isn't complete without a dip or a waterside barbecue – though you should never underestimate the ferocity of the southern **sun** (see p.73 for precautions). Some of the most picturesque beaches stretch away into salt spray from the pounding Tasman surf or Pacific rollers. **Swimming** here can be very hazardous, so only venture into the water at beaches patrolled by surf lifesaving clubs and always swim between the flags. Spotter planes patrol the most popular beaches and warn of the occasional **shark**, so if you notice everyone heading for the safety of the beach, get out of the water.

New Zealand's tempestuous coastline offers near-perfect conditions for **surfing** and windsurfing. At major beach resorts there is often an outlet renting dinghies, catamarans, canoes and windsurfers; in regions where there is reliably good surf you might also come across boogie boards and surfboards, and seaside hostels often have a couple for guests' use. If you want to get deeper under the skin of the NZ surf community, or just benefit from their local knowledge, take a squiz at ⓦwww.surf .co.nz and www.surf2surf.co.nz.

Sailing

New Zealand's numerous harbours, studded with small islands and ringed with deserted bays, make **sailing** one of Kiwis' favourite pursuits, which explains why New Zealand and Kiwi sailors have been so influential in the fate of the America's Cup (see *Adrenaline heaven* colour section). People sail year-round, but the summer months from December to March are busiest. Unless you befriend a yachtie you'll probably be limited to commercial yacht **charters** (expensive and with a skipper), more reasonably priced and often excellent **day-sailing trips**, or renting a dinghy for some inshore antics.

Scuba diving and snorkelling

The waters around New Zealand offer wonderful opportunities to scuba **dive** and **snorkel**. What they lack in long-distance visibility, tropical warmth and colourful fish they make up for with the range of diving environments. Pretty much anywhere along the more sheltered eastern side of both islands you'll find somewhere with rewarding snorkelling, but much the best and most accessible spot is the **Goat Island Marine Reserve**, in Northland, where there's a superb range of habitats close to the shore. Northland also has world-class scuba diving at the **Poor Knights Islands Marine Reserve**, reached by boat from Tutukaka, and wreck diving on the *Rainbow Warrior*, from Matauri Bay, a stack of good sites around Great Barrier Island. On the South Island, there are wrecks worth exploring off **Picton** and fabulous growths of **black and red corals** relatively close to the surface, in the south-western fiords near Milford.

For the inexperienced, the easiest way to get a taste of what's under the surface is to take a **resort dive** with an instructor. If you want to dive independently, you need to be PADI-qualified. For more information consult Ⓦwww.divenewzealand.com.

Rafting

The combination of challenging rapids and gorgeous scenery makes **whitewater rafting** one of New Zealand's most thrilling adventure activities. Visitor numbers and weather restrict the main **rafting season** to October to May, and most companies set an **age limit** at 12. You'll usually be supplied with everything except a swimming costume and an old pair of trainers and, after safety instruction, spend a couple of hours or so on the water.

Thrilling though it is, rafting is also one of the most **dangerous** of the adventure activities, claiming a number of lives in recent years. Operators have a self-imposed code of practice, but there are still cowboys out there. It might be stating the obvious but fatalities happen when people fall out of rafts: heed the guide's instructions about how best to stay on board and how to protect yourself if you do get a dunking.

Multi-day tours

Tours that are included in this section involve taking part in one or other or, in extreme cases, all of the above activities. Although New Zealand is an easy place to explore independently, tours offer specialist insight, logistical help and company along the way.

Hiking and wildlife

Active Earth Ⓦwww.activeearthnewzealand.com. Suitable for anyone who is reasonably fit and wants to see things few other tourists will. Good-humoured and informative guides take small groups tramping, climbing and wilderness camping in virtually untouched country throughout the North Island – from $745 for five nights – excluding a daily food and camp-fee kitty (around $25–35/day) and any extra adventure activities.

Fiordland Ecology Holidays Ⓦwww.fiordland.gen.nz. These wonderful trips book up months in advance and take in Doubtful, Dusky and Breaksea sounds and Preservation Inlet, where you can snorkel and scuba dive and visit dolphins and seals (3 days; $1030). All profits go into ecological projects.

Hiking New Zealand Ⓦwww.hikingnewzealand.com. Conservation-minded company, running outdoor trips and acting as agent for a number of like-minded operators that give them countrywide coverage. There's everything from hiking trips around the far north of Northland (6 days; $795) to boat trips to NZ's sub-Antarctic islands (9 days; $3212, plus $150 landing fees) – a daily camping and food fee of $25–35 applies.

Kiwi Wildlife Tours Ⓦwww.kiwi-wildlife.co.nz. Upmarket small-group birding tours (about $300/person/day, $500 single supplement).

Kiwi Wildlife Walks Ⓦwww.nzwalk.com. Expertly run guided walks in and around Fiordland National Park and Stewart Island, where they go kiwi spotting (4 days; $1795).

Real Journeys Ⓦwww.realjourneys.co.nz. Trips include an overnight cruise on the *Milford Wanderer*, taking in Doubtful Sound (from $473), with on-board kayaks.

Canoeing and kayaking

New Zealand is a paddler's paradise, and pretty much anywhere with water nearby has somewhere you can rent either canoes or kayaks. Sometimes this is simply an opportunity to muck around in boats but often there are guided trips available, with the emphasis being on soaking up the scenery. The scenic **Whanganui River** is a perennial favourite.

Jetboating

The shallow, braided rivers of the high Canterbury sheep country posed access difficulties for run-owner Bill Hamilton, who got around the problem by inventing the **Hamilton Jetboat** in the early 1960s. His inspired invention could plane in as little as 100mm of water, reach prodigious speeds (up to 80km/hr) and negotiate rapids while maintaining astonishing, turn-on-a-sixpence manoeuvrability.

The jetboat carried its first fare-paying passengers on a deep and glassy section of the Shotover River, which is still used by the pioneering Shotover Jet. **Rides** last around thirty eye-streaming minutes, time enough for hot dogging and as many 360-degree spins as anyone needs. **Wilderness trips** can last two hours or longer.

Bungy jumping and bridge swinging

For maximum adrenaline, minimum risk and greatest expense, bungy jumping is difficult to beat. For a bit of variety you could try a close relative of the bungy, **bridge swinging**, which provides a similar gut-wrenching fall accompanied by a super-fast swing along a gorge while harnessed to a cable. See the *Adrenaline heaven* colour section for locations.

Ruggedy Range ⓦwww.ruggedyrange.com. Stewart Island-based company offering enthusiastic and entertaining trips to Ulva Island and Masons Bay visiting the unique wildlife (from 1 day, 1 night; $425).

Cycling, horseriding and kayaking

Adventure South ⓦwww.advsouth.co.nz. This environmentally conscious company runs guided cycling and multi-activity tours around the South Island, with accommodation in characterful lodges or track huts – for example, 21 days cycling on the South Island ($9265). All tours carry a single supplement.

Alpine Horse Safaris, Waitohi Downs ⓦwww.alpinehorse.co.nz. Treks intended for serious riders, including food and accommodation, that follow old mining tracks well away from civilization, or at least roads (4 days; $1160).

Cycle Touring Company ⓦwww.cycletours.co.nz. Tailored self-led or guided tours of Northland, with several routes of 2–21 days, and the option to have your gear carried for you. Accommodation is in lodges and homestays (or a cheaper backpacker option) and prices are around $2433 for seven nights if you carry your gear.

New Zealand Sea Kayak Adventures ⓦwww.nzkayaktours.com. Fully catered Northland- and Bay of Islands-based guided sea kayak camping tours for six days ($1050). Trips are adventurous but they cater to a full range of abilities and offer some women-only trips.

Pacific Cycle Tours ⓦwww.bike-nz.com. Christchurch-based mountain-bike, road-bike and hiking tours round both islands with varying degrees of adventurous-ness, including a North Island bike tour (7 days; $2437).

Pakiri Beach Horseriding ⓦwww.horseride-nz.co.nz. Highly professional multi-day tours through native bush and along clifftops including an epic Coast to Coast trip (7 days; $3599).

Pedaltours ⓦwww.pedaltours.co.nz. Guided road- and mountain-biking tours of both islands, including a week-long ride around the Nelson Lakes ($2890).

Canyoning

The easiest way to get your hands on New Zealand rock is to go **canyoning** (or its near relative by the sea, **coasteering**), which involves following steep and confined river gorges or streambeds down chutes and over waterfalls for a few hours, sliding, jumping and abseiling all the way. Guided trips are available in a handful of places, the most accessible being in Auckland, Queenstown, Turangi and Wanaka.

Mountaineering

In the main, New Zealand is better suited to **mountaineering** than rock climbing, though most of what is available is fairly serious stuff, suitable only for well-equipped parties with a good deal of experience. For most people the only way to get above the snowline is to tackle the easy summit of Mount Ruapehu, the North Island's highest point, the summit of Mount Taranaki, near New Plymouth, or pay for a guided ascent of one of NZ's classic peaks. Prime candidates are the country's highest mountain, Aoraki Mount Cook (3754m), accessed from the

climbers' heartland of Aoraki Mount Cook Village, and NZ's most beautiful peak, the pyramidal Mount Aspiring (3030m), approached from Wanaka. In both cases networks of climbers' huts are used as bases for what are typically twenty-hour attempts on the summit.

Flying, skydiving and paragliding

Almost every town in New Zealand seems to harbour an airstrip or a helipad, and there is inevitably someone happy to get you airborne for half an hour's **flightseeing**. Helicopters cost around fifty percent more than planes and can't cover the same distances but score on manoeuvrability and the chance to land. If money is tight take a regular flight somewhere you want to go anyway. First choice here would have to be the journey from either Wanaka or Queenstown to Milford Sound, which overflies the very best of Fiordland.

In **tandem skydiving**, a double harness links you to an instructor, who has control of the parachute. The plane circles up to around 2500m and after you leap out together, you experience around 45 seconds of eerie freefall before the instructor pulls the ripcord.

A hill, a gentle breeze and substantial tourist presence and you've all the ingredients for **tandem paragliding**, where you and an instructor jointly launch off a hilltop, slung below a manoeuvrable parachute, for perhaps ten to twenty minutes of graceful gliding and stomach-churning banked turns. Alternatively **tandem hang-gliding** or **parasailing** are usually available.

Skiing and snowboarding

New Zealand's **ski season** (roughly June–Nov) starts as snows on northern hemisphere slopes melt away, which, combined with the South Island's backbone of 3000m peaks, the North Island's equally lofty volcanoes and the relative cheapness of the skiing means New Zealand is an increasingly popular international ski destination. Most fields are geared to the domestic downhill market, and the eastern side of the Southern Alps is littered with **club fields** sporting a handful of rope tows, simple lifts and a motley collection of private ski lodges. They're open to all-comers, but some are only accessible by 4WD vehicles, others have a long walk in, and ski schools are almost unheard of. Throughout the country there are, however, a dozen exceptions to this norm: **commercial resorts**, with high-speed chairs, ski schools, gear rental and groomed wide-open slopes. What you won't find are massive on-site resorts of the scale found in North America and Europe; skiers commute daily to the slopes from nearby après-ski towns and **gear rental** is either from shops in these or on the field.

The best up-to-date source of skiing information is the annual **Ski & Snowboard Guide** published by Brown Bear Publications (@www.brownbear.co.nz). It is freely downloadable from the website, and the printed guide can be picked up from visitor centres for a couple of bucks. For each field it gives a detailed rundown of facilities, season length, lift ticket prices and an indication of suitability for beginners, intermediates and advanced skiers. Heli-skiing is also dealt with and there's coverage of the main ski towns. Another **website** for all things skiing in New Zealand is @www.snow.co.nz.

Fishing

Kiwis grow up fishing: virtually everyone seems to have fond memories of long days out on a small boat trailing a line for snapper, if only to stock the beachside barbecue. All around the NZ coast there are low-key canoe, yacht and launch trips on which there is always time for a little **casual fishing**, but you'll also find plenty of trips aimed at more dedicated anglers. From December to May these scout the seas off the northern half of the North Island for marlin, shark and tuna. Regulations and bag limits are covered on the Ministry of Fisheries website, @www.fish.govt.nz.

Inland, the **rivers** and **lakes** are choked with rainbow and brown trout, quinnat and Atlantic salmon, all introduced for sport at the end of the nineteenth century. Certain areas have gained enviable reputations: Lake Taupo is world-renowned for its rainbow trout; South Island rivers, particularly around Gore, boast the finest brown trout; and the braided gravel-bed rivers draining the eastern slopes of the Southern Alps bear superb salmon.

A national **fishing licence** ($105 for the year from Oct 1–Sept 30, $21/24hr) covers all New Zealand's lakes and rivers except for those in the Taupo catchment area, where a local licensing arrangement applies. They're available from sports shops everywhere and directly from Fish and Game NZ (@www.fishandgame.org.nz), the agency responsible for managing freshwater sports fisheries. The website also lists bag limits and local regulations.

Wherever you fish, **regulations** are taken seriously and are rigidly enforced. If you're found with an undersize catch or an over-full bag, heavy fines may be imposed and equipment confiscated. Other fishy websites include @www.fishinginnewzealand.com and www.fishing.net.nz.

Horse trekking

New Zealand's highly urbanized population leaves a huge amount of countryside available for **horse trekking**, occasionally along beaches, often through patches of native bush and tracts of farmland. There are schools everywhere and all levels of experience are catered for, but more experienced riders might prefer the greater scope of full-day or even week-long wilderness treks (see p.61). We've highlighted some noteworthy places and operators throughout the Guide, and there's a smattering of others listed at @www.truenz.co.nz/horsetrekking.

Mountain biking

If you prefer a smaller saddle, you'll find a stack of places renting out **mountain bikes**. The main trail-biking areas around Rotorua, Queenstown, Mount Cook and Hanmer Springs will often have a couple of companies willing to take you out on **guided rides**. For information about Kiwi **off-road biking** consult @www.mountainbike.co.nz.

Spectator sports

If God were a rugby coach almost every New Zealander would be a religious fundamentalist. News coverage often gives headline prominence to sport, particularly the All Blacks, and entire radio stations are devoted to sports talkback, usually dwelling on occasions when Kiwi underdogs overcome better-funded teams from more populous nations. Kiwis are by and large an active bunch, most preferring to fish, play some form of sport or tramp.

As elsewhere, most major sports events are televised. Increasingly these are on subscription channels such as Sky TV, which encourages a devoted following in pubs.

Anyone with a keen interest in sport or just a desire to see the less reserved side of the Kiwi character should attend a rugby game. Local papers advertise games along with ticket booking details. **Bookings** for many of the bigger events can be made through Ticketek (🕸www.ticketek.co.nz), although, except for the over-subscribed internationals and season finals, you can usually just buy a ticket at the gate.

Rugby

Opponents quake in their boots at the sight of fifteen strapping **All Blacks**, the national **rugby** team, performing their pre-match *haka*, and few spectators remain unmoved. Kiwi hearts swell at the sight, secure in the knowledge that their national team is always among the world's best, and anything less than a resounding victory is considered a case for national mourning in the leader columns of the newspapers. However, the All Blacks' relative failure in the four-yearly **Rugby World Cup** – in 2007 they were knocked out by the French – means the team doesn't quite carry the respect it once merited.

Rugby (or Rugby Union, though it is seldom called this in NZ) is played through the winter, the season kicking off with the **Super 15 series** (mid-Feb to May) in which regional southern hemisphere teams (five apiece from NZ, South Africa and Australia, though controversially none from the Pacific Islands) play each other with the top four teams going on to contest the finals series.

Super 15 players make up the All Black team which through the middle of winter, hosts an international test series or two, including the annual **tri-nations series** (mid-July to Aug) against South Africa and Australia. Games between the All Blacks and Australia also contest the **Bledisloe Cup**, which creates much desired bragging rights for one or other nation for a year.

The international season often runs over into the **National Provincial Championship** (NPC), played from the middle of August until the end of October. Each province has a team, the bigger competing in the first division with the minor provinces generally filling up the second division. At the time of writing, Southland held the **Ranfurly Shield** (🕸www.ranfurlyshield .com), affectionately known as the "log of wood". Throughout the season, the holders accept challenges at their home ground, and the winner takes all. Occasionally minor teams will wrest the shield, and in the smaller provinces this is a huge source of pride, subsequent defences prompting a huge swelling of community spirit.

Domestic rugby ticket prices vary, depending on where you are in the ground but a good seat will cost around $30, while a similar seat for an international will start at around $45. To find out more, visit the NZ Rugby Union's official **website** 🕸www .nzrugby.co.nz, or the more newsy 🕸www .TheSilverFern.co.nz.

In 2011, the biggest ever **Rugby World Cup** will take place in New Zealand, with twenty nations vying for the trophy between September 9 and October 23. Battle will commence at twelve stadiums around the country, from Whangarei to Invercargill, with the final and both semi-finals taking place in Auckland. For more information check out the official website, Ⓦwww.rugbyworldcup .com. Given the clamour that accompanied the 2005 Lions Tour book absolutely everything as far in advance as possible, even if you are just visiting New Zealand with no intention of watching rugby.

Rugby league (Ⓦwww.rugbyleague.co.nz and www.nzrl.co.nz) has always been regarded as rugby's poor cousin, though success at international level has raised its profile. Rugby League's World Cup was last held in 2008 with the NZ Kiwis triumphing over Australia. New Zealand's only significant provincial team are the Auckland-based **Warriors**, who play in Australia's NRL during the March to early September season, with home games played at Ericsson Stadium, where you can buy tickets at the gate. The top eight teams in the league go through to the finals series in September.

Cricket

Attending a rugby match is something you shouldn't miss if you have the chance, but most visitors spend their time in New Zealand from October to March, when the stadiums are turned over to the country's traditional summer sport, **cricket** (Ⓦwww .nzcricket.co.nz). The national team – the **Black Caps** – hover around mid-table in international test and one-day rankings but periodic flashes of brilliance – and the odd unexpected victory over Australia – keep fans interested. You can usually just turn up at a ground and buy a **ticket** though games

held around Christmas and New Year fill up fast and internationals sell out in advance. **Tickets start at** around \$20 for an international, less for a domestic match.

Other sports

Other team sports lag far behind rugby and cricket, though women's **netball** (Ⓦwww .netballnz.co.nz) has an enthusiastic following and live TV coverage of international fixtures involving the Silver Ferns get good audiences.

Soccer in New Zealand has traditionally been thought of as slightly effete, though more youngsters play it than rugby and New Zealand's participation in the 2010 World Cup raised the game's profile nationally. NZ's only representative in the Australian National Soccer League (NSL; Ⓦwww.football australia.com.au), is Wellington Phoenix (Ⓦwww.wellingtonphoenix.com). The season runs from October to early April and home games are played at Westpac Stadium in Wellington; **tickets** (from around \$40 for a domestic match) can be bought at the gate or on the team's website.

In recent years **yachting** has attracted heightened interest: Auckland is a frequent midway point for round-the-world yacht races and has twice hosted the **America's Cup**. New Zealand's **Olympic** heritage is patchy, with occasional clutches of medals from rowing and yachting and a long pedigree of **middle-distance runners**. These days, however, multi-event championships and endurance events like triathlons and Iron Man races seem to dominate.

Culture and etiquette

Ever since Maori arrived in the land they named Aotearoa, New Zealand has been a nation of immigrants. The majority of residents trace their roots back to Britain and Ireland, and northern European culture prevails with a strong Maori and Polynesian influence. New Zealand's policy of bi-culturalism gives Maori and Pakeha (white European) values equal status, at least nominally. In practice, the operation of Parliament and the legal system is rooted in the old country, the Queen continues as head of state and beams out from all coins and the $20 note, and, along with "God Defend New Zealand", "God Save the Queen" remains one of the country's two official national anthems.

That said, **Maori** are very much part of mainstream contemporary NZ society (see *Maori in the modern world* colour section), but there's also a parallel Maori world you'll rarely see as a tourist, though some idea can be gleaned from commercial cultural tours. The racial tension that does exist mostly stays below the surface (aside from some issue-specific protests), and as a visitor you'll experience little and probably come away from New Zealand with the impression of a relatively tolerant society.

In the last couple of decades **Asian immigration** (principally from China and Korea, but also from the Indian subcontinent) has seen Asians make up around seven percent of the population (around half that of Maori) nationwide. In the Auckland region, though, this figure rises to over eighteen percent, making some form of tri-culturalism a possibility in the future.

Notwithstanding this mix, the archetypal **Kiwi personality** is rooted in the desire to make a better life in a unique and sometimes unaccommodating land. New Zealanders are inordinately fond of stories of plucky little Kiwis overcoming great odds and succeeding, perceiving the NZ persona to be rooted in self-reliance, inventiveness and bravery, tempered by a certain self-deprecating humour. Over-achieving "tall poppies" are routinely cut down.

Sport is a huge passion; the country has consistently punched above its weight in international competition, especially on the rugby field where the All Blacks are frequently at the top of the world rankings.

Despite a reputation for a rugby-playing, beer-swilling, male-dominated culture, Kiwis like to point out that they run an open-minded and egalitarian society. In 1893, New Zealand became the first country with **women's suffrage**, while generous pensions and free public health followed in the first half of the twentieth century. In 1985 New Zealand declared its waters **nuclear-free**, angering its US and Australian defence partners. Broadly liberal social attitudes prevail, with Japanese whaling and genetic modification hot topics.

New Zealand's relationship with its larger neighbour is a cause for endless entertainment on both sides of "the ditch" (the Tasman). Kiwis and **Aussies** are like siblings: there are lots of scraps (mostly verbal), especially when it comes to sport, but they're the first to jump to each other's defence in everything from military conflict to pub brawls. Mostly it's just good-natured ribbing but you won't be in New Zealand long before you hear something disparaging about Australians.

Etiquette

New Zealanders are refreshingly relaxed, low-key and free of pretension, and you're likely to be greeted with an informal "gidday!", "Kia ora!" (Hi) or "Kia ora, bro!" (Hi, mate). **Dress standards** are as informal as the greetings and unless you're on business or have a diplomatic function to attend you can leave your suit and tie at home; even the finest restaurants only require smart attire. The more pretentious nightclubs operate dress policies, mostly nothing more than a ban on work clothes and trainers. **Nudity** on beaches is pretty rare, but as long as you're reasonably discreet no one is likely to be too bothered.

The legal **drinking age** is 18, but by law you may be asked to prove your age by showing ID, which must be either a NZ driver's licence or a passport – bring it with you as foreign driver's licences aren't accepted.

Smoking is increasingly outlawed. It's banned on all public transport and in public buildings and is only permitted in outdoor areas of restaurants, cafés and bars – with petitions doing the rounds to ban it entirely on some city streets.

The Kiwi attitude to **tipping** is pleasingly uncomplicated. No tip is expected, though reward for excellent service in restaurants and cafés is appreciated.

Living in New Zealand

New Zealand is the sort of place people come for a short visit and end up wanting to stay (at least for a few months). Unless you have substantial financial backing that will probably mean finding some work. And while your earning potential in New Zealand isn't necessarily going to be great, you can at least supplement your budget for multiple bungy jumps, skydiving lessons and the like. Paid casual work is typically in tourism-linked service industries, or in orchard work.

For the last few years unemployment has remained relatively low and, providing you have the necessary paperwork finding casual work shouldn't be too difficult, while better-paid, short-term **professional jobs** are quite possible if you have the skills. Employment agencies are a good bet for this sort of work, or simply look at general job-search websites such as Ⓦ search4jobs.co.nz and the jobs section of Ⓦ www.trademe.co.nz. The **minimum wage** for all legally employed folk over the age of 16 (other than 16- and 17-year-old new entrants or trainees) is $12.50 an hour. If you'd rather not tackle the red tape you can simply reduce your travelling costs by **working for your board** (though technically the Immigration Department still considers this to be work).

Working for board and lodging

A popular way of getting around the country cheaply is to **work for your board and lodging**, typically toiling for 4–6 hours a day. **FHiNZ** (Farm Helpers in New Zealand;

Ⓦ www.fhinz.co.nz) organizes stays on farms, orchards and horticultural holdings for singles, couples and families; no experience is needed. Almost two hundred places are listed in its booklet ($25; sold online) and accommodation ranges from basic to quite luxurious. The international **WWOOF** (Willing Workers on Organic Farms; Ⓦ www.wwoof .co.nz) coordinates over a thousand proper-ties (membership, for one or a couple, with online access $40 or printed booklet $50), mostly farms but also orchards, market gardens and self-sufficiency-orientated small-holdings, all using organic methods to a greater or lesser degree. They'll expect a stay of around five nights, though much longer periods are common; you **book direct** (preferably a week or more in advance). There have been occasional reports of taskmasters; make sure you discuss what's expected before you commit yourself. Property managers are vetted but **solo women** may prefer placements with couples or families. Other organizations have fewer guarantees, though many are perfectly reputable.

A similar organization is the online **Help Exchange** (⊛www.helpx.net), which supplies a regularly updated list of hosts on farms as well as at homestays, B&Bs, hostels and lodges, who need extra help in return for meals and accommodation; you register online and book direct.

Visas, permits and red tape

Australians can work legally in New Zealand without any paperwork. Otherwise, if you're aged 18–30, the easiest way to work legally is through the **Working Holiday Scheme** (WHS), which gives you a temporary work permit valid for twelve months. An unlimited number of Brits, Irish, Americans, Canadians, Japanese, Belgian, Danish, Finnish, French, German, Italian, Dutch, Norwegian and Swedish people in this age bracket are eligible each year, plus various annual quotas of Argentineans, Brazilians, Chilean, Chinese, Czech, Estonians, Hong Kong citizens, Koreans, Latvians, Singaporeans, Malaysians, Maltese, Mexicans, Peruvians, Taiwanese, Thai and Uruguayans on a first-come-first-served basis; apply as far in advance as you can. You'll need a passport, NZ$120 for the application, evidence of an onward ticket out of New Zealand (or the funds to pay for it), and the equivalent of NZ$350 per month of your intended stay to show you can support yourself. Brits can alternatively apply for a 23-month stay. Working holiday-makers who can show they've worked in the horticulture or viticulture industries for at least three months may be eligible to obtain an extra three-month stay in New Zealand with a **Working Holidaymaker Extension** (WHE) permit. Applications are made through **Immigration New Zealand** (☏09/914 4100, ⊛www.immigration.govt.nz), which has details and downloadable forms on its website.

Some visitors are tempted to **work illegally**, something for which you could be fined or deported. However, eligible visitors over 18 (no upper age restriction) who are already in NZ can apply to **Immigration New Zealand** for a **Variation of Conditions** (VOC), allowing them to take up seasonal work in the horticulture and viticulture industries for six weeks. Alternatively, visitors already in New Zealand may be able to work for **Supplementary Seasonal Employer** (SSE) scheme employers in areas where labour shortages exist. A similar scheme, **Recognized Seasonal Employer Policy** (RSE), is open to those overseas at the time of application – contact the **Immigration Service** for details. The only other legal option is trying to gain immigrant status – not something to be tackled lightly.

Anyone working legally in New Zealand needs to obtain a **tax number** from the local Inland Revenue Department office (⊛www.ird.govt.nz); without this your employer will have trouble paying you. The process can take up to ten working days, though you can still work while the wheels of bureaucracy turn. Depending on your level of income, the tax department rakes in from 14.2 to 39.7 percent of your earnings and you probably won't be able to reclaim any of it. Many companies will also only pay wages into a **bank account**, though opening one is easy (see p.76).

Casual work

One of the main sources of casual work is **fruit-picking** or related **orchard work** such as packing or pruning and thinning. The main areas are Kerikeri in the Bay of Islands for citrus and kiwi fruit, Hastings in Hawke's Bay for apples, pears and peaches, Tauranga and Te Puke for kiwi fruit, and Alexandra and Cromwell in Central Otago for stone fruit. Most work is available during the autumn **picking season**, which runs roughly from January to May, but you can often find something just as easily in the off season. In popular working areas, some hostels cater to short-term workers, and these are usually the best places to find out what's going.

Picking can be hard-going, physical work and **payment** is usually by the quantity gathered, rather than by the hour. When you're starting off, the poor returns can be frustrating but with persistence and application you can soon find yourself grossing $100 or more in an eight-hour day. Rates vary considerably so it's worth asking around, factoring in any transport, meals and accommodation, which are sometimes included. Indoor packing work tends to be paid hourly.

Particularly in popular tourist areas – Rotorua, Nelson, Queenstown – people running **cafés**, **bars** and **hostels** often need extra staff during peak periods. If you have no luck, try more out-of-the-way locales, where there'll be fewer travellers clamouring for work. Bar and restaurant work pays minimum wage and upwards, depending on your level of experience, but tips are negligible. Generally you'll need to commit to at least three months. **Ski resorts** occasionally employ people during the June to October season, usually in catering roles. Hourly wages may be supplemented by a lift pass and subsidized food and drink, though finding affordable accommodation can be difficult and may offset a lot of what you gain. Hiring clinics for ski and snowboard instructors are usually held at the beginning of the season at a small cost, though if you're experienced it's better to apply directly to the resort beforehand.

In addition to local hostels and backpackers, handy **resources** to **look for work** include agencies such as NZ Job Search (℡09/357 3996, ⓦwww.nzjs.co.nz), which details the legalities, helps place people in jobs, and guides its clients through setting up bank accounts and dealing with the IRD. For fruit picking and the like, check out sites such as ⓦwww.seasonal work.co.nz, ⓦhttp://pickapicker.net, ⓦwww .picknz.co.nz and ⓦwww.job.co.nz.

Volunteering

A useful starting point is the online service from the UK-based **The Gapyear Company** (ⓦwww.gapyear.com), which offers free membership plus heaps of information on volunteering, travel, contacts and living abroad. The Department of Conservation's **Conservation Volunteer Programme** (search at ⓦwww.doc.govt.nz) provides an excellent way to spend time out in the NZ bush while putting something back into the environment. Often you will get into areas most visitors never see, and learn some skills while you're at it. Projects include bat surveys, kiwi monitoring and nest protection, as well as more rugged tasks like track maintenance, tree planting and hut repair. You can muck in for just a day or up to a couple of weeks, and sometimes there is a fee (perhaps $50–200) to cover food and transport. Application forms are available on the website. Programmes are in high demand and often book up well in advance, so it's worth applying before you reach New Zealand.

Travel essentials

Children

New Zealand is a child-friendly place, and while other people's kids aren't revered in the way they are in Mediterranean Europe, if you're **travelling with children** you'll find broad acceptance. In fact getting to and from New Zealand might be the most difficult part. Unless you are coming from Australia, **flights** are inevitably long so it will probably pay to break your journey, or at least make sure your airline offers plenty of distractions to keep the little ones entertained.

Once in New Zealand, **accommodation** is easy. Family rooms are almost always available at motels and hostels, and holiday parks (campsites) typically offer self-contained units where the whole family can be together. The better holiday parks also have kids' play areas and often a swimming pool. To be more self-sufficient, consider renting a medium-sized **campervan** with its own shower and toilet, though the downside is that you'll have no escape.

Travelling around you'll find **public toilets** in most towns and anywhere tourists

B

congregate – cleanliness standards are usually good.

Older kids can often join in adult **adventure activities**, though restrictions do apply. Bungy operators usually require a **minimum age** of 10, though this might rise to 12 or 13 for the bigger jumps. Whitewater rafting is typically limited to those 13 and over, though there are a few easier family-oriented trips. Similar restrictions apply to other activities, so ask when you book. **Family tickets** are often available and usually cost about the same as two adults and one child.

Children are welcomed in most cafés and **restaurants**, and most will make a reasonable effort to accommodate you.

Costs

The relatively strong Kiwi dollar means that New Zealand is no bargain, but with high standards of quality and service the country is still good value for money.

Daily costs vary enormously, and the following estimates are per person for two people travelling together. (With the prevalence of good hostels, **single travellers** can live almost as cheaply as couples, though you'll pay around thirty percent more if you want a room to yourself.)

If you are on a tight budget, using public transport, camping or staying in hostels, and cooking most of your own meals, you could scrape by on $50 a day. Renting a car, staying in budget motels, and eating out a fair bit, you're looking at more like $150 a day. Step up to comfortable B&Bs and nicer restaurants, throw in a few trips, and you can easily find yourself spending over $300 a day. Also, you can completely blow your budget on **adventure trips** such as a bungy jump ($110–240) or tandem parachuting ($250 plus), so it pays to think carefully about how to get the maximum bang for your buck.

New Zealanders are a straightforward bunch and the price quoted is what you pay. With the exception of some business hotels, the 15-percent Goods and Service Tax (**GST**) is always included in the listed price. GST refunds are available on more expensive items bought then taken out of the country – keep your receipts and carry the items as hand luggage.

Student **discounts** are few and far between, but you can make substantial savings on accommodation and travel by buying one of the backpacker or YHA cards (see p.45); **kids** (see p.69) enjoy reductions of around fifty percent on most trains, buses and entry to many sights.

Crime and personal safety

New Zealand's rates of violent crime are in line with those in other developed countries and you'll almost certainly come across some grisly stories in the media. Still, as long as you use your common sense and don't drop your guard just because you're on holiday, you're unlikely to run into any trouble. Some caution is needed in the **seedier quarters** of the larger cities where it is unwise for lone women to walk late at night. Obviously the more isolated a spot the less chance of getting help. One major safety issue is "**boy racers**" using city and town streets as racetracks for customized cars, leading to bystander fatalities. Although the police do take action they are relatively thin on the ground so be careful when out late in city suburbs.

It always pays to take precautions against petty theft, particularly from cars and campervans. When staying in cities you should move valuables into your lodging, but thieves also prey on visitors' vehicles left at trailheads and car parks. Campervans containing all your possessions make obvious and easy pickings. Take your valuables with you, put packs and bags out of sight and get good insurance. When setting out on long walks use a secure car park if possible, where your vehicle will be kept safe for a small sum.

Police and the law

As everywhere, there are cases of corruption and brutality but on the whole the police are friendly and helpful. If you do get arrested,

Emergency phone calls

☏**111** is the free emergency telephone number to summon the police, ambulance or fire service.

you will be allowed one phone call; a solicitor will be appointed if you can't afford one and you may be able to claim legal aid. It is unlikely that your consulate will take more than a passing interest unless there is something strange or unusual about the case against you.

The laws regarding **alcohol consumption** have traditionally been pretty lenient, though persistent rowdy behaviour has encouraged some towns to ban drinking in public spaces. Still, most of the time nobody's going to bother you if you fancy a beer on the beach or glass of wine at some wayside picnic area. The same does not apply to drink driving (see p.35), which is taken very seriously.

Marijuana has a reputation for being very potent and relatively easily available. It is, however, illegal and although a certain amount of tolerance is sometimes shown towards personal use, the police and courts take a dim view of larger quantities and hard drugs, handing out long custodial sentences. You'll hear extensive coverage of the country's battle with the drug known as "**P**" (methamphetamine), which is a significant problem, much of the trade controlled by gangs.

Prejudice

New Zealanders like to think of themselves as a tolerant and open-minded people, and foreign visitors are generally welcomed with open arms. Racism is far from unknown, but you're unlikely to experience overt **discrimination** or be refused service because of your race, colour or gender. In out-of-the-way rural pubs, women, foreigners, and just about anyone who doesn't live within a 10km radius, may get a frosty reception, though this soon breaks down once you get talking.

Despite constant efforts to maintain good relations between Maori and Pakeha (white New Zealanders), tensions do exist. Ever since colonization, **Maori** have achieved lower educational standards, earned less and maintained disproportionately high rates of unemployment and imprisonment. Slowly Maori are getting some restitution for the wrongs perpetrated on their race, which of course plays into the hands of those who feel that such positive discrimination is unfair.

"After all, we're all New Zealanders" is a refrain often heard.

Recent high levels of immigration from East Asia – Hong Kong, China and Taiwan in particular – have rapidly changed the demographics in Auckland, where most have settled. Central Auckland also has several English-language schools that are mostly full of Asian students. The combined effect means that in parts of Auckland, especially downtown, longer-established New Zealanders are in the minority. It is a sensation that some Maori and Pakeha find faintly disturbing. There's little overt racism, but neither is there much mixing.

Electricity

New Zealand operates a 230/240volt, 50Hz AC **power supply**, and sockets take a three-prong, flat-pin type of plug. Suitable socket adaptors are widely available in New Zealand and at most international airports; and for phone chargers and laptops that's all you'll need. In most other cases, North American appliances require both a transformer and an adaptor, British and Irish equipment needs only an adaptor and Australian appliances need no alteration.

Entry requirements

All visitors to New Zealand need a passport, which must be valid for at least three months beyond the time you intend to stay. When flying to New Zealand you'll probably need to show you have an **onward or return ticket** before they'll let you board the plane.

On arrival, British citizens are automatically issued with a permit to stay for up to six months, and a three-month permit is granted to citizens of most other European countries, Southeast Asian nations, Japan, South Africa, the US and Canada, and several other countries. Australian citizens can stay indefinitely.

Other nationalities need to obtain a visitor visa in advance from a New Zealand embassy, costing the local equivalent of NZ$130 and usually valid for three months. Visas are issued by Immigration New Zealand (@www.immigration.govt.nz). See p.68 for advice on working visas.

For **foreign embassies** and consulates in NZ see the "Listings" sections of the

Auckland and Wellington chapters, on p.122 and p.427 respectively.

Websites and contact details for all NZ embassies and consulates **abroad** can be found at ⓦwww.nzembassy.com.

Quarantine and customs

In a country all too familiar with the damage that can be caused by introduced plants and animals, New Zealand's Ministry of Agriculture and Forestry (MAF; ⓦwww.maf.govt.nz /quarantine) takes a hard line. On arrival you'll be asked to **declare any food**, plants or parts of plants, animals (dead or alive), equipment used with animals, camping gear, golf clubs, bicycles, biological specimens and hiking boots. Outdoor equipment and walking boots will be taken away, inspected and perhaps cleaned then returned a few minutes later. After a long flight it can all seem a bit of a pain, but such precautions are important and there are huge fines for non-compliance. Be sure to dispose of any fresh fruit, vegetables and meat in the bins provided or you are liable for an instant $400 fine (even for that orange you forgot about in the bottom of your bag). Processed foods are usually allowed through, but must be declared.

Visitors aged 18 and over are entitled to a **duty-free allowance** (ⓦwww.customs .govt.nz) of 200 cigarettes (or 250 grams of tobacco, or 50 cigars), 4.5 litres of wine or beer, three 1125ml bottles of spirits, and up to $700 worth of goods. There are **export restrictions** on wildlife, plants, antiquities and works of art.

Gay and lesbian travellers

Homosexuality was decriminalized in New Zealand in 1986 and the **age of consent** was set at 16 (the same as for heterosexuals). It is illegal to discriminate against gays and people with HIV or AIDS, and NZ makes no limitation on people with HIV or AIDS entering the country.

Though there remains an undercurrent of redneck intolerance, particularly in rural areas, it generally stays well below the surface, and New Zealand is a broadly gay-friendly place. The mainstream acceptance is such that the New Zealand Symphony Orchestra and Auckland Philharmonia composer, Gareth Farr, also performs as drag queen Lilith LaCroix. This tolerant attitude has conspired to de-ghettoize the gay community; even in **Auckland** and **Wellington**, the only cities with genuinely vibrant gay scenes, there aren't any predominantly gay areas and most venues have a mixed clientele. Auckland's scene is generally the largest and most lively, but the intimate nature of Wellington makes it more accessible and welcoming. Christchurch, Nelson and Queenstown also have small gay scenes.

Major **events** on the gay calendar include the annual **Vinegar Hill Summer Camp**, held 5km north of the small town of Hunterville, in the middle of the North Island, from Boxing Day to just after New Year. It's a very laidback affair, with a couple of hundred gay men and women camping out, mixing and partying. There's no charge (except a few dollars for camping), no tickets and no hot water, but a large river runs through the grounds and everyone has a great time. Queenstown's **Gay Ski Week** (ⓦwww .gayskiweeknz.com) in late August includes Friday-night skiing at Coronet Peak and a bunch of après-ski events.

The best source of on-the-ground information is the fortnightly gay newspaper *Express* (ⓦwww.expresstoday.co.nz), available free in gay-friendly cafés and venues and almost any decent bookstore.

Gay travel websites

ⓦ**www.adventureout.co.nz** Small-group outdoor adventure holidays for gay men.

ⓦ**www.gaynewzealand.com** A virtual tour of the country with a gay and lesbian slant.

ⓦ**www.gaynz.net.nz** Useful site with direct access to gay, lesbian, bisexual and transgender information including the Pink Pages, covering what's on in the gay community and a calendar of events all over the country.

ⓦ**www.gaytravel.net.nz** A gay online accommodation and travel reservation service.

ⓦ**www.rainbowtourism.com** An excellent resource for gay and lesbian travellers in both NZ and Oz, listing accommodation, events, clubs and tours.

Health

New Zealand is relatively free of serious health hazards and the most common pitfall is simply underestimating the power of nature. **No vaccinations** are required to enter the country, but you should make sure you have adequate health cover in your travel insurance, especially if you plan to take on the great outdoors (see p.59 for advice on tramping health and safety).

New Zealand has a good health service that's reasonably cheap by world standards. All visitors are covered by the accident compensation scheme, under which you can claim some medical and hospital expenses in the event of an accident, but without full cover in your travel insurance you could still face a hefty bill. For more minor ailments, you can visit a doctor for a consultation (around \$60) and, armed with a prescription, buy any required medication at a pharmacy at a reasonable price.

Sun, surf and earthquakes

Visitors to New Zealand frequently get caught out by the intensity of the **sun**, its damaging ultraviolet rays easily penetrating the thin ozone layer and reducing burn times to as little as ten minutes in spring and summer. Stay out of the sun (or keep covered up) as much as possible between 11am and 3pm, and always slap on plenty of sunblock. Re-apply every few hours as well as after swimming, and keep a check on any moles on your body: if you notice any changes, during or after your trip, see a doctor right away.

The sea is a more immediate killer and even strong swimmers should read our **surf** warning (see box below).

New Zealand is regularly shaken by **earthquakes**, but most are minor and it is not something to worry about. If the worst happens, the best advice is to stand in a doorway or crouch under a table. If caught in the open, try to get inside; failing that, keep your distance from trees and rocky outcrops to reduce the chances of being injured by falling branches or debris.

Wildlife hazards

New Zealand's wildlife is amazingly benign. There are no snakes, scorpions or other

---

Always swim between the flags

The New Zealand coast is frequently pounded by ferocious surf and even strong swimmers can find themselves in difficulty in what may seem benign conditions. Every day throughout the peak holiday weeks (Christmas–Jan), and at weekends through the rest of the summer (Nov–Easter), the most popular surf beaches are monitored daily from around 10am to 5pm. Lifeguards stake out a section of beach between two red and yellow flags and continually monitor that area: **always swim between the flags.**

Before entering the water, watch other swimmers to see if they are being dragged along the beach by a strong along-shore **current** or **rip**. Often the rip will turn out to sea, leaving a "river" of disturbed but relatively calm water through the pattern of curling breakers. On entering the water, feel the strength of the waves and current before committing yourself too deeply, then keep glancing back to where you left your towel to judge your drift along the shore. Look out too for **sand bars**, a common feature of surf beaches at certain tides: wading out to sea, you may well be neck deep and then suddenly be only up to your knees. The corollary is moments after being comfortably within your depth you'll be floundering around in a **hole**, reaching for the bottom. Note that **boogie boards**, while providing flotation, can make you vulnerable to rips, and riders should always wear fins (flippers).

If you do find yourself in **trouble**, try not to panic, raise one hand in the air and yell to attract the attention of other swimmers and surf rescue folk. Most of all, don't struggle against the current; either swim across the rip or let it drag you out. Around 100–200m offshore the current will often subside and you can swim away from the rip and bodysurf the breakers back to shore. If you have to be rescued (or are just feeling generous), a large donation is in order. Surf lifeguards are dedicated volunteers, always strapped for cash and in need of new rescue equipment.

nasties, and only a few poisonous **spiders**, all rarely seen. No one has died from an encounter with a spider for many years but if you get a serious reaction from a bite be sure to see a doctor or head to the nearest hospital, where antivenin will be available.

Shark attacks are also rare; you are more likely to be carried away by a strong tide than a great white, though it still pays to be sensible and obey any local warnings when swimming.

A far bigger problem are **mosquitoes** and **sandflies** which are a great irritant, but generally free of life-threatening diseases. The West Coast of the South Island in the summer is the worst place for these beasts, though they appear to a lesser degree in many other places across the country: a liberal application of repellent keeps them at bay.

At the microscopic level, **giardia** inhabits many rivers and lakes, and infection results from drinking contaminated water, with symptoms appearing several weeks later: a bloated stomach, cramps, explosive diarrhoea and wind. The Department of Conservation advises you purify drinking water by using iodine-based solutions or tablets (regular chlorine-based tablets aren't effective against giardia), by fast-boiling water for at least seven minutes or by using a giardia-rated filter (obtainable from any outdoors or camping shop).

The relatively rare **amoebic meningitis** is another waterborne hazard, this time contracted from hot pools. Commercial pools are almost always safe, but in natural pools surrounded by earth you should avoid contamination by keeping your head above water. The amoeba enters the body via the nose or ears, lodges in the brain, and weeks later causes severe headaches, stiffness of the neck, hypersensitivity to light, and eventually coma. If you experience any of these symptoms, seek medical attention immediately.

Insurance

New Zealand's Accident Compensation Commission (@www.acc.co.nz) provides limited medical treatment for visitors injured while in New Zealand, but is no substitute for having comprehensive **travel insurance** to cover against theft, loss and illness or injury.

Before paying for a new policy, it's worth checking whether you are already covered: some home insurance policies may cover your possessions when overseas, and many private medical schemes include cover when abroad. Students will often find that their student health coverage extends during the vacations and for one term beyond the date of last enrolment.

After exhausting the possibilities above, you might want to contact a specialist travel insurance, or consider the travel insurance deal we offer (see below). Most of them exclude so-called **dangerous activities** unless an extra premium is paid. In New Zealand this can mean scuba diving, bungy jumping, whitewater rafting, windsurfing, skiing and snowboarding, and even tramping under some policies.

Many policies can exclude coverage you don't need. If you do take medical coverage, ascertain whether benefits will be paid as treatment proceeds or only after return home, and whether there is a 24hour medical emergency number. When securing

Rough Guides travel insurance

Rough Guides has teamed up with WorldNomads.com to offer great **travel insurance** deals. Policies are available to residents of over 150 countries, with cover for a wide range of **adventure sports**, 24hr emergency assistance, high levels of medical and evacuation cover and a stream of **travel safety information**. Roughguides.com users can take advantage of their policies online 24/7, from anywhere in the world – even if you're already travelling. And since plans often change when you're on the road, you can extend your policy and even claim online. Roughguides.com users who buy travel insurance with WorldNomads.com can also leave a positive footprint and donate to a community development project. For more information go to @**www.roughguides.com/shop**.

baggage cover, make sure that the per-article limit will cover your most valuable possession. If you need to make a claim, you should keep receipts for medicines and medical treatment, and in the event you have anything stolen, you must obtain an official statement from the police.

Internet

Internet access is abundant and fairly cheap though seldom blindingly fast. You'll find coin-operated machines at most **visitor centres,** backpacker hostels, motels and campsites, generally charging around $6 an hour. Most are set up with card readers, headsets and webcams, and even loaded with things like Skype and iTunes. At more expensive accommodation there'll often be a free-use computer, and laptop connections may be available.

There's often better functionality and lower prices at the abundant **internet cafés** lining city streets, which typically charge $3–6 per hour. **Libraries** also have internet access and while some offer this service free, others charge.

Wi-fi access is increasingly widespread. Many holiday parks, hostels, motels and hotels now have a hotspot accessible using your credit card or by buying access from reception. Rates vary considerably: an hour might cost $10 but you can often get a full 24hour day for under $25. The swankier B&Bs and lodges will usually have free wi-fi in all rooms. Organizations such as Global Gossip (ⓦ www.globalgossip.com) and Zenbu (ⓦ www.zenbu.net.nz) allow you to store your purchased time for future use. Telecom also has a **nationwide network** of several hundred wireless hotspots (Starbucks and several other café chains, airports, Telecom stores, some libraries), charged at $10 per hour (or 120Mb). You just pay for the minutes you use.

Mail

NZ Post (ⓦ www.nzpost.com) runs New Zealand's reliable mail service. Stamps, postcards, envelopes, packing materials and a lot more can be bought at **post offices** (aka **PostShops**), which are open Monday to Friday 8.30am to 5pm, plus Saturday 9 or 10am to noon or 1pm in some large towns

and cities. Red and silver **post boxes** are found outside post offices and on street corners, and mail is collected daily.

There are two forms of **domestic delivery**: Standard (50¢, or $1 for larger envelopes), delivered to any destination within 2–3 days; and FastPost ($1/$1.50), delivered in 1–2 days. **International airmail** takes 3–6 days to reach Australia ($1.80), and 6–12 days to Europe, Asia and the United States ($2.30). Postcards cost $1.80 to anywhere in the world. **Parcels** are quite expensive to send overseas as everything goes by air and the economy service only saves fifteen percent for a considerably delayed delivery. Your choice is either Airmail (1kg to Australia $14, US $29, Europe $32), which takes about a week, or Economy (1kg to Australia $12, US $25, Europe $27), which takes 2–5 weeks.

One post office in each major town operates a **Poste Restante** (or **General Delivery**) service where you can receive mail; we've listed the major ones in town accounts. Most hostels and hotels will keep mail for you, preferably marked with your expected date of arrival.

There is also an independent postal system called **Universal Mail** (ⓦ www .universalmail.co.nz) which only handles international mail and uses blue boxes. It is a little cheaper but there have been reports of very slow delivery.

Maps and GPS

Specialist outlets should have a reasonable stock of **maps** of New Zealand, including Rough Guides' own two-sided, 1:1,000,000 scale, waterproof fold-out sheet, which gives a good sense of the country's terrain. **Road atlases** are widely available in NZ bookshops and service stations; the most detailed are those produced by Kiwi Pathfinder, which indicate numerous points of interest and the type of road surface. Also look out for *A Driving Guide to Scenic New Zealand* ($38) with handy angled projections giving a real sense of the lay of the land. Many car- and van-rental places have **GPS navigation systems**, usually for an additional $5–10 a day.

With a road atlas and our city plans you can't go far wrong on the roads, but more detailed maps may be required for tramping.

All the major walks are covered by the **Parkmap** series, complete with photos (around $19 from DOC offices and bookshops in NZ), while the larger-scale 1:50,000 Topo50 and 1:250,000 Topo250 (both $10) cover the whole country.

Money

The Kiwi **dollar** is divided into 100 cents. There are $100, $50, $20, $10 and $5 notes made of a sturdy plastic material, and coins in denominations of $2, $1 (both gold in colour), 50¢, 20¢ and 10¢. Grocery prices are given to the nearest cent, but the final bill is rounded up or down to the nearest ten cents. All prices quoted in the Guide are in NZ dollars.

Exchange rates fluctuate substantially, but the NZ dollar currently trades at NZ$2.25 for £1, NZ$1.44 for US$1, NZ$1.95 for €1 and NZ$1.27 for A$1. Check current rates at Ⓦ www.xe.com.

Cards, cheques and ATMs

For purchases, visitors generally rely on **credit cards**, particularly Visa and Mastercard/Bankcard, which are widely accepted, though many hostels, campsites and homestays will only accept cash. American Express and Diners Club are far less useful. You'll also find credit cards handy for advance booking of accommodation and trips, and with the appropriate PIN you can obtain **cash advances** through 24-hour ATMs found almost everywhere. **Debit cards** are also useful for purchases and ATM cash withdrawals.

Travellers' cheques can be exchanged efficiently at banks and bureaux de change all over New Zealand and replaced if lost or stolen. Recognized brands – American Express, Thomas Cook, Mastercard and Visa – are accepted in all major currencies, but travellers' cheques (even those in NZ dollars) are not accepted as cash.

Banks

The major **banks** – ASB, ANZ, BNZ, Kiwibank (found in post offices), National Bank and Westpac – have branches in towns of any size and are open Monday to Friday from 9.30am to 4.30pm, with some city branches opening on Saturday mornings (until around 12.30pm). The big cities and tourist centres also have **bureaux de change**, which are typically open from 8am to 8pm daily.

If you are spending a few months in New Zealand (and especially if you are working), you may want to open a **bank account**. A New Zealand EFTPOS (debit) card can be used just about anywhere for purchases or obtaining cash, so you can go for weeks without ever visiting a bank.

In Auckland, the branch of Westpac at 229 Queen St and the ASB at the corner of Wyndham and Hobson streets are well set up for dealing with working backpackers' needs. In Christchurch visit the ASB Migrant Banking Unit, 112 Riccarton Rd, Christchurch. An account can usually be set up within a day; remember to take your passport.

Opening hours

New Zealand's larger cities and tourist centres are increasingly open all hours, with cafés, bars and supermarkets open till very late, and shops open long hours every day. Once you get into rural areas, things change rapidly, and core **shopping hours** (Mon–Fri 9am–5.30pm, Sat 9am–noon) apply, though tourist-orientated shops stay open daily until 8pm.

An ever-increasing number of **supermarkets** (at least one in or near each major city) now open 24/7 and small "dairies" (corner shops or convenience stores) also keep long hours and open on Sundays. **Museums** and sights usually open around 9am, although small-town museums often open only in the afternoons and/or only on specific days.

Public holidays and festivals are listed on p.53.

Phones

Given the near-ubiquity of mobile phones, and the prominence of Skype (or similar services) for international calling, most people don't have much need of **public payphones**, though they are still fairly widespread across New Zealand. Coin-operated phones are now rare, but all payphones accept major credit cards, account-based phonecards and slot-in disposable PhoneCards ($5, $10, $20 and

$50). These can be bought at post offices, newsagents, dairies, garages, i-SITEs and supermarkets.

A local call on a public payphone using coins or a slot-in PhoneCard costs $1 for the first fifteen minutes, then 20¢ a minute. NZ landline calls outside the local calling area cost $1 per minute, and calls to a cell phone are $1.20 per minute.

If you are staying with friends you may get to use a **private phone**, on which local calls are generally free and national calls typically cost around $0.20 per minute depending on what pricing plan your host is on.

Phone numbers

New Zealand **landline numbers** have only five area codes. The North Island is divided into four codes, while the South Island makes do with just one (☏03); all numbers in the Guide are given with their code. Even within the same area, you may have to dial the code if you're calling another town some distance away. **Mobile numbers** start with ☏021, 022, 027 or 029, and you'll come across **freephone** numbers which are all ☏0800 or 0508. Numbers prefixed ☏0900 are **premium-rated** and cannot be called from payphones.
National directory assistance ☏018 ($0.56 from a landline, $1 from a mobile; add $0.50 to be connected directly).
International directory assistance ☏0172 ($1.67 from a landline, $1.95 from a mobile).
Emergency services Police, ambulance and fire brigade ☏111 (no charge).

International dialling codes

To call New Zealand from overseas, dial the international access code (☏00 from the UK, ☏011 from the US and Canada, ☏0011

from Australia, ☏09 from South Africa), followed by ☏64, the area code minus its initial zero, and then the number.

To dial out of New Zealand, it's ☏00, followed by the country code (see box below), then the area code (without the initial zero if there is one) and the number. Remember that there'll be a time difference between your country and New Zealand (see "Time" on p.78 to avoid rude awakenings).

Phonecards and calling cards

For **long-distance and international calling** you are best off with pre-paid account-based **phonecards** (denominations from $5 to $50) that can be used on any phone; the cost of the call is deducted from your account, which can be topped up using your credit card. There are numerous such cards around offering highly competitive rates, but be wary of the very cheap ones: they are often internet-based and the voice quality can be poor and delayed. One reliable card is Telecom's Yabba (ⓦwww .yabba.co.nz) which charges just 10¢ to landlines in Australia, Ireland, the UK, Canada, the US and South Africa. Be warned, though, that public payphones now charge an additional 24¢ per minute for use of Yabba and all other account-based phonecards, so try to use them from private phones whenever possible.

Mobile phones

NZ has three **mobile** providers: Telecom (ⓦwww.telecom.co.nz), Vodafone (ⓦwww .vodafone.co.nz) and 2degrees (ⓦwww .2degreesmobile.co.nz), all running on GSM networks. All have excellent reception in populated areas but sporadic coverage in remoter spots. Telecom also runs an ageing

Calling home

Note that the initial zero is omitted from the area code when dialling the UK, Ireland and Australia.
Australia 00 + 61 + city code.
Republic of Ireland 00 + 353 + city code.
South Africa 00 + 27 + city code.
UK 00 + 44 + city code.
US and Canada 00 + 1 + area code.

CDMA network that has broader small town and backcountry coverage.

If you're thinking of bringing your phone from home check with your service to see if your phone will roam in NZ. GSM users can save money by using their own phone, buying a New Zealand SIM card ($30 from Vodafone or Telecom, $2 from 2degrees) and going pre-pay, though you'll have to give your contacts your new NZ number. Also be sure to check that your phone isn't locked to your home network. The **cheapest rates** are with 2degrees, with 44¢ calls and 9¢ texts to all phones in NZ and most western countries (including Australia, Canada, Ireland, UK and the US).

You can rent a phone on arrival at the airport for around $25, but it is hardly worth the bother when you can buy a basic model for under $80.

Photography

Camera shops and some pharmacies will process your **digital images** onto CD (for $6–10), and increasingly hostels and hotels have some way of allowing you to review your day's snaps. Uploading to websites or a home server is usually possible but restricted by the data cap on connections.

Shopping

NZ is hardly a shoppers' paradise: you're more likely to take home fond memories than a bag full of goodies. But there is stuff worth seeking out. One of the most popular souvenirs is a curvaceous **greenstone** (jade) pendant, probably based on a Maori design. They're available all over the country, though it makes sense to buy close to the main source of raw material around Greymouth and Hokitika on the West Coast of the South Island. Most of the cheaper goods are manufactured from Chinese jade, which is regarded as inferior: for the genuine article insist on NZ *pounamu* carved locally (see box, p.647).

A variation on this theme is the **bone pendant**. Several places around the country give you a chance to work a piece of cattle bone into your own design or something based on classic Maori iconography. With a little talent and application you should be able to whip up something to be proud of in a few hours. Something similar can be made of iridescent paua shell, or you can simply buy ready-made pieces fashioned into anything from buttons to detailed picture frames.

As everywhere, gift shops come laden with tacky trinkets you wouldn't look twice at, but you will find **photo books** full of superb shots of magnificent scenery. Look out in particular for books by Craig Potton and Andris Apse, but there are many other worthy examples.

Sheepskin and **wool** products are also big, as are garments – socks, sweaters etc – at least partly made from **possum fur**. New Zealanders hate these Australian pests and will thank you for supporting any industry which hastens their demise. A quality possum-fur throw will set you back over $1000 but cushion covers come much cheaper. Sheepskins go for around $100.

On a more practical level, you may need to supplement your wardrobe of **outdoor clothing**. There's plenty of stuff around, but look out for the Icebreaker (ⓦwww .icebreaker.com), Untouched World (ⓦwww .untouchedworld.co.nz) and Glowing Sky (ⓦwww.glowingsky.co.nz) brands of stylish Merino-wool garments, which are fairly pricey but feel great, keep you warm and don't harbour nasty odours as much as synthetics.

New Zealand doesn't do budget or mid-range **fashion clothing** all that well, but some of its top designers are world-class. Garments by Karen Walker, Kate Sylvester, Trelise Cooper, Alexandra Owen, Zambesi and World are expensive for most Kiwis, but may seem quite affordable if you're travelling with a strong currency.

If you want to dress up in a more permanent fashion, you might even consider a **tattoo**. Curvilinear designs derived from ferns or based on Maori iconography are popular and you'll have little trouble tracking down skilled *moko* artists.

Time and seasons

New Zealand Standard Time (NZST) is twelve hours ahead of Greenwich Mean Time, but, from the last Sunday in September to the first Sunday in April, Daylight Saving puts the clocks one hour further forward. Throughout the summer, when it is 8pm in New Zealand, it's 6pm in Sydney, 7am in London, 2am in New York, and 11pm the day before in Los Angeles.

New Zealand follows Britain's lead with **dates**, and 1/4/2009 means April 1 not January 4.

Don't forget that the southern hemisphere **seasons** are reversed: summer lasts roughly from November to March, and winter from June to September.

Tourist information

New Zealand promotes itself enthusiastically abroad through **Tourism New Zealand**, and its extensive website ⓦ www.newzealand .com.

Many of the information centres listed below, as well as some cafés, bars and hostels, keep a supply of **free newspapers** and **magazines** oriented towards backpackers – they're usually filled with promotional copy, but are informative nonetheless. *TNT* (ⓦ www.tntdownunder .com) is about the best.

Visitor centres

Every town of any size has an official **i-SITE visitor centre**, staffed by helpful and knowledgeable personnel and sometimes offering some form of video presentation on the area. Apart from dishing out local maps and leaflets, they offer a **free booking service** for accommodation, trips and activities, and onward travel, but only for businesses registered with them. Some (usually small) businesses choose not to register and may still be worth seeking out; we've mentioned them where relevant. In the more popular tourist areas, you'll also come across places representing themselves as **independent information centres** that usually follow a hidden agenda, typically promoting a number of allied adventure companies. While these can be excellent, it's worth remembering that their advice may not be completely impartial.

Other useful resources are **Department of Conservation** (DOC; ⓦ www.doc.govt.nz) offices and field centres, usually sited close to wilderness areas and popular tramping tracks, and sometimes serving as the local visitor centre as well. These are highly informative and well geared to trampers' needs, with local weather forecasts, intentions forms and maps as well as historic and environmental displays and audiovisual exhibitions. The website contains loads of detail on the environment and the latest conservation issues plus details on national parks and Great Walks.

Travellers with disabilities

Overall, New Zealand is disabled-traveller friendly. Many public buildings, galleries and museums are **accessible**, and many tour operators will make a special effort to help you participate in all manner of activities, such as swimming with dolphins or seals. However, restaurants and local public transport generally make few concessions.

Planning a trip

A good starting point is Tourism New Zealand's ⓦ www.newzealand.com which has a "People with Special Needs" section containing several useful links. There are also organized **tours** and **holidays** specifically for people with disabilities (see the contacts below).

Independent travellers should be upfront with travel agencies, insurance companies and travel companions about your limitations. If your walking capabilities are limited, remember that you are likely to need to cover lengthy distances while travelling (often over rough terrain).

Reading your travel **insurance** small print carefully to make sure that people with a pre-existing medical condition are not excluded could save you a fortune. Your travel agent can help make your journey simpler: airline or bus companies can better cater to your needs if they are expecting you. A **medical certificate** of your fitness to travel, provided by your doctor, is also extremely useful; some airlines or insurance companies may insist on it.

Accommodation

New accommodation must have at least one room designed for disabled access and many pre-existing places have converted rooms, including most YHA hostels, some motels, campsites and larger hotels. Older buildings, homestays and B&Bs are the least likely to lend themselves to such conversions.

For listings, go straight to ⓦwww .accomobility.co.nz which has a searchable database of places that have signed up for the service.

Travelling

Few airlines, trains, ferries and buses allow complete independence. Air New Zealand provides aisle wheelchairs on International (but not domestic) flights, and the rear toilet cubicles are wider than the others to facilitate access; for more details search for "Special Assistance" on its website. Other **domestic airlines** have poorer facilities. Interislander Cook Strait **ferries** have reasonable access for disabled travellers, including physical help while boarding, if needed, and adapted toilets. If given advance warning, trains will provide attendants to get passengers in wheelchairs or sight-impaired travellers on board, but moving around the train in a standard wheelchair is impossible and there are no specially adapted toilets; the problems with **long-distance buses** are much the same.

In cities there are some **taxis** specifically adapted for wheelchairs, but these must be pre-booked; otherwise taxi drivers obligingly hoist wheelchairs into the boot and their occupant onto a seat.

Contacts in New Zealand

Access Tourism NZ ⓦwww.accesstourismnz .org.nz. Interesting advocacy site.
Disability Resource Centre 14 Erson Ave, Royal Oak, Auckland ☏09/625 8069, ⓦwww .disabilityresource.org.nz. General resource centre.
DPA Level 4/173–175 Victoria St, Wellington, NZ ☏04/801 9100 ⓦwww.dpa.org.nz. Disability advocacy organization with useful links.

Enable New Zealand ☏0800/171 981, ⓦenable .co.nz. Organization assisting people with disabilities, though not specifically focused on travellers.
Galaxy Motors ☏0800/864 252, ⓦwww .galaxyautos.co.nz. Auckland company with rental vehicle for those with special mobility needs, plus personalized tours with a guide, companion or carer.
Ucan Tours 8 Campbell St, Sumner, Christchurch ☏03/326 7881, ⓦwww.ucantours.com. Accessible group travel, customized independent tours and vehicle rental.

Women travellers

Kiwi men have fairly progressive attitudes towards women, and travelling in New Zealand doesn't present any particular problems. Of course, there are some unevolved specimens who will assume a lone female (any female) is fair game for their attentions, but this is rare and **harassment** may well be less of a problem than it is at home.

Nonetheless, dangers do exist. Just because you're on holiday and the country seems benign you shouldn't let your guard down. Always follow the usual advice about not walking down empty city streets at night and avoiding hitchhiking: a modicum of common sense and a short taxi ride can avert a disaster.

In the unlikely event of trouble, contact ⓦwww.rapecrisis.org.nz. For support, Women's Centres around the country are listed on the Ministry of Women's Affairs website at ⓦwww.mwa.govt.nz/directory. You might also consider partly organizing your holiday through **Women Travel New Zealand** (ⓦwww.womentravel.co.nz), which offers essential information for the female visitor with links to retreats, women-oriented tour operators and its newsletter. Finally, Auckland's Women's Bookshop (see p.122) is a handy resource and puts on literary events.

Guide

Guide

1 Auckland and around.. 83

2 Northland 149

3 Western North Island 205

4 Central North Island.. 257

5 The Coromandel, Bay of Plenty and the East Cape............ 307

6 Poverty Bay, Hawke's Bay and the Wairarapa 359

7 Wellington and around... 397

8 Marlborough, Nelson and Kaikoura...................................... 429

9 Christchurch and south to Otago 493

10 Central South Island 545

11 Dunedin to Stewart Island 575

12 The West Coast... 619

13 Queenstown, Wanaka and the Gold Country....................... 667

14 Fiordland 727

Auckland and around

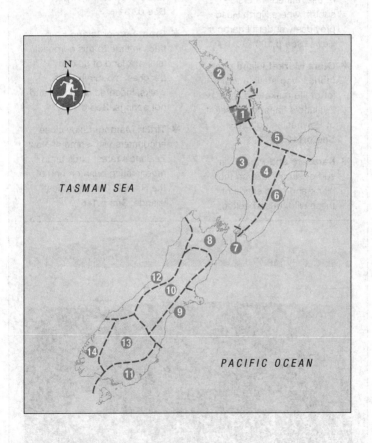

CHAPTER 1 # Highlights

* **Auckland Museum** The exemplary Maori and Pacific Island collection is the highlight of this popular museum. See p.102

* **Devonport** Stroll the streets of this refined waterside suburb where North Head provides wonderful harbour views. See p.109

* **Otara Market** Island print fabrics, veg stalls and a lot of life make this New Zealand's finest expression of Polynesian culture. See p.112

* **Karekare and Piha** Swim, surf or simply laze on the black-and-gold sands of these wild, bush-backed beaches less than an hour from the city. See p.126

* **Rangitoto Island** Make a day-trip to this gnarled lava landscape draped in pohutukawa forest with great views back to the city. See p.131

* **Great Barrier Island** Step back in time to this compact, laidback land of golden beaches, mountain bush walks, indented harbours and hot springs. See p.139

* **Tiritiri Matangi** Enjoy close encounters with some of New Zealand's rarest birds amid regenerating bush on one of the Hauraki Gulf's prettiest islands. See p.146

▲ Rangitoto Island from North Head

Auckland and around

uckland is New Zealand's largest city and, as the site of the major international airport, most visitors' first view of the country. Planes bank over the island-studded Hauraki Gulf and brightly spinnakered yachts tack through the glistening waters towards the "City of Sails". The skyscrapered downtown is surrounded by the grassy humps of some fifty-odd extinct volcanoes that ring the Waitemata Harbour, and a suburban sprawl that extends as far as the eye can see. Beyond the central business district little rises above two storeys and prim wooden villas surrounded by substantial gardens set the tone. This is one of the least densely populated cities in the world, occupying twice the area of London and yet home to just over a million inhabitants. Look beyond the glitzy shopfronts and Auckland has a modest small-town feel and measured pace, though this can seem frenetic in comparison with the rest of the country.

If Auckland stakes a claim to fame, it is as the **world's largest Polynesian city**. Around eleven percent of the population claim Maori descent while fourteen percent are families of migrants who arrived from Tonga, Samoa, the Cook Islands and other South Pacific islands during the 1960s and 1970s. Nevertheless, the Polynesian profile has traditionally been confined to small pockets, and it is only now, as the second generation matures, that Polynesia is making its presence felt in mainstream Auckland life, especially in the arts.

Many visitors only stay in the city long enough for a quick zip around the smattering of key sights, principally the **Auckland Museum**, with its matchless collection of Maori and Pacific Island carving and artefacts. A better taste of the city is gleaned by ambling around the fashionable **inner-city suburbs** of Ponsonby, Parnell, Newmarket and Devonport, and using the city as a base for exploring the wild and desolate West Coast **surf beaches** and the **wineries**, all less than an hour from the CBD. With more time, head out to the **Hauraki Gulf islands**: craggy, volcanic Rangitoto, sophisticated Waiheke, bird-rich Tiritiri Matangi and chilled-out Great Barrier.

Come September 2011, the city will be buzzing with the **Rugby World Cup**, a quadrennial extravaganza which the All Blacks haven't won since 1987, a point of national shame. The semi-finals and finals all take place at Eden Park (see map, p.89) in late October.

Auckland's **climate** is temperate and muggy, though never scorching hot, and the humidity is always tempered by a sea breeze. Winters are generally mild but rainy.

Auckland

AUCKLAND's urban sprawl smothers the North Island's wasp waist, a narrow isthmus where the island is all but severed by river estuaries probing inland from the city's two harbours. To the west, the shallow and silted **Manukau Harbour** opens out onto the Tasman Sea at a rare break in the long string of black-sand beaches continually pounded by heavy surf. Maori named the eastern anchorage the **Waitemata Harbour** for its "sparkling waters", which constitute Auckland's deep-water port and a focus for the heart of the city. Every summer weekend the harbour and adjoining Hauraki Gulf explode into a riot of brightly coloured sails.

Some history

The earth's crust between the Waitemata and Manukau harbours is so thin that, every few thousand years, magma finds a fissure and bursts onto the surface, producing yet another volcano. The most recent eruption, some six hundred years

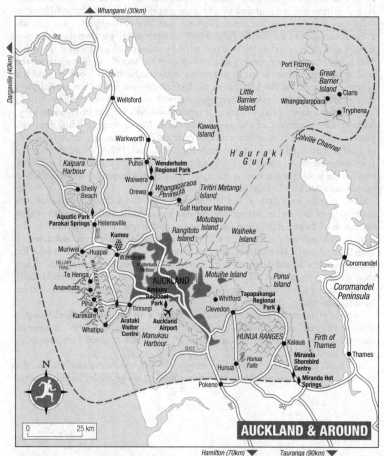

Auckland's volcanic cones

Auckland is built on around **fifty small volcanoes**, yet the city hasn't been very respectful of its geological heritage. Even the exact number seems in doubt, not least because several cones have disappeared over the last 150 years, mostly chewed away by scoria and basalt quarrying.

That might sound a Herculean feat, but Auckland's largest volcano, Rangitoto Island out in the Hauraki Gulf (see p.131), is only 260m tall, and in the city itself none is taller than Mount Eden, just under 200m. Many are pimples barely 100m high that only just poke above the surrounding housing. Early on, **Maori** recognized the fertility of the volcanic soils, and set up *kumara* gardens on the lower slopes, usually protected by fortified *pa* sites around the summit. Europeans valued the elevated positions for water storage – most of the main volcanoes have **reservoirs** in the craters.

It is only in the last few decades that volcanic features have been protected from development, often by turning their environs into parks. City ordnances dictate that some summits can't be obscured from certain angles, and yet recently the edge of one volcano was only just saved from removal for a motorway extension. Some see UNESCO World Heritage status as the best means of protection, but it is unlikely anything will happen soon.

In the meantime, the volcanoes make wonderful **viewpoints** dotted all over the city, notably from Mount Eden and One Tree Hill (see p.110), from North Head (see p.110) and from the top of Rangitoto Island (see p.131) where you can also explore lava caves.

Though it is over 600 years since the last eruption, the volcanic field remains active. No one knows when the next eruption will be, but it is unlikely to be through one of the existing volcanoes – meaning one day a new peak will emerge.

ago, formed Rangitoto Island, to the horror of some of the region's earliest Maori inhabitants, settled on adjacent Motutapu Island. Legend records their ancestors' arrival on the Tamaki Isthmus, the narrowest neck of land. With plentiful catches from two harbours and rich volcanic soils on a wealth of highly defensible volcano-top sites, the land, which they came to know as **Tamaki Makaurau** ("the maiden sought by a hundred lovers"), became the prize of numerous battles over the years. By the middle of the eighteenth century it had fallen to **Kiwi Tamaki**, who established a three-thousand-strong *pa* (fortified village) on Maungakiekie ("One Tree Hill"), and a satellite *pa* on just about every volcano in the district, but was eventually overwhelmed by rival *hapu* (sub-tribes) from Kaipara Harbour to the north.

With the arrival of musket-trading **Europeans** in the Bay of Islands around the beginning of the nineteenth century, Northland Ngapuhi were able to launch successful raids on the Tamaki Maori which, combined with smallpox epidemics, left the region almost uninhabited, a significant factor in its choice as the new capital after the signing of the Treaty of Waitangi in 1840. Scottish medic **John Logan Campbell** was one of the few European residents when this fertile land, with easy access to major river and seaborne trading routes, was purchased for £55 and some blankets. The capital was roughly laid out and Campbell took advantage of his early start, wheeling and dealing to achieve control of half the city, eventually becoming mayor and "the father of Auckland". After 1840, immigrants boosted the population to the extent that more land was needed, a demand which partly precipitated the **New Zealand Wars** of the 1860s (see p.766).

During the depression that followed, many sought their fortunes in the Otago goldfields and, as the balance of European population shifted south, so did the centre of government. Auckland lost its **capital status** to Wellington in 1865 and the city slumped further. Since then Auckland has never looked back, repeatedly ranking as New Zealand's fastest growing city and absorbing waves of migrants, initially from Britain then, in the 1960s and 1970s, from the Polynesian Islands of the South Pacific. A steady stream of rural Maori have been arriving on Auckland's doorstep for over half a century, now joined by an influx of East Asians whose tastes have radically altered the city centre. Asians now comprise almost twenty percent of Greater Auckland's population, high-rise apartments pepper the CBD and Korean, Thai, Malaysian, Chinese and Japanese restaurants are everywhere. Over 35 percent of Aucklanders were born overseas compared to a national average of 23 percent.

Arrival and moving on

As New Zealand's major gateway city, Auckland receives the bulk of **international arrivals**, a few disembarking from cruise ships at the dock by the Ferry Building downtown, but the vast majority arriving by air.

Auckland International Airport (arrival and departure info at Ⓦwww .auckland-airport.co.nz) is located 20km south of the city centre in the suburb of Mangere. The international terminal is connected to the domestic terminal by a shuttle bus (5.30am–10.20pm every 20min), but if you've a light load it's only a ten-minute walk. Before leaving the international terminal you can grab a free shower at The Collection Point (towels $5), though most travellers just head straight for the city. The well-stocked and helpful **i-SITE visitor centre** stays open for all international arrivals and will book you into a city hotel free of charge, or you can make use of the bank of courtesy phones nearby. There's also a foreign exchange office, several **ATMs**, and some **duty-free shops** open to inbound passengers.

A **taxi** into the city will set you back around $65, while the **Airbus Express** (every 15–30min 5.20am–10.15pm; $15 one-way, $22 return; backpacker cardholder, $13/20; Ⓦwww.airbus.co.nz) follows a fixed route into the city (roughly 45min). Most travellers, however, end up catching one of the door-to-door **minibuses** that wait outside the terminals. Ask at the first in line and if they're not going to the part of town where you're staying they'll point you to one that is: you'll seldom have to wait more than fifteen minutes. Fares are around $25 to downtown and $45 to Devonport; most offer small discounts to those with a backpacker card, and groups travelling to the same location get a significant reduction, adding only $6–8 per additional person. For pick-up on **departure** call Super Shuttle (☎0800/748 885) or phone a taxi company (see p.122).

Long-distance bus services run by InterCity/Newmans and Northliner arrive at the Sky City Coach Terminal under the Sky City Casino complex at 102 Hobson St. Other operators stop outside the Scenic Tours & Travel office at 172 Quay St, opposite the Downtown Ferry Terminal. Overlander **trains** arrive at the Britomart Transport Centre, at the harbour end of Queen Street.

For transport frequencies and travel times see "Travel details" on p.147.

Moving on from Auckland

When it comes time to leave, **northbound drivers** can take either SH1 directly over the harbour bridge, or go west around the head of the Waitemata Harbour past the wineries, West Coast beaches and Waitakere Ranges to meet SH1 at Wellsford. **Cyclists** must use the Devonport Ferry rather than the harbour bridge if heading north but will do well to take the western route, possibly riding a suburban train to Waitakere ($1 for the bike; travel outside peak hours).

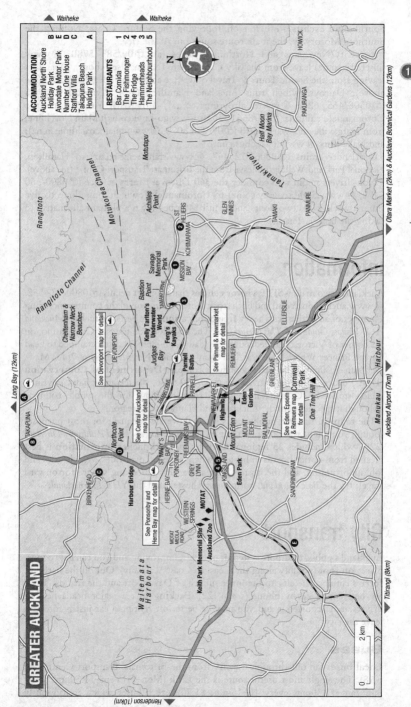

GREATER AUCKLAND

▲ Waiheke   ▲ Waiheke

See Devonport map for detail

See Central Auckland map for detail

See Parnell & Newmarket map for detail

See Ponsonby and Herne Bay map for detail

See Eden, Epsom & Remuera map for detail

ACCOMMODATION
Auckland North Shore Holiday Park   B
Avondale Motor Park   E
Number One House   D
Stafford Villa   C
Takapuna Beach Holiday Park   A

RESTAURANTS
Bar Comida   1
The Fishmonger   2
The Fridge   4
Hammerheads   3
The Neighbourhood   5

N

▲ Long Bay (12km)

Rangitoto

Cheltenham & Narrow Neck Beaches

Rangitoto Channel

Motutapu

Motukorea Channel

Waitemata Harbour

TAKAPUNA

BIRKENHEAD

Northcote Point

Harbour Bridge

DEVONPORT

Waitemata Harbour

ST MARY'S BAY

FREEMANS BAY

HERNE BAY

PONSONBY

GREY LYNN

WESTERN SPRINGS

MOTAT MEOLA ROAD

Keith Park Memorial Site
Auckland Zoo
MOTAT

KINGSLAND
Eden Park

Judges Bay
Parnell Baths
PARNELL
Kelly Tarlton's Underwater World
Ferg's Kayaks

Bastion Point

Savage Memorial Park

MISSION BAY

ST HELIERS

KOHIMARAMA

Achilles Point

NEWMARKET

Eden Garden
Highwic
MOUNT EDEN
Mount Eden ▲
BALMORAL
SANDRINGHAM

REMUERA

GREENLANE

One Tree Hill ▲
Cornwall Park

ELLERSLIE

GLEN INNES

TAMAKI

PANMURE

Tamaki River

Half Moon Bay Marina

PAKURANGA

HOWICK

Manukau Harbour

▲ Henderson (10km)

▲ Titirangi (8km)

▲ Auckland Airport (7km)

▲ Otara Market (2km) & Auckland Botanical Gardens (12km)

0   2 km

Southbound cyclists are better off following the Seabird Coast, avoiding the Southern Motorway, the main route south out of the city.

InterCity/Newmans and Northliner **buses** (all ℡09/583 5780, Ⓦwww .intercity.co.nz) leave from the Sky City Coach Terminal (see above). Operators leaving from the Scenic Tours & Travel office (see above) include: the AirBus (see above); Dalroys, which runs Auckland–Hamilton–New Plymouth–Hawera (℡0508/465 622, Ⓦwww.dalroytours.co.nz); Go Kiwi, running to the Coromandel Peninsula (℡07/866 0336, Ⓦwww.go-kiwi.co.nz); Main Coachline, from Dargaville and Warkworth (℡09/278 8070, Ⓦwww.maincoachline.co.nz); and NakedBus (Ⓦwww.nakedbus.com).

Overlander **trains** (℡0800/872 467, Ⓦwww.tranzscenic.co.nz) to Hamilton, National Park and Wellington leave from the Britomart Transport Centre (see above).

Non-drivers might also consider the 360 Discovery **ferry** service (℡0800/360 3472, Ⓦwww.360discovery.co.nz) to Coromandel Town. It runs three to five times a week, takes two hours and at just $49 one-way is a pleasant alternative to taking the bus via Thames.

Information

Auckland's two main **i-SITE visitor centres** share contact details (℡0800/282 552, Ⓦwww.aucklandnz.com) and both stock leaflets from around the country including a number of advertisement-heavy **free publications**, the best of which are *Auckland A–Z Visitors Guide* and *This is Auckland*. The branch inside the Sky City Casino, on the corner of Victoria and Federal streets (daily 8am–8pm) is a little cramped so head for the Princes Wharf branch at 137 Quay St (daily: Nov–April 8am–7pm; May– Oct 9am–5.30pm). The latter contains a compact **Department of Conservation (DOC) office** (Mon–Sat 9am–5pm; ℡09/379 6476, Ⓔaucklandvc@doc.govt.nz), which stocks DOC material and does track bookings for the whole country, although it specializes in the Auckland and Hauraki Gulf region.

The **maps** in the free publications listed above are adequate for most purposes though you might want to splash out on the *KiwiMap Auckland Pathfinder Directory* ($29), which includes 25 regional town maps. **Backpacker information** is best gleaned from notice boards in hostels, where adverts cover rides, vehicle sales and job opportunities, and the hostels offer an extensive booking service for onward travel; try the *Base Auckland*, both *Nomads* hostels and the *YHA International*.

City transport

Auckland's public transport system is poor but improving and you can get to most places **on foot** (notably along the Coast to Coast Walkway). Out on the harbour, **ferries** connect the city to the inner suburb of Devonport and the islands. **Taxis** are best contacted by phone (see p.122). **Parking** isn't a major headache, but drivers aren't courteous and you may be better off renting a car just before you leave the city.

Buses

Local buses fan out through the city from the Britomart Transport Centre (see p.98). The single most useful route is the **Link** (Mon–Fri 6am–11.30pm, Sat & Sun 7am–11.30pm; every 10–15min; $1.70), green buses which continuously

Information and transport passes

For integrated information on Auckland's buses, trains and ferries consult **Maxx** (℡0800/10 30 80, 🌐www.maxx.co.nz), which includes a timetable helpline and comprehensive journey planner. Alternatively pick up the five free *Maxx Guide* transport maps from Britomart. The most useful are the Central and Eastern regions.

For short-stay visitors, the best deal is the one-day **GetAbout Auckland Discovery Pass** ($13 from bus drivers, ferry ticket offices and the train station), which covers all the areas you're likely to want to explore and includes the Link, suburban trains and all ferries to the north shore (including Devonport), though not those to the Gulf Islands (see p.131).

loop through the city, Parnell, Newmarket, K' Road and Ponsonby; buy tickets on the bus or in the Britomart.

For buses other than the Link, **fares** are charged according to how far you travel: the inner city is $0.50, Parnell, Newmarket, Mount Eden and Ponsonby are all $1.60 per journey, Epsom is $3.20 and so on. A limited view of central Auckland can be had on the red **City Circuit** bus (daily 8am–6pm; every 10min; free) beginning on Queen Street, opposite the Britomart Transport Centre, then heading to the University before crossing back over Queen Street to explore the west side of downtown.

There's also a secure **NightRider** service (Sat & Sun 1–3am; $4.50) designed to get you home after a night out. Check the journey planner at 🌐www.maxx.co.nz.

Ferries

The Waitemata Harbour was once a seething mass of ferries bringing commuters in from the suburbs, and **ferries** remain a fast, pleasurable and scenic way to get around. The main destinations are the Hauraki Gulf islands, but there are also services calling at Devonport, run by Fullers, the principal ferry company (℡09/367 9111, 🌐www.fullers.co.nz). The **Devonport Ferry** (see box, p.110) is the cheapest of the ferries and is included in the GetAbout Auckland Discovery Pass (see above).

Trains

Few visitors will find much use for the suburban **train** services, which start from the Britomart Transport Centre and call at places that are mostly of little interest to tourists. The main exceptions are Newmarket (every 10–30min; 7min) and Kingsland (every 30–60min; 16min), the nearest station to rugby's Eden Park. **Tickets** ($1.40 to both suburbs) can be bought at Britomart or on board.

Driving

With many of the Auckland region's sights conveniently accessible on foot or by public transport, there isn't an advantage in having a car while in the city centre, though you'll need one to explore the Kumeu wineries and surf beaches of the West Coast. As the main point of entry, Auckland is awash with places to **rent a car** (see p.122 for details of outfits in the city); and if you're planning on some serious touring, you may be interested in **buying** one – see p.39 for some advice on the pros and cons, and p.122 for Auckland car markets.

Driving around Auckland isn't especially taxing, though it is worth avoiding the rush hours (7–9am & 4–6.30pm). On first acquaintance, Auckland's urban freeways are unnerving, with frequent junctions, poor signage, lane changing at whim and vehicles overtaking aggressively on all sides. Driving is on the left, though if you've just arrived after a long flight you should consider waiting a day or so before taking the plunge. Inner-city streets are metered, which means that parking is best done in the multistorey **car parks** dotted round the city; some are not open 24 hours, so check the latest exit time.

Cycling

Cycling around Auckland's hills can be a tiring and dispiriting exercise, compounded by motorists' lack of bike-awareness. However, a few areas lend themselves to pedal-powered exploration, most notably the harbourside Tamaki Drive east of the city centre, which forms part of a signposted 50km **cycle route** around the city and its isthmus.

The city has recently started a **public bike scheme** known as Next Bike ($5 registration plus $4/hr, $16/24hr, $64/week; ☏09/909 9090, ⓦwww.nextbike .co.nz), with cruiser bikes found prominently all over the central city, inner suburbs and at some hostels. Find a bike (or check the website for locations), call to register your credit card and you'll get a lock code for that bike. When you've finished, leave it at one of the numerous stations around the city centre and call again to end your rental. For **speedier bikes** downtown, visit Bike Central, 3 Britomart Place (☏09/365 1768, ⓦwww.bikecentral.co.nz), which has new city ($25/4hr, $40/day), mountain ($30/50/4hr) and road ($30/50/day) bikes.

Though less conveniently sited, Adventure Cycles, 9 Premier Ave, Western Springs (Thurs–Mon 7.30am–7pm; ☏0800/24538686, ⓦwww.adventure -auckland.co.nz), are a great resource, not just for short-term bike rental (city $20/day, MTB $25) but for **touring bikes** ($90/week; $200/month; panniers $40/week), **buy-back schemes** for long-stayers and lots of great info and repairs. Call ahead then catch bus #042, #043 or #045 from stand D8 at Britomart.

Tours

Get around the main sights on the hop-on-hop-off **Explorer Bus** (1-day pass $35, 2-day pass $55, pay the driver; ☏0800/439 756, ⓦwww.explorerbus.co.nz), which runs every half-hour (9am–4pm) and comes with a commentary. The circuit starts from the Ferry Building on Quay Street, goes along Tamaki Drive to Kelly Tarlton's Underwater World, up to Parnell and the Auckland Museum, and back via Victoria Park Market and Viaduct Harbour. Between October and April, a second loop takes in Mount Eden, MOTAT and the zoo.

More structured alternatives include **walking tours** (see p.112), **West Coast tours** (see p.123) and a Maori-led **city tour** (full day; $245) run by TIME Unlimited (☏09/446 6677 or 0800/868 463, ⓦwww.newzealandtours.travel) explaining the significance to Maori of locations around the city. The same company's Extra package ($295), includes a visit to a *marae* that's far more intimate and authentic than the mass-market extravaganzas around Rotorua, and they'll even organize *marae* stays and host Maori dinners on request.

Accommodation

With a broad range of accommodation, Auckland meets the needs of most budgets but that doesn't stop everywhere filling up at peak times, when you should **book ahead**. October 2011 will see all rooms booked months in advance for the Rugby World Cup. At other times it's less critical and through

First night accommodation

With several efficient door-to-door shuttle services into central Auckland there's hardly any reason to stay near the airport, though there are a bunch of places along Kirkbride Road, some 5km north, close to many of the car rental pick-ups. Good bets include *Airport Skyway Lodge*, 30 Kirkbride Rd (℡09/275 4443, ⓦwww.skywaylodge .co.nz; ❷, en suite ❸) and *Jet Park*, 63 Westney Rd (℡0800/538 466, ⓦwww.jetinn .co.nz; ❹, deluxe ❺, suite ❼).

If you're picking up a car or campervan near the airport after a long flight you may not fancy tangling with central city traffic. The closest appealing **campsite** is *Ambury Regional Park* (see p.97) and there are also numerous tempting **beachside spots** only an hour or two from the airport, including **Kaiaua** and **Miranda** (1hr southeast of airport, see p.130); **Muriwai** (1hr northwest of airport, see p.127); **Orewa** and Wenderholm Regional Park (1hr north of airport, see p.128 & p.129); **Piha** (1hr northwest of airport, see p.126); and **Tawharanui Regional Park** (1hr 30min north of airport, see p.155), though the latter is reached by twisty, narrow roads that might not appeal to someone driving a campervan for the first time.

the quiet winter months, from June to September, you'll be spoiled for choice and significant discounts on room rates can be had; it's worth asking. Check ⓦwww.aucklandnz.com for deals.

Auckland is a place where you might choose to stay outside the **city centre**, as most sightseeing can be done as easily from **suburbs** such as **Ponsonby**, less than 2km west of the centre, **Mount Eden**, 2km south of the centre, **Devonport**, a short ferry journey across the harbour, and **Parnell**, 2km east of the centre. All are well supplied with places to eat and drink.

The city centre remains the place to find international four- and five-star **hotels**, mostly geared towards business travellers and tour groups; walk-in rates are usually high, though there are sometimes weekend deals. Backpacker **hostels** congregate around the city centre and inner suburbs; **B&Bs** and **guesthouses** are strongest in Ponsonby, Devonport and the southern suburbs of Epsom and Remuera; and the widest selection of **motels** is just south of Newmarket in Epsom. Predictably, **campsites** are further out and not really worth the hassle.

Hotels and motels

An increasing number of **hotels** pepper the city centre and inner suburbs, ranging from budget to swanky five-star affairs. High city rents force **motels** further out and you'll see them mostly on the Great South Road in Epsom, immediately south of Newmarket, where at least a dozen nestle in one kilometre.

Central Auckland

See map on p.99.

Aspen House 62 Emily Place ℡09/379 6633, ⓦwww.aspenhouse.co.nz. Backpacker standards without the dorms or much of the spirit in this compact hotel right in the heart of the city. Rooms aren't big (and some have little natural light) but it's decent value, surprisingly quiet, includes a communal kitchen and a help-yourself continental breakfast is included. The en suites are considerably nicer. Secure parking is available for $12.50 a day. ❸/❹

Hotel DeBrett 2 High St ℡09/925 9000, ⓦwww.hoteldebrett.com. The height of Auckland chic, this classy 25-room boutique hotel references its Art Deco origins while adding bold colours and mismatched but complementary furniture. Bathrooms are gorgeous, continental breakfast and wi-fi are included and guests have access to a lovely lounge with honesty bar. There's also the *Kitchen* restaurant and a couple of excellent bars open to the public. Rooms ❽, suites ❾
Heritage 35 Hobson St ℡0800/368 888, ⓦwww .heritagehotels.co.nz. Top-class hotel partly

fashioned from the original Farmers department store. Occasional bits of aged planking and wooden supports crop up in public areas, but it is fitted out to a very high standard and many rooms have views across the harbour or into the glassed-in atrium. The outside pool has views over the city. **⑥**
Hilton Princes Wharf, 147 Quay St ☎09/978 2000, ⓦwww.hilton.com/auckland. Fabulously sited on a wharf jutting into the harbour. Beautifully decorated rooms, all with terrace or balcony, start from around $400 in summer but it is worth paying the extra $80 for a good view. If this is out of your budget, a visit to the *Bellini* cocktail bar on the ground floor will give you a taste of the high life. **⑨**
The Quadrant 10 Waterloo Quadrant ☎0800/666 611, ⓦwww.thequadrant.com. Designer hotel chic without the high prices, this four-star place has a fresh appearance and great city and harbour views from the balcony of most of its 250 rooms. Most come with kitchenette and some have washing machine and dishwasher. There's also a compact and intimate bar, a breakfast and lunch café, spa, sauna, a small gym and 10Gb of free wi-fi daily. Studio **⑤**, one-bed apartment **⑥**
Scenic Hotel 380 Queen St ☎09/374 1741, ⓦwww.scenichotelgroup.co.nz. Good mid-range hotel with lobby areas restored to their Art Deco glory. Many of the hundred rooms have city views and/or full kitchens and there's a small fitness room. Good deals (**⑤**) for advance internet bookings. **⑥**

Parnell
See map on p.105.
Parnell Inn 320 Parnell Rd ☎0800/472 763, ⓦwww.parnellinn.co.nz. Compact and simple hotel right in the heart of Parnell. Rooms are fairly small and some have ageing bathrooms, but there are some good views and kitchenettes are available. Off-street parking. **③/④**

Ponsonby
See map on p.107.
Abaco on Jervois 59 Jervois Rd ☎0800/220 066, ⓦwww.abaco.co.nz. Attractive motel close to the Ponsonby cafés, with a range of rooms and plenty of off-street parking. Budget options lack kitchens; standard rooms are much more spacious but nothing compared to the deluxe rooms, many with spa baths and distant harbour views. **③/④/⑥**

Newmarket and Epsom
See map on p.105.
Hansens 96 Great South Rd ☎0800/898 797, ⓦwww.hansensmotel.co.nz. The best-value budget motel along this strip. old but well kept. All units (except for two budget rooms) come with full cooking facilities. There's a small pool and spa, and free internet in the office. Budget **②**, units **③**
Oak Tree 104 Great South Rd ☎0800/625 8733, ⓦwww.oaktree.co.nz. Considerably swisher than most of the motels along this strip, the *Oak Tree* has nicely modernized studios with a basic kitchen, and one-bedroom apartments. Some of both have a/c. Studios **④**, apartments **⑤**
Off Broadway 11 Alpers Ave ☎0800/427 623, ⓦwww.offbroadway.co.nz. Business-oriented hotel with a/c, soundproofed en-suite studios (go for the larger ones with bathtub and balcony), and several one-bedroom suites with spa bath. There's undercover parking, a small gym and breakfast can be served in your room. Studios **④/⑤**, suites **⑥**
Siesta 70 Great South Rd ☎0800/743 782, ⓦwww.siestamotel.co.nz. Ageing but decent motel with studios (**③**) and self-catering units (**④**).
Tudor Court 108 Great South Rd ☎0800/826 878, ⓦwww.tudor.co.nz. Compact motel with small hotel-style rooms and slightly larger ones with kitchenettes. Wi-fi available. **③/④**

B&Bs and guesthouses

Auckland's stock of B&Bs and guesthouses is expanding. New places continually open, many pitching for the upper end of the market, with just a few rooms and an almost obsessive attention to detail. Places are scattered widely around the **inner suburbs** on the south side of the harbour and in the North Shore suburb of **Devonport**. Note that airport shuttle buses will drop you in Devonport for only a few dollars extra.

Central Auckland
See map on p.99.
Braemar on Parliament Street 7 Parliament St ☎09/377 5463, ⓦwww.parliamentstreet.co.nz. This very welcoming, 1901 townhouse in the heart of the city has retained its late Victorian feel.

There's a large suite, a smaller en-suite room and two rooms that share a bathroom – all baths are clawfoot – and breakfast is a major affair with dishes cooked to order. There's free internet, guest parking and a strong sustainability ethic. Rooms **⑦/⑧**, suite **⑨**

Parnell

See map on p.105.

Ascot Parnell 32 St Stephens Ave ☏09/309 9012, ⊛www.ascotparnell.com. Tranquil, comfortable Belgian-run B&B in a small, modern apartment block, with two mini-suites and a huge harbour suite. An enormous guest lounge with balcony overlooks the city and harbour, and there's a 12m pool, secure parking, free wi-fi and computer, and airport pick-up (for a small fee). Try the signature savoury Flemish toast for breakfast. Mini-suites ❽, harbour suite ❾

Chalet Chevron 14 Brighton Rd ☏09/309 0290, ⊛www.chaletchevron.co.nz. Comfortable twelve-room B&B with a range of en-suite rooms, some with distant sea views, two with baths and several well geared for singles (from $115). An all-you-can-eat breakfast is served and there's free wi-fi throughout plus a guest computer. ❼

Ponsonby

See map on p.107.

🏃 **23 Hepburn** 23 Hepburn St ☏0800/283 000, ⊛www.23hepburn.co.nz. Whites and creams are the dominant tones in this lovely three-room B&B on a quiet, leafy street a 2min walk from Ponsonby Rd. Continental breakfast ingredients are supplied in your room and are best eaten out on the sunny porch if the weather behaves. Book ahead to secure one of the larger rooms at the front. ❼

🏃 **Great Ponsonby Art Hotel** 30 Ponsonby Terrace ☏09/376 5989, ⊛www.greatpons .co.nz. This welcoming boutique hotel, in a restored 1898 villa a 3min walk from Ponsonby Rd, is the pick of the crop. Boldly decorated in ocean tones using native timbers and Pacific artworks; everyone has use of the sunny lounge and shaded garden and the breakfasts are a delight. The luxurious, en-suite rooms come with Sky TV, iPod docks and free wi-fi; there are also self-catering studio units (⑧). Rooms ❼

Devonport

See map on p.109.

108 Victoria Rd 108 Victoria Rd ☏09/445 7565, Ⓔsmj@ihug.co.nz. A B&B with two rooms overlooking a saltwater swimming pool and a cottage in lush gardens. Breakfast costs extra, there's a late checkout and both rooms can be rented as one. ❹

Devonport Garden Room 23 Cheltenham Rd ☏09/445 2472, ⊛www.devonportgardenroom .co.nz. You get your own entrance to this lovely modernized studio in an 1870s villa opening out onto a brick courtyard and leafy garden with BBQ

area and spa pool. Sumptuous breakfasts can be served under an arbour or in your room. ❻

Mahoe B&B 15b King Edward Parade ☏09/445 1515, ⊛www.mahoe.co.nz. Lovely property set back from the waterfront, in the heart of Devonport, tastefully furnished and offering either B&B in the house or a separate fully s/c apartment. Rooms ❻, apartment ❼

Parituhu Beachstay 3 King Edward Parade ☏09/445 6559, ⊛www.parituhu.co.nz. A gay-friendly budget B&B homestay in the heart of Devonport that overlooks the harbour, with just the one room, a private bath, access to a secluded garden and self-service breakfast. ❺

🏃 **Peace & Plenty Inn** 6 Flagstaff Terrace ☏09/445 2925, ⊛www.peaceandplenty .co.nz. One of New Zealand's finest B&Bs, yet relaxed, well priced and with an ethical emphasis on using local produce and services. Elegantly restored kauri floorboards lead through to a lovely veranda, past exquisite rooms filled with fresh flowers and equipped with sherry and port. Venture outside the bounds of the inn and you're right in the heart of Devonport. ❽

Birkenhead and Northcote

See map on p.89.

Number One House 1 Princes St, Northcote Point ☏09/480 7659, ⊛www.nz-homestay.co.nz. Hospitable B&B with views across the Waitemata Harbour to the city and Rangitoto Island. It has a small beach, city access by ferry (frequent weekdays, sparse at weekends), two rooms, a s/c apartment and a quirky garden with a little hobbit house. Great breakfast, plus the opportunity to go out on the owner's yacht (around $250/person/ day). Rooms & apartment ❼

Stafford Villa 2 Awanui St, Birkenhead ☏09/418 3022, ⊛www.staffordvilla.co.nz. On a quiet street in one of the North Shore's more venerable waterside suburbs, where there are several good restaurants and an excellent cinema, this top-notch place offers just two period-furnished en-suite rooms in an elegant century-old villa. Guests have access to a drawing room and a comfy library (with complimentary port), and are treated to a sumptuous breakfast. Rates are $395–445. ❾

Mount Eden and Remuera

See map on p.111.

Bavaria 83 Valley Rd, Mount Eden ☏09/638 9641, ⊛www.bavariabandbhotel.co.nz. Modest eleven-room B&B in a comfortable suburban villa. It's popular with German-speakers and there are Teutonic touches to the buffet continental breakfast. Rooms come with renovated bathrooms, some (**6**) have a deck, and there's free internet and wi-fi. Buses (#256, #258 & #267) from stand C4 on Queen St near Wellesley St pass close by. **6**

Eden Park B&B 20 Bellwood Ave, Mount Eden ⊤09/630 5721, ⦿www.bedandbreakfastnz.com. Welcoming B&B in renovated grand villa in a suburb that's very peaceful, except when there's a game on at nearby Eden Park. With chandelier, fresh flowers, home-made biscuits, three-course

breakfast and heated everything you can't go far wrong. Three en suites plus one room with a private bath and its own deep tub. **7**

Omahu Lodge 33 Omahu Rd, Remuera ⊤09/524 5648, ⦿www.omahulodge.co.nz. The spa and deep, solar-heated swimming pool is central to this four-room B&B partly in a 1940s bungalow in a refined suburb. Robes, bed turndowns, complimentary sherry and free wi-fi and internet are all part of the service. There's also a separate TV lounge and a sauna. **7**

Hostels

Auckland has stacks of **backpacker hostels** competing for your custom. Most are set up to assist new arrivals to plan onward travel, to the extent of having fully staffed on-site travel services – sometimes pushing favoured trips and activities, but generally offering impartial advice.

There's a definite trade-off between the convenience offered by **downtown** hostels and the relative quiet of places outside the centre. Most central hostels, with the exception of the YHAs, cram in the beds and, with bars and clubs only a short stagger away, cater to a party crowd. Hostels in the **inner suburbs** – Parnell, Ponsonby and Mount Eden – tend to be less boisterous, often in old, converted houses, sometimes with gardens and usually with some parking.

As you'd expect, **prices** are higher than in the rest of the country, though you can still get dorm bunks for around $22. Small dorms and four-shares hover around $25 and most doubles and twins are $60–80.

Central Auckland

See map on p.99.

Base Auckland 229 Queen St ⊤0800/227 369, ⦿www.stayatbase.com. Enormous, well-run hostel in a ten-storey converted office building. Despite the inevitable impersonality of housing around five hundred, everything runs smoothly and it seldom feels too crowded. They've thought of everything, including a downstairs bar, separate terrace bar with nightly sausage sizzle, massive internet centre, helpful travel office, laundry, gear storage and electronic key access to each floor and public areas. Mixed dorms sleep up to eight but it's worth the extra for a mixed four-bed dorm supplied with sheets or a further dollar for the separate women-only "sanctuary" with extra pampering. All sorts of evening activities, and parking nearby ($10/ overnight, $20/24hr). Big dorms $27, small dorms $29, rooms **2**, en suites with TV **3**

BK Hostel 3 Mercury Lane ⊤09/307 0052, ⦿www.bkhostel.co.nz. Well-kept, pastel-painted hostel in the heart of the lively K' Rd district, so outside rooms can be noisy. No dorms as such, just three-bed shares, doubles and twins with cheaper rates for those without windows. Common areas are spacious and security is good. Shares $25–29, rooms **1**

City Groove 6 Constitution Hill ⊤09/303 4768, ⦿www.citygroove.co.nz. Small, slightly cramped accommodation, an easy walk from both the CBD and Parnell. Relaxed atmosphere, small garden and limited parking. Dorms $24, shares $26, rooms & en suites **2**

Nomads Fat Camel 38 Fort St ⊤09/307 0181, ⦿www.nomadshostels.com. Solid downtown hostel with mixed and female dorms (some at $19; the cheapest in town), twins and doubles all arranged in small apartments, each group having its own kitchen, lounge and showers. There's a bar (very cheap meals for guests) and a travel desk. Dorms $19–25, shares $27, rooms **2**

Nomads Fusion 16–22 Fort St ⊤0508/666 237, ⦿www.nomadshostels.com. Classy conversion of a city office building into an upscale hostel on seven floors complete with rooftop kitchen and outdoor barbecue area. There's also a spa pool, sauna, good travel desk and the lively *Fusion* bar that goes off most nights (and offers very cheap meals to guests). Accommodation is in a range of mixed and female dorms (6–12 beds), and en-suite doubles and twins (the cheaper ones without windows). Dorms $22–30, en suites **3**

YHA Auckland City Corner of City Rd & Liverpool St ⊤09/309 2802, ©yha.aucklandcity@yha.co.nz.

Large and central YHA with seven floors of mostly twin and double rooms – the upper ones with fine city views – plus well-equipped common areas. No dedicated parking. Single-sex and mixed dorms $24, four-shares $28, rooms ❸

🏃 **YHA Auckland International** 5 Turner St ☎ 09/302 8200, ✉ yha.aucklandint@yha .co.nz. The pick of the two YHAs, this purpose-built 174-bed establishment comes with excellent cooking facilities, spacious rooms, separate TV and quiet lounges, a travel centre and wi-fi throughout. There are even a few free parking spaces; book early. Single-sex dorms $26, single-sex and mixed four-shares $31, rooms ❸, en suites ❹

Parnell

See map on p.105.

🏃 **City Garden Lodge** 25 St George's Bay Rd ☎ 09/302 0880, ⓦ www.citygardenlodge .co.nz. Friendly backpackers in a large, well-organized villa originally built for the Queen of Tonga, and surrounded by expansive lawns. Along with spacious dorms and some lovely doubles/twins there are little touches like hot water bottles in winter and even a yoga/meditation room (classes available). Dorms $28, shares $30, rooms ❷

International Backpackers 2 Churton St ☎ 09/358 4584, ⓦ www.aucklandinternationalbp .com. One-time home for wayward girls but now a friendly, spacious hostel in a quiet area with street parking and rejuvenated rooms. Large dorm $23, smaller dorms $25, rooms & en suites ❷

Lantana Lodge 60 St George's Bay Rd ☎ 09/373 4546 ⓦ www.lantanalodge.co.nz. Small, clean and friendly hostel with free wi-fi and a homely feel. Linen included. Dorms $24, rooms ❷

Ponsonby

See map on p.107.

Brown Kiwi 7 Prosford St ☎ 09/378 0191, ⓦ www.brownkiwi.co.nz. Compact, cosy little hostel in a restored Victorian villa on a quiet street close to the Ponsonby cafés. A patio and tiny garden at the back helps the relaxing atmosphere.

Daytime parking is poor but it's easily accessible by the Link bus. Dorms $26, share $28, rooms ❷

Uenuku Lodge 217 Ponsonby Rd ☎ 09/378 8990, ⓦ www.uenukulodge.co.nz. Comfortable, good-value hostel worked into a warren of an old boarding house just steps from the action on Ponsonby Rd and on the Link bus route. It's bright, clean and there's parking. Dorms $24, shares $26, rooms ❷

🏃 **Verandahs** 6 Hopetoun St ☎ 09/360 4180, ⓦ www.verandahs.co.nz. Welcoming and beautifully appointed backpackers in a pair of grand 1905 villas overlooking a leafy park close to the Ponsonby Rd and K' Rd nightlife. The hostel has a selection of spacious rooms (some en suite), limited off-street parking and intentionally lacks TV. Dorms $26, shares $28–30, rooms ❷/❸

Mount Eden

See map on p.111. Buses #274 and #277 run from stand D16 on Customs St East in the CBD to Mount Eden shops, passing close to all these hostels.

🏃 **Bamber House** 22 View Rd ☎ 09/623 4267, ⓦ www.hostelbackpacker.com. Spacious, well-managed hostel spread across a lovely old colonial house, a swish modern house in the grounds and several en-suite cabins that come with a kettle and fridge. There's a large lawn out front and a host of other facilities including wi-fi. Dorms $25, shares $28, rooms ❷, en-suite cabins ❸

Oaklands Lodge 5a Oaklands Rd ☎ 09/638 6545, ⓦ www.oaklands.co.nz. Run by the folk above, this large two-storey Victorian house right by Mount Eden shops has mostly dorms with beds rather than bunks, and an abundance of separate lounge areas. Dorms $23, shares $25, rooms ❷

Pentlands 22 Pentlands Ave ☎ 09/638 7031, ⓦ www.pentlands.co.nz. Appealing, recently renovated hostel in a quiet suburban street a 10min walk from Mount Eden shops and cafés. Big lounge (with piano), plenty of DVDs and loads of parking. Dorms $23, shares $25, rooms ❷

Campsites and holiday parks

You'd have to travel a long way to find a genuinely attractive spot to pitch a **tent**. There are numerous, well-equipped motor camps within the city limits that are fine for **campervans** and offer bargain **cabins**, though without your own vehicle, you'll end up spending a lot of money on buses.

Ambury Regional Park Mangere, 6km north of the airport ☎ 09/366 2000. Basic, flat sites (no power) in a sheep field overlooking the Manukau Harbour. Great location for those wanting to rest up

after flying in to NZ. Sometimes closed to vans in winter: call ahead. The adjacent farm park (with pigs, sheep, rabbits etc) has toilets and free showers. Camping $10.

Auckland North Shore Holiday Park 52 Northcote Rd, Northcote ☏ 0508/909 090, ⓦ www.nsmotels.co.nz. Well-appointed site on the North Shore just off the northern motorway, with an indoor swimming pool and extensive BBQ areas. Bus #921 from Britomart (and others) stop nearby. Tents and vans $35 per site, cabins ❷, tourist flats ❸, motel units ❹

Avondale Motor Park 46 Bollard Ave, Avondale ☏ 0800/100 542, ⓦ www.aucklandmotorpark .co.nz. Restful site 6km southwest of the city and

accessible by bus #211. Camping $14, on-site vans ❶, cabins ❷, tourist flats ❸

Takapuna Beach Holiday Park 22 The Promenade, Takapuna ☏ 09/489 7909, ⓦ www .takapunabeachholidaypark.co.nz. Small beachside caravan park on the North Shore overlooking Rangitoto and a 5min walk from Takapuna shops and restaurants. Frequent buses (#822, #839, #858 & #879) from central Auckland. Camping $32–40 per site, caravans ❷ kitchen cabins ❷, motel ❹

Central Auckland

Downtown Auckland clings to the southern shores of the **Waitemata Harbour**, its flashy waterfront restaurants and swanky apartments dotted around the bobbing yachts of the rejuvenated **Viaduct Harbour**.

Downbeat **Queen Street**, the main drag, strikes south through the **city centre**, largely sustained by banks and insurance companies. Either side is a grid of streets commemorating prime movers in New Zealand's early European history: the country's first Governor-General, William Hobson; Willoughby Shortland, New Zealand's first colonial secretary; and William Symonds, who chivvied along local Maori chiefs reluctant to sign the Treaty of Waitangi.

Specific interest comes in the form of designer shopping on the more exclusive side streets and cultural diversions in the form of the **Auckland Art Gallery**, currently undergoing a transformation (see p.101). **Albert Park**, wedged between the Gallery and the **University**, makes a nice break from the concrete jungle.

At the top of Queen Street lies **Karangahape Road**, an altogether groovier strip of cheaper shops, ethnic restaurants and more down and dirty clubs.

The Domain, an extensive swathe of parkland with trees and lawns, sweeps towards the harbour. It is Auckland's premier green space, laid out around the city's most-visited attraction, the **Auckland Museum**, exhibiting stunning Maori and Pacific Island artefacts.

Downtown and Viaduct Harbour

Auckland's waterfront was on **Fort Street** (originally Fore Street), but progressive reclamation shifted the shoreline 300m to the north, creating space for **Downtown Auckland**, which centres on the striking **Britomart Transport Centre**, located inside the neoclassical 1910 former post office at the northern end of **Queen Street**. The street ends at the dockside **Ferry Building**, a neoclassical 1912 brick structure that is still the hub of the Waitemata Harbour ferry services. The chaotic bustle of the days before the harbour bridge is now a distant memory, as the ebb and flow remains, as commuters and sightseers board speedy catamarans to Devonport and Rangitoto, Waiheke and Great Barrier islands.

A couple of hundred metres west, **Viaduct Harbour** was a scruffy fishing port until it was smartened up for New Zealand's successful defence of the **America's Cup** in 2000. Yachts still dominate a waterfront lined by exclusive apartments, flash restaurants and themed bars.

Voyager: New Zealand Maritime Museum

Anyone with the slightest interest in sailing and the sea should make straight for **Voyager: New Zealand Maritime Museum**, on the corner of Quay and Hobson

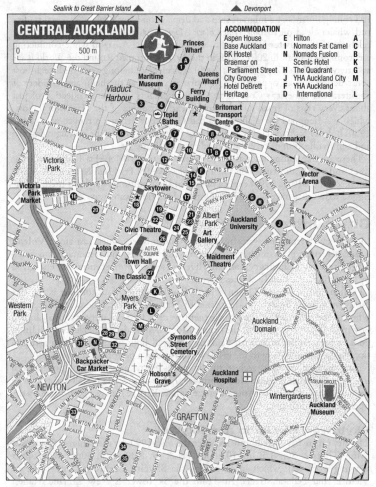

CENTRAL AUCKLAND

Sealink to Great Barrier Island ▲   ▲ Devonport

0   500 m

N

Princes Wharf

Queens Wharf

Maritime Museum

Viaduct Harbour

Ferry Building

Britomart Transport Centre

Tepid Baths

Supermarket

Victoria Park

Victoria Park Market

Skytower

Albert Park

Auckland University

Civic Theatre

Art Gallery

Aotea Centre

Maidment Theatre

Town Hall

The Classic

Myers Park

Vector Arena

Western Park

Backpacker Car Market

Symonds Street Cemetery

Hobson's Grave

NEWTON

Auckland Domain

Auckland Hospital

GRAFTON

Wintergardens

Auckland Museum

ACCOMMODATION			
Aspen House	E	Hilton	A
Base Auckland	I	Nomads Fat Camel	C
BK Hostel	N	Nomads Fusion	B
Braemar on		Scenic Hotel	K
Parliament Street	H	The Quadrant	G
City Groove	J	YHA Auckland City	M
Hotel DeBrett	F	YHA Auckland	
Heritage	D	International	L

CAFÉS & RESTAURANTS						PUBS & BARS			
Alleluya	29	French Café	34	Sri Pinang	32	Cowboy	3	Rakino's	15
Atrium Food Gallery	19	Grand Harbour	6	Tanuki	27	Flight Lounge	11	Sale St	16
Banh Mi Bale	21	Ima	13	Tony's	23	Fu Bar	9	Shakespeare Tavern	12
Bellota	18	Mezze Bar	17	Verona	30	Galbraith's Alehouse	35	Smith	8
Coco's Cantina	31	Middle East Café	22	Wildfire	2	Globe	I	Stark's	26
Corner Pancake	24	Rasoi	28			Kings Arms	33	Tabac	10
Deus Ex Machina	20	Raw Power	14			The Occidental	14	Whammy Bar	29
Euro	1	Reuben	25			O'Hagan's	3		
Food Alley	7	Soul	4			Northern Steamship Co	5		

streets (daily 9am–5pm; $16; ⓦ www.maritimemuseum.co.nz), which pays homage to the maritime history of an island nation reliant on the sea for colonization, trade and sport. The short *Te Waka* video shows an imagined Maori migration voyage, setting the scene for a display of South Pacific outrigger and double-hulled canoes. Designs for fishing, lagoon sailing and ocean voyaging include the massive 21m-long *Taratai*, which carried New Zealand film-maker and writer James Siers and a crew of thirteen over 2400km from Kiribati to Fiji in 1976. The creaking and rolling innards of a migrant ship and displays on New Zealand's coastal traders and whalers lead on to *Blue Water Black Magic*, a tribute to New Zealand's most celebrated sailor, **Peter Blake**, who was killed on the Amazon while conducting environmental work in 2001. Wins in the 1990 Whitbread Round the World Race and two America's Cups (1995 & 2000) are celebrated along with high-tech boat construction and an opportunity to work as a team at the helm and grinders of an interactive America's Cup yacht. Other highlights include: a collection of just about every class of small sailing boat; an early example of the Hamilton Jetboat, which was designed for shallow, braided Canterbury rivers; a replica of a classic 1950s holiday *bach* with great archival film footage adding to the nostalgic flavour; and a fine collection of boat figureheads and maritime art.

There are free audioguides, interesting **guided tours** (Mon–Fri 10.30am &1pm; free), and one-hour **cruises** on the *Ted Ashby* (Wed & Fri 11am & 1pm, Sat & Sun noon & 2pm; $10), a 1990s replica of one of the traditional flat-bottomed, ketch-rigged scows that once worked the North Island tidal waterways.

City centre

Moving south from the waterfront along Queen Street, duck east along **Vulcan Lane**, a former blacksmithing street now full of bars and restaurants, to reach **High Street** and **Chancery Lane**, the liveliest section of the central city energized by bookshops and trendy clothes stores.

Further south, one of Queen Street's few buildings of distinction is the Art Nouveau **Civic Theatre**, on the corner of Wellesley Street. The talk of the town when it opened in 1929, the management went as far as to import a small Indian boy from Fiji to complement the ornate Moghul-style decor, all elephants, Hindu gods, a proscenium arch with flanking red-eyed lions, and star-strewn artificial sky. Sadly, the only way to see inside it is to attend a performance (see p.120).

Bang next door, but architecturally miles away, is a chunky postmodern multiplex cinema. It flanks **Aotea Square**, home to the Town Hall and the city's foremost concert hall, the **Aotea Centre**, where Kiri Te Kanawa performed on the opening night in 1990.

Skytower, SkyJump and SkyWalk

The city centre has been dominated since the mid-1990s by the concrete **Skytower** (Mon–Thurs & Sun 8.30am–10.30pm, Fri & Sat 8.30am–11.30pm; $25, upper viewing extra $3), which sprouts from the **Skycity Casino** on the corner of Victoria and Federal streets. At 328m the Skytower is New Zealand's tallest structure and just pips the Eiffel Tower and Sydney's Centrepoint.

Along with the obligatory observation decks (192m and 220m) offering stupendous views over the city and Hauraki Gulf, there's a revolving restaurant and a couple of adventure activities. On the **SkyJump** (daily 10am–6pm; $225; booking recommended on ☎0800/759 586, ⓦwww.skyjump.co.nz) – claimed as the world's highest tower-based jump – you plummet 192m towards the ground in a kind of ten-second arrested freefall at 80kph, with a cable attached to your back. Alternatively, remain at 192m for the **SkyWalk** (daily 10am–6pm; $145; ⓦwww.skywalk.co.nz), which involves a tentative, twenty-minute circumnavigation of the Skytower exterior with just a narrow, handrail-free walkway and a rope tether to steady the nerves. The exposure feels anywhere from unsettling to terrifying, but the views are stupendous.

Albert Park and the Auckland Art Gallery

East of Queen Street, the formal Victorian-style gardens of **Albert Park** were originally the site of a Maori *pa*. The land was successively conscripted into service as Albert Barracks in the 1840s and 50s, and then as a labyrinthine network of air-raid shelters during World War II, before relaxing into its current incarnation as parkland filled with oaks and Morton Bay figs, and thronged with sunbathing students and office workers.

On Albert Park's eastern edge, the **Auckland Art Gallery** (daily 10am–5pm; free; infoline ℡09/307 7700, ⓦwww.aucklandartgallery.govt.nz) comes in two sections. While the elaborate mock-French Heritage Gallery undergoes a massive upgrade (due for a grand re-opening in mid-2011) the organization operates from the smaller **New Gallery**, across the street on the corner of Wellesley and Lorne streets. Its two floors are light and airy but provide limited scope for displaying what is the world's most important collection of Kiwi art. Works on display are frequently changed, but might include anything from original drawings by artists on Cook's expeditions and overwrought oils depicting Maori migrations through to site-specific installations by predominantly New Zealand, and particularly Maori, artists.

Much of the early collection is devoted to works by two of the country's most loved artists – both highly respected by Maori as among the few to accurately portray their ancestors. Bohemian immigrant **Gottfried Lindauer** emigrated to New Zealand in 1873 and spent his later years painting lifelike, almost documentary, portraits of *rangatira* (chiefs) and high-born Maori men and women, in the mistaken belief that the Maori people were about to become extinct. In the early part of the twentieth century, **Charles F. Goldie** became New Zealand's resident "old master" and earned international recognition for his more emotional portraits of elderly Maori regally showing off their traditional tattoos, or *moko*, though they were in fact often painted from photographs (sometimes after the subject's death).

Look out for more recent oils by **Rita Angus**, renowned for her landscapes of Canterbury and Otago in the 1940s, **Colin McCahon**, whose fascination with the power and beauty of New Zealand landscape informs much late-twentieth-century Kiwi art; and **Gordon Walters**, who draws inspiration from Maori iconography, controversially appropriating vibrant, graphic representations of traditional Maori symbols (for more on Maori design, see p.780). You'll usually find some of the excellent contemporary work by Maori painter **Shane Cotton**, and may well see one of the gallery's most expensive works, **Tony Fomison**'s, 1973 painting *Study of Holbein's "Dead Christ"*. It's typical of his later, more obsessive period, combining the artist's passion for art history and his preoccupation with mortality.

Karangahape Road

At its southern end, Queen Street climbs to vibrant and grungy **Karangahape Road**, universally known as **K' Road**. Originally home to prosperous nineteenth-century merchants, it became the heart of Auckland's Polynesian community in the 1970s, and was subsequently notorious for its massage parlours, strip joints and gay cruising clubs. For twenty years K' Road has been slated for a mainstream shopping renaissance, and while most of the strip joints are gone, K' Road remains determinedly niche. Groovy cafés, bars, music shops specializing in vinyl and clothes shops selling budget designer garb rub shoulders with colourful stores run by East and South Asians. There are no specific sights, but you can easily pass a few hours browsing the shops and eating in ethnic restaurants. In the evening, particularly at weekends, the pavements become an entertaining kaleidoscope of preening transvestites, boozed-up office workers, gay couples, spaced-out street people and the upwardly mobile in from the suburbs.

Further east, K' Road crosses Symonds Street by the somewhat neglected **Symonds Street Cemetery**, one of Auckland's earliest burial grounds, partly destroyed by the motorway which was cut through Grafton Gully in the 1960s. A patch of deciduous woodland shades the grave of New Zealand's first

Governor, William Hobson, tucked away almost under the vast concrete span of Grafton Bridge.

The Domain

Grafton Gully separates the city centre from **The Domain**, a swathe of semi-formal gardens draped over the low profile of an extinct volcano known as Pukekawa or "hill of bitter memories", a reference to the bloodshed of ancient inter-tribal fighting. Set aside in the 1840s, it is the city's finest park, furnished with mid-nineteenth-century accoutrements: a band rotunda, phoenix palms, formal flowerbeds and spacious lawns. In summer, the rugby pitches metamorphose into cricket ovals, and stages are erected in the crater's shallow amphitheatre for outdoor musical extravaganzas.

The Domain's volcanic spring was one of Auckland's original water sources and was used by the Auckland Acclimatization Society to grow European plants, thereby promoting the rapid Europeanization of the New Zealand countryside. The spirit of this enterprise lingers on in the **Wintergardens** (Nov–March Mon–Sat 9am–5.30pm, Sun 9am–7.30pm; April–Oct daily 9am–4.30pm; free), a shallow fishpond flanked by two barrel-roofed glasshouses – one temperate, the other heated to mimic tropical climes. Next door, a former scoria quarry has been transformed into the **Fernz Fernery** (same hours; free), a green dell with over a hundred types of fern in dry, intermediate and wet habitats.

Auckland Museum

The highest point on The Domain is crowned by the imposing Greco-Roman-style **Auckland Museum** (daily 10am–5pm; $10, valid for repeated entry on one day; ⓦ www.aucklandmuseum.com) which contains the world's finest collections of Maori and Pacific art and craft. Traditional in its approach yet contemporary in its execution, the museum was built as a World War I memorial in 1929 and has been progressively expanded, most recently in 2006 with the capping of a courtyard with an undulating copper dome. Below the dome, a new **Atrium Entrance** is dominated by a striking slatted Fijian kauri structure hanging from the ceiling like some upturned beehive.

At the opposite end of the building, the original colonnaded Foyer Entrance is the place to head for the thirty-minute **Maori Cultural Performance** (daily 11am, noon & 1.30pm, also Jan–March 2.30pm; $25) of song and dance, heralded by a conch-blast. If you're interested in buying Maori crafts, check out the high-quality traditional and contemporary work in the **shop** by the Foyer Entrance.

The museum is on the route of the Coast to Coast Walkway and the city tour **buses**. The Link bus stops on Parnell Road, five minutes' walk away.

Ground Floor

The superb **Maori and Pacific collections** are most easily accessed through the Foyer Entrance. The **Pacific Lifeways** room mainly concentrates on daily life and is dominated by a simple yet majestic breadfruit-wood statue from the Caroline Islands depicting **Kave**, Polynesia's malevolent and highest-ranked female deity, whose menace is barely hinted at in this serene form. Beyond, the **Maori Court** houses an extensive collection marking the transition from purely Polynesian motifs to an identifiably Maori style. This is exemplified in the **Kaitaia Carving**, a 2.5m-wide totara carving thought to have been designed for a ceremonial gateway, guarded by the central goblin-like figure with sweeping arms that stretch out to become lizard forms: Polynesian in style but Maori in concept. It was found in 1920 near Kaitaia and is estimated to date from the fourteenth or fifteenth century, predating most Maori art so far discovered.

As traditional Maori villages started to disappear towards the end of the nineteenth century, some of the best examples of carved panels, meeting houses and food stores were rescued. The main gallery is dominated by **Hotunui**, a large and wonderfully carved meeting house built in 1878, late enough to have a corrugated iron rather than rush roof. Once again the craftsmanship is superb; the house's exterior bristles with grotesque faces, lolling tongues and glistening paua-shell eyes, while the interior is lined with wonderful geometric *tukutuku* panels. Outside is the intricately carved prow and stern-piece of **Te Toki a Tapiri**, a 25m-long *waka taua* (war canoe) designed to seat a hundred warriors, the only surviving specimen from the pre-European era.

The **Pacific Masterpieces** room is filled with exquisite Polynesian, Melanesian and Micronesian works. Look out for the shell-inlaid ceremonial food bowl from the Solomon Islands, ceremonial clubs and a wonderfully resonant slit-drum from Vanuatu. The textiles are fabulous too, with designs far more varied than you'd expect considering the limited raw materials: the Hawaiian red feather cloak is especially fine.

Upper floors
The **middle floor** of the museum comprises the **natural history galleries**, an unusual combination of modern thematic displays and stuffed birds in cases. Displays like the 3m-high Giant Moa (an ostrich-like bird) and an 800kg ammonite shouldn't be missed, but there's also material on dinosaurs, volcanoes and a **Maori Natural History** display, which attempts to explain the unique Maori perspective unencumbered by Western scientific thinking. The middle floor is also where you'll find hands-on and "discovery" areas for **kids**.

Scars on the Heart occupies the entire top floor and explores how New Zealanders' involvement in war has helped shape national identity. The New Zealand Wars of the 1860s are interpreted from both Maori and Pakeha perspectives and World War I gets extensive coverage, particularly the Gallipoli campaign in Turkey, when botched leadership led to a massacre of ANZAC – Australian and New Zealand Army Corps – troops in the trenches. Powerful visuals and rousing martial music accompany newsreel footage of the Pacific campaigns of World War II and Vietnam, with personal accounts of the troops' experiences and the responses of those back home.

The suburbs

You're likely to spend more time in the suburbs than you are in the centre of the city, as the bulk of the specific sights lie outside the CBD. **Parnell** forms the ecclesiastical heart of the city, with one of Auckland's oldest churches and a couple of historical houses. Beyond lies the waterfront Tamaki Drive, running past the watery attractions of Kelly Tarlton's to the city beaches of Mission Bay and St Heliers. West of the centre, the cafés, shops and bars of **Ponsonby Road** and up-and-coming **Kingsland** give way to Western Springs, home of the **MOTAT** transport museum and the **zoo**.

Across the Waitemata Harbour the seemingly endless suburbs of the **North Shore** stretch into the distance, though you're only likely to want to spend much time in the old waterside suburb of **Devonport** and perhaps the long golden beach at **Takapuna**.

Immediately south of the centre, two of Auckland's highest points, **Mount Eden** and **One Tree Hill** with its encircling **Cornwall Park**, provide wonderful

▲ Suburban bar, Auckland

vantage points for views of the city. The main reason for heading further south is to visit Saturday's **Otara Market**.

East of the city centre

The Auckland Domain separates the city from the fashionable inner suburbs of **Parnell** and **Newmarket**, the former an established, moneyed district of restaurants, boutiques and galleries with a modest line in churches and historical houses. To the east lies Auckland's prime waterfront, traced by **Tamaki Drive**, a twisting thoroughfare that skirts eight kilometres of Auckland's most popular city beaches – **Mission Bay**, **Kohimarama** and **St Heliers**. During the summer, the waterfront is the favoured hangout of joggers and cyclists. **Kelly Tarlton's** is the only specific sight, but the harbour views out to Rangitoto and the Hauraki Gulf are excellent both from shore level and from a couple of headland viewpoints. The gentle hills behind are dotted with the secluded mansions of leafy Remuera, Auckland's old-money suburb.

Parnell

In the mid-1960s, **Parnell** narrowly escaped a high-rise-concrete fate when eccentric dreamer **Les Harvey** raised enough money to whisk the quaint but dilapidated shops and wooden villas from under the developers' noses. He then campaigned against New Zealand's strict trading laws, with the result that during the 1970s and much of the 1980s Parnell was the only place in Auckland where you could shop on a Saturday. Parnell Road soon established an enviable reputation for chic clothes shops, swanky restaurants and, most evident of all, dealer art galleries. There's also La Cigale **French-styled market**, 69 St George's Bay Rd (Sat 8am–1pm, Sun 9am–2pm), with limited produce and lots of great stuff to eat.

At the southern end of Parnell Road stands one of the world's largest wooden churches, **St Mary's** (Mon–Sat 10am–4pm, Sun 11am–5pm; free), built from native timbers in 1886. Inside, check out the series of photos taken on the dramatic day in 1982 when the church was rolled in one piece from its original site across

Parnell Road to join its more modern kin, the **Holy Trinity Cathedral** (Mon–Sat 10am–4pm, Sun 11am–5pm; free). The original Gothic chancel was started in 1959 then left half-finished until the late 1980s, when an incongruous, airy nave with a Swiss chalet-style roof was grafted on, supposedly in imitation of the older church alongside. Pop in to admire the modern stained-glass windows at the back; the bold and bright side panels symbolize Maori and Pakeha contributions to society. The most recent additions are the eighteen glass panels lining the nave, several by Maori artist Shane Cotton, who has used a unifying palette of muted reds, browns and greens.

The Gothic flourishes of the nineteenth-century church show the influence of New Zealand's prominent ecclesiastical architect, Frederick Thatcher, who designed the nearby **Kinder House**, at 2 Ayr St (Tues–Sun 11am–3pm; $4), for the headmaster of the new grammar school – a post filled by John Kinder, an accomplished watercolourist and documentary photographer. Built of rough-hewn Mount Eden volcanic rock, the house contains some interesting photos and reproductions of Kinder's paintings of nineteenth-century New Zealand. Just down the road is **Ewelme Cottage**, 14 Ayr St (Fri–Sun 10.30am–noon & 1–4.30pm; $7.50), a pioneer kauri house built as a family home in 1864 for the wonderfully named clergyman Vicesimus Lush. The appeal of the place lies not so much in the house but in its furniture and possessions, left just as they were when Lush's descendants finally moved out in 1968, the family heirlooms betraying a desire to replicate the home comforts of their native Oxfordshire.

Newmarket

The southern continuation of Parnell Road runs into Broadway, the main drag through fashion-conscious **NEWMARKET**, on the eastern flanks of Mount Eden. In recent years this has become one of the city's top shopping districts, complete with good places to eat. Just south of the shops, Great South Road is lined with motels (see p.94).

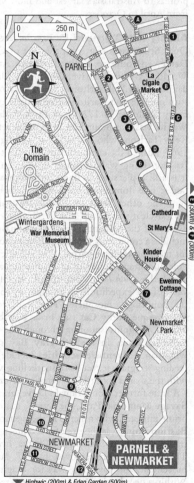

ACCOMMODATION		RESTAURANTS, CAFÉS & BARS		
Ascot Parnell	E	Asian Food	Non Solo	
Chalet Chevron	F	Hall	10	Pizza	4
City Garden		Cibo	1	Oh Calcutta!	2
Lodge	C	Di Mare	3	Otto Woo	12
International		Dunk		Rikka	9
Backpackers	A	Espresso	5	Urban Café	8
Lantana Lodge	B	Java Room	6	Zarbo	11
Parnell Inn	D	Kokako	7		

Specific sights are few in these parts, though consider visiting the Gothic timber mansion of **Highwic**, 40 Gillies Ave (Wed–Sun 10.30am–noon & 1–4.30pm; $7.50), built as a "city" property by a wealthy rural auctioneer and landowner in 1862. The estate, complete with outbuildings and servants' quarters, gives a fair indication of the contrasting lives of the time. From here it's a short walk to **Eden Garden**, 24 Omana Ave (daily: Sept–April 9am–4.30pm; May–Oct 9am–4pm; $6; ⓦwww.edengarden.co.nz), an enclave created in a former quarry. There's year-round interest with a little of everything from watergardens, cacti and proteas to Australasia's largest and most varied collection of camellias, in bloom from April to October.

Along the Tamaki Drive waterfront

Quay Street runs east from the foot of Queen Street, soon becoming **Tamaki Drive**, en route to **Kelly Tarlton's Antarctic Encounter & Underwater World**, 23 Tamaki Drive, Okahu Bay (daily 9.30am–5.30pm; $31.50 valid all day; ⓦwww.kellytarltons.co.nz). City tour **buses** and buses #745 and #769 stop outside and Tarlton's free shuttle runs from Sky City and opposite the Ferry Building at 172 Quay St (4–7 daily). Opened in 1985, **Underwater World** was the brainchild of Kiwi diver, treasure hunter and salvage expert Kelly Tarlton, who converted some huge sewage tanks that, from 1910 until 1961, flushed the city's effluent into Waitemata Harbour on the outgoing tides. Its pioneering walk-through acrylic tunnels have become commonplace, but it is still a pleasure to stand on the moving walkway and glide through two tanks: one dominated by flowing kelp beds, colourful reef fish and twisting eels; the other with smallish sharks, all appearing alarmingly close in the crystal-clear water.

Some of the remaining sewage tanks have become **Antarctic Encounter** which includes a convincing replica of the capacious hut used by Robert Falcon Scott and his team on their ill-starred 1911–12 attempt to be the first to reach the South Pole. It contains a pianola, a fully functional laboratory and a printing press – from which the *South Polar Times* rolled every few months throughout the three long years of the expedition. Contemporary footage and tales of their exploits add to the haunting atmosphere. This leads to a penguinarium visited on a naff Disneyesque **Snow Cat** ride made bearable by the close-up views of king and gentoo penguins shooting through the water and hopping around on fake icebergs. Tanks in the **Stingray Bay** section feature specimens with a 2m wingspan. **Adventure activities** include spending a few minutes in the tank feeding stingrays (extra $64), snorkelling with the reef fish (extra $64), or diving with the sharks (extra $124: certified divers only).

A little further along Tamaki Drive, grassy Bastion Point is topped by the **M.J. Savage Memorial Park**, the nation's austere Art Deco homage to its first Labour prime minister, who ushered in the welfare state in the late 1930s. More recently, **Bastion Point** was the site of a seventeen-month standoff between police and its traditional owners, the Ngati Whatua, over the subdivision of land for housing. The occupiers were removed in 1977, but the stand galvanized the land-rights movement, and paved the way for a significant change in government attitude. Within a decade, the Waitangi Tribunal recommended that the land be returned.

Bastion Point looks down on **Mission Bay**, the closest of the truly worthwhile city **beaches**, where a grassy waterside reserve is backed by an enticing row of cafés and restaurants. Swimming is best here close to high tide; at other times the water remains shallow a long way out. Similar conditions prevail at the sheltered beaches of **Kohimarama** and **St Heliers Bay**, both a short way further along Tamaki Drive.

West of the city centre

The suburbs of West Auckland developed later than their eastern counterparts, mainly because of their distance from the sea in the days when almost all travel was by ferry. The exceptions were the inner suburbs of Freeman's Bay, **Herne Bay**, **Ponsonby**, and newly fashionable **Kingsland**, which is right by the Rugby World Cup's main venue, Eden Park. Sights are scarce until you get out to **Western Springs**, infant Auckland's major water source, now home to **MOTAT**, a patchy transport and technology museum, and the city's **zoo**.

Freeman's Bay, Ponsonby and Herne Bay

Victoria Street runs west from Queen Street to **Freeman's Bay**, which was long ago reclaimed to accommodate early sawmilling operations. The land is now given over to the sports fields of Victoria Park, all overshadowed by the 38m-high chimney of **Victoria Park Market** (daily 9am–6pm; Ⓦwww.victoria-park -market.co.nz), a lacklustre knot of stalls and shops which occupies Auckland's former refuse incinerator. The **Link bus** passes on its way to Ponsonby, and city tour buses also stop here.

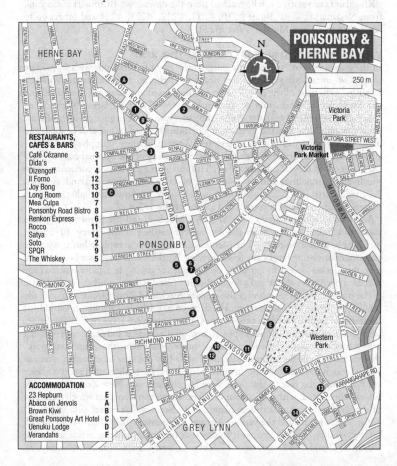

RESTAURANTS, CAFÉS & BARS	
Café Cézanne	3
Dida's	1
Dizengoff	4
Il Forno	12
Joy Bong	13
Long Room	10
Mea Culpa	7
Ponsonby Road Bistro	8
Renkon Express	6
Rocco	11
Satya	14
Soto	2
SPQR	9
The Whiskey	5

ACCOMMODATION	
23 Hepburn	E
Abaco on Jervois	A
Brown Kiwi	B
Great Ponsonby Art Hotel	C
Uenuku Lodge	D
Verandahs	F

The once fashionable suburb of **Ponsonby** had deteriorated greatly and rents were enticingly cheap by the 1960s when large numbers of immigrant Pacific Islanders made the area their home. Ponsonby took a bohemian turn in the Seventies and before long young professionals were moving in, restoring old houses and spending fistfuls of dollars in the cafés, restaurants and boutiques along Ponsonby Road. The street itself may not be beautiful, but the people sure are; musicians, actors and media folk congregate to lunch, schmooze and be seen in the latest fashionable haunt here. There's good reason to brave the poseurs, though, for some of the city's classiest clothes shopping and eating.

Kingsland

If you're in the area to see a rugby game (or cricket match) at Eden Park or just fancy time in funky shops and lively cafés, make for go-ahead **Kingsland**, 1km south of Ponsonby. Everything happens along half a kilometre of New North Road where you'll find innovative jewellery at Royal at no. 486, and Native Agent, no. 507, where Maori identity and early New Zealand colonization inform designs for clothing, soft furnishings and art. See p.117 and p.120 for café and bar listings.

Kingsland train station can be reached from the downtown Britomart station and from Newmarket West. Buses #210, #211, #212, #223, #224 and others go to Kingsland from stop M4 at 19 Victoria St.

Western Springs: MOTAT and the zoo

In the late nineteenth century the burgeoning city of Auckland, with its meagre supply of unreliable streams, was heavily reliant on the waters of **Western Springs**, 4km west of the city. The area is now devoted to attractive parkland and the **Museum of Transport & Technology** (MOTAT) on Great North Road (daily 10am–5pm; $14; ℡0800/668 286, ⓦwww.motat.org.nz), which offers a trawl through New Zealand's vehicular and industrial past in a jumble of sheds and halls. It is worth visiting for the restored Western Springs' pumphouse – where audiovisual displays run through the 100-year history of the original engine – and the Pioneers of New Zealand exhibit. This intriguing exhibition concentrates on the lives, personalities and achievements of two early New Zealand aviators: Richard Pearse (see p.536), the first man to achieve powered flight; and Jean Batten, an internationally recognized air ace of the 1930s.

Admission includes entry to the **MOTAT Meola Road** site (same hours), 1km away and linked to the main site by ancient rattling trams (every 10–30min; included in admission price). The Meola Road site is for aeroplane buffs, with the star attractions being one of the few surviving World War II Lancaster bombers and a double-decker Solent flying boat, decked out for dining in a more gracious age and used on Air New Zealand's South Pacific "Coral Route" until the early 1960s.

The tram between the two sites also stops at **Auckland Zoo**, Motions Road (daily 9.30am–5.30pm; $19; ⓦwww.aucklandzoo.co.nz), which is strong on naturalistic habitats and captive breeding programmes. The centrepiece is the trailblazing Pride-lands development with lions, hippos, rhinos, giraffes, zebras and gazelles all roaming across mock savannah behind enclosing moats. Elsewhere, the "rainforest walk" threads its way among artificial islands inhabited by colonies of monkeys, you can walk through the wallaby enclosure unhindered, and the Sealion and Penguin Shores exhibit brings you face to face with these loveable animals. New Zealand's wildlife is well represented, with a nocturnal kiwi house, a group of tuatara which form part of conservation work on offshore islands, and a large, walk-through aviary.

Plan your visit around the various **Animal Encounters** (daily 11am–3pm; details on the website). Western Springs is on city tour **bus** routes and can be reached on the #093, #113 and #163 buses from 17 Albert St, near Customs Street in the city.

The North Shore

The completion of the harbour bridge in 1959 provided the catalyst for the development of the **North Shore**, previously a handful of scattered communities linked by a web of ferries crisscrossing the harbour. By the early 1970s, the volume of traffic to the suburbs log-jammed the bridge – until a Japanese company attached a two-lane extension (affectionately dubbed "the Nippon Clip-ons") to each side. The bridge and its additional lanes can now be seen at close quarters on the Auckland Bridge Climb (see p.113).

The vast urban sprawl marches inexorably towards the Hibiscus Coast (see p.127), with most interest to be found in the maritime village of **Devonport**, at the southern end of a long string of calm swimming **beaches**. Further north, try the more open and busier **Takapuna**, a short stroll from dozens of good cafés and reached by a host of buses mostly in the #800s and #900s.

Devonport

Devonport is one of Auckland's oldest suburbs, founded in 1840 and still linked to the city by a ten-minute ferry journey. The naval station was an early tenant, soon followed by wealthy merchants, who built fine kauri villas. Some of these are graced with little turrets ("widows' watches") that served as lookouts where the traders could scan the seas for their precious cargoes and wives watch hopefully for their returning husbands. Wandering along the peaceful streets and the tree-fringed waterfront past grand houses is the essence of Devonport's appeal and there's no shortage of tempting bookshops, small galleries, cafés and restaurants along the main street to punctuate your amblings.

Call at the **i-SITE visitor centre**, 3 Victoria Rd (daily 8.30am–5pm; ⊤09/446 0677, ⓦwww.northshorenz.com), to pick up the *Old Devonport Walk* leaflet, or a map (both free). Many ferries are met by Devonport Explorer Tours (⊤09/357 6366) who do a one-hour trip ($30) around the sights and up both volcanoes.

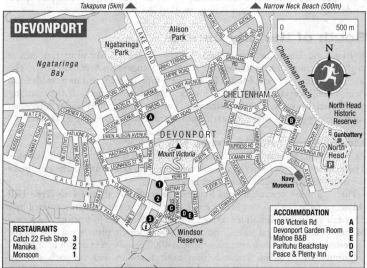

Devonport ferry

Devonport is best reached on the **Devonport ferry** (Mon–Thurs 6.10am–11pm, Fri & Sat 6.15am–1am, Sun 7.15am–10pm; every 30min; 10min journey; $10 return, bikes free), which forms part of the GetAbout Auckland Discovery Pass (see p.91). All ferries from downtown to Rangitoto, and many Waiheke Island-bound ferries also stop at Devonport.

On a fine day, take a stiff walk up one of the two ancient volcanoes that back Devonport. The closest, about fifteen minutes' walk away, is **Mount Victoria** (Taka-a-ranga; unrestricted access for pedestrians; closed to vehicles from dusk on Thurs, Fri & Sat), from where you get fabulous gulf views. The hill was once the site of a Maori *pa* and fortified village and the remains of terraces and *kumara* pits can still be detected on the northern and eastern slopes. A kilometre east, the grass- and flax-covered volcanic plug of **North Head** (Maungauika; daily 6am–10pm, vehicles 6am–8pm; free) guards the entrance to the inner harbour and makes a wonderful vantage point during yachting events or any sunny afternoon. A strategic site for pre-colonial Maori, it was later co-opted to form part of the young nation's coastal defences. In the wake of the "Russian Scares" of 1884–86, which were precipitated by the opening of the port of Vladivostok, North Head became Fort Cautley. It is now operated by DOC as the **North Head Historic Reserve** and you can amble around the peripheral remains – pillboxes, concrete tunnels linking gun emplacements and even a restored eight-inch "disappearing gun", which recoiled underground for easy reloading. The hilltop former kitchen now has a twelve-minute video (daily 8.30am–4pm; free) on the site's history.

To continue the military theme, call in at the brand new **Navy Museum** (daily 10am–4.30pm; donation; @www.navymuseum.mil.nz), due to open in late 2010 on the shores of Torpedo Bay in the southern crook of North Head.

North Head is part of the **North Shore City Coastal Walk** (free leaflet from the visitor centre). This 23km combination of clifftop and street walking starts by the Devonport ferry wharf and runs all the way north to Torbay. It forms part of the Te Araroa walkway from Cape Reinga to Bluff (see p.56).

South of the city centre

Southern Auckland, arching around the eastern end of Manukau Harbour, is neglected by most visitors, though the airport at Mangere is where most arrive. The city's most lofty volcano, **Mount Eden**, offers superb views, and its near-identical twin, **One Tree Hill**, has some of the best surviving examples of the terracing undertaken by early Maori inhabitants. Further south, Auckland's Polynesian community plies its wares early each Saturday morning at the **Otara Market**.

Mount Eden and One Tree Hill

At just 196m, **Mount Eden** (Maungawhau) is Auckland city's highest volcano. The extensive views from the summit car park, just 2km south of the city, make it extraordinarily popular with tour buses.

There's a more rewarding area 5km to the southeast around **One Tree Hill** (Maungakiekie; 183m), one of the city's most distinctive landmarks, topped by a 33m-tall granite obelisk (but no tree). For a century, until just before the arrival of Europeans, Maungakiekie ("mountain of the kiekie plant") was one of the largest *pa* sites in the country; an estimated 4000 people were drawn here by the proximity to abundant seafood from both harbours and the rich soils of the volcanic cone, which still bears the scars of extensive earthworks including the remains of dwellings and *kumara* pits. The site was abandoned and then bought by the Scottish medic and "father of Auckland", Sir John Logan Campbell, one of only two European residents when the city was granted capital status in 1840. To commemorate the 1901 visit of Britain's Duke and Duchess of Cornwall, Campbell donated his One Tree Hill estate to the people of New Zealand and named it **Cornwall Park** (daily 7am–dusk; free). The park puts on its best display around Christmas time, when avenues of pohutukawa trees erupt in a riot of red blossom. Campbell is buried at the summit where a single totara tree originally gave One Tree Hill its name. Settlers cut it down in 1852, and Campbell planted several pines as a windbreak, a single specimen surviving until the millennium. Already ailing from a 1994 chainsaw attack by a Maori activist avenging the loss of the totara, the pine's fate was sealed by a similar attack in 1999 and the tree was removed the next year.

Free leaflets outlining a trail around the archeological and volcanic sites of the hill are available from the **visitor centre** (daily 10am–4pm), which is housed in **Huia Lodge**, built by Campbell as a gatekeeper's house and now containing displays on the park and the man. Immediately opposite is **Acacia Cottage** (daily 7am–dusk; free), Campbell's original home and the city's oldest surviving building, built in 1841 and re-sited from central Auckland in the 1920s.

Fans of astronomy are better served on the southern side of One Tree Hill at the **Stardome Observatory**, where a frequently changing schedule of hour-long multimedia programmes are played out on the ceiling of the **planetarium** (Tues–Sun 8pm & 9pm; $16; T09/624 1246, W www.stardome.org.nz). Weather and darkness permitting, the shows are followed by thirty minutes of telescope viewing.

Most of Cornwall Park is closed after dark but the observatory and the summit are accessible from the southern entrance off Manukau Road, which can be reached on several **buses** including the #312 from 55 Customs St East on the corner of Queen Street.

South Auckland

Beyond Cornwall Park is **South Auckland**, the city's poorest sector and the less-than-flatteringly-depicted gangland setting of Lee Tamahori's film *Once Were Warriors*. It isn't a no-go zone, and is certainly worth a look on Saturday morning

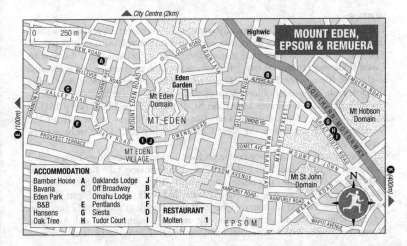

when **Otara Market** sprawls across the car park of the Otara Town Centre. Though diluted by an influx of market traders flogging cheap clothes and shoddy trinkets, it remains the largest Maori and Polynesian market in the world with displays of island-style floral print fabrics, reasonably priced Maori carvings and truckloads of cheap fruit and veg. Your best bet is the food: there are stalls where you can buy home-made cakes and Maori bread, and a van has been ingeniously kitted out to produce an ersatz *hangi*. The market gets going around 6am and runs through to noon, so get there early. Take the Otara exit off the southern motorway or catch bus #487 or #497 for the fifty-minute journey from 55 Customs St East on the corner of Queen Street.

Southbound drivers might want to spend an hour or two 8km further south at the **Auckland Botanic Gardens** (daily: late Sept to early April 8am–8pm; early April to late Sept 8am–6pm; free), well signposted right beside the motorway at Manurewa. Though only open since 1982, it is a rapidly maturing expanse with a Gondwana Arboretum, threatened native plant section, forest trails, a good visitor centre and café.

Activities

Though most visitors head out into the "real" New Zealand for a little adventure, Auckland has plenty on its doorstep. There is plenty of opportunity to explore the city and its environs on **foot**, but the city is so water-focused that it would be a shame not to get out on the harbour at some point. The easiest and cheapest way is to hop on one of the **ferries** to Devonport (see p.110) or one of the outlying islands (see "Islands of the Hauraki Gulf" from p.131), but for prolonged forays, consider one of the many **cruises** available, while a **dolphin and whale safari** or **sea-kayaking** trip offers a more intimate experience.

Two of Auckland's largest structures provide the framework for adrenaline thrills such as the **bungy jump** off the harbour bridge and SkyJump and SkyWalk off the Skytower (see p.100). If you prefer your excitement to come with wilder scenery, don't miss some excellent **canyoning** in the Waitakere Ranges.

In addition, there are sightseeing and wine **tours** to the city's Waitakere Ranges and West Coast beaches.

Walks

The most ambitious walking normally attempted by visitors to Auckland is a stroll through The Domain or a short hike up to one of the volcano-top viewpoints. The best of the sights have been threaded together as the well-marked **Coast to Coast Walkway** (16km one-way; 4hr) which straddles the isthmus. All is revealed in the free *Beyond your Backyard – Discovering Auckland City by Foot or Bike* leaflet available from the tourist offices. A route map can be found at ⓦwww.auckland-city.govt.nz. More ambitious hikers can head to Rangitoto Island (see p.131) or pick off sections of the **Hillary Trail** (see p.125) out west in the hills of the Waitakere Ranges. Most of the West Coast tours (see p.123) also include some gentle walking.

To learn more about the city centre on foot, join informative two-hour guided walks run by Auckland Walks (daily 10am; $25; booking essential ⓣ0800/300 100, ⓦwww.aucklandwalks.co.nz) or Tamaki Hikoi Tours (ⓣ0800/282 552, ⓦwww.tamakihikoi.co.nz), who offer **Maori-led walks** giving a Ngati Whatua perspective on Tamaki Makaurau. Choose from a one-hour tour of Maungawhau (Mount Eden; $30) or a three-hour trip around Maungawhau and Auckland Domain complete with Maori traditional instruments, songs and lots of stories.

Cruises and sailing

As well as their ferry services, Fullers offer a two-hour **Harbour Cruise** (daily 10.30am & 1.30pm; $35) that leaves the Ferry Building briefly visiting the Harbour Bridge, Devonport and Rangitoto Island. You can stay on Rangitoto and return on a later cruise, and the ticket gives you a free return ferry ride to Devonport.

Head around to Viaduct Harbour if you'd rather crew on America's Cup **racing yachts** *NZL 40* or *NZL 41* ($150 for a two-hour sail or $195 as part of a team in a match race between the two boats; ☎0800/397 567, ⓦwww.explorenz.co.nz). Built for New Zealand's 1995 challenge in San Diego they are now based quayside and give a real sense of power and speed.

The same company also runs a variety of more **leisurely sailing** trips on the *Pride of Auckland* including a coffee cruise (1pm & 3.45pm; 1hr 30min; $70), a lunch cruise (1pm; 1hr 30min; $85), a dinner cruise (7pm; 2hr 30min; $110) and a sail to Waiheke Island with a ferry trip back (9am; 3hr; $85).

On most **summer weekends** you can help sail the *Søren Larsen* (Dec–April Sun 10am–3pm; $125 including lunch; ☎0800/767 365, ⓦwww.sorenlarsen.co.nz), a Danish Baltic trader built of oak in 1949 and later fitted with a nineteenth-century sailing rig. This majestic vessel starred in the 1970s TV series *The Onedin Line* and led the First Fleet re-enactment that formed a part of the Australian bicentennial celebrations in 1987. Passengers are free to participate – steering, hauling sheets and climbing the rigging – though maritime instruction tends to be a larger component of the midweek trips to Hauraki Gulf and Bay of Islands (4–5 nights; $1280–1565).

Dolphin and whale watching

The Hauraki Gulf is excellent territory for spotting marine mammals, best seen on **dolphin- and whale-watching trips** run by Explore NZ (daily; 4hr 30min; $150; ☎0800/397 567, ⓦwww.explorenz.co.nz) from Viaduct Harbour. Educational and entertaining trips head out on a 20m catamaran and dolphins are spotted ninety percent of the time (you get a fifty-percent discount on a second trip if none are seen). Bryde's whales and orcas are also frequently seen.

Kayaking and kayak fishing

For **kayaking** head to Fergs Kayaks, 12 Tamaki Drive, Okahu Bay (☎09/529 2230, ⓦwww.fergskayaks.co.nz), who run guided trips 7km across the Waitemata Harbour to Rangitoto Island (departures 9.30am plus Mon–Fri 5.30pm, Sat & Sun 4pm; 6hr; $100) hiking to the summit, then paddling back. If that seems too much, opt for their 3km paddle to Devonport (same times; 3hr; $80) with a hike up North Head. In both cases, the later departure gives you a chance to paddle by moon or torchlight. If you'd rather go it alone, Fergs offer **kayak rental** in either single sea kayaks ($20/1hr, $35/half-day), doubles ($40/1hr, $70/half-day) and slightly cheaper sit-on-tops, though trips to Rangitoto and Devonport are not generally allowed.

Gorgeous bays and islands are the focus of kayak trips run by TIME Unlimited (half-day $145, full day $245; ☎09/446 6677 or 0800/868 463, ⓦwww.newzealandtours.travel). Groups are generally limited to six and (unusually for kayak operators) single kayaks are available. They even run an overnight trip ($490) with lots of fishing and camping out. Fishing takes precedence with full-day **kayak-fishing** tours ($295) on which you might expect to catch snapper, kingfish and John Dory, and swim after lunch on a gorgeous beach.

Auckland Bridge Climb and Bungy

Based on the Sydney Harbour bridge climb, A.J. Hackett's **Auckland Bridge Climb** (90min; $120; ☎0800/462 5462, ⓦwww.bungy.co.nz), gives you the opportunity to sample excellent city views from the highest point on the city's harbour, crossing some 65m above the Waitemata Harbour. There's no actual climbing involved, just strolling along steel walkways while harnessed to a cable as guides relate detail on the bridge's fulcrums, pivots and cantilevers. Reservations are essential and anyone over seven can go. Cameras are not allowed but there'll be someone on hand to take a snap and sell it to you later.

If you crave an adrenaline rush, the **Auckland Bridge Bungy** ($120; same contact details) should do the trick, with a 40m leap and a water-touch option.

Canyoning

About the most fun you can have in a wetsuit around Auckland is **canyoning**, a combination of swimming, abseiling, jumping into deep pools and sliding down rock chutes. Two companies operate in the Waitakere Ranges, both making pick-ups in Auckland. Canyonz ($175; ☏0800/422 696, ⓦwww.canyonz.co.nz) offers full-day trips in Blue Canyon including an 8m waterfall-jump or abseil. AWOL Adventures (☏0800/462 965, ⓦwww.awoladventures.co.nz) run a similar trip near Piha, with more emphasis on abseiling, particularly on their full-day trip ($155). The lower section is host to the half-day trip ($135) and **night canyoning** ($155; mostly in winter) with just a headtorch and glowworms for illumination. Both companies' trips often end up with a visit to one of the West Coast surf beaches.

Canyonz also offers day-trips down the magnificent **Sleeping God** canyon near Thames (Oct–May only; $235). In this wonderfully scenic spot you descend 300m in a series of twelve drops using slides, and abseils as long as 70m (some through the waterfall), with the opportunity to leap 13m from a rock ledge into a deep pool. It's tough enough that you'll need to be water-confident and fairly fit.

Eating

Aucklanders take their eating seriously and there is no shortage of **restaurants**. For a more casual experience, **cafés** or **pubs** (see p.118), offer decent meals for around $20. On a fine summer evening it is tempting to flock to the waterside restaurants and bars of **Viaduct Harbour**, though it can be pricey and those on a budget will do better up on **Karangahape Road**. Dedicated foodies will find the best areas for grazing in the inner-city suburbs, chiefly along **Ponsonby Road**, Auckland's culinary crucible, or **Parnell Road**, the other main eat street.

City centre and Viaduct Harbour

The needs of central Auckland office workers are met by numerous cafés, low-cost Asian restaurants and a few handy **food halls**. **High Street** and **Lorne Street** are both good hunting grounds. In the evening parts of the city feel pretty dead, though there's plenty of life around **Viaduct Harbour**. Some places are ostentatious, pricey and soulless, though the best (listed below) have great food and tempting yacht-filled vistas.

Atrium Food Gallery Elliot St. Daytime food hall that's slightly more salubrious than others, with a wide range of counters – Vietnamese, sushi, Korean, pizza, kebabs, Taiwanese – plus a bakery and decent coffee.

Banh Mi Bale 6–8 Lorne St ☏09/377 3288. The spartan decor is a poor advert for this excellent place serving superb Vietnamese dishes (mostly

$12–18) but specializing in crusty sandwiches ($8) – French bread smeared with pâté and mayonnaise then stuffed with cucumber, coriander and fillings such as lemongrass chicken or pork balls. Closed Sun.

Bellota 91 Federal St ☏09/363 6301. Fans of celebrated Kiwi chef, Peter Gordon, flock to the booths in this retro 1970s cave for his fusion take on Spanish tapas (mostly $10–16). The name means acorn, a reference to the bellota-fed pigs that participate in the menu (though there are plenty of veggie options).

Corner Pancake 10 Wellesley St at Lorne St. Bargain hole-in-the-wall serving Korean pancakes with delectable fillings such as pork, red bean, chicken and cheese, or sugar and cinnamon for $2–3 each. Mon–Fri 11.30am–7pm, Sat noon–6pm.

Deus Ex Machina Shed 5, 90 Wellesley St. Gleaming custom motorcycles, cool riding and streetwear and a short menu of breakfast and lunch dishes combine in this vast and stylish warehouse café decked out with sofas and Persian-style carpets. A little hard to find, but worth the effort, and you can watch them building bikes over an espresso.

Euro Princes Wharf ⑦ 09/309 9866. Classy, waterside à la carte dining helmed by local celebrity chef, Simon Gault. The service is always spot on and the food imaginative and tasty. Most mains are nudging $40, but the signature rotisserie chicken served with mash and peanut slaw is a modest $34.

Food Alley 9 Albert St. Spartan, inexpensive two-level food hall with twenty kitchens exhibiting a strong East Asian bias. Daily 10am–10pm.

French Café 210 Symonds St ⑦ 09/377 1911. Consistently one of the finest restaurants in the city. The ever-changing seasonal menu leans towards contemporary European cuisine and the service is faultless. Mains are $40 though there's also a superb eleven-course tasting menu ($140; matching wines add $85). Dinner Tues–Sat plus Fri lunch.

Grand Harbour 18 Customs St West ⑦ 09/357 6889. More opulent than most of the city's Chinese places and heavily patronized by the Chinese community, this bustling modern restaurant is popular for business lunches and serves great *yum cha*.

Ima 57 Fort St ⑦ 09/300 7252. Relaxed café originally set up by Israeli Yael and Palestinian Khaled. Everything they make is super-fresh, including Middle Eastern egg breakfasts ($14) and the best falafel in town ($13). Dinner, with mains around $30, is available Wed–Sat. Closed Sun.

Mezze Bar 1a Little High St ⑦ 09/307 2029. Airy café offering respite from the buzz of Queen St. Great for tapas and meze ($9–18), with broadly

Mediterranean and Middle Eastern leanings. Open for lunch and dinner with dishes such as Spanish tortilla and grilled mushroom on polenta or Moroccan meat bake (around $28), washed down with a broad selection of beers and wines.

Middle East Café 23a Wellesley St West. Tiny, simple, camel-themed eat-in or takeaway unlicensed café that's an Auckland institution, deservedly celebrated for its *chawarma* and falafel ($9–11), both cloaked in creamy garlic, spicy tomato sauce or hot chilli sauce. Closed Sat & Sun lunch .

Raw Power 10 Vulcan Lane. Great little upstairs juice bar with heaps of veggie and vegan offerings – salads, tofu burgers, falafel, curried corn fritters etc (mostly $10–18) – plus excellent fresh juices and smoothies until 4pm. Closed Sun.

Reuben 36 Lorne St, inside the New Art Gallery ⑦ 09/302 0226. Excellent daytime oasis, with a comfortable terrace for people-watching and a coffee and cake. At lunch (until 2.30pm), you can get something more substantial like a tasty risotto, fish cakes or tandoori lamb.

Soul Viaduct Harbour ⑦ 09/356 7249. An icon of Auckland's waterfront dining scene, *Soul* is perfect for classy, modern bistro meals on the terrace (mains $30–40) with fish and seafood a speciality. There's a slickness to the service and the bar where you might just nip in for a cocktail or a beer overlooking the yachts.

Tanuki 319b Queen St ⑦ 09/379 5353. Excellent *yakitori* and sake bar in a cave-like basement setting, with a more formal restaurant above. You can tuck into various delicacies – from octopus balls to teriyaki chicken, all washed down with sake or Japanese beer.

Tony's 32 Lorne St & 27 Wellesley St West ⑦ 09/373 2138. Long-standing steak restaurants, famous for good-quality, hearty mains ($30–40). The second, 27 Wellesley St address is the original.

Wildfire Princes Wharf ⑦ 09/353 7595. Flashy and popular Brazilian barbecue restaurant with some tables overlooking the water. Come for the *churrasco* (noon–3pm & 5–7pm $39, after 7pm $49), assorted tapas-style appetizers followed by a vast selection of meats and seafood marinated in herbs, roasted over manuka coals then carved off skewers at the table. If you can't face that much meat, call in for one of the fabulous *caipirinha* cocktails.

Karangahape Road and around

Karangahape Road still feels more relaxed than the city centre, with laidback cafés, an abundance of low-cost ethnic restaurants and a couple of smarter places moving in. Unless otherwise stated, these places are marked on the map on p.99.

Alleluya St Kevin's Arcade, 179 K' Rd ☎09/377 8482. You'll find some of the best city views plus good, reasonably priced food and a no-nonsense attitude at this café hidden in a pretty 1920s arcade, great for kicking back. Open daily from 9am. Licensed.

Coco's Cantina 376 K' Rd. A funky and very popular restaurant with a strong gay following. Its short, Italian-style menu might include arancini risotto balls ($10) followed by steak with anchovy butter and home fries ($28), and the outside tables are great for watching the characters along K' Rd, especially on Friday and Saturday nights. Closed Sun & Mon; no bookings.

Joy Bong 531 K' Rd ☎09/377 2218. See map, p.107. Probably the best Thai restaurant in town this Isaan place serves up dishes such as crispy fish salad and lemongrass chicken (both $23). There's also a nice little cocktail bar out back and

a hole-in-the-wall serving takeaway lunches from $10. Closed Sat lunch, & Sun.

Rasoi 211 K' Rd. It feels almost like you're in South India in this budget vegetarian café dishing up *dosas, uttappams* and *thalis* for $9–17 and there's an all-you-can-eat maharajah *thali* for $22. Great Indian sweets too.

Sri Pinang 356 K' Rd ☎09/358 3886. Simple Malaysian restaurant. Start with half a dozen satay chicken skewers and follow with perhaps *sambal* okra, beef *rendang* or clay-pot chicken rice scooped up with excellent roti. BYO only but you can buy wine and beer from the shop across the road. Closed Mon & Sat lunch, and all day Sun.

Verona 169 K' Rd. Long-standing muso hangout and general place to be seen. Drop in for an espresso or a wine in the comfy booths, grab snacks from the counter or order salads, pasta, pizza or $25 mains from the menu.

Parnell

Parnell's eating places split into two camps: established restaurants with the accent on fine dining, and trendier, cheaper cafés catering to younger devotees and backpackers. See map on p.105.

Cibo 91 St George's Bay Rd ☎09/303 9660. Fine dining a little off the main drag, worth seeking out. Reliable favourites such as steak and duck leg are available but there's always something unexpected on the menu. Popular for business lunches so probably best left for evening visits. Mains $35–38. Closed Sun.

Di Mare Shop 9, 251 Parnell Rd ☎09/300 3260. One of the best surf and turf restaurants in the city, serving delicious traditional and innovative dishes to an appreciative crowd, in an intimate, back alley courtyard restaurant off the main road. Try the ocean platter for two ($60) or the lamb Siciliana ($34). Licensed & BYO.

Dunk Espresso 297 Parnell Rd. Reliable, airy modern café with a good range of breakfasts and lunches, fresh salads and good coffee.

Java Room 317 Parnell Rd ☎09/366 1606. Intimate dinner-only restaurant serving loosely Indonesian-influenced dishes (with Malaysian, Vietnamese and Indian influences) but also prawn and pork dim sum starters ($10), chicken

laksa ($12) and Siamese snapper ($27). Closed Sun.

Kokako 492 Parnell Rd ☎09/379 2868. Join the communal table or tuck yourself away with a magazine at this modern daytime café serving Fair Trade organic coffee (including decaf) all made with organic milk. The vegetarian menu includes the likes of creamy mushrooms on spelt toast ($10) and great salads.

Non Solo Pizza 259 Parnell Rd ☎09/379 5358. As the name says, not just pizza, but they do create wonderfully thin-crust concoctions with classic Italian toppings. Also pasta and assorted *secondi piatti* served inside or on the intimate patio.

Oh Calcutta! 151 Parnell Rd ☎09/377 9090. Bronzed statues of Shiva and Ganesh look down on diners from Mogul alcoves in this classy curry restaurant which picks the best from across the subcontinent (mains $20) and imbues them with wonderfully distinct flavours. A range of lunchtime tiffin menus let you sample three curries, rice, naan and poppadoms for $25.

Newmarket and Mount Eden

There's plenty of good eating in Newmarket and Mount Eden and a couple of places warrant a special journey. See map on p.105.

Asian Food Hall Newmarket Plaza, Teed St, next to the fish market. A little slice of East Asia in Auckland with Malaysian, Thai, Japanese, Korean

and a couple of Chinese places all serving dishes at bargain prices.

Molten 422 Mt Eden Rd ☎09/638 7236. See map on p.111. All the best qualities of a top suburban bistro: comfortable and relaxed with efficient, friendly service, great food and a well-thought-out wine list. Good value, too, with generously portioned mains, such as tuna steak on rimu-smoked bacon risotto, around $35. Pop next door for a drink at *Liquid Molten*. Licensed.

Otto Woo Corner of Remuera Rd & Nuffield St ☎09/522 2272. Excellent unlicensed noodle bar, primarily for takeaways but with a few stools at stark, white tables. Choose from freshly prepared chicken bok choy, seafood laksa, satay vegetable noodles and a dozen other dishes (all $12–15) and finish off with some sweet rice balls and a fresh juice.

Rikka 73 Davis Crescent ☎09/522 5277. Beautifully presented sushi and sashimi, sizzling plates of prawns and other funky dishes in this modern Japanese place. Booking essential.

Urban Café 139 Carlton Gore Rd ☎09/966 6977. Sharp, modern café where efficient service and good coffee complement a counter full of delicious stuffed *pide*, imaginative salads and a short menu for breakfast and lunch dishes (mostly $12–17). Heaps of current mags too.

Zarbo 24 Morrow St. Great deli/café with a fabulous range of products from around the world put to good use in a delicious range of breakfast and lunch dishes ($9–20). Lunch finishes at 3pm but they stay open until 5pm for salads, cakes and coffee.

Tamaki Drive: Okahu Bay and Mission Bay

If you find yourself peckish while visiting Kelly Tarlton's or swimming at Mission Bay, try one of this selection from a long line round the bay. See map on p.89.

Bar Comida 81 Tamaki Drive. Quality version of the typical Kiwi cover-all-the-bases café/restaurant/bar with wood-fired gourmet pizza (including Rangitoto-shaped spinach pizza for $25), great coffee and desserts and a strong line in tapas and Persian flatbreads, applied to anything from BLT to grilled vegetables with hummus.

The Fishmonger 16 Polygon Rd, St Heliers ☎09/575 0537. Head one street back from the waterfront to find this top-quality chippy where

several species of fish come battered, Panko-crumbed, blackened or grilled with lemon. Perfect eaten on the beach.

Hammerheads 19 Tamaki Drive, Okahu Bay, by Kelly Tarlton's ☎09/521 4400. The perfect spot for a upmarket lunch on a sunny day or dinner, preceded by a cocktail while you admire the tremendous views over the water to the city skyline. Excellent fish and seafood mains are mostly around $37.

Ponsonby and Kingsland

At the cutting edge of Auckland's foodie scene, **Ponsonby Road** is a street where devotion to style is as important as culinary prowess. But don't be intimidated; the food is excellent and competition keeps prices reasonable. Popular daytime cafés frequently ease into more rambunctious drinking later on. All the places below are in Ponsonby and marked on the map on p.107 unless otherwise noted.

Café Cézanne 296 Ponsonby Rd. This casual, ramshackle place is a welcome retreat from the glitz of the rest of Ponsonby Rd; great for reading the papers over hearty breakfasts, excellent quiches or huge wedges of cake. Licensed & BYO.

Dida's 54 Jervois Rd ☎09/376 2813. The smart set flock to this classy tapas bar and wine lounge, sinking into the leather sofas to choose from a fantastic wine selection and an array of delectable small plates – Cloudy Bay oysters ($12), tuna and artichoke skewers ($9) etc.

Dizengoff 256 Ponsonby Rd ☎09/360 0108. Unlicensed breakfast and lunch café specializing in wonderful bagels, some Jewish deli favourites and luscious char-grilled vegetables, all at reasonable prices.

The Fridge 507 New North Rd, Kingsland. See map, p.89. The brick-lined main room and an airy outdoor deck downstairs are both great spaces to enjoy a great range of sandwiches, wraps, pies and breakfast dishes, all washed down with great coffee. Always packed at weekends.

Il Forno 55 Mackelvie St. Great daytime bakery and café, especially notable for its delectable made-on-the-premises cakes, pastries and coffee, but also doing fine sandwiches and rolls.

Ponsonby Road Bistro 165 Ponsonby Rd ☎09/360 1611. Blackboards with daily specials lend a relaxed ambience to this consistently good, casual yet sophisticated restaurant where most dishes come flexibly served as both appetizer and main. Prices are modest for the quality (most mains

$25–30), and there are $15 quick lunch specials. Closed Sun.

Renkon Express 211 Ponsonby Rd ℡09/307 8008. Just a few small tables in what is essentially a Japanese takeaway serving delicious *donburi* and noodle dishes (such as grilled eel with dry udon) for $11. It's not licensed but you can grab takeaways and sit next door over a glass of wine at *Mea Culpa* (see p.120). Daily 11.30am–3pm & 5–9.30pm.

Rocco 23 Ponsonby Rd ℡09/360 6262. There's always a lively buzz in this converted villa where Spanish-influenced dishes come with service that's sharp without being over formal. Mains – such as prosciutto-wrapped mackerel fillets or pork, monkfish and clam cazuela – are almost invariably delicious and at around $32 are good value. Closed Sun & Mon.

🏃 **Satya** 17 Great North Rd. This excellent South Indian place steps outside the usual range of curries with the likes of *bhel puri* ($8) followed by *murg badami* with almonds and marinated chicken ($18). Licensed & BYO. Lunch deals from $8.

Soto 13 St Mary's Bay Rd ℡09/360 0021. Delicate screens and a Zen garden have transformed this former fire station into a beautiful modern Japanese restaurant that's probably the finest in town. Choose from Western or Oriental low tables and select from a menu of wonderfully flavoursome dishes, all immaculately presented. Or just drop in to sample the range of sake. Closed Sun & Mon.

🏃 **SPQR** 150 Ponsonby Rd ℡09/360 1710. Dimly lit and eternally groovy restaurant/bar that's always popular for its quality Italian-influenced food (especially the pizzas). Many treat it more as a bar and venue for spotting actors and rock stars. Excellent cocktails and a wide range of wines (sold by the glass).

Devonport

Devonport has variety but few venues that live up to Auckland's better foodie hangouts. See map on p.109.

Catch 22 Fish Shop 19 Victoria Rd. On a nice evening it's hard to beat fish and chips or a straightforward burger on the beach. Pick some up at *Catch 22* and wander over. Closed Mon.

Manuka 49 Victoria Rd ℡09/445 7732. Quality restaurant specializing in pasta, wood-fired pizza ($22–28) and a few steak and chicken dishes, but good at any time of the day for light snacks and salads or just for coffee and cake.

Monsoon 71 Victoria Rd ℡09/445 4263. Value-for-money Thai/Malaysian place with tasty dishes such as fish and tiger prawns in a red curry sauce for around $18–23. Evenings only, from 5pm. Licensed & BYO.

The best way to link into the scene is to pick up the free, fortnightly *Express* magazine (Ⓦwww.gayexpress.co.nz), found in racks in gay-friendly shops, cafés and bars and at the more raunchy Out! Bookshop, 39 Anzac Ave (℡09/377 7770). Alternatively pick up a copy of the free *Gaynz.com* gig guide, which covers gay hotspots around the country.

Perhaps the best time to be in town is for the Big Gay Out (Sun in mid-Feb; Ⓦwww.biggayout.co.nz), an extravaganza of comedy, music, drag and community events that takes place in Coyle Park, Point Chevalier, just west of the zoo. It is followed by OurFest (Ⓦwww.ourfest.co.nz), ten days of events around town including comedy, quiz nights, a tennis tournament and gay films.

For counselling and support, contact the **gay and lesbian helpline** (℡09/303 3584; Mon–Fri 10am–9pm, Sat & Sun 6–9pm; Ⓦwww.outlinenz.com).

Drinking, nightlife and entertainment

With a million plus people to entertain, there's always something going on in Auckland. The best way to find out **what's on** is to look at the *New Zealand Herald*, pick up the free *Groove Guide*, or visit Ⓦwww.eventfinder.co.nz. For more specialist gig information, buy the monthly *Rip It Up* ($7.90), visit its website (Ⓦwww.ripitup.co.nz) or go to the entertainment guide section of the bFM radio station website Ⓦwww.95bfm.co.nz.

Gay and lesbian Auckland

Auckland has a fairly small but progressive and proactive **gay scene** largely woven into the café/bar mainstream of Ponsonby and the western end of K' Road, where strip clubs mingle freely with gay bars and cruise clubs. Along K' Road just about everywhere is gay friendly, but much of the action happens at *Family Bar*, 270 K' Rd, which operates as a café and bar by day and gets more raucous into the evening: expect karaoke on Wednesday and drag shows at weekends. Across the road, the *Naval & Family*, at no. 243, is Auckland's gay pub. Among the **restaurants** and **bars** of Ponsonby Road, *SPQR* (see opposite) is always a good starting point with largely gay staff and a strong gay clientele.

As elsewhere in the country, the distinction between eating and drinking places is frequently blurred. The places listed below concentrate on the **drinking** though even old-style booze barns have been dramatically smartened up and do a sideline in inexpensive counter meals. **Closing times** are relaxed, with most places staying open until 3am at weekends.

The **clubbing** torch currently burns brightest around Fort Lane and Commerce Street, where you can join the nightly flow of young things meandering between the bars and clubs. Unless someone special is on the decks or a band is playing, most clubs are free early in the week, charge $5–10 on Thursday and $10-plus on Friday and Saturday. Lots of pubs and bars double as venues for live acts, employ DJs or put on some form of entertainment.

Many of the clubs have one area set up as a stage and on any night of the week you might find top Kiwi acts and even overseas **bands** blazing away in the corner; a few pubs may also put on a band from time to time. Not many big acts from North America or Europe visit, but those who do tend to play only in Auckland, usually in the larger venues; tickets can be booked through Ticketek (℡09/307 5000, ⓦwww.ticketek.co.nz), Ticketmaster (℡09/970 9700; ⓦwww.ticketmaster.co.nz) or iTicket (℡09/361 1000; ⓦwww.iticket.co.nz). Auckland's **arts scene** is reasonably lively, and you'll usually have a choice of a couple of plays, comedy and dance or opera.

One of the best ways to see local acts is to attend one of the **free summer concerts** held in The Domain and elsewhere under the *Music in Parks* banner (Jan–March; ℡09/379 2020, ⓦwww.aucklandcity.govt.nz), mostly on Friday, Saturday and Sunday afternoons. Also check out the summertime Park Parties put on by GeorgeFM (ⓦwww.georgefm.co.nz).

All venues listed are close to the **city centre** unless otherwise specified; see map on p.99.

Viaduct Harbour, city centre and K' Road

Coherent 262 K' Rd. Lively club with a hedonistic vibe, a casual dress code and a covered area out back that links to *Ink*, the club next door. The two operate together, especially when there are biggish bands on. Open Fri & Sat until late.

Cowboy 95 Customs St West ℡09/377 7778. Small faux-Western bar where the trick is to knock back a few bourbons, tequilas or whatever, help yourself to a cowboy hat and dance around to 1980s music. In might sound cheesy but everyone has a great time.

Flight Lounge 1 Fort Lane. Basement joint with a white glass bar and penchant for funky house, electro, disco funk and hip-hop. Open on Thursday but really only gets going late on Friday and Saturday.

Fu Bar 4 Wolfe St. A cool club with a good dance-floor that kicks off about 10pm with occasional alternative and progressive sounds. Drum 'n' bass, dubstep, electronica, hip-hop. Big-name spinners hit the spot regularly, and the place often opens up into the *Zen* club next door

Globe 229 Queen St, under *Base Auckland* hostel. Long, thin, noisy backpackers-get-drunk bar that's full most nights of the week.

Kings Arms 59 France St, Newton ☎09/373 3240, ⓦwww.kingsarms.co.nz. Popular pub and second-string venue hosting local and touring acts who can't quite fill the bigger venues. Typically $10–20.

The Occidental 8 Vulcan Lane. Belgian bar serving bargain pots of mussels ($19) dressed with lobster bisque and brandy, mustard and cream, or coconut cream and lemongrass. Every item on the menu comes with a suggested libation and the beer-pouring is conducted with ritualistic zeal.

O'Hagan's 101–103 Customs St West, Viaduct Harbour. Irish-themed pub spilling out onto the Market Square. Guinness, Kilkenny and English ales on tap, a good range of meals ($19–23) and big-screen sports.

Northern Steamship Co 122 Quay St. Large, brick-walled, eclectically furnished brewbar. Early on you can settle by the fireplace for a quiet beer or quality pub meal (mostly $20–30) but things get rowdy after dark, particularly on weekends when top local DJs hold the fort. Free wi-fi.

Rakino's First floor, 35 High St. Daytime café with tables shaped like Hauraki Gulf islands. On Thursday, Friday and Saturday evenings it trans-forms into a compact venue serving up anything from acoustic and live jazz to DJs. Closed Mon.

Sale St 7 Sale St, Freeman's Bay. Big open semi-industrial space with something for everyone. Wingback chairs for a tête-à-tête, fairly formal dining, a small selection of beers brewed on site and a big sunny deck. Attracts the after-work crowd but gets progressively more glam later on.

Shakespeare Tavern 61 Albert St. Unrecon-structed Kiwi pub raised above the pack by brewing a handful of commendable ales and lagers. Best on the first-floor terrace or around the pool table.

Smith Corner of Galway & Commerce sts. Lush and classy but unpretentious bar that's so small it is almost always full, mainly with pretty things

lolling on a velvet chaise and sipping retro cocktails. Closed Sun.

Stark's 269 Queen St, City. Cool, relaxing and stylish little cocktail bar offering the best gin and tonics in town, people-watching and highly polished professional service.

Tabac 6 Mills Lane. Cool backstreet bar that takes a bit of finding. You're rewarded with a casual vibe, great cocktails and cutting-edge DJs. Occasional live bands and record launches as well. Closed Sun & Mon.

The suburbs

Galbraith's Alehouse 2 Mount Eden Rd. See map, p,000. The closest Auckland gets to an English pub, with some of NZ's finest English-style ales brewed on site plus a handful of other local brews and fifty-odd bottled varieties. A limited range of quality bar meals includes Welsh rarebit ($19) and fish and chips ($23).

Long Room 116 Ponsonby Rd, Ponsonby, See map, p.107. Cocktails are just the thing early in the evening but DJ-led dancing and occasionally live bands take over as the night wears on, when the place is usually packed. There's a big open courtyard if it all gets a bit sweaty inside.

Mea Culpa 175 Ponsonby Rd, Ponsonby. See map, p.107. There's a cosy feel to this tiny bar where you can sit outside on wrought-iron chairs on the Turkish rug.

The Neighbourhood 498 New North Rd, Kingsland. See map, p.89. A stylish, modern take on a local pub with lots of sunny outdoor seating, a full range of Mac beers on tap and big windows overlooking the north stand of Eden Park. DJs Wed–Sun.

The Whiskey 210 Ponsonby Rd, Ponsonby. See map, p.107. Stylish modern bar with something of the feel of a groovy gentleman's club, all chocolate leather sofas and white brick walls hung with superb photos of Little Richard, the New York Dolls, Jimi Hendrix and more.

Classical music, theatre and comedy

Auckland's theatre, classical music and comedy scene seldom sets the world alight, though there is usually something worth seeing, mostly at the following venues.

Aotea Centre Aotea Square, Queen St ☎09/309 2677. New Zealand's first purpose-built opera house and the home stage for the New Zealand Symphony Orchestra and the New Zealand Ballet. The sometimes edgy Silo Theatre Company performs in its Herald Theatre.

Civic Theatre Corner of Queen & Wellesley sts ⓦwww.the-edge.co.nz. Lovely theatre worth visiting if there's anything at all on – could be dance, theatre or classic movies.

The Classic 321 Queen St ☎09/373 4321, ⓦwww.comedy.co.nz. Bar and comedy venue

Festivals

As befits a city of its size, Auckland has numerous festivals and annual events. These are some of the best.

Anniversary Day (Jan, last Mon). Massive sailing regatta on Auckland's Waitemata Harbour.

Big Day Out (Jan, third Fri) ⓦ www.bigdayout.com. One-day rock/pop/dance festival, with acts from all over the world at Mount Smart Stadium in the otherwise unvisited suburb of Penrose. Tickets about $130.

International Buskers Festival (Feb, beginning) ⓦ www.aucklandbuskersfestival .co.nz. Buskers from around the world take over the city streets. Free.

Devonport Food, Wine and Music Festival (Feb, third weekend) ⓦ devonportwinefestival.co.nz. Local retailers and vintners get together to charge extra (tickets $40–45) for their wares while mostly local musicians ply their trade.

Mission Bay Jazz and Blues Streetfest (Feb, last Sun) ⓦ www.jazzandblues streetfest.com. Beachside evening bash with a stack of bands and food stalls. $10 entry.

Pasifika (March, second Sat). A massive all-day celebration of Polynesian and Pacific Island culture (music, culture, food and crafts) held at Western Springs Park. Free.

Round the Bays Fun Run (March, second or third Sun) ⓦ www.roundthebays.co.nz. Up to 70,000 people jog 9km along the Tamaki Drive waterfront.

Royal Easter Show (Easter weekend) ⓦ www.royaleastershow.co.nz. Family enter-tainment Kiwi style, with equestrian events, wine tasting and arts and crafts, all held at the ASB showgrounds along Greenlane. $18

International Comedy Festival (mid-May to early June) ⓦ www.comedyfestival .co.nz. Three weeks of performances by the best from NZ and around the world.

Auckland International Film Festival (mid- to late July) ⓦ www.nzff.co.nz. The Auckland leg of this nationwide film tour. Tickets $15.

---

hosting top local names and touring acts. Shows Mon–Sat but the best line-ups are at weekends. $20–25 for the main acts, $10–15 for the regular 10.30pm improv sessions.
Maidment Theatre Corner of Princess & Alfred sts ☏ 09/308 2383, ⓦ www.maidment.auckland.ac.nz.

Two university theatres, with mainstream works in the larger venue and more daring stuff in the studio. The Auckland Theatre Company (ⓦ www .atc.co.nz) mainly performs here.

Cinema

Multiplexes rule Auckland, but the following boutique cinemas run more inter-esting programmes. **Admission** (normally $16) is often reduced before 5pm (especially Tues); ⓦ www.flicks.co.nz has listings. The annual **NZ International Film Festival**, visits in mid-July and presses many of these cinemas into service for arthouse and foreign screenings.

Academy 44 Lorne St ☏ 09/373 2761, ⓦ www .academycinemas.com. Dedicated arthouse cinema with two screens tucked underneath the main library.
Bridgeway 122 Queen St, Birkenhead ☏ 09/481 0040, ⓦ www.bridgeway.co.nz. Intimate North Shore cinema with good foyer food and coffee and luxurious seating. Screens the smarter end of mainstream movies.

Lido 427 Manukau Rd, Epsom ☏ 09/630 1500, ⓦ www.lidocinema.co.nz. Grab a beer or wine, sink into wide seats, and enjoy mainstream and classic movies with digital sound.
Rialto 167 Broadway, Newmarket ☏ 09/369 2417, ⓦ www.rialto.co.nz. The most accessible of the fringe cinemas, showing mainstream and slightly left-field fare.

Listings

Automobile Association 99 Albert St ⑦09/966 8919, ⓦwww.aa.co.nz.

Bookshops The biggest bookshops are in the CBD: Borders at 291 Queen St (⑦09/309 3377) and Whitcoulls at 210 Queen St (⑦09/356 5400). Unity Books, 19 High St (⑦09/307 0731), is more highbrow. The Women's Bookshop, 105 Ponsonby Rd (⑦09/376 4399, ⓦwww.womensbookshop .co.nz), specializes in feminist literature and women's interest books.

Buying a car For general advice, consult Basics (see p.39), then peruse the notice boards in hostels, get the weekly *Auto Trader* or *Trade & Exchange* magazines, or visit ⓦwww.trademe .co.nz. One of the best bets is the Backpackers Car Market, 20 East St (daily 9.30am–5pm; ⑦09/377 7761, ⓦwww.backpackerscarmarket .co.nz), just off K' Rd, where backpackers buy and sell directly to each other. Alternatively head to the Auckland Car Fair, Ellerslie Racecourse, Greenlane (every Sun 9am–noon; ⑦09/529 2233, ⓦwww.carfair.co.nz), which is well organized, with qualified folk on hand to check roadworthiness.

Camping and outdoor equipment For top-quality gear visit Bivouac, 210 Queen St (⑦09/366 1966), and 302 Broadway, Newmarket (⑦09/529 2298). Kathmandu, 151 Queen St (⑦09/309 4615), and 255 Broadway, Newmarket (⑦09/520 6041), are best for low-cost clothing and gear, especially during their frequent half-price sales.

Car rental The international and major national companies all have depots close to the airport and free shuttle buses to pick you up; smaller companies are mostly based in the city or inner suburbs. In the central city, you'll find several close together along Beach Rd. The main international and local operators are listed in Basics (see p.38).

Consulates Australia ⑦09/921 8800; ⓦwww .australia.org.nz; Canada ⑦09/309 3690; ⓦwww.international.gc.ca/newzealand; Ireland ⑦09/977 2252; UK ⑦09/303 2973; ⓦwww.fco .gov.uk; US ⑦09/303 2724; ⓦwww.newzealand .usembassy.gov.

Emergencies Police, fire and ambulance, ⑦111; Auckland Central police station ⑦09/302 6400.

Internet The library (see below) has free-use computers and wi-fi (max 100Mb/day). Numerous internet cafés (many marked on our maps) have access for around $3/hr.

Laundry Suds Laundromat, 18 Fort St ⑦09/358 4370 (Mon–Fri 8am–6pm, Sat 9am–4pm).

Left luggage Lockers at the Sky City Bus Terminal, 102 Hobson St (accessible daily 7am–7.50pm), and most of the larger hostels also have long-term storage for one-time guests at minimal or no charge.

Library Central City Library, 44–46 Lorne St (Mon–Fri 9am–8pm, Sat & Sun 10am–4pm; ⑦09/377 0209).

Maps Auckland Map Centre, 209 Queen St ⑦09/309 7725, ⓦwww.aucklandmapcentre .co.nz.

Medical treatment Auckland City Hospital, Park Rd, Grafton ⑦09/367 0000; Travelcare, Level 1, 125 Queen St (Mon–Fri 9am–5.30pm, Sat 10am–5pm; ⑦0508/306 306), offers diving medicals, physiotherapy, X-rays and dental treatment; CityMed Medical Centre, corner of Albert St and Mills Lane (⑦09/377 5525, ⓦwww.citymed .co.nz), has doctors and a pharmacy (Mon–Fri 8am–6pm). Registered medical practitioners are listed separately at the beginning of the White Pages phone directory.

Newspapers and magazines Auckland's morning paper is the *New Zealand Herald* (ⓦwww.nzherald.co.nz), the closest New Zealand gets to a national daily. The best selection of international newspapers – mostly from Australia, UK and the US – is at Borders, 291 Queen St. This is also your best bet for specialist magazines, which are also sold at branches of Mag Nation (100 Queen St and 123 Ponsonby Rd, Ponsonby).

Pharmacy The most convenient late-opening pharmacy is the Newmarket Night & Day Pharmacy, 60 Broadway, Newmarket (daily 9am–11pm; ⑦09/520 6634); emergency departments of hospitals (see "Medical treatment" above) have 24hr pharmacies.

Post office The branch at 24 Wellesley St (Mon–Fri 8am–5pm; ⑦09/379 6710) has poste restante facilities.

Swimming Central pools include the indoor Edwardian-style Tepid Baths, 102 Customs St West (Mon–Fri 6am–9pm, Sat & Sun 7am–7pm; ⑦09/379 4745), and the lovely open-air saltwater Parnell Baths, Judges Bay Rd (Nov–Easter Mon–Fri 6am–8pm, Sat & Sun 8am–8pm; ⑦09/373 3561). Otherwise, simply head for one of the beaches (see "The North Shore", p.109).

Taxis Discount (⑦09/529 1000) is cheap; sustainability-oriented Green Cabs (⑦0508/447 336) use hybrids and are only a little pricier.

Women's centre Auckland Women's Centre, 4 Warnock St, Grey Lynn (Mon–Fri 9am–4pm; ⑦09/376 3227, ⓦwww.womenz.org.nz), offers counselling and health advice and has a library.

Around Auckland

Real New Zealand begins, for many, in the immediate vicinity of Auckland, where verdant hills and magnificent beaches replace towerblocks, suburbs and sanitized wharfs. The **Waitakere Ranges**, to the **west** of the city offer a viable break from urban bustle. The hills also serve to deflect the prevailing westerly winds, providing shelter for the **vineyards** around Kumeu.

Spectacular expanses of sand are found along New Zealand's western seaboard, but it is only at Auckland's **West Coast beaches** that you will find surf-lifesaving patrols in reassuring numbers. Heading north, Auckland infringes on southern Northland, making the **Hibiscus Coast** a virtual suburb. South of Auckland, the **Hunua Ranges** offer a few modest walks and provide a windbreak for the **Seabird Coast**, where low shingle banks and extensive mud flats form an excellent breeding ground for dozens of migratory species.

West of Auckland

Some of Auckland's finest scenery and best adventures can be had little more than thirty minutes' drive from downtown. The suburban sprawl peters out some 20km west of the centre among the enveloping folds of the **Waitakere Ranges**. Despite being the most accessible expanse of greenery for over a million people, the hills remain largely unspoilt, with plenty of trails through native bush. On hot summer days, thousands head over the hills to one of half a dozen thundering **surf beaches**, largely undeveloped but for a few holiday homes (known to most Kiwis as *baches*) and the odd shop. The soils around the eastern fringes of the Waitakeres

---

West Coast tours

You'll need your own transport to do justice to the beaches and most of the ranges, unless you join one of the West Coast tours, or perhaps join a canyoning trip (see p.114). All trips pick up around central Auckland.

Bush & Beach ☏0800/423 224, ⓦwww.bushandbeach.co.nz. Afternoon trips ($135) include a short bushwalk to waterfalls and kauri trees, and a visit to Piha beach. The more satisfying full-day tour ($205) has longer walks and more bushcraft.

Fine Wine Tours ☏0800/023 111, ⓦwww.insidertouring.co.nz. Phil Parker leads small-group, half-day tours visiting three Kumeu wineries and allowing time for lunch and a visit to a West Coast beach. $149.

Potiki Adventures ☏0800/692 3836, ⓦwww.potikiadventures.com. Run by a couple of passionate Ngapuhi women who bring a Maori world-view to their full-day, small-group Urban Maori Experience trips (daily 10am–6pm; $195) which include morning and afternoon tea. Tours visit Maungakiekie (One Tree Hill) before heading west to the Waitakere Ranges and Whatipu beach to learn creation stories and medicinal plant usage. Saturday trips include a visit to Otara Market.

TIME Unlimited ☏0800/868 463, ⓦwww.newzealandtours.travel. Personal service and a willingness to go the extra mile characterize these small-group tours focusing on Titirangi and Whatipu beach with an excellent bushwalk and pounding surf. Go for the half-dayer ($145) or include it as part of a full-day city and coast tour ($245). More hiking-focused trips through the Waitakeres are available at similar prices.

nurture long-established **vineyards**, mainly around Kumeu, just short of the Kaipara Harbour town of **Helensville** and the **hot pools** at Parakai.

Auckland's suburban **trains** make it as far as Henderson and Waitakere and Richies **buses** #066 & #067 run through Henderson to Kumeu and Helensville.

The Kumeu and Huapai wineries

Once a viticultural powerhouse, West Auckland has been eclipsed by bigger enterprises elsewhere. There is still some production, centred on the contiguous and characterless villages of **KUMEU** and **HUAPAI**, though much of the grape juice comes from Marlborough, Gisborne and Hawke's Bay.

As early as 1819 the Reverend Samuel Marsden planted grapes, ostensibly to produce sacramental wine, in Kerikeri in the Bay of Islands, but commercial winemaking didn't get under way until Dalmatians turned their hand to growing grapes after the kauri gum they came to dig ceased to be profitable (see p.200). Many of today's businesses owe their existence to immigrant families, a legacy evident in winery names such as Babich, Nobilo, Selak and Soljan. Today, most of the wineries source their grapes from around the country but the region's vines still produce Pinot Noir, Pinot Gris and superb Chardonnay. If you plan some serious tasting, designate a non-drinking driver or join Fine Wine Tours (see p.123).

The wineries and the **Kumeu Visitor Centre**, 49 SH16 (daily: Nov–Easter 9am–5pm, Easter–Oct 10am–4pm; ℡09/412 9886, ⓦwww.kumeuinfo.co.nz) stock the free *Kumeu Wine Country* booklet detailing the dozen **wineries** that can be visited. First up is *Soljans*, 366 SH16 (℡09/412 5858, ⓦwww.soljans .co.nz), right on the main road with free tastings and a smart but casual café. Its Pinot Gris is grown locally and it makes a fun sparkling Muscat. At *Kumeu River*, 50 SH16 (℡09/412 8415; closed Sun), a couple of kilometres north, the Brajkovich family produces several of New Zealand's finest Chardonnays, all grown hereabouts. Generous tastings, including three single-vineyard varieties, make this an essential stop.

A refreshing alternative comes in the form of *Hallertau Brewbar & Restaurant*, signposted off SH16 at 1171 Coatsville Riverhead Hwy, where a handful of beers are brewed (tasting tray for $12), and sampled at an airy bar and a casual restaurant with a range of tasting plates, tapas and full meals ($25–32).

The Waitakere Ranges and the West Coast beaches

Auckland's western limit is defined by the bush-clad **Waitakere Ranges**, rising up to 500m. The hills are a perennially popular weekend destination for Aucklanders intent on a picnic or a stroll and the western slopes roll down to the wild, black-sand **West Coast beaches**. Pounded by heavy surf and punctuated by precipitous headlands, these tempestuous shores provide a counterpoint to the calm, gently shelved beaches of the Hauraki Gulf.

The Kawerau a Maki people knew the region as Te Wao Nui a Tiriwa or "the Great Forest of Tiriwa", aptly describing the kauri groves that swathed the hills before the arrival of Europeans. By the turn of the century, diggers had pretty much cleaned out the kauri gum, but logging continued until the 1940s, leaving the land spent. The Auckland Regional Council bought the land, built reservoirs and designated a vast tract as the Centennial Memorial Park, with two hundred kilometres of walking tracks leading to fine vistas and numerous waterfalls that cascade off the escarpment.

The easiest access to the majority of the walks and beaches is via the **Waitakere Scenic Drive** (Route 24), which winds through the ranges from the dormitory

The Hillary Trail

In honour of the 2008 passing of New Zealand's mountaineering hero, Sir Edmund Hillary, Auckland has linked a series of existing walking tracks through the Waitakere Ranges into the Hillary Trail (70km; 3–4 days; Ⓦ www.arc.govt.nz). Running from the Arataki Visitor Centre via Whatipu, Karekare, Piha and Te Henga to Muriwai, it gives a great sense of the region – regenerating rainforest, stands of kauri, rocky shores, black-sand beaches and historic remains. The highest point is only 390m but it is an undulating track and moderate to good fitness is required, and be aware that occasionally slippery, steep paths and unbridged streams can make it a good deal harder in winter.

Nights are generally spent in primitive campsites ($5; book on ☎ 09/366 2000), though you can stay under a roof in Whatipu, Piha and Te Henga. The best source of on-the-ground information is the Arataki Visitor Centre.

suburb of **Titirangi**, in the foothills, to the informative **Arataki visitor centre** (Sept–April daily 9am–5pm; May–Aug Mon–Fri 10am–4pm, Sat & Sun 9am–5pm), which shows an excellent twelve-minute DVD about the area on demand (free). A felled kauri has been transformed by Kawerau a Maki carvers into a striking *pou*, or guardian post, which marks the entrance and sets the tone for several smaller carvings within. Outside, walkways forge into the second-growth forest: the ten-minute plant identification loop trail identifies a dozen or so significant forest trees and ferns; a longer trail (1hr 15min) visits one of the few mature kauri stands to survive the loggers. Arataki is also the place to pick up the *Waitakere Ranges Recreation and Track Guide* map ($8), excellent for the numerous **short walks** in the ranges.

Beyond the visitor centre, the scenic drive swings north along the range, passing side roads to the **beaches**, noted for their foot-scorching gold-and-black sands and demanding swimming conditions. Before entering the water, read the box on p.73, and heed all warning signs.

No **buses** run out this way, but Piha Surf Shuttle (☎ 0800/952 526, Ⓦ www .surfshuttle.co.nz) picks up in Auckland around 8.30am and leaves Piha for the city at 4pm (Dec–Feb daily; $60 return).

Whatipu

Whatipu is the southernmost of the West Coast surf beaches, 45km from central Auckland and located by the sand-bar entrance to Manukau Harbour, the watery grave of many a ship. The wharf at Whatipu was briefly the terminus of the precarious coastal **Parahara Railway**, which hauled kauri from the mill at Karekare across the beach and headlands during the 1870s. The tracks were continually pounded by surf, but a second tramway from Piha covered the same treacherous expanse in the early twentieth century. Scant remains are visible, including an old tunnel that proved too tight a squeeze for a large steam engine whose boiler still litters the shore.

Over the last few decades, the sea has receded more than half a kilometre, leaving a broad beach backed by wetlands colonized by cabbage trees, tall toetoe grasses and waterfowl. It's a great place to explore, particularly along the base of the cliffs to the north where, in half an hour, you can walk to the **Ballroom Cave**, fitted with a sprung dancefloor in the 1920s that apparently still survives, buried by 5m of sand that drifted into the cave in the intervening years.

The only sign of civilization now is *Whatipu Lodge* (booking essential; ☎ 09/811 8860, Ⓔ whatipulodge@xtra.co.nz; tents $15/site, rooms $45/person for one-night stays, otherwise $35). Occupying an 1870 former mill manager's house, the lodge has no mains electricity (it generates its own for limited hours), but has communal cooking facilities and hot showers. Bring a sleeping bag.

Karekare, Piha and Te Henga

Perhaps the most intimate and immediately appealing of the West Coast settlements is **KAREKARE**, 17km west of the Arataki visitor centre, with manuka, pohutukawa and cabbage trees running down to a broad beach and only a smattering of houses. In one hectic year, this dramatic spot was jolted out of its relative obscurity, providing the setting for beach scenes in Jane Campion's 1993 film *The Piano* and the inspiration for Crowded House's *Together Alone* album. The Karekare Surf Club patrols a relatively safe swimming area on summer weekends, or there is a pool below **Karekare Falls**, a five-minute walk on a track just inland from the road. There is nowhere to stay here, and no facilities.

For decades **PIHA**, 20km west of the Arataki visitor centre, has been an icon for Aucklanders. A quintessential West Coast beach with a string of low-key weekend cottages and crashing surf, it lures a wide spectrum of day-trippers and the party set, whose New Year's Eve antics hastened in a dusk-till-dawn alcohol ban on holiday weekends. Despite the gradual gentrification of the old *baches* and the opening of the swish new *Piha Café*, it is hanging onto its rustic charm.

The 3km sweep of gold-and-black sand is hemmed in by bush-clad hills and split by Piha's defining feature, 101m **Lion Rock**. With some imagination, this former *pa* site resembles a seated lion staring out to sea; the energetic climb to a shoulder two-thirds of the way up (20–30min return) is best done as the day cools. The **Tasman Lookout Track** (30–40min return) leaves the south end of the beach, climbing up to a lookout over the tiny cove of The Gap, where a spectacular blowhole performs in heavy surf.

Most **swimmers** flock to South Piha, where the more prestigious of the two surf-lifesaving clubs hogs the best **surf**. If battling raging surf isn't your thing, head for the cool **pool** below Kitekite Falls, a three-stage plunge reached on a loop track (1hr 30min) that starts 1km up Glen Esk Road, running inland opposite Piha's central Domain.

Day-trippers are catered for by a general store and surf shop, a traditional burger bar at South Piha (summer only) and the Piha Memorial RSA, 3 Beach Rd, which welcomes visitors. There's also a surf shop with a great view, Piha Surf (T09/812 8723, W www.pihasurf.co.nz), a couple of kilometres before the beach on the road in.

The best **place to stay** is *Black Sands Lodge*, 54 Beach Rd (T021/969 924, W www.pihabeach.co.nz), with three stylishly decorated *baches*: a beach cabin (⑥), and two suites (⑥/⑦) with big decks, French doors and quality furnishings and bedding. Hosts Bobbie and Julia will also prepare romantic four-course dinners, served in your suite (around $140 a head, excluding wine). Three kilometres back from the beach, with great ocean views, *Piha Lodge*, 117 Piha Rd (T09/812 8595, W www.pihalodge.co.nz; ⑥), has comfortable rooms and an outdoor pool. For budget accommodation visit *Piha Domain Motor Camp*, 21 Seaview Rd (T09/812 8815; camping $10, on-site vans ①, cabins ②), which is an easy walk from the beach. Alternatively, head inland to the Piha Surf Shop which has a range of rustic self-contained caravans and cabins (both from $30/person) with long-drop toilets and sharing a single shower.

Daytime **eating** is best at the low-key *Piha Café*. For dinner make for *Piha Surf Lifesaving Club*, overlooking South Piha beach, or the *Piha Bowling Club*, near the campsite: in both cases you just sign yourself in then tuck into good meals and cheap drinks.

The smaller and much less popular **TE HENGA** (also known as Bethell's Beach) lies at the end of a long road from Waitakere, 8km north along the coast. Less dramatic than Karekare, Piha or Muriwai, Te Henga is correspondingly less visited, making it good for escaping the crowds in the summer. There are no shops, but there is a surf club and luxurious **accommodation** in three cottages at *Bethells Beach Cottages* (☎09/810 9581, ⓦwww.bethellsbeach.com; ❽).

Muriwai

MURIWAI, the most populous of the West Coast beach settlements, lies 15km north of Piha and 10km coastwards from Huapai. Again, there's wonderful surf, and a long beach stretching 45km north to the heads of Kaipara Harbour. The main attraction is at the southern end of the beach where a **gannet colony** (best seen late Oct to mid-Feb) occupies Motutara Island and Otakamiro Point, the headland between the main beach and the surfers' cove of Maori Bay. The gannets breed here before migrating to sunnier climes, a few staying behind with the fur seals that inhabit the rocks below. Gannets normally prefer the protection of islands, this is one of the few places where they nest on the mainland, just below viewing platforms from where you get a bird's-eye view. Short paths lead up here from near the surf club and off the road to Maori Bay.

To explore the beach, dunes and pine forests to the north, join a **horse trek** run by the Muriwai Beach Riding Centre, 290 Oaia Rd ($70/2hr; ☎09/411 8480, ⓦwww.aucklandhorsehire.org.nz). To try **surfing**, visit the Muriwai Surf School (☎021/478 734, ⓦwww.muriwaisurfschool.co.nz), where you can rent gear (board and wetsuit $40/3hr), take a lesson (introductory $55, advanced $90) or muck around on sand yachts ($45/1hr), and mountain bikes ($10/1hr). Its shed is located behind *Sand Dunz café*, at the road junction close to the beach, a modern café (daily till 4.30pm) and takeaway that stays open until around 7pm in summer.

If you want to **stay**, try the shaded *Muriwai Beach Motor Camp*, (☎09/411 9262, ⓦwww.muriwaimotorcamp.co.nz; camping $12).

Helensville and Parakai

Venture beyond the vineyards of Kumeu and you'll soon find yourself in uninspiring **HELENSVILLE**, 45km northwest of Auckland but more closely associated with the Kaipara Harbour (see p.199). Kauri logs were floated here in huge rafts then loaded onto rail wagons bound for Auckland. Dairying has replaced the timber trade, but photos and displays on the town's halcyon days can be seen at the new **Helensville Pioneer Museum** (Wed, Sat & Sun 1–3.30pm; $5; ⓦwww.helensvillemuseum.org.nz), at 98 Mill Rd as you enter town from Muriwai. There's a **visitor centre**, 27 Commercial Rd (Mon–Fri 10am–5pm Sat 10am–2pm; ☎09/420 8060, ⓦwww.helensville.co.nz), in the heart of town, and *The Art Stop*, 5 Commercial Rd, is the place to go for coffee, excellent light lunches and secondhand books.

PARAKAI, 3km north of Helensville, is chiefly noted for its family-oriented Aquatic Park (daily 10am–10pm; $16, private spa $6 extra/hr; ☎09/420 8998, ⓦwww.aquaticpark.co.nz), where pools are filled by natural hot springs. Entry includes free use of a couple of buffeting water chutes, and there's an adjacent campsite.

North of Auckland

The straggling suburbs of north Auckland merge into the **Hibiscus Coast**, which starts 40km north of the city and is increasingly favoured by retirees and long-distance commuters. The region centres on the suburban Whangaparaoa Peninsula – a launching point for trips to Tiritiri Matangi Island (see p.146) – and the anodyne

Northern Gateway Toll Road

Just inland from Orewa the main Northern Motorway becomes a toll road for the final 5km before Puhoi. To avoid paying the toll, come off the motorway at Silverdale and follow the coast road through Orewa – it'll only add ten minutes to your journey.

The toll road (cars $2, motorcycles free) has no staffed booths and is monitored by cameras which read license plates. The roadside pay kiosks (northbound at a BP service station; southbound in a small lay-by) are often busy, so it is usually easier to pay using a credit card either by phone (☎0800/40 20 20; Mon–Sat 8am–6pm) or at ⓦwww.tollroad.govt.nz. Pay before or up to five days after your journey.

beachside community of **Orewa**, now mostly bypassed by an extension of the northern motorway. Immediately to the north, the hot springs at **Waiwera** herald the beach-and-BBQ scene of **Wenderholm Regional Park** and the classic old **Puhoi** pub.

Orewa and the Whangaparaoa Peninsula

The most striking of the Hibiscus Coast beaches is the 3km strand backed by **OREWA**, a predominantly retirement and dormitory town dominated by the twelve-storey Nautilus apartment block. It's a relaxing spot with plenty of swimming and sunbathing – and kitesurfing for those with their own gear – but as home to the bulk of the region's accommodation and restaurants works best as a base for exploring the area.

South of Orewa, the **Whangaparaoa Peninsula** juts out 12km into the Hauraki Gulf, its tip occupied by **Shakespear Regional Park** (8am–dusk; free), a pleasant place to swim and wander through regenerating bush spotting pukeko, red-crowned parakeets and tui. The peninsula's most enticing diversion, though, is a trip to the bird sanctuary of Tiritiri Matangi (see p.146), with boats leaving from the vast Gulf Harbour Marina just before Shakespear Park.

Practicalities

Auckland **bus** route #895 takes an hour to reach the Hibiscus Coast from the Britomart Transport Centre. These, and Northland-bound InterCity and North-liner buses, stop in central Orewa after passing the well-stocked **i-SITE visitor centre**, 214a Hibiscus Coast Hwy (daily 9am–5pm; ☎09/426 0076, ⓦwww.orewa-beach.co.nz). **Accommodation** is strung along the highway close to the beach. At the southern end, *Orewa Beach Top 10 Holiday Park*, 265 Hibiscus Coast Hwy (☎09/426 5832, ⓦwww.orewabeachtop10.co.nz; camping $18, waterfront camping $21, cabins ❶, s/c units ❸), offers good beachside camping, while *Villa Orewa*, 264 Hibiscus Coast Hwy (☎09/426 3073, ⓦwww.villaorewa.co.nz; ❻), is a classy whitewashed Greek-island-styled B&B offering airy rooms with beach-view balconies and delicious breakfasts. **Backpackers** should head towards the north end of town to *Pillows Travellers Lodge*, 412 Hibiscus Coast Hwy (☎09/426 6338, ⓦwww.pillows.co.nz; dorms $20, rooms ❶, en suites ❷), a welcoming if slightly ageing hostel with a piano in the lounge. Almost opposite is *Waves*, 1 Kohu Rd (☎0800/426 6889; ❻), the town's fanciest motel, just steps from the beach and with underfloor heating and stylish decor.

For **food**, head to *Emi Deli*, 11 Tamariki Ave, in the base of the Nautilus building, for the best muffins and quality breakfasts and lunches. **Meals** are also good at the adjacent *Pioneer* pub, 9 Tamariki Ave, or for something a little classier head to *Joust Beach Bar & Restaurant*, 268 Hibiscus Coast Hwy (☎09/426 2411), where mains of lamb rack or pan-seared salmon go for $26–31.

Waiwera and Wenderholm

The coastal highway north of Orewa (bus #895) runs through the cluster of holiday and retirement homes that make up Hatfields Beach to **WAIWERA**, 6km north of Orewa, where Maori once dug holes in the sands to take advantage of the natural hot springs. Bathing is now at **Waiwera Infinity**, Waiwera Road (daily 9am–9pm; $25; ⓦ www.waiwera.co.nz), where a network of suicidal waterslides and indoor and outdoor pools are naturally heated to between 28 and 43°C. You can enjoy all manner of spa treatments and massages, while you can stay in luxurious motel units (⑦) or a campsite by the beach ($16).

Wenderholm Regional Park, 2km north, is bordered by the Puhoi river estuary and a sweeping golden beach backed by pohutukawa-shaded swathes of grass that's often packed with barbecuing families on summer weekends. Walking tracks (20min–2hr) wind up to a headland viewpoint through nikau palm groves alive with birds that have repopulated the area from Tiritiri Matangi (see p.146). You can also take a peek at **Couldrey House Museum** (Christmas–Easter daily 1–4pm, Easter–Christmas Sat & Sun 1–4pm; $3), an 1860 colonial homestead, and stay at a water-and-toilets **campsite** ($10; reserve on ⑦ 09/366 2000) with grassy plots and a BBQ beside the mangroves. Self-contained **campervans** can stay in the main car park for up to two nights ($5/adult/night).

Puhoi

The village of **PUHOI**, 6km north of Waiwera, remains a bucolic place, settled by staunchly Catholic Bohemian migrants who arrived in 1863 from Egerland, in what was then the Austro-Hungarian Empire (now the Czech Republic). The land was poor, and settlers were forced to eke out a living by cutting the bush for timber: the horns of famed bullock teams are still ranged round the walls of the historic **Puhoi Tavern**, a colonial hotel containing a single-roomed bar festooned with pioneering paraphernalia and photos.

Few visit anywhere other than the pub, but **Puhoi Bohemian Museum** (Christmas–Easter daily 1–4pm; Easter–Christmas Sat, Sun & school holidays 1–4pm; $3) in the former Convent School, is interesting if only for the historic model of the village. Gentle activity beckons in the form of **kayaking**, or canoeing, along a tidal section of the river (1hr; double kayak or canoe $40) or downstream to Wenderholm (2hr; double kayak or canoe $80, including pick-up) with Puhoi River Canoe Hire (⑦ 09/422 0891, ⓦ www.puhoirivercanoes.co.nz; bookings essential). For refreshments, hit the pub or drive 3km north to *The Art of Cheese* **café** (daily 9am–5pm) where they make tasty cheeses.

Our coverage of Northland continues with Warkworth on p.153.

Southeast of Auckland

Most southbound travellers hurry along Auckland's southern motorway to Hamilton or turn off to Thames and the Coromandel Peninsula at Pokeno – either way missing out on the modest attractions of the **Hunua Ranges** and the **Seabird Coast** on its eastern shore. For **cyclists** in particular the coast road is an excellent way into and out of Auckland, following Tamaki Drive from the centre through Panmure and Howick to Clevedon and the coast.

Even for Auckland day-trippers the older and more rounded Hunuas play second fiddle to the more ecologically rich Waitakeres, but there are some decent walks – notably around the **Hunua Falls**. There are greater rewards further south with excellent sea-bird viewing and hot pools at **Miranda**.

The Hunua Ranges

A considerable amount of rain is dumped on the 700m-high **Hunua Ranges**, 50km southeast of Auckland, flowing down into a series of four dams that jointly supply over half the city's water. The bush surrounding the reservoirs was once logged for kauri but has largely regenerated, providing a habitat for birds rarely seen in the city. The main attraction is **Hunua Falls**, a 30m waterfall located 20km southeast of central Auckland, where the Wairoa River carves its way through the crater of an ancient volcano. There's good swimming here, or you could take the **Cossey/Massey loop** walk (3hr; 5km) which follows the Massey Track to Cosseys Dam and back down the Cosseys Gorge Track to the falls. Self-contained campervans can stay up to two nights in the Hunua Falls car park ($5 per adult).

The Miranda Sea Bird Coast

The Firth of Thames, a sheltered arm of the Hauraki Gulf separating South Auckland from the Coromandel Peninsula, borders the Hunua Ranges to the east. Its frequently windswept western littoral comprises land built up from successive deposits of shell banks; much has been converted to farmland but newer shell banks in the making can be seen along what is known as the **Sea bird Coast**. Almost a quarter of all known species of migrating shore birds visit the region, and 30,000-strong flocks of wrybill plover over-winter at this internationally significant site. During the southern summer (Sept–March) you'll see arctic migrants – notably bar-tailed godwits and lesser knots – who fly 15,000km from Alaska and Siberia.

The quiet coast road around the north and east of the Hunua Ranges winds past the **Tapapakanga Regional Park** (primitive camping $10) and **Kaiaua** (where *Kaiaua Fisheries* does good fish and chips). Some 5km south of Kaiaua self-contained **campervans** can park on the shore for up to two nights. It's a popular spot and some people camp outside the designated area (though you shouldn't). Public toilets are available in Kaiaua. It is 2km on to the excellent **Miranda Shorebird Centre** (daily 9am–5pm, and often later in the summer, when it's awash with twitchers reluctant to leave; ℡09/232 2781,

▲ Campervans at Kaiaua

W www.miranda-shorebird.org.nz); they'll fill you in on the current hot sightings and point you in the direction of the best viewing spots. With a sunny veranda for viewing, the centre also has good-value self-catering accommodation (bunks $20, flat ❷). A further 6km south are the slightly alkaline **Miranda Hot Springs** (daily 9am–9.30pm; $12.50, private spa $10 extra per 30min; W www .mirandahotsprings.co.nz), with a large, warm open pool and private kauri spa tubs. Guests at the adjacent *Miranda Holiday Park* (T 0800/833 144, W www .mirandaholidaypark.co.nz; tent sites $21, rooms ❷, s/c units ❺) have access to their own landscaped mineral pool as well as a tennis court. From here it's a twenty-minute drive to Thames (see p.316).

Islands of the Hauraki Gulf

Auckland's greatest asset is the island-studded **Hauraki Gulf**, a 70km-square patch of ocean to the northeast of the city. In Maori, Hauraki means "wind from the north" – though the gulf is somewhat sheltered from the prevailing winds and ocean swells by Great Barrier Island, creating benign conditions for Auckland's legions of yachties. Most just sail but those who wish to strike land can visit some of the 47 islands, administered by the Department of Conservation, designated either for recreational use with full access, or as sanctuaries for endangered wildlife, requiring permits.

Auckland's nearest island neighbour is **Rangitoto**, a flat cone of gnarled and twisted lava that dominates the harbourscape. The most populous of the gulf islands is **Waiheke**, increasingly a commuter suburb of Auckland, with sandy beaches and some quality wineries. Such sophistication is a far cry from laidback **Great Barrier Island**, the largest hereabouts, with its sandy surf beaches, hilly tramping tracks and exceptional fishing. The Department of Conservation's policy of allowing access to wildlife sanctuaries is wonderfully demonstrated at **Tiritiri Matangi**, where a day-trip gives visitors an unsurpassed opportunity to see some of the world's rarest birds.

Frequent **ferries** run to the more popular islands from the Downtown Ferry Terminal by Auckland's Ferry Building, at the foot of Queen Street. For more on cruising and kayaking the Gulf, see "Activities", on p.112.

Rangitoto and Motutapu islands

The low, conical shape of **Rangitoto**, 10km northeast of the city centre, is a familiar sight to every Aucklander. Yet few set foot on the island, missing out on a freakish land of fractured black lava with the world's largest pohutukawa forest clinging precariously to its crevices. Alongside lies the older, and geologically quite distinct, island of **Motutapu** or "sacred island", linked to Rangitoto by a narrow causeway. A **day-trip** is enough to get a feel for Rangitoto, make the obligatory hike to the summit (from where there are magnificent views of the city and Hauraki Gulf) and tackle a few trails, but **longer stays** are possible if you pitch your tent at the primitive campsite at Home Bay on Motutapu.

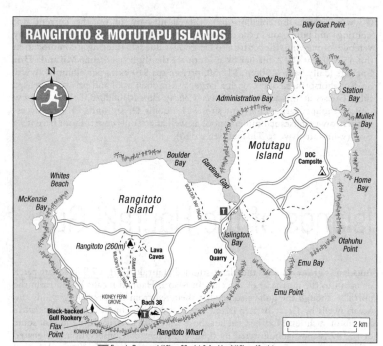

RANGITOTO & MOTUTAPU ISLANDS

N

Billy Goat Point

Sandy Bay

Administration Bay

Station Bay

Mullet Bay

Boulder Bay

Motutapu Island

DOC Campsite

Home Bay

Whites Beach

Gardiner Gap

McKenzie Bay

Rangitoto Island

Rangitoto (260m)

Lava Caves

Islington Bay

Otahuhu Point

Old Quarry

Emu Bay

Emu Point

KIDNEY FERN GROVE

Bach 38

Black-backed Gull Rookery

Flax Point

KOWHAI GROVE

Rangitoto Wharf

0   2 km

Ferry to Devonport (12km; 30 min) & Auckland (15km; 40 min)

Rangitoto is Auckland's youngest and largest **volcano**. Molten magma probably pushed its way through the bed of the Hauraki Gulf around six hundred years ago – watched by Motutapu Maori, who apparently called the island "blood red sky" after the spectacle that accompanied its creation.

Rangitoto's youth, lack of soil and porous rock have created unusual conditions for **plant life**, though the meagre supply of insects attracts few birds, making it eerily quiet. Pohutukawa trees seeded first, given a head start by their roots, which are able to tap underground reservoirs of fresh water up to 20m below the surface. Smaller and fleshier plants then established themselves under the protective canopy. Harsh conditions have led to some strange botanical anomalies: both epiphytes and mud-loving mangroves are found growing directly on the lava, an alpine moss is found at sea level, and the pohutukawa has hybridized with its close relative, the northern rata, to produce a spectrum of blossoms ranging from pink to crimson. Successful possum and wallaby clearing programmes in the 1990s allowed the pohutukawa to rebound with vigour and the recent eradication of most other mammal pests will allow DOC to introduce more native bird species – native parakeets (*kakariki*) recently bred on Motutapu for the first time in a century. Remember to check your bag for stowaway pests (mice really do find their way in) and clean your boots for seeds to prevent reintroducing invasive weeds. Check out ⓦ www.motutapu.org.nz for details of volunteering day-trips (usually Sun).

The government purchased Rangitoto for £15 in 1854, putting it to use as a military lookout point and a workcamp for prisoners. From the 1890s, areas were leased for camping and unauthorized *baches* were cobbled together on the sites. Over 100 *baches* had sprouted by the late 1930s when legislation stopped any new construction. In recent years, the cultural value of this unique set of 1920s and

1930s houses has been appreciated and the finest examples of the remaining 34 are being preserved for posterity, their corrugated iron chimneys and cast-off veranda-railing fenceposts capturing the Kiwi make-do spirit. *Bach 38*, near Rangitoto Wharf, has been restored to its 1930s condition and you're free to look around the outside. If you're lucky you might strike one of the days when the Rangitoto Island Historic Conservation Trust (Ⓦwww.rangitoto.org) opens it up for inspection – usually summer weekends.

The moment you step across the **causeway** onto **Motutapu**, the landscape changes dramatically; suddenly, you are back in rural New Zealand, with its characteristic grassy paddocks, ridge-top fencelines, corrugated iron barns and macrocarpa windbreaks. DOC's plan is to gradually restore its cultural and natural landscape, replanting the valleys with native trees – you can join the volunteer programme (see p.69) – restoring wetlands and interpreting the numerous Maori sites. Until the trees grow, Motutapu will continue to have a much more open, pastoral feel than Rangitoto, but the views of the Hauraki Gulf make time spent here worthwhile, particularly tramping the Motutapu Walkway to the campsite and beach at Home Bay (6km; 1hr 30min one-way), then back again.

Practicalities

Fullers **ferries** (3–4 daily; $25 return) take 25 minutes to reach Rangitoto Wharf, where there is a toilet block, the island's only **drinking water**, and a sun-warmed saltwater swimming pool (filled naturally by the high tide) that's great for kids. Apart from the Home Bay campsite and a couple of toilets there's nothing else on the island, so bring everything you need – including strong shoes to protect you from the sharp rocks, a sun hat and a raincoat. If you're planning a walk, carry plenty of water. Some ferries are met by the only transport on the island, a kind of tractor-drawn buggy that operates the two-hour **Volcanic Explorer Tour** ($55 including cost of ferry), a dusty summit trip with a full and informative commentary; the final 900m is on foot along a boardwalk.

DOC tries to limit the twin islands to day-trippers, but there is a primitive but pleasant beachside DOC **campsite** ($5; booking essential Christmas–Jan at Ⓦwww.doc.govt.nz), with toilets and water, at Home Bay on the eastern side of Motutapu, almost three hours' walk from Rangitoto Wharf.

Rangitoto summit walk

The best way to appreciate Rangitoto Island is on foot, but bear in mind that, though not especially steep, the terrain is rough and it can get very hot on the black lava. Consequently the best walks are those that follow shady paths to the summit. A favourite is the clockwise **Summit/Coastal Loop Track** (12km; 5–6hr; 260m ascent) around the southeast of the island. Turn left just past the toilets at Rangitoto Wharf and follow signs for the **Kowhai Grove**, a typical Rangitoto bush area with an abundance of the yellow-flowering kowhai that blossoms in September. Turn right onto the coastal road from Rangitoto Wharf then left into **Kidney Fern Grove**, which is packed with unusual miniature ferns that unfurl after rain. The well-worn **Summit Track** winds through patches of pohutukawa forest. Around three-quarters of the way to the summit, a side track leads to the **lava caves** (20min return) that probe deep into the side of the volcano. Bring a torch if you want to explore. Further along the main track a former military observation post on the **summit** provides views out across Auckland city and the Hauraki Gulf.

Continue northwards to the east–west road across the island and follow it towards Islington Bay; from there, pick up the **coastal track** south, initially following the bay then cutting inland through some little-frequented forests back to Rangitoto Wharf.

Waiheke Island

Pastoral **WAIHEKE**, 20km east of Auckland, is the second largest of the gulf islands and easily the most populous, particularly on summer weekends when day-trippers and weekenders quadruple its population of around 8000. The traffic isn't all one way, though, as the fast and frequent ferry service makes it feasible for a growing proportion of the islanders to commute daily for work in the city – a trend that has turned the western end of Waiheke into a suburb. But, with its chain of sandy beaches along the north coast, a climate that's less humid than Auckland and some great wineries, Waiheke is popular with international visitors in search of a peaceful spot to recover from jet lag or to idle away a day or two before flying home.

The **earliest settlers** on Waiheke trace their lineage back to the Tainui canoe that landed at Onetangi and gave the island its first name, Te Motu-arai-Roa, "the long sheltering island". Waiheke, or "cascading waters", originally referred to a particular creek but was assumed by **Europeans** to refer to the island. Among the first **settlers** to set foot on Waiheke was Samuel Marsden, who preached here in 1818 and established a mission near Matiatia. The island then went through the familiar cycle of kauri logging, gum digging and clearance for farming. Gradually, the magnificent coastal scenery gained popularity as a setting for grand picnics, and hamper-encumbered Victorians, attired in formal dress, arrived in boatloads.

Development was initially sluggish, but the availability of cheap land amid dramatic landscapes drew painters and **craftspeople**; others followed as access from Auckland became easier and faster.

Arrival, information and transport

Waiheke is busy on **summer weekends** and throughout January, when Aucklanders come to relax, taste wine, and dine at restaurants and bars where there's often live music. Midweek is more peaceful but fewer wineries will be open, artists occasionally close their studios and trips requiring minimum numbers are harder to organize.

Fullers operate fast **ferries** (☏09/367 9111; roughly hourly; 35min; $32 return, bikes free) from the Ferry Building in Auckland to Matiatia Wharf, just over 1km from the main settlement of Oneroa. If you're staying for a couple of days or longer, you may find it cost-effective to bring your vehicle over using the Sealink **car ferry** (roughly hourly; 45–60min; car & driver $160 return, passengers $30 return; ☏0800/732 546, ⓦwww.sealink.co.nz) from Half Moon Bay in Auckland's eastern suburbs to Kennedy Point, 4km south of Oneroa.

Waiheke's main source of information is the efficient **i-SITE visitor centre**, 2 Korora Rd, Oneroa (Mon–Sat 9am–5pm, Sun 9am–4.30pm; ☏0800/282 552, ⓦwww.waihekenz.com), where bags can be stored for $5 apiece: be sure to pick up the free *Island of Wine* map and guide. **Internet** is available at the i-SITE and next door at the library (Mon–Fri 9am–5pm, Sat 10am–4pm; free). **Shops**, a couple of **banks** and a post office are also clustered in Oneroa. The weekly *Gulf News* ($2) comes out on Thursday and has details of **what's on**, as well as a rundown of arts and crafts outlets.

Getting around

Ferry arrivals and departures connect with Fullers buses (☏09/366 6400), which run to Onetangi via Oneroa, Surfdale and Ostend, and to Rocky Bay via Oneroa, Little Oneroa and Palm Beach. Tickets ($1.50–4.10 per ride, $8 all day) are available on the bus. For more flexibility, **rent a vehicle** from Waiheke Island Adventures (☏0800/372 9777, ⓦwww.waihekeislandadventures.com) who

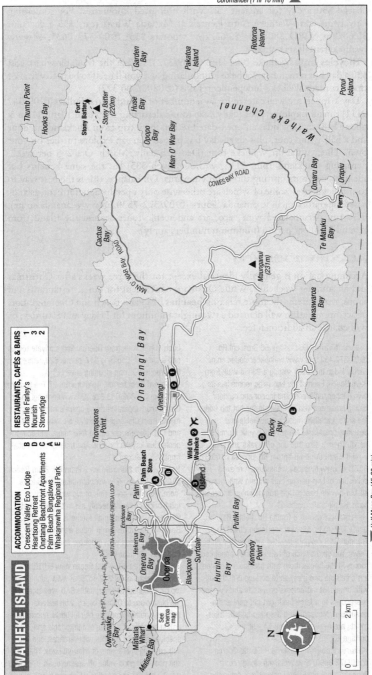

WAIHEKE ISLAND

ACCOMMODATION
- Crescent Valley Eco Lodge — B
- Heartsong Retreat — D
- Onetangi Beachfront Apartments — C
- Palm Beach Bungalows — A
- Whakanewha Regional Park — E

RESTAURANTS, CAFÉS & BARS
- Charlie Farley's — 1
- Nourish — 3
- Stonyridge — 2

charge $50 a day for ancient cars with unlimited kilometres. For something newer, go with Waiheke Auto Rentals at Matiatia Wharf (cars $55 a day plus $0.65/km; 4WD $80 plus $0.65/km; scooters $55; ℡09/372 8635, ⓦwww .waihekerentalcars.co.nz).

Bicycles from Waiheke Bike Hire (℡09/372 7937) at the Matiatia wharf cost $30 a day but remember Waiheke is undulating and you'll need to be pretty fit. For **taxis**, contact Waiheke Independent Taxis (℡0800/300 372).

Day-trippers are well catered for by a number of **island tours**. Fullers (℡09/367 9111) run an Explorer Tour (daily year-round departing Auckland 10am, 11am & noon; $48) that includes an open-dated return ferry trip from Auckland, an hour and a half island tour, plus an all-day bus pass so you can explore further on your own. Their Wine on Waiheke tour (Dec–Feb daily, March–Oct 2–5 per week, departing Auckland 1pm; $115, without lunch $85) has the same benefits but spends four hours visiting three top vineyards. On balance, this is the best way to tour the wineries, some of which are otherwise only open by appointment. Island-based operators include Ananda Tours (℡09/372 7530, ⓦwww.ananda.co.nz), who run personalized wine, eco, art and scenic tours around the island from around $100 per person (minimum numbers apply).

Accommodation

Accommodation is generally plentiful except for the three weeks after Christmas and all summer weekends. While Oneroa is convenient for buses, restaurants and shops, many prefer the more relaxing **beaches** like Palm Beach and Onetangi. Lots of accommodation will demand a two-night minimum for Friday and Saturday, or will charge an additional fee.

Crescent Valley Eco Lodge 50 Crescent Rd ℡09/372 4321, ⓦwww.waihekeecolodge.co.nz. Lovely lodge in a bush setting a 20min walk from Palm Beach. Each of the two large rooms has its own kitchen, bathroom and indoor and outdoor dining areas and you can relax in the hot tub under the stars. Excellent meals are available and delicious breakfasts are served in your room ($15 a head). There's also free use of kayaks and bikes. ❺

Fossil Bay Lodge 58 Korora Rd, Oneroa ℡09/372 8371, ⓦwww.fossilbay.webs.com. A relaxed collection of two-person huts a 5min walk from an all-but-private beach 1km from town on an organic farm. Single $35, rooms ❷

Heartsong Retreat 8 Omiha Rd, Rocky Bay ℡09/372 2039, ⓦwww.heartsongretreat.co.nz. Tranquil B&B delightfully sited amid bush with sea views. You've a choice of two elegantly appointed rooms in the house (both with breakfast included), a s/c cabana and a separate cottage ($400; both with breakfast ingredients provided), and everyone has access to a large bush-girt hot pool and a boathouse. Massage and assorted holistic treatments are available. Rooms ❼, cabana ❼, cottage ❾

Hekerua Lodge 11 Hekerua Rd, Little Oneroa ℡09/372 8990, ⓦwww.hekerualodge.co.nz. Peaceful, pool-equipped backpackers set in the

bush 10min walk from Oneroa. Some private rooms and a s/c unit. Camping $17, dorms $28, shares $36, rooms ❸, unit sleeping seven ❽

Onetangi Beachfront Apartments 27 The Strand, Onetangi ℡0800/663 826, ⓦwww.onetangi.co.nz. Only a road separates these upscale motel apartments from Onetangi Beach. All s/c with Sky TV and DVD players, access to free sauna and spa pools plus kayaks for rent. Apartments ❻, "beach-front" ❽, deluxe ❾

Palm Beach Bungalows 9 Palm Rd, Palm Beach ℡09/372 5146, ⓦwww.palmbeachbungalows .com. Hippyish collection of s/c wood and mud-brick cottages deeply set in the bush but well equipped with small kitchens and Sky TV. Romantic sojourns are a focus and the luxury bungalow comes with a double spa bath. Cottages ❻, luxury ❽

Punga Lodge 223 Ocean View Rd, Little Oneroa ℡09/372 6675, ⓦwww.pungalodge .co.nz. Delightful and hospitable B&B, well located in the bush close to Oneroa beach, with tea and muffins available from the helpful hosts. Accommodation consists of a range of comfortable and spacious en-suite doubles with verandas, and four self-catering apartments of different sizes. There's a spa pool, and good-value off-season deals. They also run the nearby *Tawa Lodge*, which has a well-priced shared-bathroom B&B and a very comfortable apartment with wonderful sea views. Ferry transfers available. Shared bath ④, B&B rooms ⑤, garden rooms ⑥, apartments ⑤–⑦

Whakanewha Regional Park Rocky Bay (reservations ℡09/366 2000). The island's only official campsite is simple but attractively sited on a tidal bay. The nearest bus stop is 3km away. $10.

Around the island

The bulk of Waiheke's population inhabits the western quarter of the island around **Oneroa**. Waiheke's finest beaches lie east of Oneroa: the almost circular Enclosure Bay for snorkelling, Palm Beach for swimming, and the more surf-oriented Onetangi. All over the island, the bays and headlands lend themselves to short, often steep **walks** (details from the i-SITE), wineries tempt, and if you're still restless, try kayaking or sailing (see p.138).

Oneroa and around

The settlement of **ONEROA** is draped across a narrow isthmus between the sandy sweep of Oneroa Bay and shallow, silty Blackpool Beach. The ridge-top main street runs from the post office past several cafés and restaurants up to the island's i-SITE (see p.134), library and cinema. Next door is the eccentric **Whittaker's Musical Experience** (daily 1–4pm; donation appreciated; ⓦwww.musical museum.org), a room full of flageolets, piano accordions, player pianos, xylophones and more, some dating back two hundred years. You're allowed to play most of them, and all are ably demonstrated during the occasional musical performances (Sat 1.30pm; $12.50).

Two excellent **vineyards** are easily accessible from Oneroa, both with wine tasting and quality restaurants (see p.139). The closest is *Cable Bay Vineyards*, 1km west at 12 Nick Johnstone Drive (tasting daily 11am–5pm; ℡09/372 5889, ⓦwww.cablebayvineyards.co.nz), a starkly modern place with sculptures dotting the lawns which have views back to Auckland. *Mudbrick*, 2km west on Church Bay Road (℡09/372 9050, ⓦwww.mudbrick.co.nz), has a more traditional feel but is no less appealing.

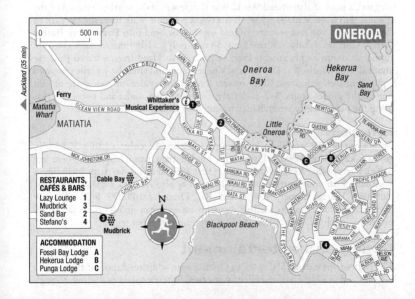

One of the island's finest **walks** is the Matiatia–Owhanake–Oneroa loop (2–3hr; undulating) which visits secluded beaches and windswept headlands, both peppered with some of New Zealand's finest modern mansions, many with sculptures visible in the grounds.

The rest of the island

What passes for a main road on Waiheke winds east from Oneroa through the contiguous settlements of Little Oneroa, Blackpool and Surfdale to **Ostend**. The island's light-industrial heart, far from any appealing beaches, Ostend is best ignored except on Saturday mornings (8am–noon) when the Ostend Hall, corner of Ostend Road and Belgium Street, is given over to the **Ostend Market**, with organic produce, arts and crafts, food stalls, massage, iridology readings and local entertainers.

Several of Waiheke's most reputable **wineries** lie between here and Onetangi, many welcoming visitors. One of the best is *Stonyridge*, 80 Onetangi Rd (daily 11.30am–5pm; ℡09/372 8822, Ⓦwww.stonyridge.co.nz), where organic, hand-tended vineyards are used to produce the world-class Larose, one of New Zealand's top Bordeaux-style reds. Most vintages are sold out (at around $220 a go) before they're even bottled so there are often limited cellar-door sales. On the weekends there's an entertaining **tour and tasting** (Sat & Sun 11.30am; $10), while at the restaurant (see opposite), wines are on offer by the glass (including Larose at $46 a pop).

There's more wine tasting, plus sampling of Waiheke Island Brewery beer, next door at *Wild On Waiheke* (Nov–April daily 11am–4pm; May–Oct Thurs–Sun 1–4pm; ℡09/372 3434, Ⓦwww.wildonwaiheke.co.nz), where four to eight samples cost $6–10.

Palm Beach, 6km east of Oneroa, takes a neat bite out of the north coast, with houses tumbling down to a small sandy beach separated by a handful of rocks from the nude bathing zone at its western end. Waiheke's longest and most exposed beach is **ONETANGI**, popular in summer with surfers, board riders and swimmers, and an occasional venue for beach horse races, usually in mid-March.

There's very little habitation east of Onetangi, just tracts of open farmland, vineyards and **Stony Batter Historic Reserve** (unrestricted entry; Ⓦwww.fsb.org.nz), a mass of abandoned World War II defences at the northeastern tip of the island 23km from Matiatia wharf. It is a twenty-minute walk from the car park to the site where you can wander around topside, or head into **Fort Stony Batter** (Feb to Christmas daily 9.30am–5pm; $8 cash only), a labyrinth of dank concrete tunnels and gun emplacements built to protect Auckland from a feared Japanese attack during World War II. The attack never came and after the war the guns and equipment were removed. Bring or rent a torch to explore on your own, or join one of the guided tours ($45 cash only, for up to two adults and two kids) that bring the place to life. Stony Batter is visited by all the island tour buses.

Activities

To get out on the water, go **kayaking** with Ross Adventures (℡09/372 5550, Ⓦwww.kayakwaiheke.co.nz) who run guided trips from Matiatia. There are half-day trips (4hr; $75), evening trips (3hr; $95), and full-day trips including a shuttle back to your starting point ($145). They also rent sea kayaks (from $35/half-day). Flying Carpet, 104 Wharf Rd, Ostend (℡09/372 5621, Ⓦwww.flyingcarpet.co.nz), offers **sailing** day-trips on an ocean-going catamaran ($160 including lunch), dinner cruises ($120) and a range of other trips.

Eating and entertainment

The bulk of the **eating** places are in Oneroa with additional spots at the various beaches and at a bunch of excellent **wineries**. Entertainment is limited, though it is worth checking listings for the Waiheke Island Community **Cinema**, 2 Koroka Rd, near the i-SITE (ⓦ www.waihekenz.com). **Live music** mostly happens at weekends, with *Sand Bar* and *The Rocks* in Ostend being worthy bets.

Charlie Farley's 21 The Strand, Onetangi. Casual licensed café with a decent range of dishes (around $20) and a deck with sea views across to Little Barrier Island – perfect for a sundowner.

Lazy Lounge 139 Oceanview Rd. A good place to hang out and watch an endless parade of local characters call in for coffee, wine, beer or food options like Thai chicken salad, pizza, breakfast burritos or a hearty slice of cake. Free wi-fi.

Mudbrick Church Bay Rd, 2km west of Oneroa ☎ 09/372 9050. White linen, polished stemware and views over the lavender beds characterize this delightful vineyard restaurant where an entrée of king scallops with salted watermelon ($24) might be followed by Waiheke lamb with celeriac purée ($40).

Nourish 3 Belgium St, Ostend. Modern café serving predominantly organic, local and seasonal produce. Along with great salads, there's an excellent chicken and avocado Turkish sandwich and free wi-fi.

Sand Bar 153 Ocean View Rd ☎ 09/372 9458. Chic little bar, great for a cocktail as the sun goes down and frequently hosting DJs at the weekend. Closed Mon & Tues.

Stefano's 18 Hamilton Rd, Surfdale ☎ 09/372 5309. Cosy little pizzeria with plenty of outdoor seating and a strong line in simply topped thin-crust pizzas (mostly $17–23) plus a few pasta dishes and great tiramisu. BYO and licensed. Closed Mon.

Stonyridge 80 Onetangi Rd ☎ 09/372 8822. Lunch alfresco, overlooking the vines, at this excellent vineyard restaurant. Expect assorted bruschetta, tasting platters and a handful of mains ($24–30) plus a great wine list and a chance to sample olive oil from their trees which date back to the 1980s, making them one of NZ's oldest olive orchards. Often acoustic music on the deck at weekends.

Great Barrier Island (Aotea)

Rugged and sparsely populated **Great Barrier Island** (Aotea) lies 90km northeast of Auckland on the outer fringes of the Hauraki Gulf and, though only 30km long and 15km wide, packs in a mountainous heart which drops away to deep indented harbours in the west and eases gently to golden surf beaches in the east. It's only a half-hour plane ride from the city but exudes a tranquillity that makes it seem a world apart. There is no mains electricity or water, no industry, no towns to speak of and limited public transport. This lends Great Barrier a sense of peace and detachment, enhanced by **beaches**, **hot springs** and tightly packed **mountains** clad in bush and spared the ravages of deer and possums.

Some history

Great Barrier is formed from the same line of extinct **volcanoes** as the Coromandel Peninsula and shares a common geological and human past. Aotea was one of the places first populated by **Maori**, and the Ngatiwai and Ngatimaru people occupied numerous *pa* sites when Cook sailed by in 1769. Recognizing the calming influence of Aotea on the waters of the Hauraki Gulf, Cook renamed it Great Barrier Island. From 1791, the island's vast stands of kauri were seized for ships' timbers, and kauri **logging** didn't cease until 1942, outliving some early copper mining at Miners Head and sporadic attempts to extract gold and silver. Kauri logging and gum digging were replaced by a short-lived whale-oil extraction industry at Whangaparapara in the 1950s, but the Barrier soon fell back on tilling the poor clay soils and its peak population of over 5000 dropped to around 1000.

Alternative lifestylers arrived in the 1960s and 1970s, and while Seventies idealism has largely been supplanted by modern pragmatism, **self-sufficiency**

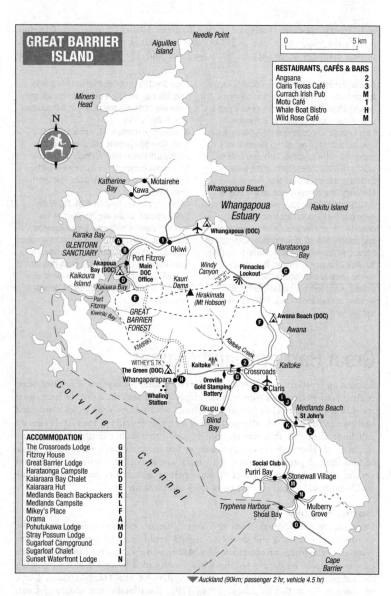

GREAT BARRIER ISLAND

RESTAURANTS, CAFÉS & BARS	
Angsana	2
Claris Texas Café	3
Currach Irish Pub	M
Motu Café	1
Whale Boat Bistro	H
Wild Rose Café	M

ACCOMMODATION	
The Crossroads Lodge	G
Fitzroy House	B
Great Barrier Lodge	H
Haratonga Campsite	C
Kaiaraara Bay Chalet	D
Kaiaraara Hut	E
Medlands Beach Backpackers	K
Medlands Campsite	L
Mikey's Place	F
Orama	A
Pohutukawa Lodge	M
Stray Possum Lodge	O
Sugarloaf Campground	J
Sugarloaf Chalet	I
Sunset Waterfront Lodge	N

Auckland (90km; passenger 2 hr, vehicle 4.5 hr)

remains, more out of necessity than lifestyle choice. People grow their own vegetables, everyone has their own water supply and the strain on diesel generators is reduced by wind-driven turbines and solar panels. **Agriculture** takes a back seat to **tourism**, however, and wealthy second-home owners are moving in. Islanders have resisted this trend but as land prices rocket, some on low incomes are forced to leave, while others head out when their kids reach high school age. Indeed, a dropping population and the need to cater for visitors means there's often **casual work** available in the summer.

Arrival, information and transport

Ferries arrive in **Tryphena**, the southern harbour and major settlement with four main bays: Shoal Bay (where ferries arrive), Mulberry Grove, Stonewall Village (the largest settlement), and Puriri Bay (a short walk along the coast from Stonewall Village). Some ferries continue up the west coast to the minuscule hamlet of **Port Fitzroy**, an ideal jumping-off point for tramps in the Great Barrier Forest.

The vast majority of visitors arrive from Auckland between Boxing Day and the middle of January, many piling in for the New Year's Eve party at the sports club at Crossroads. Most come aboard Fullers **ferries** to Tryphena and Port Fitzroy (Christmas to mid-Jan daily, plus summer long weekends; 2hr; $69 each way, bikes $10; ☎0800/385 5377).

The slower SeaLink **car ferry** (☎0800/732 546, ⓦwww.sealink.co.nz), runs year-round and carries passengers, cars and just about all the island's freight, leaving Jellicoe Street in central Auckland (5–7 weekly; 4hr 30min) for Tryphena, with one service a week (Tues) to Port Fitzroy (foot passengers $73 one-way, $120 return; bicycles free; cars $217/350).

Most flights arrive in the east at **Claris**, the island's administrative centre and convenient for the best beaches at **Medlands** and **Awana Bay**. You can **fly** to Claris from Auckland International Airport with either FlyMySky (☎0800/222 123, ⓦwww.flymysky.co.nz) or Great Barrier Airlines (GBA; ☎0800/900 600, ⓦwww.greatbarrierairlines.co.nz) which both operate at least three scheduled flights a day and charge $89–99 each way (or $169 for a fly/ferry combo). GBA also flies from the Barrier to Whangarei and Whitianga (2–3 weekly) allowing you to use Great Barrier as a stepping stone.

Packages

If you'd rather have someone else do the organizing, consider an Auckland-based fly-in day-tour with Bush & Beach ($575; ☎0800/423 224, ⓦwww.bushandbeach .co.nz) which includes a visit to the hot springs. Engaging a local company to put together a **tailor-made itinerary** can often work out cheaper than doing it yourself as they can get transport and accommodation discounts. Try Steve at Great Barrier Island Tourism (☎0800/997 222, ⓦwww.greatbarrierislandtourism.co.nz) who really knows the island.

Most of the lodges also offer packages: check out *Pohutukawa Lodge* and *Fitzroy House*.

Information and communications

There is no visitor centre on the island, but GBI Shuttle Buses run an unstaffed kiosk (daily 7am–7pm) opposite the airport in Claris and there's lots of **info** on ⓦwww.greatbarriernz.com. The helpful **DOC office** (Mon–Fri 8am–4.30pm; ☎09/429 0044) is 1km west of the Port Fitzroy wharf. Most places accept credit and debit cards, but there are no **ATMs** on the island so bring some cash. **PostShops** can be found at Tryphena, Claris and Port Fitzroy.

Internet access is fairly limited, though the *Curragh Irish Pub* in Tryphena has free wi-fi for customers. In Claris, the store has wi-fi ($8/day) and *Claris Texas Café* has an online computer ($3/15min). Tryphena and the hilltops offer the best of the fairly patchy **mobile coverage**.

Getting around

Great Barrier has no scheduled public transport though there are several **shuttle buses**. They generally meet all ferries and flights, but it's better to book in advance. From Tryphena, **fares** are around $15 to Medlands, $20 to Claris and $30 to Whangaparapara. Go with Great Barrier Buses, Tryphena (℡0800/426 832, 🆆www.greatbarriertravel.co.nz) or GBI Shuttle Buses, Claris (℡09/429 0062, 🆆www.greatbarrierisland.co.nz). For something a little different, Crazyhorse (℡0800/997 222, 🆆www.crazyhorse.co.nz) will take two of you wherever you want to go on the back of a bright-blue **custom trike**, and organize all sorts of interesting adventures.

It is often more convenient to **rent a car**: use Tryphena-based Aotea Rentals (from $55; ℡0800/426 832, 🆆www.aoteacarrentals.co.nz) or Claris-based GBI Rent A Car (from $40; ℡09/429 0767, 🆆www.greatbarrierisland.co.nz).

Mountain **bikes** can be rented from Paradise Cycles in Claris (from $20; ℡09/429 0700, 📧paradisecyces@xtra.co.nz), though the hills are steep and the roads dusty and hot in summer. Off-road mountain biking is only allowed on the Forestry Road from Whangaparapara to Port Fitzroy.

Accommodation

Accommodation on Great Barrier ranges from camping to plush lodges. **Backpackers** can choose from the three hostels listed plus one bunkroom at *Pohutukawa Lodge*. We've mentioned some of the best of the island's **self-catering cottages**, though many more excellent places are listed on sites such as 🆆www .greatbarriernz.com and 🆆www.greatbarrierislandtourism.co.nz. The owners often live close by and can arrange breakfast and sometimes dinner.

Some places **pick up** from ferries and flights, though those in Tryphena and Medlands will expect you to catch the shuttles that meet each boat or plane. Accommodation is generally more **expensive** than on the mainland, particularly from Christmas to mid-January when the island is packed – and you'll need to **book well ahead** to stand any chance of finding a place.

There are numerous, simple DOC **campsites** (all marked on our map and costing $8–9), the best of them listed below, along with one of the better-located private sites. DOC sites all have toilets, water and cold showers (except *The Green*) and fires are not allowed. Book in advance at peak periods (℡09/429 0044, 🆆www.doc.govt.nz).

Lodges, guesthouses and cottages

Fitzroy House Glenfern Rd, Port Fitzroy ℡09/429 0091, 🆆www.fitzroyhouse.co.nz. Stay inside Glenfern Sanctuary at the owner's wood-floored s/c cottage sleeping six, with views over the harbour and free access to canoes and a dinghy. Sea kayaks are $45/24hr. Check out the excellent, four-day tramping and sailing packages. Closed June–Sept. **❼**

Great Barrier Lodge Whangaparapara Harbour ℡09/429 0488, 🆆www.greatbarrierlodge.com. This harbourside lodge is pretty much all there is at Whangaparapara, and also serves as the local grocery and dive shop. Accommodation is in cottages and studio units and the main building houses a bar/restaurant. Bunkroom $45, studios & cottages **❻**

Kaiaraara Bay Chalet Kaiaraara Bay Rd, Port Fitzroy ℡09/429 0040. Modern one-bedroom self-catering unit just 30min walk from the Port Fitzroy wharf, with long sea views and room for four. Well sited for the kauri dam walk. **❻**

Orama Karaka Bay ℡09/429 0063, 🆆www .orama.co.nz. A Christian centre also operating as both a waterfront holiday park and home to the OPC outdoor centre (see p.144). There's a swimming pool, shop and access to magnificent bushwalks, fishing and diving. Camping $15–20, bunkrooms $30, cabins **❸**, s/c houses and cottages **❺**

Pohutukawa Lodge Stonewall, Tryphena ℡09/429 0211, 🆆www.currachirishpub .com. The pick of the places around Tryphena, homely, small and welcoming, with a great pub and restaurant spilling out onto the veranda, all conveniently close to the shop. There are attractive en suites plus a single four-bed backpacker room (linen supplied) that can be noisy with pub patrons leaving. Also a self-catering kitchen. Backpacker rooms $25, rooms **❺**

Sugarloaf Chalet Sugarloaf Rd, Kaitoke ℡09/429 0229. Gorgeous rustic-chic self-catering cottage with barbecue area, fire pit and solar power. It is just steps from a lovely beach and has a real outdoor flavour (complete with external shower and toilet). ⑤

Sunset Waterfront Lodge Mulberry Grove, Tryphena ☎09/429 0051, ⓦwww.sunsetlodge .co.nz. Motel-style accommodation in grassy grounds that aren't really waterfront but have close sea views. Choose from A-frames sleeping four and several smaller studios. Studio ⑥, A-frames ⑦

Hostels

The Crossroads Lodge 1 Blind Bay Rd, Crossroads ☎09/429 0889, ⓦwww.xroadslodge.com. Comfortable hostel well sited within walking distance of the airport, hot springs and island tramps. Accommodation is in cabins or double rooms. Beds $30, rooms ②

Medlands Beach Backpackers 9 Mason Rd ☎09/429 0320, ⓦwww.medlandsbeach.com. Basic, low-key backpackers with four-bed dorms, a secluded chalet and a couple of villas on a small farm 10min walk from Medlands Beach – making it popular with surfers. There are bodyboards for guests' use, but there are no meals and no shops nearby, so bring your own food. Dorms $35, room & chalet ②, villa ④

Stray Possum Lodge 64 Cape Barrier Rd ☎0800/767 786, ⓦwww.straypossum.co.nz. A little out on a limb, this bush-girt hostel has six-bed dorms, doubles, cabins and lovely s/c chalets ideal for groups of up to six. There's also a licensed pizza restaurant (nightly in Jan, plus summer weekends and by arrangement). Linen $5 for your stay, or bring a sleeping bag. Camping $12, dorms $23, rooms ②, chalets ⑤

Campsites and hut

Harataonga Campsite Harataonga. Excellent, shady DOC site 300m back from the beach and very popular with families in the fortnight after Christmas. $8–9.

Kaiaraara Hut Near Port Fitzroy. Bookable through ⓦwww.doc.govt.nz. A 28-bunk hut with water and a wood stove for heating. $10.

Medlands Campsite Medlands Beach. Attractive DOC site beside an estuary and just over the dunes from an excellent beach. Very crowded for most of Jan. $8–9.

Mikey's Place Awana ☎09/429 0140. Hospitable but primitive campsite 25km north of Tryphena that's less well located than the nearby DOC site but has hot showers, toilets and a basic cookhouse, all for $7.

Sugarloaf Campground Sugarloaf Rd, Kaitoke ☎09/429 0229. Great private campsite overlooking the southern end of Kaitoke Beach. Basics water, toilets and showers. Ask about exploring the Mermaid Pool at low tide. $8.

Around the island

Much of the pleasure here is in lazing on the beaches and striking out on foot into the **Great Barrier Forest**, a rugged chunk of bush and kauri-logging relics between Port Fitzroy and Whangaparapara that takes up about a third of the island. If you're looking for more structure to your day, a few small-time tour and activity operators can keep you entertained (see p.145).

Though **TRYPHENA** has good accommodation and places to eat, there's not much to do. Most people head straight for **Medlands Beach**, a long sweep of golden sand broken by a sheltering island and often endowed with some of the Barrier's best (un-patrolled) surf. The pretty blue and white **St John's Church** looks suitably out of place, having only been moved here from the mainland by barge in 1986 before being dragged over the dunes.

North of Medlands, the road leaves the coast for **Claris** where the post office claims to be the world's first place to have run an airmail service. The story goes that when the SS *Wairarapa* was wrecked on the northwest coast of Great Barrier in 1898, the news took a sobering three days to get to Auckland. In response the island set up a **pigeon-mail** service that was used until 1908, when a telephone was installed. Nearby, the **Milk, Honey and Grain Museum**, 47 Hector Sanderson Rd (open most days; donation), boasts a collection of memorabilia neatly organized into three categories which reveals a lot more about the island than its name suggests – a worthwhile stop if the weather's bad.

Crossroads, 2km north of Claris, is just that – the junction of roads to Okupu, Port Fitzroy and Whangaparapara. The Whangaparapara road runs past the scant roadside remains of the **Oreville gold stamping battery** (unrestricted entry) and

▲ Taking it easy on Great Barrier Island

the start of a path to **Kaitoke Hot Springs** (see box opposite). At **Whangaparapara**, a short stroll around the bay brings you to the foundations of a whaling station built here in the 1950s.

North of Crossroads, the Port Fitzroy road passes the lovely surf and swimming beach of **Awana Bay** and the roadside **Pinnacles Lookout** before reaching the start of a track to **Windy Canyon** (see opposite). The tiny settlement of **Okiwi** offers little but the appealing, daytime *Motu Café*, though it is only 5km over the hill to **PORT FITZROY**, whose harbour remains remarkably calm under most wind conditions, a quality not lost on yachties who flock here in summer. You'll find a shop, burger bar, a sporadically staffed info kiosk and a few places to stay. The northern shore of the harbour is formed by the Kotuku Peninsula, which since 2008 has been separated from the rest of the island by a 2km-long predator-proof fence forming the 2.3-square-kilometre **Glenfern Sanctuary**, Glenfern Road (guided tours daily at 11am by appointment; $40; ☎09/429 0091, ⓦwww.glenfern.org.nz). Rats have been eliminated and birdlife is slowly returning, with reintroductions of North Island robins and kokako planned. Ninety-minute tours involve a Unimog 4WD journey and a nature trail to a 600-year-old kauri where you get direct access to the treetops via a short suspension bridge.

Port Fitzroy makes the best base for **tramping** or shorter day-walks to the fine Kaiarara **kauri dam** (see box opposite). For three years from 1926, the Kauri Timber Company hacked trees out of the relatively inaccessible Kaiaraara Valley, then built dams which, when the water was released, sluiced the cut logs down to Kaiaraara Bay, where they were lashed together in rafts and floated to Auckland.

At **Karaka Bay**, 4km north of Port Fitzroy, Orama (see p.142) is home to OPC (☎09/429 0762, ⓦwww.opc.org.nz), an outdoor education school that's a great spot for renting aquatic gear (double sea kayak $65/day, dinghy $40/half-day, snorkelling gear $15) and exploring the area.

Activities

It is hard to beat spending a few hours on one of the excellent **beaches**, but at some point most visitors head out on one of the **walks** (see box below).

The harbours of the west coast are perfect for exploring by **kayak**: Tryphena-based Aotea Kayak Adventures (℡09/429 0664) run guided trips including a full-day kayak and snorkelling trip ($65); Kyak Hire (℡09/429 0987) do just that from Kaitoke; *Great Barrier Lodge* do the same from Whangaparapara; and OPC have several options up north at Karaka Bay.

Great Barrier has a enviable reputation for the quality of its **fishing** and several operators vie for your business. Skilly at Freedom Charters (℡09/429 0861) has been fishing the island for approaching fifty years and will take you out for $85 a head. He's also equipped for **scuba diving**.

You can even play **golf**, at Golf Pioneer Park, Whangaparapara Road, Claris (℡09/429 0420), a nine-hole par-three course surrounded by bush with pukeko strutting across the fairways. Green fees are $10, club rental costs $5 and there's a lively bar with cheap drinks and decent meals (Thurs & Sun).

Great Barrier walks

The **Great Barrier Forest**, New Zealand's largest stand of possum-free bush, offers a unique **walking environment**. Because the area is so compact, in no time at all you can find yourself climbing in and out of little subtropical gullies luxuriant with nikau palms, tree ferns, regenerating rimu and kauri, and onto scrubby manuka ridges with stunning coastal and mountain views. Many of the tracks follow the routes of mining tramways past old kauri dams. Tracks in the centre of the island converge on 621m **Hirakimata** (Mount Hobson) which is surrounded by boardwalks and wooden steps designed to keep trampers on the path and prevent the disturbance of nesting **black petrels**.

Harataonga/Okiwi Coastal Track (12km one-way; 5hr; undulating). Superb coastal views and easy walking along an old coast road which passes through some private property. Get one of the shuttle companies to pick you up at the far end, or just walk partway and back.

Hirakimata via Windy Canyon (6km return; 3hr; 400m ascent). The easiest way to get to the highest point on the island is via Windy Canyon (see below). Beyond, you follow a broad ridge with long coastal views, then hike boardwalks and climb stairs up though lovely, mature kauri and rimu forest to the summit.

Kaiaraara Kauri Dam (10km return; 3hr; 250m ascent). Lovely forest road and track bushwalk to NZ's best example of a kauri dam (see p.200). The hike starts at a locked gate around 2km south of the Port Fitzroy DOC office, altogether around a 40min walk from the wharf. Along the way you pass the Kaiaraara Hut (see p.143) around a 15min walk from the locked gate. From the kauri dam you can continue steeply uphill to a second, far less impressive, dam (50min on) then ascend steps to the summit of Hirakimata (a further 30–40min).

Kaitoke Hot Springs (6km return; 1hr 30min; flat). Gentle, wheelchair-accessible path that skirts the attractive wetlands of Kaitoke Swamp en route to the Kaitoke Hot Springs, where a couple of dammed pools in a stream make a great place for a soak. The best spot is 50m upstream (follow the path) where a pool is tucked into a small chasm.

Windy Canyon (1km return; 20–30min; 50m ascent). An easy walk to a narrow defile that gets its name from the eerie sounds produced by certain wind conditions. The narrow path winds through nikau palms and tree ferns to a viewpoint that gives a sense of the island's interior, as well as coastal views. Starts 4km northwest of Awana Bay.

The Aotea brochure (available from DOC in Auckland) has an adequate map and covers all the walks: we've listed some of the best below. Many of these can be combined to provide 2–3 days of rewarding tramping, making use of the campsites and the Kaiaraara Hut (see p.143). If you've come specifically to tramp, it is best to catch one of the infrequent ferries direct to Port Fitzroy. Alternatively, call one of the shuttle operators in advance to organize transport from the airport or Tryphena.

Eating and drinking

The limited number of stand-alone **restaurants** encourages lots of accommodation places to offer meals, and those that don't will almost certainly have self-catering facilities. Restaurants often close early if business is slow, so **book ahead**.

There are also **shops** in Tryphena, Claris, Whangaparapara and Port Fitzroy, where you can pick up picnic provisions. **Drinking** tends to happen in bars attached to accommodation establishments or in the social clubs at Tryphena and Claris.

Angsana 63 Gray Rd, just north of Cross-roads. A quality Thai restaurant seems incongruous for the Barrier, but the island is a better place for it. All your favourites (mains around $30) at lunch and dinner with friendly service.

Claris Texas Café Claris ☎ 09/429 0811. Reliable café with a sunny courtyard and a grassy patch for the kids. It's open daily 8am–4pm for light meals, breakfasts, panini, burgers and great desserts.

Currach Irish Pub Stonewall, Tryphena. An Irish pub that's about as traditional as you can get on a South Pacific island – a lot of the paraphernalia came from the owner's grandmother's pub, in County Kerry, which closed in 1950. Guinness and Kilkenny on tap and great hot bar meals served in the evening ($15–25). There's

often live acoustic music, especially on Thursday when anyone is welcome to jam.

Motu Café Okiwi. This new café is the best spot for daytime eating in the north of the island. The range of food is limited but the coffee's good and you can while away an hour reading magazines or discussing the island's ecology with the owners.

Whale Boat Bistro *Great Barrier Lodge*, Whanga-parapara Harbour. Bar and restaurant serving meals indoors or on the spacious deck with harbour views.

Wild Rose Café Stonewall, Tryphena. Sit on the veranda or in the garden at this daytime café specializing in organic products, fine teas and juices. Also a good range of breakfasts, burgers and light lunches.

Tiritiri Matangi

A visit to **Tiritiri Matangi** is the highpoint of many a stay in Auckland. About 4km off the tip of the Whangaparaoa Peninsula and 30km north of Auckland, Tiritiri Matangi is an "open sanctuary", and visitors are free to roam through the predator-free bush where, within a couple of hours, it's possible to see rarities like takahe, saddlebacks, whiteheads, red-crowned parakeets, North Island robins, kokako and brown teals. To stand a chance of seeing the little-spotted kiwi and tuatara, you'll have to stay overnight.

Evidence from *pa* sites on the island indicate that Tiritiri Matangi was first populated by the Kawerau-A-Maki **Maori** and later by Ngati Paoa, both of whom are now recognized as the land's traditional owners. They partly **cleared the island** of bush, a process continued by Europeans who arrived in the mid-nineteenth century to graze sheep and cattle. Fortunately, **predators** such as possums, stoats, weasels, deer, cats, wallabies and the like failed to get a foothold, so after farming became uneconomic in the early 1970s Tiritiri was singled out as a prime site for helping to restore bird populations. The cacophony of birdsong in the bush is stark evidence of just how catastrophic the impact of these predators has been elsewhere.

Since 1984, a **reforestation** programme has seen the planting of over 300,000 saplings and though the rapidly regenerating bush is far from mature, the **birds** seem to like it. Most are thriving with the aid of feeding stations to supplement diets in the leaner months, with nesting boxes standing in for decaying trees.

Four of the species released here are among the rarest in the world, with total populations of around a couple of hundred. The most visible are the flightless **takahe**, lumbering blue-green turkey-sized birds long thought to be extinct (see p.735); birds moved here from Fiordland have bred well and are easily spotted as they are unafraid of humans and very inquisitive. **Saddlebacks, kokako** and **stitchbirds** stick to the bush and its margins, but often pop out if you sit quietly for a few moments on some of the bush boardwalks and paths near feeding stations. **Northern blue penguins** also frequent Tiritiri, and can be seen all year round – but are most in evidence in March, when they come ashore to moult, and from September to December, when they nest in specially constructed viewing boxes located along the seashore path west of the main wharf.

Practicalities

Tiritiri Matangi is typically visited as a **day-trip**, giving five hours on the island; you'll need to take your own **lunch**, as there is no food available. 360 Discovery **ferries** (℡0800/360 3472, ⓦwww.360discovery.co.nz) depart from Auckland's Downtown Ferry Terminal (Christmas to mid-Jan daily 9am; rest of year Wed–Sun and public holidays 9am; $66 return) then call at Gulf Harbour (see p.128; 9.50am; $39 return) before arriving at Tiritiri around 10.10am. Boats arrive back in Auckland around 5pm.

Visitors arriving on scheduled ferries can join **guided walks** (1–2hr; $5), leaving from the wharf and led by volunteers steeped in bird-lore. They typically finish near the lighthouse at the modern **interpretation centre**. Otherwise, you're free to wander the island or indulge in a little **swimming** from Hobbs Beach, a ten-minute walk west of the wharf and the only sandy strand around.

It's also possible to **stay overnight** in a self-contained bunkhouse near the light-house. Online bookings (ⓦwww.doc.govt.nz/tiritiribunkhouse; $20) should be made as far in advance as you can (months ahead for weekends) and you'll need to bring a sleeping bag and food in sealed rodent-proof containers.

For more detail on the island go to the Supporters of Tiritiri Matangi website (ⓦwww.tiritirimatangi.org.nz).

Travel details

For more on moving on from Auckland, see p.88.

Trains	Buses
Auckland (Britomart) to: Hamilton (2–7 weekly; 2hr 30min); Kingsland (every 30–60min; 16min); National Park (2–7 weekly; 5hr 30min); Newmarket (every 10–30min; 7min); Ohakune (2–7 weekly; 6hr 30min); Otorohanga (2–7 weekly; 3hr); Palmerston North (2–7 weekly; 9hr 30min); Taihape (2–7 weekly; 7hr 30min); Wellington (2–7 weekly; 12hr).	**Auckland** to: Dargaville (1 daily, not Sat; 3hr); Gisborne (2 daily; 9hr 15min); Hamilton (17–19 daily; 2hr); Hastings (2 daily; 7hr 30min); Helensville (Mon–Fri 8 daily; 1hr 10min); Kerikeri (3 daily; 5hr); Kumeu (4–8 daily; 35min); Napier (2 daily; 7hr 15min); National Park (2 daily; 5hr 30min); New Plymouth (3–4 daily; 5hr 30min–6hr 30min); Ohakune (1 daily; 6hr 30min); Orewa (5–7 daily;

30min); Paihia (5–6 daily; 4hr 20min); Palmerston North (5–6 daily; 9–10hr); Rotorua (8 daily; 4hr); Taihape (4–5 daily; 7hr); Taupo (6–7 daily; 4–5hr); Tauranga (4–5 daily; 4hr); Thames (4 daily; 1hr 45min); Waipu (4–7 daily; 2hr 20min); Waitomo Caves (3 daily; 4hr 20min); Warkworth (4–6 daily; 1hr); Wellington (5–6 daily; 11–12hr); Whangarei (4–7 daily; 3hr); Whitianga (1 daily; 3hr).

Ferries

Auckland to: Coromandel (3 weekly; 2hr); Devonport (every 30min; 10min); Great Barrier (4–7 weekly; 2–5hr); Gulf Harbour Marina (3 daily; 50min); Rangitoto (3–5 daily; 40min); Tiritiri Matangi Island (4 weekly; 1hr 30min); Waiheke (roughly hourly; 35min).

Gulf Harbour Marina to: Tiritiri Matangi Island (4 weekly; 20min).

Half Moon Bay to: Waiheke (roughly hourly; 45min).

Flights

Auckland to: Bay of Islands (5 daily; 40min); Blenheim (4 daily; 1hr 20min); Christchurch (24 daily; 1hr 20min); Dunedin (2–3 daily; 1hr 50min); Gisborne (6–7 daily; 1hr); Great Barrier Island (6–8 daily; 40min), Hamilton (3 daily; 30min); Kaitaia (1–2 daily; 45min); Napier/Hastings (7–10 daily; 1hr); Nelson (12 daily; 1hr 20min); New Plymouth (6–8 daily; 45min); Palmerston North (7 daily; 1hr); Queenstown (6 daily; 1hr 50min); Rotorua (2–3 daily; 40min); Taupo (3 daily; 45min); Tauranga (4 daily; 35min); Wanganui (2–3 daily; 1hr); Wellington (20 daily; 1hr); Whakatane (3 daily; 45min); Whangarei (7–9 daily; 35min).

Great Barrier Island to: Auckland (6–8 daily; 40min).

2

Northland

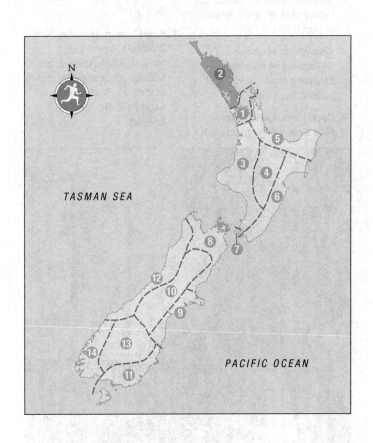

CHAPTER 2 **Highlights**

* **Poor Knights Islands** Scuba dive amid caves, fabulous rock arches, abundant fish, and a couple of navy wrecks. See p.163

* **Bay of Islands** Sail, swim with dolphins and soak up the history of Northland's tourism hot spot. See p.166

* **Whangaroa Harbour** Sail around some of New Zealand's most paradisiacal waters. See p.185

* **Cape Reinga and Ninety Mile Beach** Sandboard giant dunes and see the Pacific Ocean and Tasman Sea meeting in a maelstrom. See p.192

* **Hokianga Harbour** Watch the sun set in a fiery rainbow of orange, fuchsia and indigo. See p.196

* **Kauri forests** Marvel at New Zealand's largest tree, the majestic 2000-year-old Tane Mahuta, and see plenty more at the A.H. Reed Memorial Kauri Park. See p.199 & p.162

▲ A.H. Reed Memorial Kauri Park

Northland

Thrusting 350km from Auckland into the subtropical north, **Northland** separates the Pacific Ocean from the Tasman Sea. The two oceans crash together off Cape Reinga, New Zealand's most northerly road-accessible point. Kiwis often describe this staunchly Maori province as the "Winterless North", a phrase that rightly evokes the citrus trees, warm aquamarine waters and beaches of white silica and golden sand that make the upper reaches of the region such a magnet.

Scenically, Northland splits down the middle. The **east coast** is a labyrinth of coves hidden between plunging headlands. Beaches tend to be calm and safe, with the force of occasional Pacific storms broken by clusters of protective barrier islands. There could hardly be a greater contrast than the long, virtually straight, **west coast** pounded by powerful Tasman breakers and broken only by occasional harbours. Tidal rips and holes make swimming dangerous, and there are no lifeguard patrols. Some beaches are even designated as roads but are full of hazards for the unwary – and rental cars aren't insured for beach driving. Exploration of the undulating **interior** involves long forays down twisting side roads.

Beyond the Hibiscus Coast, on the east shore, is the rural **Matakana Coast**, popular with yachties circumnavigating Kawau Island and snorkellers exploring the underwater world of the **Goat Island Marine Reserve**. The broad sweep of **Bream Bay** runs to the dramatic crags of Whangarei Heads at the entrance to Northland's major port and town, **Whangarei**. Off the coast here lie the **Poor Knights Islands**, New Zealand's premier dive spot. Tourists in a hurry tend to make straight for the **Bay of Islands**, a jagged bite out of the coastline, dotted with islands perfect for cruising, diving and swimming with dolphins, and steeped in New Zealand history. Everything north of here is loosely referred to as **The Far North**, a region characterized by the quiet remoteness of the **Whangaroa Harbour**, **Doubtless Bay**, and the **Aupori Peninsula**, which backs **Ninety Mile Beach** all the way up to **Cape Reinga**.

The west coast is very different from the east, marked by economic neglect over the last fifty years as kauri logging ended and dairying never successfully replaced it. First stop on the way back south from Ninety Mile Beach is the fragmented **Hokianga Harbour**, one of New Zealand's largest, with spectacular sand dunes gracing the north head. South of here you're into the **Waipoua Forest**, all that remains after the depredations of the kauri loggers, a story best told at the excellent Kauri Museum at Matakohe.

The Northland website is ⓦ www.northlandnz.com.

Some history

Northland was the site of most of the early contact between Maori and European settlers, and the birthplace of New Zealand's most important document, the **Treaty of Waitangi**. Maori legend tells of how the great Polynesian explorer Kupe discovered the Hokianga Harbour and, finding the climate and abundance of food to his liking, encouraged his people to return and settle there. It was their descendants in the Bay of Islands who had the dubious honour of making the first contact with white men, as European whalers plundered the seas and missionaries sought converts. Eventually, the northern chiefs signed away their sovereignty in return for assurances on land and traditional rights, which were seldom respected. There is still a perception among some Maori in the rest of the country that the five northern *iwi* gave Aotearoa away to the Pakeha.

As more fertile farmlands were found in newly settled regions further south, rapacious **kauri loggers** and **gum diggers** cleared the bush and later, as extractive industries died away, pioneers moved in, turning much of the land to **dairy country**. Local dairy factories closed as larger semi-industrial complexes centralized processing, leaving small towns all but destitute, though the planting of fast-growing exotic trees and sporadic horticulture keep local economies ticking over.

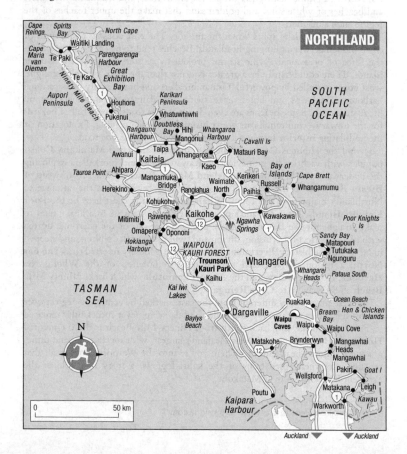

Getting around

With no trains and few airports, you'll be hitting Northland's roads. If you're driving the choices are limited to a major road up each side of the peninsula. This forms a logical loop formalized as the Twin Coast Discovery Highway: there's no need to follow it slavishly, but the brown signs emblazoned with a dolphin and curling wave make a good starting framework.

The main **bus** line is InterCity (℡09/583 5780, ⓦ www.intercity.co.nz), which also runs Northliner services, sometimes using the same bus. There is really only one route, from Auckland (SkyCity terminal) up the eastern side of the peninsula calling at Whangarei and Paihia in the Bay of Islands, where you change for Kerikeri and Kaitaia. NakedBus (premium charged ℡0900/62533, ⓦ www.nakedbus.com) also runs one bus a day between Auckland and Paihia.

Hokianga Harbour can be reached with Magic Bus (p.33), which does an anti-clockwise loop around Northland several days a week. There is also one short-range operator from Auckland: Main Coachline (℡09/278 8070), which serves Warkworth and continues on to Dargaville.

Northland has a limited number of **flights** and since distances are relatively short you're unlikely to need them, except perhaps for flights from Whangarei to Great Barrier Island with Great Barrier Airlines (ⓦ www.greatbarrierairlines.co.nz).

The Matakana Coast to Bream Bay

Around 50km north of central Auckland the city's influence begins to wane, heralding the **Matakana Coast** (ⓦ www.matakanacoast.com), a 30km stretch of shallow harbours, beach-strung peninsulas and small islands. Its individual character becomes apparent, once you pass pretty **Warkworth** and head out either to **Kawau Island**, or up the coast to the village of **Matakana** and the snorkelling and diving nirvana of **Goat Island**.

There's little to detain you on SH1 between Warkworth and Waipu as it passes the road junction at **Brynderwyn**, where SH12 loops off to Dargaville, the Waipoua kauri forest and the Hokianga Harbour. If you're heading north and want a scenic route, it's better to stay on the coast and follow **Bream Bay**, named by Cook when he visited in 1770 and his crew hauled in tarakihi, which they mistook for bream. There are no sizeable towns here, only the small beach communities of **Mangawhai Heads** and **Waipu Cove**, looking out to the **Hen and Chicken Islands**, refuges for rare birds such as the wattled saddleback.

Warkworth and around

The peaceful and slow-paced rural town of **WARKWORTH** only really comes to life in high summer when thousands of yachties moor their boats in the numerous estuaries and coves nearby. From the late 1820s for about a century, the languid stretch of river behind the town seethed with boats shipping out kauri: a boardwalk now traces its shores past the *Jane Gifford* (ⓦ www.janegifford.org.nz), a rebuilt scow which once worked the shallow waterways and now runs occasional trips (1hr; $15).

Spend a few minutes at the **Warkworth and Districts Museum**, signposted 3km south off SH1 on Tudor Collins Drive (daily: Nov–March 9am–4pm; April–Oct 9am–3.30pm, $6), which explores the region's history through re-created rooms, and a 5m-long, 130-link chain carved from a single piece of kauri. The two ancient kauri outside mark the start of two well-presented

2

twenty-minute boardwalk nature trails through the preserved bush of the **Parry Kauri Park** (9am–dusk; donation). A free leaflet at the museum's entrance explains the trees in detail.

The best outing in these parts is to the **Brick Bay Sculpture Trail**, Arabella Lane, 6km west of Warkworth (daily 10am–5pm; $10; ☎09/425 4690, ⓦwww .brickbaysculpture.co.nz), a perfect combination of art, wine and stylish architecture all delivered in an understated Kiwi fashion. An hour wandering the 2km-long bush and parkland trail past round fifty sculptures (almost all by New Zealand artists and all for sale) is rewarded by tastings of the four excellent estate-grown wines ($5) in a delightful glasshouse set over the outflow of a small lake. The rosé goes particularly well with one of the delicious antipasto platters for two ($26) or olive oil taster ($8).

Practicalities

Warkworth's **i-SITE visitor centre**, in the centre of town at 1 Baxter St (Nov–Easter Mon–Fri 8.30am–5pm, Sat & Sun 9am–4pm; Easter–Oct Mon–Fri 9am–4.30pm, Sat & Sun 9am–3pm, ☎09/425 9081, ⓦwww.warkworthnz .com), has **internet access** and is where InterCity/Northliner and Naked buses stop.

Nearby **accommodation** includes: camping at the old-fashioned, estuaryside *Sandspit Holiday Park*, 1334 Sandspit Rd (☎09/425 8610, ⓦwww.sandspitholiday park.co.nz; camping $15, cabins ❶) with free use of canoes, dinghies and a small golf course; a studio loft overlooking the vines at Cedarhouse, 450 Matakana Rd, 3km northeast of Warkworth (☎09/425 0952, ⓦwww.cedarhouse-bb.co.nz; ❺); and *Rosemount Homestead*, 25 Rosemount Rd, 4km northeast of Warkworth (☎09/422 2580, ⓦwww.rosemount.co.nz; ❼) three delightful suites (all with private bathroom) in a lovingly restored kauri homestead dating from 1900, with wraparound verandas, extensive gardens and a pool.

You can **eat** well in town (where the New World supermarket is the only one in the area), or at the nearby vineyards (see opposite). For light meals overlooking the river visit *Ducks Crossing Café*, Riverview Plaza, though the coffee's better at *Ginger*, 21 Queen St. In the evening visit *Tahi*, in the alley opposite the i-SITE, 1 Neville St, a tapas bar stocking a good range of boutique beers. Order fish and chips next door if you prefer.

Kawau Island

With a resident population of around seventy (plus lots of weekenders), **KAWAU ISLAND** is chiefly given over to holiday homes each with its own wharf. Unless you have your own boat, however, you'll most likely only visit the grand, kauri-panelled **Mansion House** (mid-Dec to Feb daily noon–3.30pm; March to mid-Dec Mon–Fri noon–2pm Sat & Sun noon–3.30pm; $4), the former private home of George Grey – then doing his second stint as New Zealand's governor – and furnished much as it would have been in Grey's time, including his writing desk, books and some silverware.

Grey's pursuit of the Victorian fashion for all things exotic resulted in **grounds** stocked with flora and fauna from all over the world, such as Chilean wine palms and coral trees. He also brought in four species of **wallaby**, which have overtaken the island and have to be regularly culled. You might even see Australian kookaburras and a white peacock. A path runs through the gardens to the tiny beach at **Lady's Bay** (5min) and on to a network of short tracks that weave through pine forest and kanuka scrub. The most popular destination is the ruins of the island's old **copper mine** (40min each way).

Practicalities

Boats to Kawau Island leave from the wharf (parking $10/24hr) at **Sandspit**, a small road-end community on the Matakana Estuary, 8km east of Warkworth. Throughout the year, Reubens (℡0800/111 616, ⓦwww.reubens.co.nz) operates the **Royal Mail Run** (daily 10.30am; 4hr; $65 return; $87 with BBQ lunch), delivering mail, papers and groceries to all the wharves on the island and giving you around an hour and a half ashore at Mansion House Bay. Reubens also runs one or two Mansion House Bay trips daily with roughly twice the time ashore ($47). Bring whatever you need to Kawau: there are no shops, though the licensed **café** at Mansion House Bay is open for lunches ($16–18) and sometimes dinner.

Matakana and around

Over the last decade or so, **MATAKANA**, 9km northeast of Warkworth, has transformed itself from an inconsequential crossroads to the heart of a burgeoning **wine** region, and minor Slow Food centre. It is close enough to Auckland to attract weekenders who arrive for the farmers' market (Sat 8am–1pm) and stick around to visit the local boutique cinema, browse the shops (heritage butchers, quality bookshop, wine-tasting boutique etc) and visit the wineries.

The catalyst for the region's development was the **Morris & James Pottery & Tileworks**, 2km west of Matakana at Tongue Farm Road (Mon–Fri 8am–4.30pm, Sat & Sun 10am–5pm; free), which has been producing handmade terracotta tiles and large garden pots from local clay since the late 1970s. You can catch a free thirty-minute tour of the pottery (daily 11.30am) before a visit to the café/bar.

The widely available *Matakana Wine Trail* leaflet details seven **wineries** offering tastings (most for a small charge). First stop should be *Heron's Flight*, 49 Sharp Rd (daily from 9am; ℡09/422 7915, ⓦheronsflight.co.nz), where Italian Sangiovese and Dolcetto have been planted with considerable success. You can dine at the lovely **restaurant** overlooking the vines, or wander through the gardens of heritage plants and Maori medicinal herbs.

We've listed local **accommodation** under Warkworth and Leigh. There's plenty of good **eating** in Matakana mostly around the main intersection. Check out the organic ice creams and great smoothies at *Blue*, or the classy dining and tapas at *Tapiano* (℡09/423 0383), both at 2 Matakana Valley Rd. A short stroll away, *Matakana Patisserie*, 70 Matakana Valley Rd, does great pies, calzone and pastries.

Tawharanui Regional Park

Just past Matakana, a side road runs about 10km southeast to **Tawharanui Regional Park** (gates open daily 6am–dusk; free) with great beaches and swathes of regenerating bush. Predators have been eradicated and native birds are returning to this designated **open sanctuary**: come to swim, snorkel, picnic and walk or bike the easy trails, but you'll have to bring everything with you. The only facilities are the **campsite** ($10; book ahead on ℡09/366 2000).

Leigh and Goat Island

East of Matakana, the road runs 13km to the village of **LEIGH**, and a picturesque harbour with bobbing wooden fishing boats. Heading a further 4km northeast brings you to the **Cape Rodney–Okakari Marine Reserve**, usually known simply as **Goat Island** for the bush-clad islet 300m offshore. In 1975, this became New Zealand's first marine reserve, with no-take areas stretching 5km along the shoreline and 800m off the coast. Some 35 years on, the undersea life is thriving, with large rock lobster and huge snapper. Feeding has been discouraged since blue maomaos developed a taste for frozen peas and began to mob swimmers and divers. Easy beach access (from the road-end parking area), clear water, rock pools on wave-cut platforms, a variety of undersea terrains and relatively benign currents combine to make this an enormously popular year-round diving spot, as well as a favourite summer destination for families: aim to come midweek if you value tranquillity.

In fine weather, join 45-minute **glass-bottomed boat tours** around the island on the *Aquador* (several trips daily; $25; ☎09/422 6334, ⓦwww.glassbottomboat .co.nz), which depart from the beach. **Snorkellers** can enjoy a lush world of kelp forest with numerous multicoloured fish; those who venture deeper find more exposed seascapes with an abundance of sponges. Rent snorkelling gear at the beach (summer only) or from **Seafriends**, about 1km along Goat Island Road (daily 9am–7pm; ☎09/422 6212, ⓦwww.seafriends.org.nz), a marine education centre with an array of **aquarium** tanks recreating different Goat Island ecosystems; it rents dive gear for use off the beach and has a small café. The highly professional Goat Island Dive, 142a Pakiri Rd, Leigh (summer daily plus winter weekends; ☎0800/348 369, ⓦwww.goatislanddive.co.nz), rents mask, snorkel and fins ($21) plus full **dive** gear and also runs trips to Goat Island Marine Reserve and beyond.

Practicalities

Facilities are limited around Leigh, and without your own wheels, your only transport option is a taxi from Matakana: Matakabs (☎0800/522 743) runs a fleet of hybrids. You can **stay** at the welcoming *Goat Island Camping & Backpackers* (☎09/422 6185, ⓦwww.goatislandcamping.co.nz; camping $18, cabins & on-site caravans ❷), about 500m back from the reserve on the way to Goat Island, which has great bay views, plus snorkel gear rental. ⚐ *The Leigh Sawmill Café*, 142 Pakiri Rd (☎09/422 6019, ⓦwww.sawmillcafe.co.nz), has five spacious en-suite doubles (❺), a self-contained cottage (❻), two dorms ($25, $40 with bedding) and a communal kitchen. The sawmill has been sensitively converted into a smart café/ bar (closed Mon–Wed in winter) serving fine gourmet pizzas and beers brewed on site; weekends typically draw touring bands.

Pakiri

There's not much to **PAKIRI**, 10km north of Leigh, except for a long, dune-backed white surf beach that makes a perfect setting for **horseriding** with the

▲ Horseriding on Pakiri Beach

wonderful Pakiri Beach Horse Rides, Rahuikiri Road (℡09/422 6275, Ⓦwww
.horseride-nz.co.nz), which operates year-round and runs a pleasant café. Rides
($110/2hr, $155/half-day, $255/full day) go along the beach, among the dunes,
across streams and through a pohutukawa glade, with excellent overnight trips
through native bush and along the tops of sea cliffs ($795) and even an epic
seven-day Coast-to-Coast ride. There's good reason to stay over in the farm's range
of attractive on-site accommodation: riverside backpacker cabins ($30), self-
contained beachside cabins for two (Ⓞ), a family cabin for seven (Ⓞ) and a
luxurious four-bedroom beach house from $500 a day for up to eight. Campers
can stay nearby at the well-sited *Pakiri Beach Holiday Park*, Pakiri River Road
(℡09/422 6199, Ⓦwww.pakiriholidaypark.co.nz; camping $15, dorms $25,
en-suite cabins Ⓞ, studios Ⓞ, beachfront cottages Ⓞ), which also has a luxury
beachfront lodge sleeping four (Ⓞ plus $50/extra adult).

Mangawhai Heads and around

Back on SH1 and heading north, your next chance to turn off towards the coast is
at the small roadside settlement of **TE HANA**, 4km north of Wellsford. Here
you'll find **The Arts Factory** (Mon–Fri 9am–5pm, Sat & Sun by appointment;
℡09/423 8069, Ⓦwww.artprimitiveandmodern.com), where artist Kerry
Strongman runs an innovative gallery specializing in work by Maori artists – check
out his giant kauri "jewellery".

From here it is 20km along winding country roads to tiny **Mangawhai**, where
the Smashed Pipi gallery, 40 Moir St (daily 9am–5.30pm), comes crammed with
colourful glass, jewellery, woven flax, ceramics and funky clothing.

The road continues 3km north to meet the coast at **Mangawhai Heads** at the
mouth of the Mangawhai Harbour, marked by holiday homes straggling over the
hillsides behind a fine surf beach. Long a Kiwi summer-holiday favourite,
Mangawhai Heads is relaxed outside the peak summer blitz and is chiefly of
interest for the scenic **Mangawhai Cliffs Walkway** (2–3hr; closed July–Sept for
lambing). Walk north along the beach for fifteen minutes then follow the orange
markers up through bush-backed farmland along the top of the sea cliffs until the
path winds back down to the beach. Provided the tide is below half, you can return
along the beach through a small rock arch.

Practicalities

For hostel **accommodation** head straight for *Coastal Cow Backpackers*, 299 Molesworth Drive (℡09/431 5246; dorms $23, rooms Ⓞ), in a pleasant modern house.
There's far more luxury at *Milestone Cottages by the Sea*, 27 Moir Point Rd
(℡09/431 4018, Ⓦwww.milestonecottages.co.nz; studio Ⓞ, cottages Ⓞ–Ⓞ), a
cluster of beautiful timber and mud-brick cottages amid sumptuous organic
gardens and coastal bush within sight of the sea; it's just a short walk to a secluded
estuary beach. All are self-catering including a BBQ deck, and there's free use of a
saltwater lap pool and kayaks. Check the website for dates of the yurt yoga and
meditation retreats in winter and spring.

At Mangawhai Heads, **eat** at the licensed *Naja Garden Café*, in a garden centre
at 5 Molesworth Drive (℡09/431 4111), which makes a fine stop for a coffee
and breakfast, or gourmet sandwiches. Back in Mangawhai, head to ⅄ *Bennetts
Café*, 52 Moir St (℡09/431 5500); it serves superb breakfasts and lunches with
considerable finesse, does fine dinners at weekends and nightly in summer, and
makes delicious chocolates on site. Around the corner, the Smashed Pipi (see
above) has a decent daytime café and a bar which serves thin-crust pizzas and
bar meals.

Lang's Beach and Waipu Cove

Surfing and swimming are superb at both **Lang's Beach**, 12km north of Mangawhai Heads, and a further 4km north at **WAIPU COVE**, just a cluster of houses, a dairy/takeaway and a few places to stay beside a sweeping stretch of Bream Bay. **Accommodation** includes the extensive, beachside (and packed in Jan) *Camp Waipu Cove*, 897 Cove Rd (T09/432 0410, Wwww.campwaipucove. com; $30–34/site, cabins ❶–❹, s/c units ❸–❺), and a dozen stylish, state-of-the-art poolside self-contained apartments at the *Waipu Cove Resort*, 891 Cove Rd (T09/432 0348, Wwww.waipucoveresort.co.nz; ❺). Alternatively, go for the modern cottages at the secluded *Waipu Cove Cottages and Camping*, 685 Cove Rd (T09/432 0851, Wwww.waipucovecottages.co.nz; tents $34, rooms ❶, cottages ❹–❺), with free use of dinghies. Half a kilometre further on, the ⚲ *Stone House* (T09/432 0432 Wwww.stonehousewaipu.co.nz; dorms $25, s/c cabin & cottage ❹) occupies a couple of lovely buildings with grounds running down to the estuary, which you can explore with the free dinghies and kayaks; there's free wi-fi and great breakfasts for $10. The *Waipu Cove Resort* is also home to the only **restaurant**, the excellent ⚲ *Beach House* (T09/432 0877; closed Mon, & Tues in winter) where menus are printed on paper bags and the succulent, "retro" fish and chips ($26) comes elegantly wrapped in newspaper. Most mains are around $30 and the restaurant opens onto a deck in warm weather.

Waipu and around

The quirky village of **WAIPU** is dominated by an Aberdeen granite monument topped by a Scottish lion rampant. It's a nod to the nine hundred Scottish settlers who followed charismatic preacher, the Reverend Norman McLeod, here in the mid-1800s. The excellent **Waipu Museum** on the main street (daily 9.30am–4.30pm; $8) tells the tale of their journey via Nova Scotia where famine and a series of harsh winters drove them on to form a strict, self-contained Calvinist community. All is admirably illustrated, with everything from McLeod's old pocket watch to genealogical records that are regularly consulted by Kiwi Scots tracing their ancestry. On New Year's Day, Waipu hosts its **Highland Games** (Wwww.highlandgames.co.nz), in which competitors heft large stones and toss cabers and sheaves in Caledonian Park. Nearby, the **Waipu Caves** make a popular excursion to view one of the longest stalagmites in New Zealand in a 200m glowworm-filled passage, in the limestone country 16km to the northwest. Obtain a free map from the visitor centre in the Waipu Museum, wear old clothes and good footwear, and take a couple of good torches. The cave is signposted from Waipu Caves Road and is impenetrable after heavy rain; you'll get muddy even in dry weather, but there's a cold shower by the caves.

North from Waipu, the road runs parallel to Bream Bay. At **Uretiti**, 6km north of Waipu, there's a wonderful long white **beach** backed by a primitive DOC camping area ($7–9), with water and cold showers, and an adjacent unofficial naturist beach.

Practicalities

InterCity/Northliner **buses** drop off and pick up on request outside the Pear Tree gift shop on the main street (T09/432 0046), which also acts as a ticket agent. NakedBus stops a block away outside the Waipu Museum which contains the town's **visitor centre** (daily 9.30am–4.30pm; T09/432 0746) and has **internet access**.

There's a better range of places to stay down the road at Waipu Cove, but you'll find welcoming budget **accommodation** here at *Waipu Wanderers*, 25 St Mary's Rd (T09/432 0532, Ewaipu.wanderers@xtra.co.nz; dorm $28, rooms ❶), which has beds in a separate house with its own kitchen and bathroom, within easy walking distance of the town centre.

The are a couple of cafés on the main street, and for tasty **meals** head for the ↟*Pizza Barn*, 2 Cove Rd (℡09/432 1011; closed April–Nov Mon & Tues and all of June) in Waipu's former post office. It serves well-priced lunches and dinners (mains $15–19), including pizzas with all sorts of elaborate topping combos. Eat in the cosy corrugated iron, timber and McLeod tartan-decorated dining room bar, or in the garden room filled with surfboards and hibiscus flower candles; and peek inside the toilets, which are a veritable art installation of 1950s kitsch.

Whangarei and around

Despite its prime gateway location to Whangarei Heads' sweeping beaches and world-class diving around the Poor Knights Islands, Northland's capital, **WHANGAREI** (pronounced Fahn-ga-ray), remains refreshingly down to earth, with a laidback local vibe and a complete absence of tourism overkill. The main focal point for visitors is the riverside Town Basin, where sleek yachts moor outside a small redeveloped settler-style shopping and restaurant complex. Elsewhere there's a smattering of museums and rewarding walks, particularly the scenic track to Whangarei Falls.

Arrival, information and accommodation

InterCity/Northliner and Naked **buses** pull up on Bank Street, the hub of the skeletal local town bus service that runs frequently on weekdays, slightly less so on Saturday, and not at all on Sunday. Several daily **flights** from Auckland arrive at Onerahi Airport, 5km east of town and linked to Whangarei by local bus and taxi firms such as Kiwi Carlton Cabs (℡0800/455 555). The main **i-SITE visitor centre** lies 2km south of town on the main route from Auckland at 92 Otaika Rd (Nov–Easter Mon–Fri 8.30am–5.30pm Sat & Sun 9am–5pm; Easter–Oct Mon–Fri 8.30am–5pm, Sat & Sun 9am–4.30pm; ℡09/438 1079, ⓦwww.whangareinz .com), and there's a more central branch in the foyer of Chapham's Clocks, Town Basin (daily 9am–5pm; ℡09/438 3993); both have **internet access**.

Accommodation in Whangarei is seldom hard to find and prices are reasonable.

Hotels, motels and B&Bs

Cypress Court Motel 29 Kamo Rd ℡0800/429 773, ⓦwww.cypresscourt.co.nz. Clean and well-maintained motel 1.5km north of the centre with spacious studios with kitchen, and a huge DVD collection. ❹

Lake House 212 Pukeatua Rd, 12km west of Whangarei along SH14 ℡09/434 8084, ⓦwww .lakehouse.net.nz. A Flemish tapestry and polished concrete floors combine in this modern, rural lodge filled with antiques. Both of its two rooms are beautifully appointed, come with farmland and lake views and include a delicious breakfast. Three-course dinners ($65 including wine) on request. ❼

Lodge Bordeaux 361 Western Hills Drive ℡09/438 0404, ⓦwww.lodgebordeaux.co.nz.

Elegant modern motel with a heated outdoor pool. All rooms come with a/c, heated tile floors, spa bath and DVD players, and some have dishwashers. Studios ❻, suites ❼

↟ **Tidesong** Beasley Rd, Onerahi ℡09/436 1959, ⓦwww.tidesong.co.nz. Peaceful and very welcoming B&B around 25min drive east of Whangarei surrounded by bush and overlooking the mangrove-filled Taiharuru Estuary. You get a spacious s/c apartment, or smaller room, free kayaks and even a putting course around the gardens. Home-cooked meals are available (lunch $10, dinner $30–35) and there's an outdoor pizza oven. Apartment ❻, room ❹

↟ **Whangarei Views** 5 Kensington Heights Rise ℡09/437 6238, ⓦwww.whangarei views.co.nz. It is hard to resist the long views

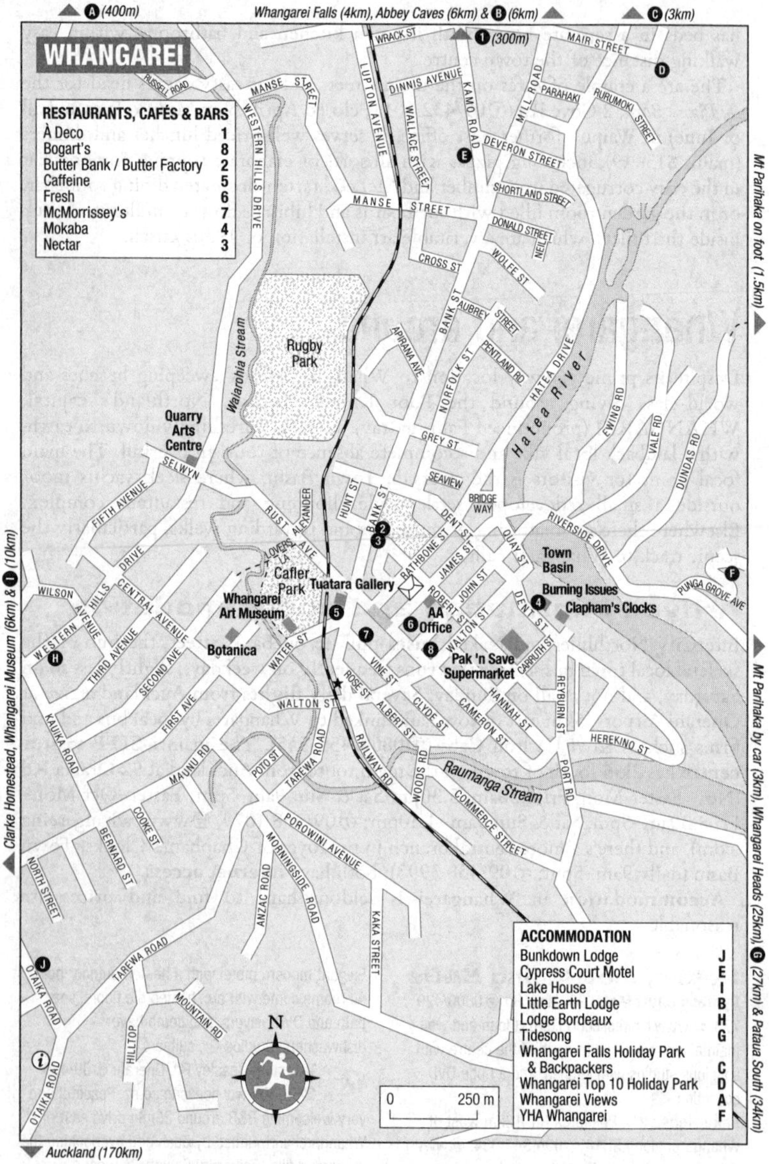

WHANGAREI
A (400m)
Whangarei Falls (4km), Abbey Caves (6km) & B (6km)
C (3km)
1 (300m)
RESTAURANTS, CAFÉS & BARS
À Deco 1
Bogart's 8
Butter Bank / Butter Factory 2
Caffeine 5
Fresh 6
McMorrissey's 7
Mokaba 4
Nectar 3
ACCOMMODATION
Bunkdown Lodge J
Cypress Court Motel E
Lake House I
Little Earth Lodge B
Lodge Bordeaux H
Tidesong G
Whangarei Falls Holiday Park & Backpackers C
Whangarei Top 10 Holiday Park D
Whangarei Views A
YHA Whangarei F
Rugby Park
Quarry Arts Centre
Cafler Park
Tuatara Gallery
Whangarei Art Museum
Botanica
AA Office
Pak 'n Save Supermarket
Town Basin
Burning Issues
Clapham's Clocks
Hatea River
Waiarohia Stream
Raumanga Stream
Mt Parihaka on foot (1.5km)
Mt Parihaka by car (3km), Whangarei Heads (25km), G (27km) & Pataua South (34km)
Clarke Homestead, Whangarei Museum (6km) & I (10km)
Auckland (170km)
0 250 m
N

over the town and modern accommodation kept tidy by a well-travelled Swiss–British couple who will share their passion for the area (and even guide tours). Choose from a comfortable en-suite room with deep bath or a fully s/c two-bedroom apartment with a deck and BBQ. Breakfast can be served in your room. Apartment ❻, room ❹

Hostels and campsites

Bunkdown Lodge 23 Otaika Rd ⓣ09/438 8886, ⓦwww.bunkdownlodge.co.nz. An ageing, low-key hostel with dorms and rooms in and around a pretty 1903 villa. There are two kitchens, a bath, piano and heaps of DVDs, and the owners go out of their way to help with local info. Dorms $25, linen rental $3, made-up rooms ❶

Little Earth Lodge 85 Abbey Caves Rd ☏ 09/430 6562, ⓦ www.littleearthlodge .co.nz. Tucked into a pastoral valley 7km northeast of Whangarei, beside Abbey Caves this hostel has one three-bed share and four double/twins, a DVD lounge, gear to explore the caves and free-range eggs if you are quick. Closed July–Sept. Dorms $28, rooms ❷

Whangarei Falls Holiday Park & Backpackers Ngunguru Rd at Tikipunga, 5km from town near Whangarei Falls ☏ 0800/227 222, ⓦ www. whangareifalls.co.nz. On the edge of the countryside, and with a pool and spa. Camping $15, dorms $23, cabins ❶

Whangarei Top 10 Holiday Park 24 Mair St ☏ 0800/455 488, ⓦ www.whangareitop10.co.nz. Small, tranquil and friendly site in a pretty setting 2km north of town with a wide range of accommodation. Free bikes. Camping $18, dorms $26, cabins ❷, en-suite cabins & s/c units ❹

YHA Whangarei 52 Punga Grove Ave ☏ 09/438 8954, ⓔ yha.whangarei@yha.co.nz. Intimate, sociable hostel a steep 15min walk from the centre of Whangarei, with expansive views over town from several rooms, and glowworms a short walk away in the bush (torches available). Accommodation is in glass-fronted cabins and four- and six-bed dorms and there's wi-fi. Reception closed 1–5pm. Dorms $25, rooms ❷

The Town

Whangarei's most appealing features are its peaceful parks and easy walks within a few minutes of the town, the best of which are outlined in the free *Whangarei Walks* leaflet, from the i-SITE. Extensive views over the harbour and town are the reward for climbing to the sheet-metal war memorial atop **Mount Parihaka** (240m), which can be approached by car along Memorial Drive or on foot along the steep Ross Track (40min ascent) from the end of Dundas Road.

Central Whangarei

Based around an 1880s villa, the redeveloped **Town Basin** is a small, prettified zone with kauri and fudge shops and the **Burning Issues Gallery** (daily 10am–5pm; free), a glass and ceramics studio where you can watch glass-blowing. The main sight is **Clapham's Clocks** (daily 9am–5pm; $8), a museum packed with 1500 clocks ranging from mechanisms taken out of church towers to cuckoo clocks, as well as work-time recorders, domestic timepieces and all manner of ornamental clocks. The collection was started by English émigré, Archibald Clapham, who delighted in anything clockwork and fun. Be sure to join the free guided tours on which you'll learn why the mouse ran up the clock in *Hickory, Dickory Dock*, and see clock mechanisms put through their paces, all to the sound of constant tick-tocking. Outside is New Zealand's largest sundial.

In the centre of town, don't miss **Tuatara**, 29 Bank St (Mon–Fri 9.30am–5pm, Sat 9am–2.30pm, plus Dec & Jan Sun 10am–3pm; free), a small design store and gallery focusing on works by emerging Maori artists, fronted by an inventive shop stocking Maori-designed goods from contemporary clothing to fine jewellery and greenstone carving. Immediately west, the well-kept **Cafler Park** is pleasant for a stroll – head for the Rose Gardens and the adjacent **Whangarei Art Museum** (Tues–Fri 10am–4pm, Sat & Sun noon–4pm; donation requested), which houses a small permanent collection of heritage and contemporary New Zealand art. A footbridge crosses the stream running through Cafler Park to the cool, restful **Botanica**, First Avenue (daily 10am–4pm; free), a conservatory and cactus house also sheltering the country's largest public collection of native ferns. From here, it's ten minutes' walk but a step back in time to the **Quarry Arts Centre**, Selwyn Avenue (daily 9.30am–4.30pm; free), an artists' co-operative for the local vibrant crafts community. You're free to wander among shacks built from adobe, timber and corrugated iron and watch the artisans at work.

The Heritage Park and around

There is a collection of museums at **Heritage Park**, 6km southwest of Whangarei on SH14 (daily 10am–4pm; $10 combined ticket only). **Clarke Homestead**, a rare example of an unrestored original homestead, was built in 1886 for a Scottish doctor, Alexander Clarke. The house was at its most vibrant in the 1930s, when Alexander's son hosted high-society parties here, and much of what you see dates from that era. The **Whangarei Museum**, housed in a modern building in the homestead grounds, has an intriguing selection of objects relating to local history, flora and fauna and a small Maori collection. The prize exhibit is the *waka tupapuka*, a sixteenth-century wooden funerary chest decorated with bird-form carvings. The museum's Kiwi House is one of the best of its kind, well laid out and with clear views of the birds.

The adjacent **Whangarei Native Bird Recovery Centre** (Mon–Fri 10.30am–4.30pm; donation requested) attempts to rehabilitate birds that have been damaged in some way and can't fend for themselves. The star attraction is Woof-Woof the tui, who mimics his keeper perfectly and whistles *Pop Goes the Weasel*.

Whangarei Falls, the Kauri Park and Abbey Caves

A broad curtain of water cascades over a 26m basalt ridge into a popular swimming hole at **Whangarei Falls**, 5km northeast of the town centre. The nicest way to get here is to walk along a bushland walking trail following the Hatea River (90min one-way) from the Parihaka Scenic Reserve on the opposite shore from the Town Basin – the i-SITE has a route map.

A couple of kilometres before Whangarei Falls, Whareora Road branches off 1.5km to the **A.H. Reed Memorial Kauri Park**, where shady paths through native bush pass 500-year-old kauri trees – look out for the ten-minute Alexander Walk, which links with a short, sinuous **canopy boardwalk** high across a creek before reaching some fine kauri. From the Elizabeth track it is possible to link up with the trail along the Hatea River to Whangarei Falls (30min one-way).

Accessed from Whareora Road, the fluted and weather-worn limestone formations of **Abbey Caves** (unrestricted access) have stalactites and stalagmites in abundance, as well as glowworms. Armed with a torch plus a moderate level of fitness you can explore them at leisure. A little scrambling is required to get into the first, Organ Cave, where you can walk a couple of hundred metres along an underground stream: avoid after heavy rain. Middle Cave and Ivy Cave are badly signposted but, once found, are also worth exploring. *Little Earth Lodge*, next to the caves (see p.161), has gear and maps for guests.

Panoramic views of Whangarei Heads are best seen by **skydiving**. Tandem jumps with Ballistic Blondes (℡0800/695 867, ⓦwww.skydiveballisticblondes .co.nz) start from $245 including pick-up from accommodation around Whangarei.

Eating and drinking

Cafés and **restaurants** cluster around the Town Basin, with some emerging hotspots in the city centre. Pak 'n Save, on the corner of Robert and Carruth streets, has the cheapest groceries.

À Deco 70 Kamo Rd ℡09/459 4957. Probably Northland's finest restaurant, set in an elegant Art Deco home 2km north of the centre. Exquisite meals, full of complex flavours and textures, that might start with a superb wild mushroom soup ($13), followed by steamed Northland flounder with aniseed bisque (mains $34–38). Closed Sun & Mon.

Bogart's 84 Cameron St. Easy-going, licensed dinner restaurant that's lively at weekends and best value for its trad and gourmet pizzas (from $17).

Butter Bank/Butter Factory 84 Bank St. Whangarei's liveliest bar often with DJs or a band at weekends. Two floors down is the *Butter Factory*, a dark wine bar (open Wed–Sat) that's all exposed rock walls, heavy beams and leather sofas.

Caffeine 4 Water St. Relaxed café with tasty muffins and wraps plus seasonal lunch mains (around $13–17) in hearty portions plus good strong coffee.
Fresh 12 James St. Airy, licensed, daytime café with a great range of focaccia and salads – roasted vegetable and quinoa, for example – with imaginative daily lunch specials mostly under $15.
McMorrissey's 7 Vine St. Northland's best (in fact only) Irish bar, generally pretty chilled and with simple and reliable bar meals (around $15). Live music at weekends.

Mokaba Town Basin. The pick of Town Basin's cafés, with outside seating overlooking the yachts, decent coffee, cool music and fresh, healthy fare (mains $14–18).
Nectar 88 Bank St ⑦09/438 8084. Stylish, contemporary café/restaurant with big windows overlooking the CBD's rooftops. Classy breakfasts ($12–18), and dishes such as tea-smoked salmon fettuccini ($18) and mussels in a Thai green sauce ($18). Closed Sun, & Mon evening.

Around Whangarei

It's worth hanging around Whangarei to explore the surrounding area, particularly to the east and north of the town where craggy, weathered remains of ancient volcanoes abut the sea. Southeast of the town, **Whangarei Heads** is the district's volcanic heartland where dramatic walks follow the coast to calm harbour beaches and windswept coastal strands. To the northeast, **Tutukaka** acts as the base for dive trips to the undersea wonderland around the **Poor Knights Islands**.

The only public transport from Whangarei to Tutukaka is with Tutukaka Shuttle ($15 each way if you're not diving; ⑦021/901 408), which are coordinated with dive trip departure and return times.

Whangarei Heads

The winding road around the northern side of Whangarei Harbour runs 35km southeast to **Whangarei Heads**, a series of small, residential beach communities scattered around jagged volcanic outcrops that terminate at Bream Head, the northern limit of Bream Bay. Stop for safe swimming at **McLeod Bay**, or continue until the road leaves the harbour and climbs to a saddle at the start of an excellent, signposted **walk** (3km return; 2hr–2hr 30min; 200m ascent) up the 430m **Mount Manaia**, crowned with five eroded pinnacles shrouded in legend, explained locally. The pinnacles remain *tapu*, but you can climb to their base through native bush, passing fine viewpoints. Beyond Mount Manaia, the road runs for 5km to **Urquharts Bay**, where a short walk (20min each way) leads to the white-sand **Smugglers Cove**. These and other walks are described in DOC's *Whangarei District Walks* leaflet, available from the i-SITE.

There's a gorgeous surf beach at the holiday community of **Pataua South**, 30km east of Whangarei, backed by the simple *Treasure Island Motor Camp* (⑦09/436 2390, ⑩www.treasureislandnz.co.nz; camping $12, peak season $18), which is treasured by in-the-know Kiwis and runs a general store/takeaway and bakery (Dec–Feb only) serving coffee and croissants. A footbridge over the estuary leads to another sweeping surf beach at Pataua North. *Tidesong* B&B (see p.159) is 6km to the southeast and serves tea, coffee and cakes to passers-by.

Tutukaka and the Poor Knights Islands

Boats set out from tiny **TUTUKAKA** – set on a beautiful, deeply incised harbour 30km northeast of Whangarei – for one of the world's premier dive locations, the **Poor Knights Islands Marine Reserve**, 25km offshore. The warm East Auckland current and the lack of run-off from the land combine to create visibility approaching 30m most of the year, though in spring (roughly Oct–Dec) plankton can reduce it to 10–15m. The clear waters are home to New Zealand's most diverse range of sea life, including a few subtropical species found nowhere else, as well as a striking underwater landscape of near-vertical **rock faces** and arches that drop almost 100m.

163

The Poor Knights lie along the migratory routes of a number of **whale** species, so blue, humpback, sei and minke whales, as well as dolphins, are not uncommon. The waters north and south of Tutukaka are home to two navy **wrecks**. The survey ship HMNZS *Tui* was sunk in 1999 to form an artificial reef, and it was so popular with divers and marine life that the obsolete frigate *Waikato* followed two years later.

Diving, snorkelling and sightseeing

Snorkellers, novice divers and experts all get a huge kick from visiting the **Poor Knights**. The largest and best operator is the thoroughly professional Dive Tutukaka, Marina Road, Tutukaka (℗0800/288 882, ⓦwww.diving.co.nz), which leaves from Tutukaka (with pick-ups from Whangarei at no extra charge) several times a day from November to April, and usually offers at least one trip a day for the rest of the year. It has several boats, so you are typically with similarly skilled divers. Two-dive trips ($130; including gear $225) also carry snorkellers and sightseers ($130), and everyone can use the on-board kayaks. Those with significant dive experience can explore the two wrecks on two-dive trips (also $130); first-timers can try a **discover scuba** dive ($275) with full gear and one-to-one instruction; a five-day PADI open-water dive qualification costs $695.

Dive Tutukaka also runs a **cruise boat** on the Perfect Day trip (5hr; $129), which takes you out for a look around the Poor Knights Islands then deep into Rikoriko Cave, the world's largest known sea cave, which penetrates 130m into the island. There's also time for snorkelling and kayaking.

Big-game fishing

Fishing for marlin, shark and tuna outside the Poor Knights Reserve (Dec–April) can be done by taking a quarter-share of a charter game-fishing boat for the day (around $250–300): for a list of operators contact the Whangarei Deep Sea Anglers Club (daily 8am–6pm during season; ℗09/434 3818, ⓦwww.sportfishing.co.nz).

Practicalities

The only amenities around the harbour at Tutukaka are **restaurants**, most notably the *Schnappa Rock Café*, Marina Road (℗09/434 3774; daily 8am–late), a groovy bar/restaurant turning out a tempting range of dishes (mains $28–34), including vegetarian, as well as bar snacks; it's buzzing with divers, and it always pays to book ahead for dinner in summer.

Accommodation is more scattered. Handiest is *Tutukaka Holiday Park*, Matapouri Road (℗09/434 3938, ⓦwww.tutukaka-holidaypark.co.nz; camping $15, dorms $25, cabins ❷), two minutes' walk from the harbour, and very busy in January and February. There's a retro feel to the 1960s *Sands Motel*, Tutukaka Block Road, Whangaumu Bay (℗09/434 3747, ⓦwww.sandsmotel.co.nz; Jan & Feb ❻, otherwise ❹), with two-bedroom units beautifully set beside a nice beach 4km off the highway; while *Pacific Rendezvous*, Motel Road, off the Tutukaka Block Road (℗0800/999 800, ⓦwww.oceanresort.co.nz; ❻), is fabulously sited on a headland overlooking Tutukaka's harbour and the Poor Knights and offers self-contained suites and apartments, as well as chalets with decks, plus pool, tennis court and two private beaches.

Matarouri and Whale Bay

MATAPOURI, 6km north of Tutukaka, is a lovely holiday settlement which backs onto a curving white-sand bay bounded by bushy headlands which separate it from the pristine **Whale Bay**, signposted off Matapouri Road 1km further north and reached by a twenty-minute bushwalk. There are virtually no facilities along this stretch apart from a shop and takeaway at Matapouri.

North to the Bay of Islands

The roads that access the coast around Tutukaka and Matapouri rejoin SH1 at **Hikurangi** 16km north of Whangarei. About 6km further north you have a choice of routes: both go to the Bay of Islands but approach from different directions. Carry straight on and you go direct to Paihia with opportunities for side trips to the Maori redoubt of Ruapekapeka Pa, and the **Hundertwasser toilets** at Kawakawa. Turn right along Old Russell Road and you twist towards the coast on the tar-sealed but winding back road to Russell.

The direct route: along SH1

Sticking with SH1, a sign 17km north of Hikurangi directs you 5km northeast to **Ruapekapeka Pa** (unrestricted access; free), the site of the final battle in the War of the North in 1846. Hone Heke's repeated flagpole felling in Russell (see p.177) precipitated nine months of fighting during which Maori learnt to adapt their *pa* defences to cope with British firepower. The apotheosis of this development is Ruapekapeka, the "Bat's Nest". Its hilltop setting, double row of totara palisades and labyrinth of trenches and interconnecting tunnels helped Hone Heke and his warriors defend the site, despite being heavily outgunned and outnumbered three to one. Signs explain the full story and trench lines and bunkers are clearly visible.

Kawakawa

The direct route follows SH1 15km north of the Ruapekapeka junction to the small town of **KAWAKAWA**, and the celebrated **Hundertwasser toilets** on the main Gilles Street. These works of art were created in 1997 by the reclusive Austrian painter, architect, ecologist and philosopher, **Friedrich Hundertwasser**, who made Kawakawa his home from 1975 until his death in 2000, aged 71. The ceramic columns supporting the entrance hint at the interior's complex use of broken tiles, coloured bottles and found objects such as the old hinges on the wrought-iron doors. A steady trickle of visitors takes a peek in both the Gents and the Ladies after suitable warning. To learn more, pop along the street to the Kawakawa Theatre where a half-hour DVD on Hundertwasser in Kawakawa (daily 9am–5pm; $5) runs continuously.

Kawakawa is New Zealand's only town with a rail track running down the main street, something exploited by the Bay of Islands **Vintage Railway** (Fri, Sat & Sun 11am, noon & 1pm plus extra services during school holidays; $10; ☎09/404 0684, ⓦwww.bayofislandsvintagerailway.org.nz), with steam- and diesel-hauled 1930s carriages trundled 5km north then back. By 2011 they hope to have the line open to the coast at Opua, a 30km round-trip that'll take two hours.

Watch the trains from the comfort of the *Trainspotters Café*, 39 Gilles St, which serves light meals and good coffee.

The back road to Russell: Whangaruru Harbour and the Cape Brett Track

With time on your hands, the most scenic way to approach the Bay of Islands is along **Old Russell Road**, which spurs off SH1 towards the coast. The narrow and winding 70km run to Russell takes around two hours, but you can spin it out over a lot longer, admiring the wonderful coastline around the **Whangaruru Harbour**, stopping for swims at numerous gorgeous bays, and perhaps a short walk in the mixed kauri forest of the **Ngaiotonga Scenic Reserve**.

Leaving SH1 you travel through 14km of farmland before reaching ⌖ *The Gallery & Café Helena Bay Hill* (daily 10am–5pm; ☎09/433 9616, ⓦwww .galleryhelenabay.co.nz), an imaginative **gallery** coupled with a great German-run daytime **café** (Easter–Sept closed Mon–Wed) with views across bush-clad

The Cape Brett Track

Northland's best overnight tramp is the challenging but rewarding **Cape Brett Track** (20km each way; 6–8hr) which follows the hilly ridge along the centre of the peninsula with sea occasionally visible on both sides: a route outlined in DOC's *Cape Brett* leaflet. The former lighthouse keeper's house at the tip of the peninsula is now a DOC **hut** (23 beds; $12, annual hut pass not valid), in a fabulous location surrounded by sea and views out to the Hole in the Rock – you might want to stay more than one night. There are gas cooking stoves but no cooking utensils, and camping is not allowed.

The track starts in Rawhiti (see below) and crosses private land, so all walkers must pay a **track fee** ($30). The Russell Booking & Information Centre is the place to pay your track fee, book the DOC hut and ask about secure parking in Rawhiti. You might also enquire about a **water taxi** from Russell to Rawhiti (around $160 for up to 6 people), Deep Water Cove, three-quarters of the way along the track ($180) or Cape Brett ($220; conditions permitting).

hills down to Helena Bay. Stop for modern café food (along with schnitzel and strudel) if you're the slightest bit peckish as there's nowhere much to eat between here and Russell.

The first settlement is 11km on at **OAKURA**, where an island-studded bay is backed by a gently curving beach and a cluster of holiday homes. Not a great deal happens here, but that's the appeal, and there's no shortage of places to swim and walk.

Along the next stretch of road, at *Coast Road Farm*, 12km north of Oakura (☏09/433 6894, ⓦwww.thefarm.co.nz; camping $12, dorms $20, rooms ❶, and en suites ❷) you can get involved with dairy farm life, ride horses or motorbikes, go kayaking and much more. Meals (breakfast & lunch $7, dinner $15) are by arrangement.

At Ngaiotonga, a further 2km north, a sealed side road runs 8km through hilly farmland to the broad sweep of **Bland Bay** with great beaches on both sides of an isthmus. Continue 2km beyond Bland Bay to reach **Whangaruru North Head Scenic Reserve**, with yet more lovely beaches, fine walks around the end of the peninsula and a DOC campsite ($7–9) with water, toilets and cold showers.

Back on the coast road it is 7km north to a road junction where you turn left for Russell (25km further) and continue straight on for the scattered and predominantly Maori village of **Rawhiti**, the start of the Cape Brett Track (see box above). Just 1km along the Rawhiti road there's shorter, easier walking in the form of the **Whangamumu Track** (4km each way; 1hr; 150m ascent), a forest path which crosses the base of the Cape Brett Peninsula to a lovely beach. Here you can see the remains of a whaling station which closed in 1940.

Following the road towards Russell for 11km you'll come across a signposted side road to some fine stands of kauri. These can be visited on the **Twin Bole Track** (around 200m; 5min) and the **Kauri Grove Walk** (1km; 20min).

The Bay of Islands

THE BAY OF ISLANDS, 240km north of Auckland, lures visitors to its beautiful coastal scenery, scattered islands and clear blue waters. There are other equally stunning spots along the Northland coast, such as the Whangaroa and Hokianga harbours, but what sets the bay apart is the ease with which you can get out among the islands, and its pivotal history. This was the cradle of European

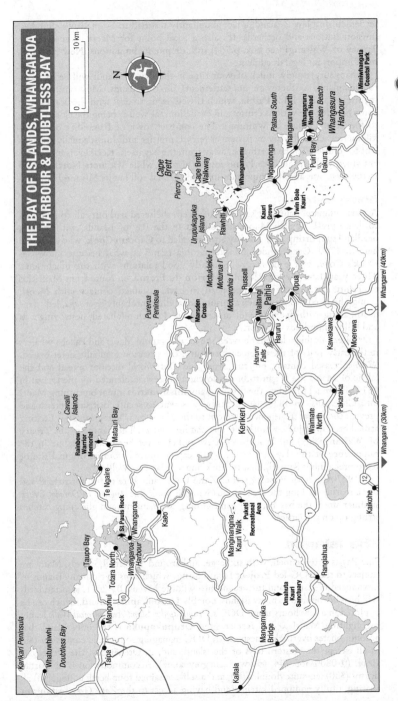

THE BAY OF ISLANDS, WHANGAROA HARBOUR & DOUBTLESS BAY

N

0   10 km

Karikari Peninsula

Whatuwhiwhi

Doubtless Bay

Taipa

Taupo Bay

Cavalli Islands

Mangonui

Totara North

Whangaroa Harbour

Matauri Bay

Te Ngaire

Rainbow Warrior Memorial

St Pauls Rock

Whangaroa

Kaeo

Manginangina Kauri Walk

Puketi Recreational Area

Omahuta Kauri Sanctuary

Mangamuka Bridge

Kaitaia

Rangiahua

Kaikohe

Kerikeri

Purerua Peninsula

Marsden Cross

Motuarohia I

Moturua I

Motukiekie I

Urupukapuka Island

Cape Brett Walkway

Cape Brett

Piercy I

Rawhiti

Kauri Grove

Twin Bole Kauri

Russell

Waitangi

Paihia

Haruru

Haruru Falls

Opua

Ngaiotonga

Whangamumu

Whangaruru North

Puriri Bay

Oakura

Pataua South

Whangaruru North Head

Ocean Beach

Whangasura Harbour

Mimiwhangata Coastal Park

Waimate North

Pakaraka

Kawakawa

Moerewa

Pakaraka

Waitangi (40km)

Whangarei (30km)

1

10

12

167

settlement in New Zealand, a fact abundantly testified to by the bay's churches, mission stations and orchards. It's also a focal point for Maori because of the **Treaty of Waitangi** (see box, p.764) still, despite its limitations, New Zealand's most important legal document.

Perhaps surprisingly, much of your time in the Bay of Islands will be spent on the mainland, as there are no settlements on the islands. Most visitors base themselves in beachside **Paihia**, which is well set up to deal with the hordes who come here for the various cruises and excursions, as well as being the closest town to the Treaty House at **Waitangi**. The compact town of **Russell**, a couple of kilometres across the bay by passenger ferry is prettier and almost equally convenient for cruises. To the northwest, away from the bay itself, **Kerikeri** is intimately entwined with the area's early missionary history, while **Waimate North**, inland to the west, was another important mission site and still has its Mission House.

Some history

A warm climate, abundant seafood and deep, sheltered harbours all contributed to dense pre-European **Maori settlement** in the Bay of Islands, with many a headland supporting a *pa*. The bay also appealed to **Captain Cook**, who anchored here in 1769. Cook landed on Motuarohia Island at what became known as Cook's Cove, where he forged generally good relations with the inhabitants. Three years later the French sailor **Marion du Fresne**, en route from Mauritius to Tahiti, became the first European to have sustained contact with Maori, though he fared less well when a misunderstanding, probably over *tapu*, led to his death, along with twenty-six of his crew. The French retaliated, destroying a *pa* and killing hundreds of Maori.

Despite amicable relations between the local Ngapuhi Maori and Pakeha whalers in the early years of the nineteenth century, the situation gradually deteriorated. With increased contact, firearms, grog and Old World diseases spread and the fabric of Maori life began to break down, a process accelerated by the arrival in 1814 of Samuel Marsden, the first of many **missionaries** intent on turning Maori into Christians. In 1833, James Busby was sent to secure British interests and prevent the brutal treatment meted out to the Maori by whaling captains. Lacking armed backup or judicial authority, he had little effect. The signing of the **Treaty of Waitangi** in 1840 brought effective policing yet heralded a decline in the importance of the Bay of Islands, as the capital moved from its original site of Kororareka (now Russell), first to Auckland and later to Wellington.

In 1927 American Western writer **Zane Grey** came here to fish for striped and black marlin, making the area famous with his book *The Angler's El Dorado*. Every summer since, the bay has seen game-fishing tournaments and glistening catches strung up on the jetties.

The islands

The Bay is aptly named, with six large, and around 140 small, islands. Many are subject to the DOC-led **Project Island Song**, which aims to rid many islands of introduced predators and turn them into wildlife havens. By 2011, assorted birds will be reintroduced to many islands, notably **Urupukapuka Island**, which can be explored in a few hours using DOC's *Urupukapuka Island Archeological Walk* leaflet highlighting Maori *pa* and terrace sites. **Urupukapuka** is the only island that accommodates overnight guests, with DOC managing some basic **campsites** ($8) in all except the western bays of the island, and, in Otehei Bay, the *Otehei Bay Resort* (℡0800/365 744, ⓦwww.zanegrey.co.nz). Accommodation is in spartan dorms ($30), en-suite doubles (ⓞ), and a self-contained four-berth cottage (ⓞ) all sharing a fully equipped kitchen and having access to the *Zane Grey* **restaurant**

and bar. The resort is run by Explore NZ, which runs regular cruises from Paihia and Russell stopping at Otehei Bay (summer only; $40 return).

Of the other large islands, by far the most popular is **Motuarohia** (aka **Roberton Island**) where DOC manages the most dramatic central section, an isthmus almost severed by a pair of perfectly circular blue lagoons. Snorkellers can explore an undersea nature trail waymarked by inscribed stainless-steel plaques.

Other sights that often feature on cruise itineraries include the **Black Rocks**, bare islets formed from columnar-jointed basalt – these rise only 10m out of the water but plummet a sheer 30m beneath. At the outer limit of the bay is the craggy peninsula of **Cape Brett**, named by Cook in 1769 after the then Lord of the Admiralty, Lord Piercy Brett. Cruises also regularly pass through the **Hole in the Rock**, a natural tunnel through Piercy Island, which is even more exciting when there's a swell running.

Paihia and Waitangi

PAIHIA is where it all happens, mostly on the 2km-long string of waterside motels, restaurants and holiday homes teeming with trip operators, backpacker hostels, party-oriented bars and hotels. Fortunately, Paihia's low-rise development is sympathetic to its three beautiful, flat bays looking towards Russell and the Bay of Islands, encircled by forested hills. A plaque outside the current St Paul's Anglican Church on Marsden Road marks the spot where, in 1831, the northern chiefs petitioned the British Crown for a representative to establish law and order. In 1833 King William IV finally addressed their concerns by sending the first British resident, James Busby. Busby built a house on a promontory 2km north across the Waitangi River in **WAITANGI** – the scene some seven years later of the signing of the **Treaty of Waitangi**, which ceded the nation's sovereignty to Britain in return for protection.

Arrival, information and getting around

InterCity/Northliner and Naked buses arrive on the Marsden Road outside the Bay of Islands' main **i-SITE visitor centre** (daily 8am–5pm, extended hours Oct–April; ℡09/402 7345, ℮paihia@visitnorthland.co.nz), which has **internet** access and books tours. Flights from Auckland arrive at the Bay of Islands **airport** 22km northwest, near Kerikeri, and are met by a shuttle bus ($55 to Paihia).

Paihia isn't big, and everywhere is within walking distance. If you've got bags to carry, engage the services of the **Paihia Tuk Tuk Shuttle Service**, based outside the i-SITE (℡027/486 6071), which will pick up and drop off two to six people pretty much anywhere in town for $5 each and run up to Haruru Falls for $8 each. Alternatively, you can rent good-quality **mountain bikes** from Bay Beach Hire, at the south end of Paihia Beach (℡09/402 6078; $15/half-day, $20/day, $25/overnight). **Parking** is tight in high season; your best bet is the pay-and-display car park opposite the 4-Square supermarket on Williams Road.

Paihia–Russell ferries

Sticking to the highways Russell is almost 100km from Paihia, but drivers can shorten that to 15km by using the small **vehicle ferry** (7am–10pm; daily every 20min; car & driver $10 each way, pedestrians $1; buy your ticket on board) across the narrow Veronica Channel at **OPUA**, 6km south of Paihia.

Foot passengers can take one of the frequent **passenger ferries** (Oct–May 7am–10pm; June–Sept 7am–7pm; $6 each way) between the main wharves in Paihia and Russell, a fifteen-minute journey.

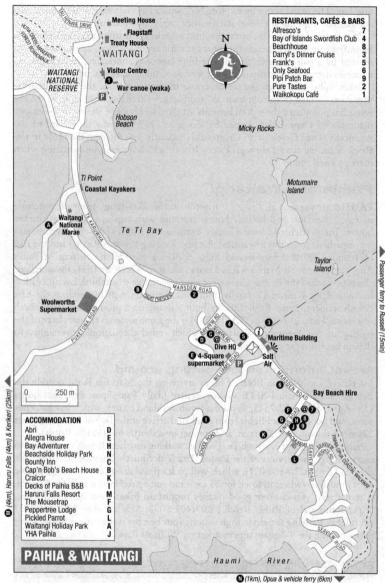

PAIHIA & WAITANGI

RESTAURANTS, CAFÉS & BARS
Alfresco's	7
Bay of Islands Swordfish Club	4
Beachhouse	8
Darryl's Dinner Cruise	3
Frank's	5
Only Seafood	6
Pipi Patch Bar	9
Pure Tastes	2
Waikokopu Café	1

ACCOMMODATION
Abri	D
Allegra House	E
Bay Adventurer	H
Beachside Holiday Park	N
Bounty Inn	C
Cap'n Bob's Beach House	B
Craicor	K
Decks of Paihia B&B	I
Haruru Falls Resort	M
The Mousetrap	F
Peppertree Lodge	G
Pickled Parrot	L
Waitangi Holiday Park	A
YHA Paihia	J

Accommodation

Paihia abounds in **accommodation** for all budgets though rates can be stratospheric during the couple of weeks after Christmas. B&Bs and homestays tend to vary their prices less than motels, and hostels maintain the same prices year-round. Motels and B&Bs are scattered, while Kings Road is a veritable backpackers' village with a selection of generally excellent places (though the street's bars make the area noisy at night). It is also worth considering **staying in**

the bay, either on Urupukapuka Island (see p.168) or taking an overnight cruise on *Ecocruz*, *Ipipiri* or *The Rock* (see p.174 for all).

Hotels, motels and B&Bs

Abri 10 Bayview Rd ☎09/402 8003, ✆www
.abri-accom.co.nz. Two high-standard individual
modern studio apartments plus a suite, in a pretty
bush setting with great views over the town and
bay from the sundecks. ❽

Allegra House 39 Bayview Rd ☎09/402
7932, ✆www.allegra.co.nz. A choice of
luxury B&B or s/c apartment in a big, light and
modern house at the top of a hill, and all with
stupendous views right out over the Bay of Islands.
All are a/c, sport their own balconies and have
access to a hot tub in native bush. B&B ❻,
apartment ❼

Bay Adventurer 28 Kings Rd ☎0800/112 127,
✆www.bayadventurer.co.nz. A kind of upmarket
backpackers resort with apartments, all nicely
laid out with an attractive pool, free bikes and
access to the nearby tennis courts (free in
winter). It is particularly good for its rooms and
fully s/c studio apartments. You can order
cooked and continental breakfasts. Dorms $26,
rooms ❸, apartments ❹

Bounty Inn Corner of Bayview & Selwyn rds
☎0800/472 444, ✆www.bountyinn.co.nz.
Pleasant, central yet quiet motel, 100m from the
beach and with ample off-street parking. Rooms
without cooking facilities, and fully equipped motel
units all come lined in timber with a sundeck or
balcony. Studios ❺, with kitchen ❻

Craicor 49 Kings Rd ☎09/402 7882, ✆www
.craicor-accom.co.nz. A couple of excellent-value
self-catering apartments, both spacious, well kept
and with limited sea views; plus an attractive
double room. Continental breakfast can be supplied
for $7.50. Room ❺, apartments ❻

Decks of Paihia B&B 69 School Rd ☎09/1402
6146, ✆www.decksofpaihia.co.nz. Welcoming
three-room B&B in a comfortable, modern house
with swimming pool set into large, sunny decks
high on the hill above Paihia. ❼

Hostels

Cap'n Bob's Beach House 44 Davis Crescent
☎09/402 8668, ✆www.capnbobs.co.nz. In Cap'n
Bob's absence, Kay runs a tight ship in this
attractive, well-maintained and homely hostel
away from the hubbub of Kings Rd. There are
good sea views and a separate women's dorm.
Dorms $26, rooms ❷, studio ❸

The Mousetrap 11 Kings Rd ☎0800/402 8182,
✆www.mousetrap.co.nz. Welcoming, nautically
themed, wood-panelled hostel that sets itself apart

from the other backpackers on this lively street.
With rooms scattered all over the site, three small
kitchens and a BBQ area it has an intimate feel,
plus there's free bike use and a decent sea view.
Dorms $23–26, rooms ❷

Peppertree Lodge 15 Kings Rd ☎09/402 6122,
✆www.peppertree.co.nz. Very clean, central hostel
with spacious eight-bunk dorms, four-bunk dorms
with own bathroom, great en-suite doubles and a
s/c flat. Guests can make use of a tennis court,
free good-quality bikes and kayaks, and there's
an excellent DVD library. Be sure to book ahead
Oct–April. Dorms $25-28, rooms ❷, flat ❹

Pickled Parrot Grey's Lane, off MacMurray Rd
☎0508/727 7682, ✆www.pickledparrot.co.nz.
Rocky the parrot presides over one of Paihia's
smaller and more relaxed hostels, tucked away in a
peaceful spot with a lovely courtyard. Secluded tent
sites; four- and six-bed dorms as well as singles,
doubles and twins, all with free continental
breakfast, plus free pick-ups, bikes and tennis
racquets. Camping $18, dorms $25, double & twin
rooms ❷

YHA Paihia Corner of Kings & MacMurray rd s
☎09/402 7487, @yha.paihia@yha.co.nz. Well-
maintained hostel with newly renovated kitchen
facilities, that attracts a friendly mix of travellers
and families. Most rooms and dorms have en
suites. Dorms $26–30, rooms ❸, apartment
sleeping six ❹

Campsites

Beachside Holiday Park SH11, 3km south of
Paihia ☎09/402 7678, ✆www.beachsideholiday
.co.nz. Small and peaceful waterside site with a
range of cabins and units, as well as dinghies and
kayaks for rent. Camping $15–18, cabins ❷,
en-suite cabins ❸

Haruru Falls Resort Puketona Rd, 4km north of
Paihia ☎0800/757 525, ✆www.harurufalls.co.nz.
Fabulous location by the river with commanding
views of Haruru Falls, offering riverside tent sites
and motel units around a pool. The resort has
outdoor games such as pétanque and volleyball, a
BBQ, and its own restaurant bar, plus kayaks and
pedalboats for rent. Camping $19, cabins ❷,
rooms & motel units ❺

Waitangi Holiday Park 21 Tahuna Rd, Waitangi
☎09/402 7866, ✆www.waitangiholidaypark
.co.nz. The closest campsite to both Waitangi and
Paihia (a 20min walk), this simple campsite has
sites overlooking the Waitangi River and four
spacious kitchen cabins. Camping $15, cabins ❷

The Town

Paihia is primarily a base for exploring the bay, and there are no sights in town itself. Fans of mangroves and estuarine scenery can tackle the gentle **Paihia–Opua Coastal Walkway** (6km; 90min–2hr one-way), which wanders along the wave-cut platforms and the small bays in between.

Waitangi Treaty Grounds

Crossing the bridge over the Waitangi River you enter the Waitangi Treaty Grounds, where in 1840 Queen Victoria's representative William Hobson and nearly fifty Maori chiefs signed the Treaty of Waitangi (see box, p.764). It's now home to the **Waitangi Visitor Centre and Treaty House** (daily: Oct–March 9am–6pm; April–Sept 9am–5pm; $20 valid for two consecutive days; free for NZ citizens), the single most symbolic place in New Zealand for Maori and Pakeha alike, and a focal point for the modern nation's struggle for identity. You can easily spend half a day here, taking in an audiovisual presentation that sets the historical framework, bolstered by a small exhibition of Maori artefacts, and perhaps a short daytime cultural performance or a guided tour (all $12), though most people give it around two hours then perhaps return for the **Culture North Night Show** (4–6 nights a week; $60; book ahead on ℡09/402 5990, ⊛culturenorth.co.nz), an excellent contemporary approach to presenting Maori culture conducted inside the traditional meeting house. Over an hour and a quarter you're introduced to an extended family as the stories of Maori life from the arrival of Kupe to the present day are enacted with verve mixing drama, song and dance with storytelling. Free pick-ups are available from Paihia.

The **Treaty House** was built in Georgian colonial style in 1833–34. Its front windows look towards Russell over sweeping lawns, where marquees were erected on three significant occasions: in 1834, when Maori chiefs chose the Confederation

The Treaty of Waitangi

The Treaty of Waitangi is the **founding document** of modern New Zealand, a touchstone for both Pakeha and Maori, and its implications permeate New Zealand society. Signed in 1840 between what were ostensibly two sovereign states – the United Kingdom and the United Tribes of New Zealand, plus other Maori leaders – the treaty remains central to New Zealand's **race relations**. The Maori rights guaranteed by it have seldom been upheld, however, and the constant struggle for recognition continues.

The treaty at Waitangi

Motivated by a desire to staunch French expansion in the Pacific, and a moral obligation on the Crown to protect Maori from rapacious land-grabbing by settlers, the British instructed naval captain William Hobson to negotiate the transfer of sovereignty with "the free and intelligent consent of the natives", and to deal fairly with the Maori. Hobson, with the help of James Busby and others, drew up both the English Treaty and a Maori "translation". On the face of it, the treaty is a straightforward document, but the complications of having two versions (see Contexts, p.764) and the implications of striking a deal between two peoples with widely differing views on land and resource ownership have reverberated down the years.

The treaty was unveiled on February 5, 1840, to a gathering of some 400 representatives of the five northern tribes in front of Busby's residence in Waitangi. Presented as a contract between the chiefs and Queen Victoria – someone whose role was comprehensible in chiefly terms – the benefits were amplified and the costs downplayed. As most chiefs didn't understand English, they signed the Maori version of the treaty, which still has *mana* (authority or status) among Maori today.

of Tribes flag, which now flies on one yardarm of the central flagpole; the meeting a year later at which northern Maori leaders signed the Declaration of Independence of New Zealand; and, in 1840, the signing of the Treaty of Waitangi itself.

The northern side of the lawn is flanked by the *whare runanga*, or **Maori meeting house**, built between 1934 and 1940 as a cooperative effort between all Maori. The interior richly carved panels represent all *iwi* (rather than the usual single tribe).

Housed in a specially built shelter in the Treaty House grounds is the world's largest **war canoe** (*waka*), the 35m-long *Ngatoki Matawhaorua*, named after the vessel navigated by Kupe when he discovered Aotearoa and built from two huge kauri. It has traditionally been launched each year on Waitangi Day, propelled by eighty warriors.

At **Haruru Falls**, 4km west of Waitangi (and accessed from the main road), the Waitangi River drops over a basalt lava flow, and though they're not that impressive by New Zealand standards, there's good swimming at their base. Haruru Falls are also reached from the Treaty House grounds via the very gentle **Hutia Creek Mangrove Forest Boardwalk** (2hr return) or on a guided **kayak** trip up the estuary and among the mangroves (see p.175).

Exploring the bay

Unless you get out onto the water you're missing the essence of the Bay of Islands. The vast majority of yachting, scuba-diving, dolphin-watching, kayaking and fishing trips start in Paihia, but all the major **cruises** and bay **excursions** also pick up in Russell. From December to March, when demand outstrips supply, everything should be booked a couple of days in advance. Most hotels and motels book these trips for you and hostels can usually arrange some sort of "backpacker" discount of around ten percent.

The treaty after Waitangi

The pattern set at Waitangi was repeated up and down the country, as seven copies of the treaty were dispatched to garner signatures and extend Crown authority over parts of the North Island that had not yet been covered, and the South Island. On May 21, before signed treaty copies had been returned, Hobson claimed New Zealand for Britain: the North Island on the grounds of cession by Maori, and the South Island by right of Cook's "discovery", as it was considered to be without owners, despite a significant Maori population.

Maori fears were alerted from the start, and as the settler population grew and demand for land increased, successive governments passed laws that gradually stripped Maori of control over their affairs – actions which led to the New Zealand Wars of the 1860s (see Contexts, p.766). Over the decades, small concessions were made, but nothing significant changed until 1973, when **Waitangi Day** (February 6) became an official national holiday. Around the same time, Maori groups, supported by a small band of Pakeha, began a campaign of direct action, increasingly disrupting commemorations, thereby alienating many Pakeha and splitting Maori allegiances between angry young urban Maori and the *kaumatua* (elders), who saw the actions as disrespectful to the ancestors and an affront to tradition. Many strands of Maori society were unified by the *hikoi* (march) to Waitangi to protest against the celebrations in 1985, a watershed year in which Paul Reeves was appointed New Zealand's first Maori Governor General and the **Waitangi Tribunal** for land reform was given some teeth.

Protests have continued since as successive governments have vacillated over whether to attend the commemorations at Waitangi.

Trips from the Bay of Islands

As the main tourist centre in Northland, the Bay of Islands acts as a staging post for forays further north, in particular for day-long bus tours to **Cape Reinga** and **Ninety Mile Beach** (see box, p.192) – arduous affairs lasting eleven hours, most of them spent stuck inside the vehicle. You're better off making your way up to Mangonui, Kaitaia or Ahipara and taking a trip from there.

Fullers Great Sights (see below) also runs Discover Hokianga (daily; 7.5hr; $93) a bus tour visiting the **Hokianga Harbour**, taking a Footprints Waipoua tour to the giant **kauri trees**, and taking a look at the **Wairere Boulders**.

Cruises, sailing and dolphin encounters

Whether you want a simple leisurely cruise, or a full-on day combining dolphin swimming, cruising and sailing, chances are you'll find something to suit. The Bay's two main operators are Fullers Great Sights, and Explore NZ/Dolphin Discoveries, both offering a wide selection of sightseeing, sailing and dolphin trips – we've listed the best below. There are also numerous smaller **yachts** which usually take less than a dozen passengers and go out for around six hours: competition is tight and standards high. Most cruises and sailing trips will give you a chance to do a little **snorkelling**, probably when anchored in some bay at lunchtime. Many also offer sit-on-top **kayaks** and **fishing** tackle.

Relatively warm water all year round and an abundance of marine mammals make the Bay of Islands a wonderful place for **dolphin watching**. You've around an eighty-percent chance of seeing bottlenose and common dolphins in pretty much any season, orca from May to October and minke and Bryde's **whales** from August to January.

Be aware that **swimming with dolphins** is never a certainty, and is forbidden when they have juveniles in tow (which can be any time of year). Generally your chances of swimming with them are about fifty percent. There's usually a money-back offer if you miss out, but check with the operator when you book.

Your best chance to see dolphins is on a cruise with one of the companies licensed to actively search for and swim with dolphins, but only eighteen people are allowed in the water at a time and since most trips carry around forty people in the peak season, you can expect to be in the water about a third of the time that the dolphins are about.

Carino ☎09/402 8040, ⊛www.sailingdolphins.co.nz. A large, fast, red catamaran based in Paihia, licensed to allow swimming with dolphins if found in the right conditions; $105, including BBQ lunch.

Ecocruz ☎0800/432 627, ⊛www.ecocruz.co.nz. A three-day sail on the 22m twin-masted *Manawanui*, which takes up to ten people around the bay with the emphasis on appreciation of the natural environment. Excellent meals are included, along with use of kayaks, snorkel gear, fishing tackle and a good deal of local knowledge and enthusiasm. Dorm bunk $595, double cabin $1350. Operates Oct–April.

The Excitor ☎0800/653 339, ⊛excitor.co.nz (2–5 trips daily; 90min; $89). The most professional of the bay's two fast boats, with 1600hp engines giving a thundering blast out to the Hole in the Rock and back at over forty knots. Add $10 for an island stopover on some trips.

Explore NZ/Dolphin Discoveries ☎0800/365 744, ⊛www.explorenz.co.nz. The pioneers of dolphin swimming in this area operate a range of cruise, sailing and dolphin trips directly competing with Fullers. Perhaps the best trip is its Dolphin/Sail Adventure Combo (Oct–May daily; 8hr; $150) which involves the morning cruising and watching dolphins ($30 extra if you get a chance to swim with them) followed by a transfer to *On the Edge*, a fast 22m twin-hulled yacht where you have a barbecue lunch in a bay (optional kayaking and snorkelling) followed by an afternoon sailing back to Paihia. There are also dedicated sailing trips aboard *On the Edge* (Oct–May daily; 6hr 30min; $115) with up to sixty others, maybe achieving speeds in excess of twenty knots.

Fullers Great Sights ☎0800/653 339, ⊛www.dolphincruises.co.nz. Long-standing operator which also runs the younger-skewed Awesome NZ brand, though the trips are little different. The Cream Trip (aka "Day in the Bay"; Oct–April daily; 6hr 45min; $99) is perhaps the best all-round trip, with a visit to the Hole in the Rock, an island stop, a chance to get wet boom-netting and a good look around as the boat delivers groceries and mail to wharves all around the bay (Mon, Wed & Sat only). You'll probably see dolphins and there is a chance to swim with them as well. There's also a dedicated dolphin-watching cruise (2 daily; 3hr; $89) and a dolphin-swimming trip (mid-Oct to April 2 daily; 4hr; $99 & $30 to swim) on the bay's smallest dolphin boat (35 passengers).

Gungha ⊤ 0800/478 900, ⓦ www.bayofislands sailing.com. A great backpacker-oriented day out with up to 25 others helping sail a 20m single-hull yacht with an island stop and lunch included. $90.

Ipipiri ⊤ 0800/653 339, ⓦ www.overnightcruise .co.nz. Fullers Great Sights-run overnight cruise in a fairly luxurious modern boat sleeping seventy. Prices are high but include comfy en-suite king or twin room, afternoon tea, buffet dinner, cooked breakfast, free use of kayaks and snorkelling gear, guided walks and a twenty-hour cruise anchoring overnight in a sheltered bay. $339.

Phantom ⊤ 0800/224 421, ⓦ www .yachtphantom.com. Only ten can board this excellent, Russell-based, NZ/US-run ocean racing sloop for six glorious hours around the bay, relaxing on deck or taking the helm. A fine lunch is served in some secluded bay. Oct–April only. $99.

R. Tucker Thompson ⊤ 0800/882 537, ⓦ www .tucker.co.nz. A beautiful Northland-built schooner sails out on day-trips into the islands (daily late Oct to April; 6hr; $135) and anchors for a swim and BBQ lunch, taking up to twenty at a time and including morning tea with freshly baked scones and cream. Also 2hr-late-afternoon sails (Nov–March Wed, Fri & Sun; $60) including an antipasto platter and glass of wine.

The Rock ⊤ 0800/762 527, ⓦ www.rocktheboat .co.nz. Backpacker accommodation and activities aboard a former car ferry converted to sleep up to 36. Board in the late afternoon and chug out to some gorgeous bays for fishing, swimming, snorkelling, kayaking, feasting on a big BBQ and then relaxing while someone plunks away on a guitar or the piano; arriving back around noon the next day. Choose from six-berth dorms ($178) and private cabins ($218), all with sea views and all with dinner and breakfast included, but not drinks. Take a sleeping bag.

Kayaking and waka paddling

Lack of experience is no impediment to **kayaking** in and around Paihia, as plenty of operators offer guided trips. If you want to go it alone, there are a couple of rental outfits to choose from.

Bay Beach Hire South end of Paihia Beach ⊤ 09/402 6078, ⓦ www.baybeachhire.co.nz. Rents sit-on kayaks (single $10/hr, $50/day; doubles $20/65), sea kayaks (singles $15/55; doubles $30/80) and catamarans ($50/hr).

Coastal Kayakers Waitangi Bridge ⊤ 09/402 8105, ⓦ www.coastalkayakers.co.nz. Open all year, running a variety of trips from half-day paddles upstream to Haruru Falls ($60) and full-day trips ($80), to three-day guided camping excursions (Nov–May; $480). Also rents out kayaks for two or more people at a time ($10/hr, $40/day).

Island Kayaks at Bay Beach Hire ⊤ 0800/611 440, ⓦ www.baybeachhire.co.nz. Operates all year, offering half-day ($55) and full-day ($90) trips exploring the inner islands and bays.

Taiamai Tours 09/405 9990, ⓦ www.taiamaitours .co.nz. Paddle your own canoe Maori-style. You and up to a dozen others will get the full works – *karakia* (prayers), *whaikorero* (speechmaking), and learn how to handle a *hoe* (paddle) – before propelling the *waka* (canoe) up the Waitangi River, getting a real feel for the Maori sense of spirituality and affinity with the land and sea. Daily at 10am & 1pm; 90min; $165.

Flights and parasailing

For a bird's-eye view of Paihia, go **parasailing** with Flying Kiwi, Paihia Wharf (⊤ 0800/359 691), which offers ten- to fifteen-minute tandem or solo flights from the back of a speedboat to around 250m ($79) or 350m ($89). More extended **flightseeing** is the preserve of Salt Air, Marsden Road, near the Maritime Building, Paihia (⊤ 0800/472 582, ⓦ www.saltair.co.nz) which runs chopper flights ($215/20min to the Hole in the Rock, $295/30min up the coast) along with fixed-wing flights to Cape Reinga (see p.195).

Scuba diving

Dive HQ, Williams Road (℡0800/107 551, ⓦwww.divenz.com), is the main **scuba-diving** outfit and will take you out in the Bay of Islands, or to the wrecks of the *Rainbow Warrior* (see p.185) and the scuttled navy frigate *Canterbury*. Two-tank dives including gear cost $215 ($275 for the wrecks if you don't have Advanced Open Water certification). Dive North (℡09/402 5369, ⓦwww .divenorth.co.nz) also does a great job, charging $235 for two dives but with no extra fee for wreck diving without AOW certification.

Fishing

Fishing trips range from a line fishing for snapper through to big-game boats in search of marlin, shark, tuna and kingfish. Ask at the i-SITE or the skippers around Paihia wharf to find a trip that suits; daily charter rates range around $90 for light tackle and $395 upwards for the big-game boats. Steve Butler (℡09/407 7165, ⓦwww.earlgreyfishing.co.nz) does great big-game charters.

Horseriding

The bay's best **horseriding** is with Horse Trek'n, Bayly Road, Waitangi (daily at 10am & 2pm; $90/2hr; reservations essential on ℡027/233 3490, ⓦwww .horsetrekn.co.nz), on well-cared-for horses across farmland, through Waitangi forest and down to the beach.

Eating, drinking and entertainment

Paihia's range of **places to eat** is unmatched anywhere in the Bay of Islands and competition keeps prices reasonable – wander around town and you'll find any number of appealing restaurants and cafés, typically specializing in seafood. The restaurants are also good places to stick around for postprandial drinking, and there are several more raucous **bars** along Kings Road.

Alfresco's 6 Marsden Rd. Relaxed café and bar that's good for a coffee, lunchtime burger-and-drink meal deals ($12–15) and dishes such as lamb fattoush ($18).

Bay of Islands Swordfish Club Marsden Rd. Private club, overlooking the bay and welcoming visitors outside the peak summer season: just sign yourself in. Simple but good-value food is served from 6pm, and "Swordy's" has some of the cheapest drinks in town.

Beachhouse 16 Kings Rd. Lively all-day café and juice bar with seating out under the shade sail and a menu of varied breakfasts, panini, and gourmet burgers ($9–15). There's the *Sand Pit* pool hall round the back, and live music most nights.

Darryl's Dinner Cruise ℡0800/334 6637, ⓦwww.dinnercruise.co.nz. Convivial and leisurely cruise (2hr 30min; $92) from Paihia Wharf up the Waitangi River to Haruru Falls, where you tuck into prawns and mussels followed by T-bone steak, lamb and fish. Catch it for a good sunset and it is a great way to spend the evening. There's a cash bar on board or BYO wine.

Frank's Marsden Rd. Chilled café, pizzeria and bar with good breakfasts, decent coffee and occasional live music.

Only Seafood 40 Marsden Rd ℡09/402 7444. Stylish restaurant located in an atmospheric villa and open nightly for seafood extravaganzas such as rare yellowfin tuna with roasted langoustine (mains around $30).

Pipi Patch Bar 18 Kings Rd. Situated at Paihia's branch of the Base backpacker chain and the liveliest bar at this end of town, always full of backpackers and locals out on the deck, often tucking into the nightly $12 BBQ and competing for trip giveaways.

Pure Tastes 116 Marsden Rd ℡09/402 0003. Ultra-fine dining restaurant at the oasis-like *Paihia Beach Resort*. Breakfasts such as French sourdough toast with caramelized apples ($16) will see you through to intricately prepared lunches (poolside in summer; mains around $20), but it comes into its own with dinner choices like pan-seared fish on squid ink tagliatelle with zucchini cannelloni and macadamia butter ($32). Also tasting menus (four-course $70, five-course $80).

Waikokopu Café Treaty House Grounds, Waitangi ℡09/402 6275. Great daytime café accessed by a track through the rainforest and surrounded by picnic-table-strewn lawns. Perfect for tucking into well-prepared breakfasts and lunches ($15–19), plus a range of cakes and great coffee. Licensed.

Russell

The isolated location of **RUSSELL** – on a narrow peninsula with poor road but good sea access – gives this small hillside settlement an island ambience. In summer, however, the place is often full of day-trippers who pile off passenger ferries from Paihia and vehicle ferries from nearby Opua to explore the village's historic buildings and stroll along its quaint waterfront.

Evenings are more peaceful and romantic – a far cry from the 1830s when **Kororareka**, as Russell was then known, was a swashbuckling town full of whalers and sealers with a reputation as the "Hell Hole of the Pacific". Savage and drunken behaviour served as an open invitation to **missionaries**, who gradually won over a sizeable congregation and left behind Russell's two oldest buildings, the church and a printing works that produced religious tracts. By 1840, Kororareka was the largest settlement in the country, but after the signing of the Treaty of Waitangi, Governor William Hobson fell out with both Maori and local settlers and moved his capital progressively further south.

Meanwhile, initial Maori enthusiasm for the Treaty of Waitangi had faded: financial benefits had failed to materialize and the Confederation of Tribes flag that flew from Flagstaff Hill between 1834 and 1840 had been replaced by the Union Jack. This came to be seen as a symbol of British betrayal, and as resentment crystallized it found a leader in **Hone Heke Pokai**, Ngapuhi chief and son-in-law of Kerikeri's Hongi Hika. Between July 1844 and March 1845, Heke and his followers cut down the flagstaff no less than four times, the last occasion sparking the first **New Zealand War**, which raged for nearly a year, during which Kororareka was destroyed. The settlement rose from the ashes under a new name, Russell, and grew slowly around its beachfront into the tranquil village of today. If you're only passing through, everything in Russell can be seen comfortably in a day.

Arrival and information

Most visitors reach Russell by **ferry** (see box, p.178), but it's also accessible along the back road described on p.165. Tourist information is available from

▲ Russell ferry

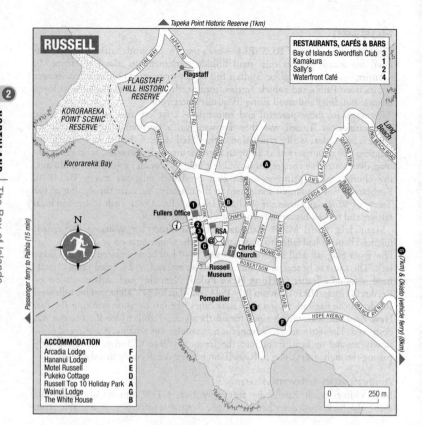

Tapeka Point Historic Reserve (1km)

RUSSELL

RESTAURANTS, CAFÉS & BARS
Bay of Islands Swordfish Club   3
Kamakura   1
Sally's   2
Waterfront Café   4

FLAGSTAFF HILL HISTORIC RESERVE

Flagstaff

KORORAREKA POINT SCENIC RESERVE

Kororareka Bay

N

Passenger ferry to Paihia (15 min)

Fullers Office

RSA

Christ Church

Russell Museum

Pompallier

G (7km) & Okiato (vehicle ferry) (8km)

ACCOMMODATION
Arcadia Lodge   F
Hananui Lodge   C
Motel Russell   E
Pukeko Cottage   D
Russell Top 10 Holiday Park   A
Wainui Lodge   G
The White House   B

0   250 m

Russell Booking & Information Centre, at the end of the wharf (daily: Nov–March 7.30am–8pm; April–Oct 8am–5pm; ☎0800/633 255, ⓦwww.russellinfo.co.nz), which makes bookings for local trips and accommodation and stocks the useful *Russell Heritage Trail* and *Bay of Islands Walks* leaflets. There's daytime **internet access** at Enterprise Russell on York Street.

Accommodation

Accommodation in Russell is much more limited than in Paihia and tends to be more upmarket, mostly B&Bs and lodges.

Arcadia Lodge 10 Florance Ave ☎09/403 7756, ⓦwww.arcadialodge.co.nz. One of Russell's gems: Brad and David bring a dash of style to this B&B in an historic wooden house

encircled by decks on a quiet hill overlooking cottage gardens and the bay. It's a 5min stroll from the village and some of the half-dozen wooden-floored suites and rooms (one not

Pick me up in Russell

Most of the bay's cruises and dolphin trips are based in Paihia but also pick up at Russell wharf (with prior reservation) around fifteen minutes later. Occasionally there are no pick-ups available, but you can catch the frequent, inexpensive passenger **ferry** between Paihia and Russell.

en suite) enjoy sea views. Much of the produce is organic and grown in the garden or locally. Free wi-fi; no children under 15 and a two-night minimum in summer. Rooms ❻, suites ❽
Hananui Lodge 4 York St ☎09/403 7875, ⓦwww.hananui.co.nz. Well-run, modernized motel-style place right by the water. The waterfront suites have the best views but even the standard units are comfortable with sea glimpses, and all get spa access. There are also new apartments across the road with big-screen TV and a/c. Units ❻, apartments ❼, suites ❽
Motel Russell 16 Matauwhi Rd ☎0800/240 011, ⓦwww.motelrussell.co.nz. Choose one of the modernized units at this simple motel with an attractive pool. Studios ❹, one-bedroom units ❼
Pukeko Cottage 14 Brind Rd ☎09/403 8498, ⓦwww.pukekocottagebackpackers.co.nz. Cute little hostel set on the hill above Russell with distant sea views. There are plenty of games and books and a selection of twins and doubles, bookable either by the room (❶) or bed ($25).

Russell Top 10 Holiday Park Long Beach Rd ☎09/403 7826, ⓦwww.russelltop10.co.nz. Central, well-ordered and spotless campsite with tent and campervan sites and an extensive range of high-standard cabins and motel units. Rates rise appreciably between Dec 20 and end of Jan. Camping $20, campervans $44–49, cabins ❸, units ❺
Wainui Lodge 92d Wahapu Rd, 7km south of Russell ☎09/403 8278, ⓦwww.bay-of-islands.pelnet.org. Tiny, five-room backpackers with morning birdsong and kayaking from its own mangrovey beach. Closed June, July & Aug. Dorm $25, room ❷
🏃 **The White House** 7 Church St ☎09/403 7676, ⓦthewhitehouserussell.com. Wonderfully relaxing B&B in a historic 1840 house that's been carefully modernized (including free wi-fi). There's a spa pool in the garden and a help-yourself buffet and cooked breakfast which you can spin out until the noon checkout. ❽

The Town

Russell's most striking building is the fascinating **Pompallier** (daily: Nov–April 10am–5pm; May–Oct 10am–4pm; $7.50), the last survivor of Russell's Catholic mission, once the headquarters of Catholicism in the western Pacific. Pompallier was built in 1842 as a printing works for the French Roman Catholic bishop Jean Baptiste François Pompallier. He had arrived three years earlier to find the Catholic word of God under siege from Anglican and Wesleyan tracts, translated into Maori. The missionaries built an elegant rammed-earth structure in a style typical of Pompallier's native Lyon. The press and paper were imported, and a tannery installed to make leather bookbindings. During the next eight years over a dozen titles of Catholic teachings were printed, comprising almost forty thousand volumes, which were some of the first books printed in Maori.

In a building now restored to its 1842 state, artisans again produce handmade books, all best understood on the **free tours** which explain the production processes in each room. You can even get your hands dirty in what is New Zealand's only surviving colonial tannery.

Nearby stands New Zealand's oldest church, the cream, weatherboard **Christ Church**, on Robertson Road, built in 1836 by local settlers – unlike most churches of similar vintage which were mission churches. In the mid-nineteenth century the church was besieged during skirmishes between Hone Heke's warriors and the British, leaving several still-visible bullet holes.

The small **Russell Museum**, York Street (daily: Christmas–Jan 10am–5pm; Feb–Christmas 10am–4pm; $7.50), shows a video telling the town's history and contains well-laid-out exhibits, including an impressive one-fifth scale model of Cook's *Endeavour*, which called in here in 1769. From the museum, a stroll along The Strand passes the prestigious *Bay of Islands Swordfish Club*, which was founded in 1924, and the *Duke of Marlborough Hotel* – the original building on this site held New Zealand's first liquor licence.

At the end of The Strand, a short track (30–40min return) climbs steeply to **Flagstaff Hill** (Maiki). The current flagpole was erected in 1857, some twelve years after the destruction of the fourth flagpole by Hone Heke as a conciliatory gesture by a son of one of the chiefs who had ordered the original felling. The Confederation of Tribes flag, abandoned after the signing of the Treaty of Waitangi, is flown on twelve significant days of the year, including the anniversary of Hone Heke's death and the final day of the first New Zealand War. From Flagstaff Hill it's a further kilometre to the **Tapeka Point Historic Reserve**, a former *pa* site at the end of the peninsula – a wonderfully defensible position with great views and abundant evidence of terracing.

Eating and drinking

Russell has a limited range of **restaurants** and prices are fairly high, but quality is good. Outside the peak summer season, things close down pretty early. For **drinking** the best bets are often the cheap private **clubs** – the *RSA* on Cass Street and the *Bay of Islands Swordfish Club* – which both welcome visitors.

Bay of Islands Swordfish Club 25 The Strand. Technically a private club but you just sign yourself in. Always a winner for cheap beer, great sunset views from the veranda and simple but good bar meals.

Kamakura 29 The Strand ⑦ 09/403 7771. Probably the finest eating in town. A modern, licensed waterfront restaurant with a strong fish and seafood bias (mains around $30), all beautifully presented.

Sally's 25 The Strand ⑦ 09/403 7652. Convivial, unpretentious and always busy day/night restaurant, strong on seafood (and especially seafood chowder; $11). It's worth booking ahead in peak season. Mains around $30.

Waterfront Café 23 The Strand. Simple café with great coffee, waterfront seating as well as all-day breakfasts and hearty lunches. Closed Mon in winter.

Kerikeri

KERIKERI, 25km northwest of Paihia, is central to the history of the Bay of Islands and yet geographically removed from it, strung out along the main road and surrounded by the orchards that form Kerikeri's economic mainstay. Two kilometres to the east of town, the thin ribbon of the Kerikeri Inlet forces its way from the sea to its tidal limit at **Kerikeri Basin**, the site chosen by Samuel Marsden for the Church Missionary Society's second mission in New Zealand.

For most of the year it's possible to get **seasonal work** weeding, thinning or picking in the subtropical orchards among citrus, tamarillos, feijoas, melons, courgettes, peppers and kiwi fruit. Work is most abundant from January to July. The best contacts are the managers of the hostels and campsites, many of which also offer good weekly rates. In recent years Kerikeri has earned itself a reputation for its high-quality **craft shops** dotted amongst the orchards.

Arrival and information

Air New Zealand **flights** from Auckland land 5km out of town towards Paihia at Bay of Islands Airport and are met by a shuttle. InterCity/Northliner **buses** stop on Cobham Road, with several services to Paihia but just one bus heading north to Kaitaia daily. There's no official visitor centre, but you can pick up **leaflets** inside the foyer of the library on Cobham Road (Mon–Fri 10am–5pm, Sat 9am–2pm, Sun 9am–1pm; ⑦ 09/407 9297); and there's a **DOC office** at 34 Landing Rd (Mon–Fri 8am–4.30pm; ⑦ 09/407 0300), which can advise on local walks and more ambitious treks into the Puketi Forest (see p.184).

Accommodation

Kerikeri has a good selection of **accommodation** in all categories, particularly budget places – a consequence of the area's popularity with long-stay casual workers. Seasonal price fluctuations are nowhere near as marked as in Paihia, though it's still difficult to find accommodation in January.

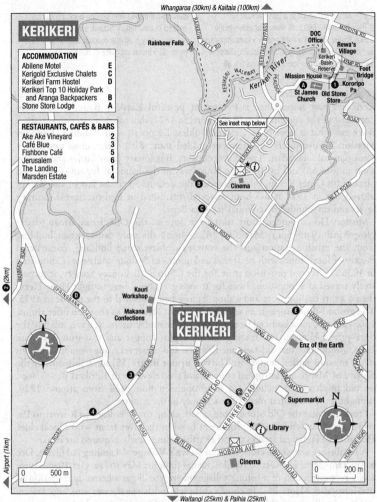

KERIKERI

ACCOMMODATION
Abilene Motel	E
Kerigold Exclusive Chalets	C
Kerikeri Farm Hostel	D
Kerikeri Top 10 Holiday Park and Aranga Backpackers	B
Stone Store Lodge	A

RESTAURANTS, CAFÉS & BARS
Ake Ake Vineyard	2
Café Blue	3
Fishbone Café	5
Jerusalem	6
The Landing	1
Marsden Estate	4

Whangaroa (30km) & Kaitaia (100km)

Rainbow Falls

DOC Office

Rewa's Village

Mission House

St James Church

Old Stone Store

Kororipo Pa

Foot Bridge

See inset map below

Cinema

CENTRAL KERIKERI

Enz of the Earth

Supermarket

Library

Cinema

Kauri Workshop

Makana Confections

Airport (1km)

Waitangi (25km) & Paihia (25km)

Abilene Motel 136 Kerikeri Rd ☎0800/224 536, ⊛www.abilenemotel.co.nz. Centrally located, older-style, ten-unit motel in a garden setting with a solar-heated pool, spa and Sky TV. Some family units. ④

Kerigold Chalets 326 Kerikeri Rd ☎0800/537 446, ⊛www.kerigoldchalets.co.nz. Modern, spacious and spotless one-bedroom chalets with kitchen, pool, barbecue area and breakfast available on request. ⑥

Kerikeri Farm Hostel SH10, 5km west of Kerikeri ☎09/407 6989, ⊛www .kkfarmhostel.blogspot.com. Top-class bunk-free hostel on an organic citrus orchard, with comfortable

dorms and rooms in a lovely wooden house. Free internet and wi-fi, outdoor pool and free-range eggs available. Dorm $25, rooms ②

Kerikeri Top 10 Holiday Park and Aranga Backpackers Kerikeri Rd ☎0800/272 642, ⊛www.aranga.co.nz. Large, beautiful streamside site on the edge of town with a spacious camping area, well-equipped standard cabins with good weekly rates, comfortable s/c units and a separate backpackers section (prices vary depending on length of stay). There's the occasional sound of kiwi in the night, and free kayaks to paddle up the river. Camping $16, dorms $25, cabins ②, units ⑥

Stone Store Lodge 201 Kerikeri Rd ☎09/407 6693, ⓦwww.stonestorelodge .co.nz. Stylish B&B in a light and airy contemporary house with views down to Kerikeri Basin. Decor is tastefully minimal, the spacious rooms are all climate-controlled with private deck. Pizzas are cooked in (and eaten around) an outdoor oven and you can enjoy a private outdoor bath amid tree ferns ($25 including glass of bubbly). ❼

Kerikeri Basin

Kerikeri's past importance is evident at peaceful Kerikeri Basin, nearly 2km northeast of the current town. It was here, in 1821, that mission carpenters started work on what is now New Zealand's oldest European-style building, **Kerikeri Mission House** (access by frequent guided tour; $10) a restrained two-storey Georgian colonial affair. The first occupants, missionary John Butler and family, soon moved on, and by 1832 the house was in the hands of lay missionary and blacksmith James Kemp, who extended the design. Since the last of the Kemps moved out in 1974 it has been restored, furnished in mid-nineteenth-century style, and surrounded by colonial-style gardens.

Mission House guided tours start next door at the **Old Stone Store** (daily: Nov–April 10am–5pm; May–Oct 10am–4pm), the only other extant building from the mission station and the country's oldest stone building, constructed mostly of local stone, with keystones and quoins of Sydney sandstone. Completed in 1836 as a central provision store for the Church Missionary Society, it successively served as a munitions store for troops garrisoned here to fight Hone Heke, then a kauri trading store and a shop, before being opened to the public in 1975. The ground-floor **store** (free) sells goods almost identical to those on offer almost 180 years ago, most sourced from the original manufacturers. You can still buy the once-prized Hudson Bay trading blankets, plus copper and cast-iron pots, jute sacks, gunpowder tea, old-fashioned sweets, and preserves made from fruit grown in the mission garden next door. The two **upper floors** ($5) admirably outline the history of Maori and European contact and the relevance of Kerikeri Basin, aided by old implements, including a hand-operated flour mill from around 1820, thought to be the oldest piece of machinery in the country.

From opposite the Old Stone Store, a path along the river leads to **Kororipo Pa**, which commands a hill on a prominent bend in the river from where local chief Hongi Hika launched attacks on other tribes using newly acquired firearms.

A footbridge across the creek leads to **Rewa's Village**, 1 Landing Rd (daily: Dec & Jan 9am–5pm; late Oct to April 9.30am–4.30pm; May to late Oct 10am–4pm; $5), a reconstruction of a fishing village where you'll get a better appreciation of pre-European Maori life. It comes complete with *marae*, weapons and *kumara* stores, as well as an authentic *hangi* site with an adjacent shell midden.

Opposite is the **Kerikeri Basin Reserve** and the start of a track past the site of Kerikeri's first hydroelectric station (15min each way) and the swimming holes at Fairy Pools (35min each way) to the impressively undercut **Rainbow Falls** (1hr each way). The latter are also accessible off Waipapa Road, 3km north of the Basin.

To explore the waters of Kerikeri Inlet, join the hour-long **steamboat cruise** (daily except Sat 2pm; $30; ☎0800/944 785, ⓦwww.steamship.co.nz; booking essential) on the charming little replica nineteenth-century *Eliza Hobson* which carries fourteen.

The rest of town

You could easily spend a day pottering around the **craft outlets** that dominate the Kerikeri hinterland, guided by the free and widely available *Kerikeri Art & Craft Trail* leaflet: most places are open daily from 10am–5pm. The Kauri Workshop, 500 Kerikeri Rd (☎09/407 9196), stocks anything you could make from **kauri**;

and next door, Makana Confections (☎0800/625 262) produces **handmade chocolates** in front of your eyes. Further out, Kaleidoscope World, 265 Waipapa Rd (☎09/407 4415, ⓦwww.scopesnz.com), makes a fabulous range of devices out of mirrors made on site and myriad coloured baubles; as well as classic swamp kauri tube **kaleidoscopes** there are wonderful jukebox kaleidoscopes and even some very 1960s soap bubble projectors.

If the crafts trail does nothing for you, help may be at hand in the form of the **Steam Sawmill**, Inlet Road, 4km east of town (Mon–Fri 9am–4pm; $7.50; ☎09/407 9707), a working steam-driven mill powered by secondhand equipment garnered from all over the country. You can take a look anytime, but it is best to join one of the tours (Mon–Fri 10.30am & 1.30pm) when the steam whistle is blown. The mill is closed from Christmas to New Year.

Eating, drinking and entertainment

For its size, Kerikeri has an impressive selection of places to **eat**, and several wineries serving meals. **Entertainment** is thinner on the ground, though there's always the lovingly restored Cathay Cinemas, on Hobson Avenue (☎09/407 4428), showing mainstream and more off-beat movies.

Restaurants, cafés and wineries

Ake Ake Vineyard 165 Waimate North Rd ☎09/407 8230, ⓦwww.akeakevineyard.co.nz. Newish vineyard producing intriguing wines (including Chambourcin, which has become a favourite with Northland grape growers) that's open for tasting (10am–5pm), vineyard tours (daily in summer 11.30am; $5, refunded with any purchase) and delicious lunches and dinners overlooking the vines (mains $20–30). Closed Mon & Tues.

🏃 **Café Blue** Kerikeri Rd, 3km west of town ☎09/407 5150. Excellent licensed café for breakfast and lunch in a pretty garden setting. Dishes include a fine range of wraps, grills, pasta dishes and lighter choices, all prepared with care. Great coffee and cakes served outside or in the airy interior.

Fishbone Café 88 Kerikeri Rd ☎09/407 6065. Great licensed café for breakfast and lunch, perennially popular for its high-quality Kiwi fusion food and top coffee.

🏃 **Jerusalem** Cobblestone Mall ☎09/407 1001. Small, friendly, licensed Israeli café beloved by Northlanders for its authentic, low-cost and wonderfully aromatic Middle Eastern dishes to eat in or take away. Closed Sun.

🏃 **The Landing** 215 Kerikeri Rd ☎09/407 8479. A fabulous setting by Kerikeri Basin and great food, from breakfast through coffee and cake to some of the classiest dinners in the north (mains around $28) served inside or on the veranda.

Marsden Estate Wiroa Rd ☎09/407 9398, ⓦwww.marsdenestate.co.nz. Makes a broad variety of reds and whites sampled through free tastings, and runs a moderately priced restaurant.

Around Kerikeri

Some 15km southwest from Kerikeri are **WAIMATE NORTH** and the colonial Regency-style **Te Waimate Mission House** (Nov–April daily 10am–5pm; May–Oct Mon, Wed, Sat & Sun 10am–4pm; $7.50; ⓦwww.tewaimatemission.co.nz), New Zealand's second-oldest European building. Now virtually in the middle of nowhere, in the 1830s this was the centre of a vigorous **Anglican mission**. Missionaries were keen to add European agricultural techniques to the literacy and religion they were teaching the Maori, and by 1834 locally grown wheat was milled at the river, orchards were flourishing and crops were sprouting – all impressing Charles Darwin, who visited the following year. The house, built by converts from local kauri in 1832, has been restored as accurately as possible to its original design. Guided tours highlight prize possessions.

The nearest substantial town to Waimate North is **KAIKOHE**, almost equidistant from both coasts. There's little reason to stop, though you might like to soak your bones at **Ngawha Springs** (daily 9am–9pm; $4), pronounced "Naf-fa

Springs" 7km southeast of Kaikohe, where eight individual pools (all with different mineral contents and at different temperatures) are enclosed by native timber but otherwise untouched by tourist trappings.

The **Puketi Kauri Forest**, 20km north of Kaikohe, comprises one of the largest continuous tracts of kauri forest in the north. Signposted routes from Kaikohe and Kerikeri lead to the **Manginangina Kauri Walk** where a five-minute boardwalk through lush forest brings you to a stand of good-sized kauri. The **Puketi Recreation Area**, 2km south, has a basic DOC campsite ($7; toilets & cold showers).

North to Doubtless Bay

North of the Bay of Islands everything gets a lot quieter. There are few towns of any consequence along the coast and it is the peace and slow pace that attract visitors to an array of glorious beaches and the lovely Whangaroa Harbour. The first stop north of Kerikeri is tiny **Matauri Bay**, where a hilltop memorial commemorates the Greenpeace flagship, *Rainbow Warrior*, which now lies off the coast. A sealed but winding back road continues north, offering fabulous sea views and passing gorgeous headlands and beaches before delivering you to **Whangaroa Harbour**, one of the most beautiful in Northland, and an excellent place to go sailing or kayaking. Further north is the idyllic surfing and fishing hideaway of **Taupo Bay**.

Continuing north brings you to the huge bite out of the coast called **Doubtless Bay**, which had two celebrated discoverers: Kupe, said to have first set foot on Aotearoa in **Taipa**; and Cook, who sailed past in 1769 and pronounced it "doubtless, a bay". Bounded on the west and north by the sheltering **Karikari Peninsula**, the bay offers safe boating and is popular with Kiwi vacationers. In January you can barely move here and you'll struggle to find accommodation, but the shoulder seasons can be surprisingly quiet, and outside December, January and February room prices drop considerably. Most of the bay's facilities cluster along the southern shore of the peninsula in a string of beachside settlements – **Coopers Beach**, **Cable Bay** and **Taipa Bay** – running west from picturesque **Mangonui**.

Matauri Bay

Some 20km north of Kerikeri, a high inland ridge provides a dramatic first glimpse of the long, Norfolk-pine-backed **MATAURI BAY** and the **Cavalli Islands** just offshore. At the northern end of the main bay a well-worn path (20min return; 70m ascent) climbs to Chris Booth's distinctive **Rainbow Warrior Memorial** which remembers the Greenpeace flagship (see box opposite), now scuttled off the Cavalli Islands. The memorial comprises a stone arch (symbolizing a rainbow) and the vessel's salvaged bronze propeller.

Missionary Samuel Marsden first set foot in Aotearoa in 1814 at Matauri Bay, where he mediated between the Ngati Kura people – who still own the bay – and some Bay of Islands Maori, a process commemorated by the quaint wooden **Samuel Marsden Memorial Church** on the road into town. The Ngati Kura tell of their ancestral *waka*, *Mataatua*, which lies in waters nearby. It was the resonance of this legendary canoe that partly led the Ngati Kura to offer a final resting place to the wreck of the *Rainbow Warrior*. Paihia-based dive operators (see p.176) run trips out to the wreck, 10 minutes offshore from Matauri Bay. The best visibility is in April; from September to November plankton sometimes obscure the view but it's still pretty good.

Accommodation in the bay is limited to the peaceful *Matauri Bay Holiday Park* (T09/405 0525, W www.matauribay.co.nz; camping $18; on-site caravans ❸;

French nuclear testing in the Pacific

Claiming that nuclear testing was completely safe, the French government for decades conducted tests on the tiny Pacific atolls of **Mururoa** and **Fangataufa**, a comfortable 15,000km from Paris, but only 4000km northeast of New Zealand.

In 1966 France turned its back on the 1963 Partial Test Ban Treaty, which outlawed atmospheric testing, and relocated Pacific islanders away from their ancestral villages to make way for a barrage of tests over the next eight years. The French authorities claimed that "Not a single particle of radioactive fallout will ever reach an inhabited island" – and yet radiation was routinely detected as far away as Samoa, Fiji and even New Zealand. Increasingly antagonistic public opinion forced the French to conduct their tests underground in deep shafts, where another 200 detonations took place, threatening the geological stability of these fragile coral atolls.

In 1985, Greenpeace coordinated a New Zealand-based protest flotilla, headed by its flagship, the **Rainbow Warrior**, but before the fleet could set sail from Auckland, the French secret service sabotaged the *Rainbow Warrior*, detonating two bombs below the waterline. As rescuers recovered the body of Greenpeace photographer Fernando Pereira, two French secret service agents posing as tourists were arrested. Flatly denying all knowledge at first, the French government was finally forced to admit to what David Lange (then Prime Minister of New Zealand) described as "a sordid act of international state-backed terrorism". The two captured agents were sentenced to ten years in jail, but France used all its international muscle to have them serve their sentences on a French Pacific island; they both served less than two years before being honoured and returning to France.

In 1995, to worldwide opprobrium, France announced a further series of tests. Greenpeace duly dispatched *Rainbow Warrior II*, which was impounded by the French navy on the tenth anniversary of the sinking of the original *Rainbow Warrior*. In early 1996 the French finally agreed to stop nuclear testing in the Pacific.

chalets ❹), which has some lovely beachfront sites and a handy small shop, but is heaving in January.

The only place for a bite to **eat** is *Matauri Top Shop*, a combined store and good-value café at the top of Matauri Bay Road, just before you descend to the bay.

Whangaroa Harbour

West of Matauri Bay, the virtually landlocked and sheltered **Whangaroa Harbour** is the perfect antidote to Bay of Islands' commercialism. The scenery, albeit on a smaller scale, is easily a match for its southern cousin and, despite the limited facilities, you can still get out on a cruise or to join the big-game fishers. Narrow inlets forge between cliffs and steep hills, most notably the two bald volcanic plugs, **St Paul and St Peter**, which rise behind the harbour's two settlements, **WHANGAROA** on the south side, and **TOTARA NORTH** opposite.

The harbour wasn't always so quiet though, being among the first areas in New Zealand to be visited by European pioneers, most famously those aboard the *Boyd*, which called here in 1809 to load kauri spars for shipping to Britain. A couple of days after its arrival, all sixty-six crew were killed and the ship burned by local Maori in retribution for the crew's mistreatment of Tara, a high-born Maori sailor who had apparently transgressed the ship's rules. A British whaler avenged the incident by burning the entire Maori village, sparking off a series of skirmishes that spread over the north for five years. Later the vast stands of kauri were hacked down and milled, some at Totara North. Even if you're just passing through, it's worth driving the 4km along the northern shore of the harbour to Totara North, passing the remains of this historic community's last sawmills, which ceased operation a few years back.

Activities

The single best thing to do around Whangaroa is to spend a day **sailing** on the 15m steel cutter, *Sea Eagle* ($90; ☎09/405 1963, ⓦwww.seaeaglecharters.com) – trips typically involve sailing out to the rugged uninhabited Cavalli Islands, stopping to let the small group of passengers snorkel, sunbathe and walk; it's great value for money. The 11m *Snow Cloud* (☎09/405 0523, ⓦwww.snowcloud .co.nz) operated equally wonderful trips and should be running again by late 2010.

Summer **kayak** trips (half-day $65; full day $85, no credit cards) can be arranged with the knowledgeable Northland Sea Kayaking, on the northeastern flank of the harbour (☎09/405 0381, ⓦwww.northlandseakayaking.co.nz); while the Whangaroa Big Gamefish Club are the people to see if you want to go out game fishing. One of the most immediately rewarding **walks** is the hike up the volcanic dome of **St Paul** (30min return; 140m ascent) from the top of Old Hospital Road in Whangaroa. The final few metres involve an easy scramble with fixed chains to assist. On the harbour's north side, DOC's **Wairakau Stream Track** (6km each way; 90min–2hr) runs from Totara North, past freshwater pools, mangroves and viewpoints to DOC's group-oriented Lane Cove Hut (whole hut bookings only at $160; ⓦwww.doc.govt.nz) on Pekapeka Bay, which sleeps sixteen people. It is accessible on foot and by boat, and has a solar-heated shower, water, toilets and plenty of sandflies. You'll need your own cooking gear.

Practicalities

Public transport reaches neither Whangaroa nor Totara North, but the daily InterCity/Northliner **bus** does pass ⚑ *Kahoe Farms Hostel*, SH10 1.5km north of the Totara North turn-off (☎09/405 1804, ⓦwww.kahoefarms.co.nz; dorm $28, rooms ❷/❸), a small and extremely hospitable backpackers on a working cattle farm with a dorm and rooms in a house with polished wood floors and rooms (some en suite) in a separate villa on the hill behind. Stefano whips up superb home-made pizza and pasta dinners, generous breakfasts and a fine espresso, plus there's kayak rental and hiking trails to some lovely swimming holes.

There's also good accommodation around Whangaroa which is where you'll find **eating** options including the *Whangaroa Big Gamefish Club* overlooking the yacht harbour.

Taupo Bay

A sealed 13km road from SH10 brings you to **TAUPO BAY**, a blissfully undeveloped holiday community with a smattering of beach shacks, and some of the best surfing and rock and beach fishing in Northland. Surfers of all levels can take lessons with Isobar Surf, 43 Mako St (☎09/406 0719, ⓦwww.isobarsurf.co.nz), with lessons starting from $65 for two hours; $180 for an "overnighter", staying at the school's surf lodge; and $690 for a five-day stay, including accommodation. Your only other accommodation option is the friendly *Taupo Bay Holiday Park* (☎09/406 0315, ⓦwww.taupobayholidaypark.co.nz; camping $15, dorm $18 cabins ❷–❹), which rents surf and boogie boards ($10 or $20/hr), kayaks ($30/hr), and sells bait and a few basic supplies at Taupo Bay's only shop. The settlement is packed in January but otherwise quiet.

Mangonui and around

With its lively fishing wharf and a traditional grocery perched on stilts over the water there's an antiquated air to **MANGONUI**, strung along the sheltered Mangonui Harbour off Doubtless Bay. A handful of two-storey buildings with wooden verandas have been preserved, some operating as craft shops or cafés, but this is still very much a working village.

Arrival and information

SH10 bypasses the Mangonui waterfront, which is reached on a 2km loop road plied by the InterCity/Northliner **bus** service, running once a day in each direction between Paihia and Kaitaia. The volunteer-staffed **visitor centre**, Waterfront Drive, opposite the 4-Square grocery (Nov–Easter daily 10am–4pm; Easter–Oct Tues–Sat 10am–3pm; ☎09/406 2046) can point you to accommodation, both here and along the coast, and has **internet access**.

Accommodation

There are some nice places to **stay** around Mangonui, but not much budget accommodation and no camping.

Beach Lodge 121 SH10, Coopers Beach ☎09/409 0068, ⊛www.beachlodge.co.nz. Five breezy yet elegant water-view apartments, each with its own deck, full kitchen and free wi-fi. No kids under 8. Summer rates from $420. ❾

Driftwood Lodge SH10, Cable Bay ☎09/406 0418, ⊛www.driftwoodlodge.co.nz. Great lodge right beside the beach with views of the Karikari peninsula from the broad deck where everyone gathers for sundowners and perhaps a BBQ. Accommodation is in fully s/c units and there's free access to dinghies, kayaks and boogie boards. Always popular, so book well ahead. Studios ❺, apartments ❻

Macrocarpa Cottage 2 Bush Point Rd, Taipa ☎09/406 1245, ✉maccottage@xtra.co.nz. An open-plan, self-catering cottage at the water's edge with one queen room, and two singles on a mezzanine, full kitchen and cable TV, plus fabulous views across the Taipa Estuary. Great for couples. ❺

Mangonui Hotel Waterfront Drive, Mangonui ☎09/406 0003, ⊛www.mangonuihotel.co.nz. Century-old, traditional hotel opposite the harbour with an upstairs veranda. Rooms (doubles are en suite) are cheerfully renovated in bright colours. Rooms with harbour views go quickly, so book ahead or arrive early. Dorms $25, single rooms ❶, double rooms ❹

Puketiti Lodge 10 Puketiti Drive, 7km south of Mangonui ☎09/406 0369, ⊛www.puketitilodge .co.nz. There's a rural feel to this modern lodge with three en-suite rooms and a deluxe dorm all with long views to the coast. Everyone has access to the huge deck and well-equipped kitchen and lounge. Dorms $40, rooms ❺

The town and around

Mangonui means "big shark", recalling the legendary chief Moehuri's *waka* which was supposedly led into Mangonui Harbour by such a fish. But it was whales and the business of provisioning **whaling** ships that made the town: one story tells of a harbour so packed with ships that folk could leap between the boats to cross from Mangonui to the diminutive settlement of Hihi on the far shore. As whaling diminished, the kauri trade took its place, chiefly around Mill Bay, the cove five minutes' walk to the west of Mangonui. To get a feel for the layout of Mangonui Harbour, take in the views at **Rangikapiti Pa Historic Reserve**, off Rangikapiti Road, between Mangonui and Coopers Beach.

The Swamp Palace & Bush Fairy Dairy

If you're staying around Doubtless Bay and have your own transport, don't miss an evening at **The Swamp Palace** (☎09/408 7040), a quirky cinema in the Oruru Community Hall, 7km south of **Taipa** in the middle of nowhere. It caters to an eclectic mix of tastes – cult and classic movies, as well as the very latest releases. Call ahead to check programmes and opening hours.

Bush Fairy Dairy, at Peria (☎09/408 5508), signposted a further 5km down Oruru Road. Brimming with local art, craft, clothing and organic produce (plus standard dairy items), this authentic, hippie-style co-op also hosts Sunday bazaars every few weeks throughout the summer, complete with poetry readings and acoustic jam sessions around the bonfire along with craft and produce markets.

In the village, don't miss the reasonably priced selection of handmade **woven flax items** and other locally made crafts at Flax Bush, 50 Waterfront Drive: the deals on woven baskets (*kete*) are among the best you'll find. You can **sample wines** from throughout Northland at the Far North Wine Centre, 60 Waterfront Drive (Dec–Feb daily 11am–4pm; fewer days in winter; ℡09/406 2485), which has a good selection and knowledgeable staff.

While ships were repaired and restocked at Mangonui, barrels were mended a couple of kilometres west at **COOPERS BEACH**, a glorious and well-shaded sweep of sand backed by a string of motels. The beach is popular in January and at weekends, but at other times you may find you have it pretty much to yourself.

Another 3km west the smaller swimming and surfing settlement of **CABLE BAY**, is separated by the Taipa River from the beachside village of **TAIPA**, now the haunt of sunbathers and swimmers, but historically significant as the spot where Kupe, the discoverer of Aotearoa in Maori legend, first set foot on land. There's a concrete memorial to him near the Shell station by the Taipa River.

Mangonui also makes a good base for organized trips to **Cape Reinga and Ninety Mile Beach** (see box, p.192).

Eating and drinking

Doubtless Bay has the best range of **places to eat** north of Kerikeri, though admittedly it doesn't have much competition. Committed **drinking** mostly happens at the *Mangonui Hotel*, which often has bands at weekends.

Coopers Café 157 SH10, Coopers Beach ℡09/406 0860. Award-winning Maori chef Michael Venner cooked his way around the kitchens of the world, before opening his relaxed fine dining restaurant. Stop in for great coffee, Belgian chocolate milkshake and impeccably prepared lunches (mains $13–23) and dinners (mains $28–35). Dinner bookings essential; closed Mon.

Fresh & Tasty Inside the *Mangonui Hotel*, Waterfront Drive, Mangonui. Rival chippy to neighbouring *Mangonui*, and much frequented by locals happy to trade location for lower prices, less waiting time and equally good tucker.

The Galley 118 Waterfront Rd, Mangonui ℡09/406 1233. Eclectic restaurant in Mangonui's

former post office serving a Mediterranean-leaning surf 'n' turf menu.

Mangonui Fish Shop 137 Waterfront Drive, Mangonui. Famed fish and chip restaurant, idyllically set on stilts over the water, that's a regular afternoon stop for returning Cape Reinga buses. Licensed and BYO.

Thai Chefs 80 Waterfront, Mangonui. Quality examples of all your favourite Thai dishes, mostly around $20.

Waterfront Café Waterfront Drive, Mangonui ℡09/406 0850. Decent café/bar with harbour views, good coffee, breakfasts, light lunches and a wide range of dinner mains including fine pizzas.

The Karikari Peninsula

Doubtless Bay to the east and Rangaunu Harbour to the west are bounded by the crooked arm of the **Karikari Peninsula** which strikes north swathed in unspoiled golden- and white-sand beaches. Outside Christmas to mid-February, they have barely a soul on them. Apart from the large and modern **Karikari Estate** golf resort, vineyard and winery, facilities remain limited. There's no public transport, and without diving or fishing gear, you'll have to resign yourself to lazing on the beaches and swimming from them – and there can be few better places to do just that.

The initial approach across a low and scrubby isthmus is less than inspiring, but 10km on, a side road leads to the peninsula's west coast and the **Puheke Scenic Reserve**, a gorgeous, dune-backed beach that's usually deserted. Another fine white strand spans the nearby hamlet of **RANGIPUTA**.

The peninsula's main road continues past the Rangiputa junction to the community of **TOKERAU BEACH**, a cluster of houses and shops at the northern end of the grand sweep of Doubtless Bay. There's **accommodation** here at *The Rusty Anchor*, 1 Tokerau Beach Rd (℡09/406 7141, Ⓦ www.rustyanchor .co.nz; camping $10, power sites $18, dorms $25, rooms ❷), and nearby at the well-run *Whatuwhiwhi Top 10 Holiday Park*, Whatuwhiwhi Road (℡0800/142 444, Ⓦ www.whatuwhiwhitop10.co.nz; camping $18 cabins & kitchen cabins ❷, units ❹, and deluxe units ❺), set back from a gorgeous beach; book ahead for summer, when prices jump considerably. Neighbouring A to Z Diving (℡09/408 3336, Ⓦ www.atozdiving.co.nz), offer **diving** off the Karikari Peninsula (two-tank dive $185), plus trips to the *Rainbow Warrior* wreck ($230), both including gear.

A kilometre north of Tokerau Beach you drive between an international-standard golf course and a hillside swathed in vines to reach **Karikari Estate winery** (℡09/408 7222, Ⓦ www.karikariestate.co.nz) the northernmost in New Zealand, which produced its first vintage in 2003. It is a great spot with lovely views, perfect for leisurely sampling the wares ($12 for 5) over an antipasto platter on the terrace.

The Karikari Peninsula saves its best until last: **Maitai Bay**, 6km north of *Karikari Estate Winery*, is a matchless double arc of golden sand split by a rocky knoll, encompassed by the *Maitai Bay Campground* ($8), Northland's largest DOC campsite, with cold showers, toilets and drinking water. Much of the site is *tapu* to local Maori, and you are encouraged to respect the sacred areas.

Kaitaia and Ahipara

KAITAIA, 40km west of Mangonui, is the Far North's largest commercial centre, situated near the junction of the two main routes north. It makes a convenient base for some of the best trips to Cape Reinga and Ninety Mile Beach (see p.192), far preferable to the longer trips from the Bay of Islands. Kaitaia has suffered from a bad rap in some media, but the town is no more or less dangerous than elsewhere. That said, there's not a great deal to see in this farming service town and with your own transport, you might want to base yourself at the magnificent beach in **Ahipara**, 15km west, to sand-toboggan the giant dunes, surf or explore the old gumfields.

If you're in the area around the third weekend of March, you can catch competitors from around the world taking part in a series of running events on Ninety Mile Beach, including the **Te Houtaewa Challenge** (Ⓦ www.newzealand-marathon .co.nz), named after the tale of a great Maori athlete. The races are preceded by the Te Houtaewa Waka Ama Surf Challenge, a series of six-man outrigger *waka* races at Ahipara, and the five-day Kai Maori Food Festival and Te Houtaewa Arts & Crafts Festival, both held in Kaitaia. Around the same time, the Snapper Classic (Ⓦ www.snapperclassic.co.nz) is among the world's biggest **surfcasting** competitions with a $50,000 prize for the largest snapper.

Arrival and information

The daily InterCity/Northliner joint **bus** service pulls up outside Kaitaia's **i-SITE visitor centre**, South Road (daily 8.30am–5pm; ℡09/408 0879, Ⓔ kaitaia @visitnorthland.co.nz), which sells bus tickets, rents sand toboggans ($10/day), stocks DOC leaflets such as *Kaitaia Area Walks* and *Cape Reinga and Te Paki Walks* and has **internet access**. Kaitaia's airport, 9km north of town near Awanui, is connected by direct **flights** to Auckland with Air New Zealand.

Accommodation

Ahipara is a more appealing **place to stay** than Kaitaia, though there is no useful public transport, supermarket or bank. Outside the post-Christmas peak, rooms are plentiful, and prices are generally lower than at the coastal resorts to the east.

Kaitaia

Historic Wireless B&B 122 Wireless Rd, 4km north of Kaitaia ☎09/408 1929, ⊛www.kaitaia-bnb.co.nz. Friendly kauri-floored homestay in a large 1912 house originally built as worker accommodation for the nearby wireless station. Shared bathrooms are comfortable and breakfast is included. ❹

Loredo 25 North Rd ☎0800/456 733, ⊛www .loredomotel.co.nz. Clean, well-maintained and ever-popular motel 1km north of the town centre with a pool, spa and barbecue area. ❹

Mainstreet Lodge 235 Commerce St ☎09/408 1275, ⊛www.mainstreetlodge.co.nz. Welcoming and well-equipped hostel, alive with folk headed for the Cape (tours pick up from the hostel). You can also do half-day bone-carving sessions here. Dorms $26, rooms & en suites ❷

Waters Edge 25b Kitchener St ☎09/408 0870, ⊛www.watersedgebandbkaitaia.co.nz. Attractive B&B in a modern suburban house with lush gardens and a pool. Dinner by arrangement. ❹

Ahipara

Ahipara Bay Motel 22 Reef View Rd ☎0800/906 453, ⊛www.ahipara.co.nz/baymotel. A choice of pleasant older motel units and six excellent luxury versions with tremendous sea views; and there's a decent on-site restaurant. Units ❺, luxury ❻

Ahipara Holiday Park 164 Takahe St ☎0800/888 988, ⊛www.ahiparamotorcamp .co.nz. The area's best camping option, just 300m from the sea, offering YHA discounts across the accommodation range. Camping $16, basic cabins ❷, en-suite double rooms & s/c cabins ❸

Beach Abode 11 Korora St ☎09/409 4070, ⊛www.beachabode.co.nz. Three well-appointed beachfront units, each with free wi-fi, full kitchen, BBQ, deck and great sea views. Kids over 12 only. Apartments ❺

🏃 **Endless Summer Lodge** 245 Foreshore Rd ☎09/409 4181, ⊛www.endless summer.co.nz. Well-managed hostel in an atmospheric 1880 timber homestead with kauri floors, right across the road from the beach. Relax in comfortable doubles, twins or two four-bed dorms; there's also a BBQ, free boogie boards, and surfboard rental; surfing instruction can be arranged. Bookings by phone only. Dorms $26, rooms ❷

The Town

A Maori village already flourished at Kaitaia when the first missionary, Joseph Matthews, came looking for a site in 1832. The protection of the mission encouraged European pastoralists to establish themselves here, but by the 1880s they found themselves swamped by the gum diggers who had come to plunder the underground deposits around Lake Ohia and Ahipara. Many early arrivals were young Croats fleeing tough conditions in what was then part of the Austro-Hungarian Empire, though the only evidence of this is a Serbo-Croat welcome sign at the entrance to town, and a cultural society that holds a traditional dance each year.

The best place to gain a sense of the area is the **Far North Regional Museum**, 6 South Rd (daily 10am–4pm; $4; ⊛www.farnorthmuseum.co.nz), with arresting displays on local life and history, including the Ahipara gumfields. It includes a copy of the twelfth- or thirteenth-century Kaitaia Carving (the original is in the Auckland Museum), a fine example of the transitional period during which Polynesian art began to take on Maori elements.

Ahipara and the gumfields

The southern end of Ninety Mile Beach finishes with a flourish at **AHIPARA**, a secluded scattered village 15km west of Kaitaia that grew up around the Ahipara gumfields. A hundred kilometres of sand recede into sea spray to the north, while to the south the high flatlands of the Ahipara Plateau tumble to the sea in a cascade of golden dunes. Beach and plateau meet at **Shipwreck Bay**, a surf and swimming beach with an underground following with surfers for its long tubes (sometimes 400m or more). The bay is named after the 1870 wreck of the *Favourite*, its paddle-shaft still protruding from the sand. At low tide you can pick mussels off the volcanic rocks and follow the wave-cut platform around a series of bays for about 5km to the dunes – about an hour's walk – although most do it by quad bike or mountain bike.

At their peak in the early twentieth century, the barren **gumfields**, on a sandy dune plateau to the south of town, supported three hotels and two thousand people. Unlike most gumfields, where experimental probing and digging was the norm, here the soil was methodically excavated, washed and sieved to extract the valuable kauri gum (see box, p.200). None of the dwellings remain on the plateau, and the gumfields are an eerie, desolately beautiful spot.

Ahipara activities

The best way to get into the dunes and gumfields is on a **quad bike** guided tour with Tua Tua Tours (T0800/494 288, Wwww.ahipara.co.nz/tuatuatours) whose excursions range from ninety minutes (single $100; double $110) to an excellent three-hour safari (single $175; double $185), which includes sandboarding. Ahipara Adventure Centre, 15 Takahe St, 100m past the store (T09/409 2055, Wwww.ahiparaadventure.co.nz), rents single-rider quad bikes ($70 for first hour, $50/hr thereafter; sand toboggan included) without a guide. It also rents out surfboards, kayaks and mountain bikes (all $25/half-day), and blo-karts ($40 for first 30min, $20/30min thereafter). Alternatively, you can saddle up with Ahipara **Horse Treks** (T027/333 8645), with two-hour rides for $60.

A short and worthwhile **walk** takes you from the western end of the beach to a **lookout** (500m, 10min return), giving spectacular views all the way to Cape Reinga. The track begins at the end of Foreshore Road. Keener hikers might fancy tackling the same area on a 6hr section of the tide-dependent **Gumfields Walk** (12km loop; free maps and tide times from the Ahipara Adventure Centre and Kaitaia i-SITE), which begins at the bridge at Shipwreck Bay and takes you into an eerie and desolate landscape of wind-sculpted dunes, then back along the beach. Let someone know where you're going, take plenty of water and look out for quad bikes.

Eating and drinking

Neither Kaitaia nor Ahipara is any great shakes for **eating**, though Kaitaia has the wider range plus the Pak 'n Save **supermarket** on Commerce Street. Ahipara just has a small store, a takeaway, a café and a restaurant.

Kaitaia

Beachcomber 222 Commerce St. Probably Kaitaia's best restaurant serving a fairly standard range of meat and fish dishes (lunches $17, dinner mains $28–32) which all come with a visit to the salad bar. Closed Sun.

Birdie's 14 Commerce St. An Old-school café, which is open from breakfast until lunch, and serves up huge portions of hearty Kiwi food at modest prices (mains $12–18). Closed Sun in winter.

Mussel Rock 75 Commerce St. Small daytime café that transforms into a fairly lively bar that is intimate compared to the town's other drinking barns.

Ahipara

Bayview At *Ahipara Bay Motel* (see opposite). Decent restaurant/bar which benefits from sea views and serves a good choice of moderately priced dishes.

Gumdiggers Café Takahe Rd. Café and takeaway that's open evenings (Thurs–Sat), especially in summer when it specializes in pizza.

Ninety Mile Beach and Cape Reinga

Northland's final gesture is the **Aupori Peninsula**, a narrow, 100km-long finger of consolidated and grassed-over dunes ending in a lumpy knot of 60-million-year-old marine volcanoes. To Maori it's known as Te Hika o te Ika ("The tail of the fish"), recalling the legend of Maui hauling up the North Island ("the fish") from the sea while in his canoe (the South Island).

The most northerly accessible point is **Cape Reinga**, where the spirits of Maori dead depart this world. Beginning their journey by sliding down the roots of an 800-year-old pohutukawa into the ocean, they climb out again on Ohaua, the highest of the Three Kings Islands, to bid a final farewell before returning to their ancestors in Hawaiiki. The spirits reach Cape Reinga along **Ninety Mile Beach** (actually 64 miles long), which runs straight along the western side of the peninsula. Most visitors follow the spirits, though they do so in modern buses specifically designed for belting along the hard-packed sand at the edge of the surf – officially part of the state highway system – then negotiating the quicksands of Te Paki Stream to return to the road. The main road runs more or less down the centre of the peninsula, while the western ocean is kept tantalizingly out of sight by the thin pine ribbon of the **Aupori**

Getting to the Cape

The best way to experience the phenomenal length of Ninety Mile Beach and the wild beauty of Cape Reinga is to take one of the **bus tours** which all make a loop up the Aupori Peninsula, travelling SH1 in one direction and Ninety Mile Beach in the other, the order being dictated by the tide. For many, the highlight is **sandboarding** on a boogie board (or in a safer but less speedy toboggan) down the huge dunes that flank Te Paki Stream.

Bus trips start from Kaitaia, Mangonui and Paihia in the Bay of Islands. Those from Paihia are the most numerous but also the longest (11hr), most leaving daily at around 7.30am. They go via Kerikeri, Mangonui and Awanui in one direction and pass Kaitaia and the kauri trees of the Puketi Forest in the other, with pick-ups along the way. Tours starting further north give you less time in the bus and more for exploring.

Going it alone on Ninety Mile Beach

Rental cars and private vehicles are not insured to drive on Ninety Mile Beach and for good reason. Vehicles frequently get bogged in the sand and abandoned by their occupants. As there are no rescue facilities near enough to get you out before the tide comes in, and mobile phone coverage is almost nil, you could end up with a long walk. Even in your own vehicle, **two-wheel-drives aren't recommended**, regardless of weather conditions, which can change rapidly.

If you are determined to take your own vehicle for the 70km spin along the beach, seek local advice and prepare your car by spraying some form of water repellent on the ignition system – CRC is a common brand. Schedule your trip to coincide with a receding tide, starting two hours after high water and preferably going in the same direction as the bus traffic that day; drive on dry but firm sand, avoiding any soft patches, and slow down to cross streams running over the beach – they often have deceptively steep banks. If you do get stuck in soft sand, lowering the tyre pressure will improve traction. There are several access points along the beach, but the only ones realistically available to ordinary vehicles are the two used by the tour buses: the southern access point at **Waipapakauri Ramp**, 6km north of Awanui, and the more dangerous northern one along **Te Paki Stream**, which involves negotiating the

Forest. The forests, and the **cattle farms** that cover most of the rest of the peninsula, were once the preserve of gum diggers, who worked the area intensively early last century.

If you've made it this far north, you'll already be familiar with the paucity of facilities in rural Northland, so the Aupori Peninsula doesn't come as much of a surprise. There's sporadic **accommodation** along the way, ranging from some beautifully sited DOC campsites to motels, lodges and hostels. Most are reasonably priced, reflecting the fact that many visitors pass through without stopping; however, all are very busy immediately after Christmas. There are a few **places to eat**, though nothing stays open after around 8pm. You can refuel at Houhora; **petrol** isn't always available in Waitiki.

Awanui

The eastern and western roads around Northland meet 8km north of Kaitaia at **AWANUI**, Maori for "Big River", though all you'll find is a bend in a narrow tidal creek that makes a relaxing setting for the daytime *Big River Café*, corner of SH10 and SH1, serving a range of light meals.

Almost all buses to Cape Reinga stop 1km north at the **Ancient Kauri Kingdom** (daily 8.30am–5.30pm, later in summer; free; ⓦwww.ancientkauri.co.nz),

quicksands of a river – start in low gear and don't stop, no matter how tempting it might be to ponder the dunes.

Tours from Kaitaia and Ahipara
Far North Outback Adventures Ahipara ⓣ09/408 0927, ⓦwww.farnorthtours .co.nz. Exclusive 4WD custom tours (8hr; $650 for up to five people) including morning tea and lunch. They go off the beaten track, taking in the white sands of Great Exhibition Bay to explore flora, fauna and archeological sites.
Harrisons Cape Runner Kaitaia ⓣ0800/227 373, ⓦwww.ahipara.co.nz/caperunner. Bargain, basic minibus tour (8hr; $45) including the Cape, beach, Kaitaia pick-up and a light lunch.
Sand Safaris Kaitaia ⓣ0800/869 090, ⓦwww.sandsafaris.co.nz. Good-value tour (8hr; $55) that's similar to Harrisons but with Ahipara pick-ups and a guided tour of the Gumdiggers Park. Light lunch included.

Tours from Mangonui
Paradise 4X4 Tours ⓣ0800/494 392, ⓦwww.paradisenz.co.nz. The standard bus tour (including pick-up from your accommodation) is $75, and there are 4WD customized tours for two to four people ($600–700) with a gourmet lunch.

Tours from Paihia
Awesome NZ ⓣ0800/653 339, ⓦwww.awesomenz.com. Cape bus trip aimed at those with an adventurous spirit, with maximum sandboarding time. Lunch and fish and chips at Mangonui are extra. $109.
Dune Rider ⓣ09/402 8681, ⓦwww.explorenz.co.nz. Upscale Cape trips in a comfortable high-clearance bus with reclining seats. Includes a tour of the Gumdiggers Park but lunch and fish and chips in Mangonui are extra.
Salt Air ⓣ0800/475 582, ⓦwww.saltair.co.nz. Fly to the Cape, landing at Waitiki, then covering the last section to Cape Reinga by 4WD. Includes refreshments at Tapotupotu Bay and sandboarding. $415.

a defunct dairy factory now operating as a sawmill, cutting and shaping huge peat-preserved kauri logs hauled out of swamps where they have lain for around 45,000 years. You can watch slabs of wood being fashioned into bowls, sculptures and breadboards but the emphasis is on the shop. Be sure to climb up to the mezzanine on the spiral staircase hewn out of the centre of the largest piece of swamp kauri trunk ever unearthed, a monster three and a half metres in diameter.

Some 10km to the north of the Kauri Kingdom and 3km off SH1, the delightfully low-key **Gumdiggers Park Ancient Buried Kauri Forest**, Heath Road (daily 9am–5.30pm summer, to 4pm winter; $10), features an easy thirty-minute nature trail through shady manuka forest. Holes have been excavated to show the methods used for gum digging, huts illustrate the living conditions and there's a small kauri gum collection. The main southern entrance to Ninety Mile Beach, the **Waipapakauri Ramp**, is just south of the park's turn-off.

Houhora and Pukenui

Around 30km north of Awanui are the Aupori Peninsula's two largest settlements: scattered **HOUHORA**, and the working fishing village of **PUKENUI**, 2km to the north, where good catches are to be had off the wharf. At Houhora, a 3km side road turns east to **Houhora Heads**.

Stay at *Pukenui Lodge*, SH1, Pukenui (T09/409 8837, Estay@pukenuilodge .co.nz; dorms $23, rooms ②, units ③), a particularly beautifully located motel and hostel with harbour views. **Diners** are often defeated by the huge burger known as PukuNui (Maori for "big stomach") at *Pukenui Pacific* on SH1 (T09/409 8816), a good-value café/bar (kitchen closes around 8pm) and the only takeaway north of Kaitaia. New Zealand's northernmost pub, the *Houhora Tavern*, is 2km north, with lawns beside the harbour, basic meals and a few campervan hook-ups ($15 per van).

The Parengarenga Harbour, Te Kao and Waitiki Landing

Some 10km north of Pukenui, a side road runs 4km east to **Rarawa Beach**, where the pure white silica sand is backed by a shady streamside DOC **campsite** ($7.50), its paradisiacal appeal tempered by abundant mosquitoes.

The beach stretches over 30km north of Rarawa to the straggling **Parengarenga Harbour**, the drop-off point for the limpet mines (delivered by yacht from New Caledonia) that were used in the 1985 sabotage of the *Rainbow Warrior*. Bends in the road occasionally reveal glimpses of the harbour's southern headland. In late February and early March, hundreds of thousands of bar-tailed godwits turn the silica sands black as they gather for their 12,000km journey to Siberia. Insect repellent is also a must here.

The Maori Ngati Kuri people own much of the land and comprise the bulk of the population in these parts, particularly around **TE KAO** where, beside SH1, you'll spot the twin-towered Ratana Temple – one of the few remaining houses of the Ratana religion, which combines Christian teachings with elements of Maori culture and spiritual belief.

The last place of any consequence before the land sinks into the ocean is **WAITIKI LANDING**, 21km from Cape Reinga. It is home to a shop, occasionally petrol, and the *Waitiki Landing Holiday Complex* (T09/409 7508; camping $12, dorms $25, en-suite cabins ②), which has received complaints, but has a campsite, timber-lined cabins, smokehouse, and restaurant/bar open until around 8pm. The complex also rents boards for riding the dunes (4hr; $10) and can arrange tramper transport (see box opposite).

From Waitiki Landing, a dirt road twists 15km to the gorgeous and usually deserted 7km sweep of **Spirits Bay** (Kapowairua), where you'll find a DOC **campsite** ($7.50) with pitches in manuka woods, cold showers and summertime mosquitoes.

The main road continues towards Cape Reinga. After 4km you pass a turn-off to the **Te Paki Stream entrance** to Ninety Mile Beach, where there's a small picnic area and parking, plus a twenty-minute **hike** to huge sand dunes ideal for **sandboarding** or **tobogganing**. Equipment can be rented at several places from Kaitaia northwards; and also by calling ahead to Ahikaa Adventures (☎09/409 8228), who often rent boards from the Te Paki road end, right by the dunes.

Cape Reinga

The last leg to **Cape Reinga** (Te Rerenga Wairua: the "leaping place of the spirits") runs high through the hills before revealing magnificent views of the Tasman Sea and the huge dunes that foreshadow it. At road-end there's just a car park with toilets and a 800m-long interpretive trail to the Cape Reinga **lighthouse**, dramatically perched on a headland 165m above Colombia Bank, where the waves of the Tasman Sea meet the swirling currents of the Pacific Ocean in a boiling cauldron of surf. On clear days the **view** from here is stunning: east to the Surville Cliffs of North Cape, west to Cape Maria van Diemen, and north to the rocky **Three Kings Islands**, 57km offshore, which were named by Abel Tasman, who first came upon them on the eve of Epiphany 1643.

The nearest shop and restaurant is back at Waitiki Landing, and the only place to stay is DOC's serene *Tapotupotu Bay* **campsite**; turn off 3km south of Cape Reinga, from where it's another 3km down an unsealed road ($7.50; toilets, cold showers and mosquitoes). Beautifully sited where beach meets estuary, it's a popular lunchtime picnic stop for tour buses.

Cape Reinga Walks

A couple of worthwhile short **walks** radiate from the Cape Reinga car park: both form part of the much longer Cape Reinga Coastal Walkway. All these walks are described in the DOC leaflet **Cape Reinga and Te Paki Walks**, containing a useful map of the area, available at Kaitaia and elsewhere. Beware of **rip tides** on all the beaches hereabouts and bear in mind the wild and unpredictable nature of the region's weather.

Cape Reinga Coastal Walkway (38km one-way; 2–3 days; constantly undulating). This spectacular and increasingly popular coastal hike starts at Kapowairua (Spirits Bay), and heads west to Cape Reinga, continues to Cape Maria van Diemen, swings southeast to the northernmost stretch of Ninety Mile Beach, and then finally past the impressive dunes of Te Paki Stream. You need to be fit and self-sufficient: the only facilities are a couple of DOC campsites, and some ad hoc camping spots with no guaranteed water. Fresh water from streams is limited and you'll need mosquito repellent. You finish a good way from where you start, but fortunately *Waitiki Landing Holiday Complex* offers a $50 drop-off and pick-up combo.

Sandy Bay (3km return; 200m ascent on the way back; 50min–90min). Eastbound walk through scrub and young cabbage trees to a pretty cove. You can continue to the lovely **Tapotupotu Bay** (a further 3km one-way; 1–2hr).

Te Werahi Beach (2.5km return; 200m ascent on the way back; 40min–1hr). Westbound walk gradually descending with Cape Maria van Diemen in your sights.

Hokianga Harbour

South of Kaitaia, the narrow, mangrove-flanked fissures of the **Hokianga Harbour** snake deep inland past tiny and almost moribund communities. For a few days' relaxation, the tranquillity and easy pace of this rural backwater are hard to beat. From the southern shores, the harbour's incredible, deep-blue waters beautifully set off the mountainous **sand dunes** of North Head. The dunes are best seen from the rocky promontory of South Head, high above the treacherous Hokianga Bar, or can be reached by boat for sandboarding. The high forest ranges immediately to the south make excellent hiking territory, and the giant kauri of the Waipoua Forest are within easy striking distance.

According to legend, it was from here that the great Polynesian explorer **Kupe** left Aotearoa to go back to his homeland in Hawaiiki during the tenth century, and the harbour thus became known as Hokianganui-a-Kupe, "the place of Kupe's great return". Cook saw the Hokianga Heads from the *Endeavour* in 1770 but didn't realize what lay beyond, and it wasn't until a missionary crossed the hill from the Bay of Islands in 1819 that Europeans became aware of the harbour's existence. Catholics, Anglicans and Wesleyans soon followed, converting the local Ngapuhi, gaining their trust, intermarrying with them and establishing the well-integrated Maori and European communities that exist today. The Hokianga area soon rivalled the Bay of Islands in importance and notched up several firsts: European boat building began here in 1826; the first signal station opened two years later; and the first Catholic Mass was celebrated in the same year.

With the demise of kauri felling and milling (see p.200), Hokianga became an economic backwater, but over the last couple of decades, city dwellers, artists and craftspeople have started creeping in, settling in **Kohukohu** on the north shore, **Rawene**, a short ferry ride away to the south, and the two larger but still small-time settlements of **Opononi** and **Omapere**, opposite the dunes near the harbour entrance.

Getting around the Hokianga and Waipoua region is difficult without your own wheels, though Magic Bus (p.33) loops past Rawene, Omapere and Tane Mahuta en route from Paihia to Auckland several days a week in summer. Note that there are **no banks** between Kaitaia and Dargaville, 170km away to the south. The ATMs in Rawene and Omapere accept a limited range of cards so bring cash.

Kohukohu and the northern Hokianga

Heading south from Kaitaia, the hilly SH1 twists its way through the forested Mangamuka Ranges for 40km to reach **Mangamuka Bridge** from where an equally tortuous road heads to **KOHUKOHU**, a waterside cluster of century-old wooden houses on the northernmost arm of Hokianga Harbour. Kohukohu was

---

Hokianga Vehicle Ferry

Apart from a lengthy drive around the head of the harbour, the only way across the Hokianga is on the **Hokianga Vehicle Ferry** (car & driver $16 one-way, $20 return, campervans & driver $30; car passengers and pedestrians $2 each way). This shuttles from Narrows Landing, 4km east of Kohukohu on the northern shores, to Rawene in the south, a journey of fifteen minutes. Departures (starting around 7.30am) are on the hour southbound (to 8pm) and on the half-hour northbound (to 7.30pm).

once the hub of Hokianga's kauri industry, but the subsequent years of decline have only partly been arrested by the recent influx of rat-race refugees. Check out the new, community-run **Village Arts** gallery, opposite the *Waterline Café* (summer daily 10am–3pm; winter Wed–Sun 10am–3pm; free; ☎09/405 5827, Ⓦwww.villagearts.co.nz), which has already made a splash promoting the Hokianga's artistic community, with exhibitions of sculpture, painting, photography and textiles at a much higher standard than you might expect for such a backwater.

Four kilometres further east, Narrows Landing is the northern terminus of the **Hokianga Vehicle Ferry** (see opposite).

Practicalities

The beauty of **staying** on the north side of the harbour is that there's almost nothing to do except relax. There's no better place to do just that than ⚓ *The Tree House*, 2km west of the ferry terminus (☎09/405 5855, Ⓦwww.treehouse.co.nz; camping $18, dorms $30, double ❷, cottage ❹). Accommodation is scattered among the trees in two spacious dorms, double and twin cabins with sundecks and a well-equipped house bus in a macadamia orchard. There's also a self-contained cottage in Kohukohu sleeping five, and you get $4 off the price of dorm and doubles if you bring your own bedding.

Kohukohu's best **eating** is ⚓ *The Waterline*, Kohukohu Road (kitchen closes 5pm Sun–Thurs, 8pm Fri & Sat), a licensed café fabulously sited on stilts over the water with panoramic harbour views from the deck. Virtually everything for the tasty breakfasts, snacks and lunches is made on the premises, including pizzas, burgers and great coffee. There's often live music such as blues session at weekends. There's also a traditional pub serving meals, and a general **store** with a modest range of groceries.

Rawene and around

Delightful **RAWENE** occupies the tip of Herd's Point, a peninsula roughly halfway up the harbour. Though almost isolated by the mud flats at low tide, Rawene's strategic position made it an obvious choice for the location of a timber mill, which contributed material for the town's attractive wooden buildings, some perched on stilts out over the water.

The town's only significant distraction, **Clendon House**, Clendon Esplanade (Nov–April Sat–Mon 10am–4pm, May–Oct Mon & Tues 10am–4pm; $5), was the last residence of British-born US Consul James Clendon, a pivotal figure in the early life of the colony. The house itself is mostly pit-sawn kauri construction. Downstairs, one room beside the veranda has been retained as the post office it once was. Clendon Esplanade leads to the **Mangrove Walkway**, a pleasant fifteen-minute return boardwalk through the coastal shallows with boards telling of inter-tidal life and the sawmill which once operated here.

The *Postmaster's Lodgings*, 1 Parnell St (☎09/405 7676, Ⓦwww.the postmasterslodgings.co.nz; ❹), offers **B&B** in a lovely century-old house with harbour views. Book ahead for dinner, or you can BBQ on the sunny deck. The low-key *Rawene Motor Camp*, 1 Marmon St, 1.5km from the ferry landing (☎09/405 7720, Ⓦwww.rawenemotorcamp.co.nz; camping $12, dorms $18, kitchenette cabins ❶), has hilltop harbour views, a pool, tent sites and cabins in bush enclaves. **Eat** at the daytime, licensed ⚓ *Boatshed Café*, on Clendon Esplanade, which is built out over the water and offers magazines to read on the sunny deck as you tuck into gourmet pizza slices or home-made muffins, soups and espresso.

Wairere Boulders

Detouring about 40km northeast of Rawene brings you to the **Wairere Boulders** (daily during daylight hours; $10 in the honesty box; ℡09/401 9935, Ⓦwww .wairereboulders.co.nz), a privately run park encompassing huge 2.8-million-year-old basalt rocks with natural fluting making them appear like carved corrugated iron. The main self-guided loop (40min) follows a narrow path weaving among boulders and across a stream with signs turning it into a kind of nature trail. There are several additional loops plus a spur trail leading through the rainforested valley and up to a good viewpoint. Wairere is a bit out of the way, so bring supplies and make an afternoon of it. The boulders are signposted 14km north of **Taheke** on SH12; the last 8km are gravel.

Opononi and Omapere

The two small villages of **OPONONI** and **OMAPERE**, some 20km west of Rawene, comprise little more than a roadside string of houses running seamlessly for 4km along the southern shore of the Hokianga Harbour, with great views across to the massive sand dunes on the north side.

Older Kiwis remember Opononi's moment of fame in the summer of 1955–56 when a wild bottlenose dolphin, dubbed "Opo", started playing with the kids in the shallows and performing tricks with beach balls. Christmas holiday-makers jammed the narrow dirt roads; film crews were dispatched; protective laws were drafted; and Auckland musicians wrote and recorded the novelty song *Opo The Crazy Dolphin* in a day. Their tape arrived at the radio station for its first airing just as news came in that Opo had been shot under mysterious circumstances. No one ever took responsibility, but amid the national mourning the song became a hit anyway. The i-SITE shows a short video in classic 1950s-documentary style which gives a sense of the frenzied enthusiasm for Opo.

Information and accommodation

In Omapere, the Hokianga **i-SITE visitor centre** (daily: Oct–April 8.30am–5pm; May–Sept 9am–5pm; ℡09/405 8869, Ⓦwww.hokianga.co.nz), stocks information on the immediate area and Waipoua Forest (see p.200), and can book **accommodation**, which is in good supply except from Christmas to the end of January.

Copthorne Hotel & Resort SH12, Omapere ℡0800/267 846, Ⓦwww.millenniumhotels.com. The best of the hotels, set opposite the dunes, with a solar-heated pool, nice bar and licensed restaurant and a range of accommodation including some beautifully appointed waterside rooms. ⑥

Globetrekkers Lodge SH12, Omapere ℡09/405 8183, Ⓦwww .globetrekkerslodge.com. Relaxing and very well-kept hostel with some harbour views. The five- and six-bed dorms and doubles are all spacious and airy, and there's a couple of nice cabins in the grounds. TV is intentionally absent and the evening BBQ usually brings everyone together. Camping $15, dorms $26, rooms ②

Hokianga Haven 226 SH12, Omapere ℡09/405 8285, Ⓦwww.hokiangahaven.co.nz. Heather only takes single-party bookings for her two attractively furnished B&B rooms with fabulous views of the dunes and the beach just steps away. Two-night minimum. ⑥

McKenzie's Accommodation 4 Pioneers Walk, Omapere ℡09/405 8068, Ⓦwww.mckenzies accommodation.co.nz. Beachside options in either a spacious room rented as a double or a twin, with a separate bathroom and private entrance, or a s/c two-bedroom cottage. B&B ④, cottage ④

Opononi Beach Holiday Park SH12, Opononi ℡09/405 8791, Ⓦopononiholidaypark.co.nz. Spacious if basic harbourside campsite. Camping $12.50, cabins ①, self-catering cabins ②

Sights and activities

If you have your own transport it is easy enough to call in at the Waipoua Forest's giant kauri (see p.201) on your way south, but it is better to join Footprints

Waipoua (℡ 09/405 8207, ⓦ www.footprintswaipoua.co.nz), which runs excellent **guided walks** to the kauri trees. The pick of its trips is the Twilight Encounter ($85) through the forest to the two largest trees. You might see giant kauri snails, eels and *ruru* (native owl), but the emphasis is more on listening to and sensing the forest under the cover of darkness leavened with a strong Maori spiritual component – story, song and music. They pick up from accommodation in Opononi and Omapere.

To get across the harbour to the **sand dunes**, use the Hokianga Express water taxi (℡ 09/405 8872 or 021/405 872; $25) which operates from 10am daily from Opononi wharf and will drop you off with sandboards and pick you up a couple of hours later. Alternatively, view the dunes from afar at **Arai te Uru Reserve**, a wonderful viewpoint reached along Signal Station Road, 1km south of Omapere.

In town, you can spend an entertaining and fruitful day making a Maori **bone carving** with Maori carver, James, at Hokianga Bone Carving Studio, 15 Ahika St ($50; ℡ 021/298 8968, ⓔ hokiangabonecarvingstudio@gmail.com). Book ahead, have a design in mind and be prepared to spend as much of the day as you need to complete your carving: you'll be well fed while you're at it.

Around 8km southeast of Opononi, **Labyrinth Woodworks**, 647 Waiotemarama Gorge Rd, (daily 9am–5pm, beep the horn if no one answers; ℡ 09/405 4581, ⓦ www.nzanity.co.nz), is one of the region's better craft shops, its wares including carved kauri pieces and excellent woodblock prints. There are also mind-bending puzzles to play with and a maturing hedge maze.

Labyrinth marks the start of the **Waiotemarama Bush Walk** (2km loop), the best and most popular of the short walks in the district, running through a lovely fern-, palm- and kauri-filled valley. A ten-minute walk leads you to a waterfall with a small swimming hole, and after a further ten minutes you reach the first kauri.

Eating and drinking

Eating options are limited with just a couple of basic cafés fleshing out the options listed below. Groceries are pricey and the range is small.

Copthorne Hotel & Resort SH12, Omapere. The best dining hereabouts, in both the elegant restaurant (mains around $30), and the *Sands* bar (mains around $22). Both have great views over the lawns and harbour to the sand dunes. Look out for dishes with a Maori influence such as local seafood or *rawena* bread and butter pudding with *titoki* liqueur ($13).
Opononi Hotel SH12, Opononi. Lively pub offering the district's best-value eating, both bar

food and à la carte. Occasional Kiwi touring bands in summer.
Opo Takeaways SH12, Opononi. Good burgers and fish and chips but closes daily at 7pm (later in summer).
Schooner Café and Restaurant Pakia Hill, SH12, 1km south of Omapere. Good coffee, light meals and weekend evening dinners including a $15 Sunday roast. The harbour views from the café and sunny deck are excellent.

The Kauri Forests and the northern Kaipara Harbour

Northland, Auckland and the Coromandel Peninsula were once covered in mixed forest dominated by the mighty kauri (see box, p.200), the world's second-largest tree. By the early twentieth century, rapacious Europeans had nearly felled the lot, the only extensive pockets remaining in the **Waipoua and Trounson kauri forests** south of the Hokianga Harbour. Though small stands of kauri can be found all over Northland, three-quarters of all the surviving mature trees grow in these two small forests, which between them cover barely 100 square kilometres. Walks provide access to the more celebrated examples, which dwarf the surrounding tataire, kohekohe and towai trees.

This area is home to the Te Roroa people who traditionally used the kauri sparingly. Simple tools made felling and working these huge trees a difficult task, and one reserved for major projects such as large war canoes. Once the Europeans arrived with metal tools, bullock trains, wheels and winches, clear felling became easier, and most of the trees had gone by the end of the nineteenth century. The efforts of several campaigning organizations eventually bore fruit in 1952, when much of the remaining forest was designated the Waipoua Sanctuary. It's now illegal to fell a kauri except in specified circumstances, such as culling a diseased or dying tree, or when constructing a new ceremonial canoe.

Further south are the muddy, mangrove-choked shores of the **Kaipara Harbour**, New Zealand's largest. The harbour once unified this quarter of Northland, with sailboats plying its waters and linking the dairy farming and logging towns on its shores. Kauri was shipped out from the largest northern town, **Dargaville**, though the fragile boats all too often foundered on the unpredictable Kaipara Bar. Many eventually washed up on **Ripiro Beach**, which just pips Ninety Mile Beach to the title of New Zealand's longest, running for 108km.

Waipoua and Trounson kauri forests

South of the Hokianga Harbour, SH12 runs 11km through farmland to Waimamaku and the daytime-only ⚜ *Morrell's Café*, the best café in the area, where you can enjoy all-day breakfasts under $15, light meals like gourmet burgers,

---

The kauri and its uses

The **kauri** (*agathis australis*) ranks alongside the sequoias of California as one of the largest trees in existence. Unlike the sequoias, which are useless as furniture timber, kauri produce beautiful wood, a fact that hastened their demise and spawned the industries that dominated New Zealand's economy in the latter half of the nineteenth century.

The kauri is a type of pine which now grows only in New Zealand, though it once also grew in Australia and Southeast Asia, where it still has close relations. Identifiable remains of kauri forests are found all over New Zealand, but by the time humans arrived on the scene its range had contracted to Northland, Auckland, the Coromandel Peninsula and northern Waikato. Individual trees can live over 2000 years, reaching 50m in height and 20m in girth, finally toppling over as the rotting core becomes too weak to support its immense weight.

Kauri loggers

Maori have long used mature kauri for dugout canoes, but it was the "rickers" (young trees) that first drew the attention of **European loggers** since they formed perfect spars for sailing ships. The bigger trees soon earned an unmatched reputation for their durable, easy-to-work and blemish-free wood, with its straight, fine grain. Loggers' ingenuity was taxed to the limit by the difficulty of getting such huge logs out of the bush. On easier terrain, bullock wagons with up to twelve teams were lashed together to haul the logs onto primitive roads or tramways. Horse-turned winches were used on steeper ground and, where water could be deployed to transport the timber, dams were constructed from hewn logs. In narrow valleys and gullies all over Northland and the Coromandel, loggers constructed kauri dams up to 20m high and 60m across, with trapdoors at the base. Trees along the sides of the

wraps and salads (all under $12) and excellent coffee, or browse the handcrafted jewellery, silk scarves and local contemporary art.

The highway then twists and turns through nearly 20km of mature kauri in the **Waipoua Kauri Forest**. Eight kilometres south of Waimamaku you reach a small car park, from where it's a three-minute walk to New Zealand's mightiest tree, the 2000-year-old **Tane Mahuta**, "God of the Forest". A vast wall of bark 6m wide rises nearly 18m to the lowest branches, covered in epiphytes. A kilometre or so further south on SH12, a ten-minute track leads to a clearing where three paths split off to notable trees: the shortest (5min return) runs to the **Four Sisters**, relatively slender kauri all growing close together; a second path (30min return) winds among numerous big trees to **Te Matua Ngahere**, the "Father of the Forest", the second-largest tree in New Zealand – shorter than Tane Mahuta but fatter and in some ways more impressive. The third path, the **Yakas Track** (3km return; 1hr), leads to Cathedral Grove, a dense conglomeration of trees, the largest being the **Yakas Kauri**, named after veteran bushman Nicholas Yakas.

Some 9km south of Tane Mahuta, **Te Rorua Waipoua Visitor Centre** (Mon–Fri 8.30am–4.30pm, Sat & Sun 9am–4pm) has displays and information on the forest and its past.

A further 9km south, *Waipoua Lodge*, SH12 (℡09/439 0422, Ⓦwww .waipoualodge.co.nz; ⑨), offers luxurious **accommodation** in former farm buildings in the tranquil grounds of a gracious kauri villa. It's pricey (from $570) but thoroughly relaxing, with a sunroom library and secluded hot tub in the grounds; you can dine on exquisite evening meals ($90) using mostly local produce. Budget accommodation is available 14km further south at the appealingly rural *Kaihu Farm Hostel*, SH12 (℡09/439 4004, Ⓦwww.kaihufarm.co.nz;

valley were felled while the dam was filling, then the dam was opened to flush the floating trunks down the valley to inlets where the logs were rafted up and towed to the mills.

Gum diggers

Once an area had been logged, the **gum diggers** typically moved in. Like most pines, kauri exudes a thick resin to cover any scars inflicted on it, and huge accretions form on the sides of trunks and in globules around the base. Maori chewed the gum, made torches from it to attract fish at night and burned the powdered resin to form a pigment used for *moko* (traditional tattoos). Once Pakeha got in on the act, it was exported as a raw material for furniture varnishes, linoleum, denture moulds and the "gilt" edging on books. When it could no longer be found on the ground, diggers – mostly Dalmatian, but also Maori, Chinese and Malaysian – thrust long poles into the earth and hooked out pieces with bent rods; elsewhere, the ground was dug up and sluiced to recover the gum. Almost all New Zealand gum was exported, but by the early twentieth century synthetic resins had captured the gum market. Kauri gum is still considered one of the finest varnishes for musical instruments, and occasional accidental finds supply such specialist needs.

The future

In recent years the kauri have been further threatened by a new disease known as PTA or **kauri dieback** (Ⓦwww.kauridieback.co.nz) with symptoms including yellowed leaves, dead branches, resinous lesions close to the ground, and eventually, death. The disease is transmitted through soil and water, so always keep to the tracks and boardwalks and clean your footwear after visiting a kauri forest.

tent site $18, dorm $28, rooms ❷) with glowworms in the bush and a 7km walk to the Trounson kauris.

Immediately south of *Waipoua Lodge*, a side road leads 7km to the **Trounson Kauri Park**, a small but superb stand of kauri where the **Trounson Kauri Walk** (40min loop) weaves though lovely rainforest. In 1997, Trounson was turned into a "mainland island" (see *Native Wildlife* colour section) in order to foster North Island brown kiwi survival. Numbers are up significantly, and you've a good chance of seeing them – along with weta and glowworms – if you stay over. Right by the park there's the simple but popular DOC **campsite** ($10), which is equipped with kitchen, toilets and hot showers; and 4km southeast you can stay at the *Kauri Coast Top 10 Holiday Park* (☏0800/807 200, ⓦwww.kauricoasttop10 .co.nz; camping $18, standard cabins ❷, kitchen cabins ❸, motel units ❹). It is easy to do a self-guided kauri walk after dark but you learn (and probably see) a lot more by joining the *Holiday Park*'s two-hour guided **night walk** (every night, weather permitting; $25, $20 for non-guests).

Kai Iwi Lakes

The **Kai Iwi Lakes**, 11km west of SH12 and 20km south of Trounson, are a real change, with pine woods running down to fresh, crystal-blue waters fringed by silica-white sand. All three are dune lakes fed by rainwater and with no visible outlet. Though the largest, **Taharoa**, is less than a kilometre across, and **Waikere** and **Kai Iwi** are barely a hundred metres long, they constitute the deepest and some of the largest dune lakes in the country. People flock here in the summer to swim, fish and waterski, but outside the first weeks in January you can usually find a quiet spot. Shallow and consequently warmer than the sea, they're good for an early-season dip.

There's no public transport to the lakes, but you'll find **accommodation** at the large and well-equipped *Kai Iwi Lakes* (☏09/439 0986; camping $12, campervans $20) which comprises the Pine Beach site on the gently shelving shores of Taharoa Lake, with water, toilets and cold showers; and the more intimate Promenade Point site with just long-drop toilets.

Dargaville and around

The sleepy dairying and *kumara*-growing town of **DARGAVILLE**, 30km south of Kai Iwi Lakes, was founded as a port in 1872, on the strongly tidal but navigable Northern Wairoa River, by Australian Joseph McMullen Dargaville. Ships came to load kauri logs and transport gum (see box, p.200) extracted by Dalmatian settlers who, by the early part of the twentieth century, formed a sizeable portion of the community.

The only specific sight is the **Dargaville Museum** (daily: Oct–March 9am–5pm; April–Sept 9am–4pm; $10), in the hilltop Harding Park, 2km west of town and marked by two masts rescued from the *Rainbow Warrior* (see box, p.185). It contains extensive displays of artefacts recovered from the shifting dunes, which occasionally reveal old shipwrecks. The only pre-European artefact is the Ngati Whatua *waka*, which lay buried under the sands of the North Head of the Kaipara Harbour from 1809 until 1972, and is a rare example of a canoe hewn entirely with stone tools. A fine collection of kauri gum gives pride of place to an 84kg piece, reputedly the largest ever found.

At the western end of town, at the **Woodturners Kauri Gallery & Working Studio**, 4 Murdoch St/SH12 (daily 9am–dark, ☏09/439 4975, ⓦwww .thewoodturnersstudio.co.nz), leading woodturner Rick Taylor demonstrates what can be done with the extraordinarily varied grains and colours of kauri, sells all manner of kauri products, and runs courses for those prepared to dedicate a day or more. This is also the best place for local **information**.

Further explorations can be made with Taylor Made Tours, who run **beach tours** ($85; ℡09/439 1576, Ⓦtaylormadetours.co.nz) on a specially designed six-wheeled, ten-passenger truck along a wild and exposed section of Ripiro Beach to the disused Kaipara lighthouse, taking in shipwrecks en route.

Practicalities

Dargaville has a modest range of **places to stay** including the fairly central *Greenhouse Hostel*, in a 1920s former school at 15 Gordon St (℡09/439 6342; Ⓔgreenhousebackpackers@ihug.co.nz; dorms $23, rooms ❶; closed June–Aug), which is old-fashioned but clean and well-run; the park-like grounds of *Dargaville Holiday Park*, 10 Onslow St (℡0800/114 441, Ⓦwww.kauriparks.co.nz; camping $14, cabins ❷, units ❷), a ten-minute walk from town; and *Kauri House Lodge*, 60 Bowen St (℡09/439 8082, Ⓦwww.kaurihouselodge.co.nz; ❼), with Dargaville's grandest rooms in an engagingly low-key yet vast kauri villa with large en-suite rooms, a billiard room, library and swimming pool.

There's adequate **eating** at *Blah Blah Blah*, 101 Victoria St, a licensed café specializing in dishes featuring Dargaville's famed *kumara*, and at *Shiraz*, 17 Hokianga Rd (℡09/439 0024; closed Sun), which does North Indian dishes plus seafood and pizza.

Around Dargaville: Baylys Beach and Ripiro Beach

A minor road runs 14km west from Dargaville to **Baylys Beach**, a conglomeration of mostly holiday homes on a central section of 100km-long **Ripiro Beach**, a strand renowned for its mobility, with several metres of beach often being shifted by a single tide, and huge areas being reclaimed over the centuries; the anchors or prows of long-lost wrecks periodically reappear through the sand. As elsewhere on the West Coast, tidal rips and holes make swimming dangerous and there are no beach patrols. Beach driving is no less fraught with danger and shouldn't be undertaken without prior local consultation; vehicles frequently get stranded. Nevertheless, it's a fine place for long walks, and spotting seals and penguins in winter. When easterlies are blowing the coastline is adorned with kites, flown out from the shore and drawing fishing lines for anything up to a kilometre. They're left for twenty minutes or so then hauled in, often heavy with fish.

You can **stay** at the well-run *Baylys Beach Holiday Park*, 22 Seaview Rd (℡09/439 6349, Ⓦwww.baylysbeach.co.nz; camping $15, caravans & cabins ❶, units & cottage ❹), a short walk from the beach and with quad bikes for rent. **Eating** is best at ⚘ *The Funky Fish*, 34 Seaview Rd (℡09/439 8883; closed Mon & Tues in winter; reserve in advance for dinner in summer and for Sun lunch all year), a groovy modern café and bar where you'll find great fish and chips, a speciality beer-battered dory with char-grilled lemon and salad, plus a range of burgers, baguettes and a varied à la carte evening menu, and a great garden bar.

Matakohe and the Kauri Museum

From Dargaville, SH12 runs 17km south through flat farmland to the knobby 180m **Tokatoka Peak**. Panoramic views unfold from the summit of this extinct volcanic plug, reached in ten breathless minutes from a trailhead 1km off SH12 near the *Tokatoka* pub.

If there's one museum you must see in the north it's the **Kauri Museum**, Church Road (daily 9am–5pm; $15; Ⓦwww.kaurimuseum.com), at tiny **MATAKOHE**, a further 30km south. One of the best small museums in the country, and deserving at least a couple of hours, it explains the way the kauri's timber and its valuable gum shaped the lives of pioneers in Northland. The displays focus on the makeshift settlements around logging camps, the gumfields, and the lives of merchants who were among the few who could afford to buy the fine kauri furniture or beautifully carved gum on show. Diagrams show how even Tane Mahuta is a midget compared to the giants of yore, and the smell of the freshly sawn timber lures you to the replica steam sawmill.

If you're travelling by public transport, visiting the museum will mean **staying** overnight. Campers should head to the *Matakohe Top 10 Holiday Park* (℡0800/431 6431, ⓦwww.matakohetop10.co.nz; camping $17, cabins ❷, motels ❹), a small, hillside campsite 500m beyond the museum offering great harbour views. *Matakohe House* (℡09/431 7091, ⓦwww.matakohehouse.co.nz; ❻), offers comfortable B&B right by the museum, with home-cooked café food, or head for *Petite Provence*, 703c Tinopai Rd, 9km south of Matakohe, (℡09/431 7552 ⓦwww.petiteprovence.co.nz; ❺), a lovely French-run B&B amid rolling farmland with views of the Kaipara, where evening meals ($45) are available. There is relatively sophisticated **dining** 5km east at Paparoa where *Sahara* (℡09/431 6833; generally closed Mon–Wed) occupies a former bank building.

Travel details

The following are direct services.

Buses

Auckland to: Dargaville (6 weekly; 3hr); Kerikeri (3 daily; 5hr); Paihia (5–6 daily; 4hr 20min); Waipu (4–7 daily; 2hr 20min); Warkworth (4–6 daily; 1hr); Whangarei (4–7; 3hr).
Dargaville to: Auckland (6 weekly; 3hr).
Kaitaia to: Kerikeri (1 daily; 1hr 40min); Paihia (1 daily; 2hr).
Kerikeri to: Auckland (3 daily; 5hr); Kaitaia (1 daily; 1hr 40min); Paihia (3 daily; 20min).
Mangonui to: Paihia (1 daily; 1hr 20min).
Paihia to: Auckland (5–6 daily; 4hr 20min); Kaitaia (1 daily; 2hr); Kerikeri (3 daily; 20min); Mangonui (1 daily; 1hr 20min); Whangarei (4–6 daily; 1hr 15min).
Waipu to: Auckland (4–7 daily; 2hr 20min); Whangarei (4–6 daily; 30min).

Warkworth to: Auckland (4–6 daily; 1hr).
Whangarei to: Auckland (4–7 daily; 3hr); Paihia (4–6 daily; 1hr 15min); Warkworth (4–6 daily; 1hr 45min).

Ferries

Kohukohu to: Rawene (hourly; 20min).
Opua to: Okiato (every 10–20min; 10min).
Paihia to: Russell by passenger ferry (every 20min; 15min).
Rawene to: Kohukohu (hourly; 20min).

Flights

Bay of Islands (Paihia/Kerikeri) to: Auckland (5 daily; 40min).
Kaitaia to: Auckland (1–2 daily; 45min).
Whangarei to: Auckland (7–9 daily; 35min); Great Barrier Island (1–2 weekly; 30min); Wellington (1 Mon–Fri; 1hr 30min).

③ Western North Island

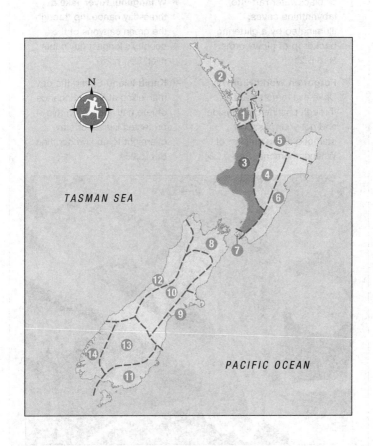

CHAPTER 3 # Highlights

* **Raglan** Surf New Zealand's finest waves or just soak up the atmosphere of this hypnotic harbourside town. See p.214

* **Waitomo** Abseil, squeeze or blackwater raft into labyrinthine caves, illuminated by a glittering backdrop of glowworms. See p.219

* **Forgotten World Highway** Drive this remote road through pristine countryside and get your passport stamped at the outpost of Whangamomona. See p.224

* **Egmont National Park** Circumnavigate or scale the conical summit of the North Island's second highest peak, Mount Taranaki. See p.232

* **Whanganui River** Take a three-day canoe trip through the green canyons of the country's longest navigable river. See p.237

* **Kapiti Island** Spend the day marvelling at the abundance of rare native birds on this protected island, or stay overnight to go kiwi spotting. See p.254

▲ Kaka on Kapiti Island

Western North Island

M uch of the appeal of the **Western North Island** is tied to its extraordinary **history** of pre-European settlement and post-European conflict. It was on the west coast, at **Kawhia**, that the Tainui people first landed in New Zealand; the *Tainui* canoe in which they arrived is buried here, and the waterside tree it was moored to lives on. Kawhia was also the birthplace of **Te Rauparaha**, the great Maori chief who led his people from here down the coast to Kapiti Island and on to the South Island, to escape the better-armed tribes of the Waikato.

Approaching the region from the north, the **Waikato**, farming country centres on the workaday provincial capital, **Hamilton**, while nearby **Raglan** has world-class surf as well as some great places to stay, eat or just unwind.

South of the Waikato, the **King Country** took its name from the King Movement (see p.218), and was the last significant area in New Zealand to succumb to European colonization. Dazzling natural features most famously include the limestone **Waitomo Caves**, where otherwordly rock formations surmount glowworm-filled caverns. Further south, the giant thumbprint peninsula of **Taranaki** is dominated by the symmetrical cone of **Mount Taranaki**, within the **Egmont National Park**. At its foot, **New Plymouth** warrants a visit for its excellent contemporary art gallery and access to a multitude of **surf beaches**.

Inland from Egmont National Park, the farming town of **Taumarunui** is one of the main jumping-off points for multi-day canoe trips along the **Whanganui River**, through the heart of the verdant **Whanganui National Park**. The river bisects **Wanganui**, a small, gracious and creative city whose river-port past can be relived on a restored paddle steamer. Some 60km to the southeast, the university city of **Palmerston North** lies at the centre of the rich farming region of **Manawatu**. A cluster of rural communities line the highway south to the **Kapiti Coast**, where laidback, beachside **Paraparaumu** is the launch point for boat trips to the paradisiacal bird sanctuary of **Kapiti Island**.

South from Auckland to Hamilton

After the motorway turns to ordinary highway south of Auckland, the first place of historical and cultural significance is at **NGARUAWAHIA**, a farming centre at the junction of the Waikato and Waipa rivers 100km south of Auckland on SH1. Both rivers were important Maori canoe routes and the **King Movement** (see p.218) has its roots here. Home to the Maori king, the town was the scene of the

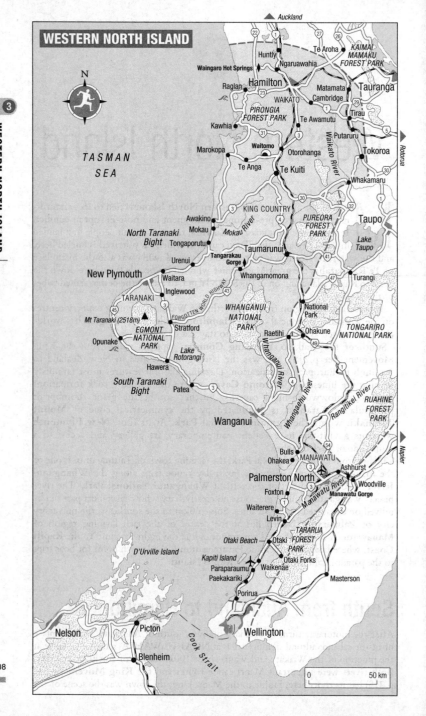

WESTERN NORTH ISLAND

N

▲ Auckland

TASMAN
SEA

Waingaro Hot Springs
Huntly
Ngaruawahia
Raglan
Hamilton
WAIKATO
PIRONGIA
FOREST PARK
Kawhia
Marokopa
Waitomo
Te Anga
Otorohanga
Te Kuiti

Te Aroha
KAIMAI
MAMAKU
FOREST PARK
Matamata
Cambridge
Tauranga
Tirau
Te Awamutu
Putaruru
Tokoroa
Whakamaru

Awakino
Mokau
Mokau River
North Taranaki
Bight
Tongaporutu
Urenui
Tangarakau
Gorge
New Plymouth
Waitara
Inglewood
TARANAKI
Mt Taranaki (2518m) ▲
EGMONT
NATIONAL
PARK
Opunake
Stratford
Lake
Rotorangi
Hawera
South Taranaki
Bight
Patea

KING COUNTRY
PUREORA
FOREST
PARK
Taupo
Lake
Taupo

Taumarunui
Whangamomona
FORGOTTEN WORLD HIGHWAY
WHANGANUI
NATIONAL
PARK
Raetihi
Whanganui River
National
Park
Ohakune
TONGARIRO
NATIONAL PARK
Turangi

Rotorua
Napier

Wanganui

RUAHINE
FOREST
PARK
Rangitikei River
Whangaehu River

Bulls
Ohakea
MANAWATU
Ashhurst
Palmerston North
Woodville
Foxton
Manawatu River
Manawatu Gorge
Waiterere
Levin
Otaki Beach
TARARUA
FOREST
PARK
Otaki
Kapiti Island
Otaki Forks
Paraparaumu
Waikenae
Paekakariki
Masterton
Porirua

D'Urville Island

Nelson
Picton
Blenheim

Cook Strait

Wellington

0   50 km

Getting around

Transport through the Western North Island is piecemeal. The **rail** line runs partly through the region, with a single daytime service in both directions between Auckland and Wellington, operating daily from mid-September to early May, and Friday, Saturday and Sunday only from early May to mid-September. Frequent commuter rail services also run between Wellington and Paraparaumu.

Most **long-haul bus** services are run by InterCity/Newmans, though there are a number of fairly short runs operated by competing companies, including Dalroy Express (℡06/759 0197, ⓦwww.dalroytours.co.nz; Auckland–Hamilton–Otorohanga–Te Kuiti–New Plymouth–Hawera), Go Kiwi (℡0800/446 549, ⓦwww.go-kiwi .co.nz; Hamilton–Auckland), Guthreys Express (℡0800/732 528, ⓦwww.guthreys .co.nz; Auckland–Hamilton–Rotorua) and Waitomo Wanderer (℡0508/926 337, ⓦwww.waitomotours.co.nz; Rotorua–Otorohanga–Waitomo Caves).

signing of the Raupatu Land Settlement (1995), whereby the government agreed to compensate Tainui for land confiscated in the 1860s.

The Maori heritage is most evident on **Regatta Day** (the closest Saturday to March 17). Watched by the Maori king, a parade of great war canoes takes place along the two rivers; with events such as hurdle races at the **Turangawaewae Marae** on River Road, off SH1 just north of the river bridge. The *marae* is only open to the public on Regatta Day; the rest of the year you can view it through the perimeter fence made of the dead trunks of tree ferns interspersed with robustly sculpted red posts and a couple of finely carved entranceways.

Twenty-three kilometres west of Ngaruawahia, on Waingaro Road at the junction with SH22, is the **Waingaro Hot Springs** complex (daily 9am–10pm; $10), with three hot-water pools and New Zealand's longest hot-water slide, as well as family-oriented **accommodation** (℡07/825 4761, ⓦwww.waingaro hotsprings.co.nz; camping $20, cabins ❷, motel rooms ❸).

Hamilton

On the banks of the languid green Waikato River, New Zealand's fourth-largest city, **HAMILTON**, functions as a regional hub rather than a major tourist destination, but it's within striking distance of some of the North Island's top spots, such as the surf beaches of Raglan and Waitomo Caves, as well as Auckland, 127km north. It's worth devoting some time to the excellent **Museum of Art and History** and the tranquil **Hamilton Gardens**, as well as a **river cruise**.

Arrival, information and city transport

Super Shuttle (℡0800/727 747; $21), connects Hamilton's international **airport** to the **Transport Centre**, on the corner of Anglesea and Bryce streets. The centre is the hub for **local and long-haul buses** and has **left luggage** lockers and a **taxi** rank; alternatively ring Hamilton Taxis on ℡0800/477 477. The **train station**, on Fraser Street (℡07/846 8353) in the suburb of Frankton, a twenty-minute walk west of the centre, is linked to the Transport Centre by bus #3. Bus and train tickets are also sold at the **i-SITE visitor centre**, at 5 Garden Place (Mon–Fri 9am–5.30pm, Sat & Sun 9.30am–3.30pm; ℡07/839 3580, ⓦwww.waikatonz .com), which also has internet access. Hut and camping passes are available from the **DOC office** at Level 5, 73 Rostrevor St (Mon–Fri 8.30am–4.30pm; ℡07/858 1000). The main post office is on Bryce Street.

Most of Hamilton's attractions are within walking distance of the centre; for those further afield (including Cambridge, Te Awamutu, Raglan and Paeroa), pick up the free Busit timetable (℡0800/4287 5463, ⓦwww.busit.co.nz). One-way fares within the city limits are $2.90 including free transfers for two hours.

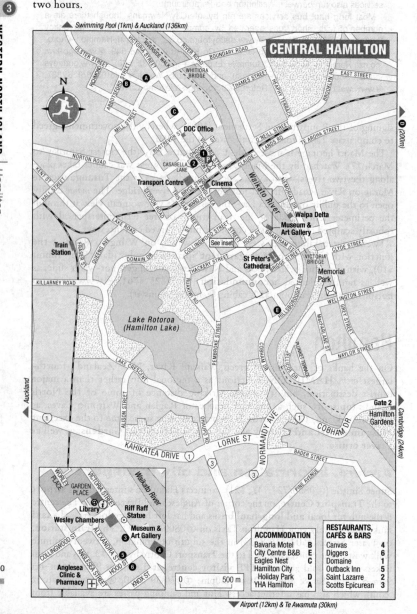

CENTRAL HAMILTON

Swimming Pool (1km) & Auckland (136km)

N

ULSTER STREET
RIVERSIDE WALK
RIVER ROAD
BOUNDARY ROAD
WHITIORA BRIDGE
THAMES STREET
EAST STREET
BROOKLYN RD
HEAPHY TERRACE
RICHMOND ST
ABBOTSFORD STREET
VICTORIA STREET

MILL STREET
O'NEILL STREET
TE AROHA STREET

DOC Office

NORTON ROAD
ROSTREVOR ST
LONDON ST
CLAUDE
LANDS RD

KENT ST
CASABELLA LANE
MEMORIAL DR

HALL ST
Transport Centre
Cinema
Waipa Delta

BRYCE STREET
Museum & Art Gallery

LAKE ROAD
SEDDON ROAD
TRISTRAM STREET
WARD ST
WAIPA ST

FRASER ST
COLLINGWOOD STREET
London STREET
HOOD ST
GRANTHAM ST
CLYDE STREET

DOMAIN DR
See inset
St Peter's Cathedral
VICTORIA BRIDGE

Train Station
QUEENS AVE
HILL ST
RUAKIWI RD
THACKERAY STREET
BRIDGE STREET
Memorial Park

KILLARNEY ROAD
WELLINGTON STREET

Lake Rotoroa (Hamilton Lake)
HILSBOROUGH TERR
MACFARLANE ST
GREY STREET
NAYLOR STREET

LAKE CRESCENT
PEMBROKE STREET
COBHAM DR
PLUNKET TERRACE

ALISON STREET
JELLICOE DR
Gate 2 Hamilton Gardens

KAHIKATEA DRIVE
LORNE ST
NORMANDY AVE
COBHAM DR
BADER STREET
PINE AVENUE

Auckland
Cambridge (24km)

INSET:
WORLEY PLACE
GARDEN PLACE
VICTORIA STREET
Waikato River

Library
Riff Raff Statue
Wesley Chambers
Museum & Art Gallery

COLLINGWOOD ST
ALEXANDRA ST
ANGLESEA ST
HOOD ST

Anglesea Clinic & Pharmacy
KNOX ST

0   500 m

ACCOMMODATION		RESTAURANTS, CAFÉS & BARS	
Bavaria Motel	B	Canvas	4
City Centre B&B	E	Diggers	6
Eagles Nest	C	Domaine	1
Hamilton City Holiday Park	D	Outback Inn	5
		Saint Lazarre	2
YHA Hamilton	A	Scotts Epicurean	3

Airport (12km) & Te Awamuta (30km)

Accommodation

Hamilton specializes in business accommodation for farm company reps in **motels**, mostly lining Ulster Street, but there are also several **B&Bs** and **hostels**.

Bavaria Motel 203–207 Ulster St ☎07/839 2520, ⓦwww.bavariamotel.co.nz. Large, comfortable s/c units with DVD players, and access to a decent library of discs. ❸

City Centre B&B 3 Anglesea St ☎07/838 1671, ⓦwww.citycentrebb.tk. Just one en-suite room with kitchenette opening out to a beautifully landscaped garden and swimming pool. B&B ❸

Eagles Nest 937 Victoria St ☎07/838 2704, ⓦwww.eaglesbackpackers.co.nz. Converted city-centre retail premises now housing six- and eight-bed dorms, plus private rooms. There's a

deck with BBQ overlooking the street. Dorms $25, rooms ❶

Hamilton City Holiday Park Ruakura Rd ☎07/855 8255, ⓦwww.hamiltoncityholidaypark .co.nz. Well-tended campsite in a park-like setting 1km east of the centre. Camping $30–32, cabins ❶, units ❸

YHA Hamilton 140 Ulster St ☎07/957 1848, ⓦwww.yha.co.nz. Contemporary urban pad with a sauna and Sky TV in its private rooms (some en suite). Dorms $28–31, rooms ❶/❷

The City

Everything of interest in Hamilton is either along or just off the main drag, **Victoria Street**, which parallels the west bank of the tree-lined Waikato River. Diagonally opposite the 1924 **Wesley Chambers** (now *Rydges Le Grand* hotel) on the corner of Collingwood Street, influenced by the buildings of boomtime Chicago, is a small open space graced by a statue of the English-born *Rocky Horror Show* creator, **Richard O'Brien** – decked out as Riff Raff, the role he played in the movie of the show – who spent his teens and early twenties hereabouts. There are regular screenings of the cult film at Skycity **cinema**, in the CentrePlace Mall on Ward Street.

At the corner of Bridge Street, the roughcast concrete **St Peter's Cathedral**, built in 1915, was modelled on a fifteenth-century church in Norfolk, England.

Waikato Museum of Art and History and the gardens

Set in a modern building that steps down to the river, the excellent **Waikato Museum of Art and History**, 1 Grantham St (daily 10am–4.30pm; donation; ⓦwww.waikatomuseum.org.nz), features a section devoted to **Tainui culture**, with woven flax, tools, ritual artefacts, carvings and the magnificent *Te Winika* war canoe.

Across the river in **Memorial Park**, various **river cruises** operated by Cruise Waikato (☎0508/426 458, ⓦwww.cruise-waikato.co.nz) include a one-hour "sausage sizzle and coffee cruise" ($25).

From Memorial Park, a riverside path heads 2km south to the huge, unfenced **Hamilton Gardens**, Cobham Drive/SH1 (free; bus #10 from the Transport Centre; ⓦwww.hamiltongardens.co.nz), with extensive displays of roses, tropical plants, rhododendrons, magnolias and cacti. Pick up a free map from the gardens' visitor centre (daily 9am–5pm; café attached).

Eating, drinking and nightlife

Hamilton's sizeable student population ensures lively term-time nightlife, and the city's food and drink scene concentrates along the southern end of Victoria Street and around the corner on Hood Street, where places start off as cafés and progressively become restaurant/bars as the day wears on. In mid-June, the annual four-day Fieldays festival (ⓦwww.fieldays.co.nz), the largest agricultural field day in the southern hemisphere, is held at Mystery Creek Events Centre just outside the city.

Canvas 1 Grantham St ⓣ07/839 2535. Stylish restaurant in the museum complex, popular for its considered menu of beautifully prepared modern Kiwi dishes, such as seared lamb in mustard sauce on five-grain toast. Lunch mains $10–22, dinners mains $25–30. Open lunch Tues–Fri, dinner Tues–Sat.

Diggers 17 Hood St. Down-to-earth drinkers' den, with a long kauri bar, liveliest at weekends, with a great atmosphere and regular gigs on Sun.

Domaine 575 Victoria St ⓣ07/839 2100. Vibrant modern restaurant with streetside seating and booths at the back, that's good for café-style

lunches and more formal evening meals (mains under $35). Closed Sun & Mon.

Outback Inn The Marketplace, off Hood St. Big boisterous student drinking hole, with pool tables and a selection of beers and snacks. Dancing Tues–Sat; DJ Wed–Sat; occasional live bands.

Saint Lazarre Casabella Lane. Chic French-run café in an elegant pot-planted alley with the best Kiwi deli food in town (filo triangles, wraps, salads and more), as well as flaky French-style pastries.

Scotts Epicurean 181 Victoria St. Bustling daytime café/restaurant, good for coffee, light meals and luscious cakes.

Southeast of Hamilton

Hamilton won't detain you long, but there's enough to soak up a couple of days' exploration in the immediate vicinity. As well as the surfers' paradise of **Raglan**, **Kawhia** is also worth a squiz for its remoteness and cultural significance. Southeast of Hamilton on SH1, there's a genteel English charm to **Cambridge**, while at **Matamata**, **Hobbiton tours** are an essential stop for *Lord of the Rings* and *Hobbit* film fans.

Cambridge

In an agricultural belt, **CAMBRIDGE**, 24km southeast of Hamilton, was founded as a militia settlement at the navigable limit of the Waikato River in 1864, and today is surrounded by stud farms. Mosaics of Cambridge-bred winners are embedded in the pavements along the town's **Equine Stars Walk of Fame**, at Cambridge Thoroughbred Lodge, 6km southeast on SH1 (Mon–Fri 10am–3pm; $12; ⓣ07/827 8118, ⓦwww.cambridgethoroughbredlodge.co.nz), you can tour stables housing prized breeds.

The town's collection of elegant **nineteeth- and twentieth-century buildings** are mapped on a heritage trail brochure (free from the i-SITE), making a pleasant hour-long stroll. Shopping in Cambridge is equally genteel; in the near-total absence of chain stores, another leaflet outlines a trail around Cambridge's locally owned **boutique shops**.

Buses operated by InterCity and NakedBus on their Auckland–Wellington routes stop beside the town hall on Lake Street. Cambridge Travel Lines (ⓣ07/827 7363) run a local service from Hamilton (Mon–Fri only) that stops by St Andrew's church. Both stops are two minutes' walk from the **i-SITE visitor centre**, at the corner of Queen and Victoria streets (Mon–Fri 9am–5pm, Sat & Sun 10am–4pm; ⓣ07/823 3456, ⓦwww.cambridgeinfo.co.nz), in a gracious building adorned with iridescent paisley wallpaper, which has **internet access** and can book accommodation.

If strolling has left you peckish, drop into *The Deli*, 48 Victoria St, a daytime venue for coffee, snacks, light meals and Devonshire teas (mains $10–17); or *Fran's Café*, 62 Victoria St (closed Sun), crammed with kitsch china ornaments and teapots, for home-baked snacks and light meals ($9.50–15).

Matamata

The dairy-farming and racehorse-breeding town of **Matamata**, 41km northeast of Cambridge, shot to prominence a few years back as the location of **Hobbiton** from the *Lord of the Rings* trilogy. All film sets were supposed to be destroyed after filming, but bad weather stopped the dismantling of seventeen hobbit-hole facades – fortuitously, as it happens, since they were rebuilt to film the forthcoming *Hobbit* movies. There are some lifelike *Lord of the Rings* character **statues** in the town centre, but the only way to visit the Hobbiton location (on a working sheep farm 15km southwest of town) is with Rings Scenic Tours' two-hour trips (daily 9.30am, 10.45am, noon, 1.15pm, 2.30pm, 3.45pm, plus 5pm in high season; $58; ℡07/888 6838, Ⓦwww.hobbitontours.com). Tour highlights include the unadorned facades of the **hobbit holes** (the interiors were filmed in Wellington studios), particularly the lake and the Party Tree (a big radiata pine). Die-hard fans will revel in the tour guides' unexpurgated tales of the filming.

Trips leave from the Matamata **i-SITE visitor centre**, 45 Broadway (daily 9am–5pm; ℡07/888 7260, Ⓦwww.matamatanz.co.nz), where the InterCity/Newmans **buses** drop off. Most people do the tour and press on, but it's worth stopping to **eat** at the funky, licensed *A Workman's Café*, 52 Broadway (℡07/888 5498; Tues–Sun breakfast till 9pm or later; mains $10–18), or have a pint at the nearby *Redoubt* **pub**.

Te Awamutu

"TA", as it's dubbed by locals, is renowned for its musical and military history. The birthplace of fraternal Kiwi music icons Tim and Neil Finn, of **Split Enz** and **Crowded House** fame, **TE AWAMUTU**, 30km south of Hamilton, has a lively town centre surrounded by rolling hills, dairy pasture and overlooked by Mount Pirongia. During the 1863 **New Zealand Wars**, Te Awamutu was a garrison for government forces and site of one of the most famous battles of the conflict, fought at the hastily constructed Orakau *pa,* where three hundred Maori stood off two thousand soldiers for three days.

InterCity and Dalroy buses on the Auckland–New Plymouth run stop at the **i-SITE visitor centre**, 1 Gorst Ave (Mon–Fri 9am–5pm, Sat & Sun 10am–4pm, extended hours in summer; ℡07/871 3259, Ⓦwww.teawamutu.co.nz). Fans can take a self-guided jaunt round places of significance in the Finn brothers' unremarkable formative years by picking up the **"Finn Tour"** booklet ($5). The i-SITE lies immediately across from Te Awamutu's extensive **rose gardens** (open access; free), on Gorst Avenue, at their best between November and May. It also holds the key to the 1854 garrison church, **St John's**, just across Arawata Street. Inside is a tribute from the British regiment, written in Maori, honouring Maori who crawled, under fire, onto the battlefield to give water to wounded British soldiers.

Te Awamutu Museum and library, 135 Roche St, ten minutes' walk west of the i-SITE (Mon–Fri 10am–4pm, Sat 10am–1pm, Sun 1–4pm; free; Ⓦwww.tamuseum.org.nz), contains an excellent collection of early, sacred Maori artefacts, displays about European settlers and the New Zealand Wars, and a *True Colours* exhibit, devoted to the Finn brothers.

The i-SITE can book **accommodation**. For daytime **food** try the small daytime French patisserie, *Salvador's*, 50 Alexandra St (closed Sun), or the *Central Café*, 201 Alexandra St. The *Redoubt Bar & Eatery*, on the corner of Alexandra and Rewi streets, is great for coffee, daytime and evening meals or just a beer.

Raglan and around

Visitors often linger far longer than they intend in **RAGLAN**, lured by the town's bohemian arts and crafts tenor and the laidback spirit of the **surfing** community, here for some of the best left-handed breaks in the world.

Raglan hugs the south side of the large and picturesque Raglan Harbour, 48km west of Hamilton. The horizon to the south is dominated by **Mount Karioi**, which according to Maori legend was the ultimate goal of the great migratory canoe *Tainui*. On reaching the mouth of the harbour a bar blocked the way, hence the name Whaingaroa ("long pursuit"). The shortened epithet, Whangaroa, was the name used for the harbour until 1855, when it was renamed Raglan after the officer who led the Charge of the Light Brigade. There's good **hiking** and **horse-riding** both here and further south at **Bridal Veil Falls**

Arrival and information

Cafés, banks and pubs line palm-shaded **Bow Street**, whose western end butts against the harbour. The surf beaches (p.216) are around 8km out of town.

The #23 Hamilton city Busit **bus** (see p.210) arrives opposite the library on Bow Street, departing from outside. By the time you're reading this the **i-SITE visitor centre** (Nov–March Mon–Fri 9.30am–5pm, Sat 10am–5pm, Sun 10am–3pm; April–Oct Mon–Fri 9am–3.30pm, Sat 10am–4pm, Sun 10am–3pm; ℡07/825 0556, ⊛www.raglan.net.nz) will share space with the local history **museum** in a new purpose-built building on Wainui Road. Both the library and Raglan Video, at 6 Bow St, have **internet access** (daily 10am–8.30pm).

Accommodation

Raglan has an abundance of **accommodation** for all budgets; the i-SITE can help with bookings including holiday cottages and apartments.

Belindsay's 28 Wallis St ℡07/825 6592, ℮belindsays@hotmail.com. Cosy backpackers in a 1930s house with polished wood floors, stained-glass windows and a deep bath as well as shower. One three-bed dorm, a single and two doubles, a sunny lounge and kitchen. Dorms $17–20, rooms ❶

Harbourview Hotel 14 Bow St ℡07/825 8010, ℮harbourviewhotel@xtra.co.nz. Pleasant rooms, including singles in the town's archetypal hotel, some with a veranda overlooking the main street. ❷/❸

Karioi Lodge, 5 Whaanga Rd, Whale Bay ℡07/825 7873, ⊛www.karioilodge.co.nz. Pleasant hostel in native bush 8km southwest of Raglan, with four-bed dorms and doubles, a communal kitchen, sauna, bike rental, mountain tracks and a flying fox, with free pick-up from Raglan. Also runs a surf school. Dorms $27, ❷

🏃 **Raglan Backpackers & Waterfront Lodge** 6 Nero St ℡07/825 0515, ⊛www .raglanbackpackers.co.nz. Hammock-strewn backpackers in the town centre, laid out round a courtyard that backs onto the estuary. Free use of kayaks, bikes, spa and sauna plus cheap surfboard

rental ($30/half-day including wetsuit). Also arranges surf lessons (p.216). Dorms $26, rooms ❷

Raglan Kopua Holiday Park Marine Parade ℡07/825 8283, ⊛www.raglanholidaypark.co.nz. Central campsite 1km by road from town also accessible by footbridge. It is well sited next to Te Kopua, the harbour's safest swimming beach. Camping $15–16, dorms $23, cabins ❷, tourist flats ❹

Sleeping Lady Lodgings Raglan Surfing School, 5 Whaanga Rd, Whale Bay ℡07/825 7873, ⊛www.sleepinglady.co.nz. The *Karioi Lodge* (see above) also has half a dozen delightful s/c holiday homes scattered through coastal bush 8km southwest of Raglan, sleeping from two to twelve ($95–240 a night for two, plus $30 for each additional person). There's a minimum two-night stay in peak season.

🏃 **YHA Raglan Solscape Eco Retreat** Wainui Rd, Manu Bay, 6km south of Raglan ℡07/825 8268, ⊛www.solscape.co.nz. Wonderfully idiosyncratic accommodation in imaginatively converted train carriages and cottages on top of a hill with panoramic views. Eco-friendly initiatives include a home-made solar water heating system, solar LED lights, tipi-style accommodation and individual earth-wood units (timber frames and roofs with mud walls) as well as free pick-ups from Raglan, and surf lessons (see p.216). Camping dorms $26–28, $15, tipis **②**, double cabooses **②**, eco units and s/c studios **④**–**⑥**

The town and its beaches

Apart from wandering the foreshore, there are few sights as such in the township except for the **museum** (opposite). Offshore, **harbour cruises** taking in pancake rock formations, historic sites and birdlife are run by Raglan Harbour Cruises (1hr; $30; ☎0274/881 215); call or check with the i-SITE for sailing times. Similar territory is covered on **guided kayak trips** with Raglan Kayak (☎07/825 8862, Ⓦwww.raglankayak.co.nz), which runs a "Kayak 'n' Coffee" tour (3hr; $70) and also rents kayaks (single/tandem/half-day $40/60).

Raglan is home to dozens of **artists** and a handful of **galleries**, including the Raglan Old School Arts Centre, Stewart Street – housed in a nineteenth-century heritage building and run by the town's creative community – which hosts a funky **market** (Ⓦwww.raglanmarket.com) every second Sunday morning.

The safest **swimming beach** is **Te Kopua**, in the heart of town, reached via the footbridge from lower Bow Street or by car along Wainui Road and Marine Parade. **Ocean Beach**, just outside the town off Wainui Road on the way to Whale Bay, gives great views of the bar of rock and sand that stretches across the mouth of the harbour and is a fine picnic spot, but strong undertows make swimming unsafe. For Raglan's renowned **surf beaches**, see box, p.216.

Eating and drinking

One of Raglan's charms is its great, relaxed café-style places for a post-surf brekkie or laidback meal. New places regularly pop up while others shut down; you'll find most around the intersection of Bow Street and Wainui Road.

Blacksand Corner of Wainui Rd & Bow St. Spacious, licensed bare-boards café with good coffee, hearty post-surf breakfasts such as cinnamon pancakes, warming soups and evening meals on Saturdays and Sundays, with all dishes under $20.

Harbour View Hotel Bow St. Reliable hotel/pub with good-value meals (mains $23–38), plus draught beer and wine by the glass.

Marlin Café & Grill 43 Rose St. Down by the wharf near the end of Wallis St, serving breakfasts/brunches until around 3pm and hearty evening meals. Steaks are a specialty (mains $26–35), but its well-stocked bar is also conducive for a sundowner or two.

Orca Restaurant & Bar 2 Wallis St. Raglan's best restaurant, serving casual brunches and standout modern Kiwi evening meals along the lines of artichoke and potato salad with truffle mayo, followed by pork belly with mustard mash or braised beef cheek (mains $17–31). The attached bar opens to a deck overlooking the estuary; regular live bands attract a cover charge of around $5–10.

🏃 **Raglan Roast** Volcom Lane. Tucked down a laneway next to GAg surf shop, this tiny, daytime hole-in-the-wall spills out to a clutch of tables. Its knockout coffee is roasted on the premises; food is limited to a pie-warmer, but you're welcome to bring your own.

🏃 **Raglan Seafoods** The wharf, Wallis St. Perched right at the end of the wharf, you can watch the day's catch being hand-filleted on site, and order some of New Zealand's finest fish and chips to take away, or wet fish to cook up yourself. Open until around 8pm; no credit cards.

Tongue and Groove Corner Bow St & Wainui Rd. Newly refurbished café/bar with a laidback vibe, steady flow of interesting locals and extensive range of imaginative food. Licensed & BYO.

Around Raglan

Sweeping views of Raglan Harbour and along the coast unfurl from the **summit** of **Mount Karioi** (755m), reached by the **Te Toto** track (8km return; 5–6hr; not to be attempted in bad weather). Starting 12km south of Raglan along Whaanga Road, the track heads up a gorge and, after a strenuous and difficult climb within a cliff-lined cut to a lookout, reaches the final, easier, section to the **summit**. A little further

Surfing Raglan

There are great waves all around the country but Raglan is New Zealand's finest **surfing** destination – the lines of perfect breakers appear like blue corduroy southwest of town. The best place for inexperienced surfers is the rock-free **Ngarunui Beach**, 5km out of Raglan. For the experienced, the main breaks, both around 8km from town, are **Whale Bay** and **Manu Bay**, which featured in the cult 1960s surf film *Endless Summer*.

The two main places for **surf lessons** are the Whale Bay-based Raglan Surfing School (T07/825 7873, W www.raglansurfingschool.co.nz), which offers a starter lesson (3hr; group/private $89/129 including gear and transport) using soft boards, plus a range of longer packages; and Manu Bay-based Solscape, which offers a range of deals (from $85 including a 2hr 30min lesson, board and wetsuit). Both places also **rent gear**, for around $35 per half-day including wetsuits, as do GAg, 9a Bow St (T07/825 8702, W www.gagraglan.com) and, in summer, a shack on Ngarunui Beach.

Alternatively, you can hit the air with **Raglan Kitesurfing** (T07/825 8702, W www .raglankitesurfing.com; $60 per 1hr land-based intro lesson, $85 per 1hr water-based lesson).

along this coast at Ruapuke, Extreme Horse Adventures (T07/825 0059, W www .wildcoast.co.nz) offer **horseriding** on their farm, through native bush and on to Ruapuke Beach ($90/person, $15 for transport from Raglan; min 4).

Twenty kilometres southeast of Raglan and signposted from the Kawhia Road, **Bridal Veil Falls** hides in dense native bush. Water plummets 55m down a sheer rock face into a green pool where rainbows appear in the spray in the sunshine. From the car park it's a ten-minute walk down to the bottom of the falls; allow twice that for the walk back up.

The Te Toto track and the falls sights can be combined on a winding gravel-road loop around the Karioi Mountain. Heading 8km east of Raglan on SH23, then 6km up Te Mata Road, and 3km up Houchen Road brings you to Magic Mountain Horse Treks, 334 Houchen Rd (T07/825 6892, W www.magic mountain.co.nz), who charge $40 for an hour's **horseriding**, or $80 for a trek to Bridal Veil Falls (advance bookings essential).

Kawhia

Far-flung **KAWHIA** slumbers on the northern side of Kawhia Harbour but wakes up when its population of around six hundred people are joined by over four thousand holidaying Kiwis flocking to **Ocean Beach**, where **Te Puia Hot Springs** bubble from beneath the black sand. Access to the springs is along the unsealed 4km Tainui–Kawhia Forest Road. At the car park a track leads over the dunes to the ocean. Go an hour either side of low tide: check times at the museum or any of the local stores, and ask for detailed directions – it's often hard to find the springs unless others have got there first to dig the shallow holes. Be warned, the black sand can scorch bare feet and dangerous rips make swimming unsafe.

The spruced-up village centre is strung along Jervois Street, where there's a petrol station, a handful of combined shop/cafés, and the **Kawhia Museum** (Oct–March Mon–Fri 11.30am–4.30pm, Sat & Sun 11am–4pm; April–Nov Wed–Sun 11am–3pm; donation; T07/871 0161), with interesting displays on local Maori culture, European settlers, and a kauri whaleboat built in the 1880s.

Legends tell of the arrival of the **Tainui** in 1350, in their ancestral **waka** (canoe), and of how they found Kawhia Harbour so bountiful that they lived on its shores for three

Maori in the modern world

Comprising some fifteen percent of the population, New Zealand's Maori are the country's largest minority, and a thriving part of this bicultural nation's identity. Maori culture fascinates and inspires with its voyaging history, strong tribal customs and contemporary take on traditional artistry, interwoven with a deep spirituality that connects the people with the natural world and their ancestors. The following is a glimpse of what it means to be Maori, and how visitors can tap into it – there's more extensive coverage on issues and culture in "Contexts" (see p.777).

Tino rangatiratanga flag and protest signs ▲

The haka ▼

Maori identity

New Zealand's Maori make up a vital part of all walks of life – as lawyers, MPs, university lecturers, sporting, musical and media identities and even as the Governor-General (the Queen's representative in New Zealand). That said, average incomes are lower than those of Pakeha, almost half of all prison inmates are Maori, only around a quarter of Maori achieve post-school qualifications and these, along with disproportionate health statistics, are among the imbalances that the **Maori Party**, a key player in New Zealand politics (see p.774), is working to redress.

Considerable **intermarriage** between Maori and Pakeha – a fact that led one academic to speculate "race relations will be worked out in the bedrooms of New Zealand" – means many Kiwis are of mixed descent. Government policy calls for a **bicultural** approach, whereby everyone lives, works and plays together, but non-Maori and Maori peoples can maintain a distinct identity.

Knowledge of **whakapapa** (tribal lineage) is central to a sense of place in the Maori world. At any formal event, elders will recite their *whakapapa*, stretching as far back as the canoes that their ancestors first came to New Zealand in, then honour the mountains, rivers, forests and seas that give meaning to their people. **Oratory**, and the ability to produce a song at a moment's notice are both highly valued. Among the more radical factions of Maoridom (see p.773), there are calls for Maori sovereignty under the banner of **Tino rangatiratanga**, meaning Maori control of all things Maori. Supporters might fly the flag at home or sport a T-shirt bearing the movement's symbol – a stylized white fern frond between fields of red and black.

Kawa, hongi and hangi

The most direct and popular introduction to Maori culture is a **concert and hangi** (feast). Virtually all visitors to Rotorua attend one of these educational and thoroughly entertaining gigs and it's also possible to visit one in Christchurch or Queenstown. Although commercial, they're also generally authentic and true to traditional customs.

Both the concert and *hangi* usually take place on a **marae**, a compound that acts as meeting place, cultural hub and spiritual home for a *hapu*, or group of extended families. **Kawa** (protocols) governing behaviour dictate that visitors must be challenged to determine friendly intent before being allowed onto the *marae*. As visitors, you elect a "chief" who represents you during this **wero**, where a fearsome warrior bears down on you with twirling **taiaha** (long club), flicking tongue and bulging eyes. Once a ritual gift has been accepted, the women make the **karanga** (welcoming call), followed by their **powhiri** (sung welcome). This acts as a prelude to ceremonial touching of noses, **hongi**, binding hosts and visitors.

And so begins the concert, performed in traditional costume. Highlights are the men's **haka**, familiar to all rugby fans, and the women's **poi dance**, in which tennis-ball-sized clumps of a kind of bulrush are swung rhythmically about the body and head. The concert is followed by the **hangi**, a feast traditionally steamed in an earth oven or, in Rotorua, over a geothermal vent.

Typically visits include learning at least a few words of the Maori **language**, one of the country's official languages (see p.807 for more).

▲ Hongi, the ceremonial touching of noses

▼ Wero – a challenge and a greeting

▼ Poi dance

Hei tiki ▲

Moko tattoo ▼

Maori tour, Kaikoura ▼

Carving and tattooing

Maori **woodcarving** is unmistakable, with a background of swirls, organic forms and fern fronds overlaid with stylized figures, often inset with paua (abalone) shell.

There's a more restrained style to carved **pounamu** (greenstone). Some of the best pieces follow ancient styles, featuring large areas of highly polished *pounamu* set off by small areas of intricately worked swirls. Several places around the country offer the opportunity to try carving yourself, usually on **bone**.

In recent years there's also been a return to the art of **moko** (tattooing), with highly symbolic patterns reflecting birthright and key achievements from a person's teens onwards. Today you'll usually see *moko* designs on arms, legs and backs, but some Maori have gone for full-face *moko*.

Experiencing Maori culture

Beyond commercial concert and *hangi* ensembles, the following tours and lodgings offer opportunities to dig deeper into Maori culture. The website ⓦhttp://inz.maori.nz is also a handy resource for finding Maori tourism operators around the country.

▶▶ **Footprints Waipoua**, Northland. See p.198.
▶▶ **Kapiti Island**, near Wellington. See p.254.
▶▶ **Maori Ngati Porou Tourism**, East Cape. See p.355.
▶▶ **Maori Tours**, Kaikoura. See p.490.
▶▶ **Maraehako Bay Retreat**, East Cape. See p.353.
▶▶ **Taiamai Tours**, Northland. See p.175.
▶▶ **Tipuna Tours**, East Cape. See p.357.

hundred years. Tribal battles over the rich fishing grounds eventually forced them inland and in 1821, after constant attacks by the better-armed Waikato Maori, the Tainui chief, Te Rauparaha finally led his people to the relative safety of Kapiti Island.

When the original *waka* arrived in Kawhia, it was tied to a pohutukawa tree, Tangi te Korowhiti, still growing on the shore on Kaora Street, near the junction with Moke Street, 800m west of the museum – reached along the waterside footpath. The *Tainui* canoe is buried on a grassy knoll above the beautifully carved and painted **meeting house** of the **Maketu Marae**, further along Kaora Street at Karewa Beach, with Hani and Puna stones marking its stern and prow.

The arrival of **European** settlers and missionaries in the 1830s made Kawhia prosperous as a gateway to the fertile King Country, though its fortunes declined in the early years of the twentieth century, owing to its unsuitability for deep-draught ships. These days the settlement is known throughout New Zealand for annual **whaleboat races** (Jan 1), when 11m-long, five-crew whaling boats dash across the bay. To sample something of this maritime spirit, join Kawhia Harbour Cruises (mid-Dec to Feb daily; $40, min 4; ☏027/350 3601) who visit the white-sand beaches and labyrinths of pancake rocks.

Practicalities

Kawhia is 55km south of Raglan and a similar distance northwest of Otorohanga, but there's **no public transport** so you'll need your own wheels. The museum acts as the town's **visitor centre**, or you can pick up information at the Otorohanga i-SITE (p.218), including details of fishing trips. If you want to **stay**, try the welcoming and well-kept *Kawhia Camping Ground*, 73 Moke St (☏07/871 0863, ⓦwww.kawhiacampingground.co.nz; camping $14, cabins ❶, caravans with awnings ❷), which also offers a ten-seater, 4WD shuttle to the hot springs ($10/person; minimum return-trip fee $40); or the waterfront *Kawhia Beachside S-cape*, 225 Pouewe St (SH31) (☏07/871 0727, ⓦwww.kawhiabeachsidescape.co.nz; camping $34–38, dorms $25, cabins ❶, units ❺), which also rents kayaks ($10/hr).

Quintessential **eating** Kawhia-style is fish and chips from one of the town takeaways on the wharf overlooking the harbour, followed with a **beer** in the very traditional *Kawhia Hotel*, *Annie's* or the *Blue Chook Inn*.

The King Country

The rural landscape inland from Kawhia and south of Hamilton is known as the **King Country**, because it was the refuge of **King Tawhiao** and members of the **King Movement** (see p.218), after they were driven south during the New Zealand Wars. The area soon gained a reputation among Pakeha as a Maori strong-hold renowned for difficult terrain and a welcome that meant few, if any, Europeans entered. However, the forest's respite was short-lived: when peace was declared in 1881, loggers descended in droves.

Tourist interest focuses on **Waitomo**, a tiny village at the heart of a unique and dramatic landscape, honeycombed by limestone caves ethereally illuminated by glowworms, and overlaid by a geological wonderland of karst. North of Waitomo is the small dairy town of **Otorohanga**, with a kiwi house and Kiwiana displays. To the south of Waitomo, **Te Kuiti** provided sanctuary in the 1860s for Maori rebel Te Kooti, who reciprocated with a beautifully carved meeting house. Further south is the **Pureora Forest**, an enclave of rich lowland podocarp forest that was the site of a conservation battle in the late 1970s, and now provides access to excellent walks and a home for the rare **kokako**, a bird that prefers walking to flight.

The King Movement

Before Europeans arrived, Maori loyalty was solely to their immediate family and tribe, but wrangles with acquisitive European settlers led many tribes to discard age-old feuds in favour of a common crusade against the Pakeha. **Maori nationalism** hardened in the face of blatantly unjust treatment and increasing pressure to "sell" land.

In 1856, the influential Otaki Maori sought a chief who might unite the disparate tribes against the Europeans, and in 1858 the Waikato, Taupo and other tribes (largely originating from the *Tainui* canoe; see p.216) chose **Te Wherowhero**. Taking the title of **Potatau I**, the newly elected king established himself at Ngaruawahia – to this day the seat of the **King Movement**. The principal tenet of the movement was to resist the appropriation of Maori land and provide a basis for a degree of self-government. Whether out of a genuine misunderstanding of these aims or for reasons of economic expediency, the settlers interpreted the formation of the movement as an act of rebellion – despite the fact that Queen Victoria was included in the movement's prayers – and tension heightened. The situation escalated into armed conflict later in 1858 when the Waitara Block near New Plymouth was confiscated from its Maori owners. The fighting spread throughout the central North Island: the King Movement won a notable victory at Gate Pa, in the Bay of Plenty, but was eventually overwhelmed at Te Ranga.

Seeing the wars as an opportunity to settle old scores, some Maori tribes sided with the British and, in a series of battles along the Waikato, forced the kingites further south, until a crushing blow was struck at Orakau in 1864. The king and his followers fled south of the Puniu River into an area that, by virtue of their presence, became known as the **King Country**.

There they remained, with barely any European contact, until 1881, when **King Tawhiao**, who had succeeded to the throne in 1860, made peace. Gradually the followers of the King Movement drifted back to Ngaruawahia. Although by no means supported by all Maori, the loose coalition of the contemporary King Movement plays an important role in the current reassessment of Maori–Pakeha relations, and the reigning Maori King is the recipient of state and royal visits.

From Te Kuiti, SH4 runs south to **Taumarunui**, with access to the Whanganui River and the start of the **Forgotten World Highway** (see p.224).

Otorohanga

Surrounded by sheep and cattle country some 30km south of Te Awamutu, **OTOROHANGA** has one main attraction: the **Kiwi House Native Bird Park**, Alex Telfer Drive, off Kakamutu Road (daily: Sept–May 9.30am–4.30pm; June–Aug 9am–4pm; $16; ☎07/873 7391, ⓦwww.kiwihouse.org.nz,), ten minutes' walk from the town centre. The grumpy little bird's lifestyle is explained in the well-laid-out nocturnal kiwi house. Outdoor enclosures contain most species of the New Zealand native bird, many in a walk-through aviary. Kiwi-feeding takes place daily at 1.30pm and 4pm.

Otorohanga celebrates all things archetypally Kiwi with street signs bearing Kiwi icons and a series of glassed-in **Kiwiana displays** along the Sir Edmund Hillary walkway, off Maniapoto Street next to the ANZ bank. Exhibits include Marmite, the pavlova and Hillary himself. Classic Kiwi items sold at many of the shops along Maniapoto Street include hats and oilskins at John Haddad Menswear Store.

Practicalities

Trains pull in behind the **i-SITE visitor centre**, 21 Maniapoto St, on the corner of Wahanui Crescent (Mon–Fri 9am–5pm, Sat & Sun 10am–2pm; ☎07/873 8951, ⓦwww.otorohanga.co.nz), **buses** stop outside on Wahanui Crescent.

There's a well-equipped central **campsite**, the *Otorohanga Holiday Park*, 12 Huiputea Drive (☎07/873 7253, ⓦwww.kiwiholidaypark.co.nz; camping from $16, cabin ❶, motel units ❸). The best bet for **eating** is the moderately priced *The Thirsty Weta*, 57 Maniapoto St, which serves hearty meals (mains $6–35) and has live music on Friday nights.

Waitomo

Some 16km southwest of Otorohanga (8km west off SH3), **WAITOMO** is a diminutive village with an outsize reputation for incredible **cave trips** and magnificent **karst features** – streams that disappear down funnel-shaped sinkholes, craggy limestone outcrops, fluted rocks, potholes and natural bridges caused by cave ceiling collapses. Below ground, seeping water has sculpted the rock into eerie and extraordinary shapes. The ongoing process of **cave creation** involves the interaction of rainwater and carbon dioxide from the air, that together form a weak acid. As more carbon dioxide is absorbed from the soil the acid grows stronger, dissolving the limestone and enlarging cracks and joints, eventually forming the varied caves you see today. Each year a further seventy cubic metres of limestone (about the size of a double-decker bus) is dissolved. Many of the caves are dazzlingly illuminated by **glowworms**.

Appropriately enough, Waitomo means "water entering shaft" and local chief **Tane Tinorau** introduced the passages to English surveyor **Fred Mace**, in 1887. The pair explored further, building a raft of flax stems and drifting along an underground stream, with candles their only source of light. Within a year, the enterprising Tane was guiding tourists to see the spectacle. The government took over in 1906 and it wasn't until 1989 that the caves were returned to their Maori owners, who receive a percentage of all revenue generated and participate in the site's management.

Arrival and information

Trains and InterCity **buses** stop in Otorohanga, from where the Waitomo Shuttle ($10 one-way; ☎0800/808 279) ferries people to Waitomo, five times daily. Great Sights buses (run by InterCity/Newmans) run daily to Waitomo on their Auckland–Rotorua run, and the Waitomo Wanderer (☎0508 926 337, ⓦwww .waitomotours.co.nz) runs daily from Rotorua (and Taupo by prior booking).

Within the Waitomo Caves Discovery Centre (see also p.221) on the main road, is the **i-SITE visitor centre** (daily: Dec 26–Feb 8.15am–7pm; March–Easter and Labour Day–Christmas 8.45am–5.30pm; Easter–Labour Day 8.45am–5pm; ☎07/878 7640, ⓦwww.waitomoinfo.co.nz). The centre is a mine of information;

Glowworms

Glowworms (*Arachnocampa luminosa*) are found all over New Zealand, mostly in caves but also on overhanging banks in the bush where in dark and damp conditions you'll often see the telltale bluey-green glow. A glowworm isn't a worm at all, but the matchstick-sized larval stage of the fungus gnat (a relative of the mosquito), which attaches itself to the cave roof and produces around twenty or thirty mucus-and-silk threads or "fishing lines", which hang down a few centimetres. Drawn by the highly efficient chemical light, midges and flying insects get ensnared in the threads and the glowworm draws in the line to eat them.

The six- to nine-month larval stage is the only time in the glowworm **life cycle** that it can eat, so it needs to store energy for the two-week pupal stage when it transforms into the adult gnat that has no mouthparts. It only lives a couple of days, during which time the female has to frantically find a mate in the dark caves (the glow is a big help here) and lay her batch of a hundred or so eggs. After a two- to three-week incubation, they hatch into glowworms and the process begins anew.

it acts as a booking agent for cave trips, trains and buses, contains a **post office** and has **internet access**. There's **no bank**, ATM, **petrol** or supermarket at Waitomo; the nearest are at Otorohanga (p.218) and Te Kuiti (p.223).

Accommodation

Backpackers are well provided for but other **accommodation** is fairly limited so **book in advance**, particularly between November and January.

Abseil Breakfast Inn 709 Waitomo Caves Rd, 400m east of the museum ☎07/878 7815, ⓦwww.abseilinn.co.nz. Pick of the B&Bs, relaxing and stylish, on top of a hill with great views. Each of the four en-suite rooms is individually decorated. ❺–❻

Rap, Raft 'n' Rock See opposite. Homey backpacker digs attached to an adventure-caving operator with brightly painted dorms sleeping just ten, a cosy lounge, kitchen and sunny courtyard. Dorms $28, rooms ❷

Te Tiro 9km west of Waitomo ☎07/878 6328, ⓦwww.waitomocavesnz.com. Cosy s/c cottages with fabulous views and a glowworm grotto. Breakfast goodies are included, but if you're cooking, bring food or something for the BBQ. ❹

Waitomo Caves Guest Lodge 7 Waitomo Caves, 100m east of the museum ☎07/878 7641, ⓦwww.waitomocavesguestlodge.co.nz. Eight comfortable, good-value rooms on a hillside with a lovely garden. ❹

Waitomo Kiwipaka School Rd ☎07/878 3395, ⓦwww.kiwipaka.co.nz. Purpose-built hostel in the heart of Waitomo with beds and rooms in a lodge, separate chalets with private bathrooms, and an

on-site café (see p.222). Dorms $29, rooms ❷, chalets ❸

Waitomo Top 10 Holiday Park 12 Waitomo Caves Rd ☎07/878 7639, ⓦwww.waitomopark.co.nz. Well-equipped campsite in the heart of town, with a swimming pool and spa. Camping $40–45, cabins ❷, en-suite cabins ❹, s/c units ❺

🏃 **World Unique Waitomo Motels** 900m up Waitomo Valley Rd, off Waitomo Caves Rd ☎07/878 6666, ⓦwww.woodlynpark.co.nz. Ingenious motel-style accommodation on the site of Billy Black's Kiwi Culture Show (see p.222). Sleep in a Bristol freighter aircraft converted into two comfortable s/c units; a 1950s railway carrlage containing a three-room unit; two hobbit holes with circular entrances sunk into a hillside and a converted World War II patrol boat. Book at least a month ahead for Dec–Feb. ❻–❼

YHA Juno Hall Waitomo Caves Rd, 1km east of Waitomo ☎07/878 7649, ⓔjunowaitomo@xtra .co.nz. Cosy, well-equipped hostel in a timber-lined building set on a low hill by a pool, BBQ deck and a tennis court, with the chance to hand-feed baby animals. Free pick-ups from town, camping $15, dorms $27, rooms ❷

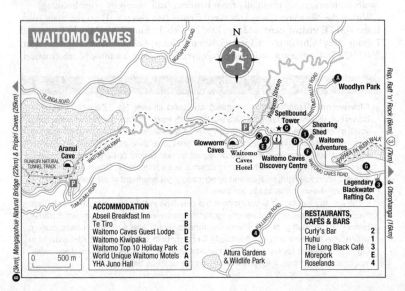

Visiting the caves

Only a fraction of the 45km of cave passages under Waitomo can be visited on **guided tours**, and the only caves you can safely explore **independently** are the Piripiri Caves, 28km west of the village (see p.223), although it doesn't have glowworms. To enhance your cave experience, stop at the **Waitomo Caves Discovery Centre** (same hours and contact details as i-SITE, p.219). Entry is $5, which is included in the price of most caving trips. The centre has informative exhibits on the geology and history of the caves, interactive displays on the life cycle of glowworms and cave wetas and a free eighteen-minute multimedia show, screened on request.

Operators lease access from farmers, so each offers the chance to explore different caves.

In all cases, **heavy rain** can lead to cancellations if water levels rise too high, so it pays to check weather forecasts and plan accordingly. To avoid the crowds, the best **tours** are the first and last of the day.

Stay-dry caving trips

Waitomo's original cave experience is **Waitomo Glowworm Caves**, 500m west of the i-SITE (daily 9am–5pm; $39; ⊛www.waitomocaves.co.nz): 45-minute **tours**, beginning on the half-hour. Paved walkways and lighting pick out the best of the stalactites and stalagmites and there's a boat ride through the grotto, where glowworms shed pinpricks of ghostly pale-green light.

The Glowworm Caves office also sells tickets for tours around the **Aranui Cave**, 3.5km west of the i-SITE (daily 10am, 11am, 1pm, 2pm & 3pm; 45min; $39). Although only 250m long, geologically it's more spectacular, with high-ceilinged chambers and magnificent stalactites and stalagmites.

At the **Ruakuri Cave** (daily 10am, 11.30am, 12.30pm, 1.30pm 2.30pm & 3.30pm; 2hr; $60, run by the Legendary Black Water Rafting Co, see below), tours draw on Maori stories of "The Den of the Dogs" (as the cave's name translates).

A **two-cave combo** of the above caves costs $65; a **three-cave combo** is $105.

Other stay-dry trips include low-impact glowworm-spotting strolls and boat rides through two caves, run by Spellbound, Waitomo Caves Road (℡0800/773 552, ⊛www.glowworm.co.nz; 4 times daily; 3hr 30min; $66; maximum twelve people); and the extraordinary Lost World trips with Waitomo Adventures (p.222).

Wet caving trips

Waitomo excels at adrenaline-fuelled **adventure-caving trips**, which should be **booked in advance**, especially for the November to January period. Most trips involve getting kitted out in a wetsuit, caver's helmet with lamp and rubber boots, and combine two or more adventure elements. **Kids** under 12 (or under a minimum weight) are not usually allowed on adventure trips, and the wilder trips are for those 15 and over.

Access to some caves is by **abseiling** (also known as rapelling or snappling). Some trips feature **cave tubing** (also known as blackwater rafting), generally involving being wedged inside the inner tube of a truck tyre for a (usually) gentle float through a pitch-black section of cave gazing at a galaxy of glowworm light overhead.

Adventure caving operators

The Legendary Black Water Rafting Co
℡0800/228 464, ⊛www.blackwaterrafting.co.nz.
Two wetsuit-clad trips in Ruakuri Cave: Black Labyrinth (3hr, 1hr underground; $110), involving a short jump from an underground waterfall and an idyllic float through a glowworm cave; and the more adventurous Black Abyss (5hr, 2–3hr underground; $215), which adds abseiling and an eerie flying-fox ride into darkness.

Rap, Raft 'n' Rock 95 Waitomo Caves Rd/SH37, 8km east of the i-SITE, 1km from the junction with SH3 ℡0800/228 372, ⊛www.caveraft.com.

Small-group trips (5hr; $135), starting with a 27m abseil into a glowworm-filled cave explored partly on foot and partly floating on a tube, and ending with a rock climb out to the starting point. **Waitomo Adventures** 1km east of the i-SITE ☏ 0800/924 866, ⊛ www.waitomo.co.nz. Popular outfit offering five trips, including its signature Lost World (4hr; $270), a glorious, spine-tingling 100m drop into the gaping fern-draped mouth of a spectacular pothole, followed by a relatively dry cave walk before climbing out on a seemingly endless ladder. Cave junkies should go for the Lost World Epic (7–8hr; $395, including lunch underground and BBQ dinner above), where an abseil is followed by several "wet" hours, navigating upstream through squeezes, behind a small waterfall and into a glittering glowworm grotto.

Other attractions and activities

If the rain hits and caving is a washout head for **Woodlyn Park**, 900m up Waitomo Valley Road from the village (☏ 07/878 6666, ⊛ www.woodlynpark .co.nz), where a rustic barn hosts the entertaining **Billy Black's Kiwi Culture Show** (daily 1.30pm, extra shows in summer; 1hr; $25), an offbeat look at the history of logging and farming with loads of audience participation.

At the **Shearing Shed**, diagonally opposite the i-SITE, you can see fluffy white angora rabbits being shorn at 12.30pm each day, followed by a rabbit fur-weaving demonstration (free).

At Altura Park, a working farm on Fullerton Road, 4km south of town (daily 9am–5pm; $12; ☏ 07/878 5278, ⊛ www.alturapark.co.nz), you can wander through the award-winning gardens, visit its diverse collection of animals, or go **horse-trekking** (30min/1hr/90min treks $50/65/80 including park entry; book in advance), with trips customized for riders of all abilities including beginners. Bring a picnic.

Waitomo Village and the Aranui Cave are linked by the **Waitomo Walkway** (total 10km; 3hr return) that starts opposite the i-SITE, disappears into the bush then follows the Waitomo Stream to the Aranui Cave. The trail then links up with the **Ruakuri Natural Tunnel** track (2km return; 45min), one of the most impressive short walks in the country. Starting from the car park for the Aranui Cave on Tumutumu Road, the track follows the Waitomo Stream on boardwalks and walkways past cave entrances. Ducking and weaving through short tunnel sections, you eventually reach a huge cave where the stream temporarily threads underground. The walk is especially magical at night when lit by glowworms in the bush. Both walks are shown on the free Waitomo Caves **map** from the i-SITE.

Eating and drinking

Waitomo has a limited range of **eating** options, particularly in winter, when opening times are restricted.

Curly's Bar Waitomo Caves Rd, immediately west of the i-SITE. Almost everyone eventually ends up at this unreconstructed Kiwi pub, either for convivial boozing or good-value meals in the steak, seafood and burger tradition. Occasional live music.

Huhu Waitomo Caves Rd, adjacent to Spellbound (p.221) ☏ 07/878 6674. Fine dining in a licensed café serving counter food and fantastic coffee, a short lunch menu and excellent evening meals ($26–35), and "small plates" (Kiwi tapas; $7–12) such as soft, chewy *rewana* (Maori bread) with herb butter, olive oil and balsamic vinegar, all with suggested matched wines by the glass. Daily from 10.30am; book in the evening.

The Long Black Café At the Legendary Blackwater Rafting Co (p.221). Cooked breakfasts, simple snacks and light lunches, served from 8am in summer (8.30am in winter) until around 3pm.

Morepork Inside the *Kiwipaka* (p.220). Licensed café open from breakfast, serving made-to-order breakfasts, lunches and evening meals including pizzas.

Roselands Fullerton Rd, 3km south of the i-SITE. Fish or steak (or vegetarian options by prior arrangement) sizzle on the barbecue on the deck of this garden-set restaurant in a beautiful hillside location. Fixed-priced menu $27. Daily 11am–2pm.

Towards the coast from Waitomo

For DIY limestone scenery, drive the Te Anga road for three free sights worth viewing in any weather. First is the **Mangapohue Natural Bridge**, 24km west of Waitomo, an easy fifteen-minute loop trail through forest to a riverside boardwalk leading into a narrow limestone gorge topped by a double bridge formed by the remains of a collapsed cave roof. It's especially dazzling at night when the undersides glimmer with constellations of glowworms. In daylight, don't miss the rest of the walk, through farmland past fossilized examples of giant oysters, 35 million years old.

Four kilometres west is **Piripiri Caves**, a five-minute walk through a forested landscape full of weathered limestone outcrops. Inside the cavern you'll need a decent torch (and an emergency spare) to explore the Oyster Room, which contains more giant fossil oysters, though there are no glowworms.

A kilometre or so on, a track (15min return) accesses one of the area's most dramatic waterfalls, the multi-tiered **Marokopa Falls**, through a jungle-like rainforest of tawa, pukatea and kohekohe trees.

Te Kuiti

The "Shearing Capital of the World", **TE KUITI**, 19km south of Waitomo, greets visitors with a 7m-high statue of a man shearing a sheep at the southern end of Rora Street, and hosts the annual New Zealand **Shearing and Wool Handling Championships** in late March or early April – details are available from the **i-SITE visitor centre** (Mon–Fri 9am–5pm, Sat & Sun 10am–4pm; ☎07/878 8077, ✉tkisite@waitomo.govt.nz), on Rora Street by the **train station**. Most buses stop here, except InterCity, whose stop is outside *Tiffany's Restaurant*.

Opposite the south end of Rora Street, on Awakino Road is a magnificently carved **meeting house**, Te Tokanganui-a-noho, left by Maori rebel Te Kooti in the nineteenth century in thanks for sanctuary.

Easily the best place to **eat** in Te Kuiti (and worth the trip from Waitomo) is the hip daytime café 🎋 *Bosco*, 57 Te Kumi Rd, a couple of kilometres north of the town centre, serving sensational coffee, cranberry smoothies, home-made muffins and slices, and a Mediterranean lunch menu that spans pumpkin cannelloni to Moroccan lamb (mains $8.50–18.50).

The SH3 from Te Kuiti to Taranaki

Southwest of Te Kuiti, **SH3** makes a beeline for the Tasman and the small coastal town of **Mokau**, noted for its run of whitebait from mid-August to November, when there are plenty of opportunities to sample it in the local cafés. It then twists its way through tiny communities, sandwiched between spectacular black beaches and steep inland ranges. Opportunities for exploration focus on walks near the **Tongaporutu** rivermouth, and there's refreshment a little further along SH3 at 🎋 **Mike's Organic Brewery** (daily 10am–6pm; ☎06/752 3676, ⊛www .organicbeer.co.nz), a craft brewery of international standing. Mike's produces four organic brews using rainwater – including Strawberry Blonde, made from whole organic strawberries. The friendly staff can usually give you a quick tour of the facilities (by arrangement). Eventually the scenery opens out onto the **Taranaki Plains** just north of New Plymouth.

Taumarunui

Surrounded by national parks and forests at the confluence of the Ongarue and Whanganui rivers, **TAUMARUNUI**, 83km from Te Kuiti at the northern end of the Forgotten World Highway (below), was one of the last places to be settled by

Europeans, who arrived in large numbers in 1908, when the railway came to town. Finding a suitable route for the track on its steep descent north towards Taumarunui from the area around the Tongariro National Park proved problematic, but surveyor R.W. Holmes' ingenious solution, the **Raurimu Spiral**, is a remarkable feat of engineering combining bridges and tunnels to loop the track over itself. The spiral, still in use, can be seen from a signposted viewpoint 37km south of Taumarunui on SH4. Rail buffs can view the model train replica in the Taumarunui **i-SITE** (daily 9am–5pm; ☏07/895 7494, ⊛www.visitruapehu .com), next to the train and bus station, which has **internet access**, books accommodation and sells Whanganui National Park Hut and Camp passes.

The Forgotten World Highway

For a taste of genuinely rural New Zealand, follow the **Forgotten World Highway** between Taumarunui and Stratford (SH43), a rugged 155m road that twists through the hills west of Taumarunui. All but a 12km stretch through the Tangarakau Gorge is sealed, but allow at least three hours for the journey, and be sure to fuel up beforehand as there's **no petrol** along the route.

The first notable stop is the **Nukunuku Museum** (see p.239), 4km down Saddler Road. Back on SH43, the road snakes through the sedimentary limestone of the **Tangarakau Gorge**, possibly the highlight of the trip, with steep bush-draped cliffs rising up above the river. At the entrance to the gorge, a small sign directs you along a short trail to the picturesque site of **Joshua Morgan's grave**, the final resting place of an early surveyor. At the crest of a ridge you pass through the dark, narrow **Moki Tunnel** before reaching Whangamomona.

Whangamomona

A steady descent brings you alongside a little-used rail line that runs parallel to the road as far as **WHANGAMOMONA**, around 90km from Taumarunui. The village's ten residents are boosted in January of every odd-numbered year during celebrations of the town's independence, declared on October 28, 1989 after the government altered the provincial boundaries, removing it from Taranaki. The **republic** swears in a president and in full party mood hosts whip-cracking and gumboot-throwing competitions, amid much drinking, eating and merriment. Celebrations revolve around the 1911 ☖ *Whangamomona Hotel* on Ohura Road (☏06/762 5823, ⊛www.whangamomonahotel.co.nz; B&B single ❷, double ❺), where year-round you can **get your passport stamped** or buy a Whangamomonian version ($3), while being entertained *Fawlty Towers*-style by the publican. Refurbished without losing any of its character (airy guest rooms share bathrooms), the **hotel** serves **meals** (daily; mains $5–15). A kilometre down the road, the simple *Whangamomona Village Motor Camp* (☏06/762 5822) offers **camping** ($10/ tent, $20/campervan) and bargain **cabins** ($20).

Leaving Whangamomona, SH43 climbs beside steep bluffs and passes a couple of saddles with views down the valley and across the **Taranaki Plains**. It then descends to flat dairy pasture, eventually rolling into **Stratford** (see p.235) as the permanently snowcapped Mount Taranaki looms into view, if the weather allows.

Taranaki

The province of **Taranaki** (nicknamed "the 'naki") juts out west from the rest of the North Island forming a thumbprint peninsula centred on **Maunga Taranaki** (aka **Mount Egmont**), an elegant conical volcano rising 2500m from the subtropical

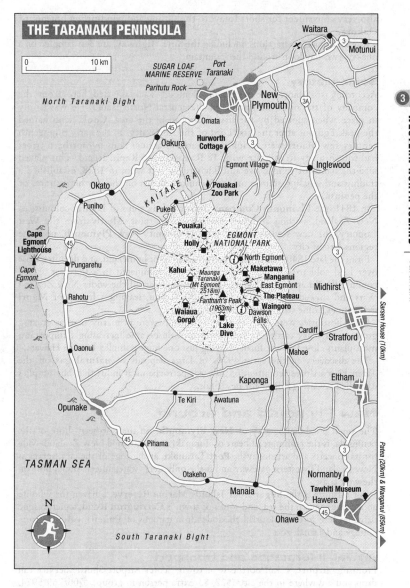

THE TARANAKI PENINSULA

0   10 km

SUGAR LOAF
MARINE RESERVE
Paritutu Rock

Port
Taranaki

North Taranaki Bight

New
Plymouth

Waitara

Motunui

3

3A

Omata

Hurworth
Cottage

Egmont Village

Inglewood

Oakura

45

3

KAITAKE RA

Okato

Pukeiti

Pouakai
Zoo Park

Punilho

Pouakai

Holly

EGMONT
NATIONAL PARK

North Egmont

Cape
Egmont
Lighthouse

45

Pungarehu

Kahui

Maunga
Taranaki
(Mt Egmont
2518m)

Maketawa

Manganui

East Egmont

The Plateau

3

Cape
Egmont

Rahotu

Fantham's Peak
(1963m)

Waiaua
Gorge

Lake
Dive

Dawson
Falls

Waingoro

Midhirst

Cardiff

Stratford

Sarsen House (10km)

Oaonui

Mahoe

Kaponga

Eltham

Te Kiri

Awatuna

Opunake

45

Pihama

TASMAN SEA

Otakeho

Normanby

Manaia

Tawhiti Museum

Hawera

45

N

Ohawe

South Taranaki Bight

Patea (20km) & Wanganui (85km)

coast to its icy summit. Taranaki means "peak clear of vegetation", an appropriate description of the upper half of "the mountain", as locals simply refer to it.

The mountain remains a constant presence as you tour the region, though much of the time it is obscured by cloud. The summit is usually visible in the early morning and just before sunset, with cloud forming through the middle of the day – the bane of summit aspirants who slog for no view.

Taranaki's vibrant provincial capital **New Plymouth** makes a good base for day-trips into the **Egmont National Park**, surrounding the mountain. It is also very convenient for short forays to the surfing and windsurfing hotspot of **Oakura**.

Rural Taranaki's attractions, including the **Surf Highway**, are best sampled on a one- or two-day loop around the mountain.

Some history

According to Maori, the mountain-demigod Taranaki fled here from the company of the other mountains in the central North Island. He was firmly in place when spotted by the first European in the area, **Cook**, who named the peak Egmont after the first Lord of the Admiralty. In the early nineteenth century few **Maori** were living in the area as annual raids by northern tribes had forced many to migrate with Te Rauparaha to Kapiti Island. This played into the hands of John Lowe and Richard Barrett who, in 1828, established a trading and whaling station on the Ngamotu Beach on the northern shores of the peninsula.

In 1841, the **Plymouth Company** dispatched six ships of English colonists to New Zealand, settling at Lowe and Barrett's outpost. Mostly from the West Country, the new settlers named their community **New Plymouth**, now the region's largest city.

From the late 1840s many Maori returned to their homeland, and disputes arose over land sold to settlers, which from 1860 culminated in a ten-year armed conflict, the Taranaki Land Wars. These formed part of the wider New Zealand Wars and slowed the development of the region, leaving a legacy of **Maori grievances**, some still being addressed.

Once hostilities were over, the rich farmlands were primarily used as grazing grounds for dairy cattle. As economies of scale became increasingly important, most plants closed down, finally leaving just one huge complex outside Hawera.

The discovery in the early 1970s of large deposits of **natural gas** off the Taranaki coast diverted attention towards petrochemical industries, but supplies dwindled, awaiting hoped-for new finds.

New Plymouth and around

The small but bustling city of **New Plymouth**, on the northern shore of the peninsula, is the commercial heart of Taranaki and renowned New Zealand-wide for its concerts and arts festivals. **Port Taranaki**, at the edge of the city, serves as New Zealand's western gateway and is the only deep-water international port on the west coast.

Just offshore is the **Sugar Loaf Islands Marine Reserve**, a haven for wildlife above and beneath the sea, and south of town is **Carrington Road**, a picturesque drive leading to the colourful rhododendron gardens of **Pukeiti**, past a historic cottage and a small zoo.

Arrival, information and transport

From the **airport**, 12km northeast of town, Scott's Airport Shuttle Service can drop you anywhere in the city ($22, $3/extra person in group; ℡06/769 5974, ⓦ www.npairportshuttle.co.nz). Shuttles meet all flights, but reserve ahead to guarantee a seat. Long-distance **buses** (InterCity/Newmans and Dalroy's) stop at the bus station at 19 Ariki St, just along from the **i-SITE visitor centre**, 65 St Aubyn St (daily 9am–6pm except Wed till 9pm, Sat & Sun till 5pm; ℡06/759 6060, ⓦ www.newplymouthnz.com), in the foyer of the **Puke Ariki museum**. The i-SITE also has Egmont National Park information and sells hut tickets. The main post office is at 21 Currie St.

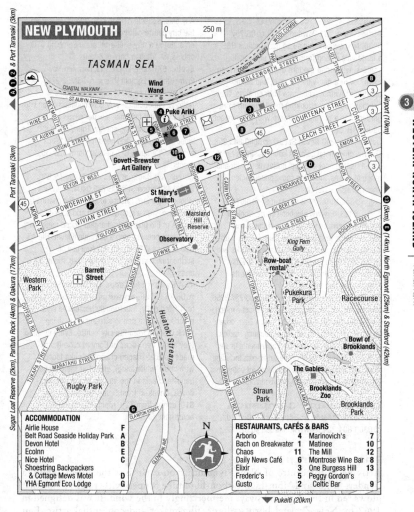

NEW PLYMOUTH

0 250 m

TASMAN SEA

Wind Wand

Cinema

Puke Ariki

Govett-Brewster Art Gallery

St Mary's Church

Marsland Hill Reserve

Observatory

King Fern Gully

Row-boat rental

Pukekura Park

Racecourse

Barrett Street

Western Park

Huatoki Stream

Bowl of Brooklands

The Gables

Rugby Park

Straun Park

Brooklands Zoo

Brooklands Park

N

Streets labelled: WOOLCOMBE, ELIOT STREET, COASTAL WALKWAY PARK, MOLESWORTH STREET, GILL STREET, ST AUBYN STREET, HINE ST, ST AUBYN ST, QUEEN ST, ARIKI STREET, DEVON ST EAST, COURTENAY STREET, CORONATION AVE, LEACH STREET, LEMON ST, CAMERON ST, KING STREET, EGMONT STREET, LIARDET STREET, GOVER ST, PENDARVES STREET, DEVON ST WEST, DAWSON STREET, BROUGHAM STREET, CARRINGTON STREET, GILBERT ST, ROGAN STREET, POWDERHAM ST, ROBE STREET, FILLIS STREET, VIVIAN STREET, FULFORD STREET, DOWNE ST, STANDISH STREET, VICTORIA ROAD, CARRINGTON STREET, WALLACE PL, FRANKLEY RD, MILL ROAD, MARATAHU STREET, TUKAPA STREET, HOLSWORTHY, BROOKLANDS RD, CLAWTON STREET, GLENPARK AVE, WEYMOUTH ST, YOUNG STREET, MORLEY ST, DEVON ST WEST, OUTFIELD RD

Left margin: ◀◀ & Port Taranaki (3km) ◀ Port Taranaki (3km) ◀ Sugar Loaf Reserve (2km), Paritutu Rock (4km) & Oakura (17km)

Right margin: Airport (10km) ▶ (5km), ⓔ (14km) North Egmont (25km) & Stratford (42km) ▶ North Egmont (25km) & Stratford (42km)

Bottom: ▼ Pukeiti (20km)

ACCOMMODATION

Airlie House	F
Belt Road Seaside Holiday Park	A
Devon Hotel	B
EcoInn	E
Nice Hotel	C
Shoestring Backpackers & Cottage Mews Motel	D
YHA Egmont Eco Lodge	G

RESTAURANTS, CAFÉS & BARS

Arborio	4	Marinovich's	7
Bach on Breakwater	1	Matinee	10
Chaos	11	The Mill	12
Daily News Café	6	Montrose Wine Bar	8
Elixir	3	One Burgess Hill	13
Frederic's	5	Peggy Gordon's	
Gusto	2	Celtic Bar	9

Local bus services are run by Tranzit Coachlines (☎06/765 5843, ⓦwww .tranzit.co.nz), but there are few useful routes and services are infrequent. A couple of companies, including Cruise New Zealand Tours (☎06/758 3222) and Taranaki Tours (☎0800/886 877), run shuttles to the mountain, costing around $50 return – the trip to the North Egmont visitor centre (p.233) takes around thirty minutes.

Accommodation

New Plymouth has a range of modestly priced **accommodation**, as well as options close to the city at the surf beach town of Oakura (see p.235), or on the flanks of the mountain (see p.233 & p.234). Motels are strung along the approach roads into the city centre.

Hotels, motels and B&Bs

Airlie House 161 Powderham St ⊕06/757
8866, ⊛www.airliehouse.co.nz. Gracious B&B in
a large villa dating from the turn of the last
century, with crisp modern decor. The "drawing
room", with a bay-window seat, and studio
apartment (with kitchen) are both en suite, the
"garden room", overlooking the flowering front
garden, has a private bathroom with a claw-foot
bath. B&B ❻

Devon Hotel 390 Devon St East ⊕0800/843 338,
⊛www.devonhotel.co.nz. A smart business hotel
with a heated pool and spa, buffet restaurant and
range of rooms, including some pricey suites.
Room ❻–❼, suite ❽

🏃 **Nice Hotel** 71 Brougham St ⊕06/758
6423, ⊛www.nicehotel.co.nz. Book in
advance to ensure you get one of the seven
unique rooms in this intimate *pied-à-terre*, with
designer bathrooms, contemporary artworks and
luxurious fittings. Its on-site restaurant, *Table*
(dinner only; mains $35), is renowned for its
French-accented cuisine. ❼

One Burgess Hill 1 Burgess Hill Rd ⊕06/757 2056,
⊛www.oneburgesshill.co.nz. Set in peaceful rolling
green hills grazed by sheep less than a 5min drive
from the city centre, these fifteen stunning studios,
one-bedroom and two-bedroom apartments (many
with log fires) have state-of-the-art fit-outs including
sleek self-catering kitchens and decadent bathrooms.
Studio ❺, one-bedroom ❻, two-bedroom ❼

Hostels and campsites

Belt Road Seaside Holiday Park 2 Belt Rd
⊕0800 804 204, ⊛www.beltroad.co.nz.

A scenic, seaside clifftop site, 20min walk from
the city centre, with camping and cabins (some
en suite) in a tidy sheltered area. Camping $16,
cabins ❷, kitchen cabins & units ❸

Ecoinn 671 Kent Rd, off SH3, between New
Plymouth and Egmont Village ⊕06/752 2765,
⊛www.ecoinn.co.nz. 3km from the Egmont
National Park boundary. Accommodation on an eco
farm with wind turbines, a water wheel and the
solar panels supplying energy. There's also a
wood-fired hot tub and good hiking. Pick-ups
available. Camping $15/person, dorm $26–30,
rooms ❶

**Shoestring Backpackers & Cottage Mews
Motel** 48 Lemon St ⊕06/758 0404, ⊛www
.shoestring.co.nz. Choose to stay in the charming
old house, with a roomy kitchen and book-filled
lounge or the bright, airy bargain-priced motel units
next door, opening onto a communal lawn. There's
also a sauna ($5/person) and free use of
surfboards. Camping $18, dorms $28, rooms ❷,
units ❹

YHA Egmont Eco Lodge 12 Clawton St
⊕06/753 5720, ⊛www.mttaranaki.co.nz. In a
fern-filled gully, this friendly hostel can also be
reached along a gentle streamside walking
track (15min) from the city centre. Every evening
they serve free slices of Egmont cake (home-
made conical-shaped chocolate cake topped
with snow-white icing), and offer the chance to
hand-feed eels in the stream or the resident
doves. Check-in from 5pm. Tent sites from
$18, dorms from $28, rooms ❷, en-suite
apartment ❸

The waterfront

Arriving in the centre of New Plymouth, you can't miss the **Wind Wand**, a
slender, bright-red, 45m-high carbon-fibre tube topped with a light globe that
glows red in the dark and sways mesmerizingly in the wind. It was designed in
1962 by New Zealand-born sculptor, film-maker and conceptual artist, **Len
Lye** (1901–80), who also created Wellington's *Water Whirler* (p.410). The wand
wasn't actually constructed until 2000, and is now a regional icon. Though a
smaller version was constructed in Greenwich Village in 1962, and a slightly
larger one at the Toronto International Sculpture Symposium in 1966, Lye's
true vision was restricted by the technology of the 1960s; more recent advances
in polymer engineering enabled the construction of the New Plymouth
full-size model. (Lye's vision was greater still, but it seems unlikely that his
forest of 125 wind wands swaying together in the breeze will be built in the
near future.)

Landscaping and pathways stretch a couple of hundred metres either side of the
Wind Wand, making a **waterfront park** that's pleasant for an evening stroll. More
ambitious walkers can follow the **Coastal Walkway** that stretches some 3km in
each direction.

City centre

The **Govett-Brewster Art Gallery**, at the corner of Queen and King streets (daily 10am–5pm; free; @www.govettbrewster.org.nz), is one of the country's finest contemporary art galleries. Home to the **Len Lye Foundation**, it owns a huge permanent collection of Lye's work. Currently there's only a small amount on display but some of Lye's films and a documentary on his life and work can usually be seen; if none are showing, ask. The gallery has no other permanent exhibits but puts on a series of temporary exhibitions,

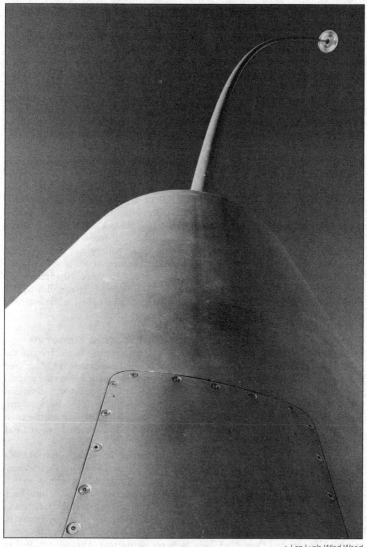

▲ Len Lye's *Wind Wand*

mostly contemporary. There's also a good art and design bookshop and an excellent café.

The other central highlight is **Puke Ariki**, St Aubyn Street (Mon–Fri 9am–6pm, Wed till 9pm, Sat & Sun 9am–5pm; free; ⊛www.pukeariki.com), a combined i-SITE visitor centre (p.226), city **library**, interactive **regional museum and exhibition space**. Upstairs, the extensive Maori section includes the canoe that brought Taranaki Maori to New Zealand, and volcanic rock carvings and woodcarvings of a style unique to Taranaki. The museum site also encompasses **Richmond Cottage** on Ariki Street (Sat & Sun 11am–3.30pm; free), an 1854 stone dwelling built for local MP Christopher William Richmond, and moved to its current site in 1962.

On Vivian Street, the Frederick Thatcher-designed **St Mary's Church** is the oldest stone church in New Zealand. Built in 1845 along austere lines with an imposing gabled dark-wood interior, it contains a striking 1972 Maori memorial with carvings and *tukutuku* panels.

Immediately behind the church, Marsland Hill Reserve contains the **Observatory**, Robe Street (Tues: summer 8–10pm; winter 7.30–9.30pm; donation), where members of the Astronomical Society volunteer to point out highlights in the night sky for visitors.

Pukekura Park and Brooklands Park

One of New Zealand's finest city parks, **Pukekura Park and Brooklands** (daily dawn–dusk; free) is split into two sections. Pukekura is mostly semi-formal, with glasshouses, a boating lake and a cricket pitch. The more freely laid out Brooklands occupies the grounds of a long-gone homestead and includes the **Bowl of Brooklands** outdoor amphitheatre, attracting big-name artists, as well as numerous mature trees, among them a 2000-year-old puriri and a big ginkgo. Nearby, a former colonial hospital from 1847 is now the **Gables** (Sat & Sun 1–4pm; free), containing an art gallery and small medical museum. On summer evenings, the Pukekura section is given over to the annual **festival of lights** (mid-Dec to mid-Feb nightly dusk–10.45pm; free), when you can stroll the gorgeously lit pathways winding between illuminated trees, and take out rowboats (around $5) festooned with lights, while listening to live music most nights.

Paritutu Rock and the Sugar Loaf Marine Reserve

New Plymouth's port sprawls 4km west of the town centre at the foot of the 200m-high **Paritutu Rock**, a feature of great cultural significance to Maori and a near-perfect natural fortress that still marks the boundary between Taranaki and Te Atiawa territories. You can ascend it from a car park on Centennial Drive, signposted off Vivian Street. It's a steep scramble (20–50min return) with a steel rope providing support, but the reward is a great view of the coast and cluster of rocky islands that comprise the DOC-administered **Sugar Loaf Marine Reserve**.

Eroded remnants of ancient volcanoes, the marine reserve's islands provide sanctuary for rare plants, little blue penguins, petrels and sooty shearwaters. The surrounding waters harbour some 67 species of fish and a wealth of multi-coloured anemones, sponges and seaweeds in undersea canyons. Humpback whales (Aug & Sept) and dolphins (Oct–Dec) migrate past and the tidal rocks are populated by New Zealand's northernmost breeding colony of fur seals. Although the islands themselves are off-limits, Chaddy's Charters run entertaining **trips** around them (2–3 daily, weather permitting; 1hr; $30; ☏06/758 9133) in an old lifeboat.

Carrington Street

If you have your own wheels follow Carrington Street (which later becomes Carrington Road) south of the city towards the Taranaki foothills. First stop, 8km south, is the charming and historic **Hurworth Cottage**, 906 Carrington Rd (Sat & Sun 11am–3pm and by appointment; $5; ☎06/753 3593). Built in 1856, its original resident was Harry Atkinson, four times Prime Minister of New Zealand, famous for advocating women's suffrage and introducing welfare benefits.

Around 20km southwest of New Plymouth **Pukeiti**, 2290 Carrington Rd (daily: Sept–March 9am–5pm; April–Aug 10am–3pm; $12; ⓦwww.pukeiti.org.nz), a rainforest garden with New Zealand's largest collection of rhododendrons and azaleas, is ablaze with colour from late October to early November during the **Taranaki Rhododendron and Garden Festival** (ⓦwww.rhodo.co.nz).

Eating, drinking and entertainment

The majority of the cafés, restaurants, bars and clubs are on the so-called "**Devon Mile**", along Devon Street between Dawson and Eliot streets. In recent times a second culinary hotspot has sprung up at Port Taranaki overlooking the water. The Skycity Cinema, 119–125 Devon St East (☎06/759 9077), screens mainstream **movies**.

New Plymouth is New Zealand's leading provincial arts hub: the biennial **Taranaki Festival of the Arts** (ⓦwww.taranakifest.org.nz) takes place every odd-numbered year at venues all over town from around late July to early August. Every year in mid-March the city hosts **WOMAD**, a three-day festival of world music (ⓦwww.womad.co.nz) with hundreds of international artists performing on six stages, workshops and a "global village" market.

Arborio In Puke Ariki, overlooking the *Wind Wand* ☎06/759 1241. A brilliant, licensed, modern café with imaginative breakfasts, including bubble and squeak, and delicious dinners ranging from steaks to clams.

Bach on the Breakwater Ocean View Parade, Port Taranaki ☎06/769 6967. Rustic *bach*-style café opening to a timber deck overlooking the port, dishing up daytime favourites like nachos and contemporary evening meals (mains $24.90–35). Closed Mon and Tues; licensed.

Chaos 36 Brougham St. Service can be slow during this artistic daytime café's lunchtime crush, but it gives you a chance to savour the funky metallic sculptures, palms and recycled timbers, and the coffee, counter fare and light meals are worth the wait.

Daily News Café Level 1 in the library, Ariki St. Small, tranquil daytime café, stocked with newspapers from across the country and around the world, serving coffee and snacks.

Elixir 117 Devon St East. Chilled café plastered with posters of upcoming festivals and gigs, serving freshly baked muffins, panini, bagels and wraps, as well as delicious mains ($16.50–26) like pecan-crumbed chicken or maple roast veggies. Licensed; closed evenings Sun & Mon.

Frederic's Corner King & Egmont sts ☎06/758 9788. A relaxed and airy restaurant with lots of Mediterranean and Mexican-influenced dishes to share ($6.50–17.50) plus individual mains ($17.50–22) like beef filet with hand-cut chips.

Gusto Ocean View Parade, Port Taranaki ☎06/759 8133. Superb-value fine-dining restaurant (mains $22–24), incongruously hidden behind the vast, bottle-green Taranaki Hunting & Fishing store and showroom, serving contemporary fare in a minimalist-chic setting.

Marinovich's 19 Brougham St ☎06/758 4749. Wonderfully old-school seafood restaurant with polished lino floors that's been going strong in New Plymouth since 1927. Fabulous fresh fish, paua and whitebait fritters and oysters and good steaks (mains $22–42.50). Lunch Mon–Fri, dinner Mon–Sat.

Matinee 69 Devon St West. A cool café and bar inside an old theatre (hence the name) that gets lively on Friday and Saturday nights with DJs and bands. Café daily until 10pm, bar Tues–Sat 4pm–3am.

The Mill 2 Courtenay St. A massive converted flour mill with several bars for the late-night crowd, a wide range of beers and snacks, and live bands (or more likely a DJ playing Top 40 hits) at weekends.

Montrose Wine Bar 49 Liardet St. An astonishing 130-plus wines by the glass, over 240 by the bottle, and 1000 more in the adjacent bottle shop, as well as carefully selected craft beers, make this wood-panelled wine bar an essential stop. Tues–Thurs 4pm–10pm, Fri & Sat 11am–11pm.

Peggy Gordon's Celtic Bar Corner Egmont & Devon sts. With an extensive range of whiskies, twelve beers on tap, inexpensive meals (Dublin chicken pie, Youghal rabbit and so on) and regular live Irish music, it's no surprise that this is a popular haunt for both locals and travellers. The *Basement Bar* showcases alternative bands.

Egmont National Park

The entire western third of the North Island is dominated by **Taranaki** (Mount Egmont) a dormant volcano that last erupted in 1755. Often likened to Japan's Mount Fuji, its profile is a cone rising to 2518m. In winter, snow blankets the mountain but as summer progresses only the crater remains white. The mountain is the focal point for **EGMONT NATIONAL PARK**, the boundary forming an arc with a 10km radius around the mountain, interrupted only on its north side where it encompasses the **Kaitake Range**, an older more weathered cousin of Taranaki.

Surrounded by farmland, the mountain's lower slopes are cloaked in native bush that gradually changes to stunted flag-form trees shaped by the constant buffeting of the wind. Higher still, vegetation gives way to slopes of loose scoria (a kind of jagged volcanic gravel) – hard work if you're hiking.

Three sealed roads climb the sides of the mountain, all on the eastern side, all ending a little under halfway up at car parks from where the park's 140km of walking tracks spread out. Of these **North Egmont** is the most easily accessible from New Plymouth but you can get higher up the mountain on the road through **East Egmont**; and there's particularly good walking (and the best alpine accommodation) around **Dawson Falls**. The i-SITE in New Plymouth has extensive **information** on the park, including short, relatively easy hikes. The main **visitor centre** is in North Egmont (see opposite).

Although the hike to the **summit** shouldn't be underestimated, it is possible in a day for anyone reasonably fit. The upper mountain is off-limits to ordinary hikers in winter, but even during the **hiking season** (Jan to mid-April) bad weather, including occasional snow, sweeps in frighteningly quickly, and hikers starting off on a fine morning frequently find themselves groping through low cloud before the day is through. Deaths occur far too often: consult the **hiking advice** in Basics (see p.59) and get further information and an up-to-date **weather forecast** from local visitor centres or DOC offices. Take **warm clothing** at any time of year, climb with at least one companion or a mountain guide, and leave a **record of your intentions**. A free DOC information sheet supplied by the visitor centres outlines the routes. Ideally carry an **ice axe**, which can be rented from Kiwi Outdoors at 18 Ariki St in New Plymouth (T06/758 4152).

Transport and guides

With accommodation close to all three major trailheads, avid hikers usually base themselves inside the park. Day visitors can easily visit the northern side of the mountain from New Plymouth, and the eastern side from Stratford, with trailheads accessible in under an hour by **car**. **Shuttle buses** run from New Plymouth (see p.227) and Stratford (see p.235).

If you'd prefer a **guided walk**, Top Guides (T0800/448 433, Wwww.topguides .co.nz), Adventure Dynamics (T06/751 3589, Wwww.adventuredynamics.co.nz) and Mac Alpine (T0800/866 484, Wwww.macalpineguides.com) all offer bushwalking, guided summit treks and a range of more technical stuff. Guides generally take up to ten clients for summer hiking and summit attempts but perhaps only two for winter expeditions, rock climbing or instruction. Guiding rates are around $300 a day, plus around $50 for each extra person.

Egmont Village and North Egmont

The easiest access point to the park, and the closest to New Plymouth, is tiny **Egmont Village**, 13km southeast of New Plymouth on SH3. From here, the 16km sealed Egmont Road runs up the mountain to **North Egmont** (960m), the best base for summit ascents. Before heading up (or out on any of the numerous easier tracks), be sure to call at the park's main information source, the **North Egmont visitor centre** (daily 8am–4.30pm; ☎06/756 0990, ⓔegmontvc@doc .govt.nz), that has displays about the mountain, maps of all the tracks, good viewing windows, weather updates and a decent café.

Short walks around North Egmont include an unusual and atmospheric **tramp** (1km loop; 45min–1hr; 100m ascent), through the hidden valley of the Goblin Forest, with its kaikawaka trees, alpine plants and gnarled trunks hung with ferns and mosses. There's also the **Veronica Loop Track** (2.5km loop; 2hr; 200m ascent) which climbs to a ridge through mountain forest and scrub, with fine views of the ancient lava flows known as Humphries Castle, and beyond to New Plymouth and the coast. Note that the supply of **water** at North Egmont is limited, so bring some with you.

There's basic but comfy backpacker-style **accommodation** at the *Camp House* (☎0800/688 2727, ⓦwww.mttaranaki.co.nz; dorms from $30; ❷), a large mountain hut built in 1891, with a heated communal lounge, full kitchen and hot showers. Check-in is at the *Mountain Café* (generally open 9am–3.30pm summer, 10am–3pm winter) in the visitor centre. For non-guests, the *Camp House* offers day-use services ($15) such as secure parking, lockers and post-hike showers. Nearby, private rooms are available at *Rahiri Cottage*, (☎0800/688 2727, ⓦwww .mttaranaki.co.nz; ❹), a 1920s "gingerbread and clinkerbrick" gatehouse by the park entrance.

East Egmont

Reached from Stratford by the Pembroke Road, the highest road on the mountain goes through **East Egmont**, a parking area and site of the *Mountain House* hotel. It then runs to **The Plateau**, a rugged and windswept spot 1172m up on Taranaki's flanks on the upper route of the Around the Mountain Circuit (p.234), which acts as the wintertime parking area for the tiny **Manganui Ski-field** (ⓦwww .skitaranaki.co.nz).

From East Egmont, the **Curtis Falls Track** (3.5km return; 2–3hr; 120m ascent) is part of the lower Around the Mountain Circuit and crosses several streams, via steps and ladders, to the Manganui River Gorge, where you can follow the riverbed (no track or signs) to the base of a waterfall. The **Enchanted Track** (3km one-way; 3hr return; 300m ascent) also begins at the car park, heading through dense vegetation before climbing to The Plateau.

Accommodation is available at the beautifully sited, revamped *Mountain House* (☎06/765 6100, ⓦwww.mountainhouse.co.nz; ❻), 846m above sea level, with en-suite rooms and self-contained chalets, as well as a **restaurant** (closed Mon & Tues) serving three-course set menus for $55. Some 5km downhill is *Anderson's Alpine Lodge* (☎06/765 6620, ⓦwww.andersonsalpinelodge.co.nz; B&B ❻), a romantic log chalet with three timber guest rooms.

Dawson Falls

The most southerly access up Taranaki follows Manaia Road to **Dawson Falls**, roughly 23km west of Stratford and 900m above sea level. Here you'll find the

Dawson Falls visitor centre (generally manned Thurs–Sun & public holidays), outside of which stands an impressive 8m-high *pou whenua* (carved pole) depicting famous Maori associated with the area.

Only experienced hikers should tackle the summit from here (see below), but several easier tracks branch off from the visitor centre, notably a short one to the historic Dawson Falls Power Station, a small hydro plant providing power for the *Dawson Falls Mountain Lodge* since 1935.

An obvious goal is the 17m-high **Dawson Falls** (600m return; 40min; 30m ascent) that plummet over the end of an ancient lava flow. This hike begins down the road and can be extended along the **Kapuni Walk** (1km return; 1hr; 50m ascent). Another walk leads to **Wilkies Pool** (1km loop; 1hr; 100m ascent), where the waters of the Kapuni Gorge rush through a staircase of rock pools, and there's a tougher hike to **Hasties Hill** (2km; 1hr 30min–2hr; 100m ascent) involving a passage across the flank of the mountain to a lookout, returning the same way.

Accommodation spans the DOC-run *Konini Lodge* (☎06/756 0990; $20), an oversized hikers' hut (bring a sleeping bag), with hot showers and a kitchen equipped with stoves and fridges to the nearby upmarket *Dawson Falls Mountain Lodge* (☎06/765 5457, ⊛www.dawson-falls.co.nz; ❼), with views from most rooms, classy and casual dining options and a bar and/or sauna for when the weather clags in.

Summit hikes and circuit hikes

There are two main **summit routes**, both requiring a full day (set off around 7.30am). Ice axes and crampons are necessary up to January if you're visiting the crater. If you want to spend longer than a day on the mountain and are happy to forgo the summit climb, the **Pouakai Circuit** or the testing **Around the Mountain Circuit** might fit the bill.

Summit routes

The **Northern Route** (10km return; 6–8hr; 1560m ascent) is the most accessible. Poled all the way, it begins at the top car park at North Egmont and initially follows the gravel Translator Road (the appropriately dubbed "Puffer") to Tahurangi Lodge, a private hut run by the Taranaki Alpine Club. A wooden stairway leads to North Ridge, after that you're onto slopes of scoria up the Lizard Ridge leading to the crater. Crossing the crater ice and a short scoria slope brings you to the summit.

The longer and poorly marked **Southern Route** (11km return; 8–10hr; 1620m ascent) is a more exacting proposition, suitable only for those with extensive mountain experience; you'll need crampons and ice axes year-round. The route starts at the Dawson Falls car park and climbs through bush before making a rapid ascent up a staircase to the Lake Dive Track. From here on, the ascent involves a steep and exhausting series of zigzags up scoria slopes.

The Around the Mountain Circuit

Dedicated hikers might consider tackling the **Around the Mountain Circuit** (44km; 3–5 days), an irregular loop around Taranaki varying in altitude from 500m to 1500m. The track is not fully maintained, so check conditions with DOC and obtain a detailed Topomap. From December through to February, the snow melts enough for hikers to occasionally loop off the main track onto the more strenuous **high-level route**, essentially making a few short cuts by heading higher up the slopes, shaving a day off the lower circuit. There are six well-spaced **huts** along the way ($15 except for the tiny Kahui hut, $5); use DOC annual hut passes (see p.58) or buy tickets from the DOC visitor centres. **Camping** ($5; free outside Kahui hut) is only allowed alongside the huts.

The Pouakai Circuit

Starting at North Egmont, the **Pouakai Circuit** (25km loop; 2 days) turns its back on the big mountain and heads north around the lower Pouakai Range, from where views of Taranaki can be wonderful. The track varies in altitude from 700m to 1300m. Get advice from DOC before embarking. The route has two huts, the 36-bed Holly Hut, which can get very busy, and the less popular 16-bed Pouakai Hut ($15). Again, camping is only allowed outside the huts ($5).

Stratford and around

Just over halfway between New Plymouth and Hawera, 23km south of the service town of Inglewood, **STRATFORD** provides direct access to the slopes of Mount Taranaki, particularly East Egmont and Dawson Falls. Eastern Taranaki Experience (T06/765 7482, Wwww.eastern-taranaki.co.nz) operates 4WD **mountain transport** ($20 to the plateau; minimum of two people) and also **rents ski and snowboard gear** (skis, boots and poles $40). If you're bound for the central North Island, Stratford marks the start of the scenic **Forgotten World Highway** (p.224).

The town's main sight is its kitsch mock-Elizabethan **clock tower** (built in 1996 to hide the 1920s version), from which a life-size Romeo and Juliet emerge to mark the hour (at 10am, 1pm, 3pm and 7pm), accompanied by recordings of Shakespearean quotes, and every street name is a character from the bard's plays.

InterCity, NakedBus and Dalroy Express **buses** stop outside the **i-SITE visitor centre** on Prospero Place (Mon–Fri 8.30am–5pm, Sat & Sun 10am–3pm; T06/765 6708, Wwww.stratford.govt.nz), in an alley opposite the clock tower.

Along SH45: the Surf Highway

The best route around Taranaki is the **Surf Highway** (SH45) from New Plymouth to Hawera, mostly travelling about 3km inland, with roads leading down to tiny uninhabited bays. It runs for about 100km, but its beachy charms can consume half a day, longer if you want to surf its consistent glassy, even breaks. **Windsurfing** is good too, with near constant onshore winds. Surf beaches are everywhere, but facilities are concentrated in the towns of **Oakura** and the quieter **Opunake**. Between the two towns is **Cape Egmont**, with its picturesque lighthouse.

Oakura

Seventeen kilometres west of New Plymouth, **OAKURA** retains a hint of counter-cultural spirit thanks to board-riders. For **surfboard rental**, visit Vertigo, 605 Main St (T06/752 7363, Whttp://thewavehaven.co.nz/), which also runs windsurfing lessons ($75/2hr). There's no visitor centre but the library, next to the TSB bank on the main road (Mon–Fri 8am–5pm, Sat 8am–noon) has local information.

If you're tempted to **stay**, try the *Oakura Beach Holiday Park*, 2 Jan Terrace (T06/752 7861, Wwww.oakurabeach.com; camping $18, cabins ❷ units ❹), with an on-site café, or ⚞ *Ahu Ahu Beach Villas*, 321 Ahu Ahu Rd (T06/752 7370, Wwww.ahu.co.nz; ❼–❽), several gorgeous self-contained villas sleeping four overlooking the ocean, built from salvaged materials with luxurious modern fittings. A clutch of funky **craft shops** and **cafés** cluster along SH45.

Cape Egmont and Opunake

At Pungarehu, about 25km southwest of Oakura, Cape Road cuts 5km west to the cast-iron tower of **Cape Egmont Lighthouse**, moved here in 1877 from Mana Island, north of Wellington. It perches on a rise on the westernmost point of the cape overlooking Taranaki's windswept coast, a great spot around sunset with the mountain glowing behind.

Some 20km on is **Opunake**, a large village with a golden beach and little to do but swim, surf and cast a line. The Opunake Surf Co (Dreamtime), at the corner of Havelock and Tasman streets arranges **surfboard rental**.

You can **stay** right by the beach at *Opunake Beach Holiday Camp*, Beach Road (℡0800/758 009, ⓦwww.opunakebeachnz.co.nz; camping $16, cabins ❷, units ❸). The best place to **eat** in these parts is the upbeat 🍴 *Sugar Juice Café*, 42–44 Tasman St (licensed; Tues–Sun daytime, plus Wed–Sat evening), which serves huge breakfasts, has a mouthwatering range of counter food (slices, muffins and more) and also does takeaways.

Hawera

Surrounded by gently undulating dairy country, **HAWERA** is the meeting point of the eastern and western routes around Taranaki. A service and administration centre for the district's farmers, Hawera is home to the world's largest **dairy complex** south of town. Year-round it handles twenty percent of the country's milk production, mostly gathered from the rich volcanic soils of Taranaki but also brought by rail from other parts of the North Island.

The town and around

Dominated by its former **water tower** (daily 10am–2pm; $2), a soaring 1914-built, 54m-high concrete structure offering fabulous views over South Taranaki, Hawera is the birthplace and hometown of one of New Zealand's most celebrated authors, **Ronald Hugh Morrieson** (see p.801), who wrote well-observed and amusing Gothic novels about small-town life and loved jazz (and a drink or two). The only – but appropriate – memorial to his existence is *Morrieson's Café and Bar*, on Victoria Street, containing a few of his books, the old staircase from his house and tabletops made from timbers salvaged from it.

Continuing the quirky theme is the **Elvis Presley Memorial Record Room**, 51 Argyle St (visits by appointment; donation, ℡06/278 7624, ⓦwww .digitalus.co.nz/elvis), a garage-shrine to the King. About ten minutes' walk west from the i-SITE, it contains thousands of rare recordings, photographs and memorabilia.

Unique and ever-expanding exhibits at the absorbing **Tawhiti Museum and Bush Railway**, 401 Ohangai Rd (Jan daily 10am–4pm; June–Aug Sun 10am–4pm; Sept–Dec & Feb–May Mon & Fri–Sun 10am–4pm; $10; ⓦwww .tawhitimuseum.co.nz), northeast of town, explore the social and technological heritage of both Maori and Pakeha using a multitude of life-size figurines modelled on local people. Other highlights include a diorama of 800 miniatures depicting the 1820s musket wars; an extraordinary account of the 1860s New Zealand Wars, seen through the eyes of a deserter from the British Army who lived out his days with the Ngati Ruanui tribe; and a small-scale **bush railway** (first Sun in the month plus public holidays; daily during school holidays; $3) that trundles 1km through displays recounting Taranaki's logging history; as well as a good on-site **café**.

For an adrenaline rush with a difference, consider **dam dropping** ($100), a variation on whitewater riding conducted by Kaitiaki Adventures (℡06/752 8242, ⓦwww.damdrop.com). You're equipped with a buoyant plastic sled, wetsuit, helmet and fins to slide 6–9m down the face of a dam. This is more fun (and less scary) than it sounds and you can do it as many times as you like before the gentle, guided, scenic float down the Wainongoro River.

Practicalities

Buses stop at the **i-SITE visitor centre**, 55 High St (Mon–Fri 8.30am–5.15pm, Sat & Sun 10am–3pm; ☎06/278 8599, ⓦwww.stdc.co.nz), at the base of the water tower.

If you want to **stay**, out of town you'll find the peaceful and charming sheep and cattle farm *Wheatly Downs Farmstay*, 484 Ararata St (☎06/278 6523, ⓦwww.mttaranaki.co.nz; tent sites from $18, dorms from $30, rooms ❸, en-suite rooms ❹), 5km past the Tawhiti Museum, with views of Mount Taranaki.

Eating options are limited – try *Morrieson's Cafe and Bar* (see opposite), or *II Chefs*, 47 High St (closed Mon & Sun).

Patea and Bushy Park

Cutting through heavily cultivated farmland, SH3 splits **PATEA**, the only major community between Hawera and Wanganui. The township has a model of the *Aotea* canoe at the western end of the main street, commemorating the settlement of the area by Turi and his *hapu*; a good **surfing beach** at the mouth of the Patea River; and a safe freshwater **swimming hole**, overlooked by the Manawapou Redoubt and *pa* site.

Some 47km southeast of Patea, 16km northwest of Wanganui, a well-signposted side road runs 8km east to **Bushy Park Homestead & Forest**, 791 Rangitatau East Rd (daily 10am–5pm; day visitors $6, children free; ⓦwww.bushypark .co.nz; dorms $25, rooms ❹), a charming historic homestead offering B&B and backpacker **accommodation** plus a licensed, moderately priced **café** (book ahead for dinner) in native bush threaded by tracks. Encircled by a 5km fence, it's now a protected **bird sanctuary** with native birds including North Island robins, moreporks, flocks of kereru and North Island brown kiwi.

Whanganui National Park

The emerald-green Whanganui River tumbles from the northern slopes of Mount Tongariro to the Tasman Sea at Wanganui, passing through the **WHANGANUI NATIONAL PARK**, a vast swathe of barely inhabited and virtually trackless bush country east of Taranaki. The park contains one of the largest remaining tracts of lowland forest in the North Island, growing on a bed of soft sandstone and mudstone (*papa*) that has been eroded to form deep gorges, sharp ridges, sheer cliffs and waterfalls. Beneath the canopy of broad-leaved podocarps and mountain beech, an understorey of tree ferns and clinging plants extends down to the riverbanks, while abundant and vociferous **birdlife** includes the kereru (native pigeon), fantail, tui, robin, grey warbler, tomtit and brown kiwi.

The best way to explore the Whanganui National Park is on a multi-day **canoe trip** along the river. A safe and reliable route to the wilderness, it's well furnished with riverside campsites and lodge accommodation. The most popular exit point for canoe trips is the small settlement of **Pipiriki**, where jetboat operators run trips upstream.

If you're not taking a river trip, you can explore the **roads** that nibble at the fringes of the park: SH43 provides limited access to the northwest, but only the slow and winding **Whanganui River Road** stays near the river for any length of

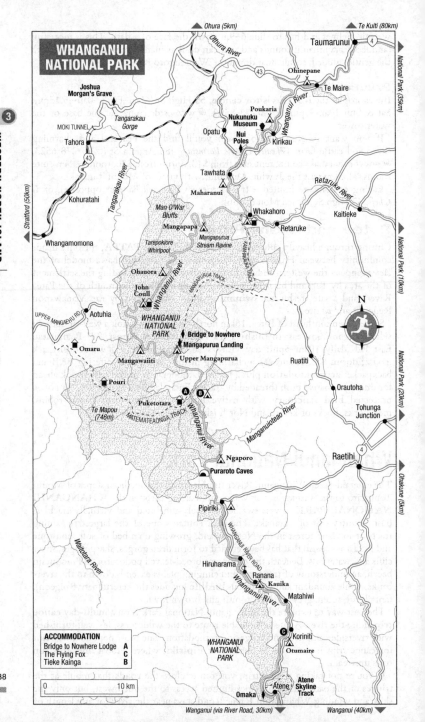

WHANGANUI NATIONAL PARK

▲ Ohura (5km)   ▲ Te Kuiti (80km)

Taumarunui

Ohinepane
Te Maire

Ohura River

Whanganui River

Joshua
Morgan's Grave

Tangarakau
Gorge

MOKI TUNNEL

Tahora

Poukaria
Nukunuku
Museum

Opatu   Nui
Poles   Kirikau

Kohuratahi

Tawhata

Maharanui

Whakahoro

Retaruke River

Retaruke

Kaitieke

Whangamomona

Man O'War
Bluffs

Mangapapa

Tarepokiore
Whirlpool

Mangapurua
Stream Ravine

Ohauora

John
Coull

Whanganui River

WHANGANUI
NATIONAL
PARK

Aotuhia

Omaru

Mangawaiiti

Pouri

Puketotara

Te Mapou
(746m)

MATEMATEAONGA TRACK

Bridge to Nowhere
Mangapurua Landing

Upper Mangapurua

A B

MANGAPURUA TRACK

Ruatiti

Orautoha

Manganuioteao River

Raetihi

Tohunga
Junction

Ngaporo

Puraroto Caves

Pipiriki

Hiruharama

Ranana
Kauika

Matahiwi

Korokiti

WHANGANUI
NATIONAL
PARK

Otumaire

Átene
Átene
Skyline
Track

Omaka

WHANGANUI
NATIONAL
PARK

Whanganui River

WHANGANUI RIVER ROAD

Waitotara River

ACCOMMODATION

Bridge to Nowhere Lodge   A
The Flying Fox   C
Tieke Kainga   B

0   10 km

N

Stratford (50km) ◀

Aotuhia

UPPER MANGAEHU RD

▶ National Park (35km)
▶ National Park (10km)
▶ National Park (20km)
▶ Ohakune (5km)

238

▼ Wanganui (via River Road, 30km)   ▼ Wanganui (40km)

time. This runs off towards Wanganui from near Ohakune on the SH4, a 70km drive south of Taumarunui.

You can also **hike** on two major tracks, both relatively easy-going despite the rugged country.

Information on the national park and the river is most readily available from the DOC office in Wanganui (see p.245) and i-SITE visitor centres in Wanganui (see p.244) and Taumarunui (see p.224), the widely available *In and Around the Whanganui National Park* booklet ($3), and online at ⓦ www.whanganuiriver.co.nz.

Some history

At 329km, the Whanganui is New Zealand's longest navigable river. It plays an intrinsic part in the lives of local **Maori**, who hold that each river bend had a *kaitiaki* (guardian) who controlled the *mauri* (life force). The *mana* of the old riverside settlements depended upon the maintenance of the food supplies and living areas: sheltered terraces on the riverbanks were cultivated and elaborate weirs constructed to trap eels and lamprey.

European missionaries arrived in the 1840s, traders followed, and by 1891 a regular boat service carried passengers and cargo to settlers at Pipiriki and Taumarunui. In the early twentieth century **tourist-carrying** paddle steamers plied the waters to reach elegant hotels en route to the central North Island.

European attempts to stamp their mark on this wild landscape have been ill-fated, however. In 1917 the **Mangapurua Valley**, in the middle of the park, was opened up for settlement by returned World War I servicemen, but, plagued by economic hardship, remoteness and difficulty of access, many had abandoned their farms by the 1930s. Although a concrete bridge over the Mangapurua Valley opened in 1936, after a major flood in 1942 the bridge was cut off, the three remaining families were ordered out, and the valley officially closed. Today, the only signs of habitation in the valley are the disappearing road, old fence lines, stands of exotic trees planted by the farmers, occasional brick chimneys and the bridge, now the poignant **Bridge to Nowhere** (see p.240).

With the coming of the railway and better roads, the riverboat tourist trade ceased in the 1920s but farms along the Whanganui continued to support a cargo and passenger service until the 1950s; thereafter the wilderness reclaimed land. This attracted recluses and visionaries, the most celebrated being poet **James K. Baxter** (p.243). The river was used extensively in Vincent Ward's 2005 movie *River Queen*.

Whanganui River trips

Canoes, kayaks and jetboats work the river, tailoring trips to your needs. The rapids are mostly Grade I with the occasional Grade II, making this an excellent paddling river for those with little or no experience. That said, the river shouldn't be underestimated: talk to operators about variations in river flows before embarking.

The navigable section of river starts at Cherry Grove in **Taumarunui**, from where it's about two days' paddle to **Whakahoro**, essentially just a DOC hut and a boat ramp at the end of a 45km road (mostly gravel) running west from SH4. Between these two points the river runs partly through farmland with roads nearby, and throws up a few rapids that are larger than those downstream. The journey also takes you past several spectacular water cascades and the **Nukunuku Museum** (entry by appointment; ☎07/896 6365). The collection was assembled by Jock Erceg (d. 2001), who spent the latter part of his life trawling the region's abandoned farmsteads, until eventually half the district started collecting ephemera for him.

▲ Getting ready to ride the Whanganui River

Further on, a former stronghold of the Hau Hau (see p.349) is the site of a couple of **nui poles**. In 1862 the Hau Hau erected a war pole, **Rongo-nui**, here, with four arms indicating the cardinal points of the compass, intended to call warriors to their cause from all over the country. At the end of hostilities, a peace pole, **Rerekore**, was erected close by.

Downstream from Whakahoro you'll see the Mangapapa Stream Ravine, the **Man-o-war Bluff** (named for its supposed resemblance to an old iron-clad battle-ship) and the **Tarepokiore Whirlpool**, that once completely spun a river steamer. At Mangapurua Landing it's an easy walk to the **Bridge to Nowhere** (1hr 15min return), a trail that becomes the Mangapurua Track (see p.242) to Whakahoro. Further downstream you come to **Tieke Kainga** (aka Tieke Marae), a former DOC hut built on the site of an ancient *pa* that has been re-occupied by local Maori; you can stay or camp here or across the river at *Bridge to Nowhere Lodge* (opposite), a terrific base for river activities. The last stretch runs past the **Puraroto Caves** and into Pipiriki, where most paddlers finish.

River information and passes

The best source of practical **information** for river trips is the free *Whanganui Journey* leaflet available from visitor centres and DOC offices in the region. The river is accessible all year, but the **paddling season** is generally from October to April, when all overnight river users must buy a **Hut and Campsite Pass**. There are two options: "Taumarunui to Whakahoro only" ($10), valid for two days on the river plus a night in one of the three campsites along the upper section of river, or the "Full Journey" ($45), allowing five days on the river, with the intervening nights spent in any combination of huts and campsites. Both carry a $15 surcharge if bought on the river itself, so it's best to prepurchase them at DOC offices or i-SITEs. Passes are generally included in the price of organized canoe trips, but it pays to check. From May to September, backcountry hut passes cost $15 (during which time the huts are serviced but not manned), and the campsites are free.

There are no shops along the river, so you need to take all your **supplies** with you: the nearest large supermarkets are in Taumarunui and Wanganui.

River accommodation

Apart from the huts and campsites, there's comfortable **accommodation** at the *Bridge to Nowhere Lodge* (☎0800/480 308, ⓦwww.rivercitytours.co.nz), accessible by the river, which it overlooks. The lodge offers home cooking, a bar, simple bunkrooms, doubles and a twin, all sharing bathrooms; you can self-cater (from $45/ person) or go for a dinner, bed and breakfast deal (from $125). Non-canoeists can get a package that includes a return jetboat (30min each way) transfer from Pipiriki, plus a Bridge to Nowhere tour, as well as accommodation and meals ($235). Across the river is the relaxing *Tieke Kainga*, where you can stay in big sleeping huts for a small donation, or camp on terraces by the river (no alcohol allowed); if any of the residents are about, you'll be treated to an informal cultural experience. You can just turn up, or pre-arrange through the *Bridge to Nowhere Lodge*.

Jetboat trips and canoe rental

The quickest way to get about on the river is on **jetboat trips** (see p.242): they all run to the start of tramping tracks, drop off for a few days' hiking and take you pretty much anywhere else you fancy going, but the main destination is the Bridge to Nowhere, which is appreciably closer to Pipiriki. With each jetboat company competing for tourist dollars, the peace and isolation for which the river is famous is sometimes elusive.

The beauty, tranquillity and remoteness of the river are best appreciated on **canoeing** and **kayaking trips**. These range from one to five days, with most operators offering both **guided trips** as well as canoe or kayak **rentals**. The operators also supply at most everything you need (except sleeping bags); trips include transport to and from the river.

Taumarunui, National Park and Ohakune are the most common **bases**. Two-day canoe and kayak trips are normally on the upper section from Taumarunui to Whakahoro, but most people prefer the more scenic three-day run between Whakahoro and Pipiriki. Five-day trips cover the whole stretch from Taumarunui to Pipiriki; few continue downstream from there.

Canoe tours and rentals

Awa Tours ☎06/385 8297, ⓦwww.wakatours .net. Excellent three-day guided canoe tours ($650) from Whakahoro on the scenic middle reaches, during which you learn about the river environment from a Maori perspective in an effort to engender a true cultural exchange, take bushwalks and stay in *marae*.
Blazing Paddles 1033 SH4, 10km south of central Taumarunui ☎0800/252 946, ⓦwww .blazingpaddles.co.nz. Gear rental for self-guided trips, with prices including drop-off, pick-up and the DOC Hut and Camp Pass, with options ranging from one hour to five days.

Bridge to Nowhere see above. The *Bridge to Nowhere Lodge* runs several well-organized combo trips jetboating upstream from Pipiriki and canoeing back down.
Wades Landing Outdoors ☎0800/226 631, ⓦwww.whanganui.co.nz. Whakahoro-based operator offering self-guided canoe and kayak trips, three days from Whakahoro to Pipiriki for $150. You can also kayak for a day downstream and catch a jetboat back ($125).
Yeti Tours ☎0800/322 388, ⓦwww .yetitours.co.nz. Guided and self-guided trips on the river from two ($375) to five days ($765), including transport to launch points or for the

tracks, a plethora of gear for rent (canoes/kayaks from $140 for two days, camping equipment packages from $35/person/day) and lots of help and advice.

Jetboat operators

Bridge to Nowhere see p.241. Popular and frequent jetboat tours from Pipiriki, principally to the Bridge to Nowhere (4hr; $115 return).
Spirit of the River Jet ☏0800/538 8687, ⓦ www.spiritoftheriverjet.co.nz. A variety of trips upriver from the Pungarehu Marae, including the Bridge to Nowhere (from $125).

Wades Landing Outdoors see p.241. Jetboating trips range from scenic joyrides and museum visits to visiting the Bridge to Nowhere (5–6hr; $150).
Whanganui River Adventures ☏0800/862 743, ⓦ www.whanganuiriveradventures.co.nz. Small jetboat operator running day-trips from Pipiriki to the Bridge to Nowhere ($115), a variety of other tours and tramper transport.
Whanganui Scenic Experience (☏0800/945 335, ⓦ www.whanganuiscenicjet.com, see opposite). Runs tours on the lower reaches of the river and Bridge to Nowhere trips (from $135).

Whanganui Park hikes

One of the few tracks that investigates the deep, rugged valleys and bush-clad slopes is the wonderful **Mangapurua Track** (40km one-way; 3 days; 660m ascent), passing through semi-open former farmland. Conditions are best from October to April; **huts and campsites** are managed by DOC. Contact the jetboat and canoe operators for more information and to arrange transport.

The Whanganui River Road

The outlying sections of the park to the south can be accessed along the partly sealed **Whanganui River Road**, from either **Raetihi**, a small town on the SH4 near Ohakune, or Wanganui (see p.244). The River Road hugs the river's left bank from the riverside hamlet of **Pipiriki** 79km downstream to **Upokongaro**, just outside Wanganui. It's a rough twisting road, prone to floods and landslips, and even in the best conditions will take a minimum of two hours.

Opened in 1934, the road is wedged between river, farmland and heavily forested outlying patches of the Whanganui National Park, and forms the supply route for the four hundred people or so who live along it. **Facilities** along the way are almost non-existent: there are no shops, pubs or petrol stations, and only a handful of places to stay. If you don't fancy the drive, consider joining one of the Wanganui-based bus tours (see box below).

The road is detailed in the free, readily available *Whanganui River Road* leaflet. The leaflet highlights points of interest and lists their **distance from Wanganui**, a convention adopted in the parentheses in the following accounts, which take the road from north to south.

The southern reaches of the Whanganui National Park are accessed from Raetihi along the winding 27km Pipiriki–Raetihi Road, meeting the river at **PIPIRIKI** (79km).

Whanganui River Road Mail Run

Ideally you'll want to spend a few days canoeing in the Whanganui National Park, but if time is short, consider taking the **Rural Mail Coach Tour** (Mon–Fri; $55; ☏06/347 7534, ⓦ www.whanganuitours.co.nz), a genuine mail-delivery service stopping frequently at houses along the way as well as points of interest. The trip starts early (accommodation pick-up can be arranged from Wanganui city) and doesn't return until mid- to late afternoon, so bring your own food or take up the $12 home-made lunch option, as there's nowhere to buy refreshments en route. Canoeing from Pipiriki, trampers' transport and jetboating can also be arranged.

Hiruharama

HIRUHARAMA (Maori for Jerusalem; 66km), 13km south of Pipiriki, was originally a Maori village and Catholic mission but is now best known as the site of the **James K. Baxter commune**, that briefly flourished in the early 1970s. Baxter, one of New Zealand's most (in)famous poets, attracted hundreds of followers to the area. A devout Roman Catholic convert, but also firm believer in free love in his search for a "New Jerusalem", he became father to a flock of his own, the *nga moki* (fatherless ones), who soon dispersed after his death in 1972. The main commune house is situated high on a hill to the northeast of the church, and Baxter is buried just below. Ask for directions from the remaining Sisters of Compassion, who still live beside the 1892 **church** (from the north head up the first driveway, with a mailbox marked "The Sisters"), which features a Maori-designed and carved altar. The renovated original wooden **convent** offers basic self-catering dorm **accommodation** (℡06/342 8190, ⓦwww.compassion.org.nz; $20, bring your own sleeping bag) for up to twenty people.

From Moutoa Island to Koriniti

Moutoa Island (60km) was the scene of a vicious battle in 1864 when the lower-river Maori defeated the rebellious Hau Hau warriors, thus protecting the *mana* of the river and saving the lives of European settlers downstream at Wanganui. A cluster of houses 1km on marks **RANANA** (London; 60km) where there's a Roman Catholic mission church that's still in use today.

The only real settlement of note in these parts is **KORINITI** (Corinth; 47km), home to a lovely small church and a trio of traditional Maori buildings, the best being a 1920s **meeting house**, all down a side road. It's a private community, so while you can enter the church, the rest you should view from the road, unless you're invited into the compound.

Immediately south of Koriniti, memorable **accommodation** is available at ⚐ *The Flying Fox* (46km; ℡06/342 8160, ⓦwww.theflyingfox.co.nz), a remote and romantic hideaway accessible by boat or aerial cableway (prior booking essential). An eclectic range of found objects and scavenged pieces of old buildings have been imaginatively combined to create three separate self-contained buildings which encourage outdoor living amid the organic gardens and bush. Wood-fired bush baths, solar-heated showers, odourless composting toilets and a few spiders keeping the mosquitoes at bay add to the appeal. Browse through a fascinating range of books, old vinyl and CDs in the James K (self-catering, sleeping five; ❼), the Brewhouse (self-catering, sleeping three; ❼), or the Glory Cart (modelled on a gypsy caravan; ❸), or camp ($15). You can self-cater or pre-arrange predominantly organic breakfasts, and book **canoeing** trips (from $85/3hr).

From Atene to SH4

Almost 10km south of Koriniti, a sign (35.5km) marks the start of the **Atene Viewpoint Walk** (5km return; 2hr; 100m ascent), affording great views of Puketapu, a hill that was once on a peninsula almost entirely encircled by the river. The river eventually cut through the isthmus to leave the hill surrounded by a dried-out oxbow. The Viewpoint Walk comprises the first few kilometres of the **Atene Skyline Track** (18km loop; 6–8hr), making a wide loop following a gently ascending ridge line that ends with a 2km walk along the road back to the start.

Further downriver are the **Oyster Shell Cliffs** (28km), roadside bluffs with oyster-shell deposits embedded in them. This is the base for Whanganui Scenic Experience (23km, see opposite), which runs jetboat tours.

Soon the winding climb begins to the summit lookout of **Aramoana** (17km), giving a last look at the river below. On a clear day you can enjoy views of the northeast horizon, dominated by Mount Ruapehu. From the junction of the River Road and SH4, it's 14km to Wanganui.

③ Wanganui

There's an old-fashioned charm to the centre of **WANGANUI**, the slow pace mirroring the speed of the river that bisects it, and museums and well-tended streetscape exuding civic pride. Founded on the banks of the **Whanganui River**, New Zealand's longest navigable watercourse, Wanganui is one of New Zealand's oldest cities and was the hub of early European commerce because of its access to the interior, and coastal links with the ports of Wellington and New Plymouth. The river traffic has long gone and the port is a shadow of what it was, but the city has given itself a facelift with an eye to its colonial past: the late Victorian and early Edwardian facades have been refurbished, and mock gas lamps installed along re-cobbled streets. The inexpensive cost of living has seen a thriving **arts community** spring up here, and it's a pleasant place to idle away some time in the renowned **art gallery**, watch a **glass-blowing** demonstration or take a class, and to ride on a restored **river steamer**.

When **Europeans** arrived in the 1830s, land rights quickly became a bone of contention with the local Maori population. Transactions that Maori perceived as a ritual exchange of gifts were taken by the New Zealand Company to be a successful negotiation for the purchase of Wanganui and a large amount of surrounding land. Settlement went ahead regardless of the misunderstanding, and it was not until the **Gilfillan Massacre** of 1847 that trouble erupted – when a Maori was accidentally injured, his tribesmen massacred four members of the Gilfillan family. Further violent incidents culminated in a full-scale but inconclusive **battle** at St John's Hill. The next year the problems were apparently resolved by a payment of £1000 to the Maori. In the 1990s, the central Moutoa Gardens became the focus of renewed tensions, while the **spelling** of the city's name also creates divisions – see box, below.

Arrival, information and city transport

Flights from Auckland and Wellington arrive at the **airport**, 5km southwest of the city; a taxi into town costs around $20–25. InterCity **buses** drop off at the Wanganui Travel Centre, 156 Ridgway St (℡06/345 4433). The **i-SITE visitor**

Wanganui or Whanganui?

Unlike the Whanganui National Park and Whanganui River, the city which bears its name, Wanganui, has long been spelt without an "h". The pronunciation of both is the same, deriving from the local Maori dialect, pronouncing the "wh" prefix phonetically (as opposed to elsewhere in the country, where the "wh" is pronounced "f"). The spelling quirk resulting from a direct transcription of the Maori name (*whanga nui* translates as "big harbour"). Following years of discussions about whether to bring the spelling of the city's name in line with the national park and river (something many locals opposed), in late 2009, authorities reached a compromise of sorts, ruling the "h" to be optional according to residents' individual preference, with either spelling accepted. For consistency with the majority of current usage, we've retained the city spelling "Wanganui" in this guide.

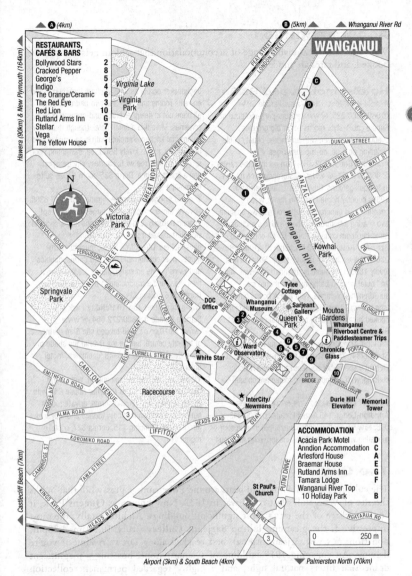

RESTAURANTS, CAFÉS & BARS

Bollywood Stars	2
Cracked Pepper	8
George's	5
Indigo	4
The Orange/Ceramic	6
The Red Eye	3
Red Lion	10
Rutland Arms Inn	G
Stellar	7
Vega	9
The Yellow House	1

ACCOMMODATION

Acacia Park Motel	D
Anndion Accommodation	C
Arlesford House	A
Braemar House	E
Rutland Arms Inn	G
Tamara Lodge	F
Wanganui River Top	
10 Holiday Park	B

WESTERN NORTH ISLAND | Wanganui

centre, due by the time you're reading this to have moved to its new riverside location at 31b Taupo Quay (Mon–Fri 8.30am–5pm, Sat & Sun 9am–3pm; ☎06/349 0508, ⓦwww.wanganui.com), has **internet access** and timetables for the local **Tranzit buses** (☎06/345 4433), who run a limited Monday to Saturday bus service round the city and to the beaches at the rivermouth, or try Rivercity Cabs (☎06/345 3333). The city centre is easily manageable on foot.

The **DOC office**, corner of St Hilland and Ingestre streets (Mon–Fri 8am–5pm; ☎06/349 2100), sells Whanganui National Park hut and camping passes. **Banks** are all on Victoria Avenue or within one block of it. The **post office** has two branches, the main one on Victoria Avenue and another at Trafalgar Square shopping mall.

Accommodation

Wanganui has a reasonable range of accommodation that seldom gets completely booked, and rates are modest.

Hotels, motels and B&Bs

Acacia Park Motel 140 Anzac Parade/SH4 ☎0800/800 225, ⓦwww.acacia-park-motel.co.nz. Simple cabin-style rooms set in big grounds overlooking the river, with an on-site beauty clinic including post-canoe-trip massages. ❸

Arlesford House 202 SH3, 7km north of the centre ☎06/347 7751, ⓦwww.arlesfordhouse.co.nz. Set in tranquil gardens, this elegant, Georgian-style 1930s country home has rimu floors, wood panelling and generously sized rooms (two en suite, two sharing a bathroom). There's also a secluded three-bedroom cottage. Room ❻/❼ cottage ❺

Braemar House B&B 2 Plymouth St ☎06/348 2301, ⓦwww.braemarhouse.co.nz. Situated in a lovely 1895 homestead surrounded by lawns. Airy and quiet, shared bathrooms front onto a sun-drenched veranda, with a YHA hostel out back (see below). Rates include continental breakfast; cooked breakfasts ($10) are available on request. Room ❹

Rutland Arms Inn Corner of Victoria Ave & Ridgway St ☎06/347 7677, ⓦwww.rutland-arms.co.nz. Elegant if somewhat soulless rooms in a historic building, with a good bar and restaurant on site. ❺

Hostels and campsites

Anndion Lodge 143 Anzac Parade ☎0800/343 056, ⓦwww.anndionlodge.co.nz. Upmarket accommodation with a range of options including luxurious backpacker dorms as well as share bathrooms, and en-suite rooms and one- and two-bedroom suites, all done out in designer black-and-crimson colour schemes. More like a small hotel, though there is a communal kitchen complete with bread-maker and dishwasher, plus a lovely BBQ area, swimming pool, spa and sauna, free wi-fi, courtesy city transport and a liquor licence. Dorm $35, room ❸, en-suite room/suite ❹–❺

Tamara Lodge 24 Somme Parade ☎06/347 6300, ⓦwww.tamaralodge.com. A large and well-kept historic building with pretty gardens and a sociable vibe that makes it popular with younger backpackers. Offers free bikes, musical instruments, neat comfortable four-bed dorms, doubles and twins (some en suite), plus a balcony with a river view, and a trampoline in the large garden. Dorms $26, rooms ❷

Wanganui River Top 10 Holiday Park 460 Somme Parade ☎0800/272 664, ⓦwww.wrivertop10.co.nz. Well-tended site 6km northeast of the city centre, beside the river in the shade of giant trees. Camping $36–48, cabins ❶, motel units ❹

YHA Braemar House (see above). Welcoming backpackers attached to *Braemar House B&B* with separate male and female dorms, private rooms out back, a kitchen and cosy lounge and a peaceful atmosphere. Camping $15, dorms $27, hostel rooms ❶

The City

The cultural heart of Wanganui beats around Pukenamu, a grassy hill that marks the site of Wanganui's last tribal war in 1832. Now known as **Queens Park**, it contains three of the city's most significant buildings. Architecturally, the most impressive is the gleaming hilltop **Sarjeant Gallery** (daily 10.30am–4.30pm; donation; ⓦwww.sarjeant.org.nz), best reached along Drews Avenue if you're driving. An engaging 1919 building of Oamaru stone, boasting a magnificent dome that filters natural light, and a highly regarded permanent collection concentrating on contemporary New Zealand art and photography, augmented by various touring exhibitions. Immediately to the north at the corner of Cameron and Bell streets, providing accommodation for artists in residence at the gallery, sits one of Wanganui's oldest buildings, the weatherboarded **Tylee Cottage**, built in 1853.

Southwest of the gallery, the Veteran Steps lead towards the centre of the city past the **Whanganui Museum** (daily 10am–4.30pm; $5). Founded in 1892, it contains an outstanding collection of Maori artefacts and three impressive canoes, all displayed in the central court. In smaller galleries hang portraits of Maori in full ceremonial dress and *moko* (traditional tattoos) by Gottfried Lindauer. Look out too for the photos of Whanganui river life, and models of ancient Maori methods of trapping eels and lampreys.

New Zealand's only **glass-blowing** school is based in Wanganui, and the city is home to around three dozen glass-blowing artists. Many work out of private studios, which open their doors to the public during March as part of the Whanganui artists open studio programme each March – dates and trails are listed at Ⓦ www.whanganuiartistsopenstudio.org.nz. The annual Wanganui **Festival of Glass** (Ⓦ www.wanganuiglass.com) takes place from late September to early October. Year-round you can see glass-blowing demonstrations in the workshop/gallery of acclaimed glass-blowers Katie Brown and Lyndsay Patterson at **Chronicle Glass Studio**, 2 Rutland St (Mon–Fri 9am–5pm, Sat & Sun 10am–3pm; free), make your own paperweight during a forty-minute short course ($100, by appointment), or book in for a weekend-long glass-blowing course ($350).

Towards the river, on Somme Parade, lie the historic **Moutoa Gardens**, a small but historic patch of grass. Traditionally Maori lived at Moutoa during the fishing season, until it was co-opted by Pakeha settlers, who renamed the area Market Square. It was here that Maori signed the document agreeing to the "sale" of Wanganui, an issue revisited on Waitangi Day 1995, when simmering old grievances and one or two more recent ones reached boiling point. Maori occupied Moutoa Gardens, claiming it as Maori land, for 83 days. This ended peacefully in the High Court, but created much bitterness on both sides. By 2001 a more conciliatory atmosphere prevailed, and the government, city council and local *iwi* agreed to share management of the gardens.

Following Ridgway Street until it meets Victoria Avenue, you reach the pretty **Watt Fountain**, which is surrounded by a number of ornate classical buildings, including the old post office and the striking Rutland Building. Continuing west you come to **Cook's Gardens**, known in New Zealand as the place where, in 1962, local hero **Peter Snell** set a new world mile record of 3min 54.4sec, on grass. There's still a running track here, along with a velodrome and the wonderful 1901 **Ward Observatory**, where every Friday evening you can look through the 24cm refractor (from around 8.30pm in summer, 8pm in winter; otherwise by arrangement through the visitor centre; $2).

The river

Wanganui's history is inextricably tied with the Whanganui River, and though commercial river traffic has virtually stopped, you can still ride the *Waimarie* **paddle steamer**, hopping aboard at Taupo Quay (late Oct to April daily 2pm; May late to Oct weekends, public & school holidays 1pm; $45; ☎0800/783 2637, Ⓦ www.riverboat.co.nz; booking advisable). New Zealand's last surviving paddle-steamer, it makes a two-hour run up a tidal stretch of the river. The huffing of the coal-fired steam engine and the slosh of the paddles make for a soothing background to an afternoon's sunning on deck, or you can retire to the wood-panelled saloon for scones and tea.

The *Waimarie* was built by Yarrow and Company of London in 1899, to a shallow-draught design with a tough hull, making it suitable for river work. It was transported to New Zealand in kit form, then put to work on the Whanganui River, where it saw service during the pre-Great War boom in tourism, when thousands from all over the world came to travel up the Whanganui River and stay at the hotel at Pipiriki. In 1949 the *Waimarie* made her last voyage and three years later sank at her moorings.

It wasn't until 1993 that the boat was salvaged and it returned to the river in 1999. The restoration took place at the **Whanganui Riverboat Centre &**

Museum (Mon–Sat 9am–4pm, Sun 10am–4pm; donation), flanked by old warehouses and stores at Taupo Quay, adjacent to the cruise departure docks. Housed in an 1881 two-storey timber-framed building, the museum concentrates on the river and its history in relation to the town.

The left bank

Crossing City Bridge to the east bank of the river leads straight towards the **Durie Hill Elevator** (Mon–Fri 7.30am–6pm, Sat 9am–5pm, Sun 10am–5pm; $2 each way). A Maori carved gateway here marks the entrance to a 213m tunnel, at the end of which a historic 1919 elevator carries passengers 66m up through the hill to the summit. At the top of the hill two excellent vantage points grant extensive views of the city, beaches and inland. The viewpoint atop the elevator's machinery room is the easy option, but the best views are 176 steps up at the top of the 33.5m-high **Memorial Tower** (daily 8am–dusk; free). Head back to town using the 191 steps to the river – it only takes about ten minutes, and provides more satisfying views.

It's about 2km south along Putiki Drive to the small, whitewashed **St Paul's Memorial Church**, Anaua Street (donation requested), which contains magnificent Maori carvings adorned with paua, a painted rib ceiling (as in Maori meeting houses), two beautiful etched-glass windows and two stained-glass, and *tukutuku* panels. The church is often locked: contact the i-SITE regarding access.

Eating, drinking and entertainment

Most of Wanganui's **cafés and restaurants** are along Victoria Avenue (which most locals simply call "the avenue") or just off it. Local artisan producers set up their stalls at the weekly Saturday morning **market**, on Taupo Quay; otherwise self-caterers can stock up at the Countdown supermarket on Trafalgar Square. The Embassy 3 **cinema**, 34 Victoria Ave (℡06/345 7958) has an impressive façade that isn't in fact Art Deco, but a polystyrene reproduction. For listings of gigs and events, check out the *Wanganui Chronicle*, New Zealand's oldest newspaper, published Monday to Saturday.

Bollywood Stars 88 Guyton St ℡06/345 9996. Top-notch spot with the usual range of curry dishes. "Express" lunch specials cost $9.90 for mains, while the evening menu ($14.90–19.90) is more extensive, including an excellent vegetarian *shahi paneer* in creamy tomato sauce.

Cracked Pepper 21 Victoria Ave. Licensed daytime café serving gourmet twists on old favourites, including lamb's fry and bacon, calamari risotto, and good chicken caesar salad, all under $25.

George's 40 Victoria Ave. A local institution, this old-fashioned fish and chip shop has an attached dining room also sells good-value wet fish. Closed Sun.

Indigo 1 Maria Place. Widely regarded by locals as the city's best restaurant (despite the patchy service), in a split-level, atrium-style glass-roofed space, serving polished contemporary fare (dishes $12–31). Closed Mon & Tues evenings. Licensed.

The Orange/Ceramic 51 Victoria Ave. A buzzing café (*The Orange*) by day, and a hip restaurant/cocktail bar (*Ceramic*) by night. Closed Sun & Mon evenings.

The Red Eye 96 Guyton St. Bohemian daytime café, with eye-brightening coffee and tasty dishes for breakfast and lunch, including great muesli cookies, sticky caramel slices and a huge range of filled bagels. Also open Fri evening, when there's often live music.

Red Lion 45 Anzac Parade. Atmospheric pulse-of-the-town pub recently repurchased by its previous long-time owners.

Stellar 2 Victoria Ave. Big, snazzy all-day bar/restaurant with a comprehensive menu (mains $23.50–32); a lively spot at weekends.

Vega Corner of Victoria Ave & Taupo Quay. Airy converted warehouse with two relaxing bars, one outdoors that backs onto the river; good-value café-style food both daytime and evening (dishes under $20) plus regular DJs.

The Yellow House Corner or Pitt & Dublin sts ℡06/345 0083. Cosy, historic timber home serving filling breakfasts, baked goodies and lunches (dishes $5–19), plus evening meals (mains $27–34; bookings essential) such as lamb with gingerbread or pecan-crusted chicken, followed by quince crumble or bitter chocolate cheesecake. Breakfast and lunch daily, dinner Thurs–Sat. Licensed.

South through Bulls

South of Wanganui, SH1 and SH3 meet at **Bulls**, 44km north of Palmerston North, worth a brief pause for its signage – the police station comes billed as Const-a-Bull, the town hall as Soci-a-Bull and so on.

Palmerston North and around

One of New Zealand's largest landlocked cities, **PALMERSTON NORTH** (so called to differentiate it from Palmerston on the South Island, and known throughout New Zealand as "Palmy") is the thriving capital of the province of Manawatu, with a population of around 78,000 residents, including a lively student population attending **Massey University**. After the arrival of the rail line in 1886, Palmerston North flourished, thanks to its pivotal position at the junction of road and rail routes, reflected today by some fine civic buildings, notably an excellent **museum** and **gallery** and a stunning **library**. Nonetheless, an unimpressed John Cleese famously claimed, "If you want to kill yourself but lack the courage, I think a visit to Palmerston North will do the trick." The town responded by naming the local rubbish dump after him.

Arrival and information

Palmerston North centres on **The Square**, a grassy expanse marred by a central car park. The **train station** is on Matthews Avenue, about 1500m northwest of the city centre. **InterCity buses** stop at the Palmerston North Travel Centre, at the corner of Pitt and Main streets, while other long-distance buses stop on Main Street, near the i-SITE. Frequent flights from Auckland, Wellington and Christchurch land at the **airport**, 3km northeast of the city, from where **taxis** (there are no buses) run into town: try Palmerston North Taxis (℡0800/355 5333; around \$20).

Local bus services also run from Main Street, near the i-SITE, in a series of loops (\$2 single). Timetables can be obtained from the **i-SITE visitor centre**, The Square (Mon–Fri 9am–5pm, Sat & Sun 10am–4pm; ℡06/350 1922, Ⓦwww .manawatunz.co.nz), which gives visitors free parking permits for the car park out front. The main **post office** is at 338 Church St.

Accommodation

Accommodation is plentiful, with motels lining the major approach roads to the city centre.

Acacia Court Motel 374 Tremaine Ave ℡0800/ 685 586, Ⓦwww.acaciacourtmotel.co.nz. Friendly, attractive spot with s/c units. ❸
Civello Accommodation 186 Fitzherbert Ave ℡06/355 3653, Ⓦwww.civellopalmerstonnorth.co .nz. Student-style singles and doubles with shared-bathrooms and a communal kitchen in a central, contemporary complex. Excellent value for money. ❶
Palmerston North Holiday Park 133 Dittmer Drive ℡06/358 0349, Ⓦwww.holidayparks.co.nz.

Spacious campsite close to the Manawatu River, with camping, cabins and tourist flats, and excellent facilities. Camping \$30, cabins ❶
Plum Trees Lodge 97 Russell St ℡06/358 7813, Ⓦwww.plumtreeslodge .co.nz. Lovely self-catering loft in a quiet suburban street, tastefully decorated, with a leafy deck where you can pick your own plums if they're ripe. An extensive breakfast hamper is supplied. ❺

The city and around

In the heart of the town's square is **Te Marae o Hine**, or the Courtyard of the Daughter of Peace, an open area graced by a couple of 5m-high Maori figures carved by renowned artist **John Bevan Ford**. The Maori name is the one suggested for the settlement's central square by the chief of the Ngati Raukawa in 1878, in the hope that love and peace would become enduring features in the relationship between the Manawatu Maori and incoming Pakeha.

Around The Square, the mishmash of architectural styles – classical Victorian and Edwardian, Art Deco and more – enhances the impact of the **City Library** (Mon, Tues & Thurs 10am–6pm, Wed & Fri 10am–8pm, Sat 10am–4pm & Sun 1–4pm), a postmodern conversion by Ian Athfield (see p.408).

Immediately west of the square lies **Te Manawa** (daily 10am–5pm; Ⓦwww .temanawa.co.nz), the city's main cultural focus. It's divided into three parts centred on the **Life Galleries** (free), a museum devoted to the history and culture of the Manawatu region. Much of the space is given over to high-quality touring exhibitions, but one room is devoted to a large impressive Maori exhibit. In the same building, **Mind Galleries** ($8) offers top-notch hands-on science-based exhibitions predominantly for kids. Adjacent stands the **Art Gallery** (free), which displays Pakeha and Maori art from its permanent collection, alongside touring exhibitions.

At the time of writing, the **New Zealand Rugby Museum**, 87 Cuba St (Mon–Sat 10am–noon & 1.30–4pm, Sun 1.30–4pm; $5), was a short stroll northwest of the square, but will be permanently relocating to Te Manawa in time for the NZ-hosted 2011 Rugby World Cup. The move will see it substantially expand its already impressive collection of rugby ephemera.

Ashhurst and the Manawatu Gorge

The semi-rural town of **ASHHURST**, 13km northeast of Palmerston North, stands at the entrance to the **Manawatu Gorge** (Te Apiti in Maori), a narrow 10km-long defile through which a rail line, SH3 and the Manawatu River squeeze. The mouth of the gorge is framed by the hills of the Ruahine and Tararua ranges, where the southern hemisphere's largest **wind farms** are a striking sight.

The gorge itself can be explored on foot along the **Manawatu Gorge Track** (3–4hr one-way; contact the i-SITE for gorge transport options), or you can see it on a hair-raising 25-minute jetboat ride with Manawatu Gorge Jet ($65; Ⓣ0800 945 335, Ⓦwww.manawatugorgejet.com).

Eating, drinking and entertainment

Thanks to its term-time student population, Palmerston North supports a vibrant **restaurant** scene. In the late evening many places morph into **bars**, some of the best lining **George Street**.

For entertainment, there's an astonishing four **theatres**: the i-SITE has details of what's playing where. For **movies**, head to the multi-screen Downtown Cinemas, on Broadway Avenue between Princess Street and The Square (Ⓣ06/355 5655).

Restaurants, cafés and bars

Barista George St. Minimalist espresso bar in a stripped industrial space of exposed pipes and concrete where they grind their own coffee and serve great cakes, snacks, and full meals (mains $10–24) such as wild mushroom risotto, along with an excellent range of NZ wines.

Café Cuba Corner of George & Cuba sts. Funky day/night café that's a local institution for breakfast, all-day brunch and lunch (under $20) and dinner (under $30). Lots of vegetarian fare, hip staff and live music on Friday nights (often with a $10 cover). Licensed & BYO.

Chokolato Downtown Complex, Main St. Late-opening café tempting post-cinema-goers with 24 flavours of its own home-made gelato (the feijoa is sublime), as well as a range of teas, coffees, hot chocolates and cakes.

High Flyers Corner of Main St & The Square. Central bar/club attracting a young crowd at night, especially to DJ dance nights Thurs–Sat, there's also bar food on offer (mains $27–38) including what they claim to be New Zealand's largest pizza, at a mammoth 24 inches (nearly 61cm).

Monsoon Asian Kitchen 200 The Square. Good-value Chinese, Malaysian and Singaporean cuisine. It isn't licensed, but they will order drinks for you from the bar across the street. From 5pm; closed Mon.

Roma 51 The Square. Italian-influenced Pacific Rim cuisine in a cosy setting with easy-going service. Many dishes available as a starter or main course. Specialities include an antipasto plate as well as thin-crust pizza. Lunch Wed–Fri, dinner daily.

Scarfies Corner David & Main sts. A three-bar extravaganza in the old *Railway Hotel*, aimed at students, with DJ entertainment Thurs–Sat.

South to the Kapiti Coast

South of Palmerston North and the Manawatu, the peaks of the rugged and inhospitable **Tararua Mountains** corral the **Horowhenua** region into a strip along the coast, where the towns of **Foxton** and Otaki merit a quick stop. Together with the Wellington commuter belt of the **Kapiti Coast**, a narrow coastal plain between the mountains and sweeping beaches peppered with dormitory suburbs and golf courses, the area is collectively referred to as the **Nature Coast**. Birdlife is prevalent throughout the region, particularly on the wonderful bush-covered bird sanctuary and marine reserve of **Kapiti Island**, 5km offshore.

The north–south rail link between Auckland and Wellington and the main bus companies serve the coastal towns but away from the rail/road corridor transport options are severely limited.

Foxton

The Horowhenua's most interesting town is **FOXTON**, 38km southwest of Palmerston North, where the old-style shop facades line the broad main street.

Archeological evidence suggests that there was a semi-nomadic **moa-hunter** culture in this area between 1400 and 1650, predating larger tribal settlements. **Europeans** arrived in the early 1800s and settled at the mouth of the Manawatu River, but struck problems with land purchases and soon retreated to found Foxton. It quickly became the **flax-milling** capital of New Zealand, adapting techniques perfected by local Maori, who had long relied on handmade flax items for their everyday needs. Flax was exported from the small river port for use in woolpacks, as binder twine, fibrous plaster lashings and carpet. To streamline the stripping and weaving processes, mills were constructed by swamps and on river-banks in Manawatu and Horowhenua.

An operational, modern, full-scale replica of a seventeenth-century **Dutch windmill** known as **de Molen** (daily 10am–4pm; $5) now dominates the townscape, offering a fifteen-minute tour on which you're taken upstairs to see its inner workings (and watch the production of its stoneground wholemeal flour when milling's underway). On the ground floor, you can buy Dutch groceries and the town's local soft drink, **Foxton Fizz**, in old-fashioned flavours like creaming soda. At the time of writing, de Molen was finalizing plans for its "bladerider", whereby you're strapped to the mill's blades and whirled through the air, fairground-style.

The broader history of the flax industry is recounted in the adjacent **Flax Stripper Museum** (daily 1–3pm; $5), behind which a 100m-long strip of river-banks contains a flaxwalk of 65 types of flax.

De Molen acts as the town's **visitor centre**. **Buses** stop outside, which is also adjacent to the old rail and tram station that contains a **horse-drawn tram** that's hauled out every summer (mainly Sun; $5) for tourist rides.

The long, sandy **Foxton Beach** is 5km away on the coast, where there's good surfing, safe swimming areas and abundant birdlife around the Manawatu river estuary.

Otaki and around

The main southbound road routes converge 19km south of Foxton at the workaday town of **LEVIN**, the administrative centre of the Horowhenua region. Some 4km south of town, off SH1, at the **Papaitonga Scenic Reserve**, a boardwalk leads to the Papaitonga Lookout (20min return) and great **views** of Lake Papaitonga. The surrounding wetlands provide a refuge for many **rare birds**, including the spotless crake, Australasian bittern, and New Zealand dabchick. In late January, Levin hosts the three-day **Organic River Festival** (Ⓦ www.ecofest.co.nz), with eco-oriented talks and stalls by day, and a stellar line-up of musicians by night. Camping spots quickly book out – tickets are sold online.

OTAKI, 20km south of Levin, sits beside a broad, braided section of the Otaki River, surrounded by market gardens. For most of the year, this is a quiet place with a strong Maori heritage (it was the first town in New Zealand to have bilingual road signs) but, like other towns along this coast, swells to bursting point for the month or so after Christmas when Kiwi holiday-makers descend en masse.

Otaki comes in three parts: the train station and i-SITE on SH1; Otaki township 2km towards the sea along Mill Road; and the **beach**, a further 3km along Mill Road, safe to swim at in summer thanks to a surf patrol. Along SH1 are well over a dozen **designer outlet stores**, particularly outdoors shops like Kathmandu, Icebreaker and so on. In the township, Te Rauparaha Street leads 200m to **Rangiatea Church**, an exact replica of the 1849 original that was widely regarded as the finest Maori church in New Zealand (Mon–Fri 9.30am–1.30pm; free; Ⓣ 06/364 6838). The church was consecrated in 2003, eight years after the original was razed in an arson attack. Inside the building is simple, with *tukutuku* panels on the walls, the pattern representing both the stars and the departed. The rafters are painted in Maori designs representing hammerhead sharks (symbols of power and privilege), and the exquisite model of the Tainui *waka*, which escaped the blaze. Outside, the simple, grey-slate headstone of the Maori chief Te Rauparaha can be found in a row of three by a decapitated Norfolk pine. Opposite the church is a memorial to the great chief.

Experienced trampers should ask the i-SITE about options for exploring the picturesque gorge of the **Otaki River** and the **Tararua Forest Park**.

Practicalities

Buses stop outside the **i-SITE visitor centre**, set in a beautiful, twice relocated 1891-built wooden courthouse at the corner of SH1 and Mill Road (Mon–Fri 9am–5pm, Sat & Sun 10am–3pm; Ⓣ 06/364 7620), which sells **hut passes** for tracks in the Tararua Forest. Two minutes' walk away is the unstaffed **train station**, served by Wellington–Palmerston North trains from Monday to Friday.

Easily the best place for daytime eating in Otaki is ⋆ *Brown Sugar*, on SH1 at the southern end of town (daily 9am–4pm), where veg frittata tops the menu, along with delicious cakes and good coffee.

Waikanae

WAIKANAE, 14km south of Otaki, is divided between the highwayside settlement and a beach community, 4km away along Te Moana Road, where the broad, dune-backed **beach** has safe swimming. If you want to stay outdoors, stop at the **Nga Manu Nature Reserve**, a large man-made bird sanctuary (daily 10am–5pm; $12; ⓦ www.ngamanu.co.nz), with easy walking tracks and some picnic spots. A circular track (1500m) cuts through a variety of habitats, from ponds and scrubland to swamp and coastal forest, which attract all manner of birds. There is also a nocturnal house containing kiwi, morepork and tuatara, plus eels, fed at 2pm daily and some walk-in aviaries where kea and kaka strut their stuff. To get here, follow Te Moana Road off SH1 for just over a kilometre and turn right at Ngarara Road; the sanctuary is a further 3km.

With over 250 vehicles in a specially built showroom, the **Southward Car Museum**, Otaihanga Road, 3km south of Waikanae (daily 9am–4.30pm; $12; ⓦ www.southward.org.nz), contains one of the largest collections of cars, fire engines and motorbikes in Australasia.

Paraparaumu and around

PARAPARAUMU, 7km south of Waikanae and 45km from Wellington, is the Kapiti Coast's largest settlement and the only jumping-off point to Kapiti Island. Locally shortened to "Paraparam", it's a burgeoning dormitory community, with commuters lured by the proximity of the long and sandy **Paraparaumu Beach**, 3km to the west along Kapiti Road, which is safe for swimming and looks out onto Kapiti Island.

The highlight of the **Lindale Centre**, 2km north on SH1 (daily 9am–5pm; free) is sampling ice cream (in rich flavours such as gingernut, and fig-and-honey) or cheese at **Kapiti Cheeses & Ice Cream**, both among New Zealand's finest. Its success has attracted a number of other food and craft shops and cafés, and farm animals to entertain the kids as part of the Lindale Kids play area ($2–8, depending on age). On Saturday mornings, a farmers' market sets up at the centre.

Around 1km south of Paraparaumu, the **Nyco Chocolate Factory**, on the corner of SH1 and Raumati Road (Mon–Sat 9am–4.30pm, Sun 10am–4.30pm; ☏ 04/299 8098, ⓦ www.chocolatesnewzealand.com) produces ninety thousand chocolates daily and sells them through a shop stuffed with goodies. Half-hour factory tours ($4; min 5 people) depart at 10.30am and 2pm Monday to Thursday (book ahead).

Practicalities

The **visitor centre**, SH1, in the Coastlands shopping centre car park (Mon–Fri 9am–5pm, Sat & Sun 10am–3pm; ☏ 04/298 8195, ⒺParaparaumu@naturecoast .co.nz), has local and DOC information. InterCity **buses** drop off at the **train station** opposite, as do local services from Wellington. **Paraparaumu airport** (ⓦ http://paraparaumuairport.co.nz), midway between SH1 and the beach, currently has scheduled services to Nelson and Blenheim with Air2There (ⓦ www.air2there.com). Plans for substantial expansion of the airport were underway at the time of writing, which would see the airport serviced by Air New Zealand flights – check for updates.

There are few genuinely tempting **places to stay**, though the welcoming YHA *Barnacles Seaside Inn*, 3 Marine Parade, Paraparaumu Beach (☏ 0800/555 856, ⓦ www.seasideyha.co.nz; dorms $28, shared bathrooms ❷), in a rambling 1923 wooden hotel, has comfortable antique-furnished rooms and overlooks the beach. Just north of town, off SH1, is the *Lindale Motor Park* (☏ 04/298 8046, Ⓔlindalemotorpark@xtra.co.nz; camping $17–30, kitchen cabins ❷, s/c unit ❸).

Restaurants and cafés cluster at the beach around the intersection of Marine Parade and Maclean Street. The pick are *Fed Up Fast Foods*, 40 Marine Parade (daily

11am–8.30pm), serving simple but stylish fresh fare including the area's best fish and chips and Kapiti ice cream, to eat in or take away; and the small, classy, evening-only *Muang Thai*, 22 Maclean St (℡04/902 9699; closed Sun).

Kapiti Island

One of the best and most easily accessible island **nature reserves** in New Zealand, the 10km by 2km **Kapiti Island** is a magical spot, its bush, once cleared for farmland, now home to birdlife that has become rare or extinct on the mainland. In 1824, famed Maori chief **Te Rauparaha** (original composer of the haka) captured the island from its first known Maori inhabitants and, with his people the Ngati Toa, used it as a base until his death in 1849. The island is considered extremely spiritual by Maori, and was designated a reserve in 1897.

Late January and February are the best months to visit, when the **birdlife** is at its most active, but at any time of the year you're likely to see kaka (bush parrots that may alight on your head or shoulder), weka, kakariki (parakeets), whiteheads (bush canaries), tui, bellbirds, fantails, wood pigeons, robins and a handful of the 250 takahe that exist in the world. The island can be explored on two fairly steep **walking tracks**, the Trig Track and the Wilkinson Track, which effectively form a loop by meeting near the island's highest point, Tuteremoana (521m). There are spectacular views from the summit, though the widest variety of birdlife is found along the lower parts of the tracks – take your time, keep quiet and stop frequently (allow about 3hr for the round-trip).

The **North End** of the island (about a tenth of its total area) is also part of the Kapiti Nature Reserve, though it's managed and accessed separately. The **Okupe Lagoon** has a colony of royal spoonbills, and there are plenty of rare forest birds and kiwi.

A wedge of sea between Kapiti Island and Paraparaumu has been designated a **marine reserve**, and its exceptionally clear waters make for great **snorkelling** around the rocks (bring your own gear, or rent it from the *Kapiti Nature Lodge*). You'll need your own gear for **scuba diving**, which is particularly good to the west and north of the island.

Practicalities

DOC manages the island and allows just fifty **visitors** a day to the main nature reserve, and a further eighteen to the North End. Obligatory **landing permits** ($11/person, valid for six months in case weather prevents a crossing) must be booked through DOC in Wellington (see p.402), though they can forward them to the Paraparaumu visitor centre for pick-up. **Book** as far in advance as you can: a few days is generally OK, but on summer weekends the main reserve is often filled three months ahead. If you're visiting both ends of the island, get two permits.

The fifteen-minute crossing from Paraparaumu Beach to Kapiti Island ($55 return) can be done with either of two **launch operators**: Kapiti Marine Charter (℡0800/433 779, ⊛www.kapitimarinecharter.co.nz), or Kapiti Tours (℡0800/527 484, ⊛www.kapititours.co.nz). Boats generally leave from the beach opposite *YHA Barnacles* around 9am and return around 3.30pm, with the option of a transfer to the North End (extra $5). DOC is understandably wary about the reintroduction of pests, so your bags are checked for any stray mammals. At the main reserve, an excellent half-hour introduction by one of the island rangers, along with the free *Kapiti Island Nature Reserve* brochure, sets you up for a few hours' exploration, though there are optional hour-long **guided tours** ($28), including tours focusing on Maori culture, and paua gathering. Facilities extend to toilets and a shelter at the landing point: take your own food and water, and bring back all rubbish.

Adjacent to the northern reserve is a small plot of private land at Waiorua Bay, owned by the descendants of Te Rauparaha, offering the only – but excellent – **accommodation** on the island. ⚐ *Kapiti Nature Lodge* (☎06/362 6606, ⓦwww .kapitiislandalive.co.nz) sleeps a maximum of ten in simple bunk-style rooms, doubles or twins. The communal feel runs through to the family-style meals, which might include fresh seafood. Rates (single $255, shared bathrooms $525/person, en-suite cabin extra $80) include breakfast, lunch and dinner and an evening kiwi-spotting walk (with high success rates – there are an estimated 1200 to 1500 on the island). Alternatively, the day tour ($322) includes the ferry, DOC permit, lunch and hour-long guided walk. Transfers can be arranged from Wellington (one-way $100).

Paekakariki and around

At the southern extent of the Kapiti Coast, the village of **Paekakariki** has a tiny but vibrant community that turns out for legendary open mic nights on the second and fourth Wednesdays of each month at the town's **café**, *Finn*, 2 Beach Rd. Paekakariki has a safe **swimming beach** just 150m from the well-appointed *Paekakariki Holiday Park*, 180 Wellington Rd (☎04/292 8292, ⓦwww .paekakarikiholidaypark.co.nz; camping $13, cabins ❶, units ❸). The holiday park is at the edge of the 6.5-square-kilometre **Queen Elizabeth Park** (daily 8am–8pm; free), which also has entrances at MacKays Crossing on SH1 and off The Esplanade in Raumati. At the MacKays Crossing entrance, the **Tramway Museum** (Sat & Sun 11am–4.30pm, daily Jan; admission free, tram rides $5; ☎04/292 8361, ⓦwww .wellingtontrams.org.nz;) runs restored Wellington trams along 2km of track to the beach. The adjacent **Stables on the Park** (Sat & Sun 10.30am–3.30pm; ☎04/298 4609, ⓦwww.stablesonthepark.co.nz) offers horse treks and pony rides for kids.

Some 22km south of Paekakariki and just 20km north of Wellington, the expanding satellite city of **Porirua** is worth a brief stop for the excellent **Pataka Museum of Arts and Cultures** (Mon–Sat 10am–4.30pm, Sun 11am–4.30pm; free; ⓦwww.pataka.org.nz), at the corner of Norrie and Parumoana streets, which hosts local and touring exhibitions by leading contemporary New Zealand artists, plus regular Maori dance performances.

If you fancy staying outside Wellington and driving (or taking the train) in from the rural hinterland, consider staying at one of two excellent **hostels**, both more appealing than most in the city. *Paekakariki Backpackers*, 11 Wellington Rd, Paekakariki (☎04/902 5967, ⓦwww.wellingtonbeachbackpackers.co.nz; dorms $28, rooms and en suites ❷; closed May–Sept), is an intimate and peaceful place close to the train station with sea views; *Moana Lodge*, 49 Moana Rd (☎04/233 2010, ⓦwww.moanalodge.co.nz; dorms $29, rooms ❷), some 12km closer to Wellington in the settlement of Moana, reliably ranks as one of New Zealand's best hostels, in a beautifully sited Edwardian villa with sea views from many rooms, free wi-fi and kayaks, and a very friendly atmosphere.

Travel details

Trains

Hamilton to: Auckland (1 daily; 2hr 30min); Ohakune (1 daily; 3hr 30min); Otorohanga (1 daily; 40min); Palmerston North (1 daily; 7hr); Te Awamutu (1 daily; 20min); Wellington (1 daily; 9hr 30min).

Otorohanga to: National Park (1 daily; 2hr 20min); Palmerston North (1 daily; 6hr 30min).

Palmerston North to: Auckland (1 daily; 9hr 30min); Hamilton (1 daily; 7hr); Wellington (1 daily; 2hr 30min).

Paraparaumu to: Paekakariki (half-hourly or more; 8min); Plimmerton (half-hourly or more; 25min); Porirua (half-hourly or more; 35min); Wellington (half-hourly or more; 50min–1hr).

Taumarunui to: Hamilton (1 daily; 2hr); Palmerston North (1 daily; 5hr); Wellington (1 daily; 7hr 30min).

Buses

Cambridge to: Hamilton (7 daily; 20min); Matamata (1–2 daily; 30min); Tauranga (1–2 daily; 1hr 30min).

Hamilton to: Auckland (14–16 daily; 2hr); Cambridge (7 daily; 20min); Matamata (2 daily; 50min); New Plymouth (3 daily; 3hr 40min–4hr 40min); Ngaruawahia (14–16 daily; 15min); Otorohanga (3–4 daily; 45min); Paeroa (1 daily; 1hr 30min); Raglan (2–3 daily; 45min); Rotorua (6 daily; 1hr 45min); Taupo (3 daily; 2hr 40min); Tauranga (2 daily; 1hr 45min); Te Aroha (1 daily; 1hr 10min); Te Awamutu (5 daily; 30min); Te Kuiti (3 daily; 1hr 30min); Thames (1–2 daily; 2hr 30min); Tirau (3 daily; 45min); Tokoroa (3 daily; 1hr 10min); Wanganui (2 daily; 6–8hr), Wellington (2 daily; 9hr).

Matamata to: Cambridge (1–2 daily; 30min); Hamilton (2 daily; 50min); Tauranga (2 daily; 1hr).

New Plymouth to: Auckland (3 daily; 5hr 30min–6hr 15min); Hamilton (3 daily; 3hr 40min–4hr 40min); Te Kuiti (3 daily; 2hr 30min); Wanganui (2 daily; 2hr 40min); Wellington (3 daily; 7hr).

Otorohanga to: Hamilton (3–4 daily; 45min); Te Kuiti (3 daily; 15min); Waitomo Caves (6 daily; 30min).

Palmerston North to: Auckland (4 daily; 9hr); Hastings (3 daily; 2hr 45min); Masterton (3 Mon–Fri; 2hr); Napier (3 daily; 3hr); Paraparaumu (6–7 daily; 1hr 30min); Rotorua (1 daily; 5hr 45min); Taupo (3 daily; 4hr); Wanganui (3–5 daily; 1hr–1hr 30min); Wellington (6–7 daily; 2hr).

Taumarunui to: Te Kuiti (1 daily; 1hr); Wanganui (1 daily; 3hr).

Te Awamutu to: Hamilton (5 daily; 30min); Otorohanga (5 daily; 20min).

Te Kuiti to: Hamilton (3 daily; 1hr 30min); New Plymouth (3 daily; 2hr 30min); Taumarunui (1 daily; 1hr).

Waitomo Caves to: Auckland (1 daily; 4hr 20min); Rotorua (2 daily; 2hr–2hr 30min).

Wanganui to: Hamilton (2 daily; 6–8hr); New Plymouth (2 daily; 2hr 40min); Palmerston North (3–5 daily; 1hr–1hr 30min); Taumarunui (1 daily; 3hr).

Flights

Hamilton to: Auckland (3 daily; 30min); Christchurch (1–2 daily; 1hr 45min); Nelson (1–2 daily; 1hr 15min); Palmerston North (3–4 weekdays; 45min); Wellington (5–10 daily; 1hr).

New Plymouth to: Auckland (5–8 daily; 45min); Nelson (1 daily; 1hr); Wellington (4–5 daily; 55min).

Palmerston North to: Auckland (5–8 daily; 1hr); Christchurch (4–6 daily; 1hr 15min); Hamilton (3–4 weekdays; 45min); Nelson (2 daily; 50min); Wellington (3 daily; 30min).

Paraparaumu to: Nelson (1–3 daily; 45min); Blenheim (1–3 daily; 40min).

Wanganui to: Auckland (3–4 daily; 1hr).

Central North Island

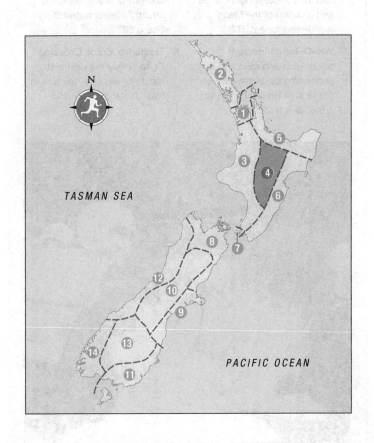

Highlights

✳ **Kaituna River** Raft this excellent short river and shoot its 7m fall. See p.270

✳ **Maori cultural performance** A delectable *hangi* feast wraps up an evening of chants, dance, songs, stories and a dollop of the Maori world-view. See p.272

✳ **Wai-O-Tapu** Iridescent pools, glooping mud and a performing geyser make this the best of Rotorua's thermal areas. See p.278

✳ **Lake Taupo** Cruise New Zealand's largest lake, haul trout out of it, or approach at speed while skydiving. See p.279

✳ **Huka Falls** For volume and power alone this is the country's finest waterfall. See p.287

✳ **Tongariro Alpine Crossing** Quite simply the best and most popular one-day hike in New Zealand. See p.298

▲ Rafting the Kaituna River

Central North Island

The **Central North Island** contains more than its fair share of New Zealand's star attractions, many the result of its explosive geological past. It is dominated by three heavyweight features: **Lake Taupo**, the country's largest; **Tongariro National Park**, with its trio of volcanoes; and the volcanic field that feeds colourful and fiercely active thermal areas, principally around **Rotorua**. If you are ticking off Kiwi icons, then time is well spent around Rotorua where boiling mud pools plop next to spouting geysers fuelled by super-heated water, drawn off to fill the hot pools around town. You'll also find the most accessible expression of Maori culture here, with highly regarded Arawa carvings and groups who'll perform traditional dances and *haka* before feeding you with fall-off-the-bone meat and juicy vegetables cooked in a *hangi* steam oven.

The dramatic volcanic scenery of Rotorua is striking for its contrast with the encroaching pines of the **Kaingaroa Forest**, one of the world's largest plantation forests, with serried ranks of fast-growing radiata (Monterrey) relishing the free-draining pumice soils. In recent years, high international milk-powder prices have fuelled a large-scale conversion to dairying, but sylviculture remain the area's chief earner.

The rest of the region is loosely referred to as the **Volcanic Plateau**, high country overlaid with a layer of rock and ash expelled two thousand years ago, when a huge volcano blew itself apart, the resultant crater and surrounds filled by **Lake Taupo**. This serene lake, and the streams and rivers feeding it, have since become a fishing mecca for anglers keen to snag brown and rainbow trout, while visitors flock to diverse sights and activities located near the thundering rapids on the Waikato River, which drains the lake. South of Lake Taupo rise three majestic volcanoes in **Tongariro National Park**, created in 1887 – a winter playground for North Island skiers and a summer destination for trampers drawn by spectacular walking trails.

The altitude of the Volcanic Plateau lends Taupo, the Tongariro National Park and environs a crisp **climate**, even in high summer. Spring and autumn are tolerably warm and have the added advantage of freedom from the summer

Getting around

Public transport around the Central North Island is limited to **buses**, mostly run by InterCity and NakedBus who ply routes from Rotorua through Taupo and on south to Turangi, Waiouru and Taihape. A bunch of minor companies service the small towns and trailheads around the Tongariro National Park (see box, p.297).

hordes, though the freezing winter months from May to October are mainly the preserve of winter-sports enthusiasts. Rotorua is generally balmier but still cool in winter, making the thermal areas steamier and hot baths even more appealing.

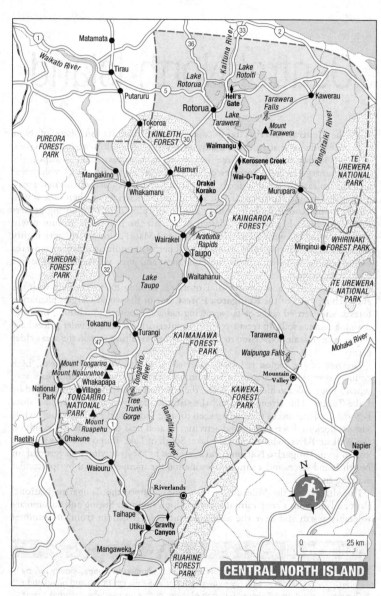

CENTRAL NORTH ISLAND

Rotorua and around

Rotorua is the North Island's tourist destination *par excellence*, so much so that locals refer to the place (only half-jokingly) as Roto-Vegas. This is one of the world's most concentrated and accessible geothermal areas, where 15m geysers spout among kaleidoscopic mineral pools, steam wafts over cauldrons of boiling mud and terraces of encrusted silicates drip like stalactites. Everywhere you look there's evidence of vulcanism: birds on the lakeshore are relieved of the chore of nest-sitting by the warmth of the ground; in churchyards tombs are built topside as digging graves is likely to unearth a hot spring; and hotels are equipped with geothermally fed hot tubs, perfect for easing bones after a hard day's sightseeing. Throughout the region, sulphur and heat combine to form barren landscapes where only hardy plants brave the trickling hot streams, sputtering vents and seething fumaroles. There's no shortage of colour, however, from iridescent mineral deposits lining the pools: bright oranges juxtaposed with emerald greens and rust reds. The underworld looms large in Rotorua's lexicon: there's no end of "The Devil's" this and "Hell's" that, a state of affairs that prompted George Bernard Shaw to ruminate on his colourful past, quipping that the Hell's Gate thermal area "reminds me too vividly of the fate theologians have promised me".

But constant hydrothermal activity is only part of Rotorua's appeal. The naturally hot water lured **Maori** to settle around Lake Rotorua and Lake Tarawera, using the hottest pools for cooking and bathing, and building their *whare* (houses) on warm ground to drive away the winter chill. Despite the inevitably diluting effects of tourism there is no better place to get an introduction to Maori values, traditions, dance and song than at one of the concert and *hangi* evenings held in and around Rotorua.

Maori-owned and -operated tour companies often make insightful and entertaining ways of exploring Rotorua's surrounding area. To the south and east, the forests are punctuated by sixteen **lakes** tucked into bush-girt hollows, many overshadowed by the shattered 5km-long massif of **Mount Tarawera**. During one cataclysmic night of eruptions in 1886 this chain split in two, destroying the region's first tourist attraction (the beautiful Pink and White Terraces), entombing the nearest settlement, Te Wairoa, now known as the **Buried Village**, and creating the **Waimangu Volcanic Valley**. The other magnificent geothermal areas around Rotorua include sophisticated **Te Puia** with its natural geysers, the adjacent **Whakarewarewa Thermal Village** where Maori still live among the boiling water, and the colourful **Wai-O-Tapu**, south of Waimangu, with vibrant colours, glooping mud and a geyser that performs on cue.

Some history

The Rotorua region is the traditional home of the **Arawa** people. According to Maori history, one of the first parties to explore the interior was led by the *tohunga* (priest), **Ngatoroirangi**, who made it as far as the freezing summit of Mount Tongariro, where he feared he might die from cold. His prayers to the gods of Hawaiki were answered with fire that journeyed underground, surfacing at White Island in the Bay of Plenty, then at several more points in a line between there and the three central North Island volcanoes. Ngatoroirangi was saved, and he and his followers established themselves around Lake Rotoiti ("small lake") and Lake Rotorua ("second lake").

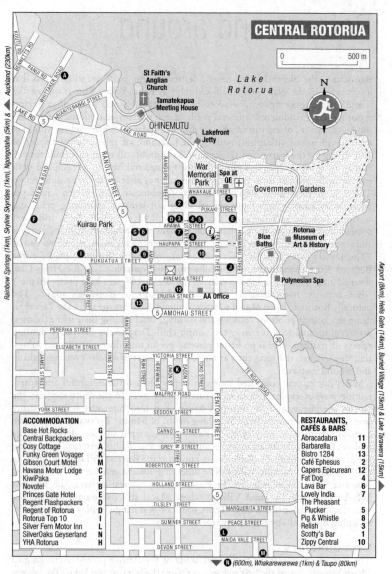

CENTRAL ROTORUA

0 — 500 m

Lake Rotorua

St Faith's Anglican Church
Tamatekapua Meeting House
OHINEMUTU
Lakefront Jetty

War Memorial Park
Spa at QE
Government Gardens

Kuirau Park

Blue Baths
Rotorua Museum of Art & History

Polynesian Spa

AA Office

Rainbow Springs (1km), Skyline Skyrides (1km), Ngongotaha (5km) & Auckland (230km)

Airport (8km), Hells Gate (14km), Buried Village (15km) & Lake Tarawera (15km)

ACCOMMODATION
Base Hot Rocks   G
Central Backpackers   J
Cosy Cottage   A
Funky Green Voyager   K
Gibson Court Motel   M
Havana Motor Lodge   C
KiwiPaka   F
Novotel   B
Princes Gate Hotel   E
Regent Flashpackers   D
Regent of Rotorua   D
Rotorua Top 10   I
Silver Fern Motor Inn   L
SilverOaks Geyserland   N
YHA Rotorua   H

RESTAURANTS, CAFÉS & BARS
Abracadabra   11
Barbarella   9
Bistro 1284   13
Café Ephesus   2
Capers Epicurean   12
Fat Dog   4
Lava Bar   6
Lovely India   7
The Pheasant Plucker   5
Pig & Whistle   8
Relish   3
Scotty's Bar   1
Zippy Central   10

(600m), Whakarewarewa (1km) & Taupo (80km)

In revenge for an earlier raid, the Northland Ngapuhi chief, **Hongi Hika**, led a war party here in 1823, complete with muskets traded with Europeans in the Bay of Islands. The Arawa retreated to Mokoia Island, in the middle of Lake Rotorua; undaunted, Hongi Hika and his warriors carried their canoes overland between lakes (the track between Lake Rotoiti and Lake Rotoehu still bears the name Hongi's Track) and defeated the traditionally armed Arawa. In the New Zealand Wars of the 1860s the Arawa supported the government. In return, colonial troops helped repulse **Te Kooti** (see box, p.372) and his people a decade later.

A few **Europeans** had already lived for some years in the Maori villages of Ohinemutu and Whakarewarewa, but it wasn't until Te Kooti had been driven off that Rotorua came into existence. **Tourists** began to arrive in the district to view the Pink and White Terraces, and the Arawa, who up to this point had been relatively isolated from European influence, quickly grasped the possibilities of tourism, helping make Rotorua what it is today.

Rotorua

You smell **Rotorua** long before you see it. Hydrogen sulphide, drifting up from natural vents in the region's thin crust, means that a whiff of rotten eggs lingers in the air, but after a few hours you barely notice it. Certainly, the odour stops no one from visiting this small city on the southern shores of **Lake Rotorua**, its northern and southern boundaries marked by two ancient villages of the Arawa sub-tribe, Ngati Whakaue: lakeshore **Ohinemutu** and inland **Whakarewarewa**. Rotorua was set up as a **spa town** on land leased from the Ngati Whakaue, and by 1885 the fledgling city boasted the Government Sanatorium Complex, a spa designed to administer the rigorous treatments deemed beneficial to the "invalids" who came to take the waters. The original **Bath House** is now part of **Rotorua Museum**, set in the grounds of the oh-so-English **Government Gardens**, which successfully and entertainingly puts these early enterprises into context.

Arrival and information

All long-distance **buses** pull up outside the **i-SITE visitor centre**, at 1167 Fenton St (daily: Nov to Easter 8am–6pm; Easter to Oct 8am–5.30pm; ☎07/348 5179, ⓦwww.rotoruanz.com), which has two efficient, often busy, desks. One deals with local tourism and the other covers DOC enquiries and New Zealand-wide travel. For a general roundup of what's happening pick up the free weekly *Thermal Air* visitor's guide, and look out for the Hot Deals (see box below).

Direct Air New Zealand **flights** from Auckland, Wellington, Christchurch and Sydney land 8km northeast of town at the lakeside airport (☎07/345 6175). Get into town with either Rotorua Taxis ($25–30; ☎07/348 1111), Super Shuttle ($19; ☎07/345 7790) or the #10 Cityride bus (every 30min; $2.20).

City and regional transport

The i-SITE has timetables for the Cityride (☎0800/442 928, ⓦwww.baybus .co.nz) urban **bus** system, centred on Pukuatua Street between Tutanekai and Amohia streets: tickets are $2.20 each way, or $7 for a day pass. The most useful services are #1 (to Skyline Skyrides, Rainbow Springs and the Agrodome) and #2 (to Te Puia): both run daily every 30min (hourly on Sun). **Renting a bike** (see p.273) is a viable way to get around the city and out onto the MTB trails in the forest.

The surrounding region is best explored by car (for **car rentals** see p.273). Alternatively, use one of the **minibus tours** which head out to the more distant sights.

Hot Deals

Visit the i-SITE to pick up its **Hot Deals** on local attractions and tours. Buying tickets here often gives ten-percent discount or throws in useful extras. Deals vary seasonally so ask about what's currently good value.

Geyser Link ☎ 0800/004 321, ⊚ www.geyserlink
.co.nz. Transport to Waimangu ($25) and Wai-O-
Tapu ($35) with small discounts for a combo trip.
Mt Tarawera NZ ☎ 07/349 3714, ⊚ www
.mt-tarawera.co.nz. The shattered line of craters
atop 1111m Mount Tarawera can only be accessed
with this Rotorua-based company who run a
half-day driving tour ($133). Get the best of both
worlds by doing a fly-drive tour: a helicopter up to
the mountain and drive back ($455).

Superia Tours ☎ 07/348 4866, ⊚ www
.superiatours.co.nz. Maori-led full-day tours
($175) include visits to Wai-O-Tapu, Waimangu,
Whakarewarewa Thermal Village and Lake
Tarawera and include a Maori cultural performance and a *marae* visit. Custom private tours also
available.
Tim's Thermal Shuttle ☎ 0274/945 508.
Transport to Wai-O-Tapu ($50 including entry) and
the Buried Village ($52 including entry).

Accommodation

There's a wide range of accommodation in Rotorua, and almost everywhere, no
matter how low-budget, has a **hot pool**, though genuine mineral-water pools are
rare. **Hostels** are all within walking distance of the city centre, while **motels**
mostly line Fenton Street, which runs south towards Whakarewarewa; competition is fierce and off-peak prices plummet. **B&Bs** and **guesthouses** are thinner on
the ground, and the **hotels**, while plentiful, generally cater to bus-tour groups and
have high "walk-in" rates.

Hotels and motels

Gibson Court Motel 10 Gibson St
☎ 07/346 2822, ⊚ www.gibsoncourtmotel
.co.nz. Welcoming motel in a quiet area with ten
one-bedroom units that are showing their age but
are great value, particularly since they each come
with a private mineral-water pool in a secluded,
leafy courtyard. ④
Havana Motor Lodge 1078 Whakaue St
☎ 0800/333 799, ⊚ www.havanarotorua.co.nz.
Quiet motel, close to the lakefront with spacious
grounds, a heated pool and two small mineral
pools. ④
Novotel Lake end Tutanekai St ☎ 0800/776 677,
⊚ www.novotel.com. Close to the lakeshore and
right by a bunch of good restaurant this top-line
hotel operates in conjunction with the adjacent *Ibis*
(⊚ www.ibishotel.com), sharing access to restaurants, pool, gym and business centre. Rates vary
wildly. *Ibis* ⑤, *Novotel* ⑥–⑦
Princes Gate Hotel 1057 Arawa St ☎ 07/348
1179, ⊚ www.princesgate.co.nz. Wooden wide-
verandaed hotel that's the sole survivor from the
days when all of Hinemaru St was lined with places
catering to folk taking the waters at the bathhouse.
Lounges and bar are delightfully creaky while the
rooms have been modernized to a high but dull
standard. Choose from rooms in the main building

or larger apartments next door. Rooms ⑤,
apartments ⑥
Regent of Rotorua 1191 Pukaki St
☎ 0508/734 368, ⊚ www.regentrotorua
.co.nz. Urban chic comes in this small hotel partly
created from a 1950s motel and partly in a modern
block with its own stylish restaurant and bar.
Accommodation is in immaculate all-white studio
suites that come with a pristine bathroom, stylish
wallpaper and furnishings straight out of the style
mags. Naturally wi-fi and iPod docking stations are
standard and you can lounge next to the heated
outdoor pool. There's also a mineral pool and a
small gym. ⑥
Silver Fern Motor Inn 326 Fenton St
☎ 0800/118 808, ⊚ www.silverfern
motorinn.co.nz. Knockout, modern, motel
with spacious, refurbished studios and
one-bedroom units, all with spa pools,
Sky TV, sunny balconies, oodles of space and
helpful staff. Free city bikes. Studios ⑤,
one-bedroom ⑥
SilverOaks Geyserland 424 Fenton St
☎ 0800/881 882, ⊚ www.silveroaks.co.nz.
Comfortable-enough business hotel where you
should book early to get a third- or fourth-floor
room with unsurpassed views of the Whakarewarewa thermal area. ⑤

A continuing problem around central Rotorua is **theft from cars**, with thieves
targeting those parked near hostels. Take any valuables into your room or ask to use
a safe.

B&Bs, lodges and guesthouses

The following are marked on the map on p.275.

Ariki Lodge 2 Manuariki Ave, Ngongotaha, 8km northwest of central Rotorua ⊕07/357 5532, ⓦwww.arikilodge.co.nz. Lawns seep down to the lake from this welcoming B&B. Two rooms, one with excellent lake view, and an enormous suite with spa bath and full kitchen. Room ❺, lake view ❻, suite ❼–❽

Aroden 2 Hilton Rd ⊕07/345 6303, ⓦwww.babs .co.nz/aroden. Comfortable suburban homestay B&B, just off the Tarawera Rd 4km from central Rotorua, with nicely appointed rooms, lush gardens and tasty breakfasts. ❻

Koura Lodge 209 Kawaha Point Rd, 5km north of central Rotorua ⊕07/348 5868, ⓦwww .kouralodge.co.nz. Go for a lakeside room in the main building at this stylish lodge equipped with secluded sauna and hot tub right on the water's edge, kayaks, tennis court and even a jetty for direct access to floatplane sightseeing. Understated rooms are tastefully furnished and well equipped, and there's a comfy guest lounge where a buffet breakfast is served. ❻

🏃 **The Lake House** 6 Cooper Ave, Holdens Bay, 7km northeast of town ⊕07/345 3313, ⓦwww.thelakehouse.co.nz. The two en suites in this luxurious but understated house open out on a sunny veranda with only lawns separating you from the lake. There's a big spa pool, free use of sit-on-top kayaks and kids can be accommodated in the built-in bunks of the Ship's Cabin. ❻

Hostels

Base Hot Rocks 1286 Arawa St ⊕0800/227 396, ⓦwww.stayatbase.co.nz. Large, lively hostel that's a perennial favourite of the backpacker tour buses, with heated outdoor spa and swimming pool and the *Lava Bar* next door. Accommodation is mostly eight-bunk dorms, each with private bathroom, plus the female-only Sanctuary dorm ($2 extra). Dorms $27, rooms ❷, en suites ❸

Central Backpackers 1076 Pukuatua St ⊕07/349 3285, ⓔrcbenquiry@slingshot.co.nz. Small, homely hostel, with beds rather than bunks in the four- and six-bed dorm rooms, plus a spa pool. Dorms $24–27, twins & doubles ❶

KiwiPaka 60 Tarewa Rd ⊕07/347 0931, ⓦwww .kiwipaka.co.nz. This well-organized complex is only a 10min walk from the town centre (on the far side of Kuirau Park), yet it's far enough away to avoid late-night party noise. Accommodation is great value and split between the "lodge", with four- or five-shares, singles, twins and doubles, and the en-suite chalets. There's also an excellent low-cost, licensed café/restaurant and small hot pool. Camping $9, four- and five-shares $27, rooms ❷, chalets ❸

Funky Green Voyager 4 Union St ⊕07/346 1754, ⓦwww.funkygreenvoyager.com. Relaxed hostel in a pair of suburban houses, 10min walk from downtown, with an easy-going communal atmosphere fostered by the idiosyncratic owner of nineteen years. Cooking facilities in particular are excellent and there's a cosy TV-less lounge. Dorms $24, doubles and en suites ❶

Regent Flashpackers 1181 Pukaki St ⊕07/348 3338, ⓦwww.regentflashpackers.co.nz. New, upscale backpackers with a stylish lounge and a couple of small mineral pools. Dorms $25, shares $30, rooms ❸

YHA Rotorua 1278 Haupapa St ⊕07/349 4088, ⓔyha.rotorua@yha.co.nz. This sparkling, purpose-built, 180-bed hostel comes with spacious tasteful communal areas plus a large kitchen and exemplary enviro credentials. Most dorms shun bunks, a female-only dorm is available and there's a great array of rooms plus s/c units for small groups. Dorms $27, rooms ❷, en suites ❸

Campsites and holiday parks

Blue Lake Top 10 723 Tarawera Rd, Blue Lake (see map, p.275) ⊕0800/808 292, ⓦwww .bluelaketop10.co.nz. Well-organized rural site 9km southeast of Rotorua, just across the road from Blue Lake, comes with games room and a spa pool. Camping $18, cabins ❶, kitchen cabins ❷, s/c units ❸, motels ❺

🏃 **Cosy Cottage** 67 Whittaker Rd ⊕07/348 3793, ⓦwww.cosycottage.co.nz. Holiday park 2km from town with an extensive range of comfortable cabins, s/c cottages, powered and tent sites, some geothermally heated – great in winter. There's a swimming pool, a couple of pleasant mineral pools, naturally fed steam boxes for *hangi*-style cooking, city bikes ($28 a day) and direct access to a lake beach where you can dig your own hot pool. Camping $17, cabins ❶, s/c cottages ❸

Rotorua Top 10 1495 Pukuatua St ⊕07/348 1886, ⓦwww.rotoruatop10.co.nz. The closest campsite to the city, with an outdoor pool, indoor hot tub, a spacious camping area ($18), basic but serviceable cabins (❷) and motel units (❹).

The town, Lake Rotorua and Whakarewarewa

Half a day is well spent on foot visiting the fine collection of Maori artefacts and bathhouse relics in the **Rotorua Museum**, located in the old bathhouse in the formal **Government Gardens**, and strolling around the shores of **Lake Rotorua** to Ohinemutu, the city's original Maori village with its neatly carved church. Afterwards, you can ease your bones with a soak in the hot pools set in a native bird sanctuary by catching a boat out to **Mokoia Island**, the romantic setting for the tale of two lovers, Hinemoa and Tutanekai.

At the southern end of town, Maori residents still go about their daily lives amid the steam and boiling pools at **Whakarewarewa Thermal Village**, while the adjacent **Te Puia** offers the region's only natural geysers, plopping mud and a nationally pre-eminent Maori carving school. Where Rotorua's northwestern suburbs peter out, Mount Ngongotaha rises up, providing the necessary slope for a number of gravity-driven activities at the **Skyline Skyrides**. In its shadow, **Rainbow Springs Kiwi Wildlife Park**, provides a window into the life cycle of trout, and an excellent **Kiwi Encounter**, while the nearby **Agrodome** fills the prescription for adrenaline junkies.

Government Gardens and around

With their juxtaposition of the staid and the exotic, **Government Gardens**, east of the town centre, are a bizarre vision of an antipodean little England. White-clad croquet players totter round sulphurous steam vents and palm trees loom over rose gardens centred on the Elizabethan-style **bathhouse**, built in 1908. Heralded as the greatest spa in the South Seas, it was designed to treat patients suffering from just about any disorder – arthritis, alcoholism, nervousness – and offered ghoulish treatments involving electrical currents and colonic irrigation as well as the geothermal baths. The bathhouse limped along until 1963, although the era of the grand spas had come to a close long before. For a modern sybaritic version of the experience head to the nearby **Polynesian Spa** or the **Spa at QE**.

The Rotorua Museum

The old bathhouse is now home to the wonderful **Rotorua Museum of Art & History** (daily: Oct to mid-March 9am–8pm; mid-March to Sept 9am–5pm; $12, free guided tours on the hour), which is currently being extended, in part to the original plans of 1908. It won't be complete until mid-2011 but the museum remains open. The spa's history is told through the *Taking the Cure* exhibit, set around the old baths themselves, complete with gloomy green and white tiling and exposed pipes. Several rooms have been preserved in a state of arrested decay while an entertaining film recreates some of the history of both the area and baths. To see more of the inner workings of the building, head for the basement – all old pipes, foundations and mud baths – which gets hotter as you walk further south, closer to the geothermal source. The remains of the original ventilation system (which quickly proved inadequate for dealing with the high humidity and hydrogen sulphide gas in the bathhouse) is on show in the roofspace, on the way up to a great rooftop viewing platform.

Don't miss the small but internationally significant **Te Arawa** display showcasing the long-respected talents of Arawa carvers who made this area a bastion of pre-European carving tradition. Many pieces have been returned from European collections, and the magnificent carved figures, dog-skin cloaks, *pounamu* (greenstone) weapons and intricate bargeboards are all powerfully presented. Prized pieces include the flute played by the legendary lover Tutanekai (see box opposite), an unusually fine pumice goddess, and rare eighteenth-century carvings executed with stone tools. A second exhibition covers the dramatic events surrounding the

Tarawera eruption. The extensive displays include an informative relief map of the region, eyewitness accounts and reminiscences, an audiovisual presentation and photos of the ash-covered hotels at Te Wairoa and Rotomahana, both now demolished. Finally there's a small but moving section on the **Maori battalion**, with an evocative half-hour video.

The Polynesian Spa, the Blue Baths and the Spa at QE

Immediately south of the Blue Baths lies the **Polynesian Spa**, Hinemoa Street (daily 8am–11pm; ☎07/348 1328, ⓦwww.polynesianspa.co.nz), a mostly open-air complex landscaped for lake views and comprising four separate areas. Most head straight for the **Adult Pools** ($20), a collection of seven pools (36–42°C) ranged around the historic Radium and Priest pools. These are off-limits, but the Priest water (claimed to ease arthritis and rheumatism) is fed into three of the pools. If you only want half an hour in the water, you're probably better served by the **Private Pools** ($18 each/30min; lake view $25) where two or three of you can soak in a shallow rock-lined pool. For a little exclusivity opt for the adjacent **Lake Spa** ($40), with landscaped rock pools along with private relaxation lounge and bar. Reserve in advance for massages, mud wraps and general pampering ($80/30min; includes Lake Spa entry). Kids are catered for in the **Family Spa** ($32 for up to two adults and four kids), with one chlorinated 33°C pool, a couple of mineral pools and a water slide.

While the main bathhouse promoted health, the adjacent **Blue Baths** (daily: Nov–March 10am–6pm; April–Oct noon–6pm; $11) promised only pleasure when it opened in 1933. Designed in the Californian Spanish Mission style, this was one of the first public swimming pools in the world to allow mixed bathing. It closed in 1982, but has since partly reopened to allow swimming in an outdoor pool (29–33°C) and soaking in two smaller pools (38–40oC). The bulk of the building is given over to private functions so is often closed at weekends.

The spirit of the original bathhouse lives on at the **Spa at QE**, 1043 Whakaue St (Mon–Fri 8am–10pm, Sat & Sun 9am–10pm, ☎07/348 0189, ⓦwww.qehealth .co.nz), where the emphasis is on cures and therapeutic treatments. It has a clinical, slightly scruffy feel but there's increasing sophistication in the areas devoted to pampering. Come for a soak in a private pool filled with alkaline water from the Rachel Spring ($12), a soothing mud bath (single $50, double $70) or an Aix massage ($50/30min), like being rubbed down while under a horizontal hot shower.

Lake Rotorua and Mokoia Island

Rotorua meets the water at Lakefront Jetty where you can rent kayaks, pedalboats and the like. This is the starting point for trips to **Mokoia Island**, 7km north of

The love story of Hinemoa and Tutanekai

The Maori love story of **Hinemoa and Tutanekai** has been told around the shores of Lake Rotorua for centuries. It tells of the illegitimate young chief Tutanekai of Mokoia Island and his high-born paramour, Hinemoa, whose family forbade her from marrying him. To prevent her from meeting him they beached their *waka* (canoe) but the strains of his lamenting flute wafted across the lake nightly and the smitten Hinemoa resolved to swim to him. One night, buoyed by gourds, she set off towards Mokoia but by the time she got there Tutanekai had retired to his *whare* (house) to sleep. Hinemoa arrived at the island but without clothes was unable to enter the village, so she immersed herself in a hot pool. Presently Tutanekai's slave came to collect water and Hinemoa lured him over, smashed his gourd and sent him back to his master. An enraged Tutanekai came to investigate, only to fall into Hinemoa's embrace.

the jetty, a predator-free bird sanctuary where a breeding programme supports populations of saddlebacks and North Island robins (often spotted at the feeder stations) and kokako. The island is better known, however, for the story of **Hinemoa and Tutanekai** (see box, p.267); the site of Tutanekai's *whare* and **Hinemoa's Pool** can still be seen on guided island visits with Mokoia Island WaiOra (2hr 30min; $120; T 0800/665 642, W www.mokoiaisland.co.nz), with the emphasis on Maori cultural interpretation and conservation.

Kawarau Jet (T 07/343 7600, W www.nzjetboat.co.nz) offers a high-octane spin around the lake (30min; $69) and trips to Lake Rotoiti (2hr 30min; $120) giving an hour at Manupirua hot springs, which can only be accessed by boat.

If it's just a lake cruise you're after try the leisurely *Lakeland Queen* (T 0800/572 784, W www.lakelandqueen.co.nz), a replica **paddle steamer** that runs a series of trips including meals (breakfast $38; lunch $45; dinner $70).

Ohinemutu

Before Rotorua the principal Maori settlement in the area was at **Ohinemutu** ($2 donation requested), on the lakeshore 500m north of the centre. Ohinemutu remains a Maori village centred on its hot springs and the small half-timbered neo-Tudor **St Faith's Anglican Church** built in 1914 to replace its 1885 predecessor. Within, there's barely a patch of wall that hasn't been carved or covered with *tukutuku* (ornamental latticework) panels. The main attraction is the window featuring the figure of Christ, swathed in a Maori cloak and feathers, positioned so that he appears to be walking on the lake. Outside is the grave of Gilbert Mair, a captain in the colonial army who twice saved Ohinemutu from attacks by rival Maori, becoming the only Pakeha to earn full Arawa chieftainship.

At the opposite end of the small square in front of the church stands the **Tamatekapua Meeting House**, again beautifully carved, though the best work, some dating back almost two hundred years, is inside and inaccessible.

To avoid feeling like a voyeur, and learn a whole lot about Maori history, life and customs in these parts, join a ninety-minute **guided tour** by Ohinemutu Village Tours (hourly 9am–4pm; $30), who operate from a kiosk at Ohinemutu.

Te Puia and Whakarewarewa Thermal Village

Rotorua's closest geothermal attractions share the **Whakarewarewa Thermal Reserve**, 3km south of the centre. Around two-thirds of the active thermal zone is occupied by **Te Puia**, SH5 (daily: Nov–March 8am–6pm; April–Oct 8am–5pm; $40 with free hour-long guided tours on the hour; W www.tepuia.com), a series of walkways past glooping pools of boiling mud, sulphurous springs and New Zealand's most spectacular geysers, the 7m **Prince of Wales' Feathers** and the granddaddy of them all, the 15m **Pohutu** ("big splash"). The latter performed several times a day until 2000, when it surprised everyone by spouting continuously for an unprecedented 329 days. It has since settled back to jetting water into the air two to three times an hour, immediately preceded by the Prince of Wales' Feathers.

The geothermal wonders are certainly impressive, but Te Puia is also home to a **nocturnal kiwi house**, a replica of a traditional **Maori village** that's used on ceremonial occasions, and an **Arts and Crafts Institute** (same hours; included with entry) where skilled artisans produce flax skirts and some enormous carvings. More portable (though expensive) examples can be bought in the gift shop. A Combo Package ($130) includes Te Puia entry and Te Po, the evening cultural show and *hangi*.

The rest of the thermal area falls under the auspices of **Whakarewarewa**: **The Thermal Village**, 9a Tukiterangi St, 3km south of central Rotorua (daily 8.30am–5pm; guided tours hourly; $25; W www.whakarewarewa.com), a living village founded in pre-European times and undergoing continual, though sympathetic, modernization. The focus here is not on geysers but on how Maori interact with this unique environment. You can stroll at leisure around the village, attend the free **cultural performance** (11.15am & 2pm), and partake in a **hangi** (served between noon and 2pm; $55; *hangi* taster $28.50). You can even buy corn cobs boiled in one of the natural cauldrons.

West of the Lake: Around Ngongotaha

Aside from visits to the thermal areas, much of Rotorua's daytime activity takes place around the flanks of **Mount Ngongotaha**, 5–10km northwest of the centre, which is increasingly being overtaken by the city's suburbs. Closest to downtown, there's all manner of gravity-driven activities at **Skyline Skyrides**, and gentler pursuits at either **Rainbow Springs** or around the mountain at **Paradise Valley Springs**. Sheep take centre stage (literally) at the **Agrodome**, while the adjacent **Agroventures** offers all manner of thrill rides.

Skyline Skyrides, Rainbow Springs and Paradise Valley

At **Skyline Skyrides**, 4km from town (daily 9am–late; $24; ℡07/347 0027, Ⓦ www.skylineskyrides.co.nz), gondolas whisk you 200m up to the station on the mountain for views across the lake and town. It is really only worth the journey if you tie it in with adventure activities such as the **luge** and the adjacent **Sky Swing** ride, which drops semi-brave daredevils from 50m. The best of various combo deals is the gondola, Sky Swing and two luge rides for $50.

At the foot of the hill lies **Rainbow Springs Kiwi Wildlife Park** (daily 8am–9.30pm, to 10.30pm in summer; $26; ℡07/350 0440, Ⓦ www.rainbowsprings.co.nz), a series of pools where you can view massive rainbow, brown and North American brook trout. These are linked by nature trails which visit several free-flight bird enclosures, a tuatara, a talkative kea and a nocturnal kiwi house. Your ticket gives you access for 24 hours, so come back after dark when the trees and pools are colourfully lit and kiwi are out and about in a naturalistic enclosure with little separating you from the birds.

Also here is the excellent **Kiwi Encounter** (daily 10am–4pm; $27.50, combo ticket with Rainbow Springs $42), an insightful celebration of the conservation work supporting the country's icon in the battle against extinction. A heartwarming 45-minute guided tour (on the hour from 10am) demonstrates egg incubation and ends with a kiwi viewing.

Trout share billing with lions at **Paradise Valley Springs**, 467 Paradise Valley Rd, 11km west of Rotorua (daily 8am–5pm; $26; ℡07/348 9667, Ⓦ www.paradisev.co.nz), a patch of mature bush where manicured pathways weave between pools of trout, an attractive wetland area, a walk-in aviary with kea, and paddocks containing tahr, wallabies and wild pigs. An elevated boardwalk nature trail gives a great introduction to New Zealand's trees, but the big draw is the breeding pride of lions which are fed daily at 2.30pm. At times they have lion cubs which, between the ages of four weeks and one year, can be petted: check the website for details.

The Agrodome and Agroventures

Just about every bus touring the North Island stops 10km north of Rotorua at the **Agrodome**, Western Road, Ngongotaha (shows at 9.30am, 11am & 2.30pm; show $26, organic farm tour and show $50; ℡07/357 1050, Ⓦ www.agrodome.co.nz), where the star attraction is a slick hour-long **sheep show**. Though undoubtedly corny, this popular spectacle is always entertaining: rams representing the nineteen major breeds farmed in New Zealand are enticed onto the podium, a sheep is shorn, lambs are bottle-fed and there's a sheepdog display. Afterwards, the dogs are put through their paces outside and you can watch a 1906 industrial carding machine turn fleece into usable wool. There's also a one-hour farm tour complete with honey tasting, a visit to an organic orchard, deer viewing and, between April and June, kiwi fruit picking.

A different market is catered for at the adjacent **Agroventures** (daily 9am–5pm), where adrenaline junkies can get fixed. Attractions include a 43m **bungy jump** ($95), the **Swoop** swing ride ($49), and the **Agrojet** ($49) where you're piloted around a short course at breakneck speed in a three-seater jetboat. The **Freefall Extreme** ($49/90sec, $85/3min) simulates a freefall skydive using a powerful vertical fan above which you hover (or at least try to). The **Shweeb** ($45/3 laps) offers a chance to race recumbent bicycles encased in clear plastic fairings and slung from an overhead monorail. Either race the clock or your mates around the undulating track. It's nowhere near as geeky as it sounds, particularly if you can get two teams together. Assorted Agroventures combo deals get you more bang for your buck.

Screams are traded for laughs at the **Zorb** ($49/wet roll, $59/dry, $108/3 runs) – another Kiwi-pioneered nutter ride located across the road. You dive into the centre of a huge clear plastic ball and roll down a 200m hill or the slower but wilder zigzag course; you can choose from wet and dry rides, the former being the more fun.

Activities

As you'd expect in a place that attracts so many visitors, numerous companies have sprung up in Rotorua to offer all manner of **adventure activities** – rafting, kayaking, mountain biking and even fishing – almost rivalling Queenstown. In addition to the activities detailed below you might want to try scenic **skydiving** with NZONE (15,000ft; $399; ☎0800/3767 9663, ⊛www.nzone.biz), although jumping out of a perfectly good aeroplane is cheaper down the road at Taupo.

Rafting, kayaking and sledging

Rotorua has a considerable reputation for its nearby whitewater rivers, which you can tackle aboard **rafts**, **kayaks** (usually tandems) or, more in-your-face, by "**sledging**" – floating down rapids clinging to a buoyant plastic sledge (really only for good swimmers). Much of the hype is reserved for the Grade IV **Kaituna River**, or at least the 2km section after it leaves Lake Rotoiti 20km north of Rotorua, which includes the spectacular 7m **Tutea's Falls** (though sledgers walk around the falls). The one to go for though, if you can get the timing right, is the Grade IV+ **Wairoa River**, 80km by road from Rotorua, on the outskirts of Tauranga, which relies on dam-releases for raftable quantities of white water (Dec–March every Sun; Sept–Nov & April–May every second Sun). This is one of the finest short trips available in New Zealand, negotiating a hazardous but immensely satisfying stretch of water.

If your tastes lean more towards appreciation of the natural surroundings with a bit of a bumpy ride thrown in, opt for the Grade III **Rangitaiki River**, which also shoots Jeff's Joy, a Grade IV drop that's the highlight of the trip. With more time and money, it's worth considering a **multi-day wilderness rafting trip** on the East Cape's **Motu River** (see box, p.350). You could also **rent kayaks** or undertake **kayaking courses** and **guided trips** on several of the larger lakes in the region, with the emphasis on scenic appreciation, soaking in hot pools and a little fishing.

Kaitiaki Adventures ☎0800/338 736, ⊛www .kaitiaki.co.nz. Rafting and sledging trips with a cultural dimension – explaining the significance of the river to Maori. Along with trips down the Kaituna (rafting $85; sledging $99) they do summer

Sunday trips down the Wairoa (rafting $99; sledging $299) with sledgers getting one-on-one guiding down this tricky river. They also do an excellent heli-in-jetboat-out half-day sledging trip down the Oreke River ($459).

Kaituna Kayaks ☎07/362 4486, 🖳www
.kaitunakayaks.com. Tandem kayaking on the
Kaituna River, including Tutea's Falls ($149) plus
whitewater kayak courses.
Raftabout/Sledgeabout ☎0800/723 822,
🖳www.raftabout.co.nz. Mostly trips down the

Kaituna either on rafts ($89) or sledges ($110),
plus summer Sunday rafting trips down the Wairoa
($120 including lunch), some trips down the
Rangitaiki ($120) and a variety of combo deals
with other adventure activities. The only company
with hot showers at its base.

Mountain biking

The North Island's best accessible **mountain biking** lies fifteen minutes' ride from central Rotorua, with large areas of the Whakarewarewa Forest's redwoods, firs and pines threaded by single-track trails especially constructed with banked turns and drops under a sub-canopy of tree ferns. Altogether there's round 70km of track, divided into over a dozen circuits graded from 1 (beginner) to 6 (death wish). There's plenty for riders of all capabilities. Entry to the forest and trails is **free** but you will need to buy the waterproof **trail map** ($5) from bike shops in town.

Access is from the obvious car park on Waipa Mill Road, 5km south of town off SH38. Either rent a bike in town (see p.273) and ride out, or drive here and rent a hardtail from Planet Bike (daily 9am–5pm except when very wet; $35/2hr, $55/ day; reserve ahead at busy times ☎07/346 1717, 🖳www.planetbike.co.nz) who have a mobile rental and repair operation based at the car park and do guided rides, including some women-only trips.

Rotorua's dedicated freeriders only hit the trails when the uphill work is handled by Southstar Shuttles (🖳www.southstaradventures.com) who operate a **shuttle service** to the top of the hill on weekends throughout the year and on Tuesday and Thursday evenings during daylight saving.

For more information visit 🖳www.riderotorua.com.

Fishing

The lakes around Rotorua have a reputation for trout fishing bettered only by the North Island rivers and streams flowing into Lake Taupo. The angling, in sixteen lakes, is both scenic and rewarding, with waters stocked with strong-fighting rainbow trout; a typical summer catch is around 1.5kg, while in winter it can creep up towards 3kg. The proximity of **Lake Rotorua** makes it a perennial favourite, reached by charter boats from the Lakefront Jetty ($160 for 2hr for up to 5 people, plus $15 for tackle).

If you are going it alone, obtain up-to-date information on lake and river conditions from O'Keefe's, 1113 Eruera St (☎07/346 0178, 🖳www .okeefesfishing.co.nz), who stock the free *Lake Rotorua & Tributaries* leaflet published by Fish & Game New Zealand, explaining the rules of the fishery and will provide contacts for fly-fishing **guides**, generally around $500 for a day. **Licences** (24hr $21, year $108) are valid for the whole country except for the Taupo fishery region and can be bought on the helpline and online (☎0800/542 362, 🖳www.fishandgame.org.nz).

Eating, drinking and entertainment

A few quality **restaurants**, most congregated along a short strip at the lake end of Tutanekai Street (known as "Eat Streat"), and lots of great cafés enliven eating in Rotorua. Unless you're part of a large group, there's little need to reserve a table. There are several good bars in Rotorua, but otherwise nightlife is limited. Most visitors spend one evening of their stay at a combined **hangi** and **Maori concert** in either a tourist hotel or, preferably, one of the outlying Maori "villages".

Restaurants and cafés

Abracadabra 1263 Amohia St. Maghrebi music provides a suitable accompaniment in this loosely Moroccan café and restaurant strung with filigree lamps and divided into intimate rooms. Come for coffee and almond cake, a falafel burger ($17), tapas ($8–10) or dinner dishes such as chicken b'stilla ($25) or lemon, olive and chicken tajine ($28). Free wi-fi. Closed Mon.

Bistro 1284 1284 Eruera St. Rotorua's best fine-dining restaurant has a relatively relaxed atmosphere despite the white-linen table-cloths, and serves the likes of fish of the day on a mussel and lemon risotto ($34). Dinner daily.

Café Ephesus 1107 Tutanekai St. Unassuming and cheap, with generous portions of Turkish, Mediterra-nean and Middle Eastern fare dished up. Chomp on traditional delights like *dolmades, guvec* or wood-fired pizza (all $17–24). Licensed & BYO. Closed Mon.

Capers Epicurean 1181 Eruera St. Large, airy, licensed café-cum-deli serving up wonderful breakfasts, from 7.30am daily, healthy salads, over-stuffed panini, and a great range of dinner mains such as twice-cooked pork belly on Asian greens ($26) or garlic chilli-crusted salmon ($27).

Fat Dog 1161 Arawa St. There's an early 1990s feel to this relaxed café/bar where hearty portions of robust food are eaten at mismatched tables. Drop in for breakfast – the Fat Dog Works ($16.50) should sort out hangovers – select from salads, panini and huge burgers for lunch ($10–20), or more substantial mains ($25–30) in the evening.

Lovely India 1123 Tutanekai St ☎07/348 4088. Authentic Indian restaurant with a sizzling mixed platter entrée for two ($18), a wide range of good-quality vegetarian dishes as well as the standard lamb kormas and tandoori chickens ($14–20). Takeaway available. Licensed & BYO.

Relish 1149 Tutanekai St. Excellent licensed café covering the bases from quality counter food, delicious cakes and coffee to dinners (mains $21–34) including porcini ravioli or salt and pepper squid plus a changing roster of tapas and a short menu of wood-fired pizza. Daily 7am–4pm, dinners Wed–Sat.

Zippy Central 1153 Pukuatua St. Groovy licensed restaurant with haphazard retro 1950s and 1960s pop decor. Serves great coffee and imaginative and well-prepared food, from salads and bagels to smoothies. Mains from $15.

Bars and clubs

Barbarella 1263 Pukuatua St. Dark late-night bar popular chiefly for underground, alternative and dance nights (hip-hop and house), visiting DJs and occasional bands. Usually Wed–Sat 11pm–3am.

Lava Bar 1286 Arawa St. Discount drinks, budget meal deals and theme nights (Sunday pyjama party, Thursday ladies' night etc), are surefire winners with assorted backpackers, rafting guides and locals. There's a happy hour (7–8pm), a pool table, and late-night music. Small cover charge on Sat.

The Pheasant Plucker 1153 Arawa St. Convivial bar chiefly notable for its good-value bar meals and nightly live music – open mic on Tues, covers bands Fri & Sat.

Pig & Whistle Corner of Haupapa & Tutanekai sts. Lively pub in a former police station with its own Swine lager on tap, a garden bar, and rock and pop covers bands Thurs–Sat ($3 cover). There's also a wide range of large bar meals (mostly $18–22).

Scotty's Bar 1104 Tutanekai St. There are just a few leaners and the bar itself in this intimate cocktail and wine bar among the restaurants.

Hangi and Maori concerts

Rotorua provides more opportunities than anywhere else to sample food steamed to perfection in the Maori earth oven or **hangi** and watch a **Maori concert**, typically an hour-long performance of traditional dance, song and chants. Although not an entirely satisfactory introduction to Maori culture, these are at least reliable and good value. The bigger hotels all put on somewhat forced extravaganzas, so go for the "Maori experiences" below. All have buses picking up at hotels and hostels ready for a start around 6pm, then run for three to four hours. They follow largely the same format, giving instruction on *marae* customs and protocol (see "Maoritanga" in Contexts, p.780) followed by a formal welcome, concert and *hangi*.

Mitai ☎07/343 9132, ⊛www.mitai.co.nz. All the standard elements are very well done, the excellent *hangi* is cooked in the ground, plus the events are conveniently sited beside Rainbow Springs, giving a chance of a night-time walk through the bush past a beautiful clear spring which feeds a stream where a fully manned *waka* arrives in flaming torchlight. $99.

Tamaki Maori Village ☎07/349 2999, ⊛www .maoriculture.co.nz. You, and several busloads, are driven out to a specially built "Maori village" south of town for a spine-chilling welcome and

▲ Unearthing a *hangi*

tales of early Maori–European interaction. Everything is so professionally done that it is hard to quibble, but its popularity has become its biggest downfall and sightlines can be restricted. The *hangi* is good, though, and the overall experience memorable. $100.
Te Po ☎07/348 9047, ⊛www.tepuia.com. Wear clean socks as it is shoes off (and men to the front)

for the thoroughly professional performance in a traditional meeting house at Te Puia. The *hangi* is top-class (with mussels and oysters to start), and the night is rounded off with a night tour of the geothermal valley, and hopefully a sight of a floodlit geyser performing. $99; $130 combined with daytime entry to Te Puia.

Listings

Bike rental Get about town with bikes from Lady Jane's Ice Cream Parlour, 1092 Tutanekai St at Whakaue St ($30/day). For off-road bikes see Rotorua Cycles, 1111 Hinemoa St ($35/3hr or $60/ day; ☎07/348 6588) or the far more extensive selection at Bike Vegas, 1275 Fenton St (hardtail $60/day, full suspension $100/day ; ☎07/347 1151). See also "Mountain biking" p.271.
Bookshops Idle Hour Book Inn, 1192 Eruera St, for secondhand books; Whitcoulls, 1238 Tutanekai St, for new.
Car rental Most of the majors are represented but the best deals and service are with Pegasus, 247 Te Ngae Rd (☎07/345 8455, ⊛www.rental cars.co.nz), which delivers and charges from $35 a day.
Cinema The local multiplex is Readings Cinema, 1263 Eruera St, but there's also the more intimate

Basement Cinema, 1140 Hinemoa St (under *Crank Backpackers*), a characterful two-screen arthouse movie theatre (22-seat and 13-seat) with a licensed café.
Internet access Coin-op at the Library ($4/hr) and several places including Cybershed, 1176 Pukuatua St.
Left luggage At Travelex, in the i-SITE ($2/24hr).
Library 1127 Haupapa St (Mon–Fri 9.30am–8pm Sat 9.30am–4pm; ☎07/348 4177).
Medical treatment For emergencies and urgent healthcare go to Lakes Care, corner of Arawa & Tutanekai sts ☎07/348 1000 (daily 8am–10pm).
Pharmacy Lakes Care Pharmacy, 1155 Tutanekai sts ☎07/48 4385 (daily 8.30am–9.30pm).
Police 64 Fenton St ☎07/348 0099.
Post office The main post office, with poste restante facilities, is at 1195 Hinemoa St.

Walks in and around Rotorua

Rotorua isn't especially well endowed with serious tramps, though there are several good day-walks and Rotorua works well as a staging post for forays into the Whirinaki Forest and further afield to Waikaremoana. The i-SITE has leaflets covering all the following.

Blue Lake (5.5km loop; 2hr; 500m ascent). This moderate loop around the Blue Lake starts by the *Blue Lake Holiday Park*, 9km southeast of Rotorua, and heads through regenerating bush, Douglas firs and past some sandy beaches perfect for a dip. The single major climb takes you away from the lake to a viewpoint.

Hamurana Springs Recreation Reserve (1.5km loop; 45min; mostly flat). On the shores of Lake Rotorua, 24km north of town, an easy trail meanders through a redwood grove to the North Island's largest spring. Almost 5 million litres an hour flow out creating a crystal-clear stream with a faint tinge that's like looking through a bottle of Sapphire gin.

Lake Okareka Walkway (5km return; 1hr plus; mostly level). Located 12km southeast of Rotorua, this lakeside interpretive trail mostly borders farmland, leavened with patches of regenerating bush and a nice boardwalk through wetlands to a bird hide.

Okere Falls Scenic Reserve (2.5km return; 40min–1hr). An easy stroll starting 18km north of Rotorua, with river views and spectacular angles on rafters shooting Tutea's Falls.

Whakarewarewa State Forest Park. Several easy trails meander through an experimental forest on the edge of Rotorua. The impressive Redwood Grove contains trees that grow three times as fast as in their native California. The forest visitor centre, Long Mile Road (Oct–March Mon–Fri 9am–5pm, Sat & Sun 10am–4pm; ☏07/350 0110), has free maps.

Around Rotorua

Many of the best attractions in the area lie outside Rotorua, among the lakes to the north and east and around the most dramatic of the volcanic zones half an hour's drive south, toward Taupo. Shuttles and tours (see p.263) mean that just about every combination of sights can be packed into a day. Independent travellers can quickly dispatch minor sights along the eastern shore of Lake Rotorua, leaving time for the seldom-crowded **Hell's Gate** thermal area and the opportunity to watch terrified rafters plunging over **Tutea's Falls**. Rewards are more plentiful to the east and south especially around Mount Tarawera which, in 1886, showered tonnes of ash on the settlement of Te Wairoa, now known as the **Buried Village**, where partly interred Maori dwellings graphically illustrate the volcano's power. As the village and the Pink and White Terraces were being destroyed the **Waimangu Volcanic Valley** was being created, and it now ranks as one of the finest collections of geothermal features in the region alongside kaleidoscopic **Wai-O-Tapu**, with its daily triggered **Lady Knox Geyser** and brilliantly coloured pools. **Kerosene Creek** has the best free hot pools around, while **Orakei Korako** offers a peaceful geothermal experience and the **Whirinaki Forest Park** presents great hiking and biking opportunities on the road to Lake Waikaremoana.

Northeast of Lake Rotorua: Hell's Gate and the northern lakes

SH30 hugs the eastern shores of Lake Rotorua, bound for Whakatane, passing through a concentration of lakes and plenty of twisting hill country. Scenery aside, there isn't a great deal to stop for along the way apart from the **Te Ngae 3D Maze**, 10km northeast of Rotorua (daily 9am–5pm; $7.50), a wooden affair with bridges linking separate sections that complicate things immeasurably: set an hour aside.

North of the maze, SH30 veers off to Whakatane while SH33 continues north towards Tauranga. Signs 6km north point down Trout Pool Road to **Okere Falls Scenic Reserve**, which surrounds the rafting mecca of the Kaituna River. From the first car park, 400m along Trout Pool, a broad track follows the river to a second car park (2.5km return; 40min–1hr) passing glimpses of the churning river below, and a viewing platform that's perfect for observing rafters plummet over the 7m **Tutea's Falls**. From here, steps descend through short tunnels in the

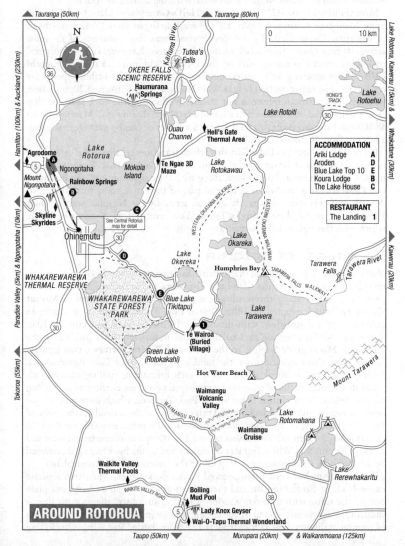

ACCOMMODATION

Ariki Lodge	A
Aroden	D
Blue Lake Top 10	E
Koura Lodge	B
The Lake House	C

RESTAURANT

The Landing	1

AROUND ROTORUA

Scenic flights

The scenery around Rotorua is breathtaking from the air, particularly the region's volcanic spine centred on Mount Tarawera. Volcanic Air Safaris (℡0800/800 848, Ⓦwww.volcanicair.co.nz) offer both **fixed-wing flights** over Tarawera ($185/30min) and **helicopter** flights with a landing at Hell's Gate ($305/1hr). Similar deals are offered by HeliPro (℡07/357 2512, Ⓦwww.helipro.co.nz), with a short flight over Mount Tarawera and the local lakes at $185 (minimum 2) and a volcano landing flight for $325.

steep rock walls beside the waterfall to **Tutea's Caves**, thought to have been used as a safe haven by Maori women and children during attacks by rival *iwi*.

Most traffic sticks to SH30, the route to **Hell's Gate** (daily: Oct–April 8.30am–5pm; May–Sept 8.30am–4.30pm; $30; Ⓦwww.hellsgate.co.nz), 14km northeast of Rotorua. The smallest of the major thermal areas, this is also one of the most active. Its fury camouflages a lack of notable features, however, and the only real highlights are the bubbling mud of the Devil's Cauldron and the hot **Kakahi Falls**, whose soothing 38°C waters once made this a popular bathing spot (now off-limits). The real attraction here is **Wai Ora Spa** (daily 8.30am–8.30pm) where you can soak in the sulphurous hot waters overlooking the park ($20) or slop rejuvenating mud over yourself in a mud bath ($75 including spa). Massages (from $80/30min) are also available and there are a number of combo packages including a bus out from Rotorua.

Beyond Hell's Gate lies **Lake Rotoiti**, which translates as "small lake", though it is in fact the second largest in the region and is linked to Lake Rotorua by the narrow Ohau Channel. This passage, along with the neighbouring **Lake Rotoehu** and **Lake Rotoma**, traditionally formed part of the canoe route from the coast. A section of this route, apparently used on a raid by the Ngapuhi warrior chief Hongi Hika, is traced by **Hongi's Track** (3km return; 1hr), a pretty bushwalk which runs through to Lake Rotoehu.

Southeast of Rotorua

Volcanic activity provides the main theme for attractions southeast of Rotorua, most having some association with **Lake Tarawera** and the jagged line of volcanic peaks and craters along the southeastern shore, collectively known as **Mount Tarawera**, which erupted in 1886. Before this, Tarawera was New Zealand's premier tourist destination, with thousands of visitors every year crossing lakes Tarawera and Rotomahana in whaleboats and *waka*, frequently guided by the renowned Maori guide Sophia, to the **Pink and White Terraces**, two separate fans of silica that cascaded down the hillside to the edge of Lake Rotomahana. Boiling cauldrons bubbled at the top of each formation, spilling mineral-rich water down into a series of staggered cup-shaped pools, the outflow of one filling the one below. Most visitors favoured the Pink Terraces, which were prettier and better suited to sitting and soaking. All this came to an abrupt end on the night of June 10, 1886, when the long-dormant Mount Tarawera erupted, creating 22 craters along a 17km rift, and covering over 15,000 square kilometres in mud and scoria. The Pink and White Terraces were shattered by the buckling earth, covered by ash and lava, then submerged deep under the waters of Lake Rotomahana.

The cataclysm had been foreshadowed eleven days earlier, when two separate canoe-loads of Pakeha tourists and their Maori guides saw an ancient *waka* glide out of the mist, with a dozen warriors paddling furiously, then vanish just as suddenly; this was interpreted by the ancient *tohunga* (priest) Tuhoto Ariki as a sign of imminent disaster. The fallout from the eruption buried five villages, including the staging post for the Pink and White Terrace trips, **Te Wairoa**, where the *tohunga* lived. In a classic case of blaming the messenger, the inhabitants refused to rescue the *tohunga* and it wasn't until four days later that they allowed a group of Pakeha to dig him out. Miraculously he lived, for a week.

The Blue and Green lakes, the Buried Village and Lake Tarawera

Around 10km southeast of Rotorua, Tarawera Road reaches the iridescent waters of **Blue Lake** (Tikitapu) with its campsite and circuit walk (see p.265 and p.274). A little further on, a ridge-top viewpoint overlooks both Blue Lake and **Green Lake** (Rotokakahi) then reaches the shores of Lake Tarawera 15km southeast of Rotorua. Just before the lakeshore, the **Buried Village** (daily: Nov–March 9am–5pm; April–Oct 9am–4.30pm; $30; ℗07/362 8287, ⓦwww.buriedvillage. co.nz) kicks off with a **museum** that captures the spirit of the village in its heyday and the aftermath of its destruction, through photos, fine aquatints of the Pink and White Terraces and ash-encrusted knick-knacks. The Maori and European settlement here was larger than contemporary Rotorua until the Tarawera eruption when numerous houses collapsed under the weight of the ash; others were saved by virtue of their inhabitants hefting ash off the roof to lighten the load. From the museum, either opt for a free **guided tour** (11am, 1.30pm & 3pm) or make your own way through the grounds.

What you see today is the result of 1930s and 1940s excavations plus some substantial reconstructions. The village itself is less an archeological dig than a manicured orchard: half-buried *whare* and the foundations for the Rotomahana Hotel sit primly on mown lawns among European fruit trees gone to seed, marauding hawthorn and a perfect row of full-grown poplars fostered from a line of fenceposts. Many of the *whare* house collections of implements and ash-encrusted household goods, and contrast starkly with the simplicity of other dwellings such as **Tohunga's Whare**, where the ill-fated priest lay buried alive for four days (see above). Look out too for the extremely rare, carved-stone *pataka* (storehouse) and the bow section of a *waka* once used to ferry tourists on the lake and allegedly brought to the district by Hongi Hika, when he invaded in 1823. Beyond the formal grounds a steep staircase and slippery boardwalk dive into the hill alongside **Te Wairoa Falls**, then climb up through dripping, fern-draped bush on the far side.

The road ends 2km on at the shore of Lake Tarawera with the mountain rising beyond. Stop for a coffee or a beer overlooking the water at the fairly mediocre *Landing* café (℗07/362 8590), and consult the staff if you fancy getting out on the water. Paddle sit-on-top **kayaks** ($25/hr) or rent a **motorboat** carrying up to ten ($125/hr) and spend a couple of hours chugging over to some shoreside natural hot pools and back.

South towards Taupo

The tussle for Rotorua's geothermal crown is principally fought between youthful **Waimangu** and the supremely colourful **Wai-O-Tapu**. Between the two lies Kerosene Creek, a wonderful spot for a hot soak free of charge.

Further south, the geysers and bubbling mud of **Orakei Korako** are a little off the beaten track and are consequently little visited.

Waimangu

At the southern limit of the volcanic rift blown out by Mount Tarawera lies, **Waimangu Volcanic Valley** (daily: Jan 8.30am–6pm; Feb–Dec 8.30am–5pm; $32.50; ⓦwww.waimangu.co.nz), 19km south of Rotorua, 5km east of SH5. This is one of the world's youngest geothermal areas, created in 1886 when a chain of eruptions racked the Mount Tarawera fault line. Pick up the comprehensive self-guided walking tour leaflet at the visitor centre then head downhill along a stream-side path, which cuts through a valley choked with scrub and native bush that has regenerated since 1886. This process has been periodically interrupted by smaller eruptions, including one in 1917 that created the magnificent 100m-diameter **Frying Pan Lake**, the world's largest hot spring. Massive quantities of hot water well up from the depths of the **Inferno Crater**, an inverted cone where mesmerizing steam patterns partly obscure the powder-blue water and are stirred and swirled by breezes across the lake. The water level rises and falls according to a rigid 38-day cycle – filling to the rim for 21 days, overflowing for two then gradually falling to 8m below the rim over the next fifteen. Steaming pools and hissing vents line the path, which passes the muddy depression where, from 1900 to 1904, the **Waimangu Geyser** regularly spouted water to 250m (and occasionally to an astonishing height of 400m) carrying rocks and black mud with it.

The path through the valley ends at the wharf on the shores of Lake Rotoma-hana, where the rust-red sides of Mount Tarawera dominate the far horizon. From here, free buses run back up the road to the visitor centre and gentle, commentated, 45-minute **cruises** (6 daily; additional $40) chug around the lake past steaming cliffs, fumaroles and over the site of the Pink and White Terraces.

Kerosene Creek

If you're looking for free, hot soaking in natural surroundings, make straight for **Kerosene Creek**, 27km south of Rotorua, a stream that's usually the temperature of a warm bath and plunges over a metre-high waterfall into a nice big pool. It is always open and sometimes attracts a party crowd at weekends. Camping in the area is banned and there have been thefts from vehicles in the car park.

To get there turn east along Old Waiotapu Road (1km south of the SH38 junction) and follow the gravel 2km to a parking area.

Wai-O-Tapu

Wai-O-Tapu Thermal Wonderland, just off SH5, 10km south of Waimangu (daily 8.30am–5pm; $30; Ⓦ www.geyserland.co.nz), is the area's most colourful and varied geothermal site. At 10.15am daily, the 10m **Lady Knox Geyser** is ignomini-ously induced to perform by a staff member who pours a soapy surfactant into the vent. If you miss the geyser your ticket allows you to come back next morning.

Everyone then drives 1km to the main site where an hour-long walking loop wends its way through a series of small lakes which have taken on the tints of the minerals dissolved in them – yellow from sulphur, purple from manganese, green from arsenic and so on. The gurgling and growling black mud of the **Devil's Ink-Pots** and a series of hissing and rumbling craters pale beside the ever-changing rainbow colours of the **Artist's Palette** pools and the gorgeous, effervescent **Champagne Pool**, a circular bottle-green cauldron wreathed in swirling steam and fringed by a burnt-orange shelf. The waters of the Champagne Pool froth over **The Terraces**, a rippled accretion of lime silicate that glistens in the sunlight.

As you drive back to the main road, follow a short detour to a huge and active **boiling mud pool** which plops away merrily, forming lovely concentric patterns.

Orakei Korako

Diverting from either SH1 (14km) or SH5 (21km), about 60km south of Rotorua is the atmospheric thermal area of **Orakei Korako** (daily: Oct–March 8am–5pm; April–Sept 8am–4.30pm; $34; Ⓦ www.orakeikorako.co.nz) characterized by its belching fumaroles, gin-clear boiling pools and paucity of tourists. A short shuttle-boat journey across the Waikato River accesses an hour-long trail which visits Ruatapu Cave, once used by Maori women to prepare themselves for ceremonies – hence Orakei Korako, "a place of adorning". Campervanners can park overnight beside the river at no extra charge and use the toilets.

Orakei Korako can also be reached by **jetboat** along the Waikato River with NZ Riverjet (⊤ 0800/748 375, ⓦ www.riverjet.co.nz), based beside SH5 at Waimahana, almost 20km south of Wai-O-Tapu. Its Riverjet Thermal Safari (daily 11am, plus 2pm on request; 3hr; $145) includes a jetboat ride and entry, while The Squeeze (same times; $130) skips Orakei Korako in favour of a fun wade up a geothermally heated stream, through a narrow chasm overhung by bush to a hot waterfall.

Whirinaki Forest Park

Midway between Waimangu and Wai-O-Tapu, 25km south of Rotorua, SH38 spurs southeast through the regimented pines of the Kaingaroa Forest towards the jagged peaks of Te Urewera National Park, a vast tract of untouched wilderness separating the Rotorua lakes from Poverty Bay and the East Cape. The Kaingaroa Forest finally relents 40km on, as the road crosses the Rangitaiki River by the predominantly Maori timber town of **MURUPARA**. DOC's **Te Urewera Area Office**, 1km southeast of town on SH38 (Nov–April Mon–Fri 8am–5pm, Sat & Sun 9am–3pm; May–Oct Mon–Fri 8am–5pm; ⊤ 07/366 1080), has stacks of information on Te Urewera National Park and Lake Waikaremoana (see p.369).

Particular emphasis is given to the wonderful but little-visited **Whirinaki Forest Park**, around 30km south, which harbours some of the densest and most impressive stands of bush on the North Island: podocarps on the river flats, and native beech on the steep volcanic uplands between them, support a wonderfully rich birdlife with tui, bellbirds, kereru and kaka. The forest is now protected, after one of the country's most celebrated environmental battles and is a wilderness paradise for hikers and mountain bikers.

You can sample some of the best of the forest on a stretch of the well-formed **Whirinaki Track** (4hr return) which passes magnificent podocarps, the Whaitinui-a-tio Canyon where the river cascades over an old lava flow and Whirinaki Falls. Go as far as you like and turn back, but the track system continues, allowing tramps of up to five days staying in some of the nine standard **huts** (all $5, except central Whirinaki; $10) that pepper the park.

The *Ride Whirinaki* leaflet ($2 from DOC visitor centres) details a couple of great **mountain-bike rides** in the area (2hr–2 days), but you'll need to have your own bike or rent one in Rotorua.

It's also possible to explore the area on a day-long guided tour with Whirinaki Rainforest Experiences ($155; ⊤ 0800/869 255, ⓦ www.whirinaki.com), who offer a Maori perspective on the forest and its history in friendly, involving trips.

Taupo and around

The burgeoning resort town of **Taupo**, 80km south of Rotorua and slap in the centre of the North Island, is slung around the northern shores of Lake Taupo, the country's largest lake. Views stretch 30km southwest towards the three snowcapped volcanoes of the Tongariro National Park, the reflected light from the lake's glassy surface combining with the 360m altitude to create an almost alpine radiance. Here, the impossibly deep-blue waters of the Waikato River ("flowing water" in Maori) begin their long journey to the Tasman Sea and both lake and river frontages are lined with parks, lending Taupo a slow pace and appealing tenor.

For decades, Kiwi families have been descending en masse for a couple of weeks' holiday, bathing in the crisp waters of the lake, fishing its depths and lounging around holiday homes that fringe the lakeshore. But there's no shortage of stuff to see and do, from the spectacular rapids and geothermal badlands north of town to **skydiving** – this is New Zealand's freefall capital – and **fishing**. The Taupo area is a most fecund trout fishery, extending south to Turangi and along the Tongariro River, with an enviable reputation for the quality of its fish. Year-round, you'll see boats drifting across the lake with lines trailing and, particularly in the evenings, rivermouths choked with fly-casters in waist-high waders.

Lake Taupo (616 sq km, 185m deep) is itself a geological infant largely created in 186 AD when the Taupo Volcano spewed out 24 cubic kilometres of rock, debris and ash – at least ten times more than was produced by the eruptions of Krakatoa and Mount St Helens combined – and covered much of the North Island in a thick layer of pumice. Ash from the **eruption** was carried around the world – the Chinese noted a blackening of the sky and Romans recorded that the heavens turned blood-red. As the underground magma chamber emptied, the roof slumped, leaving a huge steep-sided **crater**, since filled by Lake Taupo. It is hard to reconcile this placid and beautiful lake with such colossal violence, though the evidence is all around: entire beaches are composed of feather-light pumice which, when caught by the wind, floats off across the lake. **Vulcanologists** continue to study the Taupo Volcano (currently considered dormant) and treat the lake as a kind of giant spirit-level, in which any tilting could indicate a build-up of magma below the surface that might trigger another eruption.

The local Tuwharetoa people ascribe the lake's formation to their ancestor, **Ngatoroirangi**, who cast a tree from the summit of Mount Tauhara, on the edge of Taupo, and where it struck the ground water welled up and formed the lake. The lake's full name is **Taupo–Nui-A-Tia**, "the great shoulder mat of Tia" or "great sleep of Tia", which refers to an explorer from the Arawa canoe said to have slept by the lake.

Taupo

Nowhere in **TAUPO'S** compact low-rise core is more than five minutes' walk from the waters of the Waikato River or Lake Taupo, which jointly hem in three sides. The fourth side rises up through the gentle slopes of Taupo's suburbs. Most of the commercial activity happens along Tongariro Street and the aptly named Lake Terrace, which should both be much quieter once a new town bypass opens at the end of 2010.

The Tuwharetoa people had lived in the area for centuries, but it wasn't until the New Zealand Wars that Europeans took an interest with the Armed Constabulary trying to track down **Te Kooti** (see p.372). They set up camp one night in June 1869 at Opepe, 17km southeast of Taupo (beside what is now SH5), and were ambushed by Te Kooti's men, who killed nine soldiers. Garrisons were subsequently established at Opepe and Taupo, but only Taupo flourished, enjoying a more strategic situation and being blessed with hot springs for washing and bathing. By 1877, Te Kooti had been contained, but the Armed Constabulary wasn't disbanded until 1886, after which several soldiers and their families stayed on, forming the nucleus of European settlement.

Taupo didn't really take off as a domestic resort until the prosperous 1950s, when the North Island's roads had improved to the point where Kiwi families could easily drive here from Auckland, Wellington or Hawke's Bay. With the exception of a good **museum** there are few attractions within the town but Taupo makes a great base for exploring the surrounding area.

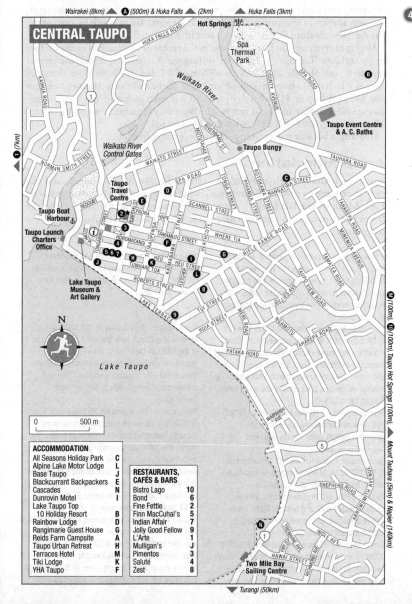

CENTRAL TAUPO

Wairakei (8km) ▲ Ⓐ (500m) & Huka Falls ▲ (2km) ▲ Huka Falls (3km)

Hot Springs

Spa Thermal Park

Waikato River

Ⓑ

Taupo Event Centre & A. C. Baths

Taupo Bungy

ⓐ (7km)

Waikato River Control Gates

Taupo Travel Centre

Ⓔ Ⓓ

Ⓒ

Taupo Boat Harbour

Taupo Launch Charters Office

ⓘ

② ③

⑤⑥⑦

Ⓕ

Ⓚ

Ⓗ

Ⓛ

Ⓘ

Ⓖ

Ⓙ

Lake Taupo Museum & Art Gallery

⑧

⑨

N

Lake Taupo

0   500 m

Ⓜ (100m), Ⓝ (100m), Taupo Hot Springs (100m) ▲ Mount Tauhara (5km) & Napier (140km)

⑤

Ⓝ

Two Mile Bay Sailing Centre

281

▼ Turangi (50km)

ACCOMMODATION		RESTAURANTS, CAFÉS & BARS	
All Seasons Holiday Park	C	Bistro Lago	10
Alpine Lake Motor Lodge	L	Bond	6
Base Taupo	J	Fine Fettle	2
Blackcurrant Backpackers	E	Finn MacCuhal's	5
Cascades	N	Indian Affair	7
Dunrovin Motel	I	Jolly Good Fellow	9
Lake Taupo Top 10 Holiday Resort	B	L'Arte	1
Rainbow Lodge	D	Mulligan's	J
Rangimarie Guest House	G	Pimentos	3
Reids Farm Campsite	A	Saluté	4
Taupo Urban Retreat	H	Zest	8
Terraces Hotel	M		
Tiki Lodge	K		
YHA Taupo	F		

Arrival, information and transport

Buses (direct connections from Rotorua, Tauranga, Hamilton, Auckland, Napier, Palmerston North and Wellington) stop at the Taupo Travel Centre bus station, 16 Gascoigne St (℗0800/222 145), in the middle of town. NakedBus stop outside the **i-SITE visitor centre** on Tongariro Street (daily 8.30am–5pm; ℗07/376 0027, ⓦwww.laketauponz.com). Almost opposite, Experience Taupo, 29 Tongariro St (daily: Oct–April 9am–7pm; May–Sept 9am–6pm; ℗07/377 0704, ⓦwww.experiencetaupo.com), also provides good information and promotes its sponsor adventure companies. Taupo's little **airport**, 10km south of the centre, has Air New Zealand flights to Auckland and Wellington.

Almost everything you'll want to visit in the centre can be reached either on foot or by taxi (see "Listings", p.287). For visiting the surrounding sights (and airport transfers), use Shuttle 2U (daily 9am–9pm; ℗07/376 7638, ⓦwww.shuttle2u.co.nz) which does a hop-on-hop-off circuit of all the main attractions and charges just $4–5 per hop or $15 for a day pass, and will even pick up from your accommodation. A similar service is run by HotBus (daily: summer 9am–4pm; winter 10am–3pm; ℗0508/468 287, ⓦwww.hotbus.co.nz).

Renting a bike or scooter (see p.287) gives greater freedom.

Accommodation

Taupo maintains a high standard of accommodation for all budgets and the only time there's a problem finding somewhere is in the crush (Christmas to end Feb). Much of the lakefront is taken up with **motels**, and grassy spots on the fringes of town given over to **campsites**, while **hostels** are abundant in the town itself.

Hotels, motels and B&Bs

Alpine Lake Motor Lodge 141 Heu Heu St ℗0800/400 141, ⓦwww.alpinelake.co.nz. One of Taupo's newest motels, *Alpine Lake* comes with underfloor heating, free broadband and spa baths in some units. ❻

Cascades 303 Lake Terrace, SH1, Two Mile Bay ℗0800/996 997, ⓦwww.cascades.co.nz. Classy, if a little aged, range of accommodation with direct access to an attractive pool and the lake. Studio and family units are spacious with a full kitchen, a mezzanine sleeping area, a patio and a spa bath. Budget ❹, mostly ❺

Dunrovin Motel 140 Heu Heu St ℗0800/386 768, ⓦwww.dunrovintaupo.co.nz. Eight upgraded budget units, mostly one- and two-bedroom. ❸

Rangimarie Guest House 165 Tamamutu St ℗07/377 0329, ⓦwww.rangimarie-bnb-taupo.co.nz. Modest, peaceful and tastefully furnished B&B with just two rooms, a large lounge, heated pool and hot tub. Add a continental breakfast and espresso coffee and it makes a great retreat. ❻

Terraces Hotel 80 Napier–Taupo Hwy ℗07/378 7080, ⓦwww.terraceshotel.co.nz. This Hilton hotel combines the beautifully restored 1889 original hotel with heritage rooms and distant lake views, and a modern wing with suites and apartments. With the classy *Bistro Lago* (see p.286) and Taupo Hot Springs on site you've got all you need for a relaxed stay. ❽

Hostels

Base Taupo 7 Tuwharetoa St ℗07/377 4464, ⓦwww.stayatbase.com. Secure 120-bed hostel in the heart of Taupo's bar zone and with a good lake-view deck, all the expected facilities, the women-only Sanctuary section ($32) and a lively bar, *Element*. Dorms $28, en-suite rooms ❸

Blackcurrant Backpackers 20 Taniwha St ℗07/378 9292, ⓦwww.blackcurrantbp.co.nz. Recently renovated hostel in what was once a motel, now with new bathroom and kitchen, great beds (mostly made-up) and always a friendly welcome. Close to bus station. Dorms $25, female-only dorm $27, en-suite double ❷

Rainbow Lodge 99 Titiraupenga St ℗07/378 5754, ⓦwww.rainbowlodge.co.nz. Spacious, relaxed backpackers spread over three buildings with a comfortable lounge, sauna, safe parking and bike rental ($20/day & $30/day). A stack of local information and little touches create a homely atmosphere. Dorms have six to nine beds and there are some particularly good-value en-suite doubles and twins with TV and patio. Free pick-ups from the bus station. Dorms $23, en-suite shares $26, rooms ❶, en suites ❷

Taupo Urban Retreat 65 Heu Heu St ☎0800/872 261, ⓦwww.tur.co.nz. A 96-bed oasis in the heart of town, this hostel comes with its own house bar (where they do a nightly $5 chilli con carne), small garden, 1hr free internet, free gym passes and bike rental ($20/half-day). Popular with the backpacker bus crowd it has great four-bunk dorms with lake views, though others are windowless. Dorms $23, en-suite dorms $27, en-suite doubles ❷

Tiki Lodge 104 Tuwharetoa St ☎0800/845 456, ⓦwww.tikilodge.co.nz. The best of the flash-packer-style hostels, purpose-built with a spacious kitchen and lounge area plus a great balcony with lake views, and a spa. Dorms $26, en-suite doubles ❷

YHA Taupo 56 Kaimanawa St ☎07/378 3311, ⓦwww.yha.co.nz. Welcoming modern YHA hostel, close to town and with good lake and mountain views from the kitchen and BBQ balcony. There's a spa pool, volleyball court and a garden with hammocks. Dorms either have eight bunks or four beds. Camping $16, dorms $23, rooms & en suites ❷

Campsites and motor parks

All Seasons Holiday Park 16 Rangatira St ☎0800/777 272, ⓦwww.taupoallseasons.co.nz. Compact site 1.5km east of town, with spa pool, hedged tent sites scattered among cabins, some with kitchens, and a range of s/c units ($5 for linen) plus budget rooms in a lodge. Camping $18, lodge ❶, cabins ❷, s/c units ❸

Lake Taupo Top 10 Holiday Resort 28 Centennial Drive, 2km northeast of town ☎07/378 6860, ⓦwww.taupotop10.co.nz. Large and super-organized site groaning with free activities including swimming pool, volleyball, tennis, games room, kids' playground and a giant chess board. The bathrooms even have heated floors and there's easy access to the A.C. Baths. Camping $23, cabins ❸, kitchen cabins ❹, en-suite rooms ❺, motel units ❻

Reids Farm Campsite 3km north of Taupo on Huka Falls Rd. Spacious free campsite right by the Waikato River just 1km upstream of the exclusive *Huka Lodge*, left to the world by a previous owner who liked backpackers. The makeshift slalom course makes it a popular spot with kayakers. Officially open late Oct to March, but no one is likely to stop you staying anytime.

The Town

Set aside at least half an hour for the **Lake Taupo Museum and Art Gallery**, Tongariro Park (daily 10am–4.30pm; $5), if only for the beautiful Reid Carvings, created in 1927–28 by the famous master carver Tene Waitere and exhibited in the form of a meeting house. They're as fine as you'll see anywhere and are supplemented with modern *tukutuku* panels and a lovely flax rain cape probably from the 1870s or earlier. Interesting displays on the geology of the area, fly-fishing and the logging industry line the way to the Tuwharetoa Gallery ranged around the decayed hull of a 150-year-old 14.5m *waka*, found in the bush in 1967. Paintings around the room include two of Ngati Tuwharetoa chiefs by local polymath Thomas Ryan, who was also a lake steamer captain and an All Black. The watercolours show the unmistakable influence of the artist's great friend Charles Goldie. Outside, the stunning **Ora Garden**, a 2004 Chelsea Flower Show winner, has been recreated in all its geothermal glory.

Two places offer geothermal bathing. Wallowing is best at the family-oriented **Taupo DeBrett Spa Resort**, 3km southeast on SH5 (daily 7.30am–9.30pm; $15; ⓦwww.taupohotsprings.com), a couple of large outdoor pools filled with natural mineral water plus private mineral pools in a range of temperatures ($3 extra); an additional $5 buys as many descents as you like on the hot-water hydroslide. Without your own vehicle, you'll find it more convenient to head for the **A.C. Baths & Taupo Events Centre**, A.C. Baths Avenue (daily 6am–9pm), a sparkling new sports hall and 12m climbing wall (harness and shoes $6, plus $10 entry), alongside the long-standing **A.C. Baths**, a complex of swimming and hot pools (swimming $6.50; private hot pools $7/person/45min/combo $12).

Nearby, the river swirls past the **Taupo Bungy**, 202 Spa Rd (daily 9am–5pm, until 7pm in summer if busy; ☎0800/888 408, ⓦwww.taupobungy.co.nz), one of New Zealand's finest bungy sites ($109) cantilevered 20m out from the bank with a 47m drop and an optional dunking. It also offers a 43m swing ($109) and a swing/bungy combo ($198). Just downstream, Spa Avenue runs to the green swathe of **Spa Thermal Park and Hot Stream** (unrestricted entry) where a small hot creek cascades through a series of wonderful soaking pools then mixes with the cool waters of the Waikato River. The stream is around 400m along the riverside walkway which continues downstream (2.8km one-way; 45min) to Huka Falls (see p.287).

Activities

Taupo offers plenty of activities to relieve you of your holiday money, primarily **skydiving**, but also **cruising** or **kayaking** on Lake Taupo, **rafting** down the raging waters of the Tongariro or Rangitaiki rivers or **fishing** the lake and rivers.

Skydiving

With great scenery and very competitive prices Taupo has become New Zealand's most popular place to go **tandem skydiving** and is claimed to be the busiest tandem drop zone in the world. At times it can feel like a production line, with three very professional companies processing dozens of people a day, each offering an array of videos, DVDs, photos and T-shirts. There's very little to choose between them – all offer jumps from 12,000ft (45sec freefall; $250) and 15,000ft (60sec freefall; $340) usually with a choice of a video shot by your jump buddy, or a "freefall" video shot by someone jumping alongside you.

Go with whoever is offering the best deal at the time, but Taupo Tandem Skydiving (℡0800/826 336, ⓦwww.tts.net.nz) has the widest array of photo and video options, and the smaller Skydive Taupo (℡0800/586 766, ⓦwww.skydivetaupo.co.nz) offers a limo pickup service.

Scenic flights and helicopter trips

For those who prefer to stay in the plane, Taupo's Float Plane offers **scenic flights** over the lake and its surrounds ($75/10min; Mount Ruapehu $295; ℡07/378 7500, ⓦwww.tauposfloatplane.co.nz); Air Charter Taupo (℡07/378 5467, ⓦwww.airchartertaupo.co.nz) offers similar trips. The best **helicopter trips** are run by Helistar Helicopters (℡0800/435 478, ⓦwww.helistar.co.nz), on the Huka Falls Road, with a variety of flights, including ones over the Huka Falls ($99/10min), while HeliPro (℡0800/HELIPRO, ⓦwww.helipro.co.nz) will also get you up and about, from $95.

Walking and horseriding

There are a few easy **walks** near town, the best covered in a DOC booklet ($2.50). The most popular is the **Great Lake Walk**, which is more modest than it sounds: just follow the lakeshore east from town, covering as much of the 7km promenade as you like. On the northern edge of town, County Avenue leads to the **Spa Thermal Park**, where there's a pleasant thirty-minute bushwalk, which can be combined with a riverbank hike to **Huka Falls** (4km; 1hr one-way), and further extended to the Aratiatia Rapids (8km; 2hr one-way), though you've then got to get back – if you set off early, you could conceivably walk back via the Volcanic Activity Centre and the Craters of the Moon (12km; 3hr).

For **horseriding**, Taupo Horse Treks, Karapiti Road (℡0800/244 3987, ⓦwww.taupohorsetreks.co.nz), do one-hour ($60) and two-hour ($120) jaunts through the pine forests around the Craters of the Moon (see p.288).

Lake cruises

Lake Taupo is best experienced on a relaxing **lake cruise**, from the Taupo Boat Harbour, setting out for the striking, modern, Maori rock carvings that can only be seen from the water at Mine Bay, 8km southwest of town. The 10m-high carvings date from the late 1970s and depict a stylized image of a man's face heavy with **moko**, together with tuatara (lizard-like reptiles) and female forms draped over nearby rocks. All trips can be booked through the Taupo Charters Office (℗07/378 3444) at the boat harbour.

The most characterful sailing trip – as much for the entertaining skipper, Dave, as the boat – is aboard *The Barbary* (daily, weather permitting, 10.30am & 2pm, plus 5pm in summer; 2hr 30min; $40; ℗07/378 3444), a 1926 ketch once owned by Eroll Flynn (who, it is claimed, won it in a card game). For a touch of gin-palace style, opt for the *Cruise Cat* (daily 10.30am & 1.30pm; 1hr 30min; $40; ℗0800/252 628), which motors up to and past the carvings while you recline. There's an entirely different feel on the *Ernest Kemp* (daily 10.30am & 2pm, plus Nov–March 5pm; 2hr; $40; ℗07/378 3444), a replica 1920s steamboat that chugs to the carvings and back in a couple of hours.

Kayaking and watersports

Much the same lakeside scenery can be seen **kayaking** with Kayaking Kiwi (℗0800/353 435, ⓦwww.kayakingkiwi.com) which runs a trip to the carvings ($108/3hr on the water), and if the weather is against you they'll sort out a rewarding alternative. Wilderness Escapes (℗07/378 3413, ⓦwww.wilderness escapes.co.nz) also offers half-day trips to the carvings ($85), sunset trips ($85), full-day trips ($210) and kayak rental ($60/day) for experienced paddlers.

There's no **whitewater rafting** on Taupo's doorstep, but the town makes a viable base for the Tongariro (covered under Turangi – see p.293), the Rangitaiki and the Wairoa. Rapid Sensations (℗0800/353 435, ⓦwww.rapids.co.nz) run the Tongariro ($135) and the Mohaka Gorge (Gd III–IV; $185), while Kiwi River Safaris (℗0800/723 857, ⓦwww.krs.co.nz) organize rafting trips to the Wairoa ($115), the Rangitaiki ($110) and a one-day Mohaka gorge trip ($175).

If this is all a bit energetic let the wind take the strain by heading for the 2MileBay Watersports Centre, Two Mile Bay (daily 9am–5pm in summer, otherwise sporadically; ℗07/378 3299, ⓦwww.sailingcentre.co.nz), who rent **catamarans** ($60/hr), **windsurfers** ($30/hr) and various other sailboats (from $50/hr) to just about anybody with rudimentary knowledge.

Fishing

New Zealand's arcane fishing rules dictate that trout can't be sold, so if you've got a taste for them you'll need to catch them yourself, and the easiest way is to fish the lake from a charter boat. First stop should be the **Taupo Launch Charters Office**, by the boat harbour (℗07/378 3444), who can quickly hook you up with something suitable such as White Striker ($210 for 2hr on their smallest charter holding up to 6; ℗07/378 2736, ⓦwww.troutcatching.com) who have a good strike rate and a wealth of local knowledge. All **boats** go out for a minimum of two hours, usually three or four, and although minimum numbers don't apply, the more on the boat the cheaper it is – **book in advance** from mid-December to February. Boat operators have all the tackle you need and will organize the mandatory Taupo District Fishing Licence ($16) for you.

Rivers flowing into Lake Taupo are the preserve of **fly-fishers**, particularly from March to September when mature rainbow trout enter the mouths of the streams and rivers and make their way upstream to shallow gravel hollows where they spawn. Brown trout are also in these waters but they tend to be more wily.

You can **rent tackle** from Taupo Rod & Tackle, 7 Tongariro St (℡07/378 5337), and pick your own spot, but average catches are much larger if you engage the services of a **fishing guide** (about $300 for half a day with gear and licence), two of the best are Chris Jolly and Will Kemp but the Taupo Charters Office has a complete list.

Mountain biking

There's great mountain biking around Taupo, much of it maintained by Bike Taupo which operates the excellent Ⓦ www.biketaupo.org.nz website. For a scenic ride, make for the **Huka Falls Walkway** heading north from Spa Thermal Park to Huka Falls (4km one-way) and on to Aratiatia Dam (additional 8km one-way). For something a little longer and harder go for the single-track **W2K ride** (16km one-way, with an additional 10km loop) which starts at Whakaipo Bay, 20km west of Taupo and finishes at Kinloch. Either plan to ride it both ways or get a friend to meet you – it's around 40km by road. There's also excellent loop riding in the **Wairakei Forest**: start by the Helistar Helicopter, 3km north of Taupo.

Either rent a bike (see opposite) or join Rapid Sensations, by the Helistar Helicopter (℡0800/353 435, Ⓦ www.rapids.co.nz) who explore the Wairakei Forest ($75/2hr) and also rent bikes ($30/2hr, $55/day).

Eating, drinking and nightlife

Taupo is groaning with good **cafés** and fairly cheap Indian and Thai restaurants, but classy **restaurants** are thinner on the ground. **Nightlife** almost all happens along the westernmost block of Tuwharetoa Street, where half a dozen lively **bars** and one **nightclub** (*The Townhouse*) vie for business until the small hours. Alternatively head out to Wairakei Terraces for the **Maori cultural experience** (see p.289).

Cafés and restaurants

Bistro Lago at the *Hilton* ℡07/377 1400. Taupo's finest dining in the beautifully modernized old wing of the hotel. Great service, immaculate presentation and delectable food that's only a few dollars more expensive than far inferior places.

Fine Fettle 39 Paora Hapi St. Taupo's wholefood central – an excellent German-run daytime café specializing in gluten-free dishes such as tasty buckwheat pancakes ($10), along with eggs Benedict ($16), mussel chowder ($8–10), panini and salads, many served with organic bread which is also available by the loaf. Slurp on an invigorating fruit smoothie. Daily from 7am.

Indian Affair 34 Ruapehu St ℡07/378 2295. Super-tasty curries in smart, modern surroundings. The Goan fish curry ($19) is particularly good. Licensed & BYO.

L'Arte 255 Mapara Rd, Acacia Bay. The pleasant 8km drive around the head of Lake Taupo to this rural sculpture garden whets the appetite for delicious daytime café meals served among quirky mosaics (one series arranged as an outdoor living room) dotted around the peaceful grounds. Great food is served inside or on a shady deck. Daily in Jan, otherwise closed Mon & Tues.

Pimentos 17 Tamamutu St ℡07/377 4549. Fairly casual, dinner-only restaurant specializing in modern takes on classic European dishes. Mains $25–30. Licensed & BYO. Closed Tues.

Saluté 47 Horomatangi St. Modern airy deli eschewing the usual Kiwi café staples and instead serving the likes of Croque Monsieur ($13) or a chorizo and mussel salad ($20). Great sandwiches, coffee, a cheese room and impeccable green credentials.

Zest 65 Rifle Range Rd. Great little daytime café out in the suburbs serving a range of tasty breakfasts (from 9am), BLTs, Caesar salads, wraps and excellent coffee. Closed Mon.

Bars and clubs

Bond 40 Tuwharetoa St. The classiest of the bars along this strip – fine for a glass of Pinot in a booth, a cocktail on the fireside sofas or smoking a Cohiba at the streetside tables.

Finn MacCuhal's Corner of Tongariro & Tuwharetoa sts. Large Irish bar that's very popular with both backpackers and locals. You come here for the Guinness, but they also do good-value steaks and fish and chips.

Jolly Good Fellow 76–80 Lake Terrace. The nearest Taupo gets to a British pub, nothing like one in style but with an excellent range of thirteen draught ales and a lively community feel. Most of the English and Irish beers on tap have travelled well. There are also pub meals in the English tradition, with toad-in-the-hole ($16.50) and all-day breakfast served including bacon butties. Lots of diners early on followed by revellers for the late shift.

Mulligan's 15 Tongariro St. Dimly lit, Irish-style bar with stout on tap, mischievous Kiwi bar staff, live music, pool table, quiz nights and massive plates of bar food including a $19 Sunday roast. Popular with both locals and tour buses.

Listings

Bike rental Most hostels have basic bikes for guests' use. *Rainbow Lodge* also rents to non-guests. Life Cycles, 16 Oraunui St (☎07/378 6117), do MTBs from $20/half-day.

Car rental Pegasus Rental Cars (☎0800/803 580, ⓦ www.rentalcars.co.nz) have the best deals, from $35 a day.

Internet Best rates at Cyber Gate, 12 Gascoigne St, and Cyber Shed, 115 Tongariro St.

Left luggage Lockers are available at the Superloo, Tongariro St, opposite the visitor centre. Daily 7.30am–5pm, 8pm in summer. $2/day.

Medical treatment Taupo Health Centre, 113 Heu Heu St ☎07/378 7060 (Mon–Fri 8am–5.30pm).

Pharmacy Mainstreet Pharmacy, corner of Heu Heu & Tongariro sts (☎07/378 2636), is open daily until 8.30pm.

Police 21 Story Place, by the museum and art gallery ☎07/378 6060.

Post office Corner of Horomatangi & Ruapehu sts (☎07/378 9090), with poste restante facilities.

Scooter rental $37/day at Global Gossip, 11 Tuwharetoa St (☎07/378 1551) – driving licence and $50 deposit required.

Taxis Top Cabs (☎07/378 9250) and Taupo Taxis (☎07/378 5100).

Around Taupo

On the outskirts of Taupo is a concentration of natural wonders, all within a few minutes of one another. Here you'll find boiling mud, hissing steam harnessed by the **Wairakei power station**, and the clear-blue Waikato River, which cuts a deep swirling course north over rapids and through deep-sided gorges. The highlights – **Huka Falls**, **Aratiatia Rapids**, **Wairakei Terraces** and the **Craters of the Moon** geothermal area – are all within 10km of Taupo and are accessible on one of Taupo's tour companies (see p.282).

Moving **south** from Taupo, SH1 follows the lakeshore to Turangi while SH5 heads east to Napier; both have worthwhile stops along the way.

Along Huka Falls Road

The bulk of the sights and activities flank the Waikato River as it wends its way north. Huka Falls Road loops off SH1 a couple of kilometres north of Taupo and passes the *Reids Farm* free campsite and *Huka Lodge* (one of New Zealand's most exclusive) en route to the first port of call, the magnificent **Huka Falls** (*hukanui*, or "great body of spray"). Here the Waikato, one of New Zealand's most voluminous rivers, funnels into a narrow chasm before plunging over a 9m shelf into a seething maelstrom of eddies and whirlpools; the sheer power of some three hundred tonnes of water per second make it a far more awesome sight than the short drop would suggest. A footbridge spans the channel, providing a perfect vantage point for watching the occasional mad kayaker making the descent, usually on weekend evenings. The car park is only open until 6pm but you can park outside and walk in at any time.

Continuing along Huka Falls Road, a large Russian helicopter marks the launch pad for Helistar flights (see p.284) en route to the cutaway hives and

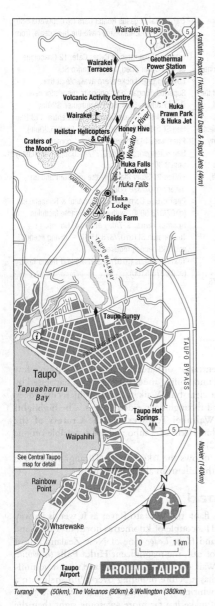

Around Taupo map labels:

Wairakei Village
Wairakei Terraces
Geothermal Power Station
Volcanic Activity Centre
Huka Prawn Park & Huka Jet
Wairakei
Helistar Helicopters & Café
Honey Hive
Craters of the Moon
KARAPITI RD
Waikato River
Huka Falls Lookout
Huka Falls
Huka Lodge
Reids Farm
TAUPO WALKWAY
Taupo Bungy
Taupo
Tapuaeharuru Bay
Taupo Hot Springs
Waipahihi
See Central Taupo map for detail
Rainbow Point
Wharewake
Taupo Airport
AROUND TAUPO
TAUPO BYPASS
N
0   1 km

Aratiatia Rapids (1km), Aratiatia Dam & Rapid Jets (4km)

Napier (140km)

Turangi ▼ (50km), The Volcanos (90km) & Wellington (380km)

educational video at the **Honey Hive** (daily 9am–5pm; free; ⓣ07/374 8553), 1km further north. Press on to the **Volcanic Activity Centre** (Mon–Fri 9am–5pm, Sat & Sun 10am–4pm; $9.50), a highly instructional museum where the dense text is alleviated by striking photos and interactive computer displays on all things tectonic. Watch one of several films run continuously then check out the seismograph linked to sensors on Mount Ruapehu, an earthquake simulator and a large relief map of Taupo Volcanic Zone, which extends from Mount Ruapehu to White Island.

The new Taupo bypass road separates you from the Wairakei geothermal power station from where excess heat is channelled into the family-oriented **Huka Prawn Park** (daily: Dec & Jan 9am–5pm; Feb–Nov 9am–3.30pm; ⓦwww .hukaprawnpark.co.nz), large open ponds where tropical prawns are raised. Stoll around the ponds and nature walk ($15), spend as long as you like fishing for prawns ($20) or combine the two ($24). If learning about a day in the life of "Shawn the Prawn" doesn't fire your imagination, graze on some of Shawn's delicious little friends (platter for two $60) in the adjacent **restaurant**, superbly set beside the Waikato River.

The peace is periodically shattered by a **Huka Jet** ($95/30min; ⓣ0800/485 2538, ⓦwww .hukafallsjet.com) roaring along the river and doing 360-degree spins on the way to the base of Huka Falls. Rapids Jet (see p.290) gives you more bang for your buck.

Craters of the Moon and the Wairakei Terraces

The Huka Falls loop road rejoins SH1 near Karapiti Road which runs west to **Craters of the Moon** (daily 8.30am–5.30pm; $6), a lively geothermal area that sprang to life in the 1950s, after the construction of the Wairakei geothermal

▲ Huka Falls

power station drastically altered the underground hydrodynamics. While it lacks geysers and colourful lakes, the area is so vigorous that you must wear closed footwear to walk the 3km of trails among roaring fumaroles and rumbling pits belching out a pungent bad-egg smell.

Some 3km north, the Wairakei power station is supplied by shiny high-pressure steam pipes which cross under SH1, twisting and bending like a giant ball-bearing racetrack. The power of mineral-laden steam is harnessed nearby at **Wairakei Terraces**, SH1 (daily: Oct–March 9am–5pm; April–Sept 9am–4.30pm; $18; ⊕07/378 0913, Ⓦwww.wairakeiterraces.co.nz), where a vigorously boiling cauldron feeds an artificial cascade of silica terraces and pools. It mimics the process that created Rotorua's Pink and White Terraces, and has grown since the late 1990s.

Paths lead through the surrounding model Maori village which comes alive for a **Maori cultural experience** (Wed 6pm, plus Fri and Sun in summer; $85) when weaving, tattooing, and stick games are demonstrated. The evening is an engagingly low-key affair (a world away from Rotorua's extravaganzas) with a good introduction to Maori culture and a *hangi* meal followed by the *haka* and dance performance.

Aratiatia Rapids and around

Around 2km downstream from the Wairakei power station the Aratiatia Dam holds back the Waikato River immediately above the **Aratiatia Rapids**, a long series of cataracts that were one of Taupo's earliest attractions. In the 1950s, plans to divert the waters around the rapids were amended by public pressure, thus preserving the rapids, though it's something of a hollow victory since they are dry most of the time, only seen in their full glory during three or four thirty-minute periods each day (Oct–March 10am, noon, 2pm & 4pm; April–Sept 10am, noon & 2pm). Stand on the dam itself or at one of two downstream viewpoints, and wait for the siren that heralds the spectacle of a parched watercourse being transformed into a foaming torrent of waterfalls and surging pressure waves, before returning to a trickle.

Tamer waters further downstream are best experienced on the exhilarating 🚤 **Rapids Jet** (normally daily at 10am, noon, 2pm & 4pm; $90; ☎0800/727 437, ⓦwww.rapidsjet.com), located on Rapids Road 3km beyond the Aratiatia Dam. This is no slick bus-them-all operation, but the North Island's only true white-water jetboating run, taking you down and up Nga Awapurua rapids during which the entire boat gets airborne. The days of boat sinkings are past, but you still need to listen closely to the safety spiel, hang on and prepare to get wet.

The Napier–Taupo Road

Travelling beyond the immediate vicinity of Taupo, SH1 hugs the lake as it heads southwest to Turangi (see p.293), while SH5 veers southeast along the **Napier–Taupo Road**, a twisting ninety-minute run through some of the North Island's remotest country. Much of the early part of the journey crosses the Kaingaroa Plains, impoverished land cloaked in pumice and ash from the Taupo Volcanic eruption and of little use save for the pine plantations which stretch 100km to the north. The history of this route is traced by the **Napier–Taupo Heritage Trail**; pick up a free booklet from either town's i-SITE. Many of the 35 stops are of limited interest but be sure to call in at **Opepe Historic Reserve**, 17km from Taupo, where, on the north side of the road, a cemetery contains white wooden slabs marking the graves of nine soldiers of the Bay of Plenty cavalry, killed by followers of maverick Maori leader Te Kooti in 1869.

Some 35km on, the Waipunga River, a tributary of the Mohaka, plummets 30m over the picturesque **Waipunga Falls**, and continues beside SH5 through the lovely Waipunga Gorge, packed with tall native trees and dotted with picnic sites which double as **campsites** with no facilities but river water. The highway descends to the Mohaka River and 🚤 *Mountain Valley*, 5km south of SH5 (☎06/834 9756, ⓦwww.mountainvalley.co.nz; camping $15, dorms $28, rooms ❷, s/c chalets ❹, cottages ❼), a little slice of rural New Zealand with a riverside bar and restaurant and the opportunity to fish the river, mountain bike, go on a farm and forest **horse trek** ($75/1hr), or do some scenic **rafting** and **kayaking** on Grade I–II stretches of the Mohaka (from $75).

Beyond the Mohaka River, the highway climbs the Titiokura Saddle before the final descent through the grape country of the **Esk Valley** into Napier.

Tongariro National Park and around

New Zealand's highly developed network of national parks owes much to Te Heu Heu Tukino IV, the Tuwharetoa chief who, in the Pakeha land-grabbing climate of the late nineteenth century, recognized that the only chance his people had of keeping their sacred lands intact was to donate them to the nation – on condition that they could not be settled or spoiled. His 1887 gift formed the core of the country's first major public reserve, **Tongariro National Park**, which became a

World Heritage Site in 1991 owing to its unique landscape and cultural significance (see box below). In the north a small, outlying section of the park centres on Mount Pihanga and the tiny Lake Rotopounamu but most visitors head straight for the main body of the park, dominated by the three great volcanoes which rise starkly from the desolate plateau: the broad-shouldered ski mountain, Ruapehu (2797m); its squatter sibling, Tongariro (1968m); and, wedged between them, the conical Ngauruhoe (2287m).

Within the boundaries of the park is some of the North Island's most striking scenery – a beautiful mixture of semi-arid plains, steaming fumaroles, crystal-clear lakes and streams, virgin rainforest and an abundance of ice and snow. The more forbidding volcanic areas were used as locations for Mordor and Mount Doom in the *Lord of the Rings* trilogy. All of this forms the backdrop to two supremely rewarding tramps, the one-day Tongariro Alpine Crossing and the three- to four-day Tongariro Northern Circuit, one of New Zealand's Great Walks. The undulating plateau to the west of the volcanoes is vegetated by bushland and golden tussock, while on the eastern side the rain shadow of the mountains produces the Rangipo Desert. Although this is not a true desert, it is still an impressively bleak and barren landscape, smothered by a thick layer of volcanic ash from the 186 AD Taupo eruption. Mount Ruapehu frequently bursts into life (most recently 1995, 1996 & 2007), occasionally emptying its crater lake down the side of the mountain in muddy deluges known as lahars. The 1995 and 1996 eruptions drastically curtailed the ski season, but there has been minimal lasting damage.

The northern approach to the region is through Turangi, not much in itself but a reasonable base both for the Tongariro tramps and for rafting and fishing the Tongariro River. It lacks the mountain feel of the service town of National Park

The Maori mountain legends

When Te Heu Heu Tukino donated Tongariro's central volcanoes to the Crown (see opposite), he was motivated by a deep spiritual need for their protection. According to Maori, the mountains at the heart of the park have distinct personalities that symbolize the links between the community and its environment. This significance was recognized in 1991 when the park became the first World Heritage Site included as a **cultural landscape**.

Legends tell of a number of smaller mountains clustered around the dominating **Ruapehu**, **Tongariro**, **Ngauruhoe** and **Taranaki**. Among these was the beautiful **Pihanga** in the northern section of the park, whose favours were widely sought. Pihanga loved only Tongariro, the victor of numerous battles with her other suitors, including one that had brought him to his knees, striking off the top of his head, giving him his present shape. Taranaki, meantime, defeated Ngauruhoe, but when he came to face Ruapehu, he was exhausted and badly wounded. He fled, carving out the Whanganui River as he made for the west coast of the North Island. Meanwhile the smaller **Putauaki** got as far north as Kawerau; but **Tauhara** was reluctant to leave and continually glanced back, so that by dawn, when the mountains could no longer move, he had only reached the northern shores of Lake Taupo, where he remains to this day, "the lonely mountain".

To the local Tuwharetoa people these mountains were so sacred that they averted their eyes while passing and wouldn't eat or build fires in the vicinity. The *tapu* stretches back to legendary times when their ancestor **Ngatoroirangi** came to claim the centre of the island. After declaring Tongariro *tapu* he set off up the mountain, but his followers broke their vow to fast while he was away and the angry gods sent a snowstorm in which Ngatoroirangi almost perished before more benevolent gods in Hawaiki saved him by sending fire to revive his frozen limbs.

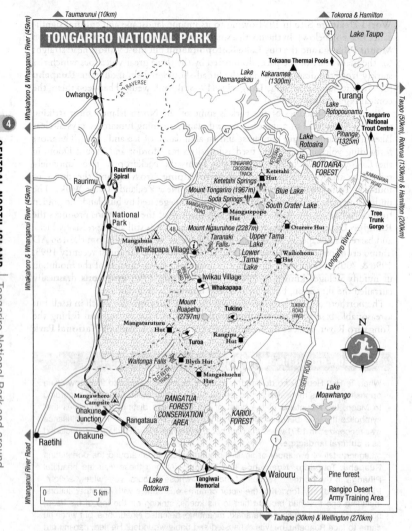

TONGARIRO NATIONAL PARK

Taumarunui (10km)

Tokoroa & Hamilton

Lake Taupo

Whakahoro & Whanganui River (45km)

Taupo (50km), Rotorua (130km) & Hamilton (200km)

Whakahoro & Whanganui River (45km)

Whanganui River Road

4

Owhango

Tokaanu Thermal Pools

Lake
Otamangakau

Kakaramea
(1300m)

Turangi

Lake
Rotopounamu

Tongariro
National
Trout Centre

Raurimu
Spiral

47

Pihanga
(1325m)

Raurimu

TONGARIRO
CROSSING
TRACK

Ketetahi
Hut

Lake
Rotoaira

46

ROTOAIRA
FOREST

KETETAHI
ROAD

KAIMANAWA
ROAD

National
Park

Ketetahi Springs

Mount Tongariro (1967m)

Blue Lake

Soda Springs

South Crater Lake

MANGATEPOPO
ROAD

Mangatepopo
Hut

Oturere Hut

Tree
Trunk
Gorge

Mangahnia

48

Mount Ngauruhoe (2287m)

Upper Tama
Lake

Whakapapa Village

Taranaki
Falls

Lower
Tama
Lake

Waihohonu
Hut

Tongariro River

Iwikau Village

Whakapapa

BRUCE
ROAD

Mount
Ruapehu
(2797m)

Tukino

TUKINO
ROAD
(4WD)

Mangaturuturu
Hut

Rangipu
Hut

DESERT
ROAD

Turoa

N

Waitonga Falls

Blyth Hut

OLD SOUTH
TRACK

Mangaehuehu
Hut

Lake
Moawhango

Mangawhero
Campsite

RANGATUA
FOREST
CONSERVATION
AREA

KARIOI
FOREST

Ohakune
Junction

Rangataua

1

Raetihi

Ohakune

0   5 km

Lake
Rotokura

Tangiwai
Memorial

Waiouru

Pine forest

Rangipo Desert
Army Training Area

Taihape (30km) & Wellington (270km)

and the alpine **Whakapapa Village**, 1200m up on the flanks of Ruapehu. The southern gateway is **Ohakune**, a more appealing place than National Park but distinctly comatose outside the ski season. Heading south, the Army Museum at **Waiouru** marks the southern limit of the Volcanic Plateau, which tails off into the pastoral lower half of the region set around the agricultural town of **Taihape**, home to the North Island's highest bungy jump.

Pretty much everyone comes to the park either to **ski** or to **tramp**, staying in one of the small towns dotted around the base of the mountains. While a **car** makes life easier, there is a reasonable network of **shuttles** plying the more useful routes and providing trailhead transport for trampers (see box, p.297). Note that this region is over 600m above sea level, so even in the height of summer you'll need **warm clothing**.

Turangi and around

Turangi, 50km south of Taupo, is small and characterless, planned in the mid-1960s and built almost overnight for workers toiling away at the tunnels and concrete channels of the ambitious Tongariro Power Scheme (see box, p.294). It doesn't even make the best of its location – Lake Taupo is 4km to the north and the town centre is separated by SH1 from its trump card, the fishing and rafting waters of the Tongariro River. Nonetheless, it is popular with trout fishers, and with good hostels and trailhead transport it makes a good base for the Tongariro Alpine Crossing (see p.298).

Arrival and information

InterCity **buses** drop at the **i-SITE visitor centre**, Ngawaka Place (daily 8.30am–5pm; ☎0800/288 726, ⓦwww.laketauponz.com), which sells bus tickets, Taupo fishing licences, maps, DOC tramping brochures and hut tickets; it also has internet access. HotBus and Tongariro Expeditions also stop when taking Taupo hikers to the Tongariro Alpine Crossing (though not if the weather is bad).

Accommodation

Turangi's need to cater to anglers, skiers and trampers bound for the Tongariro National Park has left it with a range of **accommodation**; the budget places congregate in the town centre, while plusher lodges and B&Bs line the Tongariro River to the east.

Club Habitat 25 Ohuanga Rd ☎07/386 7492, ⓦwww.clubhabitat.co.nz. Vast complex fashioned from a former workers' camp that's cheap and fairly run-down with the exception of the refurbished "executive" units. There's also a spacious games bar, dining complex, spa and sauna. Camping $12, dorms $22, rooms ❶, units ❹

Creel Lodge 183 Taupahi Rd ☎07/386 8081, ⓦwww.creel.co.nz. A simple and well-run motel comprising a cluster of s/c one- and two-bedroom units in grounds running down to the river edge with communal fish smoker and BBQ. ❹

Extreme Backpackers 26 Ngawaka Place ☎07/386 8949, ⓦwww.extremebackpackers .co.nz. Amenable hosts take good care of guests at this purpose-built backpackers with simply decorated rooms set around a central courtyard. There's also a climbing wall ($15; $10 for guests) and an amiable café. Dorms $24, rooms ❶, en suites ❷

Ika Lodge 155 Taupahi Rd ☎07/386 5538, ⓦwww.ika.co.nz. This superior homestay-cum-fishing lodge by the Tongariro River has two rooms and a two-bedroom apartment. Prices include breakfast. Double ❺, apartment ❻

Parklands Corner of SH1 & Arahori St ☎0800/456 284, ⓦwww.parklandsmotorlodge.co.nz. Extensive motor lodge with pine-lined studios and spacious modernized units plus an outdoor pool, games room and a small restaurant serving home-style dinners. Camping $15, studios ❸, units ❹

Riverstone Backpackers 222 Tautahanga Rd ☎07/3867004, ⓦwww.riverstonebackpackders .com. Lovely boutique backpackers in a converted house with lots of communal living space, both inside and out, a well-equipped modern kitchen, herbs from the garden, bike and walking-pole rentals, and a resident dog, Mogwai. Dorms $30–33, rooms & en suites ❷

Tongariro River Motel Corner of SH1 & Link Rd ☎0800/187 688, ⓦwww.tongarirorivermotel .co.nz. Simple but comfortable motel that's hugely popular with fishers, partly for its rod racks and smoker, but mainly because of the ebullient owner, Ross, who runs a lively website on everything to do with Turangi, and trout fishing in particular. ❸

Sights

The massive amount of trout fishing around Turangi makes it essential that rivers are continually restocked with fingerlings raised at hatcheries such as the **Tongariro National Trout Centre**, 4km south on SH1 (daily: Dec–April

10am–3pm; May–Nov 10am–4pm; $6; Ⓦwww.troutcentre.org.nz), set amid native bush between the Tongariro River and one of its tributaries, the Waihukahuka Stream. With an aquarium, a chance to see fingerlings being raised and lots of material on water conservation, biodiversity protection and how to fish, it's a great place to spend an hour, especially if you've got kids in tow. If you'd rather wallow in hot water, head for **Tokaanu Thermal Pools**, Mangaroa Road, 5km west of Turangi (daily 10am–9pm; $6), in tiny **Tokaanu**, which was the main settlement hereabouts in pre-European times. There's an open-air public pool and hotter, partly enclosed and chlorine-free private pools ($9/20min, including public pool access). Nearby, you can spend a very pleasurable hour or two gently paddling along a narrow, lush, bush-fringed channel, past the hot tubs and back gardens of the locals in **kayaks** rented from Wai Maori, located by the hot pools (daily 10am–5pm; $40/person/half-day; ℡0800/529 259, Ⓦwww .waimaori.com).

Hiking

Many people stay in Turangi to hike the Tongariro Alpine Crossing (see p.298), 40km to the southwest, but there are less daunting alternatives. The pleasant **Tongariro River Loop Track** (4km) is well worth the hour it takes to complete, starting from the Major Jones footbridge at the end of Koura Street on the edge of town. It follows the true right bank of the river north past a couple of viewpoints and over a bluff then crosses the river and returns along the opposite side. Ten kilometres south of Turangi, off SH47, the **Lake Rotopounamu Circuit** (5km; 90min) encircles a pristine lake surrounded by bush alive with native birds.

Fishing, rafting and mountain biking

Turangi is also famed internationally for the quality of its **trout fishing**, both on the lake and in the Tongariro River. If you're keen to haul a trout from Lake Taupo or one of the local rivers, the I-SITE will help pair you with a **fishing** guide to match your experience and aspirations as well as a licence ($16/day); expect to pay around $250 for a half-day with gear and guiding. Alternatively, Sporting Life, The Mall (℡07/386 8996, Ⓦwww.sportinglife-turangi.co.nz), sells and rents gear and has a huge amount of info on its website.

The Tongariro Power Scheme

The **Tongariro Power Scheme** provides an object lesson in harnessing the power of water with minimal impact on the environment. Its two powerhouses produce around seven percent of the country's electricity, while the outflows that feed into Lake Taupo add flexibility to the much older chain of eight hydroelectric dams along the Waikato River. Some argue it is unacceptable to tamper with such a fine piece of wilderness and while there have been some minor environmental impacts, it is surely better than a nuclear power station.

In fact, if it weren't for the scale models in visitor centres and the ugly bulk of the Tokaanu power station, only astute observers would be aware of the complex system of tunnels, aqueducts, canals and weirs unobtrusively going about their business of diverting the waters of the Tongariro River and myriad streams running off the mountain slopes, back and forth around the perimeter of the national park, using modified natural lakes for storage. Mount Ruapehu poses its own unique problems: the threat of **lahars** is ever-present and, after the 1995 eruption, abrasive volcanic ash found its way into the turbines of the Rangipo underground powerhouse, causing an unscheduled seven-month shutdown.

Rotorua and Taihape offer wilder rafting rivers but for beautiful gorge scenery, the chance to see the endangered blue duck (*whio*) and fun rapids without the white knuckles, **rafting the Tongariro River** is unbeatable. Young families should opt for the Grade II lower section but most will want to try the Grade III Access 10 section upstream. Go with local operators such as Rafting New Zealand, 41 Ngawaka Place (Ⓣ0800/865 226, Ⓦwww.raftingnewzealand.com) which goes twice a day in summer ($109/4hr) throwing in a waterfall jump and plenty of cultural interpretation. Book ahead for its excellent, summer-only overnighter ($350) which leaves late afternoon and spends the night camped beside the river with a barbecue dinner before finishing the next morning. Tongariro River Rafting, Atirau Road, near Firestone Tyres (Ⓣ0800/101 024, Ⓦwww.trr.co.nz) runs an equally good Grade III trip ($109), a family float down the Grade II section (1hr 15min on the water; $65) and **raft fishing** (Dec–May only), which involves rafting the Tongariro and stopping off at otherwise inaccessible pools to cast a fly. Rates are $650 a day for two people – little more than you'd pay for a fishing guide alone.

Tongariro River Rafting also does **mountain biking**, either rental ($40/day, or $60 for the 42 Traverse) or guided on the private Moerangi station (4hr; $99).

Eating and drinking

Eating options in Turangi are limited, though the New World supermarket is a help for self-caterers.

Bridge Fishing Lodge SH1, 800m north Ⓣ07/386 8804. Meals are served on linen tablecloths in the à la carte restaurant or in front of a big fireplace for bar meals that might include chicken fettuccini ($19), fish and chips ($19) or salmon salad ($24). Thursday is curry night.

Licorice SH1, 9km north at Motuoapa. Great little daytime café with tasty breakfasts, delicious muffins, garden seating and a plenty of magazines. Closed Mon & Tues.

Mustard Seed Café 91 Ohuanga Rd. Casual, modern licensed café with the usual range of breakfasts, panini, salads and cakes, plus good espresso.

Valentinos Ohuanga Rd Ⓣ07/386 8812. A classic Kiwi Italian place that seems like it has barely changed since the tunnellers first came to town. Pasta and meaty mains for $23–31. Closed Tues.

Whakapapa and around

Tiny **Whakapapa**, the only settlement set firmly within the boundaries of the Tongariro National Park, hugs the lower slopes of Mount Ruapehu some 45km south of Turangi on SH48, which spurs off SH47. Approaching from the north, an open expanse of tussock gives distant views of the imposing *Chateau Tongariro* hotel, framed by the snowy slopes of the volcano behind and overlooked by the arterial network of tows on the Whakapapa ski-field.

From Whakapapa, SH48 continues as Bruce Road 6km uphill to **Iwikau Village** (known locally as the "Top o' the Bruce"), an ugly jumble of ski-club chalets which from late June through to mid-October becomes a seething mass of wraparound shades and baggy snowboarders' pants. Outside the ski season, the village dies, leaving only a couple of **chairlifts** to trundle up to the brand-new *Knoll Ridge Café*, New Zealand's highest at 2020m, from where you can take **guided walks** on the mountain.

Information and accommodation

The only **bus services** to Whakapapa are the shuttle buses from Turangi (twice daily) and National Park (3–5 daily), which drop off close to DOC's helpful

visitor centre (daily: Dec–Feb 8am–6pm; March–Nov 8am–5pm; ☎07/892 3729, ✉whakapapavc@doc.govt.nz). The centre contains all the maps and leaflets you'll need and extensive displays on the park, including the tiny Ski History museum and a couple of **movies** (one for $3, both for $5) that are shown on demand – one on vulcanism hereabouts, the other combining Maori legends surrounding Tongariro with impressive footage of the landscape through the seasons.

There's not much to Whakapapa besides cafés, a pub and **places to stay**, all within a couple of minutes' walk of each other and often booked in advance. Reserve as far ahead as possible through the ski season and over the Christmas and January school holidays.

Chateau Tongariro ☎0800/242 832, ⓦwww .chateau.co.nz. Whakapapa's most prominent building is this 1929 brick edifice with gracious public areas including a huge lounge with full-size snooker table and great mountain views; it's worth a visit for a Devonshire tea even if you're not staying. Guests have use of the highest nine-hole golf course in New Zealand, tennis courts, gym and a small indoor pool, and stay in fairly anodyne rooms modernized to international hotel standard. If you're after space and good views you'll need one of the premium rooms (❼), mostly in the new wing sympathetically added in 2004. The website often advertises significant discounts in spring and autumn. ❻

Mangahuia Campsite On SH47 close to the foot of the Whakapapa access road. Simple toilets-and-water DOC campsite. $4
Skotel 100m up the hill beside the *Chateau Tongariro* ☎0800/756 835, ⓦwww.skotel.com. Hotel with woodsy, three-bunk rooms, doubles, a sauna and a restaurant/bar. Note that rates are hiked considerably in the ski season. Single $45, twin $55, en-suite rooms ❺, cabins sleeping four ❻
Whakapapa Holiday Park Opposite the visitor centre ☎07/892 3897, ⓦwww.whakapapa.net.nz. The budget option, set in a pretty patch of beech forest with tent and powered sites. Camping $17, dorms $25, cabins ❷, unit ❸

Hikes from Whakapapa

Swarms of trampers use Whakapapa as a base for short walks or long tramps. The Tongariro Northern Circuit and the Round the Mountain track (see p.300) can both be tackled from here, but there are also easier strolls covered by DOC's *Whakapapa Walks* leaflet. Three of the best of these are the **Whakapapa Nature Walk** (1km; 20–30min), highlighting the unique flora of the park; the **Taranaki Falls Walk** (6km; 2hr), which heads through open tussock and bushland to where the Wairere Stream plunges 20m over the end of an old lava flow; and the **Silica Rapids Walk** (7km; 2hr 30min), which follows a stream through beech forests to some creamy-coloured geothermal terraces.

There's much more of a vertical component to the **Ruapehu Crater Rim hike** (5–8hr return), a tough, steep slog made worthwhile by the dramatic silhouettes of Cathedral Rocks and the views west to Mount Taranaki. The walk can be done from the car park at Iwikau Village (15km return; 1000m ascent) but is much more appealing from the top of the Waterfall Express chairlift (9km return; 650m ascent), thereby avoiding a long trudge through a barren, rocky landscape. From the top of the chairlift (Jan to mid-March; $23 return) the route is poorly marked, but from Christmas until the first snows, the ascent can usually be made in ordinary walking boots without crampons.

If you are in any doubt or would appreciate some company, join a **guided crater walk** (mid-Dec to mid-April daily 9.30am; 6hr, $90 including the lift; ☎07/892 3738, ⓦwww.mtruapehu.com) which provides a commentary on geology, flora and much besides.

Getting to the Tongariro National Park treks

A couple of InterCity bus routes pass through the Tongariro National Park but most services are run by smaller companies, many associated with backpacker hostels. If you're staying in any of the towns listed below there'll be a choice of operators offering basically the same service (often with an early bus getting you to the trailhead before the masses). We've listed the larger, reliable operators: your accommodation and the various visitor centres can flesh out the options. Most companies charge $30–35 for combined Tongariro Alpine Crossing drop-off and pick-up.

From National Park: Numerous shuttle buses serve the trailheads in summer and ski-fields in winter. Try *Howard's Lodge*, *The Park*, and *National Park Backpackers* who all run their own services for $30.

From Ohakune: Matai Shuttles (☎0800/462 824, ⓦwww.mataishuttles.co.nz), run twice daily in summer calling at National Park (and sometimes Whakapapa) on the way to Mangatepopo car park.

From Taupo: Tongariro Expeditions (☎07/377 0435, ⓦwww.thetongarirocrossing .co.nz) and HotBus (☎0508/468 287, ⓦwww.hotbus.co.nz) are both good for getting to the park generally, but to attempt the Crossing from Taupo involves a ridiculously early start and puts you on it at its busiest.

From Turangi: Tongariro Alpine Crossing ($35) and ski-field shuttles year-round from *Extreme Backpackers* (see p.293) and Mountain Shuttle (☎0800/117 686, ⓦwww.tongarirocrossing.com). The latter offers several crossing shuttles, the earliest around 6pm.

From Whakapapa: several shuttles call past on their way to the Tongariro Alpine Crossing. The most frequent is Mountain Shuttle (see above).

Eating and drinking

Snacks are cheap at *Fergussons Café*, opposite the visitor centre, though you might prefer the better quality across the road at the *Chateau's Pihanga Café and T Bar*, which serve more substantial lunches and dinners. The *Skotel* serves breakfast, good-value bistro meals and has a bar. The cheapest booze and food is at the *Tussock Pub* (open at 3pm with big-screen TV) where the few locals tend to **drink**. If you want to reward yourself for the successful completion of a major tramp, the *Chateau's Ruapehu Room* has good à la carte meals at à la carte prices. Five kilometres up the hill, the basic *Lorenz's Café* is at the base of the chairlift which can whisk you up to *Knoll Ridge*, the highest café in New Zealand, with long views.

Tramping in Tongariro National Park

Tongariro National Park contains some of the North Island's finest walks, all through spectacular and varied volcanic terrain. The **Tongariro Alpine Crossing** alone is often cited as the best one-day tramp in the country, but there are many longer possibilities, notably the three- to four-day **Tongariro Northern Circuit**. Mount Ruapehu has the arduous but rewarding **Crater Rim Walk** and the **Round the Mountain Track**, a circuit of Ruapehu which offers a narrower variety of terrain and sights than the Tongariro tramps, but is consequently less used.

Practicalities

The **DOC leaflets** covering the tramps are informative and adequate for most purposes though map fans will want the region's *Parkmap* ($19).

The **weather** in the mountains (ⓦ www.metservice.co.nz/public/mountain /tongariro.html) is extremely changeable, and the usual provisos apply. Even on scorching summer days, the increased altitude and exposed windy ridges produce a wind-chill factor to be reckoned with, and storms roll in with frightening rapidity. Any time from the end of March through to late November there can be snow on the tracks, so check current conditions. Always take warm **clothing** and rain gear – and if you plan to scramble up and down the steep volcanic cone of Mount Ngauruhoe, take gloves and long trousers for protection from the sharp scoria rock. **Water** is also scarce on most tracks so carry plenty.

Whakapapa is the main **point of access** for the Tongariro Northern Circuit, and the Round the Mountain track while hikers on the Tongariro Alpine Crossing will need a shuttle bus (see p.297) to Mangatepopo Road and back from Ketetahi Road. Other than accommodation in Whakapapa, the only places to stay are **trampers huts**, all of which have adjacent **campsites**. Hut tickets can be bought in advance from DOC in Whakapapa and Ohakune, or DOC and the visitor centre in Turangi; if bought from a hut warden you pay an extra $5.

Tongariro Alpine Crossing

During the summer season (typically mid-Nov to April) the **Tongariro Alpine Crossing** (19.4km; 6–8hr; 750m ascent) is by far the most popular of the major tramps in the region, and for good reason. Within a few hours you climb over lava flows, cross a crater floor, skirt active geothermal areas, pass beautiful and serene emerald and blue lakes and have the opportunity to ascend the cinder cone of Mount Ngauruhoe. Even without this wealth of highlights it would still be a fine tramp, traversing a mountain massif through scrub and tussock before descending into virgin bush. This isn't a wilderness experience – on weekends and through the height of summer up to seven hundred people a day complete the Crossing, so it pays to aim for spring or autumn and stick to weekdays. Other ways to **avoid the crush** are to get one of the early shuttles and keep ahead of the crowds, or turn one long, arduous day into a relaxed two-day

Tramping in winter

Once the autumn snows arrive (typically in late April) ordinary tramping gear becomes inadequate for doing the Tongariro Alpine Crossing or any of the longer tramps. If you have crampons and an ice axe (and know how to use them) then winter is a great time to get out into the mountains: there are far fewer people and while the Great Walk huts along the Tongariro Alpine Crossing and Tongariro Northern Circuit lose their cooking facilities they become cheaper ($15, camping $5). Huts along the Round the Mountain Track are the same price year-round.

For those less experienced, there are **guided walks** (generally June–Oct) along large sections – though not all – of the Tongariro Alpine Crossing, which include basic instruction on how to use the ice axe and crampons provided. Tongariro Expeditions (ⓣ 07/377 0435, ⓦ www.thetongarirocrossing.co.nz) charge $125 from National Park and $135 from Turangi. National Park-based Adrift Outdoors (ⓣ 07/892 2751, ⓦ www .adriftnz.co.nz) also offers a winter Alpine Crossing ($125) and winter Ruapehu Crater Rim ascents ($195).

experience, dawdling behind the mob and staying the night at **Ketetahi Hut** ($25, camping $20; annual hut pass not valid).

Car parks at both ends of the track have a reputation for break-ins so it's a good idea to leave your vehicle in Ohakune, Turangi, National Park or Whakapapa and make use of the shuttle buses (see p.297). Almost everyone walks west to east saving 400m of ascent – all shuttle buses deposit their charges at Mangatepopo Road End car park, 6km east of SH47, between 6am and 9am and pick up at Ketetahi Road around 4.30pm.

The first hour is gentle, following the Mangatepopo Stream through a barren landscape and passing the Mangatepopo Hut. The track steepens as you scale the fractured black lava flows towards the **Mangatepopo Saddle**, passing a short side track to the **Soda Springs**, a small wildflower oasis in this blasted landscape. The Saddle marks the start of the high ground between the bulky and ancient Mount Tongariro and its youthful acolyte, **Mount Ngauruhoe**, which fit walkers can climb (additional 2km return; 2–3hr; 600m ascent) from here and still make the shuttle bus at the end of the day. The two-steps-forward-one-step-back ascent of this 35-degree cone of red and black scoria is exhausting but the views from the toothy crater rim and the thrilling headlong descent among a cascade of tumbling rocks and volcanic dust make it a popular excursion.

From the Mangatepopo Saddle, the main track crosses the flat pan of the **South Crater** and climbs to the rim of **Red Crater**, with fumaroles belching out steam, which obscures the banded crimson and black of the crater walls. Colours get more vibrant still as you begin the descent to the Emerald Lakes, opaque pools shading from jade to palest duck-egg, and beyond to the crystal-clear Blue Lake. Sidling around Tongariro's **North Crater**, you begin to descend steeply on golden tussock slopes to **Ketetahi Hut**, a major rest stop with views of Lake Rotoaira and Lake Taupo. From here you pass close to the steaming Ketetahi Springs, then begin the final descent through cool streamside bush to the car park on Ketetahi Road.

Tongariro Northern Circuit

If the Tongariro Alpine Crossing appeals, but you're looking for something more challenging, the answer is the **Tongariro Northern Circuit** (42km; 3–4 days at a gentle pace), one of New Zealand's Great Walks. In summer (roughly Oct–April), the huts – Mangatepopo, Ketetahi, Waihohonu and Oturere – are classed as **Great Walk huts** ($25, camping $20; under-18s free) and come with gas cooking stove but not pans or crockery. Hut tickets do not guarantee a bunk, so at busy times you could end up on the floor. Campers can use the hut facilities. The circuit is usually done clockwise.

Whakapapa to Mangatepopo Hut (9km; 2–3hr; 50m ascent). This section can be skipped by getting a shuttle to Mangatepopo car park. The track undulates through tussock and crosses numerous streams before meeting the Tongariro Alpine Crossing track close to Mangatepopo Hut. Can be boggy after heavy rain but is usually passable.

Mangatepopo Hut to Emerald Lakes (6km; 3–4hr; 660m ascent). You follow the Tongariro Alpine Crossing (described above), then have the choice of continuing on the Crossing to Ketetahi Hut (4km; 2–3hr; 400m descent) and returning to this point the next day or continuing to the right.

Emerald Lakes to Oturere Hut (5km; 1–2hr; 500m descent). Descend steeply through fabulously contorted lava formations towards the Rangipo Desert and Oturere Hut.

Oturere Hut to Waihohonu Hut (8km; 2–3hr; 250m descent). Initially cross open, rolling country then descend into the beech forests before a final climb over a ridge brings you to the hut, where you can drop your pack and press on for 20min to the cool and clear Ohinepango Springs.

Waihohonu Hut to Whakapapa (14km; 5–6hr; 200m ascent). The final day cuts between Ngauruhoe and Ruapehu, passing the Old Waihohonu Hut (no accommodation) that was built for stagecoaches on the old road in 1901. The path then continues alongside Waihohonu Stream to the exposed Tama Saddle and, just over 1km beyond, a junction where side tracks lead to Lower Tama Lake (20min return) and Upper Tama Lake (1hr return), both water-filled explosion craters, where you can swim, if you don't need your water warm. It is only around a 2hr walk from the saddle back to Whakapapa, so you should have time to explore Taranaki Falls before ambling back through tussock to the village.

Round the Mountain track

For something slightly more challenging (and with lower hut fees) than the Northern Circuit, opt for the **Round the Mountain Track** (71km; 4–5 days), which loops around Mount Ruapehu and is most easily tackled from Whakapapa. Most huts cost $15 (camping $5; annual hut pass valid) though the Waihohonu Hut is a Great Walk hut ($25, camping $20; under-18s free). The Round the Mountain track can also be combined with the Northern Circuit to make a mighty five- or six-day **circumnavigation** of all three mountains.

Mount Ruapehu ski-fields

Mount Ruapehu is home to the North Island's only substantial **ski-fields**, which attract around two-thirds of the nation's skiers. Every weekend from **late June to mid-October**, cars pile out of Auckland and Wellington (and everywhere in between) for the four-hour drive to Whakapapa, on the northwestern slopes of Mount Ruapehu, or Turoa, on the south side.

Whakapapa and Turoa
Both Whakapapa and Turoa have excellent reputations for pretty much all levels of skier and the orientation of volcanic ridges lends itself to an abundance of dreamy, natural half-pipes for snowboarding. Mt Ruapehu (Ⓦ www.mtruapehu.com) manages both fields, sells tow tickets ($86/day) and rents gear (skis from $38, boards from $46). For beginners there's a Discover package ($100) including ski or snowboard rental, 1hr 50min lesson and a learners' area lift pass. Several places in National Park, Ohakune and Turangi also offer competitive rates and a wide selection of equipment.

Neither field has public **accommodation** on site. Ski clubs maintain dozens of chalets at the foot of the main lifts in Whakapapa's Iwikau Village, but casual visitors (unless invited as a guest) have to stay 6km downhill at Whakapapa Village or 22km away at National Park (see opposite). Almost everyone skiing Turoa stays in Ohakune.

Whakapapa (usually late June to mid-Oct; ☎07/892 3738), is New Zealand's largest and busiest ski area, with over sixty runs (two beginner, forty intermediate, twenty advanced), a dozen major chairlifts and T-bars and the dedicated learners' area of Happy Valley. It offers 675 vertical metres of piste, plus snow-making equipment, ski schools, a huge gear operation and some café/bars. Access is along the toll-free, sealed Bruce Road. Tyre chains are sometimes required, in which case a fitting service ($25) miraculously appears at a parking area beside the road. Shuttle buses run regularly from Whakapapa Village, National Park, Turangi and Taupo.

Turoa (typically mid- to late June through to late Oct; ☎07/385 8456) offers the country's greatest vertical range of piste (720m) and a skiable area almost as extensive as Whakapapa's with wide, groomed trails (three beginner, eleven intermediate, over a dozen advanced) particularly aimed at intermediate skiers; it also offers the region's best après-ski at Ohakune. It is usually possible to drive straight up the sealed, toll-free, 17km access road from Ohakune without chains, and park for nothing. Again, the ski-field operators will fit chains ($30) when needed. Several shuttle buses run up from Ohakune, charging around $20 return.

National Park

The evocative moniker attached to **National Park**, 15km west of Whakapapa Village, belies the overwhelming drabness of this tiny settlement – a dispiriting collection of A-frame chalets sprouting from a scrubby plain with only the views of Ruapehu and Ngauruhoe to lend it grace. The place owes its continued existence to skiers and trampers bound for the adjacent Tongariro National Park, and paddlers heading for **Whanganui River trips**. With limited accommodation at Whakapapa Village, visitors often stay here, using shuttle buses (see box, p.297) to get to the tramps.

When wind and rain tempt you to stay indoors, consider the **Tupapakurua Falls Track** (4–5hr return) which winds through the bush protected from the worst of the weather. It initially follows the gravel Fisher Road from near the train station then, at a small parking area after 2km (30min) you branch left onto a track to a bench seat (additional 20min) with great views west to Mount Taranaki. A further hour's walk brings you to a small canyon with views of the slender, 50m Tupapakurua Falls.

National Park comprises a grid of half a dozen streets wedged between SH4 and the parallel rail line. **Trains** stop beside Station Road, while InterCity **buses** from Taumarunui, Turangi and Ohakune pull up nearby on Carroll Street close to the *National Park Hotel*. Bus and train tickets can be bought a further 100m up the road at *Howard's Lodge* (see below). There is an **ATM** in the petrol station on SH4 (generally daily 7.30am–7pm).

Accommodation

Accommodation is plentiful except over weekends and school holidays during the **ski season** – when prices will be at least one price code higher than those given here – and from Christmas to the end of January. Half a dozen places have a mixture of backpacker dorms and doubles (some en-suite) and everywhere either has their own **track transport** (typically $30 for drop-off and pick-up) or works closely with someone who does.

Howard's Lodge Carroll St ☎07/892 2827, ⓦwww.howardslodge.co.nz. High-standard lodge where those in the en-suite rooms get access to a plusher kitchen and lounge. There's also a spa, mountain bikes ($60/day) and a wide range of rentals for tramping, climbing, skiing and boarding. Dorms $27, rooms ❷/❸

National Park Backpackers Findlay St ☎07/892 2870, ⓦwww.npbp.co.nz. Fairly basic associate YHA with its own indoor climbing wall ($10, plus $3 for boots and harness). Camping $14, dorms $23, rooms ❷
The Park Corner of SH4 & Millar St ☎07/892 2748, ⓦwww.the-park.co.nz. The town's largest

---

The 42 Traverse

The **42 Traverse** (45km one-way; 4–6hr) mountain-bike ride – often wrongly called the 42nd Traverse – has long been popular with Kiwi riders and is gaining a wider following. It mostly follows a narrow 4WD road through some fairly remote country with great downhills (500m net descent), a couple of stream crossings and lashings of atmospheric native bush.

It isn't a particularly technical ride, but there are 300m of climbing and it will take moderately experienced and fit riders four to six hours. The traverse is best done from National Park where all lodgings will help organize pick-up and drop-off (usually $30 in total). Some lodgings have their own **bike rental**, or you can rent from Kiwi Mountain Bikes, based at the *Schnapps Bar* (☎0800/562 4537, ⓦwww.kiwimountain bikes.co.nz) – they charge $65 for the 42 Traverse and do guided rides on the mostly downhill **Fishers Track** (17km; 520m descent; $99) with van pick-up from the bottom.

lodge is a well-organized 82-room complex with a bar, restaurant, spa pool and MTB rental ($50 a day) though no mountain views from rooms. Van hook-ups $10 per vehicle, dorms $30–35, en-suite rooms ❹, deluxe ❺, apartment ❻ **Plateau Lodge** Carroll St ☏0800/861 861, ⓦwww.plateaulodge.co.nz. There's a relaxed ski-chalet feel to this wood-panelled lodge with a

broad range of accommodation and a spa. Dorms $28, rooms ❷, en suites ❸, apartments ❻ **Tongariro Crossing Lodge** Carroll St ☏07/892 2688, ⓦwww.tongarirocrossinglodge.com. This quaint, colonially furnished, former stagecoach inn has a more private feel that most of the lodges hereabouts. All rooms are en suite and breakfast (extra $17) is served. ❺

Eating and drinking

All the lodges mentioned above offer **self-catering** facilities, and *The Park* has its own **restaurant** serving good, pub-style meals. National Park's best eating is at *The Station*, at the train station (☏07/892 2881; closed Tues evenings), serving café-style dishes and great cakes and coffee before morphing into a restaurant with a range of quality meat, fish and pasta dishes (mains $26–32). Otherwise, head for the two pubs – either the traditional *National Park Hotel* on Carroll Street or the more modern, and generally livelier, *Schnapps Bar* on SH4.

Ohakune and around

Ohakune, 35km south of National Park, welcomes you with a huge fibreglass carrot, celebrating its position at the heart of one of the nation's prime market-gardening regions. This is easily forgotten once you are in town among the chalet-style lodges and ski-rental shops geared to cope with the influx of winter-sports enthusiasts who descend from mid-June to early November for the **skiing** at Turoa (see box, p.300). Outside these months Ohakune has traditionally been quiet, but restaurants and bars are increasingly open year-round to cater to summer visitors here to **hike** the Old Coach Road, get bussed to the Tongariro Alpine Crossing or prepare for the Whanganui River journey (see p.239).

Arrival and information

Ohakune is strung between two centres. The Auckland–Wellington rail line passes through **Ohakune Junction** where there's the **train station** and a cluster of hotels and restaurants mostly serving the skiing fraternity. **Central Ohakune**, the commercial heart of the town, lies 2km to the southwest, where InterCity **buses** on the Hamilton–Taumarunui–Wanganui run (daily) stop close to the **i-SITE visitor centre**, 54 Clyde St (daily 9am–5pm; ☏06/385 8427, ⓦwww .visitruapehu.com). For specific tramping information, the mountain weather forecast and a detailed low-down on local flora and fauna, make for the DOC **field centre** at the foot of Ohakune Mountain Road (Mon–Fri 9am–3pm; ☏06/385 0010, ℮ohakunevc@doc.govt.nz); the foyer stays open 24hr and contains tramping information. **Internet access** is available at PeppaTree, opposite the i-SITE. **Transport** around town and all over the region is provided by Matai Shuttles, 61 Clyde St (☏06/385 8724, ⓦwww.mataishuttles.co.nz).

Accommodation

Ohakune has stacks of **places to stay**, though several of them close outside the ski season and are packed once the snows arrive when prices get hiked up by around thirty percent more than those quoted here. Those arriving by bus will find it more convenient to stay in the main town rather than Ohakune Junction.

LKNZ Backpackers/Matai Lodge 1 Rata St, Ohakune Central ⊤06/385 9169, ⓦwww.localknowledgenz.com. Decent YHA-affiliated hostel that's been undergoing considerable renovations with all manner of new rooms and games areas planned. The owners are full of enthusiasm for the outdoors and run shuttles to help you access it. Dorms $27, rooms ❷

Mangawhero Campsite 1.5km up Ohakune Mountain Rd from the DOC field centre. A basic DOC toilets-and-water site. $4

Ohakune Top 10 Holiday Park 5 Moore St ⊤06/385 8561, ⓦohakune.net.nz. Well-kept and central campsite with a pleasant bush-girt setting. Camping $19, cabins ❷, kitchen cabins ❸, motel units ❺

Powderhorn Chateau 194 Mangawhero Terrace, at base of Ohakune Mountain Rd, Ohakune Junction ⊤06/385 8888, ⓦwww.powderhorn.co.nz. Hotel in an immense log-cabin with spacious, cosy rooms (the best with balcony and forest views), plus a large indoor hot pool ($8 for non-guests). ❻

Rimu Park Lodge 27 Rimu St, Ohakune Junction ⊤06/385 9023, ⓦwww.rimupark.co.nz. One of the most comprehensive choices, this 1914 villa contains six-bunk dorms and doubles. Along with a hot tub, the grounds are dotted with simple

cabins, en-suite units, two railway carriages fitted out as s/c units with separate lounge and sleeping quarters, some classy modern apartments and a fully s/c chalet. Dorms $25, rooms & cabins ❷, units ❸, carriages ❹, apartments ❹, chalet ❻

The River Lodge 206 Mangawhero River Rd ⊤06/385 4771, ⓦwww.theriverlodge.co.nz. Appealing lodge rooms and two cabins (most with mountain views) in a wonderfully peaceful parkland setting with mature native beech trees beside a small trout river. Well-appointed rooms are complemented by lounge areas, DVDs, books and games, and a outdoor spa pool. Continental breakfast is included and you can have dinner ($45 including a glass of wine, on request) alfresco or a BBQ by the river. Look for signs 5km out on the road to Raetihi. ❻

Whare Ora 1 Kaha St, Rangataua ⊤06/385 9385, ⓦwww.whareoralodge.co.nz. Lovely, woodsy B&B with amiable hosts in a large house 5km east of Ohakune. The downstairs room has a spa bath and overlooks a lovely garden while the immense upstairs suite comes with unsurpassed mountain views. Delicious three-course dinners are available on request ($70 including wine). ❽

The town and activities

There are numerous **walks** around Ohakune, most listed in the *Walks in and around Tongariro National Park* brochure ($3): we've detailed the best below. Most tracks are off-limits for mountain biking, but you can coast down Ohakune Mountain Road (a 1000m descent in 17km) on bikes rented from TCB, 27 Ayr St (Nov–June; $40–50/day; ⊤06/385 8433, ⓦwww.tcbskiandboard.co.nz). Matai Shuttles will take you and your bike to the top for $15.

Alternatively, let **horses** take the strain at Ruapehu Homestead, 4km east on SH49 (⊤06/385 8799), starting at $40 for an hour in the saddle.

Lake Surprise 12km return; 5hr. Tackle an undulating section of the Round the Mountain track (see p.300) to a shallow lake, from the trailhead at the 15km mark on Ohakune Mountain Road. The hike passes evidence of volcanic debris which swept down the mountain during the 1975 and 1995 eruptions.

Mangawhero Forest Walk 3km loop; 1hr. The pick of Ohakune's shorter trails following a well-marked loop through the bush from opposite the DOC field centre.

Old Coach Road 7km return; 2–3hr; 100m ascent. Excellent easy walking and mountain-bike path that combines beautiful native bush, long views over farmland and a disused tunnel with a good deal of history, all explained on wayside

panels. The route partly follows a track which, for a couple of years from 1906, allowed Auckland–Wellington rail passengers to link up the then incomplete line. This newly restored section of the Old Coach Road leads to the spindly 290m-long Hopruwhenua Viaduct (part of the original rail route but abandoned by line straightening in the 1980s) which was briefly the site of A.J. Hackett's first commercial bungy operation in 1987. By 2011 the Old Coach Road should continue a further few kilometres and link up with SH4. Starts at the end of Marshalls Rd, 2km northwest of Ohakune Junction.

Waitonga Falls Walk 4km return; 1hr 10min. Moderate bushwalk to a spectacular 39m waterfall, starting 11km up the Mountain Rd.

Eating, drinking and nightlife

During the ski season, Ohakune Junction is *the* happening place to spend your evenings, while in summer the focus switches to central Ohakune.

Cyprus Tree 19a Goldfinch St, central Ohakune. Leather sofas and a roaring fire set the tone for this café/bar/restaurant doing a modern take on classic Italian dishes – pasta, risotto, pizza (all $22–26) plus a limited range of mains and desserts.

Mountain Kebabs 29 Clyde St, central Ohakune. Succulent gourmet kebabs to take away. Winter only.

Powderhorn Chateau 194 Mangawhero Terrace, Ohakune Junction. With a woodsy après-ski feel the casual (and usually jumping) *Powderkeg* brasserie/bar is always good for burgers, pizzas ($16–22) and meaty mains ($21–32). Upstairs, the fine-dining *Matterhorn* (mains $30–35; ☎06/385 8888; closed Sun) delivers superb food in a refined but relaxed atmosphere.

Utopia 47 Clyde St, central Ohakune. Casual daytime spot for an extensive range of breakfasts, light lunches and the town's best espresso.

The Desert Road and Waiouru

South of Turangi, SH1 sticks to the east of the Tongariro National Park running roughly parallel to the Tongariro River. This is the eerily scenic **Desert Road** (SH1), which traverses the exposed and barren Rangipo Desert – not a true desert (it gets too much rainfall) but kept arid by the free-draining blanket of volcanic ash and pumice. Road cuttings slice through several metres of the stuff leaving a timeline of past eruptions.

Around 14km south of Turangi, Tree Trunk Gorge Road leads down to the Tongariro River at a spot where it squeezes and churns through a narrow fissure known as **Tree Trunk Gorge**. Back on the highway you soon climb out of the pine forest for great views of the three volcanoes off to the west and the blasted territory ahead. It is a dramatic scene, somehow made even more elemental by the three lines of electricity pylons striding off across the bleak tussock towards Waiouru.

Waiouru and the Army Museum

The Desert Road and the roads flanking the western side of Ruapehu, Ngauruhoe and Tongariro meet at **WAIOURU**, an uninspiring row of service stations and tearooms perched 800m above sea level on the bleak tussock plain beside New Zealand's major **army base**. Take cover in the three concrete bunkers of the **National Army Museum** (daily 9am–4.30pm; $12), where the *Roimata Pounamu* ("Tears on Greenstone") **wall of remembrance** comprises water (symbolizing mourning and cleansing) streaming down a curving bank of heavily veined green-stone tiles while a recorded voice recites the name, rank and place of death of each of the 33,000 New Zealanders who have died in the various wars. The chronologically arranged exhibits are manageable in scale but detailed enough to give coverage of both the campaigns, the affecting human stories behind them and the smaller details such as the display on the warrior flags Maori fought under during the New Zealand Wars of the 1860s. Accounts of the bungled Gallipoli campaign of World War I come complete with an instructive model of Anzac Cove. Nursing during WWII gets equal billing with coverage of POWs incarcerated not just in Germany but also Singapore as New Zealand's world focus begins to shift towards Asia, and eventually the Vietnam War.

There's an interesting **discovery centre** for the kids and the museum **café** is about the best around.

Taihape and around

In the 30km south of Waiouru you drop down off the volcanic plateau into the farming service town of **TAIHAPE** in the heart of the Rangitikei District. Taihape promotes itself as "New Zealand's Gumboot Capital", something it marks by a corrugated iron boot sculpture and a **Gumboot Day** (during March in even years), a tongue-in-cheek celebration of this archetypal Kiwi footwear with a gumboot-throwing competition. Get details from the **information centre**, 90 Hautapu St (daily 9am–5pm; ℡06/388 0604, ⓦwww.taihape.co.nz).

Most people hurry on by but if you fancy a **bite to eat** the main contenders here are the cottagey *Brown Sugar Café*, Huia Street, and the daytime *Soul Food Café*, 69 Hautapu St, good for coffee, excellent meals (and pizza on Fri 6–8pm only). **Places to stay** include the well-run and friendly *Stockman's Lodge*, 9 Dixon Way, 1.5km south off SH1 (℡06/388 1584, ⓦwww.stockmanslodge.co.nz; dorms $22, rooms ❷), the budget *Safari Motel*, 1km north on SH1 (℡06/388 1116; ❷), *Aspen Court*, opposite (℡0508/277 362; ❹), and *Llanerchymedd* B&B, 10 Dixon Way, 1km south (℡06/388 0283, ❸).

Activities

There is little to suggest that the hilly country to the east of Taihape hides one of New Zealand's most thrilling whitewater-rafting trips and the North Island's highest bungy jump.

The Grade V gorge section of the **Rangitikei River** is one of the toughest **whitewater-rafting** rivers in the country with ten major rapids packed into a two- to three-hour run. Trips are run from Mangaweka (see p.306), or more directly from ⚡ *River Valley*, Pukoekahu (℡06/388 1444, ⓦwww.rivervalley .co.nz), an adventure lodge right beside the river, at the pull-out point for rafting trips, some 30km east of Taihape. Morning, and occasionally afternoon, trips ($165) are run throughout the year, though if water levels are low, rafts are replaced by one- or two-person inflatable **kayaks** (also $165) launched in convoy with guides helping out tentative paddlers. *River Valley* also offers scenic rafting ($165; 5hr) down the quieter Grade II section immediately downstream of the lodge, and a four-day chopper-in-paddle-out wilderness trip ($1995; see website for dates). Its excellent **horse-trekking** trips ($105/2hr) head across farmland with great views across the rugged country hereabouts.

Customers camp ($18) or stay in six-bunk dorms ($30, linen provided), pleasant rooms (❷), or very comfortable en-suite cabins (❻). Patrons on the Kiwi Experience buses that call nightly usually use the self-catering kitchen or tuck into the celebrated roast dinners. There are also straightforward low-cost **meals** and a **bar**. Everyone also has free access to pétanque and volleyball and (for a small fee) a wood sauna, an infrared sauna, a spa pool with views of the river and massage in summer.

Adventure seekers can follow the gravel backroads from *River Valley* to Gravity Canyon (℡0800/802 864, ⓦwww.gravitycanyon.co.nz), or alternatively turn off SH1 at Utiku, 7km south of Taihape, and follow the signs 15km east. Here you'll find an 80m **bungy jump**, the country's longest and fastest **flying fox** (175m high, 1km long), on which you reach speeds of up to 160km/hr, and a **bridge swing** offering 50m of freefall. Prices are $110 for one activity and $65 for each extra. The bungy has a unique and rather pleasant water-powered lift to get you back to the bridge ($20 just to ride the lift).

Mangaweka

A DC3 airplane beside SH1 24km south of Taihape marks the dilapidated hamlet of **MANGAWEKA**, HQ of Mangaweka Adventure Co (℡0800/655 747, ⓦwww.riveradventures.net.nz), which offers a number of **whitewater-rafting** and **kayaking** trips including the Rangitikei Grade V Gorge trip ($145) and a couple of Grade II family-oriented rafting trips ($65/1hr, $95/3hr) with an overnight option ($229 including meals) camping beside the river. They also run a lovely, simple **campsite** (camping $5, powered $8) 1km east of SH1 with some riverside pitches, swimming and $2 showers. From here it's 60km to Bulls (see p.249).

Travel details

Trains

National Park to: Auckland (2–7 weekly; 5hr 30min); Ohakune (2–7 weekly; 30min); Palmerston North (2–7 weekly; 3hr 30min); Wellington (2–7 weekly; 5hr).
Ohakune to: Auckland (2–7 weekly; 6hr 30min); Wellington (2–7 weekly; 5hr 30min).
Taihape to: Auckland (2–7 weekly; 7hr 30min); Wellington (2–7 weekly; 4hr 20min).

Buses

National Park to: Auckland (2 daily; 5hr 30min); Ohakune (2 daily; 30min).
Ohakune to: Auckland (1 daily; 6hr 30min).
Rotorua to: Auckland (8 daily; 4hr); Gisborne (2 daily; 4hr 30min); Hamilton (8 daily; 1hr 30min); Kawerau (1 daily; 45min); Opotiki (2 daily; 2hr 10min); Palmerston North (3–4 daily; 5hr 15min); Taupo (7–8 daily; 1hr); Tauranga (6 daily; 1hr

30min); Waitomo (1–2 daily; 2hr 30min–3hr); Whakatane (2 daily; 1hr 30min).
Taihape to: Auckland (4–5 daily; 7hr); Taupo (5–6 daily; 2hr); Turangi (5–6 daily; 1hr 10min); Wellington (5–6 daily; 4hr).
Taupo to: Auckland (6–7 daily; 4–5hr); Hamilton (5–6 daily; 2hr 30min); Hastings (5–6 daily; 2hr 30min); Napier (5–6 daily; 2hr); Palmerston North (3–4 daily; 4hr); Rotorua (7–8 daily; 1hr); Taihape (5–6 daily; 2hr); Tauranga (4 daily; 2hr 45min); Turangi (4–5 daily; 45min); Wellington (4–5 daily; 6hr).
Turangi to: *The Chateau* (1 daily; 1hr).

Flights

Rotorua to: Auckland (2–3 daily; 40min); Christchurch (4 daily; 1hr 40min); Queenstown (1 daily; 3hr 15min); Wellington (3–4 daily; 1hr 10min).
Taupo to: Auckland (4 daily; 45min); Wellington (3 daily; 1hr).

The Coromandel, Bay of Plenty and the East Cape

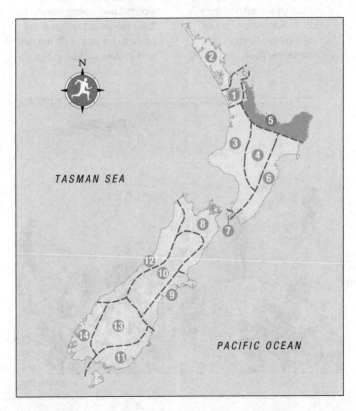

CHAPTER 5

Highlights

* **Te Aroha** Rejuvenate in the geyser-fed hot soda springs in this charming Edwardian spa town. See p.313

* **Kauaeranga Valley** Hike through the Kauaeranga's jagged landscape of bluffs and gorges to the Pinnacles overlooking both Coromandel Peninsula coasts. See p.319

* **Driving Creek Railway** Long coastal views unfold from this modern narrow-gauge line climbing high through rich Coromandel bush. See p.322

* **Hot Water Beach** Grab a shovel, stake your spot and dig into the sand to wallow in surfside hot springs. See p.330

* **White Island** Visit the otherworldly moonscape and sulphur deposits of New Zealand's most active volcano. See p.346

* **The East Cape** Rugged, isolated and solidly Maori, this little-visited region is the place to connect with the land and its people. See p.351

▲ Hot Water Beach

5

The Coromandel, Bay of Plenty and the East Cape

The long coastal sweep east of Auckland is split into three distinct areas, the Coromandel, Bay of Plenty and the East Cape. The first two are among the most popular summer-holiday destinations on the North Island; the latter one of the least-visited parts of the country. Heading from Auckland by road, you'll cut across the dairy country of the **Hauraki Plains** at the foot of the Coromandel Peninsula, with a few pleasant surprises. In the spa town of **Te Aroha** you can luxuriate in a private soda bath, while near **Paeroa** there are walks in the lush **Karangahake Gorge**, once the scene of intensive gold mining.

Jutting northward across the Hauraki Gulf from Auckland, the jagged **Coromandel Peninsula** is an area of spectacular coastal scenery, offering walks to pristine beaches and tramps in luxuriant mountainous rainforest, though its two coasts are markedly different. The west has a more rugged and atmospheric coastline, and easier access to the volcanic hills and ancient kauri trees of the **Coromandel Forest** – best explored from historic **Thames**, and from quaint **Coromandel town**, set in rolling hills beside a pretty harbour. On the east coast, **Whangamata** and **Whitianga** offer a plethora of water activities and long sandy beaches. Whitianga is also handy for **Hot Water Beach**, where natural thermal springs bubble through the sand, and the crystalline **Cathedral Cove Marine Reserve**, ideal for dolphin spotting and snorkelling.

From the open-cast gold-mining town of **Waihi**, at the base of the Coromandel Peninsula, the **Bay of Plenty** sweeps south and east to Opotiki, traced along its length by the Pacific Coast Highway (SH2), which links Auckland with Gisborne. The bay earned its name in 1769 from **Captain Cook**, who was impressed by the Maori living off its abundant resources and by the generous supplies they gave him – an era of peace shattered by the **New Zealand Wars** of the 1860s, when fierce fighting led to the establishment of garrisons at Tauranga and Whakatane.

The Bay of Plenty has the best **climate** on the North Island, making it a fertile fruit-growing region (particularly citrus and kiwi). The coast, though popular

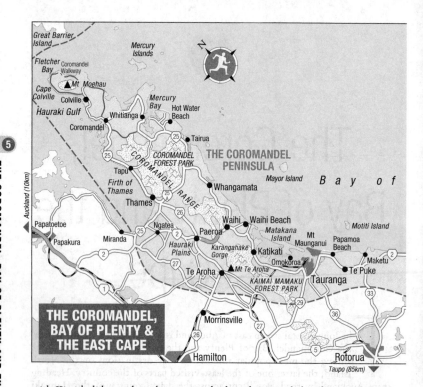

Great Barrier
Island
Mercury
Islands
Fletcher   Coromandel
Bay   Walkway
Cape
Colville   Colville
Hauraki Gulf   ▲Mt Moehau
           Whitianga
Coromandel
Mercury
Bay   Hot Water
          Beach
25 Tairua
COROMANDEL
FOREST PARK   THE COROMANDEL
                   PENINSULA
25
Tapu
Firth of
Thames   Whangamata   Mayor Island   B a y   o f
Thames   Motiti Island
26
Papatoetoe   Ngatea   Paeroa   Waihi Waihi Beach
            25   Matakana   Mt
Papakura   Miranda   Karangahake Island   Maunganui   Papamoa
                    Hauraki   Gorge   Katikati   Beach   Maketu
                    Plains   Omokoroa   2
            27   Te Aroha ▲Mt Te Aroha   Te Puke
                                   KAIMAI MAMAKU   Tauranga
THE COROMANDEL,   FOREST PARK   33
BAY OF PLENTY &   1   29
THE EAST CAPE   Morrinsville   36
                              26
                         Hamilton   27   5   Rotorua
                                                   Taupo (85km) ▼

Auckland (10km) ◀

with Kiwi holiday-makers, has remained relatively unspoiled, offering great surf beaches and other offshore activities. The western bay is home to one of the country's fastest-growing urban areas, centred on **Tauranga** and the contiguous beach town of **Mount Maunganui**. The east revolves around **Whakatane**, the launching point for boat excursions to the fuming, volcanic **White Island**, as well as dolphin swimming and wilderness rafting on the **Motu River**.

Contrasting with these two regions is the rugged and sparsely populated **East Cape**. With a dramatic coastline backed by the **Waiapu Mountains**, a rich and varied Maori history and great hospitality, this isolated region provides a taste of a more traditional way of life.

The Hauraki Plains

Stretching southeast from the Coromandel Peninsula are the fertile **Hauraki Plains**, a low-lying former swamp-turned-farming region at the peninsula's southern end, which, in typically laconic Kiwi fashion, describes itself as "flat out and loving it". The Firth of Thames, the final destination for a number of meandering rivers, borders it to the north.

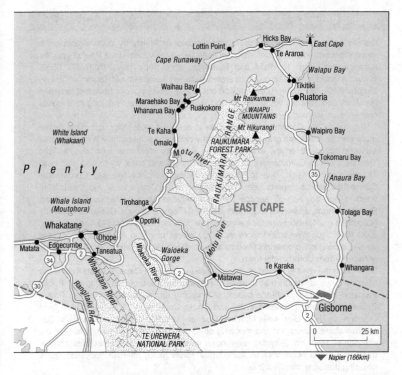

▼ Napier (166km)

The hub of the plains is **Paeroa**, not much in itself but handy for walks in magnificent **Karangahake Gorge**, running almost to Waihi.

The real gem hereabouts is **Te Aroha**, a delightful Edwardian spa town at the southern extremity of the plains, where you can hike Mount Te Aroha and soak afterwards in natural hot soda springs.

Paeroa and the Karangahake Gorge

PAEROA is "World Famous in New Zealand" as the birthplace of **Lemon and Paeroa** (L&P), an iconic home-grown soft drink founded in 1907 using the local mineral water. Its logo is emblazoned on shopfronts throughout town and a giant brown L&P bottle at the junction of SH2 and SH26. The **Paeroa Information Centre**, on the corner of Taylors Avenue and Seymour Street (daily 9am–4pm), adjoins the *L&P Café & Bar* (Mon–Tues 8.30am–3pm, Wed–Sat 8.30am–8.30pm, Sun 8.30am–8pm), selling L&P-flavoured ice cream as well as filling highway-stop fare like gourmet burgers.

Leafy **Karangahake Gorge** was the scene of the Coromandel's first gold rush. Today it's hard to envisage such frenetic activity in this tranquil spot. The steep-sided gorge begins 8km east of Paeroa along the narrow, snaking continuation of SH2 as it traces the Ohinemuri River to Waihi.

The **Karangahake Gorge Historic Walkway** (outlined in a leaflet available from the Paeroa information centre) covers 7km of a former rail line and can be accessed from several points, the best being the **Karangahake Reserve**, at the

Getting around

Getting around the **Hauraki Plains** and the **Bay of Plenty** by public transport is straightforward: InterCity runs daily services between Auckland via Paeroa and the Karangahake Gorge to Waihi and Tauranga, while Supa Travel (T 07/571 0583, W www.supatravelexpress.co.nz) operates between Auckland and Tauranga. Turley-Murphy (T 07/884 8208) runs a service once daily (except public holidays) between Hamilton and Thames via Te Aroha and Paeroa. Other local and long-haul buses converge on Tauranga – see p.335.

Negotiating the **Coromandel Peninsula** is easiest by car. Although many of the more remote roads are gravel, few pose any real danger if you take it steadily. Bus services include InterCity, which provides a regular clockwise loop service from Thames north to Coromandel, across to Whitianga and back south and across to Thames, while Magic Bus (p.33) runs anticlockwise; its two-day Coromandel Connection service departs from Thames three to five days a week. Go Kiwi (p.326) offers a hop-on, hop-off service between Auckland and numerous Coromandel Peninsula stops, as well as a Coromandel town–Rotorua service. Cut-price company NakedBus (p.34) also operates services. The 360Discovery ferry ($49 one-way; 2hr; T 09/424 5510, W www.360discovery.co.nz) leaves pier 4 in Auckland 5–7 days a week, docking in Coromandel Harbour's Hannaford's Wharf. Tickets include a shuttle service to/from Coromandel town.

Although the road is sealed all the way around the **East Cape**, it twists in and out of small bays so much that it takes a full six hours without any stopoffs. Public transport is limited to shuttle buses, all charging around $35–45 one-way. Polly's Passenger Courier (T 06/864 4728) and Cooks Couriers (T 06/864 4711) run from Gisborne to Hicks Bay, while Matakoa Courier (T 06/864 4654) run from Hicks Bay to Whakatane, picking up and stopping off virtually anywhere en route. None of the companies work on Saturday afternoons or on Sundays and timetables change frequently. From November to April, Stray Travel (p.33) offers a "Go East" pass covering the cape from Rotorua.

---

start of the gorge. Here, a pedestrian suspension bridge crosses the river to join a **loop walk** (3km; 45min), heading upstream beside the Ohinemuri River, past remnants of the gold workings and into the Karangahake Gorge, hugging the cliffs and winding through regenerating native bush. You complete the loop by crossing the river and walking through a 1km-long tunnel (partially but adequately lit), where you can spot glowworms. This walk encircles the site of the **old Karangahake township**, now reduced to the *Talisman Café* on the main road and the *Ohinemuri Estate Winery and Café*, on Moresby Street (T 07/862 8874, W www.ohinemuri.co.nz), where you can sample the wines and tuck into Mediterranean-accented café fare (Dec–Feb daily 10am–5pm; March–Nov Wed–Sun 10am–5pm), and **stay** in a smart, self-contained apartment built into the hayloft (❹), and on fine Sunday afternoons in summer there's music. Other accommodation options in the area include the comfy *Golden Owl Backpacker Lodge*, 3 Moresby Rd, Karangahake (T 07/862 7994, W www.goldenowl.co.nz; dorms $25, room ❷), and the riverside *Karangahake River Lodge & Campervan Park*, 45 River Rd (T 07/862 8481, W www.river-road.co.nz; powered site $25, lodge ❷, motel ❹).

At the eastern end of the gorge, the train station at tiny **WAIKINO** is the western terminus for the Goldfields Railway (p.334), running one to three trains daily to Waihi and back. Inside are displays on local history and walks in the area, as well as the daytime *Waikino Station Café*, with outdoor seating on the platform.

Te Aroha

On the fringes of the Hauraki Plains, 21km south of Paeroa on SH26, **TE AROHA** is home to New Zealand's only intact **Edwardian spa**. Hunkered beneath the imposing bush-clad slopes of the **Kaimai-Mamaku Forest Park**, the 954m **Mount Te Aroha** rears up immediately behind the neat little town centre, providing a reasonably challenging goal for hikers.

The town itself was founded in 1880 at the furthest navigable extent of the Waihou River. A year later, rich deposits of gold were discovered on Mount Te Aroha, sparking a full-scale **gold rush** until 1921. Within a few months of settlement, the new townsfolk set out the attractive Hot Springs Domain around a cluster of **hot soda springs** which, by the 1890s, had become New Zealand's most popular mineral spa complex. Enclosures were erected for privacy, most rebuilt in grand style during the Edwardian years. The fine suite of original buildings have been restored and integrated with more modern pools fed by the springs and nearby **Mokena Geyser**.

Arrival, information and accommodation

The town's main thoroughfare is Whitaker Street and everything of interest – banks, post office, library – is either along it or close by. The **i-SITE visitor centre** (Mon–Fri 9.30am–5pm, Sat & Sun 9.30am–4pm; ☎07/884 8052, ⓦwww.tearohanz.co.nz), at 102 Whitaker St by the entrance to the Domain, has DOC information for the area.

Te Aroha's **accommodation** includes mid-range motels and boutique hotels, bookable through the i-SITE. In a heart-warmingly cosy wooden cottage, the tiny ⚑ *YHA* on Miro Street, off Brick Street (☎07/884 8739, ⓦwww.stayyha.co.nz; dorms $20, rooms ❶), virtually unchanged since it opened in the early 1960s, is one of the oldest and simplest hostels in New Zealand. Set on the lower slopes of Mount Te Aroha, there are lovely views from the hammocks strung beneath the kanuka trees and free bikes. Campers should head 3km out on the road to Hamilton (SH26) to the well-maintained *Te Aroha Holiday Park*, 217 Stanley Rd South (☎07/884 9567, ⓦwww.tearohaholidaypark.co.nz; unpowered/powered sites $12/15, dorm $20, on-site vans and cabins ❶, flats and cottages ❶–❸), set among shady oaks, with a mineral water rock pool (open evenings).

The Town

Te Aroha's centrepiece is the **Hot Springs Domain** at the southern end of town on Whitaker Street. Within this 44-acre **thermal reserve** of gardens and rose beds, the **Spa Baths** complex is well signposted (Easter to Labour Day daily 10.30am–10pm; Labour Day to Easter Mon–Thurs 11am–9pm, Fri–Sun 10.30am–10pm; 30min; $15/person, min 2; advance bookings essential ☎07/884 8717, ⓦwww.tearohapools.co.nz), with private, bubbling enclosed pools heated to around 40°C. Choose a king-size claw-foot slipper bath if you fancy adding aromatherapy oils; otherwise the six wooden tubs are bigger. A half-hour soak in the hot soda waters is plenty. Beneficial for ailments such as arthritis, the alkaline waters are also said to extract polluting heavy metals from your system, and leave your skin incredibly soft (don't shower directly afterwards). The steaming baths are an especially popular way to warm up in winter (less so on a hot summer's day). However, because the heat can bring on unwanted effects (faintness and so on) in some people – even those who don't have precluding medical conditions – you're not permitted to enter the baths alone. The nearby outdoor **Leisure Pool** complex ($6) has a regular, chlorinated outdoor pool and toddlers' pool heated to around 32°C, and a spa (around 38°C). Nearby too are a **café** in a timber cottage and a free **foot-spa**.

Just uphill from the baths is the erratic **Mokena Geyser**, which goes off roughly every forty minutes. Due to its spa-feeding duties it doesn't always spurt to an impressive height – the best time to catch it in action each day is between noon and 2pm. From here, a **trail** leads to the top of **Mount Te Aroha** which, legend has it, was named by a young Arawa chief, Kahumatamomoe, who climbed it after losing his way in the region's vast swamp while making for Maketu in the Bay of Plenty. Delighted to see the familiar shoreline of his homeland, he called the mountain Te Aroha, "love", in honour of his father and kinsmen.

An old sanatorium, just below the spa baths in front of the croquet lawn, houses the exhibit-packed town **museum** (daily: Labour Day to Easter 11am–4pm; Easter to Labour Day 1–3pm; $3). Highlights include two finely decorated Royal Doulton Victorian lavatories, a chemical analysis of the local soda water, an early linotype machine, and over three hundred pieces of souvenir porcelain from around the world.

By the Boundary Street exit from the Domain you'll find the 1926 **St Mark's Anglican Church**, on the corner of Church and Kenrick streets, insignificant but for the incongruous 1712 organ, said to be the oldest in the southern hemisphere. Organ demonstrations can be arranged; ask at the i-SITE.

The i-SITE is also the place to pick up the *Te Aroha and Waiorongomai Walks* leaflet ($2) outlining rewarding day walks in the area.

Eating

The pick of places to **eat** is *Banco*, 174 Whitaker St, a gracious former bank adorned with antiques and shelves of gourmet groceries (at least 10am–5pm Thurs–Mon plus regular events such as tapas nights, whisky nights and so on). Filled with quirky iron sculptures, café/bar *Ironique*, 159 Whitaker St, is a good bet for brunches, snacks, and evening meals such as orange-marinated venison and pistachio-crusted pork (evening mains around $30). *Berlusconi*, 149 Whitaker St, serves fine wine along with antipasto platters and classical fare (evening mains around $30; Wed from 5pm, Thurs–Sun 10am to late). The retro-boho daytime café *Pulse*, 140 Whitaker St, offers fine coffee, free internet terminals and a rack of funky secondhand clothes, while *The Crossing*, 183 Whitaker St, serves up good-value breakfasts and its locally renowned gourmet pizza (Tues–Wed 9am–6pm, Thurs–Fri 9am–8pm, Sat–Sun 9am–4pm).

The Coromandel Peninsula

The Hauraki Gulf is separated from the Pacific Ocean by the mountainous, bush-cloaked **Coromandel Peninsula**, fringed with beautiful surf and swimming beaches and basking in a balmy climate.

Along the **west coast**, cliffs and steep hills drop sharply to the sea, leaving only a narrow coastal strip shaded by **pohutukawa** trees that erupt in a blaze of red from mid-November to January. The beaches are sheltered and safe but most are only good for **swimming** when high tide obscures the mud flats. Most tourists

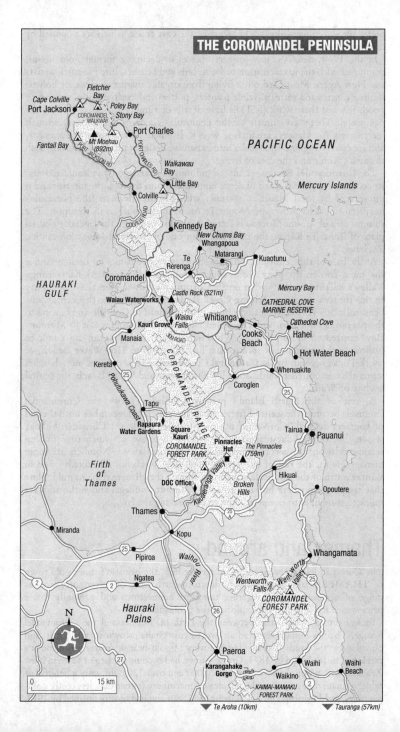

PACIFIC OCEAN

Cape Colville
Port Jackson
Fletcher Bay
Poley Bay
Stony Bay
COROMANDEL WALKWAY
Fantail Bay
PORT JACKSON RD
Mt Moehau (892m)
Port Charles
PORT CHARLES RD
Waikawau Bay
Little Bay
Mercury Islands

Colville
COLVILLE ROAD
Kennedy Bay
New Chums Bay
Whangapoua
Matarangi
Kuaotunu
Te Rerenga
Coromandel
Castle Rock (521m)
Mercury Bay
Waiau Waterworks
309 ROAD
Waiau Falls
Kauri Grove
CATHEDRAL COVE MARINE RESERVE
Whitianga
Cathedral Cove
Cooks Beach
Hahei
Manaia
309 ROAD
Hot Water Beach

HAURAKI GULF

Kereta
Pohutukawa Coast
Whenuakite
Coroglen
25

Tapu
Rapaura Water Gardens
Square Kauri
COROMANDEL FOREST PARK
COROMANDEL RANGE
Pinnacles Hut
The Pinnacles (759m)
Tairua
Pauanui

Firth of Thames
DOC Office
Kauaeranga Valley
Broken Hills
Hikuai
Opoutere

Thames
Kopu
Miranda
25
Pipiroa
2
Ngatea
2
Waihou River
Whangamata

Hauraki Plains
Wentworth Falls
Wentworth Valley
25
COROMANDEL FOREST PARK

N
26

Paeroa
27
Karangahake Gorge
Waikino
Waihi
Waihi Beach
2
KAIMAI-MAMAKU FOREST PARK

0   15 km

▼ Te Aroha (10km)   ▼ Tauranga (57km)

prefer the sweeping white-sand beaches of the **east coast**, which are pounded by impressive but often perilous **surf**.

In the 1960s and 70s, low property prices in declining former gold towns, combined with the juxtaposition of bush, hills and beaches, lured hippies, **artists** and New Agers. Most eked out a living from organic market gardens, or holistic healing centres and retreats, while painters, potters and **craftspeople**, some very good, hawked their work (i-SITEs have details of rural craft outlets all over the peninsula). These days much of the peninsula is a more commercial animal: increasingly Aucklanders are finding ways to live here permanently or commute, and are converting one-time *baches* into expensive designer properties, raising both the area's profile and the cost of living.

The **Coromandel Range** – sculpted millions of years ago by volcanic activity, its contorted skyline clothed in dense rainforest – runs through the interior and is interpreted by local Maori as a canoe, with **Mount Moehau** (the peninsula's northern tip) as its prow, and Mount Te Aroha in the south as its sternpost. The summit area of Mount Moehau is sacred, Maori-owned land, the legendary burial place of Tama Te Kapua, the commander of one of the Great Migration canoes, *Te Arawa*.

At the base of the peninsula, **Thames** showcases its gold-mining heritage and is the most convenient place from which to explore the forested **Kauaeranga Valley's** walking tracks. Further north, **Coromandel town** offers the opportunity to ride the narrow-gauge **Driving Creek Railway** and is close to the scenic trans-peninsular 309 Road. For really remote country, head to **Colville** and beyond to the peninsula's northern tip. The sealed Highway 25 continues east to **Mercury Bay**, centred on more populous **Whitianga**, near which you can dig a hole to wallow in the surfside hot springs that lure hundreds to **Hot Water Beach**, or snorkel in a gorgeous bay at **Cathedral Cove Marine Reserve**. Yet more beaches string the coast further south around **Whangamata** and **Waihi Beach**, the coastal acolyte of **Waihi**.

As one of the North Island's **principal holiday spots**, the Coromandel Peninsula becomes the scene of frenetic activity from **late December** until the end of January; dubbed "Coro-mas" not only in reference to the Christmas holiday season, but the holiday-makers who descend en masse, at which time finding accommodation can become impossible – book *well* ahead. Numbers are more manageable for the rest of the year (though long weekends fill quickly), and in **winter** much of the peninsula is deserted, though the **climate** remains mild. Note that camping anywhere but an authorized campsite is illegal and authorities are quick to issue fines to campers found to be breaking the law.

Thames and around

The Coromandel's gateway and main service hub, the historic former gold town of **THAMES** retains a refreshingly down-to-earth sense of community, and its range of accommodation, eateries, transport connections and generally lower prices make it a fine base for exploring the peninsula.

Packed into a coastal strip between the Firth of Thames and the Coromandel Range, Thames initially evolved as two towns: Grahamstown to the north, and Shortland to the south. The first big discovery of gold-bearing quartz was made in a creek-bed in 1867, and by 1871, Grahamstown had become the largest town in New Zealand, with a population of around 20,000 and over 120 pubs, only a handful of which remain today. Due to the reliance on machinery (rather than less costly gold-panning), **gold mining** tailed off during the 1880s and had mostly finished by 1913.

Its legacy forms the basis of the town's historical attractions, and you can spend at least half a day visiting them. The **Kauaeranga Valley**, a popular destination for hikers visiting the Coromandel Forest Park, is easily accessible from town.

Arrival, information and transport

Buses drop off outside the **i-SITE visitor centre**, 206 Pollen St (summer Mon–Fri 8.30am–5pm, Sat & Sun 9am–4pm; winter Mon–Fri 9am–4pm, Sat 9am–1pm, Sun noon–4pm; ⓣ07/868 7284, ⓦwww.thamesinfo.co.nz), which has **internet** access, while Pollen Street, the main shopping thoroughfare, is home to banks, travel agents and the post office. Nowhere is far from here but you can get **taxis** from Thames Taxis (ⓣ07/868 3100), or rent **touring bikes** from

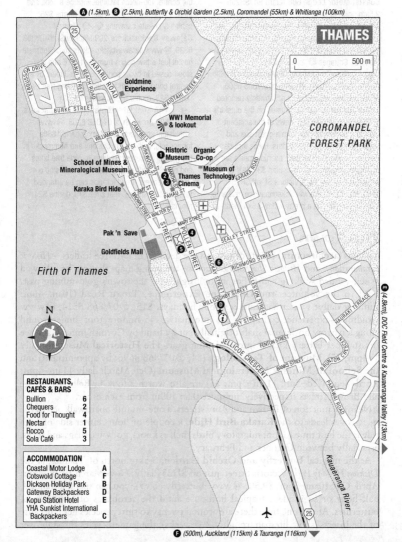

▲ Ⓐ (1.5km), Ⓑ (2.5km), Butterfly & Orchid Garden (2.5km), Coromandel (55km) & Whitianga (100km)

THAMES

0   500 m

KURANUI STREET
FERGUSSON DRIVE
BEACH ROAD
TARARU ROAD
25
WAIOTAHI CREEK ROAD

Goldmine Experience

BURKE STREET
WILLIAMSON ST
CAMPBELL ST

WW1 Memorial & lookout

COROMANDEL FOREST PARK

ALBERT ST
KIRKWOOD ST
COCHRANE ST

Historic Museum ❶
Organic Co-op

School of Mines & Mineralogical Museum Ⓒ

Museum of Thames Technology
Cinema
❷
❸
AMY ST
PAHAU ST
BROWN STREET
WALTER ST
QUEEN STREET

Karaka Bird Hide

KARAKA ROAD

MARY STREET
❹
SEALEY STREET

Pak 'n Save

POLLEN STREET
❺
❻
RICHMOND STREET
ROLLESTON STREET

Goldfields Mall

Firth of Thames

MACKAY STREET

N

WILLOUGHBY STREET
ⓓ
ⓘ
GREY STREET
FENTON STREET
HAURAKI TERRACE

JELLICOE CRESCENT
BANKS STREET
BRUNTON CRESCENT
PARAWAI ROAD

Ⓔ (4.8km), DOC Field Centre & Kauaeranga Valley (13km) ▶

Kauaeranga River

25

RESTAURANTS, CAFÉS & BARS

Bullion	6
Chequers	2
Food for Thought	4
Nectar	1
Rocco	5
Sola Café	3

ACCOMMODATION

Coastal Motor Lodge	A
Cotswold Cottage	F
Dickson Holiday Park	B
Gateway Backpackers	D
Kopu Station Hotel	E
YHA Sunkist International Backpackers	C

▼ Ⓕ (500m), Auckland (115km) & Tauranga (116km) ▼

Paki Paki Bike Shop, in the Goldfields Mall off Mary Street (℡07/867 9026, 🅦 www.pakipakibikeshop.co.nz) or **mountain bikes** from Price & Richards, 430 Pollen St (℡07/868 6157). Michael Saunders Motors (℡0800/111 110), John Davy Rentals (℡07/868 6868) and *YHA Sunkist International Backpackers* (below) all rent budget cars from around $40–65 per day and allow them onto the peninsula's roughest roads. For Kauaeranga Valley transport, see opposite.

Accommodation

Most **accommodation** in Thames is scattered away from the town centre, but the standard is generally good.

Coastal Motor Lodge 608 Tararu Rd (SH25), 2.5km north of town ℡07/868 6843, 🅦 www .stayatcoastal.co.nz. Well-equipped "cottage" units and streamlined, spacious black A-frame chalets (all s/c and designed for two) with great views over the Firth. Cottages ❹, chalets ❺

🏃 **Cotswold Cottage** 46 Maramarahi Rd, 3km south of town off SH25 ℡07/868 6306, 🅦 www.cotswoldcottage.co.nz. Lovingly restored 1920s villa set in mature grounds on the outskirts of Thames with beautiful views of the adjacent river and peninsula hills, with a guest spa and sauna and three en-suite rooms. Rates include delicious cooked breakfasts; evening meals are available on request (2-/3-course $39/49). ❻

Dickson Holiday Park Victoria St, off SH25 ℡07/868 7308, 🅦 www.dicksonpark.co.nz. Large, friendly campsite in a pretty valley 3.5km north of

the centre. Top-notch facilities include a pool, and there's bus pick-up from Thames. Dorms $26, cabins & on-site caravans ❶–❷, flats ❸

Gateway Backpackers 209 Mackay St ℡07/868 6339, 🅦 www.gatewaybackpackers.co.nz. Intimate hostel just a few paces from the i-SITE and bus stop housed in two wooden buildings linked by a central courtyard with facilities including free bikes. Dorms $23, rooms ❶, en suites ❷

🏃 **YHA Sunkist International Backpackers** 506 Brown St ℡07/868 8808, 🅦 www .sunkistbackpackers.com. Atmospheric 1860s former pub, with a wide balcony and hammocks in the garden. Excellent facilities include free bikes and on-site 4WD rental. InterCity buses stop out front on request; free pick-ups can be arranged from the bus station. Tent sites $18, dorms $24, rooms ❷

The Town

Thames' **architectural** points of interest are detailed in two free leaflets – *Historic Grahamstown* and *Historic Shortland & Tararu* – including maps that can be followed as self-guided walking tours. For more insight into the town's gold-mining past, head to the volunteer-run **Goldmine Experience**, Tararu Road (10am–4pm: summer daily; winter Sat, Sun & public holidays; $15; ℡07/868 8514, 🅦 www .goldmine-experience.co.nz) for an informative 45-minute tour underground along a narrow horizontal shaft originally cut by hand by Cornish miners, and see the stamper battery kicked into deafening gear. The **Historical Museum** (daily 1–4pm; $5), **Museum of Technology** ($4; ℡07/868 8696; by appointment) and the **School of Mines & Mineralogical Museum** (Oct–March daily 11am–4pm; April–Sept Wed–Sun, 11am–3pm; $5) are also worth a look in Bella, Cochrane and Brown streets respectively, no more than 100m from each other.

Near the junction of Brown and Amy streets, a one-minute boardwalk across the mangroves leads to the **Karaka Bird Hide**: a couple of hours either side of high tide is the best time to spot migratory birds such as knots, godwits, shags and terns, especially between October and February.

At the magical **Butterfly and Orchid Garden**, 3.5km north of Thames, at the *Dickson Holiday Park*, Victoria Street, just off SH25 (daily: Nov–March 10am–4pm; April–Oct 10am–3pm; $9.50; 🅦 www.butterfly.co.nz), you can spend a tranquil, half-hour or so inside a tropical hothouse amid the acrobatics of hundreds of butterflies. At any one time there are around twenty to thirty species here; because of the insects' short lifespan (roughly 2–3 weeks), the garden cycles through over

1000 of these exquisite winged creatures each month, about half imported as pupae, and half bred on-site.

Great sunset views extend from the hilltop **WWI Memorial and lookout**, accessed off Waiotahi Creek Road.

Kauaeranga Valley

The steep-sided **Kauaeranga Valley**, east of town, stretches towards the spine of the Coromandel Peninsula, a jagged landscape of bluffs and gorges topped by **the Pinnacles** (759m), with stupendous views to both coasts across native forest studded with rata, rimu and kauri. It's reached along a scenic and mostly sealed road snaking down the river, providing access to some of the finest walks in the Coromandel Range. *YHA Sunkist International Backpackers* and *Gateway Backpackers* (see opposite) run a shared **shuttle** service along the road ($35 return; min 2 people), or you can **drive** by heading out of the southern end of Thames, along Banks Road and onto Parawai Road which becomes Kauaeranga Road.

Kauaeranga walks

The magnificent Kauaeranga Valley has a variety of easily accessible walks, and satisfying tramps with a night spent at the large and relatively plush **Pinnacles Hut** (80 bunks; $15; advance booking essential through Kauaeranga DOC ℡07/867 9080; backcountry hut passes not valid). There are also three remote and very basic DOC **campsites** in the valley itself: one near the Pinnacles Hut, one at Billygoat Basin and another at Moss Creek ($5 each), plus more DOC campsites along the valley road (p.320). The *Kauaeranga Valley Recreation* DOC leaflet ($2) covers the basics, though you might prefer the detail provided by the 1:50,000 Hikaui Topo50 map BB35 (around $9). Both are available from the DOC office (p.320). The ease of access to these tracks can lead trampers not to take them as seriously as other tramps but in bad weather the conditions can be treacherous, so go properly prepared (see p.59).

Nature Walk to Hoffman's Pool (1.5km loop; 30min). A short, easy loop beginning 1km beyond the DOC office. Information panels make it a classic introduction to the valley's native forest. The track leads to a tranquil sand-edged pool in a river bend, an ideal picnic and swimming spot (toilets and changing sheds nearby). You return the same way or in a loop along the road.

Pinnacles–Billygoat Basin Walk (18km loop; 8hr). This upgraded track is a great way to get a taste of the region. It starts at the road-end and spends the first 2–3hr following Webb Creek along an old packhorse route (steep in places) used by kauri bushmen in the 1920s up to Pinnacles Hut. From the hut – with new ladders and steps – a steep 50min climb – reaches the Pinnacles. On the return, head south from the Hydro junction via Billygoat Basin, with information panels telling the story of the loggers. If you're after a shorter walk, you can just do a 9km loop (4–5hr) as far as the Hydro junction and back via Billygoat Basin. Alternatively, experienced hikers might want to combine part of the track with the Moss Creek Circuit (see below).

Moss Creek Tramping Circuit (23km loop; 2–3 days). After following the Pinnacles Walk and overnighting at the Pinnacles Hut (see above) about a third of the way along the Moss Creek Circuit's total length, this difficult circuit diverges north, passing the remnants of a couple of kauri dams, an old logging camp and some fine viewpoints, with Moss Creek campsite along the way. It can be muddy and difficult, involving a few unbridged stream crossings; be sure to check track updates with DOC.

Wainora Track (6km return; 2–3hr). Moderate, well-formed track to a couple of large kauri – pretty much the only accessible ones left standing hereabouts – that starts from the Wainora campsite, 7km beyond the DOC office, heading northeast.

Fourteen kilometres along you reach the refurbished **DOC office** (daily 8am–4pm; ☎07/867 9080), where you can stock up on maps, buy hut tickets and examine displays on **early kauri logging** in the valley, and store luggage ($2/bag/day). From the office, a loop track (500m; 10min) leads to a scale model of a kauri driving dam, a type once used extensively in this forest. Along the unsealed 9km beyond the DOC office to the road-end, tracks (see box, p.319) lead off into the bush containing scattered "pole stands" of young kauri that have grown since the area was logged a century ago: only a handful in each stand will reach maturity. Most of the hikes head into the bush near one of the eight simple roadside **campsites** ($9; toilets and stream water) dotting the length of the stretch.

To really get off the beaten track consider **canyoning** down the Sleeping God canyon with Canyonz (see p.114), whose trips begin in Auckland but pick up in Thames.

Eating and entertainment

In addition to the central Pak 'n Save supermarket, you can pick up **supplies** at the Organic Co-op, 736 Pollen St (Mon–Fri 9am–5pm, Sat 9am–noon), and the Saturday morning **market** (9am–noon; food, clothing and more) at the northern end of Pollen Street.

The traditional, sometimes larrikin **bars** of Thames are generally not worth the hassle, so head instead either for *Mama Gins* in town or the *Kopu Station Hotel* a few kilometres out. Films screen at the Multiplex **cinema** at 708 Pollen St. Thames has an impressive range of places to **eat**, mostly concentrated along Pollen Street.

Bullion 404 Pollen St ☎07/868 7270. Book ahead to dine at this classy spot on the likes of venison croquettes, followed by wild boar and fennel sausages on puréed white beans with avocado oil. Open from 5pm.

Chequers 710 Pollen St. Great coffee and sweet treats served at chessboard-tiled tables or at wooden tables built around the trees in the sunny courtyard. Mon–Fri 7.30am–4pm, Sat & Sun 7.30am–2pm.

Food for Thought 574 Pollen St. This central daytime spot has taken numerous NZ-wide awards for its home-made pies (especially its chicken and vegetable pie) and also has a mouthwatering range of cakes, plus excellent coffee. Open Mon–Fri 6.30am–3.30pm, Sat 7am–1.30pm.

Kopu Station Hotel Corner of SH25 & SH26, Kopu. A few km south of central Thames, "the Kopu" is a favourite local watering hole for regular live bands,

a great range of drinks (including lots of specials), grassy beer garden and laidback attitude.

Mama Gins 748 Pollen St. Cool, low-lit front-room bar with bordello-like black-and-white floral wallpaper, glossy timber tables, an eclectic mix of entertainment including live bands, big-city DJs, poetry readings and jam sessions. Open Wed–Sat 7pm till late.

Rocco 109 Sealey St, ☎07/868 8641. High-quality Spanish platters, tapas (including Coromandel mussel fritters) and substantial meals like lamb rump, served in a stylish, turn-of-the-century wooden villa. Mains around $30. Licensed; lunch daily, dinner Tues–Sun.

Sola Café 720b Pollen St. Hip bohemian daytime café serving stellar coffee and protein-packed hot vegetarian dishes, salads and counter fare, with some vegan and wheat-free options.

North to Coromandel

From Thames, SH25 snakes 58km north to Coromandel town, tracing the grey rocky shoreline of the "**Pohutukawa Coast**" (so called for its abundance of these blazing native trees) past a series of tiny, sandy bays, most with little more than a few houses and the occasional campsite. Hills and sand-coloured cliffs rise dramatically from the roadside for the first 19km to **Tapu**, where the **Tapu–Coroglen**

Road peels off to the peninsula's east coast. It is a wonderfully scenic 28km run of narrow, unsealed yet manageable driving, leaving behind the marginal farmland on the coast and climbing over the peninsula's mountainous spine. Even if you aren't tackling the traverse, it's worth making a detour 6.5km along the road to **Rapaura Water Gardens** (daily 9am–5pm, winter hours may vary; $12; ☏07/868 4821, ⓦwww.rapaurawatergardens.co.nz), a landscaped "wilderness" of bush and blooms, lily ponds and a trickling stream, threaded by paths, with philosophical messages urging you to stop and think. There are a few picnic areas and an excellent **café**. You can enjoy the gardens at night in luxury accommodation: an enchanting cottage for two (ⓖ) or a serene two-bedroom house lined with rimu (ⓞ).

The Tapu–Coroglen Road continues for 3km on to the (easily missed) **"square kauri"** signpost near the road's summit, opposite a rough lay-by and just before a small bridge. Steep steps through bush (175m; 10min) lead to this giant of a tree (1200 years old, just over 41m high and 9m wide), whose unusual, angular shape saved it from loggers. From here it's another rough and twisty 19km across the peninsula to Coroglen, linking with the main road between Whitianga and Whangamata, or 9.5km back to Tapu and the continuation of SH25 north.

Back on **SH25**, the road lurches inland soon after Kereta (about 12km north of Tapu), snaking over hills to the roadside **Manaia-Kereta Lookout** (206m), which has great views of the northern peninsula, the majestic Moehau Range and Coromandel Harbour. Beyond, the vertical cliffs of Great Barrier Island may be visible on a clear day. Along the rocky shoreline and blue-green Firth of Thames, SH25 continues for 23km before reaching Coromandel.

Coromandel

The northernmost town of any substance is charming little **COROMANDEL**, 58km north of Thames, huddling beneath high, craggy hills at the head of Coromandel Harbour, views of which extend from the **scenic railway** climbing into the hills.

The town and peninsula took their name from an 1820 visit by the British Admiralty supply ship *Coromandel*, which called into the harbour to obtain kauri spars and masts. A more mercenary European invasion was precipitated by the 1852 discovery of **gold**, near Driving Creek, in the northern part of town. The subsequent boom left a string of fine wooden buildings along the main street. There are a couple of supermarkets and petrol stations, a bank, a cluster of cafés and a broad range of accommodation.

Arrival, information and transport

The combined **i-SITE visitor centre** and **DOC office**, 355 Kapanga Rd (Nov to Easter daily 9am–5pm, Easter to Oct Mon–Sat 9am–5pm, Sun 10am–2pm; ☏07/866 8598, ⓦwww.coromandeltown.co.nz), at the northern end of town, just over the bridge, has **tide times** for Hot Water Beach and **internet access**. **Buses** pull into the car park opposite the i-SITE. **Car-rental** firms in town include the GAS service station, 226 Wharf Rd (☏07/866 8736), which allows its cars onto the unsealed roads north of Colville.

Moving on, you've a choice of striking **east to Whitianga** via the continuation of SH25 (see p.325) past the deserted beaches of Whangapoua and Kuaotunu, or the more rugged 309 Road (see p.325).

Accommodation

Coromandel offers an unexpectedly wide range of **places to stay**.

Buffalo Lodge Buffalo Rd ☏ 07/866 8960, ⓦ www.buffalolodge.co.nz. Artist Evelyne's architecturally designed home perches high up in the bush north of town, with dizzying gulf views from its three guest rooms (all with private deck). Give two days' notice for superb three-course dinners using organic produce, much of it from Evelyne's garden ($95 a head). Closed May–Sept. Not suitable for children. ❼

Coromandel Colonial Cottages 1737 Rings Rd ☏ 07/866 8857, ⓦ www.corocottagesmotel.co.nz. Eight well-kept whitewashed wooden cottages (some sleeping up to six) neatly arranged in tranquil gardens 1.5km north of town with a big solar-heated swimming pool, a kids' playground and a BBQ area. One-bedroom cottages ❸, two-bedroom cottages ❹

Coromandel Town Motel, Holiday Park & Backpackers 636 Rings Rd ☏ 07/866 8830, ⓦ www.coromandelholidaypark.co.nz. Sprawling over 3.5 acres a 3min walk north of town, this all-purpose spot combines a spick-and-span hostel with campervan facilities and well-equipped motel units. All guests have access to the swimming pool and facilities including bike rental. Dorms $25, powered sites $12, units ❸

Jacaranda Lodge Tiki Rd (SH25) ☏ 07/866 8002, ⓦ www.jacarandalodge.co.nz. A modern house in farmland 3km south of town offering B&B in extremely comfortable rooms (most en suite), a stellar collection of NZ films on DVD, and delicious continental breakfasts including home-made muesli and juices and jams from the orchards outside. ❺

Lion's Den 126 Te Tiki St ☏ 07/866 8157, ⓦ www.lionsdenhostel.co.nz. Small, funky hostel beloved by backpackers for its cosy, colourful common areas, tropical gardens and sociable share-house-style atmosphere. Dorms $24, rooms ❶

Long Bay Motor Camp 3200 Long Bay Rd ☏ 07/866 8720, ⓔ lbmccoromandel @xtra.co.nz. Laidback beachfront campsite 3km west of town with great views, safe swimming and kayak rental ($10/hr). There are additional unpowered sites at the secluded Tucks Bay, less than 1km away through the bush or a 5min walk around the headland. Tent sites $14–20, powered sites $15–25, cabins ❷

Tui Lodge 60A Whangapoua Rd, just off SH25 ☏ 07/866 8237, ⓔ tuilodge@paradise.net.nz. Good-value hostel 10min walk south of town (and on the InterCity bus route), set In a big rambling house surrounded by an orchard and tranquil garden with a large chill-out gazebo. Perks include free laundry, tea and coffee, fruit (in season), BBQ, bikes, and a sauna ($5). Tent sites $15, dorms $25, rooms ❶, en-suite rooms ❷

YHA Tidewater Tourist Park 270 Tiki Rd ☏ 07/866 8888, ⓦ www.tidewater.co.nz. Ultra-comfortable motel and attached associate YHA, 200m from town near the harbour, with BBQ area and bike and kayak rental and spacious cabin-style units sleeping up to six people. Unpowered/powered sites $12/15, dorms $25, rooms ❶, motel units ❹–❼

The town and around

Centred on a cluster of buildings left from gold-mining days, the photogenic township spreads along the main road. From the south, SH25 becomes Tiki Road and then splits into two: Wharf Road skirts the harbour and Kapanga Road immediately enters the heart of the town, lined with shops and cafés. A couple of blocks further on, it becomes Rings Road, before heading northwards out of town as Colville Road.

The main attraction in the immediate vicinity is the ingenious **Driving Creek Railway and Potteries**, Driving Creek Road, 3.5km north of town (daily 10.15am & 2pm plus up to four additional trips per day during summer; 1hr return; $20; book ahead; ☏ 07/866 8703, ⓦ www.drivingcreekrailway.co.nz). Built mostly by hand, the country's only narrow-gauge hill railway is the brainchild of Barry Brickell, an eccentric local potter and rail enthusiast who wanted to access the clay-bearing hills. The track is only 381mm wide and climbs 120m over a distance of about 3km, rewarding you with spectacular views, extraordinary feats of engineering and quirky design; at the end of the line panoramas extend from a specially constructed wooden lodge, the Eyefull Tower. The journey starts and ends at the **workshops**, where you can see various types of **pottery**: stoneware, bricks and earthenware items, and sculptures made from terracotta. There's also a video about Brickell and a sculpture garden in a wildlife sanctuary designed to protect the local and visiting birdlife.

Around 1.5km north of town is the turn-off to the **Coromandel Goldfields Centre & Stamper Battery**, another 300m or so along Buffalo Road (check tour times with the i-SITE; 1hr guided tour; $10), where the peninsula's gold-mining history is explained. The fully functional 1899 stamper battery is also briefly operated to demonstrate the processing of gold.

Three kilometres west of town, along Wharf Road, lies the beach of **Long Bay** and a pleasing **walk** through a scenic reserve (40min loop). A hundred metres inside the *Long Bay Motor Camp* (opposite), a signpost marks the track, which climbs through bush to an ancient kauri tree and on to a small grove of younger ones. Beyond, at the junction with a gravel road, turn right to Tucks Bay to follow the coastal track back.

Eating and entertainment

Little Coromandel has a disproportionate number of places to **eat**. Particularly in summer, **entertainment** is easy to come by, with a fair bit of live music.

Self-caterers can pick up fresh seafood about 5km south of town at the **Coromandel Oyster Company**, which specializes in roadside sales of mussels, mussel chowder, oysters, crayfish and scallops; and **The Coromandel Smoking Company**, at 70 Tiki Rd, in town, which smokes its own shellfish and fish.

Admirals Arms 46 Wharf St ☎ 07/866 8020. The busiest pub in town, thanks to a regular roster of DJs and bands, bar meals, and an always-buzzing good-time vibe.

Driving Creek Café 180 Driving Creek Rd, 3.5km north of town ☎ 07/866 7066. Classic Coromandel: a laidback and welcoming daytime hideaway for great coffee, snacks and meals, with beautiful hill views from the veranda and garden and occasional acoustic music.

Lure Restaurant 46 Wharf St ☎ 07/866 8020. Upstairs from the *Admirals Arms*, this impressive Scottish-run newcomer specializes in steaks (and yes, whiskies), and makes the most of the fact that it's "the only restaurant in town with sea views" with tables on the wraparound veranda.

Peppertree 31 Kapanga Rd ☎ 07/866 8211. A popular bar and restaurant open from breakfast to dinner, with an all-day snack menu. Dine indoors – there's an open fire in winter – or in the garden. Licensed and BYO; book ahead on summer weekends.

Star and Garter 5 Kapanga Rd. Airy wood-lined 1873-built bar and covered beer garden in the centre of town popular with an urbane, mixed-age crowd for the full range of Monteith's brews and some palatable vino.

The Success Café & Restaurant 102 Kapanga Rd ☎ 07/866 7100. Relaxed daytime café with a cherry-tree-shaded courtyard. In the evenings it morphs into a bistro/bar serving fine Kiwi cuisine. Licensed & BYO.

Top Pub *Coromandel Hotel*, 611 Rings Rd ☎ 07/866 8760. An easy-going spot for evening meals – seafood, steak and pizzas – that also opens for lunch in summer.

North to Fletcher Bay and Port Charles

The landscape at the tip of the Coromandel is even more rugged than the rest of the peninsula, its green hills dropping to apparently endless beaches, clean blue sea and frothing white surf. Tourist authorities have dubbed the area the **Pohutukawa Cape**, and indeed the dirt roads are lined with ancient pohutukawa trees, blazing red from early November until January. With its dairy farms long deserted, it's virtually uninhabited and there are **few facilities**: replenish supplies in Coromandel. To help deter illegal **camping**, DOC has opened five waterside **campsites** around the northern peninsula. For the two weeks after Christmas the campsites are full, but for most of the rest of the year you'll have this unspoilt area to yourself.

From Coromandel town, the road is sealed to just beyond the tiny settlement of **COLVILLE**, a quiet valley comprising little more than a post office, petrol pump and a daytime café attached to the Colville General Store (☏07/866 6805), where you can stock up on provisions for the **Coromandel Walkway** (see below). **Horse trekking** ($30/1hr, $120/5hr) is offered at the sheep and cattle property, *Colville Farm*, Colville Road, 1.5km south of Colville (☏07/866 6820), which also has **accommodation** including camping (site $10), backpacker dorms in a cottage ($23), a couple of rustic bush lodges (❷) and two self-contained houses (❸/❹) with fabulous views.

Beyond Colville, the road turns to gravel, becoming narrower, rougher and dustier the further north you go: allow an hour to reach Fletcher Bay from Colville in fine weather. Three kilometres north of Colville the road splits, the right fork heading east over the hills to Stony Bay and the southern end of the Coromandel Walkway. The left fork runs 35km north to Port Jackson and Fletcher Bay at the very tip of the peninsula, following the coast all the way. An abandoned **granite wharf** marks the halfway spot. A couple of kilometres beyond, you'll find the diminutive and lovely *Fantail Bay Recreation Reserve* ($9), the first of the DOC **campsites**, which comes equipped with basic toilets and a water supply. The road then cuts inland, over hills rising straight from the shore, to reach **PORT JACKSON**, just two houses and a 1km sandy crescent of beach. It's safe for swimming and is backed by a grassy DOC reserve, where you can **camp** ($9) with views across to Great Barrier and Little Barrier islands. From here the road deteriorates on the final 6km to **FLETCHER BAY**, probably the best beach of all, safe for swimming, its eastern end marking the start of the **Coromandel Walkway**. The beach is backed by another DOC **campsite** ($9), with flush toilets and cold showers; the cosy *Fletcher Bay Backpackers* (☏07/866 6685; dorms $25) is set on a hill 400m from the beach.

Stony Bay, at the southern end of the Coromandel Walkway, is reached by two perilously narrow and twisty gravel roads – one, via Little Bay, across the Coromandel Range from just beyond Coromandel, the other traversing the Moehau Range from just beyond Colville. The latter runs 14km from Colville to the small holiday settlement of **Port Charles**, and a further 6km to Stony Bay, where there's another DOC campsite ($9).

The Coromandel Walkway

If you're after more exertion than swimming, fishing or lolling about on the beaches, you might consider hiking from Fletcher Bay to Stony Bay along the gentle **Coromandel Walkway** (11km one-way; 3hr). The walk starts at the far end of the beach in Fletcher Bay and heads off into a no-man's-land, first following gentle coastal hills that alternate between pasture and bush, before giving way to wilder terrain as you head further south past a series of tiny bays. Several hilltop **vantage points** provide spectacular vistas of the coast and Pacific Ocean beyond. **Stony Bay** is a sweep of pebbles with a bridge across an estuary that's safe for swimming. The DOC leaflet *Coromandel Recreation Information* briefly describes the walk and shows a map, but the path is clearly marked.

From Coromandel town, the most convenient transport is the Strongman Coachlines **shuttle bus** to Fletcher Bay ($95 return; complimentary tea, coffee and biscuits; ☏0800/668 175, ⊛www.coromandeldiscovery.co.nz), dropping off walkers and collecting them at Stony Bay before returning to Coromandel, as well as stopping off for photos. It also picks up from *Fletcher Bay Backpackers* (above).

Check on the state of the **road conditions** north of Port Jackson at the Colville General Store (opposite), or the DOC office in Coromandel town (p.321) before setting out, and allow plenty of time to take it steadily.

East to Whitianga

The drive east from Coromandel to Whitianga can be done in under an hour, but you could easily stretch it out longer on either of two highly **scenic roads** that cross the mountains: the more direct, snaking **309 Road** (33km, of which 14km are gravel; no public transport) spends much of its time in the bush, while the main (and mostly sealed) **SH25** climbs through forested hills before zigzagging down to the coast, 46km away.

Coromandel to Whitianga: the 309 Road

From the junction with SH25, 4km south of Coromandel, the 309 Road twists 5km east to **Waiau Waterworks** (daily 9am–6pm; $15; ☏07/866 7191, ⓦwww.thewaterworks.co.nz), a rambling garden carved from the bush and dotted with whimsical water-powered fountains, spouts and jets, most made from recycled materials; recent additions include animals for the kids to pat. Bring a picnic, and a swimsuit for a dip in the natural swimming hole.

One hundred metres past the waterworks, a rough access road on the left crosses a ford and climbs steeply for 3km to the trailhead for the track to **Castle Rock** (2km return; 40min–1hr 30min), the most easily accessible peak on the Coromandel Peninsula. The climb gets steeper towards the final tree-root claw onto the 521m summit of this old volcanic plug, but your efforts are rewarded by fantastic views to both coasts: the Whangapoua peninsula and the Mercury Islands on the east, and Coromandel and the Firth of Thames on the west.

A further 2.5km along the 309 Road, **Waiau Falls** crash over a tiered rock face into a pool below. What the falls lack in height they make up for by being right next to the road and offering a gorgeous spot to cool off. Half a kilometre on, a car park heralds the easy bush track to the towering, magnificent **Kauri Grove** (1km return; 30min) and **"Siamese" Kauri** a little further; one of the best places in the country to appreciate their immense size. The road tops out at the 306m saddle before descending towards Whitianga.

Coromandel to Whitianga: SH25

From Coromandel, **SH25** traverses lush native forest, passing a couple of isolated but pretty beachside settlements with campsites. About 14km from Coromandel is the 5km turn-off to the secluded village and white-sand beach of **WHANGAPOUA**. At the end of the road (along the right fork into town) is a pleasing walk to the sandy beach of **New Chums Bay** (accessible at low tide only; 4km return; 1hr): from the beach, cross the estuary and follow the bushline around the headland.

Continuing along SH25, about 30km from Coromandel, you descend to diminutive **KUAOTUNU**, beside a lovely white-sand beach. A clutch of quality **places to stay** here include the shady *Kuaotunu Camp Ground*, Bluff Road (☏07/866 5628, ⓦwww.kuaotunumotorcamp.co.nz; tent sites $18, cabins ❷, units ❹), with kayak rental; upmarket budget dorms and private rooms (some en suite) at the *Black Jack Lodge*, SH25 (☏07/866 2988, ⓦwww.black-jack.co.nz; dorms $30, rooms ❷/❸), which also rents bikes and kayaks; and the welcoming *Kuaotunu Bay*

Lodge B&B, SH25 (℡07/866 4396, ⓦwww.kuaotunubay.co.nz; ❾), with en-suite doubles. Kuaotunu has a daytime café, but facilities are otherwise limited, so plan ahead.

Nine kilometres north of Whitianga on SH25, Twin Oaks Riding Ranch is the base for scenic two-hour **horse treks** (daily 9.30am & 1.30pm, plus twilight trek at 6pm Dec–Feb; $50; book ahead ℡07/866 5388, ⓦwww.twinoaksridingranch .co.nz), with breathtaking views of Mercury Bay and the northern Coromandel; transport from Whitianga can be arranged. From here, SH25 continues through farmland to Whitianga and Mercury Bay.

Whitianga and around

Pretty **WHITIANGA** clusters where Whitianga Harbour meets the broad sweep of **Mercury Bay** – named by Captain Cook in 1769 when his party of scientists stopped to observe the planet passing across the face of the sun – along **Buffalo Beach**, a long sweep of surf-pounded white sand.

Whitianga makes a central base from which to make a series of half-day and **day-trips** to wonderfully secluded spots. Just across the narrow harbour mouth and strung along Mercury Bay's eastern shore are several lovely beaches, reached by a short passenger ferry ride to **Ferry Landing**, from where you can catch a **bus** or strike out along scenic coastal tracks; an area also served by **roads** branching off the southbound SH25, which loops around the deeply indented harbour. Two highlights are **Cathedral Cove**, a stunning geological formation, and **Hot Water Beach**, with natural hot-water springs that bubble from beneath its sand. Bordering part of the eastern shore, the protected waters of **Cathedral Cove Marine Reserve** offer superb snorkelling and scuba diving. **Boat trips** to the outer reaches of Mercury Bay and the volcanically formed **Mercury Islands**, 25km offshore, explore pristine waters and shoreline and search for bottlenose **dolphins** and **whales**.

Arrival, information and transport

SH25 runs through town, becoming Albert Street along the main shopping thoroughfare, then Buffalo Beach Road along the shore. Virtually everything happens on these streets or the Esplanade, which branches off to the wharf and ferry.

Buses drop off at accommodation around town and outside the **i-SITE visitor centre** at the corner of Albert Street and Blacksmith Lane (Boxing Day to Jan daily 8am–6pm; Feb to Christmas Eve Mon–Fri 9am–5pm Sat–Sun 9am–4pm; ℡07/866 5555, ⓦwww.whitianga.co.nz), where **internet access** is available. Daily Sunair (℡07/575 7799, ⓦwww.sunair.co.nz) **flights** ($120 one-way) to/from Auckland land at the **airport**, 4km south of the town centre, reached for around $15 with Paradise Cabs (℡07/869 5555).

The surrounding **beaches** are served by ferry and buses; the **passenger ferry** to Ferry Landing (daily: 7.30am–6.30pm, 7.30am–8.30pm & 9.30am–10.30pm, later in summer; $2 each way) leaves from the Esplanade roughly every ten minutes; the crossing takes just three minutes. From Boxing Day to early February up to four **buses** daily ($2) serve Cooks Beach, Hahei and Hot Water Beach from Ferry Landing. Otherwise, Go Kiwi (℡0800/446 549, ⓦwww.go-kiwi.co.nz) and Purangi Shuttles and Tours (℡07/866 3724) run **shuttle tours** from Ferry Landing (4–5hr; $45), with services connecting with buses to Auckland and Whitianga. For more flexibility, Cooks Beach Minibuses (℡0274/432 329) can customize half-day tours of the area ($75 for 1–3 people).

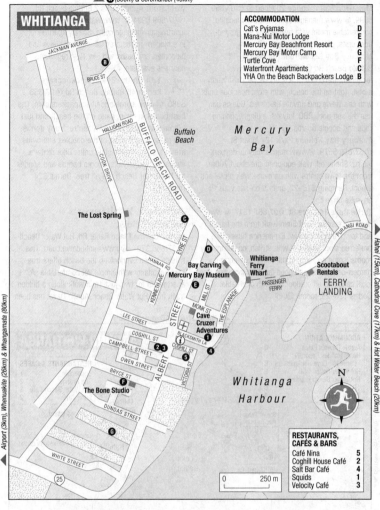

WHITIANGA

▲ Ⓐ (500m) & Coromandel (40km)

JACKMAN AVENUE

Ⓑ

BRUCE ST

HALLIGAN ROAD

BUFFALO BEACH ROAD

COOK DRIVE

Buffalo Beach

M e r c u r y B a y

Ⓒ

The Lost Spring

BYRE ST

HANNAN RD

Ⓓ

KENNETH AVE

Bay Carving
Mercury Bay Museum
Ⓔ

ALBERT STREET

MILL ST

MONK ST

Cave
Cruzer
Adventures

BLACKSMITH LA

LEE STREET

COGHILL ST

CAMPBELL STREET

Ⓐ Ⓑ ③

COGHILL ST

⑤

OWEN STREET

BRYCE ST

VICTORIA ST

④

The Bone Studio
Ⓕ

DUNDAS STREET

WHITE STREET

(25)

Ⓖ

*Whitianga
Harbour*

*Whitianga
Ferry
Wharf*

PASSENGER
FERRY

Scootabout
Rentals

FERRY
LANDING

PURANGI ROAD

N

ACCOMMODATION

Cat's Pyjamas	D
Mana-Nui Motor Lodge	E
Mercury Bay Beachfront Resort	A
Mercury Bay Motor Camp	G
Turtle Cove	F
Waterfront Apartments	C
YHA On the Beach Backpackers Lodge	B

**RESTAURANTS,
CAFÉS & BARS**

Café Nina	5
Coghill House Café	2
Salt Bar Café	4
Squids	1
Velocity Café	3

0 ———— 250 m

◀ Airport (3km), Whenuakite (26km) & Whangamata (80km)

▶ Hahei (15km), Cathedral Cove (17km) & Hot Water Beach (20km)

Ⓢ 5

Accommodation

As one of the Coromandel's main tourist centres, Whitianga has plenty of **accommodation**. Further out, beside the secluded **beaches** of Mercury Bay there's less choice, mostly at Hot Water Beach and Hahei; or there's Kuaotunu, 16km north (see p.325). In addition to advance bookings in summer, be prepared for **higher prices** than on the rest of the peninsula (especially anywhere with a sea view) and minimum stays in peak periods.

Central Whitianga

See map on p.327.

Cat's Pyjamas 12 Albert St ☏ 07/866 4663, Ⓦ www.cats-pyjamas.co.nz. Cosy central hostel a

2min walk from the town centre and beach with mural-painted common areas, a sunny courtyard and a spa, and, yes, a resident cat. Dorms $21, rooms ❶, en-suite rooms ❷

Mana-Nui Motor Lodge 20 Albert St ☎07/866 5599, ⓦwww.mananui.co.nz. Centrally located, comfortable motel with twelve fully s/c ground-floor units, plus a pool and spa. ④

Mercury Bay Beachfront Resort 111–113 Buffalo Beach Rd ☎07/866 5637, ⓦwww .beachfrontresort.co.nz. Luxurious yet kid-friendly motel, right on the beach, with eight spacious units with sea views and private balconies. Guests can use the spa pool, BBQ, kayaks, a dinghy, fishing rods and boogie boards. ⑤

Mercury Bay Holiday Park 121 Albert St ☎07/866 5579, ⓦwww.mercurybayholidaypark .co.nz. Sheltered, well-equipped site about 700m from the town centre with bargain kayak rental and a pool. Camping $18–22, units & on-site vans ②, en-suite units ④

Turtle Cove 14 Bryce St ☎07/867 1517, ⓦwww .turtlecove.co.nz. Just 5min walk from the beach and town, this is the Kiwi Experience buses' preferred stop, noisy but with stylish, contemporary rooms (some en suite) in the main building and garden-set cabins, and good facilities including free local calls and an outdoor bar with pool table. Dorms $26–29, rooms ②/③

Waterfront Apartments 2 Buffalo Beach Rd ☎07/869 5994, ⓦwww.waterfront apartmentswhitianga.co.nz. Snazzy apartments in a modern multistorey, all with sea views and balconies, spa baths and Sky TV. A registered nanny is available. ④–⑨

🏃 **YHA On the Beach Backpackers Lodge** 46 Buffalo Beach Rd ☎07/866 5380, ⓦwww.coromandelbackpackers.com. The best hostel in town, bang on the beach and just 10min walk from the town centre. Many dorms are en suite and most of the doubles and twins are in s/c apartment-style units. Bike rental's available, and kayaks, boogie boards and spades for Hot Water Beach are all free. Dorms $24, rooms ②

Around Whitianga
See map below.

Auntie Dawns Place Radar Rd, Hot Water Beach ☎07/866 3707, ⓦwww.auntiedawn.co.nz. This hillside house overlooking the beach offers true Kiwi hospitality with simple yet comfortable s/c apartments for two, just 1min walk along a hidden track from Hot Water Beach. Auntie Dawn has been

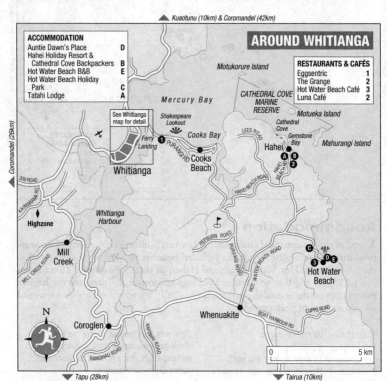

Kuaotunu (10km) & Coromandel (42km)

AROUND WHITIANGA

ACCOMMODATION
Auntie Dawn's Place   D
Hahei Holiday Resort &
  Cathedral Cove Backpackers   B
Hot Water Beach B&B   E
Hot Water Beach Holiday
  Park   C
Tatahi Lodge   A

RESTAURANTS & CAFÉS
Eggsentric   1
The Grange   2
Hot Water Beach Café   3
Luna Café   2

Motukorure Island
Mercury Bay
CATHEDRAL COVE MARINE RESERVE
Motueka Island
See Whitianga map for detail
Shakespeare Lookout
Cooks Bay
Ferry Landing
PURANGI RD
Cooks Beach
Whitianga
LEES ROAD
Cathedral Cove
Gemstone Bay
Hahei
HAHEI BEACH RD
Mahurangi Island
Coromandel (26km)
309 ROAD
KAIMARAMA RD
Whitianga Harbour
HAHEI BEACH ROAD
Highzone
Mill Creek
MILL CREEK ROAD
HEPBURN ROAD
PURANGI ROAD
HOT WATER BEACH ROAD
Hot Water Beach
N
Whenuakite
BOAT HARBOUR RD
CUPPS ROAD
KUAOTUNU ROAD
Coroglen
RANGIHAU ROAD
0   5 km

Tapu (28km)
Tairua (10km)

welcoming guests for decades, and Uncle Joe's home brew (which he regularly shares with them) is better than ever. ❹

Hahei Holiday Resort & Cathedral Cove Backpackers Harsant Ave, Hahei ☎07/866 3889, ⒲www.haheiholidays.co.nz. Located on half a kilometre of beachfront an easy walk from Cathedral Cove, close to restaurants and a shop, options range from dorms in a basic backpacker lodge to luxurious s/c beachfront villas. Powered sites from $17, dorms $28, cabins and on-site vans ❷, kitchen cabins ❷, comfy cabins ❸, cottages ❹ units ❺, deluxe villas ❻

Hot Water Beach B&B 48 Pye Place, Hot Water Beach ☎0800/146 889, ⒲www.hotwater bedandbreakfast.co.nz. Hospitable B&B sited close to the beach with great sea views. The two en-suite rooms have access to sunny decks and a spa pool, and there's even a full-sized snooker table. ❽

Hot Water Beach Holiday Park 790 Hot Water Beach Rd, Hot Water Beach ☎07/866 3116, ⒲www.hotwaterbeachholidaypark.com. Brand-new campsite with friendly owners and state-of-the-art amenities, including wi-fi in a sunny glassed-in guest lounge, an on-site shop serving fresh fish and chips. Unpowered/powered sites from $16, cabins & chalets ❹

Tatahi Lodge Grange Rd, Hahei ☎07/866 3992, ⒲www.tatahilodge.co.nz. Tranquilly set in bush and gardens footsteps from cafés and shops, with easy access to Cathedral Cove, offering s/c timber-lined units, airy backpacker accommodation, and a tucked-away cottage that sleeps five. Dorms $25, rooms ❸, units ❹, cottage ❻

The Town

Although most of the local highlights are in the surrounding area and offshore, in town you might consider a **bone-carving course**. Ian Thorne at The Bone Studio, 6b Bryce St ($100/day; book ahead on ☎07/866 2158, ⒲www.carving .co.nz), takes only a few prospective carvers at a time, gives just the right amount of guidance and encourages self-expression. Alternatively, Bay Carving, The Esplanade (☎07/866 4021, ⒲www.baycarving.com) offers shorter (2–3hr) carve-your-own courses (from $40), based on set patterns.

An old butter factory on the Esplanade houses the **Mercury Bay Museum** (daily 10am–4pm; $5), with displays on Kupe, the first Maori explorer to visit the area, the later arrival of Captain Cook and the subsequent families that settled.

If you simply want to unwind, head to the newly opened hot pools, **The Lost Spring**, 121a Cook Drive (daily 11am–10pm, seasonal hours may vary; Mon–Thurs $25/1hr 30min, Fri–Sun $25/1hr; ☎07/866 0456, ⒲www.thelostspring .co.nz). The complex is the brainchild of Alan Hopping, who – in an epic series of disasters and ultimate triumph – believed in, searched for, and finally found and tapped a local hot spring to create this extraordinary oasis. Ranging from 31°C to 40°C, the pools combine spa kitsch with recreated natural bush splendour. Book ahead to dine at the classy on-site **café**.

Ferry Landing and the beaches

The beaches across the estuary are accessible by car, by boat, or by passenger ferry (see p.326) to **Ferry Landing**, where buses continue on (see p.326). The far longer **road route** travels south along SH25, skirting the harbour and cutting inland at the signposted turn-off at Whenuakite, 26km from Whitianga. **Scooters** are available a few steps uphill from the wharf at Scootabout Rentals, 1137 Purangi Rd, Ferry Landing (car licence required; $50/2hr; book on ☎07/866 5168, ⒲www.scootabout.co.nz). **Services** at Ferry Landing are limited, so bring supplies if you're planning to stay more than a day.

From Ferry Landing, the first point of interest is **Shakespeare Lookout**, signposted 1.5km along the road and reached after another kilometre uphill to a car park. From the lookout – viewed from the sea it once supposedly resembled the Bard's profile – panoramic views stretch east to Cooks Beach and across Mercury Bay, west to Buffalo Beach, and north towards Mount Maungatawhiri.

▲ Cathedral Cove

Signposted tracks lead from the car park to the secluded Lonely Bay and onto the popular family holiday spot of **Cooks Beach** (2km one-way; 30min), also accessible from the main road 2km further east.

About 4km southeast of Cooks Beach along the main road lies the junction with Hahei Beach Road, leading 6km to the tiny beachside community of **HAHEI**, which has a store, some eateries and accommodation, and is the launch site for trips on the water (see opposite). The main attraction is **Cathedral Cove**, reached along a hilly **coastal track** that you can pick up at a car park at the western end of the village (45min to Cathedral Cove), or at Hahei Beach (1hr 30min to Cathedral Cove), a more strenuous undertaking. Although steep in places, the route affords great views out to sea. A few minutes' walk from the car park, a five-minute track descends to the rocky **Gemstone Bay**, where DOC has set up a stunning snorkelling course to show off the undersea wonders of the **Cathedral Cove Marine Reserve**. Most visitors continue to Cathedral Cove itself; striking white cliffs hug a long, sheltered and sandy beach bisected by an impressive rock arch that vaults over the strand like the nave of a great cathedral. A walk through the arch reveals a delightful beach on the other side, while offshore the remains of several arches are stranded at sea.

The area's other big draw, **Hot Water Beach**, is reached along Hot Water Beach Road (7km), which branches off the main road. The beach is split in two by a rocky outcrop that can create dangerous tidal rips (see box, p.73) – so you'll need to take care swimming – but also provides the setting for the **hot springs** bubbling beneath the sand that give the beach its name. Arrive two hours either side of **low tide** (less in rough weather; check tide times at Whitianga i-SITE or in the local paper), then dig a hole in the sand near the outcrop and relax in the hot water, refreshed by waves. You'll need a spade to dig your "spa": rent one from your accommodation, the Hot Water Beach store or *Hot Waves Café* (opposite) for $5, plus $20 deposit. For accommodation near the beach, see p.328.

Activities around Mercury Bay

The abundant waters of Mercury Bay make **dolphin and seal sightings** a common event on **boat trips from Whitianga**, along the coast to Cathedral Cove and Hot Water Beach, or out to the various island groups dotted off the coast, all of which take in the extraordinary array of volcanic features on the coastline and within the many sea caves. A variety of companies vie for your trade, with Cave Cruzer Adventures (℡0800/427 893, ⓦwww.cavecruzer.co.nz) and Whitianga Adventures (℡0800/806 060, ⓦwww.whitianga-adventures.co.nz) among the best of the bunch. Departing from the Whitianga Ferry Wharf, tours range from 75min ($50) to four hours ($125), depending on the distance travelled, features visited and wildlife spotted.

Boat trips **from Hahei** include the Hahei Explorer ($65; ℡07/866 3910, ⓦwww.haheiexplorer.co.nz), a rigid-hull inflatable that takes small groups on exhilarating hour-long sea-cave trips, visiting Cathedral Cove and an amazing blowhole, with an entertaining commentary. Alternatively, join one of the **guided sea-kayak trips** from Hahei run by Cathedral Cove Sea Kayaking (℡07/866 3877, ⓦwww.seakayaktours.co.nz), who take up to twenty people; its half-day trip ($85) visits Cathedral Cove and selected islands and caves.

Scuba diving and snorkelling in Cathedral Cove Marine Reserve can be arranged through Dive HQ, 7 Blacksmith Lane, Whitianga (℡07/867 1580, ⓦwww.divecoromandel.co.nz), or Cathedral Cove Dive (℡07/866 3955, ⓦwww.hahei.co.nz/diving), Hahei Beach Road, both of which pick up from Ferry Landing. Both companies also rent gear and run a variety of courses.

Eating and entertainment

The Esplanade, near Whitianga's marina, is the town's main **dining** hub. **Entertainment** options are surprisingly limited, but live **bands** occasionally play the *Whitianga Marina Hotel* (see *Salt Bar Café*) and *Eggcentric* in summer.

Whitianga

See map on p.327.

Café Nina 20 Victoria St. Made-to-order vegetarian and vegan food plus great coffee and home-made carrot cake at this friendly daytime café.

Coghill House Café 10 Coghill St. Relaxing spot for high-quality snacks (including great pies) or generous meals during the day. Ease yourself into the lounging area or outdoor seating.

Salt Bar Café *Whitianga Marina Hotel*, The Esplanade. Beachy-chic lunch and dinner café/bar with decking onto the marina. Known for its classical, à la carte evening mains (under $35) such as duck cooked two ways, though surprisingly few, if any, vegetarian options.

Squids 1 Blacksmith Lane. Cocktail/wine bar, good for a few drinks and good-value portions (evening mains under $35) like lamb's fry and bacon, salmon with roast *kumara* and steak with garlic mash.

Velocity Café 69 Albert St. Stylish daytime café, friendly with outdoor seating and a selection of salads, fritters and scrumptious warm, gooey chocolate brownies served with cream. Closed Sun.

Around Whitianga

See map on p.328.

Eggcentric 1047 Purangi Rd, Ferry Landing ℡07/866 0307. Quirky place with tables scattered among the sculpture-strewn gardens and in the colourful interior that comes alive in the evenings when live music vies for prominence with poetry readings, alongside simple but superb dishes like fresh scallops in rich macadamia sauce. Daily Jan, Tues–Sun Nov–Dec & Feb–April, closed May–Oct.

The Grange 7 Grange Rd, Hahei. Highly regarded licensed spot with a great range of Mercury Bay wines, open from brunch until dinner. Closed Mon & Tues.

Hot Waves Café Stylish café with airy dining areas and an attractive garden setting, serving light meals, snacks and excellent coffee. Daily 8.30am–4pm, to 8.30pm late Dec to Jan.

Luna Café 1 Grange Rd, Hahei. Cool little number where you can pick from a range of seafood and pizzas for lunch and dinner. Licensed and BYO. Closed Tues & Wed.

South to Whangamata

Brief glimpses of the coast along SH25 from Whitianga **south to Whangamata** often show overdevelopment, but unspoilt beaches can still be found, particularly the delightful **Opoutere**, a tiny harbourside retreat at the foot of a mountain with a wild sweep of beach.

Tairua

Small but with a residential density that would put some cities to shame, **TAIRUA** lies on SH25, 22km south of Hot Water Beach and 44km from Whitianga. Huddled between pine-forested hills and the estuary of the Tairua River, it's separated from the crashing Pacific breakers by two opposing and almost touching peninsulas. One is crowned by the impressive volcanic Mount Paku, the other covered by the suburban sprawl of ultra-exclusive **Pauanui**, accessible by a five-minute passenger **ferry** ride from Tairua (hourly 9am–5pm; Boxing Day to Jan 9am–midnight; $5 return, $3 one-way; check updated schedules with the information centre), or a 25km drive.

It's worth stopping briefly for a dip or to climb **Mount Paku** (10min ascent from car park, 30min ascent from beach) for spectacular views over the town, its estuary and beaches. Daily **buses** from Thames, Auckland and Whitianga drop off outside the **information centre**, 223 Main St (Mon–Fri 9am–5pm, Sat & Sun 9am–4pm; T07/864 7575, W www.tairua.info), which can book transport and accommodation.

Opoutere

Around 20km south of Tairua, a 5km side road leads to **Opoutere**, a gorgeous and usually deserted 4km-long white-sand **surf beach** backed by pines. The pohutukawa-fringed road hugs the shores of the Wharekawa Harbour where wetlands make good birdwatching spots, mud flats yield shellfish and the calm waters are good for kayaking.

From a signposted car park at the end of the sealed road, a footbridge leads to two paths, both reaching the beach in ten minutes or so: the **left-hand fork** runs straight through the forest to the beach; the **right-hand track** follows the estuary to the edge of a protected sandspit where endangered New Zealand **dotterels** breed from November to March. Opoutere Beach can have a strong undertow and there are no lifeguards, so don't swim. It's an unofficial nudist beach, but even if you're clothed, be sure to bring repellent to guard against sandflies. For a wider view over the estuary and the coastline, tackle the track up **Mount Maungarua-wahine** (2km return; 40–50min), climbing through gnarled pohutukawa and other native trees to the summit.

The summit track begins by the gate to the blissfully sited ⚑ **YHA Opoutere** (T07/865 9072, W www.yha.org.nz; dorms $24, rooms ❷), beside the estuary in a 1908 schoolhouse and surrounding wooden buildings amid mature bush alive with the calls of native birds, with free kayaks and the chance for nocturnal glowworm spotting.

About 700m towards the beach from the hostel (with direct beachfront access), also in a secluded wooded setting, sprawls the well-maintained **campsite**, *Opoutere Coastal Camping* (Labour Day weekend to April only; T07/865 9152, W www.opouterebeach.co.nz; sites $15, cabins ❸, chalets ❹ plus $15/extra person).

There's no regular **bus** service, but drop-offs can be arranged with Go Kiwi (p.326). Bring all your food as both places have only basic **provisions** for sale.

Whangamata and around

Stretching along SH25, the single-storey summer resort town of **WHANGA-MATA** is bounded on three sides by estuaries and the ocean, and on the fourth by bush-clad hills. **Ocean Beach**, a 4km-long crescent of white sand, curves from the harbour to the mouth of the **Otahu River**. The bar at the harbour end has an excellent break that's sought after by **surfers**.

The main drag, Port Road, runs straight through the small town centre, linking it with the highway. Along its length, **surf** shops, such as the Whangamata Surf Shop at no. 634 (℡07/865 8252; Mon–Fri 9am–5pm, daily in summer), rent boards and accessories and arrange surf lessons from around $50 per hour.

In the foothills of the Coromandel Range, on the edge of town, it's a pleasant **walk** to **Wentworth Falls** (10km return; 2hr) in the nearby Wentworth Valley. Take SH25 2km south to the signposted turn-off to Wentworth Valley Road and follow it 4km to the DOC campsite (see below) and the start of the track through regenerating bush past numerous small swimming holes. The route continues into the heart of the mountains, but most turn around at the two-leap falls, best viewed from a small deck.

Dedicated conservationist Doug Johansen (aka "Kiwi Dundee") runs a variety of day and multi-day **eco-tours** with Kiwi Dundee Adventures (book well in advance; ℡07/865 8809, Ⓦwww.kiwidundee.co.nz) incorporating wildlife experiences and paths off the beaten track. Full-day trips, including lunch, cost $230, including pick-ups from accommodation in Tairua, Pauanui and Whangamata.

Practicalities

Buses drop off next to the centrally located **i-SITE visitor centre**, 616 Port Rd (Mon–Sat 9am–5pm, Sun 9am–2pm; Sun until 5pm in summer; ℡07/865 8340, Ⓦwww.whangamatainfo.co.nz), which has **internet access**.

The pick of places to **stay** are *Brenton Lodge*, 2 Brenton Place (℡07/865 8400, Ⓦwww.brentonlodge.co.nz; B&B ⑨), a garden-set retreat with sea views on the edge of Whangamata, with two beautifully decorated cottages (each sleeping four) and two suites, as well as a sparkling swimming pool, spa, fresh flowers, home-made chocolates and delicious breakfasts; and *Southpacific Tourist Lodge*, on the corner of Port Road & Mayfair Avenue (℡07/865 9580, Ⓦwww.thesouthpacific.co.nz), an immaculate motel (some rooms with full kitchens) and budget lodge (dorms $24, rooms & units ③–⑦), which can organize watersports and gear and bike rental. Campers can head to the DOC **campsite** ($9) at the end of Wentworth Valley Road, 7km southwest of Whangamata, a lovely spot with streamside pitches, BBQs and coin-operated hot showers right by the start of the track to Wentworth Falls.

Considering its size and tourist credentials, there are surprisingly few standout places to **eat** in town. On Port Road ⚹ *Minato Sushi*, at no. 715, is a wonderful daytime sushi spot, with meticulously prepared fish; platters ($35) to share are a speciality. *Caffe Rossini*, at no. 646, is a contemporary daytime café serving a range of breakfasts, cakes and good coffee. *Nero's*, at no. 711 (Tues–Sat, plus Mon in summer), is an evening venue with the best pizzas in town, offering combinations such as salmon and shrimp or chicken and mango, while *Whanga Bar*, set back behind *Vibes Coffee Bar* (no. 638; closed Sun–Wed), is an intimate, licensed spot for breakfast, lunch or dinner, serving burgers, Thai fish cakes and steaks.

Entertainment spots are similarly limited, although there is a small **cinema**, at 708 Port Rd (℡07/865 6566).

Waihi, Waihi Beach and beyond

SH25 continues 30km south from Whangamata to **WAIHI**, where it meets SH2, which merits a quick stop to learn about its gold mining, both past and present.

Gold was first discovered here in a reef of quartz in 1878, but it wasn't until 1894 that a boom began with the first successful trials in extracting gold using cyanide solution. Workers flocked, but disputes over union and non-union labour ensued, and the violent Waihi Strike of 1912 helped galvanize the labour movement and led to the creation of the Labour Party. The strike is conjured up evocatively in a display in the **Waihi Arts Centre & Museum**, 54 Kenny St (Thurs–Sun 10am–3pm; $5).

The 1930s diesel engine of the **Goldfields Railway** runs scenic 6km rail trips year-round to Waikino in the nearby **Karangahake Gorge** from the wooden station at the end of Wrigley Street (trains daily 11am, 12.30pm & 2pm, returning from Waikino 45min later; 20min each way; $15 return; ⊤07/863 8640), providing spectacular views of the Ohinemuri River.

Although underground mining stopped in 1952, extraction was cranked up again in 1987 in the opencast but well-hidden **Martha Mine**. Recent exploration – and the prospect of discovering more accessible deposits – means it will continue to operate until at least 2012. **Guided tours** (Mon–Sat by arrangement; 2hr; $25; book ahead on ⊤07/863 9015, ⓌWwww.marthamine.co.nz) take you around the mine and processing areas.

A free interactive **exhibition** of current mining practice is set up in the basement of the town's central **information centre**, Upper Seddon Street (daily 9am–5pm; ⊤07/863 6715), which has **internet access**. If you want to **stay**, there's lovely homestay-style accommodation at *The Trout and Chicken*, 2km west of the centre on SH2 (⊤07/863 6964, ⓌWwww.troutandchicken .co.nz; B&B ❺), set in a blueberry orchard, which can arrange guided and independent trout fishing expeditions. The best place to **eat** in town is the *Waitete Orchard*, 31 Orchard Rd (restaurant open Thurs–Sat from 6pm, café open Tues–Sun 11am–4pm, extended hours in summer; ⊤07/863 8980), a café and ice-creamery with natural ice creams and fat-free sorbets made in the small on-site factory. By night it becomes a restaurant (mains $25.50–38) with a fine wine list.

Some 11km east of Waihi, off SH2, the golden-sand surf beach of **WAIHI BEACH**, stretching for over 9km, is one of the safest ocean beaches in the country. Although the area has something of a suburban feel, there are a couple of good campsites out this way, the best being ⚑ *Bowentown Beach Holiday Park*, Seaforth Road, Bowentown Beach (⊤07/863 5381, ⓌWwww.bowentown.co.nz; tents & powered sites from $17.50, cabins ❶, s/c cabins & units ❸–❹, motel studios & apartments ❹–❺) a secluded site right at the southern end of the beach with lots of water activities available as well as bike and kayak rental.

Waihi marks the southernmost extent of the Coromadel Peninsula. From here, the coast begins to curl eastwards into the Bay of Plenty, leaving the bush-clad mountains behind to take on a gentler, more open aspect, with rolling hills divided by tall evergreen shelter belts that protect the valuable kiwi fruit vines. In summer, numerous **roadside fruit stalls** spring up, selling ripe produce straight from the orchards, often at knockdown prices.

Some 20km after leaving Waihi you pass **KATIKATI**, an otherwise ordinary town but for the colourful and well-painted **murals** that have sprung up in the last couple of decades to catch passing traffic, many reflecting the heritage of the original Ulster settlers.

The western Bay of Plenty

The **western Bay of Plenty** centres on the prosperous port city of **Tauranga** ("safe anchorage") and its beachside neighbour, **Mount Maunganui**. This amorphous settlement, sprawled around the glittering tentacles of Tauranga Harbour, is one of the fastest-growing cities in the land. A combination of warm dry summers and mild winters initially attracted retirees, followed by telecommuters and home-based small businesses.

Both towns have a thriving **restaurant** and **bar** scene, and trips head out from Tauranga to **Tuhua (Mayor) Island**, while boats also run **harbour cruises**, full-day **sailing trips** or the chance to **swim with dolphins**. If the weather prohibits such activity head for the new **art gallery**, a fine achievement for a city with practically no cultural ambitions.

The area's charms are best appreciated if you've your own transport to access to the surrounding area, however. Beyond the city limits are opportunities to go **kayaking**, ride horses or engage in more peaceful pursuits like **wine tasting**, or picnicking beside the swimming holes at **McLaren Falls**.

Tauranga is in a major **kiwi fruit-picking region**, but be warned, it's tough and prickly work and generally you must commit yourself to a minimum of three weeks. The best time for picking is late April to mid-June, but pruning and pollen collection also takes place from mid-June to early September and again from the end of October to January. You're usually paid by the bin or by the kilo, so speed is of the essence. If this doesn't put you off, you'll find up-to-date information at the backpacker hostels, which will often help you to arrange work.

Tauranga and Mount Maunganui

Once you're through the protecting ring of suburbs, it's apparent that rampant development hasn't spoilt the narrow peninsula housing central **TAURANGA**, with several city parks and gardens backing a lively waterfront area. Progress hasn't been quite so kind to the neighbouring beach resort of **MOUNT MAUNGANUI**, huddled under the extinct volcanic cone of the same name – a landmark visible throughout the western Bay of Plenty. "The Mount", as hill and town are often known, was once an island but is connected to the mainland by a narrow neck of dune sand (a tombolo), covered with apartment blocks, shops, restaurants and houses. The Mount's saving grace is the 20km-long golden strand of Ocean Beach, wonderful for swimming and surfing. No surprise, then, that as with the Coromandel, the area is a big draw for Kiwi **holiday-makers** during summer, when Tauranga and Mount Maunganui can be overwhelming and accommodation hard to come by.

Arrival, information and transport

Daily Air New Zealand flights link Auckland and Wellington with the **airport**, which lies midway between Tauranga and Mount Maunganui (around 3km from each). Bayhopper **buses** (p.337) connect it with both towns every thirty minutes ($2.50); a taxi to either costs around $25. InterCity **long-distance buses** stop at the i-SITE visitor centres in both towns: the Tauranga **i-SITE**, at

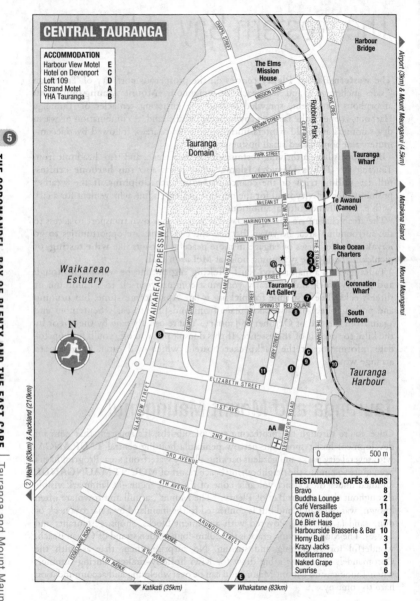

CENTRAL TAURANGA

ACCOMMODATION
Harbour View Motel E
Hotel on Devonport C
Loft 109 D
Strand Motel A
YHA Tauranga B

RESTAURANTS, CAFÉS & BARS
Bravo 8
Buddha Lounge 2
Café Versailles 11
Crown & Badger 4
De Bier Haus 7
Harbourside Brasserie & Bar 10
Horny Bull 3
Krazy Jacks 1
Mediterraneo 9
Naked Grape 5
Sunrise 6

the corner of Willow and Wharf streets (Mon–Fri 8.30am–5.30pm, Sat & Sun 9am–5pm; ☎07/578 8103, ⓦ www.bayplentynz.com), and the Mount Maunganui **i-SITE**, on Salisbury Avenue, just off Maunganui Road (daily 9am–5pm; ☎07/575 5099, ⓦ www.bayplentynz.com). There's a **DOC office**, 253 Chadwick Rd, Greerton (Mon–Fri 8am–4.30pm; ☎07/578 7677), 6km south of central Tauranga.

THE COROMANDEL, BAY OF PLENTY AND THE EAST CAPE | Tauranga and Mount Maunganui

336

Local transport

Daily **Bayhopper** (℡0800/422 9287, Ⓦwww.baybus.co.nz) bus services, cover most places in the immediate vicinity, including a half-hourly Tauranga–Mount Maunganui run ($6 all-day ticket sold on board). Apart from a handful of evening services from Monday to Friday, these dry up at around 6pm; after that you'll have to shell out for a taxi (up to $30 between Tauranga and Mount Maunganui), either from the **taxi** stand in Hamilton Street (between the Strand and Willow St) in Tauranga or by calling one of the radio-cab companies: Citicabs (℡07/571 8333) or Tauranga Mount Taxis (℡07/578 6086). From just after Christmas until Easter, Kiwi Coast Cruises' *Spirit of Tauranga* (℡07/579 1325, Ⓦwww.kiwicoastcruises .co.nz) runs a ferry service at 9am (two hourly until 5pm from Tauranga, 5.20pm from Mount Manganui; $8), to the Mount and back.

Accommodation

Tauranga has numerous **hostels** and **motels** within walking distance of the centre, and plenty more out in the suburbs. A plethora of motels line 15th Avenue, some offering good deals at slack times of year. Much of the accommodation at **Mount Manganui** is geared towards long-staying Kiwi holiday-makers, but you'll also find short-stay apartments and motels, as well as a couple of good **hostels**.

Tauranga

Ambassador Motor Inn 9 15th Ave ℡07/578 5665, Ⓦwww.ambassador-motorinn.co.nz. See map, p.343. A 5min drive from the city centre, near the estuary, this has popular, well-equipped budget units and more luxurious options. There's a heated pool, some rooms have a spa bath, and some river views. ❹

Avenue 11 Motel 26 11th Ave ℡07/577 1881, Ⓦwww.avenue11.co.nz. See map, p.343. Great-value boutique motel in a central but quiet location overlooking a small park and part of the harbour, with four spacious, sumptuously decorated units (with good views). Extra touches include personalized service, bathrobes and a spa. ❸

Bell Lodge 39 Bell St, off Waihi Rd (take Otumoetai exit off SH2) ℡07/578 6344, Ⓦwww.bell-lodge.co.nz. See map, p.343. Clean, modern and comfortable hostel with mostly en-suite rooms and units that's well set up for job seekers, particularly those after long, hourly paid contracts. It's in a peaceful spot 4km from the centre, with free pick-up and a free daily shuttle to Mount Maunganui on request. Tent sites $20, dorms $25, en-suite rooms ❷, motel-style units ❸

Harbour View Motel 7 5th Ave East ℡07/578 8621, Ⓦwww.harbourviewmotel.co.nz. Quiet and homey, just 10min walk from town and a stone's throw from the bay, with spa and free kayaks, and the chance for fishing excursions. Ideal for families. ❸

Harbourside City Backpackers 105 The Strand ℡07/579 4066, Ⓦwww.backpacktauranga.co.nz.

Large hostel bang in the middle of the action. The waterfront views and tranquil atmosphere of the rooftop garden make up for the basic rooms and noise on Friday and Saturday nights (soundproofing from neighbouring bars and rooms at the rear of the building also help). Dorms $28, rooms ❷

Hotel on Devonport 72 Devonport Rd ℡07/578 2668, Ⓦwww.hotelondevonport .net.nz. Sleek new boutique hotel with 38 ambiently lit rooms with king-size beds, angular neutral-toned decor and black-and-white photos on the walls. Higher priced rooms have city and/or harbour views. ❺–❽

Just the Ducks Nuts 6 Vale St ℡07/576 1366, Ⓦwww.justtheducksnuts.co.nz. See map, p.343. A small, friendly hostel 1.5km from the city centre up a very steep driveway, popular with workers, with great views of the harbour and the Mount and free pick-ups. Dorms $24, rooms ❶

Loft 109 109 Devonport Rd ℡07/579 5638, Ⓦwww.loft109.co.nz. Little yet central, friendly hostel in a trendy townhouse-style building with a roof deck and nautical decor. Dorms $25, rooms ❷

Silver Birch Family Holiday Park 101 Turret Rd ℡07/578 4603, Ⓦwww.silverbirch.co.nz. See map, p.343. Fairly central campsite right on the river's edge with a family atmosphere, playground and thermal pools. Unpowered/powered sites from $25/27, cabins ❶, en-suite cabins and units ❷

Strand Motel Corner of The Strand & McLean St ℡07/578 5807, Ⓦwww.strandmotel.co.nz. Budget, central and near the waterfront, but on a fairly noisy corner. You get sea views from the decks of most of the fully equipped units. ❸

YHA Tauranga 171 Elizabeth St ☎07/578 5064, ⓦwww.yha.org.nz. Well-equipped, modern and welcoming hostel in rambling, secluded grounds 5min walk from the centre, with BBQ, volleyball, a putting circuit and mini bushwalking trail. Tent sites $18, dorms $28, rooms ❷

Mount Maunganui

The following places are marked on the map on p.339.

Mount Backpackers 87 Maunganui Rd ☎07/575 0860, ⓦwww.mountbackpackers.co.nz. Small hostel right in the thick of things – close to restaurants, bars and the beach – offering job-seeking help and a full-service internet café. Dorms $26, rooms ❷

Mount Maunganui Beachside Holiday Park 1 Adams Ave ☎07/575 4471, ⓦwww.mount beachside.co.nz. A sizeable, terraced, well-equipped campsite very close to the beach in a pleasant spot beside the hot saltwater pools, right at the foot of the Mount. Camping from $40/site.

Pacific Coast Lodge Backpackers 432 Maunganui Rd ☎0800/666 622, ⓦwww .pacificcoastlodge.co.nz. Vast hostel with colourful murals on the walls and good facilities (spacious dorms, large kitchen and BBQ area), although it's about a 25min walk from the restaurants and the fashionable end of the beach. Dorms $24, rooms ❸

Tauranga city centre

You can easily spend half a day checking out the art gallery, strolling along the waterfront or lingering in the shops, restaurants and bars in Tauranga's compact **city centre**, concentrated between Tauranga Harbour and Waikareao Estuary.

Opened after a determined fifteen-year campaign to give the city a contemporary cultural attraction, the **Tauranga Art Gallery** occupies an old bank on the corner of Wharf and Willow streets, 108 Willow St (daily 10am–4.30pm, donation; ☎07/578 7933, ⓦwww.artgallery.org.nz). The building has been described by local wags as a nuclear bunker or the armadillo. Inside it's a clean-lined series of display spaces over two floors housing some excellent national and international travelling exhibitions – contact the i-SITE to find out what's on.

Next stop is the ornately carved traditional **war canoe**, *Te Awanui*, in a shelter on the corner of Dive Crescent and McLean Street; still used on ceremonial occasions on the harbour. About one block up, entered from Cliff Street, **Robbins Park** (dawn–dusk; free), is a swathe of green adorned by a rose garden and begonia house with fine views of Mount Maunganui.

At the northern end of town, on Mission Street, **The Elms Mission House** (Wed, Sat & Sun 2–4pm, and by appointment on ☎07/577 9772; $5) is one of the country's oldest homes, built from kauri between 1835 and 1847 by an early missionary, Archdeacon A.N. Brown, who tended the wounded of both sides during the **Battle of Gate Pa** (see box below). The house has maintained its original form complete with dark-wood interior and a dining table at which Brown entertained several British officers on the eve of the Battle of Gate Pa, little suspecting that over the next few days he would bury them all.

The Battle of Gate Pa

In 1864 the tiny community of Tauranga became the scene of the **Battle of Gate Pa**, one of the most decisive engagements of the **New Zealand Wars**. In January the government sent troops to build two redoubts, hoping to prevent supplies and reinforcements from reaching the followers of the Maori King (see p.218), who were fighting in the Waikato. Most of the local Ngaiterangi hurried back from the Waikato and challenged the soldiers from a *pa* they quickly built near an entrance to the mission land, which became known as Gate Pa. In April, government troops surrounded the *pa* in what was New Zealand's only naval blockade, and pounded it with artillery. Despite this, the British lost about a third of their assault force and at nightfall the Ngaiterangi slipped through the British lines to fight again in the Waikato.

Mount Maunganui

The eastern end of the 3.5km-long Tauranga Harbour Bridge is 3km from the heart of **Mount Maunganui**, reached through an industrial estate. Things improve at the northern tip where, despite the surrounding colonization by condos and apartments, the 232m Mount (Mauao in Maori) rises above the golden **beach** – an unbroken sweep stretching more than 20km east to Papamoa (p.342) and beyond. Habitually sun-kissed in summer, the Mount has a reputation as a party town, especially at New Year. The beach itself is within easy reach of good restaurants and bars where everyone gravitates for sundowners, and perfect for a day or two of volleyball, swimming and surfing.

Mount Manganui has several outfits offering **surfing lessons**, including Hibiscus (2hr group/private beginner lesson $80/120, two-/five-day surf clinic $150/350; ☏07/575 3792, ⓦwww.surfschool .co.nz), which also rents gear. Adventure Bay of Plenty (☏0800/238 267, ⓦwww .adventurebop.co.nz) runs culturally focused **sea-kayaking** trips (from $85/2hr) and **mountain-biking tours** (from $80/2hr).

A mostly level **walking track** loops around the base of the mountain (3km; 45min), offering a sea and harbour outlook from under the shade of ancient pohutukawas. The base track links with a **hike to the summit** (2km one-way; 1hr), tough going towards the top but well worth the effort for views of Matakana Island and along the coast. Both tracks start at the northern end of the beach, right by the outdoor, chlorinated **Hot Saltwater Pools**, Adams Avenue (Mon–Sat 6am–10pm; Sun 8am–10pm; public pool $9.50, private spa $15/30min; ☏07/575 0868).

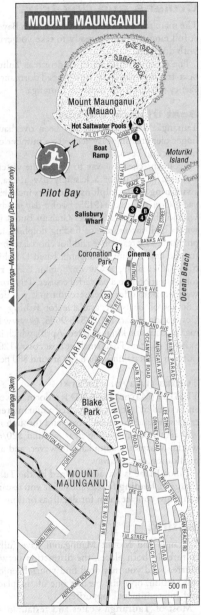

ACCOMMODATION		RESTAURANTS & BARS	
Mount Backpackers	**B**	Astrolabe	3
Mount Manganui		Mount Mellick	5
Beachside Holiday Park	**A**	Providores Urban Food Store	2
Pacific Coast Lodge	**C**	Sidetrack Café Pacifica	1
		Volantis	4

Cruises and day-trips

The main reason to come to the western Bay of Plenty is to get out **on the water**. A full range of boats is ready to take you cruising, fishing, sailing and swimming with dolphins.

The ecotourism-geared island retreat Tuhua (Mayor) is a prime Bay of Plenty boat-trip destination, a cone-shaped dormant volcano, protruding from the Bay of Plenty 40km off the coast of Tauranga.

Boat trips on the bay

Tauranga Wharf has recently been overhauled, with a barge converted into a finger pier creating easy access to a number of trips and a ferry service plying the harbour and beyond.

About the cheapest way to get on the water is with Kiwi Coast Cruises' *Spirit of Tauranga* (p.337). For a leisurely day at sea, including the bonus of seeing and **swimming with dolphins**, operators include Butler's Swim with Dolphins on the yacht *Gemini Galaxsea* ($135; book a day in advance ℡0508/288 537, ⓦwww.swim withdolphins.co.nz). Skipper Graham Butler is a good-natured sea dog and greenie with a high success rate of finding dolphins, and sometimes whales. Snorkel gear is provided, as is tea, coffee and hot chocolate, but you'll need to bring your own food for the day. Mount Maunganui-based Dolphin Seafaris, 90 Maunganui Rd ($120; ℡0800/326 8747, ⓦwww.nzdolphin.com), run half-day trips in the morning and some afternoons in a powerful cruiser. Trips run most of the year, but only in decent weather. Both offer a free second trip if you don't see any dolphins.

Scores of boats are available for **fishing charters**; try Blue Ocean Charters, Coronation Wharf (℡07/578 9685, ⓦwww.blueocean.co.nz) for game fishing for marlin, tuna and kingfish (Dec–April), which involves chartering the boat, or join an existing charter. Their smallest boat costs $1200 a day but if you go out for reef fish (snapper and tarakihi) you'll pay around $80 per person, with an extra $25 for tackle.

Tuhua (Mayor) Island

TUHUA (Mayor) ISLAND is a dormant volcano, its crater virtually overgrown and a third of its coast designated a **marine reserve**. There are some great **walking tracks** around the island's base and through its centre, and boats coming out here will rent out snorkelling gear (around $20/day) so you can explore the aquatic world. **Wasps** are abundant, however, and anyone allergic to stings should pack medication or stay away.

Tuhua Island is privately owned by the Tuhua Trust Board, and day visitors are charged a **landing fee** ($5 plus $6 if you're camping). Blue Ocean Charters (above) run trips; contact them for details as options vary.

Eating

Tauranga and Mount Maunganui have fully embraced contemporary café/bar culture. In both places, the distinction between **eating and drinking places** is blurred, and you may well find yourself enjoying a drink at one of the places in this section, or a fine meal at one of the places listed under "Drinking, nightlife and entertainment", opposite.

Most of **Tauranga**'s cafés and restaurants are in the centre – notably along Devonport Road and the Strand and the streets running back from it. **Mount Maunganui** doesn't have Tauranga's selection or culinary hotspots, but there are plenty of places on the half-dozen blocks of Maunganui Road that make up the centre, or on the waterfront strip by the mount in the lee of apartment buildings.

Fresh produce is sold at the Saturday-morning **farmers' market** from 8am, at the Compass Community Village, 17th Avenue West in Tauranga.

Tauranga

Bravo Red Square ℡07/578 4700. Cool, minimalist café and restaurant that spills onto the pedestrianized Red Square for breakfast, gourmet snacks or dinner (mains $20–30). Closed evenings Sun & Mon.

Café Versailles 107 Grey St ℡07/571 1480. Award-winning traditional French restaurant serving a wonderful range of Gallic fare from snails to bouillabaisse, taking in several inspired standards along the way, all fabulously presented with a glass of home-grown Cabernet.

De Bier Haus 109 The Strand ℡07/928 0833. Justifiably popular Belgian brasserie serving not only great beers but delicious bar snacks with which to wash them down (beer-battered frites with aoli, or soft German-style "Brezels" with garlic butter, balsamic vinegar and olive oil), as well as hearty mains (most $20–30) and incredible desserts like white chocolate cheesecake with maple and walnut.

Harbourside Brasserie & Bar Under the railway bridge at the southern end of the Strand ℡07/571 0520. Set on stilts over the harbour, with a covered deck, great views, bare boards and intriguing artwork, serving a short, stellar menu of globally inspired lunches and dinners plus weekend breakfast. Book ahead for a table on the deck or just drop in for a drink.

Mediterraneo Café and Restaurant (aka The Med) 60 Devonport Rd. Popular daytime café with great breakfasts, such as three-grain porridge, tempting counter food, and specials (written on a giant wall-mounted roll of brown paper) like pan-seared fish on grilled asparagus with toasted brioche (dishes $9–19) and some outdoor seating.

Sunrise 10 Wharf St. Intimate, friendly, funky and very popular licensed café where good breakfast standards vie with tasty chickpea and lentil burgers, salads and home-made cakes and slices. Closed Sun.

Mount Maunganui

Astrolabe 82 Maunganui Rd. Large, popular diner/drinking hole, with a beachy vibe and lively evening crowds at the weekend. Open for brunch, lunch (mains $12–23) and dinner (mains $16–37), with salads and pasta, char-grilled steak and fish, and a huge range of beers.

Providores Urban Food Store 19a Pacific Ave. Gourmet deli-style café serving inventive, often organic breakfasts and lunches (dishes $4.50–18) chalked on a blackboard (no menus) along the lines of creamy mushrooms on sourdough for breakfast, and house-smoked salmon and *kumara* cakes for lunch.

Sidetrack Café Marine Parade, under the Twin Towers. A great place to go for breakfast or morning coffee – when you can gaze across the beach to the ocean in the warming early sun – or for lunch (mains $14–18), whose quality and accommodating service sets it apart from its neighbours.

Volantis 105 Maunganui Rd. One of the best spots on the strip for a casual coffee, or snacks along the lines of gourmet burgers and panini, with several vegetarian options. Liqueur shots accompany some of the highly extravagant sundaes. Dinner mains $17.50–29.50. Licensed & BYO.

Drinking, nightlife and entertainment

Neither town pumps in the off season but Tauranga currently holds the clubbing baton, with summer revelry continuing into the wee hours along the Strand. In both Tauranga and Mount Maunganui, most restaurants (see above) double as **bars**.

Films screen at Cinema 8 on Elizabeth Street in Tauranga (infoline ℡07/577 0800) and the Rialto Cinema, Goddard Centre, 21 Devonport St (infoline ℡07/577 0445). Screening times are listed in *Bay of Plenty Times*, the best source of entertainment **listings**.

Clubs and bars

Buddha Lounge 61b The Strand. This small but cool venue with a balcony reverberates to soul, house and drum 'n' bass till 3am, with alluring sofas upstairs. Can be a bit of a squeeze on a Friday or Saturday night.

Crown & Badger Corner of The Strand & Wharf St. Lively (sometimes frenetic) English pub with a good range of beers and great-value pub-style meals.

Horny Bull 67 The Strand. Texan-style food keeps energy levels up at this jolly and often-packed bar.

Krazy Jacks 47 The Strand. Hugely fun restaurant and bar with regular acoustic evenings, electric jam nights, live local talent and above-average covers bands.

Mount Mellick 317 Maunganui Rd. Popular and friendly Irish bar with well-priced food and an exciting calendar of events including courtyard cricket, jam nights, live music, quiz nights and big-screen sports.
Naked Grape 97 The Strand. Hip wine bar with claret-coloured walls that makes a refreshing change from the pub-style places along the Strand, and also serves classy but surprisingly inexpensive breakfasts (cinnamon pancakes et al), lunches and dinners (mains $28.50–32).

Around Tauranga

In the hinterland, the suburb of **Bethlehem** is home to the Art Deco-style **tasting rooms** at Mills Reef, 143 Moffat Rd (daily 10am–5pm; Ⓦwww.millsreef.co.nz), with the chance to sample its excellent Chardonnay, Rieslings, Sauvignons and Merlots for free (and, of course, buy them), or dine at its idyllic **restaurant** (bookings Ⓣ07/576 8800; mains $23.50–33). There's live music outdoors every summer Sunday lunchtime.

The fertile countryside is backed by the angular peaks of the Kaimai-Mamaku Forest Park. Rivers, cascading down the slopes and across the coastal plain, periodically fire up **McLaren Falls**, signposted 11km south of Tauranga off SH29. Most summer Sundays, the falls become the scene of frenetic activity as hundreds of rafters and kayakers congregate to run the Grade IV–V rapids of the Wairoa River. Pretty much every day of the summer, meanwhile, locals flock here to soak in a series of shallow pools hewn out of the bedrock. A few minutes' rock-hopping should secure you a pool to yourself: bring a picnic and sunscreen.

At the coast, Mount Maunganui's Ocean Beach stretches 20km east to the **Papamoa Beach**, which is great for surfing and swimming away from the glitz of the Mount. The spotless *Papamoa Beach Top 10 Holiday Park*, off SH2 in the domain at the eastern end of Papamoa Beach Road (Ⓣ07/572 0816, Ⓦwww.papamoabeach.co.nz; camping $18, cabins ❷, units ❹, villas ❻) is right on the beachfront. Next door, the nautically decorated ⅃ᵏ *Bluebiyou* café/bar/restaurant, serves freshly prepared lunches as well as evening meals (mains $23–33) and weekend brunch; try for a seat on the covered deck overlooking the waves.

Papamoa is also home to the world's only purpose-built **blokart speedway track** at Blokart Heaven, 176 Parton Rd (from $20/15min; Ⓣ07 542 4033, Ⓦwww.blokartheaven.co.nz): think go-kart with a sail (tuition available). With a fair wind you can get up to 60km; naturally it's weather-dependent, so no wind equals no fun.

The eastern Bay of Plenty

Moving away from Tauranga toward the **eastern Bay of Plenty**, along the Pacific Coast Highway, the urban influence wanes, the pace slows and the landscape becomes more rural, with orchards and kiwi fruit vines gradually giving way to sheep country. You'll also find a gradual change in the racial mix, for the eastern Bay of Plenty is mostly Maori country; appropriate since some of the first **Maori** to reach New Zealand arrived here in their great *waka* (war canoes). In fact **Whakatane** is sometimes known as the birthplace of Aotearoa, as the Polynesian

5

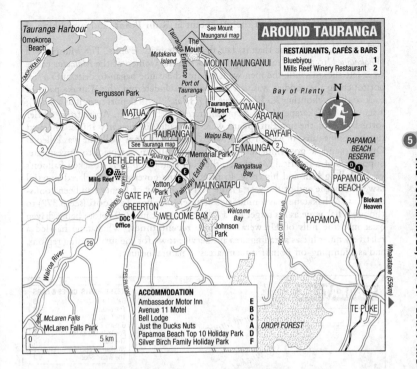

navigator **Toi te Huatahi** first landed here. The region's largest town, Whakatane makes a great base for forays to volcanic **White Island** or the bird reserve of **Whale Island**. Further east, **Opotiki** is the gateway to the East Cape and to Gisborne, as well as trips on the remote and scenic **Motu River**.

The westernmost town, **Te Puke**, is New Zealand's kiwi fruit capital, as evidenced by **Kiwi360**, 6km east of the town centre (daily: summer 9am–4pm; winter 10am–3pm; 45min guided tours $20; ℡0800/549 4360, ⓦwww .kiwi360.com). Graced by a surreal **giant kiwi fruit** slice, this massive **orchard and processing plant** operates as a kind of horticultural theme park, running informative tours as well as a souvenir emporium and a café serving kiwi fruit muffins, kiwi fruit salads, kiwi fruit wine and liqueur and full meals. **Whakatane**, 66km further along SH2, remains the largest town, and makes a great base for forays to volcanic **White Island** or the bird reserve of **Whale Island**. Further east, **Opotiki** is the gateway to the East Cape and to Gisborne, as well as providing access to interesting walks in the hills to the south and to trips on the remote and scenic **Motu River**.

Whakatane and around

Prettily set between cliffs and a river estuary, the 15,000-strong town of **WHAKATANE** sprawls across flat farmland around the last convulsions of the Whakatane River. Off the coast, you can **swim with dolphins**, or visit the bird sanctuary of **Whale Island** and volcanic **White Island**, which billows plumes of steam into the sky. Back on land, there are walks along the spine of hills above the town and to the viewpoint at **Kohi Point**, and sunbathing at **Ohope Beach**.

The area has had more than its fair share of dramatic events. The **Maori** word *Whakatane* ("to act as a man") originated when the women of the *Mataatua* canoe were left aboard while the men went ashore; the canoe began to drift out to sea, but touching the paddles was *tapu* for women. Undeterred, the Wairaka paddled back to shore, shouting *Ka Whakatane Au i Ah au* ("I will deport myself as a man"); a statue at Whakatane Heads commemorates her heroic act. Apart from a brief sortie by Cook, the first **Europeans** were flax traders in the early 1800s. The next turning point came in March 1865, when missionary **Carl Völkner** was killed at Opotiki, and a government agent, **James Falloon**, arrived to investigate. Supporters of a fanatical Maori sect, the Hau Hau (see p.349), attacked Falloon's vessel, killing him and his crew. In response, the government declared **martial law**, and by the end of the year a large part of the Bay of Plenty had been confiscated and Whakatane was a military settlement, leading **Te Kooti** (see p.372) to choose Whakatane as his target for a full-scale attack in 1869 before being driven back into the hills of Urewera. In more **recent times**, Whakatane has led a relatively quiet life as a trading area and service town for the surrounding regions, and as a jumping-off point for many areas of natural beauty.

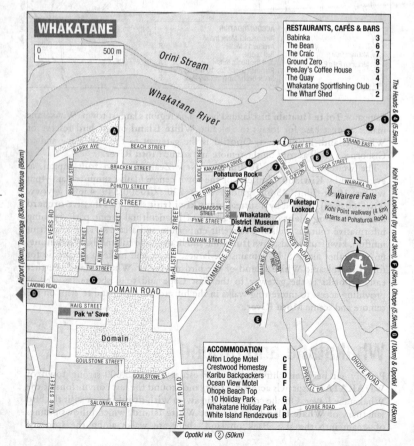

Arrival, information and transport

Long-distance **buses** running along SH2 between Rotorua and Gisborne stop twice daily in each direction outside the **i-SITE visitor centre**, on the corner of Quay Street and Kakahoroa Drive (Mon–Fri 8am–5pm, Sat & Sun 10am–4pm; ☎07/306 2030, ⓦwww.whakatane.com), which is well stocked with DOC leaflets for the local area and offers free **internet access**. The **post office** is at the corner of Commerce Street and the Strand. Flights from Auckland and Wellington arrive at Whakatane **airport**, about 10km west of the centre, connected by the Dial-A-Cab shuttle (around $25; ☎0800/308 0222). The Bayhopper **bus** service (☎0800/422 9287, ⓦwww.baybus.co.nz) serves Tauranga and Mount Maunganui (Mon–Sat), Ohope (Mon–Sat), Opotiki (Mon & Wed) and Kawerau (Tues & Fri).

Accommodation

Whakatane and nearby Ohope Beach both have a sizeable stock of **accommodation**, with an emphasis on mid-range motels.

Alton Lodge Motel 76 Domain Rd ☎0800/425 866, ⓦwww.altonlodge.co.nz. Comfortable motel with eleven spacious kitchen units and a heated indoor pool. ❹

Crestwood Homestay 2 Crestwood Rise ☎07/308 7554, ⓦwww.crestwood-homestay .co.nz. Attractive, friendly B&B in a quiet hilltop setting with scenic views, 20min walk from the town centre. Evening meals ($40 including wine) are available by arrangement. Owner Janet is a radio operator for the Whakatane Coastguard and is happy to show guests around its HQ. ❺

Karibu Backpackers 13 Landing Rd ☎07/307 8276, ⓦwww.karibubackpackers.co.nz. Suburban house converted into a big, well-maintained and welcoming hostel 1.5km from the town centre, with an attractive garden for camping and off-street parking, plus free bikes and free pick-up from the bus stop. Tent sites $14, dorms $23, rooms ❶

Ocean View Motel West End, Ohope Beach ☎07/312 5665, ⓦwww.oceanviewmotel.co.nz. Ultra-relaxing motel at the western end of the beach, with safe swimming, bushwalks and free

bikes, kayaks, boogie boards, surfboards and laundry facilities. All of its s/c units have sea views. Rooms ❸

Ohope Beach Top 10 Holiday Park Harbour Rd, Ohope, 10km east of Whakatane ☎07/312 4460, ⓦwww.ohopebeach.co.nz. Upmarket holiday park right behind Ohope Beach at the eastern end of Ohope, with a pool complex including a waterslide and a free summertime kids' programme. Camping $18, cabins ❷, s/c units ❸, motel units ❹, luxury apartments ❻

Whakatane Holiday Park McGarvey Rd ☎07/308 8694, ⓦwww.whakataneholidaypark .co.nz. A sheltered campsite 10min walk from the Strand with a summertime outdoor pool and basic but well-maintained facilities. Camping $15, cabins ❷, s/c units ❸

White Island Rendezvous 15 Strand East ☎0800/242 299, ⓦwww.whiteisland.co.nz. Spotless, Mediterranean-style multi-level motel opposite the wharf. Some rooms have spa baths, and all are equipped with Sky TV and microwave, with a popular on-site café (*PeeJay's Coffee House*; p.348). S/c units ❺

The Town

Driving into Whakatane, Commerce Street hugs cliffs that were once lapped by the sea. The junction with the Strand is effectively the town centre, marked by Whakatane's defining feature, a large rock outcrop called **Pohaturoa** ("long rock"). The place is sacred to Maori and the small park surrounding the rock contains carved benches and a black marble monument to Te Hurinui Apanui, a great chief who propounded the virtues of peace and is mourned by Pakeha and Maori alike. The site was once a shrine where Maori rites were performed, and the seed that grew into the karaka trees at the rock's base is said to have arrived on the *Mataatua* canoe. From here, it's a three-minute walk (along Canning Place, then Clifton Road and Toroa Street) to the base of **Wairere Falls**, from where

Whale Island

Whale Island (Motohora), 10km offshore from Whakatane, is a DOC-controlled haven where considerable efforts were made decades ago to eradicate goats and rats. Native bush is rapidly returning and the island has become a bird reserve and safe environment for saddlebacks, grey-faced petrels, sooty shearwaters, little blue penguins, dotterels and oystercatchers, as well as three species of lizard – geckos and speckled and copper skinks – and the reptilian tuatara; occasional visits are made by the North Island kaka and falcon, as well as fur seals.

   Access to the island itself is only by a limited number of **guided tours** (Jan & Feb only; contact Whakatane's i-SITE for details and reservations), but several operators sail around it, such as Pee Jay (opposite), which runs nature cruises (around mid-Dec to mid-Feb; 4hr; $75) and White Island Tours (4hr; $60; see opposite).

White Island

Many people ignore Whale Island in favour of the more obvious and spectacular attractions of **White Island** (Whaakari), named by Cook for its permanent shroud of mist and steam. Over twice the size of Whale Island, White Island lies 50km offshore, sometimes a rough ride. Neither this nor its seething vulcanism deters visitors, who flock to appreciate its desolate, other-worldly landscape, with billowing towers of gas, steam and ash spewing from a crater lake sixty metres below sea level. They marvel at the smaller fumaroles surrounded by bright yellow and white crystal deposits that re-form in new and bizarre shapes each day. The crystal-clear and abundant waters around the island make this one of the best **dive** spots in New Zealand.

you can rejoin The Strand and stroll a 1km section of the 4km **river walk** to the heads – a lovely late-afternoon stroll (also reached by car along Muriwai Drive) that passes two replicas of the *Mataatua waka* in a reserve, and a sprightly bronze statue of Wairaka on a rock.

   Back in town, the **Whakatane District Museum and Gallery** (Mon–Fri 10am–4.30pm, Sat & Sun 11am–3pm; donation; Ⓦwww.whakatanemuseum .org.nz) lies on Boon Street. One room is packed with well-conceived displays on geological, Maori and European history: the house collection is rich and varied with over 30,000 photographs and an important collection of Maori *taonga* (treasures) from the local *iwi*, tracing their descent from the *Mataatua* canoe. The others host travelling exhibitions.

Activities

There are several interesting **walks** in the area, all detailed in a free map or the more detailed *Discover the Walks Around Whakatane* booklet ($2) from the i-SITE. Easily the best is to Kohi Point Scenic Reserve (5.5km one-way; 4hr), combining part of the Whakatane Town Centre Walk with the Nga Tapuwae o Toi ("Sacred Footsteps of Toi") Walkway, which traverses the domain of the great chieftain Toi and continues to Kohi Point, giving panoramic views of Whakatane, Whale and White islands and Te Urewera National Park.

   You can zoom around on the local **Rangitaiki River** with Kiwi Jetboat Tours (Ⓣ0800/800 538, Ⓦwww.kiwijetboattours.com), run by an ex-world champion jetboat racer who will take you from the Matahina Dam, 25km south of Whakatane, to the beautiful Aniwhenua Falls over a number of modest whitewater

Whaakari embodies the ongoing clash between the Indo-Australian Plate and the Pacific Plate that has been driven beneath it for the last two million years. This resulted in the upward thrust of super-heated rock through the ocean floor, creating a massive **volcanic** structure. **Sulphur**, for use in fertilizer manufacture, was sporadically mined on the island from the 1880s but catastrophic eruptions, landslides and economic misfortune plagued the enterprise. The island was abandoned in 1934, and these days it is home only to 60,000 grey-faced **petrels** and 10,000 **gannets**.

From Whakatane, excellent **guided boat trips** to White Island in big boats are run by White Island Tours, also known as Pee Jay, 15 The Strand East (daily; 6hr; $175; including lunch; ☏0800/733 529, ⊛www.whiteisland.co.nz). Their two-hour tour of the island takes in the site of a 1923 sulphur-processing factory, partially submerged by a landslide, the remains being gradually eaten away by the high sulphur content of the atmosphere, and the tour progresses to an open-sided crater. Here, amid pools of bubbling mud and pillars of smoke and steam, you get the chance to study sulphur deposits and stand in the wind-driven clouds (with a gas mask on). It pays to book at least a couple of days in advance.

With plenty of cash and clement weather, you can also visit White Island by **helicopter** with Vulcan Helicopters (2hr 30min; $455/person, minimum 3 people, including a walking tour of the island; ☏0800/804 354, ⊛www.vulcanheli.co.nz), or fly over it ($175/person, minimum 3 people).

To get below the surface, contact the excellent Dive White Island, at Sportsworld, 186 The Strand (☏0800/348 394, ⊛www.divewhite.co.nz), for **dive trips** (with 2 dives; $325 including gear) in the waters off White Island, where visibility is commonly around 20m, or MV *Boston Seafire* wreck dives ($200 including gear).

sections ($85). There are also innumerable **fishing** guides, mostly working on a charter basis from the local marina; the i-SITE has a list.

The rich waters around Whakatane give abundant opportunities for **whale and dolphin watching** and **dolphin swimming** from December to March – anybody offering to take you outside those months is either wildly optimistic or less than scrupulous. The best trip from Whakatane is run by Dive Works Charters, 86 The Strand (3–4hr; 2 daily; $150; ☏07/308 5896, ⊛www .whaleislandtours.co.nz).

Ohope

Seven kilometres east of Whakatane, the tiny settlement of **OHOPE** extends along the beach in a thin ribbon to the entrance of **Ohiwa Harbour**. Ohiwa ("a place of watchfulness") is the site of a natural shellfishery for pipi and cockles, and a place of numerous *pa* sites, signifying the importance of a convenient and renewable food source to the Maori way of life.

Otherwise, this is very much a surf-and-sand beach resort, though it makes a pleasant base from which to explore Whakatane and its surroundings.

Eating, drinking and nightlife

Whakatane has a few decent spots for espressos and a couple of appealing waterside **restaurants** that are also good for an evening tipple. Pick up cheap supplies of fresh **seafood**, including mussels, oysters and smoked fish at the Ohiwa Oyster Farm (daily 9am–8pm), a shack beside Ohiwa Harbour, 1km south of Ohope beach on the road to Opotiki, with a couple of picnic tables at the water's edge.

▲ Whakatane

Entertainment is essentially limited to the **Cinema 5** multiplex, 99 The Strand (☏07/308 7623) and three bars within the *Whakatane Hotel*: *The Boiler Room* (often hosting live bands), *Spot 81* (with lounge-style acts), and *The Craic* (below).

Babinka Kakahoroa Drive ☏07/307 0009. Very popular, specially built restaurant and bar with big windows, a marine theme and a versatile menu for brunch, lunch and dinner, including a selection of curries (all under $25). Book ahead for dinner.

🏃 **The Bean** 72 Strand East. Laidback, groovy daytime café and coffee roastery, so you can be sure of a good hit; alternatively opt for an organic juice or one of the speciality teas. Mon–Fri 8.30am–4pm, Sat 9.30am–1.30pm, closed Sun.

The Craic *Whakatane Hotel*, corner of the Strand & George St. Atmospheric Irish bar furnished in mellow dark wood to include booths, serving tasty fare. Most of the town's nightlife happens here, with live bands on Friday night and some Sunday afternoons, and dancing in the bar.

Ground Zero 163 The Strand. Large, stylish daytime café with outdoor seating, specializing in quiches, filled rolls, home-made pies and muffins.

PeeJay's Coffee House Inside the *White Island Rendezvous Motel*, p000. Fine espresso helps wash down daytime snacks and light meals. Early opening hours (6.30am) make it a good spot for breakfast before a morning boat trip.

The Quay 22 Pohutukawa Ave, Ohope ☏07/312 4675. Ohope's best place to eat is this hip yet cosy licensed café which has a tempting range of cakes and cookies, gourmet fish and chips, and moderately priced evening meals from Thurs–Sun (book ahead).

Whakatane Sportfishing Club Strand East. Spacious bar with huge windows overlooking the boats and river, great for cheap drinks, good-value bar meals at lunch and dinner, and live music in the summer on most Friday evenings. It's a private club but visitors can sign in.

The Wharf Shed Strand East ☏07/308 5698. All-day café-cum-restaurant, with a mellow riverside setting in a converted wooden butter store. Good for a late breakfast, lunch or watching the sun set over the water while tucking into seafood (including delicious sesame-crusted fish), lamb or venison. Book ahead for dinner.

Opotiki

The small settlement of **OPOTIKI**, 46km east of Whakatane (via the Ohope Road), is the easternmost town in the Bay of Plenty and an effective gateway to the East Cape, making a useful stopping-off point for stocking up on supplies and petrol before heading on.

From Opotiki, SH2 strikes inland to **Gisborne**, while SH35 meanders around the perimeter of **the East Cape**, never straying far from its rugged and windswept coastline.

Arrival, information and accommodation

Buses between Whakatane and Gisborne stop outside the *Hot Bread Shop Café* (p.350), as does the Bayhopper local bus (p.345), which heads to Whakatane and Tauranga. Information on the town and the East Cape is available at the combined **i-SITE visitor centre** and **DOC office**, on the corner of St John and Elliott streets (Mon–Fri 9am–4.30pm, Sat & Sun 9am–1pm; ☎07/315 3031, ⓦwww .opotikinz.com), which has **internet** access and can book **accommodation**. The pick of Opotiki's hostels is the laidback beachside hangout, *Opotiki Backpackers Beach House*, 7 Appleton Rd, off SH2, 5km west of Opotiki (☎07/315 5117, ⓦwww.opotikibeachhouse.co.nz; dorms $28, rooms ❷; closed July & Aug), a laidback beachside backpackers with free use of kayaks and bodyboards. Good campsites in the area include the little-known gem, *Ohiwa Holiday Park*, Ohiwa Harbour Road, off SH2 (☎07/315 4741, ⓦwww.ohiwaholidays.co.nz; camping $16, cabins ❷, units & flats ❸, park motels ❹), right on the beach, with safe swimming, kayaks for rent and a "jumping pillow" – massively popular with kids (and a few adults), though note there's a two-night minimum stay on weekends (longer in peak times).

The Town

Opotiki has few sights of interest to delay your departure for the wilds of the East Cape or the more citified pursuits of Gisborne, but it is surrounded by some lush countryside and beaches. All the significant historic buildings cluster around the junction of Church and Elliot streets, including the **Opotiki Museum**, 123 Church St (Mon–Fri 10am–4pm, Sat 10am–2pm; $5), which occupies the whole block between Elliot and Kelly streets, including a nostalgic 1870s-established grocery and hardware store. Opposite, the innocent-looking white clapboard **St Stephen's Church** was once the scene of a notorious murder, for it was here, in March 1865, that local missionary **Carl Völkner** was

The Hau Hau

Zealous missionaries encouraged many Maori to abandon their belief structure in favour of **Christianity** but, as land disputes with settlers escalated, the Maori increasingly perceived the missionaries as agents for land-hungry Europeans.

When **war** broke out and the recently converted Maori suffered defeats, they felt betrayed not only by the Crown but also by their newly acquired god, and some formed the revivalist **Hau Hau** movement, based on the Old Testament. Dedicated to routing the interlopers, disciples danced around *nui* **poles**, chanting for Pakeha to leave the country. The name is derived from the **battle cry** of the warriors, who flung themselves at their enemies with their right arms raised to protect them from bullets, believing that true faith prevented them from being shot. The movement began in 1862 and by 1865, having capitalized on widespread Maori unrest, there was a *nui* pole in most villages of any size from Wellington to the Waikato. The Hau Hau were some of the most feared **warriors** and involved in the bloodiest and bitterest battles, but the movement began to fade after their **leader** and founder, Te Ua Haumene, was captured in 1866. Some of the sect's ideas were **revitalized** when the infamous rebel **Te Kooti** (see p.372) based parts of his **Ringatu** movement on Hau Hau doctrine.

Wilderness rafting on the Motu River

Some of the best **wilderness rafting** trips in New Zealand are on the Grade III–IV **Motu River**, hidden deep in the mountain terrain of the remote Raukumara Ranges, with long stretches of white water plunging through gorges and valleys to the Bay of Plenty coast. In 1981, after a protracted campaign against hydro-dam builders, the Motu became New Zealand's first designated "wild and scenic" river. Access by 4WD, helicopter and jetboat makes one- and two-day trips possible, but to capture the essence of this remote region you should consider one of the longer trips in which you'll see no sign of civilization for three days – a magical and eerie experience.

Rotorua-based Wet 'n' Wild Rafting (℡0800/462 723, ⊛www.wetnwildrafting .co.nz) starts trips from Opotiki. Trips range from two days (with helicopter access, $925), to the full five-day adventure (also $925 but without helicopter access) from the headwaters to the sea. In all cases transport and gourmet meals are provided; you can bring your own tent and sleeping bag or rent them from Wet 'n' Wild.

allegedly killed by prophet Kereopa Te Rau from the Hau Hau sect (see box, p.349). The case is far from clear-cut: it appears that Völkner had written many letters to Governor Grey espousing the land-grabbing ambitions of settlers, and local Maori claim Völkner was justly executed. Settlers used the story as propaganda, fuelling intermittent skirmishes over the next three years. The Op Shop next to the church (Mon–Fri 9am–3pm, Sat 9am–1pm) has a key for you to nip in and see the gorgeous *tukutuku* panels around the altar. Völkner's gravestone is to one side of the entrance.

A welcome retreat into the bush is given by the small and unspoiled **Opotiki (Hukutaia) Domain** (daily dawn–dusk; free), full of native flora, including a puriri tree thought to date from 500 BC and once used as a burial tree by local Maori. The bush also contains a good lookout over the Waioeka Valley and a series of short yet interesting rainforest tracks. To get here, head south from the centre of town on Church Street as far as the Waioweka River Bridge, cross it and bear left along Woodlands Road for 7km.

Activities

South of town on the **Waioeka River**, New Zealand's Best Spot (℡07/315 5553, ⊛www.newzealandsbestspot.co.nz) runs gentle **kayaking** trips down a beautiful stretch ($40/1hr, $60/2hr). On the **Motu River**, which surges through the hills to the east of Opotiki and meets the sea 45km to the northeast, there are superb backcountry **rafting trips** (see box above), and scenic flat-water **jetboating** on the lower 50km with Motu River Jet Boat Tours (℡07/325 2735, ⊛www.motujet.co.nz; $85/1hr; approximately Nov to Easter, min 2 people).

Eating

The pick of the daytime **cafés** are the *Hot Bread Shop Café*, on the corner of Bridge and St John streets, for good coffee, yummy cakes and pastries, brunch and snacks, and the excellent *Two Fish*, 102 Church St (closed Sun), with a wide range of gourmet home-made food. Traditional, if slightly pricey, **meals** are served day and evening at *Honey's* in the *Opotiki Hotel*, on the corner of Church and Kelly streets. In fine weather go for the wonderful **fish and chips** from *Ocean Seafoods Fish and Chips* at 88 Church St, to eat in or take away.

The inland route to Gisborne

From Opotiki, **SH2** strikes out south to **Gisborne**, 137km away. It's one of New Zealand's great scenic drives, dotted with tiny settlements, weaving up and down steep hills cloaked in bush and winding gingerly along the lower echelons of the plunging **Waioeka Gorge**. Following the river for 30km, the route becomes increasingly narrow and steep before emerging onto rolling pastureland on the Gisborne side and dropping to plains. From there it runs straight as an arrow through orchards, vineyards and sheep farms to Gisborne (see p.362).

The only part of the route worth breaking your journey for (or exploring from Opotiki) is the first 72km stretch to Matawai, along which a number of interesting **walks** branch off either side of the road. Ten scenic tracks through forest, ranging from fifteen minutes to ten hours one-way, are described in the DOC leaflet *Walks in Waioeka and Urutawa*, available at Opotiki i-SITE.

All that wilderness means that you need to be sufficiently prepared. The **only petrol** is at Matawai and (off the main road to the left as you're heading south) at Te Karaka, but opening hours for both are limited, so be sure to fill up in Opotiki or Gisborne.

The East Cape

Jutting into the South Pacific northeast of Opotiki and Gisborne, the little-visited **East Cape** (also known as the East Coast or Eastland) is an unspoilt backwater that's a reminder of how New Zealand once was. Between Opotiki and Gisborne, the Pacific Coast Highway (SH35) runs 330 scenic kilometres around the peninsula, hugging the rugged coastline much of the way and providing mesmerizing sea views on a fine day.

As soon as you enter the region you'll notice a change of pace, epitomized by the occasional sight of a lone horseback rider clopping along the road. **Maori** make up a significant percentage of the population – over eighty percent of land tenure here is in Maori hands, and locals are welcoming, particularly once you take time to talk to them and adjust to the cape's slower pace.

The **coast** is very much the focus here but there are also **hiking** opportunities, and just about everywhere you go there will be someone happy to take you **horse trekking**, either along the beach or into the bush. In general, the **towns**, such as they are, don't have much to recommend them and you're better off planning to stay in between towns.

Inland, the inhospitable **Waiapu Mountains** run through the area, encompassing the northeastern Raukumara Range and the typical native flora of the Raukumara Forest Park. The isolated and rugged peaks of Hikurangi, Whanokao, Aroangi, Wharekia and Tatai provide a spectacular backdrop to the coastal scenery, but are only accessible through **Maori land** and **permission** must be sought (further information is available at the DOC offices in Gisborne and Opotiki).

Services, including food stores (which are small and close at around 5pm), and petrol pumps (some of which run out from time to time) are relatively few and far between, so plan ahead.

According to legend, a great *ariki* (leader) from the East Cape was drowned by rival tribesmen, and his youngest daughter swore vengeance: when she gave birth to a son called **Tuwhakairiora**, she hoped he would make good her promise. As a young man, Tuwhakairiora travelled and encountered a young woman named **Ruataupare**; she took him to her father, who happened to be the local chief. A thunderstorm broke, signalling to the people that they had an important visitor among them, and Tuwhakairiora was allowed to marry Ruataupare and live in Te Araroa. When he called upon all the *hapu* of the area to gather and avenge the death of his grandfather, many warriors travelled to Whareponga and sacked the *pa* there. Tuwhakairiora became renowned as a warrior, dominating the area from **Tolaga Bay** to Cape Runaway, and all Maori families in the region today trace their descent from him.

Ruataupare, meanwhile, grew jealous of her husband's influence. While their children were growing up, she constantly heard them referred to as the offspring of the great Tuwhakairiora, yet her name was barely mentioned. She returned to her own *iwi* in **Tokomaru Bay**, where she summoned all the warriors and started a war against rival *iwi*; victorious, Ruataupare became chieftainess of Tokomaru Bay.

Another legend that has shaped this wild land is one of rivalry between two students – **Paoa**, who excelled at navigation, and **Rongokaka**, who was renowned for travelling at great speed by means of giant strides. At the time, a beautiful maiden, Muriwhenua, lived in Hauraki and many set off to claim her for their bride. Paoa set off early but his rival took only one step and was ahead of him; this continued up the coast, with Rongokaka leaving huge footprints as he went – his imprint in the rock at Matakaoa Point, at the northern end of Hicks Bay, is the most clearly distinguishable. En route, they created the **Waiapu Mountains**: Paoa, flummoxed by Rongokaka's pace, set a snare for his rival at Tokomaru Bay, lashing the crown of a giant totara tree to a hill; recognizing the trap, Rongokaka cut it loose. The force with which the tree sprang upright caused such vibration that Mount Hikurangi partly disintegrated, forming the other mountain peaks. Finally, Rongokaka stepped across the Bay of Plenty and up to Hauraki, where he claimed his maiden.

Campsites are the staple accommodation, and although free beachside camping is prohibited, a number of designated **"freedom camping"** sites operate from late September to early April. For these you'll need a permit ($10/two nights, $25/ten, $60/28, including one council rubbish bag per day for collection from the campsite). In general you're required to carry a chemical toilet; if you don't have one, check with the i-SITEs in Gisborne and Opotiki, which issue the permits, to discuss alternatives. **Hostels** are scattered along the route, with the occasional motel and B&B, but upmarket accommodation is almost non-existent. Apart from a couple of steak-and-chips places attached to pubs and motels, there isn't anywhere on the East Cape that you'd describe as a real **restaurant**, so you need to be prepared for self-catering or accept a diet of toasted sandwiches and fish and chips.

Opotiki to Waihau Bay

The road from Opotiki to **Waihau Bay** covers 103km, generally sticking close to the sea, but frequently twisting up over steep bluffs before dropping back down to desolate beaches heavy with driftwood. The logs have been washed down from the Raukumara Range by the numerous rivers that reach the sea here, often forming delightful freshwater swimming holes. This is probably the section of the East Cape where you'll want to spend most of your time. You'll find family campsites every few kilometres, none of them far from the beach, with a wealth of aquatic activities on offer – from boogie boards and canoes to half-day fishing and dive trips – along with horseriding and bikes to search out your own secluded cove.

Omaio and Te Kaha

Leaving Opotiki swimming beaches are initially scarce and, once past Tirohanga, the only place you're likely to want to **stay** is the hillside *Oariki Coastal Cottage*, Maraenui, almost 40km east of Opotiki (T07/325 2678; ④), a self-catering cottage for four with a log fire, surrounded by native bush overlooking the sea, with jetboating, fishing and diving opportunities (dependent upon numbers). Call ahead for directions and to arrange optional organic meals.

Continuing, you soon cross the Motu River and after 11km reach **OMAIO**, where there is a store with a petrol pump, and one of the few places in these parts where you can **camp** for free: turn sharp left onto Omaio Marae Road by the store. A further 13km on, **TE KAHA** spreads 7km along the highway in a beautiful crescent shape, with spectacular headlands and a deserted, driftwood-strewn beach that's safe for swimming. It starts by the super-relaxing *Te Kaha Homestead Lodge* (T07/325 2194, E paora@hotmail.com; dorms $30, rooms ③), a **hostel** at the water's edge with an outdoor spa, access to the beach, and opportunities for kayaking and fishing. You can self-cater or pre-arrange breakfast and dinner. A little further along the main road in an incongruous high-rise, the *Te Kaha Beach Resort* (T07/325 2830, W www.tekahabeachresort.co.nz; apartments ⑤) has streamlined apartment-style **accommodation** with full state-of-the-art kitchens, as well as a pool, and a decent **restaurant** and **bar** with 180-degree ocean views. Striking inland just after the hotel, along Loop Road to Copenhagen Road, you'll come to *Tui Lodge* (T07/325 2922, W www.tuilodge.co.nz; B&B ⑤), a secluded and spacious B&B with en-suite rooms and dinner for $35.

Whanarua Bay and Maraehako Bay

Te Kaha is about the closest land to White Island, 50km offshore, which remains in view as you continue to the communities of **WHANARUA BAY** and **MARAEHAKO BAY**, 16km further on, which make another ideal opportunity to stop and enjoy the beaches and rugged countryside. At Whanarua Bay, the peaceful *Pacific Coast Macadamias* (daily at least 10am–3pm, longer in summer; closed May–Sept), set back from the main road, has a simple but superb **café** amid the nut orchards where you can feast on delicious home-made macadamia products like muffins and ice cream as well as great coffee, and a small **shop**.

Signposted off the main road, Maraehako Bay is home to the paradisiacal *Maraehako Bay Retreat* (T07/325 2648, W www.maraehako.co.nz; tent sites $20, dorms $28, rooms ①), a beautiful, rustic waterside **hostel** in a rocky cove with a safe, private swimming beach, free kayak rental and the chance for fishing, diving, whale and dolphin watching and horse-trekking expeditions. Run by the same welcoming Maori family, the beachside *Maraehako Camping Ground* (T07/325 2047; camping $12) at the far end of Maraehako Bay, has toilets and solar-heated showers, with plenty of space to pitch up.

Waihau Bay

Still hugging the coast, SH35 winds 13km to **Ruakokere**, where a picture-perfect, white clapboard Anglican church stands on a promontory framed by the blue ocean. From here it's five minutes' drive to **WAIHAU BAY**, another sweeping crescent of sand and grass that's ideal for swimming, surfing and kayaking. The abundance of shellfish and flatfish here might encourage you to sling a line from the wharf beside the store, post office and petrol station. There are a handful of places to **stay**, including the *Waihau Bay Holiday Park* (☎07/325 3844; on-site vans $70, cabins ❸, units ❹), 3km beyond the wharf, which has its own store and contemporary daytime **café**; and *Oceanside Apartments* (☎07/325 3699, ⓦwww .waihaubay.co.nz; ❹), whose suites sleep four to seven. Continental breakfasts are included; you can order a cooked breakfast for $15, or dinner for $35. Diving, fishing trips and kayak rental can be arranged, or surfcast for snapper and kahawai off the beach out front.

Cape Runaway to Ruatoria

Beyond Waihau Bay the highway continues close to the water for a few more kilometres before veering inland at **Cape Runaway**, the East Cape's northernmost point. For the next 125km you hardly see the coast again, with the significant exceptions of **Hicks Bay**, **Te Araroa** and **East Cape**.

If you have your own transport, a worthwhile side trip is the mercurial road to **Lottin Point**, where a beautiful little bay encourages paddling and loafing. If you really fall in love with the place you could **stay** at the *Lottin Point Motel* (☎06/864 4455; ❸), which has well-equipped self-contained rooms as well as a **restaurant** and **bar**.

Hicks Bay and Onepoto Bay

The small coastal township of **HICKS BAY** (Wharekahika), 44km from Waihau Bay, shelters between headlands and coastal rock bluffs almost halfway along SH35 and makes a good base from which to visit the East Cape Lighthouse and enjoy water-based activities. Nearby are the secluded sands of **Onepoto Bay**, a safe swimming beach also popular for kayaking and surfing. Hicks Bay was named after Lieutenant Zachariah Hicks, who sighted it on Cook's *Endeavour* expedition. There are numerous *pa* sites in the area, in varying states of repair, some of which were modified for musket fighting during the 1860 Hau Hau uprising.

Entering the community along Wharf Road, off SH35, you'll find a general store and a takeaway. Continuing 2km east of Hicks Bay along SH35 brings you to *Hicks Bay Motel Lodge* (☎06/864 4880; ❸), set high above both bays with incredible views, a licensed **restaurant**, a **bar** and access to a glowworm grotto.

Horse Trekking In Hicks Bay (☎06/864 4859) offers exactly what its name suggests (from 2hr, $40; Oct–May).

Te Araroa

From Hicks Bay, SH35 climbs over a hill and drops back to the coast, 6km on, at *Te Araroa Holiday Park* (☎06/864 4873, ⓔbill.martin@xtra.co.nz; tent sites $12, powered sites $14, dorms $20, cabins ❶, tourist flats ❸, motel units ❹), which has a handy shop and a takeaway van in summer, plus sea kayaks and mountain bikes for rent.

From here it's 4km to **East Cape Manuka Oil** on SH35 (daily 9am–4pm; ☎06/864 4826, ⓦwww.manukaproducts.com) which extracts essential oils by steam distillation from the twigs of manuka trees grown in the surrounding hills. Highly valued for its healing abilities, the oil is exported all over the world.

Manuka-oil products such as soaps and medicinal creams are on sale in the small shop and café.

A further 2km on, the broad surf-washed shore of Kawakawa Bay is graced by the small village of **TE ARAROA** ("long pathway"), which marks the midway point between Opotiki and Gisborne. Te Araroa was once the domain of the famous Maori warrior Tuwhakairiora and the legendary Paikea, who is said to have arrived here on the back of a whale. Ironically, the first Europeans in the area occupied a **whaling station** not far from the present township. These days the settlement contains little more than a petrol station, two stores and a takeaway selling fresh **fish and chips**. In the grounds of the local school on Moana Parade stands a **giant pohutukawa** tree – so giant that it's easy to believe the claims that it's New Zealand's largest.

East Cape Lighthouse

The New Zealand mainland's easternmost point is marked by the **East Cape Lighthouse**, reached by a cliff-clinging unsealed 21km road from Te Araroa: follow the sign east along the foreshore. This dramatic coastal run ends in a car park, from which you climb 755 steps to the lighthouse perched atop a 140m hill – an atmospheric spot with views inland to the Raukumara Range and seaward towards East Island (a bird sanctuary), just offshore. To find the path, head 50m back down the road and go through a gate near the derelict huts.

If you're relying on public transport along SH35, you can get here at sunrise with East Cape 4WD **trips** (℡06/864 4775; 2–3hr $50 for one person, $30/person for two); contact them for pre-dawn pick-ups at accommodation in the area.

Tikitiki and Ruatoria

From Te Araroa SH35 cuts inland through 24km of sheep-farming country before reaching **TIKITIKI**, for a peek inside the modest restored Anglican **church**, on a rise as you enter the town. The plain wooden exterior hides a treasure-trove of elaborate Maori design, *tukutuku* and carving; unusually, the stained glass is also in Maori designs, and the rafters are painted in the colours of a Maori meeting house. The remote *Eastender Backpackers*, Rangitukia Road, off SH35 (℡06/864 3820), with beds in dorms ($23) and cabins (❶–❷) offers **bone carving** ($45/2–3hr) and some of the best **horse treks** in the area (2hr; $85) including a gallop on the beach.

Inland **RUATORIA**, signposted off the main highway 19km south of Tikitiki, is the largest town since Opotiki (though that's not saying much), with two petrol stations, a pub, groceries, and a serviceable daytime café, *The Village*, in a bright turquoise building on the main street, as well as evening takeaways from the roadside *Kai Kart* nearby.

The main reason to stop is to call into the information centre for the local **Maori Ngati Porou Tourism**, on the main street (Mon–Fri 8.30am–5pm; ℡06/864 8660), who have a wealth of local knowledge and arrange customized **guided trips** to 1754m **Mount Hikurangi**. Sacred to Maori as the place where Maui (p.778) beached his *waka* after fishing up the North Island, ten giant **carvings** were installed at 1000m to celebrate the new millennium, and it's the first place on the New Zealand mainland to see the sunrise. This hill country to the west of Ruatoria comes under the jurisdiction of the Raukumara Conservation Area, which includes the upper catchments of several rivers that drain into the Bay of Plenty. The desolate terrain and limited access discourage most visitors from exploring the park, but it's possible to tackle the four-hour trek up Mount

Hikurangi. The Ngati Porou control the land, so you'll need to consult the information centre for access details.

At Kopuaroa, around 15km south of Ruatoria, a loop road heads 6km to the broad sweep of **Waipiro Bay**, a busy port in its heyday, but now a beautiful and secluded inlet.

Tokomaru Bay to Gisborne

At **Tokomaru Bay** the road emerges from inland bush and pastoral country to reveal the North Island's east coast in all its glory. For the remaining 80km to Gisborne you stay mostly inland but catch frequent glimpses of yawning bays and crashing surf, accessed directly on SH35 or short side roads leading to little-visited coves.

Tokomaru Bay

TOKOMARU BAY (or just "Toko"), 11km south of Te Puia Springs, is a gorgeous spot to idle for a day, exploring the steep green hills, rocky headlands and the broad expanse of **beach**, which is dotted with driftwood, pounded by surf, and provides a good spot to swim. The Maori who settled here trace their descent to Toi te Huatahi, the great navigator and the first to arrive from the ancestral home of Hawaiki. In 1865 the Mawhai *pa* was the scene of several attacks by a party of Hau Hau, but they were repulsed by a small garrison of old men and women.

At the far northern end of town, a long wooden wharf and the ruined buildings of a freezing works (abattoir) testify to the former prosperity of this once-busy port, which thrived until improved road transport forced the factory's closure in 1953. The town now gets by on the merest hint of a craft industry: call in at the **Nga Roimata Art Gallery** on Waitangi Street (usually Mon–Fri 10am–3pm), near the general store to see and buy flax goods, possum-fur hats, pottery and more.

Backpackers can choose from two excellent **hostels**: *Footprints In The Sand*, 13 Potae St (☏06/864 5858 ⓦwww.footprintsinthesand.co.nz; tents $15, dorms $20, rooms ❷), one level block from the waterfront, with indoor and outdoor kitchens and showers, and welcoming Maori hosts; or, 100m up a steep hill, *Brian's Place*, 21 Potae St (☏06/864 5870; tents $18, dorms $28, rooms & cabins ❶), a small, friendly spot with loft-style rooms and an amazing single-person cabin perched on the hillside. Both hostels rent surfboards.

Services are limited: petrol is available, and *Te Puka Tavern* on Beach Road serves inexpensive pub **meals** in hefty portions and is the only place in town for a drink; it can get boisterous at weekends. The only other alternative is the supermarket on Waitangi Street, where you can stock up for a picnic.

Anaura Bay

Some 22km south from Tokomaru, a 6km-long sealed side road runs to rugged **ANAURA BAY**, a prized **surf** spot with a broad sweep of sand and jagged headlands. At the north end of the bay, the **Anaura Scenic Reserve** harbours a large area of mixed broadleaf bush noted for its large puriri trees and abundance of native birds. Starting near the end of the road, and signposted to the west by the reserve, the **Anaura Bay Walkway** (3.5km loop; 2hr) follows the course of the Waipare Stream into thick green bush, up a gently climbing valley and out into scrubland before turning back towards the bay and a lookout point with magnificent views.

Beside the beach immediately beyond the start of this walk there's a very basic DOC **campsite** (Dec–Feb; $5), with water but no shower. At the opposite end of the bay, superbly sited on the beach, is the *Anaura Bay Motor Camp* (☏06/862 6380; tents $12, powered sites $14). Facilities are in the former schoolhouse and there's a store selling essentials.

Tolaga Bay and beyond

TOLAGA BAY (Uawa), 36km from Tokomaru, is the first place you reach since leaving Opotiki that feels like a viable town, its population of six hundred one of the better-serviced communities on the East Cape, with a supermarket, petrol and a clutch of cafés. Once again, rugged headlands enclose the bay, the scene of a 1769 visit by Captain Cook and his crew. They're commemorated in the town's street names: Banks, Solander, Forester and, of course, Cook. Anchoring to replenish his stocks of food and water, Cook named the bay "Tolaga", a misinterpretation of the Maori name for the prevailing wind (*teraki*).

Just over 1km south of town, Wharf Road cuts seaward past the start of **Cooks Cove Walkway** (5.8km; 2hr 30min return), which involves a steep and often muddy climb through bush and birdlife, rewarding the effort with good views across the bay. Another 300m along Wharf Road you'll find the 660m-long concrete **wharf** itself, the longest concrete jetty in the southern hemisphere, jutting out past steep sandstone cliffs. Built in the late 1920s to service coastal shipping, it soon became redundant when shipping ceased in 1963, and is in a near-ruinous state, with no safety rails, though locals are rallying to save it and have it restored. It's not strong enough for vehicles, but you can wander to the end for a picturesque picnic spot.

Easily the best place to **eat** (on the entire East Cape) is ⚓ *Maria's* at the mock-Tudor *Tolaga Bay Inn*, on the corner of Solander and Cook streets, serving enormous slices of home-baked cake, knockout coffee and delicious, freshly prepared soups, salads and so forth. If you decide to stay, go for the beachfront **accommodation** at *Tolaga Bay Holiday Park*, Wharf Road (☏06/862 6716; tent sites $11, caravans & cabins ❶–❸), which has a store and great views.

The 47km stretch from Tolaga Bay to Gisborne becomes both tamer and bleaker the further south you travel, much of the land cleared for farming. The road climbs in and out of more small bays, occasionally providing panoramic vistas of sea and close-ups of the slate-grey rock shelves that characterize this coast. It passes the turn-off to **Whangara**, where the film *Whale Rider* was shot, but, as there's no direct access, there's little to see from the lookout apart from a sweep of sand and an offshore island said to be the fossilized remains of the whale that the legendary Paikea rode all the way from Hawaiki. However, for a guided introduction to the area, Tipuna Tours (from $70; ☏06/862 6118, ⓔannemcguire@xtra.co.nz) arrange enlightening trips and visit one of the three *marae* at Tolaga Bay.

After Whangara there's little to stop you heading straight for Gisborne except to ride the renowned surf at **WAINUI BEACH**, 9km from the city.

Travel details

Buses

Coromandel to: Thames (1 daily; 1hr 15min); Whitianga (2 daily; 1hr).

Opotiki to: Gisborne, via SH2 (1 daily; 2hr); Hicks Bay via SH35 (12 weekly; 3hr); Rotorua (2 daily; 2hr 10min); Whakatane (2 daily; 40min).

Paeroa to: Auckland (2 daily; 2hr 30min); Hamilton (2 daily; 1hr 30min).

Tauranga to: Auckland (2 daily; 3hr 40min); Hamilton (1 daily; 2hr); Rotorua (3 daily; 1hr 30min); Taupo (2 daily; 2hr 30min).

Te Aroha to: Hamilton (2 daily; 1hr 5min).

Thames to: Auckland (4 daily; 2hr); Coromandel (2 daily; 1hr 15min); Hamilton (1 daily; 1hr 30min); Mount Maunganui (1 daily, 2hr); Tauranga (2 daily; 1hr 45min); Whitianga (3 daily; 1hr 40min).

Whakatane to: Gisborne (3 daily; 3hr); Opotiki (2 daily; 40min); Rotorua (2 daily; 1hr 30min).

Whitianga to: Tauranga (3 daily; 3hr 45min); Thames (3 daily; 1hr 45min).

Flights

Tauranga to: Auckland (6–8 daily; 35min); Wellington (9–14 daily; 1hr 15min).

Whakatane to: Auckland (3–4 daily; 45min).

Whitianga to: Auckland (1 daily; 30min).

6

Poverty Bay, Hawke's Bay and the Wairarapa

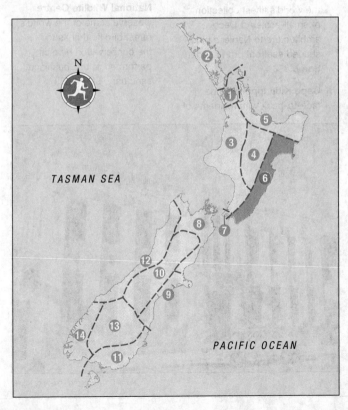

CHAPTER 6 **Highlights**

* **Gisborne** Swim with the sharks and feed the stingrays off the coast of New Zealand's easternmost city. See p.362

* **Lake Waikaremoana** Take in this picturesque lake on short hikes or the North Island's most prized multi-day tramp. See p.369

* **Napier** Wander through the world's finest collection of small-scale Art Deco architecture to Napier's pine-shaded seafront promenade. See p.373

* **Cape Kidnappers** Come face-to-beak with residents of the world's largest mainland gannet colony after a tractor ride along the beach. See p.380

* **Vineyards** Sip to your heart's content in Hawke's Bay Wine Country, or stroll to almost a dozen fine wineries from appealing Martinborough. See p.382 & p.394

* **Pukaha Mount Bruce National Wildlife Centre** Observe some of the world's rarest birdlife thanks to the conservation heroics performed at this bushland sanctuary. See p.389

▲ The Daily Telegraph building, Napier

6

Poverty Bay, Hawke's Bay and the Wairarapa

From the eastern tip of the North Island, a mountainous backbone runs 650km southwest to the outskirts of Wellington, defining and isolating the **east coast**. The Raukumara, Kaweka, Ruahine, Tararua and Rimutaka mountain ranges protect much of the region from the prevailing westerlies and cast a long rain shadow, the bane of the area's sheep farmers, who watch their land become a parched dusty brown each summer. Increasingly, these pastures are being given over to viticulture, and the regions of Poverty Bay, Hawke's Bay and the Wairarapa are now renowned the world over for their **wine**. Any tour of the wineries has to take in **Poverty Bay**, a major grape-growing region, where the main centre of Gisborne was the first part of New Zealand sighted by Cook's expedition in 1769. Finding little, other than the wary local Maori, he named it Poverty Bay and sailed south to the bay he later named **Hawke Bay** after his boyhood hero Admiral Sir Edward Hawke (the name of the surrounding province has since evolved into **Hawke's Bay**). Here Cook had a clash with Maori at **Cape Kidnappers**, now the site of an impressive gannet colony.

Hawke's Bay has long been dubbed "the fruit bowl of New Zealand", and its orchard boughs still sag under the weight of apples, pears and peaches. The district is best visited from the waterfront city of **Napier**, famed for its Art Deco buildings, constructed after the city was flattened by a massive earthquake in 1931.

Getting around

The only passenger **trains** in the region are those linking the main Wairarapa towns with Wellington. Elsewhere **buses** are more useful. InterCity (🌐 www.intercity.co.nz) run a daily service between Gisborne and Napier, and another on south to Wellington, though this goes through Palmerston North and avoids the Wairarapa. NakedBus (🌐 www.nakedbus.co.nz) run a daily service from Napier and Hastings to Wellington that also routes via Palmerston North.

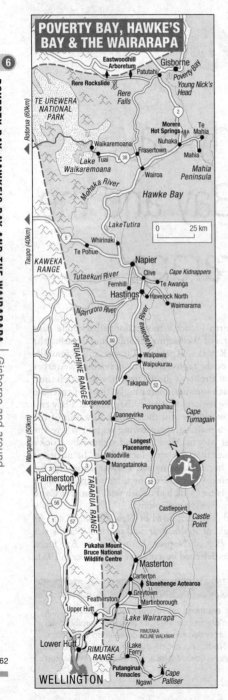

POVERTY BAY, HAWKE'S BAY & THE WAIRARAPA

Nearby Hastings suffered much the same fate and wove Spanish Mission-style buildings into the resulting Art Deco fabric, though this won't delay you long from continuing south into the sheep lands of the Wairarapa and its wonderfully accessible vineyards of Martinborough.

Access to the mountainous **interior** of this region is limited, with only six roads winding over or cutting through the full length of the ranges. The tortuous, scenic SH38 forges northwest from the small town of **Wairoa**, the gateway to the remote wooded mountains of Te Urewera National Park and beautiful **Lake Waikaremoana**, which is encircled by the four-day Lake Waikaremoana Track tramping route.

Gisborne and around

New Zealand's easternmost city, **GISBORNE**, is the first to catch the sun each new day, and, thanks to the isolating mountain ranges all about has been spared from overdevelopment. Broad streets lined with squat weatherboard houses warmed by long hours of sunshine are interspersed with expansive parkland hugging the Pacific, the harbour and three rivers – the Taruheru, Turanganui and Waimata.

It was here in October 1769 that **James Cook** first set foot on the soil of Aotearoa, an event commemorated by a shoreside statue. He immediately ran into conflict with local Maori, killing several of them before sailing away empty-handed. He named the landing site **Poverty Bay**, since "it did not afford a single item we wanted, except a little firewood". Despite the fertility of the surrounding lands, the name stuck, though many Maori prefer **Turanganui a Kiwa** – honouring a Polynesian navigator.

Early-nineteenth-century Poverty Bay remained staunchly Maori and few Pakeha moved here, discouraged by both the Hau Hau rebellion and Te Kooti's uprising (see p.372). It wasn't until the 1870s that **Europeans** headed here in numbers to farm the rich alluvial river flats. After a decent port was constructed in the 1920s, sheep farming and market gardening took off, followed more recently by the grape harvest and the rise of plantation forestry. Today Gisborne's Maori and Pakeha population is almost exactly 50:50; and the city's relaxed pace and easy-going beach culture make it one of New Zealand's more gently appealing places.

Arrival, information and tours

NakedBus and InterCity **buses** converge on the **i-SITE visitor centre**, 209 Grey St (daily: Nov to Easter 8.30am–5.30pm; Easter to Oct 8.30am–5pm; ℡06/868 6139, ⓦwww.gisbornenz.com), which has **internet access**, sells Waikaremoana hut passes and has displays on local social and natural history. For tramping information outside the area, visit the **DOC office** at 63 Carnarvon St (Mon–Fri 8am–4.30pm; ℡06/869 0460). There's free internet at the **library**, 35 Peel St (Mon, Wed–Fri 9.30am–5.30pm, Tues 9.30am–8pm, Sat 9.30am–1pm).

Direct flights from Auckland and Wellington arrive at Gisborne **airport**, on the edge of town about 2km west of the town centre, which can be reached by **taxi** for $15 – try Gisborne Taxis (℡06/867 2222). **Getting around** most of the city is easily done on foot, though **rental bikes** from Avanti Plus, corner of Gladstone and Roebuck roads ($40/day; ℡06/867 4571), are good for a spin around the wineries.

One of the best ways to explore the region is with Tipuna Tours (see p.357 for details) who run cultural interpretation tours to Whangara (see p.357; $70) visiting the locations where the movie *Whale Rider* was shot, and wider-ranging trips up to Tolaga Bay (see p.357; $120/half-day, $240/full day).

Accommodation

Despite the huge number of motels – chiefly along the main strip, palm-shaded Gladstone Road, and the waterfront Salisbury Road – **accommodation** can be hard to come by during the month or so after Christmas.

Motels and B&Bs

Beachcomber Motel 73 Salisbury Rd ℡0800/424 555, ⓦwww.beachcombergisborne.co.nz. Welcoming, well-cared-for motel with free wi-fi and a range of comfortable units 50m from the beach. ➍

🏃 **Knapdale Eco Lodge** 114 Snowsill Rd, Waihirere, 13km northwest of Gisborne ℡06/862 5444, ⓦwww.knapdale.co.nz. They take their "eco" moniker seriously at this luxurious lodge in a tranquil semi-permaculture farm with chickens, deer and horses. A dawn chorus from the nearby forest alerts you to the sumptuous breakfast, and gourmands should book one of the exquisite dinners ($75 a head). ➏

Pacific Harbour Motor Inn Corner of Reads Quay & Pitt St ℡06/867 8847, ⓦwww.pacific-harbour .co.nz. Glass bricks and panoramic windows some with harbour views flood this contemporary motel with natural light. Large, fully equipped rooms,

some with balconies and spa baths. Units ➎, apartments ➏

🏃 **Te Kura** 14 Cheeseman Rd ℡06/863 3497, ⓦwww.tekura.co.nz. There are just two guest rooms (one with a deep claw-foot bath) in this grand, beautifully timbered Arts & Crafts homestead overlooking the Waimata River in central Gisborne. Guests can relax in their own lounge, use the swimming pool and access free wi-fi, and generous hosts serve full breakfasts. ➍

Whispering Sands 22 Salisbury Rd ℡0800/405 030, ⓦwww.whisperingsands.co.nz. Beachfront motel with fourteen large modern units all with full kitchens and those on the upper level with great sea views. ➎

Hostels and campsite

Flying Nun 147 Roebuck Rd ℡06/868 0461, ⓦwww.flynun.co.nz. This slightly scruffy, hippyish former convent, a 15min walk from town, is where Dame Kiri Te Kanawa first trained her voice. Some of the spacious dorms front onto broad verandas, and although doubles can be a little cramped, singles ($38) are good value. Spacious grounds include a BBQ area and games room. No credit cards. Tents $15, dorms $23, doubles and twins ❶

Inn Paradise 13 Leith St ☎06/863 3504, ⓦwww .innparadise.co.nz. An upscale backpackers bordering on hotel standard with excellent communal kitchen and simple but tasteful rooms which mostly come with direct external access. The light industrial vicinity isn't exactly inviting but it is great value. Dorms $35, rooms ❹

Waikanae Beach Holiday Park Grey St ☎06/867 5634, ⓦwww.gisborne holidaypark.co.nz. Idyllically sited motor park right by Gisborne's main beach and 5min walk from town, with tennis courts, comfortable cabins (some en suite) and s/c units. Camping $21–28 per site, cabins ❶/❷, units ❷

YHA Gisborne Corner of Harris St & Wainui Rd ☎06/867 3269, ⓔyha.gisborne@clear.net.nz. Spacious and central hostel in a weatherboard homestead with a sunny deck, a cheery paint job and a manager switched onto the local surf hotspots. Some twins and doubles, one en suite. Dorms $26, rooms ❷

The Town

Almost everywhere in this compact city is an easy stroll from Midway Beach. Swimming, surfing and sunbathing aside, most of Gisborne's sights are connected in some way to the historical accident of James Cook's landing – and the dynamic between Maori and Pakeha cultures it engendered. The first of Cook's crew to spy the mountains of Aotearoa, a couple of days before the first landing, was 12-year-old

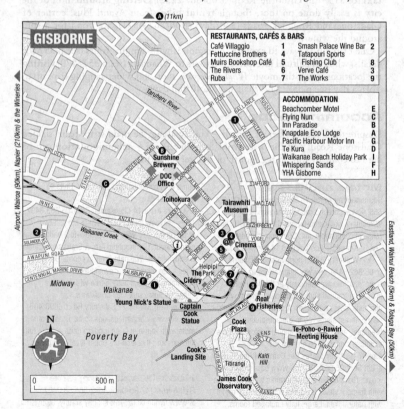

surgeon's boy Nick Young, who Cook rewarded by recording this white-cliffed promontory, 10km south of Gisborne across Poverty Bay, on his chart as Young Nick's Head. Young's keen eyes are commemorated with a pained-looking statue on the western side of the rivermouth in Gisborne. Nearby is a modern **statue of Cook** atop a stone hemisphere.

Early Maori explorers are likewise honoured with **Te Tauihu Turanga Whakamana** – a striking wooden sculpture in the centre of town depicting a Maori *tauihu* (canoe prow) carved with images of Tangaroa (god of the sea), the demi-god Maui, and Toi Kai Rakau (one of the earliest Maori to settle in New Zealand).

Across the river at the **Tairawhiti Museum**, 10 Stout St (Jan daily 10am–4pm, Feb–Dec Mon–Sat 10am–4pm, Sun 1.30–4pm; $5, free entry Mon), the *Watersheds* exhibit charts the parallel and intertwining lives of Maori and Europeans on the East Coast. There's everything from an ancient whalebone walking stick carved with Maori designs and coverage of Cook's arrival to the vibrant painting of early Ngati Porou leader Hinematioro by renowned painter Robyn Kahukiwa.

A maritime wing incorporates the original wheelhouse and captain's quarters of the 12,000-tonne *Star of Canada*, which ran aground on the reef off Gisborne's Kaiti Beach in 1912, along with exhibits on shipping, and a shrine to the local surfing. Several disused buildings from around the region are clustered outside the museum, notably the six-room 1872 **Wyllie Cottage**, the oldest extant house in town, and the **Sled House**, built on runners at the time of the Hau Hau uprising so that it could be hauled away by a team of bullocks at the first sign of unrest.

A striking modern whale-tail sculpture near the corner of Gladstone Road and Cobden Street heralds **Toihoukura** (generally Mon–Fri 9am–5pm during term times, and by appointment ☎06/868 0347; free), a school of contemporary art where existing Maori carvings are restored and students are instructed in the oral history and traditions of Maori design. Interpretations using modern materials and techniques are encouraged, and many vibrant and stunning pieces find their way into the public gallery.

If you've worked up a thirst, repair to the boutique **Sunshine Brewery**, 109 Disraeli St (Mon–Sat 9am–6pm; free), for a brief tour of the tiny brewhouse before sampling its Gisborne Gold lager, plus a pilsner, a stout and a delectable English-style ale. The beers are available in bars around town, but the shop prices are the best around. Alternatively, you can watch an industrial cider production plant, **The Cidery**, 91 Customhouse St (Mon–Fri 9am–4.30pm; free), in action, and try fresh-tasting ciders, local mead and ginger beer.

Kaiti Hill and around

An obelisk on the eastern side of the rivermouth marks **Cook's landing site**, now a couple of hundred metres inland following reclamation for the harbour. Behind, Titirangi Domain climbs the side of **Kaiti Hill** to Cook Plaza, designed around a sculpture intended to represent Cook. The hill's highest point has tremendous views across Poverty Bay to the cliffs of Young Nick's Head, and is occupied by the **James Cook Observatory**, which runs public stargazing nights on Tuesdays (Oct–March 8.30pm; April–Sept 7.30pm; $5).

On the eastern side of the hill lies **Te Poho-o-Rawiri Meeting House**, one of the largest in the country. The interior is superb, full of fine ancestor carvings, interspersed with wonderfully varied geometric *tukutuku* (woven panels). At the foot of the two support poles, ancient and intricately carved warrior statues provide a fine counterpoint to the bolder work on the walls. This is one of the most easily accessible working *marae*, but you'll need to arrange permission to enter the site (☎06/8676 0944), preferably a day or two in advance. You're pretty much left to your own devices, so remember to remove your shoes before entering the meeting house and take photographs only if you've asked permission; a *koha* (donation) is appreciated.

Outdoor activities

Gisborne offers one of New Zealand's few opportunities for heart-pounding **shark encounters**, based at Tatapouri, 14km northeast. Dive Tatapouri (Nov–March; $250; ☎06/868 5153, ⑩www.divetatapouri.com) takes small groups about 15km offshore from where, two at a time, you climb into a tough metal cage, which is partly lowered into the water where **mako sharks** lurk. Standing chest deep, you get around half an hour in the water – quite long enough – ducking down with a mask and snorkel or regulator to observe these curious 3m-long, eighty-kilo killing machines. Dive Tatapouri also offers a **reef ecology tour** ($40) on which you don waders, walk onto the reef at low tide and hand-feed stingrays, kingfish and octopi. Its Rere rockslide trips (see p000; $60) pick up at the Gisborne i-SITE.

To take advantage of Gisborne's renowned surf, go **Surfing With Frank** (private lesson $65, group lesson $45 including board and wetsuit rental; max 4 people per group; ☎06/867 0823, ⑩www.surfingwithfrank.com).

Eating, drinking and nightlife

For its size, Gisborne is surprisingly well supplied with decent **cafés** and **restaurants** for all budgets. Many are beside the city's rivers or harbour, making them ideal for an evening drink.

For **self-caterers**, affordable, straight-off-the-boat fish can be found at **Real Fisheries** shop (Mon–Fri 8.30am–5pm & Sat 8.30am–12.30pm), on the Esplanade, and fruit and vegetables are best at the bustling **farmers' market**, held each Saturday morning downtown at the Army Hall car park on Fitzherbert Street (9.30am–12.30pm). Movies are shown at the Odeon **cinema**, 79 Gladstone Rd (☎06/867 3339).

Café Villaggio 57 Ballance St ☎06/863 3895. Casual café/restaurant in a lovely Art Deco house, either on sofas around the fire in winter or spilling outside in summer. Expect lunches of BLT ($11), seafood chowder ($14) and pizza ($19) daily and dinner (mains $26–32) Thurs–Sat.

Fettuccine Brothers 12 Peel St ☎06/868 5700. Long-standing Italian restaurant (with adjacent bar), serving a full range of dishes from pasta (around $24) to substantial meat and fish dishes (around $30). Closed Sun.

Muirs Bookshop Café 62 Gladstone Rd. Airy café tucked above Gisborne's best bookshop, adjacent to the secondhand section. A sun-drenched balcony overlooks the main street, where you can enjoy panini, salads and delicious "bookshop brownies".

The Rivers Corner of Gladstone Rd & Reads Quay. Convivial Irish-ish bar with good Guinness and a range of hearty meals at good prices.

Ruba 14 Childers Rd. Modern daytime café, perfect for coffee and warm lemon curd and cream cheese muffins, or lunches like chilli squid ($19) and beef wrap ($17). Closed Mon.

Smash Palace Wine Bar 24 Banks St. Wonderfully oddball bar in a corrugated-iron barn, where

overalls from the surrounding industrial area rub shoulders with suits. Food basically comprises snacks – favourites include flaming pizzas and nachos flame-toasted with a blowtorch. Live entertainment from blues to heavy metal mostly at weekends.

Tatapouri Sports Fishing Club The Esplanade. Sociable club right on the wharf with veranda seating for seafood, steaks or gourmet burgers (all under $25). There's cheap beer, and visitors just sign in: ask at the bar.

Verve Café 121 Gladstone Rd. With rotating art exhibitions by up-and-coming local artists, this groovy but low-key daytime café and restaurant serves gorgeous, moderately priced food from savoury muffins to falafel, steak sandwiches and cakes.

The Works Corner of the Esplanade & Crawford Rd ☎06/863 1285. This former freezing works, with bare-brick walls and wood floors, is abuzz with folk in for a coffee and a snack and serious diners here for well-prepared dishes such as orange soy duck and excellent wines by the glass or bottle. Lunch mains $18–27, dinner mains $28–35.

Around Gisborne

Winery visits, gentle walks and a smattering of specific attractions make a day or so spent in Gisborne's surrounds an agreeable prospect. If you don't have a car, your best bet is to **bike** out on the flat roads to the wineries, or join Grants Wine Tours (℡06/868 6139, ✉grantsue.hughes@ihug.co.nz) for a half-day **wine tour** ($55) which includes tasting fees.

The wineries

Occupying a free-draining alluvial valley in the lee of the Raukumara Range and blessed with long hours of strong sun and cooling sea breezes, Poverty Bay's wineries (ⓦwww.gisbornewine.co.nz) have traditionally operated as a viticultural workhorse, churning out vast quantities of gluggable Chardonnay. With reduced demand for that grape, small producers are planting better cultivars (along with Viognier and Gewürztraminer) and producing quality wines. The region isn't very well set up for viticultural tourism but many wineries give a personal touch if you call in advance, and a few open for regular tastings in summer. One such is **Bushmere Estate**, 6km out at 166 Main Rd South (℡06/868 9317, ⓦwww.bushmere.com), typically open Thursday to Sunday for tastings (including a refreshing rosé), and with a good café in a pretty vineyard setting.

A further 5km southwest, **Millton**, 199 Papatu Rd, Manutuke (℡06/862 8680, ⓦwww.millton.co.nz) is one of New Zealand's few organic wineries to apply biodynamic principles. The timing of planting, harvesting and bottling are dictated by the moon's phases to produce some delicious wines (especially Chardonnay, Chenin Blanc and Viognier) that, it is claimed, can be enjoyed even by those who experience allergic reactions to other wines. Bring ingredients for a picnic among the vines and a leisurely game of pétanque on the winery's pitch.

Eastwoodhill Arboretum and Rere rockslide

A bottle of wine tucked under your arm and a groaning picnic hamper is the most conducive way to enjoy New Zealand's largest collection of northern hemisphere vegetation at **Eastwoodhill Arboretum**, Ngatapa-Rere Road, 35km northwest of Gisborne (daily 9am–5pm; $10; ⓦwww.eastwoodhill.org .nz). It was the life's work of William Douglas Cook, who grew to love British gardens and parks while recuperating in England during World War I. Concerned that war would break up the great estates of Europe and destroy their genetic stock of trees, he made it his business to import the best he could. Cook died in 1967 leaving numerous trails threading through a unique mixture of over 3500 species – magnolias, oaks, spruce, maples, cherries – brought together in an unusual microclimate in which both hot- and cold-climate trees flourish.

Some 12km further on, the Wharekopae River plunges 10m over **Rere Falls**, where a short stroll allows you to walk in behind the curtain of water. This is easily eclipsed by **Rere rockslide**, 2km upstream (unrestricted entry), where the river cascades down a 20m-wide and 60m-long rock slope that is smooth enough to provide great sport. In summer there's little water and a lot of algae making for a super-fast ride down to the pool at the bottom. The extra water in winter makes for a slower (but still exciting) and colder ride. Bring something to slide on – a boogie board, inner tube or old bit of plastic – and ask locals for advice and safety tips. Alternatively join Dive Tatapouri (see opposite) on one of its **guided trips** ($55) from Gisborne.

Mahia, Wairoa and the road to Napier

South of Gisborne, **SH2 soon leaves** the Poverty Bay vineyards behind and traverses the hill country of the Wharerata State Forest for 60km to tiny **MORERE**, and the **Morere Hot Springs** (daily 10am–5pm, late summer opening if busy; $6, private pools an extra $3 for 30min). The highly saline and pleasantly non-sulphurous waters that well up along a small stream here result from ancient seawater, warmed and concentrated along a fault line. This is also one of the east coast's last remaining tracts of native coastal forest, and grassy BBQ areas surround the pools and form the nucleus of numerous trails that radiate out through stands of tawa, rimu, totara and matai; a short streamside walk (10min) takes you to the Nikau Plunge Pools, where soaking tanks are surrounded by nikau palm groves. Also consider the Mangakawa Track (3km; 2hr) which loops from the springs through gorgeous virgin bush up to a ridge-top beech forest.

It's a wonderfully relaxing spot, so you might want to **stay** at either *Morere Hot Springs Lodge & Cabins*, SH2 (℡06/837 8824, Ⓦwww.morerehotsprings.co.nz; cabins ❷, cottage ❸), with self-contained accommodation on a working farm with a good swimming hole, or *Morere Tearooms & Camping Ground*, SH2 (℡06/837 8792, Ⓔmorere@xtra.co.nz; camping $17, cabins ❷), which in addition to its tearooms stocks a limited range of staples in its shop.

Mahia Peninsula

At Nuhaka, 8km south of Morere, the highway flirts briefly with the sea before turning sharp right for Wairoa. Mahia Road spurs east to the **Mahia Peninsula**, a distinctive high promontory that separates Hawke Bay from Poverty Bay. Surfers make good use of the rougher windward side, while the calmer beaches on the leeward side offer safe bathing and boating. Outside the mad month after Christmas it makes a relaxing place to break your journey. The peninsula's main settlement, **MAHIA BEACH**, lies 15km on. It was nationally famous throughout 2008 and 2009 when it played host to Moko, a playful bottlenose dolphin who cavorted daily with swimmers. He moved on late in 2009.

You can **stay** at the *Mahia Beach Motels & Holiday Park* (℡06/837 5830, Ⓦwww .motelscabinscampmahiabeach.com; camping $17, cabins ❷, motels ❹), with spacious camping, simple tourist cabins and flashier motel units. Eating is limited to takeaways and the lively *Sunset Sports Bar and Bistro*, which does hearty meals (steaks, crayfish etc) and often has live music at weekends.

Just over the hill, closer to the surf beaches at tiny **TE MAHIA**, you can stay at the self-contained, log-built *Cappamore Lodge*, 435 East Coast Rd (℡06/837 5523, Ⓦwww.cottagestays.co.nz/cappamore/cottage.htm; ❹), which is self-catering, though you can also eat at the licensed *Café Mahia*, 476 East Coast Rd.

Wairoa and south towards Napier

The launch pad for trips to Lake Waikaremoana, sleepy **WAIROA**, some 40km west of the Nuhaka junction, hugs the banks of the willow-lined Wairoa River a couple of kilometres from its mouth, where ships once entered to load the produce of the dairy- and sheep-farming country all around. The **Wairoa Museum**, on the riverside Marine Parade (Mon–Fri 10am–4pm, Sat 10am–1pm; donation appreciated), tells of the early days through well-presented displays (including one on the devastating cyclone Bola, which swept through the region in 1988) and has a beautifully carved Maori figure dating back to the early eighteenth century.

InterCity **buses** pick up daily at the **i-SITE visitor centre**, corner of SH2 and Queen Street (Nov–March Mon–Fri 9am–5pm, Sat & Sun 10am–4pm; April–Sept

Mon–Fri 9am–5pm, Sat & Sun 10am–11pm & 3–4pm; ℡06/838 7440, ⓦwww
.wairoadc.govt.nz), where you can arrange an on-demand shuttle inland with Lake
Waikaremoana **Shuttle Service** (℡06/837 3741) which charges $35–50 a head to
Lake Waikaremoana depending on numbers.

Accommodation is limited, though the simple and ageing *Riverside Motor Camp*,
19 Marine Parade (℡06/838 6301, ⓦwww.riversidemotorcamp.co.nz; camping
$15, backpacker bunks $20, on-site vans ❶, kitchen cabins ❷), is very clean and
well kept. The *Vista Motor Lodge*, on SH2 north of the Wairoa bridge (℡0800/284
782, ⓦwww.vistamotorlodge.co.nz; ❹), has comfy units and a heated pool; and
Café 287, 3km south on SH2 (℡06/838 6601; ❸), has attractive en-suite cabins.

The best place to **eat** during the day is *Eastend Café*, 250 Marine Parade (closed
Mon in winter) serving the likes of Thai chicken and BLT (mostly $12–16) along
with delicious cakes and coffee. Also try one of the 23 varieties of home-made pie
at *Osler's Bakery & Café*, 116 Marine Parade (Mon–Fri 4.30am–4.30pm, Sat & Sun
5am–3pm), a local institution. Alternatively, head out to *Café 287* (closed Mon &
Tues evening in winter) for hearty, home-made breakfasts, lunches and dinner
dishes from fettuccini to steaks ($17–25).

From Wairoa south to Napier, the road becomes considerably narrower, steeper
and twistier, so take it slowly and allow an hour and a half. Roughly halfway you
pass tiny **Tutira** where Pohakura Road runs 15km northwest to **Boundary
Stream Scenic Reserve**, a "mainland island" that's home to North Island brown
kiwi, kereru, North Island kaka and New Zealand falcon. There are several walks
including one to the Bell Rock viewpoint (5km return; 3hr).

Te Urewera National Park

Te Urewera National Park, 65km northwest of Wairoa, straddles the North
Island's mountainous backbone and at 2120 square kilometres encompasses the
largest untouched expanse of native bush outside Fiordland. Unusually for New
Zealand, it is almost completely covered in vegetation; even the highest peaks –
some approaching 1500m – barely poke through this dense cloak of primeval
forest, whose undergrowth is trampled by deer and wild pigs and whose rivers are
filled with trout. One road, SH38, penetrates the interior, but the way to get a true
sense of the place is to hike, particularly the celebrated Lake Waikaremoana Track
encircling **Lake Waikaremoana**, the "Sea of Rippling Waters" and the undoubted
jewel of the park. The lake's deep clear waters, fringed by white sandy beaches and
rocky bluffs, are ideal for swimming, fishing and kayaking.

Habitation is very sparse. The Tuhoe people, the "Children of the Mist", still live
in the interior of the park (the largest concentration around the village of
Ruatahuna), but most visitors make straight for **Waikaremoana**, just a visitor
centre and a motor camp right on the lakeshore. Immediately south, the quiet
former hydroelectric development village of **Tuai** provides some additional basic
services, but otherwise you're on your own.

Lake Waikaremoana

Shrouded by bushland, **Lake Waikaremoana** fills a huge scalloped bowl at an
altitude of over 585m, precariously held back by the Panekiri and Ngamoko
ranges. The lake came into being around 2200 years ago when a huge bank of
sandstone boulders was dislodged from the Ngamoko range, blocking the river
that once drained the valleys. The Maori have a more poetic explanation of the
lake's creation, involving Hau-Mapuhia, the recalcitrant daughter of Mahu, who

6

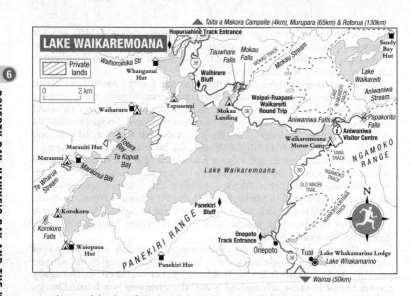

Taita a Makora Campsite (4km), Murupara (65km) & Rotorua (130km)

LAKE WAIKAREMOANA

Private lands

0   2 km

Hopuruahine Track Entrance

Waihoroihika Str

Whanganui Hut

Tauwhare Falls

Mokau Falls

MOKAU TRACK

Mokau Stream

Waihirere Bluff

Sandy Bay Hut

Lake Waikareiti

Aniwaniwa Stream

Waharuru

Tapuaenui

Mokau Landing

Waipai–Ruapani–Waikareiti Round Trip

LAKE WAIKAREITI TRACK

Aniwaniwa Falls

Papakorito Falls

Aniwaniwa Visitor Centre

Marauiti Hut

Maraunui

Te Totara Bay

Te Kopua Bay

Marauriui Bay

Lake Waikaremoana

Waikaremoana Motor Camp

TAWA TRACK

NGAMOKO RANGE

Te Wharua Stream

Korokoro

Korokoro Falls

Panekiri Bluff

NGAMOKO TRACK

OLD MAORI TRAIL

N

Waiopaoa Hut

Onepoto Track Entrance

NGAMOKO-KATAHA TRACK

PANEKIRI RANGE

Panekiri Hut

Onepoto

Tuai

Lake Whakamarino Lodge

Lake Whakamarino

Wairoa (50km)

was drowned by her father and turned into a *taniwha*, or "water spirit". In a frenzied effort to get to the sea, she charged in every direction, thereby creating the various arms of the lake. As she frantically ran south towards Onepoto, the dawn caught her, turning her to stone at a spot where the lake is said to ripple from time to time, in memory of her struggle.

The DOC-operated Aniwaniwa visitor centre and the motor camp are both well set up for helping hikers tackle the Lake Waikaremoana Track. Short visits are repaid by the opportunity to see the **Papakorito Falls**, a 20m-wide curtain of water 2km east of the visitor centre. But to really see and get a feel for the place you'll need to walk a little further afield, preferably armed with DOC's *Lake Waikaremoana Walks* leaflet ($2.50), which details the region's rewarding shorter hikes such as the easy **Hinerau Track** (1km; 20min return; 50m ascent) from the visitor centre to the double-drop **Aniwaniwa Falls**, or the **Black Beech Track** (2km; 30min one-way; 50m descent), which follows the old highway from the visitor centre to the motor camp. If you've the best part of a day to spare, take on the **Waipai–Ruapani–Waikareiti Round Trip** (17km; 5–6hr; 300m ascent), which starts 200m north of the visitor centre and winds up through dense beech forest past the grass-fringed Lake Ruapani to the beautiful and serene **Lake Waikareiti**, where you can rent rowboats (around $20/half-day, $40 bond), though you'll need to plan ahead as the key is held at Aniwaniwa visitor centre. Return down the Waikareiti Track or head on around to the northern side of the lake (3hr one-way) and stay at **Sandy Bay Hut** (18 bunks; $15).

Waikaremoana practicalities

Lake Waikaremoana is approached most easily by bus from Wairoa along SH38 which continues through the park to Murupara and Rotorua. Between Lake Waikaremoana and Murupara there is over 60km of tortuous gravel road, so approaching from the northwest is less than appealing. If you wish to travel this route contact Magic Bus (T09/358 5600, W www.magicbus.co.nz), which currently runs the Gisborne–Waikaremoana–Rotorua route on Monday and Friday, or Te Uruwera Shuttles (T0800/873 937, W www.tshuttle.co.nz), who run in both directions between Rotorua and Lake Waikaremoana on Thursday and Sunday in summer.

The main source of information on the Lake Waikaremoana and Te Urewera National Park is the **Aniwaniwa visitor centre**, right by the lake (daily: Oct–April 8am–4.30pm; May–Sept 8am–4.15pm; T06/837 3803, Eteureweravc @doc.govt.nz), the place to come for hut bookings.

The only **accommodation** inside the park itself is at the well-equipped *Waikaremoana Motor Camp*, on SH38, 2km south of the visitor centre (T06/837 3826, Wwww.lake.co.nz; cabins ❶, s/c chalets ❷), which has a compact but grassy camping area ($12); showers are available for non-guests at $5 a time. The village of Tuai, 15km south, offers *Lake Whakamarino Lodge* (T06/837 3876, Wwww .lakelodge.co.nz; rooms ❷, s/c units ❹), converted from construction workers' quarters wonderfully sited beside the trout-filled Lake Whakamarino – it's wise to book ahead. There are also a couple of DOC **campsites** along SH38: *Mokau Landing* ($5), 11km northwest of the visitor centre, and *Te Taita a Makora* (free), 11km further on.

The nearest full-time restaurant is over 60km away in Wairoa, so when it comes to **eating**, you'll largely have to fend for yourself. There's a reasonable range of groceries (and the only **petrol** between Wairoa and Murupara) at the *Waikaremoana Motor Camp*, and meals (mains around $25) are available on request at the *Lake Whakamarino Lodge*.

The Lake Waikaremoana Track

The **Lake Waikaremoana Track** (46km; 3–4 days; 1150m ascent) is one of New Zealand's "Great Walks". It is also the most popular multi-day tramp in the North Island and often compared with the South Island's renowned Routeburn and Milford tracks though, with the exception of an exhausting climb on the first day, this is a much gentler affair, with plenty of opportunities to fish, swim and listen to the melodious birdlife.

Comprehensive walking **information** is covered in DOC's *Lake Waikaremoana Track* leaflet, though **map** enthusiasts might like the two 1:50,000 Topo50 maps that cover the full circuit. Three days is enough for fit walkers, but it's normally done in four, spending nights in the five "Great Walk" **huts** ($25) and five designated **campsites** ($12) scattered around the lakeshore. Throughout the year, huts and campsites must be **booked in advance**, best done online at Wwww.doc.govt .nz, though you'll need to call in at the Aniwaniwa visitor centre to pick up your hut pass; your chances of getting a place are much better outside the busy month or so after Christmas and the week of Easter.

The winter months (June–Sept) can be cold and wet, making spring and autumn the best times to undertake the walk, though go prepared as it can snow at any point in the year. Each hut is supplied with drinking water, toilets and a heating stove, but a cooking stove, fuel and all your food must be carried. Campsites just have water and toilets.

About sixty percent of walkers prefer to travel clockwise around the lake, getting the challenging but panoramic ascent of Panekiri Bluff over with on the first day, though if the weather looks bad there's no reason why you shouldn't change your bookings (through the Aniwaniwa visitor centre) and go anticlockwise in the hope that it will improve.

If you don't fancy going it alone, consider a four-day **guided walk** with Walking Legends ($1190; T0800/925 569, Wwww.walkinglegends.com), whose accommodation is in the same DOC huts used by independent walkers. Transport from Rotorua, enthusiastic and knowledgeable guiding, excellent meals and wine are provided. All you have to do is carry a daypack. The longest day is around seven hours, and there's usually enough time for a bit of trout fishing.

Te Kooti Rikirangi

Te Kooti Rikirangi was one of the most celebrated of Maori "rebels", a thorn in the side of the colonial government throughout the New Zealand Wars of the late 1860s and early 1870s. An excellent fighter and brilliant strategist, Te Kooti kept the mountainous spine of the North Island on edge for half a decade eluding the biggest manhunt in New Zealand's history.

Born near Gisborne around 1830, Te Kooti was not of chiefly rank but could trace his ancestry back to the captains of several *waka* (canoes) that brought the Maori to New Zealand. By the middle of the 1860s, he was fighting for the government against the fanatical, pseudo-Christian Hau Hau cult that started in Taranaki in 1862. The cult spread to the east coast where, in 1866, Te Kooti was unjustly accused of being in league with its devotees. Denied the trial he demanded, he was imprisoned on the Chatham Islands, along with three hundred of his supposed allies. In 1867, he was brought close to death by a fever, but rose again, claiming a divine revelation and establishing a new religion, **Ringatu** ("the uplifted hand"), which still has some sixteen thousand believers today. Ringatu took its cues from the Hau Hau, but developed into a uniquely Maori version of Catholicism, drawing heavily on the Old Testament. Some say Te Kooti saw himself as a Moses figure – apparently given to dousing his uplifted hand in phosphorus so that it glowed in the dim meeting houses.

After two years on the Chathams, Te Kooti and his fellow prisoners commandeered a ship and engineered a dramatic escape, returning to Poverty Bay. He sought safety in the **Urewera Range**, with the Armed Constabulary in hot pursuit. Te Kooti still managed to conduct successful campaigns, exacting revenge against government troops at Whakatane on the Bay of Plenty, Mohaka in Hawke's Bay and at Rotorua. With the end of the New Zealand Wars in 1872, Te Kooti took refuge in the Maori safe haven of the King Country. He was eventually pardoned in 1883, and in 1891 was granted a plot of land near Whakatane, where he lived out the last two years of his life.

Trailhead transport

You can **drive** to the trailheads at either end of the Lake Waikaremoana Track, but there are occasional thefts and most people prefer to park free of charge at the *Waikaremoana Motor Camp*. This is the base for Homebay Water Taxi & Cruises (☎06/837 3826) who operate a reliable, on-demand **shuttle bus service** to the trailheads, often supplementing with a **water taxi** in summer. They charge $35 for a joint drop-off and pick-up package, and they'll also run a **water-taxi** service to anywhere else you might want to start or finish, enabling you to walk shorter sections by means of pre-arranged pick-ups from specified beaches. They can even organize pack transport between most huts allowing a largely luggage-free walk, though this is only economical for groups of four or more. It is also worth enquiring at the motor camp about renting **kayaks** and open **canoes** for use on the lake.

The route

When tackled clockwise, as outlined below, the first leg is the toughest; carry plenty of drinking water.

Onepoto to Panekiri Hut (9km; 4–5hr; 750m ascent, 150m descent) The track starts at a shelter by the lakeshore close to SH38 and climbs steeply past the site of a redoubt set up by soldiers of the Armed Constabulary in pursuit of Te Kooti (see box above). It then undulates along the ridge top, occasionally revealing fabulous lake views.

Wonderfully airy steps up a rocky bluff bring you to the Panekiri Hut (36 bunks), magnificently set on the brink of the cliffs that fall away to the lake far below. Camping in this fragile environment is prohibited; committed campers must press on to Waiopaoa, an exhausting 8hr walk from the start at Onepoto.

Panekiri Hut to Waiopaoa Hut (7.5km; 3–4hr; 600m descent) Descends the ridge, then rapidly loses height through an often muddy area where protruding tree roots provide welcome hand-holds. Occasional lake views and the transition from beech forests to rich podocarp woodlands make this an appealing, if tricky, section of track down to the hut (30 bunks) and campsite.

Waiopaoa Hut to Marauiti Hut (11km; 4–5hr; 100m ascent) Largely follows the lakeshore, crossing grassland and then kanuka scrub before reaching the Korokoro campsite (1hr 30min from Waiopaoa Hut). A side track leads to the pretty 20m Korokoro Falls (45–60min return). Meanwhile, the main track climbs slightly above the lake past barely accessible bays, eventually reaching the Maraunui campsite and, after ascending the low Whakaneke Spur, descends to the waterside Marauiti Hut (25 bunks).

Marauiti Hut to Waiharuru Hut (6km; 2hr; 150m ascent) Passes the lovely white-sand Te Kopua Bay and climbs an easy saddle, before dropping down to Te Totara Bay and following the lake to the large and modern Waiharuru Hut (40 bunks) and campsite.

Waiharuru Hut to Whanganui Hut (5.3km; 2–3hr; 100m ascent) A short hike across a broad neck of land to the Tapuaenui campsite and beyond, following the shore to the characterful old hut, fitted with built-in three-tier bunks (18 bunks).

Whanganui Hut to Hopuruahine (5km; 2–3hr; 50m ascent) This easy final section skirts the lake to the point where water taxis pick up (45min). The track then follows grassy flats beside the Hopuruahine River and crosses a suspension bridge to the access road to a camping area (free).

Napier and around

Seaside **NAPIER** is one of New Zealand's most likeable regional centres, thanks to its Mediterranean climate, affordable prices and the world's best-preserved collection of small-scale Art Deco architecture. With its laidback population of 54,000, Napier is Hawke's Bay's largest city, and the jumping-off point for trips out to the gannet colony at Cape Kidnappers as well as the barrel-load of world-class **wineries** on the surrounding plains.

Some history

In 1769, James Cook sailed past **Ahuriri**, the current site of Napier, noting the sea-girt Bluff Hill linked to the mainland by two slender shingle banks and backed by a superb saltwater lagoon – the only substantial sheltered mooring between Gisborne and Wellington. Nonetheless, after a less-than-cordial encounter with the native Ngati Kahungunu people he anchored just to the south, off what came

Hawke's Bay festivals

During January and February, Napier and nearby Hastings flip into festive mode. The first of the major events is the **Harvest Hawke's Bay** (last weekend in Jan; ⓦwww .harvesthawkesbay.co.nz), when food- and wine-lovers from around the country flock here for a day of drinking and entertainment at one of the wineries ($45) followed by a day touring the district's cellar doors (transport $20).

The **Mission Concert** (ⓦwww.missionconcert.co.nz) usually takes place in early February, when an internationally famous vocalist – past luminaries include Tom Jones, Eric Clapton and Rod Stewart– performs outdoors at the Mission Estate Winery to an audience of around 25,000.

In mid-February, Napier gears up for the **Art Deco Weekend** (ⓦwww.artdeconapier .com), featuring guided walks, open-house tours of domestic Art Deco architecture, vintage cars, 1930s-dress picnics, champagne breakfasts, dress balls, silent movies and the like. Heading into winter, the **Deco Decanted Jazz Festival** takes place on the third weekend in July.

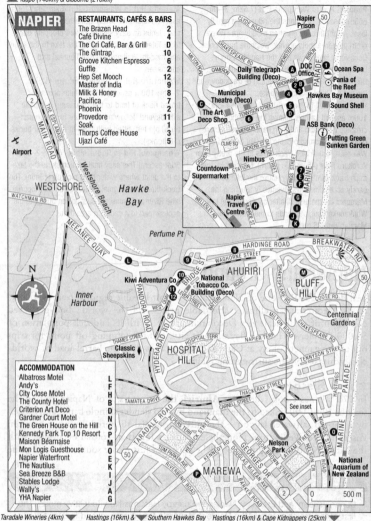

Taupo (140km) & Gisborne (210km)

NAPIER

RESTAURANTS, CAFÉS & BARS	
The Brazen Head	2
Café Divine	4
The Cri Café, Bar & Grill	D
The Gintrap	10
Groove Kitchen Espresso	6
Guffle	2
Hep Set Mooch	12
Master of India	9
Milk & Honey	8
Pacifica	7
Phoenix	2
Provedore	11
Soak	1
Thorps Coffee House	3
Ujazi Café	5

ACCOMMODATION	
Albatross Motel	L
Andy's	F
City Close Motel	H
The County Hotel	B
Criterion Art Deco	D
Gardner Court Motel	N
The Green House on the Hill	C
Kennedy Park Top 10 Resort	P
Maison Béarnaise	M
Mon Logis Guesthouse	O
Napier Waterfront	E
The Nautilus	K
Sea Breeze B&B	I
Stables Lodge	J
Wally's	A
YHA Napier	G

Taradale Wineries (4km) ▼   Hastings (16km) & ▼ Southern Hawkes Bay   Hastings (16km) & Cape Kidnappers (25km) ▼

to be known as Cape Kidnappers. Some thirty years later, when early whalers followed in Cook's tracks, Ahuriri was all but deserted, the Ngati Kahungunu having been driven out by rivals equipped with European guns. During the uneasy peace of the early colonial years, Maori returned to the Napier area, which weathered the **New Zealand Wars** of the 1860s relatively unscathed. The port boomed, but by the early years of the twentieth century all the available land was used up.

Everything changed in two and a half minutes on the morning of February 3, 1931, when the city was rocked by the biggest **earthquake** in New Zealand's recorded history, measuring a massive 7.9 on the Richter scale. More than six hundred aftershocks followed over the next two weeks, hampering efforts to rescue the 258 people who perished in the Bay area, 162 of them in Napier alone. The centre of the city was completely devastated, crumbling into smouldering rubble and consumed by the ensuing fire. The land twisted and buckled, finding a new equilibrium more than two metres higher, with 300 square kilometres of new land wrested from the grip of the ocean – enough room to site the Hawke's Bay airport and expand the city.

Napier embraced the opportunity to start afresh: out went the trams, telephone wires were laid underground, the streets were widened and, in the spirit of the times, almost everything was designed according to the precepts of the **Art Deco** movement. The simultaneous reconstruction gave Napier a stylistic uniformity rarely seen – ranking it alongside Miami Beach as one of the world's largest collections of Art Deco buildings.

Arrival, information and transport

Regular direct **flights** from Auckland, Wellington and Christchurch touch down at Hawke's Bay Airport, 5km north of town on SH2, where they are met by the Super Shuttle (℡0800/748 885, ⓦwww.supershuttle.co.nz), which charges around $15 to get into town. InterCity **buses** pull in centrally at the Napier Travel Centre, 85 Munroe St (℡06/834 2720), while NakedBus stops outside the busy **i-SITE visitor centre**, 100 Marine Parade (daily 9am–5pm; ℡06/834 1911, ⓦwww.hawkesbaynz.com), which can advise on tide times for gannet visits and has internet access. The nearby **DOC office**, 59 Marine Parade (Mon–Fri 9am–4.15pm; ℡06/834 3111), has information about walks into the remote Kaweka and Ruahine ranges to the west. Entertainment **listings** are covered in the weekday-only *Hawke's Bay Today* newspaper, especially on Thursday.

Getting around Napier's central sights is easily done on foot. The GoBay **local bus** services (not Sun; ℡06/878 9250, ⓦwww.hbrc.govt.nz) are of use primarily for visits to Hastings, Havelock North and the Mission Estate Winery (where they drop off within walking distance). To venture further afield, either join a **winery tour** (see p.384), **rent a car** (Auto Rental ℡06/834 0045 and Pegasus ℡06/843 7020 both have short-lease vehicles from $55 a day), **rent a bike** from the i-SITE ($30/day), or hop in a **taxi** with Napier Taxis (℡06/835 7777).

Accommodation

Apart from the usual shortage of rooms during the month or so after Christmas and during February's festivals (see p.373), you should have little trouble finding accommodation in Napier. There are dozens of **motels** around town, many concentrated in Westshore, a beachfront suburb a couple of kilometres from the centre, beside the northbound SH2. Right in the thick of things, Marine Parade has low-cost backpacker **hostels** and classy **B&Bs**.

Hotels and motels

Albatross Motel 56 Meeanee Quay, Westshore ℡0800/252 287, ⓦwww.albatrossmotel.co.nz. Large, good-value motel close to Westshore Beach and Ahuriri's restaurants, with a small pool, spa and free wi-fi. Studios ④, deluxe ⑤

City Close Motel 50 Munroe St ℡06/835 3568, ⓦwww.cityclose.co.nz. Good, old-school budget motel close to the bus station and city centre. ④

The County Hotel 12 Browning St ℡0800/843 468, ⓦwww.countyhotel.co.nz. Elegant, period-decorated business and tourist hotel in the Edwardian former council offices building, one of the few to survive the earthquake. Rooms are plush, and there's a good restaurant and snug bar. ⑧

Gardner Court Motel 16 Nelson Crescent ℡0800/000 830, ⓔgardencourtmotel@xtra.co.nz. Quiet, clean and reasonably central, with a solar-heated outdoor pool and standard motel rooms at bargain prices. ③

The Nautilus 387 Marine Parade ℡0508/68 845, ⓦwww.nautilusnapier.co.nz. Modern, upscale motel where all rooms get great sea views and many have hot tubs. There's a small restaurant on site and room service is available. Studios ⑥, deluxe and apartments ⑦

B&Bs and homestays

The Green House on the Hill 18b Milton Oaks, Bluff Hill ☎06/835 4475 ⓦwww .the-green-house.co.nz. Ruth goes to great lengths to make you feel truly welcome at this friendly vegetarian homestay surrounded by trees halfway up a hidden urban hill. Choose from an en suite or a two-room suite with private bathroom, both with free internet, free bus and airport pick-ups and inventive breakfasts, served on the sea-view deck when warm. ⑤

Maison Béarnaise 25 France Rd, Bluff Hill ☎0800/624 766, ⓦwww.maisonbearnaise.co.nz. Two charming open and airy en-suite doubles in a century-old villa with a lovely garden and tasty breakfasts. ⑥

Mon Logis Guesthouse 415 Marine Parade ☎06/835 2125, ⓦwww.monlogis.co.nz. Florally decorated French-run B&B in a wooden house with two rooms sharing a sea-view balcony. The tariff includes a delicious breakfast. ⑤, sea view ⑦

Sea Breeze B&B 281 Marine Parade ☎06/835 8067, ⓔseabreeze.napier@xtra .co.nz. Seafront Victorian villa with three flamboyant guest rooms – Turkish and Indian share a bathroom, Chinese is en suite (⑤). Everyone gets access to the kitchenette and the guest lounge with sea views, and there's a self-service continental breakfast. ④

Hostels

Andy's 259 Marine Parade ☎06/835 5575, ⓦwww.andysbackpackers.co.nz. Welcoming small hostel where each room comes with washbasin and TV. There's a nice sunny backyard and local pick-ups are free. Dorms $23, rooms ①, ocean view ②

Criterion Art Deco 48 Emerson St ☎06/835 2059, ⓦwww.criterionartdeco.co.nz. Spacious, airy and very central 55-bed hostel in an Art Deco former hotel with large communal areas. There are good-value dorms (some single sex) as well as doubles, some en suite. Guests get free continental

breakfast and discounts in *The Cri* café/bar downstairs. Dorms $26, rooms ②/③

Napier Waterfront 217 Marine Parade ☎06/835 3429, ⓦwww.napierbackpackers.co.nz. Breezy hostel in a weatherboard building complete with veranda overlooking Marine Parade. Cosy dorms and private rooms, good cooking facilities and regular BBQs in the garden create a relaxed vibe. Dorms $22, rooms ②

Stables Lodge 370 Hastings St ☎06/835 6242, ⓦwww.stableslodge.co.nz. Rooms ranged around a central courtyard give an intimate feel to this small, friendly and relaxed hostel with free internet, hammocks, a book exchange and good cooking facilities including a BBQ. Dorms $24–29, rooms ①

Wally's 7 Cathedral Lane ☎06/833 7930, ⓦwww .wallys.co.nz. Enthusiastically run central hostel in a pair of 1920s villas plus a cottage used as an eight-bed dorm. Good range of rooms, huge DVD collection and some off-street parking. Dorms $23, rooms ①, en suite ②

YHA Napier 277 Marine Parade ☎06/835 7039, ⓔyha.napier@yha.co.nz. Homely, spotlessly clean hostel rambling across three airy weatherboard houses right on the waterfront with some sea views. There are four-share dorms, doubles, snug singles, twins and a five-bed family room, and the sunny courtyard at the back has a BBQ. Dorms $28, rooms ②

Campsites

Bay View Snapper Park 10 Gill Rd, Bay View ☎0800/287 275, ⓦwww.snapperpark.co.nz. Beachfront campsite 9km north of Napier that provides an antidote to *Kennedy Park*'s excess. A few campervan spots and the excellent units all have sea views. See map, p.381. Camping $17, cabins ②, s/c units ③, motel units ⑤

Kennedy Park Top 10 Resort Storkey St, off Kennedy Rd ☎0800/457 275, ⓦwww .kennedypark.co.nz. This campsite on steroids, just 2km from the city centre, has acres of powered sites, a pool, BBQ area, kids' playground, a huge range of cabins and units and even a restaurant. Camping $21, cabins & kitchen cabins ③, motel units ④–⑤

The Town

Steep roads and even steeper steps switchback down the southern flank of **Bluff Hill** (Mataruahou) to the grid pattern of Napier's Art Deco **commercial centre** where, at the whim of mid-nineteenth-century Land Commissioner Alfred Domett, streets were given the names of literary luminaries – Tennyson, Thackeray, Byron, Dickens, Shakespeare, Milton and more. Bisecting it all is the partly pedestrianized main thoroughfare of Emerson Street, whose terracotta paving and palm trees run from Clive Square – one-time site of a makeshift "Tin Town" while the city was being rebuilt after the earthquake – to the Norfolk pine-fringed **Marine Parade**. The long strip of grey shingle flanking Marine Parade is Napier's main **beach**, but it is unsafe for swimming – for golden-sand swimming beaches head 30km north to Waipatiki or 35km south to Waimarama or Ocean Beach.

Around the northeastern side of Bluff Hill, about 5km from the city centre, lies the original settlement site of **Ahuriri**, its waterside warehouses now smartened up and occupied by trendy restaurants and cavernous bars.

The commercial centre: Art Deco Napier

The 1931 earthquake saw Napier rebuilt in line with the times. Although **Art Deco** embraced modernity, glorifying progress, the machine age and the Gatsby-style high life, the onset of the Great Depression pared down these excesses, and Napier's version was informed by the privations of an austere era. At the same time, the architects looked for inspiration to California's Santa Barbara – which, just six years earlier, had suffered the same fate as Napier and risen from the ashes. They adopted fountains (a symbol of renewal), sunbursts, chevrons, lightning flashes and fluting to embellish the highly formalized but asymmetric designs. In Napier, what emerged was a palimpsest of early-twentieth-century design, combining elements of the Arts and Crafts movement, the Californian Spanish Mission style, Egyptian and Mayan motifs, stylized floral designs and even Maori imagery. For the best part of half a century, the city's residents merely daubed the buildings in grey or muted blue paint. Fortunately, this meant that when a few visionaries recognized the city's potential in the mid-1980s and formed the **Art Deco Trust**, everything was still intact. The trust continues to promote the preservation of buildings and provides funding for shopkeepers to pick out distinctive architectural detail in pastel colours similar to those originally used.

You can get a sense of Art Deco Napier by wandering along the half-dozen streets of the city centre, notably **Emerson Street**. Worth special attention here is the **ASB Bank**, on the corner of Hastings Street. Its exterior is adorned with fern shoots and a mask from the head of a *taiaha* (a long fighting club), while its interior has a fine Maori rafter design. On Tennyson Street, look for the flamboyant **Daily Telegraph** building, with stylized fountains, and the **Municipal Theatre**, built in the late 1930s in a strikingly geometric form.

Marine Parade

Napier's defining feature is **Marine Parade**, a 2km-long boulevard lined with stately Norfolk pines and fashioned in the British seaside tradition (pebbly beach

---

Art Deco Napier tours and trails

Keen observers will find classic Art Deco everywhere, but for a systematic exploration of Napier's Art Deco revival, begin at **The Art Deco Shop**, 163 Tennyson St (daily 9am–5pm, ⓦwww.artdeconapier.com), where you can watch a free twenty-minute introductory video and buy a leaflet for the **self-guided Art Deco Walk** ($5), outlining a stroll (1.5km; 1hr 30min–2hr) through the downtown area. Dedicated Deco buffs meet here for the **Art Deco Afternoon Walking Tour** (daily 2pm; 2hr; $20), which brings 1930s Napier to life through anecdote-laden patter and gives you the chance to gaze around the interiors of shops and banks without feeling quite so self-conscious. The shorter **Art Deco Morning Walking Tour** (daily 10am; 1hr; $15) and **Art Deco Evening Walk** (daily end Jan to March; 1hr 30min; $18) both start at the i-SITE visitor centre. The Art Deco Trust (☎06/835 0022), based in the same building as The Art Deco Shop, operates **Vintage Deco Car Tours** (subject to availability; 1hr; $130 for a maximum of three people), and the **Deco Tour**, a minibus tour of Napier's Art Deco attractions outside the central city (daily 11.30am; 75min; $38).

and all). A popular walking and cycling path links its string of attractions. Marine Parade starts by Napier's port at the northern end of town and passes the foot of Bluff Hill before arriving at the **Ocean Spa**, 42 Marine Parade (Mon–Sat 6am–10pm, Sun 8am–10pm; $8; ☎06/835 8553), a lavish salt-chlorinated, lido-style complex of hot pools (36–38°C) overlooking the beach with bubbles, jets, spouts, steam room, sauna, massages ($35/30min), beauty treatments and a lap pool (26°C). The long hours and warm waters make it a great place for a relaxed summer evening.

A little further south you'll pass a floral clock and the ornamental Tom Parker Fountain before reaching the bronze cast of the curvaceous **Pania of the Reef**, a siren of Maori legend (see box below). Opposite, the **Hawke's Bay Museum & Art Gallery**, 65 Marine Parade (daily 10am–6pm; $10), is due to be closed for a major expansion until early 2012. Once it reopens, expect quality exhibits with an emphasis on art, design and decorative arts. During renovations the excellent exhibit on the 1931 earthquake may still be on display.

Up ahead, the curving colonnade of the Veronica Sun Bay and the **Sound Shell** stage give way to a **putting course** (daily 9.30am–4.30pm, later in summer; $8.50/18-hole round) and some attractive **sunken gardens**.

Further along the seafront lies the **National Aquarium of New Zealand** (daily 9am–5pm; $16.20; ⊛www.nationalaquarium.co.nz), the finest in the country, with distinct marine environments from Africa, Asia and Australia, plus a substantial New Zealand section. The most spectacular section is the **ocean tank** (hand-feeding at 10am & 2pm), its Perspex walk-through tunnel giving intimate views of rays and assorted sharks. There's more hand-feeding at the **reef tank** at 10am, plus "Behind the Scenes" tours (daily by reservation; $31.20) and the chance to swim with the sharks in the ocean tank (daily 2pm: snorkellers $50/30min; qualified scuba-divers $67.60, $111 with all gear).

There are also non-aquatic sections on New Zealand's reptilian tuatara, and a nocturnal **kiwi house**.

Bluff Hill and Napier Prison Tour

The city centre's northern flank butts up against the steep slopes of **Bluff Hill**, a 3km-long hummock of winding streets that houses some of Napier's more desirable suburbs. There's little to see, but at its eastern summit is **Bluff Hill Domain Lookout** (daily 7am–dusk) offering views of Cape Kidnappers to the west, and right across to the distant Mahia Peninsula in the east.

Immediately south, **Napier Prison**, 55 Coote Rd (daily 9am–4pm; ☎06/835 9933, ⊛www.napierprison.com) is an imposing sandstone-walled former clink built in 1862 and decommissioned in 1993. This is no Alcatraz but a very Kiwi jail – all weatherboard and corrugated iron – that had a chequered career, housing women, children and lunatics as well as hardened male inmates. Several cells have

Pania of the Reef

Local Maori tell the tale of **Pania**, a beautiful sea-maiden who would swim from the watery realm of Tangaroa, the god of the ocean, each evening to quench her thirst at a freshwater spring in a clump of flax close to the base of Bluff Hill, then return to her people each morning. One evening, she was discovered by a young chief who wooed her and wanted her to remain on land. Eventually they married, but when Pania went to pay a final visit to her kin they forcibly restrained her in the briny depths, and she turned to stone as what is now known as **Pania Reef**. Fishers and divers still claim they can see her with her arms outstretched towards the shore.

been left as they were, complete with gang graffiti and, reputedly, the ghosts of former inmates. Either take a 45-minute audio tour ($20) or preferably time your visit to coincide with an hour-long guided tour (daily 9.30am, 11am, 1pm & 3pm, $20). In winter there is also the R16 night tour (June–Oct Fri & Sat nights at 6pm; $65) with dinner and lots of spooky interaction.

Ahuriri

Napier's European beginnings are all around the harbourside suburb of **Ahuriri**, 5km northwest of downtown. James Cook found shelter for the *Endeavour* in the Ahuriri Estuary, and the fledgling town grew up around the harbour. When the industrial port moved around the headland Ahuriri languished, but in the last few years the old wool stores and warehouses around the inner harbour (also known as the Iron Pot) have been reborn as cavernous bars and restaurants, all typically buzzing from Thursday evening through the weekend.

During the day it's a pleasant place to stroll beside the yachts, though the only real sight is the **National Tobacco Company Building**, on the corner of Bridge and Ossian streets. Its exterior is the most frequently used image of Art Deco Napier and exhibits a decorative richness seldom seen on industrial buildings, including Art Nouveau motifs of roses and raupo (a kind of Kiwi bulrush). In one of the former wool stores, the Kiwi Adventure Co, 58 West Quay (℡06/834 3500, ⊛www.kiwi-adventure.co.nz), has an indoor **climbing wall** ($15 all day).

Unique behind-the-scenes twenty-minute tours of a **sheepskin tannery** are offered by Classic Sheepskins, 22 Thames St (daily 11am & 2pm; free; ℡06/835 9662, ⊛www.classicsheepskins.co.nz). You also have the opportunity to buy factory-priced products including Ugg boots; they'll even pick you up for free from the city centre.

Eating, drinking and entertainment

Napier has plenty of places to keep you fed and watered, with assorted **cafés** and **restaurants** scattered around the centre and harbourside Ahuriri, although the very best chefs ply their trade at the region's premier **wineries** (see box, p.383). The most central **supermarket** is the large Countdown, Munroe Street (daily 6am–midnight).

It's rare to find any really exciting entertainment, unless you hit town at **festival time** (see box, p.377), but a couple of the **bars** host live music at weekends and when touring bands pass through. Straightforward drinking happens along Hastings Street, mostly the short stretch between Browning and Emerson streets, while a trendier crowd converges on Ahuriri's converted warehouse bars.

There are mainstream **movies** at Reading Cinema, 154 Station St (℡06/831 0600), and more arthouse films at Century Cinema, 65 Marine Parade (℡06/835 7781), in the Hawke's Bay Museum building.

City Centre

The Brazen Head 21 Hastings St. Napier's best Irish-style bar with good-value grub, outdoor seating and a lively, boozy atmosphere at weekends.

🏃 **Café Divine** 53 Hastings St. Lives up to its name with enormous slices of healthy home-made slices and filos and wraps, a delicious seafood chowder ($12.50), and other inexpensive breakfasts and lunches.

The Cri Café, Bar & Grill Market St. Standard Kiwi café fare at some of the best prices in town including nightly backpackers specials under $12. The lively bar has pool tables, big-screen TVs and occasional live music.

🏃 **Groove Kitchen Espresso** 112 Tennyson St. A fine little spot with lovely café food, irresistible coffee and a great sounds, from the stereo if not from the turntables in the corner.

Breakfast and lunch daily plus dinner Fri & Sat.

Guffle 29 Hastings St. Dress up (just a little) for this diminutive cocktail and wine bar with great tunes anytime and live music on Saturday night. Closed Sun.

Pacifica 209 Marine Parade ⊤ 06/833 6335. The menu changes daily at this sophisticated, marine-blue restaurant concentrating on fish and seafood with mains around the $37–40 mark. The hapuku fillets and teriyaki gurnard are particularly good. In fine weather, head for the bamboo-screened garden. Closed Sat & Sun.

Phoenix 43 Hastings St. A real nightclub (Wed–Sat), with live bands and DJs playing breaks, hip-hop and more. Very popular with both locals and visitors.

Soak 42 Marine Parade. A glass cube of café/restaurant that's part of the Ocean Spa complex, overlooking the pools. Drop in for well-prepared Kiwi café lunches and dinners, or just a coffee.

Thorps Coffee House 40 Hastings St. Wonderfully old-school eat-in or takeaway build-your-own sandwich place also serving good breakfasts, muffins and great coffee. The interior features bevelled Art Deco detailing.

Ujazi Café 28 Tennyson St. Chilled daytime café spinning reggae and serving great breakfasts (including vegetarian) and lunch: quiches, sandwiches and salads, plus fruit sorbets and good strong Fairtrade coffee.

Ahuriri

The Gintrap 66 West Quay. The food at this cobalt-blue corrugated-iron shed is nothing to shout about, but the quantities are good and the booze flows, particularly at weekends when half of Napier's youth seems to be on the timber deck overlooking the water.

Hep Set Mooch 58 West Quay. Gaudy, relaxed daytime café in another vast warehouse, with fun, friendly staff, serving a wide range of breakfasts (such as steaming porridge with stewed apple), great muffins (sweet and savoury) and a healthy selection of salads, frittatas and filo pies.

Master of India 79 Ahuriri Shopping Centre ⊤ 06/834 3440. Atmospheric curry house with ornate gilded decor and a broad menu of vegetarian delights and goat specialities, mostly under $20. Dinner nightly; BYO & licensed. Takeaways too.

Milk & Honey *Crown Hotel*, corner of Bridge St & Hardinge Rd ⊤ 06/833 6099. Polished boards, concrete beams and fold-back windows with sea views make this smart restaurant/bar a popular spot, aided by the modern international menu (mains around $28). Or just drop in to browse the foodie books over a Syrah or an espresso.

Provedore 60 West Quay ⊤ 06/834 0189. Ahuriri's classiest dining with an intimate but spirited atmosphere and delicious food that might include lemon-infused chicken breast on sweetcorn and polenta cakes ($29) followed by white chocolate, Drambuie and macadamia tart ($14). On Tuesday they offer two courses plus a glass of wine for $35. Closed Mon.

Cape Kidnappers and the wineries

No visit to Napier or Hastings is complete without spending some time exploring the surrounding seventy or so **wineries** and the gannet colony at **Cape Kidnappers**.

Cape Kidnappers

After James Cook's ill-starred initial encounter with Maori at Gisborne, he sailed to the southern limit of Hawke Bay and anchored off the jagged peninsula known to the Ngati Kahungunu as Te Matua-a-maui, "the fishhook of Maui" – a reference to the origin of the North Island, which was, as legend has it, dragged from the oceans by Maui. Here, Maori traders noticed two young Tahitian interpreters aboard the *Endeavour*; believing them to be held against their will, the traders captured one of them and paddled away. The boy escaped back to the ship, but Cook subsequently marked the point on his chart as **Cape Kidnappers**.

Neither Cook nor Joseph Banks, both meticulous in recording flora and fauna, mentioned any gannets on the peninsula's final shark-tooth flourish of pinnacles. However, a hundred years later, twenty or so pairs were recorded,

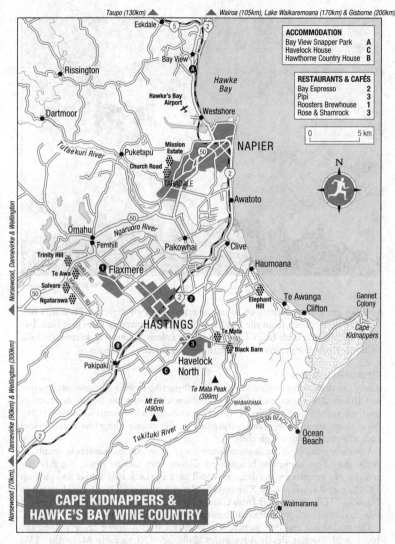

Eskdale

Bay View

Rissington

Hawke
Bay

Hawke's Bay
Airport

Dartmoor

Westshore

Tutaekuri River

Puketapu

Mission
Estate

NAPIER

Church Road

TARADALE

Awatoto

Omahu

Ngaruoro River

Fernhill

Pakowhai

Clive

Trinity Hill

Flaxmere

Haumoana

Te Awa

Salvare

Elephant
Hill

Te Awanga

Gannet
Colony

Ngatarawa

Clifton

Cape
Kidnappers

HASTINGS

Te Mata

Black Barn

Pakipaki

Havelock
North

Te Mata Peak
(399m)

WAIMARAMA
RD

OCEAN BEACH RD

Mt Erin
(490m)

Tukituki River

Ocean
Beach

CAPE KIDNAPPERS &
HAWKE'S BAY WINE COUNTRY

Waimarama

ACCOMMODATION
Bay View Snapper Park   **A**
Havelock House   **C**
Hawthorne Country House   **B**

RESTAURANTS & CAFÉS
Bay Espresso   **2**
Pipi   **3**
Roosters Brewhouse   **1**
Rose & Shamrock   **3**

0   5 km

N

Norsewood, Dannevirke & Wellington

Dannevirke (90km) & Wellington (300km)

Norsewood (70km)

and now there are over eight thousand pairs – making this the world's largest
mainland **gannet colony**.

Gannets are big birds, distinguished by their gold-and-black head markings and
their lack of fear of humans. The birds start nesting here in June, laying their eggs
from early July through to October, with the chicks hatching some six weeks later.
Once fledged, at around fifteen weeks, the young gannets embark on their
inaugural flight, a marathon, as-yet-unexplained 3000km journey to Australia,
where they spend a couple of years before flying back to spend the rest of their life
in New Zealand, returning to their place of birth to breed each year.

During the **breeding season** (July to late Oct), the cape is closed to the public,
and one colony, the Saddle, is always reserved for scientific study. At other times

▲ Gannet at Cape Kidnappers

you can get within a metre or so of the remaining two sites: the Plateau, a few hundred metres back from the Saddle, where 1500 chattering pairs nest beak-by-jowl; and the beachside Black Reef, the largest colony, a couple of kilometres back from the tip of the peninsula, where there are a further 2600 pairs.

Practicalities

There are three ways to visit the gannets, all starting from well-signposted points in **Clifton**, 20km southeast of Napier, both reached from the Napier or Hastings visitor centres with Kiwi Shuttle (booking essential; $30 return; ☎06/844 1104). Most tours are tide-dependent, travelling to the colony along the beach below rock fall-prone, 100m-high cliffs.

The most strenuous but least expensive way to get to the gannets is simply to **walk** the 11km along the beach from Clifton (late Oct to April; roughly 5hr return). No permits are needed, but you'll need to check **tide tables** and pick up DOC's useful *Guide to Cape Kidnappers* leaflet either from DOC or the Hastings or Napier i-SITEs. You set off from Clifton between three and four hours after high tide, and head back no more than ninety minutes after low tide.

The traditional and best gannet **trip** is aboard tractor-drawn trailers along the beach with Gannet Beach Adventures (daily late Oct to early May; 4hr; $38; ☎0800/426 638, ⓦwww.gannets.com), whose pace and approach give plenty of opportunities to appreciate the geology along the way and observe the birds at close quarters. These end near a DOC shelter, from where you face a twenty-minute uphill slog to the Plateau, where you'll have half an hour to admire the birds. If you don't fancy the uphill walk, go with Gannet Safaris (3hr trip; $60, plus $30 for Napier pick-up; ☎0800/427 232, ⓦwww.gannetsafaris.com), who take you right to the gannets by going **overland** through Summerlee Station.

Hawke's Bay wine country

Napier and Hastings are almost entirely encircled by the **Hawke's Bay's wine country**, one of New Zealand's largest and most exalted grape-growing regions.

Hawke's Bay wineries

There are over seventy **wineries** in the entire region. The following list represents our favourites, concentrating on those that make good lunch spots or feature some sort of attraction other than the obligatory wine tasting. Be warned that you may find it cheaper to buy the same bottle of wine at a local supermarket than at the cellar door.

Napier's closest wineries are 8km to the southwest in the suburb of **Taradale**. Closer to Hastings, there are clusters outside **Havelock North**, 5km southeast of Hastings, and 10km northwest near **Fernhill** – the fastest-growing wine district in Hawke's Bay. Winery **opening hours** are generally daily 10am–5pm in summer, but they are sometimes closed on Monday, Tuesday and even Wednesday when things are quiet.

The best of the winery restaurants are those at *Black Barn*, *Elephant Hill*, *Mission Estate* and *Te Awa*.

Black Barn Black Barn Road, Havelock North ☎06/877 7985, ⓦ www .blackbarn.com. Imaginatively designed winery that manages to remain low-key despite a great lunch bistro and café (mains around $30; closed Mon & Tues), a small art gallery, free tasting, a growers' market (mid-Nov to March Sat 9am–noon) and an amphitheatre that hosts a number of outdoor events through the summer. They also have some really lovely self-catering accommodation (⑧ & ⑨).

Church Road 150 Church Rd, Taradale ☎06/844 2053, ⓦ www.churchroad.co.nz. Renowned winery with an interesting guided tour ($12) which visits their museum, fashioned from old underground vats. Tastings (free; reserve tastings extra) often include their famed Church Road Chardonnay. Tasting platters for one or two cost $40.

Elephant Hill 86 Clifton Rd, Te Awanga ☎06/872 6060, ⓦ www.elephanthill.co.nz. A newcomer that has quickly made a splash with its architecturally dramatic winery building, single vineyard wines and fine restaurant/bar beside a calm pool. Mains are $30–35 and the restaurant is also open for dinner.

Mission Estate 198 Church Rd, Taradale ☎06/845 9350, ⓦ www.missionestate.co .nz. Noted for its pivotal role in the development of the Hawke's Bay's wine industry, New Zealand's oldest winery offers well-organized, free guided tours (daily 10.30am & 2pm) and has an excellent à la carte restaurant with lunch and dinner (mains $24–32) served on the terrace or in the old seminary building.

Ngatarawa 305 Ngatarawa Rd, Bridge Pa ☎06/879 7603, ⓦ www.ngatarawa.co.nz. An excellent first stop, a small winery with free tastings of quality tipples in a century-old stable complex with attractive picnic areas and a pétanque pitch.

Salvare 403 Ngatarawa Rd, Bridge Pa ☎06/874 9409, ⓦ www.salvare.co.nz. Little more than a one-man operation, this is the place to come for personal service, tasty wines and a couple of olive oils to try.

Te Awa 2375 SH50, Fernhill ☎06/879 7602, ⓦ www.teawa.com. Sited near the famed Gimblett Road, this winery produces exceptional reds (Merlot, Cabernet Merlot and Pinotage) that are more aromatic and livelier than many of their Hawke's Bay rivals. Lunch in what is one of New Zealand's finest winery restaurants is a treat dining inside or out on the likes of beef fillet with butternut pumpkin purée ($34) or sweetcorn and pea risotto ($25), all wine-matched, naturally.

Te Mata 349 Te Mata Rd, Havelock North ☎06/877 4399, ⓦ www.temata.co.nz. New Zealand's oldest winery on its existing site, now making a fairly small volume of premium handmade wines, notably a Bordeaux-style Coleraine, one of New Zealand's top reds. Free tastings with the added bonus of the architecturally controversial house among the grapes designed by Ian Athfield.

Trinity Hill 2396 SH50, Fernhill ☎06/879 7778 ⓦ www.trinityhill.com. Strikingly modern winery in the Gimblett Road area, producing excellent reds and Chardonnay and leading New Zealand's experimentation with the likes of Montepulciano, Tempranillo, Arneis and even make a port blended from Touriga Nacional.

Largely the province of boutique producers, it is threaded by the **Hawke's Bay wine trail**, which wends past 35-odd wineries, most offering free tastings and many with a restaurant, or at least the chance to picnic in the landscaped grounds.

Hawke's Bay is New Zealand's longest-established wine-growing region: vines were first planted in 1851 by French Marist missionaries, ostensibly to produce sacramental wine. The excess was sold, and the commercial aspect of the operation continues today as the Mission Estate Winery. Some fifty years later, other wineries began to spring up, favouring open-textured gravel terraces alongside the Tutaekuri, Ngaruroro and Tukituki rivers, which retain the day's heat and are free from moist sea breezes. In this arena the vineyards of the **Gimblett Road** – the so-called **Gimblett Gravels** – produce increasingly sought-after wines.

With a climatic pattern similar to that of the great Bordeaux vineyards, Hawke's Bay produces fine **Chardonnay** and lots of **Merlot**. **Cabernet Sauvignon** is also big but struggles to ripen in cooler summers. Many winemakers are now setting Hawke's Bay up to become New Zealand's flagship producer of **Syrah**, a subtler version of the Aussie Shiraz (though it is made from the same grape).

For the best introduction to what's on offer, visit Napier's **New Zealand Wine Centre**, 1 Shakespeare Rd (daily: Dec–Feb 8.30am–8pm; March–Nov 11am–6pm; $29; T06/835 5326, Wwww.nzwinecentre.co.nz), where you are taught how to identify wine flavours, then sit in a small cinema sampling six wines as winemakers on screen enthuse about their products.

Practicalities

If you have your own transport, head out with a copy of the *Winery Guide* leaflet (free from visitor centres), which lists wineries open to the public – see the box on p.383 for the pick of the bunch. Much of the country covered by the wine trail is also part of the region's **art and food trails**. The free *Hawke's Bay Art Guide* booklet directs you to the workshops and galleries of some of the best painters, sculptors, potters and craftspeople hereabouts, while the *Hawke's Bay Food Trail* leaflet (also free) includes a map showing the whereabouts of all manner of places producing and selling quality produce – everything from chocolate makers to olive oil producers and cheese manufacturers – along with gourmet cafés and restaurants.

If you can't find an abstemious driver, take a **wine tour**. At least half a dozen are on offer, most visiting four or five wineries over the course of a morning or afternoon. They're mainly Napier-based but will pick up in Hastings and Havelock North, usually free. Vince's World of Wine ($55; T06/836 6705, Wwww.vincestours.co.nz) is great fun, with an entertaining and knowledgeable guide and a flexible schedule. Another good bet is Grape Escape (T0800/100 489, Wwww.grapeescapenz.co.nz), which runs half-day trips ($65).

A great alternative is to **cycle** around the vineyards with On Yer Bike, 121 Rosser Rd, Hastings (T076/879 8735, Wwww.onyerbikehb.co.nz), who have put together a series of easy routes from two wineries in 14km to six in 23km. All-day bike rental (tandems available), route map, emergency mobile phone and a packed lunch are included in the $50 fee.

Hastings and around

Inland **HASTINGS**, 20km south of Napier, was once a rival to its northern neighbour as Hawke's Bay's premier city, buoyed by the wealth generated by the surrounding farmland and orchards. Napier's ascendancy as a tourist destination has put Hastings firmly in second place, though it does have an attractive core of buildings, erected after the same 1931 earthquake that rocked Napier. Hastings was saved from the worst effects of the ensuing fires, which were quenched using the artesian water beneath the city before they could take hold. As in Napier, **Art Deco** predominates and, though Hastings lacks the exuberance of its neighbour, there are some harmonious townscapes along Russell, Eastbourne and Heretaunga streets. Hastings also enthusiastically embraced the **Spanish Mission** style, and two exemplary buildings warrant a brief visit.

The area is at the heart of the wonderful Hawke's Bay wine country, and most of its vineyards are within easy reach. Apples, pears and peaches also continue to be grown in huge quantities, and the harvest, which begins in February and lasts three or four months, provides casual, hard-going, low-paying **orchard work** for those willing to thin, pick or pack fruit. The hostels are the best sources of work and up-to-the-minute information and will soon have you organized. Often there is so much work that you can be picky about what you accept. For more information about working in the region see Basics, p.67.

Hastings' neighbour is the upmarket **Havelock North**, 3km southeast and at the foot of the striking ridge line of **Te Mata Peak**. There isn't a great deal to it, and the only diversion is a drive up the peak, but the cobbled central streets lined with pavement cafés give it a village atmosphere.

Arrival and information

Long-distance **buses** pull up on Russell Street North, a few steps from the **i-SITE visitor centre**, 100 Heretaunga St East (Mon–Fri 8.30am–5pm, Sat & Sun 9am–4pm; ☎06/873 5526, ⊛www.hastings.co.nz), where you can buy tickets. There's **internet** access opposite at Hectic Netway, 102 Heretaunga St East. Local bus operator GoBay (☎06/878 9250) runs to Napier and Havelock North (Mon–Fri; limited services Sat) from the corner of Eastbourne Street East and Russell Street.

Accommodation

The availability of Hastings' budget-oriented **accommodation** is greatly affected by the **fruit-picking season**: from mid-February to May you'll struggle to find cheap accommodation, especially if you're looking for self-catering or a long-stay, unless you've booked well ahead, but nearby Napier makes a good alternative base if you're able to commute. For more luxurious accommodation, head for Havelock North, where **B&Bs** and swanky self-catering houses predominate.

A1 Backpackers 122 Stortford St ☎06/873 4285, ⊚a1backpackers@xtra.co.nz. *A1* has less of a work-camp feel than Hastings' other backpackers, making it perfect for those just passing through. It is peacefully set in a well-kept villa with a helpful owner into tramping. Free local pick-up for two-night stays. Dorms $23, rooms ❶

Hastings Top 10 Holiday Park 610 Windsor Ave ☎0508/427 846, ⊛www.hastingstop10.co.nz. Appealing campsite on the edge of Windsor Park, with tent sites, a range of modern units and good facilities, though it does get busy over the fruit-picking season. Camping $17, cabins ❷, s/c units ❹, park motel ❺

Havelock House 77 Endsleigh Rd, 3km southwest of Havelock North ☎06/877 5439, ⊛www.havelockhouse.co.nz. See map, p.381. Three large guest rooms (all with large beds, quality fittings and two with deep baths) occupy this spacious house in a quiet, woodsy setting. Guests can access a vast lounge (equipped with full-size billiard table), a tennis court and an outdoor pool, plus there's a separate two-bedroom house with deck and barbecue. Room ❻, suite ❺, house ❽

Hawthorne Country House 1420 SH2, 6km southwest of Hastings ☎06/878 0035, ⊛www.hawthorne.co.nz. Beautiful and very welcoming B&B in a grand Edwardian villa surrounded by croquet lawns and farmland. Five en-suite rooms are decorated with understated elegance and the breakfasts are delicious. See map, p.381. ❽

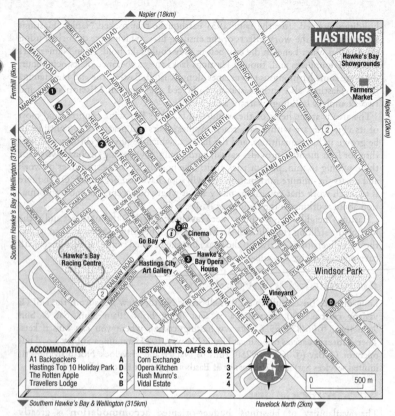

Napier (18km)

HASTINGS

Hawke's Bay Showgrounds

Farmers' Market

Fernhill (6km)

Napier (20km)

Southern Hawke's Bay & Wellington (315km)

Go Bay ★   Cinema

Hawke's Bay Racing Centre

Hastings City Art Gallery

Hawke's Bay Opera House

Vineyard

Windsor Park

N

ACCOMMODATION	
A1 Backpackers	A
Hastings Top 10 Holiday Park	D
The Rotten Apple	C
Travellers Lodge	B

RESTAURANTS, CAFÉS & BARS	
Corn Exchange	1
Opera Kitchen	3
Rush Munro's	2
Vidal Estate	4

0   500 m

Southern Hawke's Bay & Wellington (315km)   Havelock North (2km)

The Rotten Apple 114 Heretaunga St East ☎06/878 4363, ⓦwww.rottenapple.co.nz. Super-central hostel with a lively atmosphere, plenty of assistance for fruit workers and low weekly rates. Dorms $22, rooms ❷

Travellers Lodge 608 St Aubyn St West ☎06/878 7108, ⓦwww.tlodge.co.nz. Garden-set hostel in a pair of suburban houses, with a sauna, bike rental, wi-fi and off-street parking. There is a range of rooms, all with comfy beds, but these are often full Nov–May. Dorms $21, rooms ❷

The Town

After the 1931 earthquake, Hastings looked to the Californian-inspired **Spanish Mission** style of architecture: roughcast stucco walls, arched windows, small balconies, barley-twist columns and heavily overhung roofs clad in terracotta tiles. The finest examples can be seen in an hour or so, using the self-guided *Spanish Mission Hastings* walk leaflet (free from the i-SITE), but if time is short, limit your wanderings to Heretaunga Street East, where the visitor centre is located inside the **Westerman's Building**, with gorgeous bronzework and sumptuous lead lighting. The **Hawke's Bay Opera House**, on the corner with Hastings Street, was actually built fifteen years before the earthquake, but was remodelled to create the region's finest Spanish Mission facade. The i-SITE runs occasional ninety-minute Spanish Mission **guided walks** (Nov–March Sat 11am; $10).

Also worth a quick look is the **Hastings City Art Gallery**, 201 Eastbourne St East (daily 10am–4.30pm; free; ☎06/871 5095), which hosts all manner of art shows, usually well curated.

Te Mata Peak

Driving from Hastings to Havelock North, the long ridge of limestone bluffs which make up the 399m **Te Mata Peak** loom into view. The ridge is held to be the supine form of a Maori chief, Rongokako, who choked on a rock as he tried to eat through the hill – just one of many Herculean feats he attempted while wooing the beautiful daughter of a Heretaunga chief. Te Mata Peak Road winds up the hill to a wonderful vantage point that's great towards sunset. Views stretch over the fertile plains, north across Hawke's Bay and Cape Kidnappers, and east to surf-pounded Ocean Beach and Waimarama, the main swimming **beaches** for Hastings and Havelock North.

A parking area partway up Te Mata Peak Road marks the start of moderate **walking tracks** through groves of native trees and redwoods and a wetland area before reaching the summit (2–3hr return). According to legend, overcome with grief at her father's death, Rongokako's daughter threw herself off the peak – something you can emulate by **tandem paragliding** with Airplay Paragliding (⊕06/845 1977, ⓦairplay.co.nz), who ride the thermals and Pacific winds for 15min ($140). You can also head cross-country for an hour ($250), or even longer.

Eating and drinking

For a town of its size, Hastings is relatively poorly supplied with good places to **eat**, though an ever-expanding selection of places in neighbouring Havelock North bumps up the quota, and lunches at the region's **wineries** are a good option (see box, p.383). On a fine Sunday morning, skip breakfast and head straight for the **Hawke's Bay Farmers' Market** (Sun 8.30am–12.30pm; indoors in winter), at the Hawke's Bay Showgrounds on Kenilworth Road where around fifty stalls introduce you to fresh local produce, coffee and pastries while a local musician or two entertain.

Bay Espresso 141 Karamu Rd, 3km north of Hastings. See map, p.381. Rustic, daytime café (with plenty of garden seating) that's the locals' weekend home-from-home, offering superb coffee, light and healthy lunch specials around $15 as well as organic single-source beans from its own roastery ($8/200g).

Corn Exchange 118 Maraekakaho Rd, Hastings. Stylish restaurant and bar converted from an attractive 1930s grain store on the western fringes of the city, serving moderately priced lunches and dinners.

Opera Kitchen 312 Eastbourne St East, Hastings. Classy licensed café showcasing local produce through simple but delicious dishes served in stripped-back surroundings. Open daytime daily and for pre-theatre dinner when there's something on at the Opera House next door.

Pipi 16 Joll Rd, Havelock North. See map, p.381. Impressive in its pinkness, this casual and very popular café and pizza restaurant exudes casual style. Nothing matches but everything fits, and you help yourself from the drinks fridge and tell them what you've drunk when you pay. The food's great too, offering the likes of fishcakes with rocket and white bean mash ($19), great traditional pizzas (from $16) and a slew of local wines. Evening only; closed Tues.

Roosters Brewhouse 1470 Omahu Rd, 7km west of central Hastings. See map, p.381. Welcoming microbrewery offering traditional natural brews, best supped in its pleasant café or outdoors at garden tables while tucking into straightforward hearty dishes at reasonable prices. There's also free tasting of its English ale, lager and dark beers, and you can buy a flagon to take away – a wise move considering the prices elsewhere. Closed Sun.

Rose & Shamrock 15 Napier Rd, Havelock North. See map, p.381. A fair attempt at an Irish pub, with 24 Irish, English and Kiwi beers on tap, plus well-priced bar meals and occasional Irish folk bands.

Rush Munro's 704 Heretaunga St West, Hastings. A small ice-cream garden that's been packing in the locals for years. For the retro experience go for the feijoa peaked cone.

Vidal Estate 913 Aubyn St East, Hastings; book at weekends ⊕06/872 7440. Ingredients are mostly local and organic in this popular semi-formal restaurant attached to a winery set amid huge wine barrels. Dinner might include lemon and sumac-marinated chicken ($32) followed by Bakewell tart ($15). There's also an inviting bar area where tapas are served.

Southern Hawke's Bay

South of Hastings, the main road (SH2) runs through the relentless sheep stations of **Southern Hawke's Bay**, a region uncluttered by places of genuine interest. Small farming towns stand as fitting memorials to the pioneers who tamed the region, particularly Danes and Norwegians who stepped in when the New Zealand Wars of the 1860s discouraged immigration from Britain.

If time isn't too pressing, make brief stops at **"Scandinavian" settlements** such as the hilltop village of **NORSEWOOD**, little more than quiet Coronation Street, which runs from a replica Norwegian-style stave church, past *Café Norsewood* to a glassed-in boathouse containing the fishing boat *Bindalsfaering*, a gift from the Norwegian government commemorating Norsewood's centenary in 1972.

Some 20km south of Norsewood, the Danish heritage of the larger farming town of **DANNEVIRKE** is flagged by a modern windmill in Copenhagen Square on the main street, along with cut-out signs of smiling Vikings greeting and farewelling visitors. If you're after sustenance, try the *Black Stump* **café** at 21 High St.

South of Dannevirke, SH2 runs 25km to Woodville, where SH3 strikes west through the Manawatu Gorge to Palmerston North and SH2 heads south into the Wairarapa.

The Wairarapa

Most of the **Wairarapa** region is archetypal Kiwi sheep country, with white-flecked green hills stretching into the distance. In recent years, however, the southern half of the region has increasingly benefited from free-spending weekenders from Wellington visiting the boutique hotels and innovative restaurants of Martinborough and Greytown.

The establishment of New Zealand's earliest sheep station in the 1840s on rich alluvial lands close to present-day Martinborough paved the way for development by the progressive **Small Farm Association** (SFA). This was the brainchild of Joseph Masters, a Derbyshire cooper and longtime campaigner against the separation of landowner and labourer, who sought to give disenfranchised settlers the opportunity to become smallholders. He was supported by liberal governor George Grey who, in 1853, suggested that the SFA persuade Maori to sell land for the establishment of two towns – **Masterton** and **Greytown**.

Initially Greytown prospered, and it retains an air of antiquity rare among New Zealand towns, but the routing of the rail line favoured Masterton, which soon became the main commercial centre, famed chiefly today for the annual Golden

Long names and famous flutes

Visitors in search of the esoteric might want to stray along SH52, which makes a 120km tar-sealed loop east towards the rugged coastline from dull Waipukurau, 50km south of Hastings, re-emerging at Dannevirke. Almost 50km south of Waipukurau (and 6km south of Porangahau, where there is rare coastal access), a sign marks the hill known as Taumatawhakatangihangakoauauotamateaturipukaka-pikimaungahoronukupokaiwhenuakitanatahu, which, unsurprisingly, rates as one of the world's longest place names; roughly, this mouthful translates as "the hill where Tamatea, circumnavigator of the lands, played the flute for his lover".

Shears sheepshearing competition. North of Masterton, the **Pukaha Mount Bruce National Wildlife Centre** provides a superb opportunity to witness ongoing bird conservation work; to the south, **Featherston** is a base for walks up the bed of the Rimutaka Incline Railway.

The goal of many Wellingtonians and visitors is **Martinborough**, the region's wine capital and far and away its most appealing town. Back on the coast, the laidback holiday settlement of **Castlepoint** is the place for swimming and surfing, and **Cape Palliser** is a good destination for blustery mind-clearing walks and dramatic coastal scenery.

Cross the **Rimutaka Range** towards Wellington and you're into the Hutt Valley, full of commuter-belt communities, none of which really warrant a stop until you reach Petone, on the outskirts of the capital.

Tui Brewery and Pukaha Mount Bruce National Wildlife Centre

The northern half of the Wairarapa is very much a continuation of southern Hawke's Bay, but instead of speeding through this pastoral country, make a brief stop 10km south of Woodville at Mangatainoka, home to the **Tui Brewery** (Mon–Thurs 10am–4pm, Fri–Sun 10am–5pm; ℡06/376 0815, ⓦwww.tui.co.nz). This brews fairly ordinary beer that has built an enthusiastic following with its "Yeah. Right" billboard advertisements seen all over the country. The theme is explored in the small museum (free) adjacent to the café and bar serving good Kiwi tucker. You can sample several beers and keep the glass ($12.50) or join one of the **tours** (daily 11am & 2pm; $15; bookings essential), which include a visit to the distinctive seven-storey brick brewery, tastings and, again, a glass to keep.

Some 40km south of the Tui Brewery, **Pukaha Mount Bruce National Wildlife Centre** (daily 9am–4.30pm; $15; ⓦwww.mtbruce.org.nz) is one of the best places in the country to view endangered native birds. Kokako, kakariki, Campbell Island teal, hihi, kiwi, takahe and more can be found in spacious aviaries set along a 1km trail through lowland primeval forest. Beyond the trail several thousand hectares of forest are used for reintroducing birds to the wild. The generous size of the cages on the trail and the thick foliage often make the birds hard to spot, so you'll need to be patient. More immediate gratification comes in the form of a stand of Californian redwoods, a nocturnal **kiwi house**, reptilian tuatara, and a closed-circuit camera trained on the birds' nests in the breeding season (Oct–March). A twenty-minute audiovisual gives a moving account of the decline of birdlife in New Zealand, long-fin eels are fed at 1.30pm, and at 3pm each day a flock of kaka come to feed. Hour-long guided tours (daily 10.30am & 2pm; $10) add context, and you can use the picnic area or relax in the café.

High above the wildlife centre, you can **stay** at *The Hut* (℡06/375 8681, ⓦwww.thehut.co.nz; ❸), a wonderfully rustic but comfy bush cottage with an outdoor tub for a romantic bath under the stars and a log burner to cook meals. It's a steep forty-minute walk, or you can arrange four-wheeler transport with the owners for a small additional charge.

Masterton and around

Though it is Wairarapa's largest town, workaday **MASTERTON**, crouched at the foot of the Tararua Range some 30km south of Pukaha Mount Bruce, is of only passing interest. Central Masterton is bounded on its eastern side by the large **Queen Elizabeth Park**, and strolling around the formal gardens is a pleasant way to pass an hour or so. Opposite, **Aratoi**, on the corner of Bruce and Dixon streets (daily 10am–4.30pm; donation; ⓦwww.aratoi.co.nz), offers regularly changing insights into the history of the Wairarapa region along with some excellent art exhibitions.

The town's major event is the annual **Golden Shears** competition (ⓦwww .goldenshears.co.nz), effectively the Olympiad of all things woolly, held on the three days leading up to the first Saturday in March. Contestants flock from around the world to demonstrate their prowess with the broad-blade handpiece; a top shearer can remove a fleece in under a minute, though for maximum points it must be done with skill as well as speed and leave a smooth and unblemished, if shivering, beast. For a few bucks you can just walk in on the early rounds, but to attend the entertaining finals day on Saturday you'll need to book well in advance.

On a similar theme, **Shear Discovery**, 12 Dixon St (daily 10am–4pm; $5) is an excellent little museum on all things woolly. Housed in two century-old shearing sheds relocated from rural Wairarapa, it's filled with everything from sheep pens and shearing handpieces to pressed bales of wool stencilled with the marks of sheep stations. Classic 1957 footage of Kiwi shearing hero Godfrey Bowen shows how it should be done, and there's usually footage of recent Golden Shears finals, perhaps showing the super-fast handiwork of David Fagan, New Zealand's five-time world champ and winner of the Golden Shears a record sixteen times.

Draped over the hills to the west of town, the **Tararua Forest Park** offers some excellent tramping through beech and podocarp forests to the sub alpine tops, where the notoriously fickle weather can be dangerous. Serious walkers should consider the **Powell–Jumbo Tramp**, a highly worthwhile twelve-hour circuit that can be broken down into two or more manageable days by staying at **huts** (two costing $15, one $5) evenly spaced along the route. The track starts at the backcountry hut-style *Holdsworth Lodge* (tent sites $6, lodge $15; booking essential at ⓦwww.doc.govt.nz), 25km west of Masterton at the end of Norfolk Road, off southbound SH2. Day-trippers can undertake easy riverside walks (1–2hr) or head three hours across easy ground to the new and warm Atiwhakatu Hut ($5).

Practicalities

Masterton's commercial heart is strung along the parallel Chapel, Queen and Dixon streets. TranzMetro (☏0800/801 700) runs commuter services from Wellington to the **train station**, at the end of Perry Street, a fifteen-minute walk from the centre, or call Masterton Radio Taxis (☏06/378 2555). Tranzit **buses** (not Sat or Sun; ☏0800/471 227) north to Palmerston North stop at 316 Queen St, a short walk from the **i-SITE visitor centre**, on the corner of Bruce and Dixon streets (Mon–Fri 9am–5pm & Sat–Sun 10am–4pm; ☏06/370 0900, ⓦwww .wairarapanz.com), which stocks info on local hikes. Masterton's best budget **accommodation** is the spacious and attractive *Mawley Park Motor Camp*, 15 Oxford St (☏06/378 6454, ⓦwww.mawleypark.co.nz; camping $12, cabins ❶). There are clean and peaceful, old-style motel rooms at *Cornwall Park*, 119 Cornwall St (☏06/378 2939, ⓦwww.cornwallparkmotel.co.nz; ❸), 2km west of the town centre, with a pool, spa and free wi-fi. Units at *Chardonnay Motor Lodge*, 274 High St, 4km south of the centre (☏0800/222 880, ⓦwww.bkschardonnay.co.nz; ❹) are modern and well appointed.

Masterton's **eating** options are limited but adequate. The best cafés are *Entice*, at Aratoi, and *Café Cecille*, in Queen Elizabeth Park (☏06/370 1166; daytimes plus early evenings Fri & Sat), which occupies the genteel former aquarium building, with wide verandas. *Café Strada*, 232 Queen St, is also good during the day, stays open for quality, moderately priced dinners and has wi-fi.

Castlepoint

The 300km of coastline from Cape Kidnappers, near Napier, south to Cape Palliser is bleak, desolate and almost entirely inaccessible – except for **CASTLE-POINT**, 65km east of Masterton, where early explorers found a welcome break in the "perpendicular line of cliff". A lighthouse presides over the rocky knoll, which is linked to the mainland by a thin hourglass double **beach** that encloses a sheltered **lagoon** known as the Basin. Wairarapa families retreat here for summer fun and surfers ride the breakers, though when the weather turns rough it becomes a wonderfully wild bit of coastline.

The *Castlepoint Store* (T 06/372 6823) has a daytime **café**, an unreliable restaurant/bar (usually Fri & Sat evenings plus nightly in Jan) and **information** about *baches* that can be rented (some by the night). You can also **stay** at the *Castlepoint Holiday Park & Motels* (T 06/372 6705, W www.castlepoint.co.nz; camping $17–21, kitchen cabins ❸, units ❺) and a garden cottage (❺).

Carterton and Stonehenge Aotearoa

Some 15km south of Masterton, **CARTERTON** is home to **Paua World**, 54 Kent St (Mon–Fri 8am–5pm, Sat & Sun 9am–5pm; free; W www.pauashell.co.nz), an Aladdin's Cave of objects fashioned from this beautiful rainbow-swirled seashell – you can pick up anything from wonderfully kitsch fridge magnets to elegant jewellery here. The factory supplies just about every tourist knick-knack shop in the country and you can even take a brief, free self-guided tour to see how the stuff is made.

Stonehenge Aotearoa, 12km southeast of Carterton (Wed–Sun 10am–4pm; $15; guided tours Sat 2pm & Sun 11am; bookings essential T 06/377 1600, W www.stonehenge-aotearoa.com), appears like some vision of neolithic Britain on a low hill amid Wairarapa farmland. Though built on the same scale as its kin on Salisbury Plain, the similarity ends. This is a modern wood and concrete edifice, technically classed as a garden ornament by the local council when planning permission was sought. The resulting "open-sky observatory" is primarily educational and best experienced on the detailed ninety-minute tours which cover a fascinating array of information ranging from pure astronomy through Maori star stories and navigation to astrology and myth-busting comparative religion.

Some 5km south of Carterton, a rough road runs 15km west into the foothills of the Tararua Range to **Waiohine Gorge**, a picturesque chasm that's ideal for picnics.

Greytown

Laid out in 1853, the gracious settlement of **GREYTOWN**, 9km south of Carterton, still retains something of its original Victorian feel. Once the Wairarapa's main settlement, it declined when the railway bypassed the town and only revived when it became a favoured getaway from Wellington. The two-storey wooden buildings either side of the highway now house assorted art galleries, "collectibles" shops, excellent cafés and chichi B&Bs mostly geared to the weekender set but perfect for a short break.

The French Baker, 81 Main St, serves delectable sandwiches, **pastries** and cakes, or pop across the road to the reliable *Main Street Deli*, at no. 88, which serves moderately priced **meals** and sells a good range of breads and cheeses.

You can **stay** in grand style at *The White Swan*, no. 109 (T 06/304 8894, W www.thewhiteswan.co.nz; ❻) a verandahed, two-storey building moved here in pieces from Lower Hutt in 2002, or consult W www.greytown.co.nz for listings of several gorgeous **B&Bs**.

Featherston and the Rimutaka Incline

The last of the Wairarapa towns before SH2 climbs west over the Rimutaka range is **Featherston**, 13km south of Greytown. Steam buffs cross the country to visit the **Fell Locomotive Museum** on Lyon Street (daily 10am–4pm; $5), which contains the last surviving example of the locos that, for 77 years (until the boring of a new tunnel in 1955), climbed the 265m, one-in-fifteen slope of the Rimutaka Incline.

The rails have long been pulled up, but you can follow the trackbed on the **Rimutaka Rail Trail** (18km; 4–5hr; 265m ascent), which starts 10km south of Featherston at Cross Creek, passes old shunting yards and shuffles through the 576m summit tunnel before descending to Kaitoke. To save a long shuttle, most just walk up to the summit and back (4–5hr return), or do the same trip by bicycle (3hr return). Unfortunately, rental bikes from Martinborough are barely up to the job. There are three basic, grassy campsites along the rail trail.

Martinborough

Over the last couple of decades, tiny **MARTINBOROUGH**, 18km southeast of Featherston, has been transformed from a small and obscure farming town into the centre of a compact wine region synonymous with some of New Zealand's finest reds. It's within easy striking distance of Wellington, and weekends see the arrival of the smart set to load up their shiny 4WDs at the wineries. On Mondays and Tuesdays much of the town simply shuts down to recover.

Arrival and accommodation

Tranzit **buses** (℡0800/471 227), shuttling between Featherston, Masterton and Martinborough, meet the TranzMetro commuter **trains** from Wellington (℡04/801 7000) and drop off diagonally opposite the **i-SITE visitor centre**, 18 Kitchener St (Mon–Fri 9am–5pm, Sat & Sun 10am–4pm; ℡06/306 5010, ⓦwww.martinboroughnz.com), which has **internet access**.

The town's **accommodation** options lean heavily towards mid- and upper-price B&Bs and homestays, most of them in rural surroundings out of town, as well as self-contained cottages starting at around $120. Rooms are hard to find during festivals and any summer weekend: weeknights are much easier.

Kate's Place 7 Cologne St ℡06/306 9935, ⓦwww.katesplace.co.nz. Cosy, laidback homestay and backpacker combo in a weatherboard cottage on a quiet street. There's just one en-suite double plus a couple of top-quality four-share dorms with super-comfy timber bunks. Breakfast isn't served, but you can use Kate's kitchen, there are heaps of books to read and guests can borrow a bike and use the internet for free. Dorms $30, room ❸

Martinborough Motel 43 Strasbourge St ℡06/306 9408. Central budget motel with ageing but adequate units. ❷

Martinborough Village Camping 10 Dublin St West ℡06/306 8946, ⓦwww.martinboroughcamping .com. Impeccably maintained campsite 10min walk from the centre, with tent sites separate from van hook-ups, modern kitchen and showers, intentional absence of TV, and bike rental for $35/day. Camping $17, cabins ❷

The Old Manse 19 Grey St ℡06/306 8599, ⓦwww.oldmanse.co.nz. Boutique B&B in a wonderful old villa amid the vines on the edge of town. Room ❻, suite ❼

Peppers Martinborough Hotel Memorial Square ℡06/306 9350, ⓦwww.martinboroughhotel .co.nz. The attractively restored Grand Dame of Martinborough, offers rooms either upstairs in the old building (with French doors opening onto a veranda) and more contemporary rooms set around the garden. There's also a good restaurant and bar. ❻

Straw House 22–24 Cambridge Rd ℡06/306 8577, ⓦwww.thestrawhouse.co.nz. Choose from a studio or s/c two-bedroom house, both built of straw bales and stylishly decorated. Breakfast goodies are provided and there's a small reduction for second and subsequent nights. Studio ❺, house ❽

Featherston (18km)

MARTINBOROUGH

ACCOMMODATION

Kate's Place	A
Martinborough Motel	F
Martinborough Village Camping	B
The Old Manse	C
Peppers Martinborough Hotel	E
Straw House	D

Palliser

Martinborough

Margrain

Murdoch James Estate Winery (9km), Lake Ferry (35km) & Cape Palliser (65km)

KITCHENER STREET

HUANGARUA ROAD

PURUTANGA ROAD

PRINCESS STREET

PANAMA STREET

NAPIER STREET

Martinborough Wine Centre

CAMBRIDGE STREET

Ata Rangi

BROADWAY STREET

OHIO STREET

TEXAS ST

KANSAS ST

COLOGNE STREET

STRASBOURGE STREET

NEW YORK STREET

The Square

ROBERTS STREET

GREY STREET

DUBLIN STREET

VENICE STREET

KANSAS ST

CORK STREET

TEXAS ST

OXFORD STREET

SACKVILLE STREET

REGENT STREET

WELD STREET

JELLICOE STREET

DANIEL STREET

MALCOLM STREET

SUEZ STREET

REGENT STREET

Vynfields Estate Winery (100m)

| 0 | 500 m |

RESTAURANTS, CAFÉS & BARS

Café Medici	3
Est	5
Ingredient	2
Jaqs	1
The Village Café	4
Wendy Campbell's French Bistro	3

The town and wineries

Martinborough was initially laid out in the 1870s by landowner John Martin, who named the streets after cities he had visited on his travels and arranged the core, centred on a leafy square, in the form of a Union Jack. Martinborough languished as a minor agricultural centre for over a century until the first four wineries – Ata Rangi, Dry River, Chifney and Martinborough (all of which produced their first vintages in 1984) – re-invented Martinborough as the coolest, driest and most wind-prone of the North Island's grape-growing regions. With the aid of shelter belts that slice the horizon, the wineries produce some outstanding Pinot Noir, very good Cabernet Sauvignon, rich Chardonnay and wonderfully aromatic Riesling.

Martinborough promotes its viticultural prowess with several **festivals**. Tickets sell out in hours in early October for Toast Martinborough (third Sun in Nov; Ⓦwww.toastmartinborough.co.nz), a wine-oriented affair with most of the vineyards open to ticket holders, and top Wellington and local restaurants selling their wares. There's a considerably more egalitarian feel to the two Martinborough Fairs (first Sat in Feb & March; Ⓦwww.martinboroughfair.org.nz) – huge country fêtes during which the streets radiating from the central square are lined with art and craft stalls.

Outside these times, the best starting point is **Martinborough Wine Centre**, 6 Kitchener St (daily 10am–5pm; Ⓦwww.martinboroughwinecentre.co.nz), a wine shop with free tastings from a couple of local wineries and **bike rental** ($35/day)

▲ *Vynfields* winery

for a spin through the vineyards. Over a dozen wineries are accessible on foot or by bike, guided by the free and widely available *Wairarapa Wine Trail* sheet. During the summer places generally open from 11am to 4pm at weekends and shorter hours midweek. They usually charge a $5 **tasting fee**, but refund the fee with any wine purchase.

Wineries

Ata Rangi Puruatanga Rd ☏06/306 9570, ⓦwww.atarangi.co.nz. One of New Zealand's finest Pinot Noir producers also does the excellent Célèbre Merlot/Syrah blend and lovely Chardonnay. Central and a great place to start.

Margrain Vineyard Ponatahi Rd ☏06/306 9292, ⓦwww.margrainvineyard.co.nz. Good-quality wine from the relaxed cellar door plus the great little *Old Winery Café* (generally open noon–3pm) overlooking the vines with most of the well-priced dishes matched to Margrain wines.

Martinborough Vineyard Princess St ☏06/306 9955, ⓦwww.martinborough-vineyard.co.nz. A Martinborough original and still one of the largest, producing top-quality Pinot Noir and Chardonnay.

Murdoch James Dry River Rd ☏06/306 9165, ⓦwww.murdochjames.co.nz. Premium producer

some 9km south of Martinborough with a very good daytime café/restaurant and deck, a relaxed tasting room and personalized tours of the vineyard and winery ($30, booking essential).

Palliser Kitchener St ☏06/306 9019, ⓦwww .palliser.co.nz. This pioneering Martinborough winery limits its impact on the environment while producing premium wines and running cooking classes. Picnics are encouraged in the pleasant formal garden.

Vynfields 22 Omarere Rd ☏06/306 9901, ⓦwww.vynfields.com. Choose from open lawns, shady bowers or the elegant villa interior to sample flights of five wines (quarter glasses $12, half glasses $18) accompanied by antipasto platters ($28) and terrines ($15) to share. Closed weekdays in winter.

Eating and drinking

Lunch at a winery restaurant or a platter among the vines (see above) is an essential part of the Martinborough experience, though the town also caters to discerning diners with several **restaurants** charging moderate to high prices, in return for high-quality dishes.

Café Medici 9 Kitchener St. Busy breakfast and lunch café efficiently serving the likes of char-grilled veg salad, salmon and cod cakes, and delectable three-cheese tarts either inside or out. Closed Tues.

Est The Square ℡ 06/306 9665. Come to Martinborough's nineteenth-century former post office for a Chardonnay on the pavement, a Pinot Noir inside the cosy wine bar or some contemporary cuisine (mains $27–33) in the classy restaurant.

Ingredient 8 Kitchener St. The place to stock up on gourmet local produce such as wine, olives, cheese and charcuterie.

Jaqs New York St. Popular local haunt where you can cook your own BBQ and sip boutique bottled New Zealand and imported beers. Closed Mon & Tues.

The Village Café 6 Kitchener St. Daytime café with seating in the rustic-chic, barn-like interior and the pergola-covered courtyard, serving a range of tasty brunches, pizzas and salads, and good espresso.

Wendy Campbell's French Bistro 3 Kitchener St ℡ 06/306 8863. The understated frontage and eclectic decor give little indication that this place offers the finest eating in town, in classic French style but informed by seasonal Kiwi produce. Mains around $35. Booking essential at weekends.

Cape Palliser

Low-key, cosmopolitan Martinborough stands in dramatic contrast to the stark, often windswept coast around **Cape Palliser**, 60km south. The southernmost point on the North Island, the cape was named in honour of James Cook's mentor, Rear Admiral Sir Hugh Palliser. Apart from a few gentle walks and the opportunity to observe fur seals at close quarters, there's not a lot to do out here but kick back, especially since swimming is unsafe and the weather changeable.

From Martinborough, a sealed road leads 35km south to **Lake Ferry**, a tiny, laidback surfcasting settlement on the sandy shores of Lake Onoke. Here, the *Lake Ferry Hotel* (℡ 06/307 7831, ⓦ www.lakeferryhotel.co.nz; dorms $25, rooms ❷) – the southernmost on the North Island – is a great spot for fish and chips on a sunny afternoon on your way back to Martinborough. There's a traditional Kiwi public **bar** and garden, overlooking the water, and plus a slightly more formal restaurant; arrive early to grab a table on fine weekends. Nearby, the dirt-cheap *Lake Ferry Holiday Park* (℡ 06/307 7873; camping $10, cabins ❶, s/c units ❸) is a little cramped but handy for the pub.

The Cape Palliser road then twists for 13km through the coastal hills until it meets the sea near the **Putangirua Pinnacles**, dozens of grey soft-rock spires and fluted cliffs up to 50m high, formed by wind and rain selectively eroding the surrounding silt and gravel. From the parking area (where there are BBQ areas and a toilets-and-water DOC **campsite**; $6) allow a couple of hours to wander up the easy streambed to the base of the pinnacles, up to a viewpoint and then back along a pretty, ridgetop bush track.

Beyond the pinnacles, the sealed road hugs the rugged, exposed coastline for 15km to **Ngawi**, a small fishing village where all manner of **bulldozers** grind out their last days, hauling sometimes massive fishing boats up the steep gravel beach. It is five rough kilometres on to the cape proper, where a **fur seal colony**, right beside the road, is overlooked by the century-old Cape Palliser **lighthouse**, standing on a knoll 60m above the sea at the top of a long flight of some 250 steps. It's easy enough to get within 20m of the seals, but they can become aggressive if they feel threatened, and move surprisingly quickly, given their bulk – keep your distance from pups or their parents, and don't get between any seal and the sea.

Travel details

Trains

The only rail services in the region are commuter services from Wellington to Masterton.

Masterton to: Carterton (2–6 daily; 15min); Featherston (2–6 daily; 40min); Wellington (2–6 daily; 1hr 30min).

Buses

Gisborne to: Auckland (2 daily; 9hr 15min); Hastings (1–2 daily; 5hr); Napier (2 daily; 4hr); Opotiki, via SH2 (2 daily; 2hr); Rotorua (2 daily; 5hr); Wairoa (1 daily; 1hr 30min); Whakatane (2 daily; 3hr).

Hastings to: Auckland (2 daily; 7hr 30min); Dannevirke (4 daily; 1hr 30min); Gisborne (1–2 daily; 5hr); Napier (Mon–Fri hourly or better, Sat 5 daily; 1hr); Norsewood (3 daily; 1hr 10min); Taupo (4–5 daily; 2hr 30min); Wellington (3 daily; 4hr 45min).

Masterton to: Carterton (5–6 Mon–Fri, 3 Sat–Sun; 25min); Featherston (6 Mon–Fri; 1hr); Greytown (6 Mon–Fri; 30–40min); Palmerston North (1–2 daily; 2hr).

Napier to: Auckland (2 daily; 7hr 15min); Dannevirke (4 daily; 2hr); Gisborne (1–2 daily; 4hr); Hastings (Mon–Fri hourly or better, Sat 5 daily; 1hr); Norsewood (4 daily; 1hr 30min); Palmerston North (3 daily; 3hr); Taupo (4–5 daily; 2hr); Wellington (4 daily; 5hr 15min).

Wairoa to: Gisborne (1 daily; 1hr 30min); Napier (1–2 daily; 2hr 30min).

Flights

Gisborne to: Auckland (6–7 daily; 1hr); Wellington (3–4 daily; 1hr 10min).

Napier/Hastings to: Auckland (7–10 daily; 1hr); Christchurch (2 daily; 1hr 25min); Wellington (4–5 daily; 50min).

Wellington and around

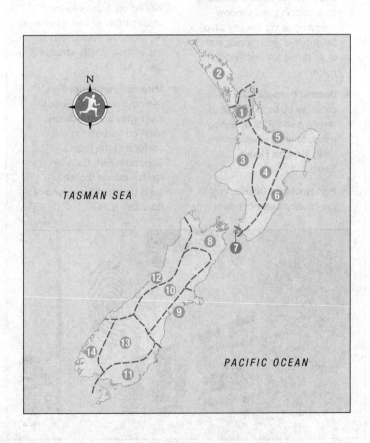

CHAPTER 7   # Highlights

✳ **Te Papa** The striking and inventive national museum showcases New Zealand's natural and bicultural history through intriguing exhibits, interactive technology and the nation's premier art collection. See p.408

✳ **Cuba Street** People-watching, café-hopping and window-shopping along the city's hip "alternative" strip give a taste of its divergent lifestyles. See p.409

✳ **Botanic Gardens** Ride the cable car up to Wellington's serene gardens for sweeping views, fragrant roses and the lovely Begonia House. See p.411

✳ **Parliamentary District** Visit the country's seat of power and associated national institutions, and view documents highlighting milestones on the country's road to nationhood including the original Treaty of Waitangi. See p.411

✳ **Zealandia: the Karori Sanctuary Experience** Native birds once again flock around Wellington, thanks to the predator-free environment and regenerating native bush at this unique wildlife sanctuary. See p.413

✳ **Miramar Peninsula** Take a behind-the-scenes peek at Wellington's film industry, feast on barbecued seafood at the iconic *Chocolate Fish Café*, or stretch out on the white-sand beach at Scorching Bay. See p.417

▲ Te Papa

Wellington and around

T he North Island finishes with a flourish at **Wellington**, New Zealand's buzzing, cosmopolitan **capital**. Wedged between glistening **Wellington Harbour** (technically **Port Nicholson**) and turbulent Cook Strait, Wellington is the principal departure point to the South Island. But, as the country's most interesting and exciting city, it warrants a stay of at least a couple of days – more if you can manage it.

Tight surrounding hills restrict Wellington to a compact core, mostly built on reclaimed land. Distinctive historical and modern architecture spills down to the bustling waterfront with its beaches, marinas and restored warehouses, overlooked by Victorian and Edwardian weatherboard villas and bungalows that climb the steep slopes to an encircling belt of parks and woodland, a natural barrier to development. Many homes are accessed by narrow, winding roads or precipitous stairways flanked by a small funicular railway to haul groceries and just about anything else up to the house. What's more, "Welly", as it's locally known, is New Zealand's **windy city**, buffeted by chilled air funnelled through Cook Strait, its force amplified by the wind-tunnelling effect of the city's high-rise buildings.

With a population of around 450,000, Wellington is New Zealand's second most populous city. And while Auckland grows more commercially important (and self-important in the eyes of much of the rest of the country), Wellington reaches for higher ground as the nation's **cultural capital**. Wellingtonians have cultivated the country's most sophisticated **café society** and **arts scene**, especially in late summer when the city hosts a series of arts and fringe **festivals** (see p.427).

Central Wellington is easily walkable and it's a pleasant stroll from the city's number one attraction, **Te Papa**, the groundbreaking national museum, along the waterfront past the Civic Square to Queens Wharf and the **Museum of Wellington City and Sea**, which recounts the city's development and seafaring traditions. Politicians and civil servants populate the streets of the **Parliamentary District**. Nearby, you can visit **Katherine Mansfield's Birthplace**, the period-furnished childhood home of New Zealand's most famous short-story writer.

The city centre is the jumping-off point for ambling or cycling along **Oriental Parade** and up to one of the city's hilltop viewpoints, such as **Mount Victoria**, or catching the stately **Cable Car** to Kelburn. From Kelburn, you can either wander down through the lovely **Botanical Gardens** or continue further out to see the ambitious and important conservation work at **Zealandia: the Karori Sanctuary**

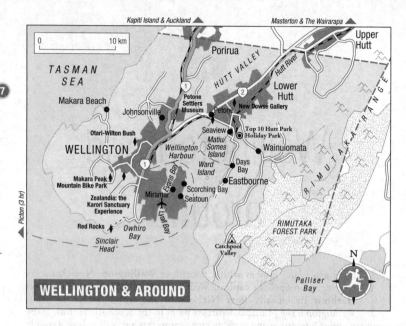

Kapiti Island & Auckland ▲   Masterton & The Wairarapa ▲

0   10 km

TASMAN SEA

Porirua

Upper Hutt

HUTT VALLEY

Hutt River

Makara Beach

Johnsonville

Petone Settlers Museum

Petone

Lower Hutt

New Dowse Gallery

Otari-Wilton Bush

WELLINGTON

Seaview

Top 10 Hutt Park Holiday Park

Wellington Harbour

Matiu/ Somes Island

Wainuiomata

Ward Island

Days Bay

Makara Peak Mountain Bike Park

Zealandia: the Karori Sanctuary Experience

Miramar

Scorching Bay

Seatoun

Eastbourne

RIMUTAKA RANGE

RIMUTAKA FOREST PARK

Red Rocks

Owhiro Bay

Lyall Bay

Evans Bay

Sinclair Head

Catchpool Valley

Palliser Bay

N

WELLINGTON & AROUND

Experience, and **Otari-Wilton's Bush**, New Zealand's last remnant of virgin bush. Zealandia and Otari-Wilton's Bush form part of the **Town Belt**, a band of greenery across the hills that encircle the city centre. Originally set aside in 1840 by the New Zealand Company for aesthetic and recreational purposes, it contains several good walks and many of the city's best lookout points. Further south, the Town Belt runs past **Wellington Zoo**; to the east it cuts the city off from the quiet suburbs and beaches of the **Miramar Peninsula**.

Superb **hiking** opportunities include the seal colony at Red Rocks, or the city's many trails, notably the **Southern Walkway**. And at some point during your stay in this harbour city, you really should get out on the water to the serene wildlife sanctuary of **Matiu/Somes Island**.

Wellington also makes a good base to explore **Kapiti Island** (p.254) and the **Wairarapa** wine district (see p.392 and p.403 for wine tours from Wellington).

Some history

Maori oral histories tell of the demigod **Maui**, who fished up the North Island, with Wellington Harbour being the mouth of the fish; and of the first Polynesian navigator, **Kupe**, discovering Wellington Harbour in 925 AD and naming the harbour's islands Matiu (Somes Island) and Makaro (Ward Island) after his daughters (see also p.000). Several *iwi* settled around the harbour, including the Ngati Tara people, who enjoyed the rich fishing areas and the protection the bay offered.

Both Abel Tasman (in 1642) and Captain Cook (in 1773) were prevented from entering Wellington Harbour by fierce winds and, apart from a few whalers, it wasn't until 1840 that the first wave of **European settlers** arrived. They carved out a niche on a large tract of harbourside land, purchased by the New Zealand Company, who set up their initial beachhead, named Britannia, on the northeastern beaches at Petone. Shortly afterwards, the Hutt River flooded, forcing the settlers to move around the harbour to a more sheltered site known as Lambton Harbour (where the central city has grown up) and the relatively level land at Thorndon, at that time just north of the shoreline. They renamed the settlement after the Iron Duke and began **land reclamations** into the harbour, a process that continued for more than a hundred years.

In 1865, the growing city succeeded Auckland as the **capital** of New Zealand, and by the turn of the twentieth century the original shoreline of Lambton Harbour had been replaced by wharves and harbourside businesses, which formed the hub of the city's coastal trade; Wellington has prospered ever since.

Arrival and moving on, information and city transport

Wellington International Airport (⊛ www.wlg-airport.co.nz), about 10km southeast of the city centre, is an important domestic hub, linking around twenty airports across New Zealand and handling international flights from Australia. There's an unstaffed information station, a bureau de change (open for all arrivals and departures), and free wi-fi.

To get into town, grab a **taxi** (see p.428) for about $30–35, or hop on the Airport Flyer **bus** (#91) outside the terminal (daily 6.30am–7.45pm; $8), which runs every

Crossing Cook Strait

To travel between the bottom of the North Island and top of the South Island you need to cross Cook Strait, either using a vehicle ferry between Wellington and Picton or flying. The latter avoids a potentially choppy ferry crossing and is much quicker but does mean missing the cruise through the beautiful Marlborough Sounds on the southern side. Most ferry services offer an audio tour about Cook Strait.

By sea

Two companies run year-round combined passenger and vehicle ferry services, both offering different fare categories with varying flexibility – check the cancellation policy of your ticket prior to booking. Be aware, too, that many rental companies don't permit their vehicles on the ferries. Companies that do allow crossings include Ace, Apex, Maui and Jucy (see p.38).

Interislander (3–5 daily; 3hr; ☏ 0800/802 802, ⊛ www.interislander.co.nz) ferries leave Wellington just over 1km north of the train station. A shuttle bus ($2) leaves the train station (by Platform 9) 50 minutes before each sailing, while a backpacker bus ($3) serves the *base* and YHA hostels, bookable through the hostels. In general, fares are around $53–73 one-way for a single passenger, $167–242 for a car and driver, and $15 for bicycles. In addition, the *Kaitaki* ship offers a refundable Kaitaki Plus ($90/229) fare, which includes the use of a private lounge and complimentary beer, wine, snacks, tea, coffee, newspapers and internet access (over-18s only).

Bluebridge (3–4 daily; 3hr 20min ☏ 0800/844 844, ⊛ www.bluebridge.co.nz) ferries operate on the same route from their terminal opposite Wellington's train station. Generally, passenger fares are $50–66 one-way; driver and car up to 5.5m $165–222; bicycles $10.

By air

Soundsair (☏ 0800/505 005, ⊛ www.soundsair.co.nz) flies between Wellington and Picton (6–8 daily; 25min; $79–89 one-way) and Wellington and Blenheim (3 daily; 40min; $79–89) and Nelson (6–10 daily; 35min; $90–104), while Air 2 There (☏ 04/904 5130, ⊛ www.air2there.com) flies between Wellington and Blenheim (2–4 daily; 40min; $90 one-way).

fifteen minutes on weekdays (every 30min on weekends) and has free wi-fi on board. The journey time to Courtney Place is fifteen minutes. Alternatively, use one of the shuttle bus companies such as Super Shuttle (℡0800/748 885 or 09/522 5100, Ⓦwww.supershuttle.co.nz), who charge, for example, $15 for the first person to a particular destination in the city centre, plus $5 for each extra person travelling to the same place.

The Overlander **train** from Auckland (see p.34) arrives at the main train station (see below), while Newmans and InterCity **buses** terminate nearby, alongside Platform 9.

Arriving and moving on by **car** is easy: from the north, State Highway 1 through Porirua and SH2 (part of the grape-signed Classic New Zealand Wine Trail) via Lower Hutt both turn into short urban motorways that merge, running scenically along the harbourside to the city centre. For details of parking see p.403.

Coming from or heading to the South Island, see p.401 for details of **crossing Cook Strait**.

Information

Wellington's **i-SITE visitor centre**, on the corner of Wakefield and Victoria streets (daily 8.30am–5.30pm, public holidays 11am–4.30pm; ℡0800/933 536, Ⓦwww.wellington.nz.com), is stocked with leaflets, maps and brochures, and shares a glass-fronted section of the Civic Centre with a café and internet terminals ($8/hr). It gives away city maps and also stocks the handy free *Wellington: Official Visitor Guide* booklet.

DOC's Wellington Visitor Centre, 18 Manners St (Mon–Fri 9am–5pm Sat 10am–3.30pm; ℡04/384 7770), has stacks of information on walks in the Wellington region and also sells hut tickets and issues permits for Kapiti Island (both also available online).

City transport

Inner Wellington is easily manageable on foot, but the city also has an efficient integrated bus, train and ferry system. The useful **Metlink Explorer** ($18) gives one day of unlimited bus and train travel throughout the Wellington region from 9am on weekdays and all day at weekends. For region-wide **train and bus information**, pick up the free *Metlink Network Map* or any of the individual timetables at the visitor centre or train station, or call Metlink (℡0800/801 700, Ⓦwww.metlink.org.nz). Cycling information is detailed on p.420.

Buses

Wellington's extensive network of **buses and trolley buses** operates from Lambton Interchange, just west of the train station, and has an After Midnight service (Sat & Sun hourly 1–3am), centred on Courtenay Place, to get revellers home safely.

All tickets and day-passes can be bought direct from the bus driver. One-way **fares** are $1–1.50 within the inner city, beyond which a zone system comes into operation: for example travelling to **Zealandia: the Karori Sanctuary Experience** costs $4. After midnight services cost $5–10. If you intend to use the transport system extensively it's worth picking the **Daytripper ticket** ($6) on the first bus you board, which covers all central city bus travel for the day, or a **Star Pass** ($12), which also includes the After Midnight buses. See p.401 for details of the Airport Flyer service.

Suburban trains

Wellington's **train station**, on Bunny Street, is the hub of Wellington's public transport network. The **suburban train service** is run by Tranz Metro

(☎04/498 3000, Ⓦwww.tranzmetro.co.nz). Trains to the Hutt Valley (p.418) and the Kapiti Coast (p.251) – leave the train station roughly every half-hour for Waterloo (for Lower Hutt; 20min; $4.50); Porirua (20min; $5.50); Plimmerton (30min; $7); and Paraparaumu (1hr; $10). The Johnsonville line ($4) provides handy access for hiking the Northern Walkway (see p.421). It's around thirty percent cheaper if you travel outside peak hours (so not before 9am or from 4–7pm).

A one-day Rover ticket ($10) gives you the run of the train network after 9am weekdays and all weekend; up to four people travelling together can save with a group Rover ticket ($25). A three-day weekend Rover ($15) is valid from 4.30am Friday to midnight Sunday. Bicycles are free. **Tickets** can be bought at the Tranz Rail Travel Centre at the main train station or on the train.

Driving and parking

Driving around the inner city is simple enough once you get used to the extensive one-way system. There's no free weekday **parking** in the city centre, but parking is free for up to two hours at a time on Saturday and all day Sunday. Car parks are plentiful, most charging around $5 an hour during weekdays (generally cheaper at night and on weekends), often with a one-day maximum of $10–12. The car park by the Te Papa museum is suitable for campervans, and there are several others nearby. If you don't want to bother with moving the vehicle all the time, some places charge $20–25 for a full 24 hours.

City tours

An ever-increasing number of clued-up local outfits offer entertaining and informative tours of the city; the best are listed below.

4WD Seal Coast Safari ☎0800/732 5277, Ⓦwww.sealcoast.com. Three-hour tours to the Red Rocks seal colony (see p.420), charging $99 for its 4WD beach driving trip (no walking involved), tea, muffins and commentary.

Flat Earth ☎0800/775 805, Ⓦwww.flatearth.co.nz. Upmarket outfit which takes very good care of you on its range of tours (from $65), including Wellington city highlights, nature and eco tours, and several specialist film tours.

Movie Tours ☎027/419 3077, Ⓦwww.adventuresafari.co.nz. Dedicated movie-theme tour options include a four-hour circuit of film locations with movie clips as well as the Weta Cave ($40).

Wairarapa Escape Tours ☎06/377 1227, Ⓦwww.tranzit.co.nz. Popular day tours of the Wairarapa (p.388) including train fares to/from Wellington, pick-up and commentary, operating daily and including lunch and wine tastings. Choose from the Wine Escape Tour ($161) or the Garden Escape Tour ($182) with visits to the area's beautiful gardens.

Wellington Rover ☎021/426 211, Ⓦwww.wellingtonrover.co.nz. Hop-on-hop-off minibus service making a loop around the city's outer sights – Mount Victoria, Red Rocks, the zoo and a couple of *LOTR* locations – three times a day ($40), with small discounts for entry to various sights along the way. The Twilight Rover ($45) trips include the south coast, Otari-Wilton's Bush and Mount Victoria.

Wild About Wellington ☎027/441 9010, Ⓦwww.wildaboutwellington.co.nz. Wellingtonian Jennifer Looman's enthusiasm for her city and its artisan produce is infectious, and her daily tours – Sights & Bites (4hr 30min; $195 with lunch) and Wild about Chocolate (4hr 15min; $50) combine sightseeing with gourmet refuelling stops. City of Style tours (3hr; $125) introduce you to local designers; Boutique Beer tours (3hr; $165) include around a dozen tastings.

Zest Food Tours ☎04/801 9198, Ⓦwww.zestfoodtours.co.nz. Superb gourmet tours taking in coffee roasteries, chocolate producers, cheese tastings, honey tastings and more (Mon–Sat; from $159 for 2hr 30min). Also wine tours through the Wairarapa.

Most inner-city streets have **parking meters** (usually Mon–Thurs 8am–6pm & Fri 8am–8pm $4/hr; otherwise free) that limit you to a two-hour stay during the metered hours. Slightly further out you get **coupon parking** (Mon–Fri 8am–4pm) where the first two hours are free, but to stay longer you have to display a coupon ($5/all day), available from dairies and petrol stations. These areas are also free outside the set hours.

Accommodation

Wellington has plenty of **accommodation** in the city centre, including some excellent **backpacker hostels**. **B&Bs** are becoming less common, but there's an increasing number of stylish self-catering serviced **apartments**. Breakfasting (or brunching) out is a quintessential Wellington experience, so you might not want a place where breakfast is included in the tariff. Central **motels** are in short supply, but many business-oriented **hotels** offer good-value deals, especially at weekends, with many major chains also represented. For a little peace and quiet, you might want to stay outside the city centre (see p.255 for example), and drive or take public transport into town. Contact the i-SITE for information on **campervan sites** in central Wellington.

The following places are shown on the map on p.406 unless otherwise stated.

Hotels, motels and apartments

Apollo Lodge Motel & Majoribanks Apartments 49 Majoribanks St ☎0800/361 645, ⓦwww .apollo-lodge.co.nz. Appealing medium-sized motel with modern rooms (some decorated in Edwardian style, others architecturally designed) 200m from Courtenay Place with off-street parking. Its adjacent apartments are well set up for longer stays. Motel ④, apartments ⑤

Halswell Lodge 21 Kent Terrace ☎04/385 0196, ⓦwww.halswell.co.nz. Comfortable, central and welcoming establishment with simple but good-value hotel rooms, relatively pricey motel units and lovely deluxe rooms (some with spa) in a lodge set back from the street. Free off-street parking. Hotel ③, motel ⑤, lodge ⑤

Trinity Hotel 166 Willis St ☎04/801 8118, ⓦwww.trinityhotel.co.nz. Freshly refurbished budget hotel with sixty rooms, all with phone, Sky TV, tea and coffee. There's an on-site restaurant, bar and parking ($15; book ahead). Weekend deals ($120) include a bottle of bubbly, cooked breakfast and late checkout. ④

Museum Hotel 90 Cable St ☎0800/994 335, ⓦwww.museumhotel.co.nz. Big, black business hotel with an intimate feel and contemporary NZ art on show, locally famous for having been trundled across the street from the Te Papa construction site on rail tracks, hence its nickname, the Museum Hotel de Wheels. Rates are reasonable for the high standards, and both self-parking and valet parking are available. Rooms ⑤, harbour view ⑦

Ohotel 66 Oriental Parade ☎04/803 0600, ⓦwww.ohtel.com. Chic, sophisticated boutique hotel opposite Waitangi Park at the city end of Oriental Parade, with on-site parking. Each of its ten rooms has decadent bathrooms with two-person baths, hi-tech entertainment systems and hand-picked 1950s, 60s and 70s vintage furniture and designer furnishings. ⑦

B&Bs and guesthouses

Austinvilla B&B 11 Austin St, Mount Victoria ☎04/385 8334, ⓦwww.austinvilla.co.nz. Two lovely and very private s/c apartments (one studio, the other with a separate bedroom and a small garden), both with bathtubs, continental breakfast and off-street parking, in an elegant villa with leafy surrounds a 10min walk from Courtenay Place. Not suitable for young children. Studio ⑤, one-bedroom ⑥

Booklovers B&B 123 Pirie St, Mount Victoria ☎04/384 2714, ⓦwww.booklovers .co.nz. For charm and comfort you can't do better than this three-bedroom literary B&B in an unfussy Victorian villa 10min walk from Courtenay Place and Mount Victoria Park with regular "authors and afternoon tea" events ($20). There are books in every room; you're even encouraged to take one away to read on your travels. A full, cooked breakfast is served any time. ⑧

Koromiko Homestay 11 Koromiko Rd, Highbury ☎04/938 6539, ⓦwww.koromikohomestay.co.nz. See map, p.414. City homestay for "gay men and their friends" in a quiet street overlooking the

Botanical Gardens and harbour. Bathrooms are shared; meals ($25 including wine) on request. ❹
The Mermaid 1 Epuni St, corner of Aro St ☎04/384 4511, ⊛www.mermaid.co.nz. A luxurious women-only guesthouse, set in a restored century-old house. The four opulently furnished rooms (one with private bathroom) all come with a view of the garden or hills. Everyone has full use of the kitchen. ❹/❺
Tinakori Lodge 182 Tinakori Rd, Thorndon ☎04/939 3478, ⊛www.tinakorilodge.co.nz. Elegant, laidback B&B in an 1868-built wooden Victorian villa, a short walk from the Parliamentary District, with nine airy rooms (some en suite) and a conservatory that looks onto a bushland reserve. ❺/❻

Hostels

Base Wellington 21–23 Cambridge Terrace ☎0800/227 369, ⊛www.stayatbase.com. Slick and well-organized 280-bed hostel converted from an office building. Facilities include cheap internet, lockable cupboards, bike rental (see p.421), decent kitchen facilities and *Basement* bar with theme nights. The women-only "Sanctuary" floor ($3 a night extra) includes towels and shampoo. Dorms $27–30, en suite ❸
Cambridge Hotel 28 Cambridge Terrace ☎0800/375 021, ⊛www.cambridgehotel.co.nz. Nicely renovated 1930s hotel that partly operates as a backpackers, with a popular, inexpensive restaurant and bar. Four- to eight-bed dorms are spacious, and the hotel rooms, while smallish, are well appointed and good value. Dorms $26, rooms & en suites ❸
Downtown Backpackers 1 Bunny St ☎04/473 8482, ⊛www.downtownbackpackers.co.nz. Large hostel in the Art Deco *Waterloo Hotel* convenient for train, bus and ferry arrivals. Dorms and rooms (some en suite) are adequate but unexciting, though there's a good bar with cheap beer and a café in this once-grand hotel's former ballroom serving cheap meals. Dorms $25, rooms ❷/❸
Nomads Capital 118 Wakefield St ☎0508/666 237, ⊛www.nomadscapital.com. Comfy 180-bed hostel (with vertigo-inducing top bunks) in the city centre with cool bar/café *Blend* attached. There

are women-only dorms for no extra charge and, best of all, plush en-suite doubles. Dorms $27, doubles ❸
Wellywood Backpackers 58 Tory St ☎0508/005 858, ⊛www.wellywoodbackpackers.co.nz. In an impossible-to-miss zebra-striped building, this welcoming independent hostel doesn't have its own bar, but is just a stone's throw from some of the city's best. One floor is devoted to common areas (internet and TV lounges, a pool table and a vast island kitchen), and staff can book you on movie and other tours. Dorms $27, rooms ❷, en suite ❸, family room sleeping up to five ❻
YHA Wellington City 292 Wakefield St ☎04/801 7280, ⓔyha.wellington@yha .co.nz. This 320-bedder is one of the best urban hostels in the country, right in the heart of the city with great harbour views from some of the upper floor rooms. It has spacious common areas including a foosball table and projector-screen TV room, a well-equipped kitchen, bike storage, an info and travel desk and social events such as regular meal nights ($6–9.50). Many of the doubles, twin, four- and six-share dorms have en suites. Dorms $31, rooms ❸/❹

Campsites

Catchpool Valley, Rimutaka Forest Park, 30km northeast of Wellington. See map, p.400. Pleasant drive-in DOC campsite beside the Catchpool stream with hot showers, toilets, water supply and barbecues. $10
Matiu/Somes Island Twelve-person DOC campsite on the Matiu/Somes Island wildlife reserve (p.400) in the middle of Wellington Harbour with great city views. There are flush toilets, and gas cooking stoves but you need to bring pots and all food. $10.
Top 10 Hutt Park Holiday Park 95 Hutt Park Rd, Lower Hutt ☎0800/488 872, ⊛www.huttpark .co.nz. See map, p.400. The capital's closest campsite, 12km north of Wellington on the harbour's northeastern shore. It's near beaches, shops and bushwalks and can be accessed on buses #81 and #83 from Courtenay Place and Lambton Interchange. Camping $17, cabins ❷, s/c units ❸, motel units ❹

The City

The heart of Wellington's **city centre** stretches south from the train station to Courtenay Place along the backbone of the central business and shopping district, Lambton Quay. The main areas for eating, drinking and entertainment are further south around Willis Street, Courtenay Place, arty Cuba Street, and down to the

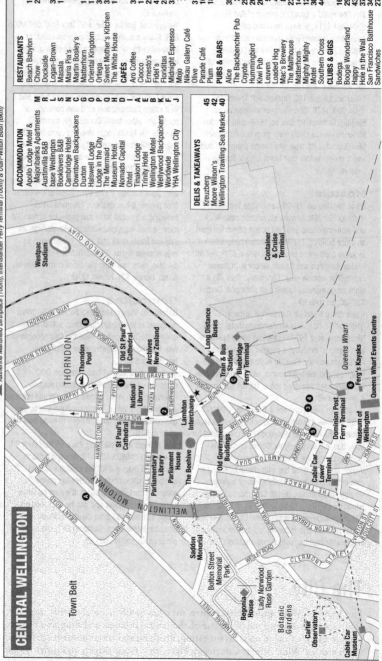

CENTRAL WELLINGTON

▲ Katherine Mansfield Birthplace (100m), Interislander Ferry Terminal (700m) & Otari-Wilton Bush (6km)

7

WELLINGTON AND AROUND

RESTAURANTS	
Beach Babylon	13
Chow	28
Dockside	6
Logan-Brown	38
Masala	19
Maria Pia's	1
Martin Bosley's	9
Matterhorn	14
Oriental Kingdom	17
Ortega	36
Sweet Mother's Kitchen	32
The White House	11

CAFES	
Aro Coffee	39
Ciocco	15
Ernesto's	22
Fidel's	41
Floriditas	24
Midnight Espresso	33
Mojo	3
Nikau Gallery Café	7
Olive	31
Parade Café	10
Plum	18

PUBS & BARS	
Alice	35
The Backbencher Pub	2
Coyote	25
Hummingbird	26
Kiwi Pub	20
Leuven	5
Loaded Hog	4
Mac's Brewery	8
The Malthouse	23
Matterhorn	14
Mighty Mighty	12
Motel	30
Southern Cross	44

CLUBS & GIGS	
Bodega	16
Boogie Wonderland	29
Happy	43
Hole in the Wall	37
San Francisco Bathhouse	34
Sandwiches	27

ACCOMMODATION	
Apollo Lodge Motel &	M
Majoribanks Apartments	R
Austinvilla B&B	L
base Wellington	S
Booklovers B&B	N
Cambridge Hotel	C
Downtown Backpackers	G
Duxton	O
Halswell Lodge	P
Lodge in the City	Q
The Mermaid	H
Museum Hotel	D
Nomads Capital	I
Ohtel	A
Tinakori Lodge	E
Trinity Hotel	B
Wellington Motel	K
Wellywood Backpackers	F
Worldwide	J
YHA Wellington City	

DELIS & TAKEAWAYS	
Kreuzberg	45
Moore Wilson's	42
Wellington Trawling Sea Market	40

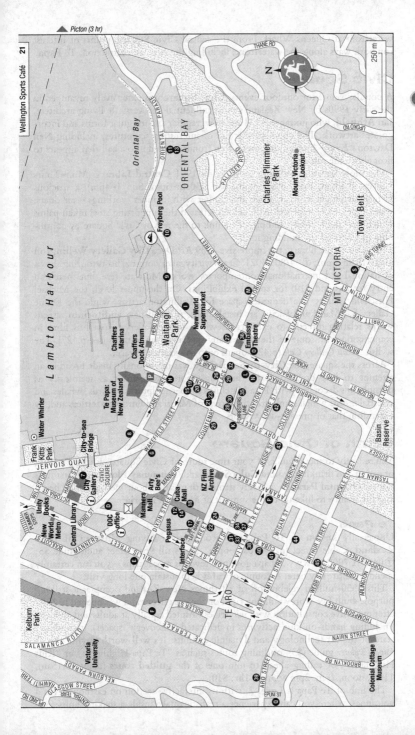

waterfront at Queens Wharf. From the central **Civic Square**, points of interest run both ways along the waterfront, including the city's star attraction, **Te Papa**.

Civic Square

A popular venue for outdoor events, **Civic Square** was extensively revamped in the early 1990s by New Zealand's most influential and versatile living architect, **Ian Athfield**, who juxtaposes old and new, regular and irregular forms and incorporates artwork. The open space is full of interesting sculptures, including Neil Dawson's *Ferns* – interlinking metal fern fronds formed into a ball that appears to float above the square.

The most arresting building is Athfield's 1991 **Central Library** (Mon–Thurs 9.30am–8.30pm, Fri 9.30am–9pm, Sat 9.30am–5pm, Sun 1–4pm), a spacious hi-tech statement in steel, stone and timber with its inner workings – air ducts, water pipes, etc – exposed. Athfield also created the supporting steel nikau palms which ring the building and provide a link to the rest of Civic Square by continuing out beyond the building itself.

Adjacent to the library, the impressive 1939 Art Deco **City Gallery Wellington** (daily 10am–5pm; ℡04/801 3021, Ⓦwww.citygallery.org.nz) hosts touring shows of national and international contemporary works. Most are free, but there's an entry fee (around $10) for special exhibitions. On the upper level, the Michael Hirscheld Gallery is a dedicated space for Wellington artists, while the Deane Gallery has Maori and Pacific art installations. A brand-new **auditorium** screens works relating directly to exhibits elsewhere in the gallery, as well as films in conjunction with some of the city's many specialist film festivals (see p.427). The stylish *Nikau Gallery Café* (p.423) opens onto an external terrace.

Across the square, the **City-to-Sea Bridge** was intentionally made broad in an attempt to link downtown to the long-ignored waterfront as seamlessly as possible. It's decorated with Para Matchitt's timber sculptures of birds, whales and celestial motifs which symbolize the arrival of Maori and European settlers and, by extension, that of present-day visitors.

South of Civic Square

You're likely to spend much of your time south of Civic Square visiting **Te Papa** or eating and drinking around **Cuba Street** and **Courtenay Place**, but don't miss out on **Oriental Parade** – a lovely stroll with great harbour views, a small beach and the chance to hike up to the summit of **Mount Victoria**.

Te Papa

Universally known as **Te Papa**, the constantly evolving **Museum of New Zealand**, Cable Street (daily 10am–6pm, Thurs till 9pm; free; audioguide $5; ℡04/381 7000, Ⓦwww.tepapa.govt.nz), rewards repeat trips – you can certainly spend an entire day here. A couple of **cafés** help sustain one long visit.

This $350-million celebration of all things New Zealand occupies a striking purpose-built five-storey building right on the waterfront and was opened in 1998 after extensive consultation with *iwi* (tribes). Aimed equally at adults and children (including hands-on kids' activities in dedicated "discovery" spaces), it combines state-of-the-art technology and dynamic exhibits. It's well worth buying the *Te Papa Explorer* guide ($3), outlining routes such as "Te Papa Highlights" or "Kids Highlights", or calling ahead to join one of the **guided tours** (daily 10.15am, 11am, noon, 1pm, 2pm & 3pm; 1hr; $10).

The hub of Te Papa is **Level 2**, with its interactive section on earthquakes and volcanoes, where you can experience a realistic quake inside a shaking house, see

Conservation in action

New Zealand is blessed with outstanding natural beauty and some unique flora and fauna. Yet if history has taught New Zealanders anything it is that their environment is fragile. Before James Cook's arrival in 1769, Maori had hunted the moa to extinction and thereafter the influx of Europeans caused the death of many more species. Most of those that remain – including the emblematic kiwi – cling precariously to survival and then only with human help. Today, New Zealand works hard to safeguard its landscape and native wildlife, and offers plenty of activities that show off its splendour to the maximum while taking the minimum toll from its natural resources.

Tararua Wind Farm, near Palmerston North ▲

Orokonui Eco Sanctuary ▼

Keeping it green

New Zealand presents itself as green and clean, an issue we cover in detail in "Contexts" (see p.793), and is taking steps, however small, to maintain its unique environmental balance. About thirty percent of all Kiwi power comes from renewable energy sources, with hydroelectric power making a considerable contribution, and wind – there are wind farms near Wellington and Palmerston North, to name but two – also playing a part.

Several organizations monitor how green New Zealand is and Tourism New Zealand has put its weight behind the Qualmark organization (Ⓦ www.qualmark.co.nz) which certifies tourism businesses, star-rates accommodation and awards three green grades: Enviro-Gold, Enviro-Silver and Enviro-Bronze.

Most organized tours do their utmost to minimize the impact they make on the environment they work in. Top of the list are wildlife-watching operations, specializing in bird – particularly kiwi – spotting and/or coastal wildlife observation, kayaking trips, whitewater-rafting operators and wildlife sanctuaries – an area in which New Zealand leads the way, with initiatives like predator-proof fencing at Wellington's Zealandia: The Karori Experience Sanctuary (see p.413).

Saving the kiwi

All species of kiwi, New Zealand's national symbol, are "threatened", two are "Nationally Critical", with only a couple of hundred birds apiece. A substantial problem is the loss of habitat, but the major issue is predation. With powerful legs and strong claws, adult kiwi are reasonably adept at defending themselves from possums, stoats and ferrets, but do less well against feral cats and dogs. A single domestic dog is thought to have killed 500 of the 900 birds in the Waitangi State forest over a six-week period in 1988. Kiwis don't actively look after their chicks, and it is estimated that where stoats are present (and that's just about everywhere on the North and South islands), the chicks have only a five-percent chance of survival. Rates increase enormously if the eggs, or newborn chicks, are retrieved from nests and reared in safe compounds or on predator-free islands until they are about six months old; the focus of Operation Nest Egg (Ⓦwww.savethekiwi.org.nz). By then the one-kilo birds can fend for themselves and are set free in the wild.

▲ Swimming with dolphins, Kaikoura

▼ Shark cage diving, Gisborne

Up close and personal

New Zealand's coast provides great wildlife-watching opportunities – everything from whales to pelagic birds – but perhaps best of all it offers the chance to experience the peculiarly affecting delights of swimming in the wild with dolphins, seals and – less commonly – sharks. Travellers returning from New Zealand often comment that what they remember most about their trip is catching the eye of a dusky, common, bottlenose, or, better, the native – and very rare – Hector's dolphin as it swam around them in ever decreasing circles. The most rewarding spots for such encounters are Kaikoura, Banks Peninsula and the Bay of Islands. Some folk prefer seal-swimming, the seals get closer are more doe-eyed and – hard though it is to believe – more mobile in the water. Both Kaikoura and Banks Peninsula offer good seal-swimming operations, as does the Abel Tasman National Park, while off the coast of Gisborne and the Marlborough Sounds you eyeball a completely different kettle of fish: blue and mako sharks.

▼ Fur seal underwater at Kaikoura

Native New Zealand

The following sanctuaries, parks and reserves are all excellent places to spot New Zealand's native wildlife. See p.785 for full details of New Zealand's conservation and wildlife organizations and websites.

Sanctuaries, parks and reserves

North Island

▶▶ **Bushy Park**, Wanganui. See p.237
▶▶ **Goat Island Marine Reserve**, Northland. See p.155
▶▶ **Kapiti Island**, near Wellington. See p.254
▶▶ **Parry Kauri Park**, Northland. See p.154
▶▶ **Poor Knights Islands Marine Reserve**, Northland. See p.163
▶▶ **Pukaha Mount Bruce National Wildlife Centre**, Wairarapa. See p.389
▶▶ **Rangitoto and Motutapu Islands**, Auckland. See p.131
▶▶ **Tiritiri Matangi**, Auckland. See p.146
▶▶ **Waipoua and Trounson Kauri Forests**, Northland. See p.200
▶▶ **Zealandia: The Karori Sanctuary Experience**, Wellington. See p.413

South Island

▶▶ **Abel Tasman National Park**. See p.458
▶▶ **Aoraki Mount Cook National Park**. See p.569
▶▶ **Awa Awa Rata Reserve**. See p.560
▶▶ **Fiordland National Park**. See p.729
▶▶ **Kura Tawhiti (Castle Hill Reserve)**. See p.554
▶▶ **Mason Bay**, Stewart Island. See p.617
▶▶ **Motuara Island**, Marlborough Sounds. See p.439
▶▶ **Oamaru Blue Penguin Colony**. See p.541
▶▶ **Orokonui Eco Sanctuary**, near Dunedin. See p.591
▶▶ **Ulva Island**, off Stewart Island. See p.615

Kapiti Island ▲

Capturing a kaka at Zealandia: the Karori Sanctuary Experience ▼

displays on the fault line that runs right through Wellington, watch Mount Ruapehu erupt on screen and hear the Maori explanation of the causes of such activity. Recent additions include the hi-tech multimedia centre **OurSpace**, where you can project your own text images onto a giant screen, The Wall, and board two **simulator rides** ($10 each, or $18 for both) – The High Ride, whirling you through the 3D world of The Wall, and the Deep Ride, journeying into a virtual underwater volcano. Level 2 also provides access to the outdoor **Bush City**, a synthesis of New Zealand environments complete with native plants, a small cave system and a swingbridge. From November to March, the hour-long Taste of Treasures tour (11am, tickets must be bought before 10.45am; $24) includes traditional Maori refreshments made from bush plants.

The main collection continues on **Level 4**, home to the excellent main Maori section including a thought-provoking display on the Treaty of Waitangi, dominated by a giant glass image of this significant document. There's also an **active marae** with a modern meeting house quite unlike the classic examples found around the country, protected by a sacred boulder of *pounamu* (greenstone). Temporary exhibitions include displays by different *iwi* showcasing that particular *iwi*'s art and culture.

Adjacent to the *marae*, look out for displays on New Zealand's people, land, history, trade and cultures including Michel Tuffery's bullock made from corned beef cans, and Brian O'Connor's paua-shell surfboard.

Level 5 is the home of New Zealand's **national art collection**, displaying a changing roster of works on paper, oils and sculpture representing luminaries of the New Zealand art world past and present – Colin McCahon, Rita Angus, Ralph Hotere, Don Binney, Michael Smither and Shane Cotton are just a few names to watch for.

Oriental Parade and Mount Victoria

Immediately east of Te Papa, **Waitangi Park** is named after a long culverted stream that has been restored to its natural course, creating a small urban wetland. At the end of Herd Street, the new **Chaffers Dock** development incorporates cafés as well as the atrium where Wellington's Sunday morning farmers' market (p.422) sets up. The park marks the start of **Oriental Parade**, Wellington's most elegant section of waterfront. Skirting **Oriental Bay**, this Norfolk-pine-lined road curls past some of the city's priciest real estate and even flanks a **beach** installed here in 2003 with sand brought across Cook Strait from near Takaka. Apart from the Freyberg pool (see "Swimming", p.428) and a few restaurants, there are no attractions as such, but you can extend a stroll into a full afternoon by continuing to Charles Plimmer Park and joining the Southern Walkway (see p.420) to the summit of **Mount Victoria**.

At 196m, **Mount Victoria Lookout** is one of the best of Wellington's viewpoints, offering sweeping views of the city, waterfront, docks and beyond to the Hutt Valley; all particularly dramatic around dusk. If you don't fancy the steep but rewarding walk, you can also reach the summit by bus (#20; Mon–Fri), the Wellington Rover (see p.403), or by car following Hawker Street, off Majoribanks Street, then taking Palliser Road, which twists uphill to the lookout.

Courtenay Place and Cuba Street

A couple of blocks south of Te Papa, the excellent **New Zealand Film Archive**, 84 Taranaki St (Mon & Tues 9am–5pm, Wed–Fri 9am–7pm, Sat 4–8pm; free; ☏04/384 7647 ⓦwww.filmarchive.org.nz), has small film-themed exhibits, but the main attraction is the ability to watch just about any New Zealand movie ever made, plus TV programmes, old commercials and assorted home movies on monitors in the media library or in the small viewing room (all free). There are also evening screenings in the cinema (Wed–Sat 7pm; $8), which on Wednesday will be an NZ feature film.

Walk a block north and you're in Wellington's entertainment heartland, centred on **Courtenay Place** and adjacent **Cuba Street**. Named for an emigrant ship (not the island after which the ship was christened, despite the Cuban-themed establishments in this part of town), Cuba Street and its offshoots comprise **Wellington's** "alternative" district, with secondhand bookshops, vintage record stores, retro and emerging-designer fashion outlets, quirky cafés, and hip bars and restaurants. Between Dixon and Ghuznee streets, Cuba Street's colourful and iconic **Bucket Fountain** was installed in 1969 and still splashes unsuspecting passers-by.

Heritage fans should press on a couple of hundred metres south to the delightful **Colonial Cottage Museum**, 68 Nairn St (Christmas to mid-Feb daily 10am–4pm; mid-Feb to Christmas Sat & Sun noon–4pm; $5; ⓦ www.colonialcottagemuseum .co.nz), central Wellington's oldest building. Though dating from 1858 (two decades into Victoria's reign), it's built in late Georgian style, and its decor gives the impression that the family has just left for Sunday church and will be back in an hour.

North of Civic Square

As the city progressively reconnects to the harbour, there's plenty of action around **Queens Wharf**, home to expensive harbour-view apartments, the Museum of Wellington City and Sea and some bars and fine restaurants, as well as the *Mojo* coffee roastery (p.423).

The business heart of Wellington beats along Lambton Quay, which runs north to the **Parliamentary District**, the city's administrative and ecclesiastical hub. Parliament marks the southern edge of **Thorndon**, Wellington's oldest suburb and home of the **Katherine Mansfield Birthplace**.

Queens Wharf and the Museum of Wellington City and Sea

North of the Civic Square lies **Frank Kitts Park**, where the mast of the *Wahine* (see below) stands sentinel on the waterfront. A few metres further along is the *Water Whirler*, a kinetic sculpture designed by Len Lye (see p.228) and opened in 2006, a quarter of a century after the artist's death. Roughly every hour (10am–10pm but not 2pm; 5–10min), it erupts into action, a sequence of complex and increasingly energetic gyrations with jets spewing water.

Near lively **Queens Wharf**, a Victorian former bond store houses the absorbing **Museum of Wellington City and Sea** (daily 10am–5pm: free; ⓦ www .museumofwellington.co.nz). The city's social and maritime history unfolds through well-executed displays on early Maori and European settlement and the city's seafaring heritage. The ground floor offers an easily digestible chronological overview of key events, while the main focus of the first floor is the poignant coverage of the **Wahine disaster**, remembering the inter-island ferry which sank with the loss of 52 lives on 10 April 1968. The *Wahine* foundered in one of New Zealand's most violent storms ever, with 734 people on board. Rescue attempts were repeatedly thwarted until the weather calmed enough for passengers to start abandoning ship, only to find the ship had listed so much that the lifeboats on the upper side were unusable. On the top floor, a hologram presentation tells the Maori legends of the creation of Wellington Harbour, while rising up through the centre of the building, a tall screen features a roster of short films. Free thirty-minute tours take place on Sundays at 2pm. It also offers several tours taking in the museum as well as other attractions, such as its popular **Ship 'n Chip tour**

(5hr; $38.50), including a ferry trip to Matiu/Somes Island (p.418) and fish and chips for lunch.

Lambton Quay and the Cable Car

Now Wellington's main commercial street, **Lambton Quay** formed the original waterfront but was cut off by the docks formed by reclamation. Head straight along Lambton Quay to the Parliamentary District, or detour up the Cable Car (see box below) and back down through the Botanic Gardens.

The Botanic Gardens and observatories

A lookout at the top of the Cable Car (see box below) provides spectacular views over the city. Here, you're also at the highest point of Wellington's **Botanic Gardens** (daily dawn–dusk; free), a huge swathe of green on peaceful rolling hills with numerous paths that wind down towards the city. Pick up the useful free map from the Cable Car Museum. The *tour de force* of the Botanic Gardens is the fragrant **Lady Norwood Rose Garden**, where a colonnade of climbing roses frames beds of over three hundred varieties set out in a formal wheel shape. The adjacent **Begonia House** (daily: Oct–March 10am–5pm; April–Sept 10am–4pm; free) is divided into two areas: the tropical, with an attractive lily pond, and the temperate, which has seasonal displays of begonias and gloxinias in summer, changing to cyclamen, orchids and impatiens in winter. There's also a good **café**.

Two minutes' walk from the upper Cable Car terminus is the revamped 1941 **Carter Observatory** (ⓦ www.carterobservatory.org) which by the time you read this should have reopened with all sorts of astronomical displays, and telesco used to give a New Zealand angle on the exploration of the southern skies Maori astronavigation through to recent planet searches. Check the details of their planetarium shows.

Parliamentary District

The northern end of Lambton Quay marks the start It is dominated by the grandiose **Old Governm** appears to be constructed from cream stone b Colonial Architect William Clayton (1823–77) from provincial to centralized government, it was s cost-cutting forced a rethink. When completed in 18 New Zealand, and except for an ornamental palace timber building in the world. It's now occupied by

---

Riding the Cable Car

Even if you never use the rest of Wellington's public transport syst short and scenic ride up to the leafy suburb of Kelburn and the upp Botanic Gardens on the **Cable Car** (Mon–Fri 7am–10pm, Sat 8.30a 9am–10pm; $3 one-way, $5 return), installed in 1902. Its shiny red ra every ten minutes from the lower terminus on Cable Car Lane, just off Lam and climb a steep, one-in-five incline, making three stops along the way a great views over the city and harbour. At the upper terminus on Upland Rc **Cable Car Museum** (daily: Easter to Nov 10am–5pm; Nov to Easter 9.30am–5. free) contains the historic winding room with the electric drive motor and a c cradle of cables. Two century-old cars are on display along with plenty of backgrou on this and other cable cars around the world. Take time, too, to catch the sho movies, particularly the one about the 400-plus mini cable cars people still use to access their properties around Wellington.

Fac.Jty, but you can usually duck inside and nip up the fine rimu staircase to see a series of photos of the building as a backdrop to various demonstrations and protests.

The Parliament Buildings

Visible across Lambton Quay are the **Parliament Buildings**, the seat of New Zealand's government, a trio of highly individual structures that nonetheless sit harmoniously together. The most distinctive is the modernist **Beehive**, a seven-stepped truncated cone that houses the Cabinet and the offices of its ministers. Designed by British (and Coventry Cathedral) architect Sir Basil Spence in 1964, it was finally completed in 1982, six years after Spence's death. The Beehive is connected directly to the Edwardian Neoclassical **Parliament House**, a suitably solid seat of government – which is more than can be said for the almost frivolous Victorian Gothic **Parliamentary Library** next door.

Informative and anecdotal hour-long guided tours (on the hour: Mon–Fri 10am–4pm, Sat 10am–3pm, Sun 11am–3pm; free; ☎04/471 9503, Ⓦwww .parliament.nz) start from a visitor centre on the ground floor of the Beehive. Highlights include the decorative **Maori Affairs Select Committee Room** with its specially commissioned carvings and woven *tukutuku* panels from all the major tribal groups in the land, and the beautifully restored 1899 Victorian Gothic library. You're led through the Debating Chamber when Parliament's not sitting; when it is, check with your guide about watching proceedings from the public gallery.

MPs venture across Molesworth Street to the **Backbencher Pub** (see p.420).

The National Library and Archives

Opposite Parliament on Molesworth Street, the **National Library of New Zealand** (Mon–Fri 9am–5pm, Sat 9am–1pm; free), is generally off-limits to all but researchers, but it is worth ducking into the large public **gallery**, which regularly hosts free exhibitions.

A stone's throw east along Aitken Street, **Archives New Zealand**, 10 Mulgrave St (Mon–Fri 9am–5pm, Sat 9am–1pm; free; Ⓦwww.archives.govt.nz), is home to the nation's most important documents. Again, much of the building is devoted to research, but you can visit the **Constitution Room**, a dimly lit, climate-controlled vault where the prize exhibit is the original Maori-language **Treaty of Waitangi** (see p.764). This barely survived a long spell lost in the bowels of the Old Government Buildings, suffering water damage and the gnawings of rodents before it was rescued in 1908. Various copies of the Treaty did the rounds of the country collecting Maori chiefs' signatures, giving a sense of how haphazard the whole process was. Other key documents include the 1835 Declaration of Independence of the Northern Chiefs and **Maori petitions** dating back to 1909, which complain of broken treaty promises. Look also for the facsimile of the 1893 **petition for women's suffrage**, put together by New Zealand's iconic suffragette, Kate Sheppard – who features on the $10 note. At this third attempt she managed to amass 32,000 signatures, a quarter of the adult female population, ushering in legislation which made New Zealand the first country to give women the vote.

The Cathedrals — old and new

From 1866 to 1964, the modest **Old St Paul's**, at the corner of Mulgrave and Pipitea streets (daily 10am–5pm; free), operated as the parish church of Thorndon, but after the houses of the Parliamentary District were taken over by government departments and foreign delegations, it was only saved from demolition in the 1960s by sustained public protest. Among the finest European timber churches in the country, it remains a consecrated building popular for weddings. You'll understand why when you see its beautiful interior, crafted in early English Gothic style (more commonly seen in stone) from native timbers that have since darkened with age to a rich mellow hue. Lovely stained-glass windows and the sheen of polished brass plaques on the walls highlight the ranks of dark pews, arches, pulpit and choral area. The church was the major work of an English ecclesiastical architect, Reverend Frederick Thatcher, who designed it for Bishop Selwyn and was vicar here for a few years.

Old St Paul's could hardly stand in greater contrast to **St Paul's Cathedral** (daily 10am–4pm; free), its modern successor, a block away on Molesworth Street. A curious mix of Byzantine and Santa Fe styles, it was designed in the 1930s by renowned ecclesiastical architect Cecil Wood of Christchurch. Queen Elizabeth II laid the foundation stone in 1954 but the cathedral wasn't complete until 1998. The cavernous interior dwarfs the dark-wood choir stalls, which look out of place among all the powder-pink concrete. The distinctive pipe organ, built in London, was originally installed in Old St Paul's.

The Katherine Mansfield Birthplace

Continue walking north through Thorndon for about ten minutes to reach the **Katherine Mansfield Birthplace**, 25 Tinakori Rd (Tues–Sun 10am–4pm; $5.50; Ⓦ www.katherinemansfield.com; bus #14 stops on nearby Park Street). A modest wooden house with a small garden, this was the childhood home of Katherine Mansfield (see box below). The house has a cluttered Victorian/Edwardian charm and avant-garde decor for its time, inspired by Japonisme and the Aesthetic Movement. An upstairs room is set aside to recount a history of the author's life and career, with some black-and-white photos of Wellington and the people that shaped her life – and videos including the excellent *A Woman and a Writer*. The connections between Thorndon and Mansfield's life and works are explored through more photos in the lean-to at the back of the house.

The suburbs

Within easy striking distance of the centre, Wellington's suburbs offer respite from the bustle of the city. The groundbreaking **Zealandia: the Karori Sanctuary Experience** is complemented by the fine stand of native bush a few kilometres north at **Otari-Wilson's Bush**, while the **Wellington Zoo** is just south of the city. A number of good walks thread through the greenery of the Town Belt or head beyond to the quiet pleasures of **Scorching Bay** on the **Miramar Peninsula**, the hub of Wellington's film industry.

Zealandia: the Karori Sanctuary Experience

A pristine oasis just 3km west of the city centre in the suburb of Karori, **Zealandia: the Karori Sanctuary Experience**, 31 Waiapu Rd (daily 10am–5pm;

Katherine Mansfield

Katherine Mansfield Beauchamp (1888–1923), is New Zealand's most famous short-story writer. During her brief life, she revolutionized the form, eschewing plot in favour of a poetic expansiveness. Virginia Woolf claimed Mansfield's work to be "the only writing I have ever been jealous of".

Mansfield lived here on Tinakori Road for five years with her parents, three sisters and beloved grandmother and the place is described in some of her works, notably "Prelude" and "A Birthday". The family later moved to a much grander house in what is now the western suburb of Karori until, at 19, Katherine left for Europe, where she lived until dying of tuberculosis in France, aged 32.

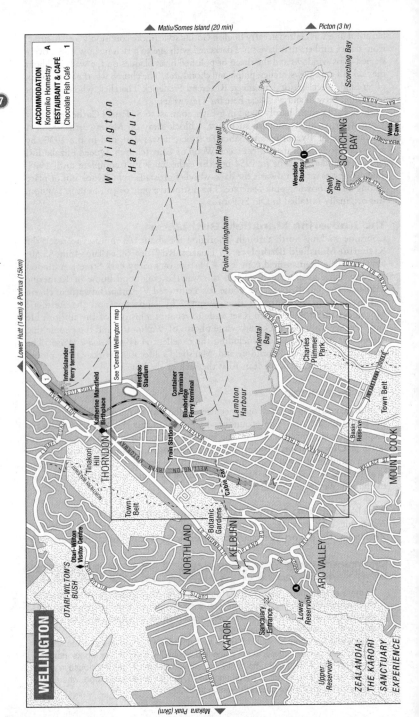

WELLINGTON

▲ Matiu/Somes Island (20 min)   ▲ Picton (3 hr)

Wellington Harbour

ACCOMMODATION	
Koromiko Homestay	**A**
RESTAURANT & CAFÉ	
Chocolate Fish Café	**1**

Scorching Bay

BAY ROAD

Point Halswell

MASSEY ROAD

Weta
Cave

Westside
Studios

SHELLY BAY ROAD

Shelly Bay

SCORCHING BAY

Point Jerningham

EVANS BAY PARADE

▲ Lower Hutt (14km) & Porirua (15km)

Interislander
Ferry terminal

AOTEA QUAY

Katherine Mansfield
Birthplace

THORNDON

Tinakori
Hill

Otari-Wilton's
Visitor Centre

OTARI-WILTON'S
BUSH

Train Station

Westpac
Stadium

Container
terminal
Bluebridge
Ferry terminal

See 'Central Wellington' map

Lambton
Harbour

Oriental
Bay

Charles
Plimmer
Park

Town Belt

Cable Car

Botanic
Gardens

Town
Belt

NORTHLAND

KELBURN

ARO VALLEY

Basin
Reserve

MOUNT COOK

Wallace St

Town Belt

Sanctuary
Entrance

Lower
Reservoir

KARORI

Upper
Reservoir

ZEALANDIA:
THE KARORI
SANCTUARY
EXPERIENCE:

▲ Makara Peak (5km)

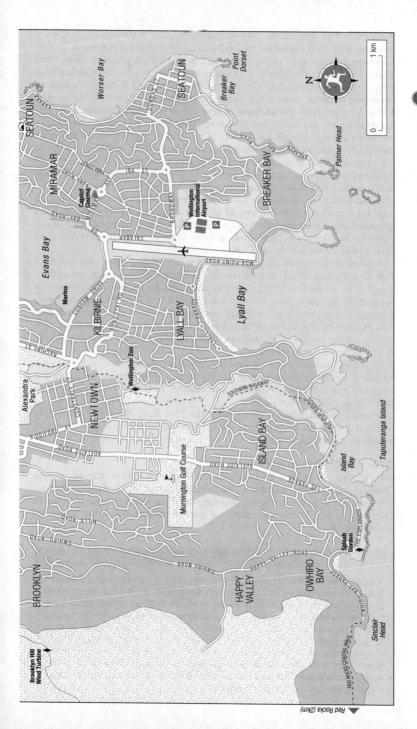

◄ Red Rocks (2km)

Brooklyn Hill Wind Turbine

BROOKLYN

HAPPY VALLEY

OWHIRO BAY

Sinclair Head

RED ROCKS COASTAL WALK

OWHIRO ROAD

HAPPY VALLEY ROAD

MILLS ROAD

OWHIRO ROAD

Splash Gordon

THE ESPLANADE

BAY PARADE

Island Bay

Taputeranga Island

ISLAND BAY

ADELAIDE ROAD

THE PARADE

Mornington Golf Course

RIDDIFORD ROAD

ADELAIDE ROAD

CONSTABLE ST

NEWTOWN

Wellington Zoo

THE ESPLANADE

SOUTHERN WALKWAY

Alexandra Park

BATHURST ST

KILBIRNIE

Marina

COBHAM DRIVE

ONEPU RD

Evans Bay

LYALL BAY

Lyall Bay

PARADE

MOA POINT ROAD

CALABAR

BROADWAY

Wellington International Airport

P   P

BAY ROAD

PARK ST

MIRAMAR

Capitol Cinema

MIRAMAR AVE

PARK STREET

IRA ST

SEATOUN

KARAKA BAY ROAD

Worser Bay

LYNDS ST

SEATOUN

BREAKER BAY ROAD

BREAKER BAY

Breaker Bay

Point Dorset

Palmer Head

N

0   1 km

April–Nov 9am–5pm; $28; ☎04/920 9200, infoline ☎04/920 2222, ⓦwww
.visitzealandia.com), named for the Zealandia microcontinent that broke away from
Gondwanaland some 85 million years ago, is successfully restoring native New
Zealand bush and its wildlife to 2.25 square kilometres of urban Wellington. Sited
around two century-old reservoirs which formerly supplied Wellington's drinking
water (and still do in times of water shortage), the managing trust first designed an
8.6km-long **predator-proof fence** to keep out all introduced mammals. As well
as restocking the area with native trees, eradicating weeds and fostering the existing
morepork and tui, the trust has introduced native birds – little spotted kiwi, weka,
saddleback, kaka, bellbird, whitehead, North Island robins, takahe and kakariki
– plus tuatara (back in a natural mainland environment for the first time in over
200 years) and the grasshopper-like weta to the sanctuary from the overspill of the
conservation and restocking programme on Kapiti Island (see p.254).

Started in the late 1990s, this far-reaching project won't be entirely complete
until the forest has matured in around 500 years. You can already walk the 35km
of paths (some almost flat, others quite rugged) listening to birdsong heard almost
nowhere else on the mainland – making it easy to understand why early arrivals to
New Zealand were so impressed with the avian chorus.

It's worth spending half a day here wandering past viewing hides, areas noted for
their fantails or saddleback, and even the first few metres of a gold-mine tunnel from
the 1869 Karori gold rush. You should seriously consider booking ahead for one of
the guided night tours (daily 30min before sunset; 2.5hr; $75 including admission),
which gives you a chance to watch kaka feeding, see banks of glowworms and hear
kiwi foraging for their dinner. With luck you'll even see one or two. The sanctuary is
already having a wider effect, with increasing numbers of tui, bellbirds and kaka
spotted in neighbouring suburbs.

Admission includes entry to Zealandia's state-of-the-art new visitor centre.
Spending around an hour touring its interactive exhibits before exploring the
sanctuary puts Zealandia's evolution into context. Also here is a scenically sited
café serving quality deli-style food.

To reach the sanctuary, either walk the 2km from the Cable Car upper
terminus or catch the #3 bus from Lambton Quay or Courtenay Place, or if you're
booked on a tour, ask about pick-ups from the city centre.

Otari-Wilton's Bush

For a glimpse of the New Zealand bush as it was before humans arrived, head to
Otari-Wilton's Bush (daily dawn–dusk; free), 6km northwest of the city centre.
The remains of the area's original podocarp-northern rata forest was set aside in
1860 by one Job Wilton and forms the core of the lush 0.8 square kilometre
preserved here.

The best view in Wellington

If the city panorama from Mount Victoria isn't enough for you, head west to **Brooklyn
Hill**, easily identified by its crowning 32m **wind turbine**. Fantastic views unfold
across the city and south towards the South Island's Kaikoura Ranges as the giant
propeller blades whirr overhead. This demonstration turbine has been harnessing
Wellington's wind since 1993, providing energy for up to a hundred homes but failing
to ignite enough interest to install more. To reach the turbine by car, take Brooklyn
Road from the end of Victoria Street and turn left at Ohiro Road, then right at the
shopping centre up Todman Street and follow the signposts (the road up to the
turbine closes at 8pm Oct–April and 5pm May–Sept). Bus #7 runs up Victoria Street
in town and drops you 3km from the summit.

At the unstaffed visitor centre, 160 Wilton Rd (daily 9am–5pm), you'll find a map of the walks, which initially follow a 100m **Canopy Walkway** of sturdy decking high in the trees across a gully. This leads to the **Native Botanic Garden**, laid out with plants from around the country, and the informative **Nature Trail** (30min), a good introduction to the New Zealand forest and its many plants. Assorted trails (all 30min–1hr) wander through the bush, one passing an 800-year-old rimu. To reach the reserve, either walk the 3km from the Zealandia: the Karori Sanctuary Experience or take bus #14 (every 30min from the Lambton Interchange).

Wellington Zoo

Sticking with natural history, you might also fancy a visit to the compact and eminently manageable **Wellington Zoo**, 200 Daniell St, around 4km south of the central city (daily 9.30am–5pm; $18; ☎04/381 6750, ⑳www.wellingtonzoo .com). As well as a nice line in exotics – the Malaysian sun bear and African wild dogs in particular – and excellent native collection, you can watch surgery being performed at its animal hospital, the Nest, or perhaps book in for a "close encounter" such as hand-feeding red pandas ($75; min age 6), or patting cheetahs ($150; min age 14). To get to the zoo, pick up the #10 bus from the train station or the #23 from Lambton Quay.

Around the Miramar Peninsula

Around 10km southeast of the city centre, Wellington's airport occupies a narrow isthmus between Evans Bay and Lyall Bay. Beyond is the **Miramar Peninsula**, a picturesque collection of suburbs and beaches, including **Scorching Bay**,

---

"Wellywood"

Wellington is the capital of **New Zealand's film industry**, which is increasingly centred on the Miramar Peninsula (above). During World War II, defence bases were set up here, and the large, long-abandoned buildings were prime for conversion into production company studios. The stunning natural setting has also been used for **film locations** for numerous films including the *Lord of the Rings*, *King Kong*, and the two upcoming *Hobbit* films (co-written and executively produced by Peter Jackson; due for release in December 2011 and December 2012).

Jackson still lives out this way, and his special effects and entertainment company, Weta, which he co-owns with Richard Taylor, Tania Rodger and Jamie Selkirk, has its base in Miramar. A visit to the workshop's **Weta Cave**, on the corner of Camperdown Road and Weka Street (daily 9am–5.30pm; free; ☎04/380 9361, ⑳www.wetanz .co.nz) includes a fascinating twenty-minute film of behind-the-scenes workshop footage, along with a peek at the small museum, and the chance to buy hand-crafted figurines and limited-edition collectibles at its shop, which also sells movie location guides (from $25). Look for the King Kong footprint in the concrete out front.

Weta partner Jamie Selkirk is also in the process of restoring Miramar's Art Deco **Capitol cinema**, on Park Road, which should be screening films again for the first time in nearly half a century by the time you're reading this.

On the western side of the peninsula at Shelly Bay, opposite the *Chocolate Fish Café* (p.418), **Westside Studios**, on Shelly Bay Road (Tues–Sun, 10am–3pm; $14) runs tours on the hour of thousands of its props, including the piano from Jane Campion's *The Piano*.

Some ten different Wellington city tour operators, including those listed on p.403, offer **movie tours** taking in the peninsula's movie-making hotspots.

To learn more about New Zealand's film industry – and to watch New Zealand films on demand for free – stop by the **New Zealand Film Archive** (p.409) in the city centre.

a crescent of white sand 13km east of the city centre, which has safe swimming and a play area. The area is the hub of New Zealand's **film industry**, dubbed "Wellywood" (see box, p.417), with plenty to interest movie buffs. The best place to eat out this way is the family-run ⋇ *Chocolate Fish Café*, on Shelly Bay Road opposite Westside Studios. In its previous Scorching Bay location, the café was famously the *Lord of the Rings* cast and crew hangout; its much-anticipated re-opening at the former Shelly Bay air force base sees it transformed into a daytime fish barbecue with alfresco and indoor seating, seafood, meat and vegetarian sandwiches hot off the grill ($10–14), and delicious home-made muffins, slices and biscuits.

Wellington Rover (see p.403) and bus #30 (Mon–Fri peak hours only) serve Scorching Bay. Take bus #2 to reach the Weta Cave. Various bus routes cover most (but not all) of the rest of the peninsula – see p.402 for more information. Alternatively, you can visit the peninsula as part of a movie tour (see box, p.403).

The harbour and the Hutt Valley

The sight of multicoloured sails scudding across the water should convince you Wellington is at its best when seen from the water. **Wellington Harbour** offers excellent sailing and kayaking (see p.420); alternatively, hop on the ferry to **Matiu/Somes Island**, isolated in the harbour's northern reaches.

Fifteen kilometres from Wellington at the northern end of the harbour, commuterland spreads along the Hutt Valley, the largest tract of flat land in these parts, accessible along SH2 and by suburban trains and buses. The original founding of Wellington is remembered in Petone's Settlers Museum, while nearby Lower Hutt has Wellington's closest campsite (see p.405), a great art gallery and is on the way to the rugged **Rimutaka Forest Park**.

Matiu/Somes Island

One of Wellington's best day-trips is to **Matiu/Somes Island**, isolated in the northern reaches of the harbour. Legendary navigator Kupe is said to have named it Matiu (meaning "peace"), in the tenth century, and his descendants lived on the island until deposed by European settlers in the late 1830s. They renamed the island after Joseph Somes, then deputy governor of the New Zealand Company that had "bought" it. For eighty years it was a quarantine station where travellers carrying diseases such as smallpox were held until they recovered or died. During both world wars anyone in New Zealand considered even vaguely suspect – Germans, Italians, Turks, Mexicans and Japanese – were interned until the end of the war, after which it became an animal quarantine station for a number of years.

In the early 1980s its conservation value was recognized and it's now managed by DOC, which oversees continued efforts to revitalize **native vegetation** and restore the historic buildings. Introduced mammalian predators have now all been eradicated and threatened native species are being introduced in an effort to save them from extinction. Already there are six types of lizard, kakariki (the red-crowned parakeet), North Island robins, little blue penguins, the cricket-like weta and the ancient reptilian tuatara. Over fifty of these ancient lizard-like creatures were captive-bred at Wellington's Victoria University and released in 1998. They seem to like it as numbers are increasing.

Access is on the **Dominion Post Ferry** (2–4 services daily; 20min each way; $21 return; ☏04/499 3339, ⓦwww.eastbywest.co.nz) which stops at the island on its cross-harbour journey to Days Bay, enabling you to explore for up to five hours before catching a ferry back to Wellington. Sailings are weather-dependent, so call ahead to confirm departures. From the wharf at the island's northeastern end, a surfaced road runs uphill for 400m to the **DOC field centre** in an old hospital, which has maps of the island, or you can pick one up in advance from the city DOC office (see p.402). A popular option is to take a picnic lunch onto the island. Note that this is a protected reserve and smoking is not allowed.

The Museum of Wellington City and Sea (p.410) and Flat Earth (p.403) also run tours here.

Petone and Lower Hutt

The northern shore of Wellington Harbour is occupied by the suburb of **Petone**, the site of the first, short-lived European settlement in the Wellington region: the **Petone Settlers Museum**, The Esplanade, Petone (Tues–Fri noon–4pm, Sat & Sun 1–5pm; free; ⓦ www.petonesettlers.org.nz), tells the tale of the early Maori life in the region and the subsequent colonial settlement. The museum is 2.5km east of the Petone train station, so access is easier on buses #81, #83 or the orange Flyer from Courtenay Place and Lambton Quay.

Some 6km north of Petone sprawls **Lower Hutt**, home to **The New Dowse**, 45 Laings Rd (Mon–Fri 10am–4.30pm, Sat & Sun 10am–5pm; free; ⓣ 04/570 6500, ⓦ www.dowse.org.nz), a progressive art museum stunningly redeveloped by Ian Athfield in 2006. It's a great modern space filled with beautiful, often challenging arts and crafts rotated from its permanent collection, with shows on fashion, photography, jewellery and wider subjects. Many works are by local artists, who bring a strong Kiwi flavour to the place, and there's an excellent café on site. The gallery is almost 2km west of the Waterloo train station; access is easiest on the same buses as the Petone Settlers Museum.

The Dowse is adjacent to the **i-SITE visitor centre**, 25 Laings Rd (Mon–Fri 9am–5pm, Sat & Sun 9am–3pm; ⓣ 04/560 4715, ⓦ www.huttvalleynz.com).

Rimutaka Forest Park

Due south of Lower Hutt is the main entrance to the **Rimutaka Forest Park**, popular among city-dwellers for its series of easy, short and **day-walks** in the attractive Catchpool Valley; there are also picnic and BBQ facilities, and a well-maintained DOC **campsite** (see p.405). Some 20km from Wellington along the Coast Road, a signpost marks the park **entrance** (gates open 8am–dusk), from where Catchpool Road winds a further 2km up the valley to the car park, the starting point for most of the walks. Keen walkers and campers will want to get as far as the braided Orongorongo River, from where a startlingly grand landscape begins; camping is free along the riverbanks. There is no convenient bus service, so you'll probably want to drive.

Pick up the *Catchpool Valley/Rimutaka Forest Park* leaflet from DOC in Wellington.

Activities

Wellington's compact size and prime location mean **outdoor activities**, land- and water-based, are on the city's doorstep.

Watersports

The harbour's reliable winds make it ideal for **windsurfing** and **kiteboarding**. Most of the action centres on Kio Bay and around the point towards Evans Bay. For lessons, try Wildwinds, Chaffers Marina, Overseas Terminal (ⓣ 04/384 1010, ⓦ www.wildwinds.co.nz), just east of Te Papa, who offer a two-hour taster lesson ($110) or a series of four sessions ($395) to really get you going. **Surfing** lessons with Mahina Surf School ($80/4hr; ⓣ 021/365 563, ⓦ www.mahinasurf.co.nz) include board and wetsuit rental, with free pick-up and drop-off in the city centre.

Kayaking along the waterfront is a great way to spend a couple of hours. Fergs Kayaks, in Shed 6, Queens Wharf (☎04/499 8898, ⓦwww.fergskayaks.co.nz), rents kayaks (single sit-on-top kayaks $20/2hr, $50/day, double sit-on-tops $35/2hr, $85/day; single sea kayaks $20/ 2hr, $60/day, doubles $40/$120), or join one of their **guided trips** such as the Lights at Night trip, with romantic city-illuminated views and a light supper (Tues 6–9pm, weather permitting; $85 each 4 or more; $105 each for 2; book 2 weeks in advance).

For sub-surface explorations, Splash Gordon, 432 The Esplanade, Island Bay (☎04/939 3483, ⓦwww.splashgordon.co.nz) offers **scuba-diving** charters on the frigate *Wellington*, scuttled a five-minute boat ride off the coast in 21m of water in 2005. Experienced divers can do two dives with all gear for $120; there are also courses for all levels including beginners.

Cycling

On a fine day there's little to beat **cycling** around the coastal roads that follow the bays east of the city. Start by heading east along Oriental Parade and follow the coast as far as you want; even right past the airport and around the northern tip of the Miramar Peninsula to Scorching Bay (see p.417) and Seatoun (25–30km one-way).

There's also a stack of **off-road riding**, much of it outlined in the *Mountain Biking in Wellington City* leaflet (available free from the i-SITE), which contains maps of key areas a short ride from the city. Highlights include the coastal track out to Red Rocks (see box below) and the single-track trails around Mount Victoria (p.409). Committed mountain bikers should head to **Makara Peak Mountain Bike Park** (ⓦwww.makarapeak.org.nz), a two-square-kilometre area of forest and farmland centred on the 412m Makara Peak, up behind Karori some

---

Walks around Wellington

With its encircling wooded Town Belt, great city views from nearby hills and the temptation of watching seals along the southern coast, Wellington offers some excellent and easily accessible walking. Pick up free detailed leaflets from the i-SITE (p.402).

Red Rocks Coastal Walk

The easy **Red Rocks Coastal Walk** (4km each way; 2–3hr return) traces Wellington's southern shoreline to Sinclair Head, where a colony of bachelor New Zealand **fur seals** takes up residence from May to October each year. The walk follows a rough track along the coastline from Owhiro Bay to Sinclair Head, passing a quarry and the eponymous **Red Rocks** – well-preserved volcanic pillow lava, formed about 200 million years ago by underwater volcanic eruptions and coloured red by iron oxide. Maori variously attribute the colour to bloodstains from Maui's nose or blood dripping from a paua-shell cut on Kupe's hand, while another account tells how Kupe's daughters cut themselves in mourning, having given up their father for dead.

The track starts around 7km south of the city centre at the quarry gates at the western end of Owhiro Bay Parade, where there's a car park. To get here by bus either take the frequent #1 to Island Bay (get off at the Parade at the corner of Reef Street and walk 2.5km to the start of the walk) or, at peak times, catch #4, which continues to Happy Valley, 1km from the track. Both head east from Courtenay Place. Alternatively join the Wellington Rover hop-on-hop-off bus or come with 4WD Seal Coast Safari (see p.403 for both).

The Southern Walkway

Offering excellent views of the harbour and central city, the **Southern Walkway** (11km; 4–5hr) cuts through the Town Belt to the south of the city centre, between

8km west of central Wellington. There's no entry fee and you'll have the run of some 40km of tracks suitable for all abilities.

Bike rental is available at Mud Cycles, 338 Karori Rd, Karori, 2km short of the bike park ($30/half-day, $45/day; ☎04/476 4961 ⓦwww.mudcycles.co.nz), who also have an outlet at *Base Wellington* (p.405) in town.

Skating and rock climbing

In-line skates ($15/2hr, $25/day) are available at Fergs Kayaks (see opposite) and are perfect for use in nearby Frank Kitts Park or around Oriental Parade. Fergs also offer an excellent and very popular indoor climbing wall ($15; harness and shoes $3 each).

Eating, drinking and entertainment

Wellington reputedly has more places to eat per capita than New York, and the standard is impressively high, whatever your budget. There's little need to venture much beyond the bounds of the central business district, though we've picked out a couple of reasons to stray. As the country's self-professed **coffee** capital (Wellington has no fewer than ten independent roasteries), you'll find the good stuff served up everywhere from cosy spots through to the *très chic*. Gastronomes might want to join a gourmet tour (see box, p.403). If you want to head further off the beaten track, local neighbourhoods worth scouting out include Newtown and the Aro Valley.

Oriental and Island bays. Despite a few steep stretches it's fairly easy going overall. Fantails, grey warblers and wax-eyes provide company, and Island Bay offers some of the city's best swimming.

The walk can be undertaken in either direction and is clearly marked by posts bearing orange arrows. To start at the city end, simply walk along Oriental Parade (or take **bus** #14 or #24) to the entrance to Charles Plimmer Park just past 350 Oriental Parade. To begin at the southern end, take the #1 bus to Island Bay and follow the signs from nearby Shorland Park.

The Northern Walkway

Extending through tranquil sections of the Town Belt to the north of the city centre, the panoramic **Northern Walkway** (16km; 4–5hr) stretches from Kelburn to the suburb of Johnsonville, it covers five distinct areas – Botanic Garden, Tinakori Hill, Trelissick Park, Khandallah Park and Johnsonville Park – each accessible from suburban streets and served by public transport. Highlights are the **birdlife** on Tinakori Hill (tui, fantails, kingfishers, grey warblers, silver-eyes); the regenerating native forest of **Ngaio Gorge** in Trelissick Park; great views across the city and the harbour and over to the Rimutaka and Tararua ranges from a lookout on **Mount Kaukau** (430m); and, in **Johnsonville Park**, a disused road tunnel hewn through solid rock.

Start at the top of the Cable Car and head north through the Botanic Garden, or join the walk at Tinakori Hill by climbing St Mary Street, off Glenmore Street, and following the orange arrows through woodland. To begin at the northern end, take a train to Raroa station on the Johnsonville line.

▲ Alfresco drinking at *Mac's Brewery*

In the streets around **Courtenay Place** and **Cuba Street** there's a plethora of local and international restaurants – from cheap curry joints and bohemian cafés through to award-winning establishments headed up by some of the finest chefs in the country. The area is also home to some of New Zealand's best **nightlife**, with a huge array of late-night cafés, bars and clubs within walking distance of each other. New places constantly spring up and tired ones quietly drop off or reinvent themselves under a different name. The partying goes on late into the next morning, and pumps hardest from Thursday to Saturday, when more secluded places nearby offer a less frenetic setting.

The **arts** are also strong, with several theatres and a lively festival season.

Eating

During the day many restaurants offer bargain lunch specials. Many pubs and bars (p.425) also serve impressive and generally inexpensive fare. For **groceries** try the three central New World supermarkets: at 68 Willis St; inside the railway station; and the largest, at the eastern end of Wakefield Street. If you're here on a Sunday morning, head down to the car park near Te Papa to the **fruit and vegetable market** and the nearby **farmers' market** in the Chaffers Dock Atrium, with stalls of artisan goods from local producers. The following are marked on the map on p.406, unless otherwise stated.

Delis and takeaways

Kruezberg Corner of Cuba & Webb sts. Black-painted caravan selling Wellington-brewed People's Coffee and snacks like haloumi or tofu burgers and smoked chicken toasted sandwiches (all under $10) to take away or eat at the striped tables in the former car-yard-turned-urban

garden. Feeding the resident stuffed-toy parrot a $1 coin gets you an underground literary story. Open until at least 4pm; often has live music or outdoor film screenings on summer nights. Licensed.

Moore Wilson's Corner of Tory & College sts. Tucked under a parking station this superb deli, charcuterie and bakery is the place to come for top-quality picnic supplies, including its own aged cheese. Fill your water bottle from the free spring water fountain out front.

Wellington Trawling Sea Market 220 Cuba St. The best fish and chip shop in the city, eat in or take away, which also sells wet fish. Daily until at least 8pm.

Cafés

Aro Coffee 90 Aro St. The pick of a village-like cluster of cafés in weatherboard buildings in the Aro Valley, serving its own hand-blended coffee roasted on the premises, along with a short, smart menu of daytime fare like bubble and squeak with poached eggs and bacon, zucchini, brie and basil omelette, and home-made pork sausages with white-bean salad (all under $20).

Ciocco 11 Tory St. Mouthwatering daytime cafè and chocolaterie selling hand-made Schoc chocolates from the Wairarapa in sixty wild flavours such as sweet basil, pink peppercorn and lime-chilli. Its hot chocolate – real melted chocolate in the bottom of a glass of steamed milk – is sipped through a metal "stroon" (combined straw/spoon).

Ernesto's 132 Cuba St. Slightly more upmarket comrade of Cuba St legend *Fidel's* (below), serving the same smooth Havana coffee in a converted clothing factory with original leadlight windows and polished timber. Creative meals under $25 include the likes of mustard-glazed pork belly with chestnut and kumara mash. Daily until 3am; licensed.

Fidel's 234 Cuba St. At the offbeat southern end of Cuba St, this eternally funky, always-busy café is plastered with revolution-era pics of Castro, and extends into the former barber's next door (in the spirit of Castro they've kept the old Super Cuts sign) and camouflage-netted courtyard. Come for locally roasted Havana coffee, vegan muffins, booze, smoothies or excellent-value meals (mains $10–24). Open till 10pm Sun–Mon, till 11pm Tues–Sat.

Floriditas 161 Cuba St ☏04/381 2212. This light, airy and stylish café is always busy, from its wonderful breakfasts ($13.50–17) to its small but clever menu which might include blue cod and fennel chowder ($12.50) followed by aged char-grilled sirloin ($34), topped off with tamarillo and marsala trifle ($10) or the house specialty amaretto afogatto ($10.50).

Midnight Espresso 178 Cuba St. Looking like a bohemian artists' squat, with posters and flyers pinned to the community notice board, artwork and murals covering the walls, and its own pinball machine, this caffeine junkie's heaven serves Havana coffee along with counter food and hot

dishes (many veggie or vegan) under $10. Daily until 3am.

Mojo 37 Customhouse Quay. Most days you can watch master roaster Lambros Gianoutsos hand-blending and roasting at the HQ of one Wellington's most successful coffee roasteries. Beans are sold at the shop (open 8am–4pm Mon–Fri, 10am–2pm Sat); the building directly behind houses *Mojo's* flagship café (open daily).

Nikau Gallery Café City Gallery Wellington, Civic Square. A stylish, contemporary daytime café with an airy setting and outdoor terrace. Excellent coffee and a high-quality yet reasonably priced menu: try the kedgeree with house-smoked fish ($20) or one of the lip-smacking desserts like lemon mousse with hazelnut praline ($11). Closed Sun.

Olive 170 Cuba St ☏04/802 5266. Elegant yet relaxed bare-boards café that sticks mainly to organic produce. Great for coffee and cake throughout the day, as well as delicious breakfasts ($5–17) like organic porridge, and lunches ($11–17) such as pan-fried haloumi; the pick of an evening (mains $23–28) is the daily changing risotto. Closed Sun & Mon evenings.

Parade Café 148 Oriental Parade. A great spot to break your Oriental Bay stroll, with fine coffee and cakes and a full range of breakfasts, lunches and dinners at moderate prices. Try the garlic calamari salad, roast pumpkin panini or gourmet bangers and mash (all $16–18). Licensed.

Plum 103 Cuba St. Elongated dark-timber café perfect for cocooning over the paper and a post-hangover "Plumster" breakfast of eggs, sausages, bacon, slow-roasted tomatoes, grilled field mushrooms and more ($19), or hot smoked salmon with hash browns, avocado and caper mayo ($15.50). Licensed.

Restaurants

Beach Babylon Ground floor, 232 Oriental Parade ☏04/801 7717. Ingeniously done out like a retro Kiwi *bach*, serving everything from casual brunches through to stylish dinners that also incorporate a retro twist: chicken supreme with whipped potato ($25.50), oven-baked lamb on bubble and squeak ($23.50), and banana splits and ice-cream sundaes (both $8) for dessert. Licensed and BYO.

Chow First floor, 45 Tory St ☏04/382 8585. Hip restaurant (one of several around the country) serving smartly presented Southeast Asian dishes. Its wide selection of "long plates" ($9–19) are ideal as side dishes or in combination as a banquet – go for the mussel fritters with coriander and chilli soy mayo.

Dockside Shed 3, Queens Wharf ☏04/499 9900. Flashy restaurant and bar in a vast historic wooden warehouse with a deck area overlooking the harbour; dress up unless you want to sit outside. The place is hot on seafood – try the Dockside fish and chips ($30) or pan-roasted whole flounder ($36), and book ahead if you want a window seat.

Logan-Brown 192 Cuba St ☎04/801 5114. Steve Logan and Al Brown are known throughout New Zealand for their TVNZ series "Hunger for the Wild" in which they drive around the country in Al's 1964 EH Holden, hunting and gathering wild ingredients. Book as far ahead as possible to dine in this colonnaded 1920s former bank on west coast turbot with crayfish or Hawke's Bay lamb rack with pea gnocchi (both $46), or Canterbury venison with parsnip mousse, asparagus and white truffle butter ($48). Lunch Mon–Fri, dinner daily.

Maria Pia's Trattoria 55 Mulgrave St ☎04/499 5590. The menu at this cosy southern Italian trattoria and wine bar varies seasonally and almost everything is cooked from scratch using mostly organic ingredients. Stop in for lunch while touring the Parliamentary District, or come back for dinner – mains start at $35. Lunch Mon–Fri, dinner Tues–Sat.

Martin Bosley's First floor, 103 Oriental Parade ☎04/920 8302. Esteemed namesake venue of one of New Zealand's most celebrated chefs. Artistically conceived and presented cuisine focuses on seafood to complement the views from the upper floor of the Port Nicholson Yacht Club. Dinner mains average $45; Bosley's *dégustation* menus ($100) have the option of matched wines ($70). Lunch Mon–Fri, dinner Tues–Sun.

Masala 2 Allen St ☎04/385 2012. Sleek banquettes and circular booths along with an ambient soundtrack offer a stylish, retro-contemporary alternative to most of Wellington's Indian restaurants. Curries (lunch mains under $13, dinner mains under $20), from the classic to the innovative, are cooked to perfection. Licensed & BYO.

Matterhorn 106 Cuba St ☎04/384 3359. At the end of a long timber-lined corridor in a 1960s coffee house, *Matterhorn* successfully merges a glam bar and a fancy restaurant. Push through the swing doors for a cocktail (try the basil and manuka honey martini) at the long bar, or beautifully done food. Evening mains ($28–36) include twice-baked gorgonzola soufflé, and caramelized slow-cooked pork belly; the Sunday night roast has cult status. Lunch Mon–Fri, brunch Sat–Sun, dinner daily.

Oriental Kingdom Left Bank ☎04/381 3303. This simple café is beloved by in-the-know Wellingtonians – so much so that it recently doubled in size to accommodate them. All of its pan-Asian fare is fresh, cheap (mains $6.50–9.50), filling and delicious, particularly its steaming laksas and roti. Licensed & BYO.

Ortega 16 Marjoribanks St ☎04/382 9559. Only steps from Courtenay Place but with the feel of a classy neighbourhood bistro, *Ortega* concentrates on superb seafood like softshell crab with smoked mussel kedgeree, served with relaxed panache. Book for dinner, or just drop in for an oloroso sherry at the bar. Mains around $30. Dinner Mon–Sat.

Sweet Mother's Kitchen 5 Courtenay Place ☎04/385 4444. Breakfast on beignets (icing sugar-doused doughnuts; $3), tuck into a Po Boy (New Orleans baguette; $8.50–9.50), warm up with a bowl of gumbo (small/large $11/15) or hickory-smoked baby back ribs ($22), and finish off with a pecan and bourbon pie ($8) or bananas foster – caramel sautéed bananas flambéed in white rum and banana liquor. Licensed; closed Mon.

The White House First floor, 232 Oriental Parade ☎04/385 8555. Harbour panoramas and exquisite food makes *The White House* one of Wellington's best and most romantic dining picks. Follow the likes of grilled venison with truffled parsnip and game pie ($45) or grilled salmon on wasabi mash with macadamia sauce ($40) with aromatic international and New Zealand cheeses (five for $45), or go the whole hog with a *dégustation* menu ($125) accompanied by paired wines (extra $65). Dinner Mon–Sat & lunch Fri (check for extended summer hours).

Drinking and nightlife

Most **pubs** and **bars** are open daily, from around eleven in the morning until midnight or later. The distinction between bars and **clubs** is often blurred, with many bars hosting free live music and dancing in the evenings, especially at weekends. Resident and guest DJs mix broad-ranging styles to create a party- or club-style atmosphere. Live **bands** (usually Kiwi but sometimes international) are a regular fixture, playing in bars, dedicated smaller venues or bigger halls like the Queens Wharf Events Centre (☎04/472 5021) and occasionally **free concerts** at the waterfront Frank Kitts Park or Civic Square. The following are marked on the map on p.406.

Pubs and bars

Alice Forresters Lane, off Tory St. At the far end of the same laneway as *Motel* (below), a neon-lit rabbit disappearing down a hole leads you down a winding corridor into this Lewis Carroll-inspired fantasyland where cocktails (such as the Mad Hatter's Tea Party – vanilla vodka and iced peppermint tea) are served in teapots and china cups. An internal door connects *Alice* with *Boogie Wonderland* (see p.426). From 6pm Wed–Fri, from 7pm Sat, until around 5am.

The Backbencher Pub Corner of Molesworth & Kate Sheppard sts. A favourite with MPs and civil servants for the satirical cartoons and outsized latex puppets of notable local politicians and sportsmen from the 1970s, and the convivial pub ambience, dozen or more draught beers and hearty meals named after current MPs.

Coyote 63 Courtenay Place. Urban Santa Fe-style bar (one of four around the country) for the hedonistic dance crowds with its own brand of commercial dance music, Kiwi-Mex dishes and drinks specials.

Hummingbird 22 Courtenay Place. Large windows opening out onto Courtenay Place allow patrons to watch – and be watched by – the passing crowds at this glossy, wood-panelled bar/restaurant. Live jazz on Sunday afternoons May–Nov.

Kiwi Pub 26 Allen St. It's a sign of New Zealand's coming of age that this former English pub (the *Courtenay Arms*) has been renamed, stripped out and refitted with Kiwiana, including board games, toys and mismatched furniture. Laidback, unpretentious vibe and good choice of beers on tap.

Leuven 135 –137 Featherston St. Belgian-style beer café in the heart of the business district, good for breakfasts of Belgian porridge and full meals such as its signature 1kg pot of mussels – but especially popular for early-evening tie-loosening sessions over a few Hoegaarden.

Mac's Brewery Corner of Cable & Taranaki sts. Central Wellington's only working brewery, in an 1800s waterfront warehouse, serves classy pub fare along with its excellent brews including Great White (wheat beer), Macs Gold (all-malt lager), Sassy Red (English-style bitter), Black Mac (dark

larger), and the knockout Hop Rocker (Pilsner); if you can't decide, order a six-beer tasting tray ($15).

The Malthouse 48 Courtenay Place. In a lounge setting with low sofas, high stools, sleek glossy timber tables and shag pile, this beer drinker's paradise has thirty different beers on tap – including some of New Zealand's finest craft brews, like the Invercargill Brewing Company's Pitch Black – plus some 150 varieties by the bottle. There are detailed tasting notes on each by top Kiwi beer commentator Neil Miller. Open 3pm–late Sun–Thurs, noon–late Fri & Sat.

Matterhorn See opposite. Uber-stylish cocktail bar, with regular live and electronic music.

Mighty Mighty First floor, 104 Cuba St. Cool, off-beam late-night bar that regularly hosts bands of just about any stripe, but might also have a weird play, a pie-eating contest, country ping pong, or hip-hop bowls – you'll just have to go and find out. There's usually a $5–10 cover. Wed–Sat until 4am.

Motel Foresters Lane. Accessed off a dingy laneway by *Chow* (p.423), this hidden, New York-style, first-floor bar, with a tiny sign, surveillance camera and an intercom to buzz visitors up – was once so exclusive it famously turned away Liv Tyler when she was shooting *The Lord of the Rings*. It still cuts it, with semi-private booths, cool sounds (mostly jazz), and serious cocktails. Open from around 6.30pm to late Tues–Sat.

Southern Cross 35 Abel Smith St. In a cavernous yet cosy contemporary space with a heated Balinese-style outdoor garden (and hot water bottles and blankets in winter), this brilliant local hosts everything from a knitting circle (Mon) to music quiz nights (Thurs), and dancing classes (Sun), plus live music at weekends. New Zealand beers are well represented on tap, and great pub grub includes snacks like bowls of cheerios (not the American breakfast cereal but Kiwi cocktail sausages).

Clubs and live music venues

Bodega 101 Ghuznee St. New Zealand's longest-running music venue hosts cutting-edge Kiwi

---

Gay and lesbian Wellington

The scene in Wellington is focused in the inner city, but for the most part it's woven seamlessly into the general café/bar mainstream. In the centre, at least, gay people openly express affection in public, and gays, lesbians, transgender and bi-folk mix freely together. For the latest information, check out the website ⓦ www.gaynz.com, or pick up national publications *Express* newspaper (ⓦ www.gayexpress.co.nz) and *OUT!* magazine (ⓦ www.out.co.nz).

Wellington's big gay event is the annual Pride Week (around late Sept), with dances, parties, films and art.

bands and the odd offbeat international act usually every Tues–Sat.

Boogie Wonderland 25 Courtenay Place. Wild and wonderfully cheesy, this retro joint is for you if you love flares, disco and mirror balls. Open Thurs–Sat 9pm until late. Cover typically $10.

Happy 118 Tory St. Underground venue on the corner of Vivian St, with live, electronic and experimental sounds. Most events free, some $5–10.

Hole in the Wall 154 Vivian St. A lively, well-respected venue with gigs and DJs most nights and everything from hardcore and garage punk to drum 'n' bass, from emerging and established artists. Occasional cover charges.

San Francisco Bathhouse 171 Cuba St. Not a bathhouse and, obviously, not San Franciscan, but the city's main indie, alternative rock and reggae venue, with a balcony looking out on the assorted life passing along Cuba St. First-rate Kiwi bands are joined on the bill by occasional international touring acts. Most gigs cost around $10–15, though some are free.

Sandwiches 8 Kent Terrace. Posher clubby venue with a focus on drum 'n' bass, with a restaurant attached, which attracts the weekend urbanites. Sometimes free, but covers can be up to $45.

Performing arts and festivals

Performing arts are strong in Wellington, which is home to several professional theatres, the Royal New Zealand Ballet, the New Zealand Symphony Orchestra and assorted opera and dance companies. The best introduction is the *Wellington – What's On* booklet, free from the i-SITE and from accommodation around the city. There are also **listings** in *The Dominion Post* (Ⓦ www.dompost.co.nz) on weekends; the city's free, weekly *Capital Times* (Ⓦ www.capitaltimes.co.nz), which you can pick up from racks around town; and the monthly *Feeling Great* (Ⓦ www.feelinggreat.co.nz), a glossy arts and entertainment guide.

Look out too for flyers about the council-sponsored Summer City festival (Jan–March) with free music and performances around town.

Classical music, theatre and cinema

The city regularly hosts **orchestral** and other performances, while four professional **theatres** stage Kiwi and international shows.

Book **tickets** direct at venues or, for a small fee, through Ticketek (Ⓣ 04/384 3840, Ⓦ www.ticketek.co.nz), which has an outlet at the St James Theatre, 77–87 Courtenay Place.

In addition to its quota of multiplexes, Wellington also has a smattering of arthouse **cinemas**: you can usually save a couple of dollars by going during the day or any time early in the week. See p.417 for details of Mirimar Peninsula's Capitol Theatre cinema refurbishment.

Theatres and concert halls

Bats Theatre 1 Kent Terrace Ⓣ 04/802 4175, Ⓦ www.bats.co.nz. Lively theatre concentrating on developmental works served up at affordable prices (usually around $15–18), with discounts for backpacker card-holders.

Circa Corner of Taranaki & Cable sts Ⓣ 04/801 7992, Ⓦ www.circa.co.nz. One of the country's liveliest and most innovative professional theatres, which has fostered the skills of some of the best-known Kiwi directors and actors.

Downstage 12 Cambridge Terrace Ⓣ 04/801 6946, Ⓦ www.downstage.co.nz. Stages its own productions and the best touring shows: a mix of mainstream and new drama, dance and comedy, with the emphasis on quality Kiwi work.

Opera House 111–113 Manners St Ⓣ 04/384 4060, Ⓦ www.stjames.co.nz. Hosts touring opera, ballet and musicals.

St James Theatre 77–87 Courtenay Place Ⓣ 04/802 4060, Ⓦ www.stjames.co.nz. This refurbished theatre in a fine 1912 building is the major venue for the Royal New Zealand Ballet and hosts opera, dance, musicals and plays. It also has a licensed café for pre- and post-performance drinks.

Westpac Stadium (Wellington Regional Stadium) Featherston St Ⓣ 04/473 3881, Ⓦ westpacstadium.co.nz. Dubbed "the cake tin" by its detractors for its iron-clad design, this modern purpose-built stadium is the venue for rugby and cricket as well as occasional rock concerts.

Cinemas

Embassy 10 Kent Terrace ℡ 04/384 7657, ⓦ www.deluxe.co.nz. Mainstream and independent movies on a single giant screen in the city centre.

The New Zealand Film Archive See p.409.

Paramount 25 Courtenay Place ℡ 04/384 4080, ⓦ www.paramount.co.nz. Central 1917-established multi-screen showing art and mainstream movies with the added indulgence of being able to watch while sipping a beer or wine.

Reading Cinemas 100 Courtenay Place ℡ 04/801 4601, ⓦ www.readingcinemas.co.nz. Mostly mainstream movies with the option of going for their plush Gold Lounge seats (from $25) which come with an in-seat food and drink service.

Festivals

Whenever you visit Wellington there's a good chance there'll be some sort of festival happening. The visitor centre has full details; the following are the biggest occasions, listed chronologically.

New Zealand International Arts Festival ⓦ www.nzfestival.nzpost.co.nz. The country's biggest cultural event is a month-long festival held in March in even-numbered years, drawing top performers from around the world. Fashioned along the lines of the Edinburgh Festival, it celebrates the huge diversity of the arts: classical music, jazz and pop, opera, puppet shows and the Grotesque, cabaret, poetry readings, traditional Maori dance, modern ballet and experimental works. Most venues are in the city centre.

Wellington Fringe Festival ⓦ www.fringe.org.nz. Vibrant affair run as a separate and roughly concurrent event to the International Arts Festival, filling the inner city with street and indoor theatre.

Wellington Film Festival ⓦ www.enzedff.co.nz. Typically held from mid-July to early Aug, with less mainstream offerings playing at cinemas around town.

Wellington International Jazz Festival ⓦ www.jazzfestival.co.nz. Five-day festival in early March bringing some of the world's best performers to town.

Wellington on a Plate ⓦ www.wellingtononaplate.com. Two-week festival in the second half of August celebrating the capital's cuisine through tastings, talks and behind-the-stoves tours as well as discounted menus at top restaurants.

World of WearableArt (WOW) ⓦ www.worldofwearableart.com. Tickets go like hot cakes for this glorious spectacle of weird costumes which runs like a bizarre fashion show over the last two weeks of Sept.

Listings

Airlines and flights For details of transport to the airport see p.401.

Automobile Association 342–352 Lambton Quay ℡ 04/931 9999.

Banks and foreign exchange Banks are dotted all over the CBD. To change money head to ANZ at 215–229 Lambton Quay, BNZ at 1 Willis St and Travelex at 120 Lambton Quay.

Bike rental See "Cycling", p.420.

Bookshops The best selection of new New Zealand and special-interest titles is at Unity Books, 57 Willis St ℡ 04/499 4245. It's also good for more mainstream fare, as are the majors: Whitcoulls, 312 Lambton Quay ℡ 04/472 1921, at 91 Cuba St and 80 Courtenay Place; and Borders, 226 Lambton Quay ℡ 04/471 1900. For secondhand books try the small but superbly stocked Pegasus, Left Bank ℡ 04/384 4733, ⓦ www.pegasusbooksnz.com; or the extensive Arty Bee's Books, The Oaks, Manners St ℡ 04/384 5339, ⓦ www.artybees.co.nz.

Camping and outdoor equipment Several good shops – Bivouac, Mountain Designs, Fairydown and Kathmandu – cluster around the junction of Willis & Mercer sts.

Car rental As well as the companies covered in Basics (see p.38) various local firms offer good deals: Nationwide, 37 Hutt Rd, Thorndon ℡ 0800/803 003, ⓦ www.nationwiderentals.co.nz; Rent-a-Dent, 24 Tacy St, Kilbirnie ℡ 0800/736 823, ⓦ www.rentadent.co.nz; and Ace Rental Cars, 126 Hutt Rd, ℡ 0800/535 500, ⓦ www.acerentalcars.co.nz.

Embassies and consulates Australia, 72 Hobson St, Thorndon ℡ 04/473 6411; Canada, 125 The Terrace ℡ 04/473 9577; UK, 44 Hill St ℡ 04/924 2888; US, 29 Fitzherbert Terrace, Thorndon (℡ 04/462 6000); for other countries, check Yellow Pages, under "Diplomatic and consular representatives".

Internet access Plenty of places, many along Courtenay Place, generally charging $4–5/hr. Interface, off the Cuba St mall on Left Bank

(Mon–Fri 10am–8pm, Sat 10am–6pm), offers a full suite of state-of-the-art facilities. There's free access at the library.

Library Wellington's Central Library (Mon–Thurs 9.30am–8.30pm, Fri 9.30am–9pm, Sat 9.30am–5pm, Sun 1–4pm; ☎ 04/801 4040), 65 Victoria St, backs onto Civic Square.

Medical emergencies For emergencies call ☎ 111. For 24hr emergency treatment, the After Hours Medical Centre is at 17 Adelaide Rd, Newtown, near Basin Reserve ☎ 04/384 4944. Wellington Hospital is on Riddiford St, Newtown ☎ 04/385 5999.

Pharmacy For late service go to After Hours Pharmacy, 17 Adelaide Rd, Newtown ☎ 04/385 8810 (Mon–Fri 5–11pm, Sat, Sun & public holidays 8am–11pm).

Photographic supplies Wellington Photographic Supplies, 11–15 Vivian St ☎ 04/384.

Police Wellington Central Police Station, corner of Victoria and Harris sts ☎ 04/381 2000. For emergencies, call ☎ 111.

Post office Several throughout the city centre; for poste restante go to 43 Manners St.

Swimming Freyberg Pool and Fitness Centre, 139 Oriental Parade (daily 6am–9pm; ☎ 04/801 4530), has a 33m indoor pool ($4 to swim), plus gym, spas, saunas, steam room, fitness classes and massage therapy. Thorndon Pool, 26 Murphy St (Oct–April Mon & Wed 6.30am–8pm, Tues, Thur & Fri 6.30am–7pm, Sat & Sun 8am–6.30pm; $5.30) is a 30.5m heated outdoor pool near Parliament.

Taxis Green Cabs (☎ 0508/447 336) use hybrids; Wellington Combined Taxis(☎ 04/384 4444) are carbon zero-certified. Authorized stands are located at the train station, on Whitmore St (between Lambton Quay & Featherston St), outside the *James Smith Hotel* on Lambton Quay, off Willis St on the Bond St corner, at the corner of Courtenay Place & Taranaki St, and at the junction of Willis & Aro sts.

Travel details

Wellington is a major transportation hub with trains and buses homing in on the ferries that cross Cook Strait to Picton and the South Island (see p.401). Direct buses and nonstop flights are listed below but there are numerous connections to further-flung places.

Ferries

Wellington to: Matiu/Somes Island (2–4 daily; 20min); Picton (5–8 daily; 3hr).

Trains

The Auckland–Wellington Overlander runs once daily Dec–April and Fri, Sat & Sun during the rest of the year.

Wellington to: Auckland (1 daily; 12hr); Hamilton (1 daily; 9hr 30min); Hutt Central/Waterloo (every 30min; 20 min); Masterton (2–5 daily; 1hr 30min); National Park (1 daily; 5hr 30min); Otaki (2 daily; 1hr 10min); Otorohanga (1 daily; 8hr 45min); Paekakariki (every 30min; 50min); Palmerston North (2 daily; 2hr–2hr 20min); Paraparaumu (every 30min; 1hr).

Buses

Wellington to: Auckland (3–4 daily; 11hr);

Masterton via the Hutt Valley (1–2 daily; 2hr); Napier (3–4 daily; 5hr 15min); New Plymouth (3–4 daily; 6hr 30min); Palmerston North (5–7 daily; 2hr); Paraparaumu (10 daily; 50min); Rotorua (5–7 daily; 7hr); Taupo (5–7 daily; 6hr).

Flights

Wellington to: Auckland (20–25 daily; 1hr); Blenheim (8–13 daily; 25min); Christchurch (15 daily; 45min); Dunedin (2 daily; 1hr 15min); Gisborne (3–4 daily; 1hr); Greymouth (5 weekly; 1hr); Hamilton (7 daily; 1hr); Kaikoura (1–2 daily in summer; 1hr); Napier/Hastings (5 daily; 50min); Nelson (6–10 daily; 35min); New Plymouth (4 daily; 50min); Palmerston North (3 daily; 30min); Picton (6–8 daily; 25min); Rotorua (3 daily; 1hr); Takaka (1 daily; 30min); Taupo (3 daily; 1hr); Tauranga (4 daily; 1hr 10min); Timaru (4 daily; 1hr 10min); Wanganui (4 weekly; 25min); Westport (1 daily Mon–Fri; 55min); Whangarei (1 daily; 1hr 30min).

Marlborough, Nelson and Kaikoura

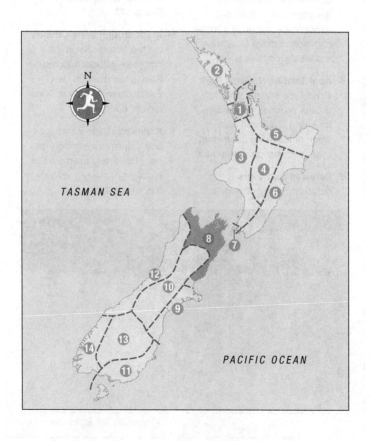

CHAPTER 8 # Highlights

❋ **The Queen Charlotte Track**
This beautiful multi-day hike is made all the more manageable by staying in great backpackers and B&Bs, and having your bags carried for you. **See p.440**

❋ **Nelson** A vibrant arts community, vineyards on the doorstep, a laidback atmosphere and great weather combine to make Nelson an essential stop. **See p.445**

❋ **Abel Tasman National Park**
Crystal-clear water and golden beaches are rewards for hiking the lush Coast Track or kayaking the myriad inlets and islands. **See p.458**

❋ **Farewell Spit tours** A surprising array of wildlife can be seen on four-wheel-drive tours along this thin strip of ocean-girt desert. **See p.471**

❋ **Heaphy Track** The huge range of dramatic scenery and final sense of achievement puts this Great Walk up with the best. **See p.472**

❋ **Marlborough Wine Country**
No trip to this area is complete without supping Sauvignon Blanc in New Zealand's most famous wine region. **See p.477**

❋ **Kaikoura** Whale-watching and dolphin-swimming trips from this pretty town are the highlight of many a visitor's trip. **See p.484**

▲ Hiking in the Abel Tasman National Park

Marlborough, Nelson and Kaikoura

The South Island kicks off spectacularly. The whole northern section is supremely alluring, from the indented bays and secluded hideaways of the Marlborough Sounds and the sweep of golden beaches around Nelson, to an impressive array of national parks, sophisticated wineries around Marlborough and the natural wonders of Kaikoura. In fact, if you had to choose only one area of New Zealand to visit, this would be a strong contender.

Most visitors travel between the North Island and the South Island by ferry, striking land at the town of **Picton** – drab in the winter, lively in the summer and surrounded by the beautiful **Marlborough Sounds**. Here, bays full of unfathomably deep water lap at tiny beaches, each with its rickety boat jetty, and the land rises steeply to forest or stark pasture.

To the west, the lively yet relaxed city of **Nelson** is the starting point for forays to wilder spots further north. Some of the country's most gorgeous walking tracks and dazzling golden beaches populate the **Abel Tasman National Park**, while yet further north the relatively isolated **Golden Bay** offers peaceful times in chilled settings. The curve of the Golden Bay culminates in a long sandy bar that juts into the ocean, **Farewell Spit**, an extraordinary and unique habitat. It borders the Kahurangi National Park, through which the rugged and spectacular **Heaphy Track** forges a route to the West Coast.

The least visited of the region's well-preserved areas of natural splendour is the sparsely populated **Nelson Lakes National Park**, principally a spot for tramping

Getting around

Ferries (see box, p.401 for details) cross Cook Strait and link up with the region's only **train**, from Picton to Christchurch. Buses fill in the gaps, many doing the same Picton–Christchurch run via Kaikoura with others running to Blenheim and Nelson where there are connections for the Abel Tasman National Park and Golden Bay. The main operators are Southern Link (☎0508/458 835, ⒲www.southernlinkkbus.co.nz), who run between Picton and Christchurch; and Atomic Shuttles (☎03/439 0697, ⒲www.atomictravel.co.nz) and InterCity/Newmans (☎03/365 1113, ⒲www.intercitycoach.co.nz), who both cover the area extensively.

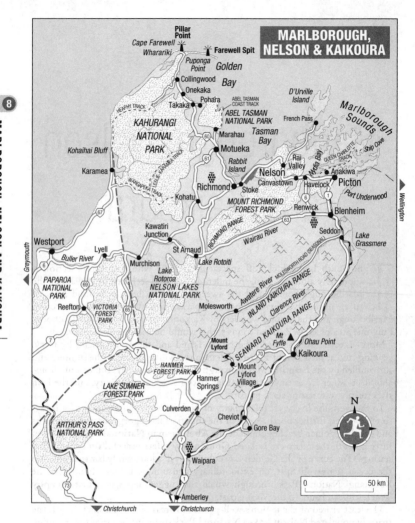

to alpine lakes or fishing, though the nearby **Buller River** also lures raft and kayak rats.

South of Picton, you can slurp your merry way through **Marlborough**, New Zealand's most fêted winemaking region centred on the modest towns of **Blenheim** and **Renwick**. A night or two in one of the rural B&Bs and some time spent around the wineries happily balances the more energetic activities of the national parks, and sets you up nicely for a few days of eco-tourism in **Kaikoura** where **whale watching** and **swimming with dolphins** and **seals** are the main draws.

The region's **weather** is some of the sunniest in the land, particularly around Blenheim and Nelson, who regularly compete for the honour of the greatest number of sunshine hours in New Zealand.

The Marlborough Sounds

The **Marlborough Sounds** are undeniably picturesque, a stimulating filigree of bays, inlets, islands and peninsulas rising abruptly from the water to rugged, lush green wilderness and open farmland. Large parts are only accessible by sea, which also provides the ideal vantage point for witnessing its splendour. The area is part working farms, including salmon or mussel farms, and part given over to some fifty-odd reserve areas – a mixture of islands, sections of coast and land-bound tracts. The Sounds' nexus, **Picton**, is the jumping-off point for **Queen Charlotte Sound** where cruises and water taxis provide access to the rewarding and very manageable **Queen Charlotte Track**. Heading west, Queen Charlotte Drive winds precipitously to the small community of **Havelock**, New Zealand's green-lipped mussel capital, before exploring the delightful **Pelorus Sound** and perhaps taking the backroads to view the swirling waters of **French Pass**.

Picton and around

Cross-strait ferries arrive at pretty little **Picton**, sandwiched between the hills and the deep, placid waters of Queen Charlotte Sound. Many people only stop for a coffee looking out over the water before pressing on, but Picton makes a great base for a few days' exploring Queen Charlotte Sound. In town, don't miss the historic *Edwin Fox* ship, or head out on excellent **cruises and kayak trips**. Water taxis buzz across the water taking trampers to various points on the **Queen Charlotte Track**. Picton also makes a decent base for exploring the **wine region** around Blenheim, half an hour's drive to the south.

There was a European settlement in the region as early as 1827 when John Guard established a whaling station, but Picton itself didn't come into being until the New Zealand Company purchased the town site for £300 in 1848. Picton flourished as a port and **service town** for the Wairau Plains to the south but predominantly as the most convenient port for travel between the islands.

Arrival and information

Interislander ferry foot passengers disembark close to the town centre, while Bluebridge foot passengers and all **vehicles** disembark on the western side of town about 1km from the centre: Bluebridge operates a free shuttle bus to the i-SITE.

Hiking around Picton

The best of the local trails run through Victoria Domain, a mostly bush-clad peninsula immediately east of Picton. As most trails link up at some point it can be a little confusing, though several free and widely available maps of town show the way.

Bob's Bay Track (1km one-way; 30min; gently undulating). Starting at Shelly Beach near the *Echo*, this extends along the shoreline to a safe swimming and picnicking beach at Bob's Bay providing great views across the water to the ferry terminal and up the Queen Charlotte Sound. From Bob's Bay a short steep path climbs away from the bay to the Harbour View parking area.

The Snout (5km one-way; 1hr 15min; 200m ascent on return). From the Harbour View parking area (see above) follow the top of the ridge past the self-explanatory Queen Charlotte View to the tip of the promontory, The Snout, whose evocative Maori name, Te Ihumoeone-ihu, translates as "the nose of the sand worm".

Tirohanga Track (3km one-way; 1hr 15min; 300m ascent). Fairly strenuous walk up the hills behind Picton passing the lovely Hilltop Viewpoint. The track starts on Newgate Street.

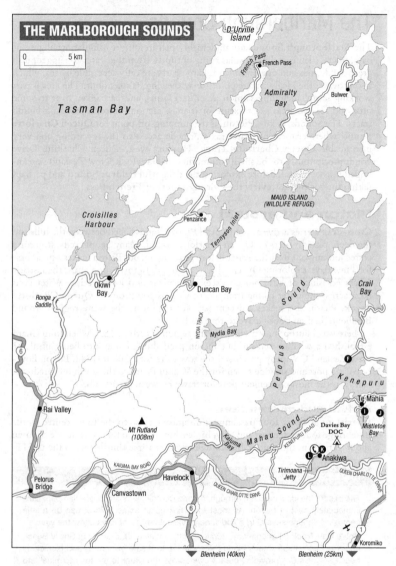

THE MARLBOROUGH SOUNDS

0   5 km

Tasman Bay

D'Urville Island

French Pass

French Pass

Admiralty Bay

Bulwer

Croisilles Harbour

Penzance

Tennyson Inlet

MAUD ISLAND (WILDLIFE REFUGE)

Okiwi Bay

Duncan Bay

Crail Bay

Ronga Saddle

NYDIA TRACK

Nydia Bay

Pelorus Sound

Kenepuru Sound

Rai Valley

Te Mahia

Mt Rutland (1008m)

Kaiuma Bay

Mahau Sound

KENEPURU ROAD

Mistletoe Bay

Davies Bay DOC

Anakiwa

KAIUMA BAY ROAD

Pelorus Bridge

Havelock

Canvastown

Tirimoana Jetty

QUEEN CHARLOTTE DRIVE

QUEEN CHARLOTTE DRIVE

6

Koromiko

6

Blenheim (40km)

Blenheim (25km)

Interislander ferry schedules work in well with the daily TranzCoastal **train** to Christchurch: one-way fares range from $59–118. **Buses** stop outside the Interislander ferry terminal and again at the i-SITE. Picton **airport**, 9km south of town, is served by Soundsair (℡0800/505 005, ⓦwww.soundsair.com), with flights from Wellington: a bus ($5 one-way) meets flights and runs into Picton.

The combined **i-SITE visitor centre** and **DOC office** (daily 9am–5pm; ℡03/520 3113, ⓦwww.destinationmarlborough.com) is on the foreshore, five minutes' walk from the ferry terminal. It is packed with leaflets on the town and the rest of the South Island, including a free Picton and Blenheim map and DOC's free *Queen Charlotte Track* visitor guide.

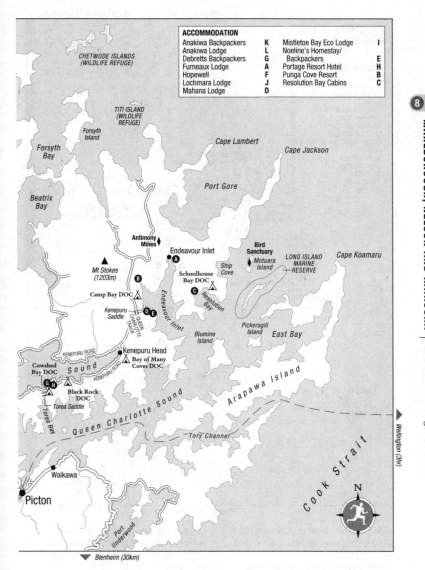

ACCOMMODATION

Anakiwa Backpackers	K	Mistletoe Bay Eco Lodge	I
Anakiwa Lodge	L	Noeline's Homestay/	
Debretts Backpackers	G	Backpackers	E
Furneaux Lodge	A	Portage Resort Hotel	H
Hopewell	F	Punga Cove Resort	B
Lochmara Lodge	J	Resolution Bay Cabins	C
Mahana Lodge	D		

CHETWODE ISLANDS (WILDLIFE REFUGE)

TITI ISLAND (WILDLIFE REFUGE)

Forsyth Island

Forsyth Bay

Forsyth Bay

Beatrix Bay

Cape Lambert

Cape Jackson

Port Gore

▲ Antimony Mines

Endeavour Inlet Ⓐ

▲ Mt Stokes (1203m) Ⓑ

Schoolhouse Bay DOC

Ship Cove

Bird Sanctuary

Motuara Island

LONG ISLAND MARINE RESERVE

Cape Koamaru

Camp Bay DOC ⚠

Ⓒ *Resolution Bay*

Kenepuru Saddle Ⓓ Ⓔ

Blumine Island

Pickersgill Island

East Bay

KENEPURU ROAD

Kenepuru Head ⚠

Bay of Many Coves DOC

Cowshed Bay DOC Ⓖ Ⓗ ⚠

KENEPURU ROAD

Sound

Black Rock DOC

Torea Bay

Torea Saddle

Queen Charlotte Sound

Arapawa Island

Tory Channel

► Wellington (3hr)

▼ Waikawa

● Picton

Cook Strait

Port Underwood

N

▼ Blenheim (30km)

Accommodation

As a major **transit centre**, Picton is well supplied with accommodation, ranging from backpacker hostels to upscale lodges.

Motels

Broadway Motel 113 Picton High St ☎0800/101 919, ⒲www.broadwaymotel.co.nz. Attractive modern motel units in the centre of town with good views from the first-floor balcony. ⑤

Harbour View Motel 30 Waikawa Rd ☎0800/101 133, ⒲www.harbourviewpicton.co.nz. Twelve spacious, tastefully appointed, s/c units, each with a balcony and with great views over the harbour. ⑥
Jasmine Court 78 Wellington St ☎0800/421 999, ⒲www.jasminecourt.co.nz. Top-of-the-line,

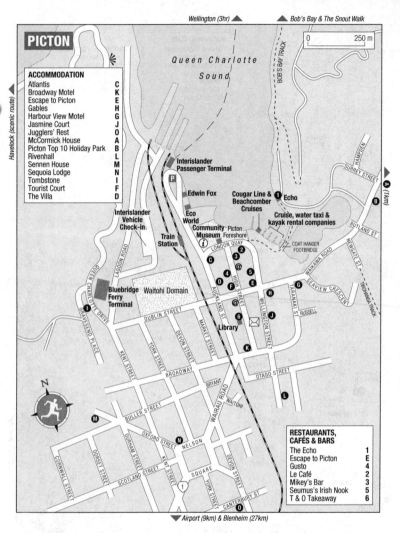

Wellington (3hr) ▲   ▲ Bob's Bay & The Snout Walk

PICTON

0   250 m

Queen Charlotte
Sound

ACCOMMODATION
Atlantis   C
Broadway Motel   K
Escape to Picton   E
Gables   H
Harbour View Motel   G
Jasmine Court   J
Jugglers' Rest   O
McCormick House   A
Picton Top 10 Holiday Park   B
Rivenhall   L
Sennen House   M
Sequoia Lodge   N
Tombstone   I
Tourist Court   F
The Villa   D

Interislander
Passenger Terminal

Edwin Fox

Cougar Line &
Beachcomber
Cruises

Echo

Cruise, water taxi &
kayak rental companies

Interislander
Vehicle
Check-in

Eco
World

Community
Museum

Picton
Foreshore

Train
Station

COAT HANGER
FOOTBRIDGE

LONDON QUAY

Bluebridge
Ferry
Terminal

Waitohi Domain

Library

Airport (9km) & Blenheim (27km)

**RESTAURANTS,
CAFÉS & BARS**
The Echo   1
Escape to Picton   E
Gusto   4
Le Café   2
Mikey's Bar   3
Seumus's Irish Nook   5
T & O Takeaway   6

modern motel with luxury units, including DVD &
CD players and sunny verandas, plus free email
and pay wi-fi. ⑥
Tourist Court 45 High St ☏0800/366 555,
ⓦwww.tourist-court.co.nz. Centrally located,
small but tolerable en-suite doubles at low
prices. ④

B&Bs and homestays
Escape to Picton 33 Wellington St ☏03/573
5573, ⓦwww.escapetopicton.com. The ante
has been upped considerably with the
opening of this chic three-suite boutique
hotel. Everything is to the highest standard

(including freestanding baths in two suites)
and breakfast is served in the restaurant (see
p.438). Rates start at $350 but are negotiable
off peak. ⑨
The Gables 20 Waikawa Rd ☏03/573 6772,
ⓦwww.thegables.co.nz. Pleasant and welcoming
B&B with three rooms in the house (one with en
suite) and a couple of s/c cottages out back where
breakfast can supplied. Children and dogs
welcome. Rooms ⑤/⑥, cottages ⑥
McCormick House 21 Leicester St ☏03/573
5253, ⓦwww.mccormickhouse.co.nz. Atmospheric
Edwardian villa with an original rimu-panelled
staircase, three luxurious, individually decorated

rooms and indulgent breakfasts made from local produce. There's a good stock of Kiwi movies and music in the lounge. ❽

Rivenhall 118 Wellington St ☏03/573 7692, ⓦwww.rivenhall.kol.co.nz. Comfortable historic homestay with two big rooms, grand views and a warm welcome from the hosts. Both rooms come with private bathroom and robes. ❻

Sennen House 9 Oxford St ☏03/573 5216, ⓦwww.sennenhouse.co.nz. Gorgeous 1886 grand villa 10min walk from town, which has been tastefully converted into a B&B with five suites, all with kitchen facilities; a welcome wine and a breakfast hamper are supplied. Smallest suite ❽, mostly ❾

Hostels and campsites

Atlantis London Quay ☏03/573 7390, ⓦwww.atlantishostel.co.nz. Central hostel close to ferry with the town's cheapest bunks, if you're prepared to share with 21 others, though there are also smaller dorms, twins and doubles plus free basic breakfast and the use of an indoor heated pool shared by the local dive school (see p.439). Dorms $20, rooms ❶

Jugglers' Rest 8 Canterbury St ☏03/573 5570, ⓦwww.jugglersrest.com. Small and relaxed shoes-off hostel a 10min walk from the ferries, with spacious dorms (no bunks) and a couple of quiet rooms in the grounds. There's a strong recycling ethic, the vegetable garden is open to all and there's home-made jam to spread on each morning's fresh bread. And you can try your hand at juggling with balls, clubs, devil sticks and even fire. Closed June–Sept. Tents $18, dorms $30, rooms ❷

Picton Top 10 Holiday Park 78 Waikawa Rd ☏0800/277 444, ⓦwww.pictontop10.co.nz.

Centrally located campsite with swimming pool, children's playground, cabins (bedding $5) and motel-style units, in a pleasant spot with sheltering trees. Camping $19, cabins ❷, kitchen cabins ❸, s/c units ❹

Sequoia Lodge 3 Nelson Square ☏0800/222 257, ⓦwww.sequoialodge.co.nz. Well-organized hostel shoehorned onto a site 10min walk from the town centre (and with free pick-ups). Beds and bunks all come with bed lights and side tables, rooms have heated towel rails, and there's a separate, en-suite female dorm. Breakfast, hammocks, spa, nightly pudding and ice cream, wi-fi and home cinema are all free, making this a great deal. Dorms $25, rooms & en suites ❷

🏃 **Tombstone** 16 Gravesend Place ☏0800/573 7116, ⓦwww.tombstonebp.co.nz. Wonderful hostel right by the town cemetery with a tastefully decorated, purpose-built accommodation block that's all carpeted and double-glazed, making it super-quiet for a place that's an easy walk from the port. A barbecue area, piano, hot tub, bikes and a continental breakfast are all available for no extra charge. Dorms are single sex, private rooms come with electric blankets and a sunny balcony, and there's a one-bedroom s/c apartment. Dorms $25, en-suite dorms $29, rooms & en suites ❷, apartment ❸

The Villa 34 Auckland ☏03/573 6598, ⓦwww.thevilla.co.nz. Youthful hostel based around a century-old house and a more modern one next door. When busy it can feel a little cramped, but it works well and there are all manner of inducements such as free bikes, apple crumble in winter and a hot tub. Dorms $25, rooms & en suites ❷

Staying out in the Sounds

The best way to soak up something of the spirit of the Marlborough Sounds is to stay in one of the swanky lodges, modest resorts or superb backpacker hostels inaccessible (or barely accessible) by road. Many of the best dot the Queen Charlotte Track but there's no need to go tramping as water taxis will get you there in a few minutes from Picton (and to a lesser extent Havelock; see p.444). As well as those listed below, consider staying at *Lochmara Lodge* and *Furneaux Lodge* (for both see p.442).

Craglee Queen Charlotte Sound ☏03/579 9223, ⓦwww.craglee.co.nz. A mermaid welcomes you to this romantic boutique lodge set in bush by the water. Rates ($450/couple) include wonderful meals, pre-dinner drinks, outdoor baths and endless relaxation. ❾

🏃 **Hopewell Kenepuru Sound** ☏03/573 4341, ⓦwww.hopewell.co.nz. A gorgeous hostel in a dreamy setting where even a couple of nights isn't enough to fully appreciate the relaxing setting, wonderfully welcoming hosts, waterside hot tub, kayaks, fishing and opportunities to visit the local mussel farm or go waterskiing. Access is either on a tortuous 2–3hr drive along Kenepuru Road, or by a sequence of water taxis from Picton ($60/person each way): call the hostel for details. Closed June–Aug. Dorms $35, rooms ❸, en suites & s/c cottage sleeping four ❹

The Town

Pretty much everything of interest in Picton is along the phoenix-palm-lined waterfront, **Picton Foreshore**. At its western end, close to the ferry terminal, the hulk of the 1600-tonne, Calcutta-built **Edwin Fox** (daily: Dec–March 9am–5pm; April–Nov 9am–3pm; $10) is the sole survivor of some four thousand "East Indiamen" that once brought migrants to New Zealand. This 1853 example also operated as a Crimean War troop carrier, transported convicts to Australia and helped establish the frozen meat trade in New Zealand before being towed to Picton in 1967. Vandalized and weather-beaten for twenty years it was finally moved to Picton Harbour, dry-docked and preserved. A small but well-designed museum prepares you for the age-blackened hull itself. Standing on the small part of the deck that remains gives a sense of what it must have been like to sail, but the best bit is below decks in the large open hold, all heavy planking partly rotted away to reveal the teak ribs.

The adjacent **Eco World** (daily: Jan & Feb 10am–7.30pm; March–Dec 10am–5.30pm; $19; Ⓦwww.ecoworldnz.co.nz) offers an insight into the flora and fauna of the Marlborough Sounds with local marine life (including little blue penguins), a few small sharks, a preserved giant squid plus tuatara and giant weta. It is best visited during feeding (11am & 2pm).

Further east, the **Picton Community Museum**, London Quay (daily 10am–4pm; $4) uses photos, a harpoon gun and some excellent examples of carved whalebone to illustrate coverage of the Perano Whaling Station, which operated in Queen Charlotte Sound until 1964.

Eating and entertainment

Picton offers enough decent **restaurants** to satisfy for a couple of days, and plenty of **cafés**, but little in the way of organized **entertainment**.

The Echo East Harbour. While this permanently moored top-sail schooner serves food, such as a seaman's snack ($18) and a cooked breakfast ($16), it's primarily a fine place for a beer on deck. Built in 1905, the *Echo* was the last ship to trade commercially under sail in New Zealand waters; spend some time looking at the maritime paraphernalia around the walls.
Escape to Picton 33 Wellington St Ⓣ03/573 5573. Wine is stored in the vault of this former bank-turned-chic-restaurant, café and bar. You can pop in for a coffee or beer, but *Escape* is really about fine dining with dinner mains such as prawn and seafood risotto going for around $40.
Gusto 33 High St. Cosy and popular daytime café dishing up delicious breakfasts along with a short menu of daily specials from pasta to open sandwiches and Thai curry, cakes and good coffee.

Le Café 14 London Quay. Bustling café and bar with pavement seating just across from the Sound, serving mouthwatering steaks with home-made chutney and all sorts of seafood. Lunch mains around $18, dinner $30. Bands occasionally play in the summer.
Mikey's Bar 18 High St. Modern bar with a pool table, and a barn-like nightclub out back where DJs are interspersed with bands trying to scrape together enough money to play somewhere bigger.
Seumus's Irish Bar Wellington St. Top Irish bar, authentically poky and with a great drinking atmosphere, large, quality bar meals ($20–25), outdoor seating, and live music several nights a week.
T & O Takeaway 85 High St Ⓣ03/573 6115. Serves the freshest and best fish and chips in town plus a variety of other fruits of the sea.

Listings

Bike rental Marlborough Sounds Adventure Co and Wilderness Guides both rent bikes for use on the QCT for $50/day.
Buses Atomic Shuttles (Ⓣ03/349 0697) run to Christchurch, Nelson, Greymouth and Fox Glacier; Richies (Ⓣ03/578 5467) go to Blenheim; InterCity

(Ⓣ03/377 0951) run to Nelson, Blenheim and Christchurch via Kaikoura. The 40min run to Blenheim costs $12.
Car rental Most major international and Kiwi companies have offices at the Ferry Terminal or around town. The i-SITE has a free sheet listing them.

Diving Dive Picton, corner of London Quay & Auckland St (☎ 0800/423 483, ⊛ www.divepicton .co.nz), offers single dives ($90 with all gear) two-tank dive days ($180–230) and two-tank wreck dive days ($280) on the *Michael Lermontov*, a Soviet cruise ship that became the southern hemisphere's largest diveable wreck when it hit rocks in 1986. For the latter you'll need experience at 30m in cold water.

Internet access Limited free access at the library, plus computers at the i-SITE and cheaper machines at United Video, 63 High St (daily 9am–9pm).

Library 67 High St (Mon–Fri 8am–5pm, Sat 10am–1pm).

Luggage storage Most lodgings store luggage while you walk the Queen Charlotte Track. The i-SITE has large luggage lockers ($4/day) and cars can be left securely with Sounds Storage, 7 Market St ($30 first two nights then $10 a night; ☎ 021/335136).

Movies Picton Cinema, by the aquarium, shows mainstream movies.

Rural Mail Bus Service You can ride the Rural Mail Bus Service (☎ 027/255 8882), essentially a minivan serving remote spots linking the main post offices in Havelock and Picton, and the southern end of the Queen Charlotte Track at Anakiwa. There are several runs each day and fares start at $15.

Taxis Gateway Taxis ☎ 03/573 7662; see also "Water taxis" below.

Water taxis Beachcomber Fun Cruises ☎ 0800/624 526, ⊛ www.mailboat.co.nz; Cougar Line ☎ 0800/504 090, ⊛ www.cougarlinecruises. co.nz; and Endeavour Express ☎ 03/573 5456, ⊛ www.boatrides.co.nz.

Winery tours Tours of the Marlborough wine country are covered in detail in "Listings" on p.480, and most companies organize Picton pick-ups for around $5 extra.

Exploring Queen Charlotte Sound

Picton is a pretty spot, but you've barely touched the region's beauty until you've explored **Queen Charlotte Sound**. This wildly indented series of drowned valleys encloses moody picturesque bays, small deserted sandy beaches, headlands with panoramic views and cloistered islands while grand lumpy peninsulas offer shelter from the winds and storms, and solitude for the contemplative fisherman or kayaker. For a taste of these labyrinthine waterways, take one of the many **day-cruises** from Picton, but to really appreciate the tranquil beauty you're far better off **kayaking** round the bays or **tramping** the Queen Charlotte Track. The relatively calm waters of the Sounds also give the opportunity for **scuba diving**, checking out the rich marine life of the huge wreck of a Soviet cruise ship (see above).

The sights

A couple of sights in Queen Charlotte Sound crop up on most itineraries, including the DOC-managed **Motuara Island**, a predator-free wildlife sanctuary that is home to the saddleback, South Island bush robin, bellbird and a few Okarito brown kiwi. All the birds are quite fearless and will rest and fly startlingly close to you. Throughout the island little blue penguins choose to nest in boxes provided, rather than build their own, and in spring (Oct–Dec), you can gently lift the top of the box and see the baby penguins inside.

Just across a channel from Motuara Island, **Ship Cove** marks the bay where Captain Cook spent a total of 168 days during his three trips to New Zealand. A large white concrete monument commemorates his five separate visits.

Cruises and tours

Water taxis are always flitting about Queen Charlotte Sound taking hikers to the Queen Charlotte Track or delivering guests to swanky lodges. If you just want to get out on the water this may be all you need but several companies also run excellent **cruises**.

Along with Rural Mail Runs (see above), Beachcomber Fun Cruises offer a cruise to Ship Cove (3hr; $69), and one to Motuara Island (3hr; $73). Some of the most sympathetic wildlife trips in the Sounds are run by Dolphin Watch Ecotours,

London Quay (Oct–April only; ☎0800/945 354, ⓦwww.naturetours.co.nz), who offer **dolphin swimming** (2–4hr; $150 to swim, $100 to watch) with dusky, common, bottlenose or the endemic Hector's dolphins. To combine dolphin watching with the Sounds' other sights, join their trips to either Motuara Island ($100) or Ship Cove ($100), both of which can be used as a drop-off for QCT walkers. Finally, there's the Birdwatchers Expedition (daily 1.30pm; $120) especially for birders.

One particularly fine way to get out on the water is with Myths and Legends **Eco Tours** (☎03/573 6901, ⓦwww.eco-tours.co.nz), run by a sixth-generation local Pakeha and his Maori wife who tour the bays in their 1930s kauri launch, explaining the history and culture of the region ($200/4hr or $250/8hr, the latter including lunch).

For something a little different, join Waterways Boating Safaris (☎03/574 1372, ⓦwww.waterways.co.nz) who guide flotillas of two-person motorboats around Kenepuru Sound (3hr; $95). You get to drive your own boat, allowing access to bushwalks and beaches. They're based 7km along Kenepuru Road (see p.443).

Kayaking

Visitors dashing across to Abel Tasman National Park often overlook the uncrowded waters and breathtaking views to be had kayaking in Queen Charlotte Sound. The friendly and professional Marlborough Sounds Adventure Company, Town Wharf (☎0800/283 283, ⓦwww.marlboroughsounds.co.nz), offers a huge range of **guided kayaking trips** including lovely half-day paddles around Picton (Oct–April daily; 4hr; $75), a gentle one-dayer (7hr; $105), a two-day trip ($160) initially guided then camping out by yourselves and paddle home the next day, and a fully guided three-day trip in the outer sounds ($520); rentals are $50 for one day, $80 for two.

Also consider the smaller Sea Kayaking Adventure Tours (☎03/574 2765, ⓦwww.nzseakayaking.com), based near Anakiwa. They have one-day guided trips ($85) as well as a three-day trip along the length of the track either camping ($300) or upgrading to fancier accommodation. Independent rentals are $50 per day, reducing to $40 per day for three days or more.

The Queen Charlotte Track

The **Queen Charlotte Track** (QCT: 71km one-way; 3–5 days; open all year; ⓦwww.qctrack.co.nz) is a spectacularly beautiful walk partly tracing skyline ridges with brilliant views across dense coastal forest to the waters of Queen

---

Delivering the mail with dolphins

Several companies run great cruises around Queen Charlotte and Pelorus sounds, but there is something special about the **Rural Mail Runs**, pulling up at a lonely wharf and having some farmer's wife (or the whole family) coming out to receive their only mail delivery of the week and perhaps a few perishable groceries. The journey includes golden beaches with bush-clad shorelines and dolphins sometimes escort the boat.

In **Queen Charlotte Sound**, Beachcomber Fun Cruises (☎0800/624 526, ⓦwww .mailboat.co.nz) run the four-hour Magic Mail Run (Mon–Sat 1.30pm; 4hr; $85) which leaves from Picton. Three routes are plied on different days of the week, but there's little to choose between them so hop on whichever is convenient. In summer, all call into Endeavour Inlet, pass a salmon farm and allow fifteen minutes ashore at Ship Cove.

Alternative postal routes explore **Pelorus Sound** from Havelock (see p.444).

Biking the QCT

Though the Queen Charlotte Track is primarily for hikers, **mountain bikers** can ride the whole thing in a couple of days. There are two steep ascents but it is not overly technical, and with pack transfers and abundant accommodation you won't need to lug heavy panniers. Most of the track is open to bikers year-round, though the northern quarter (Ship Cove–Camp Bay) is off-limits from December to February.

Marlborough Sounds Adventure Company (see opposite) operates a three-day Freedom Bike Ride ($620–720) with bike rental, transfers and comfortable accommodation at *Punga Cove* and *Portage Resort*. Alternatively it can rent you a mountain bike ($50/day) and you can organize your own trip, perhaps camping or staying in cheaper accommodation.

Charlotte and Kenepuru sounds on either side. It is broad, relatively easy going and is distinguished from all other Kiwi multi-day tramps by the lack of DOC huts and presence of some **lovely places to stay**. Access and egress is generally by boat from Picton, and your water taxi will **transport your bags** to your next destination each day, making hiking the Queen Charlotte Track a thoroughly pleasurable experience. Since boats call at numerous bays along the way, less ambitious walkers can tackle shorter sections, do day-hikes from Picton or tackle the track as part of a guided walk (see p.442). Though the track is less crowded than some, its popularity is rapidly increasing.

Queen Charlotte Sound was an important trade route and provided good shelter and bountiful food for **Maori**, who carried canoes over the low saddles of the walkway to avoid long and hazardous sea journeys. **Captain Cook** stopped at Ship Cove on five occasions and made it his New Zealand base, spending almost six months there between 1770 and 1777. The shelter and fresh water made it an ideal spot and its plentiful supplies of (what became known as) Cook's scurvy grass were particularly valued for the vitamin C content.

There is no shortage of **birds**, with tui and bellbirds in profusion, as well as the ever-friendly fantails and little piebald robins. Rocky shorelines boast an abundance of shags, gannets, terns and shearwaters, as well as the stooping oystercatchers patrolling in pairs. If you're lucky, you may spot a little blue penguin making its way to the fishing grounds in the morning.

Information and access

First stop should be Picton's i-SITE where staff will talk you through organizing your trip and hand you DOC's free *Queen Charlotte Track Visitor Guide* leaflet. Parts of the track cross private land and from late 2010 there will be a new **fee** (likely $10–15) for anyone over 15 hiking or biking the track: tickets will be sold by water taxi operators and information centres.

Trampers normally **travel north to south** from Ship Cove to Anakiwa, using **water taxis** to drop them off and pick them up. Sections of the track are also **accessible from Kenepuru Road** (see p.443), but there is no public transport and hitching or using your own vehicle seems counter to the spirit of the whole enterprise. There is no overnight parking at Anakiwa.

Water taxi companies (see p.439 for details) all offer a standard package with drop-off at Ship Cove, bag transfers and pick-up at Anakiwa for $90–95 (usually in the late afternoon). Endeavour Express ($90) is cheapest but other companies may have more convenient schedules.

Bikes are charged at $5 per journey. Equally you can just walk a short section of the track and be picked up pretty much anywhere you want: one-way transfers are $35–50.

Guided walks, combos and day-trips

Several companies around Picton offer organized encounters with the QCT with varying degrees of assistance. Marlborough Sounds Adventure Company offers **freedom walks** (4-day $610; 5-day $710) with nights spent at *Furneaux Lodge*, *Punga Cove Resort* and *Portage Resort Hotel*, which avoids booking hassles and includes a packed lunch each day. Its fully catered **guided walks** (4-day $1380; 5-day $1750) add in a knowledgeable guide accompanying you the whole way, a visit to Moturua Island and optional days spent paddling. To pack in a day each of hiking, biking and paddling, go for the excellent three-day Ultimate Sounds Adventure ($585–795 depending on accommodation).

Beachcomber Fun Cruises (see p.439) offer a series of one-day walks ($51–67), while the Cougar Line has walks from one to five hours (all $68).

Accommodation

A hot shower, a good meal and a comfy bed are three things seldom encountered on long tramps but the Queen Charlotte Track offers comfort in spades plus a good deal of backpacker-style accommodation for $30–45 a night: around twenty places in all. **Booking** is essential, not just to guarantee a bed for the night but also to ensure your water taxi company knows where to deliver your bags. A few of the smaller places don't accept EFTPOS or credit cards, so **take plenty of cash**. The six DOC **campsites** (all marked on the map on p.434) cost $6 and have water and toilets but only four have water taxi access.

The accommodation below is listed geographically from north to south, with hiking distances measured from Ship Cove.

Resolution Bay Cabins Resolution Bay, Km5 ℡03/579 9411, ✉reso@xtra.co.nz. The closest accommodation to Ship Cove, a 1920s-style mini-resort in a pretty and atmospheric spot offering swimming, kayaks and fairly rustic accommodation. Cabins $40/person, cottages for four ❻

Furneaux Lodge Endeavour Inlet, Km14 ℡03/579 8259, ⓦwww.furneaux.co.nz. One of the region's bigger lodges built in attractive grounds around a century-old homestead, with a convivial bar serving good meals and an excellent restaurant ($32 mains). Rooms range from basic backpackers (bring a sleeping bag) and made-up bunk rooms to s/c cottages, and swanky modern suites. Internet access and phone available. Dorms $30, bunk rooms $40, chalets ❻, suites ❼

Punga Cove Resort Camp Bay, Km26 ℡03/579 8561, ⓦwww.pungacove.co.nz. A large resort straggling from the boat-shed bar by the wharf, up the hillside to a classy restaurant with panoramic views; with pool, spa, sauna, fishing gear and kayaks. Dorms $40 (linen $12 extra; unavailable June–Aug), budget rooms ❸, rooms ❺, chalets ❻

Mahana Lodge Camp Bay, Km27 ℡03/579 8373, ⓦwww.mahanahomestead.com. Four en-suite rooms with decks in a modern lodge in the grounds of a century-old homestead (where $45 three-course meals are served). There's a communal TV-free lounge with great views that's perfect for relaxing. Free kayaks. ❺

Noeline's Homestay/Backpackers Near Camp Bay, Km27 ℡03/ 579 8375. A friendly welcome from the redoubtable Noeline and comfortable accommodation in a relaxing atmosphere– you may not want to leave. Linen $5. Dorms $30.

Portage Resort Hotel Kenepuru Rd, Km51, ℡03/573 4309, ⓦwww.portage.co.nz. A stylish hotel beside Kenepuru Sound, a 10min walk from the QCT at Torea Bay. Remodelled, bold-coloured rooms and designer bathrooms, along with a classy restaurant, café and bar, swimming pool and great views. Dorms have a full kitchen. Access is by car along Kenepuru Rd, or by water taxi from Picton ($35 each way). Dorms $40, backpacker en suite ❹, non-view hotel rooms ❻, view rooms ❽

Debretts Backpackers Kenepuru Rd, Km51, ℡03/573 4522, ⓦwww.stayportage.co.nz. Tranquil and well-appointed hostel sleeping six with great views of Portage Bay and Kenepuru Sound. It's a 30min walk from Torea Bay or get them to arrange a taxi. Dorms $40 (linen $5), rooms ❸

Lochmara Lodge Lochmara Bay, Km58 ℡03/573 4554, ⓦwww.lochmaralodge .co.nz. Beautiful eco-lodge with its own excellent café, restaurant and bar overlooking the still waters of Lochmara Bay. A portion of your bill goes to fund predator control and a captive breeding programme for kakariki (native parakeets) and geckos. Stroll along bush tracks past sculptures and artworks, into the kakariki aviary, past the glowworm grotto, then relax in a hammock: some waterside, others set up for stargazing. There are also free kayaks and snorkelling gear, a decadent bathhouse ($50 for two for 1hr), and massage available. All rooms are en suite but don't have TV or phone. The lodge is almost an hour's walk off the QCT or a 15min water-taxi ride from Picton ($25 each way; Picton departures daily 9am, noon, 3.15pm & 5.30pm). Closed June–Aug. Viewless twin ❸, bay-view double ❹, deluxe ❼

MistletoeBay Eco Village Mistletoe Bay, Km65 ℡ 03/573 4048, 🌐 www.mistletoebay.co.nz. Family-oriented, road-accessible rustic luxury in eight cabins (each with bathroom and beds for six; optional linen $7.50/person/stay) plus camping with a campers kitchen and coin-op showers. A small store sells home-grown organic produce,

meats, eggs and fresh coffee. Camping $15, backpackers $30, cabins ❹

Anakiwa Backpackers Anakiwa, right at the end of the track, Km71 ℡ 03/574 1388, 🌐 www .anakiwabackpackers.co.nz. Clean, simple and relaxed hostel with made-up beds, free kayaks, a windsurfer ($25), low-cost waterskiing, an espresso machine, a cat and a dog. It makes a great base for walking the southern end of the track or just hanging out. Along with a four-bed dorm and doubles there's a s/c apartment sleeping four. Dorms $33–40, rooms ❷, unit ❸

Anakiwa Lodge 9 Lady Cobham Grove, Anakiwa ℡ 03/574 2115, 🌐 www.anakiwa.co.nz. Around 400m from the end of the track, this modern associate YHA sleeps just ten and offers free internet and wi-fi, free kayaks and a spa pool (free to room guests). Dorm $30, rooms ❸, en suite ❺

The route

The track passes through some grassy farmland and open gorse-covered hills, but both ends of the track are forest reserves with lush greenery right down to the shoreline. There are a number of **detours** off the main track to places of interest, including a short walk from Ship Cove to a pretty forest-shrouded waterfall where Cook frequently bathed, a scramble down to the Bay of Many Coves, or a foray to the Antimony Mines (where there are exposed shafts – stick to the marked tracks).

To do the whole track in three days, get an early start from Ship Cove and plan to hike to Punga Cove. From there you have a fairly long day to Portage, then a relatively easy finish.

Ship Cove to Resolution Bay (4.5km; 1–2hr; 200m ascent). The track climbs steeply away from the shore through largely untouched forest to a lookout with great views of Motuara Island, before dropping down to Resolution Bay, where there's a DOC campsite and *Resolution Bay Cabins*.
Resolution Bay to Endeavour Inlet (15km; 3–5hr; 200m ascent). Follows an old bridle path over the ridge to *Furneaux Lodge* and *Endeavour Resort*.
Endeavour Inlet to Camp Bay (11.5km; 3–4hr; 100m ascent). Coastal track through regenerating forest thick with birdlife. DOC campsite and several lodges.

Camp Bay to Portage (24.5km; 6–8hr; 650m ascent). The longest stretch without convenient roofed accommodation (just two DOC campsites) is also the most rewarding, mostly following a ridge with views down to the Sounds on both sides.
Portage to Mistletoe Bay (7.5km; 3–4hr; 450m ascent). A steep initial climb is followed by a pleasant ridge walk through manuka, gorse and shrubs with the chance to break the journey at the lovely *Lochmara Lodge*, some 2km off the track.
Mistletoe Bay to Anakiwa (12.5km; 3–4hr; 100m ascent). Follows an old bridle path well above the water with great views, then finishes off through some lovely beech forest.

Queen Charlotte Drive and Kenepuru Road

With water taxis providing convenient access to fabulous out-of-the-way spots, it seems a little perverse to try to see the Marlborough Sounds by car; doubly so when you start weaving your way around the mostly paved but narrow and twisting roads – don't expect to average more than 40km/hour. In compensation, the views through the ferns to turquoise bays are magical.

The 35-kilometre Queen Charlotte Drive between Picton and Havelock is a picturesque and spectacular backroad sliding past the flat plain at the head of Queen Charlotte Sound and climbing up the hills overlooking Pelorus Sound before descending to SH6 and Havelock itself. It is a slow and winding drive, but you may want to take it even slower by stopping to wander down to a couple of sheltered coves.

Around 18km west of Picton, a narrow road heads north to **Anakiwa**, the southern end of the Queen Charlotte Track. Here you'll find a wharf used by water taxis taking hikers back to Picton, *Anakiwa Lodge* and *Anakiwa Backpackers* (see p.443 for both).

A couple of kilometres further along Queen Charlotte Drive, **Kenepuru Road** cuts right and begins its 75km journey out along the shores of Kenepuru Sound. There are no real sights along the way, though Kenepuru Road provides access to several points along the Queen Charlotte Track, and runs past a handful of DOC campsites and several places to stay – *Portage Resort Hotel*, *Debretts Backpackers* and *Punga Cove* – all listed on p.442. The road ends at the wonderful *Hopewell* **backpackers** (see p.437).

Havelock and Pelorus Sound

The sleepy town of **HAVELOCK**, 35km west of Picton, is primarily of interest for cruising the stunning **Pelorus Sound**, an intricate maze of steep-sided bays, crescent beaches and sunken sea passages surrounded by forested peaks – the largest sheltered waterway in the Southern Hemisphere. Almost every bay has a farm for green-lipped mussels, making Havelock the world capital for these choice bivalves: you simply can't leave without tucking into a plateful.

To see the best of Pelorus Sound, get aboard the ⚓ **Pelorus Mail Boat** ($120, children under 16 free; ☎03/574 1088, ⓦwww.mail-boat.co.nz), which departs from the marina on Tuesdays, Thursdays and Fridays at 9.30am and follows a different route each day. All the trips are a scenic delight, dropping in on a mussel farm and delivering mail, perishable groceries and even correspondence-school papers to the far-flung residents at a pace from a bygone age. Friday's outer sounds trip is the most comprehensive but the schedule on other days gives more flexibility for dolphin watching and time ashore. The trips return late in the afternoon so bring your own lunch.

Practicalities

Buses between Picton and Nelson all stop at Havelock, while local bus and **water taxi** operators offer services to Kenepuru and Pelorus sounds. For **information** and bookings call at the traditional *Rutherford YHA*, 46 Main Rd (☎03/574 2104, ⓦwww.havelockinfocentre.co.nz; camping $12, dorms $28, rooms ❷), which occupies a characterful old schoolhouse where pioneering atomic nucleus discoverer **Ernest Rutherford** went to school for two years from 1882. It contains the **Havelock Info Centre**, 46 Main Rd (daily 8.30am–9.30pm), which also acts as the local **DOC** agent.

Other accommodation options include *Havelock Garden Motel*, 71 Main Rd (☎03/574 2387, ⓦwww.gardenmotels.com; ❹), with fully self-contained units and helpful hosts, the small *Blue Moon Backpackers*, 48 Main Rd (☎03/574 2212, ⓔbookings@bluemoonhavelock.co.nz; dorms $25, rooms ❷), and *Havelock Motor Camp*, 24 Inglis St (☎03/574 2339, ⓦwww.havelockmotorcamp.co.nz; camping $12, cabins and on-site vans ❶), just off Main Road in the heart of town. The place to eat is the sophisticated, marina-side Slip Inn (☎03/574 2345), which does excellent mussels by the dozen ($19) topped with the likes of pesto and parmesan or sweet chilli, or a sampler of seven mussels with different toppings ($11), plus cod and chips ($25) and pizzas ($16–23). It's also fine for coffee or a sundowner. Café fare is also good at *The Wakamarinian*, 70 Main Rd, while the *Havelock Hotel*, 54 Main Rd, serves simple cuisine in massive portions for under $20. Self-caterers can buy fresh mussels from Four Square supermarket in town.

Pelorus and the road to Nelson, French Pass

It is 18km west of Havelock along SH6 to **Pelorus Bridge Scenic Reserve**, a gorgeous forested spot run through by the crystal-clear, trout-filled Pelorus River with sandy beaches, abundant swimming holes and verdant bush enlivened by tui, grey warblers and bellbirds. The place is understandably popular in summer, particularly the basic DOC **camping** area (℡03/571 6019; camping $10, cabins ❶), and a **DOC office** adjoining a modest daytime **café** (daily: Nov–March 8.30am–7pm; April–Oct 8.30am–4.30pm).

The **walking tracks** in the reserve are fairly flat, well maintained and clearly marked and there's a swingbridge to add a little extra excitement: the **Totara Walk** (1.5km return; 30min) and **Circle Walk** (1km return; 30min) routes pass through the low-lying woodland for which the area is famous, while the **Trig K Track** (2.5km one-way; 2hr), after a steady climb to 417m, offers stunning views of the whole area.

SH6 continues west past the turn off to French Pass (see below) at the small settlement of **Rai Valley** and climbs the hills past Happy Valley Adventures (see p.451) to Nelson.

French Pass

Narrow winding roads head north from Rai Valley towards French Pass, a two-hour, 60km drive through pockets of bush locked in sheep country and pine plantations. After tantalizing glimpses of inaccessible bays and coves you're finally rewarded with French Pass itself, a narrow channel between the mainland and D'Urville Island where nineteenth-century French explorer Dumont d'Urville was spun by tumultuous whirlpools. If you're here at mid-tide it is easy to understand why these seething waters were so feared. The maelstrom is best seen from a couple of short tracks in **French Pass Scenic Reserve**, 1km before the road end at **French Pass**. This tiny settlement is little more than a wharf, a shop, DOC's basic *French Pass* **campsite** ($7) and *Sea Safaris & Beachfront Villas* (℡03/576 5204, ⓦwww .seasafaris.co.nz; B&B ❼; closed June–Sept) with mostly organic meals available on request ($38). *Sea Safaris* also run all manner of dive trips, fishing charters ($360/2hr for up to 4 people), rent sea kayaks ($80 a day for a double) and take groups over to D'Urville Island for mountain biking (BYO bike) and walking (both $75), wildlife trips ($85), and dolphin and seal swimming ($135, watching $95).

Nelson and around

The thriving, small city of **Nelson**, set on the coast in a broad basin between the Arthur and Richmond ranges, is a beguiling place. Initially it is not much to look at, but it gets its hooks into you and the Nelson region has become one of the most popular visitor destinations in New Zealand. A warm, sunny climate, access to good beaches and a cluster of worthwhile wineries in the hinterland are powerful lures both to tourists and to painters and potters drawn by the sunlight, the landscape and the unique raw materials for ceramic art that lie beneath the rich green grass. Nelson is also supremely placed for accessing Golden Bay and three national parks – Abel Tasman, Kahurangi and Nelson Lakes. You can even do an **Able Tasman day-trip** from here using early buses which give you enough time for a water taxi ride and a few hours' walking along the Coast Track.

In central Nelson the **Suter Gallery** and the lively **Saturday Market** are good diversions, but you'll soon want to venture further, perhaps to **Tahunanui Beach** or the suburb of **Stoke** for the fascinating **World of WearableArt** museum. To the northwest, **Mapua** and **Upper Moutere** are starting points for notable arts, crafts and wine districts.

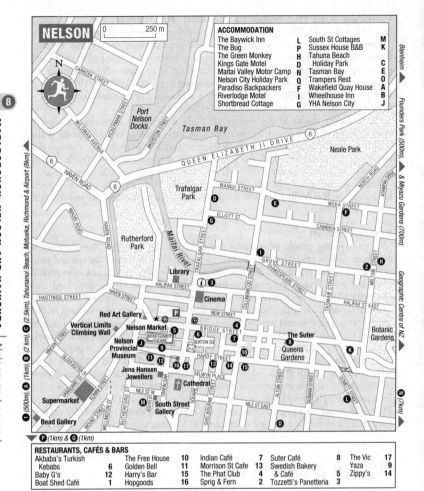

NELSON

0 .... 250 m

ACCOMMODATION

The Baywick Inn	L	South St Cottages	M
The Bug	P	Sussex House B&B	K
The Green Monkey	H	Tahuna Beach	
Kings Gate Motel	D	Holiday Park	C
Maitai Valley Motor Camp	N	Tasman Bay	E
Nelson City Holiday Park	Q	Trampers Rest	O
Paradiso Backpackers	F	Wakefield Quay House	A
Riverlodge Motel	B	Wheelhouse Inn	B
Shortbread Cottage	G	YHA Nelson City	J

Port Nelson Docks

Tasman Bay

Neale Park

Trafalgar Park

Rutherford Park

Library

Cinema

Red Art Gallery

Vertical Limits Climbing Wall

Nelson Market

Nelson Provincial Museum

Jens Hansen Jewellers

Supermarket

Bead Gallery

The Suter

Queens Gardens

Botanic Gardens

Cathedral

South Street Gallery

RESTAURANTS, CAFÉS & BARS

Akbaba's Turkish		The Free House	10	Indian Café	7	Suter Café	8	The Vic	17
Kebabs	6	Golden Bell	11	Morrison St Cafe	13	Swedish Bakery		Yaza	9
Baby G's	12	Harry's Bar	15	The Phat Club	4	& Café	5	Zippy's	14
Boat Shed Café	1	Hopgoods	16	Sprig & Fern	2	Tozzetti's Panetteria	3		

Some history

Nelson is one of the oldest settlements in New Zealand. By the middle of the sixteenth century, it was occupied by the Ngati Tumatakokiri people, some of whom provided a reception committee for **Abel Tasman**'s longboats at Murderer's Bay (now Golden Bay), where they killed four of his sailors.

By the time Europeans arrived in earnest, Maori numbers had been decimated by internecine fighting and the nearest *pa* site to Nelson was at Motueka, though this did little to prevent land squabbles, culminating in the **Wairau Affray** in 1843. Despite assurances from Maori chiefs Te Rauparaha and Te Rangihaeata that they would abide by the decision of a land commissioner, the New Zealand Company pre-emptively sent surveyors south to the Wairau Plains, the catalyst for a skirmish during which Te Rangihaeata's wife was shot. The bereaved chief and his men slaughtered twenty-two people in retaliation but the settlers continued their land acquisition as numbers were boosted by a small wave of immigrants from Germany.

Arrival, information and transport

Flights arrive at Nelson **airport**, 8km west of the centre. Super Shuttle (℡0800/748 885; $15 one person, $18 for two) meets most flights, or you can grab a taxi (℡03/548 8225; $25). Long-distance **buses** drop you near the centre of the city, within easy walking distance of most accommodation. InterCity and Abel Tasman Coachlines pull in at 27 Bridge St, while the other companies all stop outside the **i-SITE visitor centre**, on the corner of Trafalgar and Halifax streets (Mon–Fri 8.30am–5pm, Sat & Sun 9am–4pm; ℡03/548 2304, ⒲www.nelsonnz .com). The same building contains a **DOC visitor centre** (same hours; ℡03/546 9339) which does track bookings and has all the details on the local national parks, including Abel Tasman tide tables. Also check out ⒲www.backpacknelson.co.nz, with links to local accommodation, entertainment, seasonal work and much more.

You can get around most of the city sights on foot and those in the immediate vicinity with the help of a **rental car** or **bike** (see "Listings", p.453). SBL **buses** (℡03/548 1539, ⒲www.nelsoncoaches.co.nz) run local routes to Tahunanui Beach and Stoke from the terminal at 27 Bridge St, while Abel Tasman Coachlines leaves Nelson at 6.45am daily in summer for Marahau and Totaranui, via Motueka, connecting with launch services deeper into the Abel Tasman National Park. They also run a service to Takaka in Golden Bay, with links to the Heaphy Track.

Accommodation

There's a broad range of accommodation, much of it in the centre of town within reach of cultural diversions and nightlife. Classy **B&Bs** and excellent **hostels** are abundant, and there are a couple of campsites close to town, but you may want to save your camping for the prettier areas around Motueka, the Abel Tasman National Park or Golden Bay.

Motels and B&Bs

The Baywick Inn 51 Domett St ℡03/545 6514, ⒲www.baywick.com. Lovely restored two-storey villa from 1885 peacefully set overlooking the Maitai River and with luxuriously appointed rooms, two in a new cottage out back. An enthusiastic welcome includes afternoon tea, and the full cooked breakfasts are excellent. Three-course dinners by arrangement ($50–60). Free wi-fi. Room with private bath ❺, en suite ❻

Kings Gate Motel 21 Trafalgar St ℡0800/104 022, ⒲www.kingsgatemotel.co.nz. Central motel with comfortable well-kept rooms including full kitchens and a pool. ❺

Riverlodge Motel 31 Collingwood St ℡03/548 3094, ⒲www.riverlodgenelson.co.nz. One of the better motels in town, giving value for money across a range of units, all of which are clean and comfortable. ❹

South St Cottages South St ℡03/540 2769, ⒲www.cottageaccommodation.co.nz. These three gorgeous 1860s cottages in Nelson's prettiest street are let on a nightly self-catering basis with breakfast provisions supplied by the convivial and knowledgeable hosts. Accommodation is charmingly old-fashioned but with all mod cons including wi-fi at $5/day. Also a luxury two-bedroom apartment nearby. ❼

Sussex House B&B 238 Bridge St ℡03/548 9972, ⒲www.sussex.co.nz. Charming five-room B&B in a central, 1880s villa with welcoming hosts. Most rooms are en suite, including two with access to a lovely veranda. The extensive continental breakfasts are great and there's free internet. ❺/❻

Wakefield Quay House 385 Wakefield Quay ℡03/545 8209, ⒲www.wakefield quay.co.nz. Great B&B with stupendous sea views over Haulashore Island, plus a little noise from the road outside. Both rooms are beautifully turned out and come with drinks on arrival and a great breakfast. Your hosts are the enthusiastic and down-to-earth Woodi, and Johnny who runs Sail Nelson (see "Activities"). ❽

Wheelhouse Inn 41 Whitby Rd ℡03/546 8391, ⒲www.wheelhouse.nelson.co.nz. Bay views are magical from the picture windows of these nautically themed, self-catering apartments high on the hill 2km west of central Nelson. All are very private and come with full kitchen, laundry, TV/DVD, internet and BBQ. The Captain's Quarters is the largest apartment, sleeping up to six. ❻

447

Hostels

The Bug 226 Vanguard St ☎03/539 4227, ⓦwww.thebug.co.nz. Excellent and welcoming forty-bed hostel about 1km from the centre of Nelson with VW Beetle paraphernalia everywhere. Along with free bikes, free internet and wi-fi and local pick-ups they have a hammock, table football and a female dorm, and make a point of lacking a TV. Dorms $23, rooms and en suites ❷

The Green Monkey 129 Milton St ☎03/545 7421, ⓦwww.thegreenmonkey.co.nz. A quiet, boutique hostel in a converted villa that's well kept and has a relaxed atmosphere. Free internet, wi-fi and bikes. Book well in advance. Dorms $25, doubles ❷

Paradiso Backpackers 42 Weka St ☎03/546 6703 & 0800/222 572, ⓦwww.backpackernelson .co.nz. The best of the bigger hostels with up to 140 people fitting surprisingly comfortably into this large, converted villa with purpose-built outbuildings. With an outdoor pool, spa, sauna, volleyball and free wi-fi it is usually packed in summer. Dorms $25, en-suite share $28, rooms ❷

Shortbread Cottage 33 Trafalgar St ☎03/546 6681, ⓦwww.shortbreadcottages.co.nz. Boutique hostel with polished-wood floors, just thirteen beds, free internet and wi-fi and lots of home comforts. Book ahead. Dorms $25, rooms ❷

Tasman Bay 10 Weka St ☎0800/222 572 ⓦwww .tasmanbaybackpackers.co.nz. A sound choice, this comfortable purpose-built hostel, just minutes from the town centre, has clean, spacious rooms (some en suite) and enthusiastic, friendly management who ensure you always get more than you pay for. Free bikes, and free chocolate pudding nightly. Camping $18, dorms $25, rooms ❷/❸

Trampers Rest 31 Alton St ☎03/545 7477. Cosy backpackers with just eight beds in homestyle accommodation with comparatively small rooms. TV watching is by consensus only, but there's free internet and wi-fi, a tuned piano, and the wee garden boasts a hammock, avocado tree and bike storage. There are free bikes, and Alan is a real tramping enthusiast, an absolute mine of information on Nelson and all things track. Dorms $26, doubles ❷

YHA Nelson City 59 Rutherford St ☎03/545 9988, ⓔyha.nelson@yha.co.nz. Purpose-built hostel with two kitchens, plenty of communal space, informed staff and an infrared sauna. There's a wide range of accommodation, including connecting rooms for families and two disabled-access units. Dorms $29, rooms ❸

Campsites and holiday parks

Maitai Valley Motor Camp 472 Maitai Valley Rd ☎03/548 7729, ⓦwww.mvmc.co.nz. Bargain, friendly camping in a bush setting beside the Maitai River (with good swimming holes) 7km southeast of Nelson. Camping $10, cabins ❶

Nelson City Holiday Park 230 Vanguard Rd ☎0800/778 898, ⓦwww.nelsonholidaypark.co.nz. Small, very well-maintained and sited van park with limited tent space but various grades of room plus bikes at $35/day. Camping $20, cabins ❶, kitchen cabins ❷, s/c units ❹

Tahuna Beach Holiday Park 70 Beach Rd, Tahunanui ☎0800/500 501, ⓦwww.tahunabeach .co.nz. Enormous estuary-side campsite with many facilities, 5min walk from Tahunanui Beach with a wide range of accommodation. There's also a mini-golf course, kids' playgrounds and TV room. Camping $15, cabins ❶, kitchen cabins ❷, s/c units ❹

The city and around

The grid pattern streets of Nelson are dominated by the glowering, grey-stone **Christ Church Cathedral**, perched on a small hill peering down Trafalgar Street towards the sea. English architect Frank Peck's original 1924 design was gradually modified over many years due to lack of money; World War II further intervened, and even now the cathedral tower looks as if it's still under construction. The cathedral's grim exterior contrasts with its interior, illuminated by dazzling

Nelson Market

Saturday morning should involve a pilgrimage to the renowned **Nelson Market** (8am–1pm), which takes over Montgomery Square. Artists are flushed out of their rural bolt holes and stalls groan with hand-dipped candles, turned wooden bowls, bracelets made from forks and all manner of produce from the crafts community. Food stalls with mounds of fruit, endless varieties of fresh bread and fish, Thai and vegetarian dishes, preserves, coffee and cakes sustain you while you browse.

8

▲ Nelson Market

stained-glass windows, ten noteworthy examples of which are tucked away in a small chapel to the right of the main altar.

About two minutes' walk north the **Nelson Provincial Museum**, on the corner of Hardy and Trafalgar streets (Mon–Fri 10am–5pm, Sat & Sun 10am–4.30pm; $5 donation suggested; ⓣ03/548 9588, ⓦwww.nelsonmuseum.co.nz), takes a fresh, multimedia approach to local exhibits and then draws strands from them to the rest of New Zealand and the wider world. The Maori displays are each curated by the various local *iwi* with their choice of treasures from their own *marae*; witness the fine bone club, delicate flax and feather cloak, and interpretation of the designs in *tukutuku* panels. The death masks from the Mangatapu Murders highlight a grisly tale of robbery, murder and betrayal from 1866, and there's a collection of traditional Maori musical instruments whose sounds echo throughout the galleries.

Just east of the centre on Bridge Street, the pretty Victorian **Queens Gardens**, with its mature trees and well-populated duck pond, hosts **The Suter Art Gallery**, 208 Bridge St (daily 10.30am–4.30pm; $3, free on Sat; ⓦwww.thesuter .org.nz). This small public art museum is one of the finest in the South Island and hosts visiting exhibitions along with changing displays from its own collection. During the summer try to catch something of its stock of **watercolours** – especially those of John Gully whose works largely depict scenes from the surrounding area. Also look out for oils by **Toss Woollaston**, a founder of the modernist movement in New Zealand and one of a group of artists and writers who, during the 1930s and 1940s, began exploring notions of a New Zealand culture independent of colonial Britain. Another must is Gottfried Lindauer's painting of Huria Matenga, a Maori woman who helped save many lives from the wreck of the *Delaware* in 1863. Her status is indicated by feathers, bone, greenstone jewellery and the ceremonial club she holds; in the background is the foundering American ship.

Continue further east along Bridge Street to the **Botanical Reserve** where New Zealand's first ever rugby game was played in 1870. The hill behind commands a good view over the town and, it is claimed, marks the **geographical centre** of New Zealand.

About 1km north of the Botanical Gardens, **Founders Park**, 87 Atawhai Drive (daily 10am–4.30pm; $7), offers a somewhat sanitized version of early colonial history through relocated and replica buildings, while the delightful Japanese-style **Miyazu Gardens**, next door (daily 8am–dusk; free), provide a quiet oasis of reflective pools, ornamental cherry trees and restrained statuary.

Arts and crafts

Many of the region's artists and craftspeople display at galleries outside Nelson (see account from p.453) but you can get an idea of what's in store by visiting galleries in town. Good starting points are Red Art Gallery, 1 Bridge St (☎03/548 2170), which specializes in contemporary New Zealand fine art, glass and jewellery, and Catchment Gallery, 225 Hardy St (☎03/539 4100), with an emphasis on quality painting and sculpture. Also check out South Street Gallery, 10 Nile St, which specializes in local pottery. It stands on the corner of **South Street**, one of Nelson's oldest and still with a row of pretty workers' cottages.

Just southeast of the centre, the **Bead Gallery**, 18 Parere St (Mon–Sat 9am–5pm, Sun 10am–4pm; ⓦwww.beads.co.nz), is packed to the rafters with over 10,000 bead styles, all for sale. The idea is simple; you can either design your own bead-piece or have one custom-made for you using anything from 10¢ baubles to some of the most exotic anywhere in the world (up to $200 apiece). They have a particularly fine range of psychedelic century-old Venetian glass trade beads from West Africa at relatively modest prices.

Another opportunity to put your creativity to work comes in the form of **bone carving**; one-day workshops with Stephan ($65 with pick-up from your accommodation; ☎03/546 4275, ⓦwww.carvingbone.co.nz) should see you complete an attractive pendant by the end of the day.

If you're committed to exploring your artistic potential while getting closer to local practitioners then contact Creative Tourism New Zealand (ⓦwww .creativetourism.co.nz), who coordinate **creative workshops** with topics ranging from *harakeke* (flax) weaving to bone carving, wood turning and cheese making.

Lord of the Rings fans will want to visit the jeweller's Jens Hansen, at the corner of Church Street and Selwyn Place (Mon–Fri 9am–5pm, Sat 9am–2pm, Sun in summer 10am–1pm; ⓦwww.jenshansen.com), who Peter Jackson got to make **"The one ring to rule them all"**, or a few dozen of them to suit various cast members. Replicas are available, but remember what happens to the owner of such a ring.

Tahunanui Beach and WOW

Haven Road (SH6) runs northwest out of central Nelson and, after 1km, becomes **Wakefield Quay**, a popular spot for strolling along the waterfront but primarily known for the *Boat Shed Café* jutting picturesquely out over the water. Continue 3km along SH6 to reach **Tahunanui Beach Reserve**, a long golden strand backed by grassland and drifting dunes. It is where Nelson comes to relax on sunny weekends, with safe swimming, a fun park, zoo and children's playgrounds: buses run here frequently along SH6 from the city.

A further 3km out along SH6 follow signs to the **World of WearableArt and Classic Cars**, 95 Quarantine Rd (WOW; daily 10am–5pm; $18; ⓦwww .wowcars.co.nz), for a theatrical and memorable experience. It is primarily a purpose-built showcase for the best designs from the annual WearableArt show, a fashion show with a difference first put on by Suzie Moncrieff in Nelson in 1987 and now held annually in Wellington. Participants from around the world submit sculptures or pieces of art that can be worn as clothes – many made from the most unusual materials such as household junk, food, metal, stone, wood and tyres.

A thirty-minute video of past shows sets the scene for the best of the costumes themselves, all theatrically displayed. Men are often seen sloping off to peruse the shiny and desirable automobiles, both old and relatively new.

Activities

Nelson is the sort of place where sunbathing at Tahunanui might be as active as you want to get, though there is no shortage of energetic diversions. At Happy Valley Adventures, 194 Cable Bay Rd, 17km northeast of Nelson off SH6 (℡03/545 0304, ⓦwww.HappyValleyAdventures.co.nz), you explore up to 40km of track on a large forested farm using **quad bikes**, climbing hills, passing monstrous matai trees, stopping to learn a little about the forest and its stories and eventually reaching a high spot with expansive views of Cable Bay. The most popular trips are the Bayview Circuit (2hr; rider $110, passenger $30), and the Blue Hill Ride (3hr; $150, no passengers) designed for the more skilled and ambitious rider.

Some rides visit the site of the **Skywire** ($85), a four-seater cable-car chair that swoops almost 1km across a forested valley then back to the hilltop café with its panoramic deck.

For **horseriding** you'll have to head 17km southwest of Nelson through Richmond to Stonehurst Farm Horse Treks, Haycock Road (℡0800/487 357, ⓦwww.stonehurstfarm.co.nz). The majority of the shorter treks (1hr $60, 2hr 30min $95 and a summer sundowner starting at 6pm; 2hr 30min; $95) take place in the foothills of the Richmond ranges and offer great views of the coast and beyond.

To get airborne try **tandem paragliding** with Nelson Paragliding (℡0508/359 669, ⓦwww.nelsonparagliding.co.nz): a hair-raising drive up the hill to the launch site reveals a spectacular landscape, before you run like hell then glide off into the quiet up draughts for fifteen to twenty minutes of eerily silent flight. Tandem flights go for $180 and a one-day introductory lesson costs $250. For a birdlike quality to your flight, go with Nelson Hang Gliding ($165, tandem flight of roughly 15min; ℡03/548 9151, ⓦwww.flynelson.co.nz).

Paddling with Cable Bay Kayaks (℡0508/222 532, ⓦwww.cablebaykayaks .co.nz) makes a refreshing change from the mayhem around Abel Tasman. They do a half-day trip ($85) and a full-day tour ($135, $160 including lunch) which gives more time for exploring the caves of this beautiful and intricate coastline and doing a little snorkelling. They're based near Happy Valley (see above) and will pick up from Nelson.

Staying on the water, consider spending time with Johnny from Sail Nelson (℡03/546 7275, ⓦwww.sailnelson.co.nz) who runs **sailing** charters and great fully catered, **sailing courses** (two-day beginner $500; five-day improver $1495) living aboard a 10m yacht, typically around D'Urville Island and Abel Tasman. Courses run on fixed dates for two to four people.

On a wet day retreat to Vertical Limits, 34 Vanguard St ($12–16; ℡0508/837 842, ⓦwww.verticallimits.co.nz) for some indoor **rock climbing** and when the weather improves join their full-day climbing trips ($130) to Payne's Ford in Takaka.

Eating

Nelson's enviable lifestyle is reflected in the **broad choice** of eating options within easy reach of the town centre. And when you tire of these, there's always fine food on the waterfront, at Mapua Wharf or in the gorgeous settings of the **wineries**. Don't forget Nelson's pubs and bars (see p.452) for a quick snack either.

Akbaba's Turkish Kebabs 130 Bridge St. Plenty of tasty cheap kebabs and salads ($7–13) to take away, munch in the courtyard out back, or in booth seating on low floor cushions; Turkish decor and music create a lively and casual atmosphere for lunch and dinner.

Baby G's 8 Church St ☏03/545 8957. Combination café, tapas, restaurant, cocktail bar and live music venue with free wi-fi and a menu of dishes mostly under $15. Monday is improv night, Thursday is open mic, and they don't close until 3am on Fri & Sat.

Boat Shed Café 350 Wakefield Quay ☏03/546 9783. If it were only for the matchless views over Tasman Bay this converted boat shed on stilts over the water would be a hit, but you also get fabulous, fresh and simple food – perfect for romantic sunset dinners. Try the Trust the Chef menu (five small courses $55, add dessert $65).

Golden Bell 104 Hardy St. Top Thai, relaxed and with all your favourites dishes for around $20. BYO.

🏃 **Hopgoods** 284 Trafalgar St ☏03/545 7191. Nelson's finest dining is found in this airy restaurant or at tables outside on Trafalgar St. Its commitment to locally sourced, organic produce informs its range of seasonal dishes fashioned by a perfectionist chef into lovely European-influenced meals. Expect the likes of confit of lamb with sweetbreads ($35) and pineapple tarte tatin ($14). Impeccable service. Closed Sun.

Indian Café 94 Collingwood St ☏03/548 4098. The town's best curry restaurant set in a historic villa and serving all your favourites for around $16. The malai prawns are particularly good.

Morrison St Cafe 244 Hardy St. Semi-formal café with tasty brunches, lunches, snacks (many dishes dairy or gluten free) and a liberal sprinkling of local art adorning the walls. Favourites include kokoda marinated fish ($19), and chicken and soba noodle salad pilaf ($14), and there's plenty of outdoor seating.

Suter Café 208 Bridge St. Daytime café in the Suter Art Gallery with views over the Queens Gardens duck pond. The food is beautifully fresh with imaginative dishes such as pork and pistachio terrine or gurnard burrito. Plenty of salads and great cakes and coffee.

Swedish Bakery & Café 54 Bridge St. Tiny coffee joint serving genuine Danishes, Swedish marzipan treats and sandwiches including classic Swedish meatball and beetroot combos. Closed Sun.

Tozzetti's Panetteria 41 Halifax St. Great little bakery open from 7am for freshly cut sandwiches, good pies, muffins and delicious cakes. Closed Sun.

Yaza Montgomery Square. Hip, licensed café selling excellent breakfasts, lunches, coffees and the cheesiest cheese scones around. Also worth seeking out for its occasional alternative gigs – poetry, music, DJs, talks, etc.

Zippy's 276 Hardy St. If you're looking for home-baked veggie or wheat-free food, wicked vegan curries, tofu burgers, marvellous muffins and smoothies, and you can bear the purple and yellow walls then this is it. Closed Sun.

Drinking, nightlife and entertainment

While most of its suburban neighbours retire early to sip cocoa, Nelson stays up and parties – at least on Friday and Saturday. For raucous boozing and some dancing head for Trafalgar Street or the half-dozen bars on Bridge Street between Trafalgar and Collingwood streets. Pubs and **bars** of all stripes often have **live music**, karaoke and DJ **nights**; pick up the *Star Times* gig guide flyer to find out **what's on**.

Mainstream **movies** play at the State Cinema 6 (☏03/548 0808), while flicks of more minority interest turn up at the cinema in the Suter Art Gallery, 208 Bridge St (Thurs–Sun only).

Harry's Bar 306 Hardy St ☏03/539 0905. Smooth cocktail bar attached to a delightful Asian restaurant, serving everything from salmon wontons to an Indian curry and local Sauvignon Blanc to a Singapore Sling. Closed Sun & Mon.

The Free House 95 Collingwood St. Great pub in a former church fitted with the only hand pumps in town, perfect for microbrews from around the region. Ask at the bar and they'll order in pizza, and there's often live music. Open until 10 or 11pm (Sun 6pm).

The Phat Club 137 Bridge St ☏03/548 3311, ⊛www.phatclub.co.nz. The main venue for touring

bands and name DJs. Check the website or the door for what's on.

Sprig & Fern 134 Milton St. Suburban villa converted into a cosy bar with open fires and a selection of locally brewed, unpasteurized Sprig & Fern beers – crisp lagers and wheat beers to a ruby porter and a delicious pale ale – plus scrumpy, cider and a selection of local wines. Grab fish and chips from next door and bring them over. Daily until 10pm.

The Vic 281 Trafalgar St. Quality version of the Mac's brewery pubs that have sprung up all over the country. Lively atmosphere, decent beer and good-value pub meals.

Listings

Bike rental Stewarts, 114 Hardy St ☏03/548 1666, from $30/half-day, depending on type of bike.

Car rental Summer daily rates start at about $65; $45/day for week-long rentals. Try Nelson Car Hire (☏0800/283 545, ⟨w⟩www.nelsoncarhire.co.nz). Also Apex ☏03/546 9028; Hardy Cars ☏0800/903 010; Rent-a-Dent ☏03/546 9890; and Thrifty ☏03/547 5563.

Festivals The Nelson Arts Festival (twelve days in mid-Oct; ⟨w⟩www.nelsonfestivals.co.nz), presents all manner of arts, theatre, music, writers' readings and street entertainment, much of it either free or costing just a few dollars. Nelson also hosts the Nelson Jazz & Blues Festival (eight days from Jan 2; ⟨w⟩www.nelsonjazzfest.co.nz) with musicians from around the country and overseas playing various venues around the city.

Internet access Free at the library plus good rates at Aurora, 161 Trafalgar St, and Boots Off Travellers Centre, 53 Bridge St.

Library 27 Halifax St (Mon–Fri 10am–6pm, Sat 10am–1pm, Sun 1–4pm).

Left luggage Limited lockers at Boots Off Travellers Centre, 53 Bridge St.

Medical treatment Nelson Region After Hours and Duty Doctor, 96 Waimea Rd ☏03/546 8881 (daily 8am–10pm).

Pharmacy Prices Pharmacy, corner of Hardy & Collingwood sts, open daily till 8pm, 6pm on Sun.

Post office 209 Hardy St (Mon–Fri 8am–5.30pm, Sat 9.30am–12.30pm).

Taxis Nelson City Taxis ☏03/548 8225.

West of Nelson and the road to Abel Tasman

Much of the pleasure in hanging around Nelson is what lies on its doorstep, particularly the excellent **wineries** to the west. Here the vines appreciate the combination of New Zealand's sunniest climate and either the free-draining alluvial gravels of the Waimea Plains or the clay gravels of the Moutere Hills. Wineries are interspersed with the studios of a number of contemporary artists working in the Nelson region, many of whom exhibit in their own small **galleries**, showcasing ceramics, glass-blowing, woodturning, textiles, sculpture, installations and painting.

Almost everywhere of interest is located on or just off SH60, which runs north from Richmond towards Motueka through some lovely scenery big on sea views. You can sample the best of the region on an extended drive from Nelson to Motueka but the region is appealing enough to warrant a couple of leisurely days. Equip yourselves with the *Nelson Wine Guide*, *Nelson's Creative Pathways* and *Nelson Potters* leaflets: all free and available from visitor centres. A few kilometres further north, **Motueka** acts as the main base for trips into the Abel Tasman National Park.

Driving or cycling is probably the best way to get around, though you may want to join a **guided tour**, some of which combine the wineries and art galleries. Bay Tours (☏0800/229 868, ⟨w⟩www.baytoursnelson.co.nz) offer afternoon trips (four vineyards; $78) or full-day tours (five wineries; $98).

Around Waimea Inlet

Highway 6 runs 15km southwest of Nelson to Richmond where SH60 cuts north towards Motueka around the shores of **Waimea Inlet**. Be sure to stop 5km along at **Höglund Art Glass**, Lansdowne Road (daily 10am–5pm; ☏03/544 6500, ⟨w⟩www.hoglund.co.nz), an international-standard glass gallery displaying an amazing array of Scandinavian-influenced work, mostly vases. The style works best in the bigger, bolder pieces with clean lines and bright, unusual colours. Prices start around $80 (for an intricate paperweight) and range into the thousands. The glass museum introduces you to the history and techniques of handblown glass manufacture through early works by Swedish owners Ola and Marie Höglund, and from December to April you can watch the glass pieces being made.

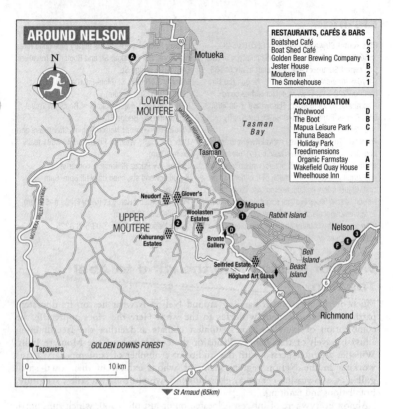

A couple of kilometres north along SH60, the Moutere Highway cuts left for **Upper Moutere**, while Redwood Road turns right past the *Seifried* winery (see both below) and on to picture-book-pretty **Rabbit Island**, one of Nelson's most popular beaches.

Back on SH60, head 5km north to the **Bronte Gallery**, Bronte Road East (daily 9am–5.30pm; Ⓦ www.brontegallery.co.nz), featuring highly individual work by internationally recognized ceramic artist, Darryl Robertson, all done on site. He also does notable abstract oils, a medium used by his partner, Lesley Jacka Robertson, whose work is on display. There's luxurious **accommodation** next door in the form of *Atholwood* (Ⓣ 03/540 2925, Ⓦ www.atholwood.co.nz; ⑨), with swimming pool, spa, mature gardens and bush running down to Waimea Inlet. Rates start at $380 a night.

The Upper Moutere wine region

A pleasant day can be spent touring Nelson's wine region, armed with the free *Nelson Wine Guide* which includes a map and lists opening hours, typically daily 11am–4.30pm in summer. The region is centred on the tiny village of **Upper Moutere**, where you'll find lots of locally produced preserves, cheeses and the like inside the Old Post Office at Moutere Gold, 1381 Moutere Hwy, and an abundance of hand-pulled and craft beers plus local wines a few steps away at the *Moutere Inn*, 1406 Moutere Hwy. It has claims as New Zealand's oldest pub and now expertly balances being both a local boozer and a shrine to fine beverages. Try a tasting flight of four beers ($10), tuck into some quality pub food ($15–20) and on summer weekends catch a band.

The wineries

Glover's Gardner Valley Rd ☏03/543 2698, ⓦwww.glovers-vineyard.co.nz. A good small-output winery run by the slightly eccentric Dave Glover, once renowned for tucking a Wagner CD into every package destined for overseas. Wagner usually plays in the background while you taste (free) European-structured wines crafted to produce highly tannic reds (Pinot Noir and Cabernet Sauvignon) and acidic whites (Sauvignon Blanc and Riesling) that stand up for themselves.

Kahurangi Sunrise Rd ☏03/543 2980, ⓦwww.kahurangiwine.com. Respected winery, offering tastings from some of the South Island's oldest commercial vines (though that's only 1973). Its stylish café is popular for alfresco dining which includes an antipasto platter for two ($40). Try the estate's own brand of olive oil.

Neudorf Neudorf Rd, Upper Moutere ☏03/543 2643, ⓦwww.neudorf.co.nz. Relaxed winery in a low-slung wooden building covered by vines with simple outdoor seating in the shade of tall ancient trees. It is a lovely spot for sampling the superb wines (mostly free), some produced from the 30-year-old vines on site – splash out ($2.50) to sample the Moutere Chardonnay, one of the country's best. Everything is available by the bottle and glass, so bring a picnic and relax in the garden.

Seifried Corner of SH60 & Redwood Rd ☏03/544 1555, ⓦwww.seifried.co.nz. The area's largest winery, offering a wide range of wines to taste. Try the Austrian Würzer and Zweigelt varietals, unique within NZ. The large restaurant does platters, great desserts and meals for kids. Restaurant open for lunch Thurs–Sun plus Fri & Sat dinners.

Woollaston Estates School Rd, Mahana ☏03/543 2817, ⓦwww.woollaston.co.nz. Swish, modern, predominantly organic winery landscaped into the Moutere Hills with tussock-roofed buildings where operations are all gravity-fed. Bring a picnic or buy a platter ($25) and enjoy tastings (free) with great views over the vines to the coast. A huge steel sculpture welcomes visitors and the art collections include works by relative Toss Woollaston (see p.449). Closed mid-April to mid-Oct.

Mapua and the Motueka road

On a sunny late afternoon, tiny **MAPUA**, a couple of kilometres off SH60 and some 34km from Nelson, is an idyllic spot with the sun catching the boats moored in the picturesque Waimea Estuary with the pines of Rabbit Island as a backdrop. Take a look in the Coolstore Gallery, but you're mainly here to eat and drink. Head straight for *The Smokehouse* restaurant (book for dinner on ☏03/540 2280), a polished affair with plenty of waterside seating and mains costing $26–32. Also consider buying some of the excellent manuka-smoked fish (of several species) and a widely acclaimed fish pâté. For something cheaper, buy fish and chips from the attached shop and enjoy them out on one of the uncluttered bits of the wharf.

After strolling around the handful of craft shops and galleries, you can revive with some top-class microbrews at the *Golden Bear Brewing Company*, (ⓦwww.goldenbearbrewing.com) where Angelino Jim concocts elegant lagers and super-hoppy pale ales and serves Cal-Mex burritos and tacos with the brewing tanks as a backdrop.

There's great beachside **camping** nearby at *Mapua Leisure Park*, 33 Toru St (☏03/540 2666, ⓦwww.nelsonholiday.co.nz; camping $16, beachfront cabins ❷, kitchen cabins ❸, motel units ❹) which includes the excellent, summer-only *Boatshed Café* and bar right on the beach, which is open to all. In February and March the place is **clothing-optional**, though plenty of non-nudists still visit at this time.

North of Mapua, SH60 runs 7km to the tiny settlement of **Tasman**, and the *Jester House* (☏03/526 6742, ⓦwww.jesterhouse.co.nz; closed Mon–Wed in winter), a rewarding licensed daytime café popular for its garden seating, rose arbours, giant chess set and **tame eels** to keep the kids entertained. The food is all home-baked and reasonably priced, and the coffee is strong. It is all very tempting and there's even **accommodation** around the back in *The Boot* (B&B; ❽), an enormous red fairy-tale boot with a luxurious lounge area, a romantic bedroom upstairs and its own little garden patio.

Motueka

The modest town of **MOTUEKA**, 47km northwest of Nelson, is primarily used as a base for exploring the Abel Tasman National Park (see p.458): there's a complete booking service, a range of accommodation and places you can rent hiking gear. The name Motueka means "island of the weka", a reference to the abundance of these edible birds which provided sustenance for Maori. European settlers arrived in 1842 and established a horticulture industry based mainly around hops, since supplemented by pip fruit and grapes. For **seasonal work**, particularly from December to March, contact the work coordinator at Work and Income at 236 High St (☎03/907 0234).

Arrival, information and accommodation

Buses pick up and drop off on Wallace Street, close to the **i-SITE visitor centre** (Dec–March Mon–Fri 8.30am–5.30pm Sat & Sun 9am–5pm; April–Nov Mon–Fri 9am–4.30pm, Sat & Sun 9am–4pm; ☎03/528 6543, ⓦwww.motuekaisite .co.nz) where staff will help you organize your visit to the Abel Tasman National Park or the Heaphy Track.

You can rent gear for **camping** and tramping from most hostels or from Abel Tasman Outdoors, 177 High St (☎03/528 8646), who offer packs ($5/day), two-person tents ($10), stove and pots ($10) and sleeping bags ($10), with discounts for multi-day rentals.

For a small town Motueka has a decent range of **accommodation**

Accommodation

Avalon Manor Motel 314 High St ☎0800/282 566, ⓦwww.avalonmotels.co.nz. Well-equipped modern motel with excellent facilities, well-tended garden and free movies. ❺

Eden's Edge 137 Lodder Lane, Riwaka, ☎03/528 4242, ⓦwww.edensedge.co.nz. Gorgeous and lovingly tended new hostel on a Braeburn apple orchard, 4km north of town, with a rural but very comfortable feel. There's a pool, bike storage and some very nicely appointed rooms (some en suite) and four-share dorms. Camping $14, dorms $26, rooms ❷

Equestrian Lodge Motel Tudor St ☎0800/668 782, ⓦwww.equestrianlodge.co.nz. Well-kept, upscale motel with units backing onto a large grassy area with a pool. ❺

Hat Trick Lodge 25 Wallace St ☎03/528 5353, ⓦwww.hattricklodge.co.nz. Conveniently located opposite the i-SITE and bus stop, this modern hostel comes with high standards and a warm welcome. Along with a spacious and well-equipped kitchen and lounge, bike rental and free gear storage, there's a separate women's dorm and a family room with its own bathroom and kitchen. Dorms $25, rooms & en suites ❷

The Laughing Kiwi 310 High St ☎03/ 528 9229, ⓦwww.laughingkiwi.co.nz. Attractive, friendly and central backpackers with a convivial atmosphere. spacious dorms and rooms, plenty of outdoor seating and a hot tub. Camping $12, dorms $24, rooms & en suite ❷

Motueka Beach Reserve Wharf Rd, 4km southeast of town. Waterside parking for s/c campervans only, though there are toilets and cold showers adjacent. One night only. $5

Motueka Top 10 Holiday Park 10 Fearon St ☎0800/668 835, ⓦwww.motuekatop10.co.nz. Verdant campsite with plenty of trees for shelter and clean, well-kept facilities (including spa pool) just 1km north of the town centre. Camping $20, cabins ❷, kitchen cabins ❸–❹, motel units ❹

The Resurgence Riwaka Valley Rd, roughly 12km northwest of Motueka ☎03/528 4664, ⓦwww .resurgence.co.nz. Hosts Clare and Peter ensure everything runs sweetly at this totally relaxing boutique lodge, tucked away near the resurgence of the Riwaka River from below Takaka Hill. The attention to detail is faultless, from the sound eco-credentials to the superb meals ($90). Facilities include an outdoor pool and spa, and there's a range of bush-set rooms and cabins priced from $445. ❾

Rowan Cottage 27 Fearon St ☎ 03/528 6492, ⊛ www.rowancottage .net. Tastefully styled cottage with two polished-floor rooms set in a lovely garden where chickens lay eggs for the full breakfast (optional). One room comes with its own secluded deck with sunken bath and everyone can use the barbecue. ④

Treedimensions Organic Farmstay Shaggery Rd, 10km west of Motueka ☎ 03/528 8718, ⊛ www .treedimensions.co.nz. Wake up to birdsong then breakfast on the deck of these attractive, modern s/c units with polished-wood floors, comfy beds and stereo. They overlook an organic orchard with 45 types of fruit and 700 species and you can usually try whatever's ripe. ④

The town and activities

Motueka is strung along SH60, with quieter streets spurring off from the main highway. Head 1km down Old Wharf Road to reach **Motueka Quay**, where the ghost of this once-busy port lingers among the scant remains of the old jetty. Here lies the rusting hulk of the Scottish-built *Janie Seddon* – named after the daughter of Richard Seddon, premier of New Zealand from 1893 until his death in 1906. The tiny **Motueka District Museum** (Dec–March Mon–Fri 10am–4pm; April–Nov Tues–Fri 10am–3pm; $2 donation) delves into the area's history through a few Maori and European artefacts, as well as the *Motueka Carvings*, a modern four-panel frieze in the foyer that skilfully depicts the livelihoods that have traditionally sustained Tasman Bay.

Motueka also offers excellent **hiking** in the hills to the west (see box below) and the opportunity to go **tandem skydiving** with Skydive Abel Tasman (☎ 0800/422 899, ⊛ www.skydive.co.nz). Based at Motueka airport, 3km southwest of town, it offers all the usual jumps ($279 from 12,000ft; $299 from 13,000ft) plus excellent scenery and helpful, friendly parachuting "buddies".

Experienced riders should make for **adventure horseriding** with Western Ranges Horse Treks (Nov–March only; ☎ 03/522 4178, ⊛ www.thehorsetrek .co.nz), around 40km southwest of Motueka on SH61: call for directions. They take you to wild and challenging places often involving river crossings: a full day ($200; no credit cards) gives you a good sense of the possibilities available on the two-dayer ($500), overnighting in a comfy hut with meals cooked outdoors over a wood fire, or even the intrepid ten-day trek ($3500).

Eating, drinking and entertainment

Motueka has several decent restaurants and somewhat arty **movies** at the intimate Gecko Theatre, opposite the i-SITE at 23b Wallace St (☎ 03/528 9996).

Walks around Motueka

Some of the best subalpine hiking in the north of the South Island is around the 1795m **Mount Arthur** and the associated uplifted plateau, the **Mount Arthur Tablelands**, all detailed in DOC's *The Cobb Valley, Mount Arthur and the Tablelands* leaflet available from the Motueka i-SITE. Traditionally, few visitors have bothered coming up this way, so what company you find will mostly be Kiwis and wildlife.

The principal starting point is the Flora car park, 930m up at the end of Graham Valley Road that leads off SH61 30km southwest of Motueka. A good 2–3hr loop heads up an easy path (1hr) to the Mount Arthur Hut ($15), from where the lowlands spread before you with Mount Arthur dominating the southern skyline. Continue along a ridge and down to Flora Hut (free) then back along a gravel road to the car park. The summit of Mount Arthur can be reached in three hours from the Mount Arthur Hut.

Chokdee 109 High St ☎03/528 0318. Reliable Thai cuisine to eat in or take away. All the usual soups, curries and noodle dishes at modest prices.

Hot Mama's 105 High St. Motueka's pick for pizza or simply hanging out over a beer or a coffee either in the breezy, bright interior or in the patio garden. The music's always interesting and at weekends it is usually live with occasional appearances by touring New Zealand folk, jazz, acoustic and rock acts.

Red Beret 147 High St. Excellent café that draws in locals for a wide range of all-day breakfasts and lunches from filo wraps to pasta dishes, gourmet burgers and excellent fish and chips.

Swinging Sultan 172 High St ☎03/528 8909. Kebab takeaway with just a couple of tables out on the pavement where you can tuck into chicken and beef kebabs and falafel (all $7–10) plus good coffee.

T.O.A.D. Hall 502 High St, 3km south of the town centre. Organic fruit-and-veg vendor and café with a flower-filled garden that's perfect for imbibing delicious made-to-order ice cream.

Abel Tasman National Park and around

The **Abel Tasman National Park**, 60km north of Nelson, is a stunningly beautiful area of golden sandy beaches lapped by crystal-clear waters and lush green bushland, all interspersed with granite outcrops and inhabited by abundant wildlife. It comes with an international reputation that draws large numbers of trampers, kayakers and day-trippers from November to March. But don't be put off. Despite being New Zealand's smallest national park – just 20km by 25km – the Abel Tasman absorbs the crowds tolerably well and packs in some real beauty.

The goal of most visitors is the coastline. Some come to hike the **Abel Tasman Coast Track** with its picturesque mixture of dense coastal bushwalking, gentle climbs to lookouts and walks across idyllic beaches. Abundant water taxis allow you to pick the sections you want to hike and get a lift back when you've had enough. Others come for the wonderful **kayaking** around the mercurial coastline spending leisurely lunchtimes on golden sands before paddling off in the late-afternoon sun to some campsite or hut. The two can be combined and you might even tack on **sailing** the limpid waters and **swimming with seals** to round off the experience. You can even stay in the park, either at one of the DOC huts and campsites, or in considerably more luxury at some attractive lodges.

With **advance trip booking** you'll be whisked from Nelson straight into the park obviating the need for nights in the surrounding gateway towns, though they're pleasant enough places to spend a little time. The service town of **Motueka**, (see p.456) is best for general organizing, but trips mostly depart from tiny **Marahau**, at the park's southern entrance. A few trips depart from diminutive **Kaiteriteri**, which might lure you to stay awhile to relax on the gorgeous beach.

The park's northern reaches are accessed from **Takaka** (see p.466) where Abel Tasman Drive leads to Wainui, Awaroa and **Totaranui**, all on the Coast Track.

Some history and natural history

Since around 1500, Maori made seasonal encampments along this coast and some permanent settlements flourished near the mouth of the Awaroa River. In 1642, **Abel Tasman** anchored his two ships near Wainui in Golden Bay and promptly lost four men in a skirmish with the Ngati Tumatakokiri, after which he departed the shores. Frenchman **Dumont d'Urville** dropped by in 1827 and explored the area between Marahau and Torrent Bay, but it was not for another 23 years that **European settlement** began in earnest. The settlers chopped, quarried, burned and cleared until nothing was left but gorse and bracken. Happily, few obvious signs of their invasion remain and the vegetation has

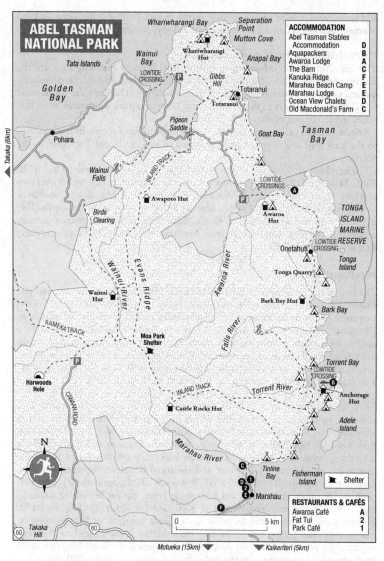

ABEL TASMAN NATIONAL PARK

ACCOMMODATION
Abel Tasman Stables
  Accommodation   D
Aquapackers   B
Awaroa Lodge   A
The Barn   C
Kanuka Ridge   F
Marahau Beach Camp   E
Marahau Lodge   E
Ocean View Chalets   D
Old Macdonald's Farm   C

Whariwharangi Bay
Separation Point
Mutton Cove
Wainui Bay
Whariwharangi Hut
Anapai Bay
Tata Islands
LOWTIDE CROSSING
Gibbs Hill
Golden Bay
Totaranui
Totaranui
Pohara
Pigeon Saddle
Goat Bay
Tasman Bay
Takaka (6km)
Wainui Falls
INLAND TRACK
Awapoto Hut
LOWTIDE CROSSINGS
TONGA ISLAND MARINE RESERVE
Birds Clearing
Awaroa Hut
Onetahuti
LOWTIDE CROSSING
Tonga Island
Tonga Quarry
Wainui Hut
Wainui River
Evans Ridge
Awaroa River
Bark Bay Hut
Bark Bay
RAMEKA TRACK
Falls River
Moa Park Shelter
Torrent Bay
Harwoods Hole
CANAAN ROAD
INLAND TRACK
Torrent River
LOWTIDE CROSSING
Anchorage Hut
Castle Rocks Hut
Adele Island
N
Marahau River
Tinline Bay
Fisherman Island
Shelter
Takaka Hill
60
Marahau
0   5 km

Motueka (15km)   Kaikeriteri (5km)

vigorously regenerated over the years. Named after the first European explorer to experience its shores, the Abel Tasman National Park was **gazetted** in 1942, following the tireless campaigning of one **Perrine Moncrieff**, a determined woman by all accounts.

Abel Tasman is full of rich and varied **plant life** with beech trees in the damp gullies and kanuka tolerating the wild and windy areas. **Birds** you might encounter include tui, native pigeons, bellbirds (their presence betrayed by their distinctive call), fantails that flutter close by feeding off the insects you disturb as you walk through the bush, and if you're lucky the bobbing, ground-dwelling weka. Along the coast you might see the distinctive orange-beaked oystercatchers and shags, who dive to great depths in search of fish. Offshore, the **Tonga Island Marine Reserve** is famous for its **fur seal colony**, sea birds and bountiful fish.

Park information and access

The main sources of **information** on the Abel Tasman National Park are the visitor centres at Nelson, Motueka and Takaka, which will all book boats, kayaks, hut and camping tickets, transport and accommodation. There are also **unmanned** DOC **display shelters** at the Marahau and Totaranui **park entrances**, with tide times and safety precautions.

Access into the park is generally on foot or by boat, but a couple of roads extend to the park entrances – principally Marahau in the south and Totaranui in the north.

The best **bus** service in the region is Abel Tasman Coachlines (Nelson ☎03/548 0285, Motueka ☎03/528 8850; ⓦwww.abeltasmantravel.co.nz), which runs two to three times daily between Motueka, Kaiteriteri and Marahau. One handy service runs from Nelson (6.45am in summer & 7.45am all year) for Motueka (1hr; $12 one-way) and Marahau (1hr 45min; $20) connecting with launch services deeper into the park. Connections leave Motueka for Takaka (7.45am in summer; $23) and Totaranui ($30).

Kaiteriteri

The tiny resort settlement of **KAITERITERI**, 15km north of Motueka and just south of the Abel Tasman National Park, ranks high in the pantheon of Kiwi summer-holiday destinations and is consequently packed to its limited gills from Christmas through to late January. There's an understandable appeal, with a golden arc of safe swimming beach looking out towards Tasman Bay where a couple of small islands add perspective. With Marahau (see below) becoming too congested for some tastes, Kaiteriteri has fashioned itself as an alternative embarkation point for Abel Tasman cruise, water taxi and kayaking trips.

Accommodation is very limited. Kiwi families flock to the beachside *Kaiteriteri Beach Motor Camp* (☎03/527 8010, ⓦwww.kaiteriteribeach.co.nz; camping $15, cabins ❶, en-suite cabins ❷: bedding $5 per bed) which is booked solid months in advance from Christmas to early February. *Kaiteri Lodge*, just back from the beach on Inlet Road (☎0508/524 8374, ⓦwww.kaiterilodge.co.nz; dorms $35, rooms ❹), is something between a motel and an upscale backpackers with modern four-share rooms and tasteful en-suite doubles plus the usual hostel accoutrements. *Bellbird Lodge*, Sandy Bay Road (☎03/527 8555, ⓦwww.bellbirdlodge.com; ❽) offers two comfortable suites, great views and welcoming hosts, but for something astonishingly relaxing and unexpected, stay at *Kimi Ora Spa Resort* (☎0508/546 4672, ⓦwww.kimiora.com; rooms ❻, suites ❼), a hillside complex set in pine forest on Martin Farm Road, signposted 1km back from the beach road, with heated indoor and outdoor pools. You can just stay, but the emphasis is on fitness (there's a MTB track around the property), therapy and indulgent massage sessions ($90/1hr).

For beach views from the terrace and pretty decent **meals** ($21–28), go for the *Shoreline* on the main road or the summer-only restaurant at *Kimi Ora*, which is open to all and serves healthy, vegetarian four-course buffet **dinners** ($35; Nov to Easter only), with a small selection of organic wines, beers and juices.

Marahau

About 8km north of Kaiteriteri, tiny **MARAHAU** is poised right at the southern entrance to the Abel Tasman National Park, something that affects almost everything that happens here. Most of the tours, water taxis and kayak operators working in the park are based here making this a very popular last or first night of civilization.

The beach road runs through the settlement to the **park entrance**, marked by an unstaffed DOC display shelter. From here, a long boardwalk across marshland leads into the national park. **Places to stay** are all geared to the needs of park visitors and are detailed below. The best place to **eat** is the licensed *Park Café*, by the start of the track (Oct–April daily 8am–late), which is legendary among appreciative walkers emerging from the park for its wholesome lunches, good coffee, restorative beers and range of delicious dinner mains ($24–29) and desserts ($11). Also check out the *Fat Tui*, at Kahu Kayaks base, a van selling excellent takeaway fish and chips and gourmet burgers.

Abel Tasman Stables Accommodation 100m along Marahau Valley Rd ☎03/527 8181, ⓦwww .abeltasmanstables.co.nz. Two in one: a two-room homestay (one en suite) plus three motel-style units. ❺

The Barn Harvey Rd ☎03/527 8043, ⓦwww.barn .co.nz. A lively backpackers by the park entrance, with beanbags scattered around an outdoor fireplace and baths in the grounds. As well as dorms they have several twins and doubles, mostly in basic, new cabins in the grounds. Also well set up for campers with an outdoor cooking area. Camping $15, dorms $25, cabins ❶, rooms ❷

Kanuka Ridge 21 Moss Rd ☎03/527 8435, ⓦwww.abeltasmanbackpackers.co.nz. Peaceful upscale hostel set on a hill back from the beach with just one dorm, several bush-backed rooms, plenty of birdsong and free wi-fi. There's bike rental ($50/day) from the enthusiastic biker, Al, who can direct you to great tracks. Closed June–Sept. Camping $15, dorms $26, rooms ❷, en suites ❸

Marahau Beach Camp Beach Rd ☎0800/808 018, ⓦwww.abeltasmancentre.co.nz.

Unpretentious but well-kept campsite with tent sites ($30 per site), backpackers $20, rooms ❶, kitchen cabins ❷

Marahau Lodge Beach Rd ☎03/527 8250, ⓦwww.abeltasmanmarahaulodge.co.nz. Studio and larger chalets scattered about the lawns give a relaxed feel to this upscale lodge with outdoor spa, sauna and breakfast delivered to your room on request. ❺

Ocean View Chalets Beach Rd ☎03/527 8232, ⓦwww.accommodationabeltasman.co.nz. Wooden planking gives a kind of alpine-chalet feel to these ten spacious units, all with balconies and distant sea views from your bed. Studio ❺, s/c unit ❻

Old Macdonald's Farm Harvey Rd, by the park entrance ☎03/527 8288, ⓦwww.oldmacs.co.nz. A family-run farm with a few cottages and a s/c studio. But it is primarily good for camping with a huge wooded area next to a couple of swimming holes. There's also secure parking ($5 a night), along with a well-stocked shop and gear storage. Camping $14, vans $40 per site, dorms $25, cabins ❸, s/c studio ❺

Exploring the Park

There is an almost infinite variety of ways to explore the Abel Tasman National Park – no matter what combination of activities you'd like to try, there's bound to be an operator who can oblige. Relatively few people tramp the **Inland Track**, most are keen to stick to the park's **Coast Track**, with its long golden beaches, clear water, spectacular outcrops and the constant temptation to snorkel in some of the idyllic bays. Also, near the coast is where you'll find a good array of **accommodation** ranging from beachside campsites to swanky lodges. **Water taxis** can take you virtually anywhere along the coast as far north as the lovely beach at Totaranui. They usually give a bit of a commentary along the way, though there are also dedicated **cruises**, some visiting the seal colony on the **Tonga Island Marine Reserve** and **Split Apple Rock**, a large apple-like boulder that has split and fallen into two halves.

The intricate details of the coast are best explored by **kayak**, either on a guided trip or by renting kayaks and setting your own itinerary. Better still, combine kayaking with walking a section of the Coast Track.

Water taxi drop-offs and guided kayaking are banned in the section of park north of Totaranui making this a much **quieter area** to hike and hang out.

Water taxis and cruises

Water taxis based in Kaiteriteri and Marahau give you the chance to walk a particular section of coast or simply ride to some gorgeous beach and get another water taxi back. They can drop you off at any of six beaches along the coast – Anchorage, Torrent Bay, Bark Bay, Onetahuti, Awaroa and Totaranui. Three main companies each do two to five scheduled runs from the south of the park to Totaranui and back and charge virtually the same price – just book whichever is going the right way at the right time or call Aquataxi (see box, p.464). Typical one-way **fares** from Marahau are to Anchorage ($32), Bark Bay ($37) and Totaranui ($44).

Any water taxi ride will give you a good look at the coast, but Wilsons (see p.464) also run **cruises** from Kaiteriteri to Totaranui and back (3 daily in summer; 3hr; $70) on a spacious and stable catamaran. There's a host of opportunities to walk a section of the track and pick up a later sailing. Probably the best is the Seals and Beach (6–8hr; $62) with a cruise around the Tonga Island seal colony, and plenty of time to walk from Tonga Quarry to Medlands Beach and swim a little. An alternative is to go with Abel Tasman Charter (Nov–April only; $215; ☎0800/223 522, ⓦ www.abeltasmancruises.co.nz), which runs a small cruise boat from near Kaiteriteri with a flexible itinerary partly determined by the guests. Doubtless there's be seal viewing, a visit to Split Apple Rock, time ashore and a good picnic lunch.

Accommodation in the park

Unlike many of New Zealand's national parks, the Abel Tasman offers a range of accommodation, accessed either by boat or the Abel Tasman Coast Path. We've listed the best below.

There are also **multi-day all-inclusive** trips to consider. Wilsons (see p.464) run two- to five-day guided walking and kayaking holidays ($800–1870) with comfortable accommodation at their two trackside lodges at Torrent Bay and Awaroa.

Many people stay at the four **DOC huts** (Oct–April $30; May–Sept $12) that are spaced around four hours' walk apart along the coast. These come with potable water, heating, good toilets, basic but comfortable bunks and most have showers, but there are no cooking facilities: bring a sleeping bag, cooking stove, pans, utensils, food and a torch. Hardened trampers will want to camp at some of the eighteen **DOC campsites** (Oct–April $12; May–Sept $8) strung along the coast, all either beside beaches or near the DOC huts (whose facilities you are not supposed to use); all sites have a water supply and toilets, but it means carrying more gear and you'll need an ocean of sandfly repellent. Huts and campsites both have a two-night maximum stay in summer and only the Anchorage and Bark Bay campsites allow **campfires**.

Bookings are required all year for all huts and campsites and should be made at least a week in advance in summer. Book online (ⓦ www.doc.govt.nz) or at an i-SITE.

The following places are listed from south to north through the park.

Aquapackers Anchorage ☎ 0800/430 744, ⓦ www.aquapackers.co.nz. Relaxed backpacker accommodation in made-up dorms and doubles aboard two converted boats moored for the summer just off the beach in Anchorage Bay: there's a free ferry from beach to boat. The package includes BBQ dinner, basic breakfast and access to a pay bar. It can be a little cramped but the stillness of the park at night and sounds of lapping water make it worthwhile. Sept–May only. Dorms $65, doubles ⑥

Catamaran Sailing Anchorage ☎ 03/547 6666, ⓦ www.sailingcharters.co.nz. Spend a night on a yacht with a little sailing, a bunk on board, dinner, wine and breakfast. Pick-up around 4.30pm and drop-off by 9am. $170/person.

Awaroa Lodge Awaroa ☏03/528 8758, ⓦwww
.awaroalodge.co.nz. Nestled in the bush with great
wetland views, this upscale lodge uses ingredients
from its organic garden in its classy restaurant
(mains $38). Hikers and casual visitors can still drop
in for a coffee or a drink by the enormous fireplace
(and access the internet), but it is really aimed at
well-heeled guests arriving by water taxi or plane
and staying in the delightful en-suite rooms and
suites. Rates from $395. Closed June–Aug. ⓐ

Totaranui Campground Totaranui. The only
car-accessible accommodation on the Abel Tasman
coast, this huge campsite (room for 850; $12) is so
busy in summer that places are obtained by lottery
for Christmas to the end of Jan. A form for booking
(required Dec 10–Feb 10) can be downloaded from
ⓦwww.doc.govt.nz. A separate section for track
hikers usually has space, though you might want to
press on.

Hiking the Coast Track

The **Abel Tasman Coast Track** (51km; 2–5 days) is one of the **easiest** of New
Zealand's Great Walks – one for people who wouldn't normally think of
themselves as trampers. You should download or buy DOC's *Abel Tasman Coast
Track* leaflet, but the track is clear and easy to follow. Lack of fitness is no
impediment as huts are never more than four hours apart (campsites 2hr) and
you can use water taxis to skip some sections or just pick the bits you fancy
walking. In dry conditions you don't even need strong boots – trainers will do
fine. All this combines to make the Coast Track extremely popular, especially
from December to the end of February when some sections seem like a hikers'
highway: heading for the section north of Totaranui can deliver a less frenetic
experience.

The **route** traverses broad golden beaches lapped by emerald waters, punctuated
by granite pillars silhouetted against the horizon and zigzagging gentle climbs
through valleys. The main planning difficulty is coping with two **tide-
dependent** sections at Onetahuti and across the Awaroa Estuary. Tide times will
help you decide which way you're going to do the track – if there are low tides
in the afternoon you'll probably want to head south, if they're in the morning,
north. Even at low tide you can expect to get your feet wet. Before setting off you
should also arrange your transport drop-offs and pick-ups (see "Water taxis and
cruises" opposite).

Marahau to Anchorage (12.4km; 4hr). Direct
access from Marahau makes this section popular.
The bush isn't the most beautiful but the access to
little golden beaches is unparalleled. The track
follows a wooden causeway across the Marahau
Estuary to Tinline Bay before rounding a point
overlooking Fisherman and Adele islands just off
the coast. As the track winds in and out of gullies,
the surroundings are obscured by beech forest and
tall kanuka trees until you emerge at Anchorage,
with its hut, campsite and summertime offshore
backpackers.

Anchorage to Bark Bay (8.7km; 3hr). Aim to
cross Torrent Bay two hours either side of low tide
or be prepared to skirt the bay (adding an hour) to
reach the few dozen houses that constitute the
settlement of Torrent Bay. Climb out of the bay
through pine trees to the gorgeous Falls River,
crossed by a 47m-long swingbridge. The Bark Bay
hut and campsites are 1hr ahead.

Bark Bay to Awaroa (11.5km; 4hr). After crossing
(or skirting) Bark Bay Estuary you cut away from

the coast only to return at Tonga Quarry where
there's a campsite and views out to Tonga Island
and its associated Marine Reserve. You soon reach
the golden beach at Onetahuti. The stream at its
northern end is tidal (cross 3hr either side of low
tide). The track then climbs to the Tonga Saddle
and descends to Awaroa Inlet and the settlement of
two dozen houses and a DOC hut with a campsite
alongside; *Awaroa Lodge* and its restaurant are
also within easy walking distance.

Awaroa to Totaranui (5.5km; 1hr 30min). You
must cross the Awaroa Estuary (2hr either side of
low tide) to reach Goat Bay then up to a lookout
above Skinner Point before reaching Totaranui with
its great arc of beach and extensive campsite.

Totaranui to Whariwharangi (7.5km; 3hr). After
rounding the Totaranui Estuary, press on over and
around rocky headlands as far as Mutton Cove then
wander through alternating shrubland and beaches,
preferably making a side trip to Separation Point,
with its lookout and fur seal colony. Continue to the
hut at Whariwharangi, a former homestead.

Whariwharangi to Wainui (5.5km; 1hr 30min). It is an easy walk to the road on the eastern side of Wainui Bay where buses pick up, but it is also possible to cross Wainui Bay (2hr either side of low tide) or following the road around the bay. If you follow the road, you can also take in the short hike up to the Wainui Falls which heads off the road at the base of Wainui Bay.

Kayaking

One of the best ways to explore the park's remoter shores is by **sea kayak**. It is hard to beat gently paddling along exploring little coves (and possibly being accompanied by seals or dolphins), stopping on a golden beach for a dip then continuing to a campsite where you cool your beer in a stream. Some campsites are only accessible from the water and have become kayakers' sites. Of course, you're not the first to discover such pleasures and in the height of summer a couple of dozen kayaks may form a brightly coloured armada at any one time.

Marahau, at the southern end of the park, is kayaking with half a dozen operators (three of them – Abel Tasman Kayaks, Ocean River and Kaiteriteri Kayak – owned by a local Maori tribal corporation). Most companies offer a broadly similar range of one- to five-day guided trips, and kayak rentals, often known as "freedom rentals". The initial stretch north of here is known as the "Mad Mile", but congestion quickly eases further north. Only Golden Bay Kayaks (see below) work from the quieter north end of the park.

Abel Tasman adventure operators

Abel Tasman Kayaks Marahau ⊕0800/732 529 ⊚www.abeltasmankayaks.co.nz. Guided kayak trip specialists based in Marahau. Their half-day ($110) and full-day ($100–135) trips include a water taxi mini-tour around the park and can be combined with seal swimming ($215). Also gourmet catered overnighters ($430) with luxury camping and a couple of longer trips.

Abel Tasman Sailing ⊕0800/467 245, ⊚www.sailingadventures.co.nz. Day-sailing trips into the park.

Abel Tasman Sea Shuttle ⊕0800/732 748, ⊚www.abeltasmanseashuttles.co.nz. Kaiteriteri-based water taxis.

Abel Tasman Seal Swim ⊕0800/732 529, ⊚www.sealswim.com. The seal swimming branch of Abel Tasman Kayaks.

Aquataxi ⊕0800/278 282 ⊚www.aquataxi.co.nz. Water taxis from Marahau and Kaiteriteri.

Golden Bay Kayaks ⊕03/525 9095, ⊚www.goldenbaykayaks.co.nz. Pohara-based company who operate in the north of the park offer rentals ($50/day) and half-day guided trips ($75). Single kayaks available and they also organize a great-value unguided overnight trip into the park ($85).

Kahu Kayaks ⊕03/527 8300, ⊚www.kahukayaks.co.nz. Independent Marahau-based kayak rentals and guided trips company that, depending on your itinerary, often comes in fractionally cheaper than the opposition. A good all-round taster is Kahu Kayaks' full-day cruise (5hr; $142), which gives you three hours paddling the Mad Mile followed by a water taxi visit to the seal colony, a short coastal walk and a water taxi back to Marahau.

Kaiteriteri Kayaks ⊕0800/252 925, ⊚www.seakayak.co.nz. Guided trips from Kaiteriteri including a half-day paddle to Split Apple Rock ($94); half a day paddling within the park plus a water taxi ride ($110); the full-day Torrent Bay walk, paddle and water taxi ($134); and assorted overnight combos.

Wilsons ⊕0800/223 582, ⊚www.AbelTasman.co.nz. A wide range of cruises, kayak trips and guided-walk packages with accommodation in quality lodges along the way.

Guided trips typically combine paddling with walking, water taxi rides, overnight stays visiting seals and more. **Multi-day** guided trips let you ease into the pace of the park even more thoroughly. Almost anything is possible and we've listed some of the best below.

For **freedom rentals** you are typically given shore-based instruction then let loose in a double kayak. You are not allowed to venture north of Abel Head at the north end of the Tonga Island Marine Reserve nor paddle solo. Conditions are generally benign and suitable for complete beginners, though if you've any doubts about your ability, opt for a guided trip. Rental **prices** are around $55–60 per person for each of the first two days, $35–40 for the third then $30–35 for each subsequent day. One-way rentals have a fee ($35–50) for returning the kayak to base by water taxi. Most companies have a range of camping **gear rental**, will store your vehicle while you are away and operate year-round, though the range of trips is reduced in winter.

Sailing and seal swimming

If you'd rather let the zephyrs of this coast propel you along, contact Abel Tasman Sailing (see box opposite) who offer small-group all-day **sailing** trips ($160) and sail-walk-seal-viewing combos ($90) using the yacht to access a four-hour coast walk.

If you love wildlife and snorkelling, don't pass up the chance to go **seal swimming** with Abel Tasman Seal Swim (Dec to mid-April only; see box opposite) – an hour with these sleek amphibians (swimming $169, watching $90) accessed by a 45-minute water taxi trip. Swimming with seals can be a lot more fun than swimming with dolphins simply because seals are more manoeuvrable and curious. The water is usually crystal-clear and the impact on the seals is minimized by ensuring that you wait for them to come and swim with you rather than just leaping in and splashing about among them.

Mountain biking

Marahau-based Abel Tasman Mountain Biking (℗0800/808 018, ⓦwww .abeltasmanmountainbiking.co.nz) runs a range of guided rides such as a half-day drip down the Rameka Track (see p.466; $152), and works with a kayaking company to offer a one-day bike and paddle combo ($203).

Hiking the Inland Track

The **Inland Track** (42km; 3 days) between Marahau and Totaranui is far less popular than the Coast Track and is strenuous enough to require moderate fitness and decent tramping gear. The track can be combined with the Coast Track to make a six- to seven-day loop and is described in a DOC leaflet.

The route climbs from sea level to **Evans Ridge** past granite outcrops and views of the coast: highlights include the **Pigeon Saddle**, the moorlands of Moa Park and the moon-like Canaan landscape, with an optional side trip to Harwood's Hole (see p.466).

Camping is not recommended on the Inland Track, but there are three, small, first-come-first-served **DOC huts** ($5; annual hut passes valid), with water and toilets but no cooking facilities.

Golden Bay

Occupying the northwestern tip of the South Island, **GOLDEN BAY** curves gracefully from the northern fringes of the Abel Tasman National Park to the encircling arm of **Farewell Spit**, all backed by the magnificence of the Kahurangi National Park. With bush-clad mountains on three sides and waves lapping at its exposed fourth side, Golden Bay's inaccessibility has kept it outside the mainstream and it can seem a world apart.

Wainui Bay, just east of the main town of **Takaka**, is most likely the spot where Abel Tasman first anchored, guaranteeing his place in history as the first European to encounter Aotearoa and its fierce inhabitants. The isolating presence of **Takaka Hill** keeps today's bayside communities very manageable and goes some way to explaining the region's spirit of **independence** and why the bay has lured such a cross section of alternative lifestylers, craftspeople and artists. The area has been particularly popular with German-speakers who now make up ten percent of the five thousand residents. Sunny, beautiful and full of fascinating sights, Golden Bay deserves a couple days of your time and has a knack of inducing you to stay longer.

For some insight into what makes the place tick, pick up the home-produced newspaper, *The G.B. Weekly* (ⓦ www.gbweekly.co.nz).

Takaka Hill

The only way to get to Golden Bay by road is on SH60, a paved but very twisty road over the **Takaka Hill** that skirts the inland border of the Abel Tasman National Park. Take it slow and stop frequently at viewpoints with glorious mountain and seascapes from Nelson north to D'Urville Island. Atop Takaka Hill, some 20km north of Motueka, you can be guided through **Ngarua Caves** (Oct–April daily 10am–4pm; 45min guided tours on the hour; $15, cash only), a modest show cave with illuminated stalactite formations and skeletons of moa who fell in through holes in the cave roof.

Half a kilometre further north, the twisting, unsealed Canaan Road runs 11km to a car park (long-drop and water supply) with access to **Harwoods Hole**, a huge vertical shaft 176m deep and over 50m in diameter, which links up to a vast cave system below. Its lip is reached by an enchanting trail (6km return; 1hr 30min; mostly level) through silver beech forest, then follows a dry rock-strewn riverbed to the hole itself. There is no viewing platform, so only the brave and foolhardy get much of a look down the hole. About 30min along the trail a side track (20min return) leads to a **clifftop viewpoint** with views down towards the Takaka Valley and the coast. A spot beside Canaan Road 3km back from the car park is one of several sites in the area used by the **Lord of the Rings** crew, in this case a scene with Strider leading the hobbits from Bree through Chetwood Forest. **Mountain bikers** are spoilt for choice here, with the excellent new Canaan Downs tracks (ask for details locally) leading off from the road-end car park, and the clearly signposted **Rameka Track** (5km; 3hr one-way; 750m descent), which follows one of the earliest surveyed routes down into the Takaka Valley with superb views of the granite outcrops and the surrounding country. Along the way it includes Great Expectations, a section of single-track designed and built by Jonathan Kennett (co-author of NZ's mountain bikers' bible; see p.804) on land set aside as a carbon sink, and being planted out in native trees. A visit here works especially well if you can find an amenable driver who can meet you at the bottom, thus avoiding the slog back up SH60 and Canaan Road.

Takaka and around

The small town of **TAKAKA**, almost 60km north of Motueka, is Golden Bay's largest settlement, and one that's increasingly pitching itself to summer tourists while continuing to cater for the local farming community and barefoot crusties who emerge from their shacks and tipis to sell their crafts and healing services. Immediately north, **Te Waikoropupu Springs** emerge from their underground lair, while to the north yawns a considerable stretch of beautiful bay, running parallel to SH60 as it rolls into Collingwood and Farewell Spit. To the east, Abel Tasman Drive winds past the safe swimming beach at **Pohara** and a few minor sights before heading into the northern section of the Abel Tasman National Park (see p.458).

Arrival and information

Golden Bay Coachlines (℡03/525 8352, ⒲www.gbcoachlines.co.nz) and Abel Tasman Coachlines (℡03/548 0285, ⒲www.abeltasmantravel.co.nz) jointly run from Nelson and continue north to Collingwood and the Heaphy Track, and east to Totaranui. Both **bus** companies drop off outside the **i-SITE** visitor centre (daily: Dec–Feb 9am–6pm; Nov, March & April 9am–5pm; May–Oct 10am–4pm; ℡03/525 9136, ⒲www.nelsonnz.com), on SH60 as you enter town from the south. It carries all DOC information, handles bookings and hut tickets for the national parks and tracks, and organizes **rental cars**.

Most of the hostels have free bikes for guests, and The Quiet Revolution, 11 Commercial St (closed Sat afternoon & Sun; ℡03/525 9555, Ⓔquietrev @hotmail.com), **rents mountain bikes** for $20 per day ($40/day for off-road use) and can sell you *Fat Tyre Fun* ($2), containing over a dozen great mountain-bike rides in Golden Bay.

Internet access is available at the library, 3 Junction St (Mon–Thurs 9.30am–5pm, Fri 9.30am–6pm, Sat 9.30am–12.30pm), and several commercial outlets on Commerce Street.

Accommodation

Golden Bay is a popular holiday spot for both Kiwis and foreign visitors; as a result there is plenty of good-quality accommodation, from backpackers to fairly swanky lodges. Camping ranges from the enormous DOC campsite at Totaranui to wayside spots where you can park your campervan overnight.

Takaka

Annie's Nirvana Lodge 25 Motupipi St ℡03/525 8766, ⒲www.nirvanalodge.co.nz. Enthusiastically run associate YHA right in town with a homely atmosphere, a nice garden with lots of seating, cheap rental bikes, and private rooms (including three attractive garden doubles). Dorms $25, rooms ❷

Autumn Farm Lodge 3km south of Takaka off SH60 ℡03/525 9013, ⒲www.autumnfarm.com. Charming gay-friendly lodge, on a sizeable plot, with comfortable rooms, a big bathhouse and a laidback (clothing optional) atmosphere. Also hosts an eight-day annual gay summer camp over New Year. Reservations essential. Camping $20, backpackers $30, B&B ❹

Golden Bay Motel 132 Commercial St ℡0800/401 212, ⒲www.goldenbaymotel.co.nz. Well-kept little motel with off-street parking and spacious rooms. ❹

Kiwiana 73 Motupipi St ℡0800/805 494 ⒲www .kiwianabackpackers.co.nz. Beautifully kept and well-run hostel in a large villa where the Kiwiana theme runs to the labelling of the airy rooms – paua, jandals, tiki, etc – and collection of books in the games room where they have pool and table

tennis. Free hot tub and BBQ in the well-tended garden plus free bikes. Closed July & Aug. Camping $18, dorms $27, rooms ❷

Mohua Motels SH60, ℡03/525 7222, ⒲www .mohuamotels.com. Takaka's newest motel, on the southern entrance to town with attractive well-appointed units, Sky TV and in-room internet. ❻

Shady Rest 139 Commercial St ℡03/525 9669, ⒲www.shadyrest.co.nz. Lovely, central B&B in a historic former doctor's house. With comfortable, wood-panelled rooms that are either en suite or with private bathroom. A generous breakfast, solar-heated outdoor bath and a lovely garden that runs down to a peaceful creek make this a treat. ❻/❼

Around Takaka

Adrift Tukurua Rd, 17km north of Takaka ℡03/525 8353, ⒲www.adrift.co.nz. Five gorgeous s/c cottages (and one studio) decorated in chic, modern style and all with direct access across lawns to the beach. All rooms have a sea view, making them perfect for a leisurely breakfast in bed. With double spa baths, free use of kayaks and a small penguin colony on site you may never want to leave. Studio ❼, cottages ❾

Golden Bay Hideaway 220 Mc Share Rd, Wainui Bay 23km east ☎ 03/525 7184, ⓦ www.golden-bayhideaway.co.nz. Wonderful spot, close to the northern end of the Abel Tasman Coast Track, comprising an eco-efficient house sleeping two, known as "Little Greenie", and a beautifully crafted house truck. Great views, an outdoor bath and cook-your-own-dinner/breakfast supplies complete the package. Truck ⑤, house ⑦

The Nook 678 Abel Tasman Drive, Pohara, 9km east ☎ 03/525 8501, ⓦ www.thenookguesthouse .co.nz. A relaxed eco-backpackers in a lovely wood-floored house where TV and internet are intentionally absent. Apart from the comfy dorms and doubles there's a fairly luxurious, straw-and-plaster cottage, rented as a s/c unit or two doubles. Free pick-up from Takaka by arrangement, bikes and a kayak are available. Camping $15, dorms $28, doubles ②, house truck ④, cottage for up to four ⑥

Pohara Beach Top 10 Holiday Park 809 Abel Tasman Drive ☎ 0800/764272, ⓦ www .poharabeach.com. A popular, well-equipped, beachfront holiday park with a broad range of accommodation. Camping $18, cabins ②, en-suite cabins ③, motels ⑤

🏃 **Sans Souci Inn** Richmond Rd, Pohara Beach, 10km east ☎ 03/525 8663, ⓦ www.sanssouciinn.co.nz. Endearing Swiss-run inn with a communal feel, in a mud-brick building with sod roof and handmade floor tiles. The six rooms share one large bathroom with shower stalls, bath and composting toilets, though there's also a s/c cottage sleeping four and an excellent restaurant (see p.470). Guests can use the kitchen or go for the delicious breakfasts ($9–15). Closed July to mid-Sept. Rooms ④, cottage ⑥

🏃 **Shambhala** SH60, 16km north at Onekaka ☎ 03/525 8463, ⓦ www.shambhala.co.nz. Welcoming shoes-off backpackers with a slightly spiritual bent, including yoga classes, located 2km down a track almost opposite the *Mussel Inn* (see opposite), from where free pick-up can be arranged. Dorms are in the main house, or there are spacious twins and doubles with lovely sea views in a separate block, with solar-heated showers and composting toilets. Lovely wild gardens and beach access. Closed June–Oct. Camping and campervans $18, dorms $28, rooms ②

Totaranui Campground (see p.463). Large and popular beachside campsite within Abel Tasman NP, 26km east of Takaka. $12.

Waitapu Bridge Pleasant riverside freedom camping site with toilets and river water 4km north of Takaka on SH60. For s/c campervans only. Maximum two nights. Free.

The town and around

Most of the action in Takaka takes place along Commercial Street (SH60 as it passes through town), where you can quickly get a handle on the spirit of the place by visiting Golden Bay Organics, at no. 47, and the Monza Gallery, at no. 25. Next, head along to the **Golden Bay Museum** (Oct–March daily 10am–4pm; April–Sept Mon–Fri 10am–4pm; free), with its detailed diorama depicting Abel Tasman's ill-fated trip to Wainui Bay in 1642, and coverage of local Maori and logging history.

The one essential site is **Te Waikoropupu Springs**, 4km north off SH60 (unrestricted access), the largest in New Zealand, set amid old gold workings and regenerating forest. Vast quantities of fresh water well up through at least sixteen crystal-clear vents, one creating Dancing Sands (where the sands, pushed by the surging water, appear to perform a jig). The colourful aquatic plant life can be seen by means of a large reverse periscope on one of the boardwalks.

Along the Anatoki

Even if you don't have kids, consider following the families flocking to the banks of the Anatoki River, 6km southeast of Takaka, specifically to **Bencarri**, McCallun Road (late Sept to April daily 10am–5pm; $12), a pretty petting farm where you can feed llamas, donkeys, emus, piglets, rabbits and more. The star attractions are the Anatoki eels who live wild in the river but have been fed here since 1914. Put some meat (provided) on a stick and the thick black eels will rise half out of the water in a desperate grab for a free lunch.

Next door, you can catch your own hatchery-raised fish at **Anatoki Salmon** (daily 9am–4.30pm; free). They'll provide you with tackle and you only pay for what you catch ($19 per kg of live fish). They'll even smoke or barbecue your catch and you can eat it overlooking the ponds.

Abel Tasman Drive

East of Takaka, **Abel Tasman Drive** threads its way past the small waterside settlement of Pohara then splits into three, each road ending at a trailhead for the Abel Tasman Coast Track: Awaroa, Totaranui and Wainui Bay – see map on p.459.

Just off Abel Tasman Drive, a poorly signed track leads to **Rawhiti Cave** (1hr 20min–2hr return; instruction sheet available from the Takaka i-SITE), its cavernous mouth hung with myriad pendulous stalactites, transparent stone straws and a discarded billy now encrusted in rock deposited from the dripping ceiling.

Seven kilometres from Takaka, follow signs to the wonderful **Grove Scenic Reserve** (unrestricted access), a mystical place that could have been transplanted straight from Arthurian legend. Massive rata trees sprout from odd and deformed limestone outcrops, and a ten-minute walk takes you to a narrow slot between two enormous vertical cliffs where a lookout reveals expansive views of the coast and beaches around Pohara.

Pohara, 10km east of Takaka, has a couple of places to stay (see p.468) and eat (see p.470) and a relaxing sandy beach but otherwise you'll want to press on past the jarring site of a former cement factory, and pretty **Tata Beach** to a trailhead for **Wainui Falls** (40min return), where Nikau palms shade the banks of the river, and a curtain of spray swathes the rather lovely falls.

The Wainui Bay road (now gravel) runs past the **Tui Community** (one of the last of several started in Golden Bay in the 1970s), and ends at the northernmost access point to the Coast Track. Other roads go to a car park at Awaroa Estuary, and the wonderful golden arc of **Totaranui Beach**. This is a common place to finish the Coast Track, right by the *Totaranui Campground* (see p.463).

Eating and entertainment

Takaka's Commercial Street has some good places to **eat**, and there are more a few kilometres out that just about justify the journey. **Drinking** and music tend to be confined to the big old hotels/pubs, the *Wholemeal Café* or *Mussel Inn* some way out of town. **Movies** are shown at the atmospheric **Village Theatre**, 32 Commercial St (T03/525 8453), where the seating includes couches and beanbags and there are cups of tea to sip during the films.

Takaka

The Brigand 90 Commercial St T03/525 9636. Relaxed restaurant and bar with lots of outdoor seating and live music several nights a week. Mains around $25.

Dangerous Kitchen 46a Commercial St (T03/525 8686 for takeaway orders). This peculiarly named café spilling out onto the pavement specializes in exotic pizzas, tasty pies, wraps and salads. Try the seafood pizza with mussels, squid and prawns. Closed Sun, Aug & Sept.

Roots Bar 1 Commercial St. Hang out around the open fire tucking into lovingly prepared Kiwi-style tapas and sipping Nelson-brewed Sprig and Fern beers and ciders as reggae, roots or drum 'n' bass music floats by. Often DJs and bands at the weekend until late. Closed Mon.

Wholemeal Café 60 Commercial St. A Takaka institution that's endearingly sloppy at times, but it's good value and makes a decent spot to hang out over a coffee and cake. Return for pizza, colourful and healthy salads, assorted fish, meat and veggie dishes ($16–25) in the cavernous interior or on the back deck. Daily until 7pm, and later in summer.

Around Takaka

Mussel Inn SH60, 18km north of Takaka. Do not miss this place – whether you want to eat, enjoy wine or ale (they brew their own, including the manuka-infused "Captain Cooker"), sit and read, play chess or soak up the lively atmosphere of a live band. The wooden building is adorned with local art and some clumpy but comfortable wooden furniture. You can always get a simple, fresh and wholesome meal; try a plate of the local mussels for around $16. Open daily, 11am until late. Closed Aug & Sept.

Penguin Café 818 Abel Tasman Drive, Pohara. Spacious modern, café/restaurant and bar that's worth the drive out from Takaka if only to sip a beer or coffee on the roadside deck which catches the sun most of the day. Well-presented

dishes might include Anatoki salmon, seafood pizza and home-made ice cream. Most mains $24–36.

Sans Souci Inn See p.468. This simple licensed restaurant has a daily set menu that can include hot smoked fish or beef fillet or a veggie option (all $31–33). There's also a choice of sumptuous freshly made desserts. Booking essential.

The road to Collingwood: arts and crafts

Many of the region's best **artists and craftspeople** live and work between Takaka and Collingwood, so the winding roads offer endless opportunities for mooching around country galleries armed with the free, widely available *Artists in Golden Bay* leaflet.

Two of the best are: Onekaka Arts, 13km north (☏03/525 7366, ⓦwww .onekaarts.co.nz), with hand-crafted silver jewellery by Peter Meares, and jade carved by Geoff Williams, and Estuary Arts (☏03/524 8466, ⓦwww.estuaryarts .co.nz), 9km further north, where Rosie Little and Bruce Hamlin produce brightly coloured and Pacific-influenced tableware and handmade low-relief art tiles, plus Rosie's evocative, almost organic, landscapes.

Collingwood and around

Golden Bay's northernmost settlement of any consequence is laidback **COLLING-WOOD**, just a store, a couple of cafés, a pub and a few places to stay that make it a useful base for tours to **Farewell Spit** (see opposite). The town occupies a thread of land wedged between the sea and Ruataniwha Inlet, a location which was briefly championed in the 1850s as the site for the nation's new capital; street plans were drawn up but as the gold petered out, so did the enthusiasm. The details are spelled out in the diminutive **Collingwood Museum** (daily 9am–6pm; donation).

The Aorere Valley runs southwest of Collingwood towards the start of the Heaphy Track. Call briefly at the **Devil's Boots**, 7km southwest, bulbous limestone overhangs that look like two feet protruding from the ground, with trees and shrubs sprouting from their soles.

Some 4km on, follow signs to ⚶ *The Naked Possum*, a great daytime café set on the edge of the bush with stacks of outside seating, some under cover around a roaring fire (always lit). High-quality café food is supplemented by wild bush tucker that forms part of the owners' ethic to reduce introduced pests in the local forest and allow the rata trees to regenerate. Try a tahr burger or a venison, mushroom and red wine pie washed down with a handle of their exclusive Stunned Possum, a rata honey beer brewed at the *Mussel Inn* (see p.469). The wild berry tart is also famed, and check out the cushions made from local possum skins naturally tanned in a bark extract. The café marks the start of the lovely **Kaituna Track** (2hr return) a bush-walk past old gold workings to the river confluence at Kaituna Forks.

It is a further 7km to Bainham and the wonderful **Langford's Store** (Tues–Sun 9am–6pm), a combined general store and post office built in 1928 by ancestors of the current owners and seemingly changed little since. Wooden shelves are stacked with goods, you can still get an assorted bag of sweets and the hand-cranked Burroughs adding machine is used to tally up your bill. Be sure to stop for coffee and cake.

Practicalities

There are a few **places to stay** in town, all within a couple of minutes' stroll of the centre. Try the *Collingwood Motor Camp* on William Street (☏03/524 8149; camping $15, cabins ❶, s/c units ❸), *Somerset House*, Gibbs Road (☏03/524 8624,

Farewell Spit tours

Two companies make an excellent job of running trips to the end of Farewell Spit (some 22km north of Collingwood). Operating since 1946, **Farewell Spit Eco Tours**, based on Tasman Street in Collingwood (℡0800/808 257, @www.farewellspit.com), run the **Farewell Spit Eco Tour** (6hr 30min; $120) which heads out along the sands of the spit to its historic lighthouse in a purpose-built 4x4. The trip comes with a bright commentary, peppered with local lore. During the day you'll see vast numbers of birds, seals and fossils, climb an enormous sand dune and maybe see the skeletons of wrecked ships if the sands reveal them.

The more eco-oriented **Gannet Colony Tour** (6hr 30min; $135), includes most of the above plus a twenty-minute walk to the massive gannet colony towards the very end of the spit. Trips operate year-round with departure times dependent on tides: check the website. On both trips lunch ($10) is optional.

Equally professional and fun trips are run by **Farewell Spit Nature Experience** (℡0800/250 500, @www.farewell-spit.co.nz) which operates from the Old School at Pakawau, 15km north of Collingwood. Its tours ($90/4hr, $110/6hr) take a strong ecology and birding angle.

@www.backpackerscollingwood.co.nz; dorms $29, rooms ❷), a low-key backpackers with estuary views, free breakfast and cheap bikes, or *Beachcomber Motels*, Tasman Street (℡0800/270 520; ❹), which back onto the river estuary.

Collingwood has a decent cheap **café**, a pub selling bar **meals** and the *Courthouse Café* (℡03/524 8025) where fine coffee, rich cakes and imaginative mains using mainly organic and local produce (around $25) are served in the atmospheric 1901 courthouse.

North to Farewell Spit

North of Collingwood the road skirts Ruataniwha Inlet, and after 10km, passes *The Innlet* (℡03/524 8040, @www.goldenbayindex.co.nz; camping $21, dorms $29, rooms ❷, s/c cottages ❸, studio apartment ❹), an excellent **hostel** with some delightful cottages plus a BBQ area and several heated outdoor baths in the bush. Ride the free bikes, rent kayaks ($35/day), hike the bush track or simply relax in the garden. The road now follows the coast 11km to **Puponga**, at the northern tip of the South Island, where you can stay at *Farewell Gardens Motor Camp* (℡03/524 8445, @www .farewellgrdens.co.nz; camping $14, cabin ❷, apartment ❺). Around 2km on, the daytime *Paddle Crab Kitchen* café acts as the **visitor centre** for the adjacent Puponga Farm Park, a coastal sheep farm open to the public. There are great views right along **Farewell Spit** – named by Captain Cook at the end of a visit in 1770 – which stretches 25km east, often heaped with tree trunks washed up from the West Coast. The whole vast sand bank is a **nature reserve** of international importance, with salt marshes, open mud flats, brackish lakes and bare dunes providing habitats for over a hundred **bird species**: bartailed godwit, wrybill, long-billed curlew and Mongolian dotterel all come to escape the Arctic winter, and there are breeding colonies of Caspian terns, and large numbers of black swans. Sadly, the unusual shape of the coastline seems to fool whales' navigation systems and beachings are common.

Short **walks** head to the outer beach (2.5km) and the inner beach (4km); both provide good views of the spit which is otherwise off-limits except on guided tours from Collingwood (see opposite).

Away from the spit, walks head through the farm park to **Cape Farewell** (the northernmost point on the South Island), to the strikingly set **Pillar Point Lighthouse**, and to the wave-lashed **Wharariki Beach**. Here, rock bridges and towering arches are stranded just offshore, while deep dunes have blocked river-mouths, forming briny lakes and islands where fur seals and birds have made a home. Visit within a couple of hours of low tide when you can access some sea caves where the seals hang out.

Nearby, the well-signposted Cape Farewell Horse Treks (℡03/524 8031, ⓦwww.horsetreksnz.com) offer some of the most visually spectacular **horse-riding** in the South Island. Trips don't actually go onto Farewell Spit, but visit Pillar Point (90min; $55), Puponga Beach (90min; $60) and Wharariki Beach (3hr; $105).

Kahurangi National Park: the Heaphy Track

The huge expanse of **Kahurangi National Park** encompasses 40,000 square kilometres of the northwestern South Island between the wet and exposed western side of the Wakamarama Range and the limestone peaks of Mount Owen and Mount Arthur. Over half of New Zealand's native **plant species** are represented in the park, as are most of its alpine species, while the remote interior is a haven for birds and **animals**, including rare carnivorous snails and giant cave spiders.

A remote and beautiful place with relatively few visitors, the park's extraordinary landscapes are best seen by walking the **Heaphy Track** (78km; 4–5 days) which links Golden Bay with Kohaihai Bluff on the West Coast. One of New Zealand's Great Walks, it is appreciably tougher than the nearby Abel Tasman Coast Track, though it compensates with its beauty and the diversity of its landscapes – turbulent rivers, broad tussock downs and forests, and nikau palm groves at the western end. The track is named after Charles Heaphy who, with Thomas Brunner, became the first Europeans to walk the West Coast section of the route in 1846, accompanied by their Maori guide Kehu. Maori had long traversed the area heading down to central Westland in search of *pounamu* for weapons, ornaments and tools.

Information, accommodation and guided walks

Download DOC's *Heaphy Track* **brochure**, or buy one at a visitor centre. It includes a schematic map that is satisfactory for hiking, though it is helpful to carry the detailed 1:150,000 *Kahurangi Park* map ($19). Along the route, there are seven **huts** that must be booked and paid for all year round (Oct–April $25; May–Sept $15), with heating, water and toilets (mostly flush): all except Brown and Gouland Downs have cooking stoves, but you need to carry your own pots and pans. There are also nine designated **campsites**, which again must be booked (Oct–April $12, May–Sept $8), mostly close to huts (though you can't use hut facilities). Before setting off, you must book online (ⓦwww.doc.govt.nz) and there is a two-night limit in each hut or campsite. Take all provisions with you, and go prepared for sudden changes of weather and a hail of sandflies.

Guided walks along the track (and elsewhere in the park) are handled admirably by the ecologically caring Bush and Beyond Guided Walks (℡03/528 9054, ⓦwww.naturetreks.co.nz) who run five-day trips ($1395).

Trailhead transport

The Heaphy Track is particularly awkward in one respect: the western end is over 400km by road from the eastern end, so if you leave gear at one end, you'll have to re-walk the track, undertake a long bus journey, or fly back to your base at Nelson, Motueka or Takaka.

The Heaphy starts at **Brown Hut**, 28km southwest of Collingwood. Golden Bay Coachlines run there from Nelson (departing 6.45am; $52), Motueka (8am; $43), Takaka (9.15am; $28) and Collingwood (9.35am; $24).

At the West Coast end of the track you'll arrive at Kohaihai shelter, 10km north of Karamea. Even with the best connections you'll need to spend nights in both Karamea and Nelson before returning to Takaka. A better solution is to base yourself in Nelson and use Trek Express (℡0800/128 735, ⓦwww .trekexpress.co.nz), who will run you direct from Nelson to Brown Hut then, several days later, pick up at Kohaihai Shelter and run you back to Nelson that evening, all for $100. Another option is Takaka-based Derry (℡03/525 9576, ⓦwww.heaphytrackhelp.co.nz) who will deliver your car to Karamea for $290 plus fuel costs. He then walks the track (very quickly) and meets you partway to give you the keys.

Flying also gives you the chance to return to your car the same day you finish the track. Remote Adventures (℡0800/150 338, ⓦwww.remoteadventures .co.nz) pick up in Karamea and fly to Takaka for $175 a head.

Track transport only runs from late October to mid-April: in **winter** months *everything* becomes more difficult, requiring taxis to reach trailheads.

The route

Ninety percent of hikers walk the Heaphy Track from east to west, thereby getting the tough initial climb over with and taking it relatively easy on subsequent days.

Brown Hut to Perry Saddle Hut (17km; 5hr; 800m ascent). A steady climb all the way along an old coach road passing the Aorere campsite and shelter, and Flanagans Corner viewpoint – at 915m, the highest point on the track.

Perry Saddle Hut to Gouland Downs Hut (7km; 2hr; 200m ascent). It's a very easy walk across Perry Saddle through tussock clearings and down into a valley (passing the famed pole strung with used tramping boots) before crossing limestone arches to the hut. This is a great little eight-bunk hut (no cooking facilities) where you might hear kiwi at night.

Gouland Downs Hut to Saxon Hut (5km; 1hr 30min; 200m descent). Crossing Gouland Downs, an undulating area of flax and tussock.

Saxon Hut to James Mackay Hut (12km; 3hr; 400m ascent). Cross grassy flatlands, winding in and out of small tannin-stained streams as they tip over into the Heaphy River below.

James Mackay Hut to Lewis Hut (12.5km; 3–4hr; 700m descent). If you have the energy it is worth pressing on to a haven of nikau palms – and less welcome sandflies.

Lewis Hut to Heaphy Hut (8km; 2–3hr; 100m ascent). It is possible to get from Lewis Hut to the track end in a day but it is more enjoyable to take your time and stop at the Heaphy Hut, near where you can explore the exciting Heaphy rivermouth: its narrow outlet funnels river water into a torrid sea, resulting in a maelstrom of sea and fresh water.

Heaphy Hut to Kohaihai (16km; 5hr; 100m ascent). This final stretch is a gentle walk through forest down the coast until you reach Crayfish Point, where the route briefly follows the beach. Avoid this section within an hour of high tide, longer if it is stormy. Once you reach Scott's Beach, you have only to climb over Kohaihai Bluff to find the Kohaihai Shelter car park on the other side – and hopefully your pre-arranged pick-up from Karamea.

Nelson Lakes National Park and around

Two glacial lakes characterize the **Nelson Lakes National Park**, around 120km southwest of Nelson, **Rotoiti** ("little lake") and **Rotoroa** ("long lake") nestled in the mountains at the northernmost limit of the Southern Alps. Both are surrounded by tranquil mountains and shrouded in dark beech forest, and jointly form the headwaters of the Buller River. **Tramping** (see box, p.475) is

▲ Lake Rotoiti, Nelson Lakes National Park

undoubtedly the main event and you could easily devote a week to some of the longer circuits, though short lakeside walks reward a briefer visit.

Anglers, kayakers and yachties mostly base themselves in tiny **St Arnaud**, draped around the northern shores of Lake Rotoiti 100km west of Blenheim.

The park's subalpine rivers, lakes, forests and hills are full of birdlife, but it has offered little solace to humans: Maori passed through the area and caught eels in the lakes, but the best efforts of European settlers and gold prospectors yielded meagre returns. Now, recreation is all.

St Arnaud

ST ARNAUD (pronounced Snt-AR-nard) is a speck of a place scattered around the north shore of Lake Rotoiti, with around a hundred residents but over four hundred houses, mostly used by holidaying Kiwis. The DOC **visitor centre**, View Road (daily 8.30am–4.30pm extended to 5 or 6pm in summer; ☎03/521 1806), has all the hiking, biking, fishing and ecology information you could need as well as local accommodation and transport listings.

Rotoiti **Water Taxis** operate on Lake Rotoiti from St Arnaud to the head of the lake, ($75 for up to 3 people, then $25/person; ☎03/521 1894, ⊛www.rotoiti watertaxis.co.nz), so if you fancy sections of hiking at the southern end of the lake there's no need to walk the whole way. Alternatively, you can pay them to take you on a scenic cruise around the lake, or they'll rent **kayaks** ($40/half-day, $60/day), rowboats and canoes ($60/half-day, $80/day).

Practicalities

Access to the region is with Nelson Lakes Shuttles (☎03/521 1900, ⊛www .nelsonlakesshuttles.co.nz) who offer an on-demand **bus** service Nelson ($30/ person, minimum $90) and also connect St Arnaud with the Mount Robert car park ($10/person, minimum $30) and Lake Rotoroa ($25/person, minimum $70).

The hub of St Arnaud is the **St Arnaud Village Alpine Store** (generally daily 7.30am–7.30pm) which sells groceries, petrol and fish and chips. Opposite, *Alpine Lodge* (☎03/521 1869, ⊛www.alpinelodge.co.nz; dorms $25, budget rooms ❷, hotel rooms ⑤) has a range of **accommodation** in modern wooden buildings plus a licensed restaurant, bar and spa pool.

About 150m up the street is the pick of the local places to stay, the combined *Nelson Lakes Motels* and *Travers-Sabine Lodge* (℡03/521 1887, ⓦwww.nelsonlakes .co.nz; dorms $26, rooms ❶, s/c units ❹): the former is a mid-sized, neat hostel with some doubles, twins and shared rooms, kitchen, TV and a wealth of information; the latter a cluster of comfortable, fully self-contained log-built chalets next door. Both have access to a hot tub ($7). Comfy B&B accommodation is available amid beech forest and rhododendrons at *Avarest*, 1 Kerr Bay Rd (℡03/521 1864, ⓦwww.avarestbnb.co.nz; ❼).

Nelson Lakes hikes

With 270km of track served by twenty huts there is no shortage of walking options. For day-walks, arm yourself with DOC's *Walks In Nelson Lakes National Park* booklet. The two multi-day tramps have their own leaflets supplemented by the 1:100,000 *Nelson Lakes National Park* map ($19). These are alpine tracks so you must be equipped with good boots, and warm, waterproof clothing – it can snow in almost any month up here – and crampons are likely to be needed from April to November. Both tracks start from the upper Mount Robert car park, 7km by road from St Arnaud.

The following hikes are listed in approximate order of difficulty.

Bellbird Walk Kerr Bay, St Arnaud (10–15min loop; flat). Easy meander through beech forest alive with the sound of tui, bellbirds and fantails thanks to the Rotoiti Nature Recovery Project, an attempt to replicate the successful offshore island pest clearances by concerted trapping and poisoning. Several of these "mainland islands" have been set up across New Zealand since the late 1990s with considerable success. Visit in the early evening when the birds (even reintroduced Great Spotted kiwi) are particularly noisy and frisky.

Honeydew Walk Kerr Bay, St Arnaud (30–45min loop; flat). An extension of the Bellbird Walk, named for the sweet excretions of the scale insect that burrows into the bark of the beech trees, its produce attracting the nectar-loving tui and bellbirds.

Whisky Falls Mount Robert trailhead (10km; 3–5hr return; 100m ascent). From a parking area on the Mount Robert Road, follow the Lakeside Trail to these 40m falls. Often shrouded in mist and fringed by hanging ferns, the falls are particularly grand after heavy rain.

Mount Robert Circuit (9km; 3–4hr loop; 600m ascent). An excellent loop around the visible face of Mount Robert starting at the Mount Robert car park, ascending the steep Pinchgut Track to the edge of the bush then traversing across to Bushline Hut ($15) before zigzagging down Paddy's Track to the start.

Angelus Hut Loop Mount Robert trailhead (28km; 2-day loop; 1000m ascent). One of the most popular overnighters, this loop follows the exposed Robert Ridge to the beautiful Angelus Basin with its shiny new hut (Oct–April bookings required $20, camping $10; May–Sept $15) and alpine tarn. Two common routes complete the loop: the steep Cascade Track and the Speargrass Track, a bad-weather escape route.

Travers-Sabine Circuit (80km; 4–7 days; 1200m ascent). This major tramp is the scenic equal of several of the Great Walks, but without that status it is far less crowded. The track probes deep into remote areas of lakes, fields of tussock, 2000m mountains and the 1780m Travers Saddle. At the height of summer, the track verges are briefly emblazoned with yellow buttercups, white daisies, sundew and harebells. The circuit requires a good level of fitness, but is fairly easy to follow with bridges over most streams. There are six huts along the track ($15; tickets from DOC) and camping is allowed – but fires aren't, so carry a stove and fuel.

A very appealing alternative is ✗ *Top House*, Tophouse Road, 8km northeast of St Arnaud (☎0800/544 545, ⊛www.tophouse.co.nz; rooms & cabins ❺) an 1887 former drovers' inn and stagecoach stop. Sitting by the fire in this earth-built hotel decorated with Victorian furniture, it can feel like you're in rural Wales. Come for a Devonshire tea, lunch on the likes of wild venison and plum pie and chips ($15) or a set evening meal ($40) and don't miss the country's smallest pub – six is a crowd – with excellent local beers. Accommodation is either in shared-bathroom inn rooms or outside in fairly modern motel-style cabins.

Finally, there are two DOC **campsites** (☎03/521 1806), both close to town overlooking the lake: *Kerr Bay* ($10–12; open all year) with pay showers, cooking facilities and a BBQ area; and the basic *West Bay* ($7–8; closed April–Nov).

The best eating is at the welcoming *Alpine Lodge Café* next door to the *Alpine Lodge*, which provides strong coffee, home-made cakes, all-day snacks and summertime dinners.

Lake Rotoroa

Pretty **Lake Rotoroa** feels a good deal more remote than the area around St Arnaud. Approached along the Gowan Valley Road which veers off SH6 some 20km northwest of St Arnaud, it ends near a self-registration DOC **campsite** (non-powered sites only $4; no showers) from where there are a few short walks. Lake Rotoroa Water Taxis ply the length of the lake ($45/person, minimum $135; ☎03/523 9199) to Sabine Hut on the Travers–Sabine Circuit (see p.475).

Murchison and around

MURCHISON, 125km southwest of Nelson and 60km west of St Arnaud is a small, former gold town now favoured by hunting and fishing types as well as rafters and river kayakers. Numerous rivers feed the Buller nearby providing excellent white water and plenty of opportunities for bagging trout.

Everything of note is on SH6 (Waller St in Murchison), or Fairfax Street that crosses it. There is no useful **bank or ATM**, but there is a **visitor centre**, 47 Waller St (Dec–April daily 10am–6pm; May–Sept Mon–Fri 10am–4pm; Oct & Nov Mon–Sat 10am–5pm, Sun 10am–4pm; ☎03/523 9350).

Tales of the gold days fill the **Murchison Museum**, 60 Fairfax St (daily 10am–4pm; donation requested), in the 1911 former post office with newspaper clippings, photographs and various oddities including gold-rush-era Chinese pottery and opium bottles.

Murchison is one of the few places in the country with public **gold panning**: pick up a pan ($10) and the *Recreational Gold Panning* leaflet from the visitor centre which lists places to try your hand. The visitor centre also stocks DOC's *Murchison Day Walks* leaflet featuring the **Skyline Walk** (3km return; 1hr 30min) which climbs through the native forest to the skyline ridge above Murchison with views of the confluence of the Buller, Matakitaki, Maruia and Matiri rivers. The track starts from the junction of SH6 and Matakitaki West Bank Road.

Once clear of Murchison, SH6 romps alongside the Buller River through the Buller Gorge to the **West Coast** town of Westport, a route covered in Chapter 12 (see p.623).

Rafting and river kayaking

There are fun **rafting** and inflatable **kayak** trips on the Buller, Mokihinui and Karamea with breathtaking scenery and swift water. During the season (early

Sept to late May) **Ultimate Descents**, 51 Fairfax St (☏0800/748 377, ⓦwww
.rivers.co.nz), regularly run the Buller (Gd III–IV; 4hr 30min; $120), spending at
least two hours on the water and including snacks and a post-trip hot tub. There
are also gentler family rafting trips (Gd II; 4hr 30min; $105), and combo trips (Gd
II–IV; 8.5hr; $220) rafting the tougher bits then kayaking down some easier
sections. Check the website for helicopter-access and multi-day trips on fabulous
West Coast rivers.

White Water Action, SH6, behind the visitor centre (☏0800/100 582, ⓦwww
.whitewateraction.co.nz), combines with Buller Adventure Tours (see p.631) for
the lively "Earthquake Slip" run down the Buller ($120).

Those keen to learn **whitewater kayaking** or brush up some skills should visit
the internationally respected New Zealand Kayak School, 111 Waller St (Oct–
April; ☏03/523 9611, ⓦwww.nzkayakschool.com); four-day intensive courses
go for $795 and include lodging at the school's hostel.

Accommodation and eating

The range of **accommodation** is adequate, and you can **eat** well at either the
relaxed *Rivers Café*, 51 Fairfax St, with good coffee and substantial main meals on
summer evenings, or the *Commercial Hotel*, 37 Fairfax St, a fairly standard Kiwi
pub with a straightforward drinkers' bar and a separate restaurant/café with
reliable bar meals.

Kiwi Park 170 Fairfax St, 1km south of the town
centre ☏03/523 9248, ⓦwww.kiwipark.co.nz.
Family holiday park with all the amenities, a small
petting zoo and a full range of accommodation.
Camping $13, cabins ❶, motel units ❸, luxury
cottages ❻

Lazy Cow 37 Waller St ☏03/523 9451,
ⓔlazycow@xnet.co.nz. Small, low-key hostel
in the centre of town with a convivial
atmosphere, nightly meals ($10–12), fresh
eggs and a large spa bath. Dorm $28, rooms ❷,
en suite ❸

Mataki Motel 34 Hotham St, ☏0800/279 088,
ⓦwww.matakimotel.co.nz. Clean and quiet motel

clearly signposted about 1km from town. Some
units have a full kitchen. ❸

Murchison Lodge 15 Grey St ☏0800/523 9196,
ⓦwww.murchisonlodge.co.nz. Very comfortable
and convivial eco-conscious lodge with airy rooms,
welcome drinks and a barbecue breakfast
including eggs laid in the grounds where you'll also
find a few cows and pigs. Free wi-fi. Private
bathroom ❺, en suite ❻

Riverview Holiday Park SH6, 1.5km east
☏03/523 9591. Simple campsite by the gurgling
Buller River, much frequented by kayakers and
rafters. Camping $12, cabins ❶, tourist flat ❸,
motel unit ❹

Blenheim and the Marlborough wine country

In the early 1970s, **BLENHEIM**, 27km south of Picton, was a fairly sleepy service
town set amid pastoral land: now it is a fairly sleepy service town completely
surrounded by some of the most fecund and highly regarded vineyards in the land
– the **Marlborough wine country**. In the intervening years Marlborough
Sauvignon Blanc single-handedly put the New Zealand wine industry on the
world map, and made this the country's largest wine region with almost sixty
percent of the national grape crop.

Many wineries go all out to attract visitors using distinctive architecture, classy
restaurants, art and gourmet foodstuffs. The profusion of weekend visitors from
Nelson, Wellington and further afield has spawned a number of smart B&Bs
throughout the district, trying to out-luxury one another. If this is what you're

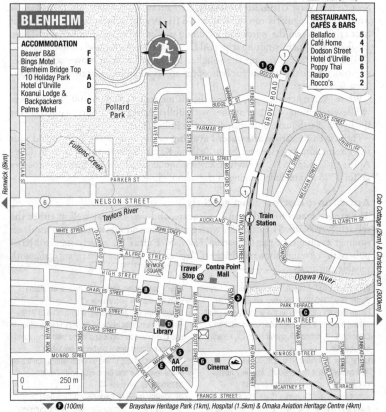

▲ Picton (27km)

BLENHEIM

N

ACCOMMODATION
Beaver B&B   F
Bings Motel   E
Blenheim Bridge Top
  10 Holiday Park   A
Hotel d'Urville   D
Koanui Lodge &
  Backpackers   C
Palms Motel   B

RESTAURANTS, CAFÉS & BARS
Bellafico   5
Café Home   4
Dodson Street   1
Hotel d'Urville   D
Poppy Thai   6
Raupo   3
Rocco's   2

◀ Renwick (8km)

Cob Cottage (2km) & Christchurch (300km) ▶

0   250 m

⑤(100m)

▼ Brayshaw Heritage Park (1km), Hospital (1.5km) & Omaka Aviation Heritage Centre (4km)

after there's little need to bother with Blenheim itself, particularly since most of the vineyards are closer to the small, unremarkable town of **Renwick**, 10km to the west.

Arrival, information and accommodation

Trains and long-distance **buses** all stop outside the **i-SITE** visitor centre, in the train station on Sinclair Street (Mon–Fri 8.30am–5pm, Sat & Sun 9am–3pm; ☏03/577 8080, Ⓦwww.destinationmarlborough.com), which stocks an assortment of **leaflets** including the *Marlborough Wine Trail* map, the *Art and Craft Trail* brochure (both free). The **airport** is 7km west of town: Marlborough Taxis (☏03/577 5511) charge $35 into town. There's bike rental at several hostels and Spokesman Cycle (see p.481). Internet is free at the library, 33 Arthur St (Mon–Fri 9am–6pm Sat10am–1pm, Sun 1.30–4.30pm) and cheap enough at the i-SITE or the Travel Stop Cyber Café, 17 Market St (Mon–Sat 10am–9pm, Sun 10am–4pm). All have wi-fi.

As befits a major wine region there's an abundance of high-priced luxury **accommodation** scattered around the district, plus more modest places in town. Budget places mostly cater to seasonal workers, though there are a couple of good hostels, particularly *Watson's Way* in Renwick.

During the first full week of February nearly all accommodation is booked far in advance for the **festival season** (see box, p.482), so either plan well ahead or steer clear of the region.

Blenheim

Beaver B&B 60 Beaver Rd ☎03/578 8401, ⓦwww.beaverhomestay.co.nz. Attractive s/c unit 10min walk from central Blenheim, with a continental breakfast supplied. ④

Bings Motel 29 Maxwell Rd ☎0800/666 999, ⓔemail@bingsmotel.co.nz. Classic older-style motel close to the centre of Blenheim with plenty of space and low rates. ③

Blenheim Bridge Top 10 Holiday Park 78 Grove Rd ☎0800/268 666, ⓦwww.blenheimtop10.co.nz. Sited a little too close to the main road and railway line but central and with all the expected facilities. Camping $32/site, cabins ②, kitchen cabins ③, s/c units ④

Hotel d'Urville 52 Queen St ☎03/577 9945, ⓦdurville.com. This former bank right in the centre of town has been turned into a chic and stylish small hotel with restaurant and cocktail bar. The best, and some say the only, place to stay in town and a good place to eat and party. Rates include continental breakfast. ⑦

Koanui Lodge & Backpackers 33 Main St ☎03/578 7487, ⓦwww.koanui.co.nz. The pick of Blenheim's fairly poor crop of hostels; modern with a well-equipped kitchen and BBQ area, plus doubles, some en suite with TV. Dorms $24, rooms ①/③

Palms Motel 68 Charles St ☎0800/256 725, ⓦwww.blenheimpalmsmotel.co.nz. Nicely decorated central motel, with Sky TV and a range of individually styled units, some with spa bath. Cooked breakfast available. ⑤

The wine region

🏃 **Cranbrook Cottage** 145 Giffords Rd, about 9km northwest of town ☎03/572 8606, ⓦwww.cranbrook.co.nz. Romantic, picture-book 1860s cottage sleeping four, set in a tree-filled paddock amid the vines. The place is s/c and breakfast (delivered to your door in a basket) is to die for. ⑦

Dry Olive Homestay 15 Dry Hills Rise ☎03/577 8648, ⓦwww.dryolivehomestay.com. Purpose-built B&B peacefully set among young olive trees, some 3km south of central Blenheim. The two bedrooms share a bathroom and living area with kitchenette and there's a separate three-bedroom family-friendly cottage. ⑦

Olde Millhouse 9 Wilson St, Renwick ☎0800/653 262, ⓦwww.oldemillhouse.co.nz. Lovely three-room B&B set among cottage gardens where a continental breakfast can be served. There is bike rental (also to non-guests), a spa pool and free bus transfers. ⑤

🏃 **St Leonard's Vineyard Cottages** 18 St Leonard's Rd ☎03/577 8328, ⓦwww .stleonards.co.nz. A broad range of former farm buildings beautifully converted into rustically luxurious s/c quarters, with access to a lovely solar-heated pool, free bikes, barbecue areas and gorgeous grounds amid the vines. Choose from The Old Dairy (④; max 2), Shearers Quarters (⑤; max 3), the Stables (⑥; max 2), the Cottage (⑦; max 3) and the Woolshed (⑧; max 5), which comes with an outdoor bath. Breakfast ingredients are supplied, often with home-laid eggs. ④–⑧

Uno Più 75 Murphys Rd ☎03/578 2235, ⓦwww .unopiu.co.nz. Run by friendly, former Italian restaurant-owner, Gino, who makes this homestay magical. It's hard to imagine being looked after any better, either in the 1917 homestead ($430) or out in the modern mud-brick self-catering cottage ($470). Breakfasts are great and excellent dinners ($80) are available by arrangement. Book in advance. ⑨

Watson's Way Backpackers 56 High St, Renwick ☎03/572 8228, ⓦwww.watsonswaybackpackers .co.nz. Easily Marlborough's best hostel: a very comfortable spot in the shade of large trees in a wonderful garden, with a public tennis court over the fence, snug rooms, made-up doubles, easy access to the wineries, low-cost bikes, an outdoor bath, BBQ and owners who can't do enough for you. Closed Sept. Tents $15, dorms $28, rooms ①, en suites ②

The Town

With the exception of the wineries, Blenheim is light on sights. Easily the most diverting is the **Omaka Aviation Heritage Centre**, 79 Aerodrome Rd (daily 10am–4pm; $20; ⓦwww.omaka.org.nz), located beside an airfield 4km southwest of Blenheim. Two large hangars contain twenty-one World War I planes, some original and still airworthy, others authentic replicas, and many set in amazingly realistic dioramas made by film-maker Peter Jackson's Weta Workshop. Indeed,

Jackson, who is a huge World War I buff, owns much of the collection and chairs the trust which set the place up and will guide its growth over the next few years. The planes are fine examples of their kind and some, such as the German Halberstadt D.IV and the American Airco DHS, are unique. Check out the crash-landing scene depicting the death of Manfred von Richthofen complete with an original fabric cross from the plane, and a group of Australian soldiers souveniring his boots. A collection of the Red Baron's own memorabilia is displayed nearby. Elsewhere there's the flight suit of US ace Eddie Rickenbacker and a mass of models, badges and love letters – the collection of an obsessive. Everything is made more poignant when you chat to the guides and interpreters, who are themselves mostly former aviators.

Other sights are minor, including **Brayshaw Heritage Park**, off New Renwick Road, 2.5km south of the town centre, a reconstruction of an early settlers' community and a collection of vintage farm machinery and vehicles. The best bit is the **Marlborough Museum** (daily 10am–4pm; $10) which has a small Maori collection and a interesting wine exhibit, covering the region's wine heritage, *terroir*, technology and how pruning techniques have been adapted to match the local conditions. The tiny 1860s **Cob Cottage**, on SH1, 3km southeast of town (daily 10am–4pm; donations requested) has been restored to house displays on the lives of early settlers.

Wine country

The gravel plains that flank the Wairau River around the towns of Blenheim and Renwick make up some of New Zealand's most prized **wine country**. The region, sheltered by the protective hills of the Richmond Range, basks in around 2400 hours of sunshine a year making it perfect for ripening the grapes for its esteemed Sauvignon Blanc. Chardonnay and Pinot Noir grapes also grow well (almost guaranteeing tasty bubbly), and the region is gaining a reputation for its light and golden olive oil.

Almost fifty wineries have cellar-door **tastings** (either free or for a small charge, which is often deducted from any subsequent purchases). Some add a short tour, tack on a restaurant or even link up with outlets hawking olive oil, fruit preserves and the like. Most of the notable wineries are around Renwick or immediately north along Raupara Road, all listed on the free *Marlborough Wine Trail* sheet (along with their opening hours and facilities), and most also feature on the more detailed *Marlborough Wineries & Wines* fold-out map ($2). **Opening hours** are generally 10am–4pm or 5pm daily, though often much reduced in winter.

Armed with these you're ready for a day among the vines, preferably with lunch at one of the winery restaurants. Few wines are available for much under $20 a bottle, and wineries like to show off with their restaurants, so although it will almost certainly be a pleasurable experience it won't be cheap. And don't be tempted to cram too many into a day; most vineyards are more suited to leisurely vineyard tastings than whistle-stop tours.

To avoid having to designate a driver, take an organized **wine tour**. Some of the cheapest are with Marlborough Wine Tours (℡03/578 9515, ⊛www .marlboroughwinetours.co.nz) who offer trips of three hours ($43), five hours ($54) and seven hours ($75) with time for lunch (not included) at one of the wineries. Sounds Connection (℡0800/742 866, ⊛www.soundsconnection .co.nz) specializes in half-day tours visiting four or five wineries ($65), a full-day circuit of six or seven wineries ($89, excluding lunch), and a full-day gourmet tour ($199) including lunch with matched wines and a visit to a chocolate factory. Tours pick up at accommodation around Picton and Blenheim.

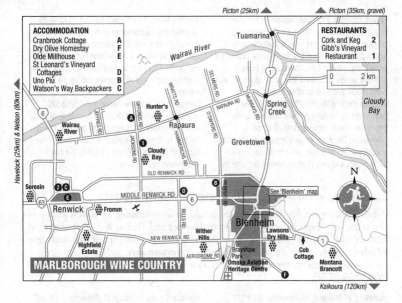

Picton (25km) ▲   ▲ Picton (35km, gravel)

ACCOMMODATION
Cranbrook Cottage **A**
Dry Olive Homestay **F**
Olde Millhouse **E**
St Leonard's Vineyard
  Cottages **D**
Uno Più **B**
Watson's Way Backpackers **C**

RESTAURANTS
Cork and Keg **2**
Gibb's Vineyard
Restaurant **1**

0   2 km

Tuamarina

Wairau River

Spring
Creek

Cloudy
Bay

Hunter's **A**

Rapaura

Grovetown

① Cloudy
Bay

OLD RENWICK RD

See 'Blenheim' map

Seresin **2 C**

MIDDLE RENWICK RD

E

N

Renwick   Fromm

Blenheim

NEW RENWICK RD

Highfield
Estate

Wither
Hills

Lawsons
Dry Hills

AERODROME RD

Brayshaw
Park

Cob
Cottage

Omaka Aviation
Heritage Centre

Montana
Brancott

F

MARLBOROUGH WINE COUNTRY

Havelock (25km) & Nelson (80km) ◄

Kaikoura (120km) ▼

Rental bikes are also a possibility, though the wineries are fairly spread out and you may find that after a couple of visits your desire to cycle diminishes rapidly. Spokesman Cycles, 61 Queen St (☎03/578 0433), offer rental for $40 a day, while Wine Tours by Bike (☎03/577 6954, ⓦwww.winetoursbybike.co.nz) charge $40 for half a day's rental ($55/full day) but include accommodation pick-ups and will come and rescue you if you have some mechanical breakdown.

Most of the wineries will **ship cases** of wine anywhere in the world, but shipping costs and high import duties mean that it seldom works out good value: expect $165 a case to the UK, $250 to the US.

The wineries

Cloudy Bay Jacksons Rd ☎03/520 9197, ⓦwww
.cloudybay.co.nz. Marlborough Sauvignon Blanc put
New Zealand on the world wine map in the late
1980s and the Cloudy Bay Sav was its flagship. It
is still drinking so well today that they can't keep
up with demand; it can be tasted (free) along with
their other top-notch wines. Cheese and charcuterie platters are $25.

Fromm Godfrey Rd ☎03/572 9355, ⓦwww
.frommwineries.com. A vineyard that is turning
winemakers' heads with a very hands-on approach
and producing predominantly red: excellent Pinot
Noir, and peppery Syrah as well as a Riesling with
echoes of the best German efforts. Visit if you're
serious about the subject and you'll taste (free) a
product that's a match for anywhere in the world,
at a price.

Highfield Estate Brookby Rd ☎03/572 9244,
ⓦwww.highfield.co.nz. Easily recognizable by its
Tuscan-inspired tower, which you can climb for

excellent views, *Highfield* offers free tastings and
lays on some of the best food in the region, with
$20–30 mains, antipasto platters ($55) that will
easily feed two and delectable desserts ($13), all
served inside or on the terrace overlooking the
vines.

Hunter's Rapaura Rd ☎03/572 8489, ⓦwww
.hunters.co.nz. Jane Hunter is recognized as one of
the world's top female winemakers. Drop by to
taste, visit the art gallery or eat in the classy,
family-friendly café which does delicious platters
($25–30) plus more formal dinners Wed–Sun.

Lawsons Dry Hills Alabama Rd ☎03/578 7674,
ⓦwww.lawsonsdryhills.co.nz. Established vines
produce stunning wines in this multi-award-
winning winery, well worth visiting for the Pinot
Gris, Gewürztraminer and Sav Blanc if nothing
else.

Montana Brancott 5km south of Blenheim on
SH1 ☎03/577 5775, ⓦwww.montanawines.co.nz.
A good starting point for your exploration of the

region. Montana effectively kicked off the wine region in the early 1970s and now operate the country's largest winery here, a favourite with coach parties. Come for free tasting, the café or the winery tour (daily 11am, 1pm & 3pm; 50min; $15.50), which includes a little wine appreciation, a short movie and structured tasting.

Seresin Bedford Rd ☎03/572 9408, ⓦwww .seresin.co.nz. Stylish winery with a distinctive primitivist "hand" logo perched on a rise overlooking the vines. Largely organic, estate-grown grapes interact with wild yeast to produce world-class wines, and they produce some killer olive oil.

Wairau River 11 Rapaura Rd ☎03/572 9800, ⓦwww.wairauriverwines.com. A splendid rammed earth and rimu timber construction by the river, at the foot of the Richmond mountain range. Free tastings and fabulous lunches served under shady vines in summer and by the fire in winter.

Wither Hills 211 New Renwick Rd ☎03/520 8270, ⓦwww.witherhills.co.nz. A striking, modern roadside winery, all concrete and tussock. Nip in for free tastings of the popular Chardonnay, Pinot Noir and Sauvignon Blanc (including the fine single-vineyard Rarangi).

Eating, drinking and entertainment

A few hours spent visiting vineyards should be accompanied by **lunch** at one of the wineries – especially *Highfield Estate*, *Hunter's* and *Wairau River* (see above). A few are also open in the evenings, but for dinner you may prefer to head into Blenheim where there's a reasonable choice of **restaurants**.

For entertainment, there's the Top Town Cinema 3, 4 Kinross St, Blenheim (☎03/577 8273).

Bellafico 17 Maxwell Rd, Blenheim ☎03/577 6072. A Blenheim staple since 1994, and it shows in the decor. But don't be fooled, there's nothing to fault the Italian-influenced food, prepared with care and served with respect. Most mains $24–30. Closed Sun.

Café Home 1c Main St, Blenheim. Primo espresso alongside the fresh sandwiches, frittata slices and cakes in modern surroundings. Closed Sun.

Cork and Keg Inkerman St, Renwick. Friendly English-style local with heavy beams, traditional games like dominoes and a good selection of South Island craft beers including those from the local Moa stable. All-day pub meals from $16.

Dodson Street 1 Dodson St, Blenheim ☎03/577 8348. Convivial bistro and ale house dishing up the likes of beef hotpot ($19) and tasty pizzas ($30–35 for a big one). Wash these down with Renaissance beers brewed on site – Scotch ale, porter and a superbly hoppy American-style pale ale. Closed Mon.

Gibb's Vineyard Restaurant 258 Jacksons Rd, 7km northwest of Blenheim ☎03/572 8048, ⓦwww.gibbs-restaurant.co.nz. Superb restaurant in a former winery building with vines all around and tables set with white linen and highly polished cutlery. You might start with celeriac and ricotta ravioli ($19) and follow with rack of lamb ($39) or veal with lemons and chorizo ($35). The

---

Marlborough festivals

Blenheim springs to life during the first full week of February. On the first Saturday, the **Blues, Brews and BBQs Festival** (ⓦwww.bluesbrews.co.nz) kicks off proceedings at the Blenheim A&P Showground with a combination of musicians and brewers from all over the country parading their wares. This is mixed in a heady cocktail with some good old-fashioned Kiwi snags, kebabs and burgers, as well as some more adventurous fare. Well worth a look if you're in party mode.

Various arts and crafts demonstrations, exhibitions, markets and special events pad out the next week, but Blenheim's big event is the annual **Marlborough Wine Festival** ($48, includes a glass for slurping; 10.30am–6pm; ⓦwww.wine-marlborough-festival .co.nz) on the second Saturday. Around 10,000 people flock to the *Montana Brancott* winery, where a vast field of marquees, containing local wines and food for purchase and consumption, throb with the sound of live music and revelry.

Richies (☎03/578 5467) run **buses** to the festival site from the town and the airport ($12.50 return), as well as from Picton ($25 return).

wine list leans heavily on Marlborough with a few quality Central Otago Chardonnays and Pinot Noirs. Dinner only and closed Sun & Mon from May–Oct.

Hotel d'Urville 52 Queen St, Blenheim ☎03/577 9945. A classy restaurant with stylish modern decor and exemplary cuisine, making the best of seasonal produce, so expect something special. Mains are $34–38, and book in advance.

Poppy Thai 31 Scott St ☎03/579 4496. The service can be sloppy and the decor is nothing to shout about but it is cheap and the meals are always tasty and delicately spiced. Lunch specials cost $8–10. Licensed & BYO.

🏃 **Raupo** 2 Symons St, Blenheim. Great café with a terrace overlooking the Opawa River, serving superb meals from 7am. Lunch (mostly $13–18) and bistro-style dinners ($25–30) are complemented by high tea, both morning and afternoon ($13).

Rocco's 5 Dodson St, Blenheim ☎03/578 6940. Enjoyable authentic Italian restaurant that could unabashedly sit on a New York or Rome street. For a blowout, order the awesome chicken Kiev alla Rocco – chicken breast filled with ham, garlic butter and cheese, all wrapped in a veal schnitzel ($28) or the fillet alla Rocco. Fresh pasta is made daily. Dinner only, closed Sun.

South from Blenheim: the Kaikoura Coast

From Blenheim it is a 130km run down between the coast and the brooding Seaward Kaikoura Range to the next place of any consequence, Kaikoura. It can be done in an hour and a half, but is best if allotted more time for frequent stops along some gorgeous stretches of coastline. Around 20km south of Blenheim a sign points inland towards **Molesworth Station** (see box below) and **Hanmer Springs**.

The highway then continues 30km to Lake Grassmere, a vast shallow salt lake which annually produces 70,000 tonnes a year of table salt. **Cyclists** may want to overnight 20km south of the salt works at the small but beautifully formed *Pedallers Rest Cycle Stop* (☎03/575 6708, ✉pedallers@callsouth.net.nz; bunks $18, camping $14) which even has a small shop: it is 1.5km off SH1; look for the water tank and sign beside the road. You're now following the coast with grey gravel beaches all the way, accessible at various points. Almost 90km out of Blenheim, the rocky Kekerengu Point juts out and makes a great place to watch the crashing waves while tucking into the delicious sandwiches, fish and chips, cakes and coffee at *The Store* (☎03/575 8600).

Another 35km on, at **Ohau Point**, you hit the best stretch of coastline, a wonderful rocky, surf-lashed strip which continues for around 30km to Kaikoura then 20km beyond. Ohau Point is home to the South Island's largest seal colony with dozens (if not hundreds) of seals lolling on the rocks not more

---

Driving through Molesworth Station

Timing is everything if you want to drive (or ride) the Acheron Road through **Molesworth Station**, at 1800 square kilometres New Zealand's largest farm. The central 59km section of road is only open to traffic for a few weeks each summer (late Dec to March). It is an impressive run through New Zealand's most accessible high country passing historic cob houses with towering mountains all around. The drive from Blenheim to Hanmer Springs (190km) takes over five hours, a couple of them on gravel, and since there are no services make sure your tank is topped up. **Camping** is only permitted at *Molesworth Cob Cottage* and *Acheron Accommodation House* (both $6). For the latest information obtain DOC's *Molesworth* leaflet ($2) and check the DOC website, ⊛www.doc.govt.nz.

Access is also possible from October to May with Molesworth Tour Company (☎03/577 9897, ⊛www.molesworthtours.co.nz) which explores the region on one-day trips ($235), overnight ($670), a three-day experience ($1130) and even a four-day guided cycle ride ($1135).

than 20m away. Immediately before Ohau Point, Ohau Stream Walk (15min return) weaves through the bush to a nice waterfall and pool where in October and November seal pups can sometimes be seen playing during the day. Approach quietly at this time.

The coastline around here is a perfect habitat for **crayfish**, which are sought by the locals and sold from roadside shacks, notably at Rakautara, 3km south of Ohau Point where you'll find *Nin's Bins* and *Cay's Crays*, roadside caravans hawking cooked crays for around $30–50.

Kaikoura and around

The small town of **KAIKOURA**, 130km south of Blenheim and 180km north of Christchurch, enjoys a spectacular setting in the lee of the Kaikoura Peninsula, wedged between the mountains and the ocean. Offshore, the sea bed drops away rapidly to the kilometre-deep Kaikoura Canyon, a phenomenon that brings sea mammals in large and varied numbers. **Whale watching** and **swimming with dolphins** are big business here, and the presence of expectant tourists has spawned a number of eco-oriented businesses offering swimming with seals, sea kayaking and hiking.

Kaikoura got its name when an ancient **Maori** explorer who stopped to eat crayfish and found it so good he called the place *kai* (food) *koura* (crayfish). Maori legend also accounts for the extraordinary coastline around Kaikoura. During the creation of the land, a young deity, Marokura, was given the job of finishing the region: first he built the Kaikoura Peninsula and a second smaller peninsula (Haumuri Bluff), then he set about creating the huge troughs in the sea between the two peninsulas, where the cold waters of the south would mix with the warm waters of the north and east. Realizing the depth of Marokura's accomplishment, the god Tuterakiwhanoa said that the place would be a gift (*koha*) to all those who see its hidden beauty – and it is still known to local Maori as Te Koha O Marokura.

The Ngai Tahu people harvested the wealth of the land and seas until they were decimated, around 1830, by the warrior Te Rauparaha. The first **Europeans** to settle in the area were whalers who came in the early 1840s, swiftly followed by farmers. The trials and tribulations of their existence are recorded in the **Kaikoura Museum** and the more evocative **Fyffe House**. Kaikoura ticked on quietly until the late 1980s when whale watching really took off and put the place on the tourism map. Since then it has steadily expanded, becoming more commercial, though without losing its South Island, small-town feel.

Arrival, getting around and information

InterCity and Atomic **buses** on the Picton–Blenheim–Christchurch run all drop off on Westend, in the town car park near the visitor centre. The TranzCoastal **train** between Picton and Christchurch arrives at the station on Whaleway Station Road. Most places in town are within walking distance, though since the town is increasingly spread out you may find use for a **taxi** (Kaikoura Shuttles ℡03/319 6166) or **bike rental**; R&R Sport, 14 Westend (℡03/319 5028) charges $20 for a half-day, $30 full. To ease the strain, opt for an electric bike ($24/1hr, $49/ half-day) rented from Seal Swim, 58 Westend.

The **i-SITE visitor centre** on Westend (Mon–Fri 9am–5pm, Sat & Sun 9am–4pm; ℡03/319 5641, ⓦwww.kaikoura.co.nz) also handles most **DOC**

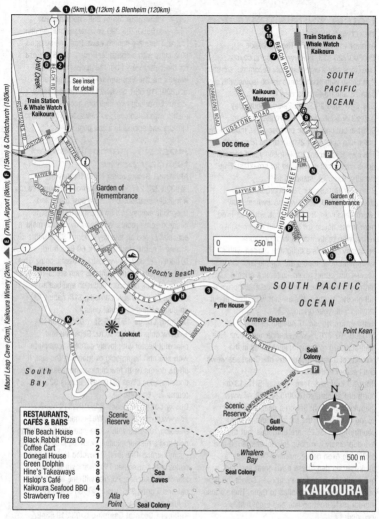

▲ ❶ (5km), Ⓐ (12km) & Blenheim (120km)

Maori Leap Cave (2km), Kaikoura Winery (2km), ▲ Ⓔ (7km), Airport (8km), Ⓕ (15km) & Christchurch (180km)

SOUTH
PACIFIC
OCEAN

Train Station &
Whale Watch
Kaikoura

Kaikoura
Museum

DOC Office

WESTEND

Garden of
Remembrance

Garden of
Remembrance

0   250 m

Train Station
& Whale Watch
Kaikoura

See inset
for detail

Lyell Creek

BEACH RD

ROBINSONS RD

LUDSTONE RD

WESTEND

BAYVIEW ST

CHURCHILL ST

SCARBOROUGH ST

THE ESPLANADE

Racecourse

Lookout

South
Bay

SOUTH BAY PARADE

Gooch's Beach   Wharf

Fyffe House

Armers Beach

AVOCA STREET

Point Kean

Seal
Colony

SOUTH PACIFIC
OCEAN

Scenic Reserve

Scenic
Reserve

KAIKOURA PENINSULA WALKWAY

Gull
Colony

Whalers
Bay

Sea
Caves

Seal Colony

Atia
Point   Seal Colony

N

0   500 m

KAIKOURA

**RESTAURANTS,
CAFÉS & BARS**

The Beach House	5
Black Rabbit Pizza Co	7
Coffee Cart	2
Donegal House	1
Green Dolphin	3
Hine's Takeaways	8
Hislop's Café	6
Kaikoura Seafood BBQ	4
Strawberry Tree	9

ACCOMMODATION

Albatross Backpacker Inn	Q	Bayview Homestay	L	Kaikoura Coastal Camping	F	Nikau Lodge	P
Alpine-Pacific Holiday Park	B	Bendamere House	N	Kaikoura Peketa Beach Holiday Park	E	Panorama Motel	I
Anchor Inn Motel	G	Dolphin Lodge	O	The Lazy Shag	M	Sunrise Lodge	C
Bay Cottages	K	Dusky Lodge	D	Miharotia	J	Waves on the Esplanade	R
		Hapuku Lodge & Tree Houses	A			YHA Maui	H

enquiries and stores luggage for $2. There's **internet** access at Global Gossip, 19 Westend (daily 9am–9pm; $4/hr), with plenty of machines and wi-fi.

Accommodation

There's a fair range of accommodation, most of it strung out along SH1 (Beach Road) immediately north of the centre, or along the Esplanade which heads out onto the peninsula east of town.

Hotels, motels B&Bs and homestays

Anchor Inn Motel 208 The Esplanade ☎0800/720 033, ⓦwww.anchorinn.co.nz. Luxurious motel with tastefully decorated, a/c units that come with every convenience (some with spa bath). Standard ❻, sea view ❼

Bay Cottages 29 South Parade, South Bay, ☎03/319 5506, ⓦwww.baycottages.co.nz. Spartan but good-value purpose-built, motel-style units, in a quiet spot 2km from the town centre. The owner is exceptionally friendly and sometimes takes guests out crayfishing for breakfast. Free laundry. Basic ❸, standard ❹

Bayview Homestay 296 Scarborough St ☎03/319 5480, ⓦwww.bayviewhomestay .wordpress.com. It is Margaret, who has lived here in the house for almost all of her eighty years, who really makes this traditional homestay. There's a delightful garden with a swimming pool, rooms are simple with external access and either an en-suite or a private bathroom, breakfasts are cooked and there's a full guests' kitchen. It's all that was great about staying with your granny. ❹

Bendamere House 37 Adelphi Terrace ☎0800/107 770, ⓦwww.bendamere.co.nz. Five high-standard rooms with kitchenette in the grounds of a large villa on the hill. Great sea views, and hearty breakfasts. ❻

Hapuku Lodge & Tree Houses SH1, 13km north of Kaikoura ☎0800/524 568, ⓦwww .hapukulodge.com. Set on a deer farm amid young olive trees, the rooms in the modern country lodge ($625) are gorgeous, but the five supremely luxurious treehouses ($530 and $700) are even better: nothing like a child's back-garden den, these have great sea and mountain views and you can even select the type of music you'd like supplied to them. There's also a great restaurant on site and breakfast is included. ❾

Miharotia 274 Scarborough St ☎03/319 7498, ⓦwww.miharotia.co.nz. Classy B&B in a modern home with three rooms, all beautifully appointed with deck access to the outside hot tub. Sea and mountain views are great and even better from the lounge, where the hosts (one a former paua diver) serve an excellent breakfast. Rates $400. ❾

Nikau Lodge 53 Deal St ☎03/319 6973, ⓦwww .nikaulodge.com. Most of the seven en-suite rooms in this lovely, wooden, 1925 house have great mountain or sea views. There's also SkyTV with in-room movies, free internet and wi-fi, an outdoor spa pool and a good breakfast.❻

Panorama Motel 266 The Esplanade ☎0800/288 299 ⓦwww.panoramamotel .co.nz. There are superb views from the stripped-pine units with a chalet feel; you'll pay $10 extra for the better view from the upper floor. ❹

Waves on the Esplanade 78 The Esplanade ☎0800/319 589, ⓦwww.kaikouraapartments .co.nz. Luxurious two-bedroom, motel-style apartments with balconies, sea views, full kitchen and laundry and access to a spa pool. ❼

Hostels, campsites and holiday parks

Albatross Backpacker Inn 1 Torquay St ☎0800/222 247, ⓦwww.albatross-kaikoura.co.nz. A friendly, spacious converted post office and telephone exchange with unusual Turkish-style decor in some rooms. Well-tended grounds make it especially good on fine days. Dorms $25, rooms ❷

Alpine-Pacific Holiday Park 69 Beach Rd ☎0800/692 322, ⓦwww.alpine-pacific.co.nz. This central, shaded park maintains high standards and offers a range of accommodation and has an outdoor pool and spa. Camping $18, cabins ❷, en-suite cabins ❹, motel units ❺

Dolphin Lodge 15 Deal St ☎03/319 5842, ⓦwww.dolphinlodge.co.nz. Secluded and peaceful hostel with lovely gardens (complete with spa and hammock) overlooking the sea. It offers dorms (with few bunks) and pleasant little doubles, plus bikes ($10/day). Dorms $23, rooms ❶, en suite ❷

Dusky Lodge 67 Beach Rd, ☎03/319 5959, ⓦwww.duskylodge.com. Well-organized hostel sleeping 100-plus with sauna, spa, large swimming pool and a restaurant along with log fires and a big sunny terrace. One level is devoted to deluxe en suites with flat-screen TVs, their own upscale lounge and kitchen. Popular with the Magic Bus patrons. Dorms $26, rooms ❶, en suites ❷, deluxe en suites ❸

Kaikoura Coastal Camping ☎03/319 5348, ⓔgoosebay@ihug.co.nz. A string of four appealing, family-oriented campsites (three beachside) strung out along SH1 around 15km south of Kaikoura. The northernmost, Paia Point, is for tents only ($8) while the others have powered sites and showers ($10–12).

Kaikoura Peketa Beach Holiday Park 665 SH1, 8km south of Kaikoura ☎03/319 6299, ⓔkaikoura@peketabeach.co.nz. A peaceful beachside campsite that's very popular with surfers who make use of the excellent waves on the doorstep. Camping $14, cabins ❶

The Lazy Shag 37 Beach Rd ☎03/319 6662, ⓔlazy-shag@hotmail.com. Modern, purpose-built hostel where guests' comfort is the priority. Rooms are warm and quiet, common rooms are spacious and well equipped, and all dorms, twins and doubles are en suite. Dorms $23, rooms ❷

Sunrise Lodge 74 Beach Rd ☎03/319 7444, ✉sunrisehostel@xtra.co.nz. Small and sociable hostel that's just a 2min walk from Whale Watch and comes without bunks and with a maximum of three to a room. Marc runs free orientational sunset bus trips nightly, is happy for you to join

him on his frequent boat fishing trips and has free bikes. The separate s/c flat sleeping four is good for families. Dorms $28, rooms and en suite ❷

YHA Maui 270 The Esplanade ☎03/319 5931, ✉yha.kaikoura@yha.co.nz. A comfortable, well-run hostel with tremendous sea and mountain views, particularly from the lounge and kitchen, and well-informed, knowledgeable staff. Dorms $32, rooms ❷, en suite ❹

The town and the peninsula

Most visitors are dead-set on seeing whales or swimming with dolphins, and the smattering of other sights and activities are often unjustly treated as ways of waiting out bad weather.

Some distraction is provided by the **Kaikoura Museum**, 14 Ludstone Rd (Mon–Fri 10am–4.30pm, Sat & Sun 2–4pm; $3), where a large rock contains the fossilized ribcage of a Cretaceous-period plesiosaur. The Maori collection illustrates the stages needed to convert a mussel shell into effective fish hooks, while out back there's an early 1900s jailhouse (complete with padded cell) that was used in Kaikoura until 1980.

Out on the peninsula, don't miss the town's oldest building, **Fyffe House**, 62 Avoca St (Nov–March daily 10am–6pm; April–Oct daily except Tues & Wed 10am–4pm; $7), an old whaler's cottage still on its original whalebone foundations. The house began life as part of the Waiopuka Whaling Station that was founded by Robert Fyffe in 1842 and was originally an unprepossessing two-room cooper's cottage. It was extended by George Fyffe in 1860, and while some rooms look now much as they did then, others reflect the condition of the place when the last resident moved out in 1980.

Avoca Street follows the edge of the peninsula round to a car park (the start of the Kaikoura Peninsula Walkway; see box, p.488) where fur **seals** often lounge on flat, sea-worn rocks watching the plentiful birdlife, gulls, shags, and black oyster-catchers, who in turn explore the rock pools full of rich tidal detritus.

South of town, SH1 runs 2km to the sea-formed **Maori Leap Cave** (35min tours daily on the half-hour 10.30am–3.30pm; $12; ☎03/319 5023), named after a Maori warrior who jumped to his death from the hills above the cave to escape capture by another tribe. Stalagmites and stalactites sprout from the floor and ceiling of the cave, and translucent stone straws seem to defy gravity by maintaining their internal water level. There are also examples of cave coral and algae that survive in the dank cave by turning darkness into energy.

Roughly 300m further south, **Kaikoura Winery** (daily: Sept–May 10am–5.30pm; June–Aug 11am–4pm; tastings $5; ⊛www.kaikourawinery .co.nz) perches on the steep hillside overlooking South Bay, a seaside location that flies in the face of conventional viticultural wisdom. Gauge how successful they've been on tours of their cellars (11am, 2pm & 4pm in summer; $15) which conclude with a tasting, or just sup a glass or two in the café.

Marine life and activities

Just 1km off the Kaikoura Peninsula the coastal shallows plummet into the 1000m-deep Kaikoura Canyon, a network of undersea troughs that funnel warm subtropical waters and cold sub-Antarctic flows into a nutrient-rich upwelling. This provides an unusually fecund habitat supporting an enormous amount and

Walks around Kaikoura

Kaikoura isn't all about spending money watching marine mammals. There's plenty to be seen on foot, best accessed on these two local walks and two longer tramps in the vicinity.

Day walks

Kaikoura Peninsula Walkway (11km loop; 3hr; undulating). A superb circuit of the peninsula covered on DOC's *The Peninsula Walkway* leaflet. Pick it up at the i-SITE and follow the route along the Esplanade past Fyffe House to the seal colony. From here it loops over the grassy cliffs to South Bay, with views down to the seals lolling on the rocks below. Several options follow paths back over the peninsula to the i-SITE. Chances are you'll see red-billed and black-backed gulls, oystercatchers, herons and shags: be warned that gulls nesting during September and October are likely to attack if they feel that their nests are threatened: steer well clear.

Mount Fyffe (16km return; 6–8hr; 1400m ascent). Several walks close to town are outlined in DOC's *Mount Fyffe and the Seaward Kaikoura Range* leaflet. The most immediately appealing is this tough hike to the 1602m summit of Mount Fyffe. Starting at a poorly signposted car park 12km northwest of town, the route climbs steadily up a 4WD road to the summit with its glorious views over the Kaikoura Peninsula and coast.

Multi-day walks

Kaikoura Wilderness Walks (Oct–March; ✆0800/945 337, ✆www.kaikoura wilderness.co.nz). A delightful combination of a guided walk in gorgeous, wild country up behind Kaikoura and the luxury *Shearwater Lodge* – far from everything on the bushline at 1000m but with crisp sheets in en-suite rooms and three-course meals. After a Kaikoura pick-up and short drive, day one (8.5km one-way; 6hr; 700m ascent) involves a steady ascent to the lodge where you're served welcome refreshments around a roaring fire followed by dinner. The hills above the lodge are explored on the second day (optional), then you wander back to the valley on the final day. Two-day option $995; more satisfying three-dayer $1395.

Kaikoura Coast Track (37km; 3 days; 600m ascent; ✆03/319 2715, ✆www .kaikouratrack.co.nz). The mixture of wild beach scenery, farmland and regenerating bush makes for a pleasant and very manageable walk, but the real pleasure here is in experiencing country life and chatting to the farming families at the two overnight stops. This self-guided, private walk starts and ends 50km south of Kaikoura at the backpacker-style *Staging Post*, 75 Hawkeswood Rd, Hawkeswood, (camping $25 for two, cabins ❶, B&B rooms ❺; Atomic buses stop within 1km) then climbs the Hawkeswood Range with spectacular views of the Seaward Kaikoura mountains. Walker numbers are limited, so book in advance. The $185 fee covers track maintenance, bag transport (so you only need carry a daypack), and three nights' accommodation in warm cottages with bunk beds, fully equipped kitchens and showers as well as fresh farm produce, milk, bread and home-cooked meals by arrangement.

variety of marine life, including fourteen species of whale. Marine mammals come for an easy meal, and tourists come to watch. You can expect to see gigantic sperm **whales** (all year), **dolphins** (all year), migratory humpback whales (June–July) and **orca** (Dec–Feb), all at relatively close quarters.

The town's aquatic activities are very popular and it pays to book well in advance though rough seas often lead to **cancellations** so it is good to allow yourself a couple of days' flexibility here. At their best, the activities can be wonderfully memorable experiences, but these are completely wild animals who may not deign to show themselves or play with you. Try not to set your expectations too high.

Whale watching

Kaikoura's flagship activity is **whale watching**, conducted by the Maori-owned and operated Whale Watch Kaikoura (2hr 30min; $145; ℡0800/655 121, 🌐www.whalewatch.co.nz). You meet at the office at the train station and are bussed around to South Bay where a speedy catamaran whisks you a few kilometres offshore (much closer than similar trips elsewhere in the world). There are typically one or two whale sightings per trip along with dolphins and sea birds: if you see no whales there's an eighty-percent refund. The office sells pills and bands to alleviate **sea sickness** – often a wise investment, particularly for afternoon trips.

An alternative is **aerial whale watching** with Wings Over Whales (℡0800/226 629, 🌐www.whales.co.nz) who have thirty-minute flights for $165; and Kaikoura Helicopters (℡03/319 6609, 🌐www.worldofwhales.co.nz) who offer a thirty-minute flight for up to three people ($600). You won't get as close to whales as you would by sea, so bring a good pair of binoculars.

Swimming with dolphins and seals

The other main reason people visit Kaikoura is to go **swimming with dolphins**, an experience many find almost spiritual. Trips are run by the highly professional Dolphin Encounter, based at 96 The Esplanade (5.30am, 8.30am & 12.30pm; swimming $165, watching $80; ℡0800/733 365, 🌐www.dolphin .co.nz) where there is a good café. Book three to four weeks in advance for the December–February peak season (though standbys do become available at short notice). You'll get most out of it if you're a reasonably confident swimmer; the more you duck-dive the more eager the dolphins will be to investigate. They seem to find it attractive listening to you humming through your snorkel – any tune will do. Don't get too carried away though: dolphins have a penchant for swimming in ever decreasing circles until lesser beings are quite dizzy and disorientated.

Seals tend to be even more curious than dolphins, so you may fancy **seal swimming** with Seal Swim Kaikoura, 58 Westend (Oct–May only; ℡0800/732 579, 🌐www.sealswimkaikoura.co.nz), with shore-based trips ($70) and more flexible trips by boat (2–2.5hr total; $90). There's a fair bit of swimming involved so it helps if you've snorkelled before. Topspot, 22 Deal St ($70; ℡03/319 5540) also runs beach-access seal swimming trips typically timed with high tide.

Birdwatching, sea kayaking and diving

Fans of sea birds won't be able to resist a rare opportunity to see endangered sea birds on trips run by **Albatross Encounter**, 96 The Esplanade (2–3 trips daily; 2–3hr; $110; ℡0800/733 365, 🌐www.oceanwings.co.nz), who take you a kilometre or two offshore in a small boat. Bait is laid to attract all manner of species – shags, mollymawks, gannets, petrels and a couple of varieties of albatross come amazingly close.

An intimate way to see wildlife close to the peninsula is **sea kayaking** with Kaikoura Kayaks (℡0800/452 456, 🌐www.kaikourakayaks.co.nz) who operate all year and often have trips when others are cancelled. You'll learn most (and probably see more wildlife) on the half-day Seal Kayaking guided trips ($85), though suitably skilled paddlers can rent kayaks ($70/half-day, $85/day). In summer, guided sit-on-top kayak fishing trips go for $120/ half-day.

To get a close look at temperate kelp forests, nudibranchs and sponges, visit Dive Kaikoura, 13 Yarmouth St (℡0800/348 352, 🌐www.divekaikoura.co.nz), which offers **scuba-diving** trips for novices ($195) and two-tank trips for certified divers ($250).

Other activities

If you'd rather stay on dry land, and learn something of the Maori culture hereabouts, join **Maori Tours Kaikoura** (℡0800/866 267, ⓌRwww.maoritours.co.nz) who offer emotionally engaging half-day tours ($115), guided by an ex-whale-watch boat driver and his family, that give a real taste of *Maoritanga* and the genuine hospitality it demands. Tours take in various local sights, storytelling, explanations of Maori ways and medicines, cultural differences and involve learning a song, that you then surprise yourself by singing.

There's great **horseriding** around 13km inland at Fyffe View Horse Treks (from $50; ℡03/319 5069), and aspiring fliers might like to **Pilot a Plane** ($120; ℡03/319 6579), a chance to take the controls for twenty minutes: an adrenaline buzz with great scenery to boot.

Still airborne, Skydive Kaikoura ($319 for 11,000ft; ℡0800/843 759, ⓌRwww .skydivekaikoura.co.nz) offers very personal **tandem skydiving** trips that are a world away from the conveyor-belt skydiving in Taupo.

Once the sun goes down, crystal-clear nights offer a great chance to experience the **Kaikoura Night Sky** (Nov–April; 1–1hr 30min; $50; ℡03/319 6635, ⓌRwww.kaikouranightsky.co.nz), with small groups clustered around a mobile 20cm telescope in the fields away from the bright lights of Kaikoura. The planets, moon craters and distant galaxies come alive with tales of celestial navigation and what the southern sky means to Maori.

Eating and drinking

Kaikoura is a small town but the steady flow of tourists helps keep a decent selection of **cafés** and **restaurants** alive. Prices are a little on the high side, especially if you're keen to sample the local crayfish, though if that's your aim, you might want to buy them ready-boiled from one of the caravans north of town (see p.484).

The Beach House 39 Beach Rd. Kaikoura's cool set hangs out here, imbibing good coffee over an extended breakfast ($10–18) or returning for lunches which include nachos, seafood chowder, quiches and panini from the cabinet. Casual atmosphere inside and out.

Black Rabbit Pizza Co 17 Beach Rd ℡03/319 6360. Quality pizzas, pasta dishes, and desserts to take away, though there are three tables. Try a spicy Red Hot Rascal ($13).

Coffee Cart SH1 Some of the best coffee in town plus muffins and free wi-fi.

Donegal House Schoolhouse Rd ℡03/319 5083, ⓌRwww.donegalhouse.co.nz. A local legend, this purpose-built Irish bar and restaurant in the middle of a farm works surprisingly well with a short but decent menu (mains $24–32) and a buzzing atmosphere, occasionally enhanced by live music. It is 10min drive north of town (follow SH1 for 4km then 2km west) so you may want to go by cab or arrange to stay in one of the numerous rooms (⑤). Daily 11am–whenever.

🏃 **Green Dolphin** 12 Avoca St ℡03/319 6666. Modern decor, large windows with sea views and excellent, casual service make this the perfect spot for an evening meal. The food is pretty damn good too with a short but well-chosen contemporary menu that usually includes a half-crayfish ($60) along with dishes half that price.

Hine's Takeaways 18 Westend. Top fish, chips and crayfish dinners. Perfect for sunset on the waterfront.

Hislop's Café 33 Beach Rd ℡03/319 6971. The pick of the cafés in Kaikoura, this lovely wooden-floored place is a must for coffee and cakes, inside or out, as well as sumptuous breakfasts, organic meals (some vegetarian or gluten-free), tasty seafood and toothsome daily fresh-baked bread. Wine by the glass, including vegan and many organic varieties. Open for breakfast ($10–20), lunch salads and sandwiches ($16–25) and dinner (mains $25–34).

Kaikoura Seafood BBQ Armers Beach ℡0327/376 3619. A few tables scattered roadside and a takeaway cart make a great setting for tucking into a range of simple seafood all served with salad and rice. Try the paua patties ($9) or half-dozen garlic scallops ($8).

Strawberry Tree 21 Westend. Convivial Irish-styled bar that's usually busy with a mix of locals and travellers. There's a seafood-heavy menu (mains $16–24).

South from Kaikoura

South of Kaikoura you have a choice of routes. It is a two- to three-hour run down SH1 to Christchurch with only relatively minor points of interest along the way. The road initially follows a 20km stretch of delightful rocky coastline then ducks inland through farming country for most of the rest of the way to Christchurch. Hikers should consider putting three days aside for the Kaikoura Coast Walk (see box, p.488) while wine drinkers will want to stop at the hamlet of **Waipara**, 130km south of Kaikoura, where paddocks full of newly planted vines announce one of New Zealand's fastest growing viticultural regions. Thanks to its long warm days, combination of alluvial gravels and limestone clays, and protection from cooling sea winds, the area produces quality wines, particularly its Pinot Noirs and Rieslings. As a wine destination it is very much in its infancy: a dozen places offer tastings and several have restaurants, but there isn't much else.

The vineyards are all within 5km of **Waipara** at the junction of SH1 and SH7 to Hanmer Springs and the Lewis Pass. Around 4km north on SH1, *Waipara Springs* (daily 11am–5pm; ☎03/314 6777, ⓦwww.waiparasprings.co.nz) was first planted in 1982 and offers tastings of its latest vintages, though they are perhaps best appreciated in the family-oriented garden **restaurant** (mains $20–30, platter for three $47) which always has wholesome fresh-baked bread to go with the daily specials. There's a considerably more upscale tenor to *Pegasus Bay*, Stockgrove Road, 4km south of the junction along SH1 then 3km east (daily 10.30am–5pm, ☎03/314 6869, ⓦwww.pegasusbay.com), where contemporary artworks surround diners in what is one of the finest **winery restaurants** in the country (daily noon–4pm; $30–35 mains). Nip in to taste some of the delicious wines or stay for lunch when each course is matched with an appropriate wine.

To experience some of the gentle limestone country hereabouts, head 11km inland along Georges Road to **Iron Ridge Quarry Sculpture Park**, 707 Ram Paddock Rd (Sun 10am–5pm; $10; ⓦwww.raymondherber.com), where dynamic steel sculptures by Raymond Herber are on display in a disused quarry. There's self-contained **accommodation** opposite at *The Shearers Quarters*, 680 Ram Paddock Rd (☎03/314 9921; $250), set on a small vineyard and truffle orchard. Simpler needs are satisfied by *Waipara Sleepers*, 12 Glenmark Drive (☎03/314 6003, ⓦwww.waiparasleepers.co.nz; camping $15, dorms $21, rooms ❷), where disused 1940s railway guards' vans have been converted into dorms and doubles, and an old station functions as a kitchen.

Some 10km south of Waipara, stop for superb café food in **Amberley** at the *Nor'wester Café*, on SH1, which is renowned for its fresh, uncomplicated dishes and great coffee. From Amberley it is only 40km down SH1 to Christchurch.

Ski Mount Lyford

In winter, consider following the scenic SH70 inland from Kaikoura and skiing **Mount Lyford** (mid-June to mid-Oct; ⓦwww.mtlyford.co.nz) which offers some of the best **skiing** in the upper South Island. It's a small field and has limited lift facilities ($65/day), but caters for a broad range of abilities (3 beginner runs, 11 intermediate, 6 advanced) and is rarely crowded. Nearby on SH70 there's **accommodation** at the *Mount Lyford Lodge* (☎03/315 6446, ⓦwww.mtlyfordlodge.co.nz; vans $25, dorms $30, rooms ❸, motels ❹), which also has a welcoming restaurant and bar.

Travel details

The following services are all direct without changes.

Ferries

Picton to: Wellington (5–8 daily; 3hr).

Trains

Picton to: Blenheim (1 daily; 30min); Christchurch (1 daily; 5hr 20min); Kaikoura (1 daily; 2hr 30min).

Buses

Blenheim to: Christchurch (4–5 daily; 4hr 45min–5hr 30min); Nelson (4 daily; 1hr 45min); Picton (8 daily; 30min).
Kaikoura to: Christchurch (4–5 daily 2hr 30min); Picton (4–5 daily; 2hr 15min).
Motueka to: Collingwood (1 daily; 1hr 30min); Heaphy Track (1 daily; 2hr 15min); Kaiteriteri (3 daily; 20min); Marahau (4 daily; 40–50min); Nelson (5 daily; 1hr); Takaka (2 daily; 1hr 10min); Totaranui (1 daily; 2hr 15min).
Murchison to: Greymouth (2 daily; 4hr); Nelson (2 daily; 2hr); Punakaiki (2 daily; 2hr 30min); Westport (2 daily; 1hr 30min).
Nelson to: Blenheim (4 daily; 1hr 45min); Collingwood (1 daily; 2hr 45min); Fox Glacier (1 daily; 9hr 30min), Franz Josef (1 daily; 9hr); Greymouth (2 daily; 6hr); Heaphy Track (1 daily; 3hr 30min); Motueka (5 daily; 1hr); Murchison (2 daily; 2hr); Picton (5 daily; 2hr); Punakaiki (2 daily; 4hr 40min); Takaka (2 daily; 2hr 15min); Totaranui (1 daily; 3hr 30min); Westport (2 daily; 3hr 30min–4hr).
Picton to: Blenheim (8 daily; 30min); Christchurch (4–5 daily; 5hr–5hr 30min); Kaikoura (4–5 daily; 2hr 15min); Nelson (5 daily; 2hr).
Takaka to: Collingwood (1 daily; 30min); Heaphy Track (1 daily; 1hr); Motueka (2 daily; 1hr 10min); Nelson (2 daily; 2hr 15min); Totaranui (1 daily; 1hr).

Flights

Blenheim to: Auckland (4 daily; 1hr 20min); Christchurch (3 daily; 50min); Wellington (10 daily; 25min).
Nelson to: Auckland (12 daily; 1hr 20min); Christchurch (4 daily; 50min); Wellington (10 daily; 35min).
Picton to: Wellington (6–8 daily; 25min).
Takaka to: Wellington (daily; 30min).

Christchurch and south to Otago

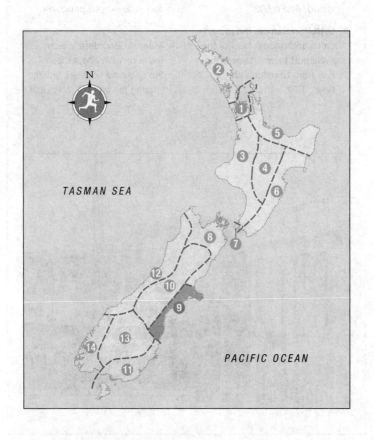

N

TASMAN SEA

PACIFIC OCEAN

Highlights

* **Christchurch Art Gallery** New Zealand's newest major gallery, with a fine collection of Kiwi art. See p.507

* **Ballooning** The Canterbury Plains are one of the best ballooning spots in the world, with views to the Southern Alps and up and down South Island. See p.509

* **Lyttelton** Sample the groovy cafés and offbeat bars of this lively port town just over the hills from Christchurch. See p.522

* **Akaroa** Stay in a fine B&B in this relaxed French-influenced village and swim with Hector's dolphins. See p.526

* **Oamaru** The fine core of Neoclassical buildings in the slowly gentrifying Historic District make this a perfect base for spotting both blue and yellow-eyed penguins. See p.537

* **Moeraki Boulders** Watch the surf crash about these 2m spherical boulders artfully littering the tide line. See p.543

▲ Lyttelton

Christchurch and south to Otago

n many ways, the South Island's east coast comes closer to expectations of New Zealand than any other part of the country. Huge sweeps of pastoral land come wedged between snowy mountains and a rugged coast. The main hub of the region is New Zealand's third city, **Christchurch**, stretched out between the Pacific Ocean and the agriculturally rich flatlands of the Canterbury Plains. It is a relaxed city with a lively café and bar scene, where parks and gardens rub shoulders with some fine Victorian architecture. **The beach suburb** of Sumner is within easy reach of the centre, and just over the bald **Port Hills** you'll find the appealing port town of **Lyttelton**. Lyttelton harbour is a drowned volcanic crater and geologically part of **Banks Peninsula**, a popular escape for city residents, its coastline indented with numerous bays and harbours. The largest settlement is the slightly twee "French village" of **Akaroa**, a great place to relax and a good base for exploring the peninsula.

South of Banks Peninsula, the main road (SH1) forges across the Canterbury Plains, a patchwork of fertile fields and vineyards bordered by long shingle beaches littered with driftwood. Further south the countryside again changes character, with undulating coastal hills and crumbling cliffs announcing the altogether more rugged terrain of North Otago. Historic settlements dotted along the coast testify to the wealth that farming has brought to the region. The first significant town is the workaday port of **Timaru**, close to a series of Maori rock paintings, evidence of a far longer history than the imposed European feel would have you believe. Further south, **Oamaru** is much more beguiling, with wonderfully accessible penguin colonies and an impressive core of nineteenth-century mercantile buildings in the process of being restored. Beyond, routes lead on towards Dunedin and the south, passing the unearthly Moeraki boulders, perfect spherical rocks formed by a combination of subterranean pressure and erosion.

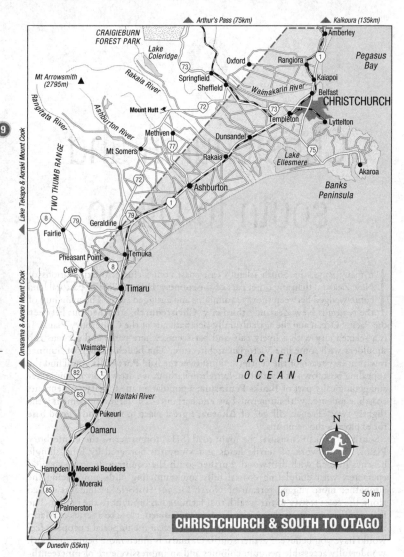

▲ Arthur's Pass (75km)   ▲ Kaikoura (135km)

CRAIGIEBURN
FOREST PARK
Lake
Coleridge
Amberley
Oxford
Rangiora
Pegasus
Bay
Rakaia River
73
Springfield
Sheffield
Kaiapoi
Waimakariri River
Mt Arrowsmith
(2795m)
Belfast
CHRISTCHURCH
Mount Hutt
72
73
Ashburton River
Templeton
Lyttelton
Methven
Dunsandel
Mt Somers
77
Rakaia
75
Lake
Ellesmere
72
Akaroa
Ashburton
Banks
Peninsula
1
8
79
Geraldine
79
Fairlie
Pheasant Point
Temuka
Cave
8
Timaru
Waimate
PACIFIC
OCEAN
82
1
83
Waitaki River
N
Pukeuri
Oamaru
Hampden Moeraki Boulders
Moeraki
0   50 km
85
Palmerston
1
CHRISTCHURCH & SOUTH TO OTAGO

▼ Dunedin (55km)

RANGITATA RIVER
TWO THUMB RANGE
◀ Lake Tekapo & Aoraki Mount Cook
◀ Omarama & Aoraki Mount Cook

Christchurch

With a population of over 350,000, **CHRISTCHURCH** is the largest city on the
South Island and capital of the Canterbury region. It exudes a palpable air of
gentility and a strong connection with the mother country. After all, it was
founded as an outpost of Anglicanism by its first settlers, was named after an
Oxford college, and has some of the feel of a traditional English university town,

with its neo-Gothic architecture and gently winding river. To some extent it pursues an archetype – the boys at Christ's College still wear striped blazers, and punts slide along the Avon – but the Englishness is largely skin-deep. In recent years the traditional conservatism of the settlement has developed a youthful and more multicultural edge, with an explosion of lively bars and restaurants and a burgeoning visual arts, theatre, music and street entertainment scene. These urban and cultural pursuits are balanced by relaxed beach life at the Pacific Ocean suburb of **Sumner**. On the southern skirts of the city, the **Port Hills** provide a playground for hikers and bikers, or a great destination for an evening drive.

The city can be used as a base for exploring further afield, with a plethora of companies offering **activities** such as rafting, ballooning and high country tours, all in the surrounding countryside (see box, p.509). Christchurch is also within a two-hour drive of several good **ski-fields** to the west, making it possible to combine a day on the pistes with an evening in the city's restaurants and bars.

Getting around

Christchurch is the hub of air, road and rail routes for Canterbury and the rest of the South Island. There are direct **flights** to Blenheim, Dunedin, Hokitika, Invercargill, Nelson, Queenstown, Wanaka and several North Island cities. Two very scenic passenger **trains** operate: the TranzCoastal to Picton (meeting ferries to the North Island) and the TranzAlpine to Greymouth (see box, p.513). Most intercity journeys are best done by **bus**. There are usually two to four services a day to most destinations, but bear in mind that journeys from, say, Christchurch to Nelson or Queenstown are likely to take up most of the day.

Akaroa French Connection ☎0800/800 575, ⊛www.akaroabus.co.nz. To Akaroa daily at 8.45am (and more in summer); free central pick-ups.

Akaroa Shuttle ☎0800/500 929, ⊛www.akaroashuttle.co.nz. To Akaroa 2–3 times daily. Departs Christchurch i-SITE and free central pick-ups.

Atomic Shuttles ☎03/439 0697, ⊛www.atomictravel.co.nz. North to Kaikoura, Blenheim and Picton; south to Timaru, Oamaru and Dunedin; west to Greymouth; and inland through Geraldine and Twizel to Wanaka and Queenstown. Departs from 88 Worcester St, but free pick-ups inside the Four Avenues.

Hanmer Connection ☎0800/242 663, ⊛www.atsnz.com. Twice daily to Hanmer Springs. Departs Cathedral Square.

Hanmer Shuttle ☎0800/800 575, ⊛www.akaroabus.co.nz. Departs daily at 9.45am to Hanmer Springs; free central pick-ups.

InterCity/Newmans ☎03/365 1113, ⊛www.intercitycoach.co.nz. North to Kaikoura, Blenheim, Picton and Nelson; south to Timaru, Oamaru, Dunedin and Invercargill; and inland to Methven, Aoraki Mount Cook, Wanaka and Queenstown. Services depart from Richies Travel at 123 Worcester St behind the cathedral.

Knightrider ☎0800/317 057, ⊛www.knightrider.co.nz. Thrice-weekly evening/ night trips to Dunedin and Invercargill. Departs from Victoria Square on Colombo Street.

Methven Travel ⊛www.methventravel.co.nz. Daily to Methven from Cathedral Square.

NakedBus ⊛www.nakedbus.com. Services operated by Atomic.

Southern Link ☎0508/458 835, ⊛www.southernlinkkbus.co.nz. Daily services to Dunedin, Queenstown and Picton from 88 Worcester St near the Square.

West Coast Shuttle ☎03/768 0028, ⊛www.westcoastshuttle.co.nz. Once daily to Greymouth. Services depart at 3pm from Richies Travel (see above).

Some history

Maori occupied scattered settlements around the region before the first Europeans arrived, establishing Lyttelton as a whaling port in the 1830s. By 1843, the Scottish Deans brothers (see p.511), were farming inland, but the real foundations of Christchurch were laid by the **Canterbury Association**, formed in 1849 by members of Oxford's Christ Church College, and with the Archbishop of Canterbury at its head. The association had the utopian aim of creating a middle-class, Anglican community in which the moralizing culture of Victorian England could prosper.

It was at Lyttelton that four ships containing nearly eight hundred **settlers** arrived in 1850, bound for the new city of Christchurch. The earliest settlers weren't all Anglicans by any means, and the millenarian aspirations upon which the city was founded soon faded as people got on with the exhausting business of carving out a new life in unfamiliar terrain. Nevertheless, the association's ideals had a profound effect on the cultural identity of the city and descent from those who came on the "four ships" still carries social cachet among members of the Christchurch elite.

Arrival and moving on

Christchurch Airport, 10km northwest of the city centre, stays open 24/7 and you may find yourself arriving at some ungodly hour. Fortunately, there are ATMs, foreign-exchange booths and a couple of **visitor centres**, at least one of which will be open. In addition, there's a freephone board for accommodation and car-rental bookings, and **left luggage** at Luggage Solutions (suitcase or backpack $6/one day, $10/overnight; daily 4.30am–6pm; ℡03/358 8027).

The City Flier bus runs into the city centre every 15–30 minutes (Mon–Fri 6am–1am, Sat 7am–1am, Sun 8am–1am; $7.50 one-way), as do buses #3, #10 & #29 (jointly Mon–Fri 5.50am–11.50pm, Sat 6.10am–11.40pm & Sun 7.30am–11.40pm; $7.50 one-way). You may find it more convenient to look out for one of the airport–city **shuttle buses** which are usually parked outside the terminal and only charge $7 to the Square (or just $5 if you catch the shuttle to *base* backpackers at twenty past the hour). Various other **shuttle** buses (such as Super Shuttle ℡0800/748 885) operate a frequent door-to-door service. There'll often be several waiting outside the terminal: hop in and once there is a viable load (this usually takes under 10min) they'll take you to your lodging (typically $20 for one, $25 for two). They pick up at most accommodation when heading **to the airport**: book the evening before. There are also $7 shuttles from the tram stop in the Square leaving for the airport roughly every 20min: take your chance.

Taxis between the airport and the CBD charge $40–50.

The **train station**, Troup Drive (train info ℡0800/872 467), is near the corner of Hagley Park, over 2km southwest of Cathedral Square. Canterbury Shuttles (℡0800/021 682, ⓦwww.canterburyshuttles.co.nz) do free CBD pick-ups for train ticket holders. Phone for a pick-up or check the website for their standard pick-up loop (mostly hostels). Post-train journey drop-offs around the city centre cost $5.

Long-distance **buses** all stop near the Square (see box, p.497).

Orientation and information

The low-rise, grid-plan city centre, together with many of its more compelling sights, is encased within the **Four Avenues** – Moorhouse, Fitzgerald, Bealey and Deans. They define a useful border round the downtown area, in the very centre of which is **Cathedral Square** (usually known as "the Square") with its landmark spire.

Christchurch's **i-SITE visitor centre**, in the former Post Office on the south side of Cathedral Square (daily: Nov to mid-Jan 8.30am–6pm; mid-Jan to March 8.30am–7pm; April–Oct 8.30am–5pm; ☎03/379 9629, ⓦwww.christchurchnz .com), stocks all manner of useful leaflets, does bookings for much of the South Island, has the latest on **festivals** (see "Listings" on p.520) and has exclusive specials on accommodation and activities. It is also the first port of call for tramping information, though there is a **DOC office** at 195 Hereford St (Mon–Fri 8.30am–5pm; ☎03/341 9102).

The i-SITE is often busy and you may find it easier to nip into the **Adventure Centre**, 69 Cathedral Square (Dec & Jan Mon–Fri 9am–9.30pm, Sat & Sun 10am–6pm; Feb–Nov 9am–6pm, Sat & Sun 10am–6pm; ☎0800/847 486, ⓦwww.adventures.net.nz), a convenient commercial enterprise which makes its money by booking trips.

City transport

You can easily see most of what Christchurch has to offer **on foot**, resorting to public transport for the odd trip out to the suburbs. The City Bus Exchange on the corner of Colombo and Lichfield streets is the hub for **bus** services run by several companies, but unified under Metro and Red Bus (info desk Mon–Fri 7.30am–6pm, Sat & Sun 9.30am–5.30pm; ☎03/366 8855, ⓦwww.metroinfo.org.nz, www.redbus.co.nz). In the immediate vicinity along Colombo Street, between the Town Hall and Moorhouse Avenue, there's the free yellow environmentally friendly **Shuttle**, running every 10–15min (7.30am–10.30pm) but it is only marginally useful. With the exception of the yellow shuttle and the Airport Bus (see opposite), the **fare** anywhere in the city's zone one, including Sumner and Lyttelton, is $2.80. If you are here for a few days, save money by buying a **Metrocard** from the Bus Exchange (min $10), which you swipe each time you board. Standard fares drop to $2.10 and once you've paid for two fares on a certain day subsequent journeys are free for the rest of the day. Most routes run from 6.30am until around midnight.

Familiarize yourself with the central city by hopping on the **Christchurch Tramway** (daily Nov–March 9am–9pm; April–Oct 9am–6pm; ⓦwww.tram .co.nz), which weaves a 3km circuit past many of the central sights, including the Arts Centre and Cathedral Square, and comes with a driver commentary. The tramway was only re-installed in 1995, but the rolling stock is largely made up of lovingly restored originals built between 1908 and 1925. Tickets ($15) give unlimited rides for two days.

Driving in Christchurch is straightforward, and even the morning and evening rush hours are pretty tame. Most central parking spaces are metered from Monday to Saturday between 7am and 6pm (otherwise free). If you have to drive into town, there's convenient **parking** in the centre of Hagley Park (Armagh Street entrance): free for the first hour and all day at weekends.

Given the city's relatively quiet roads and flat terrain, **cycling** is an ideal way of exploring some of the more out-of-the-way suburbs. Wheels 'n' Deals Cycles, 159 Gloucester St between Manchester and Colombo (Mon–Fri 8.30am–5.30pm, Sat & Sun 11am–2.30pm; ☎03/377 6655), rent mountain bikes and tourers ($18/ half-day, $25/day).

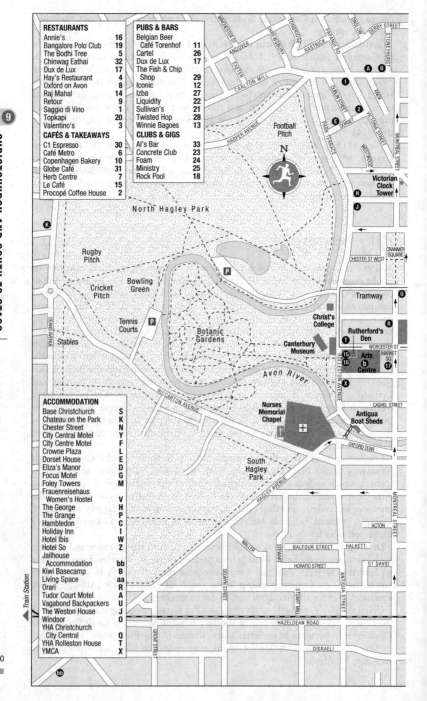

RESTAURANTS

Annie's	16
Bangalore Polo Club	19
The Bodhi Tree	5
Chinwag Eathai	32
Dux de Lux	17
Hay's Restaurant	4
Oxford on Avon	8
Raj Mahal	14
Retour	9
Saggio di Vino	1
Topkapi	20
Valentino's	3

CAFÉS & TAKEAWAYS

C1 Espresso	30
Café Metro	6
Copenhagen Bakery	10
Globe Café	31
Herb Centre	7
Le Café	15
Procopé Coffee House	2

PUBS & BARS

Belgian Beer Café Torenhof	11
Cartel	26
Dux de Lux	17
The Fish & Chip Shop	29
Iconic	12
Izba	27
Liquidity	22
Sullivan's	21
Twisted Hop	28
Winnie Bagoes	13

CLUBS & GIGS

Al's Bar	33
Concrete Club	23
Foam	24
Ministry	25
Rock Pool	18

ACCOMMODATION

Base Christchurch	S
Chateau on the Park	K
Chester Street	N
City Central Motel	Y
City Centre Motel	F
Crowne Plaza	L
Dorset House	E
Eliza's Manor	D
Focus Motel	G
Foley Towers	M
Frauenreisehaus Women's Hostel	V
The George	H
The Grange	P
Hambledon	C
Holiday Inn	I
Hotel Ibis	W
Hotel So	Z
Jailhouse Accommodation	bb
Kiwi Basecamp	B
Living Space	aa
Orari	R
Tudor Court Motel	A
Vagabond Backpackers	U
The Weston House	J
Windsor	O
YHA Christchurch City Central	Q
YHA Rolleston House	T
YMCA	X

North Hagley Park

Football Pitch

N

Rugby Pitch

Bowling Green

Cricket Pitch

Tennis Courts

Botanic Gardens

Stables

Victorian Clock Tower

CRANMER SQUARE

CHESTER ST WEST

Tramway

Christ's College

Rutherford's Den

WORCESTER ST

MARKET SQ

Arts Centre

Canterbury Museum

Avon River

CASHEL STREET

Nurses Memorial Chapel

Antigua Boat Sheds

OXFORD TERR

South Hagley Park

ACTON

BALFOUR STREET

HALKETT

HORATIO STREET

ST DAVID

HAZELDEAN ROAD

DISRAELI

Train Station

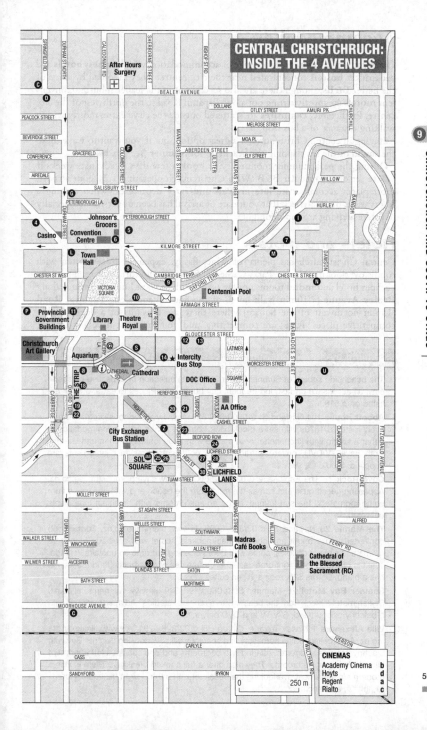

CENTRAL CHRISTCHRUCH: INSIDE THE 4 AVENUES

SPRINGFIELD RD
DURHAM ST NORTH
CALEDONIAN RD
SHERBORNE STREET
BISHOP ST RD

After Hours Surgery

C

D

BEALEY AVENUE

DOLLANS
OTLEY STREET
AMURI PK
CHURCHILL

MELROSE STREET

PEACOCK STREET
MOA PL

BEVERIDGE STREET
ELY STREET

GRACEFIELD
MANCHESTER STREET
ULSTER
ABERDEEN STREET
MADRAS STREET

CONFERENCE
COLOMBO STREET
F

AIREDALE
WILLOW

SALISBURY STREET
BANGOR

HURLEY

G
PETERBOROUGH LA. 3

Johnson's Grocers
PETERBOROUGH STREET

4
Convention Centre 6
5
I

Casino
DURHAM STREET

KILMORE STREET
7

L Town Hall
M

CHESTER ST WEST
CAMBRIDGE TERR
OXFORD TERR
CHESTER STREET
DAWSON

VICTORIA SQUARE
8
9
N

10
Centennial Pool

ARMAGH STREET

P Provincial Government Buildings 11
NEW REGENT ST
O

Library
Theatre Royal

Christchurch Art Gallery
CHANCERY LA.
Q
GLOUCESTER STREET
12
13
LATIMER
BARBADOES STREET

Aquarium
S
14 ★ Intercity Bus Stop
WORCESTER STREET

a
i
CATHEDRAL SQ
Cathedral
DOC Office
SQUARE
V
U

THE STRIP
18
W
HEREFORD STREET
WOOLSTON

19
HIGH STREET
20 21
LIVERPOOL
AA Office
Y

22
CAMBRIDGE TERR
OXFORD TERR
CASHEL STREET
CLARKSON
GILMOUR
FITZGERALD AVENUE

Z
23

City Exchange Bus Station
BEDFORD ROW
24

25 26
MANCHESTER STREET
27 28
LICHFIELD STREET
ASH

SOL SQUARE
29
HIGH ST
COLOMBO ST
30
LICHFIELD LANES
DUKE

TUAM STREET
31
32

MOLLETT STREET
ST ASAPH STREET
ALFRED

WALKER STREET
DURHAM STREET
WINCHCOMBE
COLOMBO STREET
QUILL
WELLES STREET
SOUTHWARK
WILLIAMS
COVENTRY
FERRY RD

WILMER STREET
AVCESTER
ATLAS
ALLEN STREET
Madras Café Books
Cathedral of the Blessed Sacrament (RC)

BATH STREET
33
DUNDAS STREET
ROPE
EATON
MORTIMER

MOORHOUSE AVENUE
C
d
IVERSON

CARLYLE
WAITHAM RD

CASS
CINEMAS

SANDYFORD
BYRON
Academy Cinema b
Hoyts d
Regent a
Rialto c

0   250 m

Accommodation

Christchurch has an impressive range of accommodation with **business hotels** and backpacker **hostels** concentrated near the city centre. They're joined by some of the better **B&Bs**, though there are also several out in the leafier suburbs. Convenient **motels** are mostly strung out along Papanui Road to the northwest of the city centre. Predictably, **campsites** are scattered outside the city centre, mostly within walking distance of a bus stop.

Staying in central Christchurch is a great option, but if you want to wake up to the sound of the sea slapping the beach, go for **Sumner** (see box below).

During the peak summer months try to **book** a few days in advance, weeks if you're set on a particular B&B. With Christchurch operating a 24-hour airport, most places accommodate **late arrivals** and early departures: when making a reservation, double-check that your date of arrival has been understood, especially if you're arriving around midnight.

Hotels and motels

Central Christchurch has plenty of large, flashy, expensive **hotels** often with rooms overlooking Hagley Park, Cathedral Square or Victoria Square. There are cheaper hotel and **motel** rooms not far away, with the best hunting ground along **Bealey Avenue** (a 10min walk north of the Square) and along **Papanui Road** (15min northwest of the Square) where there are upwards of a dozen highly competitive places. Rates are competitive, and you shouldn't have any trouble

---

Staying by the beach: Sumner

The beachside suburb of Sumner (see p.513) has a selection of appealing places to stay, all accessible on fast and frequent city buses (#3). Places to eat and drink are listed on p.518.

Abbott House 104 Nayland St ℡0800/020 654, ℗www.abbotthouse.co.nz. Attractively restored 1870s villa set a block back from the beach with accommodation in either a studio with kitchenette, or in a suite with large lounge, kitchen and laundry. Both have TV/DVD, private entrances and continental breakfast ingredients are supplied. Studio ❹, suite ❺

Cave Rock 16 The Esplanade ℡03/326 5600, ℗www.caverockguesthouse.co.nz. Appealing guesthouse just across the road from the beach and with sea views from some rooms and the sun lounge. Large en-suite rooms with breakfast ingredients delivered. ❺

The Marine 26 Nayland St ℡03/326 6609, ℗www.themarine.co.nz. Former pub converted into a bright and cheerful backpackers hostel with spacious four-share rooms and several doubles, some with doors opening out onto an upstairs veranda. Toast is provided for a light breakfast, there's free use of a barbecue, and the lounge has a piano. Dorms $25, rooms ❶, en suites ❷

Sumner Bay Motel 26 Marriner St ℡0800/496 949, ℗www.sumnermotel.co.nz. Stylish motel a block from the beach, with a range of studios and apartments all with a balcony or courtyard, Sky TV and DVD player. ❺

Villa Alexandra 1 Kinsey Terrace, Clifton Hill ℡03/326 6291, ℗www.villaalexandra .co.nz. An excellent-value homestay in a spacious villa overlooking Sumner Bay with a sunny veranda and turret, offering two bedrooms and one spacious loft apartment all with their own bathrooms. They also offer a full cooked breakfast. There is also a modern s/c apartment overlooking the beach let with a three-night minimum. Rooms ❹, loft ❺, apartment ❺

finding a studio for around $110 a night. In addition, many establishments offer **special deals** for weekend and long-term stays.

City centre

Chateau on the Park 189 Deans Ave ☎0800/808 999, Ⓦwww.chateau-park.co.nz. Two-hundred-room hotel, memorable for its lovely surroundings on the edge of Hagley Park, with an outdoor pool, restaurants and cocktail bar. 25min walk from the Square but they have a special shuttle. ❻

City Central Motel Apartments 252 Barbados St ☎0508/800 888, Ⓦwww.citycentral.co.nz. Modernized motel with flat-screen-TV-equipped, stylish rooms and parking just 5min walk from the city centre. It is on a busy intersection but rooms are double-glazed. ❹

City Centre Motel 876 Colombo St ☎0800/240 101, Ⓦwww.citycentremotel.co.nz. Plush modern motel with flat-screen TVs and off-street parking. Surprisingly quiet for such a central location. ❺

Crowne Plaza Corner of Kilmore & Durham sts ☎0800/154 181, Ⓦwww.crowneplaza.co.nz. Probably the best of the central business hotels, overlooking Victoria Square with a magnificent lobby plus assorted bars and restaurants. ❼

Focus Motel 344 Durham St North ☎03/943 0800, Ⓦwww.focusmotel.com. Stylish, central motel with modern studios and larger units plus a great penthouse with city views. Spa bath units $10 extra. Studios ❺, rooms ❻, penthouse ❽

Holiday Inn 356 Oxford Terrace ☎0800/154 181, Ⓦwww.holidayinn.com. Business hotel on the edge of the CBD, beside the Avon River with relaxing courtyard gardens and a high standard of rooms, plus all the expected facilities including indoor pool, restaurant and bar. ❻

Hotel Ibis 107 Hereford St ☎03/367 8666, Ⓦwww.ibishotel.com. Modern, no-frills business hotel in the heart of the city. Rooms are small and without minibar though they're tastefully decorated and have phone, fridge, tea and coffee and LCD TV, and there's a restaurant and bar on site. Parking nearby for $15/day. ❹–❺

Hotel So 165 Cashel St ☎0508/165 165, Ⓦwww.hotelso.co.nz. Central hotel where space is sacrificed for stylish lodging at budget prices. Chic rooms (all en suite) come with flat-screen TV, free wi-fi, MP3-player link to sound system, and controllable mood lighting, plus there's a small gym/sauna

and a café/bar. The tiny singles all lack windows as do some of the doubles, so you may want to step up to the slightly more spacious queen or king (both ❺). The shower/toilet combo is effectively in the room, housekeeping ($15/day) and car parking ($16) are both extra and there's a good café/bar with meal deals. Singles $69, rooms ❸

Living Space 96 Lichfield St ☎03/964 5212, Ⓦwww.livingspace.net. If you don't want to stagger more than twenty paces from the restaurants and bars of Sol Square, then this is your spot. Tidy, smallish, en-suite rooms in this converted clothing warehouse come with TV and kitchenette, and everyone has access to a communal lounge and kitchen. Noisy at weekends and parking costs $15. ❹

Tudor Court Motel 57 Bealey Ave ☎0800/488 367, Ⓦwww.tudorcourt.co.nz. Very small budget motel in a peaceful environment with simple, comfy units, about 10min walk from Cathedral Square. Continental breakfasts are available. ❹

Papanui Road

Lodgings are marked on the map on p.510.

Colonial Inn Motel 43 Papanui Rd ☎0800/111 232, Ⓦwww.colonialinnmotel.co.nz. A modern motel about 15min walk from Cathedral Square with clean and comfortable units. ❹

Diplomat Motel 127 Papanui Rd ☎0800/109 699, Ⓦwww.diplomatmotel.co.nz. Situated in the heart of Merivale, 2km north of Cathedral Square, this smart motel has large s/c units with separate kitchens, where the extra few dollars are justified by a nice outdoor pool and spa and free wi-fi. ❹

Randolph 79 Papanui Rd ☎0800/537366, Ⓦwww.randolphmotel.co.nz. Excellent modern motel in grounds overshadowed by a huge copper beech tree. Rooms with bold decor are extremely well equipped with cooking facilities, TV/DVD, stereo and in-room laundry. Deluxe rooms come with double spa bath and there's even a small gym. ❺

Strathern Motor Lodge 54 Papanui Rd ☎0800/766 624, Ⓦwww.strathern.co.nz. Spacious and well-presented modern units with kitchenette or full kitchen and free wi-fi. One unit has its own spa bath. ❹

B&Bs and guesthouses

Christchurch has a wonderful range of **B&Bs** – in the centre, in the leafy inner suburbs, and at the seaside community of Sumner. Prices start around $120.

City centre

Eliza's Manor 82 Bealey Ave ☎03/366 8584, ⓦwww.elizas.co.nz. Luxury B&B in a grand 1861 house with eight rooms all period furnished and with heat pump temperature control. Go for the spacious Heritage rooms if possible. Rooms ⑥, Heritage ⑧

The George 50 Park Terrace ☎0800/100 220, ⓦwww.thegeorge.com. One of the country's finest urban boutique hotels, recently renovated with considerable panache. There's great art, a cool bar and the chic *Pescatore* restaurant overlooking Hagley Park. Rates from $400, though check for internet specials. ⑨

The Grange 56 Armagh St ☎0800/932 850, ⓦwww.thegrange.co.nz. Good central, budget option, very popular and with eight small and modestly appointed en-suite rooms. There are also eight more spacious self-catering apartments. Room ④, B&B ⑤, apartments ⑤

🏃 **Hambledon** 103 Bealey Ave ☎03/379 0723, ⓦwww.hambledon.co.nz. Luxurious, but homely family-run B&B with plush Victorian furniture in one of the city's oldest and grandest houses, built in 1856 for one of the early city fathers. The array of high-standard, spacious suites all come with complimentary port and sherry and delicious breakfasts. ⑧

Orari 42 Gloucester St ☎03/365 6569, ⓦwww.orari.net.nz. Informally run and art-adorned B&B in a large 1893 home just steps from the Arts Centre. Ten bright, sunny rooms all have TVs, phones, artworks and either en suites or private bathrooms (one with a tub). There's wine on arrival and a full breakfast. ⑥

The Weston House 62 Park Terrace ☎03/366 0234 ⓦwww.westonhouse.co.nz. This splendid arts and crafts influenced neo-Georgian homestead opposite Hagley Park has a very intimate feel (just two guest suites), enhanced by urbane and informative hosts, Stephanie and Len. There's a fabulous library, lovely gardens, delicious breakfasts and a 1964 Cooper racing car in the garage. Rates from $395. ⑨

Windsor 52 Armagh St ☎0800/366 1503, ⓦwww.windsorhotel.co.nz. Traditional guesthouse with forty rooms in a 1907 former student hall of residence. Nothing flash and none of the rooms have en-suite bathrooms, but they are comfortable, clean and mostly quiet, the staff are friendly and the cooked breakfast keeps you going all day. Free internet and wi-fi. ⑤

Outside the Four Avenues

These lodgings are marked on the map on p.510.

Cashmere Heights 95 Longhurst Terrace ☎03/332 5211, ⓦwww.cashmereheights.co.nz. The views are only matched by the comfort and welcome at this modern, luxury B&B in the Port Hills with just two suites. Airport and train pick-ups are complimentary and breakfast is an event. ⑧

The Charlotte Jane 110 Papanui Rd ☎03/355 1028, ⓦwww.charlotte-jane.co.nz. Named for one of Canterbury's founding "Four Ships, this elegant boutique hotel has beautiful wood-panelled rooms, breakfast when you want it and an atmospheric restaurant (dinner only). Standard rooms ($395) are gorgeous but the next level up ($540) have spa baths and working fireplaces. ⑨

🏃 **Onuku** 27 Harry Ell Drive, Cashmere, 7km south of central Christchurch ☎03/332 7296, ⓦwww.onukubedandbreakfast.co.nz. Welcoming B&B in a stylish modern house high in the Port Hills with fab views of the city and great access to walking and mountain biking. Rooms are simple but tasteful with very comfy beds, pick-ups can be arranged and there's a full breakfast to set you up for the day. Private bath ④, en suite ⑤

Hostels

Most **backpacker hostels** in Christchurch are within the Four Avenues, or just beyond. Almost all are close to the action and offer excellent value for money. We've picked a range of the best: quiet modern hostels; party-oriented downtown places; and those a few blocks out with gardens and a homely atmosphere (something Christchurch specializes in). Prices don't vary a great deal, generally around $26 for dorm beds and around $65 for doubles and twins, with sheets and towels. None of the hostels listed here have tent sites.

Most hostels are prepared for late plane arrivals, and many have long-term storage for bike boxes and gear you might not need in the South Island.

base Christchurch 56 Cathedral Square ☎03/982 2225, ⓦwww.stayatbase.com. Modern 300-bed hostel in an 1880 building in the heart of the city with card-swipe entry, a café/bar, a separate women's section known as "Sanctuary" and a top-floor penthouse that's a kind of mini-hostel within a hostel. It is a fun place to stay with plenty of lounges, pool table and an Indian restaurant on the doorstep. Dorms $28, Sanctuary $30, rooms ❷, en suites ❸

Chester Street 148 Chester St East ☏03/377 1897, ⓦwww.chesterst.co.nz. With just fourteen beds this is the city's smallest hostel and feels more like a shared house with comfy doubles and a three-bed dorm. Separate TV lounge, limited off-street parking and a pleasant garden. Dorm $27, rooms ❷

🏃 **Dorset House** 1 Dorset St ☏03/366 8268, ⓦwww.dorsethouse.co.nz. Spacious hostel in a nicely renovated 1871 house located in a quiet area, with firm beds (no bunks), a strong eco-consciousness and even bathrobes to rent. There's off-street parking, Sky TV and pool in a huge lounge fitted with stained-glass windows, and free wi-fi. Also self-catering apartments in a house nearby. Dorms $27, rooms ❷, apartments ❸

Foley Towers 208 Kilmore St ☏03/366 9720, ⓔfoley.towers@backpack.co.nz. A Christchurch backpacking original from the mid-1980s, built around a couple of old houses that manages to maintain an intimate feel thanks to attentive staff, attractive gardens and an abundance of doubles and twins. Dorms $23, rooms & en suites ❷

Frauenreisehaus Women's Hostel 272 Barbados St ☏03/366 2585, ⓦwww.womenshostel.co.nz. Wonderfully relaxed and superbly well-equipped women-only hostel in an old and central house. Much loved by those looking for scented candles, mood music, spring water direct from the garden and heaps of DVDs. Dorms $26, single $43, twins ❷

🏃 **Jailhouse Accommodation** 338 Lincoln Rd ☏03/982 7777 & 0800/524 546, ⓦwww.jail.co.nz. A jail as recently as 1999, this Victorian Gothic prison has been imaginatively turned into an atmospheric hostel with mostly double and twin-bunk rooms plus some bunk-free dorms, all kauri-floored. Whimsical touches include barbed-wire inlaid toilet seats and a couple of cells left as they were. Helpful owners, bike rental ($15/day), a free Kiwi and prison-related DVD library, free pool table and good espresso round out the deal. Located almost 2km southwest of the Square: bus #7 drops off at the door. Dorms $26, rooms ❷

Kiwi Basecamp 69 Bealey Ave ☏0800/505025, ⓦwww.kiwibasecamp.com. One of the cheapest hostels in town but still maintaining a high standard. Set in a two-storey villa, it's a relaxed spot with free bikes, free shuttle service around town and free breakfast. Dorms $23, rooms ❷

The Old Countryhouse 437 Gloucester St ☏03/381 5504, ⓦwww.oldcountryhousenz.com. One of Christchurch's most peaceful hostels, fashioned from a couple of wood-floored villas with bold decor and spacious dorms. A 15min walk east of the Square (bus #21; see map, p.510). Dorms $25, rooms ❷, en suites ❸

Vagabond Backpackers 232 Worcester St ☏03/379 9677, ⓔvagabondbackpackers @hotmail.com. Very friendly place with only thirty beds, some in an annexe at the back of the house; all are well kept, quiet and clean. There's off-street parking, BBQ and a lovely garden area. There are also two doubles in a s/c apartment. Dorms $25, rooms & apartment rooms ❷

YHA Christchurch City Central 273 Manchester St ☏03/379 9535, ⓔyha.christchurchcity@yha. co.nz. Large, very central, purpose-built hostel with lots of high-quality rooms, two kitchens, two common rooms and well-informed staff that run the travel, events and booking office. If you're staying in the older wing go for one of the exterior doubles. Limited free parking. Dorms $32, rooms ❸, en suites with TV ❹

YHA Rolleston House 5 Worcester Blvd ☏03/366 6564, ⓔyha.rollestonhouse@yha.co.nz. The best-located hostel in Christchurch: opposite the Arts Centre and full of character. Plenty of dorms but a limited number of twins and doubles, so book ahead for a room. Limited parking. Dorms $33, rooms ❸, en suite ❹

YMCA 12 Hereford St ☏0508/962 224, ⓦwww .ymcachch.org.nz. Very central, state-of-the-art YMCA with spartan dorms, singles, basic doubles and deluxe en-suite doubles with phone, tea and coffee, and TV. Guests get significant discounts at the fitness centre, gym, squash courts, climbing wall and sauna, and there's an on-site café. Dorms $25, doubles ❷/❸

Campsites

Christchurch's **campsites** are well set up for tents and campervans, and offer good deals on cabins, though given their distance from the centre you might find it more convenient to stay in one of the city's excellent hostels.

The campsites are marked on the map on p.510.

Amber Park 308 Blenheim Rd, Upper Riccarton ☏03/348 3327, ⓦwww.amberpark.co.nz. Spacious, grassy site with all the expected features just 4km south of the city (bus #5 stops right outside), and handy for the train station and Canterbury University. Camping $19, en-suite cabins ❷, kitchen cabins ❸, motels ❹

Christchurch Top 10 39 Meadow St, Papanui ☎0800/396 323, ⓦwww.meadowpark.co.nz. Situated 5km north of the Square on SH74 (reached by buses #11, #12 & #13) this large campsite, close to supermarkets and restaurants, has a full range of facilities including a heated indoor pool. Camping $37 per site, cabins ❷, s/c chalets ❸, motels ❺

South Brighton Holiday Park 59 Halsey St, South New Brighton ☎03/388 9844, ⓦwww.southbright-onmotorcamp.co.nz. Handily sited near the beach 7km east of the city centre, this medium-sized site has good facilities and a limited range of cabins and flats. Camping $16, cabins ❶, s/c cabins ❷

The City

Scattered in the streets west of Cathedral Square are the city's most attractive buildings, predominantly nineteenth-century Gothic, though with some outstanding modern structures such as the **art gallery**. This is the area known as the **Cultural Precinct**, which extends to the fringes of **Hagley Park**, a focal point for leisure activities after work and at weekends. It is threaded by the placid River Avon, and there's no more relaxing way to experience some of the prettier parts of the city than by **punt**.

Outside the Four Avenues you pass into well-tended suburban districts characterized by one- and two-storey residential housing and beautifully kept gardens. Further east, **Sumner** is the most picturesque and atmospheric of the Pacific Ocean **beaches**.

Within the Four Avenues

Christchurch is centred on **Cathedral Square** a large, open, paved area typically abuzz with lunching office workers, buskers and tourists. Above it rises the Gothic Revival Anglican **Cathedral** (free guided tours Mon–Fri 11am & 2pm, Sat 11am, Sun 11.30am), designed by George Gilbert Scott, architect of London's St Pancras Station. It was begun in the 1860s and, when completed in 1904, revealed a cool and spacious interior and a 63m spire ($5 to ascend the claustrophobic 134-step staircase). On the left-hand side of the nave, look out for the Maori contribution of *tukutuku* panels made of leather and rimu wood, celebrating the Maori proverb: "What is the most important thing in life? It is people, people, people". To sample the marvellous acoustics of the building, drop by for choral evensong (Tues & Wed 5.30pm for the full choir, Fri 4.30pm for boys' choir only).

Outside stands the 1867 statue of Robert Godley, founding father of Christchurch and agent of the Canterbury Association. It is said to be the earliest public sculpture in New Zealand and is the work of Pre-Raphaelite Thomas Woolner, who was briefly in New Zealand after failing on the Australian goldfields. The vessels that brought the city's founding fathers are also remembered in the nearby *Memorial of the Four Ships*. Neither work matches the scale of Neil Dawson's *Chalice* sculpture, which looks like a monstrous ice-cream cone, silver on the outside and metallic blue on the inside, with leaf and fern patterns cut out of its higher reaches. The grandest of the buildings surrounding the Square are the Italianate 1879 **Old Post Office** and the adjacent 1901 Palladian-style former **Government Building**. Nearby is the **Southern Encounter Aquarium** (daily 9am–5pm; $16; ⓦwww .southernencounter.co.nz), where the damper habitats of the South Island are replicated and populated with native saltwater and freshwater species, with touch tanks, rock pools, plus artificial eel and salmon runs and a mock-up of a fly-fishing lodge. Come for **feeding time** (11am, 1pm & 3pm) and to be guided through a nocturnal house to view North Island **brown kiwi**.

North of Cathedral Square

The grid of streets north of the Square mostly comprise dull commercial offices though there is minor interest along **New Regent Street** where trams clank between neat rows of pastel-painted 1930s Spanish Mission-style buildings. One block west, manicured Victoria Square is bounded to the north by the languid River Avon and Christchurch's starkly modern **Town Hall**. Epicureans should nip around the corner to the venerable **Johnson's Grocers**, 787 Colombo St, a tiny treasure-trove stacked to the rafters with just about every packaged gourmet product imaginable, plus some British favourites.

Following the river a few steps to the southwest you find the 1865 **Provincial Council Buildings**, on the corner of Durham and Armagh streets (Mon–Sat 10am–4pm; free), the only provincial government buildings left in New Zealand. Built in neo-Gothic style they're the masterpiece of Christchurch's most renowned early architect, **Benjamin W. Mountfort**, notably the Gothic Revival Great Hall, magnificently decorated with an intricate ceiling and elaborate stonework.

North along Victoria Street lies the Victorian **clock tower**, which houses a clock originally imported from England in 1860 to adorn the government buildings. This area has the best of the **shopping** north of the Square, mainly antiques and homeware, with the notable exception of the Canterbury Cheesemongers, 44 Salisbury St, with a great selection of cheeses plus crusty loaves of fresh bread.

South of Cathedral Square

The area **south of Cathedral Square** has the city's greatest concentration of shops, restaurants and bars. You may well find yourself here browsing the shops or grabbing a coffee during the day, then back again for a night out. There are no sights to speak of, but **High Street** (between Cashel and St Asaph streets) comes lined with the more offbeat music and clothes shops as well as the cooler end of the café scene. With the arrival of some of the younger established clothing labels, High Street is moving slightly upscale and the edgier vibe is spilling east towards Madras Street.

After dark, make for the narrow lanes South of Lichfield, which in recent years have been dubbed **SOL Square**, the heart of Christchurch nightlife. There's a dense clusters of bars and restaurants, augmented by a second group a block east known as **Lichfield Lanes** and centred on Poplar Street.

West of Cathedral Square

Much of Christchurch's finest architecture, along with the museum, art gallery and arts centre, lies west of Cathedral Square and east of Hagley Park, an area known as the **Cultural Precinct**.

Christchurch Art Gallery

With so much neo-Gothic architecture in Christchurch it is refreshing to come face to face with the **Christchurch Art Gallery**, corner of Worcester Boulevard and Montreal Street (daily 9am–5pm & until 9pm on Wed; free; iPod tour $5; free guided tours daily at 11am & 2pm at weekends; ⓦ www.christchurchartgallery .org.nz), with its striking frontage of curving glass intersecting at odd angles. A grand staircase leads up to the historical, twentieth-century and contemporary collections where New Zealand works are the strongest, particularly those by Christchurch and Canterbury artists. The European landscape tradition comes through forcefully in nineteenth-century paintings by Charles Goldie and Dutch émigré Petrus van der Velden, such as *Mountain Stream Otira Gorge*. More recent works include Tony Fomison's compellingly dark *No!*, Rita Angus' *Cass*, depicting a lone customer on the platform of a desolate station (now on the TranzAlpine route), and Bill Hammond's primordial works liberally scattered with iconic bird-headed humanoids.

Look, too, for works from the 1930s and 1940s by Frances Hodgkins, superb glass castings by Ann Robinson and Shona Firman, and photographic works by both Neil and Fiona Pardington.

The Arts Centre

The **Arts Centre**, diagonally across from the Art Gallery, was built in 1874 as the University of Canterbury and Christchurch Girls' and Boys' High Schools. Benjamin Mountfort was at his Gothic best here using volcanic "bluestone" and Oamaru limestone. After the university decamped to suburban Ilam in 1975, the Arts Centre took over, with restaurants, food stalls, galleries, cinemas and the Court Theatre (see p.519). The leafy courtyards and grassy quadrangles make a great place to watch the world go by, especially at weekends when the Market Square on the east side is turned over to a lively **craft market**, complete with buskers and musicians. Much of what's on sale is made in workshops dotted throughout the building. To the rear of the Arts Centre a collection of ethnic food stalls (Sat & Sun 10am–4pm) offer Hungarian, Czech, Lebanese and a planet-load of other national dishes dirt-cheap. The **information centre** (daily Mon–Fri 8.30am–5.30, Sat & Sun 9am–5pm; ☏03/366 0989, ⓦwww.artscentre.org.nz) runs twenty-minute **tours** of the buildings (at 11am and on demand; free), and provides access to **Rutherford's Den** (donation) which honours Nobel Prize-winning atomic nucleus discoverer **Ernest Rutherford** – he on the $100 banknote. It is an appropriately reverential place with thoughtful displays, a look at the tiny basement laboratory where he did postgraduate research, and a fine old lecture theatre with copiously graffitied benches. Stargazers can visit the university's **Townsend Observatory** (Oct–March Fri 8–10.30pm; free) and look through the 1864 15cm refractor telescope.

Canterbury Museum

Opposite the Arts Centre, an 1870 neo-Gothic structure houses the **Canterbury Museum** (daily Oct–March 9am–5.30pm; April–Sept 9am–5pm; donation appreciated), founded by archeologist Julius Haast who supplied the museum with an Egyptian mummy bought for $24 in 1886. Christchurch's association with the Antarctic is explored with a flimsy unreliable motor tractor from Shackleton's 1914–17 expedition, a Ferguson tractor that became the first vehicle to reach the Pole as part of Edmund Hillary's push in 1958, and the far more robust Sno-Cat used by Brit Vivian Fuchs on the same expedition. Charmingly retro dioramas of penguins and Weddell seals set the tone for the Maori collection, full of great carvings but also featuring dioramas of bronzed natives going about their daily lives. Look out for **Fred and Myrtle's Paua Shell House**, a shrine to kitsch Kiwiana modelled on a house in Bluff where the famed Fluteys plastered their home with polished paua shells. After their death a few years ago, the contents were shipped here and re-assembled.

Next door stands **Christ's College**, the city's most elite private school. There are no tours, but you are free to wander round the grounds and admire the Victorian architecture.

Hagley Park and around

The Museum and Christ's College block the city off from **Hagley Park** which contains the spectacular Botanic Gardens, a golf course and playing fields, and at weekends it seems like the entire population of Christchurch is there, strolling around or playing some form of sport.

Tours and activities in and around Christchurch

Christchurch makes a good base for exploring the immediate vicinity and beyond. Here are some of the more diverting activities and tours.

Ballooning A romantic and gentle way to get airborne is with Up Up And Away (☎03/381 4600, ⊛www.ballooning.co.nz) who offer peaceful early-morning flights over Christchurch's surrounds, with spectacular views from mountains to coast for just $320. Methven-based Aoraki Balloons ($385, standby $335; ☎0800/256 837, ⊛www.nzballooning.co.nz) also offer great trips.

Cycling City Bike tour (☎0800/733 257, ⊛www.chchbiketours.co.nz) shows you the central sights via quiet streets from a comfy saddle. Daily at 2pm. $35.

Guided walking tours Central Christchurch tours (daily Oct–April 10am & 1pm; May–Sept 1pm; 2hr; $15) are led by local volunteers who really know their stuff. They start from a kiosk in Cathedral Square near the cathedral entrance.

High country tour If you want to taste the TranzAlpine train but don't fancy a whole day on board, join Hassle-free Tours (☎0800/148 686, ⊛www.hasslefree.co.nz) on their Alpine Safari (10hr; $375) which includes jetboating the Waimakariri River, going off-road across a high country station and returning by the TranzAlpine from Arthur's Pass.

Paragliding Nimbus Paragliding (☎0800/111 611, ⊛www.nimbusparagliding.co.nz) offers twenty-minute **tandem** flights on the Port Hills above Taylor's Mistake for $160.

Sightseeing Christchurch Sightseeing Tours (☎0508/669 660, ⊛www.christchurch tours.co.nz) offer a City, Beach and Harbour tour (3hr; $46); a summer-only Private Gardens tour (3hr; $40); and a Heritage Homes tour (3hr; $40).

Tank driving As unlikely as it may seem you can drive your own tank with Tanks for Everything, 980 McLeans Island Rd (☎03/359 1007, ⊛www.tanksforeverything.co.nz) near the international airport. You get a 45-minute tour of the vehicles – armoured patrol carriers, Russian Cold War-era tank, Centurion etc – followed by 15–25 minutes of instruction and time at the controls. Prices depend on vehicle $150–695.

Whitewater rafting There are no big rivers near Christchurch, but Rangitata Rafts (see p.562) run one of the most satisfying trips in New Zealand on the Grade IV–V Rangitata River with pick-ups from Christchurch. $195.

One corner is devoted to the **Botanic Gardens** (Rolleston Ave gate; daily 7am until 30min after sunset; conservatories 10.15am–4pm; free), which does all it can to live up to Christchurch's Garden City moniker. It has a collection of indigenous and exotic plants and trees unrivalled on the South Island. From summer to autumn perennials give a constant and dazzling display of colour, the herb garden, containing a variety of culinary and medicinal plants, exuding lovely aromas, and from December the rose garden proudly blooms with over 250 varieties. Best of all, though, it is just a great place to hang out on a sunny day.

The gardens are enclosed by a loop of the River Avon which you can explore by heading along to the **Antigua Boat Sheds**, 2 Cambridge Terrace (daily 9.30am–5.30pm ☎03/366 5885, ⊛www.boatsheds.co.nz) and renting a paddleboat ($20/30min for two), canoe (single $10/hr, double $20), or rowboat ($20/30min). Adjacent, **Punting on the Avon** (☎03/366 0337, ⊛www.punting.co.nz) supplies a guide nattily dressed in a striped blazer and straw boater, to **punt** you along the river ($20/person/30min).

On the southern borders of Hagley Park, Christchurch Hospital almost engulfs the tiny brick-and-slate 1928 **Nurses' Memorial Chapel**, Riccarton Avenue (Mon–Sat 1–4pm; free), dedicated to nurses who served in World War I. It was constructed after the death of three Christchurch-trained nurses aboard a torpedoed troopship in 1915, and contains four stained-glass windows by the English glass artist Veronica Whall, with an uneven texture and a variety of colours set off by the otherwise dark, low-ceilinged interior.

Beyond the Four Avenues

Inspired by a couple of hours spent in the Botanic Gardens, you might fancy a stroll across North Hagley Park to the beautiful precincts of **Mona Vale** at 63 Fendalton Rd (grounds open daily 8.30am to just before dusk; free). Originally part of the Deans' estate (see below) and now tended by the Canterbury Horticultural Society, the gardens have majestic displays of roses, dahlias, fuchsias and irises, as well as magnolias, rhododendrons and herbaceous perennials. The Bath

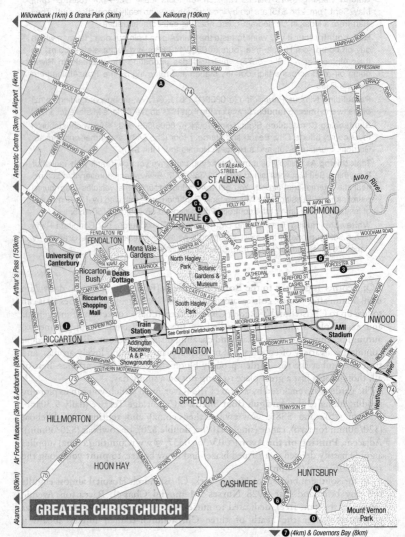

GREATER CHRISTCHURCH

House has been converted for use as a greenhouse, the old homestead is open for lunch daily and you can go **punting** ($20/person/30min).

You could hardly make a greater botanical leap than to wander ten minutes to the southwest to the suburb of Riccarton and **Riccarton Bush** (aka **Deans Bush**; daily dawn–dusk; free), an area of native forest containing several 500-year-old kahikatea trees. Access is off Kahu Road (bus #24). The survival of this valuable area of forest is largely due to Scottish brothers William and John Deans, who came here to farm in 1843 and somehow resisted the temptation to put all their property to immediate agricultural use. Today a concrete path navigates the bush, with signs pointing out the various species. The tiny black-pine **Deans Cottage** (daily 9am–dusk; free), was built by the Deans brothers on their arrival, and is furnished as it would have been when they lived there. Their descendants built the

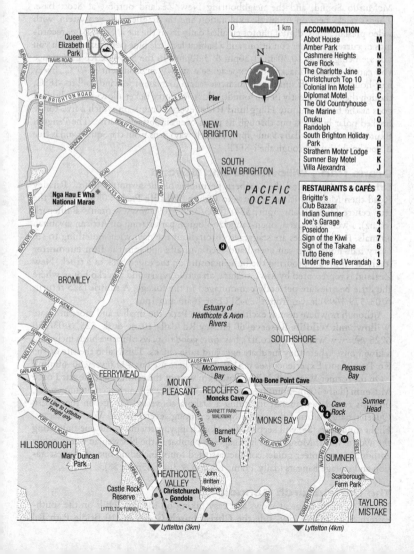

ACCOMMODATION	
Abbot House	M
Amber Park	I
Cashmere Heights	N
Cave Rock	K
The Charlotte Jane	B
Christchurch Top 10	A
Colonial Inn Motel	F
Diplomat Motel	C
The Old Countryhouse	G
The Marine	L
Onuku	O
Randolph	D
South Brighton Holiday Park	
Strathern Motor Lodge	H
Sumner Bay Motel	E
Villa Alexandra	K
	J

RESTAURANTS & CAFÉS	
Brigitte's	2
Club Bazaar	5
Indian Sumner	5
Joe's Garage	4
Poseidon	4
Sign of the Kiwi	7
Sign of the Takahe	6
Tutto Bene	1
Under the Red Verandah	3

adjacent, grand Victorian **Riccarton House** (guided tours daily except Sat, 2pm; $15; ⓦwww.riccartonhouse.co.nz), all oak panelling and stag heads. There's a Farmers' Market here on Saturday morning (9am–noon).

The International Antarctic Centre

Beyond Deans Bush, Memorial Avenue runs northwest to the airport and the **International Antarctic Centre**, 38 Orchard Rd (daily Oct–April 9am–7pm; May–Sept 9am–5pm; $55 with unlimited entry and rides; students and seniors $46; ⓦwww.iceberg.co.nz), a well-presented and dynamic exhibit concentrating on New Zealand's involvement in Antarctica. It is pricey, but you could easily spend half a day here. Since the mid-1950s, Christchurch airport has been the base of the US Antarctic programme that sponsors over 140 flights a year to its base at McMurdo Sound, and the neighbouring New Zealand outpost at Scott Base. There's stacks here on Antarctic exploration and the fragile polar ecosystem, with video presentations, digital photos emailed daily from the ice at Scott Base, recordings of current weather conditions and a habitat for little blue **penguins** (which you can see being fed at 10.30am, 1.30pm & 3.30pm). In the Snow & Ice Experience you can don a down jacket and experience a snowy environment at -5°C. Every half-hour a fairly naff simulated Antarctic storm increases the wind chill to -18°C, though the fury is mostly in the soundtrack. Your entry ticket allows you unlimited goes at the fifteen-minute **Hägglund Ride** (every 20min), on which a five-tonne tracked polar buggy is put through its paces over an obstacle course. The Penguin Express (on the hour daily 9am–5pm; $7 each way) runs from the Square and is free if you book entry through the i-SITE.

Orana Park, Willowbank and beyond

Drivers can skirt round the northern perimeter of the airport – follow Russley Road then McLeans Island Road – to **Orana Wildlife Park**, 20km west of the city centre (daily 10am–5pm; $24; ⓣ03/359 7109, ⓦwww.oranawildlifepark.co.nz), a well-organized, open-range zoological park strong on African savannah animals. Feeding times are staggered throughout the day, with something to see every half-hour. You can even hand-feed a giraffe and join the **lion encounter** (daily 2.15pm; $30) touring the lion enclosure on the caged back of a truck. New Zealand is represented by kiwi, tuatara, an active aviary and a gecko house where the little beasties are perfectly camouflaged in the foliage. A shuttle ($25 return; ⓣ03/379 1699) leaves from the i-SITE at 10am and 1pm.

Although nowhere near as exciting as Orana Park, the smaller and more intimate **Willowbank Wildlife Reserve**, 60 Hussey Rd (daily 10am–dusk; $25, ⓣ03/359 6226, ⓦwww.willowbank.co.nz), has some good displays of native birds including a kiwi house where they incubate eggs and raise chicks. This is also the site of the Ko Tane Maori Experience (see p.519). To get here use bus #11 (every 30–60min).

On the former Wigram RNZAF base 7km west of the central city, the **Air Force Museum** (daily 10am–5pm; free; ⓣ03/343 9532, ⓦwww.airforcemuseum.co.nz), presents two dozen aircraft including a Dakota converted for use on the British Queen's state visit in 1953, and a Spitfire among several World War II veterans. Flight simulators ($5) will keep the (big) kids happy, particularly the one simulating the World War II Mosquito as it engages in combat in the Norwegian fjords, while enthusiastic volunteer guides conduct assorted tours, including one of the restoration and storage hangars (daily 11am, 1.30pm & 3pm; 45min; $8).

The Christchurch Gondola

For quick access to great views and easy hiking on the Port Hills on the south-eastern flank of the city, ride the **Christchurch Gondola**, 10 Bridle Path Rd (daily 10am–10pm or later; $24 return; ⓦwww.gondola.co.nz), located by the entrance to the Lyttelton tunnel fifteen minutes' drive from Cathedral Square, and is served by the Lyttelton bus (#28) and some city tours (see p.509). The Gondola cable cars whisk you to the upper station on the 945m summit of **Mount Cavendish**. Here, time is best spent in the café admiring the 360-degree views of Christchurch, the Canterbury Plains, the volcanic outcrops of the Banks Peninsula and the Southern Alps.

From the summit, you can explore the paths that run along the ridge tops before descending back to the lower station. Alternatively try a combined gondola ride and **mountain bicycle descent** with the Mountain Bike Adventure Company ($50; reservations essential ⓣ0800/424 534, ⓦwww.cyclehire-tours.co.nz) who meet you with bikes near the top of the gondola and give you two hours to explore one of three possible descents with bird's-eye views of Sumner's beaches, Lyttelton and Banks Peninsula.

Christchurch's beaches

As the summer sun bakes the city streets it's tempting to head for the beaches, the best being Redcliffs and Sumner (both accessed by bus #3 from the City Exchange bus station). These tight beachside communities have plenty going on and a number of good places to stay and eat.

Redcliffs, 10km southeast of the city centre, lies at the mouth of the Avon estuary on and around the fractured dull red cliffs that give the community its name. The sea has eroded the base of the cliffs to leave a series of caves, the largest of which once contained moa bones indicating Maori habitation up to seven hundred years ago. As you drive along Main Road, look out for the large (but blocked-off) entrance to **Moa Bone Point Cave**, once used by European settlers.

Estuary beaches become sea beaches at **Sumner**, a Norfolk pine-backed strip of craft shops, restaurants, cafés, wine bars, surf shacks and a cinema, all

The TranzAlpine

One of the most popular day-trips from Christchurch is to ride the **TranzAlpine train** (4hr 30min each way; book well ahead for best prices; normally $113–161 one-way, $140–215 day return, ⓦwww.tranzscenic.co.nz), a tourist-oriented trip across to Greymouth on the West Coast. It is a gorgeous 231km journey – with numerous viaducts and nineteen tunnels – all seen from the train's large viewing windows and open-sided observation car. Christchurch's industrial suburbs give way to the farmland of the Canterbury Plains before climbing through braided river valleys and open tussock country into the Southern Alps. There's a pause at the beech forest high point of Arthur's Pass before descending through the 8.5km-long Otira Tunnel that burrows under the 920m pass itself to the West Coast.

The train leaves Christchurch train station at 8.15am every morning and nominally returns by 6.05pm, though years of under-funding mean that delays are fairly common. Levels of comfort and catering are also below par for what is essentially a tourist attraction, though standards are improving.

If you travel in December you will see red and white rata in bloom, but the trip is at its romantic, snow-cloaked best in the winter months (June–Aug). A good strategy for those with a vehicle is to catch the train at Darfield, 45km west of Christchurch, allowing a later start in return for missing Christchurch's industrial suburbs and a few farms. It is also worth considering alighting at Moana for a relaxed three-hour lakeside lunch before boarding for the return journey. It beats a hurried snack in Greymouth.

The trip can also form part of a high country tour (see box, p.509).

fronting a broad patch of golden sand. Named after Dr J.B. Sumner, Archbishop of Canterbury and president of the Canterbury Association in the 1850s, the suburb has become one of Christchurch's most desirable. It is a popular destination on summer weekends and a great place just to hang out anytime (see box, p.502).

The highlight of the beach is **Cave Rock** which is peppered with little caves like an enormous Swiss cheese. The lifeguard's lookout point on top can be reached by clambering up the rock. Elsewhere, you can stroll the clifftop paths around Scarborough Head (see below) or visit Urban Surf, 25d Marriner St in the heart of the village (☎03/326 6023) where you can rent boards ($20/2hr) and wetsuits ($10/2hr). They also deal with **surf coach** Doug Young (☎0800/478 734) who charges around $50 for a two-hour lesson complete with gear.

The best **surfing** is 2km south at **Taylor's Mistake** (reached along Nayland Street), a narrow beach and small community named, according to local lore, for a captain who ran aground here after mistaking the bay for the entrance to Lyttelton Harbour. The best way to get here from Sumner is to walk along the **Scarborough Head/Taylor's Mistake Walk** (1hr each way; 3km; constantly undulating), which makes its way over the headlands with great coastal views and passing a few *baches* tucked away in Hobson Bay. To get there, follow the Esplanade south onto Scarborough Road then hugging the coast onto Whitewash Head Road.

Drivers can continue beyond Sumner following the extension of Wakefield Street inland and over Evans Pass to Lyttelton, only 6km away (see p.522).

Exploring the Port Hills

On a fine evening there's no finer drive (or bike ride) in Christchurch than a traverse of the Port Hills along the **Summit Road** (see box opposite) perhaps dropping down to explore Lyttelton. Akaroa-bound drivers can even continue along a sequence of connecting backroads that forms a giant S-shaped circuit around the peninsula's two crater harbours. Designed with pedestrians and wagons in mind, it keeps as close as possible to the ridge tops marking an undulating course – with few sustained ascents – and offers stupendous views all around.

A variety of roads (see Banks Peninsula map on p.521) wind around the hills offering all sorts of variations, but this is the classic **Port Hills drive**: allow at least two hours. Start by following Colombo Street south from the city centre and when you hit the foothills continue straight ahead up **Dyers Pass Road**. This takes you past the *Sign of the Takahe* and on up to the *Sign of the Kiwi* (for both see p.518) at Dyers Pass. At the latter, turn left. You're now on the Summit Road with alternate views north down to Christchurch and south to Lyttelton and its harbour. There are numerous rocky outcrops and wayside viewpoints along this twisting 14km route to Evans Pass: many make great spots for a picnic or to watch the sun drop behind the Southern Alps.

At Evans Pass either turn right to reach **Lyttelton** and return to Christchurch through the tunnel; or turn left for the **beaches** of Sumner and Taylor's Mistake. Straight ahead is Godley Head (see p.525).

Cyclists could easily spend a day following the same route. Traffic is sparse, but what there is tends to hare round blind corners, so keep your wits about you. Mountain bikers can often get off the road on parallel tracks, which make for some excellent riding.

Walkers are also well served with paths. The lack of useful buses makes one-way hikes inconvenient, but you can stop pretty much anywhere along the ridge and find appealing walks. The *Port Hills* brochure (available free from visitor centres) shows where all the footpaths go and includes details on the **Crater Rim Walkway** (18.5km one-way; 5hr; continuously undulating), a magical path right along the crater rim.

Eating and drinking

Christchurch has more restaurants, cafés, bars and pubs than anywhere else on the South Island – everything from cheap little **ethnic** places to the **finest dining**, along with an abundance of **cool café/bars**. As ever, many places operate as restaurants during the day and bars at night, or as bars that morph into dance and club venues as night turns to morning.

Central Christchurch

There is little reason to venture beyond the Four Avenues for food and drink; you'll find most of what you need in the grid of **downtown** streets close to Cathedral Square. Areas that warrant a special mention include the southeastern end of **High Street** (around Lichfield and Tuam streets), which is particularly good for offbeat cafés and good lunch spots. **The Strip**, a section of Oxford Terrace between Cashel and Gloucester streets, overlooking the River Avon, is a great place for lunch in the sun, with a dozen or so almost indistinguishable

You can combine sightseeing with dining by clunking around Christchurch's streets on the **restaurant tram** (daily 7.30pm; from $73 for 4 courses; ☏03/366 7830, ⓦwww.tram.co.nz), offering local delicacies as well as a broader selection of Kiwi cuisine.

restaurant/bars spilling out onto the pavement. These also attract the after-work set for dinner, then settle down to serious drinking (and weekend DJs) later on. Much of the cooler action happens around **SOL Square** and the **Lichfield Lanes**, both just off Lichfield Street, where there are some great bars, many serving food. If you're **self-catering**, head for the New World **supermarket** at 555 Colombo St and the **City Seafood Market**, 277 Manchester St.

Cafés and takeaways

C1 Espresso 150 High St. Tardis-like young and funky café where filling gourmet sandwiches ($10) fight for your attention with omelettes, pizza, flatbreads, breakfasts, smoothies, juices and dynamite coffee. There's a selection of mags and papers, a mishmash of 1950s and 1960s furniture and a DJ holding forth from a little booth most evenings and weekends.

Café Metro Coner of Colombo & Kilmore sts. One of the best cafés in this part of town, right by the Town Hall with great coffee, a good range of quiches, pies, muffins and cakes, and a varied stack of up-to-date mags. Also dinner Fri & Sat.

Copenhagen Bakery 119 Armagh St. Bakery and café that's great for fresh sandwiches, croissants, quiches, quality pies, Scandinavian black bread and Danish pastries that are a world away from the over-sweet pretenders typically found outside Denmark. Open Mon–Fri 7am–5pm.

Globe Café 171 High St. Wonderful coffee spot and lunchtime hangout for students from the jazz school across the road, with a spacious interior and pavement seating. Great for teas, all manner of panini, salads, quiches and stunning cakes. Licensed.

Herb Centre 225 Kilmore St. Daytime café specializing in a range of caffeine-free drinks, smoothies, organic coffee, gluten-free nosh and quality food at lowish prices. Next door Piko Healthfoods sell organic bread and food. Closed Sun.

Le Café The Arts Centre, Worcester St ☎03/366 7722. Atmospheric, wood-beamed café that's open from 7am–midnight daily and is understandably popular for breakfast specials, focaccia sandwiches ($14), mains ($15–22), great tiramisu ($10) and scrumptious boysenberry smoothies.

Procopé Coffee House 165 Victoria St. Great little unlicensed café with shady outside seating serving delicious salads, rosti with smoked salmon ($17) and a fine lunch platter for two ($24).

Under the Red Verandah 502 Worcester St. See map, p.510. Delightful suburban daytime café 20min walk east of the centre, but worth the effort for its breakfast/brunch menu, pumpkin and corn cakes, bacon and *kumara*

frittata, organic breads and coffee served in the bare-boards interior or in the sunny courtyard. Closed Mon.

Restaurants

Annie's The Arts Centre, Worcester St ☎03/365 0566. Charming wine bar and restaurant within the polished-wood-floor confines of the Arts Centre, that spills into the sun-dappled courtyard outside. Lunches ($15–20) might include a field mushroom, feta and sweet-pepper gateau or a smoked chicken salad; dinner mains ($24–35) include herb-roasted ostrich. Licensed.

Bangalore Polo Club 136 Oxford Terrace ☎03/377 9968. The British Raj comes to The Strip in this somewhat contrived restaurant/bar that's still a good spot for a modest meal (curries yes, but also pizza, risotto, steak sandwiches) and drinking until the small hours.

The Bodhi Tree 808 Colombo St ☎03/377 6808. Casual dinner-only Burmese place that's enormously popular for dishes such as fish fillet with tamarind, coriander, chilli and tomato ($16), tempura whitebait on mango salad ($14) and yellow split-pea tofu salad ($10). Order several dishes and share. Booking almost essential. Closed Mon. Licensed & BYO.

Chinwag Eathai 161 High St. ☎03/365 7363. A substantial cut above your average Thai restaurant, this stylish, wood-panelled place serves innovative cocktails and wonderfully food fresh food such as wok-fried baby squid with garlic and ginger ($24) or green mango salad with sweet pork ($22). Takeaways available.

Dux de Lux Corner of Hereford & Montreal sts. Slightly dated but ever-popular restaurant with outdoor and indoor seating and a long-standing reputation for superb seafood and vegetarian meals at moderate prices: seafood jambalaya or gourmet pizza for under $26. Wash it down with quality beers brewed on the premises (tasting tray $14). Great for sitting outside on summer evenings, particularly Wed–Sat when there's generally live music and no cover charge.

Hay's Restaurant 63 Victoria St ☎03/379 7501. Classy restaurant that's a must for lamb aficionados: the animals are mostly reared on the owners' Banks Peninsula property. Imaginative and delicious food is accompanied by something from their wonderful wine list – mains $35–40. Closed Sun & Mon in winter.

Oxford on Avon 794 Colombo St ☏03/379 7148. Pub on the banks of the Avon, famed for its large portions of straightforward, cheap nosh (including a $17 all-you-can-eat breakfast); roast ($13 at lunch, $18 for dinner). Always busy with the food-bargain hunters.

Raj Mahal 221 Manchester St ☏03/366 0521. Excellent long-standing curry house with a strong Gujarati influence and an absence of pork or beef from the extensive menu. Try the *hara murgh* chicken cooked in a coriander cream and capsicum sauce ($19). Also takeaways. Licensed and BYO.

🏃 **Retour** 230 Cambridge Terrace ☏03/365 2888. Some of the best fine-dining meals in town are served in this romantic gem of a restaurant beautifully located in a glass-sided bandstand on the banks of the Avon. Mains ($35–40) might include caramelized duck breast with potato gratin and Asian vegetables. Lunches (served Thurs & Fri only) are much cheaper. Closed Mon.

Saggio di Vino 185 Victoria St corner of Bealey Ave ☏03/379 4006. Classy slow-food restaurant with a contemporary menu which might include loin of venison on polenta ($40) or Trumpeter fillet on saffron risotto ($35). Almost everything on the superb wine list is available by the glass, though not those in the wine library – strictly for those who know their Barolo from their Barossa. Dinner nightly.

Topkapi 185 Manchester St. Budget Turkish joint with quality kebabs ($11–14), iskenders ($18–22) and rich baklava. Licensed & BYO wine.

Valentino's 813 Colombo St ☏03/377 1886. There's always a buzz in this ever-popular traditional Italian place where delicious thin-crust pizza ($20–25) and assorted pasta ($20) and mains ($30) are served up in the interior lined with concert posters or under the streetside heaters. There's a good wine list (many by the glass) and they do lunches at weekends.

Pubs and bars

Belgian Beer Café Torenhof 88 Armagh St ☏03/377 1007. Pubby restaurant with a good range of beers, Belgian-style dishes like mussels with lemon zest and coriander ($25) or Flemish braised beef stew ($23) and a bustling atmosphere. Catch the afternoon sun on the deck overlooking the Avon.

Cartel His Lordship's Lane, 96 Lichfield St. Diminutive dark bar in the heart of the action, that spills out onto the lane where the connected get to lounge on the sofas in front of the big fire.

Dux de Lux (see opposite). Award-winning beers and live music.

🏃 **The Fish & Chip Shop** His Lordship's Lane, 96 Lichfield St. Funky and bustling bar with a retro Kiwiana theme. The subtleties might be lost on foreign visitors but you'll still enjoy the vibe and they do sell expensive fish and chips, served wrapped in newspaper at formica tables.

Iconic 200 Manchester St, corner of Manchester & Gloucester sts. Big brash sports bar with large screens, pool tables, a loud PA system, filling pub grub, special events and all sorts of drinks specials.

Izba 140 Lichfield St (off Poplar St). Go easy on trying all the flavours in this Russian vodka bar kitted out like a Russian country house (an *izba*).

Liquidity 128 Oxford Terrace. One of almost a dozen near-identical restaurant/bars along "The Strip" and as good a starting point as any. Start by dining (mains $26–35) on the pavement overlooking the Avon then head inside for DJ-led partying (Thurs–Sat from 9.30pm).

Sullivan's 150 Manchester St. Fairly traditional Irish bar with pictures of the old country, gallons of beer, live Irish-style bands from Wed–Sat, and late-night dancing towards the end of the week.

Twisted Hop 6 Poplar St. Rough concrete floor and stylish lighting gives a modern Kiwi slant to this pub selling several cask-conditioned English-style beers brewed on site. Meals run from pizzas ($21) to steak frites ($29) and fish, chips and mushy peas ($24). Grab a six-beer tasting tray ($17) and find a seat outside around the Gaudí-style fountain.

Winnie Bagoes 194 Gloucester St. Wood, metal and red-brick conversion, exuding urban chic. Tap and bottle beers, cocktails, a fair selection of wine, good pizzas and weekend DJs.

Papanui Road and Merivale

There's little culinary reason to leave the city centre and head out to the suburbs, but villagey Merivale is well placed if you are staying along Papanui Road or in the northern reaches of the city.

The following places are marked on the map on p.510.

Brigitte's Hawkesbury Building, Aikmans Rd, Merivale. Very busy but relaxed café and wine bar, serving everything from a mushroom brioche breakfast ($17) to Caesar salad ($19) and tempura fish and chips ($24). There's a sunny courtyard and they open for dinner Fri & Sat.

Tutto Bene 192 Papanui Rd ☎ 03/355 3744. Hugely popular trad Italian restaurant where hearty portions are dished up on gingham tablecloths. Pizza, pasta and risotto go for around $25 while main courses are $33. Licensed & BYO ($7 corkage). Dinner only; booking highly recommended.

Sumner

Even if you're not staying in **Sumner**, it's worth coming out to for a beach stroll, beer and bite in the evening: the #3 bus back to the city runs until gone 11pm. The following places are marked on the map on p.510.

Club Bazaar 15 Wakefield St ☎ 03/326 6155. This gourmet pizza joint has been here since 1988, and it shows in the decor, but there's no faulting the owner's dedication to thin-crust pizza and tempting pasta (around $20).

Indian Sumner 11a Wakefield Ave ☎ 03/326 4777. Good name, great curries. Dine outside on the pavement, take away or hope to get into the cramped but atmospheric interior for something from the small but well-chosen selection of mains ($12–18). Dinner only. Licensed & BYO.

Joe's Garage 19 Marriner St. Sumner's best café, always alive with folk getting their caffeine jolt (great espresso), huddled over a laptop (free wi-fi) or tucking into dishes such as crumbed beef schnitzel with chips and tomato herb sauce ($18).

Poseidon 25 The Esplanade ☎ 03/326 7090. Perfect spot for a sundowner right on the beach. They're doing good things with the food too (mains around $33), though you'll have to protect it from the seagulls.

The Port Hills

There are few places to eat when exploring the **Port Hills**, though these two should satisfy most needs. Both are in original rest stations for Harry Ell's Summit Road (see box, p.515).

Sign of the Kiwi Corner of Dyers Pass & Summit rds. Fairly basic tearoom perfectly sited on a col with great views over Christchurch to the Alps. Daily 10am–4pm.
Sign of the Takahe Dyers Pass Rd, Cashmere ☎ 03/332 4052, ⓦ www.signofthetakahe.co.nz. This grand baronial building houses two restaurants. The *Signature Restaurant* offers evening fine dining in a classy setting with long views towards the Southern Alps. A Kiwi take on French cuisine produces a menu which might

include mains ($34–39) of Akaroa salmon in chive *beurre blanc* or horopito-rubbed loin of lamb, followed by raspberry crème brûlée. The more modest *SOH* is a low-key café/bar in a stone-flagged former half-cellar (check out Harry Ell's signature on the wall) spilling out onto the lawns. Open all day for quality breakfasts, coffee, muffins and the likes of chicken Caesar salad ($19), beef stroganoff pie ($22) and a charcuterie platter ($26).

Nightlife and entertainment

Most of Christchurch's nightlife takes place along or just off Manchester Street between Gloucester and Lichfield Streets. The lanes off Lichfield Street, particularly **SOL Square**, and the **Lichfield Lanes**, have become the city's dining and partying hub.

Serious **music and drama** are centred on venues like the Town Hall and the Arts Centre, and there's a clutch of city-centre cinemas. The Go Guide in Friday's *The Press* newspaper covers theatre and live music **listings** for the whole week.

Clubs and gigs

Things are pretty quiet early in the week, but begin to rev up from Thursday when a sprinkling of places within the Four Avenues open. Some of these are full-on **clubs**, though a growing number of bars transform into dancing venues at weekends by drafting in a DJ or two. Most bars offering **live music** content themselves with a meagre diet of cover or Irish-style bands and minor local rock acts. If you want to stroll around and see where the crowds are going, make for Lichfield Street around the intersection with High Street. Alternatively, plan a night out in Lyttelton where there's usually something interesting going on. For a general idea of who is playing or spinning platters check out the fortnightly *JAGG* club guide (@www.jagg.co.nz), available free in bars.

Al's Bar 31 Dundas St ☎03/366 6877, @www.alsbar.co.nz. The most rock 'n' roll venue in town. Live gigs from local Kiwi bands and occasionally small international acts, mostly Thurs–Sun.

Concrete Club 132 Manchester St. Take a mole's-eye view of the world in this cool atmospheric basement club, with music ranging from roots to drum 'n' bass. Open Thurs–Sat.

Foam 30 Bedford Row. Laidback speakeasy-type atmosphere, smooth grooves and good cocktails.

Ministry 90 Lichfield St ☎03/379 2910. One of the biggest and liveliest of the clubs, with two dancefloors. Deep, dark and with thumping drum 'n' bass and hardcore till sunup. Also a lounge bar. Kicks off around midnight and there's usually a cover charge.

Rock Pool 85 Hereford St. A broad spectrum of imported beers, cocktails and 22 pool tables, as well as a PA rarely turned below ear-splitting level. Daily 9am till late; attached to *Mickey Finn's Irish Bar* upstairs.

Concerts, theatre, cinema and spectator sports

Christchurch runs a busy cultural calendar with shows at the various theatres, a selection of movie theatres and cricket, rugby and big gigs at AMI Stadium. Tourists are wooed with Maori cultural experiences at both Ko Tane and the Chronicles of Uitara, and the Arts Centre typically hosts a bunch of gigs and shows – and even a Ghost Walk. There is also a varied programme of music events in Hagley Park throughout the summer (@www.summertimes.org.nz).

Concerts and theatre

The Chronicles of Uitara – Lost In our own Land Ferrymead Historic Park, 8km southeast of central Christchurch ☎0508/826 254, @www.globalstorytellers.com. A hard-hitting, three-hour attempt to illustrate the impact of colonization on Maori society and how the two societies forged a path together. Actors role-play in a mock-up Maori *pa* and village where you can see traditional crafts being practised as a colonial force attacks. As you ride a tram through the relocated Victorian buildings of the Ferrymead Historic Park you're given a sense of the tensions bubbling under as Pakeha ways gradually submerge Maori values. An evening meal and short steam train ride complete the evening's entertainment. Takes place most evenings; $126.

Court Theatre 20 Worcester Blvd, Arts Centre ☎0800/333 100, @www.courttheatre.org.nz. The shining star in Christchurch's drama firmament. This long-standing and highly reputed theatre

company puts on a professional roster of mainstream and more edgy works. Tickets generally $30–50.

Ghost Walk ☎03/963 087, @www.courttheatre.org.nz. Actors from the Court Theatre lead entertaining evening strolls (Wed–Fri: Oct–March 9pm; April–Sept 8pm; $20) through the dark and creepy cloisters of the Arts Centre.

Isaac Theatre Royal 145 Gloucester St ☎03/366 6326. Concerts by touring mainstream jazz and rock acts often take place in this fine old Edwardian venue.

Ko Tane: The Maori Experience ☎03/359 6226, @www.kotane.co.nz. If you've missed your chance in Rotorua (see p.272), you can catch a Maori concert and *hangi* evening here at Willowbank Wildlife Reserve (see p.512). The basic package is the cultural performance and tour of Willowbank (once or twice nightly; $48, or $65 if you want to include a guided tour round the park) complete with *powhiri* greeting and Maori cultural performance. Or step up to the full Maori Experience ($110) with added à la carte dinner.

Town Hall Victoria Square. Performing arts venue with touring shows and a programme of classical music and ballet.

Cinema

Academy Cinema Arts Centre ☎03/366 0167, ⓦwww.artfilms.co.nz. Arthouse cinema with smaller sister cinemas, the *Academy Classic* and *Cloisters*.

Hoyts 392 Moorhouse Ave ☎0508/446 987. Major multiplex at the southern end of Manchester St.

Regent 94 Worcester St ☎0508/446 987. Four-screen multiplex right by Cathedral Square.

Rialto 250 Moorhouse Ave ☎03/374 9404, ⓦwww.rialto.co.nz. Three-screen multiplex with arty leanings.

Sport

AMI Stadium ⓦwww.amistadium.co.nz. Southeast of the centre near the junction of Moorhouse Ave & Ferry Rd. Generically known by its historic name of Lancaster Park; the main venue for the big spectator sports, hosting cricket in the summer and rugby on weekends all autumn and winter. Seven games will be played here during the 2011 Rugby World Cup.

Listings

Banks and exchange Most banks have branches and ATMs on Colombo St a block north or south of the Square or near Colombo and Hereford sts.

Bookshops Whitcoulls in the Cashel St Mall. Otherwise try: Scorpio Books, 79 Hereford St; Liberty Books, 145 Manchester St, good for secondhand paperbacks; Map World, 173 Gloucester St has the best range of maps and guides; and Madras Café Books, 165 Madras St, stocks quality books and has a good little café.

Car and campervan rental There are dozens of car and van rental places in Christchurch many of them clustered along Lichfield between Montreal and Barbados sts. From Jan to March you may have trouble landing anything if you don't book ahead; for more on car rental and contact details for international and nationwide companies, see Basics, p.36. The following are reputable local and national options with Apex and Jucy often working out the cheapest: Ace ☎0800/502 277, ⓦwww.acerentalcars.co.nz; Apex ☎0800/939 597, ⓦwww.apexrentals.co.nz; Apple ☎03/366 4855, ⓦwww.applerentalcars.co.nz; Better ☎0800/269 696, ⓦwww.betterrentals.co.nz; Explore ☎0800/447 363, ⓦwww.exploremore .co.nz; Jucy ☎0800/399 736, ⓦwww.jucy.co.nz; Nationwide ☎0800/803 003, ⓦwww.nationwide rentals.co.nz; Omega ☎0800/525 210, ⓦwww. omegarentalcars.com; Scotties ☎0800/736 825, ⓦwww.scotties.co.nz; U–Save ☎0508/112 233, ⓦwww.rental-car.co.nz.

Festivals The Christchurch City Council enthusiastically backs a number of festivals, many under the umbrella of Garden City Summer Times which runs Dec–March; check at the i-SITE for more details or consult ⓦwww.bethere.org.nz. Look out

particularly for: the free World Buskers Festival (10 days in late Jan), which is lots of fun and mostly takes place around the Arts Centre, in front of the *Dux De Lux* and in the Square; and the Ellerslie Flower Show (five days in early to mid-March) which takes place in Hagley Park.

Internet access The Central Library (see below) has free wi-fi, and internet access (free for 15min). Several internet places around the Square (mostly charging $3/hr) including Emagine, 27 Chancery Lane.

Left luggage (see p.498 for airport storage). Most hostels offer a left-luggage facility at usually no more than $5 a day. Also Emagine, 27 Chancery Lane (packs $3/calendar day; daily 8am–10pm).

Library Central Library, 89 Gloucester St (Mon–Sat 9am–10pm or later, Sun 10am–7pm).

Medical treatment In emergencies call ☎111. For a doctor at any time call The 24 Hour Surgery, corner of Bealey Ave & Colombo St (☎03/365 7777, no appointment necessary). Also High Street Medical Centre, 248 High St, ☎03/366 0235 (Mon–Fri 8am–6pm). Biggest of the hospitals is Christchurch Hospital, corner of Oxford Terrace & Riccarton Ave (☎03/364 0640).

Outdoor gear Loads of places round the junction of Lichfield St and Colombo St, notably Bivouac.

Pharmacies After-hours pharmacy at The 24 Hour Surgery (see "Medical Treatment" above; ☎03/366 4439), stays open daily until 11pm.

Police Central Police Station, corner of Hereford St & Cambridge Terrace ☎03/363 7400. Police kiosk in the Square.

Post office The main post office at 680 Colombo St (☎03/374 4381) has poste restante facilities.

Swimming The most central pool is the Centennial Leisure Centre, Armagh St (Mon–Thurs

6am–9pm, Fri, Sat & Sun 7am–7pm; ☎03/941 6853; $5). The QEII Leisure Centre in New Brighton (Mon–Fri 6am–9pm, Sat & Sun 7am–8pm; $5) has an Olympic-sized pool, diving pool and wave area.

Taxis Blue Star (☎03/379 9799) and Gold Band (☎03/379 5795) have heaps of cabs.
Travel agencies Flight Centre, 116 Cashel St (☎03/366 6371) and STA, corner of Colombo & Cashel sts (☎03/379 9098).

Banks Peninsula

Flying into Christchurch you'll be struck by the dramatic contrast between the flat plains of Canterbury and the rugged, fissured topography of **Banks Peninsula**, a volcanic thumb sticking out into the Canterbury Bight. When James Cook sailed by in 1769 he mistakenly charted it as an island and named it after his botanist Joseph Banks. His error was only one of time, as this basalt lump initially formed an island, only joined to the land as silt sluiced down the rivers from the eastern flanks of the Southern Alps.

The fertile **volcanic** soil of the peninsula's valleys sprouted totara, matai and kahikatea trees that, along with the abundant shellfish in the bays, attracted early Maori around a thousand years ago. The trees progressively succumbed to the Maori fire stick and European timber-milling interests, and the peninsula is now

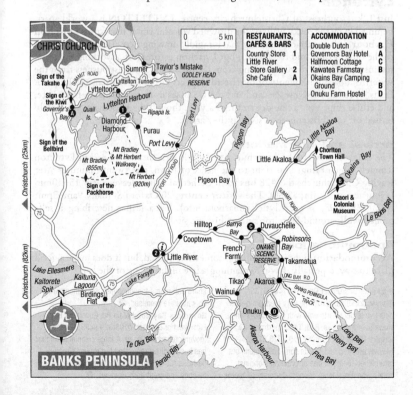

largely bald, with patches of tussock grass and small pockets of regenerating native bush.

Today, the two massive drowned craters that form Banks Peninsula are key to the commerce of the region. Lyttelton Harbour protects the port town of **Lyttelton**, disembarkation point for countless European migrants and now the South Island's major port. Its historic timeball station, harbour cruises, dolphin watching and a growing number of great cafés, bars and collectibles shops make this working port town an essential destination: catch it before the gentrification goes too far. There's an altogether more refined tone to the picturesque and visitor-oriented town of **Akaroa**; lent a gentle French influence by its founders. Elsewhere on the peninsula, a network of narrow, twisting roads wind along the crater rims and dive down to gorgeous, quiet bays once alive with whalers, sealers and shipbuilders, but now seldom visited except during the peak of summer. Despite the denuded grassland of much of the landscape, Banks Peninsula is very popular for relatively easy scenic **walks**, with panoramic views, ancient lava flows and relics from the earliest Maori and European settlers.

From Christchurch, the main route to Akaroa is **SH75**, via Lake Ellesmere and Little River, though a more picturesque journey follows the **Summit Road** from Sumner via Lyttelton, along the Port Hills and ridges of the peninsula. **Buses** from Christchurch serve only the main towns of Lyttelton and Akaroa, and to reach the smaller communities tucked into the bays you'll need your own transport. If you're planning on **cycling**, bear in mind that the peninsula is extremely hilly, and the routes linking the summit road with the various bays below can be steep.

Lyttelton

Just 12km southeast of Christchurch city centre, **LYTTELTON** is a world apart, hemmed in by the rocky walls of the drowned volcanic crater that forms **Lyttelton Harbour**. It is an attractive setting that is rapidly drawing a coterie of city escapees to the offbeat cafés and restaurants, but Lyttelton is foremost a working port that retains a raffish air: rowdy clanking from the docks and rumbustiousness from the waterfront bars, with plenty of overheard snippets of Polish, Russian and Filipino. Boats servicing the New Zealand and the US bases in Antarctica leave from here, and cruise ships visit a few dozen times a year, though the passengers are mostly bussed off to Christchurch as soon as they arrive.

Arrival and information

The quickest way from Christchurch to Lyttelton is through the 2km Lyttelton Tunnel, which brings you right to the heart of town, just twenty minutes after leaving Christchurch; the #28 **bus** from Cathedral Square leaves every 15–30min (a journey of 35min; $2.80). The **visitor centre**, 20 Oxford St (daily 9am–5pm; ☏03/328 9093, ⓦwww.lytteltonharbour.info), has a leaflet describing a self-guided **walk** around Lyttelton's many historic sites.

Accommodation

Accommodation right in Lyttelton is somewhat limited, but it does make a good place to stay, especially if you're planning a late night in one of the bars.

Dockside 22 Sumner Rd ☏027/448 8133. ⓦwww.dockside.co.nz. One very pleasant bedsit plus two larger apartments with large decks and views over the docks. Bedsit ❸, apartment ❹
Empire Hotel 9 London St ☏03/328 8202, ⓦwww.empirehotellyttelton.com. Fairly basic but refurbished rooms at one of Lyttelton's original hotels with a residents' lounge. Currently all rooms

share bathrooms though stylish renovations and en suites are promised. ❸
Governors Bay Hotel Main Rd, Governors Bay, 8km west of Lyttelton ☏03/329 9433, ⓦwww .governorsbayhotel.co.nz. A large colonial hotel that has been entirely renovated but retains simple bathless rooms above the bar with a shared balcony and great harbour views. ❹

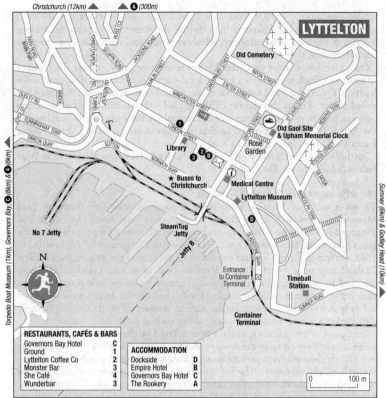

Christchurch (12km) ▲▲ ▲ ❶ (300m)

LYTTELTON

Old Cemetery

Old Gaol Site & Upham Memorial Clock

Rose Garden

Library

Buses to Christchurch

Medical Centre

Lyttelton Museum

No 7 Jetty

SteamTug Jetty

Jetty B

Entrance to Container Terminal

Timeball Station

Container Terminal

Torpedo Boat Museum (1km), Governors Bay, ❻ (8km) & ❹ (8km)

Sumner (8km) & Godley Head (10km)

N

RESTAURANTS, CAFÉS & BARS	
Governors Bay Hotel	C
Ground	1
Lyttelton Coffee Co	2
Monster Bar	3
She Café	4
Wunderbar	3

ACCOMMODATION	
Dockside	D
Empire Hotel	B
Governors Bay Hotel	C
The Rookery	A

0   100 m

▼ Diamond Harbour & Quail Island

The Rookery 9 Ross Terrace, Lyttelton
☎ 03/328 8038, ⊛ www.therookery.co.nz.
Appealing B&B imaginatively designed with
unconventional features that can make you feel
like you're aboard ship. Both main bedrooms
have private entrance and underfloor heating,
and the en suite has great harbour views and a
digital cinema. The cosy second room has Port
Hills views, and there's also a single room let for
$84. Great breakfast and convivial hosts. It is a
steep 10min walk up from town: call for driving
directions. ❺

The Town

Lyttelton's principal attraction is the **Timeball Station**, 2 Reserve Terrace (daily
10am–5.30pm; $7), a steep 1km hike up Sumner Road from the centre (though a
series of steps and paths make the journey shorter). Built in 1876, it looks like a
Gothic tower that has lost its castle. Clearly visible from all over town and
harbour, for over fifty years mariners recalibrated their on-board chronometers –
critical for accurate navigation – on the descent of a large ball down the pole on its
roof. Radio signals replaced the timeball in 1934 but the black and red ball is still
hoisted up its pole every day at 12.57pm, then, on the stroke of 1pm, it begins its
descent. Inside the station are a number of exhibits explaining the importance of
the timeball, and there are great views from the roof.

The air of a long-neglected attic pervades the **Lyttelton Museum**, Norwich
Quay (Tues, Thurs, Sat & Sun 2–4pm; donations appreciated), a former Seaman's
Institute, where an Antarctic display spotlights Scott and Shackleton, both of

whose expeditions set out from Lyttelton. Other curious artefacts have been salvaged from the small shelters built during the nineteenth century on various islands off the New Zealand shore, which were supplied with provisions to cater for unfortunate shipwrecked souls.

On a nice day, wander up Oxford Street to the rose garden where the **Upham Memorial Clock** remembers a saintly local doctor noted for his devotion to the lepers of Quail Island and his refusal to accept money from patients who could not afford to pay. This is also the site of the old jail – the remains of a couple of the cells can be seen on the northern side of the gardens. Built in 1851, the jail became the South Island's major penal institution, even accommodating sheep rustler James McKenzie (see p.565) for a time.

Further up Oxford Street you'll find the **Old Cemetery**, which featured in Peter Jackson's 1996 movie *The Frighteners*.

Boats and harbour cruises

To get a sense of Lyttelton's maritime importance, visit the **Torpedo Boat Museum** (Nov–March Tues, Thurs, Sat & Sun 1–3pm; April–Oct Sat & Sun 1–3pm; $5) reached by a five-minute shoreline walk from a car park on Charlotte Jane Quay about 1km west of town. After the Russian invasion of Afghanistan in 1885, the fear of further Russian expansion spread around the western Pacific. New Zealand responded by building a Torpedo Boat to protect Lyttelton Harbour, designed to charge up to an invading ship, detonate a charge below the waterline then scarper before it could be attacked itself. The boat was, in fact, never used and has only recently been restored after years of abandonment. Its remains are now displayed in a former powder magazine along with an entertaining video.

For a piece of living history, visit the **Steam Tug Lyttelton**, the older of only two steam tugs still operating in the country. Built in Glasgow by the Ferguson brothers in 1907, this beautiful antique boat is maintained in full working order by an impassioned bunch of volunteers. The boiler room is particularly impressive: all burnished brass and oily pistons. **Cruises** (generally Christmas to April Sun 2.30pm, 90min; $20; booking required ℡03/322 8911), steam all the way to the head of the harbour.

Apart from the regular ferry services to Diamond Harbour and Quail Island (see opposite) Black Cat Cruises (℡03/328 9078, ⓦwww.blackcat.co.nz) run a **Wildlife Cruise** (daily at 1.30pm; $60), that includes the prospect of seeing Hector's dolphins up close. There's a free shuttle from the Square in Christchurch; book in advance.

Eating and drinking

Lyttelton has a well-founded reputation for fabulous **food**, and is way livelier than you'd expect for such a small town. In fact, a trip to Lyttelton is justified solely on the intention of dining and sampling the curious pleasures of the *Wunderbar*. If you're here on Saturday morning, call in to the small **Farmers' Market** in the school grounds on Oxford Street.

Governors Bay Hotel Main Rd, 8km west of Lyttelton ℡03/329 9433. A renovated colonial hotel with outdoor seating where you can enjoy straightforward but tasty fare such as crumbed hoki or prawn laksa ($17–19).

Ground 44 London St. Great café/deli with a huge range of gourmet goodies – gelati, handmade chocolates, cheeses – along with breakfasts, soups, great pies and salads, build-your-own sandwiches (toasted or otherwise) and smoothies, all free range and organic where possible.

Lyttelton Coffee Co 29 London St. Cool, rough-hewn café with beans roasted on site and a hearty range of meals. A perfect brunch spot, with cakes, deep sofas and a sunny deck overlooking the port.

Monster Bar 29 London St ℡03/328 9166. Creepy monster drawings line the walls of this diminutive and well-hidden bar that does a fine line in skewers of yakitori bar snacks (even desserts). Great value, too.

She Café 79 Main Rd, 8km west of Lyttelton at Governors Bay ⊕03/329 9825, ⊛www.shecafe .co.nz. With tables inside and out all looking straight down Lyttelton Harbour to the sea, this makes a great place for a leisurely lunch or a cinnamon and chilli spiced Mayan hot chocolate. Prices are a little high (lunch mains $20–25), but ingredients are mostly local, free range and organic, and there's a selection of veggie and gluten-free options. Closed Mon & Tues.

Wunderbar London St ⊛www.wunderbar .co.nz. An idiosyncratic late-night drinking-hole and club, with decor ranging from crushed velour to a gruesome doll's-head lightshade, and a deck overlooking the harbour that's great for a peaceful drink if you can't take the clamour within. Entertainment ranges from 1940s and 50s cabaret nights, through poetry, live bands, stand-up comics, club and disco music, to film-noir evenings. Entry is down steps beside the supermarket, and up an iron fire escape. Check the website for upcoming events. Mon–Fri 5pm–late, Sat & Sun 1pm–even later.

Around Lyttelton Harbour

Lyttelton would be nothing without its **harbour**. Boats reach Lyttelton through "the heads", best seen from Godley Head – a moody, grass- and rock-covered promontory with steep sea cliffs offering excellent views. Across the harbour, the main destinations are the small community of **Diamond Harbour**, and **Quail Island**, a haven for birds.

Godley Head

At the northernmost tip of the harbour, **Godley Head** stands guard – a spectacular piece of land with high cliffs and excellent views, administered by DOC. Follow the signs east out of Lyttelton to the Summit Road that takes you out onto Godley Head (about 10km) and the **Godley Head Reserve**, a delightful spot for walks and picnics. The walkway network is extensive, in places stumbling across installations left behind after World War II, including dark warren-like tunnels and searchlight emplacements perched like birds' nests on the cliffs – from here, walk down to the tiny coastal settlements of Boulder Bay and Taylor's Mistake (see box, p.514).

Diamond Harbour

In bright sunlight the water sparkles like a million gems at **Diamond Harbour**, directly across the water from Lyttelton. Passenger **ferries** (sailings every 30–60min; $5 each way) make the fifteen-minute run across the harbour arriving at the Diamond Harbour wharf. Here you can generate a thirst with a 500m walk uphill, then slake it at either the *Country Store*, which does coffee, muffins and toasted sandwiches, or at **Godley House** (closed Mon) where you can grab a beer or lunch and sprawl out on the lawns overlooking Diamond Harbour.

Quail Island

Set in mid-harbour, the 0.86-square-kilometre **Quail Island** was known by the local Maori as Otamahua meaning "place where children collected seabirds' eggs". From 1907 to 1925 it housed a small leper colony and in the early days of Antarctic exploration Shackleton and Scott quarantined their dogs there before venturing to the South Pole. These days it's a venue for day-trips, swimming and walking: pack food, plenty of drinking water and rain gear. Two circular **walking tracks** (1hr & 2hr 30min), start from the island's wharf and visit safe swimming beaches along with several shipwrecks which can be seen at low tide. The island is reached with Black Cat Cruises (Oct–April daily 12.20pm with an additional boat Dec–March at 10.20am; $20 return).

Christchurch to Akaroa

With ample time on your hands and a taste for exploration consider approaching Banks Peninsula on the **Summit Road** (see box, p.515), winding around the crater rim of Lyttelton Harbour and the northern bays before finally delivering you down into Akaroa.

A much faster way of covering the 85km run **from Christchurch to Akaroa** is along SH75 that heads south from the city before curling along the southern shore of the peninsula, and over the hills to Akaroa: it takes around an hour and a half, though there are reasons to pause along the way.

Lake Ellesmere and Little River

Around 30km from Christchurch SH75 tracks the water's edge of **Lake Ellesmere** (Waihora), a vast expanse of fresh water separated from the Pacific Ocean by the 30km-long Kaitorete spit, jutting southeast from Banks Peninsula to rejoin the mainland. At the base of the spit is **Birdlings Flat**, a narrow shingle bank that has traditionally been a rich source of food for local Maori, who were granted protected fishing rights here in 1896; the accumulated shingle of the sheltering bank also provides a fossicking ground for greenstone and gems. Birdlings Flat separates the sea from **Lake Forsyth** (Wairewa), a long finger of water skirted by SH75 on the way to the tiny community of **Little River**, 53km from Christchurch, notable mainly for the *Little River Store Gallery* an excellent café, bar and bakery.

For a little exercise in these parts, consider the **Little River Railtrail** (Ⓦwww .littleriverrailtrail.co.nz), which currently runs for 24km along Lake Forsyth and Lake Ellesmere and will eventually link to Christchurch. The service station in Little River has bike rental.

Barry's Bay

From Little River, SH75 climbs over the hills that separate Akaroa Harbour from the rest of Banks Peninsula and down to the tiny community of **BARRY'S BAY**, home to the underwhelming **Barry's Bay Cheese**, SH75 (daily 9am–5pm; Ⓣ03/304 5809), where you can munch on free samples while watching cheese being made (Oct–May every second day).

There's **accommodation** nearby at *Halfmoon Cottage*, SH75 (Ⓣ03/304 5050, Ⓦwww.halfmoon.co.nz; shares $28, rooms ❷; closed June–Aug), a small and wonderfully relaxed hostel in a 1896 villa set in a pretty garden just across from the beach. There are free bikes and broadband, and low-cost kayaks for rent.

Akaroa

The small waterside town of **AKAROA** ("Long Bay"), 85km southeast of Christchurch on the eastern shores of Akaroa Harbour, comes billed as New Zealand's **French settlement**. Certainly the first settlers came from France, some of their architecture survives and the street names they chose have stuck, but that is about as French as it gets. Nonetheless, the town milks the connection with a couple of French-ish restaurants, some French-sounding boutique B&Bs and a tricolour fluttering over the spot where the first settlers landed.

Still, it is a pretty place with attractive scenery all around, a smattering of low-key activities including a unique dolphin swim, and easy access to the **Banks Peninsula Track** (see box, p.532). But Akaroa primarily pitches itself to those looking for gentle strolls followed by good food and wine before a comfy bed. These factors make the town a popular Kiwi holiday destination; a full two-thirds of its houses are *baches* (holiday homes), leaving only around 550 permanent residents.

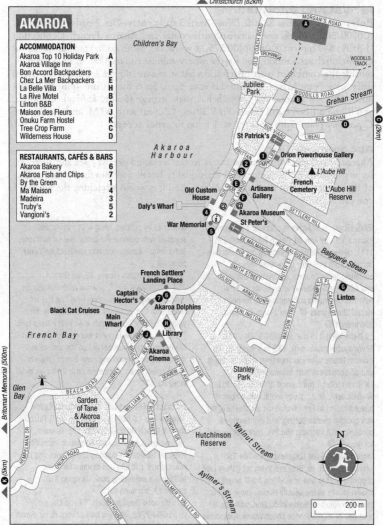

AKAROA

ACCOMMODATION

Akaroa Top 10 Holiday Park	A
Akaroa Village Inn	I
Bon Accord Backpackers	F
Chez La Mer Backpackers	E
La Belle Villa	H
La Rive Motel	B
Linton B&B	G
Maison des Fleurs	J
Onuku Farm Hostel	K
Tree Crop Farm	C
Wilderness House	D

RESTAURANTS, CAFÉS & BARS

Akaroa Bakery	6
Akaroa Fish and Chips	7
By the Green	1
Ma Maison	4
Madeira	3
Truby's	5
Vangioni's	2

The site of Akaroa was originally the domain of the Ngai Tahu paramount chief, Temaiharanui. In 1838, French Commander Jean Langlois traded goods for what he believed to be the entire peninsula and returned to France to encourage settlers to populate a new French colony. Meanwhile, the British sent William Hobson to assume the role of lieutenant-governor over all the land that could be purchased; and just six days before Lavaud sailed into the harbour, the British flag was raised in Akaroa. Lavaud's passengers decided to stay, which meant that the first formal settlement under **British sovereignty** was comprised of 63 French and six Germans.

Although Akaroa can be seen in a day-trip from Christchurch, it is far better to spend a night or two to appreciate the town and its surrounds.

Arrival and information

Buses run by Akaroa Shuttle (Nov–April 3 daily; May–Oct 2 daily; $45 return; ☎0800/500 929, ⓦwww.akaroashuttle.co.nz) and Akaroa French Connection (1 daily; $49 return; ☎0800/800 575, ⓦwww.akaroabus.co.nz) pick up at central Christchurch accommodation for the ninety-minute run to Akaroa. They drop off outside the combined **post office** and **visitor centre**, 80 rue Lavaud (Nov–April daily 9am–5pm; May–Oct Mon–Fri 9am–5pm, Sat & Sun 10am–4pm; ☎03/304 8600, ⓦwww.akaroa.com), which has pack storage ($1/hr, $5/day). Opposite, you'll find a BNZ **bank** (Mon–Fri 9.30am–4.30pm) with ATM, and the *Turenne Coffee Shop* (7am–7pm or later), which has **internet access**.

Accommodation

Akaroa's best **accommodation** caters to the weekend getaway set and there are some gorgeous B&Bs, lodges and high-quality hotels and motels. Staying in one of these seems to suit the spirit of Akaroa, and it is worth stretching the budget if you can.

B&Bs, lodges and hotels

Akaroa Village Inn 81 Beach Rd ☎0800/695 1111, ⓦwww.akaroavillageinn.co.nz. A rambling complex with probably the widest range of accommodation in town, a variety of decors and lots of self-catering apartments, several with two bedrooms and some good harbour views. Studio units ❺, apartments ❻, luxury apartments ❼

La Belle Villa 113 rue Jolie ☎03/304 7084, ⓦwww.labellevilla.co.nz. B&B in a lovely 1870s wooden house with spacious light en-suite rooms and alfresco breakfasts in summer. ❺

La Rive Motel 1 rue Lavaud ☎0800/247 651, ⓦwww.larive.co.nz. Large motel with a conical tower alluding to French chateau architecture, set in a tranquil garden setting, and eight units all containing full kitchens and TVs. Particularly good for groups. ❹

Linton B&B 68 rue Balguerie ☎03/304 7501, ⓦwww.linton.co.nz. Stay in a living art gallery (see opposite) built in and around this 1881 house known locally as the Giant's House. Large rooms (some en suite), all wildly decorated, with say, a boat bed or a greenhouse conservatory. A delicious continental breakfast is served and there are big reductions for multi-night stays. ❽/❾

Maison des Fleurs 6b Church St ☎03/304 7804, ⓦwww.holidayhouses.co.nz. Boutique accommodation in a modern two-storey cottage (you get all of it), built from peninsula-milled timbers. It's superbly appointed, plus there's a sunny balcony, wood stove for winter, and full cooking facilities. ❽

Tree Crop Farm 2km up rue Grehan ☎03/304 7158 ⓦwww.treecropfarm.com. The four "love shacks" are the only place to stay if you're looking for the sort of rustic romance offered by secluded shacks lit by candles, hung with mirrors and supplied with outdoor fire baths. Not for everyone, but a unique experience, and checkout isn't until noon. ❼

Wilderness House 42 rue Grehan ☎03/304 7517, ⓦwww.wildernesshouse.co.nz. Lovely and welcoming B&B in a fine old home with four tastefully decorated rooms, each with en suite or private bath (one with a deep tub). There's a sumptuous guest lounge with port, and breakfast is delicious, served on the terrace in good weather overlooking semi-formal grounds with English roses. They even have their own small vineyard. ❽

Hostels and campsites

Akaroa Top 10 Holiday Park Morgan's Rd, off the Old Coach Rd ☎0800/727 525, ⓦwww.akaroa-holidaypark.co.nz. Sprawling across a terraced hillside overlooking the harbour and the main street, this site has modern facilities, including a swimming pool. Camping $16, cabins ❷, s/c units ❹

Bon Accord Backpackers 57 rue Lavaud ☎03/304 7782, ⓦwww.bon-accord.co.nz. Small animal-friendly hostel (they have a dog) fashioned from two houses with a large garden. Slippers and hot water bottles are provided and there are free bikes and off-street parking. Dorms $27, rooms ❷

Chez La Mer Backpackers 50 rue Lavaud ☎03/304 7024, ⓦwww.chezlamer.co.nz. High-quality budget accommodation in a homely 1871 house complete with a lovely garden, hammock and outdoor cooking area. The staff are helpful, and offer free use of bikes and fishing rods and useful maps of local walks and points of interest. Dorms $25, rooms ❷, en suites ❸

Onuku Farm Hostel 6km south of town on the Onuku road ☎03/304 7066, ⒲www.onukufarm.com. On a hill above a bay, this wonderfully secluded spot on a sheep farm centres on the cosy main house where there are doubles and dorms (including a 6-bunk en-suite girls' dorm with hairdryer). There's no TV, and internet access is hidden away. Outside there's accommodation in a lovely brick cottage and a network of bush and farmland tracks some leading to the hammock-strung campsite equipped with outdoor kitchens and showers, and several huts and stargazers – rather like wooden tents. The hostel also runs 3–4hr guided kayaking ($45), and summer dolphin-swimming trips ($100; max 6), and encourages fishing and mussel collecting. Free pick-up around 12.30pm from Akaroa. Cash only. Closed June–Sept. Camping and small campervans $15/person, dorms $28, rooms ②

The Town

Akaroa is strung along the shore in a long ribbon easily seen on foot. For detailed exploration of the town's architectural and cultural gems, buy the *Akaroa Historic Village Walk* booklet ($10) or obtain an audioguide ($10) from the visitor centre.

Opposite the visitor centre, the **Akaroa Museum** (daily Oct–April 10.30am–4.30pm; May–Nov 10.30am–4pm; $4), stands head and shoulders above most small-town museums. Several interesting Maori artefacts and a twenty-minute film account of the remarkable history of settlement on the peninsula are backed up by a display illustrating the differences between the English version of the Treaty of Waitangi and a literal English translation of the Maori-language document signed by Maori chiefs all over Aotearoa. Other exhibits deal with the peninsula's whaling history and fascinating albums full of photographs of the original French and German settlers. Look, too, for displays on local son, **Frank Worsley**, who captained Shackleton's ship *Endurance* to Antarctica and, after disaster struck, the *James Caird* to South Georgia and safety.

The museum incorporates the early 1840s **Langlois-Eteveneaux Cottage**, thought to have been partly constructed in France before being shipped over, now filled with French nineteenth-century furniture. Also associated with the museum is the town's former **Court House**, with its original dock and bench, and the tiny **Custom House**, across rue Lavaud next to Daly's Wharf, from which spy-glass-wielding officials once kept watch on the port below.

Continuing the Gallic theme, visit the **French Cemetery** at the northern end of town, reached by a footpath that leads from rue Pompallier into the L'Aube Hill Reserve. The first consecrated burial ground in Canterbury, the cemetery was sadly neglected until 1925, when the bodies were reinterred in a central plot marked by a single monument. At the northern end of rue Pompallier, the 1864 French-inspired **Church of St Patrick**, built from large slabs of unplaned totara. The rich colours of the black pine and kauri interior complement the bold stained glass in the east window behind the altar.

Galleries and gardens

One place you shouldn't miss is **Linton**, 68 rue Balguerie (daily Christmas to March noon–5pm, April to Christmas 2–4pm; $15), home of sculptor Josie Martin and a working testament to her art. Known locally as "The Giant's House", every room, the garden and even the drive to the garage have become a canvas on which she can display her talents. Huge mosaics, concrete figures and sculpted seats tucked away in garden nooks all come with an overriding spirit of fun.

Heading north along rue Lavaud, take a peek in at the **Artisans Gallery**, at no. 45 (daily 10am–5pm), a contemporary craft gallery selling pottery, weaving, silk, jewellery, knitwear, clothing and turned wood from an 1877 cottage. Further on, a former hydroelectric plant houses the **Orion Powerhouse Gallery** (Oct–April Mon–Fri 1–4pm, Sat & Sun 11am–4pm; donation

▲ *Linton*, Akaroa

requested), a venue for modest local exhibitions of arts and crafts, as well as for concerts of acoustic music on Sundays.

One destination that divides opinion is **Tree Crop Farm**, 2km up rue Grehan (daily 10am–5pm; closed in inclement weather; $10 including a drink), a private lifestyle farm centred on a garden area with the feel of a managed wilderness. Fans love to amble along the farm tracks and through the gardens reading aphorisms written everywhere imaginable. They're initially entertaining – "the best plastic surgery is to cut up your credit cards", "old age isn't bad when you consider the alternative" – but soon become tiresome. A small café serves berry juices and coffee at relatively high prices, and there is accommodation (see p.528) in rustically romantic huts.

Activities around Akaroa

If you want to do more than sip Pinot Gris and mooch around the galleries, there is no shortage of diversions, from waterfront strolls to dolphin swimming and kayaking. One good way of exploring is to join one of two rural delivery **mail runs** that follow the peninsula's narrow roads. Akaroa Harbour Scenic Mail Run (Mon–Sat 9am; 5hr; $50; ℡03/304 7573, Ⓦwww.akaroamailrun.com) visits the settlements around the inner harbour, while the marginally preferable Eastern Bays Scenic Mail Run (Mon–Fri 9am; 5hr; $55; ℡03/304 8526) covers Okains and Le Bons bays and more.

Harbour cruises and swimming with dolphins

At 1.2–1.4m in length the native Hector's dolphins are the world's smallest breed of dolphin. They are playful, and small pods are generally happy to approach customers, particularly in summer. Three-hour **dolphin-swimming** trips with Black Cat, Main Wharf, Beach Road (Oct–April 6am, 8.30am, 11.30am, 1.30pm & 3.30pm; May–Sept 11.30am; $130, spectators $70; ℡03/304 7641, Ⓦwww.blackcat.co.nz) offer partial refunds if you can't swim with the dolphins and they have dry suits in winter. There are also dolphin-swimming trips from *Onuku Farm Hostel* (see p.529).

Black Cat also runs two-hour **harbour cruises** (Nov–March at 11am & all year at 1.30pm; $65), visiting the mouth of the harbour and back via a beautiful high-walled volcanic sea cave, colonies of spotted shags and cormorants, and caves where blue penguins can sometimes be spotted.

Akaroa Dolphins, 65 Beach Rd (daily Nov–April 10.15am, 12.45pm & 3.15pm; May–Oct 12.45pm; ☎0800/990 102, ⓦwww.akaroadolphins.co.nz) also run harbour cruises, including birdwatching ($68).

An atmospheric alternative is Fox II Sailing Adventures (late Dec to May daily 10.30am & 1.30pm; $60, BBH backpackers $50 ☎0800/369 7245, ⓦwww.akaroa foxsail.co.nz), leaving from Daly's Wharf for **sailing** trips on a wooden 1922 ketch to the outer bays of Akaroa Harbour with an excellent chance of seeing dolphins.

Kayaking

If you're just after splashing around in boats, rent aquatic playthings from Captain Hector's Canoe & Boat Hire on Beach Road, which also has sea kayaks ($60/ person/day). For something more structured, go on a small-group **guided kayaking** trip with Akaroa Guided Sea Kayaking Safari (Nov–April only; full day $195; ☎021/156 4591, ⓦwww.akaroakayaks.co.nz). There'll be swimming, a good chance of encountering Hector's dolphins, and lunch is included. Anyone can join the kayaking trips from *Onuku Farm Hostel* (see p.529).

Penguin and seal viewing

There are several opportunities to get out and see the local wildlife. Akaroa Seal Colony Safari (☎03/304 7255, ⓦwww.sealtours.co.nz) run air-conditioned 4WD vehicles to **view fur seals**, on the eastern tip of the peninsula. Tours (daily 9.30am & 1pm; $70) last over 2hr 30min and are limited to six people: pick-up at i-SITE.

Shireen and Francis Helps have been looking after white-flippered penguins (close relatives of little blues) on their farm at Flea Bay (on the Banks Peninsula Track; see p.532) for decades. You can see them close up on tours run by Pohatu Penguins (☎03/304 8552, ⓦwww.pohatu.co.nz) who offer **penguin viewing** (2–3hr; $66), 4WD nature tours ($80) and the chance to go **sea kayaking** around Flea Bay and the Pohatu Marine Reserve ($75). There are cheaper options if you can drive to the farm but the road is 4WD and steep.

Walks

For those who lack the time or inclination to tackle the **Banks Peninsula Track** (see box, p.532), there are equally rewarding shorter walks. The best is the **Round the Mountain Walk** (10km; 4hr return) circumnavigating the hills above Akaroa via the Purple Peak Road: obtain a map from the i-SITE.

For something easier, simply stroll along the waterfront Beach Road towards Glen Bay and the nineteenth-century red-and-white wooden **lighthouse** that used to stand at Akaroa Head to guide ships into the harbour, before being moved to its current location in 1980. Continuing towards Akaroa Head for about fifteen minutes, you'll come to **Red House Bay**, the scene of a bloody massacre in 1830, when the great northern chief Te Rauparaha bribed the captain of the British brig *Elizabeth* with flax to conceal Maori warriors about the vessel and then to invite Te Rauparaha's unsuspecting enemies (led by Temaiharanui) on board, where they were slaughtered. Te Rauparaha and his men then feasted on the victims on the beach.

You can also follow the inland **Onuku Road** (5km one-way; 1hr 15min) which takes you to **ONUKU**, where you'll find the *Onuku Farm Hostel* (see p.529) and **Onuku Marae** with a pretty little nineteenth-century **church**.

Eating, drinking and entertainment

Akaroa is a good place to eat well. **Expensive** establishments predominate, but there are also takeaways and cheaper cafés. Many places cut back their hours, or

The Banks Peninsula Track

The private **Banks Peninsula Track** (35km; 2 or 4 days; ⓦwww.bankstrack.co.nz; closed May–Sept) makes a wonderful alternative to DOC tracks and Great Walks. As well as a lovely combination of coastal cliff walking, volcanic landscapes, sandy swimming beaches, lush native bush and harbour views, you get to stay in some delightful, rustic accommodation and meet the locals. It is not a tramp for route-march aficionados, more a social hike best done over four days with friends keen to partake in a little botanizing, some swimming and much lazing around. Only twelve people are allowed to start the track each day on the four-dayer, and four people on the two-dayer, so **book** well in advance.

You need to be reasonably fit, but because you're guaranteed a bunk each night you can walk at your own pace. The **fee** ($230 4-day option; $150 2-day option) includes transport to the start from Akaroa and accommodation along the way in lodging with showers, full kitchen, electricity and limited food supply. Standby rates ($200 & $135 respectively) are available within five days of starting the track.

You'll need to bring a good pair of boots, sleeping bag and all-weather gear. You should also carry provisions for at least the first two days, although it is possible to buy food at small shops at Stony Bay and Otanerito Beach. There is limited scope for having your pack transported to your destination each night: see website for details.

The route

The first evening you are driven 5km south of Akaroa to Onuku where you spend the night in **Onuku hut** or in one of the stargazer huts with a view of the heavens. A home-cooked meal ($25) is available. The track proper starts the next day. From **Onuku to Flea Bay** (11km, 3hr 30min), you climb steadily to 700m (great views) then descend past a series of small waterfalls, one of which you can walk behind. Accommodation at Flea Bay is in a charming 1850s cottage with a veranda overlooking the beach. Penguin colony viewing (free) and sea kayaking around the Pohatu Marine Reserve ($20) are available.

From **Flea Bay to Stony Bay** (8km; 2hr 30min) is an exposed hike along coastal cliffs, with a seal colony providing lunchtime distraction. The night is spent in one of the gorgeous huts-cum-cottages, where there's a fire bath under the stars, indoor/outdoor shower, a small shop selling bread, tinned food, beer and wine, and a few short tracks exploring the bay.

It is another short day from **Stony Bay to Otanerito Bay** (6km; 2hr), with comfortable accommodation in a farmhouse with a great swimming beach, run by author Fiona Farrell and her husband. The final day's walk heads inland, from **Otanerito Bay to Mount Vernon Lodge** (10km; 3hr; 600m ascent), through Hinewai Nature Reserve past several small waterfalls and back to Akaroa.

even close completely, during winter. For non-blockbuster **movies**, check out the boutique Akaroa Cinema, at the corner of rue Jolie & Selwyn Avenue (ⓦwww.cinecafe.co.nz).

Akaroa Bakery 51 Beach Rd. Excellent fresh-baked bread, and a simple café serving sandwiches, pies, cakes, breakfasts and burgers. Daily 7am–5pm.

Akaroa Fish and Chips 59 Beach Rd ☎03/304 7464. Outdoor seating, a good range of fish and all the usual extras – probably the best-quality cheap grub in the town. Closes around 8pm.

By the Green 37 rue Lavaud. Smart modern café overlooking the town green, serving Akaroa's best coffee, wines, light lunches and tempting cakes.

Ma Maison 2 rue Jolie ☎03/304 7668. A lovely setting overlooking Daly's Wharf makes this a great spot for an early-evening drink though it is equally tempting for quality brunches from 10am then classy, slightly French-influenced dinners with mains around the $35 mark.

Madeira Rue Lavaud. Always jumping at weekends, this Kiwi pub offers big portions of cheapish food.

Truby's Rue Jolie. Tiny daytime café and evening bar set overlooking the water. Perfect for a sundowner.

Vangioni's 40f rue Lavaud, entrance on rue Britain ☎03/304 7714. On a warm evening the garden here is a great place to dine on excellent trattoria fare, delicious tapas and great pizza. Nightly specials are almost always tempting and the casual bar area is cosy when the weather is inclement.

Around Akaroa

A day is well spent exploring the bays around Akaroa, all reached off the wonderfully scenic **Summit Road**, which follows the ancient crater rim. Twisting roads drop down to gems of bays with deserted beaches and the remains of once thriving towns where the school or store just about hangs on. With few connecting roads between the bays, exploring the region is likely to take longer than you might expect.

Verdant **LE BONS BAY**, 20km northeast of Akaroa, is a small peaceful community with a number of holiday homes ranged behind a gorgeous sandy **beach**, framed on two sides by cliffs. Come here for moody walks along the beach and safe swimming.

Okains Bay

The next bay north from Le Bons Bay is **OKAINS BAY**, 20km from Akaroa, which has a tiny permanent population but swells with Christchurch family holiday-makers in January. The beach and the placid lagoon formed by the **Opara Stream** are excellent for swimming and boating, but the real reason to visit is the **Okains Bay Maori and Colonial Museum** (daily 10am–5pm; $7), a former cheese factory containing one of the most remarkable collections of Maori artefacts in the South Island.

Originally amassed by a local collector Murray Thacker, the collection includes a great collection of *hei tiki* (a pendant with a design based on the human form) in different styles from around Aotearoa, plus a valuable example returned here from an English collection. There's a "god stick" dating back to 1400, a war canoe from 1867 and greenstone adze heads. There's also a beautiful meeting house, with fine symbolic figures carved by master craftsman John Rua. Within the same compound, several outbuildings contain more traditional exhibitions relating to European settlement, including a "slab" stable and cottage – constructed from large slabs of totara wood.

Supplies are available at the ancient Okains Bay Store and there's some scattered **accommodation** including basic **camping** by the beach at *Okains Bay Camping Ground* (☎03/304 8789; $8), and *Double Dutch*, 32 Chorlton Rd (☎03/304 7229, ⓦwww.doubledutch.co.nz; beds $28, room and en suite ❷; closed June–Aug), a wonderfully relaxing upscale hostel in a very spacious modern house with just seven beds. It feels more like a shared house than a hostel. There's also the very welcoming *Kawatea Farmstay* (☎03/304 8621, ⓦwww.kawateafarmstay.co.nz; ❹, en suite ❺), a century-old **homestead** set in lush gardens bordered by 5km of scenic coastline with three rooms and a lovely loft. Dinners available on request (around $40).

Little Akaloa

A narrow, partly gravel road twists over the hills northwest of Okains Bay towards Little Akaloa, passing the tiny headland community of Chorlton. Here the **Old Chorlton Hall** (daily except Tues 10am–4pm; $12.50 including cream tea; ☎03/304 8726) makes an unlikely destination. Once an 1880s community hall, now a home, you sit among the overstuffed sofas, rubber plants, clocks and books of what feels like some Victorian parlour while Chris serves excellent Devonshire teas. A one-room B&B with sea views is planned: call if you fancy staying out this way.

It is 3km down to the beach at **Little Akaloa**, where the basic *Little Akaloa Reserve* (tent sites $5, campervans $10) has **camping**.

533

South to Otago

Heading south from Christchurch, SH1 forges straight across the **Canterbury Plains** connecting small farming service towns. Aside from the occasionally magnificent views of the snowcapped **Southern Alps** to the west, the drive south is through a monotonous landscape broken only by the broad gravel beds of braided rivers, usually little more than a trickle spanned by a kilometre-long bridge.

As the road passes the pottery town of **Temuka** and reaches the southern end of the Canterbury Plains, hills force it back to the shoreline at mundane **Timaru**. From here, SH8 strikes inland towards Fairlie, Lake Tekapo and Aoraki Mount Cook.

The coastal highway continues south through rolling hills to the architecturally harmonious city of **Oamaru**, and the unique and fascinating **Moeraki Boulders**. This is **penguin** country with several opportunities to stop off and spy blue and yellow-eyed penguins. From Moeraki there is little to delay you on your progress toward Dunedin, except maybe the small crossroads town of **Palmerston**, where SH85, "The Pigroot" to **Central Otago**, leaves SH1, providing another opportunity to forsake the coast and follow a historical pathway to the now defunct goldfields inland.

Rakaia, Ashburton and Temuka

Gradually leaving the suburbs of Christchurch behind, you soon hit **Dunsandel**, 40km south of the city centre, where the ⚘ *Dunsandel Store*, on SH1, does excellent coffee, cakes and deli-style meals. Almost 20km further south you cross the longest bridge in New Zealand, the 1.8km-long Rakaia River Bridge. It leads into the tiny salmon-fishing and sheepshearing settlement of **Rakaia**, where a minor road called Thompson's Track heads inland towards Methven, Mount Hutt and Mount Somers (see p.561). **Ashburton**, 27km further south, is a larger though equally quiet farming town.

TEMUKA, 150km south of Christchurch, takes its name from the Maori for "fierce oven" – indeed a large number of Maori earth ovens have been found in the area. In the twentieth century fierce ovens were used to fire **pottery**, which became a local industry following the arrival of immigrants from the "Potteries" area around Stoke-on-Trent in England. Today, sadly, only ceramics fired in China are brought here to be painted and sold at the Temuka Pottery **factory shop** on Thomas Street (Mon, Wed & Fri 1–4pm; ⓦ www.temukapottery.co.nz).

Timaru

The 28,000-strong port city of **TIMARU**, 18km south of Temuka, is at the end of a straight and flat two-hour drive from Christchurch. The city doesn't make it a vastly compelling place to stop, though it is enlivened by the **Aigantighe Art Gallery** and the **South Canterbury Museum**.

The name Timaru comes from *Te Maru*, Maori for "place of shelter", as it provided the only haven for *waka* paddling between Banks Peninsula and Oamaru. In 1837 European settlement was initiated by Joseph Price, who set up a **whaling** station south of the present city at Patiti Point. A large part of today's commercial and pastoral development was initiated by Yorkshiremen **George and Robert Rhodes**, who established the first cattle station on the South Island in 1839 and effectively founded Timaru. Land reclamation created a harbour in 1877 and helped form the fine sandy beach of Caroline Bay. For a time, Timaru became a popular seaside resort, and its annual two-week **summer carnival**, starting on Boxing Day, is still popular.

Arrival, information and accommodation

InterCity **buses** stop downtown outside the **train station**. Atomic buses stop a few steps away outside the **i-SITE visitor centre**, 2 George St (Mon–Fri 8.30am–5pm, Sat & Sun 10am–3pm (longer in summer); ☏03/687 9997, Ⓦwww.southisland .org.nz), which sells tickets. You probably won't need Timaru's Metro **bus service** (☏03/688 5544, Ⓦwww.metroinfo.org.nz), which has a flat rate of $1.50 for all journeys around the city, and $4 to Temuka. **Bikes** can be rented from The Cyclery, 106 Stafford St ($30/day; ☏03/688 8892), or use Timaru **Taxis** (☏03/688 8899).

There's **internet access** at *Off the Rail Café* (see p.537) and free at the **library**, Sophia Street (Mon, Wed & Fri 9am–8pm, Tues & Thurs 9am–6pm, Sat 10am–1pm, Sun 1–4pm).

There's a fairly limited range of accommodation, though it is rarely booked out.

Panorama Motor Lodge 52 The Bay Hill ☏0800/103 310, Ⓦwww.panorama.net.nz. Striking and hospitable motel with spacious units, all the usual facilities, as well as a sauna, spa baths, gym, off-street parking and great views over Caroline Bay. ⑤

Pleasant View 2 Moore St ☏03/686 6651, Ⓦwww.pleasantview.co.nz. Two en suites in a stylish modern house, one with great sea views, plus a guest living area. ④/⑤

Sefton Homestay 32 Sefton St ☏03/688 0017, Ⓦwww.seftonhomestay.co.nz.

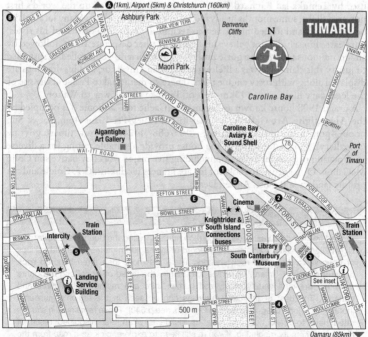

ACCOMMODATION				RESTAURANTS, CAFÉS & BARS			
Panorama Motor Lodge	D	Timaru Top 10 Holiday	B	Arthur St Café	4	Petite	3
Pleasant View	A	Park		Le Monde	1	Speights Ale House	6
Sefton Homestay	E	Wanderer Backpackers	C	Off the Rails Café	5	Sukhothai	2

Great-value B&B in a lovely, characterful 1920s house in leafy grounds. One en suite plus an equally attractive room with private guest bathroom fitted with a deep tub. There's free internet and wi-fi plus a dedicated guest lounge and discounts for cyclists. ❹

Timaru Top 10 Holiday Park 154a Selwyn St ℡0800/242 121, Ⓦwww.timaruholidaypark.co.nz. Well-kept, very high-standard holiday park offering a range of accommodation, close to the golf course and within walking distance of Maori Park. Camping $16, cabins & kitchen cabin ❷, s/c units ❸ motel units ❹

Wanderer Backpackers 24 Evans St ℡03/688 8795. Small roadside backpackers that's relatively close to town, has off-street parking, a range of rooms, a dishwasher and no check-out time. There are even occasional hunting trips and a free bus pick-up in a Beetle convertible. Camping $14, dorms $23, rooms ❶

The City

Timaru's business district centres on the 1876 **Landing Service Building**, a volcanic "bluestone" former store where goods were unloaded from the small boats that were winched up onto a shingle beach in front. It contains the i-SITE (see p.535) which, by the time you read this, should contain the new **Maori Rock Art Centre** containing displays on the **rock drawings** found in the vicinity (see box below).

A couple of hundred metres uphill, the **South Canterbury Museum**, Perth Street (Tues–Fri 10am–4.30pm, Sat & Sun 1.30–4.30pm; donation appreciated; Ⓦwww.timaru.govt.nz), contains good displays on the life of local Maori (who lived a much more hunter-gatherer lifestyle than their northern kin) and on the whaling station that occupied Patiti Point in the late 1830s and early 1840s. Hanging over the main hall of the museum is a reconstruction of the 1902 **aircraft** used by Temuka lad **Richard Pearse** in his attempt to notch up the world's first powered flight, some months in advance of the Wright brothers. Many locals claim he succeeded, and indeed his plane was technically far ahead of that of his rivals, but Pearse himself did not believe his flight – a rather desperate 100m, followed by an ignominious plunge into gorse bushes – was sufficiently controlled or sustained to justify this claim. He was a lifelong tinkerer and inventor, and his drawings are displayed along with rusty engine parts. There's a memorial to Pearse at the site of the legendary flight, about 13km west of Temuka on the way to Waitohi.

A grand 1908 house known as Aigantighe (Gaelic for "at home") is occupied by the **Aigantighe Art Gallery**, 49 Wai-iti Rd (Tues–Fri 10am–4pm, Sat & Sun noon–4pm; donation appreciated; ℡03/688 4424, Ⓦwww.timaru.govt.nz /artgallery). Original features of the house provide a suitable setting for a diverse and rotating permanent collection including five major works by native son Colin McCahon. Other artists to look out for are Frances Hodgkins, C.F. Goldie and the prolific landscape Realist, Austen Deans.

Rock art

Around five hundred years ago, Maori moa hunters visited the South Canterbury and North Otago coastal plain, leaving a record of their sojourn on the walls and ceilings of open-sided limestone rock shelters. There are more than three hundred **rock drawings** around Timaru, Geraldine and Fairlie: the faded charcoal and red ochre drawings depict a variety of stylized human, bird and mythological figures and patterns. The best of the cave drawings can be seen in the region's museums (notably the North Otago Museum in Oamaru, see p.540). Those remaining *in situ* are often hard to make out, and what is visible is often the misguided result of nineteenth-century repainting. If you're still keen to explore, pick up a map from the Timaru i-SITE and ask for directions. The best destination is Frenchman's Gully, where moa and a stylized birdman figure can be seen.

The **sculpture garden** is dominated by the results of a 1990 symposium when Kiwi, Japanese and Zimbabwean sculptors carved thirteen works from soft Mount Somers stone, which has weathered nicely. Look out for *Baboon*, carved with power tools by a Zimbabwean who had only ever carved by hand.

On a fine day, you could also spend a quiet hour ambling around the **Botanical Gardens**, Queen Street (daily 8am–dusk; free), or strolling along the low cliffs north of Caroline Bay past the wooden 1878 **Blackett's Lighthouse** to Dashing Rocks.

Eating, drinking and entertainment

Timaru's **restaurants** offer a decent range of eating options at reasonable prices, but nightlife is more limited. You can catch first-run Hollywood **movies** at Movie Max 5, on the corner of Canon and Sophia streets (Ⓣ03/684 6987), and things hot up in Timaru for the three post-Christmas weeks of the **summer carnival** (Ⓦwww .carolinebay.org.nz) when there's a circus, a fair and free concerts in Caroline Bay.

Arthur St Café 8 Arthur St. Great little café with tables outside and spread across several cosy rooms. Excellent breakfasts, veggie filo wraps, cute cakes and coffee. Closed Sun.

Le Monde 64 Bay Hill Ⓣ03/688 8550. Excellent semi-formal restaurant with views of Caroline Bay and a caring attitude to dishes such as confit of duck leg ($28) and coq au vin ($26).

Off the Rail Café 22 Station St, in the train station. Retro licensed café, housed in a 1967 former waiting room, with old booths, a jukebox, a white leather sofa, internet and a good selection of value-for-money food and zingy coffee.

Petite 16 Royal Arcade. Primarily a relaxed cocktail bar with a vast range of concoctions ($11–15) along with wine by the glass and light bites such as antipasto platters for two ($26) and pizza ($16). Closed Sun.

Speights Ale House 2 George St. Popular, cavernous bar in the Landing Service Building, offering generous pub-style lunches and dinners (mostly $15–25), plus occasional weekend live music.

Sukhothai 303 Stafford St Ⓣ03/688 4843. Good Thai restaurant serving old favourites (mostly around $15–19) plus $10 lunch specials. Closed Mon.

Oamaru and around

The former port town of **OAMARU**, 85km south of Timaru on SH1, is one of New Zealand's most alluring provincial cities, and a relaxed place to spend a day or two. The most immediate attraction is the presence of both blue and yellow-eyed **penguin colonies** on the outskirts of town, but the town itself has a well-preserved **Historic District**, a core of nineteenth-century buildings built of the distinctive cream-coloured local limestone that earned Oamaru the title "The Whitestone City". At the turn of the twentieth century it had a reputation as being the most attractive city in the South Island, and with the ongoing restoration it is regaining that status.

The limestone outcrops throughout the area once provided shelter for Maori and later the raw material for ambitious European builders. As a commercial centre for gold-rush prospectors, and shored up by quarrying, timber and farming industries, Oamaru grew prosperous. The port opened for **migration** in 1874, although many ships foundered on the hostile coastline and in the late nineteenth century wrecks littered the shore. After this boom period Oamaru declined, times evocatively recorded in work by local lass, **Janet Frame**. It is only in recent years that the town has begun to come alive again.

Arrival and information

Buses drop off at the corner of Eden and Thames streets from where it is a five-minute walk to the **i-SITE visitor centre**, 1 Thames St (mid-Dec to March daily 9am–6pm; April to mid-Dec Mon–Fri 9am–5pm, Sat & Sun 10am–4pm; ☏03/434 1656, Ⓦwww.visitoamaru.co.nz). It stocks useful free leaflets including *Janet Frame's Oamaru* and *Historic Oamaru*, and can organize amusing and highly informative **town tours** of the town with Ralph's Rambles (☏03/434 7337; $20), led by the irrepressible Ralph.

The best times to visit Oamaru are from November to January when penguins are in greatest numbers, and for the **Victorian Heritage Celebrations** over the third weekend in November when the streets of the historic district become a racetrack for penny-farthings, cheered on by local residents in Victorian attire to the tinny accompaniment of the visiting fair.

There's **internet** access at the i-SITE and free connection at the Oamaru Public Library, 62 Thames St (Mon–Fri 9.30am–5.30pm, Sat 10am–12.30pm).

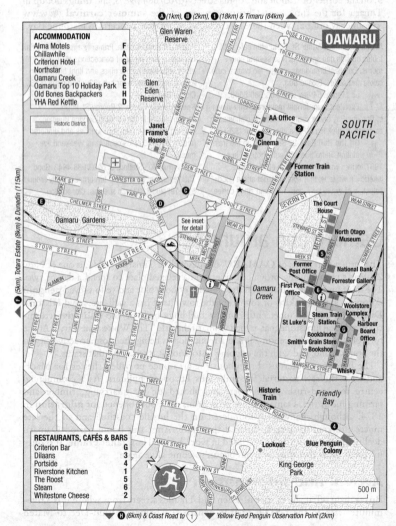

OAMARU

ACCOMMODATION
Alma Motels	F
Chillawhile	A
Criterion Hotel	G
Northstar	B
Oamaru Creek	C
Oamaru Top 10 Holiday Park	E
Old Bones Backpackers	H
YHA Red Kettle	D

Historic District

RESTAURANTS, CAFÉS & BARS
Criterion Bar	G
Dilaans	3
Portside	4
Riverstone Kitchen	1
The Roost	5
Steam	6
Whitestone Cheese	2

Ⓐ(1km), Ⓑ(2km), Ⓘ(18km) & Timaru (84km)

Ⓕ(5km), Totara Estate (8km) & Dunedin (115km)

Ⓗ(6km) & Coast Road to ① ▼ Yellow Eyed Penguin Observation Point (2km)

0 — 500 m

Accommodation

Finding a **place to stay** is seldom difficult, though it pays to book a day or two ahead from December to March. Oamaru and the area south towards Dunedin boasts a wealth of great hostels.

Alma Motels SH1, 5km south of town ☎0800/000 644, ⓦwww.almamotels.co.nz. Ageing motel with functional units and all the expected facilities; a bargain. ❸

Alpine Motel 285 Thames St ☎0800/272 710, ⓦwww.alpineoamaru.co.nz. Comfortable motel close to the town centre, with ten spacious, updated studio units, some with full kitchens. ❹

Chillawhile 1 Frome St ☎03/437 0168, ⓦwww.chillawhile.co.nz. There's a loose, chilled feel to this hostel in a rambling house 2km north of the centre. Rooms are dedicated to playing music (with guitar and organ), painting and drumming workshops. Pot luck dinners are encouraged and dorms are set up with a small sitting area to encourage sociability. Free light breakfast and bus pick-ups. Dorms $28, rooms ❷

Criterion Hotel 3 Tyne St ☎0800/259 334, ⓦwww.criterion.net.nz. Charming Victorian-styled boutique B&B in an 1877 pub right in the heart of the historic district, complete with guest kitchen and lounge. A sizeable breakfast is included. Shared bath ❹, en suite ❻

Northstar 495a SH1 ☎03/437 1190, ⓦwww.northstarmotel.co.nz. Sparkling revamped motel 3km north of the centre with stylish, new units and its own restaurant. ❹

🏃 **Oamaru Creek** 24 Reed St ☎03/434 1190, ⓦwww.oamarucreek.co.nz. Excellent

homestay B&B in what was once a maternity home – spacious and tastefully decorated rooms (some en suite) with fantastic professionally cooked organic breakfasts, dinners by arrangement ($30 for 2 courses; BYO) and a warm and friendly atmosphere, as well as knowledgeable owners who will try to put you on the right trail to a good time. ❹/❺

Oamaru Top 10 Holiday Park 30 Chelmer St ☎0800/280 202, ⓦwww.oamarutop10.co.nz. In a lovely sheltered setting close to Oamaru Gardens with a good range of accommodation. Camping $34 per site, cabins ❷, kitchen cabins ❸, motels units ❹

🏃 **Old Bones Backpackers** Beach Rd, Kakanui ☎03/434-8115, ⓦwww.oldbones.co.nz. Gorgeous, purpose-built, upscale backpackers on the coast 6km south of town (follow Wharfe Rd) with just eight doubles and twins (no dorms) opening onto a spacious, comfortable and TV-free lounge/kitchen. Everything is to the highest standard, and there's free internet and underfloor heating in the bedrooms. Closed May–Sept. Singles $43, rooms ❷

YHA Red Kettle 2 Reed St ☎03/434 5008, ⓦwww.yha.co.nz. Small and pleasant old-style hostel close to the town centre with five-bed dorms, a twin and a double room. Closed May–Sept. Dorms $27, rooms ❷

The Town

Thames Street and the knot of streets around Tyne, Itchen and Harbour streets define Oamaru's **Historic District**, a dense cluster of grand civic and mercantile buildings that sets the town centre apart from any other in the land. The key is Oamaru whitestone, a "free stone" which is easily worked with metal hand tools when freshly quarried but hardens with exposure to the elements. While keeping the prevailing Neoclassical fashion firmly in mind, the architects' imaginations ran riot, producing deeply fluted pilasters, finely detailed pediments and elegant Corinthian pillars topped with veritable forests of acanthus leaves. Oamaru was given much of its character by architect R.A. Lawson and by the firm Forrester and Lemon who together produced most of the more accomplished buildings between 1871 and 1883.

Oamaru stone is still used in modern buildings – witness the Waitaki Aquatic Centre in Takaro Park – and enthusiasts can visit its source at the **Parkside Quarry**, 7km west of town (Mon–Fri 9am–4.30pm; free; ☎03/433 9786, ⓦwww.oamarustone.co.nz), or ask about the $10 guided tours.

Along Thames Street

The majority of civic buildings are along Thames Street where the 1906 **Opera House**, Palladian **Courthouse** and classically proportioned **Athenaeum** building all line up along one side. This last served as a subscription library before providing a home for the **North Otago Museum** (Mon–Fri 10.30am–4.30pm, Sat & Sun 1–4pm; donation), with its modest selection of displays on North Otago history, Maori digs and the life of local novelist Janet Frame.

The Former Post Office, a few steps further along Thames Street, originally came without the tower, which was added by the architect's son, Thomas Forrester, in 1903. This building replaced the adjacent 1864 First Post Office, an Italianate structure which predates all the other whitestone work and is the town's only remaining example of the work of W.H. Clayton. Directly opposite the one-time post offices are two of Lawson's buildings: the imposing **National Bank** has perhaps the purest Neoclassical facade in town; while its grander neighbour now operates as the **Forrester Gallery** (daily 10.30am–4.30pm; donations welcome). This features touring exhibitions of contemporary and traditional art, plus a basement of works by iconic Kiwi artist Colin McCahon and local painter Colin Wheeler, whose cityscapes are dominated by the colour of Oamaru stone.

Tyne-Harbour Street Historic District

Continuing towards the waterfront you enter Oamaru's original commercial quarter, full of whitestone flamboyance. Gentrification is taking its time, but this is gradually becoming the place to hang out, perhaps grabbing a coffee or a beer in between browsing the bookstore, art galleries and minor museums.

Follow Itchen Street east and as you round the corner into Tyne Street you'll spot the **Woolstore Complex**, 1 Tyne St, complete with the *Woolstore Café* and the **Oamaru Auto Collection** (daily 10am–4pm; $6), with two dozen ancient and not-so-old vehicles. Upstairs, a small **market** is held every Sunday (10am–4pm).

The old **Union Offices**, 7 Tyne St, is a traditional bookbinder's workshop (Mon–Fri 2–4pm or a little later; free; ☎03/434 9277), where you can watch local character Michael O'Brien binding books and see examples of old printing and letterpress machines. Next door is the elegant **Smiths Grain Store**, built in 1881 by stonemason James Johnson, while further along you'll find Slightly Foxed, 11 Tyne St, which offers a great array of secondhand and classic **books**. Harbour Street runs parallel to Tyne Street and is lined by more rejuvenated mercantile buildings. The 1876 Venetian Renaissance-style **Harbour Board Office** was one of the first public buildings designed by the prolific Forrester and Lemon. Also worth a look is the striking 1882 Loan and Mercantile Warehouse, 14 Harbour St, once the largest grain store in New Zealand. Grain sacks have been replaced by whisky barrels at **Whisky** (daily: summer 10am–7pm; winter 10am–4pm; Ⓦ www.milfordwhisky.co.nz), home to New Zealand's only supplier of locally produced **single malts**. Wander around the heavy-beamed warehouse (free), take a guided tour ($15, on demand) or sit in the café and sample a malt whisky flight ($10–15) with four samples from barrels of differing ages, some twenty years old.

The Oamaru Gardens and Janet Frame House

Five minutes' walk west of the Historic District, **Oamaru Gardens** (daily dawn–dusk, glasshouses 9am–4pm; free) offer manicured natural beauty in a streamside setting. The rhododendron dell, fragrant garden and Victorian summerhouse give a sense of the wealth the town once enjoyed.

About ten minutes stroll to the northwest, the **Janet Frame House**, 56 Eden St (Nov–April daily 2–4pm; $5), was the modest childhood home of one of New Zealand's greatest writers. She lived here from early school days to leaving for higher education: "I wanted an imagination that would inhabit a world of fact, descend like a shining light upon the ordinary life of Eden Street…"

Even before her death in 2004 the house was being restored to 1930s style; you can explore it, get some insight from custodian, Ralph, and listen to a marvellous recording of the author reading an extract from *Owls Do Cry*, about the very sofa you'll be sitting on.

Fans of her work may want to follow the **Janet Frame Trail** (free leaflet available from the i-SITE) taking you to locations used in varying degrees of disguise in her books – the former subscription library in the Athenaeum that featured in *Faces In The Water*, or the rubbish dump that formed the symbolic centre of *Owls Do Cry*.

The penguin colonies

Oamaru is unique in having both yellow-eyed and blue **penguin colonies** within walking distance of the town centre. It is usually possible to see both colonies in one evening, since the yellow-eyes tend to come ashore earlier than the blues. Penguins are timid creatures and easily distressed, so keep quiet and still, and do not encroach within 10m of the birds. Once disturbed, the penguins may not return to their nests for several hours, even if they have chicks to feed.

Blue penguins nest under most of the waterside buildings and if you sit along the shoreline around dusk you'll probably see a few waddle past. More formal and informative viewing takes place at the **Blue Penguin Colony** (daily; best visited just before dusk; $22), fifteen minutes' walk southeast of the town centre along Waterfront Road. In the visitor centre there's a chance to see an infrared 24-hour monitor in one of the nest boxes and videos on blue penguins before being deprived of your cameras and videos and led out to the 350-seat grandstand. Come during the breeding season (June–Dec) and you'll see chicks – and hear them calling to their parents out at sea, hunting for food. When the parents return around dusk, travelling in groups known as rafts, they climb the steep harbour banks and cross in front of the grandstand to their nests. Outside the breeding season, penguins indulge in much less to-ing and fro-ing, but provide an engaging spectacle nevertheless. In the peak season (Nov to mid-Feb) you might hope to see two hundred penguins in a night, though this might drop to a dozen or so in March, June and August. It can all seem a bit of a circus so, if you'd prefer a more intimate encounter, try the self-guided **Behind the Scenes** tour (daily 10am–2hr before dark; $10, entry combo $28), which visits the breeding colony where you should see birds inside nesting boxes, maybe with chicks. This is also available guided ($17.50, combo $35).

The much larger **yellow-eyed penguins** nest in smaller numbers but keep more sociable hours, usually coming ashore in late afternoon or early evening (best

Blue penguins

Blue penguins, the smallest of their kind, are found all around the coast of New Zealand, and along the shores of southern Australia, where they are known as little penguins. White on their chests and bellies, they have a thick head-to-tail streak along their back in iridescent indigo-blue. Breeding takes place from May to January, and the parents take it in turns to stay with the eggs during the 36-day incubation period. The newly hatched chicks are protected for the first two or three weeks before both parents go out to sea to meet the increasing demand for food, returning full of fish, which they regurgitate into the chick's mouth. At eight weeks the chicks begin to fledge, but sixty percent die in their first year; the juveniles that do survive usually return to their birthplace. At the end of the breeding season the birds fatten up before coming ashore to moult: over the next three weeks their feathers are not waterproof enough for them to take to the sea and they lose up to half their bodyweight.

Oct–Feb). They mainly arrive 2km away at **Bushy Beach**, reached along Bushy Beach Road, where a hide enables you to see the yellow-eyed penguins making their way across the beach in the morning and early evening.

To facilitate both blue and yellow-eyed penguin watching, use the door-to-door **Penguin Express** (2hr 30min–3hr; $46, assorted discounts down to $40; ☎0800/304 333, Ⓦwww.penguinscrossing.co.nz), a bus tour that visits Bushy Beach and whips you around town with a bit of commentary, getting you to the blue penguins (entry included) in time for their arrival.

Eating, drinking and entertainment

Most of Oamaru's **eating and drinking** takes place close to the central Thames Street. If you're planning an outing to Moeraki Boulders consider dining at *Fleur's Place* (see opposite), and when heading north, try lunch at the *Riverstone Kitchen* (see below).

Criterion Bar *Criterion Hotel*, 3 Tyne St. With the tenor of a Victorian English pub there's a long wooden bar, some good old-fashioned beer (notably London Porter and Emersons traditional ale), plus filling inexpensive food, including bangers and mash.

Dilaans 263 Thames St. Good-value Turkish takeaway and café. Slather a couple of sauces over the chicken shish and wash it down with an apple tea. Closed Mon.

Penguin Club Emulsion Lane Ⓦwww.thepenguinclub.co.nz. A legendary back-alley venue bar hosting Friday jam nights (from 8pm), poetry, theatre and gigs by Kiwi touring bands ($10–30 cover charge): almost everyone of note in the Kiwi music biz has played here. From the *Criterion Hotel*, walk down Harbour St, and turn left down an unprepossessing alley. Entry price is low, and if you pick up a programme of events from the visitor's centre you'll be let in at the members' price.

Portside 2 Waterfront Rd ☎03/434 3400. Stylish, modern restaurant/bar by the blue penguin colony

where the airy interior is a fine place to dine (mains around $30). Or just come for a sundowner on the deck overlooking the sea. Closed Wed.

Riverstone Kitchen 1431 SH1, 19km north of Oamaru, 66km south of Timaru ☎03/431 3505. Ⓦwww.riverstonekitchen.co.nz. Some of the finest café food around, served in an uncluttered country setting. Best for lunch (around $17) when you're passing, though they also serve bistro dinners (Thurs–Sat) for around $30.

The Roost 30 Thames St ☎03/434 1165. This daytime place doesn't look that special, but the standard range of café fare is prepared and presented by people who care about what they do.

Steam 7 Thames St. Daytime purveyors of the best coffee in town, plus delicious cakes, muffins and juices. Closed Sun.

Whitestone Cheese 3 Torridge St. A deli perfect for picnic supplies, including excellent cheeses from the adjacent factory, particularly its famed, soft and creamy Windsor Blue. You can watch production from the viewing gallery at the back (best Mon–Fri before 3pm).

South of Oamaru to Moeraki and the Moeraki Boulders

South of Oamaru, most people make a beeline for the Moeraki Boulders and Dunedin, but it's worth taking half an hour or so to look around **Totara Estate**, SH1, 8km south of Oamaru (daily Nov–April 9am–5pm; May–Oct 9.30am–3.30pm; $7; 1hr tours at 11am daily in summer; $15; Ⓦwww.totaraestate.co.nz;), the birthplace of the New Zealand meat industry. Until the early 1880s New Zealand was a major wool exporter, but no one knew what to do with all the surplus meat. Meanwhile, Britain's burgeoning industrial cities were on the brink of starvation. The solution came when the Australian and New Zealand Land Company pioneered refrigeration on a sailing ship and in 1882, the three-masted *Dunedin* was refitted with coke-driven freezers and filled with lamb from Totara Estate. The estate is now a grassy historic park built around solid whitestone buildings containing a small museum along with harness room, stables, granary barn and blacksmith's forge, all appropriately equipped. The foundations and partial remains of the original slaughterhouse and carcass shed form the basis of a modern reconstruction that gives an idea of what work was like here.

A further 18km south on SH1, the family-run, TV-free ⅄ *Olive Grove Lodge & Holiday Park* (☎03/439 5830, ⓦwww.olivebranch.co.nz; camping $12, powered hook-ups $30 per site, dorms $28, rooms & en suite ❷; closed June–Aug), occupies a bend in a river with good swimming holes just 11km north of the Moeraki Boulders. Along with a hot tub, infrared sauna and hammocks there's a selection of brilliantly decorated rooms and plenty of riverside space.

Moeraki Boulders

Almost 40km south of Oamaru on SH1 the large, grey spherical **Moeraki Boulders** (some almost 2m in diameter) lie partially submerged in the sandy beach at the tide line. Their smooth skins hide honeycomb centres, which are revealed in some of the broken specimens. The boulders once lay deep in the mudstone cliffs behind the beach and as these were eroded, out fell the smooth boulders, with further erosion exposing a network of surface veins. The boulders were originally formed around a central core of carbonate of lime crystals that attracted minerals from their surroundings – a process that started sixty million years ago, when muddy sediment containing shell and plant fragments accumulated on the sea floor. They range in size from small pellets to large round rocks, though the smaller ones have all been souvenired over the years, leaving only those too heavy to shift.

Access to this strangely compelling phenomenon is either by a 300m walk along the beach from a DOC parking area (often used for ad hoc camping), or more immediately via a short private trail ($2 in the honesty box at any hour), though it is free for patrons of the adjacent **café** (daily: Oct–April 8am–6pm; May–Nov 9am–5pm).

Maori named the boulders Te Kaihinaki (food baskets), believing them to have been washed ashore from the wreck of a canoe whose occupants were seeking *pounamu*. The seaward reef near Shag Point (see p.544) was the hull of the canoe, and just beyond it stands a prominent rock, the vessel's petrified navigator. Some of the Moeraki Boulders were *hinaki* (baskets), the more spherical were water-carrying gourds and the irregular-shaped rocks farther down the beach were *kumara* from the canoe's food store. The survivors among the crew were transformed at daybreak into hills overlooking the beach.

Moeraki village

The picturesque and tranquil fishing village of **MOERAKI**, 2km south, offers access to the boulders along the beach and a chance to see yellow-eyed penguins up close. Drive to the white wooden lighthouse (1km off SH1 then 5km along an unsealed road) then follow signs down a path which leads to a hide, overlooking the beach where yellow-eyed penguins emerge after a hard day's fishing (3.30pm–nightfall), and seals loll on beaches. A second path leads to a *pa* site, its importance explained on a panel nearby.

There's limited **accommodation** in these parts, but *Moeraki Beach Motels* (☎03/439 4862; ❸) has four units facing the bay, and manages a number of holiday homes in the village (2-night minimum; ❸–❺). There's also the *Moeraki Village Holiday Park* (☎03/439 4759, ⓦwww.moerakivillageholidaypark.co.nz; tent sites $13, cabins ❶, flats & motel units ❸), and *Three Bays*, 39 Cardiff St (☎03/439 4520, ⓦwww.threebays.co.nz; ❺), a self-contained unit high on the hill with long views over the town towards the boulders.

The Moeraki Tavern does bar meals, but the best **eating** by far is at the marvellous ⅄ *Fleur's Place* (daily 9am–11pm; ☎03/439 4480, ⓦwww.fleursplace.co.nz) which lures sophisticates from Dunedin (plus the likes of Gwyneth Paltrow and Rick Stein) to a characterful converted shack for great seafood meals with fish straight off the boat (most mains $30–35), a good wine selection or an excellent coffee. Dinner bookings are essential and this could be your chance to sample muttonbird.

Most **buses** will drop you on SH1, 1.5km from the village, but Coastline Tours (☎03/434 7744) will drop you in the centre on their Oamaru–Dunedin run.

Shag Point and the road to Dunedin

Just over 10km south of Moeraki Village, a side road runs 3km to **Shag Point** and the **Matakaea Scenic Reserve**, where the rocks are often slathered with seals and a viewing platform allows distant views of yellow-eyed penguins.

A further 9km south you reach the small town of **PALMERSTON** where a hilltop **monument** marks the work of **John McKenzie** who, as Minister of Lands, Agriculture and Immigration in the early 1890s effectively laid the groundwork for modern farming by breaking up the vast holdings of absentee landlords and making them available to new immigrants. Palmerston marks the junction of two routes: the "Pigroot" (SH85) inland to the Maniototo and the historic goldfield heartland of Central Otago; and SH1 running 52km south to Dunedin. Backpackers keen on kayak fishing, spear fishing, shellfish gathering, surfing, horseriding and chilling out in front of a good movie should seriously consider a night or two at the excellent *Asylum Lodge*, 36 Russell Rd, Seacliff (☎03/465 8123; dorms $25, rooms ❷; closed May–Oct), a small, laidback hostel sited in a former psychiatric hospital on the northern outskirts of Dunedin. Most activities are free or very cheap and Frank will happily show you his collection of fifty-odd old cars – some rare, most rusty.

Travel details

Passenger trains run north of Christchurch to Kaikoura and Picton, and northwest to Arthur's Pass and Greymouth. Christchurch is the hub of the South Island's bus network: InterCity and Atomic Shuttle have the broadest networks. Only direct, nonstop flights are listed.

Trains

Christchurch to: Arthur's Pass (1 daily; 2hr 15min); Blenheim (1 daily; 4hr 45min); Greymouth (1 daily; 4hr 30min); Kaikoura (1 daily; 3hr); Picton (1 daily; 5hr 20min).

Buses

Christchurch to: Akaroa (3–5 daily; 1hr 30min); Aoraki Mount Cook (1 daily; 5hr 20min); Arthur's Pass (2 daily; 2hr 30min); Blenheim (4–5 daily; 4hr 45min–5hr 30min); Dunedin (5–6 daily; 6hr); Geraldine (4 daily; 2hr); Greymouth (2 daily; 4hr); Hanmer Springs (3 daily; 2hr); Hokitika (1 daily; 4hr 30min); Kaikoura (4–5 daily; 2hr 30min); Lyttelton (every 15–30min; 35min); Methven (4 weekly; 1hr 30min); Oamaru (7 daily; 4hr); Picton (4–5 daily; 5hr–5hr 30min); Queenstown (4 daily; 7–8hr); Tekapo (4 daily; 3–4hr); Timaru (7 daily; 2hr 30min); Twizel (4 daily; 4–5hr); Wanaka (4 daily; 7–8hr).

Oamaru to: Aoraki Mount Cook (3 weekly; 3hr); Christchurch (7 daily; 4hr); Dunedin (7–9 daily; 2hr); Omarama (3 weekly; 1hr 45min); Tekapo (4 weekly; 3hr); Timaru (7 daily; 1hr); Twizel (7 weekly; 2hr).
Timaru to: Christchurch (7 daily; 2hr 30min); Dunedin (7–9 daily; 3hr 30min); Oamaru (7 daily; 1hr).

Flights

Christchurch to: Auckland (24 daily; 1hr 20min); Blenheim (3 daily; 50min); Dunedin (8 daily; 1hr); Hokitika (3 daily; 35min); Invercargill (6 daily; 1hr 20min); Napier/Hastings (2 daily; 1hr 25min); Nelson (4 daily; 50min); Palmerston North (4 daily; 1hr 10min); Queenstown (5 daily; 50–60min); Rotorua (4 daily; 1hr 40min); Wanaka (1–2 daily; 1hr); Wellington (16 daily; 45min).
Timaru to: Wellington (2–3 daily; 1hr 10min).

Central South Island

CENTRAL SOUTH ISLAND

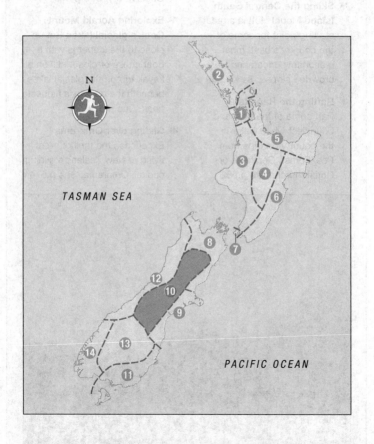

TASMAN SEA

PACIFIC OCEAN

545

CHAPTER 10

Highlights

✳ **Hiking around Arthur's Pass** Walking in this wild, rugged national park offers a jaw-dropping insight into a uniquely beautiful alpine landscape. See p.552

✳ **Skiing the Central South Island** Mount Hutt is a great starting point for some of the country's best, most reasonably priced and least-crowded slopes. See p.560

✳ **Rafting the Rangitata** Raft some of the best and bounciest white water in the country on trips from Peel Forest, Geraldine or Christchurch. See p.562

✳ **Stargazing above Lake Tekapo** After taking in the lake's incredible opaque blue waters, gaze up at the astonishingly clear star-filled night sky from Mount John Observatory. See p.565

✳ **Exploring Aoraki Mount Cook's glacial lakes** Get up close to the icebergs with a boat cruise or closer still on a kayak trip on the glacial lakes beneath the country's highest peak. See p.571

✳ **Gliding over Omarama** Experience the thrill of silent flying at New Zealand's gliding capital, Omarama. See p.574

▲ Aoraki Mount Cook

Central South Island

The **Central South Island** is one of the most varied and visually stunning areas in New Zealand, with expansive pasturelands, dense native forests and a history rich in tales of human endeavour, tinged with the toughness and idiosyncrasies of the area's settlers. The region's defining feature is the icy, white sawtooth ridge of the **Southern Alps** that forms the South Island's central north–south spine and peaks at New Zealand's loftiest summit, 3754m **Aoraki Mount Cook**.

From Christchurch to Westport, the forested **Lewis Pass** road provides access to the tranquil spa town of **Hanmer Springs** before passing the more rustic hot pools at **Maruia Springs**. Further south, both road and rail head through spectacular **Arthur's Pass**, which lies at the heart of **Arthur's Pass National Park**, with its abundance of day-walks and longer trails.

South of Christchurch, roads lead across the Canterbury Plains towards the small foothill settlement of **Methven**, the base for **Mount Hutt**-bound skiers and summertime walkers exploring **Mount Somers**.

The southern half of the region leaves behind the rolling hills for the sun-scorched grasslands of the **Mackenzie Country**, an area renowned for massive sheep runs and the unearthly blues of its glacier-fed lakes, **Tekapo** and **Pukaki**. The mightiest of the Southern Alps form an imperious backdrop. **Aoraki Mount Cook Village**, huddled at the foot of the mountain, is the starting point of numerous walks, glacial lake trips and heli-trekking and heli-skiing. An alternative base for forays to Mount Cook is the former hydro construction town of **Twizel**, less than an hour's drive south, surrounded by dams, control gates and water channels.

The Central South Island **climate** is generally hot and dry in summer with long days that sear the grasslands a tinder-dry yellow-brown. In winter, snow supplies numerous ski-fields. These alpine conditions foster unique plants and wildlife, including the Mount Cook lily, the largest white mountain daisies in the world, and the mischievous kea – the world's only alpine parrot.

Hanmer Springs and the Lewis Pass

The most northerly of the cross-mountain routes, SH7 crosses the **Lewis Pass** following an ancient Maori and early Pakeha trade route. A side road spurs off to the spa town of **Hanmer Springs**, which is also a popular base for summer walks and winter sports at the nearby **Hanmer Springs Ski Area**. Some 60km further west, you cross the **Lewis Pass** and drop down to the steaming thermal waters of **Maruia Springs**.

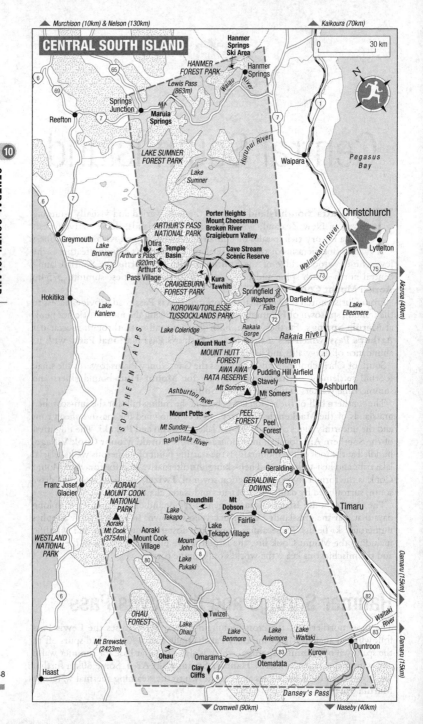

CENTRAL SOUTH ISLAND

Murchison (10km) & Nelson (130km)

Kaikoura (70km)

0   30 km

HANMER FOREST PARK

Hanmer Springs Ski Area

Hanmer Springs

Lewis Pass (863m)

Waiau River

Springs Junction

Maruia Springs

Reefton

LAKE SUMNER FOREST PARK

Lake Sumner

Hurunui River

Waipara

Pegasus Bay

Christchurch

Lyttelton

Greymouth

Lake Brunner

ARTHUR'S PASS NATIONAL PARK

Otira

Arthur's Pass (920m)

Temple Basin

Arthur's Pass Village

Porter Heights
Mount Cheeseman
Broken River
Craigieburn Valley

Cave Stream Scenic Reserve

CRAIGIEBURN FOREST PARK

Kura Tawhiti

Waimakariri River

Akaroa (40km)

Hokitika

Lake Kaniere

KOROWAI/TORLESSE TUSSOCKLANDS PARK

Lake Coleridge

Springfield

Washpen Falls

Darfield

Lake Ellesmere

SOUTHERN ALPS

Mount Hutt

Rakaia Gorge

Rakaia River

MOUNT HUTT FOREST

AWA AWA RATA RESERVE

Methven

Pudding Hill Airfield

Stavely

Mt Somers

Ashburton

Ashburton River

Mt Somers

PEEL FOREST

Mount Potts

Mt Sunday

Rangitata River

Peel Forest

Arundel

Geraldine

FRANZ JOSEF GLACIER

Franz Josef Glacier

AORAKI MOUNT COOK NATIONAL PARK

Aoraki Mt Cook (3754m)

Roundhill

Lake Tekapo

Mt Dobson

GERALDINE DOWNS

WESTLAND NATIONAL PARK

Aoraki Mount Cook Village

Mount John

Lake Tekapo Village

Fairlie

Timaru

Lake Pukaki

Oamaru (15km)

Mt Brewster (2423m)

OHAU FOREST

Twizel

Lake Ohau

Lake Benmore

Lake Aviemore

Lake Waitaki

Waitaki River

Oamaru (15km)

Ohau

Omarama

Clay Cliffs

Otematata

Kurow

Duntroon

Haast

Dansey's Pass

Cromwell (90km)

Naseby (40km)

Renowned as one of the world's most scenic **rail** journeys, the TranzAlpine (p.513), the only train serving the region, traverses the mountains from Christchurch to Greymouth via Arthur's Pass. **Bus** routes centre on Christchurch, running north to Hanmer Springs with Hanmer Connection (☎0800/242 663, ⓦwww.atsnz.com), then over the Lewis Pass to Nelson, while Atomic Shuttles (☎03/349 0697, ⓦwww .atomictravel.co.nz) run daily between Christchurch and Nelson. To continue over the Lewis Pass to Westport, the Hanmer Springs Adventure Centre Shuttle (p.551) runs to the highway junction, linking with the daily East West Coaches (☎0800/142 622) service between Christchurch and Westport. For shuttles between Kaikoura and Hanmer Springs, contact *Hanmer Backpackers* (below). Great Sights (☎09/583 5790 ⓦwww.greatsights.co.nz) make a daily run up to Aoraki Mount Cook, while the Cook Connection (☎0800/266 526, ⓦwww.cookconnect.co.nz) links Aoraki Mount Cook with Twizel and Lake Tekapo. Atomic, NakedBus and InterCity buses stop in Twizel on their Queenstown–Christchurch runs.

Hanmer Springs

About 140km north of Christchurch, a side road heads 9km north off SH7 to **HANMER SPRINGS** at the edge of a broad, fertile plain snuggled against the Southern Alps foothills, where the springs are fed by rainwater seeping through fractures in the rocks of the Hanmer Mountains, absorbing various minerals and warmed by the earth's natural heat, before rising to the surface.

Arrival, information and accommodation

Hanmer Connection **buses** (above) stop outside the **i-SITE visitor centre** on Amuri Avenue, next to the hot pools (daily 10am–5pm; ☎03/315 0020, ⓦwww.visithanmersprings.co.nz), which contains a small **bank** (Mon–Fri 10am–2pm). There's also an **ATM** outside the small but well-stocked 4-Square **supermarket** on Conical Hill Road. The town has a good spread of **accommodation** but is a popular weekend getaway so year-round it's worth booking ahead.

Accommodation

Cheltenham House 13 Cheltenham St ☎03/315 7545, ⓦwww.cheltenham.co.nz. The best B&B in town, with four large, gracious rooms set in a 1930s house with a snooker room, and two cottages in the lovingly tended garden. Evening drinks, spa and wi-fi all included; good discounts for singles. B&B ❼

Drifters Inn 2 Harrogate St ☎03/315 7554, ⓦwww.driftersinn.co.nz. Centrally located motel-cum-lodge offering comfortable, modern rooms and use of a communal lounge with log fire, kitchen and BBQ. Prices include a hearty continental breakfast. Rooms ❺

🏃 **Hanmer Backpackers** 41 Conical Hill Rd ☎03/315 7196, ⓦwww.hanmerback packers.co.nz. Heart-warmingly cosy A-frame chalet-style hostel bang in town with a snug, book-filled, TV-free lounge, hot water bottles, spotless facilities, sociable BBQ patio and lots of

free treats such as fresh fruit. Tents $16, dorms $27, doubles ❶

Hanmer Resort Motel 7 Cheltenham St ☎03/315 7362, ⓦwww.hanmerresortmotel. co.nz. Great-value central motel with a range of units (all with balcony, grassed area or private courtyard) kept to a very high standard, a kids' play area, and owners who can't do enough for you. Studios ❹, two-bedroom villas ❺, s/c family apartments ❻

Le Gîte Backpackers 3 Devon St ☎03/315 5111, ⓦwww.legite.co.nz. Cheerful, tastefully decorated hostel in a couple of converted houses and modern chalet, around 10min walk from the centre, opening to a large garden with a giant swing-sofa. Dorms $27, doubles (some en suite) ❷

Mountain View Top 10 Holiday Park Corner of Hanmer Springs Rd & Bath St ☎0800/904 545, ⓦwww.mountainviewtop10.co.nz. The closest

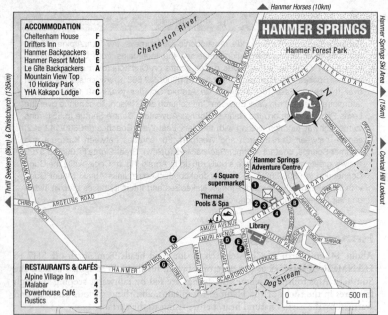

ACCOMMODATION

Cheltenham House	F
Drifters Inn	D
Hanmer Backpackers	B
Hanmer Resort Motel	E
Le Gîte Backpackers	A
Mountain View Top 10 Holiday Park	G
YHA Kakapo Lodge	C

RESTAURANTS & CAFÉS

Alpine Village Inn	1
Malabar	4
Powerhouse Café	2
Rustics	3

Hanmer Horses (10km)

HANMER SPRINGS

Hanmer Forest Park

Hanmer Springs Ski Area (15km)

Conical Hill Lookout

Thrill Seekers (8km) & Christchurch (135km)

Chatterton River

Hanmer Springs Adventure Centre

4 Square supermarket

Thermal Pools & Spa

Library

Dog Stream

0   500 m

holiday park to the town centre, with a range of motel units, cabin accommodation and campsites overlooking a riverside reserve. Bike rental $10/hr. Camping $22–35 per site, cabins ❷, kitchen cabins ❷–❸, s/c units ❸–❹, motel units ❺

YHA Kakapo Lodge 14 Amuri Ave ☎03/315 7472, ⊛www.kakapolodge.co.nz. Large, sun-filled modern hostel opening to communal balconies and courtyard areas. Dorms $28, rooms ❷, en suites & motel units ❸

The Town

Oak-lined Amuri Avenue runs past the i-SITE, shops and the shady park that gives the town its quiet, sheltered feel. The park marks the entrance to the modernized **Hanmer Springs Thermal Pools & Spa** (daily 10am–9pm; $14, two entries on same day $18, towel rental $5; ☎03/315 0000, ⊛www .hanmersprings.co.nz) complex, where you can lounge on the lawns around twelve landscaped thermal pools ranging from 33°C to 42°C, as well as two 28°C to 30°C freshwater swimming pools. Artificial streams link the pools, providing great places to wallow. Add in a waterslide ($6 extra for unlimited rides), half a dozen private pools ($24 each for 30min, min 2 people, including general entry), and the *Garden House Café* and you could stay all day. It's at its best in the evening when the crowds thin and the sun sets. Next door, the stylish **Spa** (☎03/315 0029), New Zealand's largest, offers pampering treatments including water exfoliation (40min; $110).

Hiking and biking in Hanmer Forest Park

The Black pines, Norway spruce, Douglas firs and assorted deciduous trees of **Hanmer Forest Park**, on the northern and eastern fringes of town, offer great hiking. The excellent *Hanmer Springs Walks* leaflet ($3) maps out numerous **walks** (up to 6hr), notably the **Waterfall Track** (2.5km; 2hr 30min; 400m ascent), leading to the 41m-high Dog Stream Waterfall.

Hanmer Forest is also renowned for **mountain biking**. Pick up the *Mountain Bike Tracks* leaflet ($3) and rent a bike from one of several companies in town including Hanmer Adventure Centre, 20 Conical Hill Rd (bikes $45/day; ☏0800/368 7386, Ⓦwww.hanmeradventure.co.nz) to explore the gravel roads and twisting singletrack. Alternatively, the centre can transport you to the top of Jacks Pass for a self-guided ride back ($99, including a hot pools pass).

Adventure activities

Near the turn-off from SH7, 9km south of town, the Waiau Ferry Bridge is home to Thrillseekers (☏03/315 7046, Ⓦwww.thrillseekers.co.nz), whose water-based activities include scenic two-hour-plus **rafting** trips through the Grade II Waiau River Canyon (70–90min on the water; $145), **jetboat** rides through the steep-sided gorges of the Waiau River (30min; $110), **bungy jumps** ($145) from a 35m platform midway across the Waiau Ferry Bridge, and **quad biking** (2hr; $99), with combo packages available.

Tailored **horseriding** trips with Hanmer Horses, 187 Rogerson Rd ($50/1hr, $95/2hr 30min; ☏0800/873 546, Ⓦwww.hanmerhorses.co.nz), a fifteen-minute drive northwest of town off Jacks Pass Road, often involve stream crossings. For **multi-day horseriding trips**, contact Alpine Horse Safaris (p.61).

Hanmer Springs Ski Area

The tiny **Hanmer Springs Ski Area**, (generally open mid-July to Sept; tows $55; Ⓦwww.skihanmer.co.nz) has just one rope tow and New Zealand's longest Poma-style lift, with one beginner run, six intermediate and five advanced runs. The ski-field is a forty-minute drive up the Clarence Valley Road, but the road is notoriously dicey, so take the **shuttle bus** operated by Hanmer Adventure Centre (see above; $38 return), where you can also rent ski gear. There are also rentals on the mountain, along with a **day lodge** with stoves, toasted sandwiches and tea and coffee, and basic backpacker **accommodation** ($25; BYO linen). The **Mount Lyford Ski-field** (p.491), 60km to the northeast, is also accessible from Hanmer via SH70.

Eating and drinking

Though small, Hanmer has over a dozen decent **places to eat**, many of which double as **bars**.

Alpine Village Inn 10 Jacks Pass Rd. Lively locals' bar with a good-value range of traditional fish, steak and chicken dishes, daily roasts plus an impressive array of vegetarian options (all under $25).

Malabar 5 Conical Hill Rd ☏03/315 7754. Flashy fusion restaurant with an adventurous menu with a modern twist on dishes from Asia and the subcontinent like rack of Indian lamb, tandoori chicken and seafood tempura (mains $28–36).

🏃 **Powerhouse Café** 6 Jacks Pass Rd. This funky modern café serves the best coffee in town (Christchurch-roasted Hummingbird), mouth-watering counter food (the Thai fishcakes are a house specialty), decadent breakfasts (French toast crumpets with vanilla cream, oatmeal pancakes with hazelnut syrup), and filling lunches (tropical bouillabaisse with coconut milk, calamari salad on organic soba noodles). Also open dinner Thurs–Sun in holiday periods.

Rustics 8 Conical Hill Rd ☏03/315 7274. Great little tapas restaurant with small plates of tasty treats such as pan-fried chorizo with roasted capsicum, battered monkfish or mini samosa ($11 each or four for $40).

West to the Lewis Pass and Maruia Springs

West of the Hanmer Springs turn-off, SH7 continues its climb towards the 907m **Lewis Pass**, 65km to the west, with low-yielding grassland with broom (blazing yellow in the summer), spiky matagouri, manuka and kanuka giving way to red and silver beech forest. To explore the area on foot, pick up DOC's *Lake Sumner/ Lewis Pass Recreation* leaflet from the Hanmer Springs i-SITE, which outlines almost two dozen day and multi-day **walks**.

Maruia Springs

Over Lewis Pass it's a further 8km west to **MARUIA SPRINGS**, a blissful spa grouped around Japanese-style men's and women's bathhouses, private bathhouses and natural-rock outdoor **hot pools** (daily 8am–8.30pm; pools $18, private baths $25/45min, towel rental $5), whose steaming mineral waters range from black to milky white.

If you want to **stay**, the attached hotel, *Maruia Springs Resort* (℡03/523 8840, Ⓦwww.maruiasprings.co.nz; ⑤), has simple but well-equipped rooms opening to shared or private balconies overlooking the gardens and mountains. Rates include access to the springs and its restaurant serves Japanese- and European-style **meals** (breakfast $10–23, dinner $25–35).

Arthur's Pass and around

The most dramatic of the three Southern Alps crossings links Christchurch with Greymouth, via **Arthur's Pass**, traversed by a scenic rail line and the equally breathtaking SH73 (also known as the Great Alpine Highway).

The pass is named for civil engineer **Arthur Dudley Dobson**, who heard about the route from local Maori (who had traditionally used it as a highway), and surveyed it in 1864. By 1866 horse-drawn coaches were using it to access the Westland goldfields. The railway was built in 1923, coinciding with the boom in alpine tourism worldwide.

From Christchurch to Arthur's Pass

Both road and rail routes from Christchurch to Arthur's Pass thread across the fertile Canterbury Plains beside the braided Waimakariri River before climbing to Arthur's Pass Village at 735m above sea level. En route, they traverse Springfield, where the river and the rail line veer away to the northwest while the road ascends through the Korowai/Torlesse Tussocklands Park to Porter's Pass. The road then passes the otherworldly boulders of Kura Tawhiti (Castle Hill Reserve) and the Cave Stream tunnel walk, while side roads wind into the Craigieburn range. Road and rail routes rejoin to follow the Waimakariri River towards Arthur's Pass village, in the centre of the national park. The 920m pass itself, 4km west of the village, is marked by a large obelisk to Dobson.

Springfield and around

From Christchurch the route is virtually flat for 70km west to **SPRINGFIELD**. This small village is the main base for four nearby ski-fields (see box opposite), as well as high-speed boat trips down the narrow, clear waters and waterfalls of **Waimakariri Gorge**. Waimak Alpine Jet, on Rubicon Road, off the Kowai Bush Road (from $75 for 30min; ℡03/318 4881, Ⓦwww.waimakalpinejet.co.nz), operates 22-seater jetboats, with transfers available from Christchurch (advance bookings essential). On dry land, **horseriding treks** – from beginners' treks to adventurous mountain trail rides – are offered by Rubicon Valley Horse Treks (from $50/hr; ℡0508 257 222, Ⓦwww.rubiconvalley.co.nz;), with pick-up in Springfield.

In town, a Chinese-style garden **memorial** beside SH73 remembers Springfield's best-loved son, writer, social reformer and unofficial ambassador for China, **Rewi Alley** (1897–1987).

The combined **visitor centre** and **café** on King Street (Mon–Fri 8.30am–4pm. Sat 8.30am–3pm, Sun 8.30am–2pm, longer hours in summer; ℡03/318 4000) is in the train station, signposted 500m off SH73. Springfield has a clutch of **accommodation** including one of the friendliest and most comfortable **hostels** on the South Island, the Japanese/Dutch-run ⚜ *YHA Smylies Accommodation and Tours*, SH73 (℡03/318 4740, ⓦwww.smylies.co.nz; dorms $25, rooms ❷, motel units ❸), with free Japanese baths (daily in winter, on request in summer),

---

Ski-fields around Springfield

Four **ski-fields** are easily accessible from Springfield, each offering basic, traditional Kiwi ski-club-style **accommodation** (including meals and sometimes incorporating chores – check details on the websites) as well as **equipment rental**. Although the variety of runs isn't enormous, they're inexpensive, unusual and challenging, with spectacular views, as well as reliable snow and quiet slopes. If you want someone to show you the ropes of club field skiing, contact Black Diamond Safaris (℡03/302 9696, ⓦwww.blackdiamondsafaris.co.nz), which runs 4WD **guided trips**. The **season** is generally July to September although October is often also good. For information on snow conditions visit ⓦwww.snow.co.nz.

Direct shuttles (Atomic Shuttles, ⓦwww.atomictravel.co.nz; Snowork, ⓦwww.snowork.com) run from Christchurch, while West Coast Shuttle (ⓦwww.westcoastshuttle.co.nz) heads across from the west coast on weekends. If you want to cut down on travelling, *YHA Smylie's Accommodation and Tours* (above) in Springfield runs regular shuttles (daily to/from Porters, $25 return, otherwise call for prices and times). The narrow access roads lack guardrails and are unsuitable for campervans.

The fields, described below from east to west along SH73, are part of the **multi-mountain passes** sold by Chill (ⓦwww.chillout.co.nz), along with seven other ski areas including Temple Basin near Arthur's Pass Village (opposite), and the Hanmer Springs Ski Area (p.551).

Porters 96km west of Christchurch, off SH73 via a 6km unsealed road ℡03/318 4002, ⓦwww.skiporters.co.nz. The region's main commercial field and the longest single run in the southern hemisphere. A free shuttle runs from the chain-fitting area to the main car park (bookings essential). Runs: 2 beginner; 3 intermediate; 9 advanced. Full lift pass $75/day; learners' pass $45.

Mount Cheeseman 112km from Christchurch along SH73 ℡03/344 3247, ⓦmtcheeseman.com. Well-appointed club field with good facilities, a friendly atmosphere and a wide variety of runs for intermediates, plus off-piste for those with greater experience. Runs: 2 beginner; 3 intermediate; 8 advanced. Lift passes $65/day.

Broken River 120km from Christchurch at the end of a 6km access road, off SH73 ℡03/318 7270, ⓦwww.brokenriver.co.nz. Field offering occasional night skiing and good snowboard terrain. Runs: 2 beginner; 7 intermediate; 10 advanced. Lift passes $60/day, night pass $35, instruction package $44/hr. A free inclinator (passenger-carrying goods lift) runs from the car park to the ticket office. It's possible to ski between Broken River and Craigieburn, with transferable lift passes.

Craigieburn Valley 120km out of Christchurch and another 6km up a side road ℡03/318 8711, ⓦwww.craigieburn.co.nz. This thrill-seeking field has three rope tows accessing the mostly steep runs: 0 beginner; 6 intermediate; 15 advanced. Lift passes $65/day.

a wood-fire-warmed lounge, cosy rooms and delicious three-course Japanese-and/or Kiwi-style evening meals ($20) and continental, cooked, or Japanese-style breakfasts ($10–15), as well as **ski-shuttle services** (see box, p.553). Campers can stay at the basic but cheap *Domain Campground*, next to SH73 (T03/818 4887; unpowered/powered sites $6/10 for 1–2 adults), in a sheltered spot with coin-operated showers – sign in with the caretaker signposted on the opposite side of SH73.

Porter's Pass and Kura Tawhiti (Castle Hill Reserve)

About 10km west of Springfield, the highway neatly bisects the 2.1-square-kilometre **Korowai/Torlesse Tussocklands Park**, New Zealand's first conservation park designed to protect the unique and quickly disappearing tussock grasslands of the eastern South Island.

Beyond the 932m **Porter's Pass**, SH73 turns north and runs 10km to **Kura Tawhiti** (Castle Hill Reserve), rolling grassland peppered by clusters of grey limestone outcrops of spiritual significance to Maori, with mountain daisies and Castle Hill buttercups blooming in summer, and an international reputation for the quantity and quality of its **bouldering** – a rope-free form of rock climbing. On fine days the boulderers are visible from a number of **paths** that wind among the rocks and tussock-covered hills.

Cave Stream Scenic Reserve

Some 6km westbound from Kura Tawhiti, **Cave Stream Scenic Reserve** nestles among limestone outcrops with views of the Craigieburn and Torlesse ranges. It offers a rare opportunity for an unguided **walk/wade** exploration of a **limestone cave** (362m; 1hr). Cave art, signs of seasonal camps and the discovery of an ancient wooden-framed flax backpack and other artefacts over 500 years old (now in the Canterbury Museum, p.508) indicate that Maori visited the area extensively. The cave contains bones as well as providing a home for large but harmless harvestman spiders and young eels that wriggle along the walls.

After entering at the downstream end, you'll cross a deep pool before gradually hiking upstream. If the water near the entrance is above waist-high, fast-flowing, foaming and discoloured, do not attempt the walk. At any time dress warmly, take a companion, plus at least one torch each with spare batteries and something dry to change into afterwards. There are only two major obstacles apart from the dark and cold: a 1.5m rockfall about halfway through that funnels the water and so is quite hard to climb, and a 3m waterfall at the very end. The latter is negotiated by climbing up a ladder of iron rungs embedded in the rock and crawling along a short, narrow ledge while holding onto an anchored chain.

Craigieburn Forest Park

The **Craigieburn Forest Park** lies on the eastern ranges of the Southern Alps, 42km before Arthur's Pass Village. The park is dominated by alpine scrub, tussock grasslands and dense, moss-covered mountain beech forest sprinkled with scarlet native mistletoe flowers from December to February. A variety of native birds squawk through the forest, including bellbird, rifleman, silver eye and kea and, between October and February, long-tailed and shining cuckoos join the throng. The nearby **Craigieburn Valley ski-field** (see box, p.553), within the boundaries of the forest park, is one of the most exciting accessed from Springfield.

In a signposted car park just off SH73 by Cave Stream are the **Craigieburn Picnic Area** (also a free DOC campsite) and a walkers' **shelter** with fixed maps of the local tramps. DOC's *Craigieburn Forest Park Day Walks* leaflet (from local visitor centres) details eleven day-walks in the park. Rugged hikers might fancy the **Cass–Lagoon Saddle Track** (33km, 2 days, 1300m ascent), a lovely loop with an overnight stop at Hamilton Hut (20 bunks; $15) almost exactly halfway. It starts at the east end of Cass road bridge.

High on a knoll overlooking the broad expanse of the Waimakariri River, 12km east of Arthur's Pass Village, is the historic *Bealey Hotel* (T03/318 9277, Wwww .bealeyhotel.co.nz; lodge rooms ❸, motel units ❺). Even if you don't need to stay, it's worth calling in for a drink or inexpensive, hearty **meal** in the bar filled with memorabilia of the hotel's early role as a stopoff point for Cobb & Co coaches and of moa sightings hereabouts in recent decades (hence the life-size moa sculptures standing sentinel in the grounds).

Arthur's Pass Village

Diminutive **ARTHUR'S PASS VILLAGE** nestles at 737m in a steep-sided, forest-covered U-shaped valley along the main road (SH73). The area receives over 4m of rainfall a year, and the village is often shrouded in mist or clouds, providing a moody contrast with the rich vegetation of the valley floor and slopes.

The settlement sprung up in the early 1900s to provide shelter for tunnel diggers and rail workers, and is now a superb base for walking and climbing in the surrounding **national park**. Nearby **Temple Basin ski-field**, 4km west (T03/377 7788, Wwww.templebasin.co.nz), is renowned among snowboarders for its 430m drop. Floodlit for night skiing, it offers a variety of runs (6 beginner, 10 intermediate, 8 advanced; lift passes $65) and basic, ski-club-style accommodation. *YHA Mountain House* (p.556) runs shuttles ($25 one-way for 1–6 people). Even from the drop-off point, it's still a solid hour's walk up to the ski-field, though there's a goods lift for your gear.

Regular coast-to-coast **buses** (West Coast Shuttle T07/768 0028; Atomic Shuttles T03/349 0697) and the TranzAlpine **train** (see p.513) all stop in the centre of the settlement, a short walk from everything. The excellent **DOC office** and **visitor centre** on the main street (daily: Nov–April 8am–5pm; May–Oct 8.30am–4.30pm; T03/318 9211, Wwww.arthurspass.com) has extensive displays on wildlife, plants, geology and local history, and plays a video about the trail blazed by the stagecoaches and the railway on request ($1). Outside, beneath a covered porch, you'll find weather reports and intentions cards. There are no banks or ATMs; other facilities are limited to a single **petrol pump** (the only one

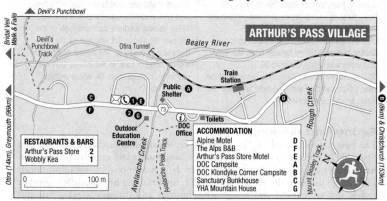

Kea: New Zealand's alpine trickster

One of the most enduring memories of a visit to Arthur's Pass and many other alpine areas of the South Island is the sight of a bright green **kea** mischievously getting its beak into something, or simply posing for the camera. With their lolloping sideways gait and inexhaustible curiosity, the world's only alpine parrots are endearing: at backcountry huts you might find kea sliding down the corrugated-iron roofing or pulling at the nails holding the roof on. Be careful where you leave your hiking boots – trampers have been known to wake up to a pile of leather strips and shredded laces.

With these playful scavenging tendencies it's hardly surprising kea traditionally got the blame for attacking sheep, and for many years were routinely shot by farmers. Recent research seems to indicate kea only attack already-weakened sheep, and shooting has long since stopped as the birds are now fully protected.

These days, however, their greatest threat is human food. These kleptomaniacs can be persistent – you'll hear the ruffle of feathers, see the flash of red beneath their wings and they'll be tearing at your lunch – but **feeding** them is forbidden as it reduces their ability to forage for themselves in winter when the summertime walkers have left town, and draws them towards the road where many are run over. As a result, the kea population is estimated to be between a mere 1000 to 5000 birds.

between Springfield and the west coast) and meagre **groceries** at the *Arthur's Pass Store*, with just a couple of places to **eat**, so stock up beforehand if you're planning to spend time in the area.

Accommodation

Good-value **accommodation** is strung out along the main road, although places fill up quickly during the high season (Dec–March).

Alpine Motel SH73 ☎03/318 9233, ⓦwww
.apam.co.nz. Comfortable motel units with kitchens, satellite TV, DVD players and free wi-fi plus an outdoor spa pool. ❹
The Alps B&B SH73 ☎03/318 9080, ⓦwww
.thealps.co.nz. Cute early 1900s cottage in the village centre, with dinner ($30) such as gourmet BBQs or African curries available by arrangement. Open Nov–March. B&B with private use of cottage ❹
Arthur's Pass Village Motel SH73 ☎03/318 9235, ⓦwww.apmotel.co.nz. Just two comfortable, modern studio units with kitchenette. ❺
DOC Campsite Next to Arthur's Pass Public Shelter, backing onto the railway. Basic site with cold water and toilets. Camping $6
DOC Klondyke Corner Campsite 8km east of the village. Free camping with long-drop toilet and river water, which should be treated.

Sanctuary Bunkhouse SH73. Unstaffed dorm-style bunk accommodation with just eight beds. Has adequate kitchen facilities, plus coin-operated hot showers and 24hr internet available to the public via honesty box payment, and bike rental can be arranged. Call the number on the door on arrival. Dorms $15
YHA Mountain House ☎03/318 9258, ⓦwww
.trampers.co.nz. Spanning a gleaming, state-of-the-art chalet and, across the road, NZ's first-ever YHA, plus two- and three-bedroom s/c 1920s railway workers' cottages high on the hill over the village (let whole or by the room), this place offers by far the largest number and widest range of beds in the village. Dorms $27, rooms ❸, cottage room ❸, whole cottage sleeping six ❼

Eating and drinking

The best places to fuel up for a hike or replenish afterwards are *Arthur's Pass Store*, SH73, which serves breakfasts, pies, sandwiches and excellent coffee, and has internet access and a bottle store (open daily 8am–6pm, longer in summer); and village linchpin the *Wobbly Kea*, SH73, for steaming hot chocolate, smooth coffee and substantial and imaginative lunches and dinners (steaks, fish and so on; all under $32), which doubles as a busy bar hosting occasional live music gigs.

Arthur's Pass National Park

Despite the spectacular views from the pass itself, you really need to take one of the many day- (or longer) walks to get a feel for the remarkable alpine landscape of **Arthur's Pass National Park**, which spans the transition zone between the wet West Coast and the much drier east: Otira, just west of the pass, gets around 6m of rain a year while Bealey, 15km to the east, gets only 2m.

Apart from a few easy walks around Arthur's Pass Village, the 950-square-kilometre national park is substantially more rugged than most in New Zealand, making it suitable only for moderately to highly experienced trampers. Most walks involve route finding (bring a compass) and unbridged river crossings – make adequate preparations (see Basics, p.59), and record your intentions with DOC. The free *Tramping in Arthur's Pass* leaflet assigns Route Guide numbers (RG) to the major tramps. You'll also need 1:50,000 topographic **maps**, available for sale ($9 each) or rent ($1 plus $20 deposit) at the DOC office, which also sells gas canisters, and offers secure gear storage ($2/item/day). The *YHA Mountain House* (opposite) operates a taxi-style **Trampers Shuttle Service** to the trailheads.

Tramps and walks

Avalanche Peak Track (5km return; 6–8hr; 1000m ascent). Strenuous day-hike that offers wonderful views of the surrounding mountains. Parts of the route are exposed; it should only be attempted by well-equipped, experienced trampers in reasonable weather. The best way is going up the spectacular Avalanche Peak Track and making a circuit by returning on the Scotts Track.

Bridal Veil Nature Walk (2.5km return; 1hr 30min; 50m ascent). Lovely walk that ascends through mountain beeches then crosses the Bridal Veil Creek before returning the same way.

Casey Saddle to Binser Saddle (RG10: 40km; 2 days; 400m ascent). Demanding loop with great views as you cross easy saddles on well-defined tracks through open beech forest, staying overnight in Casey Hut (16 bunks; $15).

Devil's Punch Bowl (2km return; 1hr; 100m ascent). The village's most popular short walk, following an all-weather climb and descent to the base of a 131m waterfall, crossing two footbridges and zigzagging up steps.

Mingha–Deception (RG6: 25km; 2 days; 400m ascent, 750m descent). A great overnighter which traces the route used for the mountain-run stage of the arduous Coast to Coast race (see p.643). Long sections are easy to follow, but there are unmarked areas requiring route finding, and 36 unbridged river crossings, so watch the water levels. If you're feeling particularly fit, add on a trip to Lake Mavis (500m ascent), a high mountain tarn with some lovely views. You can use either the Goat Pass Hut (20 bunks; $5) or the Upper Deception Hut (6 bunks; free) and ponder how mad you'd have to be to run the route competitively.

The South Canterbury foothills

The **South Canterbury foothills** mark the transition from the flat Canterbury Plains to the rugged and spectacular Southern Alps. The area is primarily known for the winter resort town of **Methven**, which serves the ski slopes of **Mount Hutt**. In summer, an ever-increasing array of activities includes skydiving, jetboating and some wonderful **walking**.

The main **route** through the area is SH72, dubbed the "Inland Scenic Route".

Methven, Mount Hutt and around

A hundred kilometres west of Christchurch on SH77, **METHVEN** is Canterbury's winter-sports capital and the accommodation and refuelling centre for the

Mount Hutt ski-field during the busy June to October **ski season**. Increasingly, it's becoming a year-round destination, providing a base for exploring the nearby Rakaia Gorge and Mount Somers. Activities accessible from town (with free pick-ups) include adrenaline-fuelled **tandem skydiving** with New Zealand's only skydiving school, Skydiving NZ (tandem jumps from $329; ☏03/302 9143, Ⓦwww.skydivingnz.com), based at the Pudding Hill Airfield, 10km northwest of town, as well as gentler **hot-air balloon** rides with Aoraki Balloon Safaris (4hr sunrise trip $345 including bubbly and breakfast; departure points depend on conditions; ☏0800/256 837, Ⓦwww.nzballooning.com) above the patchwork quilt of the Canterbury Plains and the magnificent Southern Alps that are particularly scenic in winter.

Arrival and information

Buses stop on Main Street (SH77), outside the **i-SITE visitor centre** (mid-Oct to May Mon–Fri 9am–5pm, Sat & Sun 10am–3pm; June to mid-Oct daily 8.30am–5.30pm; ☏03/302 8955, Ⓦwww.amazingspace.co.nz), which has **internet access** and books the Methven Travel shuttle to Christchurch ($36 one-way). Numerous shuttles serve the **ski-field** (p.560). At the small shopping centre around the junction of Main Street and Forest Drive you'll find banks, a post shop, a Hammer Hardware store, selling camping equipment and gas canisters, and two **ski shops** with gear rental – Wombats (☏03/302 8084) and Big Al's (☏03/302 8003); the latter operates a summertime **bike rental** and repair service.

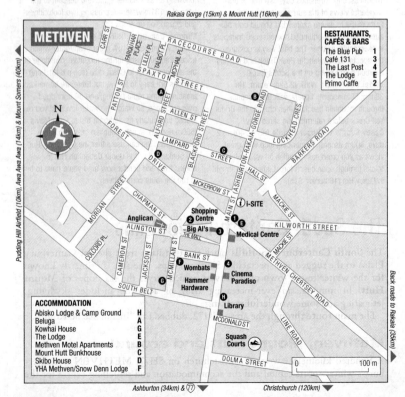

Rakaia Gorge (15km) & Mount Hutt (16km) ▲

METHVEN

RESTAURANTS, CAFÉS & BARS
The Blue Pub	1
Café 131	3
The Last Post	4
The Lodge	E
Primo Caffe	2

CARR ST
FARQUHAR PLACE
LILLEY PL
TALBOT PL
RACECOURSE ROAD
MOPHALL PL
SPAXTON STREET
PATTON ST
Ⓐ
ALFORD STREET
ALLEN ST
Ⓑ
BLACKFORD STREET
(ASHBURTON-RAKAIA-GORGE ROAD)
LOCKHEAD CRES
FOREST
LAMPARD
Ⓒ
STREET
HALL ST
BARKERS ROAD
DRIVE
Ⓓ
MCKERROW ST
N
MORGAN STREET
CHAPMAN ST
ALINGTON ST
Shopping Centre Ⓒ
Anglican
Ⓒ Big Al's Ⓒ
KILWORTH STREET
MACKIE ST
COLCORD PL
CAMERON ST
JACKSON ST
MCMILLAN ST
THE MALL
Medical Centre
ⒺⒸ i-SITE
MAIN ST
BANK ST
Ⓒ Wombats
SOUTH BELT
Ⓖ
Hammer Hardware
Cinema Paradiso Ⓒ
METHVEN CHERTSEY ROAD
Ⓗ Library
MCDONALD ST
Squash Courts
LINE ROAD
DOLMA STREET

ACCOMMODATION
Abisko Lodge & Camp Ground	H
Beluga	A
Kowhai House	G
The Lodge	E
Methven Motel Apartments	B
Mount Hutt Bunkhouse	C
Skibo House	D
YHA Methven/Snow Denn Lodge	F

Pudding Hill Airfield (10km); Awa Awa (14km) & Mount Somers (40km) ◀

Back roads to Rakaia (35km) ▶

0 — 100 m

Ashburton (34km) & ⑦ ▼   Christchurch (120km) ▼

Accommodation

There's a huge range of **accommodation** in Methven, and prices are often very reasonable in summer, but places to **eat** are fairly limited.

Abisko Lodge & Camp Ground 74 Main St ☎03/302 8875, ⓦwww.abisko.co.nz. Excellent establishment in the town centre incorporating Methven's most central campsites. Unpowered/powered sites $25/33, doubles ❸, one-bedroom apartments ❻, two- and three-bedroom apartments ❽

Beluga 40 Allen St ☎03/302 8290, ⓦwww.beluga.co.nz. Luxurious en-suite rooms in a beautifully kept house that has retained its original charm, with an outdoor hot tub in its tranquil gardens. There's also a private, self-catering "garden suite", and a delightfully renovated cottage sleeping up to four (minimum 3 nights in winter, 2 in summer). B&B ❼, garden suite ❼, cottage ❽

Kowhai House 17 McMillan St ☎03/302 8887, ⓦwww.kowhaihouse.co.nz. Comfortable, well-set-up backpackers in a converted house, with fast internet, free breakfast and an outdoor spa. Dorms $28, doubles ❸

The Lodge 1 Chertsey Rd. ☎03/303 2000, ⓦwww.thelodgenz.com. Generously sized, contemporary rooms, some with spa baths, and a popular on-site bistro and bar (below). Rooms ❺

Methven Motel Apartments 197 Main St ☎0800/468 488, ⓦwww.methvenmotels.co.nz. Sparkling new motel units, including ultra-spacious units with huge TVs and spa baths. Rooms ❺

Mount Hutt Bunkhouse 8 Lampard St ☎03/302 8894, ⓦwww.mthuttbunkhouse.co.nz. Comfortable, proudly TV-free backpacker accommodation with log fires. Dorms $28, rooms ❷

Skibo House 82 Forest Drive ☎03/302 9493, ⓦwww.skibohouse.com. Friendly B&B in a modern house. Most rooms have great mountain views, though they share a bathroom. There's an outdoor hot tub; excellent breakfasts might include Bircher muesli and porridge. B&B & s/c units ❹

YHA Methven/Snow Denn Lodge Corner of McMillan & Banks sts ☎03/302 8999, ⓦwww.methven accommodation.co.nz. Welcoming hostel spanning two adjoining A-frame buildings (one with comfy dorms, and the other a private-room "flash-packers"); each with spacious lounges and well-equipped kitchens. Freebies include breakfast, bikes, internet and an indoor hot tub. Dorms $27, rooms ❷, en suites ❸

Eating, drinking and entertainment

The Blue Pub Methven Hotel, corner of Kilworth St & Barkers Rd. Popular with the après-ski crowd and locals, this 1918-built cobalt-painted hotel has a lively bar hosting bands and weekend DJs and a highly regarded kitchen with blackboard specials like crayfish bisque, and pumpkin and ricotta tortellini.

Café 131 131 Main St. Airy wood-floored Art Deco café that's perfect for people-watching through its large stained-glass-framed windows. In addition to Methven's best coffee, there's a mouthwatering array of cakes, all-day breakfasts and filling, inexpensive lunches (including fantastic fish burgers), warming soups and summertime salads such as smoked salmon. There's also a book exchange.

Cinema Paradiso 112 Main St ☎03/302 1957. Wonderful bijou digital cinema, with two tiny rooms showing a roster of mostly arthouse flicks.

The Last Post 116 Main St ☎03/302 8259. In a former post office with a roaring open fire, Methven's finest dining features the likes of home-made cornbread and dips followed by almond-crusted yellow-fin tuna or Asian-steamed salmon parcels (mains under $40). Or just drop in for a cocktail. Closed mid-Dec to May.

The Lodge (above). Bistro fare and great gourmet pizzas, such as apricot chicken, served in a cosy room with stone-walled fire place. The attached bar hosts events including beach parties with trucked-in sand. Closed Mon Nov–June.

Primo Caffe 38 McMillan St. Quirky little café stuffed into an antique/vintage clothing/junk shop (everything is for sale), serving good coffee, home-made cakes and wholesome sandwiches.

Around Methven

Methven's main winter attraction is the nearby ski-field at **Mount Hutt**. In summer, make for the forests of the **Awa Awa Rata Reserve**, the **Rakaia Gorge** with its walkway, jetboating and beautifully sited campsite, or a unique and diverse short walk at **Washpen Falls**.

Mount Hutt ski-field

Mount Hutt, 22km northeast of Methven (℡03/302 8811, ⓦwww.nzski.com; daily lift pass $87), is widely regarded as the best and most developed ski and snowboarding field in the southern hemisphere, with a vertical rise of 683m, a variety of runs (3 beginner, 8 intermediate and 22 advanced) and, generally, the longest season (roughly June–Oct). Assorted rental and instruction packages include a one-day starter pack for adult beginners (skiing $111, boarding $140), and a ski school for kids. Rentals are available on the mountain, but there's no accommodation here, so most people **stay** in Methven, from where there are frequent **shuttle buses** (all around $27; 45min to the ski-field): buy a ticket on board or from the i-SITE, from where most of the shuttles depart.

Awa Awa Rata Reserve

Part of the Mount Hutt Conservation Area, **Awa Awa Rata Reserve**, 14km northwest of Methven, is a beautiful spot on the eastern flanks of the Southern Alps, home to tall mountain beech and snow tussock, which provides a home for a variety of native and introduced birds above the shrub line. A DOC leaflet (available from the i-SITE) details several **walking tracks** (10min–2hr). Most are accessed from the McLennans Bush Road entrance, reached by heading north from Methven on SH77 and going straight ahead onto McLennans Bush Road at the base of Mount Hutt access road. Of the 94 percent of **alpine plants** that grow only in New Zealand, 130 species can only be found on Mount Hutt, including the vegetable sheep (*Raoulia eximia*), which forms huge grey mounds that, from a distance, resemble sleeping sheep, and the *Ranunculus haastii*, a beautiful species of buttercup with blue-grey leaves and luminous yellow flowers.

Rakaia Gorge

Some 15km north of Methven, the turquoise Rakaia River emerges from the **Rakaia Gorge**, created by an ancient lava flow and now lined in many places with regenerating forest. **Maori history** tells how a *taniwha* (water spirit) lived nearby, hunting and eating moa and weka; his possessions, because of his status as a spirit, were *tapu*. While he was away searching for a hot spring one cold day the northwest wind demon flattened his property. To prevent this happening again, the *taniwha* collected large boulders and stones from the mountains to block the course of the demon and so narrowed the Rakaia River, making it flow between the rocky walls. The heat from his body melted the snow and ice on the mountains, and his perspiration fell on the rocks and formed crystals in the riverbed.

This sweaty work can be seen from the **Rakaia Gorge Walkway** (15km; 3–4hr return), which starts where SH72 crosses the river. The path leads through several forest stands and spectacular geological areas, past hardened lava flows of rhyolite, pitchstone and andesite, to the upper gorge lookout. The less committed might fancy walking as far as a fenced viewpoint high on a bluff above the river (1hr return).

Below the gorge, the river fans out into a classic example of the braided rivers so common on the eastern side of the South Island. Here you can board a high-octane **jetboat ride** with Discovery Jet ($70/30min; ℡03/318 6943), taking you to the top end of the **Rakaia Gorge** ($30; min 2 people) for a delightful and easy walk back – take a picnic to make an afternoon of it. The company also offers salmon fishing and rents rods.

On SH72, over on the south side of the river, the *Rakaia Gorge* **campsite** ($7.50) offers peaceful camping with toilets (year-round) and coin-op hot showers (summer only).

Washpen Falls

One of the area's lesser-known gems, a 25-minute drive north of Methven, 17km south of SH73, the private family farm of **Washpen Falls**, Washpen Road, Windwhistle (☎03/318 6813, Ⓦwww.washpenfalls.co.nz; self-guided walk $10, bookings essential; s/c cottage ❹), offers a wonderfully diverse meander through native bush and farmland for anyone of moderate fitness. The **walking track** (2hr 30min return) heads up to a point, and offers spectacular views of the Canterbury Plains. Along the way there's a canyon formed by an ancient volcano (used by Maori to trap moa), great examples of native-bush regeneration, and, of course, the cascading falls. The office (a corrugated-iron shed) has leaflets outlining the track's highlights. If you're tempted to **stay**, there's a rustic three-bedroom chalet overlooking the surrounding farmland and hills.

Mount Somers and around

The 1687m **Mount Somers** rises from the flatlands above the villages of **Mount Somers** and **Staveley**, encircled by the **Mount Somers Track**, which is conveniently in the rain shadow of the mountains and is often above the bushline – when it's raining in Arthur's Pass and Mount Cook's clagged in, there's still a chance you'll be able to get some hiking in here. The terrain (gentle by South Island standards) incorporates patches of regenerating beech forest, and open tussock pocked by outcrops of rock. Large areas of low-fertility soil subject to heavy rainfall turn to bog, and as a result you'll find bog pine, snow totara, toatoa, mountain flax and maybe even the rare whio (blue duck).

Staveley

The northern access point for the walkway is tiny **Staveley**, 22km southwest of Methven, where the Staveley Village Store (daily 9am–5pm) stocks last-minute supplies and serves espresso. Even if you're not keen on a multi-day hike, at least drive the 2km to the northern trailhead at the **Sharplins Falls** car park and head to the falls (1hr return) along an upgraded track and steps.

There's lovely **accommodation** nearby at 🏃 Ross Cottage, Flynns Road, a delightful 130-year-old self-catering cottage operated by Tussock and Beech Ecotours (☎03/303 0880, Ⓦwww.nature.net.nz; ❺), who offer a variety of eco-focused guided tours.

Staveley is the base for some of the South Island's best – and cheapest – **horse treks**, run by Staveley Horse Treks (from $35/hr, min 2 people; bookings essential; ☎03/303 0804, Ⓔbrucegray@clear.net.nz).

Mount Somers

Access to the southern end of the **Mount Somers Track**, near Woolshed Creek, is via the hamlet of **MOUNT SOMERS**, 8km south of Staveley. The **Mount Somers Store** sells hut tickets and a reasonable range of groceries. The cheapest place to **camp** in the village is the basic *Domain Camping Ground*, next to the local swimming pool (☎021/760 677; unpowered/powered sites $10/15), or for more comfort (including cabins), you might try the tree-filled *Mount Somers Holiday Park*, Hoods Road, 1km off SH72 (☎03/303 9719, Ⓦwww.mountsomers.co.nz; unpowered/powered sites $22/26, cabins ❶, en-suite cabins ❷). The most luxurious **accommodation** is at *Stronechrubie*, 1km south of Mount Somers on SH72 (dinner Wed–Sat, and Sun lunch; bookings essential ☎03/303 9814, Ⓦwww.stronechrubie.co.nz; chalets ❹; dinner, bed and breakfast packages $230–280), with beautiful self-contained chalets, as well as the only real **restaurant** in these parts. Its high-country cuisine spans salmon, duck and rack of lamb (mains $29–33) and an excellent wine selection.

Mount Somers Track

A strenuous but exhilarating subalpine loop round the mountain, the **Mount Somers Track** (25km loop; 2–3 days; 1000m ascent) passes abandoned coal mines, volcanic formations and a deep river canyon.

The **entire loop** is best tackled anticlockwise from the Staveley end. However, roads meet the loop in the west at Woolshed Creek (accessed from Mount Somers) and in the east at Sharplins Falls car park (accessed from Staveley), so if you don't fancy the whole thing you can **walk either half** and organize a **vehicle shuttle** through the Staveley Village Store ($35; ⊕03/303 0859). After dropping you at the trailhead, they'll keep your vehicle safe and deliver it to the car park at your finishing spot in time for your emergence from the wilds. Alternatively, Methven Travel operates a **Methven–Mount Somers shuttle service** on demand ($90 for 1–4 people to Woolshed Creek car park, $60 for 1–4 people to Sharplins Falls car park; ⊕03/302 8106).

Buy DOC **hut tickets** (two for each hut) before you start at the stores in Staveley or Mount Somers, or from i-SITEs or DOC offices. You'll need to carry a cooking stove, pots and all your food; water at the huts should be treated. Marker poles point the way adequately in most conditions but the rolling country on top of the hills is subject to disorientating fog, so bring a map and compass.

Sharplins Falls Car Park to Pinnacles Hut (5km; 3hr 45min; 470m ascent). The route initially detours to the modest Sharplins Falls then climbs steadily through beech forest, reaching the tree line at Pinnacles Hut (19 bunks; $15), nestled below rock monoliths frequently used by climbers. Pinnacles Hut to Woolshed Creek Hut (6.2km; 3hr; 265m ascent). Climb towards the 1170m saddle, now through treeless tussock with wide views into the mountains and back to the plains. On the descent, take the 5min side trip to the Water Caves, where a stream courses below a rockfall of house-sized boulders. It is then only 10min to the new Woolshed Creek Hut (26 bunks; $15), a good place to stay a couple of nights, spending the intervening day exploring the little valleys and canyons hereabouts.

Woolshed Creek Hut to the Sharplins Falls car park (13.5km; 8hr; 400m ascent). The tramp follows the South Face Route around the mountain and feels quite different. There's a less isolated feel as you gaze across the Canterbury flatlands towards the distant coast. The terrain is a mix of high-country scrub (somewhat exposed at times) and beech forest. Soon after leaving the hut, the Howden Falls side track is worth a quick squiz. You then climb a ridge before traversing tussock-covered flats, passing a new day-shelter at about the halfway point. After a steep climb up through beech forest you begin the long descent, first on a ridge with great views then down into the bush to Sharplins Falls car park.

Peel Forest and around

Peel Forest Park, 35km south of Mount Somers, encloses one of the eastern South Island's last remaining patches of original native bush, which is threaded with **walking tracks**. DOC's *Peel Forest Park* leaflet outlining walks from thirty minutes to six hours is available at the **Peel Forest Store** (⊕03/696 3567, ⊛www .peelforest.co.nz), in the hamlet of **PEEL FOREST**, 12km west of SH72, which also serves as a visitor centre, post office, takeaway and bar, and administers DOC's lovely, wooded Peel Forest Park **campsite** (unpowered/powered sites $9/13, cabins ❶).

You can explore the forest on **horse treks** offered by Peel Forest Horse Trekking ($55/1hr; ⊕0800/022 536, ⊛www.peelforesthorsetrekking.co.nz).

The highly professional Rangitata Rafts (⊕0800/251 251, ⊛www.rafts.co.nz), based 14km north of Peel Forest Store run some of New Zealand's best **white-water rafting** on the Grade IV–V high-sided gorge section of the Rangitata River (Oct–May daily at 10.30am; $185). Trips include two and a half hours on the water – with a nerve-testing optional 10m cliff jump – as well as lunch and a barbecue dinner. Pick-ups from nearby Geraldine, or from Christchurch (add 2hr at either end) cost just \$10 extra; alternatively you can **stay** at the well-equipped backpacker-style *Lodge* (camping \$10, bunks \$20, rooms ❶).

Geraldine

The prosperous farming town of **GERALDINE**, 45km south of Mount Somers and 35km north of Timaru, rewards a brief stop to browse its smattering of **craft shops, galleries**, and **specialist food stores** selling gourmet picnic ingredients like local cheeses, pickles, fruit, wine and chocolates, as well as its **museums**.

Start at the Giant Jersey, 10 Wilson St (Mon–Fri 9am–5pm, Sat & Sun 10am–4pm; donation), home to the *Guinness Book of Records'* **world's largest jersey** (weighing in at a whopping 5.5kg), as well as an array of heraldic mosaics, and a 42m-long half-scale **tableau of the Bayeux Tapestry** made entirely from tiny pieces of spring steel broken from knitting machines – the last 8m are the artist's interpretation of how the missing final section of the original might have looked.

It's worth spending a few minutes in the tiny, volunteer-staffed **Geraldine Historical Museum**, on Cox Street (generally Mon–Sat 10.30am–noon & 1.30–3.30pm, Sun 1.30–3.30pm; donation), before marvelling at the old cars and tractors amassed in the **Geraldine Vintage Car and Machinery Museum**, 179 Talbot St, (mid-Sept to May daily 10am–4pm; June to mid-Sept Sat & Sun 10am–4pm; \$7), 1km south of the town centre.

Practicalities

Buses drop off outside Geraldine's **i-SITE visitor centre**, on the corner of Talbot and Cox streets (Dec–March Mon–Fri 9am–5pm, Sat & Sun 10am–4pm; April–Nov Mon–Fri 9am–5pm, Sat & Sun 10am–3pm; ☎03/693 1006, ⓦwww.southisland.org.nz), which can help find **accommodation**, none of which is too expensive, though it's worth booking ahead in summer. Guests can rent bikes at the central, well-tended *Geraldine Holiday Park*, on Hislop Street (☎03/693 8147, ⓦwww.geraldineholidaypark.co.nz; camping \$29–30, basic cabins ❶, s/c units ❸, motel units ❹), surrounded by sheltering trees, and at the

▲ Geraldine

peaceful *Rawhiti Backpackers*, 1km from the centre at 27 Hewlings St (℡03/693 8252, ⓦ www.rawhitibackpackers.co.nz; dorms $30, rooms ❷), in an artistically decorated 1924-built former maternity hospital, with spotless rooms and common areas and expansive gardens.

By day, the best place to **eat** is the ⚘ *Verde Café Deli*, 45c Talbot St, in a secluded rose-clambered garden a block back from the main road, where classy café fare spans a great selection of counter food plus a tempting brunch menu. The *Village Inn*, at 41 Talbot St, has generous wholesome daytime and evening meals at decent prices and an attached sports bar. If time permits, catch a movie at the wonderful **Geraldine Cinema**, 84 Talbot St (typically open Thurs–Sun; $10; ℡03/693 8118), a casual sofas-and-beanbags affair with cosy duvets in winter.

Fairlie and around

Heading for the wilds of the Mackenzie Country, you first pass through the attractive town of **FAIRLIE**, 45km west of Geraldine. A statue of Mackenzie and his dog stands at the town's main intersection, but otherwise there's little reason to stop, except in winter when its clutch of places to stay make a handy base for the small **Mount Dobson** ski-field (℡03/685 8039, ⓦ www.dobson.co.nz), 26km towards Lake Tekapo. Renowned for its powder snow, long hours of sunshine and uncrowded fields, its four beginner runs, six intermediate and four advanced (lift passes $70) cater for all levels. The mountain is reached by a good 15km gravel road; with a weekend and holiday **shuttle service** from Fairlie – contact the ski office for seasonal schedules.

Aoraki Mount Cook and the Mackenzie Country

South of Fairlie SH8 shoots westward through the sheep-grazed grasslands of the **Mackenzie Country** – flanked by bright-coloured lupin and broom in the summer – to the spectacular Aoraki Mount Cook area, dominated by New Zealand's tallest mountain, the 3754m **Mount Cook**. Increasingly, it's known by its Maori name, **Aoraki**, meaning "cloud piercer", and the two names are often run together as Aoraki Mount Cook. From Aoraki Mount Cook Village, you can walk to the mountains' glaciers, notably the 27km-long **Tasman Glacier**, fed by icefalls tumbling from the heavily glaciated surrounding peaks.

North of Aoraki Mount Cook, star billing goes to the mesmerizingly blue, glacier-fed **Lake Tekapo** and **Lake Pukaki**, backed by the glistening peaks of the Southern Alps. **Twizel**, 70km south of Aoraki Mount Cook, offers an alternative base for exploring the region, including New Zealand's gliding capital, **Omarama**, 30km to its south, from where SH83 runs eastwards down the **Waitaki Gorge** to the east coast.

Lake Tekapo and around

The burgeoning village of **LAKE TEKAPO**, 42km west of Fairlie on the southern shore of its stunning namesake lake, revolves around a roadside ribbon of cafés and souvenir shops surrounded by new housing developments. Its name derives from the Maori *taka* ("sleeping mat") and *po* ("night"), suggesting that this place has long been used as a stopover. Stay overnight to fully enjoy a sunset free of day-trippers and wondrous night skies.

At an altitude of 710m, the area is reputed to have the **clearest air** in the southern hemisphere and on a good day the sharp edges and vibrant colours make

A Kiwi folk hero, **James McKenzie** lends his name (well close enough anyway) to the **Mackenzie Country**, a 180km crescent of rolling dry grassland between Fairlie and Kurow (to the south on SH83). A Gaelic-speaking Scottish immigrant of uncertain background, McKenzie is believed to have only spent a couple of years in New Zealand but his legend lives on. He was arrested in 1855 for stealing over 1000 sheep, most of them from the Rhodes brothers' Levels Run station near Timaru and grazing them in the basin of rich high-country pastureland, with the assistance of a single dog, Friday. McKenzie escaped from prison three times during the first year of his five-year sentence and when holding him became too much trouble, he was given a free pardon, after which he quietly disappeared, some say to America, others to Australia.

A poem commemorates the man and his dog in the visitor shelter at Lake Pukaki near the turn-off to Aoraki Mount Cook.

this one of the best places to photograph the Southern Alps. The most striking thing about lakes Tekapo and Pukaki, though, is their **extraordinary colour**: the light reflected from microscopic rock particles suspended in glacial meltwater lends the waters an ethereal opaque-aqua hue. Fed by the **Godley** and **Cass** rivers, Lake Tekapo covers 83 square kilometres and spills into the **Tekapo River**, wending its way across the Mackenzie Basin.

Buses linking Christchurch and Queenstown all stop outside the strip of businesses that constitute the village centre, where you'll also find the **i-SITE** Dec–March 9am–7pm; April–Nov 9am–5pm; ℡03/680 6579). Postal services are available in the nearby Kiwi Treasures souvenir shop, but there's no **bank** or ATM.

Lake Tekapo Village and Mount John

Everyone's first stop is the tiny lakeside **Church of the Good Shepherd**, Pioneer Drive (daily 9am–5pm; donation), an enchanting little stone church built in 1935 as a memorial to the Mackenzie Country pioneers. Behind the rough-hewn Oamaru stone altar, a square window perfectly frames the lake and the surrounding hills and mountains. About 100m east, the **Collie Dog Monument** was erected in 1968 by local sheep farmers to honour the dogs that make it possible to graze this harsh terrain.

Minimal light pollution presents perfect conditions for observing the night skies, and the summit of **Mount John**, 9km northwest of Tekapo, has sprouted telescope domes operated by the University of Canterbury and astronomical institutions around the world. The observatory's *Astro Café* (see p.567) is the starting point for the 30–45-minute **Observatory Day Tour** (daily 10am–4pm on request; $30; ℡03/680 6960, Ⓦwww.earthandsky.co.nz). The two-hour **Stargazing Tour** (nightly: hours dependent on nightfall, approx 8pm in winter, 10pm in summer; $80) includes an hour and a half on the cold mountain top (outfitted in enormous red parkas and sustained by hot chocolate), taking turns to look through a sixteen-inch telescope at whatever's up: the Southern Cross, the Large Magellanic Cloud, nebulae, and perhaps the glorious Jewel Box, and an "astra-photography" session with a renowned photographer in the field (bring your camera). Although you can drive up during the day, by night you'll need to catch the bus (included in the ticket price) from the booking office (which shares space with the i-SITE in the village centre), to avoid headlights disrupting the astronomers' work.

The summit can also be reached on the exhilarating **Mount John Lookout** walk (10km return; 3hr; 333m ascent), which starts at the Alpine Springs (p.566) on Lakeside Drive and climbs through a larch forest full of birds to a loop track which circles the summit.

Activities

Two **boat-trip operators** offer varied opportunities to get out on the water. Cruise Tekapo (T027/479 7675, Wwww.cruisetekapo.co.nz) runs trips ranging from a twenty-minute spin around the highlights ($35) to a two-hour trip with a barbecue (often including local salmon) on **Motuariki Island** ($105). Trips with Jetboat Experience (T021/208 5109, Wwww.originaljetboat.co.nz) range from a lakefront tour ($40/20min) to **waterskiing** ($60/30min).

Determined sightseers short of time can take a "Grand Traverse" **scenic flight** with Air Safaris, in the village on SH8 (50min; $295; T0800/806 880, Wwww .airsafaris.co.nz). The flight swoops across the Main Divide to the West Coast, providing views of the Franz Josef and Fox glaciers, the Tasman and Muller glaciers and Aoraki Mount Cook. Tekapo Helicopters, on SH8 (T0800/359 835, Wwww.tekapohelicopters.co.nz), run a range of flights over Mount Cook, all including a snow landing (25–70min; $195–500; min 3 people).

If you'd rather stick closer to the ground, guided **horse treks** with Mackenzie Alpine Trekking (Nov–April only; $50/1hr, $125/3hr 30min; T0800/628 269) traverse dramatic scenery.

To simply unwind, head to the beautiful Alpine Springs complex, at 6 Lakeside Drive (T0800/2353 8283, Wwww.alpinesprings.co.nz), which combines beautiful, state-of-the-art outdoor **hot pools** (each subtly shaped like local lakes, with heated alpine water ranging from 32°C to 40°C; $16) with a **day spa** (with treatments including a 90min "high country herbal" hot-stone massage, $195), a summertime **in-line skating rink** ($14 including blade rental), and a winter park with **ice skating** ($14 including skate rental) and **snow tubing** (from $14).

Wintertime also sees families flock to the **Roundhill** ski area (T03/680 6977, Wwww.roundhill.co.nz), 30km north of SH8. You'll find one long T-bar and a learner tow plus plenty of gentle slopes and undulating terrain incorporating two beginner and eight intermediate but no advanced runs. Lift passes cost $65, and there are good ski and board rental and instruction packages, plus tobogganing for $12 a day.

Accommodation and eating

Most **accommodation** in this tourist-oriented village is on the expensive side, with the few budget options often oversubscribed – book ahead. On a fine day you can't do better than a picnic by the lake, but there are an increasing number of decent **cafés and restaurants** in the village centre (Chinese, Thai, Italian and more).

Accommodation

The Chalet Boutique Motel 14 Pioneer Drive T0800/843 242, Wwww.thechalet.co.nz. Six individually decorated, s/c apartments, some overlooking the lake, in a pretty spot footsteps from the Church of the Good Shepherd. Rooms ⑥, family units ⑦

Lake Tekapo Motels and Holiday Park 2 Lakeside Drive T03/680 6825, Wwww .laketekapo-accommodation.co.nz. Situated at the southwestern end of Tekapo 1km from town, this large, well-equipped campsite overlooks the lake. Unpowered/powered sites from $15/18, basic cabins ③, en-suite cabins and motel units ⑤

Lakefront Lodge Backpackers Lakeside Drive T0800/840 740. Light-filled, modern chalet-style hostel with lake views from the spacious lounge

and some rooms, with bike rental ($25/half-day) and kayak rental ($25/hr). Dorms $26, rooms ②

Merino Country Farmstay SH8, 13km east of Lake Tekapo Village T03/685 8670, Wwww.merinocountryfarmstay.co.nz. Traditional Kiwi hospitality on a working sheep farm running 10,000 merinos, with romantic accommodation in the 1924-built homestead and exquisite evening meals ($38; on request) and cooked breakfasts using produce from the vegetable garden and orchard as well as freshly laid eggs. B&B ⑤

Tailor-made-Tekapo Backpackers 9 Aorangi Crescent T03/680 6700, Wwww.tailor-made -backpackers.co.nz. A 5min walk from the bus stop and shops, this friendly 1950s hostel lacks a view but does have comfy rooms with beds (no bunks) plus well-kept grounds with a BBQ area. Dorms $25, rooms and en suites **②**

YHA Lake Tekapo 3 Simpson Lane, 100m west of the village ☎03/680 6857, ⓦwww.yha.co.nz. Busy hostel with a common room framed by a floor-to-ceiling lakeview-window. Reception open 8–10am & 3.30–7pm. Dorms $33, rooms **③**

Eating and drinking

Astro Café Mt John summit. With stupendous lake and mountain views, this café atop Mt John was serving stellar cakes, sandwiches and espresso at the time of writing, but full meals are planned.

Reflections SH8 ☎03/680 6234. Local salmon, rack of lamb and peppered venison all get a run on the wide-ranging menu at this reliable restaurant that opens out to a terrace at the lake's edge, though there are few-to-no vegetarian options. Lunch mains under $20, dinner mains $26–36.

Run 77 SH8. Classy store selling elegant merino-wool clothing, gourmet deli goods (including local organic wines) that also houses the village's best daytime café, with great coffee and freshly baked sweet and savoury treats.

Towards Lake Pukaki

From Tekapo, SH8 heads southwest towards **Lake Pukaki** some 47km away. The opaque, pale-blue waters of this 30km-long lake provide a perfect foreground for views north to Aoraki Mount Cook and its icy attendants. The road then rejoins SH8 on the southern shores of Lake Pukaki, with wonderful vistas from the **Lake Pukaki visitor centre** (daily: Nov–April 9am–6pm; May–Oct 10am–4.30pm; ☎03/435 3280), which stands beside a display showcasing the Waitaki Hydro Scheme.

Another kilometre on, SH80 branches north towards Aoraki Mount Cook Village, while SH8 continues 6km to Twizel.

Aoraki Mount Cook Village

A good, fast and virtually flat road runs for 55km from the Lake Pukaki junction along the tussocklands of Lake Pukaki's western shore to Aoraki Mount Cook Village. Twelve kilometres in you'll pass **Peters Lookout**, a popular viewing point on the lake side of the road, while at 33km the *Glentanner Park Centre* (see p.569) offers accommodation, meals and flights.

On windy days, an atmospheric white dust rises from the plain at the base of the mountain as you approach **AORAKI MOUNT COOK VILLAGE**. It's a spectacular spot, at a height of 760m in an encircling horseshoe of mountains, and while the tiny village is nothing special it blends in tolerably.

Mostly you'll be wanting to get outside as much as possible, but it's worth spending some time in the **Sir Edmund Hillary Alpine Centre**, inside *The Hermitage* (daily 10am–5pm, later in summer; 24hr "Explorer Pass" for all attractions $26), which contains a **museum** showcasing the geology, mythology and

Sir Edmund Hillary

Until his death aged 88 in early 2008, surveys frequently voted **Sir Edmund Hillary** New Zealand's most admired citizen. His ascent, with Tenzing Norgay, of Mount Everest in 1953 was undoubtedly a noteworthy achievement, and his humanitarian work in the villages of Nepal was widely admired, but above all, Hillary embodied the qualities Kiwis hold most dear: hard-working, straight-talking, honest and, especially, modest. As he famously said on his return from the successful summit attempt, "Well George, we knocked the bastard off". That's what gets your face on every $5 note in the country.

Though he grew up near Auckland, Sir Ed did much of his early climbing around Aoraki Mount Cook Village, where a **bronze statue** of a youthful Hillary stands outside *The Hermitage*.

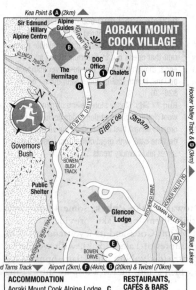

Kea Point & **Ⓐ** (2km)

AORAKI MOUNT COOK VILLAGE

Sir Edmund Hillary Alpine Centre

Alpine Guides

Ⓑ

DOC Office **ⓘ** **❶** Chalets

The Hermitage

Ⓒ **Ⓟ**

0   100 m

GLENCO TRACK

BOWEN DRIVE

Glencoe Stream

Hooker Valley Track & **Ⓓ** (3km)

Governors Bush

BOWEN BUSH TRACK

Public Shelter

GOVERNORS BUSH TRACK

Glencoe Lodge

TASMAN VALLEY RD

HOOKER DRIVE

Ⓔ

BOWEN DRIVE

80

Blue Lakes

Red Tarns Track ▼ Airport (2km), **Ⓕ** (4km), **Ⓖ** (20km) & Twizel (70km) ▼

ACCOMMODATION		RESTAURANTS, CAFÉS & BARS	
Aoraki Mount Cook Alpine Lodge	C	The Hermitage	B
DOC White Horse Hill Campground	A & D	The Old Mountaineers	1
Glentanner Park Centre	G		
The Hermitage	B		
Unwin Lodge	F		
YHA Mt Cook	E		

development of the region, along with the history of the hotel and its place in Kiwi climbing history; a state-of-the-art **3D theatre** that whizzes you through the geographical, cultural and sporting evolution of the mountains using a blend of authentic footage and computer graphics; and a **Planetarium**. Profits from the centre help fund Hillary's Himalayan Trust.

Arrival and information

All **bus** services call at *Glentanner Park Centre*, *Unwin Lodge* and *YHA Mt Cook* on request, before dropping off at the car park near *The Hermitage*, from where everything is within walking distance.

The **DOC office and visitor centre** (daily: Dec–March 8.30am–5pm; April–Nov 8.30am–4.30pm; ℡03/435 1186, ✉mtcookvc@doc.govt.nz) stocks detailed maps and contains some stunning (and free) exhibits on the natural wonders of the Aoraki Mount Cook area. There's just one unstaffed **petrol station** accepting cash or New Zealand cards (international credit card users need to organize it via *The Hermitage* hotel desk for a $5 fee), a **post office** in *The Hermitage* gift shop and **internet access** at *The Hermitage* and *The Old Mountaineers*, but **no bank** or ATM.

Accommodation

Book early from October to April, when the village often fills to capacity. Prices drop considerably during the rest of the year.

Aoraki Mount Cook Alpine Lodge 101 Bowen Drive ℡0800/680 680, ⊛www.aorakialpinelodge .co.nz. Great accommodation at a realistic price, with comfy twins and doubles, a lounge with a fantastic view, a fully equipped kitchen and internet access. Doubles **❺**, family rooms **❻**

How Aoraki Mount Cook came to be

Both the **sky father** (Raki) and the **earth mother** (Papa-tua-nuku) already had children by previous unions. After their marriage, some of the sky father's children came to inspect their father's new wife. Four brothers, Ao-raki, Raki-roa, Raki-rua and Raraki-roa, circled around her in a **canoe** called Te Waka-a-Aoraki, but once they left her shores disaster befell them. Running aground on a reef, the canoe was turned to stone. The four occupants climbed to the higher western side of the petrified canoe, where they too were transformed: **Ao-raki** became Aoraki Mount Cook, and his three younger brothers formed flanking peaks – Mount Dampier, Mount Teichelmann and Mount Tasman.

More prosaically, Mount Cook was named in honour of the English sea captain in 1851. Its summit was first reached in 1894 but, because of the peak's sacredness to Maori, climbers are asked not to step on the summit itself.

DOC White Horse Hill Campground Hooker Valley Rd. A serene and informal first-come-first-served DOC camping area with stony ground and running water in summer (which must be treated). The campsite is 2km north of the village, accessible by road or a 20min walk along the Kea Point Track. Camping $6.

Glentanner Park Centre 22km south on SH8 ☎03/435 1855, ⓦwww.glentanner.co.nz. Well-equipped site with sheltered camping, dorm-style accommodation (Oct–April only) and cabins with views of the mountains and Tasman Valley, a panoramic, sheltered BBQ area and a café. Unpowered/powered sites $16/18, dorms $25, basic cabins ❸, s/c en-suite cabins ❹

The Hermitage ☎03/435 1809, ⓦwww .mount-cook.com. Historic establishment in its third incarnation since the first premises opened in 1868, now comprising a modern complex approached through an impressive foyer. Rooms in the main building vary in luxury and come with a balcony (though not necessarily a view). Hotel rooms ❼–❾, motel units & chalets ❻–❼

Unwin Lodge near the airport turn-off, 4km from the village ☎03/435 1100. An Alpine Club hut that gives priority to NZAC members and climbers but is open to all, with ultra-basic bunkroom accommodation and massive common area with kitchen. Non-members $25.

🎿 YHA Mt Cook Corner of Bowen & Kitchener drives ☎03/435 1820, ⓦwww.yha.co.nz. Excellent 76-bed hostel in a cosy wooden building with modern, well-kept facilities, free evening saunas and bargain pizzas, and a fairly well-stocked shop. Dorms $29–34, rooms ❸–❺

Eating and drinking

Groceries don't come cheap here and the range is very limited: bring what you need from Twizel or further afield.

The Hermitage A wide range of cafés, restaurants and bars, mostly with great views: the daytime Café-Bar with a deep terrace; the Alpine Restaurant serving all-you-can-eat buffets for breakfast (continental $17.50; cooked $25), lunch ($38) and dinner ($54); and the swanky dinner-only à la carte Panorama Restaurant (☎03/435 1809; mains under $40), with priority given to hotel guests. The Snowline Bar has deep leather sofas and magic views. Packed lunches ($17) and gourmet picnic hampers (from $30) can be arranged.

🎿 The Old Mountaineers ☎03/435 1890. Undoubtedly the best place to hang out, with a log fire, real mountain-lodge feel, comfy chairs with wonderful mountain views, an internet lounge, outstanding café-style meals including hearty veggie burgers and scrumptious soups, and great coffee, beer and wine.

Exploring the Aoraki Mount Cook National Park

The 700 square kilometres surrounding the peak and extending to the north and east form the **Aoraki Mount Cook National Park**, which was designated a **world heritage site** by UNESCO in 1986. With twenty-two peaks over 3000m, the park contains the lion's share of New Zealand's highest mountains, mostly made of greywacke laid in an ocean trench 250–300 million years ago.

About two million years ago the Alpine Fault began to lift, progressively pushing the rock upwards and creating the Southern Alps. These days the process continues at about the same rate as erosion, ensuring that the mountains are at least holding their own, if not getting bigger. Aoraki Mount Cook is at the heart of a unique mountain area whose rock is easily shattered in the cold, leaving huge amounts of gravel in the valley floors. The tussock-cloaked foothills, where Mount Cook lilies, summer daisies and snow gentians thrive, contrast with the inhospitable ice fields of the upper slopes. The weather here is highly changeable, often with a pall of low-lying cloud liable to turn to rain, and the mountain air is lung-searingly fresh.

Walking and guided trekking

Scenic **walks** in the park range from gentle day-hikes on the fringes of the village to spectacular alpine treks. DOC's *Walks around Aoraki/Mount Cook village* leaflet lists ten

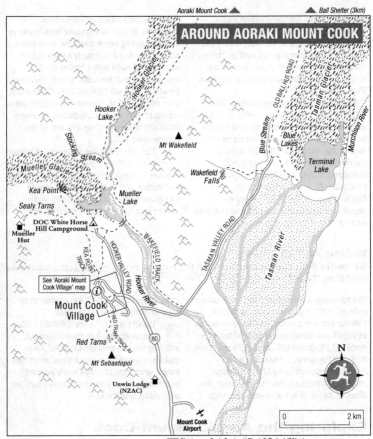

Hooker Glacier

Hooker Lake

Stocking Stream

Mueller Glacier

Kea Point

Sealy Tarns

DOC White Horse Hill Campground

Mueller Hut

Mt Wakefield

Wakefield Falls

Mueller Lake

Blue Stream

Blue Lakes

OLD BALL HUT ROAD

Tasman Glacier

Murchison River

Terminal Lake

Tasman River

TASMAN VALLEY ROAD

KEA POINT TRACK

HOOKER VALLEY ROAD

WAKEFIELD TRACK

See 'Aoraki Mount Cook Village' map

Mount Cook Village

Hooker River

Red Tarns

RED TARNS TRACK 1hr

Mt Sebastopol

80

N

Unwin Lodge (NZAC)

Mount Cook Airport

0 — 2 km

excellent shorter walks (10min–5hr) which can be extended by those with relevant experience. Don't walk on the surface of any of the glaciers unless you know what you're doing, or are in the company of someone qualified. Alpine Guides, inside *The Hermitage* (daily 8am–5pm; Ⓦwww.alpineguides.co.nz), have experienced **climbing guides** and **rent equipment** including crampons and ice axes.

For high-altitude hiking (and spectacular views), **guided trekking** can be organized with Alpine Recreation (Ⓣ0800/006 096, Ⓦwww.alpinerecreation .com), whose Ball Pass Trek ($980) involves a three-day alpine crossing close to Aoraki Mount Cook and reaching 2130m at Ball Pass, staying in comfortable huts. To experience even higher altitudes, Southern Alps Guiding (Ⓣ03/435 1890, Ⓦwww.mtcook.com) organize all-day **heli-trekking** ($700/person; minimum 2 people) with expert guides.

Tramps and walks

Blue Lakes and Tasman Glacier View (1km return; 40min; 100m ascent). A fairly gentle walk with good views of the lower sections of the Tasman Glacier, which is 600m deep at its thickest point, 3km across at its widest and moves at a rate of 20cm a day. The walk starts at the Blue Lakes shelter, 8km drive up the Tasman Valley Road, but you'll need your own vehicle as there are no shuttles.

Governors Bush Walk (1hr return; 2km). Easy walk through a stand of silver beech with good views and abundant birdlife. Sheltered in poor weather.

Hooker Valley Track (9km return; 3hr; 200m ascent). Popular and superb hike which crosses a couple of swingbridges, passes pretty Mueller Lake, skirts the Alpine Memorial with views of the western side of Aoraki Mount Cook and ends at Hooker Lake. Allow an extra hour if you start from and return to the village.

Kea Point Walk (2hr return; 7km; negligible ascent). Rewarding hike to a lookout over Mueller Lake with the hanging glaciers and icefalls of Mount Sefton above.

Mueller Hut Route (10km return; 6–8hr; 1000m ascent). This challenging route leaves the Kea Point Track just before its arrival at the glacier and climbs steeply westwards up the Sealy Tarns Track. From the tarns the route to the hut is marked by orange triangles guiding you up the final assault on loose gravel to a skyline ridge and the modern Mueller Hut (28 bunks; $35; camping outside $15). At 1800m the views are quite startling and you're engulfed by almost perfect silence, interrupted only by the murmur of running water and squawking kea. The track is often completely snow-covered in colder months, requiring crampons, ice axes and winter mountaineering experience including route-finding and using an avalanche transceiver, probe and shovel. At any time of year, consult DOC's *Mueller Hut Route* leaflet ($2), and sign the intentions book before you set out.

Red Tarns Track (4km return; 2hr; 300m ascent). This excellent and very achievable walk has one short, steep section but rewards with uninterrupted views of Aoraki, the Village and along the Tasman Valley.

Scenic flights

Scenic flights offer glimpses of areas you could never dream of reaching on foot. Book a few days ahead, but be prepared to be flexible as flights are cancelled in high winds or poor visibility. The peak season is from November to March, but in winter (June & July) the weather's often clearer and the views more dramatic.

Mount Cook Ski Planes & Helicopters (℡0800/800 702, ⓦwww.mtcookski planes.com) have operated memorable flights from the Mount Cook Airfield for the last fifty years, and helped develop the technology for snow landings; prices are the same for **fixed-wing** or **helicopter** flights – from $255 per 25min, up to the Grand Circle (55min; $495), which loops around Aoraki, briefly crossing the Main Divide, hugging the immense valley walls and then landing on the silent Tasman Glacier to wander on the breathtaking footprint-free snow.

From *Glentanner Park Centre* (p.569), 20km south of the village, the Helicopter Line (℡0800/650 651, ⓦwww.helicopter.co.nz) operates three scenic **helicopter trips** with opportunities to hover along the valley walls and peaks, or view the tumbling blocks of the Hochstetter Icefall; all include brief snow landings. Choose from the Alpine Vista (20min; $210), Alpine Explorer (30min; $295) and Mountains High (45min; $390), which circumnavigates Aoraki.

Boating, kayaking and four-wheel-driving

One of the most entertaining trips available is the three-hour-long Glacier Explorer (late Aug to late May 10am & 2pm daily; $130; ℡03/435 1809, ⓦwww .glacierexplorers.co.nz), an eerie **boat ride** on Tasman Lake, the glacial lake at the base of the Tasman Glacier. Detached icebergs drift around the lake, turned grey by the presence of ground-down rock that reflects the light; examining chunks of fallen ice up close reveals beautiful honeycombed ice cells. Wrap up warmly for the trips, which incorporate a fifteen-minute shuttle from the village, a half-hour walk then the ninety-minute boat ride.

For even more excitement, you can **kayak** among icebergs on Mueller Lake, below the Mueller Glacier, on three-hour trips with Glacier Sea Kayaking (mid-Oct to April; $110; ℡03/435 1890, ⓦwww.mtcook.com), a unique and fascinating experience aboard outrigger-stabilized kayaks with enthusiastic guides.

A good rainy-day alternative is a two-and-a-half-hour **four-wheel-drive** tour on the Tasman Glacier ($110), run by *The Hermitage* (p.569).

Skiing Aoraki Mount Cook

There are no developed ski-fields in the Aoraki Mount Cook area but choppers open up the Tasman Glacier and surrounding mountains for guided **heli-skiing and heli-snowboarding**. During the **season** (July–Sept), steep, untouched runs cater for those with strong intermediate skills or better. Southern Alps Guiding (p.570) offer all-day guided trips including lunch and one or two wilderness runs from $500/750, while five runs with Alpine Guides (☏03/435 1834, ⓦwww.wildernessheli.co.nz) costs $925 (equipment rental extra).

Twizel and around

Nine kilometres south of the junction of SH8 and SH80, **TWIZEL** (rhymes with bridle) began life in 1966 as a construction village for people working on the Waitaki Hydro Scheme (see box below). The town was due to be bulldozed flat after the project finished in 1985. Some think this would have been a kinder fate, but enough residents wanted to stay that their wishes were granted, and it's now becoming a busy summertime base for forays to Aoraki Mount Cook (a 45min drive away), scenic Lake Ohau and gliding at Omarama.

Buses stop beside the **information centre**, on Mackenzie Drive (Nov–March daily 9am–5pm; April–Oct Tues–Sat 10am–4pm; ☏03/435 3124, ⓦwww .twizel.com), next to the larger of Twizel's two 4-Square **supermarkets**. Across the road, Market Place Shopping Centre provides the town's focal point, with restaurants, postal facilities and a **bank**.

The town and around

Twizel's main attraction is the DOC-run **Kaki/Black Stilt Visitor Hide**, 3km south of the town centre on SH8, which is attempting to preserve the world's rarest wading bird from extinction, following habitat loss due to introduced plant species, the Waitaki hydroelectric project and introduced mammalian predators, by hatching eggs in captivity and raising the chicks before releasing them into the wild. Access is solely on guided tours (daily late Oct to mid-April; 1hr; $15), which must be booked through Twizel's information centre (above).

Just to the south on SH8, you can feed the salmon for free at the **High Country Salmon Farm** (daily, daylight hours), or buy the smoked product.

From Twizel, Helicopters Line (☏0800/650 652, ⓦwww.helicopter.co.nz) offers **Mount Cook flights** ($210–525): they're more expensive than those from Aoraki Mount Cook Village, but you get more time in the air.

The Waitaki Hydro Scheme

The **Waitaki Hydro Scheme** provides over a fifth of the nation's power from twelve power stations scattered along the Waitaki River and its headwaters around lakes Tekapo, Pukaki and Ohau. The scheme has its origins in the work of the engineer Peter Seton Hay, who in 1904 submitted a report to the New Zealand government indicating the extraordinary hydroelectric potential of the region. Construction began with the Waitaki power station in 1935 and continued through to 1985, when the commissioning of the Ohau C station completed one of the largest construction projects in New Zealand.

Throughout the region water is diverted along a network of canals to fill a long sequence of storage lakes held back by impressive dams, particularly the 100m-high earth-built **Benmore Dam**, 32km from Omarama in the Waitaki Valley, off SH83 en route to the east coast. You can walk or drive to the top of the dam, or take a short loop track with distant views of Mount Cook. For more on New Zealand's hydro power, see p.294.

To roar around the waterways on a **jet ski** ($120/4hr), contact Twizel Adventures (℡027/489 4935, Ⓦwww.twizeladventures.com), which also rents **kayaks** ($25/4hr) and **mountain bikes** ($25/4hr).

Accommodation and eating

Twizel has a good range of **accommodation** but its proximity to Aoraki Mount Cook means it's essential to **book ahead** from Christmas to at least the end of February. The selection of places to **eat** is more limited.

Accommodation

Aoraki Lodge 32 Mackenzie Drive ℡03/435 0300, Ⓦwww.aorakilodge.co.nz. Tasteful and welcoming B&B in the centre of town with four en-suite rooms, all with separate access, and a pretty garden. B&B ❺

Mountain Chalet Motels Wairepo Rd ℡0800/629 999, Ⓦwww.mountainchalets.co.nz. Great-value collection of light-filled, s/c A-frame chalets and adjacent lodge offering simple, comfortable backpacker accommodation. Dorms $28 ($25 with own linen), chalets ❹

Parklands 122 Mackenzie Drive ℡03/435 0507, Ⓔparklands1@xtra.co.nz. Large campsite with tent and powered sites plus some motel units and en-suite rooms which use a separate kitchen from campers. Camping $28 per site, dorms $25, rooms ❸

YHA High Country Lodge & Backpackers 23 Mackenzie Drive ℡03/435 0671, Ⓦwww .highcountrylodge.co.nz. A veritable village within a village, this huge former hydroelectric workers' camp sleeps up to 280 in barrack-style timber buildings and newer motels, but still gets booked solid in summer. Dorms $32, rooms ❷, en-suite rooms ❸, motel units ❹

Eating and drinking

Hunters Café Bar 2 Market Place ℡03/435 0303. Lively spot serving generous lunches (under $20) and evening mains such as beer-battered fish and locally farmed salmon (under $30).

Poppies 25 Market Place. Elegant wine-red space with polished concrete floors and shelves of gourmet deli goods, serving classy café fare, as well as beautifully cooked lunches and dinners ($25–35), using mostly organic produce straight from the owners' garden, such as terrine of duck, rabbit and wild mushrooms or venison and redcurrant pie, accompanied by home-made bread.

Shawty's 4 Market Place ℡03/435 3155. Good coffee, tasty breakfasts and lunches and dinners (mains under $30) including a fine line in gourmet pizzas are served in the casual interior or overlooking the village green, though portions are small.

Lake Ohau and the Ohau snow fields

The narrow road 25km west of Twizel leads to idyllic **Lake Ohau**, secluded among beech forest with distinctive natural features including kettle lakes (small depressions left when blocks of glacial ice melt) and terracing on its banks that reflects the light of summer sunsets.

Northwest of the lake, the **Ohau Forests** are crisscrossed by numerous tracks (30min–4hr), outlined in DOC's *Ruataniwha Conservation Area* leaflet. Pick it up from the *Lake Ohau Lodge* (℡03/438 9885, Ⓦwww.ohau.co.nz/index.cfm/lodge; camping $12, rooms ❸), which is a popular stop on summer bus-tour itineraries (quieter outside peak times). Guests and non-guests can book ahead for breakfast (continental/cooked $14/20) and dinner ($37.50) from a set menu, or drop by for a drink at the well-stocked bar. The only other places to **stay** in the area are a smattering of ultra-basic campsites.

The *Lake Ohau Lodge* also has petrol, and organizes a ski **shuttle service** ($20 return) to the **Ohau snow fields** (generally open late June to early Oct; ℡03/438 9885, Ⓦwww.ohau.co.nz), just 9km away. This small, high-country ski-field has reliable powder snow and uncrowded slopes, with three beginner, seven intermediate and five advanced runs. **Equipment rental** is available at the field; lift passes cost $72/day.

Omarama

SH8 traverses tussock and sheep country 30km south of Twizel to the junction settlement of **OMARAMA** (Maori for "place of light"). Prevailing westerly winds rising over the Southern Alps create a unique air-wave across the Mackenzie Country's flatlands, providing ideal **gliding** conditions. Omarama airfield was the one-time playground of Dick Georgeson, pioneer of New Zealand aviation and the South Island's first glider pilot, back in 1950. Today, Southern Soaring (℡0800/762 746, ⓦwww.soaring.co.nz) offers spectacular two-seater **glider flights**, with a chance to take the controls (30min $285; 1hr $380; 90min – including a trip to Mount Cook – $560); and – outfitted in a leather jacket, silk scarf and goggles – flights aboard a 1975-built reproduction of a 1929 **biplane** (from 10min $135).

Even if you're not taking to the skies, stop for a dip at **Omarama Hot Tubs** (daily 10am–10pm; ℡03/438 9703, ⓦwww.hottubsomarama.co.nz), ten exquisitely landscaped private outdoor tubs filled with wood-heated alpine water (2hr for 1 or 2 people $30/60) overlooking the mountains.

The most peaceful **place to stay** in the area is ⚑ *Buscot Station*, 8km north of Omarama on SH8 (℡03/438 9646; dorms $22, rooms ❷), a merino sheep farm with cosy homestead accommodation surrounded by a beautifully kept garden; they'll arrange pick-ups if you book ahead. In town, try the friendly *Ahuriri Motels*, 700m east on SH83 (℡0800/435 945, ⓦwww.ahuririmotels.co.nz; basic rooms ❶, en-suite rooms ❸).

Omarama's best **meals** are served at the licensed local landmark *The Wrinkly Rams*, SH8, which has high-class café and pub-style fare, a shop selling quality (albeit pricey) merino clothing, and regular **live sheepshearing** shows ($15; book ahead on ℡03/438 9751).

Travel details

See also p.549 for transport information in the Central South Island.

Trains

Arthur's Pass to: Christchurch (1 daily; 2hr 10min); Greymouth (1 daily; 2hr).

Buses

Aoraki Mount Cook to: Christchurch (1 daily; 5hr 30min); Lake Tekapo (1–2 daily; 1hr 30min); Oamaru (4 weekly; 3hr); Queenstown (1 daily; 4hr); Twizel (4–5 daily; 1hr).
Arthur's Pass to: Christchurch (1–2 daily; 2hr 30min); Greymouth (1–2 daily; 1hr 30min).
Fairlie to: Christchurch (3 daily; 2hr 30min); Geraldine (3 daily; 40min); Lake Tekapo (3 daily; 25min).

Geraldine to: Christchurch (5 daily; 2hr); Fairlie (3 daily; 40min).
Hanmer Springs to: Christchurch (2 daily; 2hr).
Lake Tekapo to: Aoraki Mount Cook (1–2 daily; 1hr 30min); Christchurch (4 daily; 3–4hr); Fairlie (4 daily; 40min); Twizel (5 daily; 30min).
Methven to: Christchurch (1–5 daily; 1hr 15min).
Omarama to: Oamaru (4 weekly; 1hr 45min); Queenstown (3 daily; 2hr 15min); Twizel (3–5 daily; 30min).
Twizel to: Aoraki Mount Cook (3–5 daily; 1hr); Christchurch (5 daily; 4–5hr); Oamaru (4 weekly; 3hr); Omarama (3–5 daily; 30min).

Dunedin to Stewart
Island

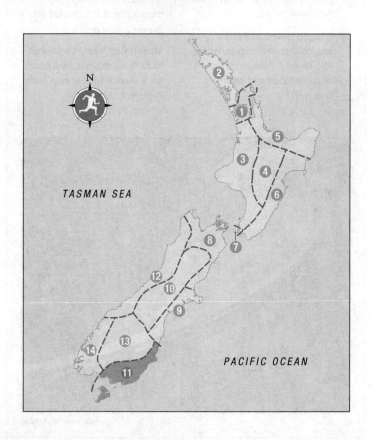

CHAPTER 11 **Highlights**

✳ **Dunedin** Check out the gallery, museums and fabulous live music scene in New Zealand's "Scottish city". See p.577

✳ **Taieri Gorge** Combine a train trip winding through the rugged Taieri Gorge with cycling the Otago Central Rail Trail. See p.590

✳ **Otago Peninsula** Paddle around this stunning coastline in a kayak to see a rich variety of landscapes and wildlife. See p.591

✳ **Curio Bay** Survey a fossilized forest, a yellow-eyed penguin colony and Hector's dolphins surfing the waves of the wild Catlins Coast. See p.603

✳ **Invercargill** Take a laidback tour before taste-testing unique brews straight from the source at the Invercargill Brewery. See p.606

✳ **Mason Bay** Tramp to Stewart Island's windswept west coast for a chance to spot rare kiwis in the wild. See p.617

▲ Train in the Taieri Gorge

Dunedin to Stewart Island

The southeastern corner of the South Island contains some of the least-visited parts of New Zealand, yet a couple of real gems are hidden here. The darkly Gothic harbourside city of **Dunedin**, 400km south of Christchurch, is a seat of learning and culture, influenced by the country's oldest university and thriving Scottish immigrant traditions. Within easy reach of the city is the windswept **Otago Peninsula**, an important wildlife haven for rare marine life and sea birds. South of Dunedin, the wild **Catlins Coast** is a protected reserve, with several rare species and dramatic scenery, from hills cloaked in native forest to a shoreline indented with rocky bays, long sweeps of sand and spectacular geological formations.

On the South Island's southern tip lies **Invercargill**, bordered by the rich pastureland of Southland's farming communities. The city is the springboard to **Stewart Island**. Relatively few visit, but those who do are rewarded by the extraordinary birdlife, particularly in **Mason Bay** and on **Ulva Island**.

Kiwis from more northern parts delight in condemning the **climate** of the southern South Island, and it's true that the further south you go, the wetter it gets. Generally, the best time to come is November to April, when you're most likely to enjoy warmer, though changeable, weather, with midsummer temperatures averaging around 19°C. You'll also catch the best of the wildlife, coinciding with the breeding season of many species.

Dunedin

The "Edinburgh of the South", **DUNEDIN** takes its name from the Gaelic translation of its Scottish counterpart, with which it shares street and suburb names. Founded by Scottish settlers, its heyday was as the commercial centre for

Getting around

Getting around is straightforward, with bus services as well as tour buses linking the major towns and crossing the island to Queenstown and the West Coast along the dramatic Southern Scenic Route. Stewart Island is accessible by air from Invercargill and sea from Bluff.

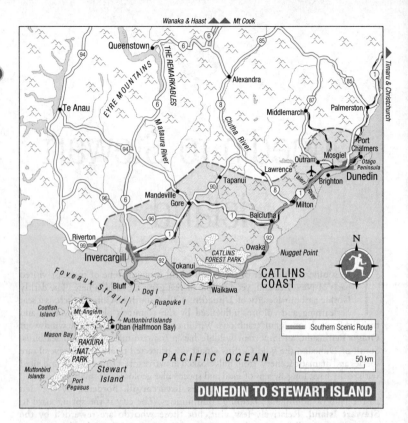

Wanaka & Haast ▲▲ Mt Cook

Timaru & Christchurch

DUNEDIN TO STEWART ISLAND

the gold-rush towns of nearby Central Otago, leaving an enduring legacy of imposing **Gothic Revival architecture** fashioned from volcanic bluestone and creamy limestone, including grand villas that climb the hills around the town. Although its population of around 115,000 spreads beyond the hills and surf beaches, Dunedin has a compact and manageable city centre.

Some 25,000 students from the 1871-established **University of Otago** – New Zealand's oldest tertiary institution – contribute to a strong **arts scene**, as well as vibrant **nightlife**, during term time, at least.

Dunedin sits at the head of **Otago Harbour**, a long and sheltered body formed ten million years ago by volcanic eruptions and now virtually encircled by rugged hills. It is home to two working ports: a small one in the heart of Dunedin, and **Port Chalmers**, a container-port whose main street consists almost entirely of tourist shops for disembarking cruise-line passengers.

Otago Harbour is protected from the Pacific Ocean by the **Otago Peninsula**, which teems with wildlife including rare penguins, seals and albatrosses. Just half an hour's drive from Dunedin, the peninsula is an easy day-trip, as is the **Orokonui Eco Sanctuary**. Ten minutes' drive from Port Chalmers, the sanctuary is a recently completed "mainland island" for the protection of indigenous plants and animals.

Some history

From around 1100 AD, **Maori** fished the rich coastal waters of nearby bays, travelling inland in search of moa, ducks and freshwater fish, and trading with other *iwi* further north. Eventually they formed a settlement around the harbour, calling it Otakou (pronounced "O-tar-go") and naming the headland at the harbour's entrance after their great chieftain, Taiaroa – today a *marae* occupies the Otakou site. By the 1820s European whalers and sealers were seeking shelter in what was the only safe anchorage along this stretch of coast, unwittingly introducing foreign diseases. The local Maori population was decimated, dropping to a low of 110, but subsequent intermarriage bolstered numbers.

The New Zealand Company selected the Otago Harbour for a planned **Scottish settlement** as early as 1840 and purchased land from local Maori, but it wasn't until 1848 that the first migrant ships arrived, led by Captain William Cargill and the Reverend Thomas Burns, nephew of the Scottish poet Robert Burns. With the arrival of English and Irish settlers the following year, the Scots were soon in the minority but their national fervour still stamped its distinct character on the town.

In 1861, a lone Australian prospector discovered **gold** at a creek near present-day Lawrence, about 100km west of Dunedin. Within three months, diggers were pouring in from Australia, and as the main port of entry Dunedin found itself in the midst of a gold rush. The port was expanded, and the population doubled in six months, trebled in three years and made the city New Zealand's most important. This new-found wealth spurred a building boom that resulted in much of the city's most iconic architecture, including the university.

By the 1870s gold mania had largely subsided, but the area sustained its economic primacy through **shipping**, railway development and farming. Decline began during the early twentieth century, when the opening of the Panama Canal in 1914 made Auckland a more economic port for British shipping. In the 1980s, the improvement in world gold prices and the development of equipment enabling large-scale recovery of gold from low-yielding soils re-established **mining** in the hinterland. Today you can visit massive operations, including one at Macraes (see p.725), an hour's drive from Dunedin.

New Zealand's "liquid gold", Speight's Gold Medal Ale, is a full-strength lager (with grassy undertones for that "southern flavour") that has been brewed in Dunedin since the late 1880s, and remains the country's biggest-selling beer.

Arrival, information and city transport

Dunedin **airport**, 5km off SH1, 30km south of town, is served by domestic flights as well as direct international flights from Australia (see p.28). Shuttle buses including Super Shuttle (☎0800/748 885, ⍟www.supershuttle.co.nz; $30) connect each flight with the city centre dropping off at accommodation; book ahead online or by phone. A taxi to the city centre will cost about $65.

Dunedin has no main-line passenger **train** service, but tourist-oriented services along the Taieri Gorge Railway and north along the coast to Palmerston leave from the Dunedin Railway Station on Anzac Avenue. This is also the terminus for Atomic Shuttles. InterCity **buses** drop off in the city centre at 205 St Andrew St.

Information

In addition to handling transport, accommodation and trips, Dunedin's **i-SITE visitor centre**, Municipal Chambers, The Octagon (Nov–March Mon–Fri 8.30am–6pm, Sat & Sun 8.45am–6pm; April–Oct Mon–Fri 8.30am–5.30pm, Sat & Sun 8.30am–5pm; ☎03/474 3300, ⍟www.dunedin.govt.nz), runs **guided walking tours** (11am daily; $25). It also stocks walks leaflets including *Walk the City* ($2.50), detailing points of interest around central Dunedin, as well as *A Walking Guide to*

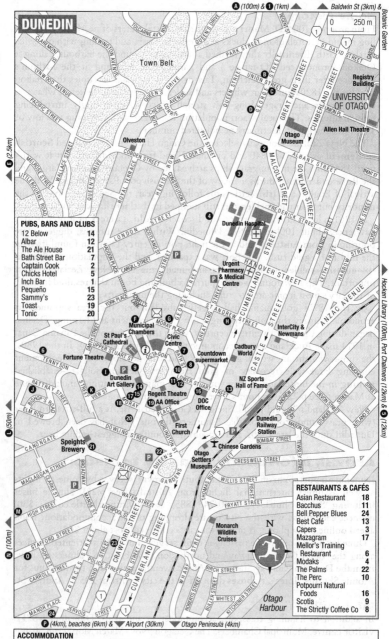

A (100m) & **①** (1km) ▲   ▲ Baldwin St (3km) &

0   250 m

Botanic Garden

PUBS, BARS AND CLUBS

12 Below	14
Albar	12
The Ale House	21
Bath Street Bar	7
Captain Cook	2
Chicks Hotel	5
Inch Bar	1
Pequeño	15
Sammy's	23
Toast	19
Tonic	20

RESTAURANTS & CAFÉS

Asian Restaurant	18
Bacchus	11
Bell Pepper Blues	24
Best Café	13
Capers	3
Mazagram	17
Mellor's Training Restaurant	6
Modaks	4
The Palms	22
The Perc	10
Potpourri Natural Foods	16
Scotia	9
The Strictly Coffee Co	8

UNIVERSITY OF OTAGO

Registry Building

Allen Hall Theatre

Otago Museum

Dunedin Hospital

Urgent Pharmacy & Medical Centre

InterCity & Newmans

Olveston

Town Belt

St Paul's Cathedral

Municipal Chambers

Civic Centre

Countdown supermarket

Cadbury World

NZ Sports Hall of Fame

Fortune Theatre

Dunedin Art Gallery

Regent Theatre

AA Office

DOC Office

First Church

Dunedin Railway Station

Speights Brewery

Chinese Gardens

Otago Settlers Museum

Monarch Wildlife Cruises

N

Otago Harbour

Hocken Library (100m), Port Chalmers (12km) & **⑤** (12km)

E (2.5km) ▲

① (50m) ▲

① (100m) ▲

P (4km), beaches (6km) & ▼ Airport (30km)   ▼ Otago Peninsula (4km)

ACCOMMODATION

858 George St Motel	A	Bluestone on		Dunedin Holiday		On Top Backpackers	F
97 Motel	I	George	D	Park	P	Sahara Guesthouse	
Aaron Lodge Top		The Brothers	J	Elm Lodge	L	& Motel	B
10 Holiday Park	E	Central Backpackers	G	Fletcher Lodge	M	Victoria	H
Allan Court Motel	C	Chalet Backpackers	N	Hulmes Court	K	YHA Stafford Gables	O

Dunedin ($3.50) for **longer walks**. You can also obtain factsheets for each walk from the **DOC** office, 77 Lower Stuart St (Mon–Fri 8.30am–5pm; ☎03/477 0677).

City transport

Dunedin's central sights, hostels, hotels and places to eat and drink are easily accessible on foot. To get further out, the city has an efficient **bus** system (ⓦ www.orc .govt.nz); check schedules at the visitor centre.

Most lines run Monday to Friday from 7.30am to 11pm with limited services on Saturday, Sunday and public holidays. Buses are not numbered but are identified by their route: the most useful is the Normanby–St Clair run, which goes from the beach right through the city, past the Botanic Garden, to the foot of Baldwin Street and beyond. **Fares** are calculated according to the number of zones crossed: the central city is one zone ($1.90), Portobello, say, is seven ($6.30). All buses start from or pass through the centre of town, stopping at different stands around The Octagon.

From March to October, you might also want to join the hop-on-hop-off **guided bus tour** with Dunedin City Explorer ($20; ☎0800/322 240, ⓦ www .otagoexplorer.com), which makes an hour-long loop of the central city sights. Tickets are valid all day, including unlimited stops. Alternatively, try the **double-decker bus tour** with First City Tours, Citisights (1hr; $20; ☎03/477 5577), departing from the visitor centre five times a day.

Drivers will soon discover the one-way system running north–south through the city and affecting Cumberland, Castle, Great King and Crawford streets. **Parking** is seldom a problem, with inexpensive meters and restricted zones in the centre but free long-term street parking a few hundred metres outside.

Accommodation

There's a broad choice of accommodation in Dunedin, most of it in or near the city centre. If you prefer something more rural, consider the **Otago Peninsula** (see p.591).

Hotels and motels

858 George St Motel 858 George St ☎0800/858 999, ⓦ www.858georgestreetmotel .co.nz. An unusual and well-executed modern design based on Victorian houses, divided into thirteen big, luxurious units. Wi-fi available. Studios ④, suites ⑥

97 Motel 97 Moray Place ☎0800/909 797, ⓦ www.97motel.co.nz. Friendly, central motel with cheerful rooms either in the motel itself or the high-rise former student accommodation behind. Good beds, good bathrooms, great value and plenty of off-street parking. ④

Allan Court Motel 590 George St ☎0800/611 511, ⓔ allan.court@earthlight.co.nz. Central, modern and comfortable, with full kitchens in all units and a guest laundry. ⑤

Bluestone on George 571 George St ☎03/477 9201, ⓦ www.bluestonedunedin.co.nz. Classy apartments with state-of-the-art kitchens, bathrooms, in-room laundries and high-speed wi-fi. ⑥

Victoria 137 St Andrew St ☎0800/266 336, ⓦ www.victoriahoteldunedin.com. Elegant, relaxed hotel in the heart of the city offering rooms, suites and a two-bedroom family apartment, plus a restaurant, a cosy bar and a café. ⑤–⑥

B&Bs and homestays

The Brothers 295 Rattray St ☎03/477 0043, ⓦ www.brothershotel.co.nz. Stylish fourteen-room boutique hotel tastefully converted from a 1920s Christian Brothers' residence. Pared-down contemporary decor and friendly service set the tone, with many of the rooms opening onto verandas with splendid views. A spacious lounge has city views, Sky TV and broadband and continental breakfast and parking are included. ⑥

Fletcher Lodge 276 High St ☎03/477 5552, ⓦ www.fletcherlodge.co.nz. Sumptuous decor and good taste abound throughout the house, an English baronial-style home of 1924 built for leading Kiwi industrialist Sir James Fletcher. A separate, more prosaic apartment guarantees independence but means you'll miss out on the splendour of the main house and the sumptuous breakfast. ⑨

Hulmes Court 52 Tennyson St ☎0800/448 563, ⓦ www.hulmes.co.nz. Two great-value homes under one management roof, (one Edwardian, the

other a grander 1860 Victorian affair), a short climb from The Octagon. Big, individually themed rooms (several en suite), off-street parking, internet access, and a continental breakfast served in the sunny drawing room. Rooms ❹, en suites ❺
Sahara Guesthouse & Motel 619 George St ☎03/477 6662, ⓦwww.dunedin-accommodation .co.nz. Roomy, 1863 guesthouse with mostly shared facilities, plus ten standard motel units with basic kitchen facilities and some new comfortable deluxe studios. Pragmatic rather than romantic. Off-street parking. ❹

Hostels

Central Backpackers 243 Moray Place ☎03/477 9985. Efficiently run, forty-bed hostel with backpack-size security lockers, a surround-sound DVD lounge and wi-fi. Guests also get discounted rates at the adjacent internet café. Dorms $25, shares $27, twins ❷, doubles ❸
Chalet Backpackers 296 High St ☎0800/242 538, ⓦwww.chaletbackpackers.co.nz. Comfortable hostel with pleasing views, good kitchen and dining facilities, four-shares rather than bunk dorms and comfy singles and doubles, plus a pool and piano room. Phone ahead in winter. Dorms $24, rooms ❶
Elm Lodge 74 Elm Row ☎0800/356 363, ⓦwww.elmlodge.co.nz. Well-run hostel spread over a couple of buildings, which still contrive to be cosy. Primary is the atmospheric 1930s house with the wood stove, made-up beds, a free spa

pool and sauna and BBQ. Dorms and shares $28, rooms ❷
On Top Backpackers Corner of Filleul St & Moray Place ☎03/477 6121, ⓦwww.ontopbackpackers. co.nz. A 100-bed hostel with eight doubles, BBQ terrace and a light, open-plan kitchen/common room above a café and bar. Dorms $25, rooms ❷
YHA Stafford Gables 71 Stafford St ☎03/474 1919, ⓦwww.yha.co.nz. Atmospheric though down-at-heel hostel in a rambling 1902 building with a rooftop garden overlooking the city and clued-in staff. Three- to six-bed dorms (some with balconies), doubles and twin rooms are generally large. Office hours 7.30am–8.30pm. Dorms $26, rooms ❷

Campsites and holiday parks

Aaron Lodge Top 10 Holiday Park 162 Kaikorai Valley Rd ☎0800/879 227, ⓦwww .aaronlodgetop10.co.nz. A sheltered, fairly spacious and well-tended site, in the hills 2.5km west of the city centre. Camping $32, cabins ❶, flats ❷, motel units ❸
Dunedin Holiday Park 41 Victoria Rd ☎0800/945 455, ⓦwww.dunedinholidaypark.co.nz. Lying alongside St Kilda Beach, this well-appointed park is 5min drive from the city centre and served by the Brockville–St Kilda bus: pick it up at The Octagon Stand 3. There's a seven-day camp store. Camping $21, cabins ❶, en-suite cabins ❷, motel units ❸

The City

Dunedin's heart is **The Octagon**, a manicured, tree-lined green space bordered by historic buildings. Restaurants, offices, banks, bars, clubs and most of the sights are within walking distance of it, and the **shopping district** stretches south along Princes Street and north along George Street. Further north is the **university** and the expansive **Botanic Garden**. To the east is the head of **Otago Harbour**, a sheltered inlet 22km long and no wider than a river in places. Just a short bus ride away, St Clair and St Kilda offer two sandy **beaches**.

The Octagon

Laid out in 1846, **The Octagon** is a blend of well-preserved buildings and more modern additions overlooking lawns and regimented trees, all presided over by a statue of Robert Burns, symbol of Dunedin's Scottish origins. Every Friday (10am–4pm), the area spills over with **market** stalls selling local crafts.

Dominating The Octagon is the 1880 **Municipal Chambers** building, a grand, classical structure with a clock tower, all constructed from limestone dramatically offset against volcanic bluestone. It's a fine example of the handiwork of Scottish architect **Robert A. Lawson**, whose influence can be seen in the design of many of Dunedin's public buildings. Beside the Municipal Chambers rise the twin white-stone spires of **St Paul's Cathedral**, one of Dunedin's finest buildings and the seat of Anglican worship in the city. This impressive Gothic Revival edifice, entirely constructed from Oamaru stone, was consecrated in 1919. Inside, the

20m-high stone-vaulted ceiling is the only one of its kind in New Zealand, and much of the stained glass in the impressive windows is original; the stark chancel and altar were added in 1971.

Continuing anticlockwise around The Octagon, Dunedin City Council architects fashioned the gleaming **Dunedin Public Art Gallery**, 30 The Octagon (daily 10am–5pm; gold coin donation, plus charges for special exhibitions) out of six Victorian buildings, all elegantly refurbished to create a light, modern split-level space with several exhibition areas. The 1996-opened structure is a contrast to the original public art gallery, founded in 1884 and the oldest in the country. The foyer of polished wooden floors, ironwork and a hundred-year-old spiral staircase is worth a look in itself. The gallery's main strength is its recently refurbished exhibition area, hosting a rotated collection of early and contemporary New Zealand pieces and temporary international travelling shows, alongside an extension of the **New Zealand Film Archive** (see p.409), where you can watch Kiwi movies, documentaries and TV programmes on individual computer screens for free.

Further around, at 17 The Octagon, is the 1874 facade of the **Regent Theatre**, a one-time hotel that was transformed into a cinema then theatre. After a smartening lick of paint in 2009, it hosts international shows and the Royal New Zealand Ballet, as well as live music. Inside, elaborate nineteenth-century plasterwork and marble staircases are juxtaposed with 1920s stained-glass windows and geometric balustrades.

Behind the Regent Theatre on Moray Place stands the 54m-high stone spire of the **First Church of Otago**, visible throughout the city. Generally recognized as the most impressive of New Zealand's nineteenth-century churches it was designed in neo-Gothic style by Robert A. Lawson. Of particular interest are a wooden gabled ceiling and, above the pulpit, a brightly coloured rose window.

South and east of The Octagon

Two hundred years of social history in Dunedin and Otago are catalogued at the engrossing **Otago Settlers Museum**, 31 Queens Gardens (daily 10am–5pm; gold coin donation), which draws from an exhaustive collection of artefacts, paintings and photographs. Highlights include the portrait gallery and "Across the Ocean Waves", an insight into the rigours (and pleasures) of emigrating to Otago by sailing ship in the nineteenth century. Look too for the "Windows on a Chinese Past" display, an insight into the lives of the legions of Chinese who left their families to seek a fortune in the Otago Goldfields. Among the exhibits in the transport wing there's a beautifully appointed 1940s caravan, a restored double-ended Fairlie steam engine and the chance to sit astride a pennyfarthing. Alongside the museum are the **Chinese Gardens**, on the corner of Rattray and Cumberland streets (daily 10am–5pm; $8; guided tour $20; Ⓦ www.dunedinchinesegarden.com), beautifully executed traditional Chinese-style gardens, a world away from the surrounding city.

Impossible to miss, thanks to its towers, turrets and minarets, the resplendent **Dunedin Railway Station**, Anzac Avenue, was constructed on reclaimed swampland in 1906. The walls of its exquisitely preserved **foyer** glisten with green, yellow and cream majolica tiles made especially for New Zealand Rail by Royal Doulton, and the mosaic floor celebrates the steam engine and consists of more than 700,000 tiny squares of porcelain. Upstairs on the balcony, a stained-glass window at each end depicts an approaching train, whose headlights gleam from all angles. The station's upper floor houses the moribund **New Zealand Sports Hall of Fame** (daily 10am–4pm; $5), a hagiographic collection of memorabilia relating to 150-odd New Zealand inductees, among them mountaineer Edmund Hillary and fast bowler Richard Hadlee. More rewarding is the Saturday-morning **farmers' market** held in the station car park.

Beyond the station is the extensive university research facility, **Hocken Library**, 90 Anzac Ave (Mon–Fri 9.30am–5pm, Tues until 9pm, Sat 9am–noon; free), whose impressive collection relating to New Zealand and the Pacific was assembled by Dr Thomas Morland Hocken, a Dunedin physician and one of the country's first historians.

Cadbury World and Speight's Brewery

Dunedin's downtown chocolate factory, just east of The Octagon, **Cadbury World**, 280 Cumberland St (full 75min tours Mon–Fri, shortened 45min tours Sat & Sun when the production lines may be stationary, booking advised; full $18, shortened $12; ℡0800/223 287, ⓦwww.cadburyworld.co.nz), is rarely less than busy. Enthusiastic guides clad in bright purple take you into the factory while showering you with free samples.

Altogether more edifying is the **Speight's Brewery Tour**, 200 Rattray St (daily: 10am, noon, 2pm, plus Mon–Thurs 7pm and Fri & Sun 4pm; $20; ℡03/477 7697, ⓦwww.speights.co.nz), an informative meander round one of New Zealand's oldest breweries, established in 1876 and delving into the alchemy of brewing, with free samples at the end. The brewery's tall, brick chimney topped by a stone barrel, a few hundred metres southwest of The Octagon, is visible from across the city. The tour entry point is beside a **water spigot** fed by the same sweet-tasting artesian liquid that is used to brew the beer: usually awash with locals filling water bottles.

North of The Octagon

The star attraction of the absorbing **Otago Museum**, 419 Great King St (daily 10am–5pm; gold coin donation; ⓦwww.otagomuseum.govt.nz) is the fascinating "Southern Land, Southern People" gallery covering aspects of life and natural history in the southern half of the South Island and the sub-Antarctic islands. Large boulders give an idea of the rock that underlies the region in displays that also draw in a fossilized plesiosaur skeleton and the influence of Oamaru stone on the region's architecture. Everything is knitted neatly together, with a discussion on climate illustrated by a Maori flax rain cape, and coverage of the region's fish calling on the experience of whitebaiters.

Elsewhere look out for the Animal Attic, a deeply Victorian amalgamation of macabre skeletons and stuffed beasts, while the special exhibitions gallery is worth a look. You can go on a guided "Highlights" tour ($10) at 11.30am, or book a specialized tour ($10) concentrating on specific elements.

Olveston

Dunedin's showpiece historic home is **Olveston**, 42 Royal Terrace (1hr guided tours only: daily 9.30am, 10.45am, noon, 1.30pm, 2.45pm & 4pm; $16; book a day ahead in summer ℡0800/100 880, ⓦwww.olveston.co.nz), ten minutes' walk northwest of The Octagon. Contained within this fine Edwardian house is a treasure-trove of art and antiques assembled by the Theomin family, who lived here from 1906 and were passionate about travel, art and music. On her death in 1966, the last-surviving family member, Dorothy, bequeathed the house and its contents to the city, and it remains just as she left it.

The University

New Zealand's oldest university, the **University of Otago** was founded by Scottish settlers in 1869. Based on the design of Glasgow University, it quickly expanded into a complex of imposing Gothic bluestone buildings, foremost among them the registry building with its **clock tower**. The visitor centre has free campus maps; a stroll through the campus from Union Street to Leith Street will take you past the best bits.

The Botanic Garden and Signal Hill

Established in 1863, the serene **Dunedin Botanic Garden** (sunrise–sunset; free) lies at the foot of Signal Hill. The steep Upper Garden contains the expansive Rhododendron Dell, where established specimens grow among native bush. It also has an arboretum, a native plant collection and an aviary, home to native birds such as kea and kaka. The flat Lower Garden features exotic trees, Winter Garden conservatories (daily 10am–4pm), an Alpine House (daily 9am–4pm), a rose garden and playground. A volunteer-run information centre (daily 10am–4pm) lies between the tea kiosk and the Winter Garden. Access to the Lower Gardens car park is from Cumberland Street, while the Upper Gardens car park is on Lovelock Avenue. Tours, specific or general (30 min; $15; ℡03/471 9275), are run by volunteers.

Just north of the Botanic Garden, Opoho Road leads up to the 393m summit of **Signal Hill**, a scenic reserve with magnificent views over Dunedin, the upper harbour and the sea from the Centennial Memorial. Apparently the nation's only monument commemorating one hundred years of British sovereignty (1840–1940) following the signing of the Treaty of Waitangi, the memorial is flanked by two powerful bronze figures symbolizing the past and the future. Embedded in the podium is a tribute to Dunedin's namesake: a chunk of the rock upon which Edinburgh Castle was built.

If you're not driving you can ride the Opoho **bus** from The Octagon Stand 7 to within 1km of the summit (the route also stops at the north end of the Botanic Garden), or walk (6km return; 1hr 30min) from the Botanic Garden.

Baldwin Street

Dunedin rejoices in the world's steepest street, **Baldwin Street**, which, with a *Guinness Book of Records*-verified maximum gradient of 1 in 2.66, has a slope of almost 19 degrees. The views from the top aren't bad, but the highlight is walking up, something achieved in about five minutes, under the bemused gaze of locals. During the annual "Gutbuster" event (generally held in late Feb as part of the Dunedin Summer Festival), contestants run to the top and back down again – the current record is one minute 56 seconds.

Baldwin Street is 5km north of the city centre: follow Great King Street until it becomes North Road then look for the tenth road on the right. The Normanby–St Clair bus from Stand 2 on Princes Street drops you at the foot of Baldwin Street.

Dunedin's beaches

Four kilometres south of the city centre, the suburbs of St Kilda and St Clair culminate in a long, wild sweep of sand enclosed by two volcanic headlands (served by frequent buses from the corner of The Octagon and Princes Street). **St Clair Beach** is excellent for surfing and is patrolled by lifeguards during the summer. For calmer waters, head to the western end where **St Clair Hot Salt Water Pool**, The Esplanade (Oct–March Mon–Fri 6am–7pm, Sat & Sun 7am–7pm; $5.50; ℡03/455 6352), offers an outdoor, heated saltwater pool beside the surf. At the opposite end of the Esplanade, by the St Clair Surf Rescue Station, the Esplanade Surf School (℡03/455 8655, ⓦwww.espsurfschool.co.nz), offer **surfing lessons** ($45/2hr for 3–6 people; 90min one-on-one lessons $90), wetsuit and board supplied.

About halfway along the strip, St Clair merges with **St Kilda Beach**, which is reasonably safe for swimming as long as you keep between the flags; it is also patrolled in summer. At the beach's eastern end, a headland separates St Kilda from the smaller **Tomahawk Beach** (not safe for swimming), often dotted with horses and buggies preparing for trotting races at low tide. The best swimming beach in the area is the blend of sand and rocky outcrops at **Brighton**, 15km south of Dunedin: catch the Brighton/Green Island bus from Stand 5 on Cumberland Street between Hanover and St Andrew streets ($6.30).

Eating

It is a tricky pleasure to choose between the excellent range of dining options spread throughout the city (especially in the vicinity of The Octagon and along George Street between Hanover and Albany streets). Kiwi cafés vie with fine dining restaurants, and budget places sit alongside those offering the gamut of world cuisine.

Quality spots for **stocking up** include the deli/café *Everyday Gourmet*, 466 George St (Mon–Fri 7.30am–5.30pm, Sat 8am–3pm, generally closed Sun), and the enticing Saturday morning **farmers' market** in the Dunedin Railway Station car park. For staples, stop by the central 24hr Countdown supermarket at 309 Cumberland St.

Cafés

Best Café 30 Lower Stuart St. Part of Dunedin folklore and in a time warp since the 1950s, this anachronism to modern dining dishes up excellent and good-value, old-school fish and chips with sliced bread and curled butter (around $18), along with oysters and whitebait patties in season. Closes at 7pm, and all day Sat & Sun.

Capers 412 George St. A loyal local following attests to good quality, with early birds after the chunky sweet and savoury scones, pancakes and heaped bacon and eggs ($8.50–14), while lunchers feast on ploughman's lunches, baked potatoes, filo parcels and quiches with a delicious salad selection. Mon–Fri 7am–4pm, Sat & Sun 7am–2pm.

Mazagram 36 Moray Place. Tiny café for bean freaks that grudgingly sells teas, gumboot and herbal, cold, soft drinks and the odd slice of tart or cake. Groovy music makes a smooth accompaniment to the wonderful coffee. Mon–Fri 8am–5pm, Sat 10am–2pm.

Modaks 318 George St. Edgy, funky, city-style café with local pop art lining the walls that has served great coffee and grub, including focaccia stuffed with avocado, hummus and sundried tomatoes and spinach and feta muffins, for years. Sadly it is up for sale.

The Perc 142 Lower Stuart St. Art Deco daytime café serving scrumptious baked goods (go early before the cinnamon pinwheels sell out), breakfasts, sandwiches and smoothies.

Potpourri Natural Foods 97 Lower Stuart St. Established daytime vegetarian café with diamond-patterned stained glass and timber pews, where wholemeal baking, a big salad bar and enormous quiche slices are the way to go. Closed Sun.

The Strictly Coffee Co 23 Bath St. If not the best coffee in town then in company with it, sold by the cup or the kilo in an industrial-chic, cherry-red daytime café filled with chrome coffee grinders. Closed Sat & Sun. A second branch on Albion Place is open daily.

Restaurants

Asian Restaurant 43 Moray Place, ☎03/477 6673. The premier Chinese joint in town with the busiest kitchen in Otago where classics and demi-classics emerge at bargain prices in a zingy, fun atmosphere. Licensed & BYO. Daily noon–2pm & 5–11pm.

Bacchus First floor, 12 The Octagon ☎03/474 0824. Respected but very expensive restaurant and wine bar with a great vantage point overlooking The Octagon. Lunch Mon–Fri; dinner Mon–Sat.

Bell Pepper Blues 474 Princes St ☎03/474 0973. Fine-dining restaurant and baby of award-winning chef Michael Coughlin where adventurous modern Kiwi cuisine is fused with mostly European flavours. Reserve for dinner (mains $30–40); Tues–Sat.

Mellor's Training Restaurant First floor, Otago Polytechnic, corner of York Place & Tennyson St ☎03/479 6172. Hit and miss cheap French/New Zealand cuisine prepared by world-class chefs or more likely their students, with one of the best city views in Dunedin. Booking essential, ideally several days ahead. Licensed & BYO. Only open March–Oct, Tues–Thurs for a set lunch (noon–2pm) and dinner (6.30–9pm).

The Palms 18 Queens Gardens ☎03/477 6534. Friendly, revamped, local favourite with picture windows overlooking Queens Gardens and a menu ranging from lamb rump to roast garlic risotto (mains $26–30). Licensed & BYO. Lunch & dinner Mon–Sat.

Scotia 199 Upper Stuart St ☎03/477 2993. Moved from the station to this new, more central location this established master dishes up some of Dunedin's finest meals in the cosy ambience of a converted Victorian terrace house. There's Emerson's on tap, a fine collection of whisky, friendly efficient service and subtle nods to Scottish culinary origins, like haggis, cullen skink and whisky, and honey and rolled oats trifle (mains around $30). The desserts are sumptuous. Daily, 3pm onward.

Drinking, nightlife and entertainment

Like all good university cities drinking is taken seriously here. A number of the city's dozens of **pubs** and **bars** serve English- and German-style beers from Dunedin's premier microbrewery, Emerson's. Local **bands** play at weekends, although once the students head home for the holidays the dancefloors can look forlorn. For entertainment and events **listings** pick up the Thursday or Friday edition of the *Otago Daily Times*, for the LOG (List of Gallery Exhibitions and Events; free), or the *Otago Gaily Times* (monthly).

To get a taste of the local culture go to a **rugby match** at Carisbrook Stadium (the "House of Pain") on Burns Street, 2.5km southwest of The Octagon. Games are usually held every second weekend during the season (roughly end Feb to end Oct). The Champions of the World shop, 8 George St, has free schedules and sells tickets.

Pubs, bars and clubs

12 Below Under the *Bennu Café Bar* (12 Moray Place), down the alley to the left. Live music and DJs ranging through soul, funk reggae, nu jazz and drum 'n' bass.

Albar 135 Stuart St. Inviting, popular Scottish-themed bar with a good selection of whiskies, European and Kiwi bottled beers and Invercargill

Brewery and Emerson's ales on tap. The otherwise authentic tapas menu includes an unusual haggis option. Mon–Sat 11am–midnight, Sun noon–10pm.

The Ale House 200 Rattray St ☎03/471 9050. Popular and spacious Speight's-owned pub, by the brewery, with good beer and food among rural

The Dunedin Sound

In the late 1970s and early 1980s an idiosyncratic style of rock music, soon dubbed the **Dunedin Sound**, began to emerge from Dunedin's local pub scene. The bands writing and producing these jangly garage tracks were isolated from the commercial mainstream but were championed by indie Christchurch label Flying Nun (now based in Auckland; ⊛www.flyingnun.co.nz) who put out early records by bands like The Chills, The Clean and The Verlaines. All saw some success in New Zealand and found a receptive (if underground) audience in Europe and the States.

As late as 1992, the *Chicago Tribune* called Dunedin the "Rock Capital of The World", but by then the scene had moved on. Some of the bands are still going (in one form or another), and in 2002 Flying Nun released its 21st birthday CD of Flying Nun covers called *Under The Influence*: ex-Pavement frontman Stephen Malkmus covered The Verlaines' wonderful *Death and the Maiden*.

The songs have certainly stood the test of time, and as the rock 'n' roll wheel turns, an updated version of the same kind of sound emanates from The Strokes and their imitators. To check out back catalogues and keep tabs on the latest bands breaking out of Dunedin, visit ⊛www.dunedinmusic.com, which also has an online music store.

kitsch decor, where tasting trays of six ales cost $14. Daily from 11.30am.

Bath Street Bar 1 Bath St. Long-established, small, edgy, mostly DJ-music venue behind a blank beige facade. Covers vary; closed Mon.

Captain Cook 354 Great King St. Thanks to a constant stream of young students or "fresh blood" this black cavern rough-house bar keeps dishing out bad cheap food, cheaper drinks and grotesque entertainments. Has to be done. "The Cook" reputedly has NZ's highest beer consumption and its own Speight's rip-off ale Cook Draught, Pride of the Cook, brewed by the conglomerate opposition.

Chicks Hotel 2 Mount St, Port Chalmers ☎03/472 8736. A bit of a schlep, but well worth it, is this up and coming live music venue and pub, in an atmospheric 1876 stone building with a hanging sign depicting a skull and crossbones.

Inch Bar 8 Bank St. Intimate watering hole with specialty beers including Emerson's on tap, and a wide range of imported brands.

Pequeño Savoy Building, Princes St. All low lighting, leather sofas and banquettes around the fire. Excellent wine and cocktails and regular live jazz, popular with suits on the pull. Closed Sun.

Sammy's 65 Crawford St ☎03/477 2185. Live music and DJ venue, more cutting-edge than most, with open-mic nights, installations and exhibitions as well as touring acts from across the globe. Doesn't get going until late; covers apply depending upon the act.

Toast 53 Princes St. Cocktail bar where they can mix any classic prohibition-era drink you care to name or a Flaming Lamborghini ($14), with DJs hitting the decks Tues–Sun 5pm–late.

🏃 **Tonic** 138 Princes St. With a beer from every decent Kiwi microbrewery you can think of, Emerson's on tap, a decent wine list, snacky platters and friendly regulars, this wonderful little bar will bring a tear to your eye. Tues–Sat 4pm–late.

Theatre, cinema and classical music

In addition to its **festivals**, Dunedin has a lively year-round **theatre** scene, several **movie houses** and **classical music** and **opera** performances. Events can be **booked** through the venue or the Ticketek office in the Regent Theatre in The Octagon (☎03/477 8597, ⓦpremier.ticketek.co.nz; Mon–Fri 8.30am–5pm, Sat 10.30am–1pm).

Regular concerts are given by the New Zealand Symphony Orchestra, the Dunedin Sinfonia (a semi-professional orchestra), and chamber music groups at the Town Hall, or the Glenroy Auditorium at the Dunedin Centre (☎03/474 3614). The Dunedin Opera Company stages two or three productions a year at the Mayfair Theatre, 100 King Edward St (☎03/455 3186), and public recitals are held by the music department of the University of Otago (check with the i-SITE).

Cinemas

Hoyts Octagon 33 The Octagon ☎03/477 3250. Mainstream multiplex.

Metropolis Cinema Town Hall, Moray Place ☎03/471 9635, ⓦwww.nzcinema.co.nz. With only 56 seats this is one of the smallest public cinemas in New Zealand, and a delightful place to watch arthouse movies. Popcorn is out, but you're welcome to take your coffee in with you. Book ahead.

Rialto 11 Moray Place ☎03/474 2200. Good for mainstream movies.

Theatres

Allen Hall Clyde St ☎03/479 8896. Campus theatre that showcases the talents of the university's drama school. Shows are often of an alternative bent and don't cost much.

Fortune Theatre 231 Stuart St ☎03/477 8323, ⓦwww.fortunetheatre.co.nz. Converted from a neo-Gothic church, the Fortune divides its

programme between new works by Kiwi playwrights, fringe theatre, popular Broadway-style plays and occasional musicals. Tickets around $30; closed Jan.

Globe 104 London St ☎03/477 3274, ⓦwww.globetheatre.org.nz. This small and intimate venue features contemporary plays, classical drama and experimental works.

Regent 17 The Octagon ☎03/477 6481, ⓦwww.regenttheatre.co.nz. The city's largest and most ornate theatre, hosting musicals, ballets, touring plays and performances by popular singers, comedians and groups.

Festivals

Dunedin Summer Festival All manner of local events, including a trolley derby, street races and the Baldwin St Gutbuster. Mid-Feb.

Fringe Festival ⓦwww.dunedinfringe.org.nz. Ten-day arts and culture festival with street performers, short films, comedy and exhibitions, generally taking place in late Sept and early Oct every even year.

New Zealand International Film Festival, Dunedin ⓦ www.enzedff.co.nz. The usual mix of oddball and pre-release mainstream movies. Late July to early Aug.

Otago Festival of the Arts ⓦ www.otagofestival .co.nz. The Fringe Festival's high-end equivalent, held concurrently (late Sept to early Oct).

Rhododendron Festival ⓦ www.rhododunedin .co.nz. Four-day celebration of Dunedin's myriad blooms, when the city's parks explode with colour and private gardens open to the public. End Oct.

Scottish Week Daily concerts, pipe bands, Highland dancing in celebration of the city's cultural roots in late Sept.

Listings

Banks and foreign exchange The major banks are clustered on George and Princes sts, all with ATMs. On Saturday morning try the ANZ, corner of George & Hanover sts, which is open to 2pm.

Bike rental There's a handy cluster of bike shops around the junction of Lower Stuart & Cumberland sts; try The Cycle Surgery, 67 Stuart St (☎03/477 7473, ⓦ www.cyclesurgery.co.nz), which does repairs, rents bikes from $20/half-day ($5 extra with panniers), and can help organize self-guided trips on the Otago Central Rail Trail, including accommodation.

Bookshops University Bookshop, 378 Great King St, opposite the Otago Museum (Mon–Fri 8.30am–5.30pm, Sat 9.30am–3pm, Sun 11am–3pm; ☎03/477 6976, ⓦ www.unibooks.co.nz), is a comprehensive independent bookshop on two floors – bargains upstairs.

Buses Dunedin is a regional hub for bus services. Atomic Shuttles (ⓦ www.atomictravel.co.nz) operate Dunedin–Christchurch, Dunedin–Queenstown–Wanaka, Dunedin–Invercargill and Invercargill–Queenstown; InterCity/Newmans (ⓦ www .intercitycoach.co.nz) operate Dunedin–Alexandra–Cromwell–Queenstown, Dunedin–Oamaru–Timaru–Christchurch, Dunedin–Gore–Invercargill, and Invercargill–Gore–Te Anau; and Wanaka Connexions (ⓦ www.wanakaconnexions.co.nz) run Dunedin–Alexandra–Cromwell–Wanaka/Queenstown and Invercargill–Lumsden–Queenstown–Wanaka. NakedBus (ⓦ www.nakedbus.com) links Dunedin and Invercargill.

Camping and outdoor equipment R & R Sport, 70 Lower Stuart St (☎03/474 1211), has the biggest range of camping, skiing, cycling and general sporting equipment. Bivouac, 171 George St (☎03/477 3679), has tramping, mountaineering, skiing and kayaking gear for rent and for sale.

Car rental As well as all the international and nationwide car rental agencies there are good local companies such as Rhodes, 124 St Andrew St (☎03/477 9950, ⓦ www.rhodesrentals.co.nz) and Ace Rentals (☎03/477 5844).

Internet access Widespread cafés and access in the library (below).

Library Dunedin Public Library, corner of John & Stewart sts (Mon–Fri 9.30am–8pm, Sat & Sun 11am–4pm; ☎03/474 3690), has excellent facilities, newspapers and slow but free internet access.

Medical treatment Dunedin Hospital, 201 Great King St (☎03/474 0999). After-hours doctors are available at 95 Hanover St (☎03/479 2900).

Pharmacy After-hours service at Urgent Pharmacy, 95 Hanover St (Mon–Fri 6–10pm, Sat & Sun 10am–10pm; ☎03/477 6344).

Post office The branches at 243 Princes St and 233 Moray Place are most convenient. The former holds poste restante (☎03/477 3517).

Taxis The handiest taxi ranks are in The Octagon, between George & Stuart sts, or call United (☎0800/829 411), which also has wheelchair-accessible taxis.

Travel agents Brooker United Travel, 346 George St ☎03/477 3383; STA, 207 George St ☎03/474 0146 & 0508/782 872.

Around Dunedin

Scenic day-trips from Dunedin include a foray into the hill country aboard the **Taieri Gorge Railway**, a trip to the tourist shops of **Port Chalmers**, or a visit to the impressive **Orokonui Ecosanctuary**, for a walk among regenerating bush and chance to spy rare native birds. Set more time aside for the **Otago Peninsula**, where you can get incredibly close to the wildlife either on foot, by bus, boat or kayak.

Taieri Gorge Railway

The **Taieri Gorge Railway** (services daily; ☎03/477 4449, ⓦ www.taieri.co.nz) stretches 77km northwest from Dunedin through rugged mountains. Constructed between 1879 and 1921, the line once carried supplies the 235km from Dunedin to the old gold town of Cromwell, returning with farm produce, fruit and livestock bound for the port. Commercial traffic stopped in 1990, and much of the route was turned into the Otago Central Rail Trail (see box, p.721), but the most dramatic section – through the schist strata of the Taieri Gorge – continues to offer a rewarding journey at any time of year.

The air-conditioned train is made up of a mix of modern steel carriages with large panoramic windows and nostalgic, refurbished 1920s wooden cars. Storage is available for backpacks and bicycles, and there's a licensed snack bar on board.

The most frequent trip is known as the Taieri Gorge Limited (4hr return; $51 one-way, $76 return), which runs to **Pukerangi** – a peaceful spot 58km from the city near the highest point of the track (250m). Less frequently, the train continues a further 19km to the old gold town of **Middlemarch** (2hr 30min one-way, 6hr return – trains stop for 1hr at Middlemarch; $58 one-way, $87 return) in the fertile Strath Taieri Plains.

Apart from these day-trips, the Railway makes an excellent way to start your journey inland towards Wanaka and Queenstown. The Track and Trail bus service meets the train at Pukerangi or Middlemarch and heads through the Maniototo (see p.722) to Queenstown ($115): book through the Taieri Gorge Railway.

Cyclists can ride the train (bikes go free) then hop straight onto the Otago Central Rail Trail. If you don't have your own bike, look into the Rail-Trail-specific deals offered by Dunedin's bike rental companies (see "Listings", p.589).

A completely different but equally picturesque rail journey leaves Dunedin Railway Station and runs along the main northbound line 66km up the coast to Palmerston: the **Seasider** (Oct–March some Wed & Sun at 9.30am; $48 one-way; $72 return), which takes four hours for the round trip.

Port Chalmers

About 12km northeast of Dunedin along the winding western shore of Otago Harbour is **PORT CHALMERS**, a small historic town arranged around a container port and cruise-ship berth. Famous for its artistic community, headed by celebrated New Zealand painter and sculptor **Ralph Hotere**, which kick-started the renovation of many of the fine nineteenth-century buildings, the town's pretty high street mostly offers expensive trinkets for cruise-ship passengers.

Chosen in 1844 as the port to serve the proposed Scottish settlement that would become Dunedin, Port Chalmers became the embarkation point for several **Antarctic expeditions**, including those of Captain Scott, who set out from here in 1901 and again for his ill-fated attempt on the pole in 1910. The first trial shipment of **frozen meat** to Britain was sent from Port Chalmers in 1882 and today the export of wool, meat and timber and reception of cruise ships is its chief business.

The Town

Container cranes loom over Port Chalmers, which occupies the hills on either side of **George Street**, a short descent to the port. Two late-Victorian churches vie for attention with the cranes: the elegant stone-spired Presbyterian **Iona Church** on Mount Street, and the nuggety bluestone Anglican **Holy Trinity**, on Scotia Street, designed by Robert A. Lawson.

George Street meets the port at its junction with Beach Street, where you'll find the small **museum** (Mon–Fri 9am–3pm, Sat 11am–2pm, Sun 1.30–4.30pm; gold coin donation) in an 1877 former post office. Brimming with maritime artefacts, models and local settler history, museum highlights include a display of navigational equipment and a working electric model of a **gold dredge**, built in 1900 by an apprentice boilermaker, who along with his brothers installed the first electric power system in the region, after a few shocks.

A further 12km north lies the small settlement of **Aramoana**, on a sand dune spit at the mouth of Otago Harbour, with wild, often deserted **beaches**.

Practicalities

By **car** from Dunedin, it's a ten-minute harbourside drive along SH88, or you can take the longer scenic route, following Mount Cargill and Upper Junction roads. From the north on SH1, take the road to Port Chalmers from Waitati. **Buses** from Dunedin to Port Chalmers leave from Stand 4 opposite the Countdown supermarket in Cumberland Street, dropping you off in George Street about 25 minutes later (sporadic service on Sun).

The **Port Chalmers Library**, 20 Beach St, carries information on the port's more historically significant buildings and local walks, the best being the **coastal walk** (4km; 1hr; mostly flat), which offers great views of the harbour and Otago Peninsula beyond.

Most people just make a day-trip from Dunedin, but you can **stay** at the isolated, quirkily designed ❂ *Billy Brown's*, 423 Aramoana Rd, Hamilton Bay, 5.5km north of Port Chalmers (☎03/472 8323, ⓦwww.billybrowns.co.nz; shares $27, rooms ❷), which has stunning views – it sleeps just eight, so book ahead.

For **eating** try local favourite, the licensed *Port Royal Cafe*, 10 George St, offering freshly baked pastries, great breakfasts and lunches; it's soon to venture into the dinner market (Thurs–Sun). Alternatively, you'll find scenic picnic spots dotted along Peninsula Beach Road, just around from the harbour. **Drinking** is best done in *Chicks* (see p.588) or 1km out of town at the 1876-built bluestone *Carey's Bay Historic Hotel*.

Orokonui Ecosanctuary

Modelled on the Karori Sanctuary in Wellington (see p.413) and situated in the hills about 3.5km behind Port Chalmers and 20km from Dunedin, the **Orokonui Ecosanctuary** on Blueskin Road near the junction with Mopanui Road (daily: summer 9.30am–4.30pm; winter 10am–3.30pm; self-guided $15, guided 90min tour $38; ☎03/482 1755, ⓦwww.orokonui.org.nz), is a recent and welcome addition to the pantheon of wildlife activities within easy reach of Dunedin. The eco-friendly purpose-built visitor centre is packed with info while the café offers wonderful views of the valley but the real treats are just the other side of the 8.7km predator-exclusion fence, protecting 2.3 square kilometres of regenerating bush, some over a century old, containing re-introduced native birds, tuatara and skinks. Among the birds you are likely to encounter are tomtit, South Island riflemen, grey warbler, brown creeper, saddleback, bellbird, tui, fantail and kaka. Although a number of organized bus tours now visit, no public buses yet ply the route. If you have your own transport it is less than thirty minutes from the city centre.

The Otago Peninsula

A 35km-long crooked finger of land running northeast from Dunedin, the **OTAGO PENINSULA** divides Otago Harbour from the Pacific Ocean. With sweeping views of the harbour, the sea and Dunedin against its dramatic backdrop of hills the peninsula offers outstanding **marine wildlife viewing** unsurpassed on the South Island.

The narrow and twisting (but smooth) harbourside road – Portobello Road and later Harington Point Road – from the city to the tip at Taiaroa Head takes less than an hour, passing a few places to stay and eat (see p.597) and stringing together most of the sights.

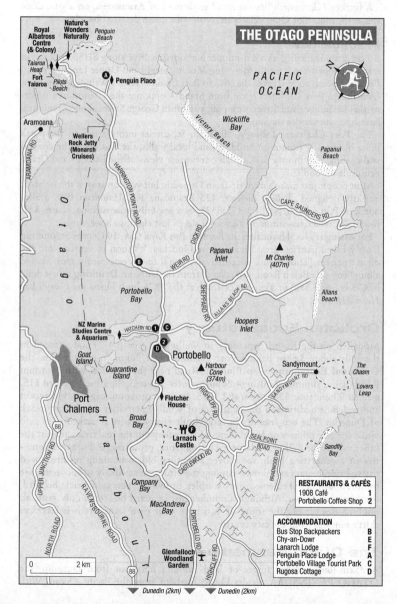

THE OTAGO PENINSULA

PACIFIC OCEAN

Royal Albatross Centre (& Colony)
Nature's Wonders Naturally
Penguin Beach
Taiaroa Head
Fort Taiaroa
Pilots Beach
A Penguin Place
Aramoana
Wellers Rock Jetty (Monarch Cruises)
ARAMOANA RD
HARINGTON POINT ROAD
Victory Beach
Wickliffe Bay
Papanui Beach
Otago
DICK RD
WEIR RD
CAPE SAUNDERS RD
B
Papanui Inlet
Mt Charles (407m)
Portobello Bay
SHEPPARD RD
ALLANS BEACH RD
Allans Beach
NZ Marine Studies Centre & Aquarium
HATCHERY RD **C**
1
2
D Portobello
Hoopers Inlet
Goat Island
Quarantine Island
Harbour Cone (374m)
Sandymount
The Chasm
Lovers Leap
E
Port Chalmers
Fletcher House
SANDYMOUNT RD
Broad Bay
HIGHCLIFF RD
Larnach Castle **F**
SEAL POINT ROAD
Sandfly Bay
88
Company Bay
CASTLEWOOD RD
BRAADWOOD RD
UPPER JUNCTION RD
RAVENSBOURNE ROAD
MacAndrew Bay
Harbour
PORTOBELLO RD
NORTH ROAD
Glenfalloch Woodland Garden
HIGHCLIFF RD
88
0   2 km

RESTAURANTS & CAFÉS
1908 Café   **1**
Portobello Coffee Shop   **2**

ACCOMMODATION
Bus Stop Backpackers   **B**
Chy-an-Dowr   **E**
Lanarch Lodge   **F**
Penguin Place Lodge   **A**
Portobello Village Tourist Park   **C**
Rugosa Cottage   **D**

▼ Dunedin (2km) ▼   ▼ Dunedin (2km)

The chief reason for visiting the peninsula is the intriguing variety and abundance of **marine wildlife** that is drawn to its shores year round. At its tip is **Taiaroa Head**, a protected area where several colonies of sea mammals and sea birds congregate. Unique among these is the majestic **royal albatross**, which breeds here in what is the only mainland albatross colony in the world. Also concentrated on the headland's shores are **penguins** (the little blue and the rare yellow-eyed) and **southern fur seals**, while the cliffs are home to other sea birds including three species of **shag**, **muttonbirds** (sooty shearwaters) and various species of gull. The peninsula's other beaches and inlets play host to a great variety of waders and waterfowl and, occasionally, New Zealand **sea lions**, while offshore, orca and other **whales** can be seen.

The best of the sights on the way to Taiaroa Head is the excellent **Marine Studies Centre & Aquarium**, though also worth a look are the woodland gardens and walks of **Glenfalloch**, renowned for their rhododendrons, azaleas and camellias; **Larnach Castle**, New Zealand's only castle, also set in flourishing gardens; and **Fletcher House**, a delightfully restored small Edwardian villa. A number of **scenic walks** cross both public and private land to spectacular views and unusual land formations created by lava flows.

With your own transport, access to the peninsula from Dunedin is easy, either via **Portobello Road**, which snakes along the western shoreline, or the inland **Highcliff Road**, which winds up and over the hills. Dunedin visitor centre supplies the free *Visitor's Guide to the Otago Peninsula*. The public Peninsula **bus** (3–9 daily; $6.30) from Stand 5 on Cumberland Street in Dunedin runs halfway along the peninsula, as far as Portobello (35min), from where it's another 14km to Taiaroa Head. On weekdays a couple of services continue to Harrington Point, within 2km of Taiaroa Head.

The road to Portobello

Around the head of Otago Harbour, **Portobello Road** shakes off Dunedin's southern suburbs and begins to weave its way along the harbour shoreline past little bays, many dotted with stilt-mounted boathouses.

Exploring the peninsula: cruises, tours and kayaking

Even if you have your own wheels there's a lot to be said for exploring the Otago Peninsula on an informative guided tour.

Elm Wildlife Tours ☏0800/356 563, ⓦwww.elmwildlifetours.co.nz. Ecologically minded guided bus tours (usually 5–6hr; $89) visit the Albatross Centre. Trips can include an Albatross Centre tour ($129), an hour-long Monarch Cruise ($134), or kayaking ($184).

Monarch Wildlife Cruises & Tours Wharf St, Dunedin ☏03/477 4276 & 0800/666 272, ⓦwww.wildlife.co.nz. A converted fishing boat with licensed galley is put to good use running one-hour cruises ($45) from the Wellers Rock jetty. These are worthwhile if you're driving out along the peninsula but it's worth considering the Peninsula Cruise (9am & 3.30pm; $85), which leaves from the wharf in Dunedin, cruises around Taiaroa Head then drops you at Wellers Rock (where you can visit the penguins or albatrosses; $45 extra) then returns to Dunedin by bus.

Wild Earth Adventures ☏03/473 6535, ⓦwww.wildearth.co.nz. For a different, often magical, perspective on the coast and its wildlife, take a sea-kayaking tour with this Dunedin-based company. The four-hour trips ($95) go around Taiaroa Head, spending around two hours on the water. Among the other trips a particular favourite is the Twilight Tour (2hr paddling; $95), with wildlife, quiet and the lights of Dunedin in the background.

Eleven kilometres from Dunedin, the peaceful **Glenfalloch Woodland Garden**, 430 Portobello Rd (daily dawn–dusk; $5; ☎03/476 1775; ⓦwww.albatross.org .nz/garden.htm), contains 1.2 square kilometres of mature garden and bush, surrounding a homestead built in 1871. Between mid-September and mid-October the garden is ablaze with rhododendrons, azaleas and camellias; you'll also find magnolias, fuchsias and roses. Near the entrance, a licensed café (generally daily 10am–5pm & evenings Thurs–Sat) serves excellent food.

Around 3km further on at **Company Bay**, Castlewood Road runs 4km inland to Larnach Castle (see below), while Portobello Road sticks to the coast past Broad Bay to **The Fletcher House**, 727 Portobello Rd (Christmas to Easter daily 11am–4pm; Easter to Christmas Sat & Sun 11am–4pm; $4; ☎03/478 0180), a small Edwardian villa lovingly restored to its original state. Built entirely of native wood, with rimu ceilings and floors, in 1909, it was the family home of the Broad Bay storekeeper.

Next up is the village of **Portobello**, 17km from Dunedin. From here, Hatchery Road leads 2km along a headland to the **NZ Marine Studies Centre & Aquarium** (daily 10am–4.30pm; $12; ☎03/479 5826, ⓦwww.marine.ac.nz), a great spot that can easily take up half a day. This is a working marine laboratory (run by the University of Otago), but although staff are round to answer your questions you're better off on the **tour** (daily 10.30am; $21 including admission), which often stretches beyond the allotted hour. The tour includes history, fish watching and sticking your hands in "touch tanks" to feel the small sea creatures and, if you keep exploring after the tour, participating in the **fish feeding** (Wed & Sat 2–3pm).

Larnach Castle

The nineteenth-century Gothic Revival **Larnach Castle** (daily 9am–5pm, last entry; grounds only $12.50, grounds & castle $25; ⓦwww.larnachcastle.co.nz) sits high on a hill commanding great views across the harbour to Dunedin. More chateau than castle, it was the sumptuous residence of Australian-born banker, politician and importer William Larnach. Designed by Robert A. Lawson and finished in 1871, materials were shipped from all over the world then punted across the harbour and dragged uphill by ox-drawn sleds. Its outer shell took three years to complete, with the ornate interior taking another nine.

After years of neglect the castle was rescued by the Barker family in the late 1960s and has since been progressively restored while remaining their home. Check out the concealed spiral staircase in the corner of the third floor, which leads up to a terraced turret.

The castle's manicured **grounds**, divided into nine gardens are of national significance and quite beautiful; keep an eye out for the handful of *Alice in Wonderland* statues, such as one of the Cheshire cat hiding in an ancient Atlas cedar tree.

Walks on Otago Peninsula

The *Otago Peninsula Tracks* leaflet (free from the Dunedin i-SITE or DOC office) briefly describes several walks on the peninsula. Bear in mind that they cover hill country and that though most tracks are well defined, some are pretty steep. Also, the weather here can turn cold or wet very quickly, even on the sunniest days.

One of the most accessible walks is the easy loop track to **Lovers Leap and the Chasm** (3km; 1hr; closed Aug–Oct), which crosses farmland to sheer cliffs dropping 200m to the sea, where you'll see collapsed sea caves and rock faces of layered volcanic lava flows.

The track begins from the end of Sandymount Road, a 25-minute drive from the centre of Dunedin.

Unless you have your own transport (or are on a tour), you'll have to take the Peninsula **bus** either to Company Bay, from where it's a 5km (signposted) walk, uphill all the way, or to Broad Bay and an even steeper walk (2km). Once here, you can stop at the café in the former ballroom, or **stay** overnight (see p.597).

Around Taiaroa Head

The peninsula's marine wildlife is mostly concentrated 10km east of Portobello around **Taiaroa Head**, 33km from Dunedin, where cold waters forced up by the continental shelf provide a rich and constant food source. Other than taking a tour, the best opportunities for seeing animals are on the beaches and inlets on either side of the headland. Southern fur seals can be seen at **Pilots Beach**, on the western side (follow the main road to the shore as it snakes past the Royal Albatross Centre) and from the **clifftops** on the eastern side of the headland. Pilots Beach is also home to a small colony of little blue penguins, which are best visited around dusk. A short signposted walk from the Royal Albatross Centre car park to a **cliff-edge viewing area** unfolds spectacular scenes of a spotted shag colony, while royal albatross in flight can be spied all year round from anywhere on the headland.

When **observing wildlife**, respect the animals by staying well away from them (at least 5m), and keeping quiet and still. **Penguins** are especially frightened by people and they may be reluctant to come ashore (even if they have chicks to feed) if you are on or near the beach and visible. In summer, keep to the track as they're extremely vulnerable to stress while nesting and moulting. Never get between a **seal** or **sea lion** and the sea; these animals can be aggressive and move quickly.

The yellow-eyed penguin

Found only in southern New Zealand, the endangered **yellow-eyed penguin**, or *hoiho*, is considered the most ancient of all living penguins, but today numbers only around four thousand. It evolved in forests free of predators, but human disturbance, loss of habitat and the introduction of ferrets, stoats and cats have had a devastating effect. The small mainland population of just a few hundred occupies nesting areas dotted along the wild southeast coast of the South Island (from Oamaru to the Catlins), while other smaller colonies inhabit the coastal forest margins of Stewart Island and offshore islets, and New Zealand's sub-Antarctic islands of Auckland and Campbell.

Male and female adults are identical in colouring, with pink webbed feet and a bright yellow band that encircles the head, sweeping over their pale yellow eyes. Standing around 65cm high and weighing 5–6kg, they have a **life expectancy** of up to twenty years. Their **diet** consists of squid and small fish, and hunting takes them up to 40km offshore and to depths of 100m.

Maori named the bird **hoiho**, meaning "the noise shouter", because of the distinctive high-pitched calls (an exuberant trilling) it makes at night when greeting its mate at the nest. Unlike other penguins, the yellow-eyed does not migrate after its first year, but stays near its home beach, making daily fishing trips and returning as daylight fails.

The penguins' **breeding season** lasts for 28 weeks, from mid-August to early March. Eggs are laid between mid-September and mid-October, and both parents share incubation duties for about 43 days. The eggs hatch in November and for the next six weeks the chicks are constantly guarded against predators. By the time the down-covered chicks are six or seven weeks old, their rapid growth gives them voracious appetites and both parents must fish daily to satisfy them. The fledglings enter the sea for the first time in late February or early March and journey up to 500km north to winter feeding grounds. Fewer than fifteen percent of fledged chicks reach breeding age, but those that do return to the colony of their birth.

The Penguin Place

For the rare privilege of entering a protected nesting area of around seventy yellow-eyed penguins, get along to the **Penguin Place**, Harington Point Road, an award-winning penguin-conservation project about 3km south of Taiaroa Head. Carefully controlled and informative tours (Oct to early April 10.15am–dusk; early April to Sept 3.15–4.45pm; 90min; up to every 30min; $40; bookings essential on ⊕ 03/478 0286, ⓦ www.penguin-place.co.nz) begin with a talk about penguins and their conservation, then a guide takes you to the beachside colony, where well-camouflaged trenches lead to several hides among the dunes. These allow extraordinary proximity to the penguins and excellent photo opportunities. Proceeds from the tours are used to fund the conservation work and unit that looks after injured penguins. You can **stay** overnight in budget accommodation on the farm (see opposite).

The Royal Albatross Centre and Historic Fort Taiaroa

The gateway to the only mainland colony of albatrosses in the world, the revamped **Royal Albatross Centre** (daily: 24 Nov–April 8.30am–8pm; May–23 Nov 9am–5.30pm; free; ⓦ www.albatross.org.nz) contains galleries with interesting displays on local wildlife and history and a café. You can buy tickets here for the centre's excellent **Royal Albatross Tour** (1hr; 24 Nov–16 Sept $40; 17 Sept–23 Nov closed for breeding season; booking essential Dec–Feb and recommended at any time on ⊕ 03/478 0499) which includes an introductory film and time to view the birds from an enclosed area in the reserve (binoculars provided), where there is also a closed circuit TV of the far side of the colony. The **best months** for viewing are generally January and February, when the chicks hatch, and April to August, when parent birds feed their chicks. By September the chicks and adults are ready to depart and new breeding pairs start to arrive.

The Centre is also the starting point for visits to the **Historic Fort Taiaroa**, a warren of tunnels and gun emplacements originally built in 1885 when an attack from Tsarist Russia was feared, and rearmed during World War II. The main attraction is the restored Disappearing Gun (operated by hydraulics), visited on either the basic thirty-minute tour (all year; $20) or the Unique Taiaroa Tour (24 Nov–16 Sept; 90min; $45), which combines with the Royal Albatross Tour.

The royal albatross

The majestic **albatross**, one of the world's largest sea birds, has long been the subject of reverence and superstition: the embodiment of a dead sea captain's soul, condemned to drift the oceans forever. A solitary creature, the albatross spends most of its life on the wing or at sea.

Second only in size to the wandering albatross, the mighty **royal albatross** has a wingspan of up to 3m. They can travel 190,000km a year at speeds of 120kph, and have a life expectancy of 45 years. The albatross mates for life, but male and female separate to fly in opposite directions around the world, returning to the same breeding grounds once every two years, and arriving within a couple of days of one another. The female lays one egg (weighing up to 500g) per breeding season, and the parents both incubate it over a period of eleven weeks.

Once the chick has hatched, the parents take turns feeding it and guarding it against stoats, ferrets, wild cats and rats. Almost a year from the start of the breeding cycle, the fledgling takes flight and the parents leave the colony and return to sea only to start the cycle again a year later.

The road beyond the albatross colony continues through the car park a further 1.5km to **Nature's Wonders Naturally** (T0800/246 446, Wwww.natures wondersnaturally.com), which offers personalized adventure conservation tours around the head on specially constructed tracks, incongruously in 8WD amphibious vehicles. The lively trips (daily; 1hr; $50) take in penguin-viewing areas, New Zealand fur seals, sea lions and old World War II relics.

Peninsula accommodation and eating

There's plenty of **accommodation** on the peninsula but good **eating** is harder to find. Portobello has a coffee shop and small supermarket and most of the main attractions have cafés, the best of which is Glenfalloch (see p.593).

Accommodation

Bus Stop Backpackers 252 Harington Point Rd, 3km north of Portobello. T03/478 0330, E backpacker@slingshot.co.nz. Accommodation in a retro-style beach house, caravan or old bus, no dorms but singles, doubles and twins. If no one's about, just let yourself in and claim a bed. Rents bikes ($20/day). Single $35, double ❷

Chy-an-Dowr 687 Portobello Rd, Broad Bay T03/478 0306, Wwww.chy-an-dowr.co.nz. Sitting on the harbourfront, this big, timber, two-storey property dates from 1905, and has three lovely doubles (one en suite, two with separate but private bath), Wi-fi available. ❼

Larnach Lodge Larnach Castle T03/476 1616, Wwww.larnachcastle.co.nz. Cosy up in the converted stables, containing six shared-bathrooms, or in the individually decorated, grander accommodation in the *Lodge*. All overnight guests get free castle admission and breakfast; you can also book a three-course dinner in the castle's dining room ($54.50/head plus wine). Stables ❺, lodge ❽

Penguin Place Lodge Harington Point Rd T03/478 0286, Wwww.penguin-place.co.nz. Simple, comfy backpackers with harbour views from many of the doubles and twins. $25/person, linen rental $5. ❶

Portobello Village Tourist Park 27 Hereweka St, Portobello T03/478 0359, E portobellopark@xtra .co.nz. Well-managed campsite with a range of accommodation and good facilities including a guest kitchen and laundry. Camping $16, budget rooms ❶, new s/c rooms ❸ and cabins ❸

Rugosa Cottage 1 Beconsfield Rd, Portobello T03/478 1076. Romantic cottage surrounded by gorgeous gardens. The Rose Room is a queen-size en suite, and the equally appealing Seafarers Cottage has a large en suite and a private garden. ❺/❻

Eating

1908 Café 7 Harington Point Rd, Portobello T03/478 0801. Elegantly set in a 1908 house with an intimate interior and outdoor seating this restaurant offers twists on traditional New Zealand mains, like lamb shank in maple syrup with orange juice. Open nightly plus weekend lunches.

The Portobello Coffee Shop 1726 High Cliff Rd, Portobello. Newish café with excellent coffee, counter food, breakfasts and lunches, including a delicious smoked fish, broccoli and creamy sauce pie. Mon–Fri 8am–5pm, Sat & Sun 9am–5pm, dinners Jan–March until 8.30pm.

South from Dunedin: Balclutha and the Catlins Coast

The rugged coastal route linking Dunedin and Invercargill is one of the less-travelled highways on the South Island, traversing some of the country's wildest scenery along the **Catlins Coast**. It is part of the **Southern Scenic Route** (Wwww.southernscenicroute.co.nz), which continues on to Te Anau in Fiordland.

The region is home to vast tracts of native forest, most protected as the **Catlins State Forest Park**, consisting of rimu, rata, kamahi and silver beech. Roaring southeasterlies and the remorseless sea have shaped the coastline into plunging cliffs, windswept headlands, white-sand beaches, rocky bays and gaping caves, many of

The **western continuation** of the **Southern Scenic Route**, from Invercargill to Te Anau via Tuatapere, is covered in the Fiordland chapter, p.753.

⑪

which are accessible. **Wildlife** abounds, including several rare species of marine bird and mammal, and the whole region rings with birdsong most of the year.

The region, one of the last refuges of the flightless moa, was a thriving hunting ground for **Maori** but by 1700 they had moved on, to be supplanted by European **whalers and sealers** in the 1830s. Two decades later, having decimated marine mammal stocks, they too departed. Meanwhile, in 1840, Captain Edward Cattlin arrived to investigate the navigability of the river that bears his (misspelt) name, purchasing a tract of land from the chief of the Ngai Tahu. Boatloads of **loggers** soon followed, lured by the great podocarp forests. Cleared valleys were settled and bush millers supplied Dunedin with much of the wood needed for housing – in 1872 more timber was exported from the Catlins than anywhere else in New Zealand. From 1879 the rail line from Balclutha began to extend into the region, bringing sawmills, schools and farms with it. Milling continued into the 1930s, but gradually dwindled and today's tiny settlements are shrunken remnants of the once-prosperous logging industry.

The only stopoff point of any size between Dunedin and the Catlins Coast is **Balclutha**, a good place to stock up before entering the relative wilderness beyond. At Balclutha, SH1 turns inland, skirting the Catlins region before turning south to Invercargill at the town of **Gore**, a centre for brown-trout fishing. Alternatively, SH92, a 126km stretch of road closer to the coast is now sealed all the way, though virtually all the Catlin's attractions are on gravel roads. Without your own transport, visit on one of several **guided tours** (see p.600).

Balclutha

The farming service town of **Balclutha**, 80km southwest of Dunedin on SH1, is cleaved in two by the **Clutha River**. There's little reason to stop longer than it takes to buy petrol and provisions and glean information on the Catlins or the approaches to Dunedin from the helpful **Clutha i-SITE visitor centre**, 4 Clyde St (roughly Nov–March Mon–Fri 8.30am–5pm, Sat & Sun 9.30am–3pm; April–Oct Mon–Fri 8.30am–5pm, Sat & Sun 10am–2pm; ☏03/418 0388, ⊛www .cluthacountry.co.nz), which has **internet access**. **Buses** stop right outside and almost everything else is within a couple of blocks along Clyde Street.

The Catlins Coast

The best way to enjoy the **Catlins Coast** is to invest at least a couple of days. From Nugget Point in South Otago (just southeast of Balclutha) to Waipapa Point in Southland (60km northeast of Invercargill), the wild scenery stretches unbroken, dense rainforest succumbing to open scrub as you cut through deep valleys and past rocky bays, inlets and estuaries. The coast is home to **penguins** (both little blue and yellow-eyed), **dolphins**, several types of sea bird and, at certain times of year, migrating **whales**. Elephant **seals**, fur seals, and increasingly, the rare New Zealand **sea lion** are found on the sandy beaches and grassy areas, and **birds** – tui, resonant bellbirds, fantails, grey warblers and colourful tree-top dwellers such as kakariki and mohua – are abundant in the mossy depths of the forest.

Outside the main settlement of Owaka you'll find a smattering of places to stay but very few places to eat or stock up. Dining and accommodation etablishments pop up and sink with monotonous regularity, so check whether they're still operating directly, or in the visitor centres. In addition to Owaka, there are

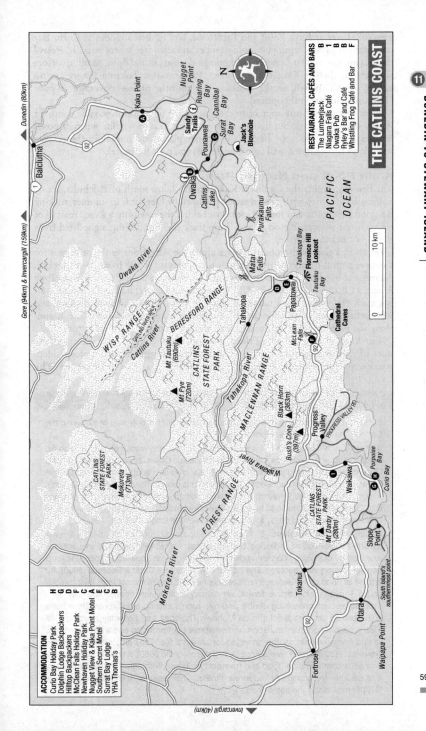

Dunedin (80km) ▲

Gore (94km) & Invercargill (159km) ▲

ACCOMMODATION
Curio Bay Holiday Park   H
Dolphin Lodge Backpackers   G
Hilltop Backpackers   D
McLean Falls Holiday Park   F
Newhaven Holiday Park   C
Nugget View & Kaka Point Motel A
Southern Secret Motel   E
Surat Bay Lodge   C
YHA Thomas's   B

RESTAURANTS, CAFÉS AND BARS
The Lumberjack   B
Niagara Falls Café   1
Owaka Pub   B
Ryley's Bar and Café   B
Whistling Frog Café and Bar F

THE CATLINS COAST

PACIFIC OCEAN

0   10 km

Invercargill (40km) ▼

general stores at Kaka Point and Papatowai, and limited supplies at Curio Bay campsite – it pays to bring your own supplies and self-cater where possible. **Petrol** stations are few and far between, and pumps close at around 5pm, so fill up before you set off, then at Kaka Point, Owaka, Papatowai or Tokanui. There are **no banks or ATMs** within the Catlins, and **mobile phone coverage** is poor (Telecom being the only option).

Those in **campervans** appreciate the abundance of peaceful wayside spots for sneaky overnight stays, but human waste poses a threat to wildlife when disposed of irresponsibly. Do your business in proper places and hopefully the relaxed attitude to free camping will continue (see Basics, p.38 for more).

Kaka Point and Nugget Point

The first stop inside the Catlins is **Kaka Point**, 22km south of Balclutha, a tiny holiday community with golden sands, patrolled by lifeguards in summer, making it a good swimming and surfing spot. Just behind the township a scenic reserve of native forest is accessible on an easy loop track (2.5km; 30min; signposted from the top of Marine Terrace).

The Point, a glass-and-wood landmark along the waterfront, is the only spot for a coffee, a meal or beer; enter through the courtyard if the front door's locked. Among the handful of places to **stay** is the comfortable *Nugget View & Kaka Point Motels*, 11 Rata St (℡0800/525 278, ⓦwww.catlins.co.nz; budget ❸, standard ❺, spa units ❻), which has a range of spacious units, almost all with decking and wonderful ocean views. The owner also offers intimate tours ($30; 2hr 30min) along the point to see penguins and seals and get a taste of the local history.

Nine kilometres south along the coast from Kaka Point, a car park marks the start of a fifteen-minute track to the dramatic **Nugget Point**, a steep-sided, windswept promontory rising 133m above the sea. Just offshore lie **The**

Tours of the Catlins

If you don't have your own transport, **guided tours** are the only way of exploring the Catlins. The two main operators are detailed here.

Bottom Bus ℡03/4370 753, ⓦwww.bottombus.co.nz or ⓦwww.catlinscoaster.co.nz. A hop-on hop-off, small-bus tour taking in the Catlins Coast, as part of its loop around Queenstown, Dunedin, Invercargill and Te Anau, used as a supplementary trip by Kiwi Experience though it attracts less of the booze-bus crowd. The bus runs from Dunedin through the Catlins to Invercargill in summer, mostly with an overnight stop at Curio Bay. Choose from Dunedin to Invercargill (recommended 3 days; $150), Dunedin to Te Anau (recommended 3 days; $199), or one of several longer options.

Catlins Wildlife Trackers 5 Mirren St, Papatowai ℡0800/228 5467, ⓦwww.catlins-ecotours.co.nz; advance bookings essential. Entertaining and inspirational tours led by committed conservationists sharing in-depth knowledge about the local ecology, history and geology. The intimate two-day tour **Catlins Ecotour** ($600), for groups of up to eight, explores remote beaches and rich rainforest from their tranquil house – overlooking native forest, an estuary, beach and ocean. You stay in a separate section containing double and twin rooms sharing a bathroom. Drive there or be picked up from Balclutha on Monday, Thursday and Saturday mornings. All meals, accommodation, transport and equipment are provided and a shuttle service to and from Dunedin can be arranged for an extra fee. They also offer the **Catlins Traverse** (Nov–March Thurs & Fri; 26km, 6 people max; $650), a two-day guided trek with all accommodation, food and transport included. With only light packs to carry it is suitable for anyone of moderate fitness. Their special seven-day experience ($1500) runs along the same lines.

Nuggets, jagged stacks of rock whose layers have been tilted vertical over time. The track ends at a still-functioning 1870 lighthouse, from where you can gaze down on lively groups of honking southern fur seals. Gannets, spoonbills and three species of shag wheel overhead and nearby Roaring Bay has a hide from which you can watch **yellow-eyed penguins** (see p.595) as they leave their nests at sunrise and descend the steep grassy cliffs to the sea or as they return two hours before dark. Their progress is slow, so you need plenty of patience, and binoculars are handy.

You'll need to backtrack a few kilometres then head out to the coast again to reach the long crescent of sand known as **Cannibal Bay**, a haul-out spot for New Zealand sea lions. Stroll along the beach for a closer look, but keep at least 5m away from them and back off quickly if they rear up and roar.

Owaka and Jack's Blowhole

The only settlement of any size within the Catlins is the farming town of **OWAKA**, 18km southwest of Kaka Point. En route, it's worth a detour down the Ahuriri Flat Road to go on a **guided walk** with Sandy Trails at 716 Ahuriri Flat Rd, Otekura (1hr 30min, $35; min 2 people; ☎03/415 8474). Judy offers a variety of walks on the family farm all of which take in the fabulous opportunity to see seals, sea lions and yellow-eyed penguins away from the bus routes and other tourists.

Little more than a crossroads, Owaka now harbours the whizz-bang new **Discover Destination Catlins** complex, on the corner of Campbell and Ryley streets (Mon–Fri 9.30am–4.30pm, Sat & Sun 10am–4pm; ☎03/415 8371, ⓦwww.catlins-nz.com). The centre contains the **Owaka Library**, the well-curated new **Owaka Museum** ($5), with evocative exhibits on local history and the **visitor centre**, which dispenses useful updates on eating and sleeping options, as well as DOC information. Staff here can also advise on practicalities, including a couple of farms offering **horseriding**, plus trailhead transport for the **Catlins River Walk** (5hr one-way).

A gravel waterside drive runs 10km southeast from Owaka to Jack's Bay, from where a farmland track (20–30min each way; closed for lambing in Sept & Oct; $1 donation appreciated) leads to **Jack's Blowhole**, an impressive 55m-deep hole in the ground, which connects though a 200m tunnel to the sea. Effectively the collapsed roof of a cave, the bottom of the hole is washed by surf at high tide, though few people have ever seen it spout.

Opening hours for eating and sleeping options in the Catlins vary seasonally and from year to year; check with the visitor centre. If you decide to **stay** overnight in Owaka check out the *Newhaven Holiday Park*, 325 Newhaven Rd, Surat Bay, 5km east of Owaka (☎03/415 8834, ⓦwww.newhavenholiday.com), for a well-kept campsite and comfy tourist flats a two-minute walk from the beach and estuary (camping $26 per site, cabins ❷, flats ❸/❹). Alternatively *Surat Bay Lodge*, on Surat Bay Road, 5km east of Owaka (☎03/415 8099, ⓦwww.suratbay.co.nz; dorms $28, rooms ❷), offers backpacker beds in a peaceful spot, where the Catlins Estuary meets the beach, free pick-ups from Owaka and bike or kayak rental. Finally, *YHA Thomas's*, on the corner of Clark & Ryley streets, right in Owaka (☎03/415 8333, ⓦwww.gaanz.co.nz; camping $10, powered sites $15, dorms $28, rooms ❷), has beds in an atmospheric rambling early 1900s building, including en-suite rooms, two TV lounges and a well-equipped self-catering kitchen.

For **eating** you can do worse than the great-value pub grub at *Ryley's Bar & Café* at the *Catlins Inn*, 21 Ryley St (year-round; daily but meals usually only Thurs–Sat). More upmarket, though still good value, is the food at the licensed *The Lumberjack*, 3 Saunders St (☎03/415 8747; mains around $20).

Southwest to Papatowai

A couple of minor waterfalls lie to the southwest, both accessed along pleasant nature trails. The three-tiered **Purakaunui Falls** lie in a scenic reserve of silver beech and podocarp, signposted off the main road 14km from Owaka. There's a picnic area here and easy track (10min) to the viewing platform.

Five kilometres south of the Purakaunui turn-off, the pretty **Matai Falls** (20min return) are reached along an easy trail through 10m-high native fuchsia trees, easily identified by their peeling pinkish bark and, in early summer, small red-and-blue trumpet flowers.

Across the estuary of the McLennan River, the small settlement of **PAPATOWAI** offers a general store, several forest and beach walks and an excellent **eco-tour** with the Catlins Wildlife Trackers (see box, p.600), plus the start of the **Catlins Top Track** (see box below). In a cheerful old bus beside the main road, The **Lost Gypsy Gallery** (hours vary, generally closed Wed & May–Aug; free – cash only for purchases), full of machines and toys ingeniously constructed from recycled materials and old electrical components, makes a quirky stop, as does the **Lost Gypsy theatre** ($5) a logical, if that is the word, extension of the gallery concept just 15m up the hill, which is full of home-made, interactive, highly amusing, what-the-butler-saw-style displays and arcade-like games. Everything is for sale, from teabag dunkers to dancing penguins and there is now a welcome coffee stall on site.

There are a few good **places to stay** including the small and delightful ⅞ *Hilltop Backpackers*, 77 Tahakopa Valley Rd (☎03/415 8028, ⓦwww.hilltopbackpackers .co.nz; dorms $25, rooms & en suite ❷), set on a farm signposted 1km inland from Papatowai, which occupies a pair of well-kept cottages with astounding views. Bring cash as they don't accept credit cards. Back on the main road, the ⅞ *Southern Secret Motel* (☎03/415 8600, ⓔsouthernsecret@xtra.co.nz; ❸), opposite the Papatowai general store, looks like an ordinary home on the outside but has four fabulous rooms done out in Pacific colours, with mosquito-net-draped wrought iron beds and a free library of over 300 videos. The same people offer *Erehwon*, a self-contained cottage with two doubles (❻) just up the road.

Waikawa and Porpoise Bay

On the main road 2.5km southeast of Papatowai, **Florence Hill Lookout** presents a fabulous panoramic view of Tautuku Bay, a magnificent crescent of pale sand backed by extensive forest. For a closer look, call in at the **Tautuku Boardwalk** (20–30min return), with a raised walkway nature trail over some lakeside marshes.

Some 11km southeast of Papatowai a turn-off leads to **Cathedral Caves** ($5), the grandest of the fifteen or so caves that punctuate this part of the coast, though these days the privately owned road is often closed. The soaring walls, created by furious seas, can only be entered two hours either side of low tide (they may also close at certain times of the year due to sand erosion): check with local visitor centres, or look at the entrance.

The Catlins Top Track

The longest and most varied walk in the region is the **Catlins Top Track** (22km loop), which begins and ends at Papatowai and crosses sweeping beaches, farmland and privately owned bush, delivering fascinating geology, a great variety of flora and fauna, and true tranquillity. It can be walked in a day (9–10hr; $25) but is better appreciated in two days ($45 including accommodation). The track is managed by Catlins Wildlife Trackers (☎0800/228 5467, ⓦwww.catlins-ecotours.co.nz). All walkers are given an excellent booklet that details each section of the walk accompanied by a map. Bring your own food, drinking water and sleeping bag.

A kilometre or so further along the main road, Rewcastle Road runs 3km to the car park for the picturesque **McLean Falls** (30min return), reached along a rainforest walk. The most impressive of the falls hereabouts, it is best in the late afternoon when sun strikes the main cascade. Just past the turn-off from the main road to the falls is *McLean Falls Holiday Park*, 29 Rewcastle Rd (℡03/415 8338; ⓦwww.catlinsnz.com; camping $38, shares $32, cabins, rooms & cottages ❸–❺), whose on-site *Whistling Frog Café & Bar* offers breakfast, lunch and dinner for guests and non-residents.

About 20km on, off the SH92, is the licensed 🍴 *Niagara Falls Café*, the best place to eat in the Catlins, serving sophisticated home-made café fare such as veggie burgers, blue cod risotto, great breakfasts and seafood chowder (daily 9am–5pm; ℡03/246 8577) and open for dinner if they get bookings. Nearby, the fishing village of **WAIKAWA** is home to the small **Waikawa District Museum** (daily 10.30am–4.30pm; gold coin donation), with an interesting exhibition on seafarers and logging and a small case containing a bible with a bullet hole and the bullet, which penetrated the unfortunate World War I rifleman carrying it. The museum also doubles as the area's visitor centre, with material on the Hector's Dolphins (see box, p.604) which come in close to the shore at nearby **Porpoise Bay**.

Curio Bay and Slope Point

At the western end of Porpoise Bay, a headland is occupied by the *Curio Bay Holiday Park* (℡03/246 8897; camping $15 per site, powered sites $25, showers $2), a friendly year-round campsite with a tiny store, sites sheltered by flax, and wonderful views east along Porpoise Bay and west into **Curio Bay**. Hector's dolphins cavort in the surf of Porpoise Bay, while yellow-eyed penguins can be viewed (mostly at sunrise and at the end of the day) on the Curio Bay side, from the top of McColgan's Loop. As always, keep your distance from the animals.

A few hundred metres west along Curio Bay, a wave-cut platform reveals a fine **petrified forest**, its fossilised Jurassic trees clearly visible at low tide. Over 180

▲ Curio Bay

million years ago, when most of New Zealand still lay beneath the sea, this would have been a broad, forested floodplain. Today, the seashore, composed of several layers of forest buried under blankets of volcanic mud and ash, is littered with fossilized tree stumps and fallen logs.

Apart from the campsite, you can stay nearby at *Dolphin Lodge Backpackers*, 529 Curio Bay Rd (℡03/246 68 579, ⓔlodge@yahoo.co.nz; dorms $22, linen rental $3, rooms ❶), a beautifully sited hostel on the dunes from where you can watch the waves roll in. Alternatively try ⚲ *Catlins Surf Beachfront Rentals* (℡03/246 8552, ⓦwww.catlins-surf.co.nz; ❺–❼), who rent out a variety of beachfront houses at very reasonable prices. The operation is coordinated by Nick Smart who also heads up the excellent **Catlins Surf School** (packages from 90min, $50 including wetsuit and board).

From Curio Bay it's 16km along unsealed roads to **Slope Point**, where a farmland walk (40min return; closed Sept & Oct for lambing) brings you to the South Island's southernmost point. Continuing west, a ten-minute drive takes you to **Waipapa Point**, 26km beyond Curio Bay, the site of New Zealand's worst

The New Zealand sea lion and Hector's dolphin

Two extremely rare species – the New Zealand or **Hooker's sea lion** (*Phocarctos hookeri*) and **Hector's dolphin** (*Cephalarhynchus hectori*) – are found only in New Zealand waters.

Hooker's sea lions mostly live around the sub-Antarctic Auckland Islands, 460km south of the South Island, but some breeding also takes place on the Otago Peninsula, along the Catlins Coast and around Stewart Island. The large, adult male sea lions are black to dark brown, have a mane over their shoulders, weigh up to 400kg and reach lengths of over 3m. Adult females are buff to silvery grey and much smaller – less than half the weight and just under 2m. Barracuda, red cod, octopus, skate and, in spring, paddle crabs make up their diet, with Hooker's sea lions usually diving 200m or less for four or five minutes – although they are capable of achieving depths of up to 500m. Pups are born on the beach, then moved by the mother at about six weeks to grassy swards, shrubland or forest, and suckled for up to a year.

Sea lions prefer to haul out on sandy beaches and in summer spend much of the day flicking sand over themselves to keep cool. Unlike seals they don't fear people. If you encounter one on land, give it a wide berth of at least 5m (30m during the Dec–Feb breeding season) and if it rears up and roars, back off quickly – they move swiftly.

The **Hector's dolphin**, with its distinctive black and white markings, is the smallest dolphin in the world and, with a population under 4000, is also one of the rarest. It's only found in New Zealand inshore waters – mostly around the coast of the South Island – with eastern concentrations around Banks Peninsula, Te Waewae Bay and Porpoise Bay, plus western communities between Farewell Spit and Haast. They roam up to 8km from shore in winter, but in summer prefer shallow waters within 1km of the coastline, catching mullet, arrowsquid, red cod, stargazers and crabs. Female dolphins are typically a little larger than the males, growing to 1.2–1.4m and weighing 40–50kg. They give birth from November to mid-February, and calves stay with their mothers for up to two years.

In summer and autumn, the tiny resident population at Porpoise Bay regularly enters the surf zone and even comes within 10m of the beach. Hector's Dolphins are shy and being disturbed can impact on feeding, which in turn affects their already low breeding rate. If you're spending time around them, be sure to follow DOC rules (posted locally), which essentially forbid, touching, feeding, surrounding and chasing dolphins and encourage you to keep a respectful distance. Swimming around pods with juveniles is also forbidden, and in summer most pods will have juveniles.

civilian shipwreck, in 1881, when 131 lives were lost on SS *Tararua*. The lighthouse that now stands on the point was erected soon after and you may now see fur seals and sea lions on the golden beach and rocky platform at its foot.

Back on the main road, it is another 10km to the windswept trees of **Fortrose**, before a bland 60km stretch of SH92 takes you to Invercargill.

Gore and around

The quiet Southland farming town of **GORE**, 71km west of Balclutha, is a pleasant transit point at the intersection of routes from Dunedin to Te Anau and Invercargill. Dominated by the Hokonui Hills, Gore spans the Mataura River ("reddish swirling water"), and claims to be the **brown trout capital** of the world – celebrated by an enormous fish statue in the town centre. During the fishing season (Oct–April) you can pit your wits against a brown trout with tackle rented from B&B Sports, 65 Main St (☎03/208 0801), and a licence from the visitor centre ($21/24hr).

As New Zealand's home of **country music**, Gore comes alive for eight days in autumn for the Gold Guitar Awards (late May & early June; ☎03/208 1978, ⓦwww.goldguitars.co.nz), when hundreds of would-be country stars and a few established performers roll into town.

Stop by the **Hokonui Heritage Centre**, on the corner of Norfolk Street and Hokonui Drive (Mon–Fri 8.30am–5pm, Sat & Sun 9.30am–4pm), which contains the **i-SITE visitor centre** (same hours; ☎03/203 9288, ⓦwww.gorenz.com), a small local **history museum** (gold coin donation), and the entertaining **Hokonui Moonshine Museum** ($5), detailing decades of illicit whisky distillation deep in the local bush-covered hills, which began in 1836 and reached a peak during a regional fifty-year-long local Prohibition from 1903.

Across the street, the **Eastern Southland Art Gallery** (Mon–Fri 10am–4.30pm, Sat & Sun 1–4pm; free) has a nationally significant collection of art bequeathed by expat Kiwi sexologist, Dr John Money, who amassed works including some majestic African carvings and career-spanning pieces from the private collection of Ralph Hotere.

Fans of vintage aircraft should head 17km west along the road to Queenstown (SH94) to the **Old Mandeville Airfield**, where you can take to the air on joyrides ($85/10min–$140/20min; contact Croydon Aircraft Company ☎03/208 9755) in a Tiger Moth, Fox Moth or Dragonfly. You're welcome to look around the hangar where renovation is constantly in progress on all sorts of aircraft, and take a more leisurely stroll round the brand-new **museum** containing all sorts of beautiful aeroplanes (daily 10am–5pm; around $15). Adjacent is *The Moth* (☎03/208 9662), a recently renovated restaurant/bar that's as stylish as the aircraft it's named after.

Gore lies on the major bus route between Dunedin, Invercargill and Te Anau. Buses drop off at the visitor centre, where you can book **accommodation** and **transport** and pick up information on the area. There are two worthwhile places to stay. First is ⚮ *Wentworth Heights*, 86a Wentworth St (☎03/208 6476, ⓦwww .wentworthheights.co.nz; ❺), offering comfortable en-suite doubles, fabulous breakfasts and dinners (by arrangement) and a warmth of welcome few can match; if you have time Barry is also a fishing guide (ⓦwww.flyfishmataura.co.nz). Meanwhile at the budget end of the scale is the more prosaic but very comfortable *Fire Station Backpackers*, 19 Hokonui Drive (☎03/208 1925, ⓦwww.thefirestation .co.nz, dorms $25, rooms ❶). Most **eating** options concentrate around Main Street, including *Howl at the Moon*, 2 Main St, a café/bar with a Kiwi cowboy feel, serving a good range of snacks and bigger meals for under $28. The bar hots up Friday and Saturday nights. Fine dining entails a 1km walk to *Casa Bella*, 81 Hokonui Drive (☎03/208 0154; dinner Tues–Sat), while for café staples try the *Table Top Café*, 76 Main St (Mon–Fri 8am–5pm, Sat 9am–2pm).

Invercargill and around

Many visitors pass straight through **INVERCARGILL**, regarding it as little more than a waystation en route to Stewart Island or the Catlins Coast. But the city warrants a little more time. Settled in the mid-1850s it sprawls over an exposed stretch of flat land at the head of the New River Estuary. In 2000, community contributions allowed its main centre of learning, the Southern Institute of Technology (SIT), to offer free tuition for New Zealand and Australian residents (with lower than usual fees for international students) on all of its courses. As a result, Invercargill's population swelled to 54,000, and its arts scene and nightlife gained new life. More recently, the discovery of a possible oil source nearby has led to some new investment in the town, and the prospect of more to come.

To the south, at the tip of a small peninsula, lies **Bluff**, the departure point for ferries to **Stewart Island** (see p.611).

Arrival, information and city transport

Direct domestic flights from Christchurch and Stewart Island land at Invercargill's **airport**, 2.5km southwest of the city centre. Blue Star taxis (☎03/218 6079; $20) provide transport into town; an airport shuttle service is provided by Executive Rental Cars (☎03/214 3434, $15/passenger). Knightrider **buses** from Christchurch pull up at the corner of Tay and Jed streets, but all others stop outside the excellent **i-SITE visitor centre**, 105 Gala St (daily 8am–5pm; ☎03/211 0845, ⓦwww.visitinvercargillnz.com), in the foyer of the Southland Museum, where you can pick up the *Event time in Southland* (good for local events listings) and get coin-operated **internet access**. While here, pick up the Invercargill Bus Timetable outlining the city's dozen **bus** routes (☎03/218 7170), which mostly make loops out from the centre. There are also a couple of free bus circuits; a notice board outside the library on Dee Street posts schedules.

The city's **DOC office**, on Level 7 of the State Insurance Building on Don Street (Mon–Fri 9am–4.30pm; ☎03/214 4589), has information on walks and wildlife in the Catlins, Stewart Island and Fiordland.

Accommodation

Accommodation prices this far south are reasonable, and there's a fair choice close to the transport links, but note, Tuesday and Wednesdays fill up quickly when business reps converge on the town.

295 on Tay 295 Tay St ☎0800/295 295, ⓦwww.295ontay.co.nz. Modern and palatial motel with all mod cons including broadband Internet access and full kitchens, some rooms have spa baths. ❹

Admiral Court Motor Lodge 327 Tay St ☎0800/111 122, ⓦwww.admiralcourt.co.nz. Ten spotless, fully s/c units with extras including breakfast delivered to your door, plungers with freshly ground coffee, wi-fi, and transport to and from the airport; a handful of units also have spa baths. ❹

Invercargill Top 10 Holiday Park 77 McIvor Rd, 9km north of the city centre ☎0800/486 873,

ⓦwww.invercargilltop10.co.nz. Upscale campsite with a high standard of facilities. Camping $36 per site, cabins ❷, tourist cabin ❸, unit ❹

Kackling Kea 225 Tweed St ☎03/214 7950 ⓦwww.kacklingkea.co.nz. Thick duvets, the aroma of freshly baked bread, muffins and fewer than twenty guests make this hostel feel more like a home. Dorms $26, shares $28, room ❷

Safari Lodge 51 Herbert St ☎03/0800 885 557, ⓦwww.safarilodge.co.nz. Swanky B&B in a 107-year-old, mock-Tudor mansion, full of mementos of the owner's Mozambique travels, with tastefully decorated rooms and some lovely vintage cars in the garage. ❽–❾

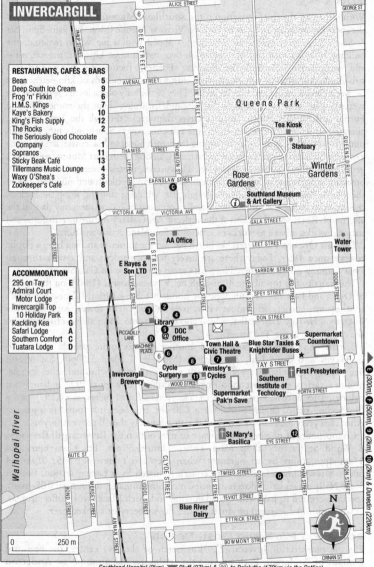

Ⓐ *(100m)*, ▲ Ⓑ *(7km)*, *Anderson Park (7km)*, *Te Anau (160km) & Queenstown (180km)*

INVERCARGILL

RESTAURANTS, CAFÉS & BARS

Bean	5
Deep South Ice Cream	9
Frog 'n' Firkin	6
H.M.S. Kings	7
Kaye's Bakery	10
King's Fish Supply	12
The Rocks	2
The Seriously Good Chocolate Company	1
Sopranos	11
Sticky Beak Café	13
Tillermans Music Lounge	4
Waxy O'Shea's	3
Zookeeper's Café	8

ACCOMMODATION

295 on Tay	E
Admiral Court Motor Lodge	F
Invercargill Top 10 Holiday Park	B
Kackling Kea	G
Safari Lodge	A
Southern Comfort	C
Tuatara Lodge	D

Airport *(2.5km)*, Ⓑ *(8km) & Oreti Beach (9.5km)*

Ⓜ *(300m)*, Ⓕ *(500m)*, Ⓖ *(2km)*, Ⓙ *(2km) & Dunedin (220km)*

Southland Hospital (2km), ▼ *Bluff (27km) &* 92 *to Balclutha (172km via the Catlins)*

Southern Comfort 30 Thomson St ☎03/218 3838, ⒺDcoupers@xtra.co.nz. Suburban hostel in a beautifully kept Victorian villa set among manicured lawns. Recently revamped with an excellent kitchen (with a dishwasher!) and free luggage storage for those tramping on Stewart Island. Dorms $27, rooms ②

🏃 **Tuatara Lodge** 30 Dee St ☎0800/488 282, ⓦwww.tuataralodge.co.nz. Friendly, spacious, recently repainted hostel in a converted bank building, right in the heart of town. Immaculate rooms, limited off-street parking and good security, plus an excellent café on the ground floor. Dorms $25, rooms ②, en suites ④

The City

Within the city the chief attraction is the **Southland Museum and Art Gallery**, at the southern entrance to Queens Park on Victoria Avenue (Mon–Fri 9am–5pm, Sat & Sun 10am–5pm; gold coin donation). Capped with a big white pyramid, the building houses a well-laid-out collection over two storeys. Upstairs, the extensive and imaginative "Beyond the Roaring Forties" focuses on New Zealand's **sub-Antarctic islands**, tiny windswept clusters lying hundreds of kilometres apart between New Zealand and the Antarctic. They're the only obstacles in the path of the westerly gales that rage through these latitudes, earning them the names Roaring Forties and Furious Fifties. Displays cover shipwrecks through the ages, wildlife, climate and so on. The remainder of the museum covers Southland's history, both human and natural, with exhibits ranging from moa bones to Maori artefacts via some excellent films of the city's various speed freaks, among them Burt Monro (see below), getting it on down at the local beaches. Downstairs, there's coverage of a successful breeding programme of **tuatara** – small, dinosaurian reptiles found nowhere else in the world. You can observe them through glass windows running along the back of the museum facing the park – they usually come out of hiding on sunny days in the afternoon. Rotating exhibitions at the adjacent **Art Gallery** feature international and national works, as well as works by emerging Southland artists and films.

The vast **Queens Park** stretches north behind the museum and has been a public reserve since 1869. Today there are lovely formal gardens and a walk-through aviary among other delights. The park's main entrance is on Gala Street.

The stairs to the top of the 40m-high brick **water tower** (1889), on the corner of Doon and Leet streets (Sun & public holidays 1.30–4.30pm; $2) near the park's southeastern corner, offer great views over the city. The tower features on the *Invercargill Heritage Trail* leaflet, which also details some distinctive **architecture** in the city centre along Tay Street.

Behind one Art Deco facade and another slightly more prosaic exterior is **E. Hayes and Sons Ltd**, 168 Dee St (Mon–Fri 7.30am–5.30pm, Sat & Sun 9am–4pm), a giant hardware store which, amongst the wrenches and lathes for sale, houses a variety of historic motorbikes, including the original 1922 Indian Scout belonging to Burt Monro (subject of *The World's Fastest Indian*, see p.797), and a functioning petrol engine made, for a £20 bet, from detritus found in a garage. After two years the bet was won and if you ask nicely they'll prove it to you.

Connoisseurs of fine beer won't want to miss out on the **Invercargill Brewery**, 8 Wood St (factory shop Mon–Thurs 11am–5.50pm, Fri 11am–6pm, Sat 11am–4pm, tours by arrangement when they aren't brewing; $15; ☏03/214 5070, ⓦwww.invercargillbrewery.co.nz), followed by a tasting session. Brewer Steve Nally makes half a dozen varieties, including Biman (pronounced BEE-man), specially created to pair with spiced curries, and Pitch Black, with coffee aromas, as well as limited seasonal productions like boysenberry or smoked beer.

Anderson Park and Oreti Beach

On the outskirts of Invercargill, 7km north of the city centre, the beautiful grounds of **Anderson Park** provide the setting for the atmospheric **Anderson Park Art Gallery** (daily 10.30am–5pm; gold coin donation during special exhibitions, otherwise free), housed in a 1925 neo-Georgian mansion built for a local businessman. Designed by Christchurch architect Cecil Wood, it was constructed from reinforced concrete and set against a backdrop of forest. During October, a spring exhibition of recent Kiwi art replaces the permanent collection, one of the most interesting independent collections in NZ, of traditional and contemporary New Zealand art, including Houtere, McCahon, Bevan Ford and Frizell. Behind the gallery, **The Maori House**, built in the early 1920s and used for dances, has a doorway and porch decorated with carvings by Tene Waitere, a renowned Rotorua carver. There is no bus service out here; a taxi will cost about $25 one-way or you could rent a bike (see below).

Oreti Beach, 10km west of the city centre, is a beautiful broad expanse of fine sand, sweeping 30km right around to the seaside resort of Riverton to the west, and giving great views of Stewart Island and Bluff. Burt Munro of *The World's Fastest Indian* movie fame used the beach for many of his speed motorbike trials. In summer, it's popular for swimming (surf patrols operate when busy), yachting and waterskiing, but windy days cause violent sandstorms.

Eating and drinking

Invercargill has enough cafés to keep you sated but few really top-notch places so make do instead with **local produce**; award-winning sheep's cheese from the Blue River Dairy, 111 Nith St (Ⓦwww.blueriverdairy.co.nz); baked goods (including bargain-priced bags of broken biscuits) at Kaye's Bakery, 19 Onslow St; creamy ices (including some made from the Invercargill Brewing Company's Pitch Black beer) from the factory/HQ of Deep South Ice Cream, 122 Rockdale Rd; and fine handmade chocolates from The Seriously Good Chocolate Company, 147 Spey St (Ⓦwww.seriouslygoodchocolate.com), which has an attached tearoom. Also worth a look, on Sundays, are the farmers' market at Southland Boys School (from 10am) and, in the afternoon (2–4pm). The *Sticky Beak Café*, on the way to the beach on Viner Road, Oatara, has the best apricot, prune and walnut loaf and "wobbly" marmalade.

Look out for local **seafood**, including excellent Bluff oysters (fresh April–Oct) and blue cod, as well as **muttonbird**. You can buy the fresh seafood on display at *King's Fish Supply*, 59 Ythan St (Mon–Tues 8.30am–7.30pm, Wed–Sat 8.30am–8.30pm, Sun 4–8.30pm) to take away (priced by weight) or have it cooked to order while you wait (extra $1); they also do incredibly cheap, delicious fish and chips ($6).

A number of the city's **bars** transform into dance venues as the evening wears on, though the town is usually quiet until Thursday night. Check *The Southland Times* for gigs by **local bands**. There are also a handful of **nightclubs**, which are at their liveliest during university term time. The five-screen Reading **cinema** at 29 Dee St (☎03/211 1555) has reduced ticket prices on Tuesday.

Bean 73 Dee St. Functional breakfast and lunch café which is popular with locals because of excellent cakes and breakfasts and some zingy coffee. Mon–Fri 7am–4pm, Sat 8.30am–2pm.

Frog 'n' Firkin 31 Dee St. Popular pub that's positively hopping after midnight late in the week when it turns into a fun dance venue.

H.M.S. Kings 80 Tay St ☎03/218 3443. Seafood restaurant stocked by King's Fish Supply where you can try fresh Bluff oysters in season and excellent local fish in a glossy timber nautical dining room. Dinner mains around $35. Closed Sat & Sun lunch.

The Rocks Courtville Place, 101 Dee St ☎03/218 7597. A small, arty restaurant with a varied menu. Tues–Sat 11am–2pm & 5pm onward.

Sopranos 33 Tay St. Decently priced Mafia-themed gourmet pizza joint. Closed Mon.

Tillermans Music Lounge 16 Don St ☎03/218 9240. Popular bar with pool tables, and a focal point for (often fairly offbeat) live music on Sat nights.

Waxy O'Shea's 90 Dee St. Convivial and more convincing than average Irish bar with good music, occasionally live.

Zookeeper's Café 50 Tay St. Cool split-level bar/café easily identified by the corru-gated-iron elephant on the roof outside. Serves brunch, bar food, snacks (including an outstanding seafood chowder) and meals from $15–30, as well as local beers and wines.

Listings

Bike rental Cycle Surgery, 2l Tay St (☎03/218 8055) rents good-quality mountain bikes for $35 while Wensley's Cycles, corner of Tay & Nith sts

(☎03/218 6206) rents from $35/day, while the i-SITE has them at $15/4hr.

Left luggage At the i-SITE ($2/day).

Library Invercargill Public Library is at 50 Dee St (Mon–Fri 9am–8pm, Sat 10am–1pm, Sun 1–4pm; ℡ 03/218 7025).

Medical treatment Southland Hospital, on Kew Rd (℡ 03/218 1949), has a 24hr accident and emergency department. For illness and minor accidents outside surgery hours, contact the Urgent Doctor Service at 103 Don St (℡ 03/218 8821; Mon–Fri 5–10pm; Sat, Sun & public holidays 24hr).

Pharmacy Inside the Countdown supermarket (Mon–Thurs & Sat–Sun 8.30am–8pm, Fri 8.30am–9pm).

Police The central police station is at 117 Don St (℡ 03/211 0400).

Post office The main post office is at 51 Don St, near the junction with Kelvin St (Mon–Fri 8.30am–5pm, Sat 10am–12.30pm).

Shopping Glowing Sky, with shops in Wellington, Stewart Island, Auckland, Invercargill and Wanaka this Stewart Island company have become the premier maker of merino wool gear, perfect for outdoor pursuits and frighteningly fashionable to boot. Prices are fab and if you need something to keep warm on the tracks these are the boys to see.

Bluff

Twenty-seven kilometres south of Invercargill (a 20min drive down SH1), overlooking Foveaux Strait, is the small run-down fishing town of **BLUFF** and its man-made harbour. This is the departure point for ferries to **Stewart Island** (see opposite). You won't need more than a couple of hours to get a good look at the place, but without a car this will involve a good deal of walking, as the town spreads along the shoreline for about 6km.

Continuously settled since 1824, Bluff is the oldest European town in New Zealand. It's showing its age a little, but the busy **harbour** exports Southland's meat, timber, aluminium, fish and wool, and imports a variety of goods from overseas. In addition Foveaux Strait yields a highly sought-after delicacy – the sweet **Bluff oyster**. This deepwater shellfish is dredged from April until September then processed in local oyster sheds before being sent all over the country. Between June and August you can buy them direct at factory prices from several places on the waterfront including Johnson's Oysters (daily 8am–5pm; ℡ 03/212 8665). The annual **Bluff Oyster and Southland Seafood Festival** celebrates these slimy bivalve molluscs on the third weekend in May, the event is now back in the hands of the local community and details are currently in short supply, but it'll be at the Bluff Events Centre.

Doubling as the town's **visitor centre**, Bluff's small **Maritime Museum** (Mon–Fri 10am–4.30pm, Sat & Sun 1–5pm; $2), on Foreshore Road as you enter town from Invercargill, has historical displays focusing on whaling, the harbour development, oyster harvesting and shipwrecks. Pride of place is given to a triple-expansion steam engine, and the 1909 oyster boat, *Monica*, which sits outside the building.

Although Bluff isn't the South Island's most southerly point (that's Slope Point in the Catlins), at **Stirling Point** a multi-armed signpost balancing the one at the other end of the country at Cape Reinga marks the distance to major cities around the world, as well as the equator (5133km) and the South Pole (4810km). Before you get to the signpost is an anchor chain disappearing into the sea – it is connected to Stewart Island, the South Island's anchor stone, according to Maori lore. From the car park at the end of the road you can set out on a couple of easy walks: the **Foveaux Walkway** (6.6km; 2hr one-way; mostly flat) which follows the coast back to town; and the **Topuni Track** (2km one-way; 45min; 265m ascent) which climbs to **Bluff Hill Lookout**, with 360-degree views encompassing Stewart Island, 35km away. The lookout is also accessible by road from Bluff: follow Lee Street, opposite the ferry wharf for 3km.

Stewart Island Experience (℡ 0800/000 511) runs a regular bus service from Invercargill ($18 each way), to connect with the ferry. For details on ferry sailings to Stewart Island, see opposite.

Stewart Island

New Zealand's third main island is the relatively unknown **STEWART ISLAND**, separated from the mainland by Foveaux Strait. Most of it is uninhabited and characterized by bush-fringed bays, sandy coves, windswept beaches and a rugged interior of tall rimu forest and granite outcrops. With the creation of **Rakiura National Park** in 2002 a full 85 percent of the island is now protected. Stewart Island's Maori name is Rakiura ("The Land of Glowing Skies"), although the jury is still out on whether this refers to the aurora australis – aka **southern lights** – occasionally seen in the night sky throughout the year, or the fabulous sunsets.

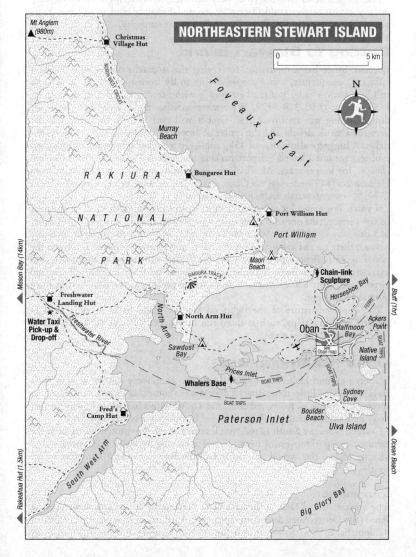

Captain Cook came by in 1770 and erroneously marked a peninsula on his charts. The island was later named after William Stewart, the first officer on a sealing vessel that visited in 1809. With the arrival of Europeans, felling rimu became the island's economic mainstay, supporting three thousand people in the 1930s. Now almost all of Stewart Island's three hundred and sixty residents live in the sole town, **Oban**, surviving on **conservation** work, **fishing** (crayfish, blue cod and paua), **fish farming** (salmon and mussels) and tourism.

The slow island ways can quickly get into your blood and you may well want to stay longer than you had planned, especially if you're drawn to serious wilderness **tramping**, sea **kayaking**, and abundant **wildlife** in unspoilt surroundings.

The island is never crowded (with only around 35,000 overnight visitors a year), but if you visit between mid-December and mid-February book in advance. Year-round, come prepared for all weathers (often in the same day).

Getting to Stewart Island

Foveaux Strait has a reputation for trying the stomachs of even the hardiest sailors. Consequently, many people choose to **fly** from Invercargill (which can still be a bumpy ride) and the best way is with Stewart Island Flights (3 daily; $185 return; ℡03/218 9129, ⓦwww.stewartislandflights.com) but check for deals. Getting out to Invercargill airport will cost $15 by taxi; the transfer between Oban's airfield and the centre of town is included in the price of your ticket. A **luggage allowance** of 15kg applies, per person applies and camping gas canisters are not allowed. Airport parking costs about $8 for the first 24 hours; cheaper for longer stays. Alternatively you could choose to use Stewart Island Helicopters ($195 one-way to Oban, other destinations' prices vary; ℡03/212 7700, ⓦwww.stewartislandhelicopters.co.nz).

If you're bringing a lot of luggage, want to carry camping stove fuel or just need to save money, take one of the **ferries** run by Stewart Island Experience (2–4 daily; $63 one-way ℡03/212 7660 or 0800/000 511; ⓦwww.stewartislandexperience .co.nz); there's a fast catamaran on the hour-long journey between Bluff and the wharf in Oban. Boats typically leave Bluff at 9.30am and in the late afternoon, with extra services in summer. A connecting bus picks up from Invercargill city and airport, and costs $20 each way. There's secure parking at the Bluff terminal for around $10 a night.

The dispersed nature of the sights on Stewart Island make it well suited to **guided walking trips**, such as those run by Ruggedy Range (℡03/219 1066, ⓦwww.ruggedyrange.com).

Oban (Halfmoon Bay)

Scattered around Halfmoon Bay, **OBAN** (also commonly known as Halfmoon Bay) comprises little more than a few dozen houses, a visitor centre, a tiny museum, a couple of stores and cafés, and a hotel with a bar. More houses straggle away up the surrounding hills, surrounded by bush alive with native birds.

Coming from the South Island, you'll **arrive** at the downtown wharf or at the tarmac airstrip 3km west of town. If you're coming by water taxi, perhaps after visiting Mason Bay, you'll pull up at **Golden Bay** just over a kilometre to the southwest.

Information

The Stewart Island **DOC office/Rakiura National Park visitor centre**, Main Road (late Dec to April daily 8am–5pm; mid-April to late June Mon–Fri 8.30am–4.30pm, Sat & Sun 10am–2pm; late June to Nov Mon–Fri 8.30am–4.30pm, Sat &

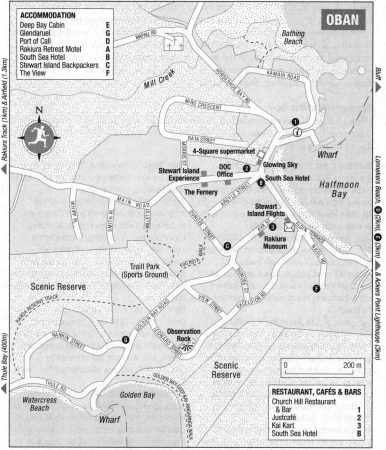

Moturau Moana Gardens (1km), Ⓐ (1.7km), Horseshoe Bay (2km) & ▲ Rakiura Track & North West Circuit (3.5km)

OBAN

ACCOMMODATION
Deep Bay Cabin   E
Glendaruel   G
Port of Call   D
Rakiura Retreat Motel   A
South Sea Hotel   B
Stewart Island Backpackers C
The View   F

RESTAURANT, CAFÉS & BARS
Church Hill Restaurant
 & Bar   1
Justcafé   2
Kai Kart   3
South Sea Hotel   B

0   200 m

▼ Water taxi & launch routes to Ulva Island, Millars Beach & Ocean Beach

Sun 10am–noon; ☎03/219 0009, ⓦwww.doc.govt.nz), has excellent displays on the island's tracks and natural history, supplies local maps and information, and sells DOC hut passes, as well as screening free videos about the island. The centre also has **luggage lockers** (small $5, large $10; for as long as you like).

Bear in mind that there are **no banks or ATMs** on Stewart Island. Many businesses take credit cards, and visitors with New Zealand bank accounts can use EFTPOS, but it is wise to bring plenty of cash. Note too that only Telecom has **mobile phone coverage** on parts of the island.

The **post office** is in the Stewart Island Flights depot, Elgin Street, on the water-front near the junction with Ayr Street (Oct–March Mon–Fri 7.30am–6pm, Sat & Sun 8.30am–5pm; April–Sept daily 8.30am–5pm), where stamps are still cancelled by hand. For **internet access** try the *South Sea Hotel*, and *Stewart Island Backpackers*.

Local transport

Oban is a pleasant place to **walk** around and unless you are staying in one of the more distant lodges you won't need any land transport. To get a feel for the lay of the land, join Stewart Island Experience's Village and Bays **tour** (1–3 daily; 1hr 30min; $35; T 03/219 0056; W www.stewartislandexperience.co.nz).

For independent transportation, rent a car ($80/day) or motor scooter ($40/2hr, $60/8hr), all including fuel, from Stewart Island Experience. Once away from the small road system you'll need the aid of **water taxis**, typically speedboats with powerful outboard motors carrying six to ten. Four companies offer a broadly similar service, including Stewart Island Water Taxi (T 03/219 1394).

Accommodation

Oban's range of **accommodation** is broadish, although finding a place in high season can be difficult: **book** before you arrive. There's a new fifty-plus-bed YHA due to be built in the next two years.

Deep Bay Cabin Deep Bay T 03/219 1219, E wanjengell@xtra.co.nz. Snug s/c wooden cabin hidden in the bush with four bunks, kitchen and shower, and a year-round pot-bellied stove. Roughly a 20min walk from town and a great spot for resting after the longer tracks. **2**

Glendaruel 38 Golden Bay Rd T 03/219 1092, W www.glendaruel.co.nz. Comfortable and welcoming B&B 10min walk from town, surrounded by native bush. Rooms are all en suite, guests get their own lounge, and owner Raylene will do her best to ensure you have a great time on the island. **7**

Port of Call Jensen Bay T 03/219 1394, W www.portofcall.co.nz. A boutique B&B in a large, beautifully designed sun-filled contemporary house overlooking the bay 2.5km east of town, plus a couple of gorgeous separate self-catering cottages, one of which accommodates three people. Everything is beautifully appointed and there's free transport to and from town. Cottages **6**/**7**, B&B **8**

Rakiura Retreat Motel 156 Horseshoe Bay Rd T 03/219 1096, W www.rakiuraretreat.co.nz. Great views over Halfmoon Bay from a hill just outside

Oban, 2km from the wharf (a 25min walk). Decor in the five well-maintained units reflect the island's Maori traditions. Free transfers. **6**

South Sea Hotel 25 Elgin Terrace T 03/219 1059, W www.stewart-island.co.nz. Century-old waterfront pub with rooms upstairs, all sharing bathrooms, and a nice lounge overlooking the wharf. Some have sea views but others are directly above the noisy bar. There are also more modern motel units and rooms in a cottage out the back. Rooms and cottage **5**, sea-view rooms and units **4**

Stewart Island Backpackers corner of Ayr & Dundee sts T 03/219 1114, W www.stewart -island.co.nz/shearwater. Central, large and fairly basic hostel with loads of pleasant shared-bath doubles and twins and four-share dorms plus camping ($10) with use of hostel facilities. Dorms $25, rooms **2**

The View Nichol Rd T 03/219 1328. Friendly, warm, spacious and clean, this small backpackers is just 500m from the wharf at the top of a bloody great hill (hence the name), with a double and four-share dorm. Closed May–Sept. Dorm $30, rooms **3**

The Town

Oban's sights are limited, though you should devote a few minutes to the **Rakiura Museum** on Ayr Street (Mon–Fri 9am–1.30pm, Sat 10am–1.30pm, Sun noon–2pm; $2), which focuses on local history. The small Maori collection boasts a rare necklace of dolphin teeth, while the whaling display has two giant teeth from a sperm whale.

Less than ten minutes' walk away you'll find **The Fernery**, 20 Main St (Sept–May daily 10am–6pm; reduced hours in winter; T 03/219 1453), a cornucopia of souvenirs and gifts inspired by the island and handmade by New Zealand artists and craftspeople, while in town is the fabulous **Glowing Sky** (see p.610) outlet, by the supermarket, where New Zealand merino wool clothes have reached the height of fashion and practicality. Up the hill on Leonard Street is **Observation Rock** (25min from the centre), with its hilltop panorama of Paterson Inlet and the island's highest peak, Mount Anglem. As the sun sets you may be treated to a dozen or so kaka screeching and flying about.

North of Halfmoon Bay, twenty minutes' walk along Horseshoe Bay Road, are the secluded **Moturau Moana gardens**. Picnic tables, BBQS and a viewing platform looking out across the bay to Oban are set amid lawns, native plants and dense virgin forest.

Eating and drinking

Oban only has a few **places to eat**. Last dinner orders tend to be around 8.30pm – even earlier when the town is quiet. For self-caterers, groceries are available from the small 4-Square **general store**, 20 Elgin Terrace, which also sells prepared lunch-boxes ($11). It closes around 7pm in summer, 6.30pm the rest of the year. A new service might interest some – an evening meal delivered to your accommodation by Stewart Island Moveable Feast, with three courses costing $60 (☏027/444 1802).

Church Hill Restaurant & Bar 36 Kamahi Rd ☏03/219 1323. Fine views of Halfmoon Bay from the deck of this century-old house help make this one of the best places to eat in town but the quality does vary.
Justcafé 6 Main Rd. Daytime café with great espresso, light meals, cakes and cookies, the owners of which also operate a spa with a range of treatments like hot stone massage and a seaweed body wrap (from $85). Café and spa open Oct–April.

Kai Kart Ayr St. Billy Connolly once stopped by this fabulously quirky old Pie Kart (aka glorified caravan), which has recently been decked out with leadlights and decoupaged tables. You can order superb blue cod fish and chips or burgers to eat inside or at the outdoor picnic tables, or take them to the adjacent beach. Mid-Oct to mid-April.
South Sea Hotel Elgin Terrace. The island's pub is very much its social centre, with a restaurant offering reasonably priced lunches and early evening meals.

Paterson Inlet and Ulva Island

The birdlife in Oban is pretty special, but **Ulva Island** – an open wildlife sanctuary 2km south of Oban in the flooded valley of **Paterson Inlet** – goes one better with cacophonous birdsong and the chance to see endangered saddleback and rare red-crowned parakeets on a series of easy walks through dense rainforest to secluded beaches. The former Norwegian **Whalers Base** is another wildlife-rich destination, and can be included on guided **kayaking trips**.

Ulva Island

Tremendous local effort has rid the long, low **Ulva Island** (daylight hours; free) of introduced predators and it is now an **open sanctuary** where you'll see more native birdlife than almost anywhere else in New Zealand. The place is full of birdsong, its thick vegetation alive with weka, bellbirds, kaka, yellow- and red-crowned parakeets, tui, fantails, pigeons and robins, who approach visitors with fearless curiosity.

Access is mainly by **water taxi** (10min each way; $25 return from Golden Bay). Armed with DOC's *Explore an Island Paradise: Ulva Island* booklet ($2), you can follow easy trails across a forest floor, but the best way to appreciate this haven is on a **guided tour** such as that run by Ulva Goodwillie of ⅍Ulva's Guided Walks (approx 3hr; $95, including water taxi fees; ☏03/219 1216, ⓦwww.ulva.co.nz), who was named after the island and imparts local Maori stories.

Water taxis and cruises arrive at **Post Office Bay**, whose former post office, over 100 years old, is a remnant from the days when the island was the hub of the local community. A web of trails crisscrossing the island leads first to nearby **Sydney Cove**, where there's a pleasant picnic shelter on the beach.

Whalers Base

On the shores of Paterson Inlet is **Whalers Base**, an over-wintering spot for Norwegian whalers near **Millars Beach**, about 7km west of Oban. It's only accessible by water taxi (around $55 return), and most operators will leave you there for a few hours and pick you up later. From Millars Beach, an easy twenty-minute coastal walk heads north from the beachside picnic shelter through native bush to the whaling base. Several eerie relics remain from 1924–32 when a fleet of Antarctic whaling ships was repaired here, and the beach is littered with objects left behind: old drums, cables, giant iron propellers, a boiler out in the water and, at the far end, a wrecked sailing ship deliberately sunk by the whaling company to create a wharf.

Activities

Both Ulva Island and Whalers Base form part of various **tours** and kayak trips that take in Paterson Inlet and beyond. Adventurous visitors can explore more thoroughly by **sea kayaking** around the scattered inlets and islands. On extended trips you can even paddle out to the four water-accessible **DOC huts** around the inlet. Bottlenose dolphins and fur seals are frequent visitors and the tidal flats attract wading birds. Bear in mind that the waters around Stewart Island are changeable and May to August brings the most settled weather; only extremely experienced kayakers should venture into these waters unaccompanied.

There's also a chance to see **kiwi in the wild** without crossing the island to Mason Bay, and some great short **walks**. Longer hikes are covered opposite.

Adventure trips and tours

Bravo Adventure Cruises ℡03/219 1144, ⓔphilldismith@xtra.co.nz. Cruises geared around spotting the Stewart Island brown kiwi (a subspecies of the mainland birds) in remote areas around the shores of Paterson Inlet. Four-hour trips ($100) leave from the wharf in Halfmoon Bay around dusk, but are weather dependent and extremely popular, so it's essential to reserve well ahead – even then a tour can't be guaranteed. You'll need warm clothing, sturdy footwear, a torch and reasonable fitness, as the outing entails a short boat trip and up to 2hr walking, including some steep sections, in the dark to a windswept beach, where the kiwi feast on tiny crustaceans. Great care is taken to avoid disturbing these timid birds.

Rakiura Kayaks ℡03/219 1160, ⓦwww.rakiura .co.nz. Excellent half-day ($65) and full-day ($85) guided trips, as well as overnighters with the option of staying in a house on an offshore island (price negotiable), plus kayak rental.
Stewart Island Experience ℡03/219 0034, ⓦwww.stewartislandexperience.co.nz. Two trips, the first a leisurely Paterson Inlet Cruise (Oct–April 1–3 daily; 2hr 30min; $75) taking in the main sights including Whalers Base and a 45min guided walking tour of Ulva Island. The Underwater Explorer tour (Oct–April 1–3 daily; 45min: $35) in a semi-submersible takes you through forests of bladder kelp. You'll see butterfish, blue cod, moki, sea tulips and curious filter-feeding animals.

Short walks around Oban

Over a dozen short **walks** around Oban are covered in the DOC's *Day Walks* leaflet; a couple of the nicest are right in town.

Fuchsia Walk/Raroa Track (2km one-way; 30min). This little-used trail winds through fuchsia forest filled with tui, bellbirds, kaka and pigeons then comes out at Trail Park. Cross this and head down through rimu forest to the beach.
Golden Bay–Deep Bay–Ringaringa (6km loop; 1hr 30min–2hr). Skirting east from Golden Bay, the track follows the coast to Deep Bay and then over the hill to Ringaringa Beach. From here, follow the signs over a stile to Ringaringa Point and the graves of early missionaries.

Harrold Bay and Ackers Point Lighthouse (3km return; 40min). An easy, well-graded coastal walk with a chance to see little blue penguins and muttonbirds returning to their nests at dusk (Nov–Feb). Near the start of the track, you can follow a brief diversion to Harrold Bay, the site of a simple stone house built in 1835, making it one of the oldest European buildings in New Zealand. The main track continues through coastal forest to a lighthouse and lookout point from where you can watch the penguins arduously climbing to their nests hidden in the bush. You'll need a torch to find your way around after dusk, but it's important to keep the beam pointed to the ground to avoid disturbing the birds. Follow the signs from Leask Bay, 2.5km east of town.

The rest of Stewart Island

There are no roads outside the immediate vicinity of Oban, so straying further afield requires planning. Essentially you have to fly, take a water taxi or walk.

As ever, **trampers** need to be ready for whatever the New Zealand weather conjures up, doubly so on Stewart Island, which is exposed to winds coming straight across the southern ocean from Antarctica. Take several layers of clothing to cope with sun and rain (often at almost the same time), and don't forget sandfly repellent. Huts can be busy from November through to March, so it's a good idea to bring a tent.

Mason Bay

Stewart Island has become synonymous with **kiwi spotting** in the wild, something that is difficult to do on mainland New Zealand. Tours from Oban include kiwi spotting, but most people are keen to get to **Mason Bay**, on the west coast, where they stay overnight in the 20-bunk DOC hut ($5; camping outside free) and head out after dark in the hope of finding these elusive creatures. You'll almost certainly hear them, and have a fair chance of seeing them provided you don't go crashing about in the bush: just pick a spot and wait. Take a torch, but keep the beam pointed to the ground to avoid disturbing the birds.

For hardy visitors, the cheapest way to visit is to **walk** (37km one-way; 13–15hr) along the southern leg of the North West Circuit (see below), probably staying overnight at Freshwater Landing Hut ($5). You can save a lot of time by catching a **water taxi** from Oban to Freshwater Landing Hut ($55 each way) then walking to Mason Bay (14km; 3–4hr; flat but often flooded – check conditions before you head out). Alternatively, Stewart Island Flights and one of the water taxi companies work together, allowing you to complete a "Coast to Coast" **loop**, flying from Oban to the beach at Mason Bay, staying a night or two there, walking to Freshwater Landing, then getting a water taxi back to Oban (or vice versa). It costs $195 for the flight and water taxi combo (hut accommodation extra), with a two-adult minimum.

Rakiura Track

Stewart Island's most popular overnight track is the relatively gentle **Rakiura Track** (36km loop; 2–3 days), one of New Zealand's Great Walks. This makes a circuit starting and finishing in Oban, though you can shave 7km off the route by getting someone to drop you off and pick you up at the road-ends. DOC's *Rakiura Track* leaflet is adequate for route finding, and you'll need to pre-purchase a **Great Walks Pass** from DOC for the two huts ($15 a night) and three campsites ($5) along the track. The huts are equipped with mattresses, wood stoves for heating only, running water and toilets, so you'll need your own cooker. You can walk in either direction at any time of the year and there is no limit on the number of nights you can stay.

The majority of people walk anticlockwise. Starting through bush, the track gets the best coastal walking in early around Maori Bay and Port William, site of the first hut. From Port William to the North Arm hut the track climbs over a 300m forested ridge, where a viewpoint gives the only really long views of the tramp, across Paterson Inlet and beyond to the Tin Range.

North West Circuit

It is a very big step up from the Rakiura Track to the **North West Circuit** (130km; 8–12 days) around the island's northern arm: only the hardiest (masochistic) trampers should consider attempting it. The boggy terrain is energy sapping even in good weather: thigh-deep mud is not uncommon. And unless you organize a boat or charter flight to drop food at one of the coastal huts, you'll have to carry all your supplies.

The track itself alternates between open coast and forested hill country, offering a side trip (11km return; 6hr) to the 980m summit of Mount Anglem. DOC's *North West and Southern Circuit Tracks* leaflet gives a good overview, pinpointing the ten huts (mostly sited on the coast: there are no campsites). Most huts cost $5 a night (annual hut pass valid), but Port William and North Arm huts are both Great Walks huts ($15) so it will probably pay to buy a **North West Circuit Pass** ($50), which entitles you to a night in each hut on the circuit.

Travel details

There are no genuine passenger **train** services in the region, though the Taieri Gorge Railway can be useful for linking Dunedin with the Maniototo. Fairly frequent **buses** ply the main Christchurch–Dunedin–Invercargill route and the inland route from Dunedin to Queenstown, with a few other services plugging the gaps.

Trains

Dunedin to: Middlemarch (summer Fri & Sun only 1 daily; 2hr 30min); Pukerangi (1 daily, 2hr).

Buses

Dunedin to: Alexandra (2 daily; 3hr); Balclutha (4–5 daily; 1hr 30min); Christchurch (5–6 daily; 5–6hr); Cromwell (3 daily; 3hr 15min); Gore (4–5 daily; 2hr 30min); Invercargill (4–5 daily; 3hr 30min); Lawrence (3 daily; 1hr 30min); Oamaru (5–6 daily; 2hr); Queenstown (3 daily; 4–5hr); Ranfurly (1 daily; 1hr 30min); Te Anau (1 daily; 4h 45min); Wanaka (2–3 daily; 4hr).
Invercargill to: Balclutha (2–4 daily; 2hr 30min); Dunedin (3–4 daily; 3hr 30min); Gore (2–4 daily;

1hr); Queenstown (2 daily; 2hr 30min); Te Anau (1 daily; 4hr); Wanaka (1 daily; 4hr).

Flights

Bluff to: Stewart Island (2–4 daily; 1hr).
Stewart Island to: Bluff (2–4 daily; 1hr).

Planes

Dunedin to: Auckland (1 daily; 1hr 50min); Christchurch (6–8 daily; 1hr); Wellington (3 daily; 1hr 10min).
Invercargill to: Christchurch (5–7 daily; 1hr 15min); Stewart Island (3 daily; 20min).
Stewart Island to: Invercargill (3 daily; 20min).

12

The West Coast

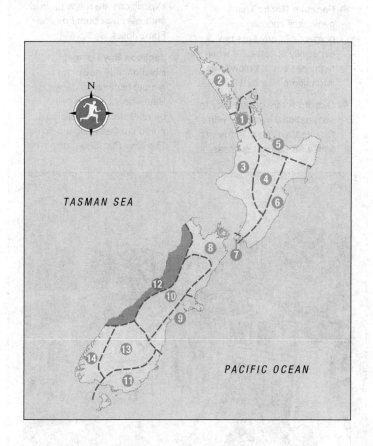

CHAPTER 12 **Highlights**

* **Oparara Basin** Set a day aside to explore caves harbouring moa bones, vast limestone arches and placid streams that are great for cooling off. See p.635

* **Pancake Rocks** This geological curiosity is gorgeous at any time but especially spectacular when high seas set the blowholes into action. See p.638

* **Okarito** A rare opportunity to spot national symbols, with Okarito Kiwi Tours, in the wild, with a 98-percent success rate, and/or kayak with Okarito Nature Tours on the seductive lagoon. See p.650

* **Glacier exploring** Hiking out onto the glacier is an awe-inspiring experience, and expeditions are run with great enthusiasm at both Fox and Franz Josef. See p.651

* **Jackson Bay** For real isolation, ride down the remote highway to Jackson Bay, where your trip will be rewarded by a delicious portion of fresh-cooked fish at *The Cray Pot*. See p.662

▲ Pancake Rocks, Punakaiki

The West Coast

he Southern Alps run down the backbone of the South Island, both defining and isolating the **West Coast**. A narrow, rugged and largely untamed strip 400km long and barely 30km wide, it is home to just 32,000 people. Turbulent rivers cascade out of the mountains though lush bush, past crystal lakes and dark-green paddocks before spilling into the Tasman Sea, its coastline fringed by atmospheric, surf-pounded beaches and backed by the odd tiny shack or, as frequently, nothing at all.

What really sets "the Coast" apart is the interaction of settlers with their environment. **Coasters**, many descended from early gold and coal miners, have long been proud of their ability to coexist with the landscape – a trait mythologized in their reputation for independent-mindedness and intemperate drinking, fuelled by Irish migrants drawn to the 1860s gold rushes. Stories abound of late-night boozing way past closing time, and your fondest memories of the West Coast might be chance encounters in the pub.

Cook sailed up this way in 1770, describing the Coast as "an inhospitable shore … As far as the eye could reach the prospect was wild, craggy and desolate". Little here then for early **European explorers** such as Thomas Brunner and Charles Heaphy, who made forays in 1846–47, led by Kehu, a Maori guide. They returned without finding the cultivable land they sought, and after a shorter trip in 1861 Henry Harper, the first bishop of Christchurch, wrote, "I doubt if such a wilderness will ever be colonized except through the discovery of **gold**". Prophetic words: within two years reports were circulating of flecks in West Coast rivers and a year later Greymouth and Hokitika were experiencing gold rushes. The boom was soon over but mining continued into the twentieth century with huge dredges working their way up the gravel riverbeds by the spent tailings.

As gold was worked out, **coal** took its place and laid the foundation for more permanent towns; the West Coast still produces half the country's output. Kiwis and immigrants alike also took advantage of the abundant open space and relatively low land prices nurturing a thriving **alternative culture** – from behind the trees you will spot tin smokestacks on bus conversions and eco lodges nosing out from behind native bush. In the last twenty years, however, everything has been turned upside down by the challenge of increasing **tourism** and a greater awareness of the Coast's fragile **ecosystems**, a situation that over the last decade gave rise to tension between the Coasters and the government, particularly regarding native timber felling and its impact on the area's unique environment.

No discussion of the West Coast would be complete without mention of the torrential **rainfall**, which descends with tropical intensity for days at a time; every rock springs a waterfall and the bush becomes vibrant with colour. Such soakings have a detrimental effect on the soil, retarding decomposition and producing a

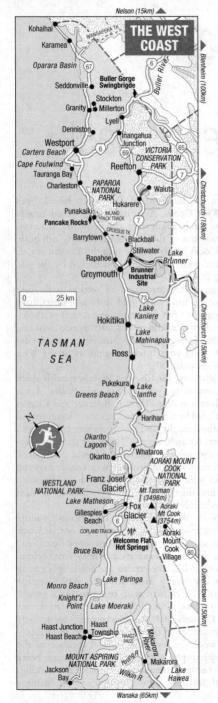

peat-like top layer with all the minerals leached out. The result is **pakihi**, scrubby, impoverished and poor-looking paddocks that characterize much of the West Coast's cleared land. But the abundant sunshine that alternates with the downpours produces excellent conditions for **marijuana** cultivation, an undeclared component of the local economy. Enthusiasm for dope growing is topped only by the springtime rush to catch **whitebait**, when fishers line the riverbanks on rising tides trying to net this epicurean holy grail.

The boom-and-bust nature of the West Coast's mining has produced scores of ghost towns and spawned its three largest settlements – **Westport**, **Greymouth** and **Hokitika**. The real pleasure of the West Coast, though, lies in smaller places, where the Coasters' indomitable spirit shines through: places such as **Karamea**, on the southern limit of the Kahurangi National Park, or **Okarito**, by a seductive lagoon. With the exception of a couple of decent museums and a handful of sights, the West Coast's appeal is in its scenic beauty – the drive, either up or down the coast, is iconic, matching any great road trip in the world. The **Oparara Basin**, near Karamea, and the **Paparoa National Park**, south of Westport, exhibit some of the country's finest limestone formations, including huge arched spans and the famous Pancake Rocks, while in the Westland National Park the frosty white tongues of the **Franz Josef** and **Fox glaciers** poke down the flanks of the Southern Alps toward dense emerald bush and the sea.

Since this is New Zealand there's no shortage of activities, particularly the exciting fly-in **rafting** trips down the West Coast's steep

The simplest and best way to see the West Coast is with your own **vehicle**. The prevalent northerly wind makes **cycling** a chore but that said the distances between towns aren't off-putting and you can always find somewhere to camp. Public transport is fairly restrictive, **trains** only penetrate as far as Greymouth, **bus services** are few and though they call at all the major towns won't get you to most of the walks. However, with patience and forward planning it is possible to see much of interest, especially if you are prepared to walk. For details of transport routes see "Travel details" on p.665.

rivers. The limestone bedrock makes for some penetrative adventure **caving**, and there's plenty of **hiking**, with the Heaphy Track to the north, the Inland Pack Track near Punakaiki and a stack of tramps around the glaciers.

Most people visit from November to April, but in **winter** temperatures are not so low, there are greater numbers of cloud-free days and pesky **sandflies** are less active. The West Coast never feels crowded but in the off season accommodation is plentiful and cheaper though many adventure trips and scenic **flights**, which require minimum numbers to operate, may be harder to arrange.

The northern approaches: along the Buller and Grey rivers

Stretching 169km from its source at Lake Rotoiti in the Nelson Lakes National Park to its mouth at Westport, the **Buller River**'s blue-green waters reflect sunlight dappled through riverside beech forests as they swirl through one of the grandest of New Zealand's river gorges. The Maori name for the Buller is Kawatiri, meaning "deep and swift", qualities which lure rafters to several stretches. Gold was discovered along the Buller in 1858, sparking a gold rush centred on **Lyell**, now a ghost town whose outlying remains can be visited on the **Lyell Walkway**.

The Buller lies between the Lyell and Brunner ranges, and is traced by SH6 from Kawatiri Junction to Westport through Inangahua Junction, where Greymouth-bound travellers turn south towards **Reefton**. From Reefton, SH7 hugs the **Grey River**, a far less dramatic watercourse, as it flows through a wide valley to the east of the granite tops of the Paparoa Range past more evidence of the gold and coal industries, principally at **Blackball** and the **Brunner Industrial Site**.

The Buller Gorge

SH6 from Nelson passes through Murchison (see p.476) and follows the Buller River 11km to **O'Sullivan's Bridge**, where you turn right to remain on SH6 as it enters the Upper Buller Scenic Reserve. After 6km, the road passes the **Buller Gorge Swingbridge** ($5; ☎03/523 9809, ⓦwww.bullergorge.co.nz), an adventure heritage park hybrid, accessed by New Zealand's longest (110m) pedestrian swingbridge. Crossing high above the river, it parallels a fun 160m-long **flying fox** (zipwire) on which you can ride sitting ($30), tandem ($30 each), or prone, Superman-style ($45). On the far side of the swift-flowing water, the heritage park has a variety of **bushwalks** (15min–2hr) taking in an earthquake fault line, gold mine workings and the Ariki Falls (1hr round trip).

You can also pan for gold ($12.50) or catch a jetboat ride ($75/45min), taking in the bridge.

Twenty kilometres on, the road passes the grassy site of **Lyell**, a former gold-mining town high above the Buller on flats beside Lyell Creek. In its 1890s heyday it supported five hotels, two banks, two churches and a newspaper, all serving a population of three thousand. Fires and the gradual decline in gold mining saw off the settlement but the few remains can be visited via the short but strenuous **Lyell Walkway**, which passes terraces where huts stood, sobering slabs askew in the cemetery (15min return), and the ten-hammer Croesus quartz stamping battery (1hr 30min return). The roadside site of the former township itself is now a peaceful DOC **campsite** ($6).

At **Inangahua Junction**, 17km to the west, SH69 cuts south to Reefton, while SH6 continues west towards Westport through the **Lower Buller Gorge**, the narrowest and most dramatic section. The road hugs the cliff face in places, most notably at **Hawks Crag**, where the rock has been hewn to form a large overhang – the fact that the water level rose several metres above this carved-out section during a 1926 flood will give you some idea of the volume of water that can surge down the gorge. A few kilometres on you pass Buller Adventure Tours (see p.631) who run rafting trips on the river.

Reefton and around

Located beside the Inangahua River at the intersection of roads from Westport, Greymouth and Christchurch, **REEFTON** owes its existence to rich gold-bearing quartz reefs. These were exploited so heavily in the 1870s that some considered Reefton "the most brisk and businesslike place in the colony". It was also the first place in New Zealand, and one of the first in the world, to install electric street

---

Westland's endangered forest

If gold and coal built the West Coast's foundations, the **timber industry** supported the structure. Ever since timber was felled for sluicing flumes and pit props, Coasters relied on the seemingly limitless forests for their livelihood. Many miners became loggers, felling trees which take from three hundred to six hundred years to mature and which, according to fossil records of pollen, have been around for 100 million years.

Few expressed any concern for the plight of Westland's magnificent stands of **beech** and **podocarp** until the 1970s, when environmental groups rallied around a campaign to save the Maruia Valley, east of Reefton, which became a touchstone for forest conservation. It wasn't until the 1986 **West Coast Accord** between the government, local authorities, conservationists and the timber industry that some sort of truce prevailed. In the 1980s and 1990s most of the forests were selectively logged, often using helicopters to pluck out the mature trees without destroying those nearby. While it preserved the appearance of the forest, this was little comfort for New Zealand's endangered **birds** – particularly kaka, kakariki (yellow-crowned parakeet), morepork (native owl) and rifleman – and long-tailed **bats**, all of which nest in holes in older trees.

In 1999, Labour leader Helen Clark honoured her election pledge and banned the logging of beech forests by the State-owned Timberlands company. Precious West Coast jobs were lost and the government stepped in with the $100 million fund, which helped restart the local economy. Thousands still felt betrayed in this tradition-ally Labour-voting part of the world, but a resurgent farming sector, higher property prices and increased tourism gave Clark breathing space, until the economic downturn and 2008 general election.

lighting powered by a hydroelectric generator. Such forward thinking abated and Reefton weathered poorly, though the reopening of an old gold mine on the outskirts of town has brought new hope and money. That said once you've exhausted the local cafés you'll probably want to head for Waiuta or press on down the Grey Valley.

Two walks link the specific points of interest around town, both the subject of brochures available from the visitor centre. The elegiac **Historic Walk** (40min) meanders around Reefton's grid of streets, visiting once-grand buildings – some ripe for preservation, others partway there. The pleasant **Powerhouse Walk** (40min) is slightly more uplifting in recalling an illustrious past, perhaps because of its course along the Inangahua River. In the centre of town, on the corner of Walsh and Broadway, the so-called "Bearded Miners" entertain visitors at an old **miner's cottage** and smithy (daily, pretty much when they feel like it; donation) by firing up the forge and helping you pan for gold.

The water for Reefton's original hydroelectric scheme was diverted 2km from Blacks Point, where the **Blacks Point Museum**, SH7 towards Springs Junction (Oct–April Wed–Fri & Sun 9am–noon & 1–4pm, Sat 1–4pm; $5), occupies a former Wesleyan Chapel. The museum charts the district's cultural and mining history and shows a DVD, on request, promoting the modern mining operation, namechecking the **guided mine tour** (1.45pm; 3hr; booked via Reefton's i-SITE). Outside, an ancient five-hammer stamper battery is cranked into action, also on request. The informative *Walks in the Murray Creek Goldfield* leaflet, available in the museum and at the i-SITE, details nearby mining **trails**.

Practicalities

Buses all stop on Broadway, Reefton's main street. Within sight of the helpful **i-SITE visitor centre** and **DOC office**, 67–69 Broadway (daily: Nov–March 8.30am–5pm; April–Oct Mon–Fri 9am–5pm, Sat & Sun 10am–3pm; ☏03/732 8391, ⓦwww.reefton.co.nz), which has **internet access**, a small replica gold mine (gold coin donation), rents out gold pans ($2/day) and has a winding machine that splutters into life if you feed the coin box two bucks.

The best and friendliest place to **stay** in town is *Reef Cottage B&B Inn*, 51–55 Broadway (☏0800/770 440, ⓦwww.reefcottage.co.nz; ❹/❺), with four beautifully decorated Victorian- and 1920s-style doubles (two en-suite, two with separate bathrooms), while Reefton's former nurses' home, *The Old Nurses Home*,104 Shiel St (☏03/732 8881, ⓔreeftonretreat@hotmail.com; rooms ❶ en suites ❸), is popular with domestic tourists, offering a wide range of twins and doubles with communal bathrooms. *Reefton Domain Motor Camp*, 1 Ross St, at the top of Broadway (☏03/732 8477; camping $10, cabins ❶), is a central **campsite** with hook-ups and swimming in the Inangahua River, while *Slab Hut Creek* is a primitive DOC site ($6) 8km south on SH7 down the Grey Valley and 1km east.

For **eating**, head to Broadway, where both *Alfresco's* at no. 16 and *Reef Cottage Café* at no. 53 do light meals and coffee by day and are open evenings during the summer. The homey *Diggers Cafe* at no. 68 offers filling grub plus internet and wireless access (daily from 7am in summer and 9am–4pm in winter).

The Grey Valley

Southwest of Reefton, SH7 follows the Grey Valley, cut off from the Tasman Sea by the rugged Paparoa Range and hemmed in by the Southern Alps. From both sides, the bush is gradually reclaiming the mine workings that once characterized the region. Nothing has stepped in to replace them and the small communities tick over, eking a living from inquisitive tourists keen to explore the former mining towns of **Waiuta** and **Blackball** and to walk the **Croesus Track**.

Waiuta

The first diversion of any consequence is 21km south of Reefton, where **Hukarere** marks the junction for **WAIUTA**, a ghost town seventeen partly sealed kilometres east. This was the last of the West Coast's great gold towns, reaching a population of 6000 in the 1930s.

Its end came when a mineshaft collapsed in 1951, burying large deposits of gold-bearing reef-quartz, almost 900m down, where it was uneconomic to extract them. Miners left for jobs on the coast, Australian companies bought most of the mining equipment and many houses were carted off, but the town wasn't completely abandoned; a few cottages are still occupied and there are several more buildings scattered around, including the original post office. The rolling country, pocked by waste heaps, is slowly being colonized by gorse and bramble, but the cypresses and poplars that once delineated gardens and the fruit trees that filled them remain; sadly the rugby field, whippet track, croquet lawns and swimming pool fared less well. Wonderfully atmospheric for just mooching around, guided by the invaluable **Waiuta** leaflet (from Reefton i-SITE) and strategically placed interpretive panels, you can see the lot in a couple of hours.

Blackball

Both the Grey River and SH7 meander through inconsequential small towns until they reach **Stillwater**, 11km short of Greymouth, where side roads lead to Blackball and Lake Brunner.

Languid **BLACKBALL** is a former gold- and coal-mining village spread across a plateau at the foot of the Paparoa Range, 11km northeast of Stillwater. Here, commuters, neo-hippies and gnarled part-time hunters and prospectors coexist. Blackball owes its existence to alluvial gold discovered in Blackball Creek in 1864, but gold returns diminished and it was left to coal to save the day. This supported Blackball until the mine's closure in 1964, along the way staking the town's place in New Zealand's history as a birthplace of the **labour movement**.

During the first three decades of the twentieth century, the whole of the Grey Valley was a hotbed of doctrinaire socialism, as organizers moved among the towns, pressing unbending mine managers to address atrocious working conditions. An impasse resulted in the crippling 1908 "cribtime strike", when Pat Hickey, Bob Semple and Paddy Webb requested an extension of their "crib" (lunch) break from fifteen to thirty minutes. Management's refusal sparked an illegal ten-week strike – the longest in New Zealand's history – during which the workers' families were fined £75 for their action. None could pay and although the bailiffs tried to auction their possessions, the workers banded together refusing to bid – one then bought all the goods for a fraction of their worth and redistributed them to their original owners. This spirit eventually won the day: the workers returned to the mine and crib time was extended, but the £75 was extracted from their subsequent wages.

The struggle led to the formation of the Miners' Federation, which later transformed itself into the **Federation of Labour**, the country's principal trade union organization. Eric Beardsley's historical novel **Blackball 08** gives an accurate and passionate portrayal of the strike. These days Blackball's rustic tranquillity is the main draw, abetted by excellent walking through the gold workings of Blackball Creek and up onto the wind-blasted tops of the Paparoa Range along the **Croesus Track** (see opposite).

Practicalities

With no regular public transport, you'll have to find your own way to Blackball, where social life revolves around the welcoming, low-key ⚑ *Formerly The Blackball Hilton*, Hart Street (℡0800/425 225, ⓦ www.blackballhilton.co.nz; B&B ④). The

The Croesus Track

Prospectors seeking new claims gradually pushed their way up Blackball Creek. The scant remains of decades of toil now provide the principal interest on the **Croesus Track**, the first half of which is easily explored in a day from Blackball. The whole track over the 1200m Paparoa Range to Barrytown, on the coast 30km north of Greymouth, takes two gentle days or one eight-hour slog. DOC's informative *Central West Coast* leaflet shows adequate detail for walkers, and the NZMS's 1:50,000 *Ahaura* Topomap is the one for map enthusiasts.

Access and accommodation

The track **starts** at Smoke-ho car park, at the end of a rough but passable road 7km north of Blackball, and **finishes** opposite the *All Nations Tavern* on SH6 in Barrytown, where buses pass twice daily in each direction. The most convenient approach is with Kea Tours (☎0800/532 868) who do a Blackball drop-off and Barrytown pick-up combo for $40 (minimum 2). The only hut is the first-come-first-served **Ces Clarke Hut** (24 bunks; $15), with panoramic views and a coal-burning stove.

The track

Much of the track was designed to accommodate tramways, so you get a gentle, steady grade as you wind through native podocarps interspersed with ferns, mosses and vines, gradually giving way to hardier silver beech and eventually alpine tussock and herbfields above the treeline. Sea mist commonly cloaks the tops during the middle of the day. Half an hour from the Smoke-ho car park, a side path (10min return) leads to the former site of the **Minerva Battery**. Immediately after the junction, the main path crosses Clarke Creek on a modern wire bridge above the remains of an old wooden bridge. Another half-hour on, a detour leads to two clearings that once contained **Perotti's Mill** (10min return) and the **Croesus Battery** (50min return). After almost an hour, another side path leads to the primitive **Garden Gully Hut** (5min return) and the **Garden Gully Battery** (40min return). The main track turns sharply west before reaching the **Ces Clarke Hut**, on the treeline: fill your water bottles here, as there is no other supply. The top of the ridge near Mount Ryall (1220m) lies two undulating hours beyond, a little more if you run off to climb **Croesus Knob** (1204m). The broad ridge offers wonderful views of the coast, reached in under three hours by a steep but well-marked path diving into the bush.

---

last of the mining-era **hotels**, it opened as the *Dominion* in 1910, subsequently operated as the *Hilton* – ostensibly named for the former mine manager remembered in Hilton Street nearby – until challenged by the international hotel chain of the same name. Apart from lively drinking with locals, the hotel offers the annual World of Unwearable Arts Exhibtion (Oct–Nov), Blackball's cheeky riposte to The World of WearableArt (see p.427) and accommodation – doubles and twins with shared bathrooms. The emphasis is on character rather than creature comforts, but guests have use of an indoor hot tub. The restaurant is open for guests' breakfast, coffee, lunches ($10–16) and dinners ($18–28), which might include Blackball salami.

For picnic supplies, call in at the excellent Blackball Salami Co (Mon–Fri 8am–4pm, Sat 9am–3pm) up the street from the *Hilton* to feast on delicious venison sausages, chorizo, various salamis (of which 150 go to Antarctic bases every year) and other delectable morsels; or pop across the road for fish and chips from the dairy.

Lake Brunner

From SH7 near Blackball, a sealed road runs 55km south to link up with SH73 between Greymouth and Arthur's Pass. Along the way it passes Lake Brunner

(Moana Kotuku), a filled glacial hollow celebrated for its trout fishing. The shoreline village of **MOANA** is popular with holidaying Kiwis and second-home owners but not brimming with diversions. By late summer the lake is surprisingly warm and makes for good **swimming**, or you can head out on foot along a couple of easy paths. At the end of town, beyond the motor camp a slender swingbridge over the fledgling Arthur River provides access to the riverside **Rakaitane Track** (30min return) and the **Lake Side Track** (20–60min return), with good mountain views.

The TranzAlpine **train** makes a daily stop at Moana. Facilities here are limited, but there's **accommodation** at the *Lake Brunner Resort*, Ahau Street (T03/738 0083, W www.lakebrunnerresort.net.nz; ⑤), which has a block of swanky modern units, some with lake views. The licensed *Station House Café*, Koe Street (T03/738 0158), offers the best **eating**, with lunches from $14 and dinners from $29.50 (booking essential).

Brunner Industrial Site

Back on SH7, a couple of kilometres past Stillwater, a tall brick chimney marks the **Brunner Industrial Site** (unrestricted access). Recently smartened up roadside information panels mark the path to a fine old suspension bridge (now strengthened and refurbished but still only open to foot traffic), which crosses the swirling river to the remaining buildings and the ruins of the skilfully crafted beehive coking ovens.

On his explorations in the late 1840s, Thomas Brunner noted a seam of riverside coal, and by 1885 the site was producing twice as much as any other mine in the country and exporting firebricks throughout Australasia. In 1896 New Zealand's worst mining disaster (with 69 dead) heralded its decline. The site was finally abandoned in the 1940s and only exhumed from dense bush in the early 1980s.

Westport and around

Like a proud fly caught in amber **WESTPORT**, despite government and tourist money and the council's zealous desire to modernize, remains fixed in time. Diversions are scarce, except at the seal colony at **Cape Foulwind**, on the brain-clearing walk to the old lighthouse beyond or exploring the ghostly former coal towns of the **Rochford Plateau**. Were Westport, once known as *Worstport*, not a transport interchange, few would stay in this workaday fishing port as the temptations of the Heaphy Track and Karamea, 100km north, are too strong. However stay some must and their time is made tolerable by good-value accommodation, an engaging museum, some adventure activities and the very hospitable locals.

Westport was the first of the West Coast towns, established by one **Reuben Waite** in 1861 as a single store beside the mouth of the Buller River. He made his living provisioning Buller Gorge prospectors in return for gold but when the miners moved on to richer pickings in Otago, Waite upped sticks and headed south to help found Greymouth. Westport turned to coal and, while the mining towns to the north were becoming established, engineers channelled the river to scour out a **port**, which fast became the largest coal port in the country, but now lies idle. Westport battles on, with a respectable-sized fishing fleet and the odd ship laden with the produce of New Zealand's largest cement works, at Cape Foulwind, fuelled by coal from the opencast mine at Stockton.

Arrival, information and transport

Almost everything of consequence in Westport is around Palmerston Street. The helpful **i-SITE visitor centre**, 1 Brougham St (daily: Christmas to April

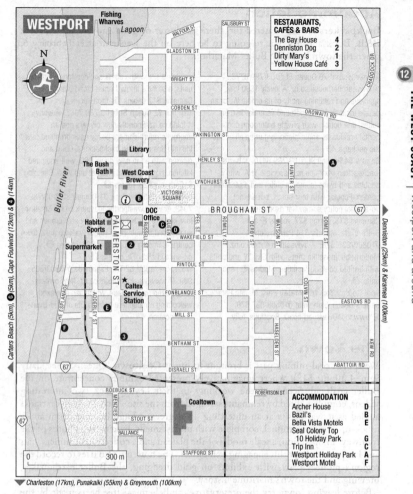

WESTPORT

Fishing
Wharves
Lagoon

N

Carters Beach (5km), ◉ (5km), Cape Foulwind (12km) & ④ (14km)

Buller River

RESTAURANTS,
CAFÉS & BARS
The Bay House   4
Denniston Dog   2
Dirty Mary's   1
Yellow House Café   3

BALFOUR ST
SALISBURY ST
GLADSTON ST
BRIGHT ST
COBDEN ST
OROWAITI RD
PAKINGTON ST
CRADOCK DR

Library
HENLEY ST
HUNTER ST
Ⓐ

The Bush
Bath
LYNDHURST ST
West Coast
Brewery
VICTORIA
SQUARE
ⓘ Ⓑ
BROUGHAM ST
67
DOC
Office
Ⓖ Ⓓ
WAKEFIELD ST
DERBY ST
WATSON ST
DOMETT ST
Habitat
Sports ❶
PALMERSTON ST
RUSSELL ST
PEEL ST
ROMILLY ST
Dennision (25km) & Karamea (100km)
❷
Supermarket
RINTOUL ST
★ Caltex
Service
Station
FONBLANQUE ST
COLVIN ST
EASTONS RD
THE ESPLANADE
ADDERLEY ST
Ⓔ
MILL ST
HASELDEN ST
KEW RD
Ⓕ
❸
BENTHAM ST
67
DISRAELI ST
ABATTOIR RD

ROEBUCK ST
ROBERTSON ST
ACCOMMODATION
Archer House   D
Bazil's   B
Bella Vista Motels E
Seal Colony Top
  10 Holiday Park   G
Trip Inn   C
Westport Holiday Park A
Westport Motel   F
Coaltown
67
MENZIES ST
STOUT ST
BALLANCE ST
STAFFORD ST

0   300 m

▼ Charleston (17km), Punakaiki (55km) & Greymouth (100km)

9am–5pm, later if the clamour demands; May–Oct Mon–Fri 9am–4pm, Sat &
Sun 9.30am–3.30pm; Nov to Christmas, Mon–Fri 9am–5pm, Sat & Sun
9am–4.30pm; ℡03/789 6658, ⓦwww.westport.org.nz), is the place for
tramping information and internet access. Book your Heaphy Track hut tickets
online, or let the i-SITE, do it for a $5 supplement. For less-walked tracks
consult the **DOC office**, 72 Russell St (Mon–Fri 8am–noon & 1–5pm;
℡03/788 8008).

Karamea Express **buses** stop outside the i-SITE; Atomic Shuttles and Nelson
Lakes Shuttles drop off in town or by accommodation and InterCity and East–
West stop outside the Caltex service station at 197 Palmerston St. Westport is
compact enough for you to **get around** on foot, though to reach the nearby
attractions you'll need your own transport or Buller Taxis (℡03/789 6900).
Bike rental is available from Habitat Sports, 204 Palmerston St ($35–45/day;
℡03/788 8002).

Accommodation

Backpackers are well catered for, there's a cluster of good **motels** and a decent **B&B**. Book ahead if you're going to be here on the weekend after February 6, when the town hosts the Buller Marathon.

Archer House 75 Queen St ☎03/789 8778, ⓦwww.archerhouse.co.nz. A lovely 1890 villa, spacious and retaining many of its ornate Victorian details including a wraparound veranda. Two en suites, one double with private bathroom, continental breakfasts and a pleasing garden all add to the package. ⑥

Bazil's 54 Russell St ☎03/789 6410, ⓔbazils .backpackers@xtra.co.nz. Associate YHA, with doubles and twins (some en suite) and a pleasant garden. Popular with tour buses, but a strict no-alcohol policy somewhat dissipates the lariness. Camping $13, dorms $27, rooms ②/③

Bella Vista Motels 314 Palmerston St ☎0800/235 528, ⓔbvwestport@xtra.co.nz. Modern, businesslike motel with Sky TV and units with limited cooking facilities. Studios ④, spa units ⑤

Seal Colony Top 10 Holiday Park Marine Parade, Carters Beach, 6km west ☎0508/937 876, ⓦwww.top10westport.co.nz. Spacious, fully equipped site, with cabins and comfortable motel units, a stone's throw from a broad beach. Camping $17 cabins ②, motel units ④

Trip Inn 72 Queen St ☎03/789 7367, ⓦwww .tripinn.co.nz. Friendly new owners and an energetic refurbishment policy have breathed new life into this rambling backpackers. Quiet and relaxed with a fab new deck, BBQ, well-equipped kitchen, home cinema, internet and wi-fi. Camping $15, dorms $26, rooms ②

Westport Holiday Park 31 Domett St ☎03/789 7043, ⓦwww.westportholidaypark.co.nz. Smallish, low-key site partly hemmed in by native bush and surrounded by suburbia, 10min walk from the town centre. Camping $15, dorms $26, cabins ②, en-suite chalets ③, motels ⑤

Westport Motel 32 The Esplanade ☎0800/805 909, ⓦwww.westportmotel.co.nz. New owners have jazzed up the place, which has a relaxed, welcoming atmosphere befitting its off-the-main-drag location. ③

The Town

Westport's coal-mining past is brought to life at **Coaltown**, Queen Street (daily 9am–4.30pm; $12), where imaginatively presented exhibits concentrate on the Buller coalfield. Scenes of the workings in their heyday pack two interesting videos, complemented by remnants salvaged from the site – a coal wagon on tracks angled as it was *in situ* at an unsettling 45 degrees, a huge braking drum and a mock-up of a mine tunnel, complete with musty smells. Fascinating photos of the tramways in operation, a scale model of the plateau and a collection of miners' hats and lamps round out this engaging exhibition. The museum also tries to record the region's pioneer past, with exhibits on gold dredging, the Buller earthquakes, brewing and the town's maritime history.

Before leaving town, try the preservative- and chemical-free beers made by the co-operatively run **West Coast Brewery**, 10 Lyndhurst St (Mon–Fri 10am–5.30pm, Sat 8.30am–5pm; ☎03/789 6201), which distributes its wares throughout the northern half of the South Island, sponsors Hokitika's Wildfoods Festival and offers free tastings.

In true entrepreneurial West Coast spirit the owner of a soap shop at 114 Palmerston St has transformed his back block into **The Bush Bath** (1hr 15min; double $40; ☎03/789 8828,), the surrounds decorated with ferns imported from the bush outside town. It's not the best location but you have to admire his gall and the locals love it.

Walks and activities

Once again we have Captain Cook, battling heavy weather in March 1770, to thank for the naming of Westport's most dramatic and evocatively titled stretch of coastline, **Cape Foulwind**, 12km west of town. The name also lends itself to the undulating 4km **Cape Foulwind Walkway**, which runs over exposed headlands, airing superb coastal views. It is perfect for sunset ambling between the old lighthouse, a replica of Abel Tasman's astrolabe and the **Tauranga Bay Seal Colony**, where platforms overlook New Zealand's most northerly breeding colony of fur seals. The animals, at the southern end of the walkway, are at their most active and numerous from October to January, often numbering four hundred or more, a sign of the welcome recovery from the decimation of 150 years of sealing. Don't be tempted by the beach at Tauranga Bay, it is treacherous.

For something wilder still, go **rafting** with Buller Adventure Tours (℡0800/697 286, ⓦwww.adventuretours.co.nz), located 8km east of Westport on SH6, heading into the Buller Gorge. Throughout the year they run the six major rapids of the Grade IV "Earthquake Slip" section of the **Buller River** around Lyell, spending nearly three hours on the water for $120. They also offer **jetboat rides** through the Lower Buller Gorge (1hr 15min; $79), **horse trekking** through bush and along a river beach (from $80/2hr) and ninety-minute guided rides on sports quad bikes ($140).

Eating, drinking and nightlife

Foodies head for the *Yellow House Café* or out of town to *The Bay House*, while those in need of a "feed" hit the local **pubs**, which adhere to the West Coast tradition of aggressive edginess at the weekends. **Nightlife** of any quality is absent since the council demolished the atmospheric, historic cinema.

The Bay House Tauranga Bay ℡03/789 7133, ⓦwww.bayhousecafe.co.nz. Restaurant/café beyond the southern end of the Cape Foulwind Walkway, serving great coffee, breakfast, brunch, lunch and excellent dinners (mains around $30) – such as fillet of beef with bacon and puy lentils, locally caught turbot, at least one veggie option and mouthwatering desserts – served in the cosy interior or on the terrace, overlooking the bay. Licensed.

Denniston Dog 18 Wakefield St ℡03/789 7640. The only café/bar that isn't just a pub with a percolator offers a good range of beers, coffee and some excellent light and main meals ($11–32). Try the King salmon or venison hotpot.

Dirty Mary's 198 Palmerston St. Daily, from 8.45am until 8pm, this unassuming café dishes out filling breakfasts, home-made pies, soups and chowder, fish and chips and decent coffee at low prices.

Yellow House Café 243 Palmerston St ℡03/789 8765. Don't let the bright yellow and red walls of this converted house put you off, instead decorate your own paper tablecloth with crayon and tuck into delicious cakes during the day and the likes of artichoke dip ($14), whitebait patties and chocolate gormandise in the evening (mains $24–29), all cooked to order from mostly local ingredients. Licensed.

Around Westport

Westport historically thrived on supplying inhospitably sited coal-mining towns where fresh vegetables were hard to grow and sheep almost impossible to raise. Foremost among them was **Denniston**, located high on the **Rochford Plateau**. Since coal mining stopped in the late 1960s houses have been carted away and the bush has rapidly engulfed what remains, which makes it an intriguing place to explore for half a day, or longer if you want to tackle the **Denniston Incline Walk**. All the other deep mines have gone the same way, leaving a legacy of inclines, tramways and rusting machinery that can be visited on a number of walks, the **Charming Creek Walk** being the best.

Outwest Tours (℡0800/688 937, ⓦwww.outwest.co.nz) run trips out this way. Their **Denniston Tour** (daily 9.30am–4pm; $95) visits the town and plateau, while the coal-company-sponsored **Stockton Mine Tour** (daily 10am–4pm; $10) gives an insight into a working opencast mine.

Denniston

The Karamea Road runs north from Westport to Waimangaroa, 17km away, where a steep 9km road wends its way 600m up to the semi-ghost town of **DENNISTON**, the setting for Jenny Pattrick's 2003 bestselling historical novel *The Denniston Rose*.

John Rochford discovered the rich Coalbrookdale Seam in 1859 and the plateau was soon humming with activity, spurred on by the construction of the **Denniston Self-Acting Incline** in 1879. This impressive, gravity-powered tramway was the steepest rail-wagon incline in the world, lowering coal-filled wagons 518m over 1.7km and hauling up empty ones. Throughout its 88-year lifespan, over a thousand tonnes of coal a day would rattle at a prodigious 70km/hr down to Conn's Creek for the trip into Westport. Initially goods, machinery and even people came up the incline but after four unfortunates were flung to their death, a path was constructed in 1884, easing some of the hardship of living on the plateau.

The region peaked at around 2500 inhabitants in 1910, but the accessible coal eventually played out and the incline closed in 1967. All that's left now is the post office, a fire station, half a dozen scattered houses, three or four of them occupied, and a treasure-trove of industrial archeology centred on a gaunt winding derrick. The views are great in fine weather, but a blanket of cloud and damp fog adds a suitably ethereal quality.

The old schoolhouse here has been turned into a small "Friends of the Hill" **museum** and **visitor centre** (Jan daily plus Sun all year 10am–3pm; free), containing historical photos and old mining machinery. It all comes alive when you talk to curator Gary James (℡03/789 9755), who is usually happy to open up.

At Conn's Creek, 2km inland from Waimangaroa, fit and ambitious visitors can tackle the **Denniston Walk** (2km one-way; 2–3hr; 520m ascent), which follows the 1884 path roughly parallel to the incline.

North of Waimangaroa

North of Waimangaroa, SH67 runs 7km to **Granity** – where you can break your journey for a coffee and home-made pie (try the buttered chicken) from the *Blue Zephyr Café* – and then continues 2km to **Ngakawau**. Here, a coal depot signals the start of the lovely **Charming Creek Walk** (5km one-way; 2hr; 100m ascent), which follows an old railway, used for timber and coal extraction between 1914 and 1958. The first half-hour is dull, but things improve dramatically after the S-shaped Irishman's Tunnel, which has great views of the boulder-strewn river below and, after a swingbridge river crossing, the Mangatini Falls. From here to the picnic stop by the remains of Watson's Mills is the most interesting section of the walk and is as far as most people get (2–3hr return).

Ngakawau merges imperceptibly with **Hector**, where you can stay comfortably at *The Old Slaughterhouse*, 2km north of the village on SH67 (℡03/782 8333, Ⓦwww.oldslaughterhouse.co.nz; dorms $30, rooms ❷). This relaxing **hostel** in a lovely wooden house perches on the hillside with vast ocean views, welcoming hosts, good bushwalks and Hector's dolphins regularly playing in the surf below. It would be a crime to shatter the peace with TV, internet, washing machines or hairdryers, so they don't. Access is a steep ten-minute walk off SH67, though the owners will carry your bags on a quad bike.

There's more accommodation 15km further north and 3km down a side road at the *Gentle Annie* (℡03/782 1826, Ⓦwww.gentleannie.co.nz; camping $10, dorms $25, rooms ❷, cottages sleeping 6 ❹). A relaxed, beautifully sited spot near the mouth of the Mokihinui River, beside Gentle Annie Beach. Accommodation ranges from camping to well-equipped, romantic, self-contained cottages with sea or river views.

Karamea and the Oparara Basin

The northwestern corner of the South Island competes with Fiordland as the least developed and most inaccessible region in the country, a distinction acknowledged by the formation of the **Kahurangi National Park** in 1996. The second-largest park in the country, it embraces a wilderness of spectacular hill country, supporting alpine meadows, the high Matiri ("Thousand Acre") Plateau, New Zealand's finest karst landscape, dramatic windswept beaches and a coastal strip warm enough to support extensive stands of nikau palms. Charles Heaphy and Thomas Brunner surveyed the region in 1846, paving the way for European and Chinese gold miners, who came twenty years later. Pioneers established themselves at **Karamea**, now the base for visiting the fine limestone country of the **Oparara Basin** and the last bit of the **Heaphy Track**.

The road north from Westport runs parallel to the coast, pinched between the pounding Tasman breakers and bush-clad hills as it passes through meagre hamlets with barely a shop or a pub. The journey takes almost two hours if you don't stop, though there are plenty of opportunities to pause, not least at the coal towns around Westport (see opposite). North of the **Mokihinui River**, the road leaves the coastal strip, twisting and climbing over **Karamea Bluff** before descending again into a rich apron of dairying land. Rainfall begins to drop off and humidity picks up, promoting more subtropical vegetation characterized by marauding cabbage trees and nikau palms. At the foot of the bluff, **Little Wanganui** marks the turn-off for the start of the **Wangapeka** and **Leslie–Karamea** tracks (jointly 52km; 3–5 days), which traverses the southern half of the Kahurangi National Park to Tasman Bay near Motueka.

Karamea

Without losing its sleepy identity **KARAMEA**, 100km north of Westport, has expanded to cater to the needs of a growing number of tourists. Despite being an isolated spot, virtually at the end of the road (to continue any distance north you'd have to go on foot along the Heaphy Track), there's no shortage of things to do, the southern section of the **Kahurangi National Park** easily justifying a day or two of exploration and the **Oparara Basin** rewarding closer inspection.

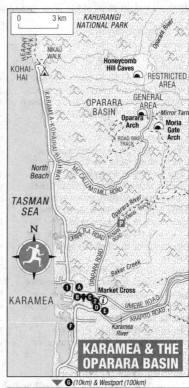

KARAMEA & THE OPARARA BASIN

▼ ⑥ *(10km)* & Westport *(100km)*

ACCOMMODATION		RESTAURANTS	
Karamea Domain	B	Karamea Village Hotel	1
Karamea Lodge	F	The Last Resort	C
Karamea Motels	D	Riverstone Restaurant	E
The Last Resort	C	Saracens Café	2
Riverstone Restaurant	E		
Rongo	A		
Wangapeka Backpackers	G		

Back in 1874, this was very much **frontier territory**, with the Karamea River port providing the only link with the outside world. Settlers eked a living from **gold** and **flax**, but after a couple of fruitless years realized that the poorly drained *pakihi* soils would barely support them. They pushed on, opening up the first road to Westport just in time for the upheavals of the 1929 Murchison **earthquake**, which altered the river flow and permanently ruined the harbour. Logging finally ceased in 2000, leaving tourism, agriculture and fruit-growing as the town's lifeblood. The **visitor centre** is at Market Cross, 2km east of the centre (Jan–April daily 9am–5pm; May–Dec Mon–Fri 9am–5pm & Sat & Sun 9am–noon; ℡03/782 6652, Ⓦwww .karameainfo.co.nz), with helpful staff and **internet access;** you can **book huts** for the **Heaphy Track** online here, or get staff to do it for you for $5 extra. The **Heaphy Track** is generally walked from north to south and is covered on p.472.

Karamea Express **bus** services ply the Westport–Karamea route (Nov–March Mon–Sat; April–Oct Mon–Fri; $30 each way; ℡03/782 6757), running south to Westport in the early morning and setting off around 11.30am for the return journey. Buses connect with ongoing services in Westport. Karamea Express also serves the **Heaphy Track** trailhead at Kohaihai (Nov–March daily around 2pm; $12; in winter on demand) and drops off at the Wangapeka trailhead on the Westport–Karamea run.

Accommodation

Increased tourism means there are now quite a few **places to stay** in Karamea, and some good **camping** spots.

Karamea Domain On SH67 between *The Last Resort* and the *Karamea Village Hotel* ℡03/782 6069. Basic site utilizing the showers and toilets of the town's sports field. Camping $15 per site, hook-ups $16, dorms $12.

Karamea Lodge SH6, 5km south of town ℡03/782 6034, Ⓦwww.karamealodge.co.nz. Luxury units with decks, sea views, kitchen and lounge and continental breakfast. ❺

Karamea Motels 17 Wharf Rd ℡03/782 6838, Ⓦwww.karameamotels.co.nz. Run by the same people as Rongo (see below) and along the same lines, with units about 100m toward the estuary and a viewing platform that works best if you stay stood up. Dorms $30, rooms ❸, motel units ❸

The Last Resort 71 Waverly St (SH67) ℡0800/505 042, Ⓦwww.lastresort.co.nz. Based around an imaginatively styled main lodge with an on-site restaurant and bar, comfortable accommodation in dorms (no bunks, no linen: bring a sleeping bag), simple but attractive lodge rooms (some en suite), motel-style studios and

well-appointed "cottages" sleeping four. Shares $30, lodge ❹, studios ❹, cottages ❺ **Riverstone Restaurant** (see "Eating and drinking"). Purpose-built, comfortable chalet accommodation behind and up the hill from the restaurant, with good views of the river. ❻

Rongo 130 Waverle St (SH67) ℡03/782 6667, Ⓦwww.livinginpeace.com. Welcoming, rainbow-painted hostel in spacious grounds with an organic veggie garden, fab cactus garden and comfy wood-floored rooms and dorms. Art and music play a big part in the hostel's daily life, and it even runs a community radio station (107.5FM). If you stay three nights you get the fourth free. The same folk run a funked-up, comfy motel units (see above). Dorms $27, rooms ❸

Wangapeka Backpackers Wangapeka Rd ℡03/782 6663, Ⓦwww.wangapeka.co.nz. Cosy homestay on a working farm with native bush and welcoming, well-informed hosts, who will ensure you make the most of the beautiful surroundings. $20 a bed, $45 if you join your hosts for breakfast and dinner.

Eating and drinking

Karamea's **eating scene** is limited and there is only one small **supermarket** at Market Cross.

Karamea Village Hotel Corner of Waverley St & Wharf Rd. Karamea's revamped pub dishes up cheap takeaways, straightforward bar meals and a selection of "Wild Food" dishes.

The Last Resort (see "Accommodation"). Good semi-formal dining (mains around $18–30) and a relaxing bar.

🍴 **Riverstone Restaurant** 3.5km south of Karamea's centre on the main road, just after the river bridge ☎03/782 6640, ⓦwww .rivstone.co.nz. Fine dining comes to town in style with this beautifully sited restaurant with river views and a mouthwatering menu, including duck confit, chicken curry and home-made cheeses, one of which is Caerphilly tangy.

Saracens Café Opposite the visitor centre. Relaxed spot serving coffee, pies, enormous sausage rolls and sandwiches in a craft gallery or outside.

The Oparara Basin and Kohaihai

Kahurangi's finest limestone formations lie east of the Karamea–Kohaihai Highway in the **Oparara Basin**, a compact area of **karst** topography characterized by sinkholes, underground streams, caves and bridges created over millennia by the action of slightly acidic streams on the jointed rock. This is home to New Zealand's largest native **spider**, the harmless, 15cm-diameter gradungular spider (found only in caves in the Karamea and Collingwood area, where it feeds off blowflies and cave crickets), and to a rare species of ancient and primitive carnivorous **snail** that grows up to 70mm across and dines on earthworms. Tannin-stained rivers course gently over bleached-white boulders and, in faster-flowing sections, the rare whio (blue duck) swims for its supper. If your interest in geology is fleeting, the Oparara Basin still makes a superb place for day **walks** or a **picnic**.

Ten kilometres north of Karamea, the steep, narrow and gravel McCallums Mill Road runs 14km east to the Oparara Basin, where the **Honeycomb Hill Caves** have become a valuable key to understanding New Zealand's fauna. The sediment on the cave floor has helped preserve the ancient skeletons of birds, most of them killed when they fell through holes in the roof. The bones of over fifty species have been found here including those of the Haast eagle, the largest eagle ever known with a wingspan of up to 4m.

The cave system can only be visited on the excellent and educational **Honeycomb Hill Caves Tour** (daily 10am & 2pm on demand, min 2 persons; $85; ☎03/782 6652, ⓦwww.oparara.co.nz) which explores just some of the 15km of passages. Tours depart from the end of McCallums Mill car park, close to the cave, and take two and a half hours. If you don't have your own transport, a ride can be organized for $25 return. Cave trips can be combined with the **Honeycomb Hill Arch Kayak Tour** (mid-Dec to Aug; $85), a gorgeous paddle through bush and under a broad limestone arch.

As is common in limestone areas, the watercourses alter frequently, leaving behind dry caves such as the **Crazy Paving and Box Canyon caves** (about 10min return) near the Honeycomb Caves. Both are accessible along a five-minute track from the car park and are good for spider- and fossil-spotting: take a torch each, and watch the slippery floors.

The two most spectacular examples of limestone architecture lie at the end of beautiful, short bushwalks signposted from a car park 3km back down the road towards Karamea. The largest is the **Oparara Arch** (40min return), a vast two-tiered bridge 43m high, 40m wide and over 219m long, which appears magically out of the bush but defies any attempt at successful photography. The lovely **Moria Gate Arch** was named decades before *Lord of the Rings* movie fever swept the land. It is reached on a track (1hr return) through the untouched, high-canopy native forest then through a short cave (torch handy but not really needed). This can be combined with a visit to peaceful **Mirror Tarn** (90min for both).

Kohaihai

Visitors with no aspirations to tramp the full length of Heaphy Track can sample the final few coastal kilometres from the mouth of the Kohaihai River, 17km north of Karamea, where there is river (but not sea) swimming, a beautifully sited DOC **campsite** ($6) and an abundance of sandflies. In the heat of the day, you're much better off across the river in the cool of the **Nikau Walk** (30–40min loop), which winds through a shady grove dense with nikau palms, tree ferns and magnificent gnarled old rata dripping in epiphytes. When it cools off, either continue along the Heaphy to **Scott's Beach** (1hr 30min return), or stick to the southern side of the Kohaihai River and the **Zig-Zag Track** (35min return), which switchbacks up to an expansive lookout.

Paparoa National Park and around

South of Westport lies the Paparoa Range, a 1500m granite and gneiss ridge inlaid with limestone that separates the dramatic coastal strip from the valleys of the Grey and Inangahua rivers. In 1987, the coastal limestone country was designated the **Paparoa National Park**, one of the country's smallest and least-known parks. The highlight is undoubtedly **Pancake Rocks**, where crashing waves have forced spectacular blowholes through a stratified stack of weathered limestone. But to skip the rest would be to miss out on a mysterious world of disappearing rivers, sinkholes, caves and limestone bluffs best seen on the **Inland Pack Track**, but also accessible on shorter walks.

Maori often stopped while travelling the coast in search of *pounamu* (greenstone) and early **European explorers** followed suit seeking agricultural land. Charles Heaphy, Thomas Brunner and two Maori guides came through in 1846, finding

Paparoa walks and the Inland Pack Track

The best way to truly appreciate the dramatic limestone scenery of the Paparoa is on the **Inland Pack Track** (27km; 2–3 days; see map, p.638), but this should only be undertaken by folk with plenty of hiking experience. Most of the terrain is easy going, but there are no bridges for river crossings, and while the water barely gets above your knees in dry periods, the rivers can become impassable after rain. With less time or greater demand for comfort, some of the best can be seen on two day-walks. The delightful **Punakaiki–Pororari Rivers Loop** (12km; 3hr 30min; 100m ascent) follows the initial stretch of the Inland Pack Track as far as the Pororari River, which is then followed downstream between some magnificent limestone cliffs to return to Punakaiki. The **Fox River Cave Walk** (10km; 2hr 30min; 100m ascent) traces the last few kilometres of the Inland Pack Track from the Fox Rivermouth as far as the caves and returns the same way.

Practicalities

DOC's *Inland Pack Track* leaflet provides enough information for the tramp, but you might also fancy the 1:50,000 *Paparoa National Park* map.

The track is best walked south to north, which eliminates the risk of missing the critical turn-off up Fossil Creek. There are no huts along the way, just a massive rock **bivvy** known as the Ballroom Overhang at the end of a long first day. You're advised to carry a **tent** for protection from voracious sandflies, and to avoid a wet night in the open if the rivers flood. **Campfires** are permitted at the Ballroom Overhang, but DOC recommends carrying a stove as most of the usable wood has already been burned. Be sure to check the **weather forecast** with DOC and fill out an **intentions form**.

Base yourself in Punakaiki and call Green Kiwi Tours (☎03/731 1843, ⓦwww .greenkiwitours.co.nz), who will drop off or pick up a vanload (1–8 people) at Fox River for $50, so get a group together.

little to detain them, but within twenty years this stretch was alive with **gold** prospectors at work on the black sands at **Charleston**.

Visitor interest is centred on **Punakaiki**, close by the Pancake Rocks, where bus passengers get a quick glimpse and others pause for the obligatory photos. A couple of days spent here will be well rewarded with a stack of wonderful walks, horseriding or canoeing up delightful limestone gorges.

Westport to Punakaiki

South of Westport, SH67 crosses the Buller River and picks up SH6, the main West Coast road. There's little specific reason to stop except for some lovely **places to stay**. Around 17km south of Westport, ⚘ *Beaconstone*, Birds Ferry Road (☏027/431 0491, ⓦwww.beaconstone.co.nz; closed June–Sept; shares $28, rooms ❶, cottage ❷), is one of the best hostels on the coast, great value, friendly, with a few doubles, one triple, a separate cottage with mountain views and a new communal area. Eco-friendly features include composting toilets and solar power, and it's set in 120 acres of native bush threaded by various trails.

Six kilometres further along SH6 is **Mitchells Gully Gold Mine** (usually 9am–4pm; $10; ☏03/789 6553), a family-run mine working dating back to 1866, which demonstrates the time-honoured methods used to extract fine gold held in a cement-like mass of oxidized ironsand. Along with mining paraphernalia, you can see a restored overshot wheel driving a stamping battery, and working water races and tunnels.

The most intensive mining went on 3km to the south at **CHARLESTON**, once a rollicking boomtown of around 18,000 people, but now a one-horse town without

The Inland Pack Track

The Inland Pack Track starts 1km south of the Punakaiki visitor centre beside the south bank of the Punakaiki River. From **Punakaiki River to Bullock Creek** (9.5km; 4hr; 220m ascent, 100m descent), the track rises to a low saddle then descends to ford the Pororari River, continuing with views inland to the Paparoa Range before reaching Bullock Creek. This should be forded with care – in flood conditions it is impassable. From **Bullock Creek to Fox River** (10km; 3–4hr; 100m ascent, 150m descent), you skirt swampland then climb to a ridge before descending gradually to Fossil Creek, which is followed wading from pool to pool, occasionally clambering over fallen tree trunks. After half an hour of this, Fossil Creek meets the main tributary of the Fox River, Dilemma Creek, by a small sign – keep your eyes peeled. This is the most dramatic section of the trip but potentially the most dangerous, with eighteen fords to cross between gravel banks in the bed of Dilemma Creek: if you have any doubts about the first crossing, turn back, as they only get worse. The lower river has carved out a deep canyon between gleaming white vertical cliffs and, if you can find a patch of sun, this makes a great place to rest. The track resumes by a sign on the true left bank just above the confluence with the Fox River; a steep bluff on the right makes a useful landmark.

A signposted track crosses to the true right bank of the Fox River below the confluence, then crosses several more times to the vast limestone **Ballroom Overhang** (1km; 30min each way; negligible ascent) with its 100m-long lip. It could easily provide shelter for a hundred or more campers, and has a long-drop toilet. Return the same way to the confluence, from where the track runs to the **Fox Rivermouth** (5km; 2hr; 100m descent). A short distance along, a sign points across the river to the interesting **Fox River Cave** (30min). Meanwhile, the Inland Pack Track crosses to the car park by the Fox Rivermouth, some 12km by road from your starting point; southbound **buses** currently pass around 11.45am and 3.55pm.

the horse. From the **Charleston Tavern** Underworld Adventures (☎0800/116 686, Ⓦwww.caverafting.com) run the adult- and child-pleasing **Nile River Rainforest Train** (3–4 daily; $20) a 25-minute interpretive journey on a modern narrow-gauge bush train through native bush, masking interesting limestone features. The train journey forms part of the hugely enjoyable Underworld Rafting **caving trip** (4hr; $145) which also involves a bushwalk through a dramatic valley of limestone bluffs before delving underground decked out in wetsuit and caver's helmet accompanied by a rubber inner tube. An informative guided walk through the Metro cave system finishes with a final drift down a fabulously illuminated, flooded, glowworm cave and out through a gorgeous ravine into the Nile River, where depending on water levels you can shoot the rapids or just drift. For the more timid there's the **Glowworm Cave Tour** (3hr; $90), while adrenaline seekers should opt for the full-on **Adventure Caving** (5hr; $295) which explores the Te Tahi cave system by means of a 30m abseil, plus numerous tight squeezes, scrambles and climbs.

If they stay at all, many choose to **free camp** beside Constant Bay, where there are toilets and water. The *Charleston Tavern* serves West-Coast Kiwi fare including whitebait or steaming seafood chowder.

Some 20km south of Charleston rise the 50m cliffs of Te Miko – tagged Perpendicular Point by Charles Heaphy, who in 1846 recorded climbing the cliff on two stages of ladders constructed of shaky and rotten rata vines while his dog was hoisted on a rope. Te Miko remained an impenetrable barrier to pack animals until 1866, when a new Westport–Greymouth telegraph line prompted the forging of the **Inland Pack Track** (see p.636). The coast road, finally completed in 1927, now climbs over Te Miko, passing the **Iramahuwhero Point Lookout**, with stupendous views along the coast past the layered rocks of the Te Miko cliff.

Punakaiki and the Pancake Rocks

The **Pancake Rocks** and blowholes at **PUNAKAIKI** are often all visitors see of the Paparoa National Park, as they tumble off the bus opposite the twenty-minute paved

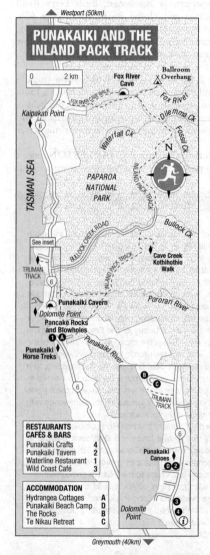

loop track which leads to the rocks. Here layers of limestone have weathered to resemble an immense stack of giant pancakes, the result of **stylobedding**, a chemical process in which the pressure of overlying sediments creates alternating durable and weaker bands. Subsequent uplift and weathering has accentuated this effect to create photogenic formations. The edifice is undermined by huge sea caverns where the surf surges in, sending spumes of brine spouting up through vast **blowholes**: high tide with a good swell from the south or southwest sees the blowholes at their best.

More shapely examples of Paparoa's karst landscape are on show on a number of walks. Inside the **Punakaiki Cavern**, 500m to the north, you'll find a few glow-worms (go after dark: torch essential) and, 2km beyond that, the **Truman Track** (30min return) runs down from the highway to a small beach hemmed in by wave-sculpted rock platforms.

There's good **river swimming** in the Pororari and Punakaiki rivers, and **sea bathing** at the southern end of Pororari Beach, a section also good for point-break **surfing**. Keeping with aquatic pursuits, Punakaiki Canoes (℡03/731 1870, Ⓦ www.riverkayaking.co.nz) rent out **kayaks** ($35/2hr, $55/day) from their base beside the Pororari River and run guided trips from $70. There's also **horseriding** with Punakaiki Horse Treks (Oct–April; ℡03/731 1839), who charge $125 for two and a half hours of bush, rivers and beach. A range of **caving** and **environmental tours** with Green Kiwi Tours (℡03/731 1843, Ⓦ www.greenkiwitours .co.nz), start at $60/hr per group.

North- and south-bound **buses** run by InterCity and Southern Link K Bus stop for half an hour outside the **Wild Coast Café**, giving enough time for a quick look at the Pancake Rocks across the road. DOC's **Paparoa National Park visitor centre** is now also an **i-SITE** (daily: Dec–April 9am–6pm; May–Nov 9am–4.30pm; ℡03/731 1895, Ⓦ www.punakaiki.co.nz) with displays on all aspects of the park, information on activities, walking maps, leaflets, helpful staff and the wherewithal to do bookings.

Accommodation

Punakaiki is a tiny place, but its popularity is growing, spawning a slew of places to stay.

Hydrangea Cottages SH6 ℡03/731 1839, Ⓦ www.pancake-rocks.co.nz. Four gorgeous cottages set above the road, most with sea views. The real appeal, though, is the self-catering cottages themselves (studio, one- & two-bedroom), all constructed with native timbers and local stone. Studios ⑥, suites ⑧

Punakaiki Beach Camp SH6 ℡03/731 1894, Ⓔ beachcamp@xtra.co.nz. Attractive, grassy campsite with campervan hook-ups close to the beach and pub. Camping $15, cabins ①, kitchen cabins ②

The Rocks Hartmount Place ℡03/731 1141, Ⓦ www.therockshomestay.com. Welcoming homestay, with three comfortable en-suite rooms, all with bush or sea views, and a lounge with a broad seascape. The same folk manage the luxurious *Flax Haven*, sleeping up to seven. B&B ⑥, Flax Haven ⑦

Te Nikau Retreat Hartmount Place, 200m north of the Truman Track and 3km north of the i-SITE ℡03/731 1111, Ⓦ www.tenikauretreat .co.nz. Associate YHA hostel which must rank as one of the most relaxing backpackers in the country, carved out of bush that's peppered with nikau palms. The ever-growing smattering of buildings includes small dorms, rooms, separate houses, rustic en-suite cabins for couples and a beneath-the-stars option that's like a wooden sleeping bag with a viewing window. Fresh bread, muffins and eggs are sold, and there's internet access. Dorms $26, shares $28, rooms ②, en suites and cabins ③

Eating

Punakaiki has a limited supply of worthwhile **restaurants**. There's no decent shop for supplies, so if you're self-catering, bring everything.

Punakaiki Crafts SH6, by the visitor centre. The best espresso in town, percolated by an ex-Londoner.

Punakaiki Tavern SH6, 1km north of the i-SITE. No-frills pub with good-value, simple, well-portioned meals (mostly $18–35).

Waterline Restaurant *Punakaiki Rocks Hotel*, SH6, 700m south of the i-SITE ☏03/731 1167.

Easily the fanciest place in Punakaiki, with à la carte dining in a room overlooking the sea. Open for lunch and dinner, and very expensive.

Wild Coast Café SH6, by the i-SITE. Popular with the tour buses, this place serves "West Coast" breakfasts and hangover cures (a mass of bacon, eggs and hash browns), panini and salads until sunset.

Punakaiki to Greymouth

Punakaiki to Greymouth is a spectacular drive, pushed onto the sea cliffs by the intrusive ramparts of the Paparoa Range. Except to take photos, the only reason to stop is to visit the **Barrytown knife maker** (2662 Coast Rd, SH6; $120; ☏03/731 1053), who will guide you through the intricacies of making your own blade, from hot steel to honed slicer, in a day.

Tiny **RAPAHOE**, 30km south of Punakaiki, has about the safest bathing beach on the coast and a reputation for gemstones. Follow the track to the excellent vantage point of **Point Elizabeth** (2hr return).

Greymouth

The Grey River forces its way through a break in the coastal Rapahoe Range and over the treacherous sand bar to the sea at workaday **GREYMOUTH**, the West Coast's largest town. It's not the highlight of most visitors' itineraries, but is the end of the line for the TranzAlpine Railway and a convenient stop for drivers. Take the time and trouble to dig beneath the surface and you might be pleasantly surprised by high-quality greenstone carving, worthwhile **adventure activities** and a cool bar. That said, do what you came for and move on, particularly in winter when **The Barber**, a razor-sharp cold wind whistling down the Grey Valley envelops the town in thick icy fog.

Greymouth began to take shape during the early years of the **gold rush** on land purchased in 1860 by James Mackay, who bought most of Westland from the Poutini Ngai Tahu people for 300 gold sovereigns. The town's defining feature is the river, which is deceptively calm and languid through most of the summer but awesome after heavy rains. Devastating **floods** swept through Greymouth in 1887, 1905, 1936, 1977 and 1988; since the last great flood, the Greymouth Flood Protection Scheme has successfully held back most of the waters.

Arrival, information and transport

The stylish way to arrive in Greymouth is on the TranzAlpine **train** from Christchurch (see p.496), which pulls in at the station on Mackay Street and is met by InterCity and Atomic **buses** (tickets from the i-SITE or the travel centre inside the station; ☏03/768 7080, Mon–Fri 9am–5pm, Sat & Sun 10am–3pm), running south to Hokitika and Franz Josef, or north to Westport and Nelson. Southern Link K Bus (☏0508/458 835) also finish their daily run from Picton here, but don't synchronize with the trains. Greymouth's **airport** offers scenic flights with Air West Coast (☏03/738 0524, ⓦwww.airwestcoast.co.nz).

The **i-SITE visitor centre**, inside the Regent Theatre on the corner of Mackay and Herbert streets (Nov to Easter Mon–Fri 8.30am–6pm, Sat 9am–5pm, Sun

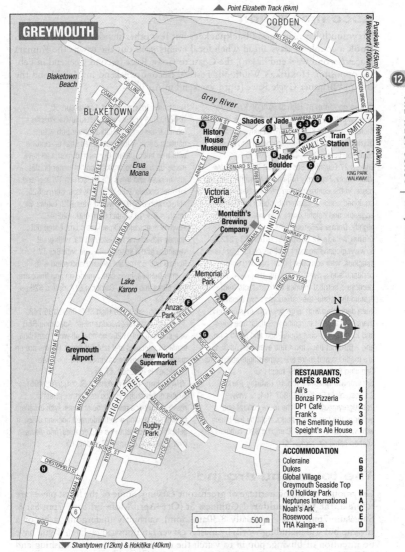

GREYMOUTH

Point Elizabeth Track (6km)

COBDEN

Punakaiki (45km) & Westport (100km)

Reefton (80km)

THE WEST COAST | Greymouth

12

Blaketown Beach

Grey River

BLAKETOWN

Erua Moana

History House Museum

Shades of Jade

Jade Boulder

Train Station

KING PARK WALKWAY

Victoria Park

Monteith's Brewing Company

Lake Karoro

Memorial Park

Anzac Park

Greymouth Airport

New World Supermarket

Rugby Park

Greymouth Seaside Top 10 Holiday Park

Shantytown (12km) & Hokitika (40km)

N

0   500 m

RESTAURANTS, CAFÉS & BARS

Ali's	4
Bonzai Pizzeria	5
DP1 Café	2
Frank's	3
The Smelting House	6
Speight's Ale House	1

ACCOMMODATION

Coleraine	G
Dukes	B
Global Village	F
Greymouth Seaside Top 10 Holiday Park	H
Neptunes International	A
Noah's Ark	C
Rosewood	E
YHA Kainga-ra	D

10am–4pm; Easter to Oct Mon–Fri 8.30am–5.30pm, Sat & Sun 9am–5pm; ☏03/768 5101, ⓦwww.greydistrict.co.nz), has **internet access** and provides the *Grey District* visitor guide, containing a good street map. You might want to check out **tours** to the Pancake Rocks (see p.638: 2.15pm; 2hr 30min; $95), run by Kea Tours.

Folk planning to **rent a car** in the South Island are increasingly riding the TranzAlpine train then picking up a rental in Greymouth. All the majors have **car-rental** offices either at the train station or nearby, though it's cheaper with NZ Rent A Car (☏03/768 0379) – who often charge little or no fee for long-term rentals dropped off in Queenstown or Christchurch.

641

Accommodation

Greymouth has many good **backpackers** but few other standout **places to stay**. **Book** a couple of days ahead when local events pack out the town: the Kumara Races (second weekend in Jan), the Coast to Coast Race (second weekend in Feb; see opposite), Hokitika's Wildfoods Festival (second weekend in March) and the Around Brunner Cycle Race (third weekend in April).

see opposite

Coleraine Motel 61 High St ℡0800/270 077, ⓦwww.colerainemotel.co.nz. Units in this sparkling motel come with Sky TV, CD/DVD players, double glazing to keep the road noise down and some have spa baths. Units ⑤, executive ⑤

Dukes 27 Guinness St ℡03/768 9470, ⓦwww.duke.co.nz. Smoothly organized, vibrantly colourful hostel in the centre with an intimate bar, well-equipped doubles, comfortable beds and knowledgeable and helpful hosts who make tasty soup nightly. Dorms $25, rooms ❷

Global Village 42 Cowper St ℡03/768 7272, ⓦwww.globalvillagebackpackers.co.nz. Light and spacious, well-equipped hostel backing onto parkland and a river. The rooms are imaginatively decorated in tribal themes with artefacts from around the world, the bathrooms have recently been decorated with large colourful mosaics, and there's a range of tempting activities: free bikes and kayaks, low-cost sauna, spa and small gym, and a BBQ out back most fine evenings. All beds are made up and there are some single-sex dorms. Camping $15, dorms $25, rooms ❷

Greymouth Seaside Top 10 Holiday Park 2 Chesterfield St ℡0800/867 104, ⓦwww.top10greymouth.co.nz. The more central and better of the two motor parks, right by the beach with very good facilities. Camping $20, cabins ❷, kitchen cabin ❷, motels ❹

Neptunes International 43 Gresson St ℡0800/003 768, ⓦwww.neptunesbackpackers.co.nz. Excellent hostel in a former pub with nautical decor, a free hot tub and baths supplied with free bubble bath. Dorms and rooms all have made-up beds (no bunks) and hot water bottles, just in case and there's a big-screen TV, pool and internet access. Free train pick-ups. Dorms $25, non-powered $10, powered sites $12, rooms ❷

Noah's Ark 16 Chapel St ℡0800/662 472, ⓦwww.noahsarkbackpackers.co.nz. Large but homey hostel in a two-storey villa, with great verandas and a spacious lounge with Sky TV. Rooms and dorms are lavishly decorated with animal themes, beds come made up and there are free bikes and a spa. Camping $17, dorms $25, rooms ❷

Rosewood 20 High St ℡0800/185 748, ⓦwww.rosewoodnz.co.nz. Appealing B&B in a characterful 1920s home – all wood panelling, leadlight windows and tasteful decor. Rooms are en suite or have private bathroom and a cooked breakfast is included. ❻/❼

YHA Kainga-ra 15 Alexander St ℡03/768 4951, ℮yha.greymouth@yha.co.nz. Former priest's residence, now a relaxed, quiet hostel with excellent facilities, including a well-informed booking office, a selection of dorms, twins and doubles, and views over the town. Dorms $27, rooms ❷

The town and around

Greymouth has a long heritage of greenstone carving. Some of the finest pieces are found at the **Jade Boulder**, 1 Guinness St (Oct–April Mon–Fri 8am–7pm Sat & Sun 9am–7pm; May–Sept daily 8.30am–5pm), currently undergoing a bit of a revamp but still including works by master carver Ian Boustridge. Even if you have no intention of buying, pop in to watch the cutting, grinding and polishing and visit the **Jade Trail** (free), which tells the parallel stories of jade from a Maori mythological and geological perspective.

Also poke your head into the tiny **Shades of Jade**, 16 Tainui St (Mon–Fri 8.30am–5pm, Sat 10am–2.30pm, Sun noon–2.30pm), a charming spot where the local carvers keep the prices down because they own the shop and make their own stock using New Zealand *pounamu*. There is jade carving daily and they'll often show you stones they've picked up on the beaches and in the rivermouths.

Greymouth's **History House Museum**, Gresson Street (Mon–Fri 10am–4pm; $5; ℡03/768 4028), makes a good shot at relating the Grey District's history through maritime memorabilia and a stack of photos depicting the town's heyday. The townspeople's long struggle to combat the floods is also given a thorough going over.

Book ahead and be sure to wear closed footwear if you want to go on a 45-minute **brewery tour** at Monteith's Brewing Company, on the corner of Turumaha and Herbert streets (daily 11.30am, 2pm, 4pm & 6pm; $15; ℡03/768 4149). Age-old recipes have been revived to produce flavoursome brews popular along the coast, and you get to taste them.

Choose a fine evening for a pleasant walk: the **Point Elizabeth Track** starts 6km north of town and follows the coast through stands of nikau to a lookout (5km return, 90min). You can continue to Rapahoe (see p.640; another 3km) and pick up a bus from there back to town (2 daily).

Activities

Activities around Greymouth are predominantly aquatic, subterranean or both. Some of the best are run by Wild West Adventures (℡0508/286 877, Ⓦwww .fun-nz.com), notably their Taniwha Cave Rafting (5hr, 90–120min underground; $145), an undemanding **caving** trip where wetsuits and cavers' lamps are the order of the day because of long sections on inner tubes under glowworms. They also offer even gentler, family-friendly, **Rain Forest Boat Cruising** (3hr; $135), plying placid waterways with kayaks and pontoons dressed up like jungle canoes and they run a bunch of rafting and **heli-rafting** trips, as do Eco-Rafting (see p.648).

Eating and drinking

The spectrum of eating and drinking in Greymouth has broadened but not enough to make a rainbow, with most places sticking to hale and hearty rather than colourful. Evening **entertainment** is limited to *Frank's* (see below), though numerous pubs compete for loudness and mainstream **movies** flicker at the Regent Theatre, on the corner of Herbert and Mackay streets. If you have a hankering for some unique and delicious **goat's cheese** check out Gaalburn Dairy Goat Farm, 18km south of Greymouth (℡03/736 9784, Ⓦwww.gaalburncheese.co.nz), where they make fabulous saanen, a sort of cheddar, among others.

The Coast to Coast Race

Kiwis are mad on multisport and punch above their weight on the international circuit, and every weekend you'll see scores of people honing their biking, running and paddling skills. The ultimate goal of all true multisporters is the gruelling 243km **Coast to Coast Race** (second weekend in Feb; Ⓦwww.coasttocoast.co.nz), which requires a pre-dawn start from the beach near Kumara Junction, 15km south of Greymouth. A 3km run leads to a 55km cycle uphill to Otira where jelly-kneed contenders tackle the most gruelling section, a 33km run up and down the boulder-strewn creek beds of the Southern Alps, before kayaking for several hours down Canterbury's braided Waimakariri River and then cycling the final stretch to Sumner.

From humble beginnings in 1983 – when it was the world's first major multisport event – the Coast to Coast has blossomed into a professional affair with over a thousand competitors. Serious contenders engage a highly organized support crew and specialized gear; only the most high-tech bikes will do and designers build racing kayaks especially for Waimakariri conditions. Most competitors take two days, but around 150 elite triathletes compete in "The Longest Day", the same course in under 24 hours. Mere mortals – though admittedly extremely fit ones – can also compete by forming two-person teams sharing the disciplines.

The event remains largely a macho spectacle that draws considerable press interest and correspondingly generous sponsorship – a vehicle manufacturer is usually coaxed into offering a car or truck to the winner if they break a certain time. The course record is an astonishing 10hr 35min, set in 1994.

Ali's 9 Tainui St ☎03/768 5858. Unpretentious, licensed café serving snacks, lunches and dinners (except Sun, closes 3pm); including good burgers, sweetcorn fritters, and steak and fries for only $23.
Bonzai Pizzeria 31 Mackay St. Cheerful licensed restaurant with tearoom staples through the day, including pastries and quiches and a broad range of reasonably priced and tasty pizzas served daytime and evening.
DP1 Café 108 Mawhera Quay. Cool café, with internet access, serving snacks and tasty coffee.
🏃 **Frank's** 115 Mackay St ☎03/768 9075. Funky first-floor late-night lounge with inventive nibbles like Momo dumplings, Thai

chicken curry and Blackball sausages, where live music, comedy, poetry and art events add a little class, from 5pm, Thurs, Fri & Sat.
The Smelting House 102 MacKay St. Owned and run by a dietitian, but don't let that put you off – this smashing little daytime café serves enormous sausage rolls, muffins and tasty veggie pies. Closed Sun.
Speight's Ale House 130 Mawhera Quay. Big and bustling restaurant/bar in a 1909 Edwardian Baroque former government building with a good menu of hearty dishes, perhaps including lamb shanks ($24), rump steak ($25) and sausage and mash ($17), mostly matched to beers from the Speight's range.

Hokitika and around

South from Greymouth, SH6 hugs a desolate stretch of coast with little of abiding interest until **HOKITIKA**, 40km away. "Hoki" (soon to be Hokitika Beach if the council get its way), is marginally more interesting than Greymouth, due to its proximity to a beach, a couple of engaging activities – bone carving and the strangely seductive sock-making machine museum – and good bushwalks.

Like the other West Coast towns, Hokitika owes its existence to the **gold rushes** of the 1860s. Within months of the initial discoveries near Greymouth in 1864, fields had been opened up on the tributaries of the Hokitika River, and Australian diggers and Irish hopefuls all flogged over narrow passes from Canterbury to get their share. Within two years Hokitika had a population of 6000 (compared with today's 4000), streets packed with hotels, and a steady export of over a tonne of gold a month, mainly direct to Melbourne. Despite a treacherous bar at the Hokitika rivermouth, the **port** briefly became the country's busiest, with ships tied up four deep along Gibson Wharf. As gold grew harder to find and more sluicing water was needed, the enterprise eventually became uneconomic and was replaced by dairying and the timber industry. The port closed in 1954, only to be smartened up in the 1990s as the focus for the town's Heritage Trail.

In the last decade or so, Hokitika has become synonymous with the annual **Wildfoods Festival** (second Sat in March; advance tickets $35; ⓦwww .wildfoods.co.nz), when the population quadruples to celebrate bush tucker. Around fifty stalls in Cass Square sell delicacies like stir-fried possum, marinated goat kebabs and smoked eel wontons, all washed down with home-brewed beer and South Island wine. The gorging is followed by an evening hoe-down, the Wildfoods Barn Dance ($10). If food still takes your fancy, look out for the farmers' market on Saturdays but if you feel a bit more artistic pop along to the annual **Wet West Film Festival** (ⓦwww.wetwestfilmfest.com), which takes place in early October and celebrates all things watery, from moody art flicks to extreme kayaking. The town's other intriguing shindig is in mid-January, the **Driftwood and Sand Competition**, where entrants compete to produce the most original and aesthetic construction from detritus found on the beach.

Arrival and information

Air New Zealand **fly** daily to Hokitika from Christchurch, arriving 2km east of the centre. Buses from Christchurch and along the coast stop outside the

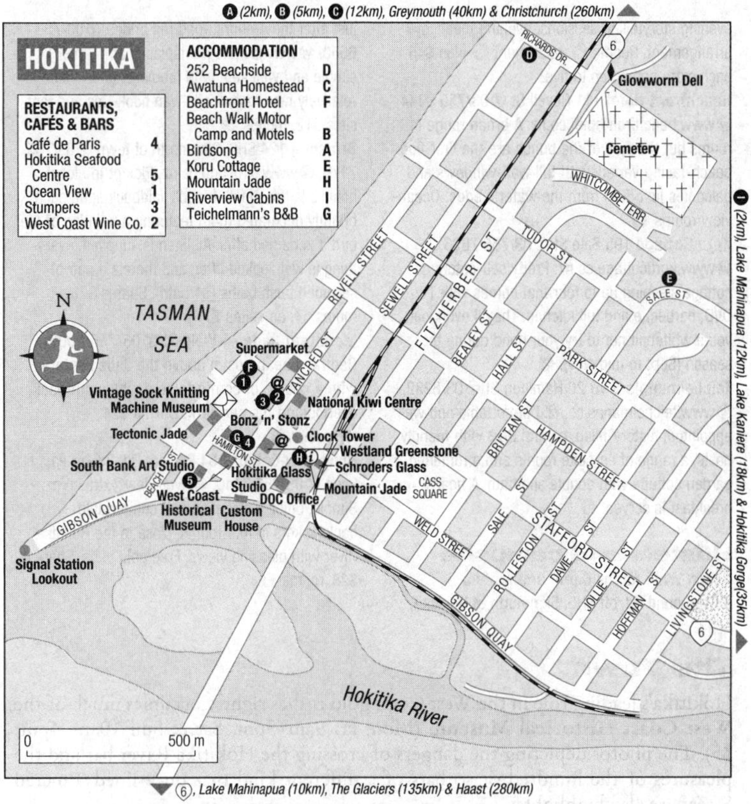
A (2km), B (5km), C (12km), Greymouth (40km) & Christchurch (260km)
HOKITIKA
ACCOMMODATION
252 Beachside D
Awatuna Homestead C
Beachfront Hotel F
Beach Walk Motor Camp and Motels B
Birdsong A
Koru Cottage E
Mountain Jade H
Riverview Cabins I
Teichelmann's B&B G
RESTAURANTS, CAFÉS & BARS
Café de Paris 4
Hokitika Seafood Centre 5
Ocean View 1
Stumpers 3
West Coast Wine Co. 2
N
TASMAN SEA
Supermarket
Vintage Sock Knitting Machine Museum
Tectonic Jade
South Bank Art Studio
Bonz 'n' Stonz
National Kiwi Centre
Clock Tower
Westland Greenstone
Schroders Glass
Hokitika Glass Studio
Mountain Jade
DOC Office
West Coast Historical Museum
Custom House
CASS SQUARE
Signal Station Lookout
GIBSON QUAY
BEACH ST
HAMILTON ST
TANCRED ST
REVELL STREET
SEWELL STREET
FITZHERBERT ST
BEALEY ST
HALL ST
BRITTAN ST
SALE ST
ROLLESTON ST
DAVIE ST
JOLLIE ST
HOFFMAN ST
LIVINGSTONE ST
WELD STREET
STAFFORD STREET
HAMPDEN STREET
PARK STREET
TUDOR ST
SALE ST
WHITCOMBE TERR
RICHARDS DR.
Glowworm Dell
Cemetery
Hokitika River
0 500 m
I (2km), Lake Mahinapua (12km), Lake Kaniere (18km) & Hokitika Gorge(35km)
6, Lake Mahinapua (10km), The Glaciers (135km) & Haast (280km)

National Kiwi Centre at 64 Tancred St (☎03/755 5251): Atomic buses also stop outside the museum (see p.646). The **i-SITE visitor centre**, 26 Weld St (Dec–March daily 8.30am–8pm; April–Nov Mon–Fri 8.30am–5pm, Sat & Sun 10am–4pm; ☎03/755 6166, Ⓦwww.hokitika.org), does DOC bookings while the **DOC office**, on Sewell Street (Mon–Fri 8am–4.45pm; ☎03/756 8282), stocks leaflets on local walks. If you're heading south note that the **banks** here are the last before Wanaka, more than 400km away over the Haast Pass.

Accommodation

Accommodation in Hokitika is seldom hard to find, though you should book ahead during the Kumara Races (second weekend in Jan), for all of February including around the Coast to Coast race (see p.643) and during the Wildfoods Festival (see opposite).

Hotels, motels and B&Bs

252 Beachside 252 Revell St ☎0800/252 252, Ⓦwww.252beachside.co.nz. Spacious motel and campervan park offering a range of comfortable units and campervan hook-ups, 10min walk from the centre. $30 per van, cabins ❷, units ❹

Awatuna Homestead SH6, 13km north of Hokitika ☎0800/006 888, Ⓦwww.awatunahomestead.co.nz. Welcoming B&B with three tasteful, comfortable rooms and one self-catering apartment. A relaxing spot with assorted animals, home-grown veggies, plenty of books, outdoor bath, a track down to the beach and evening storytelling sessions; evening meals by arrangement. Rooms ❽, apartment ❽ plus $45 each extra person up to five.

Beachfront Hotel 111 Revell St ☎03/755 8344, ⓦwww.beachfronthotel.co.nz. A broad range of rooms but the pick of the bunch are the first-floor, beach-facing variety with full wall-windows and balconies just 50m from the water's edge. Ocean-view rooms ❽

Koru Cottage 195 Sale St ☎03/755 7636, ⓦwww.korucottage.co.nz. Pretty self-catering cottage sleeping up to four that comes with TV/DVD, barbecue and full kitchen. They'll even loan you a whitebait net to try your hand during the season (Sept to mid-Nov). ❺

Teichelmann's B&B 20 Hamilton St ☎03/8232, ⓦwww.teichelmanns.co.nz. Comfortable and well appointed, history-filled, central B&B with friendly hosts, a range of en-suite rooms and a romantic garden cottage with double spa bath. A hearty breakfast is served. ❻

Hostels and campsite

Beach Walk Motor Camp and Motels 8 Greyhound Rd, off SH6, 5km north of Hokitika, just after the Arahura, road/rail bridge ☎03/755 6550, ⓦwwwjacquiegrantsplace.com. Small, simple and well kept with fabulous, good-value, relatively new motel units. Van hook-ups and tent sites $12, motels ❷

Birdsong 124 SH6, 3km north of town ☎03/755 7179, ⓦwww.birdsong.co.nz. Pick of the local hostels is this small, friendly laidback spot, each brightly decorated room featuring a painting of the bird it is named after. All linen is supplied, everything is well looked after, and there's a pair of secluded bush baths ($4/bath). Shares $28, rooms ❷, en suites ❸

Mountain Jade 41 Weld St ☎03/755 8007. Central, cheap hostel above the Jade Factory with a couple of comfortable doubles out back, overlooking the car park. Dorms $21, rooms ❷/❸

Riverview Cabins 154 Kaniere Rd, 3.5km east of town ☎03/755 7440, ⓔriver-view@xtra.co.nz. Simple, quiet, welcoming and comfortable backpackers in four rooms, close to the Hokitika River with pleasing views. Free gold pans. Shares $28, rooms ❷

The Town

Hokitika's leading role in the West Coast gold rushes rightly occupies much of the **West Coast Historical Museum** (Mon–Fri 9am–5pm, Sat & Sun 10am–4pm; $5). The photos depicting the dangers of crossing the Hokitika River bar and the pleasures of the hundred or so bars of a different kind that once lined Tancred Street are also highlights.

With interest suitably kindled, grab the free **Hokitika Heritage Walk** leaflet, detailing the town's historic landmarks including the **clock tower** commemorating the Boer War, and the Gibson Quay area. This restored former riverside dock makes for a pleasant evening stroll – from the spit-end **Signal Station Lookout** to the 1897 **Custom House**, via an ugly memorial to ships lost on the bar – finished off with takeaway fish and chips from the riverside *Hokitika Seafood Centre* (see p.648).

For an entirely different, charming and quirky experience pop into the **Vintage Sock Knitting Machine Museum**, 75 Revell St (daily 9am–5pm; free; ⓦwww.autoknitter.com), which doubles as a commercial outlet for all things woolly. The friendly, knowledgeable staff will give you a rundown on the largest collection of fully restored sock knitting machines known to man, some capable of knocking up ten pairs in an hour.

Only visit the **National Kiwi Centre**, 64 Tancred St (daily 9am–5pm; $14), a privately run aquarium and nocturnal house combo with tuatara, eels and kiwi if you must.

Arts and crafts

Despite its atmospheric beach, Hokitika is primarily renowned for its crafts scene. On almost every street corner someone will offer to show you how to weave, carve (greenstone or bone) or blow glass, or try to sell you the products of their labours. For those in buying mode, there are quality pieces to be found,

Greenstone

Maori revere **pounamu** (hard nephrite jade) and **tangiwai** (the softer, translucent bowenite), usually collectively known as **greenstone**. In Aotearoa's pre-European culture, it took the place of durable metals for practical, warfaring and decorative uses: adzes and chisels were used for carving, *mere* (clubs) for combat, and pendants were fashioned for jewellery. Charles Heaphy observed a group of Maori producing a *mere* in 1846, noting that they "saw the slab with a piece of mica slate, wet, and afterwards polish it with a fine sandy limestone which they obtain in the vicinity. The hole is drilled with a pointed stick with a piece of Pahutanui flint. The process does not appear so tedious as has been supposed; a month sufficing, apparently, for the completion."

In Maori, the entire South Island is known as **Te Wahi Pounamu**, "the place of greenstone", reflecting the importance of its sole sources, the belt from Greymouth through the rich Arahura River area near Hokitika south to Anita Bay on Milford Sound – where the beautifully dappled *tangiwai* occurs – and the Wakatipu region behind Queenstown. When the Poutini Ngai Tahu arranged to sell most of Westland to James Mackay in 1860, the Arahura River, their main source of *pounamu*, was specifically excluded.

Its value has barely diminished. Mineral claims are jealously guarded, the export of greenstone is prohibited and no extraction is allowed from national parks; penalties include fines of up to $200,000 and two years in jail. **Price** is heavily dependent on quality, but rates of $100,000 a tonne are not unknown – and the sky's the limit when the stone is fashioned into sculpture and jewellery. Many of the cheaper specimens are quite crude, but pricier pieces (a minimum of $100 for something aesthetically pleasing, and over $1000 for anything really classy), exhibit accomplished Maori designs; at the other end of the scale, pendants can be picked up for as little as $20.

Hokitika is the main venue for greenstone shoppers: keep in mind that the larger **shops** and **galleries** are firmly locked into the tour-bus circuit so prices are high. Big shops are fine for learning about the quality of the stone and competence of the artwork but smaller places have more competitive deals. Buyers should ask about the origins of the raw material – insiders suspect that lots of greenstone sold in NZ is cheaper jade sourced overseas. Specific shopping **recommendations** are given below.

and the southwestern end of Revell Street is becoming a bit of an artists' enclave. **Greenstone** (see box above) is big business, with shops all over town. For some of the finest work, visit Tectonic Jade, 67 Revell St, or the Traditional Jade Company, 2 Tancred St. If you want to **carve** a piece for yourself, pop along to the excellent Bonz 'n' Stonz Carving Studio, 16 Hamilton St (T0800/214 949, Wwww.bonz-n-stonz.co.nz), where you can learn to carve (6hr; jade $125, bone $85, shell $75). The friendly and estimable Steve Gwaliasi guides you through the design and execution in what is a personal and very memorable experience.

Glass-blowing is another long-standing Hoki tradition, best seen on weekdays (9am–5pm), at the Hokitika Glass Studio, 9 Weld St. And don't miss the South Bank Art Studio, 32 Revell St, where **sculptures** are cut and shaped from heat-treated **copper** sheet.

Activities

If carving seems a little sedate, Eco-rafting (see box, p.648) can take you **whitewater rafting** on some lumpy local rivers, while Wilderness Wings, at the airport (T0800/755 8118, Wwww.wildernesswings.co.nz), offer a number of **scenic flights**, principally around Mount Cook and the glaciers (1hr 15min; $300).

Eating and drinking and entertainment

Reasonably priced **eating** isn't in short supply in Hokitika, though the town lacks a cool **bar**. For free evening entertainment, stroll to the **Glowworm Dell** about 1km north of the centre beside SH6. If you're prepared to flash the cash there's always the movies: mainstream at the Regent, 23 Weld St, arthouse and alternative at the Crooked Mile Talking Movies, 36 Revell St (T03/755 5309, Wwww.crookedmile.co.nz).

Café de Paris 19 Tancred St T03/755 8933. Relaxed, to the point of clueless, service but the good food redeems it, with an extensive selection of moderately priced breakfasts, lunches and more formal dinners based on a French theme (mains around $30). Book in the evenings. Licensed & BYO.

Hokitika Seafood Centre Corner of Gibson, Wharf & Quay sts. The best fish and chip shop in town, with good riverside noshing daily (mostly from 11am–8pm, later at weekends).

Ocean View 111 Revell St T03/755 8344. Hotel restaurant with à la carte evening dining (mains $28–35) and great sea views from window tables and the deck.

Stumpers Corner of Weld & Revell sts. Modern sports bar and daytime café with live bands and passable bar meals.

West Coast Wine Co. 108 Revell St T03/755 5417. Tiny bar in a wine shop with a nice courtyard, where good wine is complemented by excellent coffee and supplemented by moreish cheese and meat platters and very un- "Yorkshire Pork Pies".

Rafting the wild West Coast rivers

In recent years kayakers and rafters have realized that some of the most thrilling and scenic whitewater trips are on New Zealand's West Coast, where dramatically steep rivers spill out of the alpine wilderness, fed by the prodigious quantity of rain that guarantees solid flows most of the time. The steepness of the terrain means you're in constantly thrilling if not downright scary territory (rivers in this area are mostly Grade IV, sliding either one up, or down). If you enjoy rafting and want more, this is a good place to come.

Few of these rivers had been kayaked or rafted until the 1980s, when helicopters were co-opted to reach them. Most rafting trips still require **helicopter access**, so costs are relatively high, and what you pay will often depend on numbers, so getting, say, six people together will save you a packet.

Though their popularity is increasing, trips are still relatively infrequent and you should **book** as far in advance as possible. The main **season** is November to April, and there is a minimum age of 13 years (15 for some of the more frightening runs).

The **most commonly rafted rivers** are (from north to south) the Karamea (Gd III+), the Mokihinui (Gd IV), the Arahura (Gd IV), the Whitcombe (Gd V), the Hokitika (Gd III–IV), the Wanganui (Gd III), the Perth (Gd V) and the Whataroa (Gd IV). The best companies, with a sample of trips, are:

Eco-Rafting Hokitika T0508/669 675, Wwww.ecorafting.co.nz. Uses rafting to introduce customers to the nature and social history of the places visited. A full-day heli-raft on the Perth is $500, three days on the Karamea $1500.

Ultimate Descents 51 Fairfax St, Murchison T0800/748 377, Wwww.rivers.co.nz. One-day heli-rafting trips on the Karamea ($450) and two-day trips on the Mokihinui ($850), among others.

Wild West Adventures Greymouth T0508/286 877, Wwww.fun-nz.com. These guys offer a wide range of trips from hard-man heli-rafting ($575) to relatively tame rafting ($185), on most of the above rivers.

Adrenaline heaven

With an extraordinary range of climatic conditions and geographical phenomena spread over both islands, New Zealand is a true playground for adrenaline junkies and outdoor enthusiasts. Couple this with the often innovative Kiwi approach to adventure activities, and you can easily find yourself overwhelmed. The quick, big-buck thrills of bungy jumping and skydiving compete with stomach-churning days canyoning or whitewater rafting. For the cost of a day heli-skiing you could go scuba diving, swimming with dolphins and kayaking. Or shun the lot and spend your whole time tramping through some of the world's most gorgeous scenery.

The Abel Tasman National Park ▲

The Kepler Track ▼

Tremendous tramps

New Zealand is crisscrossed by thousands of kilometres of walking tracks. Eight of New Zealand's finest tramps, and one river journey, have been classified as **Great Walks**; even the most well-trodden of these reveal magnificent natural wonders in the raw.

On the North Island

▶▶ The gentle **Lake Waikaremoana Track** (3–4 days; see p.371) circumnavigates one of the country's most beautiful lakes.

▶▶ The **Tongariro Northern Circuit** (3–4 days; see p.299) takes in magnificent volcanic and semi-desert scenery.

▶▶ The **Whanganui River Journey** (2–4 days; see p.239) is best explored by canoe and a series of highly atmospheric short walks.

On the South Island

▶▶ The **Heaphy Track** (4–5 days; see p.472) passes through the Kahurangi National Park, balancing subalpine tops and surf-pounded beaches.

▶▶ The **Abel Tasman Coast Track** (2–4 days; see p.463) skirts beaches and crystal-clear bays, ideally explored by sea kayak.

▶▶ The world-famous **Milford Track** (4 days; see p.745) accesses stunning glaciated alpine scenery and stupendous waterfalls.

▶▶ The **Routeburn Track** (3 days; see p.700), one of the country's finest walks, spends quality time above the bushline.

▶▶ The **Kepler Track** (4 days; see p.736) is renowned for ridge walks and virgin beech forest.

For more on outdoor activities in New Zealand see pp.55–63.

▶▶ The **Rakiura Track** (3 days; see p.617), on Stewart Island, follows the rainforest-bordered coast and provides opportunities to see kiwi in the wild.

Wet and wild

Torrents of water cascade from the high mountains of the North and South Islands, and there's enormous fun to be had by joining the gurgling whitewater mass.

Rafting is a perennial favourite, with both **Rotorua** and **Queenstown** offering an enviable selection of river runs. Less frequented but equally exciting rafting areas include Canterbury's **Rangitata River** and the **West Coast** of the South Island, which offers the best rafting in the land – often accessed by chopper.

Sea kayaking is at its best around the **Abel Tasman National Park**, **Marlborough Sounds**, **Fiordland** and **Kaikoura**, where there's always the chance of bumping into fur seals, penguins and rare sea birds. **River kayakers** can enjoy a relaxing paddle on the Whanganui River Journey or take on fast-flowing white water, best tackled at the kayak school in **Murchison**.

Jumping mad

Diving off tall towers with vines tied around the ankles has been a rite of passage for centuries in the South Pacific islands of Vanuatu, but commercial bungy jumping was pioneered by Kiwi speed skiers A.J. Hackett and Henry Van Asch. They began pushing the bungy boundaries, culminating in Hackett's jump from the Eiffel Tower in 1987. He was promptly arrested, but the publicity sparked worldwide interest that continues to draw bungy aspirants to New Zealand's sites – some of the world's

▲ Rafting the Kaituna River, Rotorua

▼ Sea kayaking, Abel Tasman National Park

▼ Bungy jumping

Sliding down an ice tunnel, Franz Josef ▲

Skiing, South Island ▼

best, with bridges over deep canyons and platforms cantilevered out over rivers. The first commercial operation was set up just outside Queenstown on the 43m **Kawerau Suspension Bridge**. Its accessible location and the chance to be dunked in the river make this the most popular jump of many on both the South and North islands.

Winter wonderland

Most people visit New Zealand in the summer, but in winter there's first-class skiing and snowboarding. The main **North Island ski-fields** include the country's two largest and most popular skiing destinations, **Turoa** and **Whakapapa**, both on the volcanic Mount Ruapehu. Along with the chance to ski a dormant volcano, visitors can take advantage of some beautiful, virtually deserted **tramps**, including the Tongariro Alpine Crossing, where frozen lakes and vibrant colours are thrown into relief by steaming fumaroles.

On the **South Island**, the west coast of the Southern Alps offers a variety of glacier-climbing experiences on the **Franz Josef and Fox glaciers**. On the other side of the Alps you can shoot up to **Mount Cook** and take a boat or a kayak to the foot of a glacier and watch the ice crumble. Mix all this in with the party atmosphere and uncrowded runs on the commercial **ski-fields** – Coronet Peak and The Remarkables by **Queenstown**; Treble Cone, Cardrona and the Waiorau Snow Farm near **Wanaka**; and further north, Porter Heights and Mount Hutt, both within two hours' drive of **Christchurch** – and you're guaranteed a memorable time, as well as some of the most spectacular snow-dusted scenery you'll ever see.

Around Hokitika

Some of the best bush scenery and **walks** are 30km inland where the dairying hinterland meets the foothills of the Southern Alps. Minor roads (initially following Stafford Street out of town) make a good 70km scenic drive, shown in detail on DOC's **Central West Coast: Hokitika** leaflet. The road passes the fishing, waterskiing and tramping territory of **Lake Kaniere**, a glacial lake 18km from Hokitika with several picnic sites and primitive camping ($6) along its eastern side. The most popular walk is the **Kaniere Water Race Walkway** (9km one-way; 3hr; 100m ascent), starting from the lake's northern end and following a channel that used to supply water to the goldfields, through stands of regenerating rimu. The eastern-shore road passes the attractive **Dorothy Falls** and continues to a side road leading to the **Hokitika Gorge**, 35km from Hoki, where a short path leads to a swingbridge over the tranquil Hokitika River.

Immediately south of Hokitika, SH6 runs 5km south to a relatively hidden landing where gentle paddleboat **cruises** (10am, 2pm & 5pm; 90min; excellent value at $30; ☎03/755 7239) take you along the Mahinapua Creek to the lake. A couple of kilometres on, the **Mahinapua Walkway** (16km return; 4hr; mainly flat; leaflet from DOC), offers easy walking with picnic opportunities at a lakeside beach. A further 2km south along SH6 the **Mananui Bush Walkway** (30min return) leads through coastal forest remnants to dunes and there's a particularly nice basic **camping** spot at **Lake Mahinapua**, accessed off SH6 1km south ($6).

From Hokitika to the glaciers

The main highway leaves the coast **south of Hokitika** and snuggles in close to the Southern Alps for most of the 135km to the glacier at Franz Josef. The journey through dairy farms and stands of selectively logged native bush is broken by a series of small settlements –Ross, Pukekura and Harihari. The most popular attractions along the way are **Whataroa**, to visit the **White Heron** colony, and **Okarito**, where the relaxed charms of the lagoon and **kiwi-spotting** trips may give you pause.

Ross

At the tiny village of **ROSS**, 30km south of Hokitika, a lake-filled hole is all that remains of the rich opencast mine that sought alluvial **gold** until 2004. The mining company has moved to a new site nearby, but would dearly love to get at the gold-bearing gravels underneath the town. The government has given consent provided all the townspeople agree to move off the land.

Though Ross had over 3000 residents at its gold-rush peak, things had slowed considerably by 1909, when a couple of diggers prospecting less than 500m from the current visitor centre turned up the largest gold nugget ever found in New Zealand, the 3.1-kilo "**Honourable Roddy**", named after the then Minister of Mines. The nugget was bought by the government and given as a coronation gift in 1910 to Britain's George V, who melted it down to make royal tableware. A replica of the fist-sized lump resides in the 1885 **Miner's Cottage**, Bold Street (daily: Dec–March 9am–4pm; April–Nov 9am–3pm; free), surrounded by gold-rush photos.

Leave time for the well-signposted **Water Race Walk** (4km loop, 1hr 30min) and check out the Jade Studio at 23 St James St (daily noon–5pm), one of the best small **jade** galleries around.

The **visitor centre**, 4 Aylmer St (daily: Dec–March 9am–4pm; April–Nov 9am–3pm; ℡03/755 4077, 🌐www.ross.org.nz), shows an interesting **video** (free) on the 1865 gold rush and rents gold pans ($10).

Pukekura

A giant model sandfly at the hamlet of **PUKEKURA**, 23km south of Ross, marks the **Bushman's Centre** (daily 9am–5.30pm; free; ℡03/755 4144, 🌐www.pukekura.co.nz). The centre's **museum** ($4) takes a light-hearted approach to timber milling, live deer capture, possum trapping and harvesting sphagnum moss for East Asian orchid growers, and there's also a café. The rest areas around beautiful (and often warm) **Lake Ianthe**, 6km south, make good picnic stops.

Harihari

Some 17km further south, tiny **HARIHARI** was the marshy landing site of **Guy Menzies**, who flew solo from Sydney to New Zealand in 1931, becoming the first to do so. Menzies ended up strapped in upside down in the mud of La Fontaine swamp, 10km northwest of town, a site now marked by explanatory panels. A replica of Menzies' plane resides near the southern entrance to town in **Guy Menzies Park**. You might also want to turn onto Whanganui Flat Road and drive 20km (partly gravel) coastwards past the Menzies' landing site to the delightful **Hari Hari Coastal Walkway** (8km loop; 2–3hr; negligible ascent), which runs past elaborate whitebaiting stands to the Doughboy Lookout (60m) with great views of the coast and the Southern Alps. After a short stretch of dramatic coastline you return though kahikatea forest and along the line of a tram track once used by loggers.

What with the park and the walk you may decide to **stay**, in which case treat yourself to the very welcoming 🏕 *Flaxbush Motel*, SH6 (℡03/753 3116, 📧flaxbush123@xtra.co.nz; cabins ❸, motel studios ❸, cottages & family units ❹). A Noah's ark for unwell and injured wildlife, boasting a variety of farm animals and New Zealand's only licensed pet possum, with his own room in the house. Within walking distance a passable **cheap feed** can be washed down with a jug of ale at the *Harihari Motor Inn*, which also commemorates Menzies' unscheduled stopover.

Whataroa

From October to late February, New Zealand's entire adult population of the graceful white heron (*kotuku*) arrives to breed at the Waitangiroto Nature Reserve near **WHATAROA**, 30km south of Harihari. Sitting across the river, in a hide, gazing on forty or so nesting pairs of herons (plus slightly larger numbers of royal spoonbills), going about their daily business of preening, fishing and mating is a truly memorable if slightly surreal experience that ends all too quickly. The only way to visit is with the highly professional **White Heron Sanctuary Tours**, SH6, in the centre of Whataroa (Oct–Feb 3–6 daily; 2hr 30min; $110; booking advised ℡0800/523 456 or 03/753 4120, 🌐www.whiteherontours.co.nz). The trip includes a scenic jetboat ride on the pretty Waitangiroto River and about half an hour ogling the birds; binoculars are provided.

Okarito

In 1642, Abel Tasman became the first European to set eyes on Aotearoa at **Okarito**, now a secluded hamlet dotted round the southern side of its eponymous lagoon and reached by a 10km side road, 15km south of Whataroa. The discovery of gold in the mid-1800s sparked an eighteen-month boom that saw fifty stores and hotels spring up along the lagoon's shores. Timber milling and flax production stood in once the gold had gone but the community foundered, leaving a handful of holiday homes, a few dozen permanent residents and a lovely beach and lagoon, used as the setting for much of Keri Hulme's Booker Prize-winning novel, *The Bone People*.

Okarito Lagoon is hard to appreciate from the shore, but Okarito Nature Tours (T 03/753 4014, W www.okarito.co.nz) run great-value guided **kayaking trips** (2hr; $75; min 2) and rent double kayaks for half a day ($50) or overnight ($80), camping at a remote beach. Call first to check tide conditions, but plan to go out early in the morning when the water is calmest and the birds are active and abundant.

If you don't want to paddle, opt for Experience Okarito Boat Tours (Oct–May daily; T 03/753 4223, W www.okaritoboattours.co.nz), who **cruise** leisurely through the lagoon and its feeder streams. Early tours (2hr; $75), concentrate on spotting birds while afternoon tours (1hr; $45), mainly focus on the seductive scenery.

Wildlife of a different feather can usually be seen on the excellent, low-impact Okarito Kiwi Tours (book well in advance, T 03/753 4330, W www.okarito kiwitours.co.nz), who'll take you into the bush **kiwi spotting** (2–3hr; around $65). If it goes well you'll start about ninety minutes before sunset and catch a glimpse of some of the extremely rare Okarito brown kiwi. To maximize the already high (98-percent) success rate, wear quiet clothes and sturdy boots.

The most popular walks are: the **Okarito Trig Walk** (1hr 30min return; 200m ascent) at the southern end of town, climbing to a headland with fabulous mountain and coastal views; and the **Pakihi Walk**, 5.5km back towards SH6 (2km return; 20–30min; 50m ascent), a good gravel path leading to a lookout with long views of Okarito Lagoon.

Practicalities

Okarito only has one road, inaptly named the Strand, and the community's limited **accommodation** is on it: there is **no shop** or café, so bring provisions. The widest range of **accommodation** is at the *Okarito Beach House* (T 03/753 4080, W www. okaritobeachhouse.com; dorms $25, doubles & en suites ❷, cottage ❸) a huddle of buildings which include comfy rooms and a romantic self-contained cottage. A memorial commemorating Tasman's sighting stands next to the associate ⚐ **YHA Okarito** (T 03/544 4799, W www.holidayhomes.co.nz; $60 for 2, $10 per extra person; book well in advance, closed June–Aug), a simple two-room affair in an 1860 schoolhouse, with twelve made-up bunks. There is no shower so you'll need to wander across the street to the shady **campsite** ($10; no powered sites), where showers take $1 coins. Alternatively, back on SH6, 4km south of the Okarito junction, DOC's fine *MacDonalds Creek* **campsite** ($6) is at Lake Mapourika.

The glaciers

Around 150km south of Hokitika, two white rivers of ice force their way down towards the thick rainforest of the coastal plain – ample justification for the inclusion of this region in Te Wahipounamu, the South West New Zealand World Heritage Area. The glaciers form a palpable connection between the coast and the highest peaks of the Southern Alps. Within a handful of kilometres the terrain drops from over 3000m to near sea level, bringing with it **Franz Josef glacier** and **Fox glacier**, two of the largest and most impressive of the sixty-odd decent-sized

Glaciers for beginners

The existence of a **glacier** is a balancing act between competing forces: snowfall at the **névé**, high in the mountains, battles with rapid melting at the **terminal** lower down the valley, the victor determining whether the glacier will advance or retreat. Snowfall, metres thick, gradually compacts to form clear **blue ice**, accumulating until it starts to flow downhill under its own weight. Friction against the valley walls slows the sides while ice in the centre slips down the valley, giving the characteristic scalloped effect on the surface, which is especially pronounced on such vigorous glaciers as Franz Josef and Fox. Where a riverbed steepens, the river forms a rapid: under similar conditions, glaciers break up into an **icefall**, full of towering blocks of ice known as **seracs**, separated by **crevasses**.

Visitors familiar with grubby glaciers in the European Alps or American Rockies will expect the surface to be mottled with **rock debris** which has fallen off the valley walls onto the surface; however, the glaciers here descend so steeply that the cover doesn't have time to build up and they remain pristine. Rock still gets carried down with the glacier though, and when the glacier retreats, this is deposited as **terminal moraine**. Occasionally retreating glaciers leave behind huge chunks of ice which, on melting, form **kettle lakes**.

The most telling evidence of past glacial movements is the location of the **trim line** on the valley wall, caused by the glacier stripping away all vegetation. At Fox and Franz Josef, the advance associated with the Little Ice Age around 1750 left a very visible trim line high up the valley wall, separating mature rata from scrub.

glaciers that creak off the South Island's icy backbone, together forming the centrepiece of the rugged **Westland National Park**. Legend tells of the beautiful Hinehukatere who so loved the mountains that she encouraged her lover, Tawe, to climb alongside her. He fell to his death and Hinehukatere cried so copiously that her tears formed the glaciers, known to Maori as Ka Riomata o Hinehukatere – "The Tears of the Avalanche Girl".

The area is also characterized by the West Coast's prodigious **precipitation**, with upwards of 5m being the typical yearly dump. These conditions, combined with the rakish angle of the western slopes of the Southern Alps, produce some of the world's fastest-moving glaciers; stand at the foot for half an hour or so and you're bound to see a piece peel off. But these phenomenal speeds haven't been enough to counteract melting, and both glaciers have receded over 3km since Cook saw them at their greatest recent extent, soon after the Little Ice Age of 1750. Glaciers are receding worldwide, but the two here sometimes buck the trend by advancing from time to time, typically around five years after a particularly big snowfall in the mountains.

The glaciers were already in full retreat when travellers started to battle their way down the coast to observe these wonders of nature. They were initially named "Victoria" and "Albert" respectively but, in 1865, geologist Julius von Haast renamed Franz Josef after the Austro-Hungarian emperor, and following a visit by prime minister William Fox in 1872, the other glacier was bestowed with his name.

Activity in the glaciers focuses on two small **villages**, which survive almost entirely on tourist traffic. Both lie close to the base of their respective glacier and offer excellent plane and helicopter **flights**, guided **glacier walks** and **heli-hiking**. With your own transport, it makes sense to base yourself in one of the two villages and explore both glaciers from there. If you have to choose one, Franz Josef has a wider range of accommodation, restaurants, and offers the most comprehensive selection of trips, while Fox is quieter.

Franz Josef Glacier

FRANZ JOSEF GLACIER (Waiau) is the slightly larger of the two glacier villages, with a wider range of places to stay and eat. The Franz Josef glacier almost licks the fringes of the village, the Southern Alps tower above and developers have done what they can to create an alpine character with steeply pitched roofs and pine panelling. It is an appealing place, and small enough to make you feel almost like a local if you stay for more than a night or two – something that's easily done, considering the number of fine walks and the proximity of the glaciers.

Arrival and information

First stop in Franz Josef should be the excellent combined **DOC office** and **visitor centre** on SH6 (daily: Nov–March 8.30am–6pm; April–Oct 8.30am–noon and 1–5pm; ☎03/752 0796, ⓔwestlandnpvc@doc.govt.nz), which has stacks of leaflets on walks in the area and first-class glacier and geology displays plus a diverting documentary (every 20min; $3) on the whole South West New Zealand World Heritage Area. The centre also gets **weather reports** at 3pm daily, so check with them before starting any serious walks.

There is an **ATM** but no banks. **Internet access** is most reliable at Ferg's Kayaks on Cron Street.

You can walk everywhere in town and Glacier Valley Eco Tours (☎0800/999 739, ⓦwww.glaciervalley.co.nz) offer a **shuttle service** to the glacier road-end ($12 return) and a series of local tours, such as Lake Matheson (3hr; $70) and a Lake Matheson combo with Fox glacier (5 hr; $100). Other than that, getting around is a pain.

Accommodation

With the region's popularity and a bus schedule that forces many people to overnight here, accommodation in Franz Josef is tight throughout the summer. Between November and March (and particularly February), you should aim to make **reservations** at least a week in advance, more like six months for swankier places.

▲ Helicopter on Franz Josef glacier

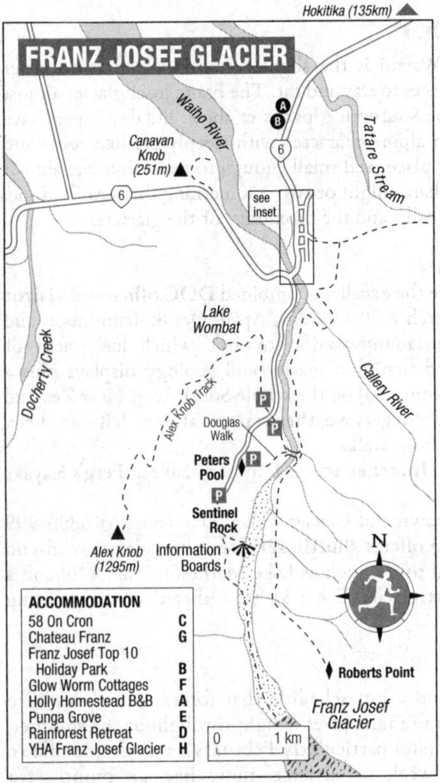
Hokitika (135km)
FRANZ JOSEF GLACIER
Fox Glacier (25km) & Haast (165km)
Waiho River
Tatare Stream
Canavan Knob (251m)
see inset
6
Lake Wombat
Docherty Creek
Alex Knob Track
Callery River
Douglas Walk
Peters Pool
Sentinel Rock
Alex Knob (1295m)
Information Boards
N
Roberts Point
Franz Josef Glacier
0 1 km
ACCOMMODATION
58 On Cron C
Chateau Franz G
Franz Josef Top 10 Holiday Park B
Glow Worm Cottages F
Holly Homestead B&B A
Punga Grove E
Rainforest Retreat D
YHA Franz Josef Glacier H

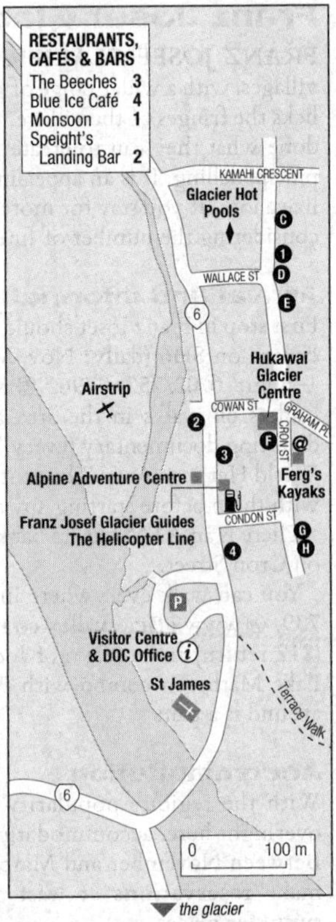
RESTAURANTS, CAFÉS & BARS
The Beeches 3
Blue Ice Café 4
Monsoon 1
Speight's Landing Bar 2
KAMAHI CRESCENT
Glacier Hot Pools
WALLACE ST
6
Hukawai Glacier Centre
Airstrip
COWAN ST
GRAHAM PL
CRON ST
Ferg's Kayaks
Alpine Adventure Centre
CONDON ST
Franz Josef Glacier Guides
The Helicopter Line
Visitor Centre & DOC Office
St James
Terrace Walk
0 100 m
the glacier

58 On Cron 58 Cron St ☎03/752 0627, ⓦwww.58oncron.co.nz. Stylish, great-value units, some with spa bath, plus BBQs, and friendly, helpful staff. 6/7

Chateau Franz 8 Cron St ☎0800/728 372, ⓦwww.chateaufranz.co.nz. A wide range of accommodation from budget dorms and smaller en-suite dorms to full-blown motel units via summer caravans, one called the "love shack". Free spa, free soup nightly and TVs and VCRs everywhere. Dorms $22, rooms & en suites 2, motels 3

Franz Josef Top 10 Holiday Park SH6, 1km north of town ☎0800/467 897, ⓦwww.mountainview.co.nz. High-spec rural campsite with a good range of tent and powered sites, cabins and units. Camping $21, cabins 2, kitchen cabins 3, units 4

Glow Worm Cottages 27 Cron St ☎0800/151 027, ⓦwww.glowwormcottages.co.nz. Small, homely hostel with a well-equipped kitchen, six-bed dorms and four-shares with their own bathrooms, plus comfy doubles and motel-style en suites. Free soup and spa. Dorms $25, rooms 1, en suites 4

Holly Homestead B&B SH6, 1.5km north of town ☎03/752 0299, ⓦwww.hollyhomestead.co.nz. Comfortable, to the point of indulgence, with welcoming hosts who provide B&B in an attractive two-storey 1920s home, just outside town with five en-suite rooms (one with bathtub), including a suite ($420). There's a deck with mountain views, and rates include a delicious full breakfast. Only suitable for those 12 and over. 8–9

Punga Grove 40 Cron St ☎0800/437 269, ⓦwww.pungagrove.co.nz. Stylish, modern luxury motels, all nicely furnished and with Sky TV. Rainforest studios back onto the bush and come with gas fires, underfloor heating and spa bath. Motel 6, studios 8

Rainforest Retreat 46 Cron St ☎0800/873 346, ⓦwww.rainforestretreat.co.nz. Large lodge and campervan park with gravel pads (good for campervans; OK for tents) and access to a communal lodge. Also backpacker dorms and en-suite rooms, spacious studio motels, atmospheric log cabins on stilts, luxurious lodges, a spa and sauna. Camping $14–18, dorms $25, en-suite four-shares $27, rooms ②, motels ⑤, log cabins ⑥, lodges ⑦

🛖 **YHA Franz Josef Glacier** 2–4 Cron St
☎03/752 0754, @yha.franzjosef@yha
.co.nz. Modern, well-run hostel on the edge of town

with the southernmost rooms facing bush and subject to a joyful dawn chorus. Spacious kitchen, clean comfortable rooms (some en suite), BBQ area and free sauna make this the best value around.
Dorms $26, rooms ③

The Town

In Franz Josef you can hike to the glacier, join a guided walk on the glacier, kayak on a nearby lake or take a scenic flight. Guided glacier walks and kayaking happen in most weathers but on misty and very wet days you'll find that scenic flights and heli-hikes are cancelled and alternatives limited. At such times, the best bet is is a soak in the new, specially constructed **Glacier Hot Pools** on Cron Street (45min; main pools $22.50, private pool $40; ☎0800 044044, Ⓦwww.glacierhotpools .co.nz). Artificially heated to 36°C, 38°C and 40°C respectively, the three public pools are covered in semi-porous canopies and surrounded by native bush, most of which has been transported to the site. Private pools come with cabana-type sheds containing a shower and some complimentary bits and pieces. Although a pleasure in their own right, the pools' restorative qualities come into their own when you need to banish the aches of hiking or yomping about on a guided glacier walk (combo deals are available with Franz Josef Glacier Guides, see below).

The enormous **Hukawai Glacier Centre**, on the corner of Cowan and Cron streets, was once a combined interpretive centre and indoor (real) ice climbing wall. It has closed, and although plans exist to refloat it, it doesn't look set to reopen anytime soon.

If you fancy a stroll, the pretty, half-timbered **St James Church** (always open), which once framed the glacier in the altar window, is a couple of hundred metres' trudge along SH6, south of the village. Sadly the ice retreated from view in 1953 and the church nearly did the same in 1995 when the flooded Waiho River scoured away the alluvial bank and left it precariously poised on a cliff. Opposite, the **Terrace Walk** (30min return; mostly flat) meanders through the bush to a pleasant viewpoint overlooking the Waiho River.

Glacier hiking, heli-hiking and ice climbing

It is possible to walk to the face of the Franz Josef glacier independently, but to walk on the ice you'll need to take a **glacier-walking** trip with Franz Josef Glacier Guides, SH6 (☎0800/484 337, Ⓦwww.franzjosefglacier.com). A half-day trip (2–3 daily; $105) involves a hike across the braided riverbed below the glacier, fitting your crampons, then a little over an hour on the ice, snaking up ice steps cut by your guide. For a more tangible sense of adventure, fork out for the full-day trip ($160) which gives around five hours on the ice, hopefully finding ice tunnels to explore, deep blue crevices into which to stare and a general sense of wonder and other worldliness. They also offer **heli-hiking** (1–2 daily; 3hr; $390), which combines a short helicopter flight with a couple of hours on a fascinating section of ice caves, pinnacles and seracs that you couldn't hope to reach on foot in a day. Try to be clear about your aspirations and abilities and you can be matched up with a party of like-minded folk. For an even more active day, go **ice climbing** (7–8hr; $250) – an instructional roped-up and tiring day in plastic boots with crampons and ice tools on steep ice.

Scenic flights

On any fine day the skies above Franz Josef are abuzz with choppers and light planes. Safety demands that specific flight paths must be followed, limiting what can be offered and forcing companies to compete on price; ask for youth, student, YHA, BBH, senior or just-for-the-sake-of-it discounts, most readily given if you can band together in a group of four to six and present yourselves as a ready-to-go plane or chopper load.

Most people go by **helicopter**, with all operators regularly landing on a snow-field high above the glacier where the rotors are left running – hardly serene. The cheapest are Fox and Franz Josef Heliservices (℡0800/800 793, Ⓦwww.scenic-flights.co.nz), who offer one glacier and landing (20min; $200), two glaciers and landing (30min; $275), and two glaciers, landing and Mount Cook (40min; $390).

Planes give you a longer flight with greater range for less money while a skiplane landing on a snowfield is very rewarding, particularly the silence after they switch the engine off. Mount Cook Ski Planes (℡0800/368 000, Ⓦwww.mtcookskiplanes.com) run to both glaciers (40min with 10min landing; $315) and a scenic option including the glaciers, landing on the Tasman Glacier and a squiz at Mount Cook (60min; $395). Air Safaris (℡0800/723 274, Ⓦwww.airsafaris.co.nz) might be a smidgen cheaper but don't do landings: try their Grand Traverse (50min; $295).

Walking, kayaking and quad biking

Top of everyone's list of **walks** is the one from the glacier car park, 5km south of the village, to the face of the Franz Josef glacier (6km return; 1hr 30min; flat), a roped-off and ever-changing wall of ice with the Waiho River sloshing out from beneath. The rough track crosses gravel beds left behind by past glacial retreats, giving you plenty of opportunity to observe small kettle lakes, the trim line high up the valley walls and a fault line cutting right across the valley (marked by deep gullies opposite each other). One of the best viewpoints is from the top of the glacier-scoured hump of **Sentinel Rock**, a ten-minute walk from the car park.

Worthwhile walks off the access road include the circular **Douglas Walk** (1hr) past Peter's Pool, a serene lake left by a retreat in the late eighteenth century. For the more adventurous there is the **Roberts Point Track** (12km return; 5.5hr; 950m ascent), carrying on from a point on the Douglas Walk loop past the Hendes Hut (a good lunch stop) to Roberts Point, high above the ice with stunning views. It's a bit of a slog and often slippery but well worth the effort. Alternatively try the other side of the glacial valley and the **Alex Knob Track** (12km return; 8hr; 1000m ascent), which climbs high above the glacier through several vegetation zones and offers more fine views up the valley. The only way to actually walk on the glacier surface is with a guide (see p.655).

If you'd rather spend an active few hours sitting down, join one of the marvellous **guided kayaking** trips offered by Glacier Country, 20 Cron St (℡0800/423 262, Ⓦwww.glacierkayaks.com). The most popular ($75) is on the black waters of the kahikatea- and flax-fringed Lake Mapourika, 8km north of town. Trips run in the morning, afternoon and early evening, spending about three hours on the water and offer loads of photo opportunities in sun and/or rain. There's also a heli-paddle option ($450).

The last resort, when all else fails, is **quad biking** with Glacier Country ($150/90min; ℡0800/234 288, Ⓦwww.acrosscountryquadbikes.co.nz); it too offers a heli-quad option ($365).

Eating, drinking and entertainment

Franz Josef has a lot of accommodation and a commensurate number of **places to eat** and drink, but the relatively remote location keeps prices high. Even if you are self-catering you can expect to pay over the odds for a limited stock of **groceries**. Entertainment here is about as rare as a cheap cucumber, so you'll be relying on the local cinema which shows the promotional film *Flowing West* ($12), DVDs in your accommodation or a good book: Take Note, just south of the *Blue Ice Café* (daily 8am–7pm in summer) offers a variety of reading matter at decent prices and has an on-site jade carver.

The Beeches SH6. Quality café good for coffee and lunches during the day and a broad range of reasonably priced dinners (mains around $25–34); all available indoors or out.

Blue Ice Café SH6. The modern and airy restaurant at street level serves imaginative and tasty mains for $27–35 and a range of gourmet pizzas from $16, to take away or eat in the unreconstructed upstairs bar, where the free pool table and rowdy music draws in a lively crowd most nights.

Monsoon 46 Cron St. Convivial café/bar (happy hour 7–9pm), offering the like of steak dinners at $29 a pop and a backpacker meal deal on selected menu items.

Speight's Landing Bar SH6, at the corner with Cowan St. Busy, popular and swish-looking café/bar, with loads of outdoor seating, serving substantial mains and the eponymous ale.

Fox Glacier

Fox Glacier, 25km south of Franz Josef, lies scattered over an outwash plain of the Fox and Cook rivers, and services the local farming community and passing sightseers. Everything of interest is beside SH6 or Cook Flat Road, which skirts the scenic Lake Matheson on the way to the former gold settlement and seal colony at Gillespies Beach. The foot of the Fox glacier is around 6km away.

Arrival, information and getting around

Fox is subject to the same **bus** schedule as Franz Josef (see p.653) and consequently has similar shortages of accommodation through the summer months. If you come unstuck, seek help at the **DOC office**, SH6 (Mon–Fri 9am–noon & 1–4.30pm ☏03/751 0807, ✉foxsouthwestlandao@doc.govt.nz), which also has displays concentrating on lowland forests and glaciation.

If you don't have **transport**, use Fox Glacier Shuttles & Tours (☏0800/369 287) to get to the glacier ($13 return) and Lake Matheson ($17 return). They also run to Gillespies Beach, for a look at the seal colony (price on demand, depending on numbers but pay no more than $40).

Accommodation

Fox's range of places to stay is more limited than Franz Josef's but is generally pretty good; **book** as far ahead as you can and be prepared for resort prices. The basic and free DOC **campsite** at Gillespies Beach (see p.659) is popular in summer.

Fox Glacier Holiday Park Kerrs Rd ☏0800/154 366, ⓦwww.foxglacierholidaymotelpark.co.nz. Fairly basic campsite with tent sites, cabins and s/c units. Camping $17, cabins ❷, units ❸

Fox Glacier Lodge Sullivan Rd ☏0800/369 800, ⓦwww.foxglacierlodge.co.nz. A pine-lined alpine chalet with attractively furnished en-suite rooms sharing a communal kitchen. A buffet breakfast is included, and there are campervan hook-ups. Also self-catering apartments. Powered sites $15, rooms ❻, apartments ❼

The Homestead Cook Flat Rd, 700m off SH6 ☏03/751 0835, ✉foxhomestead@slingshot.co.nz. Friendly homestay in a pleasant old house within walking distance of town, with occasional views of

Mount Cook, pleasant en suites and a continental and/or cooked breakfast. ❺

Ivory Towers Sullivan Rd ☏03/751 0838, ⓦwww.ivorytowerslodge.co.nz. Fox's only genuine backpackers is friendly, clean, colourfully decorated and is about to grow in size, Most dorms have both beds and bunks, while doubles all have TV. The kitchen is spacious, there's a sauna ($8), internet access, a small cinema for those rainy afternoons and bikes to rent ($24/day). Dorms $28, rooms ❷, en suites ❸

Mountain View B&B 1 Williams Drive, 2km off SH6 ☏03/751 0770, ⓦwww.foxglaciermountain view.co.nz. Welcoming modern B&B with three en suites and a separate s/c cottage in its own

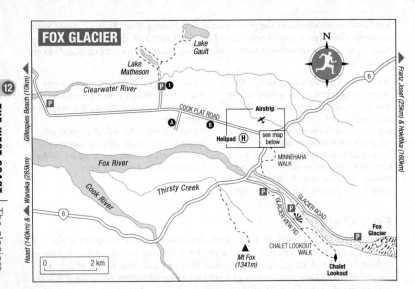

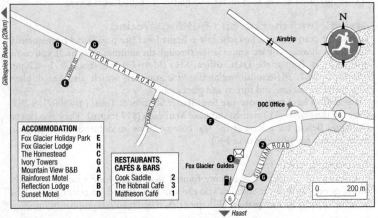

grounds on the edge of town with great mountain views. You get tasteful decor in well-equipped rooms plus a full breakfast. ⑥

Rainforest Motel 15 Cook Flat Rd, 200m off SH6 ☎0800/724 636, ⒲www.rainforestmotel .co.nz. Log cabins with attractive and well-priced studios and larger one-bedroom units. ⑤

Reflection Lodge Cook Flat Rd, 1.5km off SH6 ☎03/751 0707, ⒲www.reflectionlodge.co.nz. So named because of the glorious reflection of the

mountains in the large garden pond, this romantic homestay offers reasonably priced accommodation in comfortable, spacious and friendly surroundings (dinner by arrangement). ⑦

Sunset Motel Cook Flat Rd, 1km off SH6 ☎0800/751 006, ⒲www.sunsetmotels.co.nz. The best of the upmarket motels, tastefully decorated and with all rooms boasting wi-fi and great views of Mount Cook and Mount Tasman. ⑥

Glacier hiking, heli-hiking and ice climbing

Glacier walking on the Fox glacier, as on Franz Josef, gets better the longer you spend on the ice, despite Fox being accessed from the side and giving more immediate access to crevasses and seracs. Fox Glacier Guides (℡0800/111 600, Ⓦwww.foxguides.co.nz), are a smaller concern than those operating on the Franz Josef which means there are less folk on the ice at any one time, but half-day walks (2–4 daily; $95) only allow an hour on the ice so it's worth stepping up to a full-day trip ($145), giving over three hours. They also offer **heli-hiking** ($395), with two and a half hours of icy hiking, and **ice climbing** (8–9hr; $235), which gives you the chance to get vertical for a few hours.

Scenic flights
The Fox Glacier airport and helipad are slightly less busy than those at Franz Josef, but a similar range of flights are on offer. Again, Fox and Franz Josef Heliservices (see p.646) are the cheapest **chopper flights** with the same deals as in Franz. The only company offering **plane flights** from Fox is Mt Cook Ski Planes (see box, p.656), which has flights for much the same prices as from Franz Josef.

Walks and activities
It would be a shame to miss the Fox glacier just because you have already seen Franz Josef: the **approach walks** are different and their characters distinct, the Fox valley being less sheer but with more impressive rockfalls. The approach, imaginatively named Glacier Road, crosses the wide bed left by glacial retreats and is occasionally re-routed as "dead" ice under the roadway gradually melts. From the car park, 6km from the town, a track leads to the foot of the glacier in half an hour, crossing a couple of small streams en route. Partway back along Glacier Road, **River Walk** (2km; 30min) crosses a historic swingbridge to the Glacier Valley Viewpoint on Glacier View Road, which runs 3km along the south side of the Fox River. From here, the **Chalet Lookout Walk** (4km; 1hr 15min return; 150m ascent) climbs relatively moderately for stupendous glacier and mountain views.

It's difficult to imagine a New Zealand calendar or picture book without a photo of Mount Cook and Mount Tasman mirrored in **Lake Matheson**, 5km west of town along Cook Flat Road. A well-signposted boardwalk through lovely native bush encircles the lake, which was formed by an iceberg left when the Fox glacier retreated 14,000 years ago. It takes around an hour and gives everyone a chance for that perfect image, especially those who venture out for sunrise. The *Matheson Café*, by the Lake Matheson car park, is well located and serves good posh nosh.

About 5km beyond Lake Matheson, **Peak Viewpoint** is ideal for fabulous fine-day views of the top of the Fox glacier and the snowcapped mountains. Continue 10km further along Cook Flat Road to reach **Gillespies Beach**, a former gold-mining settlement with a small cemetery and a primitive DOC campsite (free). From the campsite an excellent **walk** threads north parallel to the beach, past the scant remains of an old gold dredge (30min return) to Gillespies Lagoon (1hr 15min return), a short Miners' Tunnel (1hr 40min return) and the Galway Beach Seal Colony (3hr 30min return).

Back in Fox, fill an empty half-hour with a stroll around the flat **Minnehaha Walk** (1km; 20min loop), which winds through lush bush that's cool and shady on a summer day, or dank and brooding in the rain. Come after dark to see **glowworms**. If all this leaves you unruffled try a **tandem skydive** (℡0800/751 0080) from 12,000ft ($295).

Eating and drinking
Fox Glacier caters for the hungry with a tiny selection of **cafés** that double as **bars**, and one proper, lively **pub**.

Cook Saddle SH6. A local favourite, this Western-inspired, all-wood saloon dishes out massive portions of good-quality food at goofily low prices, from stuffed veggie wraps to whopping great steaks. There's regular live music in the summer and if the language is sometimes a bit fruity, it's all the more charming for it. Daily from 11am.

The Hobnail Café SH6. In the alpine-chalet surroundings of Fox Glacier Guides, this workaday café has disturbing New Zealand tearoom tendencies, but offers a wide range of cheapish breakfasts, salads, sandwiches, soups and burgers.

Matheson Café Cook Flat Rd. Stylish, architecturally engaging daytime café at the start of the walk around Lake Matheson, with mountain views through big picture windows. The breakfasts ($7–14) reward an early walk, lunches are well presented, including a particularly fine lamb burger, and afternoon coffee and cake usually coincide with the sun catching the mountains. Dinners from early Nov to end Feb (mains $29–36).

South Westland and Makarora

South from the glaciers, the West Coast feels even more remote. There wasn't a road through here until 1965 and the final section of tarmac was not laid on the Haast Pass until 1995. SH6 mostly runs inland, passing the start of the hike to the **Welcome Flat Hot Springs** (see box below) and through kahikatea and rimu forests as far as **Knight's Point**, where it returns to the coast along the edge of the Haast Coastal Plain, whose stunning **coastal dune systems** shelter lakes and some fine stands of kahikatea. The plain continues south past the scattered township of **Haast** to the site of the short-lived colonial settlement of **Jackson Bay**. From Haast, SH6 veers inland over the Haast Pass to the former timber town of **Makarora**, not strictly part of the West Coast but moist enough to share some of its characteristics and a base for the excellent **Gillespie Pass** Tramp.

South to Haast

Many visitors do the run from the glaciers to Wanaka or Queenstown in a day, missing out on some fine remote country. Facilities aren't completely absent: many accommodation and eating places are clustered around Haast, but there are an increasing number of other pit stops along the way. One place you might like to break your journey is **Bruce Bay**, 45km south of Fox Glacier, where the road briefly parallels a long driftwood-strewn beach perfect for an atmospheric stroll.

Welcome Flat Hot Springs

The most popular two-day hike in the region is the in-and-back jaunt to the **Welcome Flat Hot Springs**, a series of open-air pools where you're bound to find a spot that's just the right temperature for easing those bones. Almost everyone spends the night at DOC's adjacent **Welcome Flat Hut** (31 bunks; $15; no reservations; annual pass not valid). Be warned that during the summer the hut is very popular and you may just get a mattress on the floor or be forced to camp ($5).

The track (detailed on DOC's *Copland Track* leaflet) starts by a car park on SH6, 26km south of Fox Glacier: Atomic and InterCity **buses** will drop off, and pick up pre-booked customers. From **SH6 to Welcome Flat** (17km; 6–7hr; 450m ascent) is a fairly tough tramp (far less defined than any of the Great Walks) following the true right bank all the way to Welcome Flat, crossing numerous creeks by hopping from rock to rock or wading. If the creeks are high, as they commonly are, you may have to use the flood bridges, which will add an hour or so. After heavy rain, the track becomes impassable: take plenty of extra supplies in case you get held up for a day or two.

Recently tour bus drivers have been stopping long enough for their occupants to erect small cairns, most of which are thankfully obliterated by high tide or good wind.

Some 17km further south, the road crosses the **Paringa River**, where a plaque marks the southern limit of Thomas Brunner's 1846–48 explorations. He recorded in his diary the desire to "once more see the face of a white man, and hear my native tongue". Buses stop nearby at the *Salmon Farm* for an overpriced snack or lunch. A better bet is to pick up some delicious hot or cold smoked salmon to take away and continue 8km south to the northern shores of **Lake Paringa** and DOC's simple but beautifully sited Lake Paringa **campsite** ($6).

Around 18km south of Lake Paringa, the **Monro Beach Walk** (5km; 1hr 30min return) leads through lovely forest to a spot where you might see rare **Fiordland crested penguins** – mainly during the breeding season (July–Dec), but also occasionally in February, when they come ashore to moult. Ample wallets can gain a deeper appreciation of the fragile ecosystems of south Westland by staying nearby at the exclusive *Wilderness Lodge Lake Moeraki* (☏03/750 0881, Ⓦwww.wildernesslodge.co.nz; ❾) where, for around $490 per person per day, you get lodge **accommodation**, all meals, free canoe use and guided nature walks and safaris.

The highway finally returns to the coast 5km on at **Knight's Point**, where a roadside marker commemorates the linking of Westland and Otago by road in 1965. Ahead lies the **Haast Coastal Plain**, which kicks off at the tea-coloured **Ship Creek**, 10km on, where a picnic area and information panels by a beautiful long surf-pounded beach mark the start of two lovely walks: the twenty-minute **Kahikatea Swamp Forest Walk** up the river through kahikatea forest to a lookout and the **Mataketake Dune Lake Walk** (2km; 30min return) along the coast to the dune-trapped Lake Mataketake.

From Ship Creek it's only another 15km to the 700m-long Haast River Bridge, the longest single-lane bridge in the country, immediately before Haast Junction.

Haast

Haast is initially a confusing place, with three tiny communities all taking the name: Haast Junction, at the intersection of SH6 and the minor road to Jackson Bay, Haast Beach, 4km along the Jackson Bay Road (see p.662) and Haast Township, the largest settlement, 3km along SH6 towards Haast Pass and Wanaka.

At Haast Junction, the distinctive **Haast Visitor Centre** (daily: early Nov to April 9am–6pm; rest of year 9am–4.30pm; ☏03/750 0809, Ⓔhaastvc@doc .govt.nz) serves as the local information centre and has informative displays on all aspects of the local environment. The short *Edge of Wilderness* film is shown on demand ($3). To explore deeper, join a **jetboat safari** with Waiatoto River Safaris (daily on demand; $199; ☏0800/538 723, Ⓦwww.riversafaris.co.nz), a two-hour wilderness ride from the coast into the heart of the mountains with the emphasis firmly on appreciating history and scenery. Alternatively, try Heliventures (☏03/750 0866, Ⓦwww.heliventures.co.nz), who offer **flights** to the Lost Valley (35min; $260, min 3 people), or Mount Aspiring (1hr; $525, min 3 people), including a snow landing.

Even if you're just passing through you'll probably want to **eat**, but don't expect much. At Haast Township the **Fantail Café** does adequate teas, snacks and takeaways and the locals' favourite, *Hard Antler Bar*, offers ample bar meals and cheap jugs of beer. There's a small and fairly expensive supermarket for supplies.

Accommodation in and around Haast

Those wanting to **stay** have an increasing range of choices, but Haast gets busy from Christmas to the end of February so book ahead.

Collyer House Okuru, 13km south of Haast Junction ☎03/750 0022, ⓦwww.collyerhouse .co.nz. Appealing luxury accommodation with four modern en suites, all with distant sea views. A great welcome, sizeable cooked breakfast and evening meals, by arrangement, seal the deal. ❽

Haast Beach Holiday Park Okuru, 15km south of Haast Junction ☎03/750 0860. Ⓔhaastpark @xtra.co.nz. Simple holiday park close to the beach and the Hapuku Estuary Walk. Tents $15, dorms $25, cabins ❶, kitchen cabins ❸, motel units ❹

Heritage Park Lodge Haast Township ☎0800/526 252, ⓦwww.heritageparklodge.co.nz.

Motel offering comfortable studios, some with self-catering facilities, all with TV. ❸

Wilderness Accommodation Haast Township ☎03/750 0029, Ⓔwhitesnalex@xtra.co.nz. Comfortable, welcoming and great-value spot combining a backpacker hostel with four-shares and made-up doubles, and a series of motel studio units, all with access to a wilderness-themed common area and kitchen. They also have scooter rental for $25/half-day, ideal for trips to Jackson Bay. Dorms $25, backpacker rooms ❷, units ❺

The road to Jackson Bay

A modest number of inquisitive tourists make it 50km south of Haast to the fishing village of Jackson Bay. Leaving Haast Junction, the canopies of windswept roadside trees bunch together like cauliflower heads down to and beyond **Haast Beach**, 4km south, where there's a small shop and petrol supplies.

Ten kilometres on, there's accommodation in the form of *Collyer House* (see above) and, a couple of kilometres beyond, *Haast Beach Holiday Park* (see above). Opposite, the **Hapuku Estuary Walk** (20min loop) follows a raised boardwalk over a brackish lagoon and through kowhai forest that gleams brilliant yellow in October and November. Sand dunes support rimu and kahikatea forest, and there are occasional views to the **Open Bay Islands**, now a **wildlife sanctuary** and a major breeding colony for fur seals and Fiordland crested penguins.

The road continues 35km to **JACKSON BAY**, a former sealing station tucked in the curve of Jackson Head, which protects it from the worst of the westerlies. In 1875 it was chosen as the townsite to rival Greymouth and Hokitika. Assisted migrants – Scandinavians, Germans, Poles, Italians, English and Irish – were expected to carve a living from tiny land allocations, with limited and irregular supplies. Sodden by rain, crops rotted, and people soon left in droves; a few stalwarts stayed, their descendants providing the core of today's residents, who eke out a meagre living from lobster and tuna fishing.

Try the **Wharekai Te Kou Walk** (40min return) across the low isthmus behind Jackson Head to a beach where Fiordland crested penguins may be seen from July to November. The **Smoothwater Track** (3hr return) has great coastal views on the way to the Smoothwater River.

There are no **facilities** in Jackson Bay except for 🍴 *The Cray Pot* (daily: summer 11am–8pm; winter closes at 3pm), a kind of diner on wheels. Here you can get fantastic fresh-cooked fish (usually blue cod) and chips, seafood chowder or some form of meat and mugs of tea or coffee, away from the sandflies, while gazing at the sea-tossed fishing boats through fake leadlight windows.

Haast Pass and Makarora

From Haast it is nearly 150km over the **Haast Pass** (at 563m, the lowest road crossing of the Southern Alps) to Wanaka – a journey from the rain-soaked forests of the West Coast to the parched, rolling grasslands of Central Otago. Ngai Tahu

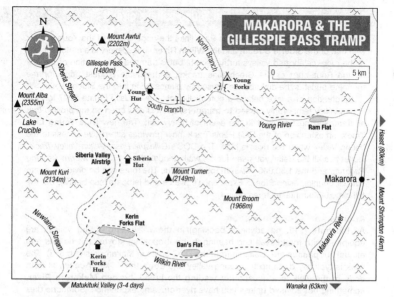

used the pass as a greenstone-trading route and probably introduced it to gold prospector Charles Cameron, the first Pakeha to cross in 1863; he was closely followed by the more influential **Julius Von Haast**, who modestly named it after himself. The pass was finally opened as a vehicular route in 1965.

The road starts beside the broad **Haast River**, which, as the road climbs, narrows to a series of churning cascades. Numerous short and well-signposted walks, mostly to waterfalls on tributaries, spur off at intervals. The most celebrated the **Thunder Creek Falls**, the roadside **Fantail Falls**, and the **Blue Pools Walk**, where an aquamarine stream issues from a narrow, icy gorge: swim if you dare. Though there are few specific sights, it is a great area to linger a while, **camping** in one of the DOC's toilets-and-water sites ($6/person): *Pleasant Flat*, 45km from Haast, *Cameron Flat* 10km short of Makarora.

Makarora

The hamlet of **MAKARORA** lies roughly midway between Haast and Wanaka, on the northern fringe of Mount Aspiring National Park. If you're aching for the comforts of Wanaka and Queenstown there's little reason to stop, but casual hikers, and keen trampers with a few days to spare, should consider tackling the local walks.

In the nineteenth century the dense **forests** all about and the proximity of Lake Wanaka made Makarora the perfect spot for marshalling cut logs across the lake and coaxing them down the Clutha River southeast to the fledgling North Otago **gold towns** of Clyde and Cromwell. The creation of the national park in 1964 paved the way for Makarora's increasing importance as the main northern access point to a region of majestic beauty, alpine vegetation and dense beech-filled valleys.

All you'll find here is a motor camp, a restaurant/bar, a shop and a **DOC office** (Dec–April daily 8am–5pm; May–Nov Mon–Fri occasionally staffed; ☎03/443 8365), the place to go for information and hut tickets for tramps. The main justification for stopping is to head out on the Gillespie Pass tramp (see p.664) or to

⑫

Gillespie Pass: the Wilkin and Young valleys circuit

This tramp over the 1490m Gillespie Pass links the upper valley of the **Young River** with that of the **Siberia Stream** and the **Wilkin River**. The scenery is a match for any of the more celebrated valleys further south, but is tramped by a fraction of the folk on the Routeburn or the Greenstone tracks; perhaps the biggest gripe for the tramping purist is the disturbance caused by planes flying into the Siberia Valley.

The creation of a lake behind a potentially unstable landslip in late 2007 left the Young Valley temporarily **closed to trampers**, but it is now open on the proviso that all trampers must avoid it in the event of heavy rain. The new **Blue-Young Link Track**, an extension of the Blue Pools Track, now provides alternative access to the Young Valley when the river is high. The DOC's *Gillespie Pass, Wilkin Valley Tracks* leaflet has all the detail you need for the walk, though the 1:160,000 *Mount Aspiring Parkmap* and the 1:50,000 *Wilkin* maps are useful. The route can be divided up into smaller chunks, using Siberia Experience's planes and jetboats (see below), but the full circuit (58km) takes three days.

Access and accommodation

All the **huts** ($15; no advance booking) in the Wilkin and Young valleys are equipped with mattresses and heating (but not cooking) stoves; hut **tickets** and annual hut **passes** are available from the DOC office in Makarora (see p.663). The walk is typically done up the Young Valley and down the Wilkin. **Access** at both ends of the walk is a question of **wading** the broad, braided **Makarora River**, something not advised unless you have river-crossing experience. Someone dies almost every year.

It is a good idea to use the Blue-Young Link Track to access the walk and arrange a **pick-up** by jetboat from Kerin Forks at the far end of the walk, unless you want to take your chances with river crossings or a stand-by backflight out of Siberia Valley.

The route

Start from the Blue Pools car park, heading through forest and open country, with bridges crossing the Makarora and Blue rivers and the Ore and Leven streams. The Young Valley is signposted on the left of SH6. Cross the stile and follow orange poles to the confluence of the Young and Makarora rivers. From the **confluence to Young**

join Southern Alps Air's excellent four-hour **Siberia Experience** ($310; ☏0800/345 606, ⓦwww.siberiaexperience.co.nz), which includes a flight into the remote Siberia Valley, a three-hour tramp to the Wilkin River and a jetboat ride back to Makarora, the same deal but with an added helicopter flight is $330.

Finally, if the longer hikes seem a little daunting, there are a couple of **shorter walks** close to Makarora, the **Makarora Bush Nature Walk** (15min loop), which starts near the DOC office and, branching off this, the **Mount Shrimpton Track** (5km return; 4–5hr; 900m ascent), which climbs steeply up through silver beech to the bushline, then to a knob overlooking the Makarora Valley.

If you need **accommodation** try the *Makarora Wilderness Resort*, SH6 (☏03/443 8372, ⓦwww.makarora.co.nz; camping $12, dorms $30, doubles ❷, kitchen cabins ❸, chalets ❹). The shop sells limited supplies and there's a wood-beamed café/bar serving sandwiches and buffet lunches or basic steak, chicken and veggie dinners.

Continuing towards Wanaka, a couple of lovely DOC **campsites** are the only real reasons to break your journey: *Boundary Creek* ($6) beside Lake Wanaka, or *Kidds Bush* ($6) beside Lake Hawea, 6km down a side road off SH6 at The Neck, where lakes Wanaka and Hawea almost meet.

Hut (20km; 6–7hr; 500m ascent), the easy-to-follow track traces the true left bank through beech forest to Young Forks, where there is a campsite (free). After the fork, the track follows the South Branch, climbing steeply (100m), before traversing a series of unstable slips to reach Stag Creek. From here it's a steady climb up through forest to the new Young Hut (20 bunks).

Suitably rested, you've another strenuous day ahead from **Young Hut to Siberia Hut** (12km; 6–8hr; 700m ascent, 1000m descent), first up to the treeline overlooked by the 2202m Mount Awful, apparently named in wonder rather than horror. Then it's over the Gillespie Pass, a steep and lengthy ascent eventually following snow poles to a saddle; it'll take three hours to reach this fabulous, barren spot with views across the snowcapped northern peaks of the Mount Aspiring National Park. Grassy slopes descend steeply to Gillespie Stream, which is followed to its confluence with the Siberia Stream, from where it's a gentle, undulating hour downstream to Siberia Hut (20 bunks). Keen types might tag on a side trip to **Lake Crucible** (4–5hr return) before cantering down to the hut. Those with more modest aspirations can spend two nights at Siberia Hut and do the **Lake Crucible side trip** (13km; 6–7hr return; 500m ascent) on the spare day.

From the Siberia Hut, follow the true left bank of the Siberia Stream a short distance until you see Crucible Stream cascading in a deep gash on the far side. Ford Siberia Stream and ascend through the bush on the true right bank of the stream. It is hard going, and route-finding among the alpine meadows higher up can be difficult, but the deep alpine lake tucked under the skirts of Mount Alba and choked with small icebergs is ample reward. Planes fly in and out of the **Siberia Valley airstrip**, and you can take your chance on "backloading" **flights out**. To continue tramping from **Siberia Hut to Kerin Forks** (8km; 2–3hr; 100m ascent, 300m descent), enter the bush at the southern end of Siberia Flats on the true left bank of Siberia Stream and descend away from the stream then zigzag steeply down to the Wilkin River and the **Kerin Forks Hut** (10 bunks), where many trampers arrange to be met by a jetboat. If it has rained heavily, fording the Makarora lower down will be impossible, so don't forgo the jetboat. The alternative is to walk from **Kerin Forks to Makarora** (17km; 5–6hr; 100m ascent, 200m descent), following the Wilkin River's true left bank, then crossing the Makarora upstream of the confluence.

Travel details

The main West Coast bus route is InterCity/Newmans' service from Nelson to Fox Glacier via Westport, Greymouth, Hokitika and Franz Josef. A second service starts in Franz Josef and stops in Fox Glacier, Haast and Makarora on the way to Wanaka and Queenstown. This setup enforces a night in either Franz Josef or Fox. To travel straight through, go with Atomic (W www.atomictravel.co.nz), who run daily between Greymouth and Queenstown. Several other companies service smaller places.

Trains

The only passenger train service is the TranzAlpine, running from Christchurch to Greymouth in the morning and back each afternoon.
Greymouth to: Arthur's Pass (1 daily; 2hr 15min); Christchurch (1 daily; 4hr 20min).

Buses

Fox Glacier to: Franz Josef (3 daily; 30min); Greymouth (3 daily; 3hr 45min–4hr 30min); Haast (3 daily; 2hr 40min–3hr); Hokitika (3 daily; 3hr); Makarora (3 daily; 4hr 30min); Queenstown (3 daily; 6hr–7hr 30min); Wanaka (3 daily; 5–6hr).

Franz Josef Glacier to: Fox Glacier (3 daily; 30min); Haast (3 daily; 3hr–3hr 30min); Greymouth (3 daily; 3hr–3hr 30min); Hokitika (3 daily; 2hr 30min); Makarora (3 daily; 4hr 20min–5hr); Queenstown (2 daily; 7–8hr); Wanaka (2 daily; 6–7hr).

Greymouth to: Arthur's Pass (3 daily; 1hr 30min); Christchurch (3 daily; 4hr 30min); Fox Glacier (3 daily; 3hr 45min–4hr 30min); Franz Josef (3 daily; 3hr–3hr 30min); Hokitika (3 daily; 30min); Murchison (1 daily; 2hr 15min); Picton (1 daily; 7hr); Punakaiki (3 daily; 30min); Queenstown (2 daily; 9–10hr); Wanaka (2 daily; 8hr–8hr 30min); Westport (3 daily; 1hr 30min–2hr 15min).

Hokitika to: Arthur's Pass (1 daily; 1hr 45min); Christchurch (1 daily; 4hr 30min); Fox Glacier (3 daily; 3hr); Franz Josef (3 daily; 2hr 30min); Greymouth (3 daily; 30min); Ross (3 daily; 25min); Whataroa (3 daily; 1hr 30min).

Westport to: Greymouth (3 daily; 1hr 30min–2hr 15min); Karamea (2 daily; 1hr 40min–2hr); Murchison (3 daily; 1hr 15min–1hr 45min); Nelson (3 daily; 3hr 30min–4hr); Punakaiki (3 daily; 1hr); St Arnaud (1 daily; 1hr 45min).

Flights

Greymouth to: Wellington (4 weekly; 1hr).
Hokitika to: Christchurch (2–4 daily; 35min).
Westport to: Wellington (1 daily Mon–Fri; 50min).

13

Queenstown, Wanaka and the Gold Country

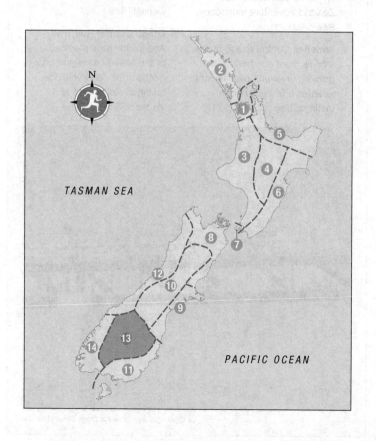

TASMAN SEA

PACIFIC OCEAN

N

CHAPTER 13 **Highlights**

* **Nevis Highwire Bungy** Test your nerve on the Nevis; one of New Zealand's biggest elasticated leaps from a hut suspended high above a canyon. See p.681

* **Shotover River** Take a jetboat ride down through an iconic part of the New Zealand adventure landscape. See p.681

* **Wineries** Central Otago is the world's most southerly wine-growing area with over twenty wineries offering sublime tastings. See p.688 & p.719

* **The Routeburn Track** Lush bush and alpine scenery combine to make this one of New Zealand's best tramps. See p.700

* **Canyoning** Get intimate with one of the Matukituki Valley's verdant canyons – about the most fun you can have in a wetsuit. See p.707

* **Otago Central Rail Trail** Absorb the rural pleasures of the Maniototo region on a gentle three-day cycle ride, taking in old tunnels and viaducts. See p.721

▲ Crossing a viaduct on the Otago Central Rail Trail

13

Queenstown, Wanaka and the Gold Country

Wedged between the sodden beech forests of Fiordland, the fertile plains of south Canterbury and the sheep country of Southland lies Central Otago; a region encompassing **Queenstown**, **Wanaka** and the surrounding **Gold Country**. Deserted hills to the east give way to the mountains around Queenstown and Wanaka, rubbing shoulders with the glaciated Southern Alps. Meltwater and heavy rains course out of the mountains into the 70km lightning bolt of **Lake Wakatipu**, draining east through the Kawarau River, which carves a rapid-strewn path through the Kawarau Gorge. Along the way it picks up the waters of the Shotover River from the goldfields of Skippers and Arrowtown. To the north, the pristine, glassy lakes of Wanaka and Hawea feed the **Clutha River**, which joins with the Kawarau at Cromwell and high-tails it to the coast through the heartland of the Otago Gold Country.

Queenstown is the region's flawed jewel, with a legendary setting looking across Lake Wakatipu to the craggy heights of the Remarkables range. Otherwise known as Screamstown, New Zealand's self-proclaimed adventure capital can take on the atmosphere of a high-priced theme park, offering the chance to indulge in just about every adrenaline-fuelled activity imaginable: bungy jumping, jetboating, rafting, skydiving and paragliding, all honed into well-packaged, forcefully marketed products. The wonderful scenery has provided the background for major feature films such as *The Vertical Limit*; *The Lion, The Witch and The Wardrobe*; and the highest concentration of locations from *The Lord of the Rings* trilogy.

Neighbouring **Arrowtown** wears its gold heritage well. There is something to delay most folk amid quaint streets, intimate restaurants, cool bars, indie cinema, historic Chinese and gold settlements and day-long walk to the defunct gold mines around **Macetown**. All this provides a welcome break from Queenstown's high-pitched ambience but perhaps the perfect antidote is the great outdoors. Some of the country's most exalted multi-day tramps start from nearby Glenorchy, from which well-organized track transport will drop you at the trailheads of the magnificent **Routeburn Track**, the match of any in the country; the green and beautiful **Caples** and **Greenstone** tracks (combined to make a satisfying five-day circuit); and the rugged **Rees–Dart Track**, which opens the challenging Cascade Saddle Route.

Glacially scoured, the three-sided pinnacle of Mount Aspiring, "the Matterhorn of the South", forms the centrepiece of the **Mount Aspiring National Park**.

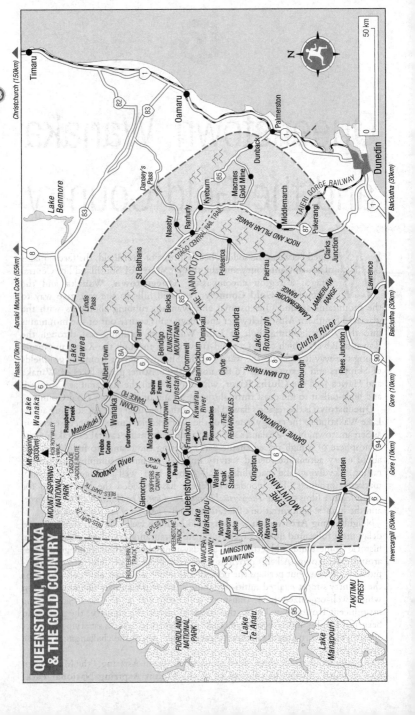

QUEENSTOWN, WANAKA
& THE GOLD COUNTRY

Getting around the region is easily done: frequent buses link the main towns, supplemented by shuttle buses to trailheads and minibuses between hotels and the various adventure activities.

Permanently snowcapped, this alpine high country is linked by the alluring Matukituki Valley to the small and expanding resort town of **Wanaka**, draped around the placid waters of its eponymous lake. Wanaka's laidback atmosphere stands in marked contrast to frenetic Queenstown, though there's no shortage of adventure operators vying to thrill you.

Queenstown and Wanaka lie on the fringe of the **Otago Goldfields**, which stretch east towards the coast at Dunedin. Most of the gold has long since gone and the area is largely deserted, but there are numerous interesting reminders of New Zealand's gold-rush days. Queenstown and Arrowtown were two of the biggest gold towns but to the east are the more modest centres of **Cromwell**, **Alexandra** and **Roxburgh**. All scattered along the banks of the Clutha River, which once provided Maori with the easiest route to the greenstone fields of the West Coast. Gold miners subsequently used the same paths, fanning out to found tiny towns such as **St Bathans** and **Naseby**, enjoyable places to idle among the boom-time remains.

From June to October the region's focus switches to **skiing**, with Queenstown acting as a base for the downhill resorts of **Coronet Peak** and **the Remarkables**, while Wanaka serves the **Cardrona** and **Treble Cone** fields, as well as the **Snow Farm** Nordic field.

Queenstown

The faint screams of adrenaline activity junkies pierce **QUEENSTOWN**'s, tranquillity while, in the evenings, the base thump of music and shrill whistle of the TSS *Earnslaw* provide the backdrop. Kiwis and visitors complain that the town is too loud, crowded, expensive, big for its boots and the victim of devil-may-care development, but this is, after all, New Zealand's most popular commercialized resort. Yet somehow Queenstown, attractively set by deep-blue Lake Wakatipu and hemmed in by craggy mountains, still has the air of a small-town idyll. Furthermore, it offers a great selection of restaurants, some of the flashiest (and most highly priced) accommodation in the country, and nightlife that will either suck you in or drive you away.

Best taken in small doses, Queenstown is well worth using either as a base from which to plan lengthy forays into the surrounding countryside, or as a venue for sampling all manner of adventure activities. The most prominent of these is undoubtedly **bungy jumping**. The town's environs boast three of the world's most gloriously scenic bungy sites, visited either in isolation or as part of a package, perhaps including **whitewater rafting** and **jetboating** on the Shotover River.

Visitors after a more sedate time plump for **lake cruises** on the elegant TSS *Earnslaw*, the last of the lake steamers, or aboard an America's Cup yacht; the **gondola ride** to Bob's Peak, which commands magnificent vistas from a cable car over Queenstown and the Remarkables range; and **wine tours** around some of the world's most southerly vineyards (see p.688). Formal lakeshore gardens and hillside viewpoints provide the focus for easy local **walks**, with heartier multi-day tramps starting at **Glenorchy** (see p.694) at the head of the lake. For details on visiting **Milford Sound** from Queenstown, see the box on p.746.

Frantic summers are nothing in comparison to winter, when Kiwi and international skiers descend on **Coronet Peak** and **the Remarkables**, two fine ski-fields within half an hour of Queenstown, particularly during the annual **Queenstown Winter Festival**, late June and early July.

Arrival, information and city transport

Queenstown's main downtown area is concentrated around Rees Street, Shotover Street, Camp Street and the pedestrianized Mall, which runs from the Main Town Wharf northeast to Ballarat Street. **Buses** arrive close to the junction of Camp and Shotover streets, from where it's less than fifteen minutes' walk to most hotels and hostels. Just outside Frankton, 7km northeast of central Queenstown, is the city's **airport** (ⓦ www.queenstownairport.co.nz). Most flights are met by the door-to-door Super Shuttle (around $15), and you can also get into town using the Connectabus (see "City transport" opposite). Taxis (ⓣ 03/442 6666 or 442 7788) charge around $25 for the ride in. Most major car rental companies have offices at the airport.

The **i-SITE visitor centre**, on the corner of Camp and Shotover streets (daily: Dec–April 7.30am–6.30pm; May–Nov 7.30am–6pm; ☎03/442 4100, ⓦwww .queenstowninformation.co.nz), organizes bookings and offers impartial advice. Shotover Street is awash with rival visitor centre-cum-booking offices. Perhaps the most prominent is **The Station**, on the corner of Camp and Shotover streets, which acts as the nerve centre and the main pick-up spot for A.J. Hackett bungy and the Shotover Jet. A few steps away, the **Info&Track Centre**, 37 Shotover St (daily 7am–9pm; ☎03/442 9708, ⓦwww.infotrack.co.nz), is a handy backpacker-oriented booking office.

The **DOC visitor centre**, 38 Shotover St (Oct–April daily 8.30am–5.30pm; May–Sept daily 9am–5pm; ☎03/442 7935, Ⓔqueenstownvc@doc.govt.nz), on the first floor of the Outside Sports shop, comes stacked with leaflets and operates a Great Walks Booking Desk.

Tourist **publications** worth seeking out include the free *iTAG* guide (ⓦwww .itag.co.nz) and the *Mountain Scene* newspaper for an insight into what's currently making Queenstown tick.

City transport

Everywhere you are likely to want to go in central Queenstown can be reached **on foot**. Most activities take place out of town but operators run courtesy buses to the sites, usually picking up from accommodation en route. There are **taxi ranks** on Camp Street, at the top end of the Mall, and on Shotover Street; alternatively, book a taxi with Alpine Taxi (☎0800/442 6666) or Queenstown Taxis (☎0800/488 294).

The only useful bus service is Connectabus, from Camp Street outside McDonald's *McCafé* (daily departures hourly 8am–11pm; ☎03/441 4471, ⓦwww .connectabus.com), which runs out to Frankton ($6 each way), the airport ($6) and on to Arrowtown ($8; day pass $19).

Drivers will have no problem negotiating Queenstown's streets; although **parking** can be tight in the centre of town, you'll usually find a free all-day spot a few streets away.

Accommodation

Queenstown has the widest selection of **places to stay** in this corner of New Zealand but such is the demand in the middle of summer or the height of the ski season, that rooms can be hard to come by and prices high. Accommodation at both ends of the spectrum is excellent, but things are tougher in the middle where there are few modestly priced, convenient **motels** and **B&Bs**. Boutique **lodges** are abundant, but expensive, while big **hotels** offer good deals in what passes for Queenstown's off season (essentially April, May & Nov) but in general you'll do better in smaller places. The best budget deals are at the many **hostels**, which compete fiercely for trade, frequently offering high-standard rooms (some en suite) at relatively modest prices. The Queenstown district also has a few compact **campsites** with attendant cabins.

With a few exceptions, all the accommodation is packed into a compact area less than fifteen minutes' walk from the centre of town. If a less ear-piercing atmosphere – and lower prices – appeal, it's well worth considering **Arrowtown** (see p.689) or **Glenorchy** (see p.694).

Hotels

Browns Boutique Hotel 26 Isle St ☎03/441 2050, ⓦwww.brownshotel.co.nz. Appealing downtown establishment with ten rooms, comfortable and well appointed, with small balconies overlooking the town or the lake and a luxurious guest lounge with an open fire. ❽

The Dairy Corner of Brecon & Isle sts ☎03/442 5164, ⓦwww.thedairy.co.nz. This thirteen-room boutique hotel has delightful common areas hung

Frankton (3km), Airport (5km), Arrowtown (20km) & Milford Sound (290km) ▲

Queenstown Hill (907m) ▲

◀ Arthurs Point (5km), Coronet Peak (16km) & Skippers Road (16km)

Fernhill (2km), ◀ (10km), ◀ (28km) & Glenorchy (50km)

ACCOMMODATION

Alpine Lodge	X
Base Discovery Lodge	A
Black Sheep	E
Browns Boutique Hotel	U
Bumbles	H
Butterfli Lodge	K
Caples Court	G
The Chalet	M
Creeksyde	B
The Dairy	T
Four Seasons Motel	I
Hippo Lodge	D
Hurley's	L
Little Paradise Lodge	R
The Lodges	J
Nomads	C
Pinewood	V
Queenstown Lakeview	O
Holiday Park	U
Queenstown Motel	H
Apartments	K
The Stonehouse	F
Southern Laughter	M
Hostel	B
Twelve-Mile Delta	T
Reserve	I
YHA Central	Q
Queenstown	W
YHA Queenstown	P
Lakefront	P

RESTAURANTS, CAFÉS & BARS

@ Thai	18
Aggy's Shack	23
Altitude	1
Atlas Bar	22
Bardeaux	15
Bombay Place	9
Bunker	10
The Cow	7
Destination	4
Organic	17
Debajo	6
Dur de Lux	21
FergBurger	2
Finz	19
Halo	16
Kappa	8
Mini Bar	14
Patagonia Chocolates	12
Pig and Whistle	5
Pog Mahone's	13
Pub on Wharf	10
Solera Vino	3
Vudu	20
Wai	11
Winnies	21
World Bar	2

CENTRAL QUEENSTOWN

0 — 250 m

N

Lake Wakatipu

Frankton Arm

Queenstown Bay

Queenstown Gardens

St Omer Park

See inset map for detail

Skyline Gondola

Bob's Peak

Kiwi & Birdlife Park

Library

Courthouse & Old Stone Library

Freshchoice

Alpine Foodcenter

Wine Toasties

DOC Office

Eichardt's Hotel

Main Town Pier

Steamer Wharf

with quality New Zealand artworks (several original) where you might sup something delightful from the extensive honesty bar. The rooms (some with bathtubs) are well appointed and tastefully decorated in modern styles. Breakfast and afternoon tea are served in the original dairy (corner shop). Rates start at $450 but pay the extra $30 for a lake view. ⑨

Hurley's Corner of Frankton Rd & Melbourne St ☎0800/589 879, ⓦwww.hurleys.co.nz. Tasteful, luxuriously appointed apartments and studios close to the centre, each equipped with a full kitchen, TV, CD player and spa baths and with free access to two saunas and a full gym. Studios ⑤, apartments ⑦

Motels and apartments

🏃 **Caples Court** 20 Stanley St ☎0800/282 275, ⓦwww.caplescourt.co.nz. Delightful, comfortable motel with more spirit to its decor than most, and each room done in a different style. Most have a kitchen and a balcony and seven of the nine units have views over the town and/or lake. The other two are tucked peacefully away beside a quiet garden. Garden units ④, lake view ⑤

Four Seasons Motel 12 Stanley St ☎03/442 8953, ⓦwww.queenstownmotel.com. Upgraded downtown motel with off-street parking, good kitchens, mountain views, an outdoor swimming pool (unfortunately beside the main road), a spa and a range of units. ⑤

The Lodges 8 Lake Esplanade ☎0800/284 356, ⓦwww.queenstownthelodges.co.nz. New owners are sprucing up these lakeside apartments with kitchen, laundry and parking. ⑥

Queenstown Motel Apartments 62 Frankton Rd ☎0800/661 668, ⓦwww.qma.co.nz. Good-value motel close to town with functional older units and twelve newer ones, all pale wood, bold colours and tasteful artworks. There's a strong environmental stance, with energy-saving light bulbs, and recycling bins in the kitchenettes. Old ③, new ⑤, new lake view ⑥

B&Bs, homestays and lodges

The Chalet 1 Dublin St ☎03/442 7117, ⓦwww .chaletqueenstown.co.nz and **The Stonehouse** 47 Hallenstien St ☎03/442 7177, ⓦwww.historic stonehouse.co.nz. Undoubtedly the best B&Bs in Queenstown, both owned by the same people, in quiet locations; the first a Swiss-style building with grand views, the other a relaxing historic stone getaway. The decor in both is immaculate, the hosts welcoming, the service close to perfection and the food worth staying in for. ⑧

🏃 **Little Paradise Lodge** Meilejohn Bay, 28km along Glenorchy Rd ☎03/442 6196, ⓦwww.littleparadise.co.nz. Eccentric, alternative and charming guesthouse close to the lake where almost everything is made from logs cut or stone hewn by the Swiss owner, Thomas, including the non-chlorinated swimming pool fed by its own stream and complete with water lilies. The real joy is the garden – the smells and blooms are captivating. Accommodation is in standard rooms and an en-suite chalet. You can cook for yourself, and there's kayak rental ($10) and free fishing gear. Dorms $45, rooms ④/⑤

Hostels

Alpine Lodge 13 Gorge Rd ☎03/442 7220, ⓦwww.alpinelodgebackpackers.co.nz. Small and welcoming hostel with separate movie and quiet lounges. They also operate the adjacent *Turner Lodge*, which has spacious en suites and its own lounge and cooking area that's less frenetic than the main hostel. Dorms $26, rooms ②, lodge en suites ③

Base Discovery Lodge 47 Shotover St ☎03/441 1185, ⓦwww.basebackpackers.co.nz. Massive (300-plus beds), lively hostel with an inadequate kitchen, but that doesn't matter because you'll probably end up eating and drinking in their bar and booking your tours at their travel desk. However, dorms have secure lockers, a toilet and shower and there's a decent range of en-suite doubles and twins with TV. Dorms $28, rooms & en suites ③

Black Sheep 13 Frankton Rd ☎03/442 7289, ⓦwww.blacksheepbackpackers.co.nz. Licensed backpackers converted from a motel, with three- to seven-bed dorms, BBQ near the spa pool, a bar (4–10pm). Dorms $28, rooms ②, deluxe ③

Bumbles 2 Brunswick St ☎03/442 6298, ⓦwww .bumblesbackpackers.co.nz. Refurbished hostel, well sited on the lakefront road, offering great views from most rooms and common areas, a spacious kitchen, a BBQ area and off-street parking. Dorms $28, ②

Butterfli Lodge 62 Thompson St ☎03/442 6367, ⓦwww.butterfli.co.nz. A small house overlooking the lake, with a friendly atmosphere and cosy accommodation for a limited number of people. Book early; two-night minimum. Dorms $26, rooms ②

Hippo Lodge 4 Anderson Heights ☎03/442 5785, ⓦwww.hippolodge.co.nz. A couple of suburban houses imaginatively converted into four sections, each with its own bathroom, kitchen and living area. Several of the rooms and lounges have fabulous views over Queenstown.

They're one of the few hostels to offer work (2–3hr/day) for accommodation. Tent sites $18, dorms $28, rooms ❷, en suite ❸

Nomads 5–11 Church St ☎03/441 3922, ⓦwww.nomadqueenstwon.com. Massive, very new, quite posh hostel with piddly kitchen, but excellent rooms, a female-only area and central parking. Dorms $25, rooms ❷, en suite ❸

🏃 **Pinewood** 48 Hamilton Rd ☎0800/746396, ⓦwww.pinewood .co.nz. An extensive collection of new and older renovated s/c buildings (all surrounded by lawns) a 10min walk from the centre, this friendly hostel has a spa bath with views ($5/30min) and en suites which collectively have their own kitchen and lounge areas. Dorms $25, rooms ❷, en suites ❸

Southern Laughter Hostel 4 Isla St ☎03/441 8828, ⓦwww.kiwi-backpackers.co.nz. Split over three buildings with a surprisingly large variety of rooms and a free spa, this hostel makes up for not being flash by being friendly. Dorms $25, rooms ❷, en suite ❸

YHA Central Queenstown 48a Shotover St ☎03/442 7400. Not as popular as its lakeside counterpart, this workaday hostel is right in the thick of it, and provides comfy rooms and adequate kitchen facilities. Dorms $25, rooms ❷ en suite ❸

YHA Queenstown Lakefront 88 Lake Esplanade ☎03/442 8413, ⒺChisholm.queenstownlakefront@yha .co.nz. One of NZ's flagship YHAs in an excellent, quiet location 7min walk from town. The feel is surprisingly homely and accommodation is in spacious, mostly four- to eight-bed dorms plus twins and doubles, many with good lake views. Dorms $25, rooms ❷ en suite ❸

Campsites and motor parks

Creeksyde 54 Robins Rd ☎03/442 9447, ⓦwww .camp.co.nz. Well-organized, spotlessly clean Top 10 holiday park 10min walk from town with shaded sites, many used by campervans. A central building houses a spa bathroom and sauna (both $15/30min for two), a ski store and drying rooms. Camping $20, shared bathrooms ❷, en suites ❹, s/c units ❺

Queenstown Lakeview Holiday Park Brecon St ☎0800/482 735, ⓦwww.holidaypark.net.nz. Enormous site that sprawls over the base of Bob's Peak with grassy, though not well-shaded, tent and van sites (showers $1) to kitchenless studios and fully s/c units sleeping up to five. Facilities are of a high standard. Camping $18, studios ❹, units ❺, flats ❻

Twelve-Mile Delta Reserve 12km west of Queenstown towards Glenorchy. Lakeside DOC campsite with facilities limited to basic toilets and running water. Camping $7.

The Town

Central Queenstown has little to show for its gold-rush past. At the top of the Mall, Ballarat Street crosses a small stream spanned by an 1882 stone bridge to reach the **Courthouse** and **Old Stone Library** (now offices), both built in the mid-1870s and since dwarfed by century-old giant sequoias. At the opposite end of the Mall, the waterfront **Eichardt's Hotel** is a super-expensive affair dating partly from 1871. Around the corner on Marine Parade, the 1866 **Williams Cottage** retains many original features and now operates as a shop cum café. Marine Parade continues east to **Queenstown Gardens** (unrestricted entry), an attractive parkland retreat that covers the peninsula separating Queenstown Bay from the rest of Lake Wakatipu.

If you don't have time to head out to the wineries (see p.688), call in at **Wine Tastes**, 14 Beach St (daily noon–10pm; ☎03/409 2226, ⓦwww.winetastes.com), where over eighty wines are dished out by sophisticated vending machines. Simply obtain a charge card or run a tab, sample what you fancy in – half- or full-glass quantities ($2–32) then hang out on the leather chairs, perhaps with a cheeseboard.

North of town, Brecon Street heads for Bob's Peak past Queenstown's **cemetery** – the final resting place of Queenstown pioneer Nicholas von Tunzelmann, as well as Henry Homer, discoverer of the Homer Saddle – on the Milford Road. Almost opposite, the **Kiwi & Birdlife Park** (daily: Nov–Feb 9am–6pm; March–Oct 9am–5pm; $35 including audio tour; ☎03/442 8059, ⓦwww.kiwibird.co.nz), is an expanse of ponds, lawns, native bush and aviaries, which house some of New

Zealand's rare birds. Though more zoo than wildlife park it does a good job of presenting morepork, kea, kereru (native pigeons), kakariki (native parakeets) and black stilt (one of the world's most endangered bird species, see p.790), alongside the products of captive-breeding programmes for the North Island brown kiwi. Time your visit to coincide with the twenty-minute **Conservation Show** (daily 11am & 3pm; free), when you get up close and personal with kereru, kea and tuatara, or the **Maori Performance** (11.15am & 3.15pm; free).

Bob's Peak

The best views of Queenstown, Lake Wakatipu, the Remarkables and Cecil and Walter peaks are from **Bob's Peak**, rising up immediately behind the town. Accessible from the sedate **Skyline Gondola**, Brecon Street (daily from 9am, last entry 9.30pm; $23 return; Ⓦwww.skyline.co.nz), which deposits you at the Skyline Complex, the peak can also be reached on foot, by following Lomond Crescent for about an hour.

The conifer-clad slopes are a launch pad for **paragliders** throughout the day, while the Skyline Complex plays host to the Ledge bungy and swing (see p.681), and the **Luge** (gondola plus one ride $30); a twisting concrete track negotiated on a wheeled plastic buggy with a primitive braking system – take it easy on your first run, then let rip once you've got the hang of it. If all this kickstarts your appetite the complex has a café and a buffet-style "taste of New Zealand" restaurant (lunch $32, dinner $55).

Cruising Lake Wakatipu

The coal-fired **TSS Earnslaw**, the last of the lake steamers, is one of Queenstown's most enduring images. Wherever you are, the encircling mountains echo the shrill sound of the steam whistle as the beautifully restored relic slogs manfully out from Steamer Wharf.

Launched in 1912, the 51m-long craft was the largest and most stately steamer to ply the lake. Burnished brass and polished wood predominate even around the gleaming steam engine, which is open for inspection. Crowds usually cluster around the piano at the back of the boat for a surprisingly popular music-hall singsong that can make the return journey seem interminable.

The *Earnslaw*, operated by Real Journeys (Ⓣ0800/656 501, Ⓦwww.real journeys.co.nz), runs from Queenstown across the lake to **Walter Peak High Country Farm** (3–6 daily between 10am and 6pm; 1hr 30min; cruise only $48 return), a tourist enclave nestling in the southwestern crook of Lake Wakatipu. The Walter Peak homestead, a convincing replica of a building which burnt down in 1977, is beautifully sited among lawns that sweep down to the lakeshore, and plays host to a **farm tour** – an entertaining if sanitized vignette of farm life, with demonstrations of dog handling and sheepshearing. The tour can be combined with tea and scones ($68 including cruise), a BBQ meal ($93) or a carvery buffet dinner (6pm; $115). The boat trip itself can be combined with a horse trek, tea and scones (3hr 30min; $105). There's also a Heritage Tour (4pm; $75) combining a cruise with a historic tour of the house and gardens and a little wine tasting.

By taking your own bike ($5) with you on the boat, you can continue along the remote and unsealed 80km road up the Von River past Mavora Lakes to SH94 at Burwood, 27km east of Te Anau.

If you'd prefer the excitement of windpower, board a converted **America's Cup yacht** with Sail Queenstown ($150/2hr; Ⓣ03/442 7517 or 021/724 579, Ⓦwww .sailqueenstown.co.nz), who take you out on the lake, conditions permitting, and give you a chance to help sail or just sit back and enjoy.

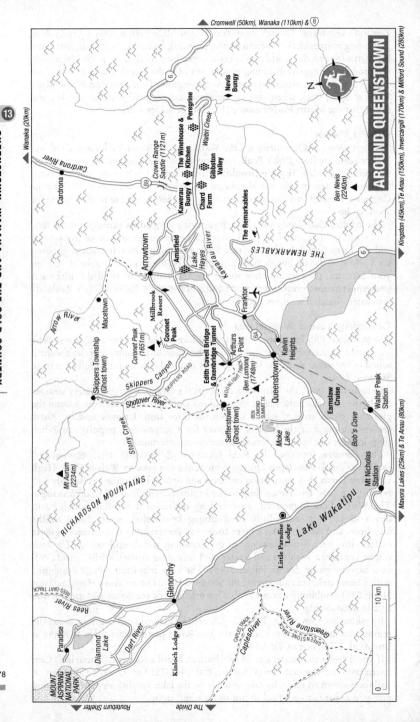

AROUND QUEENSTOWN

N

▲ Cromwell (50km), Wanaka (110km) & ⑧

◀ Wanaka (20km)

Cardrona River

Cardrona

Crown Range Saddle (1121m)

The Winehouse & Kitchen

Peregrine

Kawerau Bungy

Nevis Bungy

Waitiri Creek

Gibbston Valley

Chard Farm

Ben Nevis (2240m) ▲

Arrowtown

Amisfield

Lake Hayes

Kawarau River

The Remarkables

Frankton

THE REMARKABLES

6

▶ Kingston (45km), Te Anau (150km), Invercargill (170km) & Milford Sound (280km)

Arrow River

Macetown

Millbrook Resort

Coronet Peak (1651m)

Coronet Peak

Skippers Township (Ghost town)

Skippers Canyon

SKIPPERS ROAD

Edith Cavell Bridge & Oxenbridge Tunnel

Arthurs Point

MOONLIGHT TRACK

Ben Lomond (1748m) ▲

BEN LOMOND SUMMIT TK

6A

Kelvin Heights

Shotover River

Stony Creek

Sefferstown (Ghost town)

Moke Lake

Queenstown

Earnslaw Cruise

Bob's Cove

Walter Peak Station

Mt Aurum (2234m) ▲

RICHARDSON MOUNTAINS

Mt Nicholas Station

Lake Wakatipu

▶ Mavora Lakes (25km) & Te Anau (80km)

Little Paradise Lodge

Rees River

REES–DART TRACK

Glenorchy

Greenstone River

GREENSTONE TRACK

CAPLES TRACK

Caples River

Paradise

Diamond Lake

Dart River

MOUNT ASPIRING NATIONAL PARK

Kinloch Lodge

▲ Routeburn Shelter

▲ The Divide

0   10 km

The Shotover River and Skippers Canyon

The churning **Shotover River** is inextricably linked with Queenstown, the valley echoing with the screams from the majority of the town's adventure-based trips – bungy jumping, rafting, jetboating, mountain biking and more (see "Activities", p.680). The Shotover rises in the Richardson Mountains north of Queenstown and picks up speed to surge through its deepest and narrowest section, **Skippers Canyon**, and into the Kawarau River downstream from Lake Wakatipu. Tributaries run off Mount Aurum, beneath which is the mother lode of the Shotover goldfields, first discovered when a couple of pioneer shearers, Thomas Arthur and Harry Redfern, found gold in 1862 at Arthur's Point, 5km north of Queenstown. Word spread that prospectors were extracting over ten kilos a day, and within months thousands were flocking from throughout New Zealand and Australia to work what was soon dubbed "The Richest River in the World".

The river-edge gravels had been all but worked out by 1864, necessitating ever more sophisticated extraction techniques. With the introduction of gravity-fed water chutes, mechanical sieves and floating dredges, the construction of a decent road became crucial. From 1863, Chinese navvies spent over twenty years hacking away with pick and shovel at the Skippers Road; those who stuck out the harsh conditions began building quarters more substantial than the standard-issue canvas tents. Meanwhile, entrepreneurially minded pioneers began to exploit the boom, building 27 hotels along the 40km of road, and selling fresh fruit and vegetables at extortionate prices to miners often suffering from scurvy. By the turn of the century the river was worked out, though a few stayed on. Even today a couple of die-hards make a living from gold panning and sluicing, and in 1999, for a few days after flooding, happy prospectors were panning up to $600 worth in a couple of hours.

The Skippers Road

If you are willing to risk the treacherous **Skippers Road**, there are gold-rush relics worth exploring, but frankly the narrow, winding ribbon is best left to experienced drivers. Locals tend to hare around, leaving little space for oncoming traffic; besides, rental cars aren't insured for Skippers. Being driven to the start point for the Shotover rafting trips (see p.682) gives you a good chance to survey the area.

The Skippers Road, which follows the Shotover River only in its upper reaches, branches off Coronet Peak Road 12km north of Queenstown. It is approached along Malaghans Road through **Arthur's Point**, 5km north of Queenstown, marked by the historic but mundane *Arthur's Point Hotel*, the only one of the Skippers Road hotels still operating. Half a kilometre on, the Edith Cavell Bridge spans a gorge where the Shotover Jet (see p.681) performs its antics, its upstream progress limited by the Mother-in-Law rapid and the 1911 **Oxenbridge Tunnel**.

Skippers Road soon begins to shadow the river, negotiating Pinchers Bluff, where Chinese and European navvies cut the road from a near-vertical cliff face. Upstream, the 1901 **Skippers Bridge** was the first high-level one built – and consequently survived the winter floods, which had swept away all past efforts. For the first time, the township of Skippers had reliable access, though this did little to prevent the exodus that saw a population of 1500 dwindle to nothing once the gold ran out. The old schoolhouse has been restored and there are ruins of a few more buildings scattered around making it a bleak, haunted place. You can **camp** here at a toilets-and-water site for $7.

The best way to get up here is with Skippers Canyon Jet (see p.681), which offers flexible packages with the added bonus of guides who have lived in the area for over twenty years. Either take its 4WD **tour** (4hr; $120) which explores the region and visits Winky's Museum, or go on its jetboat.

Activities

Most of Queenstown's activity companies now have a presence in or an association with one of the myriad **information** and **booking offices** that line Shotover Street. Virtually every booking office will book any trip as will most accommodation. Prices don't usually vary but check for backpacker discounts and deals. Almost all booking offices are open daily, usually to around 8pm.

With so much on offer, it's tempting to be frugal elsewhere and blow the budget in Queenstown, but in reality most activities here are more **expensive** than in other parts of the country. To get the most action for the least money, check out one of the numerous **combination deals** knitting together two to five adventure trips.

Bungy jumping

Even visitors who had no intention of parting with a large wad of cash to dangle on the end of a thick strand of latex find themselves **bungy jumping** in Queenstown. A combination of peer pressure, magnificent scenery and zealous promotion gets to most people and, let's face it, historic bridges high above remote rivers beat a crane over a supermarket car park any day. A.J. Hackett (℡0800/286 495, Ⓦwww.bungy.co.nz) operates three sites around Queenstown, and all can be combined in the "Thrillogy" ($450). If you want a record of your fifteen minutes of hair-raising fame you can pay to download photos or a film from its website (about $15–20).

A.J. Hackett's original, most famous and frequently jumped bungy site is **Kawarau Bungy** (43m; daily 9am–5pm; $175, including a certificate and T-shirt;

Walks around Queenstown

When hard-sell adventure activities in Queenstown get a bit oppressive, a few hours away can be wonderfully therapeutic. The majority of the walks outlined below – listed in ascending order of difficulty – are well covered by DOC's *Queenstown walks and trails* leaflet. Serious multi-day tramps in the region are centred on Wanaka and Glenorchy (see p.694 & p.702 respectively).

One Mile Creek Walkway (6km return; 1hr 30min; 50m ascent). Fairly easy walk heading through a gully filled with beech forest before following a 1924 pipeline from Queenstown's first hydroelectric scheme. The route starts on the lakefront by the Fernhill roundabout and offers an opportunity to acquaint yourself with fuchsia, lancewood and native birds – principally fantails, bellbirds and tui.

Queenstown Hill Walk (5km return; 2–3hr; 500m ascent). Starting from the top of Belfast Street, this is a fairly steep climb through mostly exotic trees to panoramic views from the 907m Queenstown Hill.

Ben Lomond Summit Track (11km return; 6–8hr; 1400m ascent). A full-day tramp scaling Ben Lomond, one of the highest mountains in the region (1748m) and consequently subject to inclement weather, especially in winter when the track can be snow-covered. Start by the One Mile Creek Walk or use the Skyline Gondola and walk up past the paragliding launch site to join the track, which climbs through alpine tussock to reveal expansive views. Gentler slopes approach Ben Lomond Saddle, from where it's a steep final haul to the summit.

Ben Lomond–Moonlight Track (16km one-way; 8–10hr; 1400m ascent). A demanding, difficult-to-follow route (especially in snow) combining the ascent to Ben Lomond Saddle with a poled sub alpine route to the site of the former gold town of Sefferstown and the eastern section of the Moonlight Track to Arthur's Point. Organize someone to pick you up at Arthur's Point or endure a 5km slog back to Queenstown.

transport $30 extra), beside SH6, 23km east of Queenstown. In the only place around Queenstown where you can get dunked in a river, the scene, at busy times, is a ghoulish production line of bungy initiates being trundled out and tour buses disgorging spectators to fill the viewing platforms. The best views are from the Kawarau Bungy Centre (free entry), where you can learn more than you thought there was to know about bungy jumping on the Secrets Behind Bungy Tour (45min; $45), an interactive leap through bungy history and the jump experience.

At The **Ledge Bungy** (47m; summer generally 1–7pm; winter 4–9pm; $175, including T-shirt) at the top of the Skyline Gondola, it feels like you are diving out over Queenstown. Unlike at other sites, you're fitted with a body harness allowing you to do a running jump, and if they aren't too busy you may be able to jump with all manner of "toys" (surfboards, bikes and the like) to add that extra dimension. Night jumps in winter make for yet another variation on the theme.

Some say that with bungy jumping it is only the first metre that counts, but when it comes down to it, size does matter. A.J. Hackett has pulled out all the stops with **Nevis Highwire Bungy** (134m; Queenstown departures daily at 8am, 10am, noon & 2pm; $250, including T-shirt), which gives about eight seconds of falling. Jumpers launch from a partly glass-bottomed gondola strung way out over the Nevis River, a tributary of the Kawarau some 32km east of Queenstown. Access is by 4WD through private property so spectators have to fork out $50, though this does give you a ride out to the launch gondola and a wonderful view.

Swinging

Swinging presents an alternative to bungy jumping but still includes that stomach-in-your-mouth freefall sensation, with the bonus of a massive swoop through the air on the end of a rope. The 109m **Canyon Swing** (6–8 departures daily; $199, second swing $39; ℡0800/279 464, ⓦwww.canyonswing.co.nz) sweeps a huge arc over the Shotover River including a 60m fall. If you time it right you'll have rafts full of spectators below on the river as you launch – forwards, backwards, cartwheel, seated in a chair or even with a bin over your head. At 125m, **A.J. Hackett**'s Nevis Arc, by the bungy in the Nevis Valley ($170; see above), is now the world's highest swing, while the company also runs the tiddly 47m Ledge Sky Swing above Queenstown, at the bungy site ($120).

Jetboating

Commercial **jetboating** kicked off in Queenstown way back in 1965 and remains high in the adrenaline hierarchy. There are strong arguments for spending your jetboating dollar on better-value wilderness trips elsewhere – the Wilkin River Jet, Waiatoto River Safaris and trips down the Wairaurahiri River spring to mind – but Queenstown does offer the most thrilling of these rides, the **Shotover Jet** (daily 8.30am–5pm; 30min; $109; ℡0800/746 868, ⓦwww.shotoverjet.com), which thrusts downstream along the Shotover Canyon from Arthur's Point, 5km north of Queenstown. Perilously close shaves with rocks and canyon walls plus several 360-degree turns and periodic dousings guarantee that a twenty-minute trip is enough for most. Courtesy minibuses take customers to Arthur's Point from The Station (see p.673).

There's no doubting the lure of the Shotover Jet, but you get better value for money with **Skippers Canyon Jet** (3 daily, starting at 8.30am; 4hr 30min; $109; ℡0800/226 966, ⓦwww.skipperscanyonjet.com), who drive you along the Skippers Road and take you jetboating among the ancient gold workings of the upper Shotover River, meaning the thrills come with plenty of fascinating heritage (see "Skippers Canyon", p.679).

Rafting

The majority of jetboat operators stick to flat water, leaving the rough stuff for **whitewater rafting** on the Kawarau and Shotover rivers. Although there appear to be three rafting companies, each with assorted packages and combo deals, all rafts are in fact operated by Queenstown Rafting (☎0800/723 8464, ⓦwww .rafting.co.nz).

The more reliable of the two rivers is the large-volume **Kawarau River** (4hr with around 1hr on the water; $175) a 7km section of which negotiates four Grade III rapids (exciting but not truly frightening) ending with the potentially nasty Chinese Dog Leg, said to be the longest commercially rafted rapid in New Zealand. Being lake-fed, its flow is relatively steady, though it peaks in spring and drops substantially towards the end of summer.

In contrast, the **Shotover River** (5hr with almost 2hr on the water; $175; heli-rafting $259) is more demanding: the rapids, revelling in names such as The Squeeze, The Anvil and The Toilet, reach their apotheosis in the Mother-in-Law rapid, usually bypassed at low water by diverting through the 170m Oxenbridge Tunnel (see p.679). The 14km rafted section of the river (Grade III–IV) flows straight out of the mountains and its level fluctuates considerably. In October and November, snowmelt ensures good flows and a bumpy ride; by late summer low flows can make it a bit tame for hardened rafters, though it is still scenic and fun for first-timers. In winter the lack of sunlight reaching the depths of the canyon makes it too cold for most people, though you can elect to do a much shorter trip by accessing the rapids by helicopter. The same people also run three-day, fly-in wilderness trips on the **Landsborough River**.

Rafting is usually limited to those aged 13 or older, but by tackling an easier (Grade I–II) stretch of the Shotover, **Family Adventures** (☎0800/472 384, ⓦwww.familyadventures.co.nz) can take all ages. Their trips (adults $155, kids $110) include a drive into Skippers Canyon and ninety minutes floating in rafts. You don't even need to paddle.

Family fun is also available on the Kawarau with **Flow** (adults $89, kids $49; ☎03/442 4922, ⓦwww.nzraft.co.nz), which offers gentle (Grade I–II) trips in either rafts or inflatable canoes, followed by a barbecue.

River surfing and whitewater sledging

From mid-October to April, two sections of the Kawarau River are used for the parallel sports of whitewater sledging and river surfing – the "Dog Leg" section by the rafters, and the "Roaring Meg" run, a few kilometres downstream, by the sledgers. For both sports small groups are equipped with a board or sledge, a wetsuit, a helmet and fins, then led downstream and encouraged to view their independence and freedom of movement as virtues rather than hazards. While rafters bob around high up on their inflatable perches, river surfers and sledgers get right in the thick of it: what look like ripples to rafters become huge waves and the serious rapids can be thoroughly daunting, as froth engulfs you on all sides: things work best if you are both confident in water and a decent swimmer.

River surfing involves floating downstream, grasping a foam boogie board and surfing as many as possible of the rapids' standing waves. Serious Fun ($155; ☎0800/737 468, ⓦwww.riversurfing.co.nz), run two-and-a-half-hour trips down either the "Dog Leg" or "Roaring Meg", depending on the conditions.

Mad Dog River Boarding ($149; ☎0508/623 364, ⓦwww.riverboarding.co.nz) does just one run on Roaring Meg, adding in a flat-water stretch with rope swings, rock jumps (up to 23m if you're really keen), waterslide and jet-skiing. Largely the same techniques are used in **whitewater sledging**, which involves grasping the handles of a foam or plastic "sledge" and snuggling arms and upper body down into a streamlined shape. The extra buoyancy gives a better ride over the waves and greater manoeuvrability for catching eddies, though surfing waves is more difficult. Frogz ($149; ☎0800/437 649, ⓦwww.frogz.co.nz) offers double runs down the Roaring Meg section, with pick-ups in Queenstown and Wanaka.

Canyoning

Fans of river surfing and whitewater sledging may also be drawn to **canyoning**, in which small groups are led down narrow canyons to walk in streams, swim across

---

Winter in Queenstown

Two ski-fields – **Coronet Peak** and the smaller **Remarkables** – within easy reach of numerous quality hotels, good restaurants and plenty of après-ski combine to make Queenstown New Zealand's premier **ski destination**. The highlight of the season is the ten-day **Queenstown Winter Festival** (ⓦwww.winterfestival.co.nz), around the end of June or early July, which, as well as all the conventional ski/snowboard events, has snow sculpture, ski-golf and great entertainment. Of the various other events, the family-oriented **Remarkables Spring Fling**, in the first week of the September school holidays, is one of the best.

Both ski areas (and Mount Hutt) are run by the same company, whose website (ⓦwww.nzski.com) has snow reports and plenty of other practical information. One-day lift passes are specific to each area, but there are various **multi-day tickets,** which are valid at all three fields (around $237).

Neither ski area has **accommodation** on site, but frequent shuttle buses run to and from Queenstown ($10), where the supply is plentiful – except during school holidays. For **ski rental** visit the excellent (if pricey) Browns, 39 Shotover St (☎03/442 4003, ⓦwww.brownsnz.com), who charge $44 a day for mid-range skis, boots and poles ($44 for a snowboard); or Outside Sports, 36 Shotover St (☎03/441 2111, ⓦwww .outsidesports.co.nz), who offer similar deals.

Coronet Peak

When it opened in 1947, **Coronet Peak** (☎03/442 4640), 18km north of Queenstown, became New Zealand's first true ski destination. The most sophisticated snow-making equipment in Australasia extends its season into spring, when cobalt blue skies and stunning scenery earn it an enviable reputation. Its range of **runs** (3 beginner, 16 intermediate, 12 advanced) for skiers and riders of all abilities, and over 400 vertical metres of skiing, only add to its popularity. Throughout the season, which typically starts in early June and sometimes makes it into October, **buses** from Queenstown shuttle back and forth along the sealed access road (no toll). **Passes** for daytime skiing (9am–4pm) cost $93; floodlit skiing (July–Sept Fri & Sat 4–9pm) goes for $48.

The Remarkables

The Remarkables (☎03/442 4615), 28km east of Queenstown, occupies three mountain basins tucked in behind the wrinkled face of the Remarkables. It is best known for learner and intermediate terrain, but there are also good **runs** (3 beginner, 8 intermediate, 18 advanced) for advanced skiers, and rapid access to some excellent country for off-piste ski touring. A **day pass** costs $87. Though the bottom of the lifts is 500m higher than at Coronet Peak, more snow is required to cover the tussock, giving a slightly shorter season (late June to early Oct). At 320m, the total vertical descent from the lifts is also less than at Coronet, but you gain an extra 120m by taking the Homeward Run – a long stretch of off-piste with sparkling scenery – to the 14km unsealed **access road** (no toll), where frequent free buses shuttle you back up to the chairlift.

pools, slide down rocks and jump off cliffs, protected only by a wetsuit, helmet and climbing harness. Canyoning.co.nz (Oct–April; ☎03/441 3003) runs two trips. **Canyoning Queenstown** (3hr, 90min in the water; $155) involves morning and afternoon trips to Twelve Mile Delta just out of town; for a longer day out requiring a bit more commitment on your part, go **Canyoning Routeburn** (7hr with over 3hr in the water; $215), which involves walking the first twenty minutes of the Routeburn Track then launching yourself into a water-sculpted, narrow canyon full of jumps and slides.

The Rung Way

If the mountains around Queenstown look tempting but you don't have the skills or equipment to go rock climbing, you can get a sense of the experience with **Rung Way** (☎0800/786 4929, ⓦwww.rungway.co.nz), which runs Via Ferrata, a system originally used in Europe to move troops quickly across mountainous terrain during the two world wars. Suitably harnessed up, you make your own way up a trail of steel rungs drilled into a series of cliff faces just above Queenstown, clipping yourself into a long steel cable, which runs beside the rungs. Previous experience isn't necessary, and more demanding routes are available for the gung-ho. Climbs take place daily at 9am and 1pm (4hr; $159), and the company also offers more conventional rock-climbing trips and courses.

Paragliding and hang-gliding

A fine day with a little breeze is all it needs to fill the skies above Queenstown with **tandem paragliders** descending from Bob's Peak. Taking to the skies with G Force Paragliding ($199, before 10am $169, both including Gondola; ☎0800/759 688, ⓦwww.nzgforce.com;) works like a taxi rank, so if you want a go, simply stand in line until it is your turn. How many acrobatic manoeuvres are executed during the ten to fifteen minutes you're airborne is largely down to you, your jump guide and the conditions. If you don't see anyone in the air during the main operating times (9am–5pm), don't bother with the gondola ride, as the weather's probably being uncooperative.

Three companies operate from just out of town, usually running off Coronet Peak. Extreme Air (☎0800/727 245, ⓦwww.extremeair.co.nz) offers paragliding from 1300m ($195). If you want to fly with a three-time New Zealand champion and his crew, try Coronet Peak Tandems (from $179; ☎0800/467 325, ⓦwww .tandemparagliding.com). Both should give you around fifteen minutes in the air. If all this pretending to be a bird becomes addictive, Elevation (☎0800/359 444, ⓦwww.elevation.co.nz) runs a full-day session ($240) which will teach you controlled flight up to 20m above the ground and can lead on to full solo flights the following day.

Paragliding while being towed behind a boat goes by the name of **parasailing**, offered by Paraflights, Main Town Pier (☎0800/225 520, ⓦwww.paraflights .co.nz). For $129 you are winched out on a rope until you reach a height of 100m above the lake surface and, after ten minutes admiring the scenery, you're winched back in again, still dry.

There's notably more of a birdlike quality to **tandem hang-gliding**, where you and your instructor are harnessed in a prone position under the wing of a hang-glider and execute a number of progressively steeper turns as you soar down from Coronet Peak to the Flight Park on Malaghans Road 700m below. Skytrek ($210 for 12–15min in the air; ☎0800/759 873, ⓦwww.skytrek .co.nz) runs several flights a day throughout the year, sometimes launching from the Remarkables.

Skydiving and aerobatics

Queenstown is an expensive place to go **tandem skydiving**, but the scenery does partly compensate. NZone (℡0800/376 796, Ⓦwww.nzone.biz) run jumps from 12,000ft (45 seconds freefall; $299) and 15,000ft (65 seconds; $399), all taking place over Lake Wakatipu and landing by the foot of the Remarkables. Another airborne possibility includes a twenty-minute spin in a Pitt Special **biplane**, with all the usual loop the loops, with Jagiar ($290; ℡0800/524 247, Ⓦwww.jagair.co.nz).

Horseriding

Queenstown is a great place to go **horseriding**. First-timers can visit Shotover Stables on Malaghans Road, 7km north of town (℡03/442 7486), whose gentle treks (1hr riding; $65) emphasize local history and explore gold-mining relics down by the Shotover riverbed. With more experience, try Ben Lomond Station (℡0800/236 566, Ⓦwww.nzhorsetreks.co.nz), whose horses head backcountry, or the Walter Peak High Country Farm (see p.677).

Mountain biking

Queenstown's exhilarating **mountain-biking** trips predominantly feature downhill riding. Fat Tyre Adventures (℡0800/328 897, Ⓦwww.fat-tyre.co.nz) have a variety of single-track mountain-biking packages with up to four hours in the saddle, including an excellent trip in the Dunstan Mountains above Cromwell (5hr; $195). The company also operates all-day trips to locations accessed by helicopter ($349–499), which are scenic, challenging and great fun. Gravity Action (℡03/442 5277 1021, Ⓦwww.gravityaction.com) offers relatively cheap thrills ($149 for over 2hr in the saddle) descending almost 600m down a narrow track which, until a better road was pushed through in 1888, was the only route into Skippers Canyon, or a steep ride down from the top of the gondola in Queenstown (2hr 30min; $149).

Off-road and 4WD tours

Guided **off-road driving** trips with Off Road Adventures (℡03/442 7858, Ⓦwww.offroad.co.nz) allow participants to learn to control quad bikes or motorbikes on a variety of terrains. Packages range from straightforward, family-oriented affairs (allow 3hr, 1hr riding; $189) to the tougher Adventure Tour (3hr, 1hr 55min riding; $219), including steep trails on a high-country station.

For those wishing to relinquish control, there are a number of **4WD** vehicles on offer where the driver/guide takes a gentler, more informative approach to the countryside, some focusing on *LOTR* locations. Easily the biggest operator is Nomad Safaris ($149; ℡0800/688 222, Ⓦwww.nomadsafaris.co.nz), who do trips into Skippers Canyon (see p.679), cross the Arrow River over twenty times on the run into Macetown (see p.689), and offer a couple of "Safari of the Scenes" *LOTR* trips (see box, p.672). They'll also let you get behind the wheel for some real off-roading ($260).

Scenic flights and ballooning

To get high above Queenstown, enlist the services of Alpine Choppers (20min; $160; ℡03/451 0001, Ⓦwww.alpinechoppers.co.nz), who also run scenic flights with a landing at the top of the Remarkables (20min; $180), or even further afield.

A more peaceful approach is in a **hot-air balloon** with Sunrise Balloons (3hr including around 1hr flight time; $375; ℡0800/468 247, Ⓦwww.ballooningnz .com). After an early start, you climb as high as 2000m to gawp at the mountain scenery (on a clear day you can see Mount Cook), before landing for a champagne breakfast.

Eating

Queenstown has stacks of restaurants, lots of them very good and correspondingly expensive. Many are increasingly making the most of the town's climate and spilling out onto the pedestrianized streets and along the waterfront, where you can sit and watch the *Earnslaw* glide in. **Breakfast** and **snack** places generally close by 6pm, though some serve early **dinners**, while restaurants often double as bars as the evening wears on.

Cafés and snack bars

Aggy's Shack Corner of Marine Parade & Church St. You'll get the best fish and chips in town as well as local smoked eel, marinated raw fish, sea urchin and all manner of fish, to enjoy at outdoor benches. Open daily 11am–late.

Destination Organic Corner of Camp & Earl sts. Organic deli and daytime café dishing up home-made muesli, eggs on toast (using their own bread), great salads, an organic platter, home-made cakes and absolutely fabulous coffee. Closed Sun.

Halo Camp St. Relaxed, licensed café with de rigeur good espresso and a worthy breakfast burrito ($15.50). Gourmet burgers ($15–17), many vegetarian, and prawn fritters are served at outdoor seating beside an old church.

Patagonia Chocolates 50 Beach St. Waterside café notable for rich hot chocolate drinks (ginger, lavender, chilli), luscious cakes, delectable gelato and handmade chocolates. Free wi-fi.

Vudu 23 Beach St. It has seen many a worthy challenger come and go, but this relaxed daytime and evening café remains the town's best. Comfy booths, magazines, inexpensive breakfasts, quiches, scrumptious muffins and good coffee, plus more substantial fare like chicken wraps, steak sandwiches and pasta. The breakfast quesadilla is a local favourite ($15).

Restaurants

@ Thai Third Floor, AirNZ Building, Church St ☏ 03/442 3683. The best of the town's Thai places, with good chicken satay and attentive service. Takeaway available.

Bombay Place 68 Shotover St ☏ 03/441 2886. Authentic-ish, Indian with Bollywood on the screen, serving the likes of prawn masala ($19), chicken sagwala ($16.90), plus some tempting veggie options. Takeaway available.

The Cow Cow Lane. Long standing, popular pizzeria (be prepared to share a table), offering reasonably priced grub ($20–25 a head). BYO & licensed. Daily noon–midnight.

Ferg Burger 42 Shotover St. This extremely popular shopfront burger bar, all swift and sweaty with little seating, dispenses massive, broad-ranging variations on meat in a bun, or non-meat in a bun, plus fries and/or a beer or plonk. Daily from 8am until late.

Finz Steamer Wharf ☏ 503/442 7405. Overlooking the lake, this semi-formal eatery offers a great view and good-value seafood, a classic bouilla-baisse ($22.50), green-lipped mussels ($20) and pan-seared calamari salad ($19.50).

Kappa 36a The Mall. Cheapish, no-nonsense Japanese place on the first floor. Nip in for sushi ($4–7), a bowl of soba or udon noodles ($9–15), or one of the specials – perhaps nori-flavoured blue cod and asparagus tempura ($15).

Solera Vino 25 Beach St ☏ 03/442 6082. This small and elegant, fine-dining restaurant is the best in town by a mile. It offers delectable French Mediterranean dishes including a sumptuous bouillabaisse (mains around $35), and has a wine list as long as a baguette. Very popular, so booking is advisable. Dinner-only.

Wai Steamer Wharf ☏ 03/442 5969. Fine-dining, waterfront restaurant with outdoor seating on the wharf. Mains ($34–48) include roasted mahi mahi with scallops and sautéed bok choy, but it is worth considering setting the whole evening aside for the slightly pretentious, trencherman's delight, *dégustation* menu ($135, $210 with wine matches).

Winnies 7 The Mall. Popular for pasta and gourmet pizzas, made from local ingredients, with a better-than-average à la carte and blackboard menu and reasonable prices, this is a decent spot with balcony seating and friendly service.

Drinking and nightlife

Despite its high profile and large number of visitors, Queenstown is still essentially a small town with a TGIF attitude and a lot of binge drinking at the weekend. There's no highbrow culture, some of the **clubs** border on being backpacker cattle markets and decent touring bands are rare. Still, if you are in the mood, it can be fun (some spots have happy hours to get the evening rolling), and there is no shortage of chic hideaway **cocktail bars**. As a result of the raucous nature of the nightlife the local council has imposed a 4am curfew on all the bars and clubs.

The free *Mountain Scene* newspaper, found all over town, has up-to-date **listings**, including the **movies** shown at the Reading Cinemas, 11 The Mall (T03/442 9990). About the only regular entertainment is Kiwi Haka ($53; reservations essential T03/441 0101, Wwww.skyline.co.nz), a **Maori concert and hangi** performance, which takes place several times each evening up at the Skyline Complex.

Bars and clubs

Altitude 47 Shotover St. A party bar attached to *Base* (see p.675); boozy with nightly adventure-trip giveaways, concentrating on cheap food and fleecing the sheep off the backpacker bus tours.

Atlas Bar Steamer Wharf, Beach St. Cosy bar, popular with the locals who sit in the windows to watch the *Earnslaw* as she comes in to dock, where you can enjoy a variety of beers, including Emerson's, and some inventive tapas.

Bardeaux 5 Eureka Arcade. A funky little cocktail bar, with big sofas, a roaring fire and a broad selection of excellent whisky and wine. Relaxed early on, but picks up big time after 11pm and often stays open until 4am.

Bunker Cow Lane. A stylish upstairs cocktail bar with cool music – anything from jazz to ambient.

Debajo Cow Lane. Catholic-icon-filled late-night Spanish bar that likes to bill itself as Queenstown's "home of house". Killer cocktails too.

Dux de Lux 14 Church St. The only brewpub in town, serving half a dozen excellent beers and frequent Kiwi live music – mostly rock, reggae and blues – until late, plus an entertaining midweek quiz. Underneath is the World Bar, currently considered the town's premier night spot.

Mini Bar Eureka Arcade, opposite *Bardeaux* (see above). Personable little bar serving an enormous selection of beers from all over the known universe.

Pig and Whistle 41 Ballarat St. A bustling, English-style pub, with a large beer garden, open fire and good-value food; popular in the early evening.

Póg Mahone's 14 Rees St. One of the better Irish bars you'll come across, typically crowded with folk clamouring for draught Guinness and loosely Irish bar meals (mains from $16–26) or warming themselves by the open fire. It's even fuller for the live Irish-style music on Thurs, Fri & Sat. Outdoor lakeside seating.

Pub on Wharf 88 Beach St. Busy boozer, particularly early in the evening, where cheap food and good wharf-watching seats are the order of the day.

Listings

Airlines Air New Zealand Travel Centre, Church St T03/441 1900.

Banks and exchange All major banks have a branch and ATM around the centre.

Bike rental Several places rent out low-spec bikes good for getting around town and the lakeside trails. Queenstown Bike Rentals, corner of Marine Parade & Church St (T0800/557 232, Wwww.discount rentals.co.nz), is among the cheapest ($10/ hr or $35/day), and has tandems ($30/hr). The company also rents out kayaks ($20/2hr) and scooters ($40/2hr, $60/day). For real off-road use, Dr Bike at Outside Sports, 36 Shotover St (T03/441 0074), rents out a variety of mountain bikes (from $30/ half-day $50/full). Vertigo and Gravity Action also offer rentals (see mountain biking, p.685).

Buses Atomic Shuttles (T03/322 8883) runs to Christchurch, Dunedin and up the coast to Greymouth; InterCity (T03/474 9600) operates the most extensive services to all major destinations; Southern Link Shuttles (T03/358 8355) runs from Queenstown to Nelson via Wanaka and Christ-church, over two days; and Connexions (Wwww .time2.co.nz) runs the most direct service to Wanaka, plus Invercargill and Dunedin.

Camping and outdoor equipment At Small Planet, 17 Shotover St (T03/442 6393; daily 9am–8pm), you can pick up new and used gear, including snowboards, ski gear, climbing, camping and tramping stuff and boots – all at good prices and with competitive buy-back deals. The company also does rentals, and if you've got something to get rid of, will hawk it for 25-percent commission. Alpine Sports, 39 Shotover St (T03/442 7099, Wwww.alpinesports.co.nz), has heaps of rental camping gear.

Car rental Numerous companies around town offer good deals: look for advertised rates.

Library Corner of Shotover St & Gorge Rd (Mon–Sat 10am–5pm), with internet access.

Medical treatment Queenstown Medical Centre, 9 Isle St (T03/441 0500), and Lakes

District Hospital, 20 Douglas St, Frankton (☎03/441 0015).
Pharmacy Wilkinsons Pharmacy, corner of The Mall & Rees St (daily 8.30am–10pm, ☎03/442 7313).
Police 11 Camp St (☎03/441 1600).

Post office The main post office, 13 Camp St (Mon–Fri 8.30am–6pm, Sat 9am–4pm), has poste restante facilities.
Supermarket Fresh Choice, 64 Gorge Rd; Alpine Foodcentre, corner of Shotover & Stanley sts.

⑬

The Gibbston wineries

Grapes have only been grown commercially in the Central Otago district since the 1980s, but local winemakers have already garnered a shelf-full of awards. The vineyards of what is the world's most southerly wine-growing region lie close to the forty-fifth parallel in a landscape detractors pooh-poohed as too cold for wine production, despite the fact that the Rhône Valley in France lies on a similar latitude. A continental climate of hot dry summers and long cold winters prevails, which tends to result in low yields and high production costs, forcing wineries to go for quality boutique wines sold at prices which seem high (mostly $25–40) until you taste them.

The steep schist and gravel slopes on the southern banks of the **Kawarau River** were recognized as potential sites as early as 1864, when French miner Jean Désiré Feraud, bored of his gold claim at Frenchman's Point near Clyde, planted grapes from cuttings brought over from Australia. His wines won awards at shows in Australia, but by the early 1880s he'd decamped to Dunedin. No more grapes were grown until 1976, when the Rippon vineyard was planted, outside Wanaka (see p.706). It was another five years before the Kawarau Gorge was recognized as ideally suited to the cultivation of Pinot Gris, Riesling and particularly Pinot Noir grapes. As an added bonus, the dry conditions inhibit growth of fungus and mildew; the dreaded phylloxera has been kept at bay so far.

Altogether, over twenty wineries are open for tasting in Central Otago. There are concentrations around Bannockburn (see p.719) and Clyde (see p.719), but those closest to Queenstown are on the southern slopes above the Kawarau Gorge, 20km northeast of the town along SH6.

You can drive to them all, but you'll learn a lot more if you join one of the **wine tours** that depart from Queenstown. For expert guidance and a chance to see a fair bit of the local area, Appellation Central Wine Tours (☎03/442 0246, ⓦwww .appellationcentral.co.nz), run informative and fun small-group tours calling at wineries in Gibbston and around Bannockburn and Cromwell. Their afternoon Boutique Wine Tour ($160) includes lunch at one of the four wineries, but enthusiasts will want to go for the more leisurely, full-day Gourmet Wine Tour ($195) taking in four vineyards, a mid-morning cheese tasting and a visit to The Big Picture (see p.719).

Wineries

The following are listed in increasing distance from Queenstown.

Amisfield 10 Lake Hayes Rd ☎03/442 0556, ⓦwww.amisfield.co.nz. Chic modern winery, artfully combining local schist with big windows and recycled timbers. Tasting is $5 (daily 10am–6pm), or you can blow the budget and a few hours on a "trust the chef" lunch option with seven dishes served over three courses ($55; with wine match and dessert $100).

Chard Farm Chard Rd ☎0800/843 327, ⓦwww .chardfarm.co.nz. Free tasting of a wide range of wines, most notably the Chardonnay, Pinot Noir and Pinot Gris. It's reached down a precipitous 2km dirt road off SH6 opposite the Kawarau Bungy. Mon–Fri 10am–5pm, Sat & Sun 11am–5pm.
Peregrine SH6 ☎03/442 4000, ⓦwww .peregrinewines.co.nz. Nestled under a huge steel

and plastic structure designed to mimic both the peregrine's wing and the angled layering of the local schist, this stylish winery has free tasting with views of the elegantly industrial barrel room. Daily 10am–5pm.

Gibbston Valley SH6 ☎03/442 6910, ⓦwww .gvwines.co.nz. The most highly evolved of the region's wineries, with tasting ($5), a popular

daytime restaurant (the $26–30 Mediterranean platter is excellent) and an on-site cheesery selling a wine-washed Monk's Gold, among others. The Winery & Cave Tour (hourly 10am–4pm; 30min; $10) explores not especially impressive cellars burrowed into the hillside, and includes an informative tasting session.

Arrowtown and Macetown

ARROWTOWN, at the confluence of the Arrow River and Bush Creek 23km northeast of Queenstown, still has the feel of an old gold town, though on busy summer days any lingering authenticity is swamped by the tourists prowling the sheepskin, greenstone and gold of its souvenir shops. Nonetheless the town manages to retain the spirit of a living community, with grocers' shops, pubs and a post office coexisting alongside the gift-wrapped centre. Arrowtown has a permanent (and increasingly wealthy) population of around 3000, but in summer, when holiday homes are full and tourists arrive in force, it comes close to regaining the 7000-strong peak attained during the **gold rush**.

There is some debate as to whether American William Fox was actually the first to discover alluvial gold in the Arrow River in 1862, but he dominated

▲ Arrowtown Chinese Settlement

13

Arrowtown's hidden Chinese history

The initial wave of miners who came to Arrowtown in the early 1860s were fortune-seekers intent on a fast buck. When gold was discovered on the West Coast, most of them hot-footed it to Greymouth or Hokitika, leaving a much-depleted community that lacked the economic wherewithal to support the businesses which had mushroomed around the miners.

The solution was to import **Chinese labour**; the first Chinese arrived in Otago in 1866, their number reaching 5000 by 1870. The community settled along Bush Creek, its **segregation** from the main settlement symptomatic of the inherent racism of the time – something which also manifested itself in working practices that forced the Chinese to pick over abandoned mining claims and work the tailings of European miners. Even Chinese employed on municipal projects such as the Presbyterian church got only half the wages paid to Europeans doing the same job.

A ray of light is cast amid the prevailing bigotry by contemporary newspaper reports, which suggest that many citizens found the Chinese business conduct "upright and straightforward" and their demeanour "orderly and sober" – perhaps surprisingly in what was an almost entirely male community. Most came with dreams of earning their fortune and returning home so, initially at least, few came with their families; a process of chain **migration** later brought wives, children and then members of the extended family. Few realized their dreams, but around ninety percent did return home, many in a box, sent to an early grave by overwork and poor living conditions. Many more were driven out in the early 1880s when recession brought racial jealousies to a head, resulting in the enactment of a punitive poll tax on foreign residents. There was little workable gold by this time and those Chinese who stayed mostly became market gardeners or merchants and drifted away, mainly to Auckland, though the Arrowtown community remained viable into the 1920s. Once the Chinese had left or died, the Bush Creek settlement was abandoned and largely destroyed by repeated flooding.

proceedings, managing to keep the find secret while recovering over 100kg. Jealous prospectors tried to follow him to the lode, but he gave them the slip, on one occasion leaving his tent and provisions behind in the middle of the night. The town subsequently bore his name until Foxes gave way to Arrowtown. The Arrow River became known as the richest for its size in the world – a reputation which drew scores of Chinese miners (see box above), who lived in the now partly restored **Arrowtown Chinese Settlement**. Prospectors fanned out over the surrounding hills, where brothers Charley and John Mace set up **Macetown**, now a ghost town.

The best way to appreciate Arrowtown itself is to linger on after the crowds have gone – there's plenty of accommodation. If your visit is in late April you can partake in the **Autumn Festival** (Ⓦ www.arrowtownautumnfestival.org.nz), with all manner of historic walks, street theatre and hoedowns.

Arrival and information

The Connectabus **bus** (Ⓦ www.connectabus.com; hourly; 25min; $8 one-way) departs from the top of the Mall on Camp Street in Queenstown and runs via Frankton, the airport and Lake Hayes to Ramshaw Lane in Arrowtown.

Arrowtown's **i-SITE visitor centre** is in the foyer of the Lakes District Museum at 49 Buckingham St (daily 8.30am–5pm; ☎03/442 1824, Ⓦ www .museumqueenstown.com), where you can pick up the *Historic Arrowtown* booklet ($2), and the informative *Arrowtown Chinese Settlement* booklet ($3). It also has **internet access**.

Accommodation

Most of Arrowtown's accommodation is of a high standard and usually less busy than in Queenstown.

Motels

Settlers Cottage Motel 22 Hertford St ☏ 0800/803 801, ⓦ www.settlerscottagemotel.co.nz. A lace-and-Laura Ashley place with decor based on traditional pioneer motifs. Studios and one- and two-bedroom units all come with microwaves and hairdryers. ④

Shades of Arrowtown Corner of Buckingham & Merioneth sts ☏ 03/442 1613, ⓦ www.shadesof arrowtown.co.nz. Tastefully decorated modern motel set in leafy surrounds in the heart of town.

There's a good range of units (most with kitchenette or full kitchen), plus a s/c cottage sleeping six ($175). ④–⑤

Viking Lodge Motel 21 Inverness Crescent ☏ 0800/181 900, ⓦ www.vikinglodge.co.nz. One of Arrowtown's best-value motels, featuring an outdoor pool and a cluster of one- and two-bedroom A-frame chalets with well-equipped kitchens and Sky TV. There's also a children's play area featuring a trampoline. ③–⑤

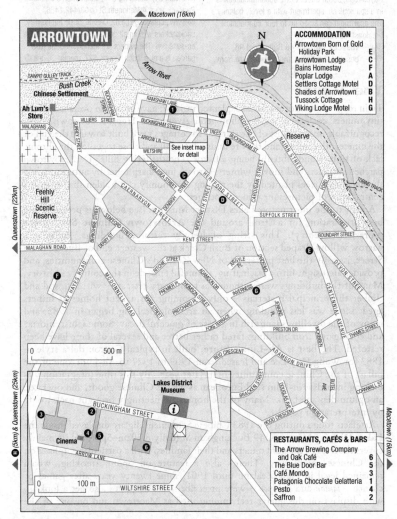

▲ *Macetown (16km)*

ARROWTOWN

N

ACCOMMODATION
Arrowtown Born of Gold Holiday Park	E
Arrowtown Lodge	C
Bains Homestay	F
Poplar Lodge	A
Settlers Cottage Motel	D
Shades of Arrowtown	B
Tussock Cottage	H
Viking Lodge Motel	G

SAWPIT GULLEY TRACK
Bush Creek
Chinese Settlement
Ah Lum's Store
Arrow River

Reserve
TOBINS TRACK

Feehly Hill Scenic Reserve

◀ Queenstown (22km)

0 — 500 m

◀ (5km) & Queenstown (25km)

Lakes District Museum
Cinema
BUCKINGHAM STREET
ARROW LANE
WILTSHIRE STREET

0 — 100 m

Macetown (16km) ▶

RESTAURANTS, CAFÉS & BARS
The Arrow Brewing Company and Oak Café	6
The Blue Door Bar	5
Café Mondo	3
Patagonia Chocolate Gelatteria	1
Pesto	4
Saffron	2

B&Bs and homestays

Arrowtown Lodge 7 Anglesea St
☎03/442 1101, ⓦwww.arrowtownlodge
.co.nz. Four comfortable and tastefully furnished
cottages built from recycled nineteenth-century
mud bricks. Each is en suite and offers mountain
views. Breakfast can be served out on the sunny
deck, and transport to Macetown and the airport
can be arranged. There's also free internet and free
laundry. ❺

Bains Homestay R32 Butel Rd ☎03/442 1270,
ⓦwww.dotco.co.nz/bainshomestay. Set in peaceful
green surroundings just off the Arrowtown–Lake
Hayes road, 300m out of town, accommodation is
in a spacious s/c apartment with a lovely balcony.
The apartment can sleep up to four, continental
breakfast included. ❺

Tussock Cottage 48 Rutherford Rd,
beside Lake Hayes and around 5km from
town ☎03/442 1449, ⓦwww.tussockcottage
.co.nz. A fab, luxuriously equipped, romantic,
two-room s/c cottage, of strawbale construction
with a tussock-covered roof, with bikes and
kayaks for guests' use and welcoming and
informed hosts. ❻

Hostel and campsite

Arrowtown Born of Gold Holiday Park 12
Centennial Ave ☎03/442 1876, ⓦwww
.arrowtownholidaypark.co.nz. Spacious campsite
with a tennis court near the community swimming
pool. It has a modern kitchen and ablutions block
(showers $1). Camping $17, studios ❹, s/c flats ❺

Poplar Lodge 4 Merioneth St ☎03/442 1466,
ⓦwww.poplarlodge.co.nz. Central, basic but homely
backpackers with small dorms, rooms and a separate
en-suite unit. The owners are friendly, and the rose
garden is a nice touch. Dorms $27, rooms ❷, unit ❹

The Town

Twin rows of sycamores and oaks, planted in 1867, have grown to overshadow the
tiny miners' cottages along the photogenic **Avenue of Trees**, Arrowtown's most
recognizable image. Most of the sixty or so cottages were built towards the end of
the nineteenth century and they're unusually small and close together, the chronic
lack of timber undoubtedly being a factor. The sheltering hills give Arrowtown
parched summers and snowy winters, thrown into sharp relief by autumn, when
the deciduous trees planted by the mining community cast golden shadows on a
central knot of picturesque miners' cottages.

A visit to the informative Lakes District Museum (see below) is probably the
best preparation for a stroll around the **Arrowtown Chinese Settlement**
(unrestricted entry). This string of heavily restored buildings, hugging a
narrow willow-draped section of Bush Creek at the western end of Buckingham
Street, is easily the best preserved of New Zealand's Chinese communities, and
provides an insight into a fascinating, shameful episode in the country's history.
Many of the buildings were intended as temporary retreats – with tin, sod and
timber the principal materials – only becoming permanent homes as miners
aged. Little was left standing when an archeological dig began in 1983, and
many of the dwellings languish in a state of graceful decay. Some schist, mortar
and corrugated iron buildings fared rather better and several of these have been
restored. The best is **Ah-Lum's Store**, built in typical Canton delta style in
1883 for Wong Hop Lee and leased from 1909 to 1927 to Ah-Lum, one of the
pillars of the Chinese community in its later years. By this time integration was
making inroads: Ah-Lum sold European as well as Chinese goods, and operated
an opium den and bank. Many of the homes are fleetingly brought back to life
by interpretation panels.

Artefacts found during the 1983 Chinese Settlement dig are displayed inside the
Lakes District Museum, 49 Buckingham St (daily 8.30am–5pm; $6). It mainly
covers the lives of the gold miners and their families, with a particular emphasis on
the Chinese community. There's also a feature on opium smoking, which
remained legal in New Zealand until 1901, some twenty years after games of
chance – *fantan* and *pakapoo* – were proscribed. Technophiles also get a look in,
with displays on the quartz-reef mining used at Macetown and on one of the

country's earliest hydro schemes, which once supplied mining communities in Skippers and Macetown with power. Down in the basement are displays on the old brewery, a bakery, a print room and a school room.

Walks

Half a dozen good **walks**, listed in the free *Discover Arrowtown* leaflet available from the visitor centre, allow exploration of Arrowtown's history as well as its natural surroundings. Telltale poplar, rowan and willows in the valleys are relics of settlement by prospectors pushing further up Arrow and Bush creeks. Scattered communities sprang up along the banks, but were abandoned just as suddenly; where settlers' cottages once stood, **fruit trees** have colonized the riverbanks, and in autumn apples, pears and plums weigh down the branches, and bushes of blackberry, blackcurrant, gooseberry, raspberry and elderberry become rampant. There are few specific sights, but you can spend a lazy afternoon gorging on fruit and trying to identify the overgrown sites of houses. The surrounding hills are speckled with **rose bushes**: according to folklore, these were planted by miners seeking vitamin C (rosehips are one of the richest sources); others contend that they were planted primarily for their root systems, which could be fashioned into briar pipes.

Of the walks, the **Sawpit Gully Trail** (7km loop; 2–3hr) is a local favourite; parts of it overlap with the eight-hour Macetown–Arrowtown circuit (see p.694), and it takes in a *Lord of the Rings* location (part of the "Ford of Bruinen"), goldmining remains and some great views of the Remarkables and Lake Hayes.

Eating, drinking and entertainment

Arrowtown's small but booming **eating** scene has plenty to offer while about the best entertainment venue is *Dorothy Brown*'s, off Buckingham Street (T 03/442 1964, W www.dorothybrowns.com), a small, two-screen, high-quality independent **cinema** and bar that's almost too good to be true. Mainstream and arty films can be seen from stupendously comfortable seats (40-seater $18, 15-seater $15) and you take your wine and snacks in with you.

Cafés, restaurants and bars

The Arrow Brewing Company and Oak Café 6–7 Oak Arcade, 48–50 Buckingham St. Open daily from 11am until late is this ruby in the dust, a boutique brewery producing excellent beers, the odd wine of its own and some delicious, well-priced gourmet pies and burgers.

The Blue Door Bar Buckingham St, beside *Pesto*. Stylish, intimate and cool (not particularly cheap), bar in a 130-year-old cellar with a log fire. An informal affair with irregular live jazz, blues and folk.

Café Mondo Ballarat Arcade, 14 Buckingham St. Relaxed café with lots of outside seating and great

muffins, and home-made pies, with breakfast or lunches at around $15–18.

Patagonia Chocolate Gelatteria Ramshaw Lane. Sumptuous chocolates and hot chocolates, ice creams and sorbets.

Pesto 18 Buckingham St T 03/442 0885. Gourmet pizza and pasta restaurant with mains under $25. If they're busy they'll retrieve you from the *Blue Door Bar* (which they also own), when your table's ready. Daily 5pm–late.

Saffron 18 Buckingham St T 03/442 0131. Owned by the same folk as *Pesto* and *The Blue Door Bar* (see above), this is the posh arm of the trio. Superfine, formal meals will set you back $24–30 for a lunch main, $36–45 for a dinner main.

Macetown

As gold fever swept through Otago in the early 1860s, prospectors fanned out, clawing their way up every creek and gully in search of a flash in the pan. In 1862, alluvial gold was found at Twelve Mile, sparking the rush to what later became

The Arrowtown–Macetown Circuit

The 16km 4WD road up the Arrow Creek from Arrowtown to Macetown is the district's premier biking and trekking route. Walkers include the road as part of the strenuous, full-day **Arrowtown–Macetown Circuit** (8hr loop; 32km; 700m ascent), best done in the months from **Christmas to Easter**, after the melting snows have subsided – making the 22 river crossings on the Arrow Creek a little easier, though even in summer, access can be problematic after rain. The *Macetown and the Arrow Gorge* booklet makes a good companion for the route.

The walk starts by the confluence of the Arrow River and Bush Creek, following the northern bank of the latter westwards, then skirting the base of German Hill and branching up Sawtooth Gully. The gully emerges through open hill country and leads to Eichardt's Flat. (At this point, about an hour out of Arrowtown, you can pursue the **Sawpit Gully variation** east down Sawpit Gully to meet the Arrow River road and Arrowtown, making a 2–3hr circuit.)

From the Sawpit Gully junction, the Macetown path contours gradually around to the **Big Hill** saddle, with its expansive views back to Lake Hayes and **the Remarkables**. The route then drops steeply towards Eight Mile Creek, the path becoming indistinct – marked by infrequent poles – as it traverses soggy and potentially ankle-twisting country. After three or four hours, you stumble across the Arrow Creek road, just a couple of kilometres short of **Macetown**. When you've had your fill of Macetown, follow the Arrow Creek road back to Arrowtown; for respite from the dust, you can occasionally divert onto paths that run parallel to the road.

known as **Macetown** (unrestricted entry), now a ghost town and a popular destination for mountain bikers, horse trekkers and trampers. The best way to experience the place's unique atmosphere is to arrive with tent and provisions and spend a day or two exploring.

Macetown's story is one of boom and bust. At its peak, it boasted a couple of hotels, a post office and a school, but when the gold ran out, it couldn't fall back on farming in the way that Arrowtown and Queenstown did and, like Skippers (see p.679), it died. All that remains of the town are a couple of stone buildings – the restored schoolmaster's house and the bakery – and a smattering of wooden shacks. On first acquaintance, it isn't massively exciting, but the grassy plateau makes a great free camping spot, sheltered by low stone walls and willow, sycamore and apple trees. The only facilities are long-drop toilets and river water. The surrounding creeks and gullies are littered with the twisted and rusting remains of gold batteries, making a fruitful hunting ground for industrial archeology fans; the area is covered in some detail in the *Macetown and the Arrow Gorge* booklet ($3, available from the i–SITE in Arrowtown).

Macetown is a full-day (or overnight, if you want to camp) outing either on foot (see box above), by **mountain bike** (you'll need to rent one from Queenstown), or on a **4WD** trip with Queenstown-based Nomad Safaris (4hr; $149; ℗0800/688 222), who can pick you up in Arrowtown.

Glenorchy and the major tramps

The tiny mountain-girt town of **GLENORCHY**, at the head of Lake Wakatipu 50km northwest of Queenstown, is quiet and supremely picturesque, making it a perfect retreat from screaming Queenstown. For many visitors, Glenorchy is simply a staging post en route to some of the finest **tramping** in New Zealand – a circuit of the Rees and Dart rivers, the Routeburn Track and the Greenstone and Caples **tracks**.

The Glenorchy region's fantastic scenery owes a debt to beds of ancient sea-floor sediments laid down some 220–270 million years ago and metamorphosed into the grey-green schists and *pounamu* (greenstone) of the Forbes and Humboldt mountains. The western and northern flanks of the Forbes Mountains were shaped by the Dart Glacier, now a relatively short tongue of ice which, at its peak 18,000 years ago, formed the root of the huge glacial system that gouged out the floor of Lake Wakatipu. For a map of the area, see p.696.

In pre-European times the plain beside the combined delta of the Rees and Dart rivers was known as **Kotapahau**, "the place of revenge killing", a reference perhaps to fights between rival *hapu* over the esteemed *pounamu* which littered an area centred on the bed of the Dart River. There's still greenstone up there, but most is protected within the bounds of the Mount Aspiring National Park.

The first **Europeans** to penetrate the area were gold prospectors, government surveyors and nearby run-holders in search of fresh grazing. The fledgling community of Glenorchy served these disparate groups, along with teams of sawmillers and workers from a mine extracting scheelite, a tungsten ore used in armaments manufacture. Despite the lack of road access, **tourists** began to arrive early in the twentieth century, cruising across Lake Wakatipu on the TSS *Earnslaw* before being decanted into charabancs for the 20km jolt north to the Arcadia homestead at **Paradise**. Paradise has been deemed stunning enough to act as movie backdrops for the Rockies, the European Alps and Middle Earth, though the jury is out on whether it draws its name from its idyllic qualities or the abundance of paradise ducks.

The **road from Queenstown** was eventually pushed through in 1962, opening up a fine lakeside drive that passes **Bob's Cove**, the best place to observe the lake's **seiche**, a phenomenon which causes the lake level to fluctuate by around 150mm every five minutes. Glenorchy remains defiantly rural with only the Dart River Jet disturbing the bucolic atmosphere. Most walkers base themselves at Glenorchy, from where there are **buses** to the trailheads and Queenstown.

Arrival, information and accommodation

Track Transport (☎03/442 9708, ⓦwww.infotrack.co.nz) run **buses** between Queenstown and Glenorchy (Oct–April daily; 1hr; $20). All buses stop outside the Glenorchy **visitor centre**, 2 Oban St (☎03/441 0303), one of several warring info centres in town. The others are at the pub, the hotel and the excellent Trading Post, a check-in point for a daily boat to *Kinloch Lodge* (2.45pm; $10). All provide limited **internet** access and **groceries** but it makes more sense to bring most of your supplies with you. Glenorchy has a range of **accommodation** to suit most budgets.

Accommodation

Glenorchy Holiday Park 2 Oban St ☎03/441 0303. Well organized, with spacious tent and powered sites, plus cabins sleeping up to four. Non-residents can shower here for $5. Camping $10, dorms $20, cabins ❷

Glenorchy Lake House Mull St ☎03/442 4900, ⓦwww.glenorchylakehouse.co.nz. Central two-room lodge with sumptuous fittings and bedding, deep baths, a spacious lounge with mountain views and a big hot tub room. Guests have the place to themselves but someone will miraculously appear to cook a delicious breakfast. Room with private bath ❽, en suite ❾

Kinloch DOC campsite A small affair tucked away in the trees by *Kinloch Lodge*, with a toilet, BBQ area, picnic table and stream water (not suitable for drinking without treatment). $7.

Kinloch Lodge 862 Kinloch Rd ☎03/442 4900, ⓦwww.kinlochlodge.co.nz. Located 26km from Glenorchy but close to the trailheads for the Greenstone, Caples and Routeburn tracks, this makes an excellent, peaceful retreat before or after some hard tramping, not least because of the free spa with great lake views ($10 for non-guests). Enthusiastically run, the original 1868 Heritage Lodge houses very comfortable rooms with shared bathrooms, and there's an

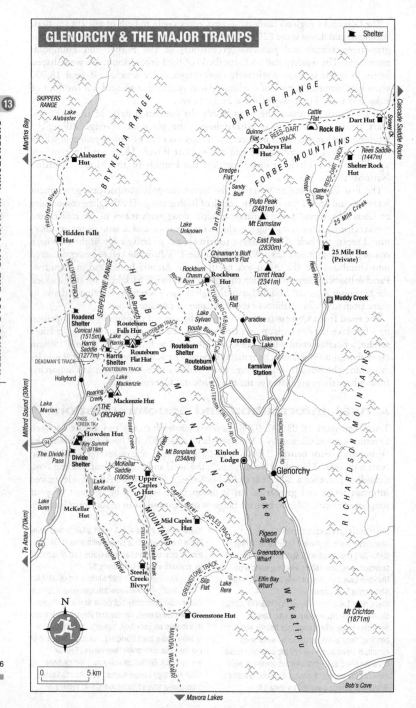

GLENORCHY & THE MAJOR TRAMPS

■ Shelter

SKIPPERS RANGE

Lake Alabaster

BARRIER RANGE

Cattle Flat

Cascade Saddle Route

Snowy Ck

Martins Bay

Quinns Flat

Rock Biv

Dart Hut

Daleys Flat Hut

REES-DART TRACK

FORBES MOUNTAINS

Rees Saddle (1447m)

Shelter Rock Hut

Alabaster Hut

Dredge Flat

Sandy Bluff

Hunter Creek

Clarke Slip

REES-DART TRACK

25 Mile Creek

Hollyford River

BRYNEIRA RANGE

Pluto Peak (2481m)

Dart River

25 Mile Hut (Private)

Hidden Falls Hut

Lake Unknown

Mt Earnslaw

East Peak (2830m)

Chinaman's Bluff

Chinaman's Flat

Rees River

SERPENTINE RANGE

HOLLYFORD TRACK

HUMBOLDT

North Branch

Rockburn Chasm

Rock Burn

Rockburn Hut

Turret Head (2341m)

Mill Flat

Muddy Creek

Roadend Shelter

Conical Hill (1515m)

Routeburn Falls Hut

Lake Harris

ROUTEBURN TRACK

Route Burn

Lake Sylvan

SYLVAN-ROCKBURN TRACK

Paradise

Harris Saddle (1277m)

Harris Shelter

Routeburn Flat Hut

Routeburn Shelter

Arcadia

Diamond Lake

DEADMAN'S TRACK

ROUTEBURN TRACK

Routeburn Station

Earnslaw Station

Hollyford

Lake Mackenzie

Roaring Creek

Mackenzie Hut

MOUNTAINS

ROUTEBURN-KINLOCH ROAD

Lake Marian

THE ORCHARD

PASS CREEK TK

Fraser Creek

Milford Sound (30km)

Howden Hut

Key Summit (919m)

Mt Bonpland (2348m)

Kinloch Lodge

GLENORCHY PARADISE RD

The Divide

Divide Shelter

McKellar Saddle (1005m)

Upper Caples Hut

Kay Creek

Glenorchy

Lake McKellar

ALLSA

Caples River

CAPLES TRACK

Te Anau (70km)

Lake Gunn

McKellar Hut

MOUNTAINS

Mid Caples Hut

STEELE CREEK RTE

Pigeon Island

RICHARDSON MOUNTAINS

Lake Wakatipu

Greenstone River

Steele Creek

GREENSTONE TRACK

Steele Creek Bivvy

Slip Flat

Lake Rere

Greenstone Wharf

Elfin Bay Wharf

Mt Crichton (1871m)

Greenstone Hut

MAVORA WALKWAY

Bob's Cove

N

0   5 km

Mavora Lakes

excellent, separate self-catering backpacker section, the *Wilderness Lodge*, with bunks and neat rooms (one en suite). Delicious meals are served (see p.698). They can arrange boat transport from Glenorchy ($10), bike rental, guided kayak trips and transport to the track ends. Dorms $30, backpacker rooms ❸, backpacker en suite ❹, B&B rooms ❻

Mount Earnslaw Motels 87 Oban St ☎03/442 6993. Glenorchy's only motel has well-kept, spacious cabin-style units with a homely feel and helpful management. ❹

The town and activities

While it is growing to meet the ever-increasing number of tourists, Glenorchy still only has a petrol station, a post office, a couple of pubs and cafés, some accommodation and a grocery shop. Just about every local operator plasters its promotional material with *Lord of the Rings* location imagery, but if you need to see specific shooting sites, join the Queenstown-based Safari of the Scenes trips run by Nomad Safaris (see p.672). To get a feel for the area, follow the pleasant **Glenorchy Walkway** (2km loop; 30–40min; flat) from the wharf at the end of Islay Street along the edge of Lake Wakatipu and through the wetlands around the lagoon.

Almost all the **activities** in and around town are pitched at the Queenstown crowd, but you can always link up with groups when they arrive in Glenorchy. Durations and prices quoted here are from Glenorchy: most companies charge around $20–30 for transport to and from Queenstown and Queenstown-based trips are two hours longer.

Jetboating

Busloads are transported from Queenstown for the excellent **jetboating** on the **Dart River**, which fully utilizes the vessel's shallow-water capabilities, picking routes through braided riverbeds amid grand snowcapped mountains on the edge of Mount Aspiring National Park. **Dart River Jet Safaris** (year-round; ☎0800/327 853, ⓦwww.dartriverjetsafaris.com) run three trips, priced the same whether you join them in Glenorchy or Queenstown. Pure enthusiasts should go on the **Jetboat Safari** (2hr 30min–3hr; $229), which travels to the national park boundary and back, jetboating all the way but with an optional (delightful) walk up the Beansburn. Their combination **Wilderness Safari** (3hr; $199) involves a ninety-minute jetboat ride, a bushwalk and a ride in a 4WD coach through some magnificent scenery, including *Lord of the Rings* locations. Better still, you can combine an upstream jetboat ride with canoeing downstream in their **Funyaks** (7hr; $279), two- or three-person inflatable canoes. Suitable even for absolute beginners, this is a gentle trip with no rapids and little likelihood of an enforced swim. The highlight is the brief stop to walk into **Rockburn Chasm**, where a small tributary of the Dart has carved out a narrow, twisting canyon filled with calm, clear water.

Other activities

Glenorchy has always been a horsey town, and you can have a go at Dart Stables (☎0800/474 3464, ⓦwww.dartstables.com), which runs **horseriding** trips ($145/2hr; Ride of the Rings tours, $165/90min; overnight rides $595) through the surrounding countryside.

More of the local area can be seen with Mountainland Rovers (☎0800/246 494, ⓦwww.mountainlandrovers.co.nz), whose **Land Rover tours** (3hr; $139) head up the Rees Valley to the spectacular Lennox Falls or hit the much-viewed *LOTR* circuit. The emphasis is on appreciating the scenery and history of the area, and driver Dick Watson spins a good yarn.

Guided kayaking trips on moody Lake Wakatipu are run from *Kinloch Lodge* ($40 for 1hr or a sunset trip), who use sit-on-top kayaks and include local history, in the form of a visit to a remote old sawmill, and delicious home baking, topped off with a dip in the outdoor hot tub.

Eating

The **eating** scene in Glenorchy is pretty limited. *Glenorchy Café & Bar* (open Fri & Sat evenings in summer), in the former post office on Mull Street, is an excellent, very popular café serving breakfasts, soups, flat breads, gourmet pizzas and other home-made treats (check out the ludicrously large cookies), and has a stylish wee bar out back. The cosy restaurant at the *Kinloch Lodge* (see p.695) serves a range of great grub from breakfasts and espressos (8–9.30am), casual lunches (noon–3pm), to more formal dinners (6.30–7.30pm; reservations required in winter) with an à la carte menu (mains around $30–35).

The major tramps

The fame of the **Routeburn Track** is eclipsed only by that of the Milford Track (see p.745), yet arguably it is superior, with better-spaced huts, more varied scenery and a route mostly above the bushline, away from sandflies. The Routeburn is one of New Zealand's finest walks, straddling the spine of the Humboldt Mountains and providing access to many of the southwestern wilderness's most archetypal features: forested valleys rich with birdlife and plunging waterfalls are combined with river flats, lakes and spectacular mountain scenery. The nature of the terrain means that the Routeburn is usually promoted as a moderate tramp and the short distance between huts eases the strain. Fit hikers might consider doing it in two long days, though that doesn't leave much time for soaking up the scenery.

To return along SH94 and SH6 from the end of the Routeburn to the start is a journey approaching 300km, so to avoid backtracking anyone with a day or two to spare should consider returning to Glenorchy by hiking either the **Greenstone** or **Caples tracks**. Both are easy, following gently graded, parallel river valleys where the wilderness experience is moderated by grazing cattle from the high-country stations along the Lake Wakatipu shore. The Greenstone occupies the broader, U-shaped valley carved out by one arm of the huge Hollyford Glacier. The Caples runs over the subalpine McKellar Saddle and down the Caples Valley, where the river is bigger and the narrow base of the valley forces the path closer to it.

The **Rees–Dart Track** is the toughest of the major tramps in the area, covering rugged terrain and requiring six to eight hours of effort each day. It follows the standard Kiwi tramp formula of ascending one river valley, crossing the pass and descending into another, but adds an excellent side trip to the Cascade Saddle.

In **winter** the Routeburn takes on a different character and becomes a much more serious undertaking. The track is often snowbound and extremely slippery, the risk of avalanche is high and the huts are unheated. Return day-trips from Routeburn Shelter to Routeburn Falls Hut and from The Divide to the Lake Mackenzie Hut are much better bets. The lower-level Greenstone and Caples tracks also make a less daunting prospect, the huts are heated by wood-burning stoves that can be used throughout the year, though the McKellar Saddle is often snow-covered. The Rees–Dart Track in winter is really only for mountaineers.

Practicalities

Tramping **information** is best sought at the **DOC visitor centre** in Queenstown (see p.673), where you can fill in intentions forms (not required for the

Routeburn), get the latest weather forecast, get the latest on track conditions and buy maps. DOC's *The Routeburn Track* and *The Greenstone and Caples Tracks* leaflets, together with the 1:65,000 *Routeburn, Caples & Greenstone Parkmap* ($19), cover these three walks. For the Rees–Dart Track, the *Dart and Rees Valleys* leaflet and *Mount Aspiring Parkmap* are good, but the more detailed 1:50,000 *Aspiring* and *Earnslaw* Topomaps are better.

The information below assumes you're starting from Glenorchy, but it's also possible to hike the Greenstone/Caples and Routeburn combination from The Divide (north of Te Anau) with the luxury of *Kinloch Lodge* (see p.695) as your third night. The management runs transport from the Greenstone car park to the lodge then on to Routeburn Shelter.

Trailhead transport

During the summer tramping season there's little difficulty in getting transport to or from either end of the tracks. Track Transport (Oct–April; ☎03/442 9708, ⓦ www.infotrack.co.nz) runs a **bus service** to the trailheads, as follows: Queenstown to Glenorchy ($20) then on to the start of the Routeburn (another $20); Glenorchy to the Greenstone car park ($30); Glenorchy to the start of the Rees–Dart ($30); Glenorchy to Chinaman's Bluff (at the end of the Rees–Dart; $30). Trampers wanting to be dropped off or picked up at The Divide (the western end of the Routeburn) can hop on buses running between Te Anau and Milford Sound (ask visitor centres or the companies on p.746 for schedules) or arrange a pick-up from The Divide back to Queenstown, usually about $77. Most buses hit The Divide at 10.15am and 3.15pm, plus one Te Anau-bound buses ($37) at 5.45pm; Milford-bound buses ($32) pass at 8am, 10.55am, 1.30pm and 2.15pm. To save backtracking, trampers can arrange to have their **bags** sent from Queenstown to Te Anau or Milford Sound, with Track Transport (see above).

Hut and campsite bookings

The **Routeburn Track** is one of New Zealand's Great Walks and has a compulsory system for booking **accommodation passes** for the four huts and two campsites for the duration of its tramping season (late Oct to April). The system allows people to walk in either direction, retrace their steps and stay up to two nights in a particular hut. Numbers are limited, so book as far ahead as possible – three months if you need a specific departure date or are part of a large group. This way you get a guaranteed bed in a hut equipped with flush toilets, running water (which must be treated), heaters and gas rings: you'll need to carry your own pans and plates. The cost is $45 per person per night.

It is easiest to **book** online (ⓦ www.doc.govt.nz) from July 1 for the following season, though it is also possible to book by mail and in person at DOC visitor centres. If the track is closed due to bad weather or track conditions, full refunds are given; however, new bookings can only be made if there is space. Changes can be made to existing bookings ($10 per alteration) before you start, again, if space allows. **Outside the season** the huts ($15) cannot be booked and annual hut passes are valid.

A limited number of **campsites** (with pit toilets and water; $15) exist close to the Routeburn Flats and Mackenzie huts; campers are not allowed to use hut facilities.

The **Greenstone and Caples tracks** are less popular, and there is no booking system. Each trail has two $15 huts, but none of them has gas rings. Although it's better to buy hut tickets in advance (unless you have an annual hut pass), wardens may be able to sell you hut tickets. Free **camping** is allowed in both valleys along the fringes of the bush (though not on the open flats), but as ever

> Note that all **times** and **distances** given in the following accounts are **one-way**, unless otherwise stated.

you're encouraged to camp close to the huts and use the outside facilities. If you use the hut facilities but sleep outside you pay half the hut fee. Camp at least 50m away from the track if you're sleeping elsewhere.

The three **Rees–Dart** huts (each $15) cannot be booked. Trampers should carry an annual hut pass or buy hut tickets in advance.

Guided walks

If you just want a **one-day hike** to sample the Routeburn and avoid the tyranny of shuttle buses, consider joining Ultimate Hikes (T0800/659 255, Wwww .ultimatehikes.co.nz) on their one-day **Routeburn Encounter** ($155), which includes transport from Queenstown, gear and lunch. Full Routeburn aspirants who aren't confident about their level of fitness or prefer not to lug heavy backpacks can also join an organized group. The pace is fairly leisurely and walkers only carry their personal effects (no food or camping equipment); daily hikes are typically 5–6 hours, occasionally on rough terrain, so anyone unused to hillwalking should still do a good deal of preparatory hiking. **Accommodation** is in privately run huts, which are by no means luxurious, but do have hot showers and duvets on the bunks, and you'll be served breakfasts and dinners with wine.

There's a high **price** to pay for all this pampering: Ultimate Hikes' **Routeburn Guided Walk** (Nov–April; see above for contact details), including return transport from Queenstown and three days' walking, with two nights' accommodation in huts, costs $1240 (Nov & April $1050); the **Grand Traverse**, a five-day, six-night walk combining the Routeburn and Greenstone tracks, will set you back $1575 (Nov & April $1625). The Routeburn can also be combined with the Milford Track Guided Walk (see p.749).

The Routeburn Track

Most people walk the **Routeburn Track** (32km; 2–3 days) westwards from Glenorchy to The Divide; it can also be combined with the Greenstone and Caples tracks to make three- to five-day loops. The Routeburn isn't for everyone, but anyone of moderate fitness who can carry a backpack for five or six hours a day should be fine. That said, the track passes through subalpine country and snowfall and flooding can sometimes close it, even in summer.

Trailhead buses drop off at **Routeburn Shelter** mid-morning, mid- and late afternoon giving flexibility to hike to either Routeburn Flats hut or continue to Routeburn Falls huts, and even offering ample opportunity to explore the North Branch of Route Burn.

Routeburn Shelter to Routeburn Flats Hut (7km; 2–3hr; 250m ascent). The route follows Route Burn steadily uphill on a metre-wide track, though it's never strenuous and has an even shingle surface. Because Route Burn is a tributary of the Dart River, you are following a side valley and will have experienced a wide variety of scenery – river flats, waterfalls and open beech forest – by the time you reach the Routeburn Flats Hut (20 bunks). The nearby *Routeburn Flats* campsite is superbly sited on the edge of wide alluvial flats, at the end of a short path a couple of hundred metres beyond the hut. Only a few tents are permitted and campers can make use of an open fireplace and a small shelter, the run-off from which provides water for cooking.

Routeburn Flats Hut to Routeburn Falls Hut (2km; 1hr–1hr 30min; 300m ascent). Hut users are better off making the first day a little longer and tackling this next leg, which is considerably steeper and rougher, the extra exertion rewarded by a stay at the magnificently sited Routeburn Falls Hut (48 bunks), perched on the bushline above a precipice with eastward views looking back to Routeburn Flats and Sugar Loaf (1329m).

Routeburn Falls Hut to Mackenzie Hut (11km; 4–6hr; 300m ascent, 350m descent). This is the longest stretch and covers the most exposed section of the track. Most of the day is spent above the bushline among the subalpine snow tussock of the Harris Saddle (1255m) and passing through bog country, where sundews, bladderworts and orchids thrive. You might even catch sight of chamois clambering on the rocks to either side of the saddle. The track climbs gradually enough to the Harris Saddle Shelter (2–3hr), which offers respite from the wind and has toilets; on a clear day, drop your pack here and climb up to the 1515m summit of **Conical Hill** (2km return; at least 1hr; 260m ascent) for superb views down into the Hollyford Valley and along it to Martin Bay and the Tasman Sea. Continuing from the Harris Saddle Shelter, you cross from the Mount Aspiring National Park into the Fiordland National Park and skirt high along the edge of the Hollyford Valley, before switchbacking down through silver beech, fuchsia and ribbonwood to Mackenzie Hut (50 bunks). The campsite is a short way from the hut, near the lake.

Lake Mackenzie Hut to Howden Hut (9km; 3–4hr; 250m descent). The track continues along the mountainside through a grassy patch of ribbonwood, known as The Orchard, and past the cascading Earland Falls to the Howden Hut (28 bunks) at the junction of three tracks. The Greenstone and Caples tracks (handy for turning the tramp into a five-day Glenorchy-based circuit) head south, while the Routeburn continues.

Howden Hut to The Divide (3km; 1hr–1hr 30min; 50m net descent). This stretch initially climbs for 20min to a point where you can make a half-hour excursion to Key Summit for views of three major river systems – the Hollyford, the Eglinton and the Greenstone. From the **Key Summit** (919m) turn-off, the track descends through silver beech to the car park and shelter at The Divide.

The Greenstone Track

Trampers starting on the **Greenstone Track** (36km; 2–3 days) at The Divide first cover the short section to Howden Hut (described above), then walk south as follows.

Howden Hut to McKellar Hut (7km; 2hr–2hr 30min; 50m descent). After 20min the track passes the primitive but free *Greenstone Saddle* campsite. The Greenstone continues beside Lake McKellar to McKellar Hut ($15; 12 bunks), just outside the Fiordland National Park.

McKellar Hut to Greenstone Hut (17km; 4hr 30min–6hr 30min; 100m descent). This easy track starts by crossing the Greenstone River and follows the true left bank down a broad, grazed valley mostly along river flats and through the lower slopes of the beech forests. A swingbridge then crosses Steele Creek, and the track continues for two more hours to the Greenstone Hut, a good base for exploring the gentle Mavora Walkway to the south. It will take you 2–3 days, passing through open tussock country and beech forest, to reach Mavora Lakes (see p.677); a couple of huts provide accommodation en route ($5).

Greenstone Hut to Greenstone car park (10km; 3–5hr; 100m descent). The track follows the true left bank as the valley narrows and the river heads into a long gorge. The river soon meets the Caples River, an enticing series of deep pools that make great swimming holes. A swingbridge gives access to the left bank of the Caples River and the Caples Track; turn right to Greenstone Wharf (20–30min), or left to Mid Caples Hut (see below).

The Caples Track

The Caples Track (27km; 2 days) follows the Greenstone Track from **The Divide to Howden Hut** and then the first half of the section from Howden Hut to McKellar Hut, turning off an hour south of Howden Hut and beginning the very steep bush-clad zigzag up the **McKellar Saddle** (1005m).

The Divide to Upper Caples Hut (17km; 7–9hr; 500m ascent, 550m descent). Try to assess your capabilities beforehand as many find this first part of the walk too too much for one day, but are obliged to push on, as camping is neither pleasant nor permitted on the saddle's fragile bogland and open tussock. The descent mostly follows snow poles, crossing and recrossing the infant Caples River before regaining beech forest and the Upper Caples Hut ($15; 12 bunks).

Upper Caples Hut to Mid Caples Hut (7km; 2hr–2hr 30min; 50m descent), On this stretch you mainly cross grassland to the hut ($15; 12 bunks). Greenstone Wharf is within a day's walk of here, though you can break it into two sections, starting with this one.

Mid Caples Hut to Greenstone Wharf (7km; 2–3hr; 100m descent). The path reaches a short but dramatic gorge, crosses it and follows the true left bank, continuing alongside the bush edge and crossing grassy clearings before arriving at the junction with the Greenstone Track, from where it is only 20min to Greenstone Wharf car park.

The Rees–Dart Track

Transport timetables make it most convenient to tackle the Rees–Dart Track (58km; 3–4 days) by walking up the Rees and down the Dart.

Muddy Creek car park to Shelter Rock Hut (17km; 6–7hr; 400m ascent). The track follows a 4WD track across grass and gravel flats on the true left bank of the braided lower Rees and requires a couple of foot-soaking stream crossings. Press on past the Otago Tramping Club's Twenty-five Mile Hut (private), across Twenty-five Mile Creek and over more river flats for another hour or so, with Hunter Creek and the peaks of the Forbes Mountains straight ahead. Just past Hunter Creek, the Rees Valley steepens appreciably and becomes cloaked in beech forests, which continue sporadically until just below the treeline, where the path passes the site of the old Shelter Rock Hut. Head on for 1km until you hit tussock country, where one final crossing of the Rees River, now a large stream, takes you back to the left bank and the Shelter Rock Hut ($15; 22 bunks).

Shelter Rock Hut to Dart Hut (9km; 4–6hr; 600m ascent, 450m descent). The second day is the shortest but one of the toughest, scaling the 1447m Rees Saddle. Stick to the true left bank of the Rees, traversing subalpine scrub and gravel banks for a couple of kilometres, before crossing the river and climbing to a tussock basin and the saddle. Descend across snow grass beside Snowy Creek, which churns down a narrow gorge to your right. A kilometre or so later the track crosses a swingbridge to the true right bank, commencing a loose and rocky descent past a long series of cascades to another crossing of Snowy Creek, just above its confluence with the Dart River.

There are camping spots in the grassy areas on the true right bank and accommodation in the form of the Dart Hut ($15; 32 bunks); many stay two nights here, giving time to explore the Cascade Saddle route (see "Walks in the Matukituki Valley" box on p.714).

Dart Hut to Daleys Flat Hut (16km; 5–7hr; 450m descent). The track from Dart Hut climbs high above the river and stays there for 3km, passing through beech forest before dropping to Cattle Flat, 5km of grassed alluvial ridges traced by a winding and energy-sapping but easy-to-follow route. At the end of Cattle Flat, the track returns to the bush and runs parallel to the river until it reaches the beautiful grassy expanse of Quinns Flat (lovely in late-afternoon light), where the track turns inland. Within half an hour you reach the sandfly-ridden Daleys Flat Hut ($15; 20 bunks), redeemed by its pleasant location on the edge of a clearing.

Daleys Flat Hut to Chinaman's Bluff (16km; 5hr–6hr; 100m ascent, 150m descent). The walk skips through the bush for around 4km until Dredge Flat, where you make your own track, looking for markers on the left that indicate where you re-enter the bush. The track then climbs steeply over Sandy Bluff before dropping to river level for an easy walk across the flats and along the river to Chinaman's Bluff. Track Transport pick up from here, though you can continue on foot from Chinaman's Bluff to Paradise car park (6km; 2hr; negligible descent) along a 4WD track.

Wanaka

Pronounced evenly as Wa-Na-Ka, **WANAKA**, only 55km northeast of Queenstown but over an hour and a half by road, once languished in the shadow of its brash southern sibling. Thanks to a similar combination of beautiful surroundings and robust adventure activities, it is now one of New Zealand's fastest growing towns, with extensive developments and new housing subdivisions popping up everywhere. Situated at the point where the hummocky, poplar-studded hills of Central Otago rub up against the dramatic peaks of the Mount Aspiring National

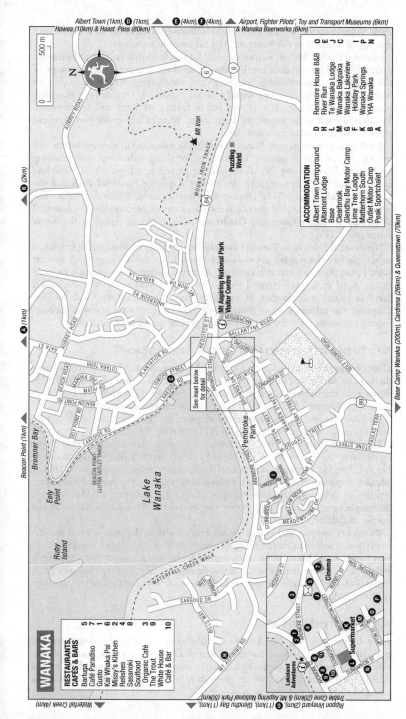

Albert Town (1km), **D** (1km), ▲ **E** (4km), **F** (4km), ▲ Airport, Fighter Pilots', Toy and Transport Museums (6km)
Hawea (10km) & Haast Pass (80km) & Wanaka Beerworks (6km)

B (2km) ▲

A (1km) ▲

Beacon Point (1km) ▲

ACCOMMODATION

Albert Town Campground	Renmore House B&B	D
Altamont Lodge	River Run	O
Base	Te Wanaka Lodge	H
Clearbrook	Wanaka Bakpaka	E
Glendhu Bay Motor Camp	Wanaka Lakeview	J
Lime Tree Lodge	Holiday Park	C
Matterhorn South	Wanaka Springs	G
Outlet Motor Camp	YHA Wanaka	F
Peak Sportchalet		K
		B
		A
		I
		P
		N
		M
		L

Mt Iron

MOUNT IRON TRACK

Puzzling World

Mt Aspiring National Park Visitor Centre

BALLANTYNE ROAD

▼ Base Camp Wanaka (200m), Cardrona (26km) & Queenstown (70km)

Lake Wanaka

Ruby Island

Bremner Bay

Eely Point

WATERFALL CREEK WALK

WANAKA

RESTAURANTS, CAFÉS & BARS

Barluga	5
Café Paradiso	7
Gusto	1
Kai Whaka Pai	6
Missy's Kitchen	2
Relishes	4
Sasanoki	8
Soulfood	3
Organic Café	3
The Trout	9
White House Café & Bar	10

Waterfall Creek (4km) ▲

Rippon Vineyard (2km), **6** (1km), Glendhu Bay (11km), ▲ Treble Cone (20km) & Mt Aspiring National Park (50km)

500 m

N

See inset below for detail

Cinema

Supermarket

Lakeland Adventures

Park, Wanaka commands the shore of the willow-girt lake of the same name, with the jagged summits of the Southern Alps mirrored in its waters.

Founded in the 1860s as a service centre for the local run-holders and itinerant gold miners, the town didn't really take off until the prosperous middle years of the twentieth century, when camping and caravanning Kiwis discovered its warm, dry summer climate. Wanaka remains a small, eminently manageable place, with the tenor of a village and a feeling of light and spaciousness. Promoting itself as an adventure destination, Wanaka is primarily an excellent place in which to relax for a few days.

A half-day spent exploring Wanaka's intriguing **maze** and modest **museums** will leave plenty of time to laze on the beach, go kayaking, jetboating, rock climbing or, best of all, canyoning. Wanaka is also the perfect base from which to explore the surrounding region, notably the **Mount Aspiring National Park** and the **Cardrona Valley** (see p.712). During the winter months, Wanaka's relative calm is shattered by the arrival of skiers and snowboarders eager to explore the downhill **ski-fields** of **Treble Cone** and **Cardrona**, and the Nordic terrain at the **Snow Farm** (see p.713).

Stones are thrown into Wanaka's peaceful waters again on New Year's Eve when seemingly half the teenage population of South Island make a pilgrimage here, at which time the town is worth avoiding. A very different vibe is palpable in town in late April during the biennial Festival of Colour (odd years; Ⓦwww.festival ofcolour.co.nz), a celebration of visual art, dance, music, theatre and the like. Likewise the relatively new WanakaFest (mid-Oct; Ⓦwww.wanakafest.co.nz) mostly celebrates food and booze, accompanied by a variety of musical acts.

Arrival, information and transport

Direct **buses** from Christchurch, Dunedin, Queenstown and Franz Josef all arrive daily, close to the i-SITE (see below). Southern Link K Bus (Ⓣ0508/458 835, Ⓦwww.southernlinkkbus.co.nz), go to Queenstown ($14 each way), as does Atomic ($30 return; Ⓣ03/349 0697, Ⓦwww.atomictravel.co.nz).

Air New Zealand flights arrive at the **airport**, on SH6, 9km east of the centre and Alpine Coachlines meet the flights ($15; Ⓣ0800/754 926).

The **i-SITE visitor centre**, 100 Ardmore St (daily: Jan–March 8.30am–6pm; April–Nov 8.30am–5.30pm; Ⓣ03/443 1233, Ⓦwww.lakewanaka.co.nz) is helpful, but for tramping and general backcountry information, go to DOC's **Mount Aspiring National Park visitor centre** (Nov–March daily 8am–5pm; April–Oct Mon–Fri 8.30am–4.30pm, Sat 9.30am–4pm; Ⓣ03/443 7660, Ⓔmtaspiringvc@doc.govt.nz), 500m east of central Wanaka on SH84 at the corner of Ballantyne Road.

Wanaka is compact and you can **walk** everywhere in the centre. Most accommodation is less than fifteen minutes' away on foot, but longer excursions are best made with **bicycles** or **cars** rented from around town (see "Listings", p.710); or for short trips into the surrounding area there's always Wanaka Taxis (Ⓣ03/443 7999). There are several **banks** around town, with foreign-exchange facilities and ATMs.

Accommodation

For a diminutive place, Wanaka has experienced an explosion of accommodation, particularly luxury lodges. **Rates** are marginally lower than Queenstown, but reflect the town's resort status. You should have no problem finding a bed, except during the peak months of January, February, July and August, when **booking** is essential and prices rise.

Hotel and motel

Altamont Lodge 121 Mount Aspiring Rd, 2km west of Wanaka ℡03/443 8864, ⓦwww.altamontlodge .co.nz. Tramping-cum-ski lodge, with a pine-panelled alpine atmosphere, communal cooking and lounge areas, a spa pool, drying rooms and ski-tuning facilities. Rooms are functional, with shared bathrooms and good rates for singles. Bring your own bed linen or pay $5 extra/bed. ❷

Clearbrook Corner of Helwick & Upton sts ℡0800/443 441, ⓦwww.clearbrook.co.nz. Classy, great-value motel with tastefully decorated luxury units (studios, plus one- and two-bedroom apartments) ranged along the burbling Bullock Creek. All units have TV, stereo, full kitchen with dishwasher, laundry and balconies with mountain views. There are also separate three-bedroom houses sleeping six ($370). ❺

B&Bs, homestays and lodges

Lime Tree Lodge Ballantyne Rd, 6km south of Wanaka on SH6 ℡03/443 7305, ⓦwww.limetreelodge.co.nz. Five-star B&B accommodation and treatment at a fabulous, purpose-built lodge, spread over two wings containing six rooms and two suites. Individually decorated rooms, refreshing personal touches and delicious food all go to make you stay longer than you intended and the hosts are friendly, knowledgeable and determined that you should enjoy every moment. Rooms ❾, suites ❾

Peak Sportchalet 36 Hunter Crescent, 2km north of town ℡03/443 6990, ⓦwww.peak-sportchalet .co.nz. Purpose-built s/c studio and two-bedroom chalet, run by charming Germans who provide a buffet breakfast ($10 extra). Great for a family or two couples. Studio ❹, chalet ❺

Renmore House B&B 44 Upton St ℡03/443 6566, ⓦwww.renmore-house.com. Large purpose-built house, centrally located beside the burbling waters of Bullock Creek, with three plush en-suite rooms all fitted out to a high standard. There are bikes for guests' use and the hosts are genial and welcoming. ❼

River Run Halliday Rd, 5km east of Wanaka ℡03/443 9049, ⓦwww.riverrun.co.nz. Stylish lodge sited on ancient river flats with trails leading down to the Clutha River. The modern house, built using lots of recycled timber, was thoughtfully conceived by the owners and contains five well-appointed en-suite rooms, sunny verandas and a common dining area where most guests stay for three-course dinners ($85) that are the match of any restaurant in Wanaka. Rates include breakfast and pre-dinner drinks. ❾

Te Wanaka Lodge 23 Brownston St ℡0800/926252, ⓦwww.tewanaka.co.nz. One of the best B&Bs in town, with thirteen luxurious en-suite rooms all with private entrances and Sky TV. A cedar hot tub shares the peaceful garden with a delightful small cottage. There's a sumptuous buffet breakfast and even a house bar with a good wine selection. The owners are friendly and highly knowledgeable about all things outdoors. ❼

Wanaka Springs 21 Warren St ℡03/443 8421, ⓦwww.wanakasprings.com. Classy, purpose-built, boutique lodge with comfortable, beautifully decorated rooms, stylish communal areas, free liqueurs and a spa pool in the native garden. The hosts have good local knowledge. ❽

Hostels

Base 73 Brownston St ℡03/443 4291, ⓦwww .staybase.com. More and more hostels are opening in Wanaka and this relatively new one is typical of Base hostels throughout NZ and Australia; good rooms, tiny, poorly equipped kitchen, pushy booking desk and attached bar with meal deals for residents and a reputation for late nights. Dorms $25 rooms ❷, en suites ❸

Matterhorn South 56 Brownston St ℡03/443 1119, ⓦwww.matterhornsouth.co.nz. Combined hostel and budget lodge, with an appealing backpacker section featuring dorms of various sizes and a free spa. The more upmarket section has modern, en-suite four-shares with TV and fridge, and access to an excellent kitchen and comfortable lounge. Dorms $24, rooms ❷, en suites ❸

Wanaka Bakpaka 117 Lakeside Rd ℡03/443 7837, ⓦwww.wanakabakpaka.co.nz. Low-key hostel 5min walk from town and with great lake and mountain views, a peaceful atmosphere, summer BBQs and bike rental ($20/day). Go for the nicer, newer rooms if you have a choice. Dorms $26, rooms ❷

YHA Wanaka 94 Brownston St ℡03/443 1880, ⓦwww.yha.co.nz. YHA have taken over what was the *Purple Cow*, a large, spacious hostel in a former hotel with dorms of up to six beds, many in separate blocks with their own lounge, bathroom and TV. Also en-suite doubles, some with lake view and TV/DVD. Sit and gaze at the fabulous lake view through the big picture windows. They've retained their old hostel at 181 Upton St (℡03/443 7405) to deal with any overspill. Dorms $26, rooms ❷, en suites ❸

Campsites and motor parks

Albert Town Campground 6km northeast of Wanaka on SH6. Open, informal camping area, with water and toilets, on the banks of the swift-flowing Clutha River. $7

Glendhu Bay Motor Camp Mount Aspiring Rd, 12km west of Wanaka ☎03/443 7243, ⓦwww .glendhubaymotorcamp.co.nz. Beautifully situated, lakeshore family campsite with fabulous views across to Mount Aspiring, a boat-launching ramp, canoe rental ($10/hr) and a motorboat ($100/hr, plus fuel). Camping $14, bunks $20, cabins ❶

Outlet Motor Camp Lake Outlet Rd, 6km from Wanaka ☎03/443 7478. Spacious and stunningly sited campsite at the point where Lake Wanaka becomes the Clutha River, in a great position for strolls along the lake or river frontage. Along with tent and powered sites there are on-site s/c tents with real beds. Camping $12, tents ❷

Wanaka Lakeview Holiday Park 212 Brownston St ☎03/443 7883, ⓦwww.wanakalakeview .kiwiholidayparks.com. A convenient, 10min walk from central Wanaka, with tent sites and all the usual facilities, including rooms in a lodge which has bathrooms and kitchen under the same roof and s/c tourist flats. Camping $16, dorms $20, standard cabins ❶, flats ❸

The Town

Though central Wanaka is a pleasant place to hang out, there are no sights as such. For attractions you'll either need to head east to Puzzling World and the museums around the airport or venture 3km west to the small **Rippon Vineyard**, Mount Aspiring Road (daily: Dec–April 11am–5pm; July–Nov 1.30–5.30pm; ☎03/443 8084, ⓦwww.rippon.co.nz). Tastings are free (try the Pinot Noir and the rare Osteiner Riesling hybrid) and you'll struggle to find a more spectacular picnic spot, so pack a few sandwiches and sit back in the sun. The best approach to the vineyard from Wanaka is on foot, along the lakefront Waterfall Creek Walk (see box, p.708), though it is easy to go too far; to avoid this, turn up a track after the first block of vines. Alternatively let something with four legs take the strain on the very civilized **Vineyard Trail Ride** run by Timber Creek Equestrian Centre ($90; ☎027/210 9098) – a gentle, scenic ride through the country and vines, followed by a wine tasting and then a gentler still ride back. Every even year, in February, the Ripon Vineyard plays host to the one-day Rippon **open-air music festival** (ⓦwww.ripponfestival.co.nz) with top Kiwi bands and lively after-party.

The solid lump of Mount Iron rises immediately east of town, pointing the way to **Stuart Landsborough's Puzzling World**, almost 2km away on SH84 (daily 8.30am–5.30pm; $9 for the Maze or the Illusion Rooms, or $12.50 for both; ☎03/443 7489, ⓦwww.puzzlingworld.co.nz). The star attraction is "The Great Maze", a complex wooden structure comprising 1500m of dead-end passageways packed into a dense labyrinth, with overhead bridges linking the two halves. Your mission is to reach all four corner towers, either in any order (30min–1hr) or in a specific sequence (at least 1hr), then find your way out again. Other attractions are Illusion Rooms, including holograms; a "Tilted House", which revels in tricks of perspective; and the "Hall of Following Faces", an octagonal room with seven of the sides made up by arrays of moulded images of famous people. As you walk around the faces appear to turn towards you. Yet more fun can be had, and some of Peter Jackson's hobbit-realizing tricks understood, in the Ames Forced Perspective Room, which has been carefully manipulated to make you appear either ent- or hobbit-sized. Leave time to play with the frustrating puzzles in the café.

The airport area

Wanaka's airport is the base for a number of aerial activities (see p.709) and the **New Zealand Fighter Pilots Museum** (daily 9am–4pm; $10; ⓦwww.nzfpm .co.nz), which honours Kiwi pilots and ground crew who fought in the two world wars. This homage to the New Zealand contingent contains hagiographic profiles of the men and blow-by-blow descriptions of the major campaigns, all accompanied by rousing war anthems. The museum also features interactive story screens, plus two displays on the Battle of Britain and the Fall of Germany, as told by NZ pilots who survived them. Over Easter in even-numbered years the airport plays host to the three-day **Warbirds over Wanaka** air show ($395 for a gold pass, $165 for a standard for 3 days or $70 for Saturday, the main event; Ⓦwww .warbirdsoverwanaka.com), which sees over 100,000 people watch all manner of airborne craft take to the air.

A similar theme is explored in the adjacent and expanding (new buildings are currently under construction) **Wanaka Transport and Toy Museum** (daily 8.30am–5pm; $8), an astonishing hoard of cars, planes, trucks and bikes preserved by Wanaka's dry climate. Some machines are well-kept examples of stuff still puttering around New Zealand roads, but there's also exotica such as a Centurion tank, Velocette and BSA bikes, a yellow-fur-covered Morris Minor and the Solar Kiwi Racer, an aluminium and glass-fibre bullet-shaped car powered by solar panels on its roof. Also on display are all manner of toys, including an impressive *Star Wars* collection, not to mention more than five hundred Barbies.

Next to the museum, the **Wanaka Beerworks** (daily 9am–4pm or later; Ⓣ03/443 1865, Ⓦwww.wanakabeerworks.co.nz) is an award-winning micro-brewery (simple tours daily at 2pm) which produces a golden malt, a pilsner and a dark ale, all three of which can be sampled for $6, and are are sold through bars and restaurants around Central Otago.

Activities

Wanaka's relatively low profile and the absence of the hard sell and conveyor-belt style that characterizes Queenstown's operations add up to a more relaxed approach – and frequently better value for money. Most accommodation and numerous agents around town handle **bookings**, or you can contact the activity operator direct.

Canyoning

If you like water and don't mind heights then the best activity around Wanaka is **canyoning** with Deep Canyon (Nov–March daily; Ⓣ03/443 7922, Ⓦwww .deepcanyon.co.nz), who take small groups into narrow canyons following a creek downstream with heaps of jumps, slides and abseils. Warm, protective clothing helps ease the sense of vulnerability, and the day is rounded off with a picnic and strong coffee. First-timers are best opting for the **Niger Stream trip** (7–8hr; $225), down a pretty stream with plenty of jumping into deep pools. It helps if you've had some abseiling experience to get the best from **Big Nige** (7–8hr; $290), which kicks off by rappelling down a waterfall. Plan ahead for **Wilkin Wilderness** (12hr; $890), which combines a helicopter flight, a fabulous canyon and jetboating on the Wilkin river.

Rock climbing and mountaineering

Wanaka's dry, sunny climate is ideal for **rock climbing**. The best starting point is the Base Camp Wanaka Climbing Centre, 50 Cardrona Valley Rd (daily 9am–6pm; Ⓣ03/443 1110, Ⓦwww.basecampwanaka.co.nz), 2km south of the town centre. Try Clip 'N Climb ($18/1hr; bring trainers), where a top-rope system gives you the freedom to try all sorts of artificial climbs – against the clock, a face-to-face race, in the dark with UV-lit holds etc. For something closer to the real thing, have a go on the indoor wall, or the superbly sculpted outdoor wall ($15 without gear, about $18 if you need everything), which is pretty close to climbing

Walks around Wanaka

Included here are the best local treks; no special gear is required, just robust shoes, wet-weather gear, sun protection and DOC's *Wanaka Walks and Trails* leaflet, which has a good map.

Mount Iron Track (2km; 1–2hr; 240m ascent). The most accessible of Wanaka's hilltop walks climbs a 549m glacially sculpted outcrop, its western and northern slopes ground smooth by the glacier that scoured its southern face. The path through farmland and the bird-filled manuka woodland of the Mount Iron Scenic Reserve starts 1500m east of Wanaka on SH84, climbing the steep southern face to the summit. Here you can enjoy magnificent panoramic views, before following the path down the east face of Mount Iron towards the entrance to Puzzling World (see p.706).

Roy's Peak Track (16km; 4–6hr; 1100m ascent). A more challenging prospect, winding up to the summit (1578m), for wonderful views over Lake Wanaka and surrounding glaciers and mountains. The path starts 7km west of Wanaka on the Mount Aspiring Road, but is closed during the lambing season (1 Oct–10 Nov).

Diamond Lake Track (7km; 2hr 30min; 400m ascent). A fine local walk with great lake and mountain views, starting at the car park 18km west of Wanaka on the Mount Aspiring Road. There are a couple of short variations – but to get the views, you'll need to tackle the summit of Rocky Mountain (775m).

Beacon Point–Clutha Outlet Circuit (16km; 3–5hr; mostly flat). Long but undemanding riverbank and lakeside walk which starts from Wanaka and follows the shore to Eely Point (15min), a sheltered bay popular for boating and picnics. Beyond Eely Point is Bremner Bay and the continuation of the waterfront path to Beacon Point (a further 30min). Either return the same way or continue along Beacon Point Road to the *Outlet Motor Camp* and pick up the Outlet Track, which runs 4km to Alison Avenue, then down to SH6 not far from the Albert Town bridge. By following SH6 this can be turned into a loop back to Wanaka, passing the base of Mount Iron.

Waterfall Creek Walk (3km one-way; 35min; negligible ascent). The westbound equivalent of the Beacon Point–Clutha Outlet Circuit leaves Roy's Bay, heading through Wanaka Station Park and past Rippon Vineyard to a car park at Waterfall Creek. From here the path continues as the Millennium Walkway (5km each way; 1hr; 100m ascent), following lakeside terraces to Ironside's Hill. Both of these are open to bikers.

on real rock. If you're new to the game they'll teach you how to belay safely and leave you to it.

For **tuition** and guiding, try Wanaka Rock (☎03/443 6411, ⓦ www.wanaka rock.co.nz), which runs full-day introductory courses involving top-roping, seconding and abseiling for 2–4 people ($190 each for a full day) and get a copy of *Wanaka Rock* ($30, available from Good Sports – see p.711) for added inspiration.

Professional **mountaineering** packages are offered by Adventure Consultants (☎03/443 8711, ⓦ www.adventureconsultants.co.nz). They do five-day ascents of Mount Aspiring (from $4100) as well as excellent seven-day mountaineering courses ($5390) including ice climbing, snow-cave building and all the basic skills, plus several summit ascents.

Biking

Wanaka abounds with shops (see p.710) renting out all-terrain bikes and selling the *Lake Wanaka Cycling Map* ($2), which details local off-road rides. The lakeside tracks (see box, p.708) are open to riders, and the "Sticky Forest" has a particularly dense knot of excellent single track. Alternatively get out to the Dirt Park in the

Cardrona Valley (day pass $30), right by the Snow Farm (see p.713), where there's chairlift access to all manner of freestyle terrain.

Skydiving and paragliding

Magnificent scenery, clear skies and competitive prices make Wanaka an excellent place to get airborne. A ten-minute scenic flight can be combined with 45–60 seconds of freefall on a **tandem skydive** with Skydive Lake Wanaka, Wanaka Airport ($295 from 12,000ft, $395 from 15,000ft; T0800/786 877, Wwww .skydivenz.co.nz).

A less fraught approach to viewing the tremendous scenery is to go **tandem paragliding**. Flights take off from the Treble Cone ski-field with Wanaka Paragliding (800m descent; 2hr with 15–25min in the air; $190, including transport; T0800/359 754, Wwww.wanakaparagliding.co.nz).

Scenic flights

Scenic flights to Milford Sound (see p.742) from Wanaka tend to be a few dollars more expensive than those from Queenstown, but they do spend half an hour more flying over a wider range of stunning scenery, including Mount Aspiring, the Olivine Ice Plateau and the inaccessible lakes of Alabaster, McKerrow and Tutoko. Most local accommodation receives daily bulletins on Milford weather and flight conditions. Wanaka Flightseeing (T0800/105 105, Wwww .flightseeing.co.nz) offers a range of flights, including the wonderful journey over the Southern Alps to link up with a boat cruise on Milford Sound (4hr; $435). There's also a **helicopter** option with Alpine Helicopters ($780/2hr; T03/443 4000, Wwww.alpineheli.co.nz). Alternatively, nip to Makarora for the **Siberia Experience** (see p.664).

Cruises and boat activities

With a beautiful lake and a number of decent rivers there's plenty of opportunity for getting wet in style. Lakeland Adventures, in the i-SITE building (T03/443 7495, Wwww.lakelandadventures.co.nz), lay on all manner of waterborne activities, the most leisurely being **lake cruises**, particularly to Stephensons Island (2hr; $70) where you can stroll briefly.

From October to April, Alpine Kayak Guides (T03/443 9023, Wwww .alpinekayaks.co.nz) run half-day **kayaking** trips on the Clutha River (Grade II; 4hr; $149): trips depart from the i-SITE in Wanaka.

For thrills and spills, the best **jetboat ride** is with Wanaka River Journeys (3hr; $220; T0800/544 555, Wwww.wanakariverjourneys.co.nz), who thunder up the Mutukituki River, providing great views of Mount Aspiring, the Avalanche Glacier, Mount Avalanche and the rest, with a knowledgeable guide and bushwalk.

A far cry from Queenstown's boisterous Kawarau and Shotover rivers are the **rafting trips** run by Pioneer Rafting (Sept–April daily; $135/half-day; T03/443 1246, Wwww.ecoraft.co.nz). Pitched at families, the emphasis is on appreciating the scenery, swimming and gold panning as you drift down the Upper Clutha (Grade II–III).

Fishing

Lake Wanaka and nearby lakes and rivers are popular territory for quinnat salmon and brown and rainbow trout **fishing**. There's a maximum bag of six fish per day and you'll require the sport fishing licence ($21/day, $105 for the season), obtainable direct (Wwww.fishandgame.org.nz) or from tackle shops. Unless you really know your bait, you'll have a better chance of catching your supper with a fishing

guide – the i-SITE has reams of names, all with access to boats, rods, reels and lures but they don't come cheap.

Eating and drinking

Skiers and the healthy influx of summer tourists have determined the style and number of places to **eat and drink** in Wanaka, and some of them are quite good. Unless you strike it lucky and catch a band passing through, the only entertainment is the wonderful Paradiso **cinema**, on the corner of Ardmore Street and Ballantyne Road ($12; ☎03/443 1505, ⓦwww.paradiso .net.nz), where you sit in sagging old sofas, armchairs, airline seats or even a bisected Morris Minor. The films range from Hollywood to arthouse, and there's always an interval during which everyone tucks into cookies, ice cream, coffee or booze from the on-site café (see below). Sadly the cinema's lease is up soon but hopefully the council will not redevelop the site. There are lots of bars, but the only real **nightclub** is the *Red Rock* on Ardmore Street (Fri & Sat 8.30pm until whenever; ☎03/443 5545), which is lively and loud and serves entertaining snacks.

Barluga Tucked away off Ardmore St on Post Office Lane. Little wine bar with leather sofas, armchairs, a log fire and courtyard, with a giant sideways clock and a broad range of quality local wine.

Café Paradiso Corner of Ardmore St & Ballantyne Rd. Groovy licensed café attached to its cinema namesake, serving excellent coffee, popcorn, cookies and cake, plus home-made ice cream that's free of additives and wondrously fruity ($3.50), curries and pizzas (from $18) – available in the evening – and cinema-friendly local brews.

Gusto 1 Lakeside Rd. Café-style dining for ladies who lunch, with interesting platters, good coffee, a wide range of fresh juices and some generous salads and all-day breakfasts.

🏃 **Kai Whaka Pai** Corner of Ardmore & Helwick sts. Wanaka's liveliest daytime eating spot is a favourite with locals who come for chocolate cookies, breakfasts and fine coffee. In the evening the emphasis is on beer, wine, noise and uncomplicated meals.

Missy's Kitchen 80 Ardmore St ☎03/443 5099. Fine dining, with a select menu (mains $26–32) and extensive wine list that is best appreciated on the balcony on balmy summer nights.

Relishes 99 Ardmore St ☎03/443 9018. Pretension-free café/restaurant serving good-quality lunches ($16–19) and dinners ($26–35). Try the

home-made burger (around $20), and don't skimp on dessert.

Sasanoki 139 Ardmore St ☎03/443 6474. Japanese kitchen, more take away than eat in, unless you are a sardine, serving excellent udon noodles, endame, sashimi and donhuri, all at a snip. Daily 11.30am–2.30pm & 5–8pm.

🏃 **Soulfood Organic Café** 74 Ardmore St. Wonderful, unpretentious indoor and courtyard eating in this deli cum café. Excellent coffee, quality grub, delicious home-made cheeses (brie, halloumi and feta), filling breakfasts – bacon and eggs, ben's eggs with miso, pancakes – or stop for lunch and enjoy focaccia with salads, quiches, cakes and tarts, all for less than it costs to get the waiter's attention in some joints. Mon–Fri, 8am–5pm, Sat & Sun 8am–4pm.

The Trout 151–153 Ardmore St. Probably the least up-itself bar in town, with a good selection of ales and some cheap bar snacks.

🏃 **White House Café & Bar** 33 Dunmore St ☎03/443 9595. The owner is a character, the menu tiny and the attitude relaxed, particularly where building maintenance is concerned, but it is a culinary adventure – sometimes good, sometimes dreadful. If you take a chance and it's on form the honest mains ($26–36) of local ingredients with a Mediterranean influence will compensate for much, and the wine list and desserts will add a glow.

Listings

Bike rental Numerous places around town rent bikes and many hostels and B&Bs have machines for guests' use. For more specialized needs visit

Thunderbikes, 48 Helwick St (☎03/443 2558), for hardtails ($20/4hr, $40/day) and long-travel fully sprung models ($50/$75), or Outside Sports, 17–23

Dunmore St (☎03/443 7966), who offer a similar range.

Camping and outdoor equipment Wanaka Sports, 8 Helwick St, rent out fishing tackle ($25/day), while Outside Sports (see above) stocks pretty much everything else.

Car rental Aspiring Car Rentals, Mt Aspiring Rd (☎03/443 7883), have the cheapest cars in town, starting at around $45/day, with unlimited kilometres and insurance.

Medical treatment Wanaka Medical Centre, 21 Russell St ☎03/443 7811.

Pharmacy Wanaka Pharmacy, 33 Helwick St (☎03/443 8000) and Aspiring Pharmacy, corner of Helwick and Dunmore sts (☎03/4337986).

Police Helwick St ☎03/443 7272.

Post office 39 Ardmore St (Mon–Fri 8.30am–5.30pm, Sat 9am–noon).

Ski rental Racers Edge, 99 Ardmore St (☎03/443 7882, ⓦwww.racersedge.co.nz), rents out skis ($36–47/day) and snowboards ($42), and also run a ski-tuning and repair service – as do Good Sports on Dunmore St (☎03/443 7966).

Around Wanaka

Wanaka is the only town of any size within a huge area of western Central Otago, and the only resort with easy access to tramps in the **Mount Aspiring National Park**. Consequently, it's a popular base for exploring the surrounding countryside, principally the open and mountainous areas to the north and west, the Haast Pass road over to the West Coast, and the tortuous **Crown Range Road**, the most direct route to Queenstown, passing through the **Cardrona Valley**.

▲ Treble Cone ski-field, Wanaka

Winter in Wanaka

In May Wanaka gets geared up for **winter**, mountain-bike rental shops switch to ski rental (see "Listings", p.711), watersports instructors don baggy snowboarder pants, pot-bellied stoves replace parasols at restaurants, and frequent shuttle buses run up to the ski-fields. If you plan to drive up to the ski-fields, you'll need tyre chains, which can be rented at petrol stations in Wanaka.

Cardrona

Cardrona Alpine Resort (late June to early Oct; T03/443 7411, Wwww.cardrona .com) sprawls over three basins on the southeastern slopes of the 1934m Mount Cardrona, the 12km unsealed toll-free access road branching off 24km south of Wanaka and just short of the hamlet of Cardrona. Predominantly family-oriented, Cardrona is noted for dry snow and an abundance of gentle **runs** (5 beginner, 13 intermediate, 9 advanced). There are quads and several learner tows, and a maximum vertical descent of 390m and snowboarders have the run of three terrain parks. An adult **lift pass** costs \$85.

You'll need snow chains to negotiate the access road to the base facilities halfway up the field. Non-drivers can get **buses** from Wanaka, and from Queenstown, an hour and a half away. The resort offers **accommodation** on the mountain – in luxury, fully self-contained studios for two (⓪), or two- and three bedroom apartments which sleep up to eight (\$310–620).

Treble Cone

More experienced skiers tend to frequent the steep slopes of **Treble Cone** (late June to early Oct; T03/443 7443, Wwww.treblecone.co.nz), 22km west of Wanaka, accessed by a 7km toll-free road. Its appeal lies in open uncrowded **runs** (4 beginner, 16 intermediate, 19 advanced), spectacularly located high above Lake Wanaka, and a full 700 vertical metres of skiing with moguls, powder runs, gully runs

The Cardrona Valley

William Fox's unwitting discovery of gold at Arrowtown in 1862 quickly brought prospectors along the Crown Range and into the **Cardrona Valley**, where gold was discovered later that year. Five years on, the Europeans legged it to new fields on the West Coast, leaving the dregs to Chinese immigrants, who themselves had drifted away by 1870.

The **Crown Range Road** (SH89) through the valley is the most direct (though not necessarily the quickest) route from Wanaka to Queenstown. Reaching an altitude of 1120m, it is one of New Zealand's highest public roads and is windy enough in places to discourage anyone towing a caravan or trailer. Nonetheless, on a fine day the drive past the detritus of the valley's gold-mining heyday is a rewarding one, with views across the tussock high country.

Around 24km out of Wanaka lies a petrolhead's playground, the **Cardrona Adventure Park** (year-round, but call ahead outside the summer season; T0800/102 122, Wwww.adventurepark.co.nz). For a leisurely start, go quad biking across farmland (\$160/2hr), then, if you must, upgrade to a **monster truck** and drive (\$250) over an obstacle course.

Two kilometres further on, tiny **CARDRONA** comprises little more than a few cottages, a long-forgotten cemetery and the *Cardrona Hotel* (T03/443 8153, Wwww.cardronahotel.co.nz; B&B rooms ⓪), which stands in a state of arrested decay. Built in 1863, it survived the floods of 1878 that destroyed most of the old town, battling on until 1961. After years of neglect it was reopened in 1984, and although it looks the same on the outside the interior has

and plenty of natural and created half-pipes. Three new groomed trails make it much better for beginners than previously and snowboarders will have a ball. Day **lift passes** go for $89.

Morning **buses** leave from Wanaka, and a shuttle bus takes skiers from the start of the access road on Mount Aspiring Road up to the tows. Backcountry tours are also available from Treble Cone, with Aspiring Guides (℡03/443 9422, ⓦwww .aspiringguides.com).

Snow Farm
With so many Kiwi skiers committed to downhill, it comes as a surprise to discover the **Snow Farm** (℡03/443 0300, ⓦwww.snowfarmnz.com), a cross-country ski area across the valley from Cardrona, 24km south of Wanaka, then 13km up a winding dirt road. At $35 for access to the field and $25 for ski rental, it's an inexpensive way to get on the snow, from July to September, negotiating the 55km of marked Nordic trails.

Heli-skiing
Heli-skiing is not cheap, but there's no other way of getting to runs of up to 1200 vertical metres across virgin snow on any of six mountain ranges. From June to October Harris Mountains Heli-Ski (℡03/442 6722, ⓦwww.heliski.co.nz), offers almost 400 different runs on 150 peaks – mainly in the Harris Mountains between Queenstown's Crown Range and Wanaka's Mount Aspiring National Park.

Strong intermediate and **advanced skiers** get the most out of the experience, where **conditions** are more critical than at the ski-fields, but on average there's heli-skiing seventy percent of the time, typically in four- to five-day weather windows. Of the multitude of packages, the most popular is "The Classic" ($825), a four-run day.

been spruced up and the beer garden's not bad either; it's now a popular watering hole for skiers, and a good spot for bar and restaurant **meals** (mains $23–32).

South from here, the road twists and turns a further 26km through grassy flanks of bald, mica-studded hills to a great viewpoint overlooking Queenstown and Lake Wakatipu, before it switchbacks down towards SH6 and Queenstown.

The Matukituki Valley and Mount Aspiring National Park

The **Matukituki Valley** is Wanaka's outdoor playground, a 60km tentacle reaching from the parched Otago landscapes around Lake Wanaka to the steep alpine skirts of Mount Aspiring, which at 3030m is New Zealand's highest mountain outside the Mount Cook National Park. Extensive high-country stations run sheep on the riverside meadows, briefly glimpsed by skiers bound for Treble Cone, rock climbers making for the roadside crags, Matukituki-bound kayakers, and trampers and mountaineers hot-footing it to the **Mount Aspiring National Park**.

The park, mooted in 1935 but not created until 1964, is one of the country's largest, extending from the Haast Pass (where there are tramps around Makarora; see p.663) in the north, to the head of Lake Wakatipu (where the Rees–Dart Track and parts of the Routeburn Track fall within its bounds) in the south. The pyramidal Mount Aspiring forms the centrepiece of the park, rising with classical

DOC's *Matukituki Valley Tracks* and *Rees–Dart Tracks* leaflets are recommended for these walks, along with the detailed *Mount Aspiring National Park* map ($19). The routes are manageable for fit and experienced trampers, but the climatic differences in the park are extreme – the half-metre of rain that falls each year in the Matukituki Valley does not compare with the six metres that fall on the western side of the park, so go prepared.

Several huts in this area are owned by the New Zealand Alpine Club (NZAC) but are open to all: pay at the DOC visitor centre in Wanaka.

Raspberry Creek to Aspiring Hut
The popular and mostly pastoral day-walk from **Raspberry Creek to Aspiring Hut** (9km one-way; 2hr 30min–3hr; 100m ascent) starts along a 4WD track which climbs from the Raspberry Creek car park beside the western branch of the Matukituki River, only heading away from the river to avoid bluffs en route to Downs Creek, from where you get fabulous views up to the Rob Roy Glacier and Mount Avalanche. Bridal Veil Falls is a brief distraction before the historic Cascade Hut, followed 20min later by the relatively luxurious stone-built **Aspiring Hut** (NZAC; 38 bunks; $15, with gas), a common base camp for mountaineers off to the peaks around Mount Aspiring, which is wonderfully framed by the hut's picture windows. There's **camping** ($6) near the hut.

Rob Roy Valley
The **Rob Roy Valley Walk** (6km one-way; 2hr; 400m ascent) is shorter and steeper than the walk to Aspiring Hut and more spectacular, striking through beech forest to some magnificent alpine scenery, snowfields and glaciers. From the Raspberry Creek car park, follow the true right bank of the Matukituki for 15min to a swingbridge; cross to the true left bank that leads on to the Rob Roy stream, which cuts through a small gorge into the beech forest. Gradually the woods give way to alpine vegetation – and the Rob Roy Glacier nosing down into the head of the valley.

Aspiring Hut to the head of the valley
For an excellent day out from Aspiring Hut, explore the headwaters of the Matukituki River to the north. The **Aspiring Hut to Pearl Flat** (4km; 1hr 30min; 100m ascent) stretch follows the river as it weaves in and out of the bush to Pearl Flat. From **Pearl Flat to the head of the valley** (3.5km; 1hr 30min; 250m ascent) the path follows the right bank, crosses a huge avalanche chute off the side of Mount Barff and climbs

beauty over the ice-smoothed broad valleys and creaking glaciers. It was first climbed in 1909 using heavy hemp rope and without the climbing hardware used by today's mountaineers, who still treat the mountain as one of the grails of Kiwi mountaineering ambition.

Travelling along the unsealed section of the Mount Aspiring Road beside the Matukituki River, you don't get to see much of Aspiring, as Mount Avalanche and Avalanche Glacier get in the way. Still, craggy mountains remain tantalizingly present all the way to the **Raspberry Creek**, where a car park and public toilets mark the start of a number of magnificent tramps (see box above) into the heart of the park.

Buses operated by Mount Aspiring Express ($35 one-way; ☏0800/186 754), and Alpine Coachlines (same prices; ☏0800/754 926, ⓦwww.alpinecoachlines. co.nz) run 55km along Mount Aspiring Road to the national park's main trailhead at Raspberry Creek.

high above the river through cottonwood and into open country. Scott Rock Bivvy, marked on some maps, is little more than a sheltering rock 50m east of the river, reached by a bridge.

An alternative, initially following the same route, goes very steeply from **Aspiring Hut to French Ridge Hut** (9km; 4hr; 1000m ascent); the hut (NZAC; 20 bunks; $15) has great mountain views but is only below the snowline from December to March.

Cascade Saddle Route

The most challenging of the local tramps connects the Matukituki Valley to the Rees–Dart Circuit centred on Glenorchy (see p.694), via the arduous **Cascade Saddle Route** (4–5 days one-way), a magnificent alpine crossing with panoramic views of the Dart Glacier and the Barrier Range. However, DOC warn this route should not be attempted in adverse weather and are adamant that parties need to be well prepared, preferably with alpine experience. Long stretches of exposed high country and a finishing point 150km from the start mean that the route is not to be undertaken lightly. Cascade Saddle can only be negotiated without specialized mountaineering equipment for around four months a year (typically Dec–March), and requires full waterproofs, while a tent gives you the option of breaking the longest day by spending a night just beyond the alpine meadows at the saddle.

The first part of the route follows the track from **Raspberry Creek to Aspiring Hut** (9km; 2hr 30min–3hr; 100m ascent – see description opposite). From **Aspiring Hut to Dart Hut** (13km; 8–11hr; 1350m ascent), views of Mount Aspiring improve as you rise above the treeline onto the steep tussock and snow-grass ridge above. The route is marked by orange snow poles, which lead you to a steel pylon (1835m) that marks the top of the ridge, down to Cascade Creek and across it before climbing gently to the meadows around Cascade Saddle (1500m; 4–6hr). Non-campers will have to press on another four or five hours to the Dart Hut, some 500m lower down, along the upper **Dart Valley**. The initial steep descent beside snow-poles is treacherous when wet, but on a warm afternoon enjoys expansive views towards the mouth of the rubble-topped Dart Glacier, where chunks of ice periodically crash into the milky river that surges beneath it. In 1914, the terminus of the glacier crept to within a kilometre of Dart Hut, but it is now retreating an average of 50m a year. After following lateral moraine, rounding bluffs and fording streams, you eventually reach the new **Dart Hut** ($15; 32 bunks), from where it is two days to Glenorchy, following either the Dart or Rees river valleys.

The Central Otago goldfields

Their mining past is one of the main attractions of the **Central Otago goldfields**, a historically rich region east of Queenstown and Wanaka, centred on the middle reaches of the **Clutha River**. This barren, rugged, peculiarly beautiful high country is where, from the 1860s to the end of the century, gold was panned from the streambeds, dredged from the deeper rivers, and eventually mined and blasted from the land. Small-time panners still extract "colour" from the streams, but for the most part the gold has gone, leaving a landscape littered with abandoned mines, perilous shafts and scattered bits of mysterious-looking machinery.

Towns that boomed in the 1860s were mostly moribund by the early twentieth century, but a few struggled on mostly growing **stone fruit**, and later grapes for what has become a burgeoning **wine region** full of unique flavours (see p.719).

Gold from dirt

The classic image of the felt-hatted old-timer panning merrily beside a stream is only part of the story of gold extraction, but it's a true enough depiction of the first couple of years of the Otago gold rush. Initially all a miner needed was a pick and shovel, a pan, and preferably a special wooden box known as a "rocker" for washing the alluvial gravel. As the easily accessible gravel beds were worked out, all manner of ingenious schemes were devised to gain access to fresh paydirt. The most common technique was to divert the river, and some far-fetched schemes were hatched, especially on the Shotover River: steel sheets were driven into the riverbeds with some success, landslides induced to temporarily dam the flow, and a tunnel was bored through a bluff.

When pickings got thinner miners turned to **sluicing guns** that blasted the auriferous gravel free, ready for processing either by traditional hand-panning or its mechanical equivalent, where "riffle plates" caught the fine gravel and carpet-like matting trapped the fine flakes of gold. Eventually the scale of these operations put individual miners out of business and many pressed on to fresh fields.

To get at otherwise inaccessible gravel stock, larger companies began building **gold dredges**, great clanking behemoths anchored to the riverbanks but floating free on the river. Buckets scooped out the river bottom, then the dredge processed the gravel and spat the "tailings" out of the back to pile up along the riversides.

Otago's alluvial gold starts its life underground embedded in quartz reefs, and when economic returns waned, miners sought the mother lode. Reef quartz mining required a considerable investment in machinery and whole towns sprang up to tunnel, hack out the ore and haul it on sledges to the stamper batteries. Here, a series of water-driven (and later steam-powered) hammers would pulverize the rock, which was then passed over copper plates smeared with mercury, and onto gold-catching blankets, before the remains were washed into the berdan – a special kind of cast-iron bowl. Gold was then separated from the mercury, a process subsequently made more efficient by using cyanide.

The reconstructed nineteenth-century boom town of **Cromwell**, 50km east of Queenstown, probably won't delay you long, but is a good jumping-off point for the former mining settlement of **Bendigo** and the wineries of **Bannockburn**. The twin towns of **Clyde** and **Alexandra** have fashioned themselves as bases for the popular Otago Central Rail Trail, which penetrates the wild and open **Maniototo** region to the northeast. The dilapidated former gold towns of **St Bathans**, **Naseby** and **Ranfurly** are also quietly resurgent, while **Macreas Flat** still has a working mine. Back beside the Clutha River, SH8 dives southeast of Alexandra through dull **Roxburgh** and **Lawrence**, where the gold rush started, to the coast.

You need your own vehicle to explore this region, but there is some **public transport**. The Taieri Gorge Railway (see p.590) runs from Dunedin to Middlemarch and is met by Track & Trail buses (☎03/477 5577, ⓦ www.transportplace .co.nz), to Queenstown; Catch-A-Bus (☎03/479 9960) runs (daily except Sat) between Wanaka and Dunedin; and buses frequently scoot along SH8 between Queenstown and Dunedin.

Some history

New Zealand's greatest gold rush kicked off in 1861 when Gabriel Read, an Australian, unearthed flakes of the precious metal beside the Tuapeka River, south of Lawrence. Within weeks Dunedin had all but emptied and thousands were camping out on the **Tuapeka goldfield** around **Gabriels Gully**. In the winter of 1862 Californian prospectors Horatio Hartley and Christopher Reilly teased their first flakes out of the Clutha River, bagging a 40kg haul in three months. This sparked off an even greater gold rush, this time centred on **Cromwell**, which mushroomed. Later in 1862, Thomas Arthur and Harry Redfern struck lucky at what is now Arthur's Point on the Shotover River, sparking a mass exodus for the fresh fields of what soon became known as "the richest river in the world". Miners flooded into **Skippers Canyon** and later **Arrowtown**, the last of the major gold towns. Within a few years returns had dwindled and as traders saw profits diminishing, **Chinese miners** were co-opted to pick over the tailings (discarded bits of rock and gravel) left behind by Europeans.

Though the boom-and-bust cycle was rapid, some form of mining continued for the best part of forty years and the profits fuelled a South Island economy, which dominated New Zealand's exchequer. Dunedin's economy boomed, and the golden bounty funded the majority of the grand civic buildings there.

Many claims were eventually abandoned – not for lack of gold, but because of harsh winters, famine, war, a dip in the gold price, lack of sluicing water, or just disinterest. Although returns are far from spectacular, there are still people eking out a living from gold mining all over the province. There's very little appliance of science: instinct counts for much and fancy mining theories not at all. Bigger capital-intensive companies occasionally gauge the area's potential, and as one mining engineer pithily put it, "there's still a shitload of gold out there".

Cromwell

East of Arrowtown, SH6 runs for 40km through the scenic Kawarau Gorge, past the Gibbston wineries (see p.688) to **CROMWELL**, a dull service town whose gold-mining roots are waterlogged below the shimmering surface of the **Lake Dunstan** reservoir. Formed by the Clyde Dam 20km downstream (see p.719), Lake Dunstan swamped much of Cromwell's historic core. The present-day town centre is uninspiring, but the region is beginning to find its place on the tourist map thanks to its cluster of quality wineries, fruit orchards and old gold diggings.

Soon after Hartley and Reilly's 1862 discovery of **gold** beside the Clutha River, a settlement sprouted at "The Junction" at the fork of the Kawarau and Clutha

▲ Old Cromwell Town

rivers. Local stories tell that it was later renamed when a government survey party dubbed it Cromwell to spite local Irish immigrant workers. Miners low on provisions planted the first fruit trees in the region, little expecting Cromwell to become centre of the Otago **stone fruit** orchard belt.

On arrival, head straight for **Old Cromwell Town** (unrestricted entry), an historic reserve on Melmore Terrace, where Lake Dunstan now laps the increasing number of restored old shopfronts, most of which would now be submerged had they not been dismantled and rebuilt on the water's edge. You can spend a pleasant hour browsing the art, craft and gourmet food shops before retiring for a libation to the *Grain & Seed Café*.

Practicalities

Queenstown- or Wanaka-bound **bus** travellers may well have to change in Cromwell, using the stop on Lode Lane right by The Mall. The **i-SITE visitor centre** was still at 47 The Mall at the time of writing (daily: Nov–March 9am–6pm; April–Oct 9am–5pm; ℡03/445 0212, Ⓦwww.centralotago.co.nz), though it's due to move to a site on SH8B beside the fruit sculpture. It provides the free and comprehensive *Discover Cromwell* and *Walk Cromwell* leaflets and contains a small **museum** packed with gold-mining memorabilia.

Cromwell has a limited range of **accommodation**. On the edge of town, *Cromwell Top 10 Holiday Park*, 1 Alpha St (℡0800/107 275, Ⓦwww.cromwell holidaypark.co.nz), is a large campsite, with camping ($18), cabins (❷), en-suite cabins (❸) and motel units (❹). Out in the backcountry, 4km north of town on SH8, *Quartz Reef Creek*, (℡03/445 0404, Ⓦwww.quartzreefcreek.co.nz; ❺) offers two sunny rooms in a fabulous garden by a modern lakeside house with great views of the water and a welcoming and knowledgeable host – a bargain. **Places to eat** include *Feast*, 26 The Mall (℡03/445 3020; closed Sun & Mon), a quality daytime café that's also one of the few reliable places open in the evening; *Grain & Seed Café*, overlooking Lake Dunstan in Old Cromwell Town, offering good coffee and a range of light meals ($8–12); *The Big Picture* SH6, 4km west of Cromwell (see opposite), a good daytime café in a vineyard that stays open on Friday and Saturday evenings, serving reasonable food and classy wine; and the excellent *Juice Café*, on SH8B close to the bridge over Lake Dunstan, specializing in fresh juices squeezed from its own orchards.

Around Cromwell

Big tour buses disgorge at the half-dozen **fruit stalls** that encircle Cromwell. Pick of the bunch is Jones' Fruit Orchards, 5km west on SH6, which is stacked with fresh and dried fruit, the former blended to make wonderful fruit ice creams, best consumed in the adjacent rose garden. The best **winery** locally is *Wooing Tree*, Shortcut Road, Cromwell (℡03/445 4142, Ⓦwww.wooingtree.co.nz), one of the little family-run wineries where everything is done by hand – and all the more charming for it, offering $5 tastings (daily 10am–5pm) of excellent Pinot Noir, particularly Beetlejuice and some crisp Pinot Gris.

The only other tourist attraction around Cromwell is the **Goldfields Mining Centre** (daily 9am–5.30pm; ℡0800/111 038, Ⓦwww.goldfieldsmining .co.nz), approached by footbridge over the Kawarau, 7km west of Cromwell on SH6. You can walk around by yourself in an hour or so ($20), but it is far more informative to join the fifty-minute guided tour (departs on the hour; $25). Apart from the tour the most engaging part of the centre is the Chinese Village, ironically constructed as a film set in the early 1990s. On the **guided tour** you get to handle some large gold nuggets, see a stamper battery cranked up using a water-powered Pelton wheel and try your hand at extracting a flake or two.

A good **café** provides distraction, as does Goldfields **Jet Boat Rides** ($85/40min; ☎0800/111 038, ⓌWwww.goldfieldsjet.co.nz), who run trips that actually negotiate rapids.

Dedicated ruin hounds can head out to remote clusters of cottage foundations such as those in the Carrick Range or the Nevis Valley (both south of Cromwell), or 15km north of Cromwell towards the Lindis Pass, where you'll find the quartz-mining district of **Bendigo** and its acolytes Logantown and Welshtown.

Bannockburn and the wineries

For goldfield aficionados the best bet is **BANNOCKBURN**, a scattered hamlet 9km southwest of Cromwell. Armed with the *Walk Cromwell* leaflet from the Cromwell i-SITE, make for the **Bannockburn Sluicings** (unrestricted entry), a tortured landscape that was once home to two thousand people, washing away the land to reveal the gold-rich seams below. A two-hour **self-guided trail** dotted with information boards starts 1500m along Felton Road and weaves up to Stewart Town, home to dilapidated mud-brick huts and ageing pear and apricot trees.

All this exploring is thirsty work, and you'll welcome the chance to sample the Bannockburn **wineries**. Since the early 1990s, the warm, north-facing hillsides around the sluicings have been increasingly planted in grape vines, and the vintages from them – primarily Pinot Noir and Pinot Gris – have garnered considerable praise. Eight wineries are open for tasting (call in advance if you're visiting in winter), all listed on the free *Central Otago Wine Map*. For informed guidance, join Queenstown-based Appellation Central Wine Tours (see p.688).

A good starting point is **The Big Picture**, on SH6 4km west of Cromwell (Mon–Thurs & Sun 9am–6pm, Fri & Sat 9am–10pm; $20; ☎03/445 4052, ⓌWwww.bigpicturewine.com) where you sniff all manner of aromas used to describe wine – citrus, clove, leather, truffle, liquorice, etc. You then venture into a small movie theatre where you find six wines waiting to be sampled. The film rolls and you are transported around Central Otago by helicopter, introduced to the landscape – the *terroir* – and lastly the winemakers themselves, who discuss the making and qualities of their wine as you taste it. There's also a good café/restaurant (see opposite).

One of the finer wineries is **Olssens**, 306 Felton Rd (summer daily 10am–5pm; ☎03/445 1716, ⓌWwww.olssens.co.nz), which offers tasting ($4, refundable with purchase). Alternatively give **Carrick**, Cairnmuir Road, Bannockburn (☎03/445 3480, ⓌWwww.carrick.co.nz), a crack for a good lunch in the garden if the weather is sunny, and $5 tastings (daily 11am–5pm) of the more acidic Sav Blanc, Rieslings and tannin-rich Pinot Noir.

Clyde

SH8 cuts southeast from Cromwell through 20km of the bleak and windswept **Cromwell Gorge**, hugging the banks of Lake Dunstan to peaceful **Clyde**. This former gold town contains good places to stay and eat, mostly as a result of the Otago Central Rail Trail (see box, p.721).

Since the mid-1980s, the town has been dominated by the giant grey hydro-electric **Clyde Dam**, 1km north of town on SH8, which generates five percent of New Zealand's power and provides water for irrigation. Initially controversial, the dam is nevertheless considered something of an engineering marvel, with special "slip joints" providing the dam wall with flexibility in case of earthquakes.

The 1864 stone courthouse on Blyth Street now operates as the **Clyde Museum** (Tues–Sun 2–4pm; $3), worth a peek for its intriguing coverage of Clyde's botched Great Gold Robbery of 1870 when one George Rennie tried to make off with £13,000 in bullion and banknotes. The **Briar Herb Factory Complex**, corner of Fraser and Fache streets (Tues–Sun 2–4pm; $3), was established in the 1930s as New Zealand's first herb factory, and thrived by making use of the common thyme, which still grows wild in abundance hereabouts.

Practicalities

Buses stop in Clyde on demand, pulling up on Sunderland Street, which is where you'll find most things. Clyde is the northern terminus for the Otago Central Rail Trail (see box opposite), and Trail Journeys, on the corner of SH8 and Springvale Road (☎0800/724 587, ⓦwww.trailjourneys.co.nz), organize pretty much everything to do with riding the trail and excursions off it: they **rent bikes** (around $35/day) and panniers ($5/day), can pick you up from the far end, and book accommodation along the way.

The town's best **accommodation** option is ⚑ *Dunstan House*, 29 Sunderland St (☎03/449 2295, ⓦwww.dunstanhouse.co.nz; ❺/❻), a comfy B&B in a former stagecoach waystop, with bags of character. Rooms are imaginatively decorated (half en suite and some with claw-foot bath), some opening out onto a wraparound veranda on the first floor, where miners once rode their horses, after a glass or two. There's plenty of bike storage, and a piano in the lounge. *Clyde Holiday and Sporting Complex*, Whitby Street (☎03/449 2713, ⓔcrrc@ihug .co.nz; camping $17, cabins ❶), is a campsite surrounding a sports ground, with fully self-contained cabins and several on-site caravans, plus a pool.

The *Post Office Café*, on the corner of Blyth and Matau streets, housed in an 1865 former post office, serves the best **food** in town in the evenings and has a **bar** serving delicious Post Office Dark ale. Otherwise, *The Bank Café*, 31 Sunderland St, is a good and central café, offering great coffee and a friendly smile, and is sometimes open in the evening. Out of town, 4km south at 68 Boulton Rd, *The Packing Shed* (☎03/449 2757; lunches Thurs–Sat) is a semi-formal, rural café in a large garden serving good daytime food; to get there, head across the river bridge opposite the *Post Office Café* and follow Earnscleugh Road.

Alexandra and around

A large white clockface – visible from as far away as 5km – looms out of the cliff backing **ALEXANDRA** (affectionately known as Alex), 10km southeast of Clyde. Alexandra sprang up during the 1862 gold rush, and flourished for four years before turning into a quiet prosperous service town for the fruit-growers of Central Otago.

A huge water wheel marks Alexandra's main point of interest, the fascinating **Alexandra Museum and Art Gallery** (which also contains a cinema), in Pioneer Park, on Centennial Avenue (daily 9am–5pm; donation), which houses displays on the region's natural and social history, the heartrending mystery of James Horn, whose deathbed letter will bring a lump to your throat, and coverage of the sorry tale of the rabbits, introduced into the area in 1909, who did what rabbits do – so well that they became a menace throughout the South Island. To combat the problem, the town holds an **Easter Bunny Shoot** every year, and hunters from all over New Zealand congregate on Good Friday for the slaughter.

In the early years, the only way across the Manuherikia River was by punt, but in 1879 the town built the **Shaky Bridge**, a suspension **footbridge**, which connects with the *Shaky Bridge Café* (see p.722) and a **lookout point** (2km one-way; 40min) high above the town on Tucker Hill, affording great views of the whole area.

Activities

Its abundance of treeless hills makes Alex a good base for **mountain biking**. Head along to Altitude Adventures, 88 Centennial Ave (ⓣ03/448 8917, ⓦwww .altitudeadventures.co.nz), who specialize in guided single-track tours; half-day local trips from $60, more for longer excursions. They're also well set up for getting you on the Otago Central Rail Trail (see box below) and rent bikes from around $30 a day.

Practicalities

Buses all stop outside the **i-SITE visitor centre**, 21 Centennial Ave in Pioneer Park (daily: Oct–March 9am–6pm; April–Sept 9am–5pm ⓣ03/448 9515). Good **accommodation** is hard to find. Cheapest option is *Marj's Place*, 5 Theyers St (ⓣ03/448 7098, ⓦwww.marjsplace.co.nz; dorms $25, hostel rooms ❷, rooms ❸), a hostel cum homestay in two houses in a quiet street 1km from the centre. The sleek *117 Avenue Motels*, 117 Centennial Ave (ⓣ0800/758 899, ⓦwww.avenue-motel.co.nz; units ❹, suites ❺), has tastefully decorated units and suites (some with spa bath and Xbox), while the swanky choice is *Rocky Range*, SH8, 2km southeast of town (ⓣ03/448 6150, ⓦwww.rockyrange.co.nz; ❾), a French provincial-style lodge perched on a hill amid schist outcrops with stunning panoramic views. Rooms (from $350 a night) are sumptuous and there's a great spa pool amid the rocks. Meals are $65 (including wine).

Otago Central Rail Trail

One of the finest ways to explore the Maniototo is on the **Otago Central Rail Trail** (ⓦwww.otagocentralrailtrail.co.nz), a largely flat 150km route from Clyde to Middlemarch that passes through all the main towns except for St Bathans and Naseby. Open to walkers, cyclists and horseriders, it follows the trackbed of the former Otago Central Branch railway line and includes modified rail bridges and viaducts (several spanning over 100m), beautiful valleys and long agricultural plains. At Middlemarch it meets the Taieri Gorge Railway (see p.590), though unless you arrive on Friday or Sunday, you'll have to cycle 18km along the road to Pukerangi for the daily train.

Passenger trains ran through the Maniototo until 1990, but it wasn't until February 2000 that the trail opened, galvanizing a dying region. Most people **cycle**, and all sorts of accommodation has sprung up to cater to bikers' needs. Pubs and cafés located where the trail crosses roads aren't shy to advertise the opportunity to take a break.

The comprehensive and widely available *Otago Central Rail Trail* leaflet (free) outlines the route, with further context available in Gerald Cunningham's *Guide to the Otago Central Rail Trail* (Reed Outdoors; $25). The route is generally hard-packed earth and gravel, making it possible to ride most bikes, though fat tyres make for a more comfortable journey. The trail takes most people three days, but if you're just out to pick the choicest bits (or are walking and don't fancy the whole thing) aim for a couple of 10km stretches, both with tunnels, viaducts and interesting rock formations: Lauder–Auripo in the northern section, and Daisybank–Hyde in the east. A torch is handy (though not essential) for the tunnels.

Bikes and customized packages with **accommodation** can be organized through various agencies. The best bets are Cycle Surgery in Dunedin (see p.609), *Blind Billy's Holiday Camp* in Middlemarch (see p.725), Trail Journeys in Clyde (see p.720) and Altitude Adventures in Alexandra (see above).

A couple of commercial **websites**, ⓦwww.otagorailtrail.co.nz and ⓦwww.railtrail .co.nz, offer practical information.

Of the **places to eat**, the licensed *Courthouse Café*, 8 Centennial Ave, serves delicious home-baked food at reasonable prices, including snacks and substantial lunches; in summer it stays open until 9pm (Fri & Sat). For sophistication wander across the Shaky Bridge to *Shaky Bridge Café*, Graveyard Gully Road (T03/448 5111; closed Mon), and try the wines, coffee, muffins, contemporary brunches or sumptuous dinners. *Monteith's Brewery Bar*, 26 Centennial Ave, is a lively **bar** that serves hearty meals, but most people come here to drink on the sunny terrace.

The Maniototo

The most interesting route to the east coast from Alexandra is through the **Maniototo**, a generic name for the flat high country shared by three shallow valleys – the Manuherikia River, the Ida Burn and the Taieri River – and the low, craggy ranges that separate them. Despite easy road access, the Maniototo is a windswept, ambient world apart, largely ignored until the **Otago Central Rail Trail** (see box, p.721) caught on.

Predictably, Europeans first came to the area in search of gold. They found it near **Naseby**, but returns swiftly declined and farming on the plains became more rewarding. This was especially true when **railway** developers looking for the easiest route from Dunedin to Alexandra chose a way up the Taieri Gorge and across the Maniototo. In 1898, the line arrived in **Ranfurly**, which soon took over from Naseby as the area's main administrative centre.

Former gold-mining communities such as **St Bathans** and **Naseby** are worth a brief visit for their calm seclusion and subtle reminders of how greed transforms the land. In between you'll see dozens of small cottages, many abandoned – a testimony to the harsh life in these parts.

The main public **transport** is the Catch-a-Bus service (T03/479 9960; daily except Sat) between Dunedin and Wanaka, which leaves Dunedin at 8am (Mon–Thurs), arriving in Wanaka at noon and starting the return journey at 1pm. Friday's service leaves Dunedin at 4pm (arrive Wanaka 8pm) and Sunday's departure is 10am (arrive Wanaka 2pm). Visitors planning to use the Taieri Gorge Railway (see p.590) may appreciate the Track & Trail buses (T03/477 5577, Wwww.transportplace.co.nz) that meet the train and go to Queenstown.

Omakau and Ophir

Heading northeast from Alexandra, you're immediately in the high-country plain, passing through inconsequential hamlets until you reach the twin settlements of **Omakau** (where the *Muddy Creek Café* does good coffee) and **Ophir**, 2km to the south. The latter was the original gold town hereabouts and still has its imposing, still-operational 1886 **Post & Telegraph Office** (Mon–Fri 9am–noon) and the nice little **suspension bridge** across the Manuherikia River, 1km further south.

Grahame Sydney

Many New Zealanders only know the Maniototo through the works of Dunedin-born realist painter **Grahame Sydney** (Wwww.grahamesydney.com), who spends much of his time in the region. His broad, big-sky landscapes of goods sheds amid parched fields and letterboxes at lonely crossroads are universally accessible, and instantly recognizable to anyone visiting the region.

Prints and postcards of his work are found throughout the Maniototo and beyond, and originals hang in most of the country's major galleries. At first glance many of the works are unemotional renditions, but reflection reveals great poignancy. As he says, "I'm the long stare, not the quick glimpse".

St Bathans

The first place with genuine appeal is the minute former gold town of **ST BATHANS**, 80km north of Alexandra and accessed 17km along St Bathans Loop Road from Becks. St Bathans boomed in 1863, but when the gold ran out in the 1930s everything went with it. These days it's virtually a ghost town, with just a handful of residents and an attractive straggle of ancient buildings along the single road. Some of the locals manage the atmospheric 1882 *Vulcan Hotel* (T03/447 3629; ⦿), where local farmers and visitors prop up the wooden bar, which serves St Bathans Gold, a single malt once bottled on the premises. With its garden bar and good café/restaurant, the pub makes a great place to stay; room 1 is reputed to be haunted.

The prettiest thing about the area is the striking **Blue Lake** right beside the town, where mineral-rich water has flooded a crater left by the merciless sluicing of Kildare Hill, once 120m high but now entirely washed away. A short track leads from the *Vulcan* to a vantage point over the azure lake, now used for waterskiing, swimming and picnics.

Naseby

The small settlement of **NASEBY**, 25km east of St Bathans and 9km off SH85, clings to the Maniototo some 600m above sea level. At its 4000-strong peak in 1865, Naseby was the largest gold-mining town hereabouts, but today numbers have dropped to around 200 huddled in a collection of small houses (many of them originally built of sun-dried mud brick by miners), with a shop, a garage, a couple of pubs, a café and a campsite.

The town's story is told through two tiny museums, both at the junction of Earne and Leven streets. The **Maniototo Early Settlers Museum** (Dec–May Tues–Sun 1.30–3.30pm) is packed with black-and-white photos of past residents and also contains a small collection of items left by Chinese miners, while the **Jubilee Museum** (daily 10am–5pm; $1 token available from the general store across the street) houses the remains of an old watchmaker's shop together with displays on the local gold rush of the 1860s and 1870s. Naseby's **visitor centre** (daily 11am–2pm; T03/444 9961) is in the former post office on Derwent Street. The best places to **stay** are the *Old Doctors Residence*, 58 Derwent St (T03/444 977, W www.olddoctorsresidence.co.nz; ⦿), a fabulous B&B where the customers get treated like prodigal children, the accommodation is luxurious and the food sumptuous; and the delightful *Naseby Trail Lodge*, on the corner of Derwent and Oughter streets (T03/444 8374; ⦿), a recently built eco-lodge with a fine-dining restaurant open to non-residents. Alternatively the *Ancient Briton* and the nearby *Royal Hotel* both offer hearty **meals**, while the *Black Forest Café* on Derwent Street does reasonable snacks and coffee.

In summer, visitors are either cooling off at the shaded **swimming dam**, ten minutes' walk up Swimming Dam Road, or exploring the surrounding **Naseby Forest**, which is one of New Zealand's best destinations for single-track **mountain biking**. You can rent bikes and obtain a trail map from Kilas Bike Shop, 20 Derwent St ($25/half-day, $50/full-day; T03/444 9088). The best of the local **walks** is the **One Tree Hill Track** (1600m; 1hr return), which starts on Brooms Street in town and snakes uphill along the eastern side of Hogburn Gully, past dramatic honey-coloured cliffs entirely carved by water – leaflet available from the visitor centre.

Naseby is New Zealand's home of **curling** (a sort of lawn bowls on ice). This traditionally took place outdoors in winter but you can now try your hand at the indoor Naseby Curling International (daily 9am–5pm; $15/hr). Instruction is usually available.

Dansey's Pass

The gravel Kyeburn Diggings Road runs east out of Naseby over **Dansey's Pass** (about 40km from Naseby), to Duntroon to the north. It is a narrow, barren and beautiful route that's reasonably well maintained but sometimes closed in summer and often shut in winter: check in Naseby before setting out. Old gold workings are visible from the roadside, where water-jets from sluices have distorted the schist and tussock landscape, leaving rock dramatically exposed. Along the way you pass the charming *Dansey's Pass Coach Inn*, 16km east of Naseby. Built from local schist stone in 1862 (the stonemason was reputedly paid a pint of beer for each stone laid), it's the only relic of the once two-thousand-strong gold-rush community and offers good beer and affordable lunches.

Ranfurly

Back on SH85 and 5km southeast of the Naseby turn-off lies **RANFURLY**, the largest settlement on the Maniototo. It's a compact place enjoying a resurgence thanks to the popularity of the rail trail, and a rather desperate attempt to brand itself as New Zealand's **Rural Art Deco** centre (ⓦ www.ruralartdeco .co.nz). In truth, there's only a handful of noteworthy buildings, but Ranfurly goes all out to make the best of what it has, particularly during the Rural Art Deco Weekend at the end of February. The **Art Deco Gallery**, 1 Charlemont St East (Tues–Sun: Nov–April 1–3.30pm; May–Oct 11am–4pm; $2 donation), contains all manner of Deco furnishings and houseware, but the star is the building itself, the 1948 Centennial Milk Bar. Opposite the visitor centre, the *Ranfurly Lion Hotel* and the Ranfurly Auto Repairs shop both exhibit a few Art Deco features, but elsewhere much is achieved with imaginative paint jobs and period signage.

In summer, anyone with a 4WD or high-clearance vehicle can set out from Ranfurly to explore part of the magnificent **Old Dunstan Road** (closed June–Sept), the original route to the Central Otago goldfields across the Rock and Pillar and Lammerlaw ranges. Ask for directions and current conditions.

Practicalities

The **visitor centre** is housed in the former train station on Charlemont Street East (Oct–May daily 9am–6pm; June–Sept daily 9am–5pm; ⓣ 03/444 1005, ⓦ www.maniototo.co.nz), which has a free audiovisual show on the region and pictorial displays tracing the history of the town and the Otago Central Railway. Ranfurly's range of **accommodation** is limited: central are *Old Po Backpackers*, 11 Pery St (ⓣ 03/444 9588, ⓦ www.oldpobackpackers.co.nz; dorms $23, rooms ❷), with bargain accommodation and good facilities, and *Ranfurly Holiday Park*, Reade Street (ⓣ 0800/726387, ⓦ www.ranfurlyholidaypark.co.nz; camping $14, cabins ❶, motel units ❸). *Komako*, 3km south of town at 634 Waipiata-Naseby Rd (ⓣ 03/444 9324, ⓔ grant.heather@xtra.co.nz; ❼), offers three gorgeous cabins right by the Rail Trail, surrounded by great views (plus blooming peonies Oct–Dec). There's not much **eating** either – two places on Charlemont Street East are the daytime *E-Central Café*, at no. 14, which does bikers' breakfasts, decent coffee and a range of light meals, and *Ranfurly Lion Hotel*, at no. 10, a good hotel restaurant in Art Deco surroundings.

Macraes Gold Mine, Middlemarch and south to Dunedin

At Kyeburn, 15km east of Ranfurly, the slow route to Dunedin (SH87) branches south off SH85 and twists through the eastern Maniototo, a barren yet scenic landscape squeezed between the towering Rock and Pillar Range and the

Taieri River. Fifty kilometres south of Kyeburn you'll reach the tiny community of **MIDDLEMARCH**, the Friday- and Sunday-only terminus of the **Taieri Gorge Railway**, which makes a delightful two-hour run between here and Dunedin (see p.590 for details). Anyone planning to tackle the Otago Central Rail Trail from east to west should definitely consider starting by riding the railway either to Middlemarch or to **Pukerangi** (the weekday turnaround point), 18km to the south.

For useful visitor **information** on Middlemarch, check out ⓦwww.middle march.co.nz. Most cyclists **stay** at *Blind Billy's Holiday Camp*, Mold Street (ⓣ03/464 3355, ⓦwww.middlemarch-motels.co.nz; camping $11, dorms $22, on-site vans ❷, cabins ❷, s/c cabins ❸, motel units ❹), a campsite with cooking facilities in a converted railway carriage and a wide range of cabins and motel units. Alternatively, try the private house offered by *Quench*, the town's new café/ bar at 29 Snow Ave (ⓣ03/464 3077; ❻), which is quiet, well appointed and two minutes from the bar. Otherwise **eating** is limited – *Quench* does well-priced, well-presented food but otherwise it's a desert.

The most renowned of Otago's operating gold mines, the huge opencast **Macraes Gold Mine**, lies on windswept hills between Ranfurly and Palmerston and can be visited on a two-hour **tour** (daily 10am & 2pm; $25; reservations essential on ⓣ0800/465 386, ⓦwww.oceanagoldtours.com), which also takes in a historic reserve and a fully operational stamper battery.

Roxburgh and Lawrence

The fastest route from Alexandra to the coast is **SH8**, which follows the meandering course of the Clutha River, passing through rugged hill country between the Old Man and Lammerlaw ranges to the east, and the Knobby Blue Mountain range to the west. Along the way are **Roxburgh** and **Lawrence**.

Roxburgh

Almost 30km south of Alexandra, a **viewpoint** overlooks the large, concrete **Roxburgh Dam** and the shimmering turquoise of Lake Roxburgh, which backs up for over 30km. Eight kilometres south of the dam, the bland former gold town of **ROXBURGH** sits hemmed in by vast orchards which yield bountiful crops of peaches, apricots, apples, raspberries and strawberries, all harvested by an annual influx of seasonal pickers. The season's surplus is sold from a phalanx of roadside stalls from early December through to May.

If you decide to stop, head for the one-size-fits-all ♪ *Lake Roxburgh Lodge*, SH8, 8km north (ⓣ03/446 8220, ⓦwww.lakeroxburghlodge.co.nz; ❹), which offers a warm welcome, a relaxed atmosphere, wonderful en-suite motel-style rooms and an excellent licensed **restaurant**.

Lawrence

From Roxburgh, SH8 runs 32km south to **Raes Junction** (where SH90 spurs off southwest to Tapanui and Gore), and continues 26km to **LAWRENCE**, Otago's original gold town. It's hard to believe that this sleepy farming town, its population barely nudging 550, was once the scene of frenetic activity, as twelve thousand gold-seekers scrambled to try their luck in the gold-rich Gabriel's Gully. This short-lived boom (it was over in barely a year) is recalled in a smattering of Victorian buildings, hastily constructed in a variety of materials and styles. A few have now been converted into chichi **galleries** that provide some reason to linger.

The combined **visitor centre** and **Goldfields Museum** on Ross Place/SH8 (Mon–Fri 9.30am–4.30pm, Sat & Sun 10am–4pm; ⓣ03/485 9222, ⓦwww .lawrence.co.nz) brings something of those heady days to life through imaginative displays. From here, a 3.5-km drive along Gabriel's Gully Road passes the **Pick and Shovel Monument** commemorating the pioneer miners, en route to **Gabriel's Gully Goldfield Park**, where a series of plaques explaining the old workings should take you an hour or so to explore. A climb up the steep rise of **Jacob's Ladder** gives a good view of the gully, long since filled with tailings that reach nearly 20m in depth. It is possible to visit Gabriel's Gully as part of a loop walk from town (8.5km loop; 2hr 30min) returning along a ridge.

After something to **eat** from *Jimmy's Pies*, 143 Scotland St, the original Jimmy's Pie Shop, world famous in New Zeland, where the now ubiquitous pies were first baked, you'll probably want to press on.

Travel details

Buses

The following are direct scheduled bus services in summer. In winter services are cut back considerably.

Alexandra to: Dunedin (3 daily; 3hr); Lawrence (3 daily; 1hr 15min); Queenstown (3 daily; 1hr 30min); Ranfurly (daily except Sat; 1hr).

Arrowtown to: Queenstown (hourly).

Cromwell to: Alexandra (3 daily; 30min); Dunedin (3 daily; 3hr 40min); Lawrence (3 daily; 2hr); Queenstown (7–9 daily; 1hr); Wanaka (7–9 daily; 45–60min).

Glenorchy to: Queenstown (2–4 daily; 1hr).

Lawrence to: Alexandra (3 daily; 1hr 15min); Cromwell (3 daily; 2hr); Dunedin (3 daily; 1hr 20min).

Queenstown to: Alexandra (3 daily; 1hr 30min); Aoraki Mount Cook (2 daily; 4hr); Arrowtown (hourly); Christchurch (6 daily; 7hr–9hr); Cromwell (7–9 daily; 1hr); Dunedin (3 daily; 4–5hr); Franz Josef Glacier (2 daily; 7–8hr); Glenorchy (2–4 daily; 1hr); Greymouth (1 daily; 10hr); Kingston (3–4 daily; 1hr); Milford Sound (1 daily; 5hr 40min); Te Anau (3 daily; 2hr 15min); Wanaka (7–9 daily; 1hr 45min).

Wanaka to: Christchurch (6 daily; 7hr–9hr); Cromwell (8–9 daily; 45min–1hr); Dunedin (3 daily; 4hr–4hr 30min); Franz Josef Glacier (2 daily; 6–7hr); Queenstown (7–9 daily; 1hr 45min); Ranfurly (daily except Sat; 3hr).

Trains

Middlemarch to: Dunedin (summer Fri & Sun only 1 daily; 2hr 30min)

Pukerangi to: Dunedin (1 daily, 2hr).

Flights

Queenstown to: Auckland (5 daily; 1hr 45min); Christchurch (6 daily; 50min).

Wanaka to: Christchurch (1 daily; 1hr).

Fiordland

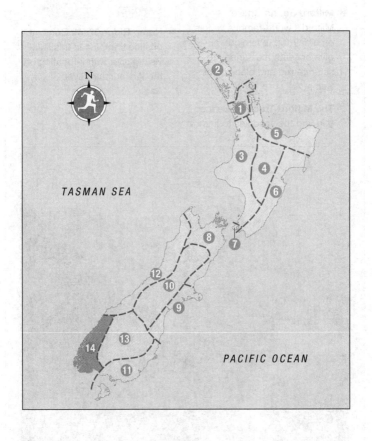

CHAPTER 14 **Highlights**

❋ **Te Anau** Watch the
inspirational film *Ata Whenua:
Shadowlands*, shot from a
helicopter above the region's
landscapes, then book a heli-
flight to see for yourself.
See p.734

❋ **Milford Sound** Cruise
Milford's world-famous waters
on a day-trip, overnight, or
dive beneath the surface to
see rare red and black coral.
See p.742

❋ **The Milford Track** Brave the
rain and the sandflies to find

out why this beautiful four-day
tramp is iconic. See p.745

❋ **Doubtful Sound** Experience
scenic grandeur and superb
wildlife at sea level from a
kayak, without the tourist
bustle of Milford Sound.
See p.752

❋ **Hump Ridge Track** Combine
pristine tramping in this little-
visited area with jetboating on
the Wairaurahiri River.
See p.756

▲ The Milford Track

Fiordland

F or all New Zealand's grandeur, no other region matches the concentration of stupendous landscapes found in its southwestern corner, **Fiordland**, a fact acknowledged by the United Nations, who gathered almost the entire environ – along with Mount Aspiring National Park, parts of Westland and the Aoraki Mount Cook area – into the **Te Wahipounamu World Heritage Area**.

The **Fiordland National Park**, incorporates almost the entire region and most of the area covered in this chapter, stretching from Martins Bay, once the site of New Zealand's remotest settlement, to the southern forests of Waitutu and Preservation Inlet, where early gold prospectors set up a couple of short-lived towns. Its 12,500 square kilometres embrace a raw, heroic landscape, with two of New Zealand's deepest lakes, its highest rainfall, fifteen hairline fiords and some of the world's rarest birds.

Maori legend tells how the **fiords** were formed at the hands of the great god Tu-to-Rakiwhanoa. Scientists point to complex geology, which evolved over the last 500 million years. When thick layers of sea-bed sediment were compressed and heated deep within the earth's crust, crystalline granite, gneiss and schist were formed. As the land and sea levels rose and fell, layers of softer sandstone and limestone were overlaid; during glacial periods, great ice sheets deepened the valleys and flattened their bases to create the classic U shape which was invaded by the sea.

After experiencing the challenging ambience created by Fiordland's copious rainfall and vicious **sandflies** (*namu*), you'll appreciate why there is little evidence of permanent Maori settlement, though they spent summers hunting here and passed through in search of greenstone (*pounamu*). **Cook** was equally suspicious of Fiordland when, in 1770, he sailed up the coast on his first voyage to New Zealand: anchorages were hard to find; the glowering sky put him off entering Dusky Sound; slight, shifting winds discouraged entry into what he dubbed Doubtful Harbour; and he missed Milford Sound altogether.

Paradoxically for a region that's now the preserve of hardy trampers and anglers, the southern fiords region was once the best charted in the country. Cook returned in 1773, after four months battling the southern oceans, and spent five weeks in Dusky Sound, and his midshipman, George Vancouver, returned in 1791, bloodthirsty sealers and whalers hot on his heels. Over the mountains, **Europeans** seized, or paid a pittance for, land on the eastern shores of Lake Te Anau and Manapouri though it offered meagre grazing, while **explorers** headed for the interior, conferring their names on the passes, waterfalls and valleys they came across – Donald Sutherland lent his name to New Zealand's highest waterfall and Quintin McKinnon scaled the Mackinnon Pass (but failed to persuade cartographers to spell his name correctly).

One persistent feature of Fiordland is the **rain**. Milford Sound is particularly favoured, being deluged with up to 7m of rainfall a year – the second highest in the world. Fortunately the area's settlements are in a rain shadow and receive less than half the precipitation of the coast. Despite its frequent soakings, **Milford Sound** sees the greatest concentration of traveller activity – in fact, the Sound is particularly beautiful when it's raining, with ribbons of water plunging from hanging valleys directly into the fiords where colonies of red and black coral grow

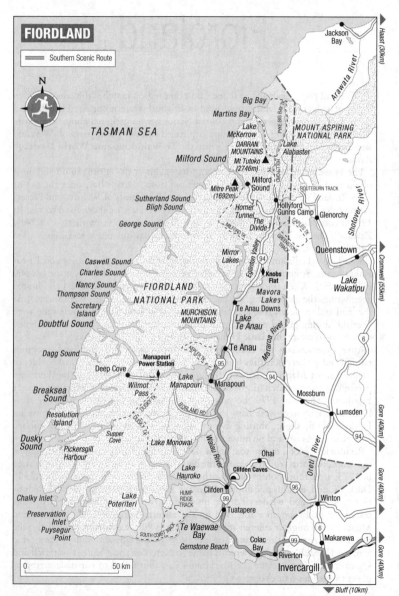

FIORDLAND

Southern Scenic Route

N

TASMAN SEA

Jackson Bay

Arawata River

Big Bay

Martins Bay

Lake McKerrow

DARRAN MOUNTAINS

Lake Alabaster

MOUNT ASPIRING NATIONAL PARK

PYKE BIG BAY TK

HOLLYFORD TK

Milford Sound

Mt Tutoko (2746m)

Milford Sound

Mitre Peak (1692m)

Sutherland Sound
Bligh Sound

George Sound

Homer Tunnel

The Divide

MILFORD TK

ROUTEBURN TRACK

Hollyford
Gunns Camp

CAPLES TK

Glenorchy

GREENSTONE TRACK

Shotover River

Eglinton Valley

Mirror Lakes

94

Knobs Flat

Queenstown

Caswell Sound
Charles Sound
Nancy Sound
Thompson Sound

Secretary Island

Doubtful Sound

FIORDLAND NATIONAL PARK

MURCHISON MOUNTAINS

Mavora Lakes

Te Anau Downs

Lake Te Anau

Maraora River

Lake Wakatipu

6

Dagg Sound

Deep Cove

KEPLER TK

Manapouri Power Station

Wilmot Pass

Te Anau

95

94

Mossburn

Lumsden

94

Breaksea Sound

Resolution Island

Dusky Sound

Pickersgill Harbour

Supper Cove

DUSKY TK

Lake Manapouri

Manapouri

BORLAND RD

Lake Monowai

Waiau River

Ohai

Oreti River

Gore (40km)

Gore (40km)

Chalky Inlet

Preservation Inlet
Puysegur Point

Lake Poteriteri

HUMP RIDGE TRACK

Lake Hauroko

Clifden Caves

Clifden

99

Tuatapere

Winton

96

6

Makarewa

Gore (40km)

SOUTH COAST RD

Te Waewae Bay

Gemstone Beach

Colac Bay

Riverton

Invercargill

99

1

0 _____ 50 km

Haast (30km)

Cromwell (55km)

Bluff (10km)

Almost all **buses** in Fiordland ply the corridor from Queenstown through Te Anau to Milford Sound: most are tour buses, stopping at scenic spots and regaling passengers with a jocular commentary, others are scheduled services that disgorge trampers at the **trailheads**. Unless you are very pushed for time don't be persuaded to visit Milford from Queenstown, as it is an arduous journey that will lessen the Milford Sound experience – much better to stay overnight in Milford, if you can, or visit from Te Anau. The main bus routes are Queenstown via Te Anau to Milford Sound, and Te Anau to Invercargill via Manapouri, Tuatapere and Riverton. If you are interested in tramping then the specialist buses and some tour services pick up and drop off at The Divide. Elsewhere, services are skeletal. The only **flights** you are likely to take are scenic jaunts returning from Milford Sound to Te Anau or Queenstown.

14

FIORDLAND | Te Anau and around

and dolphins, fur seals and Fiordland crested penguins cavort. Many visitors on a flying visit from Queenstown see little else, but a greater sense of remoteness is gained by driving along the achingly scenic **Milford Road** between the sound and the lakeside town of **Te Anau**. Better still, trudge the **Milford Track**, widely promoted as the "finest walk in the world", though others in the region – particularly the **Hollyford Track** and the **Kepler Track** – shouldn't be overlooked. A second lakeside town, **Manapouri**, is the springboard for trips to the West Arm hydroelectric power station, **Doubtful Sound** and the isolated fiords to the south. From Manapouri, the Southern Scenic Route winds through the western quarter of Southland via minor towns along the southwestern coast.

Te Anau and around

Ringed by snowcapped peaks, the gateway town to Fiordland, **TE ANAU** (pronounced Teh AHN-ow), stretches along the shores of its eponymous lake, one of New Zealand's grandest and deepest. To the west, the lake's watery fingers claw deep into bush-cloaked mountains, so remote that their most celebrated inhabitant, the takahe, was thought extinct for half a century. Civilization of sorts can be found on the lake's eastern side, home to a population of around 1500. The main way-station on the route to Milford Sound, Te Anau is an ideal base and recuperation spot for the numerous tramps, including several of the most famous and worthwhile in the country. Top of most people's list is the **Milford Track**, which starts across the lake, as does the **Kepler Track**. To the north, the Milford Road passes The Divide, the western end of the Routeburn, Greenstone and Caples tracks (see p.700); beyond that is the Hollyford Valley and a tramp to the Tasman Sea, while at the southeastern end of the national park lies the privately run Hump Ridge Track.

Arrival, information and transport

Buses drop off around town or stop on the town's main shopping and restaurant street, known, imaginatively, as Town Centre. The best source of general information is the **i-SITE visitor centre**, at the junction of Town Centre and Lake Front Drive (daily 8.30am–5.30pm; ☎03/249 8900, ✉fiordland-isite@realjourneys .co.nz), run in conjunction with the booking office of Real Journeys. For all things track and field hit DOC's, **Fiordland National Park Visitor Centre**, 500m south along Lake Front Drive (daily: late Oct to late April 8.30am–5pm, rest of year

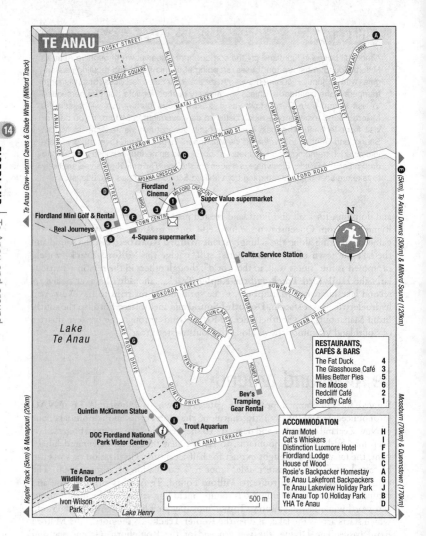

8.30am–4.30pm, ⓔfiordlandvc@doc.govt.nz), which contains a **Great Walks Booking Desk** (☎03/249 8514, ⓔgreatwalksbooking@doc.govt.nz). Also check out its summer-visitor programme of talks and full-day, conservation-themed trips in the forests (book in advance; prices begin at about $10 but depend greatly on length, transport and who is giving them).

The **post office** and **banks** with ATMs are along Town Centre. While away on the tracks, trampers can usually **store gear** (for a small fee) at their accommodation, though it helps if you're staying there on your return. Tramping **gear rental** is available from several places, including Bev's Tramping Gear Hire, 16 Homer St (☎03/249 7389, ⓦwww.bevs-hire.co.nz). Individual items are charged by the day (pack $10, sleeping bag $10 etc). The Great Walks Package Special ($130) contains everything you need – including food for four days – except boots.

Local transport

Getting around Te Anau is no problem: everywhere is walkable, and there's a plethora of transport to the trailheads. **Bikes** can be rented from backpackers and Fiordland Mini Golf, Quadricycles & Bike Hire, 7 Mokonui St ($20/half-day, $25/day; ℡03/249 7211). Scenic Shuttle (℡0800/277 483) runs to Manapouri in the morning, and Tracknet (℡0800/483 2628, ⊛www.tracknet.net) operates buses to Milford Sound, Queenstown and the Kepler and Routeburn trailheads. Taking an organized trip is generally cheaper, but you can rent a **car** from Rent-a-dent ($89/day; ℡03/249 8576), at the Caltex station on Luxmore Drive.

Accommodation

Motels dominate the length of Lake Front Drive and Quintin Drive, a block back. At most accommodation **rates** drop dramatically between June and August, and may be negotiable in the shoulder seasons (mid-April to May & Sept). Commercial **camping** is central, but many people head around 25km north to a couple of lakeside DOC campsites ($5) near Te Anau Downs.

Hotels and motels

Arran Motel 64 Quintin Drive ℡0800/666 911, ⊛www.arranmotel.co.nz. Attractive en-suite rooms, some with cooking facilities. Rates can vary, so check ahead to see what's on offer. ❹

Distinction Luxmore Hotel Town Centre ℡0800/589 667, ⊛www.luxmorehotel.co.nz. The posh tour-bus favourite is a large central hotel with standard and (newer) superior doubles and twins with en suites, as well as a variety of eating options. Standard ❻, deluxe ❽

Fiordland Lodge 472 Te Anau–Milford Hwy, 5km north ℡03/249 7832, ⊛www.fiord landlodge.co.nz. Swanky accommodation, set on a hill with great lake views. In addition to spacious lodge suites there are some luxurious "cabins" sleeping up to five. All rooms are done

on a dinner, bed and breakfast basis and start at $680 for two. ❾

B&Bs and homestays

Cat's Whiskers 2 Lake Front Drive ℡03/249 8112, ⊛www.catswhiskers.co.nz. A house facing the lake with welcoming hosts and four en-suite rooms: one with a bath, and all with TV, wi-fi and good, full cooked breakfast. Courtesy drop-offs around town. ❻

House of Wood 44 Moana Crescent ℡03/249 8404, ⊛www.houseofwood.co.nz. Designed like an alpine chalet, with timber en-suite rooms. Guests share the hosts' cosy lounge. Only a 2min walk from the town centre, or borrow a mountain bike to get around. Filling breakfasts are included and dinners can be organized ($45 with wine). ❺

Tu-to-Rakiwhanoa and Te Namu

Fiordland came into being when the great god **Tu-to-Rakiwhanoa** hewed the rough gashes of the southern fiords around Preservation Inlet and Dusky Sound, leaving Resolution and Secretary islands where his feet stood. His technique improved further north, where he cut the more sharply defined Nancy Sound, Caswell Sound and Milford Sound (Piopiotahi), the peak of Tu's achievement.

After creating this spectacular landscape, he was visited by Te-Hine-nui-to-po, goddess of death, who feared the vista created by Tu was so wonderful that people would want to live here for ever. To remind humans of their mortality, she freed *namu* (**sandflies**), at Te Namu-a-Te-Hine-nui-te-po (Sandfly Point), at the end of the Milford Track. And the pesky bugs have certainly had the desired effect. In 1773, when Cook entered Dusky Sound, he was already familiar with the sandfly:

The most mischievous animal here is the small black sandfly which are exceedingly numerous and are so troublesome that they exceed everything of the kind I ever met with ... The almost continual rain may be reckoned another inconvenience attending this Bay.

Hostels and campsites

Rosie's Backpacker Homestay 23 Tom Plato Drive ☏ 03/249 8431, ✉ backpack @paradise.net.nz. Small, relaxed and welcoming backpackers in a family home with lake and mountain views, along with musical instruments for guests to play. Book early as it fills up fast. Closed June & July. Dorms **$2**

Te Anau Lakefront Backpackers 48 Lake Front Drive ☏ 03/249 7713, ⓦ www.teanaubackpackers .co.nz. Ageing but friendly with small dorms, mostly with their own bathroom and kitchen. They're well set up for trampers, with free gear storage and a hot tub for when you get back. Dorms from $29, rooms **$2**

Te Anau Lakeview Holiday Park 1 Manapouri Rd, 1km south ☏ 0800/483 2628, ⓦ www.teanau .info. Well-equipped complex with spacious tent and campervan areas, modern facilities including a sauna, and a wide range of cabins and units. Camping $15.50, dorms $27, singles $35, backpacker rooms & cabins **$2**, kitchen cabin **$3**, en-suite cabins **$3**, tourist flats **$4**, motel units **$5**

Te Anau Top 10 Holiday Park 128 Te Anau Terrace ☏ 0800/249 746, ⓦ www.teanautop10 .co.nz. Excellent on-site accommodation and abundant facilities including underfloor-heated bathrooms, wi-fi, jacuzzi and kids' playground, all tightly packed into a central campsite. Book ahead. Camping $44 per site, cabins **$2**, en-suite units **$4**, s/c units **$5**, motels **$6**

YHA Te Anau 29 Mokonui St ☏ 03/249 7847, ✉ yha.teanau@yha.co.nz. Modern, comfortable, two-storey hostel close to the town centre with large dorms, double rooms (including en suites), free gear storage, helpful staff, separate TV lounge and BBQ area. There's even a self-catering family cottage with double and twin rooms rented separately or together. Dorms $28, rooms **$3**, en suite **$4**, cottage **$4**

Sights and activities

There's little in Te Anau to distract you from simply admiring the scenery across the lake or taking gentle strolls along its shore. Ten minutes' walk south, a statue of Milford Track explorer Quintin McKinnon heralds DOC's Fiordland National Park visitors centre, which contains fascinating displays on the natural history of Fiordland National Park.

Nearby is DOC's **Te Anau Wildlife Centre** (unrestricted entry; $1 donation), where you can amble through the park-like setting and catch glimpses of injured or captive-bred native birds such as kakariki (parakeets), whio (blue duck), kea, kaka (indigenous parrots) and the celebrated takahe (see box opposite).

Te Anau's main paying attraction is Real Journeys' **Te Anau Glowworm Caves** (daily: Nov–March 2pm, 5.45pm, 7pm & 8.15pm; April–Sept 2pm, 7pm and some additional tours; around 2hr 15min; $63). The town's full Maori name, Te Ana-au, means "cave with a current of swirling water" and it was a search for the town's namesake which led to their rediscovery in 1948. It has been slightly spruced up and although the tour feels a little processed it remains old-fashioned in spirit and is worth the ferry ride. Key elements are a short underground boat ride through glittering glowworms and a couple of noisy waterfalls. Boats leave from the jetty adjacent to the visitor centre and head to the western side of Lake Te Anau, where cave guides lead you underground in small groups, spending thirty minutes in a 200m length of the Aurora cave system which stretches under the Murchison Mountains.

Alternatively try a one-hour **jetboat ride** past *Lord of the Rings* locations on the placid Waiau River with Luxmore Jet ($95; ☏ 0800/253 826, ⓦ www.luxmorejet .co.nz), or **quad biking** with High Ride Four Wheeler Adventures (☏ 03/249 8591, ⓦ www.highride.co.nz), who offer a three-hour ride ($145, including the shuttle from Te Anau), taking in the high country and stunning views of lakes Manapouri and Te Anau. No prior experience is necessary. High Ride also offers **horseriding** ($80), taking about three hours, including the shuttle from Te Anau.

Don't leave town without visiting the 🎬 **Fiordland Cinema**, The Lane (☏ 03/249 8812, ⓦ www.fiordlandcinema.co.nz), which presents the 32-minute *Ata Whenua: Shadowlands* (5–10 screenings daily 10am–9pm; $10). Filmed mostly from a helicopter, it shows Fiordland at its majestic best with wonderful cinematography, an original soundtrack and no ponderous voiceover. You'll want to go straight out for a heli-flight (bookable in the foyer). Screenings are interspersed with a selection of mainstream movies, the chairs are big and comfy and you can take espresso, beer or a wine in with you.

Day-walks from Te Anau

Kicking around Te Anau before a big tramp provides a good opportunity to explore some of the local **short walks**. Those not doing the Milford Track might entertain a one-day guided walk at its southern end, though walks along the Milford Road are more rewarding (see box, p.741).

DOC visitor centre to Control Gates (4km one-way; 50min; flat). Easy lakeside walk past the Te Anau Wildlife Centre to the point where the Waiau River leaves Lake Te Anau for Lake Manapouri. The Control Gates mark the start of the Kepler Track (see p.736).

Control Gates to Brod Bay (5km one-way; 1hr 30min; gently undulating). The first section of the Kepler Track goes to Dock Bay (30min) where there's good swimming, and on through mountain and silver beech forest, past some limestone bluffs, to the campsite at Brod Bay.

Control Gates to Rainbow Reach (9.5km one-way; 2hr 30min–3hr 30min; mostly flat).

Following the course of the Waiau River through red and mountain beech. By using the Tracknet buses to the Control Gates and back from Rainbow Reach (see "Kepler Track" account) you can make this walk over 5–7hr, perhaps going 3km beyond Rainbow Reach to a wetland viewing platform.

Milford Track Real Journeys (℡0800/656 501) and Trips 'n' Tramps (℡03/249 7081) jointly run easy day-walks (Nov to mid-April daily 9.15am; $190) beside the Clinton River at the start of the Milford Track. Trips involve a bus to Te Anau Downs, boat to Glade Wharf, 5–6hr hiking and relaxing including lunch at Clinton Hut and return.

The takahe

For half a century the flightless blue-green **takahe** (*Notornis mantelli*) was thought extinct. These plump, turkey-like birds – close relatives of the pukeko – were once common throughout New Zealand, but after the arrival of Maori their territory became restricted to the southern extremities of the South Island and by the time Europeans came, only a few were spotted, by early settlers in Fiordland. No sightings were recorded after 1898; the few trampers and ornithologists who claimed to have seen its tracks or heard its call in remote Fiordland valleys were dismissed as cranks.

One keen birder, **Geoffrey Orbell**, pieced together the sketchy evidence and concentrated his search on the 500 square kilometres of the **Murchison Mountains**, a virtual island surrounded on three sides by the western arms of Lake Te Anau and on the fourth by the Main Divide. In 1948, he was rewarded with the first takahe sighting in fifty years. However, the few remaining birds seemed doomed: deer were chomping their way through the grasses on which the takahe relied. Culling averted the immediate crisis and, despite periodic setbacks from harsh winters, management programmes have brought takahe numbers to 227.

Meanwhile, studies at the **Burwood Bush** rearing facility (closed to the public), in the Red Tussock Conservation Area east of Te Anau, have shown that takahe often lay three eggs but seldom manage to raise more than one chick. DOC officers now enter the Murchison Mountains each November to manipulate the **egg quota** so that each pair has only one viable egg to hatch. Any "surplus" eggs are removed to Burwood Bush, where rearing techniques pioneered here are employed to raise takahe for release back into the wild. Taped takahe noises encourage the chicks to hatch; then, to prevent them imprinting on their carers, the chicks are fed using **hand puppets** designed to look like adult takahe.

Afraid of having all their eggs in one basket, DOC has established several populations on predator-free sanctuary islands – Maud Island in the Marlborough Sounds, Mana Island and Kapiti Island northwest of Wellington, and Tiritiri Matangi in Auckland's Hauraki Gulf – where the birds are breeding well.

Lake cruises and kayaking

A highlight of visiting Te Anau is **getting on the lake**. If you're going tramping, this is accomplished en route to the start of the Kepler or Milford tracks (see below & p.745). Operators who provide trailhead transport also offer a number of scenic trips.

Cruise Te Anau ☎03/249 8005, ⊛www .cruiseteanau.co.nz. Scenic cruises aboard a restored kauri motor launch (summer daily 10am, 1pm & 5pm; 2hr 30min; $80) plus overnight cruises including dinner and breakfast (4pm–9.30am; $250). They also offer summer track transport to Brod Bay at the start of the

Kepler ($25), and off-season transport to the start and end of the Milford (April–Nov only; $170). **Fiordland Wilderness Experiences** ☎0800/200 434, ⊛www.fiordlandseakayak.co.nz. Guided paddles on Lake Te Anau and Manapouri (no solos; $135/day) as well as an array of trips in the sounds (see p.745).

Flights

The best operators in terms of value, reliability and experience are listed here; each has its own speciality but all will guarantee a jaw-dropping spectacle – provided they take off, of course.

Air Fiordland ☎03/249 7505, ⊛www.air fiordland.com. One of the best deals offered by this company is a flight over the Milford Track to Milford Sound, a cruise and a bus back (7hr 30min; $460). **Southern Lakes Helicopters** Lake Front Drive ☎0508/249 7167, ⊛www.southernlakes helicopters.co.nz. Helicopter flights from a waterside helipad start at $190 for 25min and range up to a couple of hours including flights to Milford, Doubtful and Dusky sounds with landings in a narrow canyon or on snow high in the hills.

They also do flight/walk/cruise combinations and offer drop-offs for the tracks. **Wings & Water** Lake Front Drive ☎03/249 7405, ⊛www.wingsandwater.co.nz. Seaplane flights are ideal for an aerial view of southern Fiordland. Local loops (10min; $95), Kepler Track overflights (20min; $210), Doubtful Sound overflights (40min; $295) are among the options. One worthwhile combo involves jetboating down the Waiau River to Lake Manapouri and then flying back to Te Anau via the hidden lakes (1hr; $225).

Eating and drinking

Eating options are improving in Te Anau, while **self-caterers** have two well-stocked supermarkets to explore. Given that most visitors are embarking on or coming off tramps, **drinking** is low-key, and entertainment is mostly BYO.

The Fat Duck 124 Town Centre. Swish bar/restaurant with passable, if pricey, breakfasts, brunches, good dinners and desserts and a cocktail-bar feel. Closed Mon & Tues in winter.
The Glass House 1 Milford Crescent ☎03/249 4305. Eat in full view of passers-by at this new, fully glass-fronted fine-dining café with excellent food, from fulsome breakfasts, some with home-made hollandaise, to a slim dinner menu of delicious ingredients (mains around $30–35). Expect it to get better and better. Open daily 7am–10pm.
Miles Better Pies Corner of Milford Rd & Town Centre. Good coffee, better pies, to eat in or take to the lakefront. Open daily 6am–3pm.

The Moose 84 Lakefront Drive. Rambunctious locals' haunt with cheap Kiwi grub and drinks deals, plus live music summer weekends in the evening.
Redcliff Café 12 Mokonui St ☎03/249 7431. A cosy timber cottage housing a semi-formal fine-dining restaurant serving modernized Kiwi classics (mains around $35–40) with a garden bar, occasional live bands and a well-stocked front-of-house bar. Daily from 5pm.
Sandfly Café 9 The Lane. Laidback daytime café specializing in home-baked slices, various bagels and cakes. Closed Mon in winter.

The Kepler Track

The **Kepler Track** (45–70km; 3–4 days), finished in 1988, was intended to take the load off the Milford and Routeburn tracks and its success has, ironically, made it equally popular. Tracing a wide loop through the Kepler Mountains on the western side of Lake Te Anau, the track has one full day of exposed subalpine ridge walking, some lovely virgin beech forest and has the advantage of being accessible on foot from Te Anau. Typically walked anticlockwise, getting most of the climbing out of the way early, the track ranges from as little as 45km – if you use boats and buses – to 70km for the full Te Anau–Te Anau walk.

Well graded and maintained throughout, to the extent that you barely need to look where you are treading, it is still strenuous, because of its length and the long haul up to Luxmore Hut. Some sections can be closed after snowfall but DOC's *Kepler Track Independent Tramping* leaflet (free) is adequate for the most part, though for detailed information consult the 1:60,000 *Kepler Track Trackmap* ($15).

Access and accommodation

The Kepler Track is one of New Zealand's Great Walks and through the summer season (late Oct to late April) its three main **huts** ($45/night) – Luxmore (55 bunks), Iris Burn (50 bunks) and Moturau (40 bunks) – have a warden, gas rings and flush toilets. During this time it's essential to book in advance, either online at Ⓦ www.doc.govt.nz or through the Great Walks booking desks in Te Anau, Glenorchy or Queenstown. In winter, these huts lose their warden and gas rings, go back to pit toilets, and revert to serviced hut status ($15). Trampers are discouraged from using the simple and very small Shallow Bay Hut, just off the track beside Lake Manapouri.

Camping ($15) is permitted at only two places, Brod Bay and Iris Burn, making for one very short and two very long days – assuming you walk anticlockwise – getting the bulk of the climbing over on the first day.

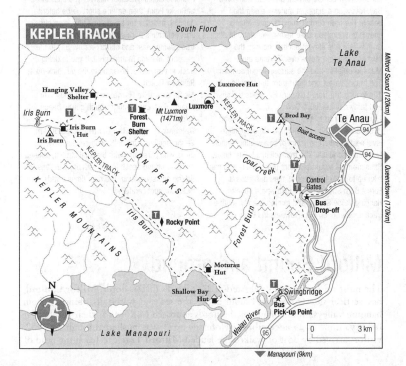

Trailhead transport

The Kepler Track starts at the Control Gates, 5km southwest of Te Anau. It is a pleasant enough walk around the southern end of the lake, but most people get the Tracknet **bus** (Oct–April only; $6; ℡0800/483 262, ⓦwww.tracknet.net), which picks up at accommodation around town at around 8.30am and 9.30am and drops off at the Control Gates. On the return leg, most trampers stop 11km short of the Control Gates at the swingbridge over the Waiau's Rainbow Reach. Tracknet pick up at Rainbow Reach at 10am, 3pm and 5pm and charge $10 back to Te Anau.

You can skip another 5km of lakeside walking (and make a relaxed start) by **boating** across Lake Te Anau from Te Anau wharf to Brod Bay with Kepler Water Taxi (8.30am & 9.30am or by arrangement; around $20; ℡03/249 8364).

The route

If you're walking from Te Anau, head south along Lake Front Drive, then right, following the lakeshore and take the first right to the Control Gates.

Control Gates to Brod Bay (5.6km; 1hr–1hr 30min; flat). The track follows the lakeshore around Dock Bay and over Coal Creek, passing through predominantly beech and kamahi forests but with a fine stand of tree ferns. Brod Bay has good swimming off a sandy beach and makes a lovely place to camp.

Brod Bay to Luxmore Hut (8.2km; 3–4hr; 880m ascent). Non-campers must press on from Brod Bay, following a signpost midway along the beach. The path climbs fairly steeply; after a couple of hours you sidle below limestone bluffs, from where it is almost another hour to the bushline and fine views over Te Anau and Manapouri lakes and the surrounding mountains. The hut is almost one hour from the bushline. A 10min side trip from Luxmore Hut visits the short and fairly dull Luxmore Cave.

Luxmore Hut to Iris Burn Hut (14.6km; 5–6hr; 300m ascent, 900m descent). An exposed, high-level section where any hint of bad weather should be treated seriously. The track climbs to just below the summit of Mount Luxmore (from where you can hike up to the 1471m peak), then descends to Forest Burn Shelter before following a ridge to Hanging Valley Shelter and turning sharply south to trace another open ridge towards Iris Burn –

reached by zigzagging west into the forested Hanging Valley then following the stream to the hut and campsite in a large tussock clearing. It's worth doing the easy walk to the Iris Burn waterfall (40min return).

Iris Burn Hut to Moturau Hut (16.2km; 4–6hr; 300m descent). The track from the Iris Burn Hut descends steadily through beech forest and riverside clearings. About halfway you pass toilets at Rocky Point, then enter a short gorge before hugging the river for several magical kilometres. Just before Iris Burn spills into Lake Manapouri, the track swings east and skirts Shallow Bay to the pleasant lakeside Moturau Hut. If you're doing the track in three days, press on to the bus pick-up at Rainbow Reach.

Moturau Hut to Rainbow Reach (6km; 1hr 30min; flat). Easy walk through gentle beech forest.

Rainbow Reach to the Control Gates (9.5km; 2–3hr; negligible ascent). Another easy walk for those who persevere with the final stretch, through mature lowland beech forest with opportunities for fishing and swimming. The river flows swiftly, so pick your spot carefully.

Milford Sound and around

The most northerly and celebrated of Fiordland's fifteen fiords, **Milford Sound**, has vertical sides towering 1200m above the sea and waterfalls plunging from hanging valleys. While many of the fiords approach Milford for their spectacular **beauty**, none is as **accessible**. Before the road was pushed through in 1952, visitors arrived by boat or walked the lauded **Milford Track** to reach the head of the fiord, but the opening of the Homer Tunnel paved the way for the phalanxes of buses that disgorge tourists onto cruises. The tiny airport hardly rests as planes buzz in and out, while the crowds – all day in the summer and around the middle of the day in spring and winter – can certainly detract from the grandeur. But don't let that put you off: even torrential rain adds to the atmosphere of this magical place, as ethereal mists descend, periodically lifting to reveal waterfalls at their thunderous best.

Like the other sounds, Milford is a drowned glacial valley rather than a river valley, which, technically, makes it a fiord. Maori know it as **Piopiotahi** ("the single thrush"), and attribute its creation to the god Tu-to-Rakiwhanoa, who was called away before he could carve a route into the interior, leaving high rock walls. These precipitous routes are now known as the Homer and Mackinnon passes, probably first used by Maori who came to collect *pounamu*. The first European known to have sailed into Piopiotahi was sealer John Grono who, in 1823, named the fiord Milford Haven after his home port in south Wales. The main river flowing into the Welsh Milford was the Cleddau, so naturally the river at the head of the fiord is so named.

The earliest settler was Scot **Donald Sutherland**, who arrived with his dog, John O'Groat, in 1877; he promptly set a series of thatched huts beside the freshwater basin of what he called the "City of Milford", funding his explorations by guiding small numbers of visitors who had heard tell of the scenic wonder.

The predations of today's influx of visitors and the operation of a small fishing fleet have necessitated strategies to preserve the **fragile ecosystem**. Like all fiords, Milford Sound has an entrance sill at its mouth, in this case only 70m below the surface – by comparison, the deepest point is almost 450m. This effectively cuts off much of the natural recirculation of water and hinders the mix of sea water and the vast quantities of fresh water that pour into the fiord. The less-dense tannin-stained fresh surface layer (up to 10m deep) builds up, further diminishing the penetration of light, which is already reduced by the all-day shadow cast by the fiord walls. The result is a relatively barren inter-tidal zone that protects a narrow – but wonderfully rich and extremely fragile – band of light-shy red and black **corals**; these normally grow only at much greater depths, but thrive here in the dark conditions. Unfortunately, Milford's fishing fleet use crayfish pots, which tend to shear off anything that grows on the fiord's walls. A marine reserve has been set up along the northeastern shore, where all such activity is prohibited, but really this is far too small and conservation groups are campaigning for its extension.

The road to Milford Sound

The 120km **Milford Road** (SH94), from Te Anau to Milford Sound, is one of the world's finest, though this hasn't stopped folk, mostly Queenstowners, from hatching outlandish plans to circumvent it (including a proposed tunnel from Glenorchy to The Divide, all in an effort to reduce the length of the journey from Queenstown). As things stand, this two-hour drive can easily take a day if you grab every photo opportunity, and longer if you explore some of the excellent hiking trails outlined on the *Milford Road* leaflet, available free from the i-SITE in Te Anau. Anywhere else the initial drive beside Lake Te Anau would be considered gorgeous, but it is nothing compared to the Eglinton Valley, where the road penetrates steeper into bush-clad mountains, winding through a subalpine wonderland to the bare rock walls of the seemingly impassable head of the Hollyford River. The Homer Tunnel cuts through to the steep Cleddau Valley before the road descends to Milford Sound.

Milford Road safety

The subalpine section of the Milford Road is one of the world's most **avalanche-prone**. Since the last death on the road, in 1984, a sophisticated monitoring system has been put in place and explosives are dropped from helicopters to loosen dangerous accumulations of snow while the road is closed. This mostly happens between May and November, when motorists are required to carry chains (available from service stations in Te Anau for around $30); you'll be stopped at the small kiosk five minutes' drive out of Te Anau to make sure that you have them and know how to fit them – and sent back to Te Anau if you don't. It's not uncommon for people to be stuck in Milford if the road does close. Always check weather forecasts with the DOC office in Te Anau before you set out; weather reports are also regularly updated on ⓦwww.milfordroad.co.nz.

Whatever the season, drivers should bear in mind that there is heavy bus traffic; Milford-bound from around 11am to noon and Te Anau-bound between 3 and 5pm. Apart from the store in the Hollyford Valley, 8km off your route, there is nowhere to buy food until you reach Milford, so go prepared. There is a pump in Milford, but it often runs out of petrol, so fill up in Te Anau before you leave.

Maori parties long used this route on their way to seek *pounamu* at Anita Bay on Milford Sound but no road existed until two hundred unemployment-relief workers with shovels and wheelbarrows were put on the job in 1929. The greatest challenge was to puncture the headwall of the Hollyford Valley: work on the 1200m **Homer Tunnel** began in 1935, but was badly planned from the start. Working at a one-in-ten downhill gradient, the builders soon hit water and were forced to pump out continuously; a pilot tunnel allowing the water to drain westwards was finished in 1948. After a concerted push, the road was completed in 1953 and officially inaugurated the following year, opening Milford Sound to road traffic for the first time. Each April, uninhibited locals compete in a race through the tunnel naked (apart from running shoes).

Campers will want to spend a night in one of the dozen simple DOC **campsites** ($5) along the way, most with giardia-free stream water, long-drop toilets and fireplaces. Two are between Te Anau and Te Anau Downs, and the remaining ten along the next 50km, either on the grassy flats of the Eglinton Valley or the bush nearby. Mackay Creek, Totara Creek and East Branch Eglinton, all around 50km north of Te Anau, are particularly good.

Driving to Milford Sound

Heading north from Te Anau, there's little reason to stop in the first 30km to the harbour at **Te Anau Downs**, where boats leave for the start of the Milford Track. The road then cuts east away from the lake, before veering north into the **Eglinton Valley** through occasional stands of silver, red and mountain beech, interspersed with open flats of red tussock grass. Surprisingly in a national park, these plains are grazed, an anomaly resulting from pre-national park leases. Particularly picturesque mountains hem the valley and, when the weather is calm, are reflected in the roadside **Mirror Lakes**, 56km north of Te Anau. There's excellent self-catering **accommodation** in the valley at *Knobs Flat* (☏03/249 9122, ⓦwww.knobsflat.co.nz; studio ❹), a bush bath and no TV or cell-phone reception. Half-day **guided walks** ($70) take you through the valley. Around 20km north, the *Cascade* campsite marks the start of the **Lake Gunn Nature Walk**.

As you get nearer to the head of the valley, the road steepens to **The Divide**, 84km north of Te Anau, at 532m the lowest east–west crossing of the Southern

Alps. This is the start/finish of the Greenstone, Caples and Routeburn tracks, the last of which can be followed to Key Summit (see below). The car park has toilets and a walkers' shelter with a notice board advertising the times of passing buses, although it is better if hikers prearrange a pick-up.

Pressing on a couple of kilometres towards Milford, you descend into the valley of the Hollyford River, best seen from a popular viewpoint just before the Hollyford Road shoots off north. The Milford Road continues west towards the Hollyford's source, the huge glacial cirque of the Gertrude Valley.

A kilometre further on, the entrance to the **Homer Tunnel** is home to many curious **kea** (do not to feed them, as it could kill them). Despite recent improvements the tunnel remains rough-hewn, steep, narrow and dark. During peak periods in the summer traffic lights dictate one-way traffic (expect a wait of up to 15min), but for the rest of the time you'll need to look out for oncoming vehicles.

The tunnel emerges at the top of a series of switchbacks down to the Cleddau River. Almost 10km on from the tunnel all buses stop at **The Chasm**, while their passengers stroll (15min return) to the near-vertical rapids where the Cleddau has scoured out a deep, narrow channel. Tantalizing glimpses through the foliage reveal sculpted rocks hollowed out by churning water or eroded into freestanding ribs that resemble flying buttresses. From here it is another 8km to Milford Sound.

The Hollyford Valley

The Milford Road drops down from The Divide into the **Hollyford Valley**, which runs 80km from its headwaters in the Darran Mountains north to the Tasman Sea at Martins Bay. The 16km gravel Lower Hollyford Road provides access to the Hollyford Track and the Lake Marian walk, plus a couple of other diversions.

The only habitation is 8km along the valley road at Hollyford, *Gunns Camp* (no phone, ⓔgunnscamp@ruralinzone.net; camping & vans $30/person bunks $20, twin & double cabins ①), a huddle of simple 1930s cabins which served as married families' quarters for the long-suffering road-builders, and the subject of an ongoing sympathetic revamp. Cabins generally have a double room and four-berth bunk room, linked by a kitchen/lounge with a wood/coal range. Trampers' supplies (along with postcards, books, maps, some rare bowenite greenstone pendants and souvenirs) are sold in the **shop** (daily 8.30am–8pm). There's also a **museum** (shop hours; $1, free to guests) containing photos, pioneer artefacts and

---

Hikes from the Milford Road

Old-timers grumble about tourists wasting their time, effort and money on prize tramps like the Milford and the Routeburn when so many excellent, easily accessible walks are on the Milford Road. There are challenging hikes off this road but we've stuck with commonly tackled **day-walks**. For tougher stuff, go to the DOC office in Te Anau.

Lake Gunn Nature Walk (3km loop; 45min; negligible ascent). Wheelchair-accessible nature walk with interpretive panels. Starts 74km north of Te Anau.

The Divide to Key Summit (5km return; 2–3hr; 400m ascent). Panoramic views, when it's not raining, over three valley systems are the reward for this tramp along the western portion of the Routeburn Track. Starts 84km north of Te Anau.

Lake Marian (5km return; 2–3hr; 400m ascent). Picturesque ascent to a scenic alpine lake, passing pretty cataracts (30–40min return), where boardwalks are cantilevered from the rock. Starts 1km along Lower Hollyford Road, 88km north of Te Anau.

some interesting paraphernalia relating to the one-time community at Martins Bay, the devastating floods that periodically afflict the region and the building of the Milford Road and the Homer Tunnel.

The road runs 8km beyond the camp to the Road End – the beginning of the Hollyford Track. It is also the start of a shorter walk to **Humboldt Falls** (20–30min return), a three-step cascade tumbling 200m.

Milford Sound

To appreciate the best of Milford Sound see it from the water. The smattering of buildings that comprise the **settlement** do not stand comparison, but do look out over the edge of a basin where the Cleddau and Arthur rivers surge into the fiord – a scene dominated by the iconic, triangular, glaciated pinnacle of **Mitre Peak** (1694m), named for its resemblance to a bishop's mitre.

Arrival and getting around

If you choose to **walk** to Milford Sound, along the Milford Track (see p.745), you will see the best of the place, though **drivers** and **cyclists** do get the freedom to stop, sightsee and camp along the dramatic road from Te Anau (see p.739). Failing either, you can fly, hop on a bus, or do a combination of both, often with a cruise on the fiord thrown in (see box, p.746 for a rundown).

Milford Sound, the settlement, is a small airstrip, fishing harbour, out-sized cruise terminal, post office, pub and café. Although they're only a few hundred metres apart, a free **shuttle bus** connects them all.

▲ Milford Sound

Accommodation and eating and drinking

The prominent *Mitre Peak Lodge* is only open to Milford Track guided walkers. The only other **accommodation**, overnight cruises on the sound aside, is 犬 *Milford Sound Lodge* (☎03/249 8071, ⓦwww.milfordlodge.com; camping $15–18, dorms $28, rooms ❷, units ❼) a well-run backpackers with spacious dorms, twins and doubles (with shared bathrooms), a cramped kitchen, bar, comfortable lounge and pricey shop. Out back are specially designed, plush new double units with a full glass wall looking out on the river. It is almost 2km back from the wharf (linked by a courtesy bus).

The settlement's sole **place to eat** is the *Blue Duck Café & Bar* (café daily 8.30am–4.40pm, bar 11am–late; ☎03/249 7982), where you can enjoy sandwiches and pies, or full meals (most under $35) while watching the weather sweeping along the fiord. There's also an **information desk**, owned by one of the cruise lines.

Around Milford

You're pretty much surrounded by water here, and should waste little time getting out on it. However, if tales of his pioneering days have inspired you, pay homage at **Donald Sutherland's grave**, hidden among the staff accommodation behind the pub. Alternatively take a five-minute stroll up to a **lookout** behind *Mitre Peak Lodge*, or the **Piopiotahi Foreshore Walk**, which leads from the car park to the settlement along the edge of the fiord (5–10min; flat).

About a third of the way along the fiord is the wonderful, recently revamped **Milford Deep Underwater Observatory** (☎03/249 9442, ⓦwww.milford deep.co.nz) accessible from several of the major cruise lines (about a 20min stop; $29 more than the equivalent non-observatory cruise). The observatory consists of a floating platform moored to a sheer rock wall in Harrison Cove, part of the marine reserve. A spiral staircase takes you 9m down through the relatively lifeless freshwater surface layer to a circular gallery where windows look out into the briny heart of the fiord. Sharks and seals occasionally swim by, but most of the action happens immediately outside in window-box "gardens", specially grown from rare locally gathered **coral** and plant species. Lights pick out colourful fish, tubeworms, sea fans, huge starfish and rare red and black coral. Unless you're an experienced diver this is the only chance you'll get to see these corals, which elsewhere in the world grow only at depths greater than 40m.

Day cruises

The dramatic view from the shore of Milford Sound pales beside the spectacle from the water, with waterfalls plunging hundreds of metres into the fiord. It's difficult to grasp the heroic scale of the place, unless your visit coincides with that of one of the great cruise liners – even these formidable vessels are totally dwarfed.

The majority of cruises explore the full 22km of Milford Sound, all calling at waterfalls, a seal colony and overhanging rock faces; at **Fairy Falls**, boats nose up to the base of the fall, while suitably attired passengers are encouraged to edge out onto the bowsprit and collect an earful of water. Longer trips sometimes anchor in **Anita Bay** (Te-Wahi-Takiwai, "the place of Takiwai"), a former greenstone-gathering place at the fiord's mouth, but still sheltered from the wrath of the Tasman Sea.

The simplest option is one of the twenty-odd two- to four-hour **day cruises** (best booked a few days in advance in summer) either on one of the large, fast and comfortable boats or one of the more intimate small boats. Trips cost from $55 to

The Hollyford Track

Long, but mostly flat, the **Hollyford Track** (56 km; 3–4 days one-way; DOC leaflet) is open year-round, though it's muddy after rain. Running from the end of the Hollyford Valley road to Martins Bay, the track follows Fiordland's longest valley but suffers from being essentially a one-way tramp, requiring four days' backtracking – unless you're flash enough to fly out from the airstrip at Martins Bay or tough enough to continue around a long, difficult and remote loop known as the **Pyke–Big Bay Route** (9–10 days total; consult DOC's *Pyke–Big Bay Route* leaflet for details). The joy of the Hollyford is not in the sense of achievement that comes from scaling alpine passes, but in the appreciation of the dramatic mountain scenery and the kahikatea, rimu and matai **bush** underlayed by wineberry, fuchsia and fern. At Martins Bay, Long Reef has a resident **fur seal** colony, and from September to December you might spot rare Fiordland crested **penguins** (tawaki) nesting among the scrub and rocks.

Trampers who hate carrying a big pack and prefer comfortable lodgings and having hearty meals cooked for them should opt for a **guided walk** with Hollyford Track (⊕0800/832 226, ⊛www.hollyfordtrack.com): small groups are led by knowledgeable guides, and nights are spent at the relatively luxurious *Martins Bay Lodge* and the *Pyke River Lodge* (3 days plus fly-out $1655).

Accommodation and access

The six DOC **huts** (mostly 12 bunks; $15) are equipped with bunks, mattresses, water and toilets and do not need to be booked, though hut tickets or an annual hut pass should be bought in advance.

Buses from Te Anau to Milford drop off at Marian Corner, where the Hollyford and Milford roads part, and 16km from Road End, but it is best to go with Tracknet (⊕0800/483 262) who run right to Road End (Nov–April Mon, Wed & Fri; $47).

Hollyford Track cooperates with local air companies to offer **flights** (which must be

around $85 depending on the duration and size of the boat. The operators are Cruize Milford (⊕0800/500 121, ⊛www.cruizemilford.co.nz), Mitre Peak Cruises (⊕03/249 8110, ⊛www.mitrepeak.com), Real Journeys (⊕0800/656 501, ⊛www.realjourneys.co.nz) and Red Boat or Southern Discoveries Cruises (⊕03/441 1137, ⊛www.redboats.co.nz).

Overnight cruises

Only Real Journeys run **overnight trips** on Milford Sound. Three of the vessels used for day cruises are equipped with beds, and each offers a slightly different experience, though all involve a leisurely cruise around, a chance to go kayaking, good meals and a night spent at anchor in some sheltered cove. The backpacker-oriented, 61-berth *Milford Wanderer* (Nov–March daily 4.30pm–9.30am, $230; April–Oct same hours, $161) is a motor-driven replica of a sailing scow, complete with cosmetic sails. On-board accommodation is cramped four-bunk rooms equipped with sheets, duvets and towels, but a hearty three-course meal (drinks extra) helps iron out the kinks.

The more luxurious sixty-berth *Milford Mariner* (Nov–March daily 4.30pm–9.15am, $470; Oct & April daily 4.30pm–9.15am, $329, May & Sept daily 4.30am–10.15am, $329) has comfortable private, twin-share cabins with en suites and serves a higher class of meal.

Kayaking and scuba-diving

The elemental nature of Milford Sound can best be appreciated by **kayaking**. If you'd rather go below surface (and are PADI- or SSI-certified), join a fascinating

pre-booked) between Milford Sound and Martins Bay. Most people choose to fly out from Martins Bay ($580/plane for 1–4 people and packs).

Finally, you can avoid most of the long day's walk beside the attractive but samey Lake McKerrow with Hollyford Track's **jetboat service** between Martins Bay and the head of Lake McKerrow (Nov–April; around $110).

The route

Road End to Hidden Falls Hut (9km; 2–3hr; negligible ascent). The track follows a disused section of road which crumbles into track and then some riverbank before arriving at Hidden Falls Hut.

Hidden Falls Hut to Alabaster Hut (10km; 3–4hr; 100m ascent). Keen walkers may want to push on from Hidden Falls Hut through ribbonwood and beech to Little Homer Saddle and past Little Homer Falls.

Alabaster Hut to Demon Trail Hut (15km; 3–4hr; negligible ascent). Leaving Alabaster Hut, you pass a side track to the nicely sited McKerrow Island Hut, before continuing beside Lake Alabaster to Demon Trail Hut.

Demon Trail Hut to Hokuri Hut (10km; 5–6hr; 100m ascent). Probably the toughest day on the walk, following the shore of Lake McKerrow on rough ground with some tricky stream crossings, to the twelve-bunk Hokuri Hut.

Hokuri Hut to Martins Bay Hut (13km; 4–5hr; negligible ascent). Passing the scant remains of Jamestown, a cattle-ranching settlement that prospered in the 1870s, and the small airstrip served by Hollyford Track's flights, you'll stumble across some of the dozen dwellings that comprise Martins Bay; whitebaiters and hunters stay here occasionally, although there are no permanent residents. Continuing parallel to Martins Bay, and occasionally glimpsing the Hollyford River through wind-shorn trees, you reach the Martins Bay Hut.

scuba-diving trip. The tannin-stained freshwater surface layer darkens the water quickly, making the flora and fauna think it's deeper than it really is. Consequently, black coral (white but with a black skeleton), brachiopods (ancient shellfish), purple and white nudribranchs, scarlet wrasse and telescope fish are all visible at modest depths.

Fiordland Wilderness Experiences
℡ 0800/200 434, ⊚ www.fiordlandseakayak
.co.nz. Ecologically oriented 4–5hr guided trips
($125 from Milford).

🚶 **Rosco's Milford Sound Sea Kayaks**
℡ 03/249 8500, ⊚ www.roscomilford
kayaks.co.nz. Extensive range of Milford Sound-
based kayaking trips with expert if characterful

guides, including a wonderful 7am Morning Glory
(7hr; $169), a 3.30pm Twilighter (5hr; $159), a
paddle and stroll along the Milford Track (4hr; $89)
and various combos. Trips are mostly mid-Oct to
mid-April, though the Sunriser runs all year.
Tawaki Dive ℡ 03/249 9006, ⊚ www.tawakidive
.co.nz. Two guided dives cost $189 from Te Anau or
$159 from Milford plus $99 for gear rental.

The Milford Track

More than other Great Walk, the **Milford Track** is a Kiwi icon and unlike other major tramps, New Zealanders are in the majority here. Its exalted reputation is part accident and part history. It is likely that **Maori** paced the Arthur and Clinton valleys in search of *pounamu*, but there is little direct evidence. The first **Europeans** to explore were Scotsmen Donald Sutherland and John Mackay who, in 1880, blazed a trail up the Arthur Valley from Milford Sound. The story goes that while working their way up the valley they came upon the magnificent Mackay Falls and tossed a coin to decide who would name it,

Milford Sound is on most visitors' itineraries, and there are plenty of operators to get you there from almost anywhere in the country.

Bus trips **from Te Anau** are the best bet – they are appreciably shorter, generally taking a leisurely eight hours, allowing you to concentrate on the most interesting section of the Milford Road and usually include a cruise on the sound – see p.743 for a rundown of the cruise lines.

From Queenstown, streams of luxury **buses** make the tiring five-hour-plus drive via Te Anau to Milford. There are frequent photo-opportunity stops and a relentless commentary and passengers are then decanted into various cruises before at least another five hours' return journey – a hurried twelve- to thirteen-hour day. This so-called coach-cruise-coach format is too much for many, so they opt for fly-cruise-coach trips (which may be cancelled by bad weather), or coach-cruise-fly variations (which guarantee you get there, though may mean a coach back in bad weather).

From Te Anau

The cheapest trips are those which don't include cruises – good value if you're going kayaking: try track-transport specialists Tracknet (Oct–April; 3 daily; ☎03/249 7777 ⊛www.tracknet.net), who will get you there for $47, although you'll have to put up with detours to the trailheads. The big boys, such as Real Journeys (☎0800/656 501), InterCity (☎03/379 9020) and Great Sights (☎0800/744 487), all run luxury **bus and cruise** packages from around $153, though there are small reductions for backpackers and substantial standby **discounts** outside the peak season.

More interesting are full-day trips with Fiordland Wilderness Experiences (see p.753), which cost $155 round-trip from Te Anau including kayaking from October to May; or go walking year-round with Trips 'n' Tramps (☎03/249 7081, ⊛www .tripsandtramps.co.nz), whose guide-led nature trips ($158) concentrate on short relaxed bushwalks before joining a cruise.

From Queenstown

If you don't have the time to stay in Te Anau and visit Milford from there and you are a masochist, you'll have to opt for a **coach-cruise-coach** day-trip from Queenstown. Starting at 7am and usually returning around 8pm there are countless companies offering trips, the best value being the backpacker-oriented BBQ Bus (⊛www .milford.net.nz; $174; ☎03/442 1045), which runs full-day trips with stops for short bushwalks and a BBQ in the Hollyford Valley.

More upmarket tours using air-conditioned vehicles, complete with multilingual commentary or interpretation material, are offered by several companies, including Real Journeys ($230; ☎0800/656 501), whose unusual wedge-profiled coaches give the best all-round views.

Many visitors shy away from such a long day and opt instead for a more expensive package involving the forty-minute **flight** to Milford's small airfield, a **cruise** and a **return flight**: Air Fiordland (☎0800/103 404, ⊛www.airfiordland.com) charges around $395. A good compromise, giving you a chance to see the scenery from the road in one direction, is a **fly-cruise-coach** combo. Most of the bigger bus and flight companies offer these, including Air Fiordland, which charges $540 to coach in and fly out.

Travellers locked into the Kiwi Experience circuit (see p.33) have to pay extra to do the Milford Sound leg.

on the understanding that the loser would name the next waterfall. Mackay won the toss but rued his good fortune when, days later, they stumbled across the much more famous and lofty Sutherland Falls. They may well have climbed the adjacent Mackinnon Pass, but the honour of naming it went to **Quintin McKinnon** who, with his companion Ernest Mitchell, reached it in 1888 after having been commissioned by the Otago Chief Surveyor, C.W. Adams, to cut a path up the Clinton Valley.

The route was finally pushed through in mid-October 1888 and the first **tourists** followed a year later, guided by McKinnon. The greatest fillip came in 1908 when a writer submitted her account of the Milford Track to the editor of London's *Spectator*. She had declared it "A Notable Walk" but, in a fit of editorial hyperbole, the editor retitled the piece "The Finest Walk in the World". From 1903 until 1966 the government held a monopoly on the track, allowing only guided walkers; the huts were supplied by packhorses, which weren't finally retired until 1969.

Wider **public access** was only achieved after the Otago Tramping Club challenged the government's policy by tramping the Milford in 1964. Huts were built in 1966 and the first independent parties came through later that year.

Practicalities

There's no doubt that the Milford Track (54km; 4 days) is wonderful and includes some of Fiordland's finest scenery, but some disparage it as over-regimented, expensive and not especially varied, while others complain that the huts are badly spaced and lurk below the tree line among the sandflies. While these criticisms aren't unfounded – the tramp costs around $280 in hut and transport **fees** alone – the track is well managed and maintained, the huts clean and unobtrusive, and because everyone's going in the same direction you can go all day without seeing a soul. The Milford is also tougher than many people expect, packing the only hard climb and a dash for the boat at Milford Sound into the last two days. DOC's *Milford Track Independent Tramping* **leaflet** (free) is adequate for route-finding, though the 1:70,000 *Milford Track Trackmap* ($15) provides much more information.

Booking and accommodation

As with the Kepler and Routeburn tracks, **independent walkers** tackling the Milford Track during the late October to late April tramping season are subject to a rigid system of advance-booking **accommodation passes** for the three special category huts. You can only walk the track from south to north, spending the first night at Clinton Hut, the second at Mintaro and the third at Dumpling. No backtracking or second nights are allowed and there is **no camping**. Numbers are limited to forty per day, so you'll need to book well in advance; a couple of months if you are adaptable, six if you need a specific departure date or are part of a large group, but this does have the advantage of guaranteeing you a bed.

Huts all have wardens and are equipped with flush toilets, running (but not drinking) water, heaters and gas rings, but not pans and plates; the **cost** is $135 for the three nights, and family discounts of twenty percent apply throughout the season. **Bookings** are taken for the following season from July 1 and can be made online at Ⓦ www.doc.govt.nz, or through the Great Walks Booking Desk, DOC (PO Box 29, Te Anau Ⓣ03/249 8514, Ⓔgreatwalksbooking@doc.govt.nz); pick up your accommodation passes from Te Anau before 11am on the day of departure. If the track is closed due to bad weather or track conditions full refunds are made.

Outside the season the huts revert to serviced hut status ($15), unstaffed with no heating, clothes-drying or cooking facilities; bookings are not required and annual hut passes are valid. However, due to the presence of avalanche zones along the track, anyone walking out of season should check conditions with DOC before setting out.

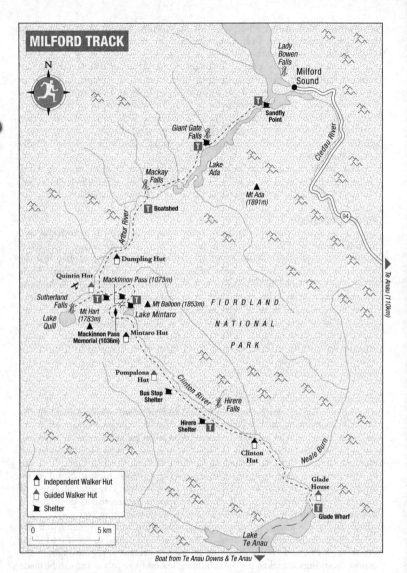

MILFORD TRACK

N

Lady Bowen Falls

Milford Sound

Sandfly Point T

Giant Gate Falls T

Lake Ada

Mt Ada (1891m)

Cleddau River

Mackay Falls

Arthur River

T Boatshed

94

Dumpling Hut

Quintin Hut

MacKinnon Pass (1073m)

Sutherland Falls

Lake Quill

T

Mt Hart (1783m)

T

▲ Mt Balloon (1853m)

Lake Mintaro

F I O R D L A N D

MacKinnon Pass Memorial (1036m)

Mintaro Hut

N A T I O N A L

Te Anau (110km) ▶

Pompalona Hut

Clinton River

P A R K

Bus Stop Shelter

Hirere Falls

Hirere Shelter T

Clinton Hut

Neale Burn

Glade House

Independent Walker Hut
Guided Walker Hut
Shelter

Glade Wharf T

0   5 km

Lake Te Anau

Boat from Te Anau Downs & Te Anau ▼

Trailhead transport

Both ends of the Milford Track can only be realistically approached **by boat**, and arrangements must be made at the same time as accommodation passes are issued. Independent walkers need to catch the Tracknet bus (30min; $22) from Te Anau to the harbour at Te Anau Downs, 30km north of Te Anau, then the Real Journeys launch across Lake Te Anau to Glade Wharf (1hr; $65). There are early departures but since the first day's walk is very easy, it makes sense to make a late start using the 1.15pm bus and the 2pm launch.

At the Milford end of the track, catch either the 2pm or the 3.15pm launch from the aptly named Sandfly Point (Nov–April; $36.70) for the journey to Milford

Sound (20min). Tracknet **buses** back to Te Anau can be picked up at 9.30am, 2.30pm and 5pm (3hr; $47).

Guided walks

For many years, the only way to walk the Milford Track was on a **guided walk**. Some argue that this is still the best approach, with just your personal effects to carry and comfortable beds in clean, plain huts with hot showers, duvets on the bunks, three-course dinners with wine and cooked breakfasts. Staff prepare the huts, cook the meals, make up the lunches and tidy up after you, but all this mollycoddling comes at a price. The **Milford Track Guided Walk** (Nov–April daily departures; ℡0800/659 255, Ⓦwww.ultimatehikes.co.nz) is a four-night, five-day affair and costs $1950. For that you get a pre-track briefing in Queenstown, transport from there to the trailhead, accommodation and food on the track, a night at the *Mitre Peak Lodge*, a Milford Sound cruise and a return bus ride to Queenstown. Accommodation on the walk is in shared bunkrooms but for $2350 you can upgrade to a double en suite ($600 extra single supplement). The same company runs a variety of other guided walks including the Routeburn Track.

Anyone wanting a taste of the track without having to walk more than a couple of kilometres can join a Milford Track day-walk from Te Anau.

The route

The track starts at the head of Lake Te Anau and follows the Clinton River into the heart of the mountains, climbing over the spectacular Mackinnon Pass before tracing the Arthur River to Milford Sound.

Glade Wharf to Clinton Hut (5km; 1–2hr; 50m ascent). The first day is a doddle, starting along a 2km 4WD track which serves Glade House (guided walkers only). The path then crosses a swingbridge to the right bank of the gentle, meandering Clinton River; keen anglers can spend an hour or two fishing for trout in the deep pools. The track runs through dense beech forest, only occasionally giving glimpses of the mountains ahead beyond Clinton Hut.

Clinton Hut to Mintaro Hut (16.5km; 4–6hr; 350m ascent). The track follows the true right bank of the Clinton River to its source, Lake Mintaro, right by the Mintaro Hut. Again it's easy going and by the time you reach a short side track to Hidden Lake, Mackinnon Pass should be visible. The track steepens a little to Bus Stop Shelter, flattens out to Pompolona Hut (guided), and is a further hour to Mintaro Hut where, if it looks like it will be a good sunset, you should drop your pack and head up Mackinnon Pass.

Mintaro Hut to Dumpling Hut (14km; 5–6hr; 550m ascent, 1030m descent). The walk so far does little to prepare you for the third day. Though the surface of the broad path is firm and well graded, less experienced bushwalkers will find the haul up to Mackinnon Pass (1hr 30min–2hr) very strenuous. Long breath-catching pauses provide an opportunity to admire the wonderful alpine scenery,

notably the headwall of the Clinton Valley, a sheer glacial cirque of grey granite. As the bush drops away behind you, the slope eases to the saddle at Mackinnon Pass, a great place to eat lunch, though you'll have the company of kea and the incessant buzzing of pleasure flights from Milford. A memorial to McKinnon and Mitchell marks the low point of the saddle, from where the path turns east and climbs to a day shelter (with toilets and, in summer, a gas ring) just below the dramatic form of Mount Balloon. From here it's all downhill, and steeply too, initially skirting the flank of Mount Balloon then following the path beside the picturesque Roaring Burn and down to the Arthur River. The confluence is marked by Quintin Hut (guided), which was originally built by the Union Steamship Company as an overnight shelter for sightseers from Milford visiting the Sutherland Falls. Though it remains a private hut, toilets and shelter are provided for independent walkers – who mostly dump their packs for the walk to the base of the 560m Sutherland Falls (4km return; 1hr–1hr 30min; 50m ascent), the highest in New Zealand. Dumpling Hut is another hour's walk from Quintin Hut.

Dumpling Hut to Sandfly Point (18km; 5–6hr; 125m descent). You're in for an early start and a steady walk to meet your launch or kayak at 2 or 3.15pm. After rain this can be a magnificent walk, the valley walls streaming with waterfalls and the

Arthur River in spate. The track follows the tumbling river for a couple of hours to the Boatshed (toilets), before crossing the Arthur River by swingbridge and cutting inland to the magnificent MacKay Falls. More a steep cascade than a waterfall, they are much smaller than the Sutherland Falls but equally impressive, particularly after rain. Don't miss Bell Rock, a water-hollowed boulder that you can crawl inside. The track subsequently follows Lake Ada, created by a landslip 900 years ago, and named by Sutherland after his Scottish girlfriend. A small lunch shelter midway along its shore heralds Giant Gate Falls, which are best viewed from the swing-bridge that crosses the river at the foot of the falls. From here it is roughly an hour and a half to the shelter at Sandfly Point.

Manapouri, Doubtful Sound and the southern fiords

New Zealand has no shortage of beautiful lakes, but even among them, Lake Manapouri shines, its long, indented shoreline contorted into three distinct arms and clad with thick bushland tangled with ferns. The lake sits at 178m and has a vast catchment area, guzzling all the water that flows down the Upper Waiau River from Lake Te Anau and unwittingly creating a massive hydroelectric generating capacity – something which almost led to its downfall.

The one good thing to come from the hydroelectric project has been the opening up of **Doubtful Sound**, following the construction of the Wilmot Pass supply road. What was previously the preserve of the odd yacht and a few deerstalkers and trampers is now accessible to anyone prepared to take a boat across Lake Manapouri and a drive over the Wilmot Pass. Costs are unavoidably high and you need to be self-sufficient (no corner shops here), but any inconvenience is easily outweighed by glorious isolation and pristine beauty. Wildlife is a major attraction, not least the resident pod of sixty-odd bottlenose dolphins, who frequently come to play around ships' bows and cavort near kayakers. Fur seals slather the outer islands, Fiordland crested penguins come to breed here in October and November, and the bush, which comes right down to the water's edge, is alive with kaka, kiwi and other rare bird species.

Cook spotted Doubtful Sound in 1770 but didn't enter, as he was "doubtful" of his ability to sail out again in the face of winds buffeted by the steep-walled fiord. The breeze was more favourable for the joint leaders of a Spanish expedition, Malaspina and Bauza, who in 1793 sailed in and named Febrero Point, Malaspina Reach and Bauza Island.

In fact, Cook seemed more interested in **Dusky Sound**, 40km south, where he spent five weeks on his second voyage in 1773, while his crew recovered from an arduous crossing of the Southern Ocean. On Astronomer's Point nearby, it is still possible to see where Cook's astronomer had trees felled so he could get an accurate fix on the stars; not far from here is the site where 1790s castaways built the first European-style house and boat in New Zealand. Marooned by the fiord's waters, Pigeon Island shelters the ruins of a house built by Richard Henry, who battled from 1894 to 1908 to save endangered native birds from introduced stoats and rats.

Manapouri

The scattered community of **MANAPOURI**, 20km south of Te Anau, wraps prettily around the shores of the lake of the same name which, in the 1960s, became a cause célèbre for conservationists (see box opposite). Its contentious power station can be visited on day-trips.

Electricity, aluminium and brickbats

Lake Manapouri's **hydroelectric** potential had long been recognized, but nothing was done until the 1950s. Consolidated Zinc Pty of Australia wanted to smelt their Queensland bauxite into **aluminium** – a power-hungry process – as cheaply as possible, and alighted upon **Lake Manapouri**. They approached the New Zealand government, who agreed to build a power station on the lake, at taxpayers' expense, while Rio Tinto's subsidiary Comalco built a smelter at Tiwai Point, near Bluff, 170km to the southeast.

The scheme entailed blocking the lake's natural outlet into the Lower Waiau River and chiselling out a vast powerhouse 200m underground beside Lake Manapouri's West Arm, where the flow would be diverted down a 10km tailrace tunnel to Deep Cove on Doubtful Sound. By the time the fledgling **environmental movement** had rallied its supporters, the scheme was well under way, but the government under-estimated the anger that would be unleashed by its secondary plan to boost water storage and power production by raising the water level in the lake by more than 8m. The threat to the natural beauty of the lake sparked **nationwide protests**, though the 265,000-signature petition prepared by the "Save Manapouri Campaign" failed to change the government's mind. It was only after the 1972 elections, when Labour unseated the National Party that the policy was changed and the lake saved. The full saga is recounted in Neville Peat's *Manapouri Saved* (see "Books" in Contexts, p.803).

The **Manapouri Underground Power Station** took eight years to build. Completed in 1971, it remains one of the most ambitious projects ever carried out in New Zealand. Eighty percent of its output goes straight to the **smelter** – which consumes around fifteen percent of all the electricity used in the country, and it is widely perceived to be an unnecessary drain on the country's resources. Because of the unexpectedly high friction in the original tailrace tunnel the power station had always run below 85-percent capacity and to boost power production a second parallel tailrace tunnel was built in the late 1990s.

Arrival and information

To get to Manapouri without your own transport, hop on the Te Anau–Inver-cargill Scenic Shuttle (☎03/249 7654, ⓦ www.scenicshuttle.co.nz), which leaves Te Anau at 7.30am and returns from Manapouri to Te Anau mid-afternoon. Real Journeys buses connecting with boats to West Arm and Doubtful Sound may also take extras ($12.60), but only if their cruise passengers don't fill the bus.

The road from Te Anau reaches Manapouri as Cathedral Drive and then becomes Waiau Street, passing most things of interest on the way to Pearl Harbour and the Real Journeys office (daily: Nov–Feb 7.30am–8pm; March–Oct 8am–5.30pm; ☎0800/656 501, ⓦ www.realjourneys.co.nz), the closest thing the village has to an information centre, and the jumping-off point for lake cruises. The sole shop and the post office both occupy the same building as the *Cathedral Café* on Cathedral Drive – find one and you've found the lot.

Accommodation and eating

Though most people prefer to base themselves in Te Anau, Manapouri has a reasonable selection of **places to stay**. Best bet is the attractive 🦣 *Freestone Backpackers*, SH99, 3km east of Manapouri (☎03/249 6893, ⓔ freestone@xtra .co.nz; dorms $20, rooms ❷), in a series of comfy wooden chalets, each with great mountain and lake views from the veranda, a pot-bellied stove and basic cooking facilities; the ultra-friendly hosts sometimes lay on classical recitals. Otherwise, *The Cottage*, Waiau Street (☎03/249 6838, ⓦ www.thecottagefiordland.co.nz; ❺), has two pleasant en suites with decks, in a cutesy house with a cottage garden close to the wharf; continental breakfast is included. Finally, *Possum Lodge* 13 Murrell Ave (☎03/249 6623, ℮possumlodge@xtra.co.nz; tent & powered sites $15, dorms $21, rooms & cabins ❷, motel units ❸), is an appealingly old-fashioned, peaceful and well-maintained campsite and hostel, right where the Waiau River meets the lake.

You'll find far and away the best of the limited **eating** options in the weatherboard church of *Café 23*, 23 Waiau St, which does breakfasts from 7am, lunches, loads of home-made baked goods for mid-morning or afternoon snacks, and will stay open until 7.30pm, if you ring ahead. Otherwise try the *Cathedral Café*, Cathedral Drive, which serves light meals ($10–24) until around 6.30pm in summer, or venture to the *Lakeview Café*, 68 Cathedral Drive, at the *Manapouri Lakeview Motor Inn*, for bar meals until around 9pm.

Around town

The several dozen houses that constitute Manapouri cluster at the outlet of the Waiau River, which the hydroelectric shenanigans have turned into a narrow arm of the lake now known as Pearl Harbour.

Apart from cruises and kayak trips, the only thing to do in Manapouri is to saunter along the **walking trails** detailed in DOC's *Manapouri Tracks* leaflet (from the DOC in Te Anau), such as the **Pearl Harbour to Fraser's Beach** trail (45min), which follows an easy track through lakeshore beech forest with fantails and silvereye flitting about the undergrowth. For other tracks, you'll need to row across the Waiau River in a boat rented from Adventure Kayak & Cruise, 33 Waiau St, next to the Mobil station (daily 8am–8.30pm; ☎03/249 6626, ⓦwww.fiordlandadventure.co.nz). It costs $10 a day and you pay an extra charge to stay on the other side overnight, either camping or in one of the two DOC huts (each $5).

The most frequently walked route is the **Circle Track** (7km; 3hr loop; 330m ascent), which contours west around the lake before turning southeast to climb the ridge to a point with stupendous views over the lake, then heads north back to the start.

The lake: cruises and kayaking

Most of the lake cruises are operated by Real Journeys (see p.751), who are the only operator to run trips across Lake Manapouri to the impressive, if controversial, **Manapouri Underground Power Station** (Oct–April tours 12.30pm daily; $65). After crossing the lake, a bus takes you down a narrow, 2km-long tunnel to a viewing platform in the Machine Hall. All you see are the exposed sections of seven turbines, but there's an interesting model of the whole system and panels assaulting you with statistics before you're whisked back to the bus. In addition to these three- to four-hour trips, Real Journey's Doubtful Sound day cruises include a visit to the power station.

For greater independence, you'll need **kayak rental**: Adventure Kayak & Cruise (see above) rent singles and doubles (1 day $50, 3 days $125); while Te Anau-based Fiordland Wilderness Experiences (see opposite), rent out better boats for a fraction more.

Doubtful Sound and the southern fiords

To fully appreciate the beauty and isolation of the **southern fiords**, you need to spend a few days among them, travelling by boat or kayak. If time is limited, plump for a full-day or overnight trip to **Doubtful Sound**; with more time, spend a few days weaving between the mystical waterways.

For an in-depth encounter with the fiords, book several months in advance for one of the superb **multi-day trips** organized by Fiordland Ecology Holidays (see p.60). A similar ethical vein flavours the energetic and awe-inspiring **kayaking trips** run by ⚑ Fiordland Wilderness Experiences (☎0800/200 434, Ⓦwww .fiordlandseakayak.co.nz), who run popular two-day trips ($380) and longer explorations in remoter areas. From May to September, the *Milford Wanderer* also runs multi-day trips, taking in such remote spots as Dusky Sound ($1750) and Preservation Inlet ($2350).

Real Journeys (see p.751) run two trips to Doubtful Sound, the cheapest, the full-day **Wilderness Cruise** (1–2 daily; $275, lunch $15), includes a boat trip across Lake Manapouri and a bus ride for the 20km ride over Wilmot Pass to Deep Cove. Here you board a three-hour cruise out to the mouth of the fiord, where fur seals loll on the rocks, and into serene Hall Arm, where bottlenose dolphins sometimes congregate. Most trips visit the power station before boating you back across the lake.

Spectacular though the day cruise is, it's no substitute for an **overnight cruise** on the *Fiordland Navigator* (Nov–March daily at 12.30pm, Oct, April & Sept 12.30am; quad-share $365, twin-share $675, single $1181), a modern cruiser designed to look like a traditional sailing scow. The trip doesn't visit the power station but you're away from Manapouri for a full 24 hours, time enough to immerse yourself in this extraordinary landscape by joining a nature walk, kayaking or even swimming. Food and accommodation are excellent and there are savings of around twenty percent in October and mid-April to mid-May, and a ten-percent YHA discount throughout the summer.

The Southern Scenic Route

Don't miss out on the beautiful fringe country, where the fertile sheep paddocks of Southland butt up against the remote country of Fiordland National Park. The region's towns are linked by the underrated, pastoral charms of the **Southern Scenic Route** (Ⓦwww.southernscenicroute.co.nz), a series of small roads where sheep are the primary traffic hazard. From Te Anau it runs via Manapouri to SH99, following the valley of the Waiau River to the cave-pocked limestone country around **Clifden**. A minor road cuts west to Lake Hauroko, access point for the Dusky Track, while the Southern Scenic Route continues south through the small service town of **Tuatapere** (the base for hiking the Hump Ridge Track, and home of the track information office), to estuary-side **Riverton** and on to Invercargill.

Scenic Shuttle **buses** (☎0800/277 483, Ⓦwww.scenicshuttle.co.nz) do the trip from Te Anau through Manapouri, Tuatapere and Riverton to Invercargill and back daily (departing Te Anau 7.30am; $49).

Clifden and Lake Hauroko

At the junction with the main highway, it is 32km further south to **CLIFDEN**, which is barely a town at all but is of some interest for the historic **Clifden Suspension Bridge**, one of the longest in the South Island, built over the Waiau River in 1899 and in use until the 1970s. Maori once camped on summer foraging trips at the **Clifden Caves** (unrestricted access), which are signposted both around 1km north of the bridge along SH96 and 1km down Clifden Gorge Road. With no one to guide you there's a palpable sense of adventure when tackling this 300m-long labyrinth lined with flowstone and stalactite formations and dotted

The **eastern continuation** of the **Southern Scenic Route**, along the Catlins Coast to Dunedin, is covered in the Dunedin to Stewart Island chapter, p.597.

with glowworms. The passages are not tight but you'll need to crouch, scramble and climb a ladder, following a series of reflective strips. Let the Hump Ridge Track booking office and information centre (see opposite) know your intentions, and go with at least one other person. Wear clothes you don't mind getting dirty and take at least two torches.

Lake Hauroko, at the end of a dirt road, 30km west of Clifden, is New Zealand's deepest lake (462m), and far enough off the beaten track that you can skinny dip. Low bush-clad hills surrounding the lake create the "sounding winds" immortalized in its name. There are no facilities at First Bay, the road-end, though there is a primitive campsite midway between Clifden and Lake Hauroko. At the north end of the lake, the DOC Hauroko Burn Hut ($5) is accessible by boat, or on foot via the **Dusky Track** – one of the longest and most remote in New Zealand, and much tougher than any of the Great Walks. Experienced trampers considering tackling it should obtain information and condition reports from DOC offices in the region.

To explore this beautiful wilderness area, engage one of the companies running wilderness **jetboating trips** on the lake and along the 27km of the Grade III **Wairaurahiri River** down to the coast. Hump Ridge Jet (T0800/270 556, W www.humpridgejet.com) runs a one-day adventure ($190), allowing four hours to relax or hike into the impressive Percy Burn viaduct then jetboating back. Wairaurahiri Jet (T0800/376 174, W www.wjet.co.nz) charges more for a similar trip.

Tuatapere and around

Two sawmills and one feeble stand of beech and podocarp forest is the only evidence that **TUATAPERE**, on the banks of the Waiau River 14km south of Clifden, could once have justified its epithet of "The Hole in the Forest". As the largest town in southwestern Southland, Tuatapere makes a good geographical base (though it is limited in terms of services) for exploring the southern limits of Fiordland. To fight the apparent stagnation, the community banded together to create the **Hump Ridge Track**, to encourage travellers to the area. The South Coast Track visits come of the same area, and both can be combined with jetboating along the Wairaurahiri River, based nearby at Clifden.

The Town

Maori legend records the great war canoe *Takitimu* being wrecked on the Waiau River bar at Te Waewae Bay some six hundred years ago. Maori set up summer foraging camps along the river and used these as way-stations on the route to the *pounamu* fields around Milford Sound, but Tuatapere only came into being when European **pioneers** arrived around 1885. By 1909 the **railway** had arrived from Invercargill, bringing with it increasingly sophisticated steam-powered haulers that made short work of clearing the surrounding bushland. More recently, foresters' attention shifted west to the fringes of the Fiordland National Park where, in the 1970s, the Maori owners proposed clear felling stands of rimu. Environmentalists prevailed upon the Conservation Minister who eventually, in 1996, agreed to pay compensation in return for a sustainable management policy. The bush makes a last stand at a riverside clump of beech, kahikatea and totara on The Domain – staff at the information centre will point the way. For a

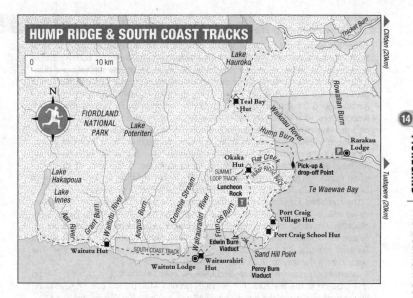

HUMP RIDGE & SOUTH COAST TRACKS

0   10 km

N

FIORDLAND
NATIONAL
PARK

Lake
Hauroko

Lake
Poteriteri

Thicket Burn

Clifden (20km)

Teal Bay
Hut

Waikoau River

Hump Burn

Rowallan Burn

Rarakau
Lodge

P

Okaka
Hut

Flat Creek

SUMMIT
LOOP TRACK

HUMP RIDGE TRACK

Pick-up &
drop-off Point

Tuatapere (20km)

Lake
Hakapoua

Lake
Innes

Aan River

Grant Burn

Waitutu River

Angus Burn

Crombie Stream

Wairaurahiri River

Francis Burn

Luncheon
Rock

Te Waewae Bay

Port Craig
Village Hut

Port Craig School Hut

Waitutu Hut

SOUTH COAST TRACK

Waitutu Lodge

Wairaurahiri
Hut

Edwin Burn
Viaduct

Sand Hill Point

Percy Burn
Viaduct

rose-tinted version of pioneer history, visit **Bushman's Museum**, accessed through the information centre (see below; same hours; gold coin donation).

Practicalities

Tuatapere is a small town thinly spread on both sides of the Waiau River. On the eastern side, the **Hump Ridge Track booking office and information centre**, 31 Orawia Rd (Nov–April daily 8.30am–5.30pm; May–Oct Wed–Sun 10.30am–3.30pm; ℡03/226 6739), is primarily set up for hikers heading off for the Hump Ridge Track. They can store valuables while you're on the tramp, but will also help with local accommodation, transport and the like.

Accommodation is limited, with the comfortable *Tuatapere Motel*, 73 Main St (℡0800/009 993; ④) also operating *Shooters Backpackers* (dorms $28, rooms ②) next door.

The best **eating** around is at the 🍴 *Yesteryear Café*, in the old bakery at 3a Orawia Rd (open daily 7.30am–6pm in summer, much less in the winter), where generous lunches ($10) of sausage casserole or mince on toast are accompanied by albums your gran would like on the 1970s turntable and home baking is prized above all else. Alternatively try the bar in the pragmatic *Waiau Hotel*, 47 Main St, or buy some of the sausages (particularly venison) that made Tuatapere the "sausage capital of New Zealand" – from the century-old Tuatapere Sausage Shop, 75 Main St.

Colac Bay and Riverton

South of Tuatapere, SH99 follows the wind-ravaged cliffs behind the wide and moody Te Waewae Bay, where fierce southerlies have sculpted the much-photographed macrocarpa trees into compact forms. Beyond the small town of Orepuki, the road cuts inland, regaining the sea 45km southeast of Tuatapere, at the quiet community of **Colac Bay**, with a nationally renowned surf break.

For non-surfers, there's no reason to stop before **RIVERTON** (Aparima), a further 12km on and one of the country's oldest settlements. Frequented by whalers as early as the 1790s, the town was formally established in 1836 by another

The Hump Ridge and South Coast tracks

Tuatapere is the base for two markedly different hiking experiences: the traditional **South Coast Track** and the **Hump Ridge Track**, with its engaging combination of coastal walking, historic remains, subalpine country and relatively sophisticated huts.

Both tracks share historically interesting kilometres of coastal walking, following a portion of the 1896 track cut 100km along the south coast to gold-mining settlements around the southernmost fiord of Preservation Inlet. This paved the way for woodcutters, who arrived en masse in the 1920s. Logs were transported to the mills on tramways, which crossed the burns and gullies on viaducts – four of the finest have been faithfully restored, including the 125m bridge over Percy Burn that stands 35m high in the middle. The remains of the former mill village of **Port Craig** – wharf, rusting machinery, crumbling fireplaces – are equally fascinating and can be visited using the DOC brochure, available locally. The only habitation at Port Craig now is DOC's Port Craig School Hut and the Hump Ridge's Port Craig Village Hut.

The **trailhead** for both tracks is the Rarakau car park, 20km west of Tuatapere, accessible by bus (around $25 one-way) organized through the Hump Ridge Track office; there's secure parking here ($5/day). Hump Ridge walkers can also travel from Tuatapere to Track Burn ($50 one-way, $80 return), which continues 8km west from Rarakau along a 4WD track, saving about 2hr at the beginning and/or end. The section from Rarakau to Track Burn costs $30.

Jetboat operators (see "Clifden and Lake Hauroko" account on p.753) will pick up and drop off at the Wairaurahiri rivermouth (around $150/person one-way), allowing you to walk sections of the tracks combined with a ride on the Wairaurahiri River.

The South Coast Track

The historic **South Coast Track** (covered on DOC's *Waitutu Tracks* leaflet) slices through the largest area of lowland rainforest in New Zealand. Although it is easy going it takes the best part of four days to reach Big River and you'll just have to turn around and walk back unless you prearrange a jetboat out from the Wairaurahiri Hut (see p.754). A popular alternative is to make a three-day excursion, staying at DOC's Port Craig School Hut ($15), and exploring the environs. Two more huts ($5 each) spaced four to seven hours' walk apart provide accommodation, and camping is free.

Walking the South Coast Track

Rarakau to Port Craig School Hut (17km; 5–7hr; negligible ascent). The first leg follows either the old logging road or, tide permitting, the beach – which should shave half an hour off your walking time.

Port Craig School Hut to Wairaurahiri Hut (16km; 4–6hr; 200m ascent). Here the track follows the old tramway, crossing all four of the restored viaducts, before dropping down to the Wairaurahiri River. There is alternative accommodation on the banks of the Wairaurahiri River in the form of the private *Waitutu Lodge* (book through the Tuatapere information centre): take sleeping bag and food.

Wairaurahiri Hut to Waitutu Hut (13km, 4–6hr, negligible ascent). This section of the path largely follows the coastal flats across Maori land. Fit trampers with camping equipment might want to continue from Waitutu Hut to Big River (12km; 5–7hr; negligible ascent), the end of the track; note there are no facilities at Big River.

whaler, John Howell – who is also credited with kick-starting New Zealand's now formidable sheep-farming industry. Strung along a spit between the sea and the Jacob's River Estuary (actually the mouth of the Aparima and Pourakino rivers), where fishing boats still harbour, Riverton has a blissfully relaxed feel.

A 5m-high paua shell (made from concrete though lined with real paua) underlines the town's reputation as a paua capital, with several shops selling the polished

The Hump Ridge Track

The privately managed **Hump Ridge Track** (book in advance ☎0800/486 774, ⓦwww.humpridgetrack.co.nz or at the office in Tuatapere, see p.755) is done in three days with nights spent at two comfortable forty-bunk huts ($90) equipped with lights, gas cookers, cooking pots and eating utensils, cold running water, six-bunk rooms, and ablution blocks with flush toilets and washbasins, and even porridge each morning cooked by the summer season hut manager. So-called **Freedom walkers** still need to bring a sleeping bag and food. The tramp requires a good level of fitness and isn't for beginners or kids under 10.

If this still sounds too difficult you can arrange for helicopter **bag transfer** (max 15kg) to the next hut. Either go for the full package ($180) or just have your stuff lifted up the steep climb to the first hut on the first day when the pack is heaviest ($65): everything, including empty bottles, must be carried out. Hikers can even upgrade to a double or twin room with sheets and duvet (add $50/person).

In addition there's a **Freedom Plus** package ($455), which includes one night's backpacker accommodation in Tuatapere, full heli-packing, return transport to Track Burn and hot showers.

The trip can also be done as a **guided walk** with Kiwi Wilderness Walks (☎0800/733 5494, ⓦwww.NZwalk.com), who run a four-day, three-night trip ($1395) including all meals, superior accommodation at the huts, hotel accommodation in Tuatapere and return transport from Te Anau or Invercargill.

Despite 8km of boardwalks, to protect the fragile alpine environment on the tops and preserve your feet from long stretches of mud, you can still expect to encounter mud, and when off the boardwalks it feels like a real "tramper's" track.

Walking the Hump Ridge Track

Everyone walks the track in the same direction either starting at Rarakau or catching transport to Track Burn.

Rarakau to Okaka Hut (18km; 6–9hr; 900m ascent). Starts along the coast but turns inland along boardwalks through open forest with a thick undergrowth of crown ferns. It's hard work once you start climbing but you're rewarded with views though breaks in the beech forest, until you finally burst out onto the open tops. You're soon at the Okaka Hut on the Hump Ridge, with fabulous views back the way you came. Allow time to explore the adjacent Summit Loop Track (1hr) along boardwalks past picturesque sandstone tors and lovely alpine plants.

Okaka Hut to Port Craig (19km; 6–9hr; 100m ascent, 900m descent). The track follows the Hump Ridge, staying high for several hours with magical views. Following lunch with a panoramic view, you descend along Edwin Burn to meet the South Coast Track. After crossing the Edwin Burn Viaduct, follow the old tramway (sleepers and spikes still intact) to the more majestic Percy Burn Viaduct then to the hut at Port Craig Village (or DOC's Port Craig School Hut).

Port Craig to Rarakau (11km; 5–7hr; undulating). Wanders through towering coastal rimu and down on to sandy beaches, and back to the Track Burn pick-up point (or on two more hours to Rarakau).

shells by the score. The oldest and best of these is the Fiordland Gift Studio, 166 Palmerston St (☎03/234 8153); you can also visit its factory on Bath Road for some great bargains.

Many boat charters are available to take you out trout or saltwater **fishing**. Information is available from the **Riverton Heritage and Tourist Centre**, 172 Palmerston St (☎03/234 8698), which is also a brilliant **museum** (daily 10am–5pm;

$10) stuffed with exhibits and interactive doodahs on the Maori and European history of the region.

Surprisingly for such a pretty spot, Riverton lacks worthwhile **accommodation** but it does have a fabby eatery, the ꝗ *Beach House Café*, 126 Rocks Hwy (☎03/234 8274), which has sweeping sea views and a cosy timber-lined dining room warmed by an open fire. It's great for coffee and cake but better for impeccably cooked fish and seafood (mains $25–35; lunch & dinner daily).

Beyond Riverton, SH99 heads into the hinterland of Invercargill, 40km away.

Travel details

Fiordland is off the main transport routes, with no trains or scheduled flights from the main airlines, and even buses are scarce. The i-SITE offices in the region keep updated transport schedules.

Bus companies

The main bus routes are Queenstown via Te Anau to Milford Sound, and Te Anau to Invercargill via Manapouri, Tuatapere and Riverton.
InterCity/Newmans ☎09/623 1504 ⓦwww .intercitycoach.co.nz: Queenstown–Te Anau–Milford and back daily; Te Anau–Gore–Balclutha–Dunedin daily.
Scenic Shuttle ☎0800/277 483, ⓔscenicshuttle@xtra.co.nz: Te Anau–Manapouri–Tuatapere–Riverton–Invercargill daily both directions.
Tracknet ☎0800/483 2628 ⓦwww.tracknet.net: Queenstown–Te Anau–Milford and back three times daily plus Kepler Track shuttles from Te Anau.

Bus routes

The Divide to: Milford Sound (5 daily; 1hr 15min); Te Anau (5 daily; 1hr).

Manapouri to: Clifden (1 daily; 1hr 30min); Invercargill (1 daily; 3hr 30min); Riverton (1 daily; 3hr); Te Anau (1 daily; 20min); Tuatapere (1 daily; 2hr).
Milford Sound to: The Divide (5 daily; 1hr 15min); Queenstown (7 daily; 4hr 45min–5hr 30min); Te Anau (7 daily; 2hr 15min–2hr 45min).
Queenstown to: Milford Sound (7 daily; 4hr 45min–5hr 30min); Te Anau (7 daily; 2hr 15min).
Te Anau to: The Divide (2–4 daily; 1hr); Dunedin (1 daily; 4hr 45min); Invercargill (1 daily; 4hr); Manapouri (2 daily; 20min); Milford Sound (7 daily; 2hr 15min–2hr 45min); Queenstown (7 daily; 2hr 15min).
Tuatapere to: Invercargill (1 daily; 2hr 30min); Riverton (1 weekly; 1hr 30min).

Flights

Milford Sound to: Queenstown (at least 20 daily; 35min).
Te Anau to: Queenstown (3–4 daily; 30min).

Contexts

Contexts

History...761

Chronology of New Zealand.............................775

Maoritanga...777

Landscapes and wildlife.................................785

Film and music 795

Books..798

History

M any New Zealanders of European descent have long thought of their country as a model of **humanitarian colonization**. Maori often take a different view, however, informed by the repeated theft of land and erosion of rights that were guaranteed by a **treaty**. Schoolroom histories have generally been faithful to the European view, even to the point of influencing Maori mythology. In the last couple of decades, however, revisionist historians have largely discredited what many New Zealanders know as fact. Much that is presented as tradition turns out to be the late-nineteenth-century scholarship of historians who bent research to fit their theories and, in some cases, even destroyed evidence. What follows is inextricably interwoven with Maori legend and can be understood more fully with reference to the section on *Maoritanga* (see p.777).

Pre-European history

It's thought that the ancestors of modern **Maori** arrived from Polynesia in double-hulled canoes between 1200 and 1300 AD. Their journey was planned to the extent that they took with them the *kuri* (dog) and food plants such as taro (a starchy tuber), yam and *kumara* (sweet potato). The notion of a legendary **"Great Fleet"** of seven canoes arriving in 1350 AD seems most likely to be a Victorian adaptation of Maori oral history, which has been readopted into contemporary Maori legend.

The Polynesians found a land so much colder than their tropical home that many of their crops and plants wouldn't grow. Fortunately there was an abundance of marine life and large flightless birds, particularly in the South Island, where most settled. The people of this **Archaic Period** are often misleadingly known as "Moa Hunters" and while some undoubtedly lived off these birds, the moa wasn't present in other areas. By around 1350 settlements had been established all around the coast, but it was only later that there's evidence of horticulture, suggesting a later migration bringing plants for cultivation, or the beginning of successful year-round food storage, allowing a settled living pattern rather than the earlier hunters' short-lived campsites.

Either way, this marks the beginning of the **Classic Period** when *kainga* (villages) grew up close to the *kumara* grounds, often supported by *pa* (fortified villages) where the people could retreat when under attack. As tasks became more specialized and hunting and horticulture took up less time, the arts – particularly

Polynesian migration

Modern scholarship suggests that humans from Southeast Asia first explored the South Pacific around five thousand years ago, gradually evolving a distinct culture as they filtered down through the Indonesian archipelago. A thousand years of progressive island-hopping got them as far as Tonga and Samoa, where a distinctly **Polynesian** society continued to evolve, honing seafaring skills to the point where lengthy sea journeys were possible. Around a thousand years ago, Polynesian culture reached its classical apotheosis in the **Society Islands** west of Tahiti, widely thought to be the hub for a series of migrations heading southwest across thousands of kilometres of open ocean, past the Cook Islands, eventually striking land in what is now known as New Zealand (Aotearoa).

carving and weaving (see p.782) – flourished and warfare became endemic, digs revealing an armoury of *mere*, *patu* and *taiaha* (fighting clubs) not found earlier. The decline of easily caught birdlife and the relative ease of growing *kumara* in the warmer North Island marked the beginning of a northward population shift. When the Europeans arrived, 95 percent of the population was located in the North Island, mostly in the northern reaches, with coastal settlements reaching down to Hawke's Bay and Wanganui.

C European contact and the Maori response

Many **Europeans** were convinced of the existence of a *terra australia incognita*, an unknown southern land that counterbalanced the northern continents. In 1642, the Dutch East India Company, keen to dominate any trade with this new continent, sent Dutchman **Abel Tasman** to the southern oceans where he became the first European to catch sight of Aotearoa. He anchored in Golden Bay, where a small boat being rowed between Tasman's two ships was intercepted by a Maori war canoe and four sailors were killed. Without setting foot on land Tasman turned tail and fled up the west coast of the North Island, going on to add Tonga and Fiji to European maps. He named Aotearoa "Staten Landt", later renamed Nieuw Zeeland after the Dutch maritime province.

Nieuw Zeeland was ignored for over a century until 1769, when **James Cook** (see box below) paid the first of three extensive visits. Cook and his crew found Maori a **sophisticated people** with a highly formalized social structure and skills to turn stone and wood into fabulously carved canoes, weapons and meeting houses – yet they had no wheels, roads, metalwork, pottery or animal husbandry. After an initial unfortunate encounter near Gisborne (see p.362) and another off Cape Kidnappers, near Napier (see p.380), Cook managed to strike up friendly, constructive relations. The original settlers now found that their tribal allegiance wasn't enough to differentiate them from the Europeans and subsequently began calling themselves **Maori** (meaning "normal" or "not distinctive") while referring to the newcomers as **Pakeha** ("foreign").

Offshore from the Coromandel Peninsula, Cook deviated from instructions and unfurled the British flag, claiming formal possession without the consent of Maori, but was still able to return twice in 1773 and 1777. The French were also interested – on his 1769 voyage Cook had passed **Jean François Marie de Surville** in a storm without either knowing of the other's presence.

James Cook

Yorkshireman Lieutenant (later Captain) **James Cook** was a meticulous **navigator** who sailed his barque *Endeavour* into the Pacific to observe the passage of Venus across the sun. Following Admiralty instructions he then continued west, arriving at "the Eastern side of the Land discover'd by Tasman" where he observed the "Genius, Temper, Disposition and Number of the Natives" and encouraged his botanists, Banks and Solander, to collect numerous samples.

On three voyages between 1769 and 1777 Cook spent a total of ten months around the coast of Aotearoa, leaving his mark with numerous place names. Some of his **charts** were in use well into the twentieth century, and his only significant errors were to show Banks Peninsula as an island and Stewart Island as a peninsula.

Hongi Hika from Ngapuhi *iwi* of the Bay of Islands was the first Maori chief to appreciate the value of firearms, and had already acquired several when missionary Thomas Kendall met him in 1814. By this time he was encouraging his people to grow crops that could be traded with Pakeha for guns.

In 1820 Hongi Hika travelled to England with Thomas Kendall to work on *A grammar and vocabulary of the language of New Zealand*. While he was there he briefly became the toast of London society and was presented to George IV as an "equal". Having little use for most of the gifts showered upon him, he traded them for 300 muskets. Eager to emulate the supreme power of the imperial king, Hongi Hika set about subduing much of the North Island, using the often badly maintained and inexpertly aimed guns to rattle the enemy, who were then slaughtered with the traditional *mere*. Warriors abandoned the old fighting season – the lulls between hunting and tending the crops – and set off to settle old scores, resulting in a massive loss of life.

The establishment of the Botany Bay penal colony in neighbouring Australia aroused the first commercial interest in New Zealand and from the 1790s to the 1830s New Zealand was part of the Australian frontier. By 1830 the coast was dotted with semi-permanent **sealing** communities which, within thirty years, had almost clubbed the seals into extinction. The British navy rapidly felled giant kauri trees for its ships' masts, while others supplied Sydney shipbuilders. By the 1820s **whalers** had moved in, basing themselves at Kororareka (now Russell), where they could recruit Maori crew and provision their ships. This combination of rough whalers, escaped convicts from Australia and all manner of miscreants and adventurers combined to turn Russell into a lawless place populated by what Darwin, on his visit in 1835, found to be "the very refuse of Society".

Before long, the Maori way of life had been entirely disrupted. **Inter-tribal fighting** soon broke out on a scale never seen before. Hongi Hika (see box above) was the first off the mark, but the quest for new territory also fuelled the actions of Ngati Toa's **Te Rauparaha** (see p.254), who soon controlled the southern half of the North Island.

The huge demand for **firearms** drove Maori to sell the best of their food, relocating to unhealthy areas close to flax swamps, where flax production could be increased. Even highly valued tribal treasures – *pounamu* (greenstone) clubs and the preserved heads of chiefs taken in battle – were traded. European **diseases** swept through the Maori population, European-introduced alcohol and tobacco became widespread, Maori women were prostituted to Pakeha sailors, and the tribal structure began to crumble.

Into this scene stepped the **missionaries** in 1814, the brutal New South Wales magistrate **Samuel Marsden** arriving in the Bay of Islands a transformed man with a mission to bring Christianity and "civilization" to Maori, and to save the souls of the sealers and whalers. Subsequently Anglicans, Wesleyans and Catholics all set up missions throughout the North Island, ostensibly to protect Maori from the worst of the exploitation and campaigning in both London and Sydney for more policing of Pakeha actions. In exchange, they destroyed fine artworks considered too sexually explicit and demanded that Maori abandon cannibalism and slavery; in short Maori were expected to trade in their *Maoritanga* and become **"Europeans"**. By the 1830s, self-confidence and the belief in Maori ways was in rapid decline: the *tohunga* (priest) was powerless over new European diseases which could often be cured by the missionaries, and some Maori had started to believe Pakeha that the Maori race was dying out.

763

The push for colonization

Despite Cook's discovery claim in 1769, imperial cartographers had never marked New Zealand as a British possession and it was with some reluctance – informed by the perception of an over-extended empire only marginally under control – that New South Wales law was nominally extended to New Zealand in 1817. The effect was minimal; the New South Wales governor had no official representation on this side of the Tasman and was powerless to act. Unimpressed, by 1831 a small group of northern Maori chiefs decided to petition the British monarch to become a "friend and the guardian of these islands", a letter that was later used to justify Britain's intervention.

Britain's response was to send the less-than-competent **James Busby** as British Resident in 1833, with a brief to encourage trade, stay on good terms with the missionaries and Maori, and apprehend escaped convicts for return to Sydney. Convinced that New Zealand was becoming a drain on the colony's economy, the New South Wales governor, Bourke, withheld guns and troops, and Busby was

The Treaty of Waitangi: in English and Maori

The main points set out in the **English treaty** are as follows:
- The chiefs cede sovereignty of New Zealand to the Queen of England.
- The Queen guarantees the chiefs the "full exclusive and undisturbed possession of their Lands and Estates Forests Fisheries and other properties which they may collectively or individually possess".
- The Crown retains the right of pre-emption over Maori lands.
- The Queen extends the rights and privileges of British subjects to Maori.

However, the **Maori translation** presents numerous possibilities for misunderstanding, since Maori is a more idiomatic and metaphorical language, where words can take on several meanings. The main points of contention include the following:
- The preamble of the English version cites the main **objectives** of the treaty being to protect Maori interests, to provide for British settlement and to set up a government to maintain peace and order. On the other hand, the main thrust of the Maori version is that the all-important rank and status of the chiefs and tribes will be maintained.
- The concept of **sovereignty** in the Maori version is translated as *kawanatanga* (governorship), a word Maori linked to their experience of the toothless reign of James Busby (see p.168). It seems unlikely that the chiefs realized just what they were giving away.
- In the Maori text, the Crown guaranteed the *tangata whenua* (people of the land) the possession of their properties for as long as they wished to keep them. In English this was expressed in terms of **individual rights** over property. This is perhaps the most wilful mistranslation and, in practice, there were long periods when Maori were coerced into selling their **land**, and when they refused, lands were simply taken.
- **Pre-emption** was translated as *hokonga* – a term simply meaning "buying and selling", with no explanation of the Crown's exclusive right to buy Maori land, which was clearly spelled out in the English version. This has resulted in considerable friction over Maori being unable to sell any land that the government didn't want, even if they had a buyer.
- The implications of **British citizenship** may not have been well understood: it is not clear whether Maori realized they would be bound by British law.

unable to enforce his will. Busby was also duped by Baron de Thierry, a Briton of French parents, who claimed he had bought most of the Hokianga district from Hongi Hika and styled himself the "sovereign chief of New Zealand", to "save" Maori from the degradation he foresaw under British dominion. In a panic, Busby misguidedly persuaded 35 northern chiefs to proclaim themselves as the "**United Tribes of New Zealand**" in 1835. As far as the Foreign Office was concerned, this allowed Britain to disclaim responsibility for the actions of its subjects.

By the late 1830s there were around two thousand Pakeha in New Zealand, the largest concentration around Kororareka in the Bay of Islands. Most were British, but French Catholics also consolidated their tentative toehold, and in 1839 British-born James Clendon was appointed American consul. Meanwhile, **land speculators** and colonists began taking an interest. The Australian emancipationist, William Charles Wentworth, had "bought" the South Island and Stewart Island for a few hundred pounds (the largest private land deal in history, subsequently quashed by government order) and British settlers were already setting sail. The British admiralty finally took notice when the Australian convict settlements, originally intended simply as an out-of-sight, out-of-mind solution to their bulging prisons, looked set to become a valuable possession.

A combination of these pressures and Busby's exaggeration of the Maori inability to manage their own affairs goaded the British government into action. The result was the 1840 **Treaty of Waitangi** (see box opposite & p.172), a document that purported to guarantee continued Maori control of their lands, rights and possessions in return for their loss of sovereignty, a concept open for misinterpretation. The annexed lands became a dependency of New South Wales until New Zealand was declared a separate colony a year later.

Settlement and the early pioneers

Even before the Treaty was signed, there were moves to found a settlement in Port Nicholson, the site of Wellington, on behalf of the New Zealand Company. This was the brainchild of **Edward Gibbon Wakefield**, who hoped to stem American-style egalitarianism and use New Zealand as the proving ground for his theory of "scientific colonization". This aimed to preserve the English squire-and-yokel class structure but ended up encouraging absentee landordism.

Between 1839 and 1843 the New Zealand Company dispatched nearly 19,000 settlers to "**planned settlements**" in Wellington, Wanganui, Nelson and New Plymouth. This was the core of Pakeha immigration, the only substantial non-Wakefield settlement being **Auckland**, a scruffy collection of waterside shacks which, to the horror of New Zealand Company officials, became the capital after the signing of the Treaty of Waitangi.

The company couldn't buy land direct from Maori, but the government bought up huge tracts and sold it on, often for ten or twenty times what they paid for it. In 1850 the New Zealand Company foundered, leaving settlements which, subject to the hard realities of colonial life, had failed to conform to Wakefield's lofty theories and were filled with sturdy workers from labouring and lower-middle-class backgrounds.

In 1852 New Zealand achieved self-government and divided the country into six **provinces** – Auckland, New Plymouth, Wellington, Nelson, Canterbury and Otago. In addition to taking over land sales, it encouraged migrants with free passage, land grants and guaranteed employment on road construction schemes – a call heeded by those hoping for a better life away from the drudgery of working-class Britain. Maori still held the best land, growing potatoes and wheat for both local consumption and export to Australia, where the Victorian gold rush had created a huge demand. Pakeha were barely able to compete, and the slump in export prices in the mid-1850s saw many look to **pastoralism**. The Crown helped by halving the price of land, allowing poorer settlers to become landowners but simultaneously paving the way for the creation of huge pastoral runs and putting further pressure on Maori land.

Maori resistance and the New Zealand Wars

The first five years after the signing of the Treaty were a disaster, first under governor Hobson then the ineffectual FitzRoy. Relations between Maori and Pakeha began to deteriorate immediately, as the capital was moved from Kororareka to Auckland and duties were imposed in the Bay of Islands. The consequent loss of trade from passing ships precipitated the first tangible expression of dissent, a famous series of incidents involving the Ngapuhi leader **Hone Heke**, who repeatedly felled the most fundamental symbol of British authority, the flagstaff at Russell. The situation improved to some degree with the appointment of **George Grey**, the most able of New Zealand's governors, who did more than anyone else to shape the country's early years. Soon Maori began to adapt their culture to accommodate Pakeha – selling crops, operating flour mills and running coastal shipping. Grey encouraged the process by establishing mission schools, erecting hospitals where Maori could get free treatment, and providing employment on public works. In short, he upheld the spirit of the Treaty, thereby gaining enormous respect among Maori. Sadly, he failed to set up any mechanism to perpetuate his policies after he left for the governorship of Cape Town in 1853.

Under **New Zealand's constitution**, enacted in 1852, Maori were excluded from political decision-making and prevented from setting up their own form of government; although British subjects in name, they had few of the practical benefits and yet were increasingly expected to comply with British law. By now it was clear that Maori had been duped by the Treaty of Waitangi: one chief explained that they thought they were transferring the "shadow of the land" while "the substance of the land remains with us", and yet he now conceded "the substance of the land goes to the Europeans, the shadow only will be our portion". Growing **resistance** to land sales came at a time when settler communities were expanding and demanding to buy huge tracts of pastoral land. With improved communications Pakeha became more self-reliant and dismissive of Maori, who began to lose faith in the government and fell back on traditional methods of handling their affairs. Self-government had given landowners the vote, but since Maori didn't hold individual titles to their land they were denied suffrage. Maori and Pakeha aspirations seemed completely at odds and there was a growing **sense of betrayal**, which helped replace tribal animosities with a tenuous unity. In 1854, a month before New Zealand's first parliament, Maori held inter-tribal meetings to discuss a response to the degradation of their culture and the rapid loss of their land. The eventual upshot was the 1858 election of the ageing **Te Wherowhero**, head chief of the Waikatos, as the Maori "King", the leader of the **King Movement** (see box, p.218) behind which Maori could rally to hold back the flood of Pakeha settlement. Most were moderates making peaceful overtures that Pakeha chose to regard as rebellious.

Matters came to a head in 1860, when the government used troops to enforce a bogus purchase of land at Waitara, near New Plymouth. The fighting at Taranaki soon consumed the whole of the North Island in the **New Zealand Wars**, once known by Pakeha as the Maori Wars and by Maori as *te riri Pakeha* (foreigners' anger). Maori were divided, with some settling old grievances by siding with the government against their traditional enemies. Through the early 1860s the number of Pakeha troops was tripled to around 3000, providing an effective force against less coordinated Maori forces. Though there were notable Maori successes, the final result was inevitable. Fighting had abated by the end of the 1860s but peace wasn't finally declared until 1881.

British soldiers had been lured into service with offers of land and free passage and, in a further affront to defeated Maori, many were settled in the solidly Maori Waikato. Much of the most fertile land was **confiscated** – in the Waikato, the Bay of Plenty and Taranaki – with little regard to the owners' allegiances during the conflict. By 1862 the Crown had relinquished its right of pre-emption and individuals could buy land directly from Maori, who were forced to limit the stated ownership first to ten individuals and later to just one owner. With their collective power smashed, voracious land agents lured Maori into debt then offered to buy their land to "save" them.

Between 1860 and 1881, the **non-Maori population** rose from 60,000 to 470,000, swamping and marginalizing Maori society. An Anglo-Saxon worldview came to dominate all aspects of New Zealand life, and by 1871 the Maori language was no longer used for teaching in schools. Anthony Trollope in 1872 wrote of the defeated people: "There is scope for poetry in their past history. There is room for philanthropy as to their present condition. But in regard to their future – there is hardly a place for hope."

Meanwhile, as the New Zealand Wars raged in the North Island, **gold fever** had struck the South, with discoveries near Queenstown in 1861 and later along the West Coast. For the best part of a decade, gold was New Zealand's major export, but its most noticeable effect was on population distribution: by 1858 the shrinking Maori population had been outstripped by rapidly swelling Pakeha numbers, most settling in the South Island where relations with Maori played a much smaller part.

Consolidation and social reform

The 1870s were dominated by the policies of Treasurer Julius Vogel, who started a **programme of public works** funded by borrowing on a massive scale. Within a decade previously scattered towns in separately governed provinces were transformed into a single country unified by improved roads, an expanding rail system, 7000km of telegraph wires and numerous public institutions. Almost all the remaining farmable land was bought up or leased from Maori and acclimatization societies sprang up with the express aim of Anglicizing the New Zealand countryside and improving **farming**. With no extensive market close enough to make perishable produce profitable, **wool** became the main export, stimulated by the development of the Corriedale sheep, a Romney-Lincoln cross with a long fleece. Wool continued as the mainstay until 1882, when the first **refrigerated meat shipment** left for Britain, signalling a turning point in the economy and the establishment of New Zealand as Britain's offshore larder, a role it maintained until the 1970s.

Accidental suffrage

In 1893, New Zealand became the first nation on earth to grant women the vote. Other territories (South Australia, Wyoming etc) had led the way with limited **women's suffrage**, but New Zealand threw the net wider. It is something New Zealanders are inordinately proud of even though it came about more by accident than any free-thinking principle.

When a radical electoral reform bill was up for consideration, Prime Minister Seddon let an amendment pass on the assumption that it would be rejected by the Legislative Council (an upper house which survived until 1950). Seddon then ordered a Liberal Party councillor to change his vote, his interference causing the ire of two other councillors who then voted for the bill, allowing it to pass by twenty votes to eighteen. It's also contended that female suffrage was approved in response to the powerful quasi-religious temperance movement, which hoped to "purify and improve the tone of our politics"; effectively giving married couples double the vote of the unmarried man, who was often seen as a drunken layabout.

Regardless of the rationale, New Zealand set a precedent and other major Western nations eventually followed suit – Finland in 1906, all Australian states by 1908, Britain in 1918, and the US in 1920. It wasn't until 1919, however, that New Zealand women were given the right to stand for parliament, and they were not eligible to be appointed to the New Zealand Legislative Council until 1941.

From 1879 until 1896 New Zealand slid into a "long depression", mostly overseen by the conservative "Continuous Ministry" – the last government composed of colonial gentry. During this time **trade unionism** began influencing the political scene and bolstered the Liberal Pact (a Liberal and Labour alliance). In 1890 the alliance wrested power and ushered in an era of unprecedented social change. Its first leader, **John Ballance**, firmly believed in state intervention and installed socialist **William Pember Reeves** as his Minister of Labour. Reeves was instrumental in pushing through sweeping reforms to working hours and factory conditions that were so progressive that no further changes were made to labour laws until 1936. Too radical for most of his colleagues, he only remained in office until 1896. When Ballance died in 1892 he was replaced by **Richard "King Dick" Seddon**, a blunt Lancastrian who introduced a graduated income tax and repealed property tax, hoping to break up some of the large estates. New Zealand was already being tagged the "social laboratory of the world", but more was to come.

In 1893, New Zealand was the first nation in the world to enact full **female suffrage**, undoubtedly in line with the liberal thinking of the time, but apparently an accident nonetheless (see box above). In 1898 Seddon further astonished the world by weathering a ninety-hour continuous debate to squeeze through legislation guaranteeing an **old age pension**. Fabian Beatrice Webb, in New Zealand that same year, declared that "it is delightful to see a country with no millionaires and hardly any slums".

By the early twentieth century, Pakeha could rest easy in the knowledge that their standard of living was one of the highest in the world. But things were not so rosy for Maori, whose numbers had plummeted from an estimated 200,000 at Cook's first visit to around 50,000 in 1896. However, as resistance to European diseases grew, numbers started rising, accompanied by a new confidence buoyed by the rise of Maori parliamentary leadership. **Apirana Ngata**, **Maui Pomare** and **Te Rangi Hiroa (Peter Buck)**, all alumni of Te Aute College, an Anglican school for Maori, were committed to working within the administrative and legislative framework of government, convinced that the survival of *Maoritanga* depended on shedding those aspects of the traditional lifestyle that impeded their acceptance of the modern world.

Seddon died in 1906 and the flame went out of the Liberal torch, though the party was to stay in power another six years. This era saw the rise of the "**Red Feds**", international socialists of the Red Federation who began to organize Kiwi labour. They rejected the arbitration system that had kept wage rises below the level of inflation for a decade, and encouraged **strikes**. The longest was at Blackball on the West Coast, where prime movers in the formation of the Federation of Miners, and subsequently the Federation of Labour, led a three-month stoppage.

The 1912 election was won by William Massey's Reform Party, with the support of the farmers or "cow cockies". Allegiances were now substantially polarized and 1912 and 1913 saw bitter fighting at a series of strikes at the gold mines of Waihi, the docks at Timaru and the wharves of Auckland. As workers opposed to the arbitration system withdrew their labour, owners organized scab labour, while the hostile Farmers' Union recruited mounted "special constables" to help the government. Protected by naval and military forces, they decisively smashed the Red Feds. The Prime Minister even handed out medals to strike-breaking dairy farmers.

Coming of age

Though New Zealand had started off as the unwanted offspring of Mother England, it had soon transformed itself into a devoted daughter who could be relied upon in times of crisis. New Zealand had supported Britain in South Africa at the end of the nineteenth century and was now called upon to do the same in **World War I**. Locally born Pakeha now outnumbered immigrants and, in 1907, New Zealand had traded its self-governing colony status for that of a Dominion. This gave the country control over its foreign policy, but did not stop New Zealanders flocking to the war effort. Altogether ten percent of the population was involved, 100,000 fighting in the trenches of Gallipoli, Passchendaele and elsewhere. Seventeen thousand were killed.

At home, the **Temperance Movement** was back in action, attempting to curb vice in the army brought on by drink. Plebiscites in 1911, 1914 and 1919 narrowly averted national prohibition but the "wowsers" succeeded to the point that from 1917 pubs would close at 6pm for the duration of the war, though it wasn't repealed until 1967. This "**Six o'clock swill**" – frenetic after-work consumption in which the ability to tank down as much beer as possible was raised to an art form – probably did more to hinder New Zealand's social development than anything else (and the emphasis on quantity over quality encouraged breweries to churn out dreadful watery brews).

The wartime boom economy continued until around 1920 as Britain's demand for food remained high. Pakeha **returned servicemen** were rehabilitated on newly acquired farmland; in contrast, Maori returned servicemen got nothing.

New Zealand continued to grow, with ongoing improvements in infrastructure – hydroelectric dams and roads – and enormous improvements in farming techniques, such as the application of superphosphate fertilizers, sophisticated milking machines and tractors. Yet it was ill-prepared for the **Great Depression**, when the Wall Street Crash sent shock waves through the country. The already high national debt skyrocketed as export income dropped and the Reform government cut pensions, health care and public works' expenditure. The budget was balanced at the cost of producing huge numbers of unemployed. Prime Minister Forbes dictated "no pay without work" and sent thousands of men to primitive rural relief camps for unnecessary tasks such as planting trees and draining swamps, resulting in lines of ragged men awaiting their relief money, malnourished children in schools and former soldiers panhandling in the streets.

Throughout the 1920s the Labour Party had gradually watered down some of its socialist policies in an attempt to woo the middle-ground voter. In 1935 it was swept to power and ushered in New Zealand's second era of massive social change, picking up where Seddon left off. Labour's leader **Michael Joseph Savage** felt that "Social Justice must be the guiding principle and economic organization must adapt itself to social needs", a sentiment translated by a contemporary commentator as aiming "to turn capitalism quite painlessly into a nicer sort of capitalism which will eventually become indistinguishable from socialism". Salaries reduced during the depression were restored; public works programmes were rekindled, with workers on full pay rather than "relief"; income was redistributed through graduated taxation; and in two rapid bursts of legislation Labour built the model **Welfare State**, the first in the world and the most comprehensive and integrated. State houses were built and let at low rental, pensions were increased, a national health service provided free medicines and health care, and family benefits supplemented the income of those with children.

Maori welfare was also on the agenda and there were moves to raise their living standards to the Pakeha level, partly achieved by increasing pensions and unemployment payments. Legal changes paved the way for Maori land to be farmed using Pakeha agricultural methods, while maintaining communal ownership. In return, the newly formed **Ratana Party**, who held all four of the Maori Parliamentary seats, supported Labour, keeping them in office until 1949.

New Zealand's perception of its world position changed dramatically in 1941 when the Japanese bombed Hawaii's Pearl Harbor. The country was forced to recognize its position half a globe away from Britain and in the military sphere of America. As in World War I, large numbers of troops were called up, amounting to a third of the male labour force, but casualties were fewer and on the home front the economy continued to boom. By the 1940s New Zealand was the world's most prosperous country, with an enviable quality of life and welfare safety net.

More years of prosperity

The Reform Party and the remnants of the Liberals eventually combined to form the National Party which, in 1949, wrested power from Labour. With McCarthyite rhetoric, National branded the more militant unionists as Communists and succeeded in breaking much of the power of the unions during the violent and emotional 1951 **Waterfront Lock-out**. From the late 1940s until the mid-1980s, **National** became New Zealand's party of government, disturbed only by two three-year stints with Labour in power. The country's underlying conservatism had now found its expression. Most were happy with the government's strong-arm tactics, which emasculated the militant unions.

Notions of this prosperous life (see box opposite) had huge appeal for Brits still suffering rationing after World War II, and between 1947 and 1975, 77,000 British men, women and children became "**ten pound poms**", making use of the New Zealand government's assisted passage to fill Kiwi job vacancies.

By most measures New Zealand's wealth was evenly spread, with few truly rich and relatively few poor. The exception were Maori. Responding to the urban labour shortages and good wages after World War II many now took part in a **Maori migration** to the cities, especially Auckland. Yet by the 1970s, unemploy-

The Kiwi ideal

Novelist C.K. Stead described the 1950s **Kiwi ideal** as "to live in a country with fresh air, an open landscape and plenty of sunshine; and to own a house, car, refrigerator, washing machine, bach, launch, fibre-glass rod, golf clubs, and so on". This ideal had a flipside. Historian Tony Simpson recalls "we used to run a smug little society in which all was forbidden unless it was specifically permitted, in which case it was compulsory".

ment, unrest and a disproportionate prison population were exposing weaknesses in the widely held Pakeha pride in Maori bravery, skill, generosity, sporting prowess and good humour that was nonetheless unable to set aside the discrimination which kept Maori out of professional jobs.

On the economic front, major changes took place under **Walter Nash**'s 1957–60 Labour government, when New Zealand embarked on a programme designed to relieve the country's dependence on exports. A steel rolling mill, oil refinery, gin distillery and glass factory were all set up and an aluminium industry was encouraged by the prospect of cheap power from a hydroelectric project on Lake Manapouri (see box, p.751). When **Keith Holyoake** helmed the next National government, in 1960, Britain was still by far New Zealand's biggest export market but was making overtures to the economically isolationist European Common Market. Britain was no longer the guardian she once was and in the **military** sphere New Zealand began to court Pacific allies, mainly through the ANZUS pact, which provided for mutual defence of Australia, New Zealand and the US.

Dithering in the face of adversity

In 1972 Britain finally joined the Common Market. Some other export markets had been found but New Zealand still felt betrayed. Later the same year **oil prices** quadrupled in a few months and the treasury found itself with mounting fuel bills and decreasing export receipts. The Labour government borrowed heavily but couldn't avoid electoral defeat in 1975 by National's obstreperous and pugnacious **Robert "Piggy" Muldoon**, who denounced Labour's borrowing and then outdid them. In short order New Zealand had dreadful domestic and foreign debt, unemployment was the highest for decades, and the unthinkable was happening – the standard of living was falling. People began to leave in their thousands and the "brain drain" almost reached crisis point. Muldoon's solution was to **"Think Big"**, a catch-all term for a number of capital-intensive petrochemical projects designed to utilize New Zealand's abundant natural gas to produce ammonia, urea fertilizer, methanol and synthetic petrol. It made little economic sense. Rather than use local technology and labour to convert vehicles to run on compressed natural gas (a system already up and running), Muldoon chose to pay international corporations to design huge prefabricated processing plants which were then shipped to New Zealand for assembly, mostly around New Plymouth.

Factory outfalls often jeopardized traditional Maori shellfish beds, and a new **spirit of protest** saw *iwi* win significant concessions. Throughout the mid-1970s Maori began to question the philosophy of Pakeha life and looked to the Treaty of Waitangi (see box, p.764) to correct their grievances. These were aired at occupations of traditional land at Bastion Point in Auckland and at Raglan, and through a petition delivered to parliament after a march across the North Island.

Maori also found expression in the formation of **gangs** – particularly Black Power and the Mongrel Mob – along the lines graphically depicted in Lee Tamahori's film *Once Were Warriors* (see p.796), which was originally written about South Auckland life in the 1970s. Fortified suburban homes still exist and such gangs continue to be influential among Maori youth.

Race relations were never Muldoon's strong suit and when large numbers of illegal **Polynesian immigrants** from south Pacific islands – particularly Tonga, Samoa and the Cook Islands – started arriving in Auckland he responded by instructing the police to conduct random "dawn raids" checking for "over-stayers", many of whom were deported. Muldoon opted for a completely hands-off approach when it came to sporting contacts with apartheid South Africa and in 1976 let rugby administrators send an All Black team over to play racially selected South African teams. African nations responded by boycotting the Montréal Olympics, making New Zealand an international pariah. New Zealand signed the 1977 Gleneagles Agreement requiring it to "vigorously combat the evil of apartheid" and yet in 1981 the New Zealand Rugby Union courted a **Springbok Tour**, which sparked New Zealand's greatest civil disturbance since the labour riots of the 1920s.

Economic and electoral reform

Muldoon's big-spending economic policies proved unsuccessful, and in 1984 Labour was returned to power under **David Lange**. Just as National had eschewed tradi-tional right-wing economics in favour of a "managed economy", Labour now changed tactics, addressing the massive economic problems by grasping the baton of Thatcherite economics. Under Finance Minister Roger Douglas's **Rogernomics**, the dollar was devalued by twenty percent, exchange controls were abolished, tariffs slashed, the maximum income tax rate was halved, a Goods and Services Tax was introduced and state benefits were cut. Unemployment doubled to twelve percent, a quarter of manufacturing jobs were lost, and the moderately well-off benefited at the expense of the poor; nevertheless, **market forces** and enterprise culture had come to stay. As one of the world's most regulated economies became one of the most deregulated, the long-standing belief that the state should provide for those least able to help themselves was cast aside.

In other spheres Labour's views weren't so right-wing. One of Lange's first acts was to refuse US ships entry to New Zealand ports unless they declared that they were nuclear-free. The Americans would do nothing of the sort and withdrew support for New Zealand's defence safety net, the **ANZUS** pact. Lange also gave **legal recogni-tion to the Treaty of Waitangi**, for the first time since the middle of the nineteenth century. Now, Maori grievances dating back to 1840 could be addressed.

The rise in apparent income under Rogernomics created consumer confidence and the economy boomed until the **stock market crash** of 1987, which hit New Zealand especially hard. In 1990 National's **Jim Bolger** took the helm, and throughout the deep recession National continued Labour's free-market reforms, cutting welfare programmes and extracting teeth from the unions by passing the **Employment Contracts Act**, which established the pattern of individual workplaces coming to their own agreements on wages and conditions. By the middle of the 1990s the economy had improved dramatically and what for a time had been considered a foolhardy experiment was seen by monetarists as a model for open economies the world over. Meanwhile, the gap between rich and poor continued to widen.

Modern New Zealand

In 1996, New Zealand experienced its first MMP election (see box below), which brought a new Maori spirit into parliament, with far more Maori MPs than ever before.

Bolger's poor handling of the first MMP coalition government saw his support wane, and he was supplanted in a palace coup, with **Jenny Shipley** becoming New Zealand's first female prime minister. In the 1999 election, the **Green Party** came out of left field, long-sidelined but newly resurgent under MMP. They racked up six seats and helped form a government with Labour and the Alliance under **Helen Clark** – the first female prime minister to win an election in her own right. The 1999 election brought New Zealand's first Rastafarian MP, **Nandor Tanczos**, resplendent in waist-length dreads and a hemp suit, and **Georgina Beyer**, the world's first transgender MP.

The Labour-led coalition stopped logging of beech forests on the West Coast and replaced the Employment Contracts Act with more worker-friendly legislation

C

CONTEXTS | History

First-past-the-post, MMP and Maori seats

Ever since New Zealand achieved self-government from Britain in 1852, it had maintained a first-past-the-post Westminster-style of Parliament, with the exception of the scrapping of the upper house in 1950.

In the troubled economic times of 1993, when dissatisfaction with both major parties was running high, New Zealand voted for **electoral reform**. They chose Mixed Member Proportional representation (MMP), a system the country still struggles to fully understand. The debate as to how well it works continues, but it does give smaller parties an opportunity to have a greater influence, and New Zealand's Parliament has become all the more colourful for it.

Of the 120 MPs elected, around half represent their own area of the country ("electorate" or "seat") and half are elected from party lists. Voters get **two votes**. The first is for a person, who you hope will become your electorate MP. The second is for a party and is generally considered the more important as it determines the overall make-up of Parliament. A party's representation in Parliament is made up from the number of electorate seats they win plus a number of their list MPs determined by their percentage of the party vote.

To get any seats at all, small parties must exceed the threshold of five percent of the party vote, or win a constituency seat. If they win a seat, their representation is proportional to their party vote even if it's under five percent.

To further complicate matters, Maori voters can choose to vote either within the general system described above, or for one of the seven **Maori seats** which cover the country. All parties are entitled to field candidates in both general and Maori constituencies, though parties championing Maori concerns tend to win.

After taking office, Prime Minister John Key announced a **referendum** on New Zealand's electoral system, held at the same time as the general election due in late 2011. Voters will be asked two questions, firstly if they wish to change the system, and, if so, what electoral system they would like, with four alternatives: First Past the Post, the Preferential Voting system, Single Transferable Vote system or Supplementary Member system. Key has said he doesn't anticipate that voters will change from the current MMP system. However, if a majority of voters do, a second, binding referendum will be held with the 2014 general election, to choose between MMP and the preferred option from the first referendum. If the majority then vote for change, the 2017 general election will be held under the chosen system.

but failed to deliver on education and health care. Still, Labour was returned with an increased majority after the 2002 election.

Labour's popularity remained high until the 2003 **foreshore and seabed debate** in which Labour forced through legislation ostensibly guaranteeing beach-access to all, by declaring that the land in question was owned by the Crown. Maori perceived this high-handed action as an affront to their sovereignty, and traditionally Labour-supporting Maori voters turned to the July 2004-established **Maori Party**, co-led by former Labour MP **Tariana Turia**. In November 2004, the Foreshore and Seabed Act was passed into law, and at the 2005 election the Maori Party won four of the seven Maori seats. Still, Labour was able to cobble together a coalition without Maori Party support, and continue in power though with a much reduced majority.

This, combined with the perception of the Labour government having outstayed its welcome after nearly a decade in power, saw a resurgent National Party, under former currency trader **John Key**, form a minority government following the 2008 election, with the support of the Maori Party (which repeated its electoral success of 2005 and picked up a fifth seat), as well as ACT New Zealand and United Future. Labour's **Phil Goff**, who held a number of ministry portfolios under his party's previous government including Defence, took over the leadership of the Labour opposition.

Key's government has agreed in principle with the Maori Party to **repeal the Foreshore and Seabed Act**. Various options on the table at the time of writing include one of "no ownership". As Key said in 2010, "it is a concept where you don't get into the emotional debate of ownership . . . no one owns the air, no one owns the sea and we live happily in that sort of environment". Maori reaction has been mixed, and, for now, the debate continues, as it does over the MMP system, which will be put to a referendum during the 2011 general election.

Chronology of New Zealand

1200–1300 AD ▶ Arrival of first **Polynesians**.

c.1350 ▶ The traditional date of arrival of the "Great Fleet" from Hawaiki.

1642 ▶ Dutchman **Abel Tasman** sails past the West Coast but doesn't land.

1769 ▶ Englishman **James Cook** circumnavigates both main islands.

1772 ▶ French sailor **Marion du Fresne** and 26 of his men killed in the Bay of Islands.

1814 ▶ Arrival of **Samuel Marsden**, the first Christian missionary.

1830s ▶ Sealing and whaling stations dotted around the coast.

1833 ▶ James Busby installed as British Resident at Waitangi.

1835 ▶ Independence of the United Tribes of NZ proclaimed.

1840 ▶ **Treaty of Waitangi** Capital moved from Kororareka to Auckland.

1840s ▶ Cities of Auckland, Christchurch, Dunedin, Nelson, New Plymouth, Wanganui and Wellington established.

1852 ▶ NZ becomes a self-governing colony divided into six provinces.

1858 ▶ Settlers outnumber Maori.

1860–65 ▶ **Land Wars** between Pakeha and Maori.

1860s ▶ Major gold rushes in the South Island.

1865 ▶ Capital moved from Auckland to Wellington.

1867 ▶ Maori men given the vote.

1870s ▶ **Wool** established as the mainstay of the NZ economy.

1876 ▶ Abolition of provincial governments. Power centralized in Wellington.

1882 ▶ First **refrigerated meat shipment** to Europe. Lamb becomes increasingly important.

1890 ▶ NZ become "social laboratory" with introduction of compulsory arbitration and graduated income tax.

1893 ▶ Full **women's suffrage**; a world first.

1898 ▶ Old age pension introduced.

1910s ▶ Rise of organized labour under the socialist Red Federation. Strikes at Blackball, Waihi and Auckland.

1914–18 ▶ NZ takes part in WWI with terrible loss of life.

1917 ▶ **Temperance Movement** closes pubs at 6pm. Only repealed in 1967.

1920s ▶ Initial prosperity evaporates as the Great Depression takes hold.

1935 ▶ M.J. Savage's Labour government ushers in the world's first **Welfare State** with free health service, family benefits and increased pensions.

1941 ▶ Bombing of Pearl Harbor and WWII begins NZ's military realignment with the Pacific region.

1947 ▶ New Zealand becomes fully independent from Britain.

1950 ▶ Parliament's upper house abolished.

1951 ▶ NZ joins **ANZUS** military pact with the US and Australia.

1950s ▶ NZ comfortable as one of the world's most prosperous nations.

1957–60 ▶ Infrastructure improvements: steel mill, oil refinery, and numerous hydroelectric power stations built or planned.

1960s ▶ Start of **immigration from Pacific Islands**. Major **urbanization of Maori** population.

1972–75 ▶ NZ economy struggles to cope with huge oil price hikes and Britain's entry into the Common Market.

1975 ▶ **Waitangi Tribunal** established to consider Maori land claims.

1975–84 ▶ National's Robert "Piggy" Muldoon tries to borrow NZ out of trouble, investing heavily in ill-considered petrochemical projects.

1976 ▶ African nations boycott Montréal Olympics because of NZ's rugby contacts with South Africa.

1977 ▶ NZ signs Gleneagles Agreement banning sporting ties with South Africa.

1981 ▶ **Springbok Tour**. Massive protests as a racially selected South African rugby team tours NZ.

1984 ▶ The "Hikoi" land march brings Maori grievances into political focus.

1984 ▶ Labour regains power under David Lange. Widespread privatization and deregulation of NZ's protectionist economy. Refusal to allow American nuclear warships into NZ ports severely strains US–NZ relations.

1985 ▶ French secret service agents bomb Greenpeace flagship the **Rainbow Warrior** in Auckland Harbour.

1987 ▶ New Zealand becomes a **Nuclear-Free Zone**.

1990–96 ▶ Jim Bolger leads National government, pressing on with Labour's free-market reforms and further dismantling the welfare state.

1996 ▶ First **MMP election** returns an alliance of National and NZ First.

1997 ▶ Jenny Shipley ousts Bolger to become NZ's **first woman Prime Minister**.

1999 ▶ **Labour** regain power under Helen Clark in coalition with the Alliance and the Green Party.

2000 ▶ British knighthoods replaced by NZ's own honours system.

2003 ▶ Privy Council in London replaced by a Supreme Court as NZ's highest legal body.

2003 ▶ NZ population reaches four million. Continued immigration from East Asia brings the Asian population up to ten percent of the nation.

2004 ▶ Maori Party formed as a result of the debate over the rights to the foreshore and seabed.

2005 ▶ The Maori Party Maori parliamentary seats in the general election.

2008 ▶ The **National Party**, led by **John Key**, forms a minority government with the support of the Maori Party – which retained its four seats and gained a fifth – along with ACT New Zealand and United Future.

2009 ▶ Prime Minister John Key announces the return of knighthoods to the New Zealand Honours system, with past recipients of the New Zealand Order of Merit eligible to receive titles.

2011 ▶ New Zealand hosts the Rugby World Cup.

Maoritanga

When the Pakeha first came to this Island, the first thing he taught the Maori was Christianity. They made parsons and priests of several members of the Maori race, and they taught these persons to look up and pray; and while they were looking up the Pakehas took away our land.

Mahuta, the son of the Maori King Tawhiao,

addressing the New Zealand Legislative Council in 1903.

The term **Maoritanga** embodies Maori lifestyle – the Maori way of doing things, embracing social structure, ethics, customs, legends, art, and language (see p.807). Despite New Zealand's Anglo-European-dominated society, contemporary Maori culture has seen a dramatic resurgence in recent decades. Maori make up around fifteen percent of the population, with Maori–Pakeha marriage since the early nineteenth century creating a complex interracial pool, with innumerable Pakeha claiming Maori forebears. Maori ancestry remains the foundation of Maoridom but a sense of belonging is increasingly important.

Many Pakeha have long cited scenes of Maori and Pakeha elbow-to-elbow at the bar and Maori rugby players in the scrum alongside their Pakeha brothers as evidence of a harmonious existence. Yet this has ignored an undercurrent of Maori dissatisfaction over their treatment since the arrival of Europeans; the policy of **assimilation** relied on Maori conforming to the Pakeha way of doing things, making no concession to *Maoritanga*. Maori adapted quickly to European ways but were rewarded with the near-loss of their language (see p.807), and the loss of their **land**. It is impossible to overestimate the importance of this: Maori spirituality invests every tree, hill and bay with a kind of supernatural life of its own, drawn from past events and the actions of the ancestors. It is by no means fanciful to equate the loss of land with the diminution of Maori life force.

It's only really since the 1980s that the paternal Pakeha view has been challenged, with the country adopting **biculturalism**. As Maori rediscover their heritage and Pakeha comprehend what has been around for generations, knowledge of *Maoritanga* and some understanding of the language is seen as desirable and advantageous. Recent governments have increasingly fostered a take-up in the learning of Maori language, resurgence in Maori arts and crafts and a growing pride in the culture by both Maori and Pakeha.

For some **Pakeha**, however, there is unease over Treaty of Waitangi land claims (see box, p.172). So far, reaction to the strengthening Maori hand in this climate of conciliation has only been voiced quietly but just how this scenario will pan out remains to be seen.

The sluggish pace of change, coupled with ongoing debate over the Foreshore and Seabed Act (see p.774), has led to an increase in Maori activism. The debate effectively led to the birth of the Maori party, which is growing in strength and influence, but even this change is too little for some – as evidenced by the October 2007 raids of an alleged paramilitary training camp in the North Island. A group of mostly Maori activists led by Tame Iti were arrested as terrorists, although the charges were commuted to firearms offences. The reaction of the Labour government, including the "lock-down" of the community at nearby Ruatoki, heightened calls for greater self-determination.

Maori legend

Maori culture remains primarily oral with chants, storytelling and oratory central to ceremonial and daily life. Different tribal groups had different sets of stories, or at least variations on common themes, but European historians with pet theories often distorted the tales they heard and destroyed conflicting evidence, creating their own Maori folklore. Over time many of these stories have been taken back into Maori tradition, resulting in a patchwork of authentic and bowdlerized legends and helping create a common Maori identity.

Creation

From the primal nothingness of **Te Kore** sprang **Ranginui** the sky father and **Papatuanuku** the earth mother. They had numerous offspring, including: **Haumia Tiketike**, the god of the fern root and food from the forest; **Rongo**, the god of the *kumara* and cultivation; **Tu Matauenga**, the god of war; **Tangaroa**, the god of the oceans and sealife; **Tawhirimatea**, the god of the winds; and **Tane Mahuta**, the god of the forests. Through long centuries of darkness the brothers argued over whether to separate their parents and create light. Tawhirimatea opposed the idea and fled to the skies where his anger is manifested in thunder and lightning, while Tane Mahuta succeeded in parting the two, allowing life to flourish. Ranginui's tears filled the oceans, and even now it is their grief that brings the dew, mist and rain.

Having created the creatures of the sea, the air and the land, the gods turned their attentions to humans and, realizing that they were all male, decided to create a female. They fashioned clay into a form resembling their mother and **Tane** breathed life into the nostrils of the Dawn Maiden, **Hinetitama**.

Maui the trickster and Kupe the navigator

Maori mythology is littered with demigods, none more celebrated than **Maui-Tikitiki-a-Taranga**, whose exploits are legend throughout Polynesia. With an armoury of spells, guile and boundless mischief, Maui gained a reputation as a trickster, using his abilities to turn situations to his advantage. Equipped with the powerful magic jawbone of his grandmother, he set about taming his world,

Maui fishes up the North Island

Maui's greatest work was the creation of **Aotearoa**. Because of his reputation for mischief, Maui's brothers often left him behind when they went fishing, but one morning he stowed away, revealing himself far out to sea and promising to improve their catch. Maui egged them on until they were beyond the normal fishing grounds before dropping anchor. In no time at all Maui's brothers filled the canoe with fish, but Maui still had some fishing to do. They scorned his hook (secretly armed with a chip of his grandmother's jawbone) and wouldn't lend him any bait, so Maui struck his own nose and smeared the hook with his blood. Soon he hooked a fabulous fish that, as it broke the surface, stretched into the distance all around them. Chanting an incantation, Maui got the fish to lie quietly and it became the North Island, Te ika a Maui, the fish of Maui. As Maui went to make an offering to the gods, his brothers began to cut up the fish and eat it, hacking mountains and valleys into the surface. To fit in with the legend, the South Island is often called Te waka a Maui, the canoe of Maui, and Stewart Island the anchor, Te punga o te waka a Maui.

believing himself invincible. He even took on **the sun**, which passed so swiftly through the heavens that people had no time to tend their fields. Maui, with the aid of his older brothers, plaited strong ropes and tied them across the sun's pit before dawn. The sun rose into the net and Maui set upon the sun with his magic jawbone, beating the sun and imploring it not to go so fast. The sun weakened and agreed to Maui's request. Maui's legendary antics extend to the creation of Aotearoa (see box opposite).

Maori trace their ancestry back to **Hawaiki**, the source of the Polynesian diaspora, for which the Society Islands and the Cook Islands are likely candidates. According to legend, the first visitor to Aotearoa was **Kupe**, the great Polynesian navigator. He was determined to kill a great octopus that kept stealing his bait; drawn ever further out to sea in pursuit, he finally reached landfall on the uninhabited shores of Aotearoa, the "land of the long white cloud". He named numerous features of the land before returning to Hawaiki with instructions for retracing his voyage.

Social structure and customs

Maori society is **tribal**, though the deracination resulting from the move from tribal homelands to cities has eroded many close ties. In urban situations the finer points of *Maoritanga* have been rediscovered and the basic tenets remain strong, with formal protocol ruling ceremonies from funeral wakes to meetings.

The most fundamental grouping in Maori society is the extended family or **whanau** (literally "birthing"), spanning immediate relatives to cousins, uncles and nieces. A dozen or so *whanau* form localized sub-tribes or **hapu** (literally "gestation or pregnancy"), perhaps the most important group, comprising of extended families of common descent. *Hapu* were originally economically autonomous and today continue to conduct communal activities, typically through *marae* (see p.780). Neighbouring *hapu* are likely to belong to the same tribe or **iwi** (literally "bones"), a looser association of Maori spread over large geographical areas. The thirty-odd major *iwi* are tenuously linked by common ancestry, traced back to semi-legendary canoes, or *waka*. In troubled times, *iwi* from the same *waka* would band together for protection. Together these are the **tangata whenua**, "the people of the land", a term that may refer to Maori people as a whole, or just to one *hapu* if local concerns are being aired.

The literal meanings of *whanau*, *hapu* and *iwi* can be viewed as a metaphor for the Maori view of their relationship with their ancestors or **tupuna**, existing through their genetic inheritors, the past forming part of the present. Hence the respect accorded the **whakapapa**, an individual's genealogy tracing descent from the gods via one of the migratory *waka* and through the *tupuna*. The *whakapapa* is often recited on formal occasions such as **hui** (meetings).

Maori traditional life is informed by the parallel notions of **tapu** (taboo) and **noa** (mundane, not *tapu*). This belief system is designed to impose a code of conduct: transgressing *tapu* brings ostracism, ill fortune and sickness. Objects, places, actions and people can be *tapu*, demanding extra respect; the body parts of a chief, especially the head, menstruating women, sacred items, earrings, pendants, hair combs, burial sites, and the knowledge contained in the *whakapapa* are all *tapu*. There is a practical aspect too, with the productivity of fishing grounds and forests traditionally maintained by imposing *tapu* at critical times. The direct opposite of *tapu* is *noa*, a term applied to ordinary items that, by implication, are considered safe; a new building is *tapu* until a special ceremony renders it *noa*.

People, animals and artefacts, whether *tapu* or *noa*, possess **mauri** (life force), **wairua** (spirit) and **mana**, a term loosely translated as prestige but embodying wider concepts of power, influence, charisma and goodwill. Birthright brings with it a degree of *mana* that can then be augmented through brave deeds or lost through inaction. Wartime cannibalism was partly ritual and by eating an enemy's heart a warrior absorbed his *mauri*; likewise personal effects gain *mana* from association with the *mana* of their owner, accruing more when passed to descendants. Any slight on the *mana* of an individual was felt by the *hapu*, who must then exact **utu** (a need to balance any action with an equal reaction), a compunction that often led to bloody feuds, sometimes escalating to war and further enhancing the *mana* of the victors. Pakeha found this a hard concept to grasp and deeds that they considered deceitful or treacherous could be considered correct in Maori terms.

The responsibility for determining *tapu* falls to the **tohunga** (priest or expert), the most exalted of many specialists in *Maoritanga*, conversant with tribal history, sacred lore and the *whakapapa*, and considered to be the earthly presence of the power of the gods.

Marae

The rituals of *hapu* life – *hui*, **tangi** (funeral wakes) and **powhiri** (formal welcomes) – are conducted on the **marae**, a combined community, cultural and social centre where the cultural values, protocols, customs and vitality of *Maoritanga* find their fullest expression. Strictly, a *marae* is a courtyard, but the term is often applied to a whole complex, comprising the **whare runanga** (meeting house, or *whare nui*), *whare manuhiri* (house for visitors), *whare kai* (eating house) and an old-fashioned **pataka** (raised storehouse). *Marae* belonging to one or more *hapu* are found all over the country, while pan-tribal urban *marae* exist to help Maori who have lost their roots.

Visitors, whether Maori or Pakeha, may not enter *marae* uninvited, so unless you're personally invited, you're most likely to visit on a commercially run **tour**. Invited guests are expected to provide some form of **koha** (donation) towards the upkeep of the *marae*, usually included in tour fees. Remember, the *marae* is sacred and due reverence must be accorded the **kawa** (protocols).

Following long tradition, **manuhiri** (visitors) approaching the *marae* are ritually challenged, to determine intent, by a **wero**, where a fearsome warrior bears down with twirling **taiaha** (long club), flickering tongue and bulging eyes. The women then make the **karanga** (welcoming call), followed by the **powhiri** (sung welcome), breaking the *tapu* and acting as a prelude to touching noses, **hongi**, binding the *manuhiri* and the *tangata whenua* physically and spiritually. On commercial trips, the welcome ceremony is followed by a concert comprising songs, dances, chants, and a **hangi** (feast cooked in an earth oven).

Arts and crafts

The origins of **Maori art** lie in eastern Polynesia but half a millennium of isolated development has resulted in unique forms of expression. Eastern Polynesia has no suitable clay, so Maori forebears had no skills for pottery and focused on wood, stone and weaving, occasionally using naturalistic designs but more often the **stylized forms** that make Maori art unmistakable.

As with other *taonga* (treasures), many examples were taken by Victorian and later collectors, but there is determined effort by *iwi* and Te Puni Kokiri (the Ministry of Maori Development) to restore *taonga* to New Zealand, including severed heads scattered through museums around the world – some were recently returned by the Victoria & Albert Museum in London.

Woodcarving

Maori handiworks' greatest expression is **woodcarving**. The essence of great Maori woodcarving is that as much care is given to the production of a humble water bailer as to the pinnacle of Maori creativity, *waka* (canoes) and *whare whakairo* (carved houses). Early examples of woodcarving feature the sparse, rectilinear styles of ancient eastern Polynesia, but by the fifteenth century these were replaced by the cursive style, employed by more traditional carvers today. In Northland, kauri wood was used, while elsewhere durable, easily worked totara was the material of choice. Carvers worked with shells and sharp stones in the earliest times, but the artist's scope increased with the invention of tools fashioned from **pounamu** (greenstone, a form of jade; see p.647). Some would say that the quality of the work declined after European arrival: not just through the demand for quickly executed "tourist art", but as a consequence of pressure to remove the phallic imagery found obscene by missionaries. As early as 1844, carving had been abandoned in areas with a strong missionary presence, and it continued to decline until the 1920s when Maori parliamentarian Apirana Ngata established Rotorua's pan-tribal **Maori Arts and Crafts Institute** – a foundation on which *Maoritanga* could be rebuilt.

The role of carver has always been highly respected, with seasoned and skilled exponents having the status of *tohunga* and travelling the country to carve and teach. The work is *tapu* and *noa* objects must be kept away – cooked food is not allowed nearby, and carvers have to brush away shavings rather than blow them – though women, previously banned, can now become carvers.

Maori carving exhibits a distinctive **style**. Relief forms are hewn from a single piece of wood with no concession to natural form, shapes or blemishes. Landscapes are symbolized not actually depicted, perspective is not represented, and figures stand separately. Unadorned wood is rare, carvers creating a stylistic bed of swirling spirals, curving organic forms based on fern fronds or seashells and interlocking latticework. Superimposed on this are key elements, often inlaid with paua shell.

The most common is the ancestor figure, the **hei tiki**, a distorted human form, either male, female or of indeterminate gender. Almost as common is the mythical *manaia*, a beaked birdlike form with an almost human profile. Secondary motifs include the *pakake* (whale) and *moko* (lizard).

While the same level of craftsmanship was applied to all manner of tools, weapons and ornaments, it reached its most exalted expression in *waka taua* (**war canoes**), the focus of community pride and endeavour. Gunwales, bailers and paddles are fabulously decorated but the most detailed work is reserved for the prow and sternpost, usually a matrix of spirals interwoven with *manaia* figures. As guns and the European presence altered the balance of tribal warfare in the 1860s, the *waka taua* was superseded in importance by the *whare whakairo* (carved meeting house).

Whare

Originally the chief's residence, the *whare* gradually adopted the symbolism of the *waka* – some incorporated wood from *waka*. Each meeting house is a tangible manifestation of the *whakapapa*, usually representing a synthesis of the ancestors: the ridge-pole, the backbone; the rafters, the ribs; the interior, the belly; the gable, the head; and the barge-boards, the arms, often with finger-like decoration. Inside, all wooden surfaces are carved and the spaces filled with intricate woven-flax panels, *tukutuku*.

Greenstone carving

Maori carvers also work in **pounamu** (greenstone), supplied by pre-European trade routes originating in the West Coast and Fiordland – indeed, the South Island became known as Te Wai Pounamu, the Greenstone Water. The stone was fashioned into adzes, chisels and clubs for hand-to-hand combat; tools that took on a ritual significance and demanded decoration. *Pounamu*'s hardness dictates a more restrained carving style and *mere* and *patu* tend to be only partly worked, leaving large sweeping surfaces ending in a flourish of delicate swirls. Ornamental pieces range from simple drop pendants worn as earrings or neck decoration to *hei tiki*, worn as a breast pendant. Like other personal items, especially those worn close to the body, an heirloom *tiki* possesses the *mana* of the ancestors and absorbs the wearer's *mana*, becoming *tapu*.

Tattooing

A stylistic extension of the carver's craft is exhibited in *moko*, ornamental and ceremonial **tattooing** that almost died out with European contact. Women had *moko* on the lips and chin, high-ranking men had their faces completely covered, along with their buttocks and thighs; the greater the extent and intricacy of the *moko*, the greater the status. A symmetrical pattern of traditional elements, crescents, spirals, fern fronds and other organic forms, was gouged into the flesh with an *uhi* (chisel) and mallet, then soot rubbed into the wound. In the last couple of decades the tradition of full-face *moko* has been revived, as a symbol of *Maoritanga* and an art form in its own right; since 1999, *moko* artists have been eligible for government funding.

Weaving and clothing

While men carved, women concentrated on weaving and producing clothing. When Polynesians arrived in these cool, damp islands their paper mulberry plants didn't thrive and they were forced to look for alternatives. They found *harakeke* (New Zealand **flax**), the foundation of Maori fibre-work. The long, strong and pliable fibres, growing on marshy land all over the country, were used as fishing lines, as cordage for axe-heads and as floor matting. With the arrival of the Pakeha, Maori adopted European clothes, but they continued to wear cloaks on formal occasions and today these constitute the basis for contemporary designs.

Used in something close to their raw form for *raranga* (plaiting) they made *kete*, handle-less baskets for collecting shellfish and *kumara*, triangular canoe sails, sandals and *whariki*, patterned floor mats still used in meeting houses. For finer work, trimming, soaking and beating flax, a laborious process, produced stronger and more pliable fibre.

Most flax was neutral but Maori design requires some **colouring**: black is achieved by soaking in a dilute extract of *hinau* tree bark then rubbing with a black swamp sediment, *paru*; red-brown ranges of colours require boiling in dyes derived from the tanekaha tree bark and fixing by rolling in hot ashes; while the less popular yellow tint is produced from the bark of the Coprosma species. These days synthetic dyes are used to create green.

Natural and coloured fibres are both used in *whatu kakahu* (**cloak-weaving**), the crowning achievement of Maori women's art, the finest cloaks ranking alongside prized *taonga*; the immense war canoe now in the Auckland Museum was once exchanged for a fine cloak. The technique is sometimes referred to as finger-weaving as no loom is used. The women work downwards from a base warp strung between two sticks. Complex weaving techniques produce a huge array of different textures, often decorated with *taniko* (coloured borders), cord tags tacked onto the cloth at intervals and, most impressively, **feathers**. Feather cloaks (*kahu hururu*) don't appear to have been common before European contact, though heroic tales often feature key players in iridescent garments. The appeal of the bright yellow feathers of the huia probably saw to its demise, and most other brightly coloured birds are now too rare to use for cloaks, so new feather cloaks are rarely made.

You'll come across some fine examples in museums, the base cloth often completely covered by a dense layer of kiwi feathers bordered by zigzag patterns of tui, native pigeon and parakeet. More robust, *para* (rain capes) were made using the water-repellent leaves of the cabbage tree and a form of coarse canvas that could reportedly resist spear thrusts was used for *pukupuku* (war cloaks). Some *pukupuku* were turned into *kahu kuri* (dog-skin cloaks) with the addition of strips of dog skin, arranged vertically so that the natural fur colours produced distinctive patterns.

Weaving and plaiting are again popular; cloaks are an important element of formal occasions, whether on the *marae* for *hui* and *tangi*, or elsewhere for receiving academic or state honours. Old forms are reproduced directly or raided as inspiration for contemporary designs that interpret traditional elements in the light of modern fashion.

The haka, Maori dance and Maori music

The use of the *haka* (see box below) by what are often predominantly Pakeha sides might seem inappropriate but it is entrenched in Kiwi culture; there was a considerable backlash in 1996 when the All Black coach suggested the *haka* should be

The haka

Before every international rugby match, New Zealand's All Blacks put the wind up the opposition by performing an intimidating thigh-slapping, eye-bulging, tongue-poking chant. Traditionally this has been the Te Rauparaha *haka*, just one of many such Maori posture dances, designed to display fitness, agility and ferocity. The Te Rauparaha *haka* was reputedly composed early in the nineteenth century by the warrior Te Rauparaha (p.254), who was hiding from his enemies in the *kumara* pit of a friendly chief. Hearing noise above and then being blinded by light he thought his days were numbered, but as his eyes became accustomed to the sun he saw the hairy legs of his host and was so relieved he performed the *haka* on the spot.

Touring teams have performed the *haka* at least since the 1905 All Black tour of Britain, and since the 1987 World Cup for home matches as well. The performance is typically led by a player of Maori descent chanting:

Ringa pakia Slap the hands against the thighs

Uma tiraha Puff out the chest

Turi whatia Bend the knees

Hope whai ake Let the hip follow

Waewae takahia kia kino Stamp the feet as hard as you can

After a pause for effect the rest of the team join in with:

Ka Mate! Ka Mate! It is death! It is death!

Ka Ora! Ka Ora! It is life! It is life!

Tenei te ta ngata puhuru huru This is the hairy man

Nana nei i tiki mai Who caused the sun to shine

Whakawhiti te ra Keep abreast!

A upane ka upane! The rank! Hold fast!

A upane kaupane whiti te ra! Into the sun that shines!

changed to mollify those Maori *iwi* who had been decimated by Te Rauparaha. The new, specially written *Kapa O Pango haka* was unveiled in 2005 but it hasn't completely replaced the Te Rauparaha version.

At commercial **Maori concerts** (in Rotorua, Christchurch, Queenstown and elsewhere) there will invariably be a *haka*, usually the Te Rauparaha version, usually performed by men. Though women aren't excluded, they normally concentrate on **poi dances**, where balls of *raupo* (bulrush) attached to the end of strings are swung around in rhythmic movements, designed to improve co-ordination and dexterity.

The drums of eastern Polynesia didn't make it to New Zealand, so both chants and the *haka* go unaccompanied. Along with the traditional bone flute, Pakeha added the guitar to accompany **waiata** (songs), relatively modern creations whose impact comes from tone, rhythm and lyrics. The impassioned delivery can seem at odds with music that's often based on Victorian hymns: perhaps the best known are *Pokarekare ana* and *Haere Ra*, both post-European-contact creations. Outside the tourist concert party, Maori music has developed enormously in recent years to the point where there are tribal and Maori-language music stations almost exclusively playing music written and performed by Maori, often with a hip-hop or R&B influence and a Pacific twist. For more on music, see box, p.797.

Landscapes and wildlife

Despite its size, New Zealand is bursting with enormous diversity: subtropical forests, volcanic basins, boiling mud pools, geysers, rugged white-silica and gold-sand fringed coastlines and spectacular alpine regions. These landscapes support an extraordinary variety of animals and plant life, with almost ninety percent of the flora not found anywhere else in the world. Many habitats, plants and wildlife are easily accessible, protected within national parks and scenic reserves.

The Shaky Isles

The earliest rocks are thought to have originated in the continental forelands of Australia and Antarctica, part of Gondwanaland, a massive supercontinent to which New Zealand belonged. Oceanic islands were created by continental drift, the movement of the large plates that form the earth's crust, which created an island arc and oceanic trench about 100 million years ago.

Roughly 26 million years ago, New Zealand rose further from the sea and today's landscape evolved, through **volcanic** activity and continuous movement along fault lines, particularly the Alpine Fault of the South Island. On the boundary between the Australian and Pacific tectonic plates, New Zealand's North Island has the two plates crashing into one another, the Pacific plate pushed beneath the Australian to produce prolific volcanic activity. Conversely under the South Island the Pacific plate rides over the Australian, causing **mountain building** and creating the Southern Alps. This unique island combination generates about four hundred **earthquakes** a year, although only a quarter are big enough to be noticed, and has earned New Zealand the nickname "the Shaky Isles". The volcanoes on the North Island periodically become impressively active: White Island (just off the coast of the Bay of Plenty) blows steam, while Mount Ruapehu erupted in 2006 and 2007.

The end of isolation

New Zealand's flora and fauna evolved untouched until the first human reached Aotearoa, reportedly around a thousand years ago. Before the arrival of Maori, the land was covered in thick **forest** composed of hundreds of tree species and the only mammals were seals, whales and dolphins round the coast, and a couple of types of **bat**. Land mammals were non-existent, a unique situation, which allowed **birds** to take their place in the food chain; with no predators, many gradually lost

---

Conservation and wildlife organizations and websites

Department of Conservation ⓦ www.doc.govt.nz. Government department charged with conserving New Zealand's natural and historic heritage.

Forest and Bird Protection Society ⓦ www.forestandbird.org.nz. New Zealand's leading independent conservation organization.

NZ Birds ⓦ www.nzbirds.com. Comprehensive site on everything feathery.

Save The Kiwi ⓦ www.savethekiwi.org.nz. Department of Conservation and Bank of New Zealand effort to save this iconic bird from extinction.

the ability to fly. When Maori came, with their dogs and rats, and then Pakeha, with all their introduced species, the birds could not compete. Those that survived (see box, p.790) now cling precariously to existence.

Maori impact pales in comparison with the devastation wreaked by **Europeans**. Cook's first exploratory visits left a legacy of wild pigs, sheep and potatoes, while in the early 1800s whalers and sealers bloodied the coastal waters, while logging campaigns cleared vast tracts of native trees for grazing cattle. Pioneers continued to tamper with the delicately balanced ecosystem in an attempt to create a "New England". **Acclimatization societies** sprung up in the late 1800s to introduce familiar animals and plants from settlers' European homelands – New Zealand would never have become the successful pastoral nation it is without the grasses, pollinating birds, bees and butterflies, sheep and cattle. But many releases were disastrous, either out-competing native plants and birds or killing them.

The lowlands

Archetypal paddocks full of **sheep**, often backed by shelter belts of macrocarpa trees, are within sight of the airports. Sheep number about 40 million, roughly half the population of thirty years ago, with much of their grazing land turned over to

---

The scourge of the bush: mammalian pests

Since human habitation began, 43 indigenous bird species have become extinct and New Zealand is now home to about eleven percent of the world's most endangered species. People settling and the introduction of non-native plants and animals are responsible for devastating this country's unique ecosystem.

Possums

Visitors to New Zealand soon become familiar with the nocturnal **possum**, if only as road-kill. Live specimens usually show up when you are tramping, their eyes reflecting your torchlight around huts at night. Although they look cute they are a pest, causing enormous damage to flora and fauna, stunting trees by munching new shoots, eating native birds' eggs and killing chicks. Consequently, New Zealanders have an almost pathological hatred of this introduced Australian marsupial and greenies who would never dream of wearing any other fur happily don possum-skin slippers.

Before the start of controlled European migration in 1840, enterprising individuals were liberating **brushtail opossums** (*Trichosurus vulpecula*, more commonly known as **possums**) in New Zealand, with the aim of establishing a fur industry. Releases stopped around 1930 but control measures were not introduced until 1951, when a bounty was paid on all possums with their skins intact. Until the late 1980s possums were killed for their fur, but successful anti-fur lobbying saw prices plummet. Hunting tailed off and possum numbers skyrocketed. There are now in excess of **seventy million** possums, who currently eat their way through some 21,000 tonnes of vegetation every night, and are known carriers of bovine TB – endangering the dairy, beef and deer industries.

Possums are so widespread that hunting barely has any effect and the government is forced to spend around $100 million a year on possum control. The most cost-effective is aerial drops of **1080 poison**, a controversial substance banned in almost every other country in the world. Farmers claim it kills their stock and the native birds it is designed to protect. Certainly native birds do die, but the decimation of the possum population allows such an increase in avian breeding success that bird numbers exceed their pre-poisoning levels.

other uses: dairying, deer farming or, less commonly, ostriches. Elsewhere, land has been redeveloped for horticulture or **vineyards**, which continue to crop up, particularly around Gisborne, Hastings, Martinborough, Blenheim, Nelson, Waipara and Cromwell. Vintners are co-producing **olives** – with increasing success – and optimistic souls plant oak and hazel trees in the hope of creating a truffle industry.

Throughout both farmed and forested New Zealand you'll see native **cabbage trees** (*ti kouka*) with thin grey trunks (up to 10m high) topped by spear-shaped leaves and clusters of white flowers. Captain Cook and his men ate the leaf shoots, finding them vaguely cabbage-like.

Lowland forests

Much of the thick forest that greeted Maori and early settlers was burned, logged, or cleared for farming, but pockets of **native bush** survive. The forests of Northland, the Coromandel Peninsula, the west coasts of both islands, around Wellington and on Stewart Island contain a wonderful variety of native trees. There are also sixty endemic native flowering plant species in lowland areas, whose blooms are almost all white or yellow. With no pollinating bees to attract there was little need for vibrant petals.

New Zealand's best-known tree, the **kauri**, is found in mixed lowland forest, particularly in Northland. With a lifespan of two to four thousand years, this

Wild pigs, deer, tahr and chamois

When James Cook sailed around New Zealand in the 1770s he released **pigs** so that on return voyages there would be something tasty to eat. These feral pigs (known as "Captain Cookers") are still out there rooting up the ground, although pig hunting keeps numbers down.

Seven **deer** species were successfully established for sport from 1851 up to the 1930s, and even today there are illegal releases of deer by hunters. Authorities are reluctant to advocate complete removal because of the political strength of the hunting lobby. In the first half of the twentieth century, the government also introduced the Himalayan **tahr**, a goat-like animal, and European **chamois**, both of which inhabit the high country of the South Island.

Rabbits and mustelids

Rabbits were introduced to New Zealand from the 1840s and though they don't pose a particular threat to native wildlife, the means used to try and stem the population certainly does. In the 1880s **ferrets** were introduced, but instead of targeting rabbits, these members of the mustelid family found the flightless birdlife easier prey. Along with **weasels**, **stoats** were also introduced to combat the rabbit plague, but instead they became the number-one enemy of native species.

Dogs, cats, rats and mice

Uncontrolled **dogs** can't resist playing with any flightless birds they might come across and studies suggest they are responsible for 76 percent of adult brown kiwi deaths alone. There are an estimated 1.2 million **cats** in New Zealand, a quarter of them feral, and they kill numerous birds and lizards.

The *kiore* or Polynesian **rat** has been largely displaced by more aggressive Norway and ship rats, living everywhere from the treetops to the leaf litter, who ravage small bird and insect populations as well as devouring plant seeds and suppressing growth in the bush. **Mice** play a similarly devastating role.

magnificent king of the forest rises to 30m, two-thirds of it straight, branchless trunk. Greatly revered by Maori canoe-builders, who enacted solemn ceremonies before hacking them down, and European shipbuilders, who used them for masts and timbers, many kauri were more prosaically turned into frames, cladding and floorboards for wooden houses. The tree is also the source of kauri gum, dug and exported in the late nineteenth and early twentieth century.

Open spaces along forest edges and riverbanks are often alive with tui (see p.791) sucking nectar from golden clusters of **kowhai**, the national flower, which hang from trees, whose wood was once fashioned into Maori canoe paddles and adze handles.

The North Island and the top third of the South are home to New Zealand's only native palm, the **nikau**. Its slender branchless stem bears shiny leaves, up to 30cm, long pink spiky flowers and red berries, used by European settlers as pellets in the absence of ammunition.

Irregularly branched, growing to 20m, the **pohutukawa** is found as far south as Otago, in forests around the coast and at lake edges. Typically it bears festive bright crimson blossoms around Christmas. Another well-known red-blooming

The kiwi

Flightless, dull brown in colour and distinctly odd looking, the kiwi is New Zealand's much-loved, national symbol. Stout, muscular, shy and nocturnal, it is a member of the ratite family – which includes the ostrich, emu, rhea, cassowary and the long-extinct moa – and is one of the few birds in the world with a well-developed sense of **smell**. At night you might hear them snuffling around, using the nostrils at the end of their bill to detect earthworms, beetles, cicada larvae, spiders and koura (freshwater crayfish), berries and the occasional frog. Armed with sensitive bristles at the base of its bill and a highly developed sense of hearing, the kiwi can detect other birds and animals on its territory and will readily attack them with its claws. The females are bigger than the males and lay huge eggs, weighing a fifth of their body weight. After eighty days, the eggs hatch and the chicks live off the rich yolk; neither parent feeds them and they emerge from the nest totally independent. They sleep for up to twenty hours a day, which explains why they normally live to the age of 20 or 25.

Sadly there are probably fewer than 70,000 birds left and numbers in the wild are dropping. Kiwi are most easily seen in **kiwi houses** around the country in places such as Auckland Zoo, Otorohanga, Napier, Wellington and Hokitika. The best opportunities for seeing **kiwi in the wild** are:

Trounson Forest, Northland (see p.200).

Tiritiri Matangi, Auckland (see p.146).

Kapiti Island, near Wellington (p.254).

Okarito, near Franz Josef (p.650).

Mason Bay, Stewart Island (see p.617).

Kiwi species

Kiwi have traditionally been divided into three species – Brown, Little Spotted and Great Spotted – but genetic research in the 1990s subdivided three new species off from the Brown Kiwi.

Great Spotted Kiwi Going by the Maori name *roa*, this is the largest kiwi species, with adults males averaging 2.4kg and females 3.3kg. They are the most rugged kiwi,

tree is the gnarled **rata**, found mostly in South Island forests but occasionally popping up around the North Island.

New Zealand is also known for its unusual family of pine species, or **podocarps**. One such is the majestic **rimu** (red pine), which grows to 60m, with small green flowers, red cones and tiny green or black fruit. It was heavily milled for its timber (the charcoal was mixed with oil and rubbed into Maori tattoo incisions) but is still widespread throughout mixed forests. Other podocarps include **matai** (black pine), **miro** (brown pine), **kahikatea** (white pine), and **totara**, which grow for up to a thousand years. The trunks were used by Maori to make war canoes while strips of the thick brown bark were woven into baskets.

Below the canopy of these trees you'll find an enormous variety of **tree ferns**, many hard to tell apart. The most famous, adopted as the national emblem, is the **ponga** (silver fern). Reaching about 10m in height, its long fronds are dull green on top and silvery white underneath.

The lowland forest is prime habitat for the bulk of New Zealand's endangered birds (see box, p.790).

and are happiest in subalpine regions with wet, mossy vegetation. Smaller birds range down into lowland and coastal beech forests. European explorers told stories of kiwi the size of a turkey with powerful spurs on its legs, whose call was the loudest. Their harsh home has also helped keep them relatively safe from mammalian pests. Numbers seem fairly stable around 17,000 birds, mostly in the northern half of the South Island.

Little Spotted Kiwi Also known as Kiwi Pukupuku, this is the smallest of the kiwi, with adults weighing 1100–1300g. The main population (around 1000 birds) is on Kapiti Island. Mellow and docile by nature, pairs often share daytime shelter, going their separate ways to feed, grunting to one another as they pass. They rarely probe for food, instead finding prey on the ground or in the forest litter. The best time to hear them is just after dark from high points around an island. Listen carefully for the male's shrill whistle and the female's gentle purr.

Brown Kiwi These medium-sized kiwi are the most widespread, particularly in the central and northern North Island. They are famous for their big nose, bad temper and for being tough fighters of intruders on their territory. They live in a wide range of vegetation, including exotic forests and rough farmland on the North Island.

Rowi (aka Okarito Brown). Originally considered a subspecies of the Brown Kiwi, this is the rarest kiwi, with only around 250 surviving in the wild, all in the 10,000-hectare south Okarito Forest in South Westland. They're greyish in colour often with patches of white feathers on their face. Males and females share incubation – unlike most kiwi, where the male does the lion's share.

Haast Tokoeka These very rare birds only number around 300, unsurprisingly mostly around Haast in south Westland. They range from the shoreline to alpine tops but are most common around the bushline and in subalpine grasslands, even digging their burrows in snow.

Southern Tokoeka Totalling around 30,000 and the most common kiwi, with a stable population on Stewart Island where there are no mustelids. Also found in Fiordland, they are one of the most primitive and the most communal, sometimes seen poking about along the tideline within a few metres of one another.

Rivers, lakes and wetlands

High mountains and plentiful rain mean that New Zealand is not short of rivers. Canterbury and the Waitaki sport distinctive **braided rivers**, their wide shingle beds and multiple channels providing a breeding ground for many birds, insects, fish and plants. Numerous lakes provide rich habitats; many of New Zealand's **wetlands**, on the other hand, have been drained for agriculture and property development, although some are preserved as national parks and scenic reserves.

New Zealand's rare and endangered wildlife

New Zealand has 43 animals and many more plants on the IUCN Red List of Globally Threatened Species compiled by Birdlife International (ⓦ www.redlist.org). Among developed countries, only the United States has more. Of the birds, some 22 percent of New Zealand species are regarded as globally threatened, including the following.

Birds

Bellbird (*korimako*). Relatively common in forest and shrub, the shy, pale green bellbird is noted for its distinctive musical call.

Black stilt (*kaki*). This thin black bird with round eyes and long red legs is incredibly shy – if you do see one in the wild, keep well away. It is one of the world's rarest wading birds. Usually found in swamps and beside riverbeds, the best place to see them is in the specially created reserve near Twizel (see p.572).

Blue duck (*whio*). Uniquely among ducks, the *whio* (sometimes known as the torrent duck) spends most of its time in mountain streams, where it dives for food. One of four endemic species with no close relatives anywhere in the world, you can spot it by its blue-grey plumage, with chestnut on both breast and flanks. It also has an unusual bill with a black flexible membrane along each side, and yellow eyes (as seen on the $10 note). Its Maori name represents the male bird's call.

Fantail (*piwakawaka*). Relatively common forest dweller, seen constantly opening and closing the tail that gives it its name. It often flies alongside walkers on trails, not out of a desire for company but to feed on the insects disturbed.

Kaka Large parrot closely related to the kea, though it does not venture from its favoured lowland forest environments. You can recognize the bird by its colour: bronze with a crimson belly and underside of the tail and wings.

Kakapo The world's only flightless parrot, kakapo were once so widespread they were kept as pets. Now there are less than a hundred birds left, all on a couple of predator-free islands off the coast of Fiordland (off-limits to tourists).

Kakariki Bright green parakeets which come in yellow-crowned, red-crowned and the newly identified orange-crowned varieties. Found at most wildlife sanctuaries and on offshore islands.

Kea The world's only alpine parrot. See box, p.556.

Kereru (aka *kukupa*). With adults weighing in around 650g, this is the world's second largest pigeon. Its metallic green, purple and bronze colouring and pure white breast is often seen flashing through low-lying forests with its distinctive noisy wing-slaps. It is a very ancient New Zealand species, which seems to have no relatives elsewhere.

Kiwi See box, p.788.

Kokako Rare slate-grey bird with distinctive blue wattles (patches of skin) on each cheek. An abysmal flyer, it lives mainly in protected forests and mainland islands where trapping keeps predator numbers low. Closely related to the saddleback (see opposite) and featured on the $50 note.

It's in low wetland areas that you're likely to come across the tallest of the native trees, the kahikatea (white pine), which reaches over 60m. There's a particularly fine stand on the North Island close to Te Awamutu (see p.213).

One bird you're bound to see in the vicinity of a lake is the **pukeko** (swamp hen), a bird still in the process of losing the power of flight. Also found in parts of Australia, the pukeko is mostly dark and mid-blue with large feet and an orange beak, and lets out a high-pitched screech if disturbed.

New Zealand is renowned for its freshwater fishing, with massive brown and rainbow **trout** and **salmon** swarming through the fast-flowing streams. All intro-

Morepork (*ruru*). New Zealand's only native owl, this small brown bird is usually heard in the bush at night, and occasionally in town and city gardens. Both Maori and Pakeha names are supposed to represent its call.

NZ falcon (*karearea*). Seen occasionally in the north of the North Island but more often in the high country of the Southern Alps, Fiordland and the forests of Westland. New Zealand's only native raptor has a heavily flecked breast, chestnut thighs and a pointed head (as seen on the $20 note). Conservationists and winegrowers hope to reintroduce it to the Marlborough Plains where it may deter smaller, nuisance birds.

Robin. There are three species of native robin, all glimpsed as they flit around the forest, often fearlessly pecking the dirt around your feet. They range from black with a cream or yellow breast to all black. Their prolonged and distinctive song lasts for up to thirty minutes, with only brief pauses for breath.

Saddleback (*tieke*). This rare but pretty thrush-sized bird is mostly black except for a tan-coloured saddle.

Stitchbird (*hihi*). Small with a slightly curved beak and distinctive yellow and white patches on its sides. There are thought to be a few left, some on Kapiti Island and Tiritirii Matangi where you can see them using the feeding stations.

Takahe Rare turkey-sized bird once thought extinct (see p.735).

Tui With its white throat and mostly green and purple velvet-like body, the tui is renowned for mimicking the calls of other birds and for its copious consumption of nectar and fruit. Its song has greater range than the bellbird and contains rather unmusical squeaks, croaks and strangled utterances.

Weka About the most common flightless native, the weka is a little like a kiwi but slimmer, far less shy, and generally dark brown with marked golden flecks, especially on its heavily streaked breast. Like the kiwi, the weka grubs around at dusk but can be seen regularly during the day: many are bold enough to approach trampers and take titbits from their hands. The bird's whistle is a loud and distinctive "kooo-li". There are four subspecies found in a variety of habitats throughout the country.

Other endangered species

Tuatara This nocturnal lizard-like creature is a throwback to the age of dinosaurs and remains little changed over 260 million years. The tuatara lives on insects, small mammals and birds' eggs, a diet that sees them grow to 60cm in length and keeps them alive for well over a hundred years. Best viewed in a zoo or kiwi house.

Weta A relatively common grasshopper-like insect that has lived in lowland forests for 190 million years. Several species live in the bush but they're hard to spot so you're most likely to see them in caves or zoos. The most impressive species is the giant weta (*wetapunga*), which ranks as the heaviest insect in the world, weighing up to 71g, and is said to have been the inspiration for Ridley Scott's *Alien*.

duced species, these fish have adapted so well to their conditions that they grow much larger here than other places in the world; as a result, many native species have been driven out. Another delicacy found in New Zealand's waters are native **eels**, who despite spending most of their lives in New Zealand rivers, migrate over 2000km to breed in the waters off Fiji.

Keeping the fishermen company along the riverbanks of the Mackenzie country and Canterbury are the perilously rare **black stilts** (see box, p.790). The **common pied stilt**, a black-and-white bird, has been more successful in resisting introduced predators.

Another inhabitant of the Canterbury braided riverbank is the **wrybill**. This small white and grey bird uses its unique bent bill to turn over stones or pull out crustaceans from mud. The wrybill's close cousin, the **banded dotterel**, favours riverbanks, lakes, open land with sparse vegetation and coastal lagoons and beaches. A small, brown and white bird with a dark or black band around its neck, it breeds only in New Zealand, though it does migrate to Australia. Around fast-flowing streams you might see the increasingly rare **blue duck** (see box, p.790).

The highlands

With most of the lowland forests cleared for farming, you need to get into the hills to appreciate the picture that greeted Maori and early European immigrants. The best bets are the Tongariro, Whanganui, Taranaki, Nelson Lakes, Arthur's Pass and Aoraki Mount Cook national parks – all cloaked in highland forests, particularly native beech trees, that unlike northern hemisphere varieties, are evergreen. The 20m-high **mountain beech** (tawhairauriki) grows close to the top of the treeline and has sharp dark leaves and little red flowers. Also at high altitudes, often in mixed stands, are **silver beech** (tawhai), whose grey trunks grow up to 30m. Slightly lower altitudes are favoured by black and red beech. Often mixed in with them, the thin, straggly **manuka** (tea tree) grows in both alpine regions and on seashores.

New Zealand has five hundred species of flowering alpine plant that grow nowhere else in the world. Most famous are the large white-flowered yellow-centred **Mount Cook lilies**, the world's largest buttercup. It flowers from November to January. On the high ground of the South Island is the **vegetable sheep**, a white hairy plant that grows low along the ground and, at a great distance, could just about be mistaken for a grazing animal.

Among alpine caves and rock crevices you might come across the black **alpine weta** (also known as the "Mount Cook flea"). Fewer species of birds inhabit the high country, but those that do are a fascinating bunch. In the Southern Alps you'll hear and see the raucous **kea** and perhaps the **New Zealand falcon** (for both see p.790). Subalpine areas host smaller birds like the yellow and green **rock wren** and the **rifleman**, a tiny green and blue bird with spiralling flight. Such areas are also the natural home of two of the country's rarest birds, the **takahe** and the **kakapo** (see p.790), neither seen outside a couple of tightly controlled areas.

The coast, islands and sea

New Zealand's indented coastline, battered by the Tasman Sea and the Pacific Ocean, is a meeting place for warm and cold currents, which makes for an environment suited to an enormous variety of fish. The warm currents, populated by hoki, kahawai, snapper, orange roughy and trevally, attract tropical fish like barracuda, marlin, sharks and tuna. The cold Antarctic currents bring blue and red cod, blue and red moki, and fish that can tolerate a considerable range of temperatures, such as the tarakihi, grouper and bass.

Marine mammals also grace these waters: the rare **humpback whale** is an occasional visitor to Kaikoura and Cook Strait, while **sperm whales** are common year-round in the deep sea trench near Kaikoura. **Orca** are seen regularly wherever there are dolphins, seals and other whales. Another frequent visitor is the **pilot whale**: up to two hundred pass by Farewell Spit each year; they're also seen in Cook Strait and the Bay of Plenty.

Common dolphins congregate all year round in the Bay of Plenty, Bay of Islands and around the Coromandel Peninsula. Of the three other species seen in New Zealand, **bottlenose dolphins** hang around Kaikoura and Whakatane most of the year, while **dusky dolphins**, the most playful, can be spotted near the shore of the Marlborough Sounds, Fiordland and Kaikoura from October to May. At any time of year you might get small schools of tiny **Hector's dolphins** accompanying your boat around Banks Peninsula, the Catlins and Invercargill.

Until recently there were few opportunities to see the Hooker's (or "New Zealand") **sea lion** except on remote Antarctic islands, but these rare animals, with their round noses and deep, wet eyes now appear around the Catlins and Otago Peninsula. The larger New Zealand **fur seal** is in much greater abundance around the coast. You're most likely to come across them in the Sugar Loaf Marine Reserve off New Plymouth, around the Northland coast, in the Bay of Plenty, near Kaikoura, around the Otago Peninsula and in the Abel Tasman National Park. Both seals and sea lions can become aggressive during the breeding season (Dec–Feb), so remember to keep your distance (at least 30m). **Elephant seals** still breed in the Catlins; more extensive colonies exist on the offshore islands.

Also drawn by the coast's fish-rich waters are a number of visiting and native sea birds, the most famous being the graceful and solitary **royal albatross**, found on the Otago Peninsula and, just offshore, the smaller **wandering albatross**. A far more common sight are **little blue penguins**, which you'll see on any boat journey. The large **yellow-eyed penguin** is confined to parts of the east coast of the South Island, from Christchurch to the Catlins, while the **Fiordland crested penguin**, with its thick yellow eyebrows, is rarely seen outside Fiordland and Stewart Island. Other common sea birds include **gannets**, their yellow heads and white bodies unmistakable as they dive into shoals of fish; and **cormorants** and **shags** (mostly grey or black), usually congregating on cliffs and rocky shores. On and around islands you're also likely to see the **sooty shearwater, titi** (also known as "muttonbirds"), while the **black oystercatchers** and the black-and-white **variable oystercatchers**, both with orange cigar beaks and stooping gait, can be spotted searching in pairs for food on the foreshore.

Green issues

New Zealand comes with an enviable reputation for being **clean and green**, but this is more by accident than design. With a population of just over four million and a relatively short recorded history, you might expect human impact to be limited, but in less than a thousand years (mostly the last 150) humans have converted three-quarters of the land to farming and commercial forestry. Just ten percent of native forest remains, while generous winds and flushing rainfall conveniently dispose of much of the country's **pollution**.

Land usage

European settlers and, later, returning WWI veterans spent years taming steep bush-covered hills only suitable for raising sheep. These **farms** were profitable when wool and lamb prices were high, but in recent years have become uneconomic, thus some areas are being allowed to revert to their natural state, through the **tenure review** process, opening them up to the public as parks and reserves. Far more often marginal lands are planted with introduced **pines** and logged every 25 years, reducing them to barren fields of stumps. Meanwhile, the ever-growing need for housing, roads and associated infrastructure gobbles up productive farmland and threatens fragile wetland.

Pollution

In large parts of New Zealand you can inhale lungfuls of fresh air and dapple your fingers in crystal-clear lakes and rivers, but all is not idyllic. Due to poor public transport New Zealand's **car ownership** rates are some of the highest in the world. New Zealand also imports huge numbers of secondhand cars from Japan that would not be allowed off the boat in other countries and there is no requirement for regular vehicle emission testing.

Mountains streams and alpine tarns look so clean and fresh you'll be tempted to drink straight from them. In most cases this is fine, but the water might also harbour **giardia**, an intestinal parasite that can easily ruin your holiday. It is best to treat all drinking water. Freshwater rivers have recently become prey to the **didymo** algae (*Didymoshenia geminata*); boaties, fishers and kayakers should thoroughly clean all their gear before moving to another river to prevent it spreading. Additionally, modern intensive **farming** techniques, particularly the use of fertilizers, have polluted many rivers and streams. On the bright side, **industrial pollution** is a relatively minor issue, but only because there is little manufacturing.

The search for power

With a population growing ever more power-hungry and a lack of major investment over the last thirty years, New Zealand's power supplies are inadequate. Green **hydro** and **geothermal power** account for only two-thirds of electricity supply, compared to eighty percent in the late twentieth century and even these clean generation methods are contentious: hydro reservoirs have destroyed natural habitats, especially riverbanks where threatened birds live. More geothermal stations are planned but over-extraction detrimentally affects geysers and boiling mud pools.

Building coal power stations (and converting to oil and gas stations) could make New Zealand electricity self-sufficient for over a hundred years, but at a considerable cost to the environment. Clean emission technologies are strenuously debated. **Wind energy** meets resistance from those complaining of noise and visual pollution, and installed capacity is very low. For decades no one dared suggest New Zealand should invest in **nuclear power** but the power pinch and the need to follow Kyoto commitments is eroding long-held resistance.

The good news is that, despite government vacillation and the paramount interests of big business, an ever-increasing number of New Zealanders are working to preserve the country's unique environment.

Film and music

n the wake of *The Lord of the Rings* films, shot in New Zealand, the Kiwi film industry enjoyed one of its intermittent revivals, previously most notable from 1988–1994 when *The Navigator, An Angel at my Table, The Piano, Once Were Warriors* and *Heavenly Creatures* all gained international recognition. Yet, while the directors involved went on to eminence, the renaissance faded like a closing shot. Like most small countries, New Zealand lacks the resources, infrastructure and finances to sustain a large-scale film industry on a permanent basis. More often, the country is used as a relatively inexpensive backdrop for American TV series and for movies that need big outdoors scenes, such as *The Chronicles of Narnia*. As a result the local film industry, with a few notable exceptions, is known mainly for technical backup and providing extras – unless of course you count the one-man New Zealand film saviour, Peter Jackson. He is bringing the *Hobbit* movie series to New Zealand; the first will kick off soon and be released in 2012. Whether Jackson can repeat the miracle of the *Lord of the Rings* trilogy and kickstart another "golden age of Kiwi cinema" with less source material remains to be seen but it's probably not wise to bet against him.

An Angel at my Table Jane Campion, 1990. Winner of the Special Jury prize at the Venice Film Festival. One of the most inspiring films New Zealand has produced, based on the brilliant autobiographies of Janet Frame (see p.540).

Bad Blood Mike Newell, 1981. A New Zealand/British collaboration set in New Zealand in World War II that relates the true story of Stan Graham, a Hokitika man who breaks the law by refusing to hand in his rifle. The ensuing events give rise to a discussion of the Kiwi spirit.

Bad Taste Peter Jackson, 1988. Winner of the special jury prize at the Paris Film Festival. Aliens visit earth to pick up flesh for an inter-galactic fast-food chain and have a wild old time.

Came a Hot Friday Ian Mune, 1984. The best comedy to come out of New Zealand, concentrating on two incompetent confidence tricksters whose luck runs out in a sleepy country town.

Crush Alison Maclean, 1992. A competitor at Cannes. Offbeat, angst-ridden psychological drama set around Rotorua, where the boiling mud and gushing geysers underline the tensions and sexual chaos that arise when an American femme fatale enters the lives of a New Zealand family.

Desperate Remedies Peter Wells and Stewart Main, 1993. This winner of the Certain Regard Award at Cannes comments wryly on the intrigues and desires of a group of people whose lives somehow interconnect.

Eagle Versus Shark Taika Waititi, 2007. A low-key, well-realized love story starring Jemaine "Flight of the Conchords" Clement, with similar quirky humour.

Fifty Ways of Saying Fabulous Stewart Main, 2005. Clever adaptation of the book of the same name (see p.799) that grabs the spirit of the original and rings out lots of laughs as well as poignancy.

Forgotten Silver Peter Jackson, 2000. Jackson, at his tongue-in-cheek best, constructs a fake documentary about a Kiwi movie pioneer, who invents film, sound, colour and the biblical epic, from flax, in the bush on the West Coast.

Goodbye Pork Pie Geoff Murphy, 1980. A much-loved comedy/road movie following the adventures of two young men in a yellow mini, the cops they infuriate, and the mixed bag of characters they encounter.

Heavenly Creatures Peter Jackson, 1994. Winner of the Silver Lion at Venice and an Oscar nominee. This account of the horrific Parker/Hulme matricide in the 1950s follows the increasingly self-obsessed life of two adolescent girls. An evocative and explosive film that brings all Jackson's subversive humour to bear on the strait-laced real world and the girls' fantastic imaginary one. Kate Winslet's film debut.

In My Father's Den Brad McGann, 2004. Depicts an emotional rough ride for an exhausted war journalist (Matthew Macfadyen) who returns home and becomes involved in an unexpected and engrossing journey of discovery. From a novel by Maurice Gee (see p.800).

The Navigator Vincent Ward, 1988. A well-received competitor at Cannes, this atmospheric and stylistically inventive venture employs all Ward's favourite themes and characters, including the innocent visionary, in this case a boy who leads five men through time from a fourteenth-century Cumbrian village to New Zealand in the twentieth century in a quest to save their homes.

Once Were Warriors Lee Tamahori, 1994. A surging fly-on-the-wall style comment on the economically challenged Maori situation in modern south Auckland, bringing to mind the British kitchen-sink dramas of the 1950s and 1960s. More a study of class than a full-blown racial statement, it revels in ordinary drudgery and despair, with a warts-and-all story about human weakness and strength of spirit against a background of urban decay. Based on a novel by Alan Duff (see p.800).

Out of the Blue Robert Sarkies, 2006. Based on the true events of the Aramouna Massacre, in which thirteen people lost their lives to a local unemployed gun collector. A dark tale concentrating on the heroism of the out-gunned seaside town police and inhabitants.

Patu Merata Mita, 1983. A powerful documentary recording the year of opposition to the 1981 Springbok rugby tour of New Zealand, which goes some way to showing the extraordinary passions ignited.

The Piano Jane Campion, 1993. With Holly Hunter, Harvey Keitel, Sam Neill and Anna Paquin. This moody winner of the Cannes Palme d'Or (and three Oscars) made Campion bankable in Hollywood. Its mixture of grand scenes and personal trauma knowingly synthesizes paperback romance, erotica and Victorian melodrama – and includes Keitel's stab at the worst Scottish accent of all time.

River Queen Vincent Ward, 2005. Production problems on the Whanganui River saw Ward depart before the project was finished but what's left is a beautifully shot, over-simplified and uneven film worth a look just for the locations.

Scarfies Robert Sarkies, 2000. Surprise hit of the year in NZ and arthouses worldwide, a darkly funny story about students taking over a deserted house in Dunedin only to discover a massive dope crop in the basement. Things get progressively more unpleasant when the dope grower returns.

Sleeping Dogs Roger Donaldson, 1977. Perhaps the birth of the real New Zealand film industry, based on C.K. Stead's book *Smith's Dream*. Sam Neill plays a paranoid anti-hero hunted by repressive state forces. A slick thriller, that rushes to a violent conclusion.

The Ugly Scott Reynolds, 1996. Shown at the 1997 Cannes Film

Contemporary Kiwi music

New Zealand's musical traditions stretch back to the instruments played by the earliest Maori arrivals (see p.761), and have been a defining part of the nation's culture ever since.

Known for breaking new ground (such as the distinctive "Dunedin Sound", p.587), the country has produced formative artists such as **Neil and Tim Finn**, first with the success of Split Enz (in the 1970s and early 1980s), and later with Crowded House (from the early 1980s, who reformed in 2006 and are still recording and performing), as well as successful solo careers. Today, Neil's son, Liam Finn, is one of New Zealand's most talented singer-songwriters and multi instrumentalists.

The new millennium saw an explosion of Kiwi roots, reggae, dub and electronica with Pacifica influences, with artists such as Katchafire, Trinity Roots, Salmonella Dub, the Black Seeds and Fat Freddy's Drop among the greatest success stories.

Even more recently, there's a growing resurgence of hard-edge rock – from established names like the Mint Chicks, to the high-energy live shows of emerging Queenstown-based three-piece The Flaming Drivers.

Catching a **gig** is one of the best ways to tap into the country's music scene – the website ⓦ www.amplifier.co.nz lists upcoming shows, has downloads and sells CDs.

Perhaps the artist who truly provides the "soundtrack of the nation" is **Dave Dobbyn**. Best known outside the country for the catchy *Slice of Heaven*, recorded with the band Herbs (often considered New Zealand's unofficial national anthem), Dobbyn also formed the bands Th' Dudes and DD Smash – as well as an enduring solo career. Several of his songs appear on *The Great New Zealand Songbook* (Sony; 2009), a double CD – "Last Century" and "This Century" – that showcases a diverse cross section of Kiwi artists. For details of Kiwi radio stations, see p.52.

Festival, and winner of rave reviews in the US, this edgy comment on incarceration, reform and mistrust revolves around a serial killer who has been locked away and wants to convince the world he is cured.

Utu Geoff Murphy, 1983. One of the official selections at Cannes, this portrays a Maori warrior in the late 1800s who sets out to revenge himself on the conquerors of New Zealand, in the form of a Pakeha farmer. A tense, well-acted representation of modern and historic issues.

Vigil Vincent Ward, 1984. A Cannes competitor, this dark, rain-soaked story portrays a young girl's coming of age and her negative reaction to a stranger who is trying to seduce her mother, adding tension to her own sexual awakening.

Whakataratara Paneke Don C. Selwyn, 2001. The Maori *Merchant of Venice*, with English subtitles, an ambitious home-grown film that brings much local acting talent to the screen in an involved, if overly long, epic.

We're Here to Help Jonothan Cullinane, 2007. Inspiring film based on a true story about a man victimized by the Revenue Department who fought back and won.

The World's Fastest Indian Roger Donaldson, 2005. Feel-good movie about old codger Burt Munro, who in real life proved you don't have to be young to achieve your dreams – though being barmy helps. Anthony Hopkins in the lead role is marvellous and even does a passable Invercargill accent.

Books

K iwis publish extensively, including a disproportionate amount of glossy picture books and wildlife guides. Modern authors, inheritors of an increasingly confident tradition, regularly produce excellent novels, poems and factual material. Almost all of the following titles can be found in bookstores or online. Books that are especially recommended are marked 🐦.

History, society and politics

Mark Beehre *Men Alone – Men Together*. Photographer and oral historian Mark Beehre documents the diverse lives of 45 gay men, recounting key events in their lives and those in New Zealand's social history before, during and after homosexual law reform.

James Belich *The New Zealand Wars*. Well-researched, in-depth study re-examining the Victorian and Maori interpretations of the colonial wars. A book for committed historians. *Paradise Reforged* is a history of New Zealanders from 1880 to 2000, concentrating on their relationship with the outside world.

Alistair Campbell *Maori Legends*. A brief, accessible retelling of selected stories with some evocative illustrations.

R.D. Crosby *The Musket Wars*. Account of the massive nineteenth-century upsurge in inter-*iwi* conflict, exacerbated by the introduction of the musket, which led to the death of 23 percent of the Maori population, a proportion greater even than that suffered by Russia in World War II.

Alan Duff *Out of the Mist and Steam*. Duff, author of *Once Were Warriors* (see p.796), has created a vivid memoir of his life that falls short of autobiography but gives the reader a good idea where the material for his novels came from.

A.K. Grant *Corridors of Paua*. A light-hearted look at the turbulent and

fraught political history of the country from 1984 to the introduction of MMP in 1996.

Mark Inglis *Legs on Everest*. In 1982 Mount Cook Search and Rescue mountaineer Inglis became stuck in an ice cave for fourteen days, losing both legs below the knees to frostbite. In 2006, on artificial limbs, he was the first double amputee to climb to the summit of Mount Everest. An inspirational read.

Hamish Keith *The Big Picture A History of New Zealand Art from 1642*. A fascinating and rewarding tome for anybody interested in the progression from early Maori art through European influence to today's fusion of styles.

🐦 **Michael King** *The Penguin History of New Zealand*. Published in 2003, this is a highly readable general history of New Zealand, from Maori oral history to uneasy Maori–Pakeha relations and the Maori renaissance. *Death of the Rainbow Warrior* is a brilliant account of the farcical, and ultimately tragic, efforts of the French secret service to sabotage Greenpeace's campaign against French nuclear testing.

Hineani Melbourne *Maori Sovereignty: The Maori Perspective*; and its companion volume *Maori Sovereignty: The Pakeha Perspective* by Carol Archie. Everyone from grass-roots activists to statesmen gets a voice in these two volumes, one airing the widely divergent Maori visions of sovereignty, the other covering equally disparate Pakeha views. They assume a good understanding of Maori structures and recent New Zealand history but are highly instructive nonetheless.

🏃 Claudia Orange *The Story of the Treaty*. A concise illustrated exploration of the history and myths behind what many believe to be the most important document in New Zealand history, the Treaty of Waitangi.

Margaret Orbell *A Concise Encyclopaedia of Maori Myth and Legend*. A comprehensive rundown on many tales and their backgrounds that rewards perseverance, though a little dry.

Jock Phillips *A Man's Country? The Image of the Pakeha Male*. Classic treatise on mateship and the Kiwi bloke. Thorough exploration through the formative pioneering years, rugby, wartime camaraderie and the family-man ideal.

Anne Salmond *Amiria: The Life Story of Maori Women*. Reprinted classic describing the traditional values passed on to the author, set against a background of tribal history and contemporary race relations.

D.C. Starzecka (ed) *Maori Art and Culture*. A kind of Maori culture primer, with concise and interesting coverage of Maori history, culture, social structure, carving and weaving.

K. Taylor and P. Moloney *On the Left: Essays on Socialism in New Zealand*. Comprehensive collection of political essays spanning over a century that shows why New Zealand society has such a strong egalitarian spine.

Chris Trotter *No Left Turn*. Wonderful episodic history of New Zealand, that convincingly argues that the country has been continuously shaped by "greed, bigotry and right-wing politics".

Dorothy Urlich Cloher *Hongi Hika*. Compelling biography dealing with the foremost Maori leader at the time of the first contact between Maori and the Europeans, and his subsequent participation in the Musket Wars.

Mere Whaanga *A Carved Cloak for Tahu*. Tells the story of the northern Hawke's Bay *hapu* of Ngai Tahu Mata Whaiti, including history, tradition and an overview of religions and the effects of those elements on modern development.

Fiction

Graeme Aitken *Fifty Ways of Saying Fabulous*. Extremely funny book about burgeoning homosexuality in a young farm boy, who lives in a world where he is expected to clean up muck and play rugby.

Eric Beardsley *Blackball 08*. Entertaining and fairly accurate historical novel set in the West Coast coal-mining town of Blackball during New Zealand's longest ever labour dispute.

🏃 Graham Billing *Forbrush and the Penguins*. Described as the first serious novel to come out of

Antarctica, this is a compelling description of one man's lonely vigil over a colony of penguins.

Samuel Butler *Erewhon*. Initially set in the Canterbury high country (where Butler ran a sheep station), but increasingly devoted to a satirical critique of mid-Victorian Britain.

Nigel Cox *Tarzan Presley*. Amusing reworking of the Tarzan myth where the hero grows up in New Zealand and then becomes the king of rock'n'roll – nothing if not ambitious.

Ian Cross *The God Boy*. Widely considered to be New Zealand's equivalent to *The Catcher in The Rye*, about a young boy trapped between two parents who hate each other and the violent consequences.

Barry Crump *A Good Keen Man*; *Hang on a Minute Mate*; *Bastards I Have Met*; *Forty Yarns, The Adventures of Sam Cash and a Song*. Just a few of the many New Zealand bushman books by the Kiwi equivalent of Banjo Patterson, who writes with great humour, tenderness and style about the male-dominated world of hunting, shooting, fishing, drinking, and telling tall stories. Worth reading for a picture of a now-past New Zealand lifestyle.

Alan Duff *Once Were Warriors*. Shocking and violent social-realist book set in 1970s south Auckland and adapted in the 1990s for Lee Tamahori's film of the same name. Well intentioned and passionate.

Janet Frame *An Angel at My Table*. Though one of New Zealand's most accomplished novelists, Frame is perhaps best known for this three-volume autobiography, dramatized in Jane Campion's film which, with wit and a self-effacing honesty, gives a poignant insight into both the author and her environment. Her superb novels and short stories use humour alongside highly disturbing combinations of events and characters to overthrow readers' preconceptions. For starters, try *Faces in the Water*, *Scented Gardens for the Blind*, *Towards Another Summer* and *Owls Do Cry*.

Maurice Gee *Crime Story*; *Going West*; *Prowlers*; *The Plumb Trilogy*. Novels from an underrated but highly talented writer. Despite the misleadingly light titles, Gee's focus is social realism, taking an unflinching, powerful look at motivation and unravelling relationships.

Patricia Grace *Potiki*. Poignant, poetic and exquisitely written tale of a Maori community redefining itself while its land is threatened by coastal development. *Baby No Eyes* is a magical weaving of real events with stories of family history told from four points of view. *Dogside Story*, shortlisted for the 2001 Booker Prize, is a wonderful story about the power of the land and the strength of *whanau* at the turn of the Millennium. *Tu* is an astonishing novel about the Maori Battalion fighting in Italy in WWII, drawn from the experiences of the author's father and other relatives.

Peter Hawes *Leapfrog with Unicorns* and *Tasman's Lay*. Two from an unsung hero, cult figure and probably only member of the absurdist movement in New Zealand, who writes with great energy, wit and surprising discipline about almost anything that takes his fancy. Hawes has also written the not-to-be-missed *Inca Girls Aren't Easy*, a series of joyous, sad and slippery tales, under the name W.P. Hearst. A brilliant late addition to Hawes' eccentric canon, *Royce, Royce the People Choice*, is a sort of *Old Man and the Sea* mixed with *Moby Dick*.

Keri Hulme *The Bone People*. The winner of the 1985 Booker Prize, and an extraordinary first novel, set along the wild beaches of the South Island's West Coast. Mysticism, myth and earthy reality are transformed into a haunting tale peopled with richly drawn characters.

Witi Ihimaera *Bulibasha – King of the Gypsies*. The best introduction to one of the country's finest Maori authors. A rollicking good read, energetically exploring the life of a rebellious teenager in 1950s rural New Zealand, it's an intense look at adolescence, cultural choices, family ties and the abuse of power, culminating in a masterful twist. Look out also for the excellent *The Matriarch* and *The Uncle Story*, the brilliant *Whale Rider* and *Star Dancer* by the same author.

Lloyd Jones *Mister Pip*. Intriguing, engaging 2007 Booker-shortlisted novel dealing with an unreported war on a remote South Pacific island where the schoolchildren's futures are entwined with a boy called Pip and a man named Dickens. Jones' 2009 collection of short stories, *The Man In The Shed*, showcases his sharp observations about contemporary NZ life.

Shonagh Koea *The Grandiflora Tree*. A savagely witty yet deeply moving study of the conventions of widowhood, with a peculiar love story thrown in. First novel from a journalist and short-story writer renowned for her astringent humour.

🏃 **Katherine Mansfield** *The Collected Stories of Katherine Mansfield*. All 73 short stories sit alongside fifteen unfinished fragments in this 780-page tome. Concise yet penetrating examinations of human behaviour in apparently trivial situations, often transmitting a painfully pessimistic view of the world, and startlingly modern for their time.

Craig Marriner *Stonedogs*. Frenetic, feral, culturally fraught tale of gang-controlled drug running between Rotorua, Auckland and Northland, portraying "a New Zealand the tourists and executives had better pray they never stumble upon".

🏃 **Ngaio Marsh** *Opening Night*; *Artists in Crime*; *Vintage Murder*. Just a selection from the doyenne of New Zealand crime fiction. Since 1934 she has been airing her Anglophile sensibilities and killing off innumerable individuals in the name of entertainment, before solving the crimes with Inspector Allen. Perfect mindless reading matter for planes, trains and buses.

Owen Marshall *Drybread*. Sparingly written novel set between Christchurch and Central Otago that examines love and loss through its two protagonists:

a mother returning to New Zealand to flee a court order from the US, and an emotionally scarred local journalist pursuing her story.

🏃 **Ronald Hugh Morrieson** *Came a Hot Friday*. Superb account of the idiosyncrasies of country folk and the two smart spielers who enter their lives, in a visceral gothic comedy thriller focusing on crime and sex in a small town.

Frank Sargeson *The Stories of Frank Sargeson*. Though not well known outside New Zealand, Sargeson is a giant of Kiwi literature. His writing, from the 1930s to the 1980s, is incisive and sharply observed, with dialogue true to the metre of New Zealand speech. This work brings together some of his finest short stories. *Once is Enough, More than Enough* and *Never Enough!* make up the complete autobiography of a man sometimes even more colourful than his characters; Michael King wrote a fine biography, *Frank Sargeson: A Life*.

🏃 **Maurice Shadbolt** *Strangers and Journeys*. On publication in 1972 this became a defining novel in New Zealand's literary ascendancy and its sense of nationhood. A tale of two families, with finely wrought characters whose lives interweave through three generations. Very New Zealand, very human and not overly epic. Later works, which have consolidated Shadbolt's reputation, include *Monday's Warriors*. *Season of the Jew* and *The House of Strife*.

C.K. Stead *The Singing Whakapapa*. Highly regarded author of many books and critical essays who is little known outside New Zealand and Australia. This powerful novel focuses on an early missionary and a dissatisfied modern descendant searching for meaning in his own life. *All Visitors Ashore* is a masterpiece based around the harbourfront strike of 1951 and slyly alluding to Stead's literary contemporaries, while *Mansfield* is an evocative fictional musing about New Zealand's most famous short-story writer.

🏃 **Damien Wilkins** *The Miserables*. One of the best novels to come out of New Zealand, shorn of much of the colonial baggage of many writers. Surprisingly mature for a first novel, it sharply evokes middle-class New Zealand life from the 1960s to the 1980s through finely wrought characters.

Anthologies

Warwick Brown *100 New Zealand Artists*. Companion to the *Picador Book of Contemporary New Zealand Fiction* but also allowing room for sculptors, printmakers, photographers and graphic artists.

James Burns (ed) *Novels and Novelists 1861–1979, a Bibliography*. A sweeping and comprehensive introduction to the history of the New Zealand novel and the characters who have made it such a powerful art form.

Bill Manhire (ed) *100 New Zealand Poems*. A very manageable selection that provides an excellent introduction to the poetry of the nation.

🏃 **Owen Marshall (selected by)** *Essential New Zealand Short Stories*. A truly representative collection of fascinating tales by some of New Zealand's finest, including Frame, Ihimera, Mansfield, Shadbolt, Stead and Gee.

🏃 **Ian Wedde and Harvey McQueen (eds)** *The Penguin Book of New Zealand Verse*. A comprehensive collection of verse from the earliest European settlers to contemporary poets, and an excellent introduction to Kiwi poetry; highlights are works by James K. Baxter, Janet Frame, C.K. Stead, Sam Hunt, Keri Hulme, Hirini Melbourne and Apirana Taylor.

Reference and specialist guides

Angie Errigo *Rough Guide to The Lord of the Rings*. An essential companion for background on the whole J.R.R. Tolkien phenomenon with exhaustive detail about the man, the books, the films, fan websites and even the books' influence on 1970s prog rock.

Rosemary George *The Wines of New Zealand*. Entertaining and informative look at New Zealand's most important wine regions, the history, the people and the product.

John Kent *North Island Trout Fishing Guide* and *South Island Trout Fishing Guide*. Laden with information on access, seasons and fishing style, and illustrated with maps of the more important rivers.

Flora, fauna and the environment

D.H. Brathwaite *Native Birds of New Zealand*. Brilliant colour photographs and lots of information pinpointing thirty rare birds that, with a little effort and some patience, you can observe while travelling around.

Andrew Crowe *Which Native Tree?* Great little book, ideal for identifying New Zealand's common native trees – though not tree ferns – with diagrams of tree shape, photos of leaves and fruit and an idea of geographic extent.

Susanne & John Hill *Richard Henry of Resolution Island.* Comprehensive and very readable account of a man widely regarded as New Zealand's first conservationist. The book also serves as a potted history of this underpopulated area of Fiordland, peopled by many of the key explorers.

Geoff Moon *The Reed Field Guide to New Zealand Birds.* Excellent colour reference book, with ample detail for species identification. *The Reed Field Guide to New Zealand Wildlife,* by the same author, is stuffed with colour photos.

Rod Morris & Hal Smith *Wild South: Saving New Zealand's Endangered Birds.* A fascinating companion volume to a 1980s TV series following a band of dedicated individuals trying to preserve a dozen of New Zealand's wonderfully exotic bird species, including the kiwi, kakapo, takahe and kea.

Neville Peat *Manapouri Saved.* Full and heartening coverage of one of New Zealand's earliest environmental battles when, in the 1960s, a petition signed by ten percent of the country succeeded in persuading the government to cancel its hydroelectric plans for Lake Manapouri.

Kerry-Jayne Wilson *Flight of the Huia.* Focusing on Jurassic frogs and bizarre creatures such as the Alpine parrot, this book studies faunal change in New Zealand and current conservation issues.

Tramping

Pearl Hewson *New Zealand's Great Walks.* Hewson is a no-nonsense DOC officer working out of the Wellington Office and what she doesn't know about the Great Walks isn't worth knowing. This is a practical, concise guide that concentrates her experiences into a useful aid to trampers.

Moir's Guide. Probably the most comprehensive guide to tramping in the South Island. It is divided into two volumes: North, covering hikes between Lake Ohau and Lake Wakatipu; and South, which concentrates on walks around the southern lakes and fjords including the Kepler Track, plus the less popular Dusky and George Sound tracks.

Cycling and adventure sports

Mike Bhana *New Zealand Surfing Guide.* Pragmatic handbook to the prime surf spots around the New Zealand coast, with details on access, transport, the best wind and tide conditions and expected swells.

Graham Charles *New Zealand Whitewater: 120 Great Kayaking Runs.* A comprehensive and entertaining guide to New Zealand's most important kayaking rivers. River maps and details on access are supplemented by quick reference panels with grades, timings, and handy tips like which rapids not to even think about running.

Bruce Ringer *New Zealand by Bike.* The definitive Kiwi cycle-touring guide, with fourteen regional tours (with many side trips) which can be knitted together into a greater whole. Plenty of maps and altitude profile diagrams.

Nigel Rushton *Pedallers' Paradise*. Separate lightweight North Island and South Island volumes covering recommended routes.

Marty Sharp *A Guide to the Ski Areas of New Zealand*. Exactly what you'd expect, with full descriptions of the fields complete with tow plans and information on access, local towns and ski rental.

Paul, Simon and Jonathan Kennett *Classic New Zealand Mountain Bike Rides*. All you need to know about off-road biking in New Zealand, with details of over four hundred rides. Simon runs the ⓦwww.mountainbike .co.nz site.

Language

Language

Maori 807

Glossary 810

Language

E nglish and *te reo Maori*, the Maori language, share joint status as New Zealand's official languages, but on a day-to-day basis all you'll need is English, or its colourful Kiwi variant. All Maori's speak English fluently, often slipping in numerous Maori terms that in time become part of everyday Kiwi parlance. Mainstream TV and radio coverage of any event that has significance to Maori is likely to be littered with words totally alien to foreigners, but well understood by Anglophone Kiwis. It is initially confusing, but with the aid of our glossary (see p.810) you'll soon find yourself using Maori terms all the time.

A basic knowledge of Maori pronunciation will make you more comprehensible and some understanding of the roots of place names can be helpful. You'll need to become something of an expert to appreciate much of the wonderful oral history, and stories told through *waiata* (songs), but learning a few key terms will enhance any Maori cultural events you may attend.

To many Brits and North Americans, **Kiwi English** is barely distinguishable from its trans-Tasman cousin, "Strine", sharing much of the same lexicon of slang terms, but with a softer accent. Australians have no trouble distinguishing the two accents, repeatedly highlighting the vowel shift which turns "bat" into "bet", makes "yes" sound like "yis" and causes "fish" to come out as "fush". There is very little regional variation; only residents of Otago and Southland – the southern quarter of the South Island – distinguish themselves with a rolled "r", courtesy of their predominantly Scottish forebears. Throughout the land, Kiwis add an upward inflection to statements, making them sound like questions; most are not, and to highlight those that are, some add the interrogative "eh?" to the end of the sentence, a trait most evident in the North Island, especially among Maori.

Maori

For the 50–100,000 native speakers and additional 100,000 who speak it as a second tongue, **Maori** is very much a living language. It is gaining strength all the time as both Maori and Pakeha increasingly appreciate the cultural value of *te reo*, a language central to *Maoritanga* and forming the basis of a huge body of magnificent songs, chants and legends, lent a poetic quality by its hypnotic and lilting rhythms.

Maori is a member of the Polynesian group of languages and shares both grammar and vocabulary with those spoken throughout most of the South Pacific. Similarities are so pronounced that Tupaia, a Tahitian crew member on Captain Cook's first Pacific voyage in 1769, was able to communicate freely with the Aotearoa Maori they encountered. The Treaty of Waitangi was written in both English and Maori, but *te reo* soon began to lose ground to the point where, by the late nineteenth century, its use was proscribed in schools. Maori parents keen for their offspring to do well in the Pakeha world frequently promoted the use of English, and Maori declined further, exacerbated by the mid-twentieth-century migration to the cities. Though never on the brink of extinction, the language reached its nadir in the

1970s when perhaps only ten percent of Maori could speak their language fluently. The tide began to turn towards the end of the decade with the inception of *kohanga reo* **pre-schools** (literally "language nests") where **Maoritanga** is taught and activities are conducted in Maori. Originally a Maori initiative, it has now crossed over and progressive Pakeha parents are increasingly introducing their kids to biculturalism at an early age. Fortunate *kohanga reo* graduates can progress to the small number of state-funded Maori-language primary schools known as *kura kaupapa*. For decades, Maori has been taught as an option in secondary schools, and there are now state-funded tertiary institutions operated by Maori, offering graduate programmes in Maori studies.

The success of these programmes has bred a young generation of Maori speakers frequently far more fluent than their parents who, shamed by the loss of their heritage, are attending Maori evening classes. Legal parity means that Maori is now finding its way into officialdom too, with government departments all adopting Maori names and many government and council documents being printed in both languages. Maori-language **radio stations** are now commonplace in the northern half of the North Island where most Maori live, but the real boost came in 2004 with the launching of **Maori Television**. Substantially government funded, it still has relatively low ratings but is well worth tuning into for a very different take on what's going on. Partly in English, partly in Maori and occasionally a synthesis of the two, there's a wonderful cross-fertilization of styles. You can expect everything from movies and sitcoms to discussion panels on Maori issues and lifestyle programmes such as *Kai Time on the Road* (a cooking and Maori food show), and an animated show for pre-schoolers.

In your day-to-day dealings you won't need **to speak Maori**, though both native speakers and Pakeha may well greet you with *kia ora* ("hi, hello"), or less commonly *haere mai* ("welcome"). On ceremonial occasions, such as *marae* visits, you'll hear the more formal greeting *tena koe* (said to one person) or *tena koutou katoa* (to a group).

Maori words used in place names are listed below, while those in common use are listed in the general glossary (see p.810). If you are interested in learning a little more, the best handy reference is Patricia Turoa's *The Collins Maori Phrase Book*, which has helpful notes on pronunciation, handy phrases and a useful Maori–English and English–Maori vocabulary.

Maori place names

The following is a list of some of the most common words and elements you will see in **town and place names** throughout New Zealand.

Ao	Cloud	Manu	Bird
Ara	Road or path	Mata	Headland
Awa	River or valley	Maunga	Mountain
Hau	Wind	Mihi	Speeches
Ika	Fish	Moana	Sea, lake
Iti	Small	Motu	Island or anything isolated
Kai	Food, or eat		
Kainga	Home, village	Muri	End
Kare	Rippling	Nui	Big
Kino	Bad	O	The place of
Ma	White, clear	One	Sand, beach
Manga	Stream	Pa	Fortified settlement

Pae	Ridge	Tahu	Light
Papa	Flat, earth, floor	Tai	Sea
Patere	Chants	Tane	Man
Puke	Hill	Tapu	Sacred
Puna	Spring	Tara	Peak
Raki	North	Te	The
Rangi	Sky	Tomo	Cave
Roa	Long, high	Wai	Water
Roto	Lake	Waka	Canoe
Rua	Hole, cave, pit, two	Whanga	Bay, body of water
Runga	Top	Whenua	Land or country

Pronunciation

Laziness and arrogance have combined to give Pakeha – and consequently most visitors – a distorted impression of Maori pronunciation, which is usually mutated into an Anglicized form. Until the 1970s there was little attempt to get it right, but with the rise in Maori consciousness since the 1980s, coupled with a sense of political correctness, many Pakeha now make some attempt at Maori pronunciation. As a visitor you will probably get away with just about anything, but by sticking to a few simple rules and keeping your ears open, apparently unfathomable place names will soon trip off your tongue.

Maori was solely a spoken language before the arrival of British and French missionaries in the early nineteenth century, who transcribed it using only fifteen letters of the Roman alphabet. The eight **consonants**, **h**, **k**, **m**, **n**, **p**, **r**, **t** and **w**, are pronounced much as they are in English. The five **vowels** come in long and short forms; the long form is sometimes signified in print by a macron – a flat bar above the letter – but usually it is simply a case of learning by experience which sound to use. When two vowels appear together they are both pronounced, though substantially run together. For example, "Maori" should be written with a macron on the "a" and be pronounced with the first two vowels separate, turning the commonly used but incorrect "Mow-ree" into something more like "Maao-ri".

Here are a few **pronunciation** pointers to help you get it right:

• Long compound words can be split into syllables which all end in a vowel. Waikaremoana comes out as Wai-ka-re-mo-ana. Scanning our list of place name elements should help a great deal.

• All syllables are stressed evenly, so it is not **Wai**-ka-re-mo-ana or Wai-ka-re-**mo**-ana but a flat Wai-ka-re-mo-ana.

• Maori words don't take an "s" to form a plural, so you'll find many plural nouns in this book – kiwi, tui, kauri, Maori – in what appears to be a singular form; about the only exception is Kiwis (as people), a Maori word wholly adopted into English.

• **Ng** is pronounced much as in "sing".

• **Wh** sounds either like an aspirated "f" as in "off", or like the "wh" in "why", depending on who is saying what and in which part of the country.

Glossary

ANZAC Australian and New Zealand Army Corps; every town in New Zealand has a memorial to ANZAC casualties from both world wars.

Aotearoa Maori for New Zealand, the land of the long white cloud.

Ariki Supreme chief of an *iwi*.

Bach (pronounced "batch") Holiday home, originally a bachelor pad at work camps and now something of a Kiwi institution that can be anything from shack to palatial waterside residence.

Back-blocks Remote areas.

Bludger Someone who doesn't pull their weight or pay their way, a sponger.

Bro Brother, term of endearment widely used by Maori.

Captain Cooker Wild pig, probably descended from pigs released in the Marlborough Sounds on Cook's first voyage.

Chilly bin Insulated cool box for carrying picnic supplies.

Choice Fantastic.

Chook Chicken.

Chunder Vomit.

Coaster (Ex-) resident of the West Coast of the South Island.

Cocky Farmer, comes in "Cow" and "Sheep" variants.

Crib South Island name for a *bach*.

Cuz or **Cuzzy** Short for cousin, see "bro".

Dag Wag or entertaining character.

Dairy Corner shop selling just about everything, open seven days and sometimes 24 hours.

Dob in Reporting one's friends and neighbours to the police; there is currently a dobber's charter encouraging drivers to report one another for dangerous driving.

DOC Department of Conservation. Operators of the national parks, conservation policy, track administration and much more.

Docket Receipt.

Domain Grassy reserve, open to the public.

Eftpos Card-based debit system found in shops, bars and restaurants.

Feijoa Fleshy, tomato-sized fruit with melon-like flesh and a tangy, perfumed flavour.

Footie Rugby, usually union rather than league, never soccer.

Freezing works Slaughterhouse.

Godzone New Zealand, short for "God's own country".

Good as (gold) First rate, excellent.

Greasies Takeaway food, especially fish and chips.

Greenstone A type of nephrite jade known in Maori as *pounamu*.

Haka Maori dance performed in threatening fashion before All Black rugby games.

Handle Large glass of beer.

Hangi Maori feast cooked in an earth oven (see p.49).

Hapu Maori sub-tribal unit. Several make up an *iwi*.

Harakeke Flax.

Hard case See "dag".

Hogget The meat from a year-old sheep. Older and more tasty (though less succulent) than lamb, but not as tough as mutton.

Hollywood A faked or exaggerated sporting injury used to gain advantage.

Hongi Maori greeting, performed by pressing noses together.

Hoon Lout, yob or delinquent.

Hori Offensive word for a Maori.

Hot dog A battered sausage on a stick, dipped in tomato ketchup. What the rest of the world knows as a hot dog is known here as an American hot dog.

Hui Maori gathering or conference.

Iwi Largest of Maori tribal groupings.

Jafa Just Another Fucking Aucklander. Semi-derogatory term now (over)used as a noun. "He's a bloody Jafa".

Jandals Ubiquitous Kiwi footwear, thongs or flip-flops.

Jug Litre of beer.

Kiwi fruit In New Zealand they are always called kiwi fruit, never "kiwis". Golden-fleshed kiwi fruit are also available, and less acidic than their green counterparts.

Lucked in In luck. What "Lucked out" means elsewhere in the world.

Lucked out Out of luck. The meaning completely reversed on its way across the Pacific.

Kai Maori word for food, used in general parlance.

Kaimoana Seafood.

Kainga Village.

Karanga Call for visitors to come forward on a *marae*.

Kaumatua Maori elders, old people.

Kawa-Marae Etiquette or protocol on a *marae*.

Kete Traditional basket made of plaited harakeke.

Kiore Polynesian rat.

kiwi The national bird and mascot of NZ, always set lower case.

Kiwi An alternative label for a New Zealander.

Koha Donation.

Kohanga Reo Pre-school Maori language immersion (literally "language nest").

Kuia Female Maori elder.

Kumara Sweet potato.

Kuri Polynesian dog, now extinct.

Lay-by Practice of putting a deposit on goods until they can be fully paid for.

Mana Maori term indicating status, esteem, prestige or authority, and in wide use among all Kiwis.

Manaia Stylized bird or lizard forms used extensively in Maori carving.

Manuhiri Guest or visitor, particularly to a *marae*.

Maoritanga Maori culture and custom, the Maori way of doing things.

Marae Place for conducting ceremonies in front of a meeting house – literally "courtyard". Also a general term for a settlement centred on the meeting house.

Mauri Life force or life principle.

Mere War club, usually of greenstone.

Metalled Graded road surface of loose stones found all over rural New Zealand.

MMP Mixed Member Proportional representation – New Zealand's electoral system.

Moko Old form of tattooing on body and face that has seen a resurgence among Maori.

Muttonbird Gull-sized sooty shearwater that was a major component of the pre-European Maori diet and tastes like oily and slightly fishy mutton – hence the name.

Ngati Tribal prefix meaning "the descendants (or people) of". Also Ngai and Ati.

OE Overseas experience, usually a year spent abroad by Kiwis in their early twenties.

Pa Fortified village of yore, now usually an abandoned terraced hillside.

Paddock Field.

Pakeha A non-Maori, usually white and not usually expressed with derogatory intent. Literally "foreign" though it can also be translated as "flea" or "pest". It may also be a corruption of *pakepakeha*, which are mythical human-like beings with fair skins.

Pashing Kissing or snogging.

Patu Short fighting club.

Paua The muscular foot of the abalone, often minced and served as a fritter, while the wonderful iridescent shell is used for jewellery and decoration.

Pavlova Meringue dessert with a fruit and cream topping.

Pike out To chicken out or give up.

Piss Beer.

Pissed Drunk.

Podocarp Family of pine, native to New Zealand including rimu, kahikatea, matai, miro, totara etc.

Pohutukawa Gnarled native tree found around the coast of the upper North Island.

Blooms bright red in mid-December and is sometimes known as New Zealand's Christmas Tree.

Poms Folk from Britain; not necessarily offensive.

Pounamu New Zealand greenstone, a unique type of jade.

Powhiri Traditional welcome onto a *marae*.

Puku Maori for stomach, often used as a term of endearment for someone amply endowed.

Puha Maori term for "sow thistle", a leafy plant traditionally gathered by Maori and eaten like spinach.

Rangatira General term for a Maori chief.

Rapt Well-pleased.

Rattle your dags Hurry up.

Root Vulgar term for sex.

Rooted To be very tired or beyond repair, as in "she's rooted, mate" – your car is irreparable.

Rough as guts Uncouth, roughly made or operating badly, as in "she's running rough as guts, mate".

Sealed road Bitumen-surfaced road.

Section Block of land usually surrounding a house.

She'll be right Everything will work out fine.

Shout To buy a round of drinks or generally to treat folk.

Skull To knock back beer quickly.

Smoko Tea break.

Snarler, snag Sausage.

Squiz A look, as in "Give us a squiz".

Stoked Very pleased.

Sweet Cool.

Taiaha Long-handled club.

Tall poppy Someone who excels. "Cutting down tall poppies" is to bring overachievers back to earth – every Kiwi's perceived duty.

Tamarillo Slightly bitter, deep-red fruit, often known as a tree tomato.

Tane Man.

Tangata whenua The people of the land, local or original inhabitants.

Tangi Mourning or funeral.

Taniwha Fearsome water spirit of Maori legend.

Taonga Treasures, prized possessions.

Tapu Forbidden or taboo. Frequently refers to sacred land.

Te reo Maori Maori language.

Tikanga Maori customs, ethics and etiquette – the Maori way of doing things.

Tiki Maori pendant depicting a distorted human figure.

Tiki tour Guided tour.

Togs Swimming costume.

Tohunga Maori priests, experts in *Maoritanga*.

True Left On the left facing downstream.

True Right On the right when facing downstream.

Tukutuku Knotted latticework panels decorating the inside of a meeting house.

Tupuna Ancestors; of great spiritual importance to Maori.

Ute Car-sized pick-up truck, short for "utility".

Varsity University.

Vegemite or **Marmite** dark, savoury yeast-extract spreads. There's always debate between those that love Vegemite (Australian) and those that prefer Kiwi Marmite – sweeter and more appealing than its British equivalent – and of course those that loathe all the above.

Wahine Woman.

Waiata Maori action songs.

Wairua Spirit.

Waka Maori canoe.

Waratah Stake, a term used to describe snow poles on tramps.

Wero Challenge before entering a *marae*.

Whakapapa Family tree or genealogical relationship.

Whanau Extended family group.

Whare Maori for a house.

Whare runanga Meeting house.

Whare whakairo Carved house.

Wop-wops Remote areas.

Travel

Andorra The Pyrenees, Pyrenees & Andorra Map, Spain

Antigua The Caribbean

Argentina Argentina, Argentina Map, Buenos Aires, South America on a Budget

Aruba The Caribbean

Australia Australia, Australia Map, East Coast Australia, Melbourne, Sydney, Tasmania

Austria Austria, Europe on a Budget, Vienna

Bahamas The Bahamas, The Caribbean

Barbados Barbados DIR, The Caribbean

Belgium Belgium & Luxembourg, Bruges DIR, Brussels, Brussels Map, Europe on a Budget

Belize Belize, Central America on a Budget, Guatemala & Belize Map

Benin West Africa

Bolivia Bolivia, South America on a Budget

Brazil Brazil, Rio, South America on a Budget

British Virgin Islands The Caribbean

Brunei Malaysia, Singapore & Brunei [1 title], Southeast Asia on a Budget

Bulgaria Bulgaria, Europe on a Budget

Burkina Faso West Africa

Cambodia Cambodia, Southeast Asia on a Budget, Vietnam, Laos & Cambodia Map [1 Map]

Cameroon West Africa

Canada Canada, Pacific Northwest, Toronto, Toronto Map, Vancouver

Cape Verde West Africa

Cayman Islands The Caribbean

Chile Chile, Chile Map, South America on a Budget

China Beijing, China, Hong Kong & Macau, Hong Kong & Macau DIR, Shanghai

Colombia South America on a Budget

Costa Rica Central America on a Budget, Costa Rica, Costa Rica & Panama Map

Croatia Croatia, Croatia Map, Europe on a Budget

Cuba Cuba, Cuba Map, The Caribbean, Havana

Cyprus Cyprus, Cyprus Map

Czech Republic The Czech Republic, Czech & Slovak Republics, Europe on a Budget, Prague, Prague DIR, Prague Map

Denmark Copenhagen, Denmark, Europe on a Budget, Scandinavia

Dominica The Caribbean

Dominican Republic Dominican Republic, The Caribbean

Ecuador Ecuador, South America on a Budget

Egypt Egypt, Egypt Map

El Salvador Central America on a Budget

England Britain, Camping in Britain, Devon & Cornwall, Dorset, Hampshire and The Isle of Wight [1 title], England, Europe on a Budget, The Lake District, London, London DIR, London Map, London Mini Guide, Walks In London & Southeast England

Estonia The Baltic States, Europe on a Budget

Fiji Fiji

Finland Europe on a Budget, Finland, Scandinavia

France Brittany & Normandy, Corsica, Corsica Map, The Dordogne & the Lot, Europe on a Budget, France, France Map, Languedoc & Roussillon, The Loire, Paris, Paris DIR,

Paris Map, Paris Mini Guide, Provence & the Côte d'Azur, The Pyrenees, Pyrenees & Andorra Map

French Guiana South America on a Budget

Gambia The Gambia, West Africa

Germany Berlin, Berlin Map, Europe on a Budget, Germany, Germany Map

Ghana West Africa

Gibraltar Spain

Greece Athens Map, Crete, Crete Map, Europe on a Budget, Greece, Greece Map, Greek Islands, Ionian Islands

Guadeloupe The Caribbean

Guatemala Central America on a Budget, Guatemala, Guatemala & Belize Map

Guinea West Africa

Guinea-Bissau West Africa

Guyana South America on a Budget

Holland see The Netherlands

Honduras Central America on a Budget

Hungary Budapest, Europe on a Budget, Hungary

Iceland Iceland, Iceland Map

India Goa, India, India Map, Kerala, Rajasthan, Delhi & Agra [1 title], South India, South India Map

Indonesia Bali & Lombok, Southeast Asia on a Budget

Ireland Dublin DIR, Dublin Map, Europe on a Budget, Ireland, Ireland Map

Israel Jerusalem

Italy Europe on a Budget, Florence DIR, Florence & Siena Map, Florence & the best of Tuscany, Italy, The Italian Lakes, Naples & the Amalfi Coast, Rome, Rome DIR, Rome Map, Sardinia, Sicily, Sicily Map, Tuscany & Umbria, Tuscany Map,

Venice, Venice DIR, Venice Map

Jamaica Jamaica, The Caribbean

Japan Japan, Tokyo

Jordan Jordan

Kenya Kenya, Kenya Map

Korea Korea

Laos Laos, Southeast Asia on a Budget, Vietnam, Laos & Cambodia Map [1 Map]

Latvia The Baltic States, Europe on a Budget

Lithuania The Baltic States, Europe on a Budget

Luxembourg Belgium & Luxembourg, Europe on a Budget

Malaysia Malaysia Map, Malaysia, Singapore & Brunei [1 title], Southeast Asia on a Budget

Mali West Africa

Malta Malta & Gozo DIR

Martinique The Caribbean

Mauritania West Africa

Mexico Baja California, Baja California, Cancún & Cozumel DIR, Mexico, Mexico Map, Yucatán, Yucatán Peninsula Map

Monaco France, Provence & the Côte d'Azur

Montenegro Montenegro

Morocco Europe on a Budget, Marrakesh DIR, Marrakesh Map, Morocco, Morocco Map,

Nepal Nepal

Netherlands Amsterdam, Amsterdam DIR, Amsterdam Map, Europe on a Budget, The Netherlands

Netherlands Antilles The Caribbean

New Zealand New Zealand, New Zealand Map

DIR: Rough Guide **DIRECTIONS** for short breaks

Available from all good bookstores

Nicaragua Central America on a Budget
Niger West Africa
Nigeria West Africa
Norway Europe on a Budget, Norway, Scandinavia
Panama Central America on a Budget, Costa Rica & Panama Map, Panama
Paraguay South America on a Budget
Peru Peru, Peru Map, South America on a Budget
Philippines The Philippines, Southeast Asia on a Budget,
Poland Europe on a Budget, Poland
Portugal Algarve DIR, The Algarve Map, Europe on a Budget, Lisbon DIR, Lisbon Map, Madeira DIR, Portugal, Portugal Map, Spain & Portugal Map
Puerto Rico The Caribbean, Puerto Rico
Romania Europe on a Budget, Romania
Russia Europe on a Budget, Moscow, St Petersburg
St Kitts & Nevis The Caribbean
St Lucia The Caribbean
St Vincent & the Grenadines The Caribbean
Scotland Britain, Camping in Britain, Edinburgh DIR, Europe on a Budget, Scotland, Scottish Highlands & Islands
Senegal West Africa
Serbia Montenegro Europe on a Budget
Sierra Leone West Africa
Singapore Malaysia, Singapore & Brunei [1 title], Singapore, Singapore DIR, Southeast Asia on a Budget
Slovakia Czech & Slovak Republics, Europe on a Budget
Slovenia Europe on a Budget, Slovenia
South Africa Cape Town & the Garden Route, South Africa, South Africa Map
Spain Andalucía, Andalucía Map, Barcelona, Barcelona DIR, Barcelona Map, Europe on a Budget, Ibiza & Formentera DIR, Gran Canaria DIR, Madrid DIR, Lanzarote & Fuerteventura DIR Madrid Map, Mallorca & Menorca, Mallorca DIR, Mallorca Map, The Pyrenees, Pyrenees & Andorra Map, Spain, Spain & Portugal Map, Tenerife & La Gomera DIR
Sri Lanka Sri Lanka, Sri Lanka Map
Suriname South America on a Budget
Sweden Europe on a Budget, Scandinavia, Sweden
Switzerland Europe on a Budget, Switzerland
Taiwan Taiwan
Tanzania Tanzania, Zanzibar
Thailand Bangkok, Southeast Asia on a Budget, Thailand, Thailand Map, Thailand Beaches & Islands
Togo West Africa
Trinidad & Tobago The Caribbean, Trinidad & Tobago
Tunisia Tunisia, Tunisia Map
Turkey Europe on a Budget, Istanbul, Turkey, Turkey Map
Turks and Caicos Islands The Bahamas, The Caribbean
United Arab Emirates Dubai DIR, Dubai & UAE Map [1 title]
United Kingdom Britain, Devon & Cornwall, Edinburgh DIR England, Europe on a Budget, The Lake District, London, London DIR, London Map, London Mini Guide, Scotland, Scottish Highlands & Islands, Wales, Walks In London & Southeast England
United States Alaska, Boston, California, California Map, Chicago, Colorado, Florida, Florida Map, The Grand Canyon, Hawaii, Los Angeles, Los Angeles Map, Los Angeles and Southern California, Maui DIR, Miami & South Florida, New England, New England Map, New Orleans & Cajun Country, New Orleans DIR, New York City, NYC DIR, NYC Map, New York City Mini Guide, Oregon & Washington, Orlando & Walt Disney World® DIR, San Francisco, San Francisco DIR, San Francisco Map, Seattle, Southwest USA, USA, Washington DC, Yellowstone & the Grand Tetons National Park, Yosemite National Park
Uruguay South America on a Budget
US Virgin Islands The Bahamas, The Caribbean
Venezuela South America on a Budget
Vietnam Southeast Asia on a Budget, Vietnam, Vietnam, Laos & Cambodia Map [1 Map],
Wales Britain, Camping in Britain, Europe on a Budget, Wales
First-Time Series FT Africa, FT Around the World, FT Asia, FT Europe, FT Latin America
Inspirational guides Earthbound, Clean Breaks, Make the Most of Your Time on Earth, Ultimate Adventures, World Party
Travel Specials Camping in Britain, Travel with Babies & Young Children, Walks in London & SE England

ROUGH GUIDES
Don't Just Travel

Computers Cloud Computing, FWD this link, The Internet, iPhone, iPods & iTunes, Macs & OS X, Website Directory
Film & TV American Independent Film. British Cult Comedy. Comedy Movies, Cult Movies, Film, Film Musicals, Film Noir, Gangster Movies, Horror Movies, Sci-Fi Movies, Westerns
Lifestyle Babies & Toddlers, Brain Training, Food, Girl Stuff, Green Living, Happiness, Men's Health, Pregnancy & Birth, Running, Saving & Selling Online, Sex, Weddings
Music The Beatles, The Best Music You've Never Heard, Blues, Bob Dylan, Book of Playlists, Classical Music, Heavy Metal, Jimi Hendrix, Led Zeppelin, Nirvana, Opera, Pink Floyd, The Rolling Stones, Soul and R&B, Velvet Underground, World Music
Popular Culture Anime, Classic Novels, Conspiracy Theories, Crime Fiction, The Da Vinci Code, Graphic Novels, Hidden Treasures, His Dark Materials, Hitchhiker's Guide to the Galaxy, The Lost Symbol, Manga, Next Big Thing, Shakespeare, True Crime, Tutankhamun, Unexplained Phenomena, Videogames
Science The Brain, Climate Change, The Earth, Energy Crisis, Evolution, Future, Genes & Cloning, The Universe, Weather

For more information go to www.rough guides.com

Small print and
Index

A Rough Guide to Rough Guides

Published in 1982, the first Rough Guide – to Greece – was a student scheme that became a publishing phenomenon. Mark Ellingham, a recent graduate in English from Bristol University, had been travelling in Greece the previous summer and couldn't find the right guidebook. With a small group of friends he wrote his own guide, combining a highly contemporary, journalistic style with a thoroughly practical approach to travellers' needs.

SMALL PRINT

The immediate success of the book spawned a series that rapidly covered dozens of destinations. And, in addition to impecunious backpackers, Rough Guides soon acquired a much broader and older readership that relished the guides' wit and inquisitiveness as much as their enthusiastic, critical approach and value-for-money ethos.

These days, Rough Guides include recommendations from shoestring to luxury and cover more than 200 destinations around the globe, including almost every country in the Americas and Europe, more than half of Africa and most of Asia and Australasia. Our ever-growing team of authors and photographers is spread all over the world, particularly in Europe, the US and Australia.

In the early 1990s, Rough Guides branched out of travel, with the publication of Rough Guides to World Music, Classical Music and the Internet. All three have become benchmark titles in their fields, spearheading the publication of a wide range of books under the Rough Guide name.

Including the travel series, Rough Guides now number more than 350 titles, covering: phrasebooks, waterproof maps, music guides from Opera to Heavy Metal, reference works as diverse as Conspiracy Theories and Shakespeare, and popular culture books from iPods to Poker. Rough Guides also produce a series of more than 120 World Music CDs in partnership with World Music Network.

Visit www.roughguides.com to see our latest publications.

Rough Guide credits

Text editor: Ann-Marie Shaw
Layout: Pradeep Thapliyal
Cartography: Animesh Pathak
Picture editor: Jj Luck
Production: Rebecca Short
Proofreader: Karen Parker
Cover design: Dan May, Chloë Roberts
Photographer: Paul Whitfield
Editorial: London Andy Turner, Keith Drew, Edward Aves, Alice Park, Lucy White, Jo Kirby, James Smart, Natasha Foges, Róisín Cameron, James Rice, Lara Kavanagh, Emma Traynor, Emma Gibbs, Kathryn Lane, Monica Woods, Mani Ramaswamy, Harry Wilson, Lucy Cowie, Alison Roberts, Eleanor Aldridge, Ian Blenkinsop, Joe Staines, Matthew Milton, Tracy Hopkins, Ruth Tidball; **Delhi** Madhavi Singh, Lubna Shaheen, Jalpreen Kaur Chhatwal
Design & Pictures: London Scott Stickland, Dan May, Diana Jarvis, Mark Thomas, Nicole Newman, Sarah Cummins, Emily Taylor; **Delhi** Umesh Aggarwal, Ajay Verma, Jessica Subramanian, Ankur Guha, Sachin Tanwar, Anita Singh, Nikhil Agarwal, Sachin Gupta

Production: Liz Cherry
Cartography: London Ed Wright, Katie Lloyd-Jones; **Delhi** Rajesh Chhibber, Ashutosh Bharti, Rajesh Mishra, Jasbir Sandhu, Karobi Gogoi, Alakananda Roy, Swati Handoo, Deshpal Dabas
Online: London Faye Hellon, Jeanette Angell, Fergus Day, Justine Bright, Clare Bryson, Aine Fearon, Adrian Low, Ezgi Celebi; **Delhi** Amit Verma, Rahul Kumar, Narender Kumar, Ravi Yadav, Debojit Borah, Rakesh Kumar, Ganesh Sharma, Shisir Basumatari
Marketing & Publicity: London Liz Statham, Jess Carter, Vivienne Watton, Anna Paynton, Rachel Sprackett, Laura Vipond; **New York** Katy Ball, Judi Powers; **Delhi** Ragini Govind
Digital Travel Publisher: Peter Buckley
Reference Director: Andrew Lockett
Operations Assistant: Becky Doyle
Operations Manager: Helen Atkinson
Publishing Director (Travel): Clare Currie
Commercial Manager: Gino Magnotta
Managing Director: John Duhigg

SMALL PRINT

Publishing information

This seventh edition published September 2010 by
Rough Guides Ltd,
80 Strand, London WC2R 0RL
11 Local Shopping Centre, Panchsheel Park, New Delhi 110017, India
Distributed by the Penguin Group
Penguin Books Ltd,
80 Strand, London WC2R 0RL
Penguin Group (USA)
375 Hudson Street, NY 10014, USA
Penguin Group (Australia)
250 Camberwell Road, Camberwell, Victoria 3124, Australia
Penguin Group (Canada)
195 Harry Walker Parkway N, Newmarket, ON, L3Y 7B3 Canada
Penguin Group (NZ)
67 Apollo Drive, Mairangi Bay, Auckland 1310, New Zealand
Cover concept by Peter Dyer.
Typeset in Bembo and Helvetica to an original design by Henry Iles.

Printed in Italy by L.E.G.O. S.p.A, Lavis (TN)

840pp includes index
A catalogue record for this book is available from the British Library
ISBN: 978-1-84836-523-0

1   3   5   7   9   8   6   4   2

Help us update

We've gone to a lot of effort to ensure that the seventh edition of **The Rough Guide to New Zealand** is accurate and up-to-date. However, things change – places get "discovered", opening hours are notoriously fickle, restaurants and rooms raise prices or lower standards. If you feel we've got it wrong or left something out, we'd like to know, and if you can remember the address, the price, the hours, the phone number, so much the better.

Please send your comments with the subject line **"Rough Guide New Zealand Update"** to ⓔ mail@roughguides.com. We'll credit all contributions and send a copy of the next edition (or any other Rough Guide if you prefer) for the very best emails.

Have your questions answered and tell others about your trip at ⓦ www.roughguides.com

Acknowledgements

Catherine Le Nevez: Cheers/*Kia ora* to all the locals, fellow travellers and tourism professionals who provided insights, assistance and good times along the way. In particular, huge gratitude goes out once again to Claire Allred and team at YHA HQ and the fantastic hostel managers throughout NZ; Tony Lyons and everyone at the aptly named Ace Rental Cars; and my "Kiwi bro" Carsten for the flat in Wellington and awesome catch-ups around the country – as well as Minnie, John and family on Kapiti Island; Craig, Cheryl, Spiderman and the firies; Anna in Te Aroha; the East Cape *whanau*; and the Murray family in Lake Tekapo (a true testament to the kindness of strangers!). At Rough Guides, major thanks to editors Keith Drew and Annie Shaw, and co-authors Paul and Tony. As ever, *merci surtout* to my family.

Tony Mudd: Thanks to all of the operators, travellers and other general good eggs I met while completing research for this edition; your help, advice and tips are invaluable. Special mention must be made of Tony Lyons, of Ace, and his team, Gerry Hill of the Great Pons and all the helpful souls at YHA NZ. Thanks particularly

to the editorial staff of Rough Guides and the team behind the production of this edition, especially Annie. Lastly my eternal gratitude to Don, Vi, Anne and John, my friends in NZ and at home, my wife Alison (who makes all of this possible and fun) and the restorative powers of the beer in my local, *The White Hart*.

Paul Whitfield: Thanks to everyone I met on research trips throughout the land, especially those who suggested great restaurants to check out, waxed lyrical about hotels and hostels and shared experiences. Special thanks go out to: Andrea, Jo and others at Tourism Auckland; Andrea at the Napier i-SITE; Cécile Dransart in Christchurch; Garry, Hillary and clan in Napier; and Richard and Raewyn in Wellington. Cheers too to: Bruce Fairless for sharing the high seas and acting as a photo model; Jenny, Jo and Jarvie for culinary explorations of Martinborough; Marion, Allan, Colin, John, Martin, Jed, Kirsten, Sarah for allowing the faces, legs, back of heads of whatever to appear in various shots. Lastly, huge gratitude is due to Marion for helping with the wine tasting and restaurant sampling, and hanging in there through long absences.

Readers' letters

Thanks to all the readers who have taken the time to write in with comments and suggestions (and apologies if we've inadvertently omitted or misspelt anyone's name):

Nelleke Aben and Kasper van der Valk, Jules Adam, Ian Allen, Kitty Arbuthnot, Finn Arnesen, Jerry Baston, Joy and Paul Biggin, Shona Billings, Bobbie Caroll, Lindy Clarbull, Susan Frances Edwards, Jenny Farmer, Gillian and Keith Gillanders, Fiona Griffiths, Steve Hamilton, Rob Henderson, Alex and Phil Hide, Libby Jellie, Warren Jowett, Joanna Kirby, Edward Knowles, Ann Lee, Tony McManus, Melvin, Michaela, Michael Midgley, M. Miller, Wendy Milmine, Steve and Chrissy Moon, Gerard Ng, Christian Nommesen, Vince Picone, Ben Regan, Hugh Rennie, Harry and Sally Sargent, Richard Sedding, Rebecca Trengove, D. Walker, Trevor Weir, Maggie Wright

SMALL PRINT

Photo credits

All photos © Rough Guides except the following:

Things not to miss

01 Cruise boat, Milford Sound © Holger Leue/ Tourism New Zealand

02 Thermal mud, Wai-O-Tapu © Philippe Bourseiller/Getty

03 Poolburn Tunnel, Otago Rail Trail © Peter Andrews/www.otagorailtrail.co.nz

11 Emerald Lakes on the Tongariro Crossing © Christian Kober/Corbis

16 Nugget Point, Catlins © Darryl Torckler/Getty

17 Farewell Spit © M.L. Harris/Getty

18 Moa and Haast's eagle exhibit, Te Papa © Te Papa

20 Whale © Whale Watch, Kaikoura

22 Yellow-eyed penguin, Dunedin © Penguin Place

25 Mount Aspiring, Routeburn Track © Ian Cumming/Getty

26 Flat Stream Viaduct, Taieri Gorge Railway © Taieri Gorge Railway

27 Black water rafting, Waitomo Caves © Tourism Holdings/Tourism New Zealand

29 Kaka, Zealandia: the Karori Sanctuary Experience © Paul Ramos Little

30 Diving, Poor Knights Islands Marine Reserve © Kim Westerkov/Tourism New Zealand

Adrenaline heaven colour section

Jetboating on the Shotover River © Paul Thompson/Corbis

Bungy jump © Jochem D. Wijnands/Getty

Man sliding down ice tunnel, Franz Josef © Aurora Open/Keri Oberly/Getty

Craigieburn Valley, South Island © Jack Moscrop/ Getty

Conservation in action colour section

Kiwi © Zealandia: the Karori Sanctuary Experience

Tararua Wind Farm © Danita Delimont/Getty

Swimming with dolphins, Kaikoura © Dennis Buurman

Shark cage diving, Surfit, Gisborne © Surfit

Fur seal underwater at Kaikoura © Kim Westerskov/Getty

Taking photo of kaka, at Zealandia: the Karori Sanctuary Experience © Paul Ramos

Maori in the modern world colour section

Haka © Tim Graham/Getty

Pendant in the form of the god Hei-Tiki © The Bridgeman Art Library/Getty

Moko tattoo © Frans Lemmens/Getty

Black and whites

p.449 Nelson Market © Marcus Jackson

p.474 Jetty on the shores of Lake Rotoiti, Nelson National Park © Peter Bush/Getty

p.546 Aoraki Mount Cook © Marcus Jackson

p.563 The Crown Hotel, Geraldine © Marcus Jackson

p.576 Taieri Gorge Railway © Taieri Gorge Railway

p.603 Horseriding, Curio Bay, Catlins, © Frans Lemmens/Getty

p.620 Pancake Rocks, Punakaiki © Marcus Jackson

p.653 Helicopter on Franz Josef glacier © Janie Airey/Getty

p.668 Prices Creek Viaduct, Otago Rail Trail © Peter Andrews/www.otagorailtrail.co.nz

p.689 Chinese Settlement, Arrowtown © Marcus Jackson

p.728 Overlooking Arthur Valley, Milford Track © Colin Monteath/Getty

p.742 Cruise boat, Milford Sound © Peter Hendrie/Getty

Index

Map entries are in colour.

309 Road......................325
42 Traverse..................301

A

A.H. Reed Memorial
  Kauri Park..........150, 162
Abbey Caves..............162
Abel Tasman Coast Track
 463
Abel Tasman Drive........469
Abel Tasman Inland Track
 465
**Abel Tasman National
  Park**.............16, 458–466
Abel Tasman National Park
 459
acclimatization societies
 786
accommodation.............42
adventure sports.........see
  Adrenaline heaven colour
  section
Agrodome.....................269
Ahipara.......................189
airlines............................30
  domestic............................32
Akaroa.................526–533
Akaroa..........................527
albatrosses..................489,
  596, 793
Alexandra.....................720
Alley, Rewi...................553
America's Cup..............98,
  100, 113
Anakiwa........................444
Anatoki River................468
Anaura Bay...................356
Anderson Park..............608
Angelus Hut Loop.........475
Angus, Rita..........101, 507
Aniwaniwa Falls............370
**Aoraki Mount Cook
  National Park**....569–572
Aoraki Mount Cook,
  around.......................570
**Aoraki Mount Cook
  Village**.............567–572
Aoraki Mount Cook
  Village.......................568
Arataki Visitor Centre....125
Aratiatia Rapids............289

Arrowtown..........689–693
Arrowtown....................691
Arrowtown–Macetown
  Circuit tramp..............694
Art Deco Napier......23, 377
Arthur's Pass.......555–557
Arthur's Pass National
  Park..........................557
Arthur's Pass ski-fields
 555
Arthur's Pass Village.....555
Arthur's Pass Village 555
Ashburton.....................534
Ashhurst.......................250
astronomy...................111,
  489, 565
Atene...........................243
Athfield, Ian.................250,
  383, 408
AUCKLAND.........84–122
Auckland and around
 86
Central Auckland...........99
Devonport....................109
Mount Eden, Epsom and
  Remuera....................111
Parnell and Newmarket
 105
Ponsonby and Herne Bay
 107
Acacia Cottage...............111
accommodation...........92–98
activities...................112–114
airport..............................88
airport accommodation.....93
Albert Park.......................100
Aotea Centre...................100
Aotea Square...................100
Auckland Art Gallery........100
Auckland Botanic Garden
 112
Auckland Cathedral.........105
Auckland Museum...........102
Auckland Zoo..................108
B&Bs...............................94
backpackers.....................96
bars................................118
Bastion Point...................106
bridge climb....................113
bungy jumping................113
bus station.......................88
buses...............................90
cafés..............................114
campsites.........................97
canyoning.......................114
Central Auckland........98–103
cinema...........................121

city centre.......................100
city tours...........................92
Civic Theatre...................100
clubs...............................119
Coast to Coast walkway
 112
comedy...........................120
concerts...........................120
Cornwall Park..................111
cruises.............................113
cycling.............................92
Devonport.......................109
Devonport ferry...............110
DOC office.......................90
dolphin watching.............113
Domain, the....................102
downtown........................98
drinking, nightlife and
  entertainment........118–121
driving.............................91
eating.......................114–118
Eden Garden...................106
Ewelme Cottage...............105
ferries..............................91
festivals...........................121
Freeman's Bay.................107
gay Auckland...................119
gigs.................................119
guesthouses.....................94
Herne Bay.......................107
Highwic...........................106
history..............................86
holiday parks....................97
hostels.............................96
hotels..............................93
Huia Lodge......................111
Karangahape Road.........101
kayaking..........................113
Kelly Tarlton's.................106
Kinder House...................105
Kingsland........................108
Kohimarama....................106
lesbian Auckland.............119
listings............................122
Maungakiekie..................110
Maungawhau....................110
Mission Bay....................106
MOTAT...........................108
motels..............................93
Mount Eden....................110
Mount Victoria.................110
moving on from Auckland
 88
Navy Museum..................110
Newmarket......................105
North Head......................110
North Shore.....................109
North Shore City Coastal
  Walk..........................110
Once Were Warriors........111
One Tree Hill....................110

Otara Market................... 112
parking 92
Parnell 104
planetarium 111
Ponsonby 108
pubs 118
restaurants 114
Rugby World Cup 85,
    92, 107
sailing 113
SkyJump 100
Skytower 100
SkyWalk 100
South Auckland.............. 111
St Heliers....................... 106
Stardome Observatory..... 111
suburbs, the.............103–112
Symonds Street Cemetery
    101
Takapuna........................ 109
Tamaki Drive................... 106
theatre............................ 120
trains 91
transport passes 91
Viaduct Harbour............... 98
Victoria Park Market 107
visitor centre 90
volcanoes......................... 87
Voyager: New Zealand
    Maritime Museum........... 98
walks............................... 112
Western Springs.............. 108
whale watching 113
Wintergardens 102
Aupori Peninsula 192
aurora australis............. 611
Awa Awa Rata Reserve
    560
Awanui........................... 193

B

B&Bs.............................. 43
backpacker buses........... 33
backpackers................... 44
Balance, John................ 768
Balclutha....................... 598
ballooning.....509, 558, 685
banks.............................. 76
Banks, Joseph......380, 521
Banks Peninsula
    521–533
Banks Peninsula........... 521
Banks Peninsula Track
    532
Bannockburn................ 719
Barry's Bay 525
Barrytown...................... 640
Batten, Jean 108
Baxter, James K. ...239, 243
Bay of Islands 166–184

Bay of Islands and
    Whangaroa Harbour
    167
Bay of Plenty....... 335–351
Baylys Beach................ 203
Beehive, The................. 412
beer 50
bellbird...................254, 790
Bendigo 719
Bethell's Beach............ 126
Bethlehem 342
biculturalism 777
bicycle touring.............. 41
biking...............see cycling
biosecurity 72
Black Rocks 169
Blackball 626
Bland Bay..................... 166
Blenheim............. 477–483
Blenheim...................... 478
blue duck...................... 790
Blue Lake..................... 277
Bluff............................. 610
Bob's Cove................... 695
Bolger, Jim................... 772
Bone People, The
    ....651, 800
books 798–804
Boundary Stream Scenic
    Reserve...................... 368
boutique hotels............. 43
Brick Bay Sculpture Trail
    154
Bridge to Nowhere
    ....239, 240
Broken River ski-field
    553
Bruce Bay..................... 660
Brunner Industrial Site
    628
Brunner, Thomas 472,
    621, 628, 633, 636, 661
Buck, Peter................... 768
Buller Gorge 623
Buller River 623
Bulls............................ 249
bungy jumping.........19, 61,
    113, 270, 283, 305, 551,
    680, Adrenaline heaven
    colour section
Buried Village 277
Busby, James......168, 169,
    172, 764
buses............................ 32
Bushy Park 237
Butler, John 182

C

cabins........................... 45
Cable Bay.................... 188
Cambridge................... 212
Campbell, John Logan
    111
campervan rental........... 38
camping......................... 45
canoeing.........61, 129, 241
Canterbury Association
    498
canyoning......62, 114, 320,
    683, 707
Cape Brett.................... 169
Cape Brett Track 166
Cape Egmont................ 236
Cape Foulwind 630
Cape Kidnappers 380
Cape Kidnappers and
    Hawke's Bay wine
    country 381
Cape Palliser 395
Cape Reinga................. 195
Cape Reinga Coastal
    Walkway 195
Cape Reinga tours 192
Cape Rodney–Okakari
    Marine Reserve 155
Cape Runaway............. 354
Caples Track................ 701
car buying...................... 39
car rental....................... 36
Cardrona...................... 712
Cardrona ski-field......... 712
Cardrona Valley 712
Carterton 391
Cascade Saddle Route
    715
Castle Hill Reserve 554
Castlepoint 391
Cathedral Caves (Catlins)
    602
Cathedral Cove 330
Catlins Coast 19,
    598–605
Catlins Coast 599
Catlins Top Track.......... 602
Catlins tours 600
Cavalli Islands 184
Cave Stream Scenic
    Reserve...................... 554
caving 23, 221, 638, 643
chamois........................ 787
Charleston................... 637
Charming Creek Walk ..632
children......................... 69
Chinaman's Bluff 702

CHRISTCHURCH
.... 496–521
Christchurch and south to
  Otago 496
Central Christchurch
  500–501
Greater Christchurch
  510–511
accommodation 502–506
Air Force Museum 512
airport 498
Antigua Boat Sheds 509
Arts Centre 508
B&Bs 503
backpackers 504
Botanic Gardens 509
bus station 499
cafés 516
campsites 505
Canterbury Museum 508
Cathedral 7, 506
Cathedral Square 506
Cave Rock 514
Christchurch Art Gallery
  .... 18, 507
Christchurch Gondola 512
Christ's college 508
cinema 520
city transport 499
clubs 519
concerts 519
cycling 499
Deans Bush 511
Deans Cottage 511
driving 499
eating and drinking 515–518
gigs 519
guesthouses 503
Hagley Park 508
High Street 507
history 498
hostels 504
hotels 502
information 498
International Antarctic Centre
  512
Lichfield Lanes 507
listings 520
Mona Vale 510
motels 502
New Regent Street 507
nightlife and entertainment
  518
Nurses' Memorial Chapel
  509
Orana Wildlife Park 512
parking 499
Port Hills 514
Provincial Council Buildings
  507
Redcliffs 513
restaurants 516
Riccarton Bush 511
Riccarton House 512
SOL Square 507
Summit Road 514

Sumner 513
takeaways 516
Taylor's Mistake 514
theatre 519
train station 498
tram 499
TranzAlpine train 513
Willowbank Wildlife Reserve
  512
Christchurch Art Gallery
  .... 18, 507
chronology 775
cigarettes 67
Claris 143
Clark, Helen 773
Clifden 753
Clifden Caves 753
Clifton 382
climate 13
Clyde 719
Coast to Coast race 643
coffee 51
Colac Bay 755
Collingwood 470
Colville 324
Company Bay 595
Conical Hill 701
conservation organizations
  .... 785, *Conservation
  in action* colour section
consulates 71
Cook, James (Captain)
  .... 139, 168, 309,
  326, 357, 362, 373, 379,
  380, 395, 400, 439, 441,
  471, 521, 612, 630, 729,
  750, 762, 763, 786, 810
Cook Strait, crossing 401
Cooks Beach 330
Cooks Cove Walkway 357
Coopers Beach 188
Coromandel 321–323
Coromandel, Bay of Plenty
  and East Cape
  310–311
Coromandel Peninsula
  314–334
Coromandel Peninsula
  315
Coromandel Walkway
  324
Coronet Peak ski-field
  683
costs 70
Coudrey House Museum
  129
Craigieburn Forest Park
  554
Craigieburn Valley ski-field
  553

Craters of the Moon 288
credit cards 76
cricket 65
crime 70
Croesus Track 627
Cromwell 717
Crossroads 143
Crown Range 712
cruises 174, 285, 524,
  571, 709, 743
Curio Bay 603
customs regulations
  72
cycling 41, 708
cycling tours 62

D

dam dropping 236
dangers 73
Dannevirke 388
Dansey's Pass 724
Dargaville 202
dates 78
Dawson Falls 233
de Surville, Jean Francois
  Marie 762
debit cards 76
Denniston 632
Department of
  Conservation 55, 79
Desert Road, the 304
dialling codes 77
Diamond Harbour 525
Diamond Lake 708
disabilities, travellers with
  79
discrimination 71
Divide, the 701, 741
diving .... see scuba diving
DOC 55, 79
DOC huts 57
dolphin watching and
  swimming 113, 174,
  340, 347, 440, 489, 530
dolphins 793
Doubtful Sound 752
dress standards 66
drinking 50
driving 35
Driving Creek Railway
  322
drugs 71
du Fresne, Marion
  .... 168, 775
DUNEDIN 577–589
Dunedin 580

Dunedin to Stewart Island
.............................578
  accommodation 581
  airport............................... 579
  B&Bs 581
  backpackers..................... 582
  Baldwin Street.................. 585
  bars 587
  Cadbury World 584
  cafés................................ 586
  camping 582
  cinema 588
  city transport.................... 581
  clubs 587
  drinking, nightlife and
    entertainment..........587–589
  Dunedin Botanic Garden
  585
  Dunedin Public Art Gallery
  583
  Dunedin Railway Station
  583
  eating 586
  festivals 588
  First Church of Otago 583
  history 579
  Hocken Library................. 583
  holiday parks.................... 582
  homestays........................ 581
  hostels............................. 582
  hotels 581
  information 579
  listings 589
  motels 581
  NZ Sports Hall of Fame ... 583
  Octagon, the 582
  Olveston 584
  Otago Museum 584
  Otago Settlers Museum ... 583
  pubs 587
  Regent Theatre 583
  restaurants 586
  rugby............................... 587
  Signal Hill 585
  Speight's Brewery............ 584
  St Clair Beach.................. 585
  St Kilda Beach 585
  theatre............................. 588
  University of Otago 584
Dunedin Sound, the 587
Dunsandel 534
Dusky Track.................. 754
duty free 72

E

earthquakes............. 73, 785
East Cape 15, 351–357
East Cape Lighthouse
  355
East Egmont.................. 233
Eastwoodhill Arboretum
  367

EFTPOS......................... 76
Egmont National Park
  232–235
Egmont Village 233
electricity 71
Ell, Harry 515
email 75
embassies 71
emergency calls 70
etiquette 66
exchange rates............... 76

F

Fairlie 564
falcon, NZ.............. 791,792
fantails 790
Farewell Spit........... 20, 471
Farewell Spit tours 471
farming 786
farmstays....................... 44
Featherston 392
ferries............................. 41
festivals ...53, 373, 482, 588
film 8, 795–797
Fiordland 729–758
Fiordland.......................730
Firman, Shona 508
fishing 63, 164,
  176, 271, 285, 340, 709
Flagstaff Hill.................. 179
Fletcher Bay 324
Fletcher House 594
flights
  from Australia.................... 28
  from Canada 27
  from Ireland....................... 27
  from South Africa.............. 30
  from the UK....................... 27
  from the US........................ 27
  flights within NZ 31
flightseeing 62, 175,
  276, 284, 566, 571, 655,
  661, 685, 709, 736
Fomison, Tony 101, 507
food 47
football (soccer).............. 65
Forgotten World Highway
  224
Fortrose 605
Fox Glacier 657–660
Fox Glacier.....................658
Foxton 251
Foxton Beach................ 251
Frame, Janet 540
Franz Josef Glacier
  653–657
Franz Josef Glacier 654

French Pass.................. 445
fruit picking................... 180

G

Gabriel's Gully 725
gannets......... 127, 381, 793
Gate Pa 338
gay New Zealand 72
geothermal power 794
Geraldine 563
getting around 31
geysers..... 12, 267, 278, 314
giardia...................... 74, 794
Gibbston........................ 688
Gillespie Pass tramp
  664
Gillespies Beach........... 659
Gisborne 362–367
Gisborne 364
glacier hiking 17,
  655, 658
glaciers 17, 652
Glade Wharf 748
Glenfalloch Woodland
  Garden...................... 594
Glenorchy 694–698
Glenorchy & the major
  tramps 696
gliding............................ 574
glossary 810–812
glowworms.........158, 202,
  219, 638, 659, 734, 753
Goat Island Marine Reserve
  155
Godley Head 525
gold mining................... 716
Golden Bay.......... 465–473
Goldie, Charles..... 101, 507
Gore.............................. 605
Govett-Brewster Art Gallery
  229
GPS 75
Granity 632
Great Barrier Island
  139–146
Great Barrier Island 140
Great Fleet..................... 761
Great Walks....................57,
  Adrenaline heaven colour
  section
green issues 793
Green Lake 277
greenstone.......... 647, 782
Greenstone Track 701
Grey, George 154,
  445, 766

Grey, Zane 168
Grey River..................... 623
Greymouth.......... 640–644
Greymouth 641
Greytown 391
Grove Scenic Reserve
.... 469
GST 70

H

Haast 661
Haast Beach................. 662
Haast Pass 662
Haast River.................. 663
Hahei 330
haka 783
Halfmoon Bay.............. 612
Hamilton 209–212
Hamilton, central 210
Hamilton Gardens 211
Hammond, Bill.............. 508
Hamurana Springs 273
hang-gliding 684
hangi 17, 49, 272, 687
Hanmer Forest Park 550
Hanmer Springs
...........................549–551
Hanmer Springs............ 550
Harihari 650
Haruru Falls 173
Harvey, Les................... 104
Harwoods Hole............. 466
Hastings 384–387
Hastings........................ 386
Hau Hau, the 349
Hauraki Gulf................. 131
Hauraki Plains..... 310–314
Havelock 444
Havelock North............. 385
Hawera 236
Hawke's Bay 362
Hawke's Bay
wine country 362
Hawke's Bay
wine country 381
Hawks Crag.................. 624
hazards........................... 73
health............................. 72
Heaphy, Charles 472,
621, 633, 636, 638, 647
Heaphy Track 472
Heavenly Creatures 796
Hector........................... 632
Hector's dolphins 604
Heke, Hone.................. 165,
177, 766

Helensville 127
heli-hiking 572, 655,
658, 713
Hell's Gate 274
Henry, Richard.............. 750
herons........................... 650
Hibiscus Coast, the...... 127
Hicks Bay 354
hihi .... see stitchbird
Hika, Hongi........... 262, 763
hiking 56,
see also tramping
hiking tours..................... 61
Hikurangi 165
Hillary Trail 125
Hillary, Edmund 125,
567, 584
Hinemoa 267
Hiroa, Te Rangi............. 768
Hiruharama................... 243
history 761–776
Hobbit, The...............8, 213
Hobbiton....................... 213
Hobson, William 102,
172, 177
Hodgkins, Frances 508
hoiho............................ 595
Hokianga ferry 196
Hokianga Harbour 20,
196–199
Hokitika 644–648
Hokitika 645
Hokitika Gorge.............. 649
Hole in the Rock........... 169
holiday parks 45
holidays 53
Hollyford Track 744
Hollyford Valley............. 741
Holyoake, Keith 771
Homer Tunnel 740, 741
homestays...................... 44
Honeycomb Hill caves
.... 635
Hongi's Track................ 276
horseriding..................... 63,
127, 156, 176, 191, 215,
284, 305, 324, 326, 451,
457, 472, 489, 551, 562,
631, 639, 685, 697
horseback tours 62
hostels............................ 44
hot pools/springs 12,
127, 129, 131, 144, 183,
209, 216, 267, 313, 330,
339, 368, 550, 552, 566,
655, 660
Hot Water Beach
.........................308, 330
hot-air ballooning 558

hotels.............................. 43
Hotere, Ralph 590
Houhora........................ 194
Huapai 124
Huka Falls..................... 287
Humboldt Falls.............. 742
Hump Ridge Track 756
Hump Ridge Track........ 755
Hundertwasser toilets
.... 165
Hundertwasser, Friedrich
.... 165
Hunua Falls.................. 130
Hunua Ranges, the....... 130
hydroelectricity 751, 794

I

Inangahua Junction...... 624
Inland Pack Track......... 636
insurance....................... 74
internet access.............. 75
Invercargill.......... 606–610
Invercargill 607
Iwikau Village................ 295

J

Jack's Blowhole 601
Jackson Bay.................. 662
Jerusalem 243
jetboating.........21, 61, 241,
288, 290, 560, 631, 661,
681, 697, 709, 754

K

kahikatea 789, 791
Kahurangi National Park
.... 472
Kai Iwi Lakes 202
Kaiaua.......................... 130
Kaikohe........................ 183
Kaikoura 13, 484–490
Kaikoura 485
Kaikoura Coast Track ... 488
Kaikoura Peninsula
Walkway 488
Kaikoura Wilderness Walks
.... 488
Kaitaia.......................... 189
Kaitake Range 232
Kaiteriteri 460

Kaiti Hill 365
Kaituna River 258, 270
kaka 254, 369, 790
Kaka Point 600
kakapo 790
kakariki 790
kaki .... see stilt, black
Kaki/Black Stilt visitor hide
.... 572
Kapiti Island 254
Karamea 633–635
Karamea 633
Karangahake Gorge 315
karearea ......see falcon, NZ
Karekare 126
Karikari Peninsula, the
.... 188
Karori Sanctuary 24, 413
Katikati 334
Kauaeranga Valley 319
kauri 166, 202, 325, 787
Kauri Forests, the 199
kauri gum 191, 226
kauri museum 200, 203
Kawakawa 165
Kawau Island 154
Kawerau River 717
Kawhia 216
kayak fishing 113
kayaking 61, 113,
    129, 175, 241, 285, 331,
    440, 451, 464, 476, 489,
    531, 571, 616, 639, 656,
    709, 736, 745, 752,
    Adrenaline heaven colour
    section
kayaking tours 62
kea 556, 790
Kemp, James 182
Kenepuru Road 444
Kepler Track 736
Kepler Track 737
kereru 790
Kerikeri 180–183
Kerikeri 181
Kerikeri Mission House
.... 182
Kerosene Creek 278
Key, John 774
King Country, the 217
King Movement
.... 218, 766
kitesurfing 216
kiwi 202, 369,
    506, 617, 788, 789,
    Conservation in action
    colour section
Knight's Point 661
Kohaihai 635

Kohukohu 196
kokako 147, 790
korimako .... see bellbird
Koriniti 243
Kororareka 177
Kororipo Pa 182
Korowai/Torlesse
    Tussocklands Park 554
kotuku 650
kowhai 788
Kuaotunu 325
Kumeu 124
Kupe 188, 196, 400, 778
Kura Tawhiti 554

L

Lady Knox Geyser 278
Lake Brunner 627
Lake Dunstan 719
Lake Ellesmere 525
Lake Ferry 395
Lake Gunn 741
Lake Hauroko 753
Lake Ianthe 650
Lake Kaniere 649
Lake Mackenzie 701
Lake Mahinapua 649
Lake Manapouri 750
Lake Marian 741
Lake Matheson 659
Lake Ohau 573
Lake Paringa 661
Lake Pukaki 567
Lake Rotoiti 276, 473
Lake Rotoroa 267, 476
Lake Tarawera 276
Lake Taupo 280
Lake Tekapo 564
Lake Tekapo Village 565
Lake Waikareiti 370
Lake Waikaremoana
.... 369–373
Lake Waikaremoana
.... 370
Lake Waikaremoana Track
.... 371
Lake Wakatipu 11
Lang's Beach 158
Lange, David 185, 772
Langford's Store 470
language 806–812
Lawrence 725
Lawson, Robert A 582,
    583, 590, 594
Le Bons Bay 533
Leigh 155

lesbian New Zealand 72
Levin 251
Lewis Pass 551
Lindauer, Gottfried 101
*Lion, the Witch and the
    Wardrobe, The* 8
Lion Rock 126
Little Akaloa 533
Little River 525
living in NZ 67
lodges 43
Lord of the Rings 8, 213,
    291, 672, 466, 685, 697,
    734
Lower Hutt 419
Lye, Len 228, 410
Lyell Walkway 624
Lyttelton 522–533
Lyttelton 523

M

Macetown 693
MacKay Falls 745, 750
Macraes Gold Mine 724
magazines 53
Mahia Beach 368
Mahia Peninsula 368
mail 75
Maitai Bay 189
Makarora 663
Makarora and the Gillespie
    Pass Tramp 663
Manapouri 750–752
Manawatu Gorge 250
Mangamuka Bridge 196
Mangapurua Track 242
Mangapurua Valley 239
Mangatainoka 389
Mangaweka 306
Mangawhai 157
Mangawhai Heads 157
Mangonui 186
mangroves 197
Maniototo, The 722–725
Mansfield, Katherine 413
Manu Bay 216
manuka 910
Maori
    arrival 761
    arts and crafts 780–784
    concerts 272, 687
    culture .... see *Maori in the
        modern world* colour section
    customs 779
    language 807–809
    legend 778
    Maoritanga 777–784

maps....................................75
Mapua 455
marae...............................780
Maraehako Bay 353
Marahau 460
Marlborough Sounds
.............................433–445
Marlborough Sounds
...........................434–435
Marlborough wineries.... 480
Marlborough wineries
...................................481
Marlborough, Nelson and
Kaikoura....................432
Marokopa Falls.............223
Marsden, Samuel 168,
184, 763
Martin's Bay...................744
Martinborough 392–395
Martinborough 393
Maruia Springs 552
Mason Bay 617
Masterton 389
matai..............................789
Matakaea Scenic Reserve
...................................544
Matakana.......................155
Matakana Coast 153
Matakohe.......................203
Matamata 213
Matapouri 164
Matauri Bay 184
Matukituki Valley...........713
Maui...............................778
Mavora Lakes...............677
Mavora Walkway 701
Mayor Island.................340
McCahon, Colin............101
McKenzie, James 565
McKinnon, Quintin.......729,
734, 746
McLaren Falls 342
McLeod Bay 163
media..............................52
Medlands Beach 143
Mercury Bay 326
Methven................557–561
Methven 558
Middlemarch.........590, 725
Milford Road..................739
Milford Sound 14,
739–750
Milford Track 728,
745–750
Milford Track................748
Miranda 130
miro 789
Mirror Lakes 740
Mitre Peak 742
Moana 627

mobile phones...............77
Moeraki...........................543
Moeraki Boulders....16, 543
Mokau............................223
Mokoia Island 267
Molesworth Station 483
money..............................76
Monro Beach.................661
morepork 791
Morere 368
Morrieson, Ronald Hugh
...................................236
mosquitoes....................74
motels..............................43
motorbiking 40
motorhome rental...........38
Motoua Gardens 247
Motu River............270, 350
Motuara Island 439
Motuarohia 169
Motueka 456–458
Motutapu Island 131
Mount Aspiring National
Park 713
Mount Bruce.................389
Mount Cheeseman ski-field
...................................553
**Mount Cook National
Park**................... 569–572
Mount Cook Village
............................567–569
Mount Cook Village 568
Mount Cook, around
...................................570
Mount Cook, walks around
...................................570
Mount Dobson ski-field
...................................564
Mount Fyffe 488
Mount Hikurangi...........355
Mount Hutt ski-field.....560
Mount Iron 708
Mount John 565
Mount Karioi 215
Mount Lyford 491
Mount Manaia 163
Mount Maunganui
............................335–342
Mount Maunganui 339
Mount Ngauruhoe 291
Mount Ngongotaha 269
Mount Paku...................332
Mount Ruapehu............291
Mount Somers...............561
Mount Somers Track 562
Mount Tongariro 291
mountain biking.....63, 271,
279, 285, 301, 465, 466,
513, 551, 685, 721, 723
mountaineering.......62, 708

Mountfort, Benjamin....507,
508
Moutoa Island...............243
mud pools 12
Muldoon, Robert 771
Murchison.....................476
Muriwai 127
Murupara 279
Museum of New Zealand
.......................20, 389, 408
music....................587, 797
mustelids 787
muttonbirds 793

N

Napier 373–380
Napier............................374
Napier–Taupo Road......290
Naseby 723
Nash, Walter.................771
National Park................301
Nelson.................. 445–452
Nelson 446
Nelson, around 454
**Nelson Lakes National
Park**.................... 473–476
Nelson Market..............448
netball..............................65
New Plymouth..... 226–232
New Plymouth 227
New Zealand Wars 767
newspapers 53
Ngaiotonga Scenic Reserve
...................................165
Ngakawau......................632
Ngarua Caves...............466
Ngaruawahia 207
Ngata, Apirana 768
Ngawha Springs...........183
Ngawi 395
nikau palm....................788
Ninety Mile Beach
.............................21, 192
Norsewood....................388
North Egmont...............233
North Island 4
North Island, central.... 260
North West Circuit........617
Northern Gateway Toll
Road 128
Northland............. 150–204
Northland 152
nuclear power...............914
nudists...........................455
Nugget Point 600
Nukunuku Museum 224,
239

O

Oakura 235
Oakura (Northland) 166
Oamaru 537–542
Oamaru 538
Oban 612
Oban 613
Ohakune 302–304
Ohau ski-field 573
Ohinemutu 267
Ohope 347
Okains Bay 533
Okarito 650
Okere Falls Scenic Reserve
   274
Old Russell Road 165
Old Stone Store 182
Omaio 353
Omakau 722
Omapere 198
Omarama 574
Once Were Warriors 111,
   772, 798
Onepotu Bay 354
Oneroa 137
Oneroa 137
Onetangi 138
Oparara Arch 635
Oparara Basin, the 635
opening hours 76
Ophir 722
Opononi 198
Opotiki 348–350
Opoutere 332
Opua 169
Opunake 236
Orakei Korako 278
Oreti Beach 608
Orewa 128
Orokonui Ecosanctuary
   591
Ostend 138
Otago Central Rail Trail
   .... 15, 668, 721
Otago Peninsula
   591–597
Otago Peninsula 592
Otaki 251
Otaki Gorge 289
Otorohanga 218
Owaka 601

P

Paekakariki 255
Paeroa 315

Paihia 169–176
Paihia and Waitangi 170
Paihia—Russell ferry 169
pakihi 622
Pakiri 156
Palm Beach 138
Palmerston 544
Palmerston North
   249–251
Pancake Rocks 620, 638
Pania of the Reef 378
Papakorito Falls 370
Papamoa Beach 342
Paparoa National Park
   636–640
Papatowai 602
Paradise 695
Paradise Valley 269
paragliding 62, 451,
   509, 684, 709
Parakai 127
parakeets 254
Paraparaumu 253
parasailing 175
Pardington, Fiona 508
Pardington, Neil 508
Parengarenga Harbour
   194
Paringa River 661
Paritutu Rock 230
Parry Kauri Park 154
Patauta South 163
Patea 237
Paterson Inlet 615
paua 10
Peel Forest 562
Pelorus Bridge Scenic
   Reserve 445
Pelorus Sound 444
Penguin Place, The 596
penguins 21, 147,
   531, 541, 544, 595, 596,
   762, 793
phonecards 77
phones 76
photography 78
Piano, The 126, 796
Picton 433–439
Picton 436
Piha 126
Pihanga 291
Pilots Beach 595
Pink and White Terraces
   276
Pinnacles, the 319
Pipiriki 242
piwakawaka ...... see fantails
Pohara 469
pohutukawa 788
Point Elizabeth 739

Point Elizabeth Track
   643
police 70
pollution 794
Pomare, Maui 768
Pompallier 179
ponga 789
Poor Knights Islands 24,
   163
Porirua 255
Porpoise Bay 602
Port Chalmers 590
Port Charles 324
Port Craig 868
Port Fitzroy 144
Port Jackson 324
Port Nicholson 399
Porter's Pass 554
Porters ski-field 553
Portobello 594
   Larnach Castle 594
post 75
Pouakai Circuit 235
pounamu 647, 782
Poverty Bay 362
Poverty Bay, Hawke's Bay
   and the Wairarapa 362
power supply 71
prejudice 71
price codes 43
pronunciation 809
public holidays 53
Puhoi 129
Pukaha Mount Bruce
   National Wildlife Centre
   389
pukeko 791
Pukekura 650
Pukekura Park 230
Pukenui 194
Pukerangi 590, 725
Puketi Kauri Forest 184
Punakaiki 620, 638
Punakaiki and the Inland
   Pack Track 638
punting 509, 511
Puponga 471
Pureora Forest Park 217
Putangirua Pinnacles 395

Q

quad biking 451, 656
Quail Island 525
Queen Charlotte Drive
   443
Queen Charlotte Sound
   439–444

Queen Charlotte Track
.....................................440
QUEENSTOWN ... 671–688
Central Queenstown.... 674
Queenstown, around.... 678
Queenstown, Wanaka and
   the Gold Country 670
   accommodation 673–676
   activities 680–685
   airport............................ 672
   Bob's Peak...................... 677
   drinking and nightlife 686
   eating 686
   gondola 677
   information 673
   Lake Wakatipu 677
   listings........................... 687
   Shotover River 679
   Skippers Canyon 679
   Skippers Road 679
   tours............................. 672
   transport....................... 673
   walks around Queenstown
   680
   Walter Peak 677
   winter in Queenstown 683

R

racism.............................. 71
radio 52
rafting 60, 270, 305,
   306, 350, 476, 509, 562,
   631, 648, 682, 709
Raglan............ 17, 214–216
Rai Valley 445
Rainbow Falls 182
Rainbow Springs 269
Rainbow Warrior, the ... 184,
   185, 194
rainfall 13
Rakaia Gorge................ 560
Rakaia........................... 534
Rakiura Track........ 466, 617
Ranana 243
Ranfurly 724
Rangiputa 188
Rangitaiki River 270, 346
Rangitata River 562
Rangitikei River 305, 306
Rangitoto Island
   131–133
Rangitoto and Motutapu
   islands 132
Rapahoe 640
Rarawa 194
Raspberry Creek 714
rata 789
Rawene.......................... 197

Rawhiti Cave 469
Redcliffs....................... 513
Reefton 624
Rees-Dart Track 702
Reeves, William Pember
   768
Remarkables ski-field.... 683
Rere Falls..................... 367
Rere rockslide............... 367
restaurants.................... 48
rifleman......................... 792
rimu 789
Rimutaka Forest Park... 419
Rimutaka Rail Trail........ 392
Ripiro Beach................. 203
river surfing................... 682
Riverton 755
Roberton Island............ 169
robin 791
Robinson, Ann.............. 508
rock art 536
rock climbing........ 554, 707
Ross 649
Rotorua............... 261–274
Rotorua, around 275
Rotorua, central........... 262
Roundhill ski-field........ 566
Routeburn Track..... 22, 700
Roxburgh...................... 725
Royal Albatross Centre
   596
Royal albatross.............. 596
Roy's Peak.................... 708
Ruakokere 353
Ruakuri Natural Tunnel
   222
Ruapehu Crater Rim hike
   296
Ruapekapeka Pa 165
Ruatahuna 369
Ruatoria 355
rugby 64, 65, 587
ruru .... see morepork
Russell 177–180
Russell 178
Rutherford, Ernest
   .... 444, 508

S

saddleback........... 147, 791
sailing 59, 113, 174, 186,
   464, 791
St Arnaud 474
St Bathans.................... 723
St Clair.......................... 585
St Kilda 585

sandflies 74, 733
Sandfly Point................ 748
Sarjeant Gallery............ 246
Savage, Michael Joseph
   .... 106, 770
scuba diving 24, 59,
   164, 176, 254, 331, 378,
   489, 745
sea lions 604
Seabird Coast, the 130
seal colonies................. 631
seal swimming.............. 464
seals 6, 793
seasons 11, 78
Seddon, Richard 768
self-catering.................. 49
Shag Point.................... 544
Shakespear Regional Park
   128
shark encounters.......... 366
sharks........................... 74
sheep............................. 7
Sheppard, Kate 412
Ship Cove............ 439, 441
Ship Creek.................... 661
Shipley, Jenny 773
shopping....................... 78
Shotover River............. 679
Siberia Experience 664
six o'clock swill 769
ski-fields 233
skiing 62, 572, 300,
   491, 551, 553, 560, 564,
   566, 573, 683, 712
Skippers Canyon.......... 679
Skippers Road............. 679
skydiving 62, 270, 284,
   457, 489, 558, 685, 709
sledging........................ 682
Slope Point................... 603
smoking......................... 67
Smugglers Cove........... 163
snakes 74
snorkelling 59, 164, 174
Snow Farm ski-field 713
snowboarding................ 62
soccer............................ 65
South Coast Track........ 756
South Coast Track........ 755
South Island................... 5
South Island, central.... 548
southern lights.............. 611
Southern Scenic Route
   (east)........................... 597
Southern Scenic Route
   (west) 753–758
specialist tours 61
spiders........................... 74
Spirits Bay 195

Split Apple Rock........... 461
sports 64
Springbok Tour 772
Springfield 552
Staveley 561
Stewart Island 611–618
Stewart Island:
  the northeast 611
stilt, black 790
stitchbird 147, 791
Stonehenge Aotearoa... 391
Stony Batter Historic
  Reserve 138
Stratford 235
student discounts 70
Sugar Loaf Marine Reserve
  230
Summit Road 514
Sumner 513
sunburn 73
Surf Highway 235
surfing 16, 59, 216,
  235, 236, 339
Sutherland Falls 746
Sutherland, Donald 729,
  739, 745
swimming 59, 106
swimming safety 73
swimming with seals 489
swinging 61, 681
Sydney, Grahame 722

T

tahr 787
Tahunanui Beach 450
Taiaroa Head 595
Taieri Gorge Railway 23,
  576, 590, 725
Taihape 305
Taipa 188
Tairua 332
takahe 147, 254,
  735, 791
Takaka 466–470
Takaka Hill 466
Tane Mahuta 201
tank driving 509
Tapapakanga Regional Park
  130
Tapeka Point 180
Tapu 320
Taranaki 224–237
Taranaki Around the
  Mountain Circuit 234
Taranaki Peninsula 225
Taranaki summit hikes
  234

Tararua Forest Park 252
Tasman 455
Tasman, Abel 400, 446,
  458, 650, 762
tattooing 782
Taumarunui 223
Taupo 279–287
Taupo, around 288
Taupo, central 281
Taupo Bay 186
Tauranga 335–342
Tauranga and around
  343
Tauranga, central 336
Tauranga Bay 631
Tawharanui Regional Park
  155
taxes 70
Taylor's Mistake 513
Te Anau 731–736
Te Anau 732
Te Anau Downs 740
Te Araroa, East Cape 354
Te Araroa hike 56
Te Aroha 313
Te Awamutu 213
Te Hana 157
Te Henga 126
Te Kaha 353
Te Kao 194
Te Kooti 262, 280,
  344, 372
Te Kuiti 223
Te Mahia 368
Te Mata Peak 387
Te Matua Ngahere 201
Te Paki Stream 195
Te Papa 20, 389, 408
Te Puke 343
Te Rauparaha 251, 254,
  446, 763
Te Urewera National Park
  369–373
Te Waikoropupu Springs
  468
Te Wairoa 277
tea 51
temperature 13
Temple Basin ski-field
  555
Temuka 534
Thames 316–320
Thames 317
Thatcher, Frederick
  .... 105, 230
Three Kings Islands 195
tieke .... see saddleback
Tikitiki 355
Timaru 534–537
Timaru 535

time zones 78
tipping 67
Tiritiri Matangi 146
Titirangi 125
Tokaanu 294
Tokerau Beach 189
Tokomaru Bay 356
Tolaga Bay 357
toll road 128
Tonga Island 461
Tongaporutu 223
Tongariro Alpine Crossing
  .... 18, 298
Tongariro Around the
  Mountain track 300
Tongariro National Park
  290–304
Tongariro National Park
  292
Tongariro Northern Circuit
  299
Tongariro Power Scheme
  294
totara 789
Totara Estate 542
Totara North 185
Totaranui 460, 461,
  462, 463, 465, 467, 469
Tourism New Zealand 79
trains 34
tramping 56
tramping equipment 58
tramping safety 59
tramping tours 61
tramps
  Abel Tasman Coast Track
    463
  Abel Tasman Inland Track
    465
  Angelus Hut Loop 475
  Arrowtown–Macetown Circuit
    694
  Banks Peninsula Track 532
  Ben Lomond Summit Track
    680
  Ben Lomond–Moonlight Track
    680
  Cape Brett Track 166
  Cape Reinga Coastal
    Walkway 195
  Caples Track 701
  Cascade Saddle 715
  Casey Saddle to Binser
    Saddle 557
  Catlins Top Track 602
  Croesus Track 627
  Gillespie Pass tramp 664
  Great Barrier Island 145
  Greenstone Track 701
  Heaphy Track 472
  Hillary Trail 125
  Hollyford Track 744
  Hump Ridge Track 756

Inland Pack Track 637
Kaikoura Coast Track....... 488
Kaikoura Wilderness Walk
.... 488
Kauaeranga walks........... 319
Kepler Track 736
Lake Waikaremoana Track
.... 371
Mangapurua Track 242
Milford Track 745
Mingha–Deception 557
Mount Hikurangi 355
Mount Somers Track....... 562
Mueller Hut route 571
North West Circuit 617
Pouakai Circuit................ 235
Queen Charlotte Track..... 440
Rakiura Track 617
Rangitoto Summit walk.... 133
Rees–Dart Track............... 702
Routeburn Track 700
Ruapehu Crater Rim hike
.... 296
South Coast Track 756
Taranaki Around the Mountain
Circuit 267
Taranaki summit hikes 234
Te Araroa........................ 56
Tongariro Alpine Crossing
.... 299
Tongariro Northern Circuit
.... 341
Tongariro Round the
Mountain track............. 300
Travers-Sabine Circuit...... 475
Welcome Flat Hot Springs
.... 660
Whirinaki Track................ 279
Wilkin and Young valleys
circuit........................... 664
TranzAlpine train........... 513
travel agents................... 30
travel passes 34
travellers' cheques 76
Travers-Sabine Circuit
.... 475
Treaty of Waitangi
.... 172, 764
Treble Cone ski-field..... 712
tree ferns 17, 789
trekking (see also tramps)
.... 56
Trounson Kauri Park 202
trout 791
Tryphena........................ 143
Tuai 369
Tuatapere....................... 754
tuatara 608, 791
Tuhua Island 340
tui................................... 254, 791
Turanganui a Kiwa........ 362
Turangi............. 293–295
Turoa ski-field................ 300
Tutanekai 267

Tutea's Falls.................. 270
Tutira............................. 369
Tutukaka 163
TV 52
Twizel............................ 572

U

Ulva Island.................... 615
Upper Moutere 454
Urquharts Bay 163
Urupukapuka Island 168

V

vaccinations 73
van der Velden, Petrus
.... 507
vegetarian food 48
vehicle buying 39
vehicle rental 36
Via Ferrata 684
visas 71
visitor centres 79
Volcanic Plateau........... 259
voluntary work.............. 69

W

Waiatoto River 661
Waihau Bay 353
Waiheke Island.... 134–139
Waiheke Island 135
Waihi............................. 334
Waihi Beach 334
Waikanae...................... 252
Waikawa 602
Waikino......................... 312
Waimakariri Gorge........ 552
Waimangu...................... 277
Waimate North 183
Waimea Inlet................. 453
Waingaro Hot Springs...209
Wainui Beach 357
Wainui Falls 469
Waioeka Gorge............. 351
Waioeka River............... 350
Waiohine Gorge............ 391
Wai-O-Tapu 15, 278
Waiouru 304
Waipapa Point 604
Waipara 491
Waipiro Bay 356

Waipoua Kauri Forest...200
Waipu 158
Waipu Caves................. 158
Waipu Cove 158
Waipunga Falls 290
Wairakei Terraces 289
Wairarapa, The.... 388–395
Wairarapa, The 362
Wairere Boulders 198
Wairoa 368
Wairoa River 270, 342
Waitakere Ranges 124
Waitaki Hydro Scheme
.... 572
Waitangi......................... 172
Waitangi Treaty Grounds
.... 172
Waitangi Treaty House
.... 172
Waitangi, Treaty of........ 172
Waitiki Landing............. 194
Waitomo 219–222
Waitomo....................... 220
Waiuta........................... 626
Waiwera......................... 129
Wakefield, Edward Gibbon
.... 765
Walters, Gordon 101
Wanaka 702–711
Wanaka 703
Wanaka walks 708
Wanganui............. 244–248
Wanganui 245
Warkworth 153
Washpen Falls 561
Waterfall Creek 708
weather........................... 11
weka 254, 791
Welcome Flat Hot Springs
.... 660
WELLINGTON 398–428
Central Wellington
.... 406–407
Wellington 414–415
Wellington and around
.... 400
accommodation 404–405
airport............................ 401
Archives New Zealand 412
B&Bs 404
bars 425
Beehive, The 412
Botanic Gardens 411
Brooklyn Hill................... 416
Bucket Fountain.............. 410
buses 402
Cable Car........................ 411
Cable Car Museum.......... 411
cafés................................ 423
campsites........................ 405
Carter Observatory 411

cathedrals 412
Central library.................. 408
cinema 427
City Gallery Wellington..... 408
city tours 403
city transport.................... 402
Civic Square..................... 408
clubs 425
Colonial Cottage Museum
      410
concerts 426
Courtenay Place 409
crossing Cook Strait 401
Cuba Street...................... 410
cycling.............................. 420
delis................................. 422
DOC office 402
Dowse, New..................... 419
driving 403
eating, drinking and
      entertainment........421–427
ferry terminals 401
festivals 427
Frank Kitts Park 410
gay and lesbian Wellington
      425
gigs 425
guesthouses..................... 404
history 400
hostels............................. 405
hotels 404
Karori Sanctuary 413
Katherine Mansfield
      Birthplace 413
kayaking........................... 420
kiteboarding 419
Lambton Quay 411
listings............................. 427
Matiu Island 418
Miramar Peninsula 417
motels 404
Mount Victoria Lookout 409
Museum of New Zealand
      .... 389, 408
Museum of Wellington City
      and Sea 410
National Library of New
      Zealand........................ 412
New Dowse....................... 419
Oriental Parade 409
Otari-Wilton's Bush 416
parking 403
Parliament Buildings 412
Parliamentary District....... 411
Petone.............................. 419
pubs 425
Queens Wharf 410
restaurants 423
Scorching Bay.................. 417
scuba diving..................... 420
Somes Island 418
surfing 419
takeaways 422
Te Papa 389, 408
theatre.............................. 426

Thorndon.......................... 413
trains 402
visitor centre 402
Waitangi Park................... 409
walks 420
Water Whirler 410
Wellington Zoo 417
"Wellywood"...................... 417
Weta Cave........................ 417
windsurfing....................... 419
Zealandia.......................... 413
Wenderholm Regional Park
      129
Wentworth Falls............... 333
West Coast beaches 124
West Coast, the...620–666
West Coast, the........... 622
Western North Island ...208
Westport.............. 628–631
Westport 629
weta.....................791, 792
wetlands 790
Whakahoro 239
Whakapapa 295
Whakapapa ski-field..... 300
Whakarewarewa State
      Forest Park 274
Whakarewarewa Thermal
      Reserve....................... 267
Whakatane 343–348
Whakatane................... 344
Whale Bay (Northland)
      164
Whale Bay (Waikato) 216
Whale Island.................. 346
Whale Rider 357
whale watching 20, 113,
      347, 489
Whalers Base 615
whales 793
Whanarua Bay.............. 353
Whangamata 333
Whangamomona 224
Whangamumu Track 166
Whanganui 244–248
Whanganui National Park
      237–244
Whanganui National Park
      238
Whanganui River 19, 239
Whanganui River Road
      242
Whangaparaoa Peninsula
      128
Whangaparapara.......... 144
Whangapoua 325
Whangara 357
Whangarei 159–163
Whangarei................... 160

Whangarei Heads 163
Whangaroa 185
Whangaroa Harbour 165,
      185
Whararariki Beach 471
Whataroa 650
Whatipu 9, 125
whio .... see blue duck
Whirinaki Forest Park ...279
Whirinaki Track 279
white herons 650
White Island.............22, 346
whiteheads 254
Whitianga 326–331
Whitianga...................... 327
Whitianga, around 328
wi-fi.................................. 75
Wildfoods Festival 644
wildlife tours 61
wildlife, rare and
      endangered 790,
      Conservation in action
      colour section
Wilkin and Young valleys
      circuit.......................... 664
wind energy................... 794
Wind Wand...........228, 229
windsurfing..................... 59
wine 19, 51
wineries123, 124, 137, 138,
      154, 367, 383, 449, 455,
      487, 688, 706, 719
WOMAD 231
women travellers 80
women's suffrage 768
Woollaston, Toss 449
work........67, 180, 385, 456
working visas.................. 68
World of WearableArt ...450
wrybill 792
WWOOF 67

Y

yachting........................... 65
yellow-eyed penguins ..595
YHAs 44

Z

Zealandia.................24, 413
zorbing........................... 270

Map symbols

maps are listed in the full index using coloured text

---	Chapter boundary	◆	Point of interest
-----	International boundary	ⓘ	Tourist office
--- ··	Provincial boundary	⟙	Gardens
	Motorway	⟙	Lighthouse
─①─	National highway	⊞	Hospital
	Pedestrianized street	⊠	Post office
===	Road	@	Internet access
⊞⊞⊞	Steps	ⓒ	Telephone
)·······(	Underpass	🚻	Toilet
───	Unpaved road	🏊	Swimming pool
-----	Path	⚑	Ski area
───	River	⚠	Campsite
─ ─	Ferry route	◉	Accommodation
─■─	Railway	⊠	Gate
●---●	Cable car	♜	Castle
)(	Bridge/tunnel	⛳	Golf course
🞃	Mountain range	🍷	Winery
▲	Peak	🔅	Viewpoint
⌇⌇⌇	Cliff	∴	Ruins
🗻	Gorge	♦	Museum
🗻	Waterfall	⊙	Statue
🗻	Spring	➤	Boat
🗻	Surf/beach	⚓	Church (regional maps)
◓	Cave	╋	Church (town maps)
⚓	Boat stop	◯	Stadium
★	Bus stop	■	Building
✈	International airport	⊞	Cemetery
✕	Domestic airport	▨	Park/forest
🛢	Fuel station	⚏	Swamp
P	Parking	▦	Beach
⌂	Hut	▨	Glacier